江苏 2007 统计年鉴

JIANGSU STATISTICAL YEARBOOK

（总第24期 №.24）

江苏省统计局 编

Compiled by

Jiangsu Provincial Statistics Bureau

中国统计出版社

China Statistics Press

(京)新登字 041 号

图书在版编目(CIP)数据

江苏统计年鉴.2007/江苏省统计局编.—北京:中国统计出版社,2007.6

ISBN 978-7-5037-5140-0

Ⅰ.江... Ⅱ.江... Ⅲ.统计资料—江苏省—2007—年鉴 Ⅳ.C832.53-54

中国版本图书馆 CIP 数据核字(2007)第 051671 号

江苏统计年鉴—2007

作　　者 / 江苏省统计局
责任编辑 / 郑淼淼
E-mail / yearbook@ stats. gov. cn
执行编辑 / 张　平　刘学军
封面设计 / 薛　佩
出版发行 / 中国统计出版社
通信地址 / 北京市西城区三里河月坛南街 75 号　中国统计出版社
邮　　编 / 100826
电　　话 /(010)63376907
印　　刷 / 南京人民印刷厂
经　　销 / 新华书店
开　　本 / 889×1230 毫米　1/16
字　　数 / 153 万字
印　　张 / 45.375
印　　数 / 1-4000 册
版　　别 / 2007 年 7 月第 1 版
版　　次 / 2007 年 7 月第 1 次印刷
书　　号 / ISBN 978-7-5037-5140-0/F·2440
定　　价 / 360.00 元

编者说明

一、《江苏统计年鉴一2007》(以下简称《年鉴》)是一部全面、系统反映江苏省2006年及历史重要年份国民经济和社会发展情况的资料性年刊,收录了江苏省及各地区大量的经济社会发展统计信息。

二、《年鉴》分为二十二个部分,1. 行政区划和自然资源;2. 综合;3. 人口就业;4. 人民生活;5. 固定资产投资;6. 物价;7. 农业;8. 工业、能源;9. 建筑业;10. 交通运输、邮电业;11. 国内贸易;12. 对外经济贸易和旅游;13. 财政、金融、保险;14. 科技、教育;15. 文化、体育、卫生、环保;16. 档案、司法、社会福利、其他;17. 城市经济与建设;18. 部分区经济社会基本情况;19. 区域经济;20. 市县社会经济;21. 县(市)经济发展序列;22. 乡镇基本情况。另附:2006年国民经济和社会事业发展的各类统计公报、全国分省主要指标和企业排序。每部分末附有《主要统计指标解释》。

三、《年鉴》资料大部分来自年度统计报表,一部分来自抽样调查等。全国分省资料来自国家统计局出版的有关统计资料。

四、《年鉴》中所使用的度量衡单位均采用国际统一标准计量单位。

五、《年鉴》中国民经济行业分类按2002年国家标准《国民经济行业分类》(GB/T4754-2002)执行。

六、《年鉴》表中"..."表示数据不足本表最小单位数;"空格"表示该项统计指标数据不详或无该项数据;"#"表示其中的主要项。

《年鉴》的编辑出版得到了国家统计局江苏调查总队和省级有关部门的大力支持和协助,在此表示感谢。欢迎国内外读者提出宝贵意见,使《年鉴》的形式和内容更趋完善。

COMPLIER'S NOTES

Ⅰ. Jiangsu Statistical Yearbook 2007 (abbreviated as Yearbook hereafter) is an annual publication which provides comprehenisive and systematic data series about the national economy and social development in Jiangsu Province in 2006 and some selected data series in historically important years. It includes much statistical information on social and economic development in the province and in various regions.

Ⅱ. The Yearbook contatins the following twenty-two parts, 1. Division of Administrative Districts and Natural Resources; 2. General Survey; 3. Population and Employment; 4. Peopl's Livehihook; 5. Investment in Fixed Assets; 6. Price; 7. Agriculture; 8. Industry and Energy; 9. Construction; 10. Transportation, Postal and Telecommunications Services; 11. Domestic Trade; 12. Foreign Economy and Trade and Tourism; 13. Government Finance, Banking and Insurance; 14. Science, Technology and Education; 15. Culture, Sports, Health Care and Environmental Protection; 16. Archives, Judgement, Social Welfare and Others; 17. Urban Economy and Construction; 18. Basic Situation of Economy and Society of Part Districts; 19. Regional Economy; 20. Social Economy of Cities(Counties); 21. Social Economic Development Alignment of Cities(Counties); 22. Basic Situation of Towns and Townships. Besides, there are appendixes for statistics communique on naitonal economic and social development of 2006, national major indicators grouped by provinces and alignment of enterprises. Appended at the end of every part, there are explanatory notes to major statistical indicators.

Ⅲ. The major data sources of this publication are obtained from annual statistical reports, and some from sample surveys. National major indicators grouped by provinces are obtained from relative statistical data published by the National Bureau of Statistics of China.

Ⅳ. The units of measurement used used in the Yearbook are all internationally standard measurement units.

Ⅴ. The classification of national economic industry used in the Yearbook is the national standard of 2002's "The Classification on National Economic Industry", i. e. (GB/T4754 – 2002).

Ⅵ. In the Yearbook, "…" indicates that the figure is not large enough to be measured with the samllest unit in the table; (blank) indicates that the figure is not available, "#" indicates the major component items.

We express thanks to NBS Survey Office in Jiangsu or other provincial relative departments for supporting and helping to the work of complication and publication of the Yearbook. We sincerely welcome conitinued valuable suggestions from the general readers so that the form and content of the Yearbook can be further improved.

目 录

CONTENTS

3　人口、就业

POPULATION AND EMPLOYMENT

4　人民生活

PEOPLE'S LIVELIHOOD

5 固定资产投资
INVESTMENT IN FIXED ASSETS

6 物 价
PRICE

7 农 业
AGRICULTURE

8 工业、能源

INDUSTRY AND ENERGY

9 建筑业

CONSTRUCTION

10 交通运输、邮电

TRANSPORTATION, POSTAL AND TELECOMMUNICATIONS SERVICES

11 国内贸易

DOMESTIC TRADE

12 对外经济贸易和旅游

FOREIGN ECONOMIC, TRADE AND TOURISM

13　财政、金融、保险

GOVERNMENT FINANCE, BANKING AND INSURANCE

14　科技、教育

SCIENCE, TECHNOLOGY AND EDUCATION

15 文化、体育、卫生、环保

CULTURE, SPORTS, PUBLIC HEALTH AND ENVIRONMENTAL PROTECTION

16 档案、司法、社会福利、其他

ARCHIVES, JUDGEMENT, SOCIAL WELFARE AND OTHERS

17 城市经济与建设

URBAN ECONOMY AND CONSTRUCTION

18　部分区经济社会基本情况

BASIC SITUATION OF ECONOMY AND SOCIETY OF PART DISTRICTS

19　区域经济

REGIONAL ECONOMY

20 市县社会经济

CITY(COUNTY)SOCIAL ECONOMY

21 县（市）社会经济发展序列

COUNTY(CITY) SOCIAL ECONOMIC DEVELOPMENT ALIGNMENT

22　乡镇基本情况

BASIC CONDITIONS OF COUNTRY AND TOWN

附录一　全国分省主要指标

APPENDIX Ⅰ MAJOR INDICATORS BY REGION

附录二 统计公报

APPENDIX Ⅱ STATISTICS COMMUNIQUES

附录三 单位选介

APPENDIX Ⅲ THE UNITS INTRODUCTION

江苏省2006年国民经济和社会发展统计公报

江苏省统计局　国家统计局江苏调查总队

（2007年3月1日）

2006年是"十一五"发展的开局之年。在省委、省政府的正确领导下，全省上下紧紧围绕富民强省、"两个率先"目标，全面落实科学发展观，认真贯彻宏观调控各项政策措施，坚持率先发展、科学发展、和谐发展，统筹推进改革发展稳定的各项工作，经济社会发展取得新成绩，和谐社会建设收到新成效，全面小康社会建设跃上新台阶，较好地完成了年初制定的各项目标。

一、综　合

全省经济保持稳定较快增长。初步核算，全年实现地区生产总值21548.36亿元，比上年增长14.9%。其中，第一产业增加值1544.90亿元，增长5.0%；第二产业增加值12186.46亿元，增长16.0%；第三产业增加值7817.00亿元，增长15.5%。人均生产总值28685元，按当年汇率折算达3598美元。经济结构调整和增长方式转变取得新进展。三次产业增加值比例为7.2:56.5:36.3。高新技术产业产值10370亿元，占规模以上工业的比重达24.9%，比上年提高0.7个百分点。服务业（包括农林牧渔服务业）实现增加值7894.52亿元，比上年增长15.4%，占生产总值的比重为36.6%，提高0.8个百分点。所有制结构中，非公有制经济增加值在生产总值中的份额达60.9%，其中私营个体经济比重为35%，分别提高1.4个和0.8个百分点。节能降耗和污染减排工作取得明显成效，部分城市和地区环境质量有所改善。城市化水平进一步提高。年末全省城市化水平达51.9%，提高1.4个百分点。产业布局调整取得新进展，沿沪宁线、沿江、沿东陇海线和沿海产业带发展态势良好。进一步加大"四项转移"力度，积极推进南北共建苏北开发区。苏北、苏中一些主要经济指标的增幅高于全省平均水平。

市场物价总水平保持基本稳定。全年居民消费价格上涨1.6%，涨幅比上年回落0.5个百分点。商品零售价格上涨0.8%。原材料、燃料、动力购进价格上涨6.4%，工业品出厂价格上涨1.5%，农业生产资料价格上涨1.7%。

表1. 居民消费价格比上年上涨情况（%）

指标	全省	城市	农村
居民消费价格	1.6	1.6	1.7
食品	2.6	2.7	2.6
#粮食	3.5	3.7	3.1
烟酒及用品	-0.1	-0.3	0.1
衣着	0.9	1.1	0.4
家庭设备用品及服务	1.4	1.6	1.1
医疗保健及个人用品	1.5	1.2	2.0
交通和通信	-0.4	-1.3	1.6
娱乐教育文化用品及服务	-0.7	-0.4	-1.2
居住	4.5	4.7	4.1

就业再就业工作继续加强。年末全省城乡从业人员4564.76万人，比上年末增加54.64万人。通过多种途径使43.04万城镇下岗失业人员实现了再就业。年末城镇登记失业率为3.4%，比上年末下降0.2个百分点。新增农村劳动力转移62.6万人。

各项改革逐步推进。重点领域和关键环节的改革取得新进展，发展环境继续改善。以转变政府职能为重点，深入推进行政管理体制改革，政府社会管理和公共服务职能得到加强，事业单位改革取得阶段性成果。国有企业改革重组力度加大，国有控股上市公司股权分置改革基本完成，国有资本实力和带动力增强。民营经济发展加快，年末全省工商部门登记的私营企业达60万户，新增9.3万户，总注册资本达9717.07亿元；工商部门登记的个体户187.01万户。深入推进财政、金融改革，省级机关全面实行非税收入统一管理，农村信用社改革继续深化，江苏银行开业运营，地方股份制保险公司组建工作进展顺利。积极推进农村综合改革，乡镇机构改革试点、农村义务教育改革、县乡财政管理体制改革有序展开。

经济社会发展中还存在一些突出的矛盾和问题：一是农业发展和农民持续增收的难度加大。农业产业化进程不快，农村公共服务水平不高，促进农民持续增收的长效机制还没建立；二是经济结构性矛盾依然突出。主要表现为产业结构不够合理，自主创新能力不强，投资与消费比例不够协调，服务业比重偏低，工业产品附加值偏低；三是经济社会发展与资源环境的矛盾更显尖锐。粗放型增长方式尚未得到根本改变，资源环境压力较大，如期完成"十一五"期间节能减排指标和保护生态环境，任务相当艰巨；四是影响社会和谐稳定的因素依然存在。社会发展仍然滞后于经济发展，人民群众对环境污染治理、稳定物价、看病就医、道路交通、教育收费等方面还有不满意的地方，部分城乡居民生活比较困难，等等。

二、农林牧渔业

农业稳定发展。认真落实一系列支农惠农政策，加上有利的气候条件，粮食增产、农业增效、农民增收保持良好势头。全年粮食总产量达3041.44万吨，比上年增加206.85万吨，增长7.3%。其中夏粮总产量939.14万吨，比上年增长11.2%；秋粮总产量2102.30万吨，增长5.6%。种植业结构发生变化，全年粮食种植面积为498.51万公顷，比上年增加7.56万公顷；棉花、油料种植面积分别为35.49万公顷、81.23万公顷，分别减少1.34万公顷和3.46万公顷。蔬菜面积117.36万公顷，下降1.7%。优质、高效、安全和生态农业发展较快。

林牧渔业生产稳定。全年造林面积6.65万公顷。多数畜产品产量持平，肉类总产量346.73万吨，与上年持平，其中猪牛羊肉产量242.10万吨，禽肉产量103.71万吨；禽蛋总产量185.54万吨，增长1.9%；牛奶总产量60.81万吨，增长7.4%。全年水产品总产量405.45万吨，增长4.3%；其中淡水产品286.37万吨，海水产品119.08万吨，分别增长4.1%和5.0%。

表2. 主要农产品产量情况

产品名称	产量(万吨)	比上年增长(%)
粮食	3041.44	7.3
棉花	38.14	18.2
油料	218.18	1.0
油菜籽	149.40	-5.8
花生	66.82	20.5
蚕茧	12.56	18.6
茶叶	1.34	11.5
水果(含瓜果类)	210.02	3.9
肉类	346.73	持平
水产品	405.45	4.3

农村产业结构调整继续加快。农村工业、建筑业、运输业、批发零售贸易业、餐饮业产值占农村社会总产值比重保持在90%以上。全省农田有效灌溉面积达380.40万公顷；新增节水灌溉面积3.88万公顷；年末全省农业机械总动力3279万千瓦，比上年末增长4.6%。

社会主义新农村建设开局良好。农业投入增加，促进了农村发展。全年省财政安排“三农”支出181亿元，增长20.4%。启动实施新一轮农村五件实事工程，建成农村公路1.1万公里，新改建农村公路大中桥梁1050座，完成279万名农村劳动力培训任务，乡镇卫生院改造、乡村综合文化站室建设和以“三清一绿”为重点的环境整治等工作均取得成效，农村生产生活条件进一步改善。

三、工业和建筑业

工业生产保持较快增长。全年完成工业增加值11047.52亿元，比上年增长16.6%。规模以上工业企业完成增加值10015.12亿元，增长21.4%。轻、重工业增加值3283.17亿元、6731.95亿元，分别增长18.4%和22.9%。国有控股工业增加值1548.51亿元，增长14.5%；其中国有工业增加值680.85亿元，增长15.5%。集体工业增加值444.65亿元，增长21.2%。私营工业增加值2671.25亿元，增长24.2%。股份制工业增加值4266.31亿元，增长20.6%。外商港澳台投资工业增加值3994.28亿元，增长22.8%。大中型工业增加值5969.22亿元，增长16.5%。

新兴行业和高技术行业增长加快。坚持走新型工业化道路，现代制造业发展水平进一步提高。全省通讯设备、计算机及其他电子设备制造业产值6316.72亿元，比上年增长19.0%；化学原料及化学制品制造业产值3967.00亿元，增长25.4%；纺织业产值3674.94亿元，增长18.0%；黑色金属冶炼及压延加工业产值3728.61亿元，增长24.7%；通用设备制造业产值2588.64亿元，增长30.6%；电气机械及器材制造业产值2984.96亿元，增长35.8%。产品结构继续优化，工业新产品产值3023.04亿元，比上年增长42.0%。主要工业产品产量多数保持增长，在列统的75种主要工业产品中，保持增长的有58种，下降的有17种。

表3. 主要工业产品产量情况

产品名称	单位	产量	比上年增长(%)
纱	万吨	350.56	13.9
布	亿米	64.95	15.5
化纤	万吨	665.14	15.9
卷烟	亿支	845.41	3.6
彩色电视机	万部	248.25	-27.4
家用电冰箱	万台	408.80	10.0
房间空调器	万台	473.29	-7.5
原煤	万吨	3047.53	8.1
原油	万吨	188.49	3.2
发电量	亿度	2216.40	19.7
钢	万吨	4202.31	23.3
钢材	万吨	5816.26	26.3
十种有色金属	万吨	31.89	-2.2
水泥	万吨	10880.77	13.9
硫酸	万吨	403.21	13.6
纯碱	万吨	247.23	11.6
乙烯	万吨	140.17	25.5
化肥(折100%)	万吨	254.66	5.7
汽车	万辆	27.48	-9.8
#轿车	万辆	14.60	0.2
发电设备	万千瓦	372.45	-8.2
集成电路	万块	1146504.00	36.6
程控交换机	万线	11.94	-76.1
微型电子计算机	万部	4712.14	62.7
移动通讯设备	信道	503012.00	163.5
光通信设备	万部	2.06	29.1

工业经济运行质量和效益提高。全省规模以上工业企业实现产品销售收入41030.19亿元,比上年增长26.1%;产品销售率98.5%,提高0.4个百分点;实现利税3157.15亿元,增长31.3%,其中利润1901.83亿元,增长36.5%。亏损企业亏损面11.9%,下降1.7个百分点;亏损额148.43亿元,下降8.4%。工业经济效益综合指数为189.98,提高17.6个百分点。

建筑业保持较快发展。全年省内完成建筑业增加值1138.94亿元,增长10.5%。全省建筑企业实现利税总额301.73亿元,增长19.4%。全员劳动生产率14.0万元/人,增长8.5%。全年共完成建筑业总产值5154.48亿元,增长18.1%;竣工产值3878.57亿元,增长13.7%,竣工率达75.2%。建筑业企业房屋建筑施工面积60617.16万平方米,增长19.5%;房屋建筑竣工面积28138.96万平方米,增长7.7%,其中住宅竣工面积15689.86万平方米,增长9.1%。

四、固定资产投资

固定资产投资稳定增长。全年完成全社会固定资产投资10063.65亿元,比上年增长20.3%。其中,城镇固定资产投资完成7473.7亿元,增长20.2%;农村固定资产投资2589.95亿元,增长20.7%。在全社会投资中,国有及国有控股投资2528.37亿元,下降0.3%;外商、港澳台经济投资1727.58亿元,增长16%;民间投资5807.7亿元,增长33.8%,其中私营个体经济投资3110.67亿元,增长36.6%。民间投资占全社会投资的比重达57.7%,比上年提高5.8个百分点。

投资结构进一步调优。在城镇固定资产投资中,第一产业投资15.45亿元,比上年增长21.9%;第二产业投资3439.08亿元,增长22.3%;第三产业投资4019.17亿元,增长18.4%。工业投资3391.17亿元,增长22.2%;其中通信设备、计算机及其他电子设备制造业472.14亿元,交通运输设备制造业197.71亿元,通用设备制造业投资248.59亿元,分别增长50.4%、40.7%和56.2%。第三产业投资中,房地产开发投资1901.01亿元,增长23%;交通运输仓储和邮政业投资548.51亿元,增长2.5%;水利、环境和公共设施管理业投资673.25亿元,增长17%;教育投资139.96亿元,增长5.6%;卫生、社会保障和社会福利业投资56.22亿元,增长39.2%。重点调控行业投资明显下降,城镇投资中钢铁工业完成投资130.71亿元,下降17.5%;水泥工业投资24.76亿元,下降13.2%;纺织工业投资273.87亿元,增长31.5%,增幅下降15.6个百分点。

重大基础设施和重大产业项目建设得到加强。沿海、宁淮、盐徐高速公路建成通车,新增高速公路469公里,累计通车里程达到3355公里,在全国率先实现联网畅通。水运事业发展加快,港口、航道建设投资分别增长83.1%和66.1%,全省港口集装箱运输量达到424万标箱,增长38.8%。淮河入海水道工程全面建成,南水北调东线一期、新一轮淮河治理、重点海堤达标、京杭运河扩容和苏通大桥、南京过江隧道、南京地铁2号线等工程建设进展顺利。无锡海力士集成电路、昆山龙腾光电等一批重大产业项目建成投产。

固定资产投资成果明显。全年城镇固定资产投资建成投产项目7337个,项目建成投产率为53.2%;新增固定资产

5730.2 亿元，固定资产交付使用率为 76.7%。

五、国内贸易

消费品市场稳中趋旺。全年实现社会消费品零售总额 6623.18 亿元，比上年增长 16.2%。分城乡看，城市消费品零售额 4822.93 亿元，增长 17.1%；农村消费品零售额 1800.25 亿元，增长 13.7%。分行业看，批发零售贸易业零售额 3813.78 亿元，增长 15.9 %；住宿和餐饮业零售额 746.51 亿元，增长 18.0%；其他行业零售额 60.89 亿元，增长 19.6%。限额以上批发零售贸易企业经营状况良好，全年实现商品销售 6417.97 亿元，比上年增长 12.6%，其中批发业 4575.95 亿元，零售业 1842.02 亿元，分别增长 6.8% 和 30.1%。以住房、汽车、信息通讯、旅游等为代表的热点消费保持较快增长，居民消费结构升级加快。全年实现商品房销售额比上年增长 24.2%，其中住宅销售额增长 23.4%；限额以上批发零售贸易企业汽车类零售额增长 56.1%，通讯器材类零售额增长 23.1%，文化办公用品类零售额增长 22.7%。

各类商品市场较快发展。年成交额在亿元以上的商品交易市场 486 家，成交额 5823.8 亿元。其中年成交额在 10－50 亿元的有 77 家，成交额 1471.1 亿元；年成交额在 50－100 亿元的有 15 家，成交额 1118.9 亿元；年成交额在 100 亿元以上的有 12 家，成交额 2098.7 亿元。新型流通业态以及现代经营方式均有较快发展。

六、开放型经济

对外贸易平稳较快增长。全年进出口总额 2840.0 亿美元，比上年增长 24.6%。其中，出口总额 1604.2 亿美元，增长 30.5%；进口总额 1235.8 亿美元，增长 17.7%。出口商品结构不断优化。机电产品、高新技术产品出口额占出口总额的比重分别为 69.4% 和 43.6%。其中计算机与通信技术出口 568.7 亿美元，占高新技术产品出口额的 81.3%，增长 31.0%。农产品出口额 12.2 亿美元，增长 33.1%。外商投资企业出口占出口总额的比重为 77.1%。私营企业出口较快增长，出口额为 165.3 亿美元，增长 63.2%。对欧盟、美国、日本、香港特别行政区的出口分别为 381.2 亿美元、363.8 亿美元、180.6 亿美元和 155.7 亿美元，增长 32.5%、33.5%、12.9% 和 14.5%；从东盟、韩国、台湾省进口额 171.8 亿美元、223.5 亿美元和 249.8 亿美元，增长 29.2%、3.0% 和 18.2%；对俄罗斯、拉丁美洲、非洲出口额 11.4 亿美元、53.4 亿美元和 26.9 亿美元，分别增长 49.4%、62.7% 和 47.6%。

表 4. 进出口贸易主要分类情况

指　　标	绝对数(亿美元)	比上年增长(%)
出口总额	1604.2	30.5
#一般贸易	531.5	30.8
加工贸易	1061.3	29.4
#工业制成品	1583.1	30.4
初级产品	21.1	33.5
#机电产品	1113.8	32.6
#高新技术产品	699.6	33.4
#外商投资企业	1236.2	31.2
国有企业	157.9	9.9
进口总额	1235.8	17.7
#一般贸易	282.7	10.1
加工贸易	740.2	14.1
#工业制成品	1121.9	17.8
初级产品	113.9	17.3
#机电产品	864.5	19.3
#高新技术产品	505.5	25.3
#外商投资企业	1074.0	18.7

利用外资水平和质量提高。全年新增工商注册外资企业 6541 家，新增工商注册协议外资 387.8 亿美元，比上年增长 93.9%；实际外商直接投资 174.3 亿美元，增长 32.3%。全省新批总投资 3000 万美元以上的大项目 214 个，9000 万美元以上大项目 53 个。全年服务业新批外商直接投资项目 1304 个，协议注册外资 97.4 亿美元，实际到帐外资 29.2 亿美元，分别增长 15.6%、28.8% 和 71.4%。

开发区加快向集约化发展方向转变。按业务管理口径统计，125 家开发区完成进出口总额 2095.7 亿美元，其中出口总额 1138.4 亿美元，占全省总量的 73.8% 和 70.9%；新批外商投资企业 3725 家，实际到帐注册外资额 138.8 亿美元，占全省总量的 79.6%。

“走出去”取得积极成效。全年新签对外承包工程和劳务合作合同金额 46.8 亿美元，增长 41.4%；完成营业额 43.5 亿美元，增长 36.2%；新派出人员 47882 人次，增长 8.4%；期末在外人数 112421 人，增长 12.1%。全年新批境外投资项目 222 个，中方协议投资3.32亿美元。

七、交通、邮电业和旅游业

全年交通运输仓储邮政业、电信和其他信息传输服务业实现增加值900.76亿元和384.15亿元,分别比上年增长10.7%和31.1%。

交通运输业发展较快。全年完成旅客运输量、货物运输量分别比上年增长11.1%和10.8%,旅客周转量、货物周转量增长11.9%和18.8%。完成港口货物吞吐量8.5亿吨,增长16.4%,其中外贸货物吞吐量1.35亿吨,增长18.2%。年末全省公路里程12.69万公里,新增3200公里;铁路营业里程1602.7公里,铁路正线延展长度2301.1公里。年末民用汽车保有量240.8万辆,增长25.3%;其中本年净增汽车48.55万辆,增长56.3%。年末私人汽车保有量148.37万辆,其中本年净增汽车38.94万辆,分别增长35.6%和24.7%。年末私人轿车保有量90.11万辆,其中本年净增轿车29.36万辆,分别增长48.3%和45.9%。

表5. 各种运输方式完成运输量

运输方式	货物周转量		货运量		旅客周转量		客运量	
	绝对数(亿吨公里)	比上年增长(%)	绝对数(万吨)	比上年增长(%)	绝对数(亿人公里)	比上年增长(%)	绝对数(万人)	比上年增长(%)
总 计	3644.6	18.8	125114.0	10.8	1366.8	11.9	161320.9	11.1
铁 路	497.2	3.5	5169.2	1.6	267.9	9.2	7288.7	9.5
公 路	542.1	18.1	84319.0	10.5	1062.6	12.1	153725.0	11.2
水 路	2515.1	22.3	32862.0	12.3	0.1	-5.4	27.0	-27.0
民 航	0.6	10.9	4.8	11.5	36.2	27.4	280.2	26.2
管 道	89.6	24.8	2759.0	23.4	—	—	—	—

邮电通信业较快增长。全年邮电业务总量997.16亿元,比上年增长36.8%。其中邮政业务总量62.54亿元,电信业务总量934.62亿元,分别增长18.1%和38.2%。邮电业务收入516.35亿元,比上年增长13.9%。其中邮政业务收入49.35亿元,电信业务收入467亿元,增长10.9%和14.2%。年末局用交换机总容量4578.68万门。年末固定电话用户3224.71万户,新增165.36万户;其中城市电话用户2226.34万户,乡村电话用户998.37万户。住宅电话用户2344.24万户,新增25.52万户。年末移动电话用户2847.61万户,新增297.18万户。全省电话普及率达80.4部/百人,比上年增加5.25部。长途光缆线路总长度2.64万公里,新增0.09万公里。年末互联网用户575.99万户。

国内国际旅游业稳定发展。全年国内旅游人数19935.8万人次,比上年增长15.7%;国内旅游收入2012.2亿元,增长23.8%。全年境外入境旅游人数445.2万人次,比上年增长17.7%,其中外国人314.9万人次,增长20.1%,港澳台同胞130.3万人次,增长12.2%。国际旅游外汇收入27.9亿美元,增长23.3%。旅行社组织公民自费出境旅游31.31万人次,增长21.8%。

八、财政、金融、证券和保险业

财政收入较快增长。全年实现地方财政一般预算收入1656.68亿元,增收334.01亿元,增长25.3%;基金收入731.9亿元,增长34.2%,一般预算收入加上基金收入、上划中央四税1547.29亿元,财政总收入为3935.87亿元(不含海关税收等612.28亿元),增长25.9%。税务部门征收的税收中,外商及港澳台投资企业、私营企业分别完成999.75亿元和570.93亿元,比上年增长26.0%和31.7%。

表6. 全年财政收入分项情况

指 标	绝对数(亿元)	比上年增长(%)
一般预算收入	1656.68	25.3
#增值税(25%)	329.43	24.0
营业税	431.81	26.0
企业所得税(40%)	220.87	24.3
个人所得税(40%)	81.73	23.5
契税	105.44	30.4
上划中央四税	1547.29	23.1
#国内消费税	114.72	16.1
增值税(75%)	988.30	24.0
基金预算收入	731.90	34.2
财政总收入(不含海关税收等)	3935.87	25.9

财政支出结构继续调整。一般预算支出 1987.59 亿元，增支 314.19 亿元，可比增长 15.2%；基金预算支出 705.52 亿元，增支 162.70 亿元，增长 30.0%。全年农林水气象支出 119 亿元，增长 22.0%；社会保障补助支出 80.84 亿元，增长 26.9%；医疗卫生支出 88.74 亿元，教育支出 297.96 亿元，科学支出 10.56 亿元，分别增长 18.2%、17.2% 和 32.8%；基本建设拨款 184.09 亿元，企业挖潜改造资金 71.65 亿元，行政管理费 229.37 亿元，分别增长 19.8%、13.1% 和 17.7%。

金融运行平稳。年末广义货币供应量（M2）余额、狭义货币供应量（M1）余额和流通中现金（M0）余额为 29024.09 亿元、11018.20 亿元和 3501.85 亿元，分别比上年增长 17.8%、21.7% 和 15.4%。年末全省金融机构人民币贷款余额 18485.02 亿元，比年初增加 3203.77 亿元，同比多增 1062.26 亿元；其中短期贷款增加 1471.44 亿元，同比多增 785.16 亿元。年末全省金融机构人民币存款余额 25860.47 亿元，比年初增加 3994.14 亿元，同比多增 375.46 亿元；其中，居民储蓄存款增加 1605.39 亿元，同比少增 112.51 亿元；企业存款增加 1517.18 亿元，同比多增 739.88 亿元。

表 7. 金融机构人民币存贷款情况

指 标	绝对数（亿元）	比上年增加（亿元）	比上年末增长（%）
年末各项存款余额	25860.47	3994.14	17.5
#企业存款	9011.29	1517.18	19.6
居民储蓄存款	12183.47	1605.39	15.1
年末各项贷款余额	18485.02	3203.77	20.1
#短期贷款	9281.57	1471.44	18.8
#工业贷款	3330.94	610.57	47.0
商业贷款	1117.73	122.09	12.5
农业贷款	745.92	98.79	10.9
私营企业及个体贷款	214.79	78.11	34.1
中长期贷款	7395.33	1705.48	30.0
#消费贷款	2131.48	475.71	31.5
#个人住房贷款	1802.09	438.26	31.8

证券市场加快发展。全省在境内外上市公司达到 138 家，新增 21 家。年末全省境内上市公司由上年末的 90 家增加到 99 家，在上海、深圳证券交易所筹集资金 51.92 亿元，其中通过发行股票筹集资金 26.25 亿元，分别比上年增加 35.24 亿元和 17.43 亿元。全年证券经营机构股票交易量 11612.86 亿元，期货经营机构代理交易量 17053.62 亿元，分别增长 197.6% 和 73.6%。境内上市公司总股本 391.99 亿股，比上年末增长 8.1%；市价总值 2595.17 亿元，增长 50.1%。年末共有证券营业部 208 家；期货经纪公司营业部 25 家；证券投资咨询机构 3 家。

保险事业发展平稳。全年保费收入 502.83 亿元，比上年增长 15.0%。其中，财产险收入 120.42 亿元，寿险收入 337.83 亿元，健康险和意外伤害险收入 44.58 亿元，分别增长 28.6%、9.5% 和 26.4%。赔付额 159.17 亿元，比上年增长 33.9%。其中财产险赔付 78.70 亿元，增长 47.7%；寿险赔付 64.36 亿元，增长 21.0%；健康险和意外伤害险赔付 16.11 亿元，增长 30.7%。

九、科学技术和教育

自主创新步伐加快。全省科学研究与技术开发机构 3889 个，其中政府部门属独立研究与开发机构 190 个，高等院校属科研机构 569 个，大中型工业企业办科研机构 1272 个。科技队伍迅速壮大，从事科技活动人员 36 万人，其中研究与发展人员 10.5 万人。拥有中国科学院和中国工程院院士 90 人。全省已建国家及省级高技术研究重点实验室、工程技术研究中心、科技公共服务平台 224 个，比上年增加 58 个。其中，重点研发机构 12 个。经国家认定企业技术中心 10 个。全年科技活动经费支出 725 亿元，增长 16.6%，其中研究与发展活动经费支出 330 亿元，占全省生产总值的 1.55%。全社会科技创新投入大幅度增长，省科技成果转化专项资金投入增长 60%。技术公共服务、技术成果交易、创新创业融资和社会化人才服务四大平台建设得到加强。

科学研究成果显著。全省有 28 项成果获国家科技奖，其中自然科学奖 3 项、发明奖 2 项、科技进步奖 23 项；省科技进步奖 180 项，其中一等奖 11 项、二等奖 49 项、三等奖 120 项。技术市场较为活跃，全年共签订各类技术合同 1.12 万项；技术合同成交额 119.53 亿元，增长 18.5%。知识产权工作取得明显进展，专利申请量跃居全国第二位，全年专利申请量 53267 件，比上年增长 53%，其中发明专利 10214 件，增长 55.2%；专利授权量 19352 件，增长 42.5%。

高新技术产业化进程加快。高新技术产业产值比上年增长 30.8%。组织实施省科技项目 2112 项，其中高技术研究及重大科技攻关项目 311 项、科技成果转化专项资金项目 83 项、火炬计划项目 603 项、星火计划项目 350 项。全省高新技术企业达 3397 家，新批国家高新技术企业 75 家，当年认定省级高新技术产品 1693 项，国家重点新产品 222 项。已建国家级高新技术特色产业基地 49 个，其中当年新建 4 个。新建国家级大学科技园 2 家。全省国家级和省级高新技术产业开发区实现技工贸总收入 11051.42 亿元，创汇 670.58 亿美元，分别比上年增长 28.5% 和 73.8%。

质量检验工作进一步加强。全省共有产品质量检验机构155个，国家检测中心9个；监督抽查产品132种，比上年上升11.7%。共有产品质量、体系认证机构7个，完成强制性产品认证的企业4400个；法定计量技术机构189个，强制检定计量器具401.67万台件，比上年增长12.9%；制定、修订地方标准287项，下降5.9%。

优先发展各级各类教育。全省共有普通高校119所，普通高等教育招生35.91万人，在校生130.62万人，毕业生25.73万人。研究生教育招生3.18万人，在校研究生8.91万人，毕业生1.93万人。高等教育毛入学率达35.6%。全省职业教育在校生达到145万人。初中毕业生升学率93.5%。小学学龄儿童入学率99.8%。特殊教育招生0.39万人，在校生3万人。幼儿园在园幼儿150.15万人。农村办学条件进一步改善，农村义务教育阶段学生学杂费全部免除。

表8. 各类教育招生和在校生情况(单位:万人)

指　标	招生数		在校生数		毕业生数	
	绝对数	比上年增加	绝对数	比上年增加	绝对数	比上年增加
研究生教育	3.18	0.31	8.91	1.12	1.93	0.44
普通高等教育	35.91	-0.24	130.62	14.64	25.73	2.76
中等职业教育	45.2	4.02	119.36	13.29	23.82	4.1
普通高中教育	53.69	1.44	152.57	7.23	44.97	2.32
普通初中教育	99.06	-6.24	318.71	-27.51	121.35	1.02
小学教育	63.75	1.82	455.75	-29.78	97.75	-7.7

十、文化、卫生和体育

文化事业和文化产业加快发展。扶持文化事业和文化产业发展，南京图书馆等一批文化重点项目相继建成或开工建设，公共文化服务体系、文化市场体系、文化创新体系建设取得新进展。文艺创作、广播影视、新闻出版和哲学社会科学事业取得新成绩。年末全省共有艺术表演团体127个，文化馆115个，公共图书馆103个，博物馆100个，档案馆170个，向社会开放档案216万卷(件)；共有广播电台14座，广播发射台和转播台21座，电视台14座，广播人口综合覆盖率和电视人口综合覆盖率分别达100%和99.9%。有线电视用户1227.72万户，比上年增长14%，其中农村有线电视用户新增130多万户。生产故事影剧片7部。全年报纸出版26.23亿份，比上年下降2.1%；期刊出版9065万册，增长3.7%；图书出版43918万册，增长3.2%。文化遗产保护工作得到加强。

卫生事业进一步加强。加大对农村卫生的扶持力度，改造乡镇卫生院，新型农村合作医疗人口覆盖率达到90.5%，培训农村医疗卫生技术和管理人员2.59万名；大力发展社区卫生服务，社区卫生服务覆盖城市居民65%。年末共有各类卫生机构16100个，其中医院、卫生院2504个，卫生防疫和防治机构203个，妇幼卫生保健机构109个。各类卫生机构拥有病床20.5万张，其中医院、卫生院病床18.94万张。共有卫生技术人员26.22万人，其中执业医师、执业助理医师11.06万人，注册护师8.28万人，卫生防疫和防治机构卫生技术人员0.75万人，妇幼卫生机构卫生技术人员0.4万人。乡镇卫生院0.14万个，床位5.3万张，卫生技术人员6万人，乡村医生和卫生员5.9万人。

体育事业蓬勃发展。全面实施万村体育健身工程，全省运动员在国内外重大赛事中取得优异成绩。在重大国际国内比赛中，获世界冠军15项，创世界纪录3项，创亚洲纪录3项；有33人次获金牌，29人次获银牌，40人次获铜牌。成功承办了第三届全国体育大会，顺利举办了第十六届全省运动会。

十一、环境保护和安全生产

环境保护工作力度加大。认真落实环保目标责任制，突出抓好重点行业和企业污染减排工作，以“三清一绿”为重点的环境整治工作完成年度目标。年末全省共有环境监测站609个，设立自然保护区38个，其中国家级自然保护区3个，自然保护区面积86.18万公顷。建成烟尘控制区171个，面积达0.35万平方公里；建成环境噪声达标区193个，面积为0.29万平方公里。城市污水集中处理率50%，比上年提高12.8个百分点。工业废水排放总量29.91亿吨，工业废气排放总量21206.4亿标立方，工业粉尘排放量31.86万吨。着力推进重点流域水污染防治、区域环境综合整治，“绿色江苏”和生态省建设取得重要进展，全省新增造林面积157.8万亩，全国首批6家国家生态市我省有4家，占全国的2/3。

全年发生各类事故42626起，死亡7634人，同比事故起数下降10.7%，死亡人数下降10.5%。亿元GDP生产安全事故死亡人数为0.35人，下降25.5%。

十二、人口、人民生活和社会保障

人口总量继续保持增长态势。全年人口出生率9.36‰，上升0.12个千分点；人口死亡率7.08‰，上升0.05个千分点；人口自然增长率2.28‰，上升0.07个千分点。年末全省常住人口7549.5万人，比上年末增加75万人。

人民生活水平继续提高。根据对5000户城镇住户的抽样调查，全年城镇居民人均可支配收入14084.26元，比上年增长14.3%，考虑物价因素，实际增长12.5%；人均消费性支出9628.59元，增长11.7%，其中食品支出占人均消费性支出的比重为36.0%。根据对3400户农村住户的抽样调查，全年农村居民人均纯收入5813元，比上年增长10.2%，考虑物价因素，实际增长8.4%；人均生活消费支出4135元，增长15.9%，其中食品支出占人均生活消费支出的比重为41.8%。城乡居民居住条件进一步改善。城镇居民人均住房建筑面积为29.68平方米，农村居民人均住房使用面积为40.8平方米。

社会保障覆盖面进一步扩大。城镇企业职工基本养老保险、基本医疗保险、失业保险参保人数分别增加107.4万人、147.7万人、62.6万人，覆盖面均达92%以上。在全省范围内调高了最低工资标准、企业退休人员基本养老金标准、优抚对象抚恤补助标准和城乡居民最低生活保障补助水平。切实帮助困难群众解决生产生活中的实际问题，省级社会保障支出和帮扶困难群众支出达到66.5亿元，增长37.7%。全省城乡“低保”实现全覆盖，141.5万困难群众实现应保尽保。年末全省参加城镇企业职工基本养老保险职工1059.67万人，参加基本养老保险的离退休人员301.97万人，参加基本医疗保险的职工933.3万人，参加基本医疗保险的退休人员338.5万人，参加失业保险职工901.1万人。城乡特困群众临时生活救助和医疗救助制度初步建立。新增敬老院床位2.7万张，农村五保户集中供养率达到55%左右。年末全省各类福利院拥有床位12.11万张，收养8.95万人；建立城镇各种社区服务设施24550个，其中社区服务中心528个；城乡居民最低生活保障对象143.44万人，筹集福利资金7.28亿元，接受社会捐赠3亿元。

注：本公报使用的数据为快报数。

STATISTICAL COMMUNIQUE OF JIANGSU PROVICE ON 2006 NATIONAL ECNOMIC AND SOCIAL DEVELOPMENT

Jiangsu Provincial Statistics Bureau
NBS Survey Office in Jiangsu
03/01 2007

2006 was the beginning year of the 11th five – year plan. Under the correct leadership of the Provincial Party Committee and the Government, people all over the province overall implemented the view point of scientific development, conscientiously carried out the policies of macro – control, while surrounded closely with the targets of enriching the people, strengthening the province and two "leading achievements" They also adheared to the leading development, scientific development and harmonious development; comprehensively arranged and pushed on all the tasks of reform, development and stability. Therefore new achievements and results were made in economic and social development. The construction of an all – round comfortable society leaped onto a new level. The targets, fomulated at the beginning of this year, were better fulfilled.

I General Survey

Jiangsu's economy kept a stable and faster growth. Preliminary statistics showed that the annual regional gross product reached 2154. 836 billion yuan, an increase of 14. 9% over 2005. Of this total, the added value of primary industry was 154. 490 billion yuan, increased by 5%; that of the secondary industry, 1218. 646 billion yuan, increased by 16%; tertiary industry, 781. 70 billion yuan, increased by 15. 5%. Per capita gross product was 28685 yuan (i. e. $ 3598, converted at current foreign exchange). New progresses were made in the readjustment of econmic structure and the change of economic growth mode. Added value of three industries recorded a ratio of 7. 5: 56. 5: 36. 3. Output value of new – high tech industries was 1037. 0 billion yuan, accounting for 24. 9% of the output value of the over – scale industry, 0. 7 percentage points higher than 2005. Added value of service industries (including serve for agriculture, forestry, animal hiusbandry and fishery) was 789. 452 billion yuan, increased by 15. 4% over 2005, accounting for 36. 5% of the gross product, 0. 8 percentage points higher than 2005. In ownership structure, added value of non – public owned economy accounted for 60. 9% of the gross product; in which the private and individual economy reached 35%, 1. 4 and 0. 8 percentage points higher than 2005. Obvious efficiency was made in the task of energy saving, consumption decreasing, and emission reducing of pollution. The environmental quality in part of cities and districts was improved in some extent. The level of urbanization had a further improvement, and reached 51. 9% by the end of 2006, 1. 4 percentage points higher than 2005. New progress was seen in industrial distribution. There was a good development pattern in the industrial belts along the Nanjing – Shanghai line, Yangtze River, east Long – Hai line and the sea. "Four transferring items" were further stressed, so as to push forward actively the construction of north – Jiangsu's development zones through the joint force of south and north areas. The growth range of some major indicators of north – Jiangsu and middle – Jiangsu was higher than the average level of the whole province.

The general level of market prices maintained basic stability. Annual consumer prices of residents rose by 1. 6%, the growth rang fell 0. 5 percentage points than 2005; retail prices rose by 0. 8%; purchasing prices of raw material, fuel and power, rose by 6. 4%; ex – factory prices of industrial products rose by 1. 5%; prices of means of agricultural production rose by 1. 7%.

Table 1. Consumer Price Increased Over Previous Year(%)

Item	Province	City	Countryside
Consumer Price	1. 6	1. 6	1. 7
Food	2. 6	2. 7	2. 6
Grain	3. 5	3. 7	3. 1
Tobacco, Liquor and Articals	-0. 1	-0. 3	0. 1
Clothing	0. 9	1. 1	0. 4
Household Facility Articals and services	1. 4	1. 6	1. 1
Medicine, Health Care and Individual Articals	1. 5	1. 2	2. 0
Means of Transportation and Telecommunication	-0. 4	-1. 3	1. 6
Recreation, Education, Cultural Articals and services	-0. 7	-0. 4	-1. 2
Residence	4. 5	4. 7	4. 1

The task of employment and reemployment continued to strengthen. By the end of 2006, there were 45. 6476 million persons employed in urban and rural area, an increase of 546. 4 thousand persons over 2005; 430. 4 thousand urban unemployment and laid off personnels were reemployed through various ways. By the end of 2006, the rate of registered unemployment in cities and towns was 3. 4%, 0. 2 percentage points lower than 2005. Newly increased rural transferring labor forces reached 626 thousand persons.

Various reforms were pushed forward step by step. There were new progresses in the reform of major fields and key links. The development circumstance continued to improved. The functions of social management and public service of the government were enhanced, phasic results were got in the reform of institutions in taking the function transferring of the government as the focus to deeply carry on the reform of administrative system. Reform and reorganization of state – owned enterprises were intensified. Reform of stock right putting divided of the state share holding listed corporation was basically fulfilled. The strength and driving force of state – owned capital were stressed. Mass – run enterprises developed rapidly. By the end of 2006, there were 600 thousand private enterprises registered in the industrial and commercial administrative departments, newly increased by 93 thousand households, with a total of 971. 707 billion yuan registered capital. There were 1. 8701 million households of self – employed laborers registered in industrial and commercial administrative departments. The innovation of finance and monetary was deeply pushed on. Centralized management was overall realized for the non – taxes income in the provincial level organs. The reform of rural credit cooperative continued to deepen. Bank of Jiangsu had begun to put into operation. The constitution of local stock system insurance corporation progressed smoothly. Comprehensive innovation in rural area was pushed on actively. Reform of experiment of township institutions, of rural compulsory education and of financial managent in counties and townships spread orderly.

The outstanding contradictions and problems existing in economic and social development were as follows: 1. There were more difficulties in agricultural development and the successively increasing of farmers' income. The course of agricultural industrialization was not fast. The level of rural public service was not favourable. The long – term effective machanism to increase the farmers' income successively had not yet established. 2. The contradiction of economic mix still was prominent, mainly expressed in: industrial structure was unreasonable; the capacity of brazing new trail in one's own hand was not strong; the ratio between investment and consumption was not coordinate enough; the proportion of service industry was on the low side, so did the extra value of industrial products. 3. The contradiction between economic development and resource environment became more acute; extensive growth mode had not yet changed fundamentally; there were more presure on resource environment; the task was very hard to complete the targets of energy saving and emission reducting of pollution, as well as the ecological environment protection during the period of 11th five year plan as scheduled. 4. The factors, which had effected the harmonious and stability, were still existing; the social development was still lagged behind the economic development; the masses of people were not satisfied with the treatment of pollution, stability of price, medical service, road and transportation and fees collection of educational departments. In addition, part of urban and rural residents still lived a poor life, and so on.

II Farming, Forestry, Animal Husbandry and Fishery

Agriculture developed stably. Owing to the seriously carrying out of a series of preferencial policies for supporting agriculture and the favourable climate condition, the output of grain increased, the agricultural efficiency expanded and the farmers' increased income maintained a fine momentum. In 2006, the annual total grain output reached 30. 4144 million tons, 2. 0685 million tons more than 2005, or an increase of 7. 3%. The total output of summer grain was 9. 3914 million tons, up by 11. 2%; that of the autumn grain, 21. 0230 million tons, up by 5. 6%. There was a change in the mix of farming cultivation. The cultivated area of grain was 4. 9851 million hectares, increased by 75. 6 thousand hectares; that of the cotton, oil – bearing crops reached 354. 9 thousand hectares and 812. 3 thousand hectares respectively, dropped by 13. 4 thousand hectares and 34. 6 thousand hectares. Cultivated area of vegetables was 1. 1736 million hectares, decreased by 1. 7%. Good quality, high efficiency, safety and ecological agriculture developed rapidly.

The production of forestry, animal husbandry and fishery was stable. Annual afforested area was 66. 5 thousand hectares. The output of most animal products kept the same level of that in 2005.

Total output of meat was 3. 4673 million tons, unbiased with 2005; of this total, pork, beef and mutton, 2. 4210 million tons; poulty, 1. 0371 million tons; eggs, 1. 8554 million tons, up by 1. 9%; total output of milk, 608. 1 thousand tons, up by 7. 4%. Annual total output of aquatic products was 4. 0545 million tons, up by 4. 3%. Of which, the output of fresh water products was 2. 8637 million tons, that of the marine products was 1. 1908 million tons, up by 4. 1% and 5. 0% respectively.

Table 2. Output of Major Farm Products

Item	Output(10000 tons)	Increased Over Previous Year(%)
Gain	38. 14	7. 3
Cotton	3041. 44	18. 2
Oil – Bearing Crops	218. 18	1. 0
Rapseeds	149. 40	–5. 8
Peanuts	66. 82	20. 5
Silkworm Cocoons	12. 56	18. 6
Tea	1. 34	11. 5
Fresh Fruits(Including Melon Fruits)	210. 02	3. 9
Meat	346. 73	unbiased
Aquatic Products	405. 45	4. 3

The adjustment of rural industrial structure continued to accelerate. Output value of rural industry, construction, transportation, wholesale and retailsale trade, and catering industry accounted for above 90% in the rural total output value. In Jiangsu, the area of effective irrigated farm land reached 3. 804 million hectares; newly increased area of water – saving irrigeted farm land was 38. 8 thousand hectares. By the end of 2006, the aggregated power of farm machinery was 32. 79 million kilowatts, increased by 4. 6% over 2005.

There was a good start in the construction of new socialist village. The agricultural input was expanded, so as to promote the rural development. In 2006, expenditure for agriculture, countryside and the farmer arranged by the provincial finance reached 18. 1 billion yuan, up by 20.4%. The implementation of a new round rural five reality affairs project was started, such as 11 thousand kilometers of rural highways were built; 1050 large and medium bridges on the rural highways were newly built and replaced; 2790 thousand rural labor forces training was fulfilled; also achievements were found in the transformation of township commune hospitals; in the construction of rural comprehensive cultural stations and the treatment of environment in taking the "three clear and one green" as the focal point. The condition of rural production and livelihood was further improved.

Ⅲ Industry and Construction

Industrial production kept a faster growth. The industrial added value in 2006 was 1104.752 billion yuan, increased by 16.6% over 2005. The added value of over – scale industrial enterprises was 1101.512 billion yuan, grew by 21.4%. The added value of light and heavy industry was 328.317 and 673.195 billion yuan, up by 18.4% and 22.9% respectively. The added value of state shareholding industry was 154.851 billion yuan, grew by 14.5%; of which the state – owned industry was 68.085 billion yuan, grew by 15.5%. The added value of collective industry was 44.465 billion yuan, up 21.2%; that of the private industry, 267.125 billion yuan, up by 24.2%; shareholding system industry, 426.631 billion yuan, up by 20.6%. The added value of foreign, HongKong, Macao and Taiwan invested industry was 399.428 billion yuan, up by 22.8%. Added value of large and medium—sized industry was 596.922 billion yuan, up by 16.5%.

The emerging and high tech industry showed a faster growth. Jiangsu adheared to take the road of new type industrialization. Development level of modern manufacturing industry was further improved. In Jiangsu, the output value of communication equipment, computer and other electronic equipment manufacturing industry was 631.672 billion yuan, went up by 19.0%; that of the chemical raw material and chemical products, 396.700 billion yuan, up by 25.4%; textile industry, 367.494 billion yuan, up by 18.0%; smelting and pressing ferrous metals industry, 372.861 billion yuan, up by 24.7%; ordinary equipment industry, 258.864 billion yuan, up by 30.6%; electrical machinery and equipment industry, 298.496 billion yuan, up 35.8%. The product mix continued to optimize. Output value of new industrial products was 302.304 billion yuan, increased by 42.0% over 2005. Output of most major industrial products kept increasing. Of the 75 major industrial products that were listed in statistics, the output of 58 products remained expanding, while 17 products dropped.

Table 3. Output of Major Industrial Products

Item	Unit	Output	Increased Over 2005(%)
Yarn	10^4 tons	350.56	13.9
Cloth	10^8 meters	64.95	15.5
Chemical Fiber	10^4 tons	665.14	15.9
Cigarettes	10^8 pieces	845.41	3.6
Color TV sets	10^4 sets	248.25	-27.4
Refrigerators	10^4 units	408.80	10.0
Air Conditioners	10^4 units	473.29	-7.5
Coal	10^4 tons	3047.53	8.1
Crude Oil	10^4 tons	188.49	3.2
Electricity	10^8 kWh	2216.40	19.7
Steel	10^4 tons	4202.31	23.3
Rolled – Steel	10^4 tons	5816.26	26.3
Ten Kinds of Nonferrous Metals	10^4 tons	31.89	-2.2
Cement	10^4 tons	10880.77	13.9
Sulphuric Acid	10^4 tons	403.21	13.6
Caustic Ash	10^4 tons	247.23	11.6
Ethylene	10^4 tons	140.17	25.5
Chemical Fertilizers(100% effectiveness)	10^4 tons	254.66	5.7
Motor Vehicales	10^4 units	27.48	-9.8
Cars	10^4 units	14.60	0.2
Generated Equipments	10^4 RW	372.45	-8.2
Integrated Circuit	10^4 pieces	1146504.00	36.6
program controlling switchboard	10^4 lines	11.94	-76.1
Mini Electronic Computer	10^4 sets	4712.14	62.7
Mobil Telecommunication Equipments	10^4 circuits	503012.00	163.5
Opitical Communication Equipments	10^4 sets	2.06	29.1

The performance quality and results of industrial economy was improved. In Jiangsu, the product sales revenue of over – scale industrial enterprises was 4103.019 billion yuan, grew by 26.1% over 2005; the rate of product sales was 98.5%, 0.4 percentage points higher than 2005. In 2006, 315.715 billion yuan of profits and taxes were realized, went up by 31.3; of which profits were 190.183 billion yuan, went up by 36.5%. The scope of loss – making enterprises was 11.9%, dropped by 1.7 percentage points; deficits value was

14. 843 billion yuan, decreased by 8. 4%. The compehensive index of industrial economy results was 189. 98, up 17. 6 percentage points.

Construction industry developed rapidly. 2006 in Jiangsu, the added value of construction industry was 113. 894 billion yuan, grew by 10. 5%. 30. 173 billion yuan of gross profits and taxes were competed by construction enterprises, went up by 19. 4%. The whole staff labor productivity was 140 thousand yuan/person, grew 8. 5%. Annual total output value of construction industry reached 515. 448 billion yuan, an increase of 18. 1%. Output value of completed projects recorded 387. 857 billion yuan, up 13. 7%; the completion rate was 75. 2%. The floor space of housing under construction by construction enterprises was 606. 1716 million square meters, rose by 19. 5%; the floor space of housing completed was 281. 3896 million square meters, rose by 7. 7%. Of this total, the residence was 156. 8996 million square meters, rose by 9. 1%.

Ⅳ Investment in Fixed Assets

Investment in fixed assets expanded stably. The completed total investment in fixed assets in 2006 was 1006. 365 billion yuan, increased by 20. 3% over 2005. Of which, investment in cities was 747. 37 billion yuan, up by 20. 2%; in rural area was 258. 995 billion yuan, up by 20. 7%. Among the total investment, investment completed by state and state shareholing economy was 252. 837 billion yuan; down by 0. 3%; by foreign, HongKong, Macao and Taiwan invested economy was 172. 758 billion yuan, up 16%; by mass – run economy was 580. 77 billion yuan, rose by 33. 8%; in mass – run economy, investment by private and individual economy was 311. 067 billion yuan, rose by 36. 6%. The proportion of mass – run investment in total investment was 57. 7%, 5. 8 percentage points higher than that in 2005.

Investmet structure was further optimized. In cities and towns, investment for primary industry was 1. 545 billion yuan, rose by 21. 9% over 2005; for secondary industry was 343. 908 billion, rose by 22. 3%; for tertiary industry was 401. 917 billion yuan, rose by 18. 4%. Industrial investment was 339. 117 billion yuan, rose by 22. 2%. Of this total, investment in communication equipment, computer and other electronical equipment manufacturing industry was 47. 214 billion yuan; in transportation equipment manufacturing industry was 19. 771 billion yuan; in ordinary equipment manufacturing industry was 24. 859 billion yuan; grew by 50. 4%, 40. 7% and 56. 2% respectively. Of the total investment in tertiary industry, real estate development took 190. 101 billion yuan, grew by 23%; transportation, storage and post took 54. 851 billion yuan, grew by 2. 5%; water conservancy, enviroment and public facilities management took 67. 325 billion yuan, grew by 17%; education took 13. 996 billion yuan, grew by 5. 6%; public health, social security and social welfare took 5. 622 billion yuan, up 39. 2%. However, the investment in major controlled industries dropped sharply. Among the total urban investment, iron and steel industry was 13. 071 billion yuan, dropped by 17. 5%; cement industry was 2. 476 billion yuan, dropped by 13. 2%; textile industry was 27. 387 billion yuan, grew by 31. 5%, but the growth range dropped by 15. 6 pecentage points.

Construction of major infrastructure and other industrial items was reinforced. Highway along the sea, Nanjing – Huai'an and Yancheng – Xuzhou express ways were completed and put into traffic. Newly expanded express ways reached 469 kilometers. Total length of express ways in operation reached 3355 kilometers accumulately. The internet was first unimpeded in China. Water ways transportation developed rapidly. Investment in the construction of harbour and channel went up by 83. 1% and 66. 1% respectively. In Jiangsu, the container traffic volume reached 4. 24 million standardized boxes, increased by 38. 8%. The project of water way flowing to the sea from the Huaihe River was overall completed. In addition, the contruction of the South – North Water Transmission project eastern line first phase; a new round treatment of Huaihe River; major sea wall target hitting; Beijing – Hangzhou canal expanding; Suzhou – Nantong Yangtze River bridge; Nanjing Yangtze River crossing turnel; Nanjing No. 2 metro line ect. all progressed smoothly. A group of major industrial intems such as Wuxi Hailis integrated circuit, Kunshan Longtun photoelectricity were completed and put into production.

Obvious achievements were made in the investment of fixed assets. Annual urban investment in fixed assets completed and put into production reached 7337 items; the rate of completion and put into production reached 53. 2%; newly increased fixed assets came to 573. 02 billion yuan, the rate of availability of such assets reached 76. 7%.

Ⅴ Domestic Trade

Consumer goods market was stable and tending to brisk. Annual total retail sales of consumer goods was 622. 318 billion yuan, up by 16. 2% over 2005. Analysed by urban and rural markets, the ratail sales in cities was 482. 293 billion yuan, rose by 17. 1%. On the other hand, sales on the rural market was 180. 025 billion yuan, rose by 13. 7%. In terms of industries, retail sales from wholesale and retail trade was 581. 578 billion yuan, rose by 15. 9%; from accommodation and catering industry was 74. 651 billion yuan, rose by 18. 0%; from other industries was 6. 089 billion yuan, rose by 19. 6%. The management of above designated – size wholesale and retail trade enterprises was in a good condition. Annual total sales value of commodities was 641. 797 billion yuan, grew by 12. 6% over 2005; of this total, that of the wholesale trade was 457. 595 billion yuan, while the retail trade was 184. 202 billion yuan, grew by 6. 8% and 30. 1%. Carazy consumption, represented by residence, motor vehicale, information, communication and tourism, remained a faster growth; the consumptive structure of residents upgraded rapidly. Annual sales value of commercial houses grew by 24. 2%; of which the residence sales value grew by 23. 4%, The retail sales value of motor vehicles from above designated wholesale and retail trade enterprises grew by 56. 1%; that of the communication equipments, increased by 23. 1%; cultural articals and stationery for the use of handling official business, increased by 22. 7%.

Various commodity markets developed rapidly. There were 486 commodity transaction markets, each with more than 100 million yuan of annual transaction value, whose annual total transaction value ammounted to 582. 38 billion yuan. Of these total markets, there were 77 ones, each with more than 1 – 5 billion yuan of annual transaction value, whose annual total transaction value ammounted to

147. 11 billion yuan; 15 ones, each with more than 5 – 10 billion yuan of annual transaction value, whose annual total transaction value reached 111. 89 billion yuan; 12 ones, each with more than 10 billion yuan of annual transaction value, whose annual total transaction value reached 209. 87 billion yuan. New type circulation form and modern management pattern both recorded a faster development.

VI Opening Oriented Economy

Foreign trade appeared a stable and faster development. Annual import and export volume totalled 284. 0 billion US dollars, rose by 24. 6% over 2005. The total value of export was 160. 42 billion US dollars, rose by 30. 5%, and the total value of import was 123. 58 billion US dollars, rose by 17. 7%. The commodity structure of the export was optimized continuously. The proportion of electromechanical products and new – high tech products in the total export accounted for 69. 4% and 43. 6% respectively. Of which, the export of computer and communication technological equipment was 56. 87 billion US dollars, accounting for 81. 3% of the total export value of new – high tech products, grew by 31. 0%. Export value of the agricultural products reached 1. 22 billion US dollars, increased by 33. 1%. Export value of foreign invested enterprises accounted for 77. 1% in the total export value. Export of private enterprises expanded rapidly, with the export value of 16. 53 billion US dollars, grew by 63. 2%. Export to EU, America, Japan, HongKong Special Administrative region was 38. 12, 36. 38, 18. 06 and 15. 57 billion US dollars respectively, rose by 32. 5%, 33. 5%, 12. 9% and 14. 5%. Import from the Association of Southeast Asian Nations, South Korea and our Taiwan province reached 17. 18, 22. 35, 24. 98 billion US dollars, respectively, increased by 29. 2%, 3. 0% and 18. 2%. Export to Russia, Latin America, Africa reached 1. 14, 5. 34 and 2. 69 billion US dollars, increased by 49. 4%, 62. 7% and 47. 6%.

Table 4. Imports and Exports by Major Type of Trade, Category and Ownership

Item	Absolute Value (100 million US dollars)	Increased Over 2005 (%)
Total Export	1604. 2	30. 5
#General Trade	531. 5	30. 8
Processing Trade	1061. 3	29. 4
#Manufactured Goods	1583. 1	30. 4
Primary Goods	21. 1	33. 5
#Electromechanical Goods	1113. 8	32. 6
#High – New Tech Goods	699. 6	33. 4
#Foreign Invested Enterprises	1236. 2	31. 2
State – Owned Enterprises	157. 9	9. 9
Total Import	1235. 8	17. 7
#General Trade	282. 7	10. 1
Processing Trade	740. 2	14. 1
#Manufactured Goods	1121. 9	17. 8
Primary Goods	113. 9	17. 3
#Electromechanical Goods	864. 5	19. 3
#High – New Tech Goods	505. 5	25. 3
#Foreign Invested Enterprises	1074. 0	18. 7

The level and quality of foreign capital utilization were upgraded. In 2006, the number of newly increased foreign enterprises, registered in the commericial and industrial administrative departments was 6541, with newly increased 38. 78 billion US dollars of foreign capital agreements, rose by 93. 9% over 2005. The actual foreign direct investment was 17. 43 billion US dollars, rose by 32. 3%. In Jiangsu, the number of newly approved large items was 214, each item with a total of over 30 million US dollars investment; so did there were 53 large items, each item with a total of over 90 million US dollars investment. 1304 foreign direct investment projects for service industry were approved; the agreement of registered foreign capital reached 9. 74 billion US dollars; the actually booked foreign capital was 2. 92 billion US dollars, increased by 15. 6%, 28. 8% and 71. 4%.

Development zones were accelerated to expand in an intensive direction. Total import and export value of 125 development zones was 209. 57 billion US dollars, counted in accordance with the business management standard; of which, the export value was 113. 84 billion US dollars, accounting for 73. 8% and 70. 9% of Jiangsu's total. The newly approved foreign invested enterprises were 3725, the actually booked and registered foreign capital recorded 13. 88 billion US dollars, accounting for 79. 6% of Jiangsu's total.

Active results were got in "going out". Annual newly signed contracts of foreign project and labor service cooperation were 4. 68 billion US dollars, up by 41. 4%; a turnover of 4. 35 billion US dollars was completed, up by 36. 2%. Newly dispatched out personnels were 4788. 7 person – times, up by 8. 4%. By the end of 2006, there were 112421 persons working abroad, up by 12. 1%. Newly approved overseas projects were 222 units, 332 million US dollars of agreed investment belonged to China.

Ⅶ Transportation, Post and Telecommunication Services and Tourism

The annual added value of transportation, storage, post and telecommunication plus other information transmission services was 90. 076 billion yuan and 38. 415 billion yuan, went up by 10. 7% and 31. 1% over 2005 respectively.

A faster development was seen in transportation. In 2006, the volume of passenger traffic and freight traffic increased by 11. 1% and 10. 8% respectively over 2005. The turnover volume of passenger and freight traffic increased by 11. 9% and 18. 8%. The volume of cargo handled at harbours was 850 million tons, up by 16. 4%, of which 135 million tons was completed by foreign trade, up by 18. 2%. By the end of 2006, the length of high ways in operation was 126. 9 thousand kilometers, newly increased by 3200 kilometers. The length of railways in operation was 1602. 2 kilometers. The length of main railways extended 2301. 1 kilometers. By the end of 2006, the number of possession of civil vehicles was 2. 408 million units, rose by 25. 3%; of which 485. 5 thousand was netly expanded in 2006, rose by 56. 3%. By the end of 2006, the number of possession of private vehicles was 1. 4837 million units; of which, 389. 4 thousand was netly increased in this year, up by 35. 6% and 24. 7% respectively. By the end of 2006, the number of possession of private sedans was 901. 1 thousand units; of which, 293. 6 thousand was netly increased in 2006, up by 48. 3% and 45. 9%.

Table 5. Total Volume of Traffic by Various Means of Transportation

Means of Transportation	Turnover Volume of Freight Traffic		Volume of Freight Traffic		Turnover Volume of Passenger Traffic		Volume of Passenger Traffic	
	Absolute Volume (100 million ton kms)	+ - % over 2005	Absolute Volume (10000 tons)	+ - % over 2005	Absolute Volume (100 million person kms)	+ - % over 2005	Absolute Volume (10000 persons)	+ - % over 2005
Total	3466. 6	18. 8	125114. 0	10. 8	1366. 8	11. 9	161320. 9	11. 1
Railway	479. 2	3. 5	5169. 2	1. 6	267. 9	9. 2	7288. 7	9. 5
Highway	542. 1	18. 1	84319. 0	10. 5	1062. 6	12. 1	153725. 0	11. 2
Waterway	2515. 1	22. 3	32862. 0	12. 3	0. 1	-5. 4	27. 0	-27. 0
Civil Aviation	0. 6	10. 9	4. 8	11. 5	36. 2	27. 4	280. 2	26. 2
Pipeline	89. 6	24. 8	2759. 0	23. 4	—	—	—	—

Post and telecommunication service industry expanded rapidly. The annual total business volume was 99. 716 billion yuan, went up by 36. 8%; that of the postal service was 6. 254 billion yuan; while the telecommunication service was 93. 462 billion yuan, grew by 18. 1% and 38. 2%. The business income of post and telecommunication was 51. 635 billion yuan, 13. 9% increase over 2005; that of the post was 4. 935 billion yuan, telecommunication was 46. 7 billion yuan, up by 10. 9% and 14. 2%. By the end of 2006, the total office switchboard capacity was 45. 7868 million sets. By the end of 2006, the fixed telephone users reached 32. 2471 million households, newly increased by 1. 6536 million; in which, the urban users were 22. 2634 million households, rural users were 9. 9837 million users. Residence telephone users were 23. 4424 million households, newly expanded by 252. 2 thousand. By the end of 2006, mobile telephone users reached 28. 4761 million households, newly increased by 2. 9718 million. The popularized rate of telephone in Jiangsu was 80. 4 sets/100 persons, increased by 5. 25 sets over 2005. Total length of long - distance optical circuit ammounted to 26. 4 thousand kilometers, newly extended by 900 kilometers. By the end of 2006, there were 5. 7599 million internet users.

Domestic and international tourism developed stably. In 2006, the number of domestic tourists was 199. 358 million person times, went up by 15. 7% over 2005. Revenue from domestic tourism reached 201. 22 billion yuan, went up by 23. 8%. The number of overseas tourists entering to Jiangsu was 4452 thousand person times, up by 17%; of which, foreigners, 3149 thousand person times, up by 20. 1%; HongKong, Macao and Taiwan compotriots, 1. 303 million person times, up by 12. 2%. Foreign exchange income earning from international tourism reached 2. 79 billion US dollars, up by 23. 3%. The number of tourists, with one's own expense and organized by the travel service to go abroad, was 313. 1 thousand person times, up by 21. 8%.

Ⅷ Government Financing, Banking, Securities and Insurance

A fast increasing was found in the government financial revenue. Annual local general budgetary revenue reached 165. 668 billion yuan, rose by 33. 401 billion yuan, or grew by 25. 3%; foundation revenue was 73. 19 billion yuan, grew by 34. 2%; general budgetary revenue plus foundation revenue and turnover to the central government four taxes reached 154. 729 billion yuan, the total financial revenue was 393. 587 billion yuan (excluded 61. 228 billion yuan of tariff of customs) rose by 25. 9%. Among the tax revenue collected by tax department from foreign, HongKong, Macao and Taiwan invested enterprises and private enterprises reached 99. 975 billion yuan and 57. 093 billion yuan respectively, rose by 26. 0% and 31. 7% over 2005.

Table 6. Annual Financial Revenue by Items

Item	Absolute Volume (100 million yuan)	Increased Over 2005 (%)
General Budgetary Revenue	1656. 68	25. 3
Added Value Tax(25%)	329. 43	24. 0
Run Tax	431. 81	26. 0
Enterprises Income Tax(40%)	220. 87	24. 3
Individual Income Tax(40%)	81. 73	23. 5
contracted Tax	105. 44	30. 4
Turnover to the central Government Four Taxes	1547. 29	23. 1
Taxes on Domestic Consumption	114. 72	16. 1
Added Value Tax(75%)	988. 30	24. 0
Foundation Budgetary Revenue	731. 90	34. 2
Total Financial Revenue(excluded tariffs of customs ect.)	3935. 87	25. 9

The structure of financial expenditure continued to improve. The general budgetary expenditure was 198. 759 billion yuan, increased by 31. 419 billion yuan, a comparable increase of 15. 2%; foundation budgetary expenditure was 70. 552 billion yuan, increased by 16. 270 billion yuan, or grew by 30%. The annual expenditure for agriculture, forestry, water conservancy and meteorology was 11. 9 billion yuan, grew by 22. 0%; for social security subsidy, 8. 084 billlion yuan, grew by 26. 9%; for medical service and health care, 8. 874 billion yuan, for education, 29. 796 billion yuan; for science, 1. 056 billion yuan, grew by 18. 2%, 17. 2% and 32. 8% respectively. Expenditure for capital construction allocation was 18. 409 billion yuan; for tapping potentialities and transformation of the enterprises, 7. 165 billion yuan; for adminstrative expense, 22. 937 billion yuan, increased by 19. 8%, 13. 1% and 17. 7% respectively.

The monetary performance was stable. By the end of 2006, the balance on currency supply in broad sense(M_2), in narrow sense (M_1) and in cash of circulation (M_0) reached 2902. 409 billion yuan, 1101. 820 billion yuan and 350. 185 billion yuan, increased by 17. 8%, 21. 7% and 15. 4% over the end of 2005 respectively. By the end of 2006, the balance on loans of RMB in monetary organizations of Jaingsu was 1848. 502 billion yuan, an increase of 320. 377 billion yuan over the beginning of 2006, the increased value was 106. 226 billion yuan more than the same period of 2005. Of the total loans balance, the short term loans increased by 147. 144 billion yuan, the increased value was 78. 516 billion yuan more than the same period of 2005. By the end of 2006, the balance on deposits in monetary organizations of Jiangsu was 2586. 047 billion yuan, an increase of 399. 414 billion yuan over the beginning of 2006, the increased value was 37. 546 billion yuan more than the same period of 2005. Of this total deposits balance, the residents' saving deposits increased by 160. 539 billion yuan, but the increased value was 11. 251 billion yuan less than the same period of 2005, while the deposits of enterprises increased by 151. 718 billion yuan, the increased value was 73. 988 billion yuan more than the same period of 2005.

Table 7. Deposits and Loans Balance(RMB) of Monetary Organizations

Item	Absolute Volume (100 billion *yuan*)	Increased Over the End of 2005	
		Volume Added (100 million *yuan*)	Growth Rate (%)
Year End Deposits Balance	25860. 47	3994. 14	17. 5
#Deposits of Enterprises	9011. 29	1517. 18	19. 6
Saving Deposits	12183. 47	1605. 39	15. 1
Year End Loans Balance	18485. 02	3203. 77	20. 1
#Short - term Loans	9281. 57	1471. 44	18. 8
#Industrial Loans	3330. 94	610. 57	47. 0
Commercial Loans	1117. 73	122. 09	12. 5
Agricultural Loans	745. 92	98. 79	10. 9
Loans for Private Enterprises and Individuals	214. 79	78. 11	34. 1
Medium - term and Long - term Loans	7395. 33	1705. 48	30. 0
#Loans for Consumption	2131. 48	475. 71	31. 5
#Individual Housing Loans	1802. 09	438. 26	31. 8

The development of securities market was accelerated. There were 138 listed firms on stock market within or out of Jiangsu province, newly increased by 21 firms. By the end of 2006, the listed firms on stock market in Jiangsu went up from 90 ones in the end of 2005 to 99 ones, which had collected 5.192 billion yuan of funds from Shanghai and Shenzhen securities exchanges; in this collected funds, 2.625 billion yuan were collected by issuing the stock, increased by 3.524 billion yuan and 1.743 billion yuan over 2005. The annual transaction volume of stocks by the securities managerial organizations was 1161.286 billion yuan; that of completed by the futures organizations was 1705.362 billion yuan through agency, went up by 197.6% and 73.6% respectively. The total equity capital of the listed firm on stock markets within Jiangsu reached 39.199 billion shares, up by 8.1% over the end of 2005, with a total value (market price) of 259.517 billion yuan, up by 50.1%. By the end of 2006, there were altogether 208 securities managerial departments, 25 business offices of futures broker companies and 3 insultation organizations for investment.

Insurance cause developed stably. The annual premium revenue totalled 50.283 billion yuan, went up by 15.0% over 2005. Of which, property insurance was 12.042 billion yuan; life insurance, 33.783 billion yuan; health care and accidential injury insurance, 4.458 billion yuan, increased by 28.6%, 9.5% and 26.4% repectively. The case of indemnity was 15.917 billion yuan, increased by 33.9% over 2005. Of which, property insurance was 7.87 billion yuan, rose by 47.7%, life insurance, 6.436 billion yuan, rose by 21.0%; health care and accidential injury insurance 1.611 billion yuan, rose by 30.7%.

Ⅸ Science, Technology and Education

The step of brazing new trails in one's own hand was accelerated. In Jiangsu, there were 3889 scientific research and technological development institutions. Among which, 190 were independent research and development institutions under the government departments; 569 were scientific research institutions under the colleges and universities; 1272 were scientific research institutions run by the large and medium - sized enterprises. Scientific and technical personnel grew in size quickly. There were 360 thousand persons engaged in scientific and technical activities; of whom, 105 thousand were research and development personnels. Jiangsu held 90 academicians of the Academy of Science of China and the Academy of Engineering of China. In whole province, 224 national and provincial level items, including the high technical research major laboratories, engineering technical research centres, scientific and technical public service platefroms had been established, rose by 58 ones over 2005; of which, 12 were major research and development institutions. 10 technical centres of enterprises were affirmed by the state. The annual expenditure for scientific and technical activities was 72.5 billion yuan, rose by 16.6%; of which expenditure for research and development activities were 33.0 billion yuan, accounting for 1.55% of Jiangsu's gross product. The input for brazing new trails in science and technology of the whole society expanded in a big margin. The input of special funds for the transferring of scientific and technical achievement increased by 60%. The construction of four large platforms such as the technical public service, technical result transaction, financing for brazing new trails and pioneering work, and socialized service for talents was intensified.

Remarkable achievements were made in scientific research. In whole province, the national scientific and technical prizes were won by 32 achievements; of which, 3 were natural science prizes, 2 were invention prizes, 23 were scientific and technical progress prizes. Provincial scientific & technical progress prizes were won by 180 achievements; of which, 11 were first class, 49 were second class, 120 were third class. The technical market became more brisk. In 2006, 11.2 thousand various technical contracts were signed, with 11.953 billion yuan of transaction value, grew by 18.5%. Significant progress was shown in the work of protection on intellectural property rights. The volume of patent application jumped up to the second place in China. 53627 patent applications were applied for in 2006, up by 53% over 2005; of which, 10214 were invention patents, grew by 55.2%; 19352 patent applications were authorized, grew by 42.5%.

The course of high - new tech industridization was accelerated. Output value of high - new tech industries grew by 30.8%. 2112 provincial scientific and technical items were organized and implemented, including 311 high tech research and tackling key projects of science and technology; 83 special funds items for the transferring of scientific and technical achievements; 603 "touch plan" as well as 350 "spark plan" items. There were 3397 high - new tech enterpries throughout the province; 75 national high - new enterprises were newly approved; 1693 provincial high - new tech products and 222 national major new products were affirmed in 2006. 49 state grade industrial bases with high - new tech characteristies had been set up; of which 4 were set up in 2006. 2 state grade scientific and technical parks of the universities were newly established. In Jiangsu, 1105.124 billion yuan of gross revenus and 67.058 billion US dollars of foreign exchanges were realized by the state and provincial grade high - new tech industrial development zones from technology, industry and trade, grew by 28.5% and 73.8% respectively over 2005.

The task of quality inspection was further stressed. There were 155 product quality examining institutions, 9 national inspection centres; 132 categories of product were selectly examined under supervision, 11.7% more than 2005. There were altogether 7 product quality and system attesting institutions, 4400 enterprises fulfilled the product compulsory attestation. There were 189 legal calculating technical institutions; 4.0167 million sets of utensiles were tested through compulsion, rose by 12.9% over 2005; 287 local classification of various types were formulated or amended, a decrease of 5.9%.

Priority development was given for various levels and categories education. In Jiangsu, there were 119 regular institutions of higher education, which took in 359.1 thousand students, the number of total enrolled students reached 1.3062 million, and the graduates reached 257.3 thousand. The enrollment of the postgraduates was 31.8 thousand, the number of total enrolled students reached 89.1 thousand, and the graduates reached 19.3 thousand. The gross rate of graduates from senior secondary school entering into the higher educational institutions was 35.6%. There were 1.45 million students studying in professional schools. The rate of graduates from junior secondary school entering into the senior secondary schools was 93.5%. The enrollment rate of primary school age children was 99.8%. Special education took in 3900 students, with a total of 30 thousand students studying in the schools. There were 1.5015 million children in kindergartens. The condition of running the rural schools was further inproved. The tuition and other sundry fees were all free of charge for the students in the stage of rural compulsory education.

Table 8. Enrollments and the Total Number of Students of Various Education (10000 persons)

Item	Enrollments		Total Number of Students		Graduates	
	Absolute Number	+ - Over 2005	Absolute Number	+ - Over 2005	Absolute Number	+ - Over 2005
Post Graduate Education	3. 18	0. 31	8. 91	1. 12	1. 93	0. 44
University and College Education	35. 91	-0. 24	130. 62	14. 64	25. 73	2. 76
Secondary Professional Education	45. 2	4. 02	119. 36	13. 29	23. 82	4. 1
Regular Senior Middle Education	53. 69	1. 44	152. 57	7. 23	44. 97	2. 32
Regular Junior Middle Education	99. 06	-6. 24	318. 71	-27. 51	121. 35	1. 02
Primary School	63. 75	1. 82	455. 75	-29. 78	97. 75	-7. 7

X Culture, Public Health and Sports

The development of cultural undertakings and cultural industry was accelerated. In order to support the development of cultral undertakings and cultural industry, a group of major cultural items, including Nanjing laboratory and other projects had built up or begun to construct one after another. New progress was seen in the construction of public cultural service system, cultural market system and cultural new creation system. New achievements were made in literary and artistic creation, broadcasting, film & television, news publication, philosophy and social science. By the end of 2006, there were 127 art performing groups, 115 cultural stations, 103 public labraries, 100 museums, 170 archives, from where 2. 16 million volume(piece) files were opened to public. There were 14 broadcasting stations, 21 transmitting and relaying stations, 14 television stations. The comprehensive population coverage rate of broadcasting and television reached 100% and 99. 9%. There were 12. 2772 million cable television users, grew by 14% over 2005; of which, rural cable television users were more than 1. 3 million. Jiangsu produced 7 feature movies and issued 2. 623 billion copies of newspapers, down by 2. 1%; 90. 65 million copies of periodicals, grew by 3. 7%; 439. 18 million copies of books, grew by 3. 2%. The task of cultural inheritance protection was strengthened.

Public health undertaking was further enhanced. Jiangsu enlarged the supporting momentum for rural public health and engaged in the reform of rural commune hospital. The population coverage rate of new type rural cooperative medical service reached 90. 5%. 25. 9 thousand rural medical & health technicians and managerial personnels were trained. Also, the medical service of community was developed with great effort. the urban resident coverage rate of medical service of community was 65%. By the end of 2006, there were 16. 1 thousand various public health institutions, including 2504 hospitals and commune hospitals, 203 sanitation and antiepidemic stations, 109 maternity and child health care centres. There were 205 thousand hospital beds in various public health institutions, of this total, 189. 4 thousand beds belonged to hospitals and commune hospitals. There were 262. 2 thousand sanitation technicians, including 110. 6 thousand practitioner doctors and practitioner assistant doctors; 82. 8 thousand registered nurses; 7500 sanitation and antiepidemic technicians; 4000 maternity and child health care technicians, There were 1400 township commune hospitals, with 53 thousand hospital beds, 60 thousand sanitation technicians, 59 thousand village doctors and paramedics.

A great vitality was shown in the development of sports. The sports health projects were overall implemented in 10000 villages. Excellent successes were got by the Jiangsu's athlets in domestic and international major competitions. In major international and domestic compititions, 15 world champions were won by them. Jiangsu's athlets had created 3 world records, 3 Asian record; there were 33 person - times won the gold medals, 29 person - times won the sliver medals and 40 person - times won the bronze medals. Jiangsu had successfully hosted 3th national sports meeting, and also had smoothly held the 16th provincial games.

XI Environmental Protection and Safety Production

The strength of environmental protection was enhanced. The target responsibility system of environmental protection was conscientiously carried out. The task of pollution emission decreasing in major industries and enterprises was conspicuously grasped. The annual goal of environmental treatment was fulfilled in taking the "three clear and one green" as the focal point. By the end of 2006, there were 609 environmental monitoring stations in Jiangsu, 38 natural reverses were set up; of which, 3 were the state natural reverses; the area of natural reverses was 861. 8 thousand hectares. 171 smoking and dust controlling zones were established, with an area of 3500 square kilometers; also 193 environmental noice standardized zones were established, with an area of 2900 square kilometers. The rate of urban waste water centralized treatment was 50%, 12. 8 percentage points higher than 2005. The total volume of discharged industrial waste water reached 2. 991 billion tons; the total volume of industrial waste gas emission was 2120. 64 billion standardized cubic meters; the total volume of discharged intustrial dust was 318. 6 thousand tons. Jiangsu stressed to push forward the treatment and prevention of pollution on the major river basin's water, as well as the comprehensive treatment of regional environment. Important progress was obtained in "green Jiangsu" and the construction of a ecological province. The newly increased area of afforestation was 1. 578 million mu in Jiangsu. Among the national first group of 6 ecological cities, Jiangsu had 4 cities, accounting for 2/3 of the country. There were 42626 various accidents occured in 2006, the number of deads was 7634 persons, dropped by 10. 7% and 10. 5% respectively. The number of deads per 100 million GDP was 0. 35 persons, down by 25. 5%.

XII Population, People's Livelihood

Total volume of population witnessed a momentum of continuous growth. In 2006, the birth rate of population was 9. 36‰, rose by 0. 12 per thousand points, the death rate was 7. 08‰, rose by 0. 05 per thousand points; the natural growth rate was 2. 28‰, rose by 0. 07 per thousand points. By the end of 2006, the permanent population reached 75. 495 million persons, 750 thousand more than that in the end of 2005.

People's living standard continued to improve. According to sample survey for 5000 urban households, the annual per capita disposable income of the urban residents was 14084. 26 yuan, increased by 14. 3%, or an actual increase of 12. 5%, if the price factors were excluded. Per capita consumptive expenditure was 9628. 59 yuan, increased by 11. 7%; of which, the proportion of food expenditure accounted for 36%. According to sample survey for 3400 rural households, the annual per capita net income of rural residents was 5813 yuan, increased by 10. 2%, or an actual increase of 8. 4%, if the price factors were excluded. The per capita living expenditure was 4135 yuan, increased by 15. 9%; of which, the proportion of food expenditure accounted for 41. 8%. The housing condition was further improved. The per capita construction floor space of urban residence was 29. 68 square meters, while the per capita utilized living floor space of rural residence was 40. 8 square meters.

The coverage scope of social security was further enlarged. The number of workers of urban enterprises who took part in basic old age insurance, basic medical insurance and unemployment insurance was 1. 074 million, 1. 477 million and 626 thousand persons respectively, the coverage scope was above 92%. Jiangsu upgraded the standard of the minimun wages, the basic old pensions of the retired personnels of enterprises, the subsidies for special care masses and minimun living guarantee of urban and rural residents. In order to solve the actual problems of the needy masses in production and living, the expenditure of provincial level for social security and supporting the needy masses reached 6. 65 billion yuan, grew by 37. 7%. In urban and rural area, the "low insurance" was overall covered throughout the province. There were 1. 485 million needy masses, who were ought to be insured, all enjoyed the insurance. By the end of 2006, 10. 5967 million workers of the enterprises and 3. 0197 million retired personnels were involved in basic old age insurance in urban area; 9. 333 million workers and 3. 385 million retired personnels were involved in the basic medical insurance; 9. 011 million workers took part in the unemployment insurance. The system of temparary succour for the living of urban and rural special needy masses and the medical succour were initiatively established. In addition, 27 thousand beds were newly expanded for the old folk's home. The rate of contralized providing for the rural five – guarantee households (enjoying the guarantee of food, clothing, medical care, housing and burial expenses) reached 55% or so. By the end of 2006, there were 121. 1 thousand beds in various welfare institutions, in which 89. 5 thousand people were adopted; 24550 various facilities were set up in urban communities, of which 528 were community service centres. There were 1. 4344 million urban and rural residents who were affirmed as the minimum living standard guarantee objects. Besides, 728 million yuan of welfare funds were collected, 300 million yuan of contribution funds were accepted.

notes: The data of this communque were from statistical flash.

JIANGSU STATISTICAL YEARBOOK

第 1 篇

行政区划和自然资源

DIVISIONS OF ADMINISTRATIVE AREAS AND NATURAL RESOURCES

1　行政区划和自然资源
DIVISIONS OF ADMINISTRATIVE AREAS AND NATURAL RESOURCES

自 然 概 况

位　置

江苏简称苏，位于我国大陆东部沿海中心，介于东经 116°18′－121°57′，北纬 30°45′－35°20′之间。东濒黄海，西连安徽，北接山东，东南与浙江和上海毗邻。

江苏地处美丽富饶的长江三角州，平原辽阔，主要有苏南平原，江淮平原、黄淮平原和东部滨海平原，自然条件优越，经济基础较好。

面　积

全省面积 10.26 万平方公里，占全国总面积的 1.1%。其中平原面积 7.06 万平方公里，水面面积 1.73 万平方公里。海岸线长 954 公里，耕地面积 474 万公倾。

河　流

全省境内河川交错，水网密布，长江横穿东西 400 多公里，大运河纵贯南北 690 公里，西南部有秦淮河，北部有苏北灌溉总渠、新沭河、通扬运河等。有大小湖泊 290 多个，全国五大淡水湖，江苏得其二，太湖和洪泽湖象两面大明镜，分别镶嵌在水乡江南和苏北平原。

资　源

江苏以地形地势低平，河湖众多为特点，平原、水面所占比例之大，在全国居首位，成为江苏一大地理优势。水产资源丰富，有广阔的海涂、浅海，东部沿海渔场面积达 15.4 万平方公里，其中包括著名的吕泗、海州湾等四大渔场，盛产黄鱼、带鱼、昌鱼、虾类、蟹类及贝藻类等。江苏也是全国河蟹、鳗鱼苗的主要产地。内陆水面 2600 多万亩，养殖面积近 800 万亩，有淡水鱼类 140 余种，已利用的有 40 多种。矿产资源分布广泛，品种较多，已发现的有 120 种。能源矿产主要有煤炭、石油和天然气；非金属矿产有硫、磷、钠盐、水晶、兰晶石、蓝宝石、金刚石、高岭土、石灰石、石英砂、大理石、陶瓷粘土；金属矿产有铁、铜、铅、锌、银、金、锶、锰等。粘土类矿产、建材类矿产、化工原料矿产、冶金辅助原料矿产、特种用途矿产和有色金属矿产，是江苏矿产资源的优势。

气　候

全省气候具有明显的季风特征，处于亚热带向暖温带过渡地带，大致以淮河—灌溉总渠一线为界，以南属亚热带湿润季风气候，以北属暖温带湿润季风气候。全省气候温和，雨量适中，四季分明。

DIVISIONS OF ADMINISTRATIVE AREAS AND NATURAL RESOURCES

LOCATION

Jiangsu (Short for Su) lies in the east of the country. It is situated in the center of the costal area, between 116°18′ – 121°57′E and 30°45′ – 35°20′N, with Yellowsea on the east, Anhui province on the west, Shandong on the north, and Zhejiang and Shanghai as its neighbours on the southeast.

Jiangsu seats on the beautiful and abundant Yangtze River Delta. Composed of vast plains, mainly South – Su, Jianghuai, Huanghuai and eastern plain by the sea, the province provides favorable natural conditions and good economic bases.

AREA

The area of Jiangsu is 102.6 thousand square kilometres, occupied 1.1 % of the total national area, among which 70.6 thousand square kilometres are plain areas, 17.3 thousand square kilometres are water surface. The coastline of the province is as long as 954 kilmetres, and the 4740 thousand hectares are cultivated land.

RIVERS AND LAKES

In Jiangsu, there are rivers crisscrossing throughout the province, and distributes the network of waterways. The Yangtze River travels the whole area of Jiangsu, from west to east, for more than 400 kilometres. The Grand Canal flows south to north for 690 kilometres. There are Qinhui River in the southeast of Jiangsu, Subei general irrigation canal, Xinshu River and Tongyang canal etc. in the north part.

Among the 290 lakes of varying size in Jiangsu, the Taihu Lake and Hongzehu Lake are both listed among the national "Five Large Fresh Water Lakes", like two bright mirrors inlaid respectively into the southern region of the Changjiang River and Subei Plain.

RESOURCES

The province is characteristic of topographical features in low and flat terrains, with numerous rivers and lakes. The proportion of plain and watersurface area is so large that it ranks the first in China and become a geographical superiority proportion. There are plentiful aquatic resources, vast shallow sea beaches and epeiric seas. There are 154 thousand square kilometres of fishing grounds on the eastern coastal area, composed of the four famous fishing grounds such as Lusi and Haizhouwan etc., abound in yellow croaker, hairtail, butterfish, shrimp and crab, and shellfish and algae. Jiangsu is also a main production area of crabs and young eels in the country.

There are more than 26 million mu of interior water surface, with 8 million mu of aquatic farm. Among 140 kinds and more of flesh water fishes, over 40 are utilized. Numerous varieties of mineral resources are widely dispersed, 120 kinds of them have been discovered. The main sources of energy and minerals dispersed in Jiangsu are coal, petroleum and natural gas. Nonmetallic minerals contain sulphur, phosphorus, sodium, crystal, dyanite, sapphire, diamond, kaolin, limestone, quartzite, marble and pottery clay. Metallic minerals contain iron, copper, lead, zinc, silver, gold, strontium and manganese. The minerals as clay, construction materials, sand, chemical raw materials, metallurgical assistance raw materials, special purpose minerals and non-ferrous metal minerals become a mineral superiority of Jiangsu.

CLIMATE

Located in a transition area from subtripical zone to temperature zone, Jiangsu shows a distinct characteristic of monsoon. Taking the Huaihe river to general irrigation canal as an approximate line of demarcation, the climate to the south of the line belongs to monsoon of tropical moist zone, while the climate to the north of the line belongs to monsoon of warm moist zone. Jiangsu has a warm climate, with moderate rainfall and distinct seasons.

1－1 主要城市月平均气温（2006年）
MONTHLY AVERAGE TEMPERATURE OF MAJOR CITIES (2006)

单位:摄氏度 (℃)

市 名 City	1月 Jan	2月 Feb	3月 Mar	4月 Apr	5月 May	6月 June	7月 July	8月 Aug	9月 Sept	10月 Oct	11月 Nov	12月 Dec	年平均气温 Yearly Average
南京市 Nanjing	3.9	4.3	11.3	17.1	21.2	26.5	28.7	29.5	22.5	20.3	12.8	5.3	17.0
无锡市 Wuxi	5.1	5.3	11.7	17.0	21.2	26.6	29.4	30.1	23.2	21.5	14.5	7.0	17.7
徐州市 Xuzhou	1.3	3.0	10.4	16.7	21.1	26.8	27.5	27.6	21.6	19.7	11.2	2.9	15.8
常州市 Changzhou	4.4	4.5	11.1	16.6	20.9	26.4	29.0	29.6	22.4	20.7	13.5	5.9	17.1
苏州市 Suzhou	5.3	5.5	11.6	16.9	21.2	26.2	29.6	30.3	23.4	21.8	14.8	7.2	17.8
南通市 Nantong	4.9	4.9	10.7	15.8	20.6	25.6	28.6	29.6	22.8	21.1	14.7	7.1	17.2
连云港市 Lianyungang	2.4	2.3	9.1	15.0	20.0	25.3	26.9	27.7	22.0	20.1	12.1	3.6	15.5
淮安市 Huaian	2.5	3.0	9.6	15.3	19.9	26.1	27.4	27.8	21.1	19.3	12.0	3.6	15.6
盐城市 Yancheng	2.7	2.5	8.6	14.1	18.9	24.5	27.5	27.6	21.2	19.1	12.2	4.0	15.2
扬州市 Yangzhou	3.5	4.0	10.9	16.4	20.8	26.5	28.4	29.2	22.2	20.5	13.1	5.0	16.7
镇江市 Zhenjiang	3.8	4.0	10.8	16.2	20.6	26.1	28.4	29.2	22.2	20.4	13.1	5.6	16.7
泰州市 Taizhou	3.5	3.6	9.7	15.0	19.7	25.4	27.9	28.5	21.8	20.0	13.1	5.2	16.1
宿迁市 Suqian	1.5	2.6	9.5	15.4	19.9	25.6	26.4	27.2	20.7	18.9	11.2	3.0	15.2

1－2 主要城市月降水量(2006年)
MONTHLY PRECIPITATION OF MAJOR CITIES(2006)

单位:毫米 (mm)

市 名 City	1月 Jan	2月 Feb	3月 Mar	4月 Apr	5月 May	6月 June	7月 July	8月 Aug	9月 Sept	10月 Oct	11月 Nov	12月 Dec	全年累计 Yearly Total
南京市 Nanjing	107.1	61.2	12.1	132.2	90.9	155.7	248.2	106.7	72.4	9.3	101.2	9.8	1106.8
无锡市 Wuxi	146.7	68.0	22.9	140.9	74.2	72.8	289.2	50.3	88.9	17.3	119.3	6.4	1096.9
徐州市 Xuzhou	19.5	14.9	0.0	45.8	56.4	243.3	220.4	145.2	30.4	0.0	76.5	27.4	879.8
常州市 Changzhou	122.3	71.3	22.2	129.0	80.2	118.1	161.2	128.6	91.2	14.8	102.2	7.9	1049.0
苏州市 Suzhou	152.8	77.1	38.5	115.8	98.2	65.7	145.3	87.0	85.0	4.3	133.0	15.8	1018.5
南通市 Nantong	137.3	59.0	26.8	98.9	88.8	145.7	395.7	74.7	71.4	21.4	118.1	7.4	1245.2
连云港市 Lianyungang	15.5	22.9	12.6	41.6	24.0	114.0	325.6	210.5	42.6	6.5	55.3	26.8	897.9
淮安市 Huaian	29.3	31.6	5.0	64.3	54.3	190.4	371.1	155.4	94.9	16.8	97.3	24.7	1135.1
盐城市 Yancheng	33.9	32.5	5.3	47.4	108.1	157.1	411.8	200.3	57.6	20.3	96.3	17.5	1188.1
扬州市 Yangzhou	109.8	58.8	15.6	90.3	70.7	113.5	379.3	51.8	70.1	9.3	110.6	10.8	1090.6
镇江市 Zhenjiang	134.1	68.5	24.1	88.7	87.3	111.1	220.0	68.1	80.7	11.0	116.3	8.0	1017.9
泰州市 Taizhou	112.6	49.5	18.9	87.5	80.6	125.2	265.4	32.4	60.5	8.9	120.6	8.2	970.3
宿迁市 Suqian	21.1	22.9	0.3	46.4	62.2	150.5	279.3	124.3	59.5	3.0	75.2	22.1	866.8

1-3 行 政 区 划 (2006年)
ADMINISTRATIVE DIVISIONS(2006)

单位:个 (unit)

市 名 City		各级市单位数 Number of Cities at All Levels	县级单位数 Number of Counties	县 County	县级市 Cities at County Level	市辖区 Districts Under the Jurisdiction of Cities
全 省	**Total**	**40**	**106**	**25**	**27**	**54**
南京市	Nanjing	1	13	2		11
无锡市	Wuxi	3	8		2	6
徐州市	Xuzhou	3	11	4	2	5
常州市	Changzhou	3	7		2	5
苏州市	Suzhou	6	11		5	6
南通市	Nantong	5	8	2	4	2
连云港市	Lianyungang	1	7	4		3
淮安市	Huaian	1	8	4		4
盐城市	Yancheng	3	9	5	2	2
扬州市	Yangzhou	4	7	1	3	3
镇江市	Zhenjiang	4	6		3	3
泰州市	Taizhou	5	6		4	2
宿迁市	Suqian	1	5	3		2

1-3 续表 Continued

单位:个 (unit)

市 名 City		镇 Town	乡 Township	街道办事处 Subdistrict Office	居民委员会 Neighbourhood Committee	村民委员会 Village Committee
全 省	**Total**	**994**	**109**	**285**	**5381**	**17303**
南京市	Nanjing	39		75	824	647
无锡市	Wuxi	50		35	499	924
徐州市	Xuzhou	114		40	412	2255
常州市	Changzhou	64		16	261	1092
苏州市	Suzhou	61		32	712	958
南通市	Nantong	121	4	13	406	1812
连云港市	Lianyungang	53	30	17	194	1437
淮安市	Huaian	92	24	10	225	1441
盐城市	Yancheng	129	9	9	453	1975
扬州市	Yangzhou	70	7	12	303	1168
镇江市	Zhenjiang	41		10	296	605
泰州市	Taizhou	85	6	12	397	1895
宿迁市	Suqian	75	29	4	399	1094

1-4 按行政区域分水资源总量(2006年)
WATER RESOURCES BY DIVISIONS OF ADMINISTRATIVE AREAS(2006)

单位:亿立方米 (100million cu. m)

市名 City		水资源总量 Total	地表水资源量 Surface Water Volume	地下水资源量 Underground Water Volume	地下水与地表水重复计算量 Duplicated Computation Volume of Surface Water and Underground Water	年降水量 Annual Precipitation
全省	**Total**	**404.40**	**314.70**	**110.73**	**21.03**	**1041.05**
南京市	Nanjing	24.57	20.78	4.23	0.44	73.84
无锡市	Wuxi	19.60	17.29	4.50	2.19	48.59
徐州市	Xuzhou	33.76	18.42	17.58	2.24	83.62
常州市	Changzhou	15.60	13.29	2.94	0.64	46.68
苏州市	Suzhou	24.66	19.68	7.10	2.11	89.49
南通市	Nantong	27.24	19.31	9.65	1.72	97.98
连云港市	Lianyungang	24.74	19.03	6.80	1.09	59.96
淮安市	Huaian	59.08	46.15	15.08	2.15	120.16
盐城市	Yancheng	81.36	66.13	17.81	2.58	169.88
扬州市	Yangzhou	29.51	25.24	6.31	2.04	75.32
镇江市	Zhenjiang	14.00	12.41	2.14	0.55	42.77
泰州市	Taizhou	20.76	16.26	5.50	1.01	60.54
宿迁市	Suqian	29.51	20.73	11.07	2.28	72.20

1-5 按流域区域分水资源总量(2006年)
WATER RESOURCES BY DRAINAGE AREA(2006)

单位:亿立方米 (100million cu. m)

域名 Region		水资源总量 Total	地表水资源量 Surface Water Volume	地下水资源量 Underground Water Volume	地下水与地表水重复计算量 Duplicated Computation Volume of Surface Water and Underground Water	年降水量 Annual Precipitation
合计	**Total**	**404.40**	**314.70**	**110.73**	**21.03**	**1041.05**
淮河上中游区	District of Upper and Middle Reaches of Huaihe River	42.34	31.67	12.12	1.45	90.44
淮河下游区	District of Lower Reach of Huaihe River	148.99	122.53	31.55	5.09	334.10
沂沭泗河区	Yishusi River Districet	83.67	56.61	32.49	5.43	205.65
长江下游干流区	District of Lower Reach of Changjiang River Mainstream	61.77	47.02	18.79	4.03	206.68
太湖区	Taihu Lake District	67.63	56.88	15.78	5.03	204.19

主要统计指标解释

行政区划　指国家对行政区域的划分。根据宪法规定，我国的行政区域划分如下：(1)全国分为省、自治区、直辖市，(2)省、自治区分为自治州、县、自治县、市；(3)自治州分为县、自治县、市；(4)县、自治县分为乡、民族乡、镇；(5)直辖市和较大的市分为区、县；(6)国家在必要时设立的特别行政区。

气候　指地球与大气之间长期能量交换与质量交换所形成的一种自然环境状态，它是多种因素综合作用的结果。气候既是人类生活和生产的环境要素之一，又是供给人类生活和生产的重要资源。气温、降水、湿度等气象要素的多年平均值是用来描述一个地区气候状况的主要参数，而各种气象要素某年、某月的平均值(或总量)则可以反映出该时期天气气候状况的重要特征。

自然资源　指人类可以直接从自然界获得，并用于生产和生活的物质资源。自然资源一般可以分成可再生资源和非再生资源两大类。可再生资源指在较短时间内可以再生、可以循环利用的资源，包括土地资源、水资源、气候资源、生物资源和海洋资源等。非再生资源指在使用后不能再生的资源，包括矿产资源和地热能源。

耕地面积　指经过开垦用以种植农作物并经常进行耕耘的土地面积。包括种有作物的土地面积、休闲地、新开荒地和抛荒未满三年的土地面积。

水资源　水在自然界中以固体、液体和气态三种聚集状态存在，分布于海洋、陆地(包括土壤)以及大气之中，通过水循环形成水资源。水资源包括经人类控制并直接可供灌溉、发电、给水、航运、养殖等用途的地表水和地下水，以及江河、湖泊、井、泉、潮汐、港湾和养殖水域等。水资源是发展国民经济不可缺少的重要自然资源。

地表水和地下水　陆地上的水因空间分布不同，分为地表水和地下水。地表水指分别存在于河流、湖泊、沼泽、冰川和冰盖等水体中水分的总称，又称陆地水。地下水指储存在地面以下饱和岩土孔隙、裂隙及溶洞中的水。

矿产资源　矿产指由地质作用形成，富集于地壳中或出露于地表达到工农业利用要求的有用矿物。矿产是一种重要的自然资源，是社会发展的重要物质基础。

矿产保有储量　指探明的矿产储量(包括工业储量和远景储量)，扣除已开采部分和地下损失量后的年末实有储量。

气温　指空气的温度，我国一般以摄氏度(℃)为单位表示。气象观测的温度表是放在离地面约 1.5 米处通风良好的百叶箱里测量的，因此，通常说的气温指的是离地面 1.5 米处百叶箱中的温度。其统计计算方法为：

月平均气温是将全月各日的平均气温相加，除以该月的天数而得。

年平均气温是将 12 个月的月平均气温累加后除以 12 而得。

降水量　指从天空降落到地面的液态或固态(经融化后)水，未经蒸发、渗透、流失而在地面上积聚的深度。其统计计算方法为：

月降水量是将全月各日的降水量累加而得。

年降水量是将 12 个月的月降水量累加而得。

Explanatory Notes on Main Statistical Indicators

Administrative Division　refers to the division of administrative areas by the state. The Constitution of the People's Republic of China stipulates that the administrative areas in China are divided as: 1) The whole country is divided into provinces, autonomous regions and municipalities directly under the central government; 2) Provinces and autonomous regions are divided into autonomous prefectures, counties, autonomous counties and cities; 3) Autonomous prefectures are divided into counties, autonomous counties and cities; 4) Counties and autonomous counties are divided into townships, nationality townships and towns; 5) Municipalities and large cities are divided into districts and counties, 6) The state shall, when necessary, establish special administrative regions.

Climate　refers to the natural environmental status formed by the long-term exchange of energy and mass between the earth and the air, and is the results of interaction of many factors. Climate is both one of the environment factors and the important resources for the living and production activities of the human being. The average values across several years of meteorological factors such as temperature, rainfall and humidity are used as important parameters to describe the climate of a region, while the average values (or total values) of a given year or month of meteorological factors reflect the key characteristics of climate for that period of time.

Natural Resources　refer to material resources that could be obtained from the nature by human being and used for production and living. Natural resources in general can be classified as renewable resources and non-renewable resources. Renewable resources refer to resources that could be renewed and recycled during a relatively short period of time, including land resource, water resource, climate resource, biology resource and marine resource. Non-renewable resources include resources that could not be renewed, such as minerals and geothermal resource.

Area of Cultivated Land refers to area of land reclaimed for the regular cultivation of various farm crops, including crop-cover land, fallow, newly reclaimed land and land laid idle for less than 3 years.

Water Resource Water exists in the nature in solid, liquid and gaseous states, is distributed in the ocean, land (including earth) and air, and constitutes the water resource through the circulation of water. Water resource includes the surface water and underground water that is controlled by the human being for irrigation, power-generation, water supply, navigation and cultivation. It also includes rivers, lakes, wells, springs, tides, gulf and water area for cultivation. Water resource as an important natural resource is indispensable for the development of the national economy.

Surface Water and Underground Water Water on earth can be divided into surface water and underground water according to its distribution. Surface water refers to moisture exists in rivers, lakes, swamps, glaciers, icecaps and so on. It is also called land water. The underground water refers to water deposited underground in the cranny and the hole of saturated rock soil and in the water-eroded cave.

Mineral Resources refer to useful minerals that can be used for industrial or agricultural purposes enriched in lithosphere or on earth due to the geological process. Minerals are important natural resources, and important material base for social development.

Ensured Mineral Reserves refer to the actual mineral reserves, which equal to the proven mineral reserves (including industrial reserves and prospective reserves) minus extracted parts and underground losses.

Temperature refers to the air temperature. China uses centigrade as the unit. The thermometry used for weather observation is put in a breezy shutter, which is 1.5 meters high from the ground. Therefore, the commonly used temperature refers to the temperature in the breezy shutter 1.5 meters away from the ground. The calculation method is as follows:

Monthly average temperature is the summation of average daily temperature of one month divided by the actual days of that particular month.

Annual average temperature is the summation of monthly average of a year divided by 12 months.

Volume of Precipitation refers to the deepness of liquid state or solid state (thawed) water falling from the sky to the ground that has not been evaporated, infiltrated or run off. The calculation method is as follows:

Monthly precipitation is the summation of daily precipitation of a month.

Annual precipitation is the summation of 12 months precipitation of a year.

JIANGSU STATISTICAL YEARBOOK

第 2 篇

综 合

GENERAL SURVEY

2 综 合
GENERAL SURVEY

从数字看 2006 年的江苏
JIANGSU IN STATISTICS'2006

江苏的地位
POSITION OF JIANGSU IN THE COUNTRY

地区生产总值	Gross Domestic Product	占全国	10.3%
#第三产业	Tertiary Industry	占全国	9.5%
人均地区生产总值	Per Capital GDP	高于全国	12730 元
全社会固定资产投资总额	Total Investment in Fixed Assets	占全国	9.2%
社会消费品零售总额	Total Retail Sales of Consumer Goods	占全国	8.7%
进出口总额	Total Imports and Exports	占全国	16.1%
#出口总额	Total Exports	占全国	16.6%
实际外商直接投资	Actual Foreign Direct Investment	占全国	25.1%
粮食产量	Output of Grain	占全国	6.1%
钢产量	Output of Steel	占全国	12.3%
发电量	Output of Electricity	占全国	7.8%
城镇居民人均可支配收入	Per Capita Disposable Income of Urban Residents	高于全国	2325 元
农村居民人均纯收入	Per Capita Net Income of Rural Residents	高于全国	2226 元

江苏的人口
POPULATION OF JIANGSU

年末人口	Population	7549.50	万人	(10000 persons)
从业人员	Employment	4564.76	万人	(10000 persons)
#在岗职工人数	Staff and Workers Employed	645.71	万人	(10000 persons)
出生人口	Births	70.31	万人	(10000 persons)
死亡人口	Deaths	53.18	万人	(10000 persons)
结婚人数	Marriages	59.23	万对	(10000 couples)
离婚人数	Divorces	13.80	万对	(10000 couples)
人口密度	Density of Population	736	人/平方公里	(person/sq. km)
人口平均期望寿命(2005 年)	Life Expectancy	75.32	岁	(year)

江苏的经济发展
ECONOMIC DEVELOPMENT OF JIANGSU

		1953－1978年 平均增长(%) 1953－1978 Average Annual Growth Rate(%)	1979－2006年 平均增长(%) 1979－2006 Average Annual Growth Rate(%)
地区生产总值	Gross Domestic Product	5.2	12.6
第一产业	Primary Industry	2.5	4.8
第二产业	Secondary Industry	12.3	14.3
#工业	Industry	12.4	14.4
第三产业	Tertiary Industry	3.9	14.6
全社会固定资产投资	Total Investment in Fixed Assets	11.6	24.5
财政收入	Government Revenue	8.8	16.0
货物运输量	Freight Traffic	9.0	8.0
社会消费品零售总额	Total Retail Sales of Consumer Goods	6.3	16.8
出口总额	Total Exports		23.7

江苏的一天
ONE DAY IN JIANGSU

地区生产总值	Groos Domestic Product	59.30	亿元	(100 million yuan)
第一产业	Primary Industry	4.23	亿元	(100 million yuan)
第二产业	Secondary Industry	33.56	亿元	(100 million yuan)
#工业	Industry	30.44	亿元	(100 million yuan)
第三产业	Tertiary Industry	21.50	亿元	(100 million yuan)
财政收入	Government Revenue	10.78	亿元	(100 million yuan)
货物运输量	Freight Traffic	342.78	万吨	(10000 tons)
竣工房屋面积	Floor Space of Residential Housing Completed	78.67	万平方米	(10000 sq. m)
社会消费品零售总额	Total Retail Sales of Consumer Goods	18.15	亿元	(100 million yuan)
出口总额	Total Exports	4.40	亿美元	(USD 100 million)
出版报纸	Newspapers Published	732.33	万份	(10000)
邮寄函件	Letters Delivered	107.95	万件	(10000)

2-1 全省法人、产业活动单位数及从业人员数(2006年)
NUMBER OF CORPORTIONS, INDUSTRIAL ACTIVITIES UNITS AND EMPOLYMENT (2006)

项 目	Item	法人单位 Corporation Units		产业活动单位 Economic Activities Units	
		单位数(个) Number of Units (unit)	从业人员(万人) Employees (10000 persons)	单位数(个) Number of Units (unit)	从业人员(万人) Employees (10000 persons)
总 计	**Total**	**536112**	**2188.65**	**77974**	**288.08**
按隶属关系分	**Grouped by Type of Adiministrative Relationship**				
中央	Central	1229	48.44	4433	31.07
省(自治区、直辖市)	Province	3681	66.32	7269	35.38
市(区、市州、盟)	Municipality	16173	148.46	8189	42.67
县(区、市、旗)	County(District,City)	42587	272.07	18737	52.92
街道	Subdistrict Office	5161	11.98	969	1.70
镇	Town	31178	139.87	9345	18.74
乡	Township	2407	10.28	478	0.55
居委会	Neighbourhood Committee	3847	5.88	524	1.08
村委会	Village Committee	19696	34.26	1848	4.00
其他	Others	410153	1451.09	26182	99.97
按登记注册类型分	**Grouped by Type of Registration**				
内资	Inner Funded	512307	1844.02	75738	267.56
国有	State-Owned	59190	286.92	20417	86.24
集体	Collective-Owned	31012	122.72	16780	23.70
股份合作	Share Holding Cooperative	11308	46.05	1759	4.62
国有联营	State Joint-owned	189	1.23	34	0.27
集体联营	Collective Joint-owned	481	1.88	180	0.21
国有与集体联营	Stale-owned and Collective Joint Funded	207	1.75	95	0.17
其他联营	Other Joint Funded	2917	5.54	102	0.17
国有独资公司	State-owned Solely Funded Co.	574	26.66	513	14.88
其他有限责任公司	Other Responsibility Co. Ltd.	30282	320.37	8522	59.62
股份有限公司	Share Holding Co. Ltd.	6125	88.59	5810	29.02
私营独资	Private Solely Funded	116202	221.16	2897	2.53
私营合伙	Private Partnership	17221	38.29	727	0.88
私营有限责任公司	Private Responsibility Co. Ltd.	203228	633.05	12049	38.30
私营股份有限公司	Private Responsibility Co. Ltd.	7521	28.00	671	2.03
其他	Others	25850	21.79	5182	4.94
港澳台商投资	Hongkong, Macao and Taiwan Funded	10537	134.49	862	7.85
与港澳台商合资经营	Join with Hongkong, Macao and Taiwan Funded	4024	52.96	430	3.63

2－1 续表 Continued

项目	Item	法人单位 Corporation Units		产业活动单位 Economic Activities Units	
		单位数（个）Number of Units (unit)	从业人员（万人）Employees (10000 persons)	单位数（个）Number of Units (unit)	从业人员（万人）Employees (10000 persons)
与港澳台商合作经营	Cooperate with Hong Kong, Macao and Taiwan Funded	315	3.36	26	0.15
港澳台商独资	Hong Kong, Macao and Taiwan with Solely Funded	6046	75.20	369	2.57
港澳台商投资股份有限公司	Hong Kong, Macao and Taiwan Share Holding Co. Ltd.	152	2.98	37	1.50
外商投资	Foreign Funded	13268	210.13	1374	12.68
中外合资经营	Sino－Foreign Joint Furded	4881	64.98	719	7.06
中外合作经营	Sino－Foreign Cooperative Funded	383	4.70	37	0.18
外资企业	Foreign Solely Funded	7814	136.71	604	5.42
外商投资股份有限公司	Foreign Funded Share Holding Co. Ltd.	190	3.75	14	0.03
按行业分	**Grouped by Sector**				
农、林、牧、渔业	Farming, Forestry, Animal Husbandry and Fishery	2662	3.12	99	0.26
采矿业	Mining and Quarrying	1869	22.82	108	12.11
制造业	Manufacturing	241821	1190.57	4378	71.72
电力、燃气及水的生产和供应业	Power, Gas and Water Production and Supply	2829	12.86	698	1.65
建筑业	Construction	18990	400.58	1739	65.29
交通运输、仓储和邮政业	Transportation, Storage and Post	9339	44.90	2875	15.64
信息传输、计算机服务和软件业	Informaiton Transmmision, Computer Service and Software	7858	10.06	1490	3.75
批发和零售业	Wholesale and Retail Sales	101462	130.02	29141	30.72
住宿和餐饮业	Hotel and Catering	6796	30.49	1632	5.17
金融业	Banking	1169	22.59	9961	20.03
房地产业	Real Estate	12020	25.53	1377	2.47
租赁和商务服务业	Leasing and Commercial Services	25289	34.42	2064	5.46
科学研究、技术服务和地质勘查业	Scientific Research, Polytechnical Service and Geological Prospecting	10134	18.27	825	3.14
水利、环境和公共设施管理业	Water Coservancy, Environment and Public Facility Management	3898	12.34	431	1.63
居民服务和其他服务业	Resident Services and Others	8002	10.57	1192	1.85
教育	Education	12879	87.99	3632	14.71
卫生、社会保障和社会福利业	Health Care, Social Security and Social Welfare	9754	33.93	7020	11.57
文化、体育和娱乐业	Culture, Sports and Recreation	4669	8.17	666	1.48
公共管理和社会组织	Public Management and Social Organizations	54672	89.43	8646	19.42

注：表中的“产业活动单位”仅指多产业法人单位所属的产业活动单位。

Note: In this table, “economic activities units” only referred to the economic activities units under the multi-industry corporation units.

2-2 江苏国民经济占全国的比重（2006年）
PERCENTAGE OF JIANGSU'S NATIONAL ECONOMY IN THE COUNTRY (2006)

指标		Item		全国 Country	江苏 Jiangsu	江苏占全国的比重（%） Percentage to the Country of Jiangsu
土地面积	（万平方公里）	Land Area	(10000 sq. km)	960	10.26	1.1
年末总人口	（万人）	Year-end Total Population	(10000 persons)	131448	7549.50	5.7
地区生产总值	（亿元）	Domestic Gross Product	(100 million yuan)	210871	21645.08	10.3
第一产业		Primary Industry		24737	1545.01	6.2
第二产业		Secondary Industry		103162	12250.84	11.9
第三产业		Tertiary Industry		82972	7849.23	9.5
人均地区生产总值	（元）	Per Capita GDP	(yuan)	16084	28814	高12730元
全社会固定资产投资	（亿元）	Total Investment in Fixed Assets	(100 million yuan)	109870	10071.42	9.2
#城镇投资		Urban Inveslment		93472	7481.80	8.0
#房地产开发		Real Estate Developmer		19382	1906.71	9.8
财政收入	（亿元）	Government Revenue	(100 million yuan)	38371	3935.87	10.3
财政支出	（亿元）	Government Expenditures	(100 million yuan)	40213	2726.77	6.8
社会消费品零售总额	（亿元）	Total Retail Sales of Consumer Goods	(100 million yuan)	76410	6623.18	8.7
进出口总额	（亿美元）	Total Exports and Imports	(USD 100 million)	17607	2839.95	16.1
#出口		Exports		9691	1604.19	16.6
实际外商直接投资	（亿美元）	Actual Foreign Direct Investments	(USD 100 million)	695	174.31	25.1
普通高等学校本专科在校生	（万人）	Students Enrollment in Institutions of Higher Education	(10000 persons)	1739	130.62	7.5
医院卫生院床位数	（万张）	Hospital Beds	(10000 units)	327	19.58	6.0
卫生技术人员	（万人）	Medical Technical Personnel	(10000 persons)	462	27.54	6.0
#执业(助理)医师		Practitioner (Assistant) Doctors		200	11.46	5.7
在岗职工平均工资	（元）	Average Wages of Staff and Workers Employed	(yuan)	21001	23782	高2781元
城镇居民人均可支配收入	（元）	Per Capita Disposable Income of Urban Residents	(yuan)	11759	14084	高2325元
农村居民人均纯收入	（元）	Per Capita Net Income of Rural Residents	(yuan)	3587	5813	高2226元
居民人均储蓄	（本外币,元）	Per Capita Savings Deposit of Residents	(yuan)	12676	16498	高3822元
工农业主要产品产量	（万吨）	Output of Major Industrial and Agricultural Products	(10000 tons)			
粮食		Grain		49748	3041.44	6.1
棉花		Cotton		675	38.14	5.7
油料		Oil-Bearing Crops		3059	218.18	7.1
粗钢		Rough Steel		42266	4202.31	9.9
钢材		Rolled Steel		47340	5816.26	12.3
原煤		Coal		238200	3047.53	1.3
发电量	（亿千瓦小时）	Electricity	(100 million kWh)	28344	2216.40	7.8
水泥		Cement		123500	10880.77	8.8
农用化肥	（折100%）	Chemical Fertilizers	(convert into 100 %)	5593	254.66	4.6
化学纤维		Chemical Fibers		2026	665.14	32.8
布	（亿米）	Cloth	(100 million)	550	64.95	11.8
汽车	（万辆）	Moter Vehicles	(10000 units)	728	27.48	3.8

2－3　国民经济和社会发展总量与速度指标

指标	Item	总量指标 1978	1990	1995	2000
人口与就业	**Population and Employment**				
人口　（万人）	**Population　(10000 persons)**				
年末人口	Population at the Year-end	5834.32	6766.90	7066.02	7327.24
市镇人口	Urban	800.77	1458.94	1929.09	3040.81
乡村人口	Rural	5033.55	5307.96	5136.93	4286.43
就业　（万人）	**Employment　(10000 persons)**				
就业人数	Employment	2777.72	4225.02	4385.17	4418.14
#职工人数	Staff and Workers	581.50	879.85	915.98	673.25
#国有单位	State-Owned Units	366.37	536.88	576.24	411.40
年末城镇登记失业人数	Unemployment Registered in Urban Area		22.52	20.13	30.36
宏观经济	**Macroeconomy**				
国民核算　（亿元）	**National Accounting (100 million yuan)**				
地区生产总值	Gross Domestic Product	249.24	1416.50	5155.25	8553.69
第一产业	Primary Industry	68.71	355.17	866.24	1048.34
第二产业	Secondary Industry	131.09	692.59	2715.26	4435.89
第三产业	Tertiary Industry	49.44	368.74	1573.75	3069.46
支出法地区生产总值	Gross Domestic Expenditures				
#最终消费	Final Consumption Expenditure	130.55	717.36	2250.66	3710.72
居民消费	Resident Consumption	115.15	608.29	1806.43	2815.51
政府消费	Government Consumption Expenditure	15.40	109.07	444.23	895.21
资本形成总额	Gross Capital Formation	77.98	588.44	2479.30	4044.78
固定资本形成	Fixed Capital Formation	40.40	374.12	1756.88	3225.42
存货增加	Changes in Stock	37.58	214.32	722.42	819.36
固定资产投资　（亿元）	**Investment in Fixed Assets (100 million yuan)**				
全社会固定资产投资总额	Total Investment in Fixed Assets	21.75	356.30	1680.17	2995.43
#国有单位	State-Owned Units	20.70	134.86	602.70	1200.01
集体单位	Collective-Owned Units	1.05	74.87	491.08	455.86
#房地产开发	Real Estale Development		11.71	240.85	358.72
财政　（亿元）	**Public Finance　(100 million yuan)**				
财政收入	Government Revenue	61.09	136.20	350.08	865.00
地方财政支出	Local Government Expenditures	28.38	100.97	253.49	645.57

AGGREGATE INDICATORS ON NATIONAL ECONOMIC AND SOCIAL DEVELOPMENT AND THEIR INDICES AND GROWTH RATE

Aggregate Data		速度指标 Indicies and Growth Rate								
2005	2006	2006年比下列各年增长(%) Index (2006 as percentage of the following years)					年平均增长(%) Average Annual Growth Rate			
		1978	1990	1995	2000	2005	1979 ~ 2006	1991 ~ 2006	1996 ~ 2006	2001 ~ 2006
7474.50	7549.50	29.4	11.6	6.8	3.0	1.0	0.9	0.7	0.6	0.5
3774.62	3918.19	389.3	168.6	103.1	28.9	3.8	5.8	6.4	6.7	4.3
3699.88	3631.31	-27.9	-31.6	-29.3	-15.3	-1.9	-1.2	-2.3	-3.1	-2.7
4510.12	4564.76	64.3	8.0	4.1	3.3	1.2	1.8	0.5	0.4	0.5
602.93	645.71	11.0	-26.6	-29.5	-4.1	7.1	0.4	-1.9	-3.1	-0.7
273.43	268.41	-26.7	-50.0	-53.4	-34.8	-1.8	-1.1	-4.2	-6.7	-6.9
41.63	40.40		79.4	100.7	33.1	-3.0		3.7	6.5	4.9
18305.66	21645.08	2654.2	684.4	258.2	110.9	14.9	12.6	13.7	12.3	13.2
1461.48	1545.01	270.4	97.8	51.8	21.0	5.0	4.8	4.4	3.9	3.2
10355.04	12250.84	4086.0	937.2	310.4	132.9	16.0	14.3	15.7	13.7	15.1
6489.14	7849.23	4436.3	810.7	278.9	110.3	15.5	14.6	14.8	12.9	13.2
7538.04	9005.61	2234.2	706.8	254.2	116.1	16.1	11.9	13.9	12.2	13.7
5339.09	6236.42	1663.5	554.2	206.5	99.9	13.8	10.8	12.5	10.7	12.2
2198.95	2769.19	7253.3	1582.5	446.9	166.7	21.7	16.6	19.3	16.7	17.8
9313.16	10673.86	4506.6	670.2	254.0	109.8	11.8	14.7	13.6	12.2	13.1
8739.71	10021.43	9373.3	1072.8	353.9	150.6	11.9	17.6	16.6	14.7	16.5
573.45	652.43	307.2	6.8	-31.3	-50.0	11.5	5.1	0.4	-3.4	-10.9
8739.71	10071.42	46205.4	2726.7	499.4	236.2	15.2	24.5	23.2	17.7	22.4
2077.97	2144.93	10262.0	1490.5	255.9	78.7	3.2	18.0	18.9	12.2	10.2
445.16	441.57	41954.3	489.8	-10.1	-3.1	-0.8	24.1	11.7	-1.0	-0.5
1545.15	1906.71		16182.7	691.7	431.5	23.4		37.5	20.7	32.1
3124.83	3935.87	6342.7	2789.8	1024.3	355.0	26.0	16.0	23.4	24.6	28.7
2216.21	2726.77	9508.1	2600.6	975.7	322.4	23.0	17.7	22.9	24.1	27.1

指　标　Item		总量指标			
		1978	1990	1995	2000
物价　（上年=100）	**Price　(preceding year=100)**				
商品零售价格总指数	General Retail Price Index	100.2	102.3	114.3	98.6
居民消费价格指数	General Consumer Price Index	100.1	103.2	115.8	100.1
工业品出厂价格指数	Ex-Factory Price Index of Industrial Products			114.2	101.1
利用外资　（亿美元）	**Utilization of Foreign Capital (USD 100 million)**				
合同外商直接投资	Contracted Foreign Direct Investment		2.44	129.70	106.11
实际外商直接投资	Actual Foreign Direct Investment		1.41	47.81	64.24
产　业	**Industry**				
农业	**Agriculture**				
农林牧渔业劳动力　（万人）	Number of Persons Engaged in Farming, Forestry, Animal Husbandry and Fishery (10000 persons)	2030.67	1714.49	1541.33	1480.22
农林牧渔业总产值　（亿元）	Gross Output Value of Farming, Forestry, Animal Husbandry and Fishery (100 million yuan)	105.87	580.53	1686.78	1869.73
主要农产品产量　（万吨）	Output of Major Farm Products (10000 tons)				
粮食	Grain	2400.65	3264.15	3286.30	3106.63
棉花	Cotton	47.54	46.42	56.15	31.45
油料	Oil-Bearing Crops	37.44	112.39	159.46	225.65
糖料	Sugar Crops	6.88	22.26	23.37	28.26
蚕茧	Silkworm Cocoons	2.63	12.00	18.62	9.01
猪牛羊肉	Pork, Beef and Mutton		158.38	217.82	227.41
水产品	Aquatic Products	39.76	118.25	219.47	308.79
工业	**Industry**				
全部工业增加值　（亿元）	Added Value of All Industties (100 million yuan)	117.10	634.13	2467.63	3848.52
主要工业产品产量　（万吨）	Output of Major Industrial Products (10000 tons)				
粗钢	Steel	54.51	190.18	360.40	617.16
钢材	Rolled-Steel	60.31	203.01	787.89	1401.83
发电量　（亿千瓦小时）	Electricity　(100 million kWh)	126.42	404.47	700.41	909.69
原煤	Coal	1707.02	2407.79	2650.72	2479.02
农用化肥（折100%）	Chemical Furtilizers	72.18	145.90	191.85	192.38
化学农药	Chemical Pesticide	4.92	4.51	12.18	17.23
水泥	Cement	444.10	1532.89	3966.42	4599.52
化学纤维	Chemical Fiber	2.11	40.76	102.20	190.99
彩色电视　（万台）	Color Television Sets　(10000 units)	0.03	36.64	11.45	127.66
家用电冰箱　（万台）	Household Refrigerators　(10000 units)		83.18	250.72	285.17
建筑业	**Construction**				
建筑业企业职工平均人数（万人）	Average Number of Employed Persons (10000 persons)		124.31	232.94	221.48
建筑业总产值　（亿元）	Gross Output Value　(100 million yuan)		147.23	998.11	1546.17
施工房屋面积　（万平方米）	Floor Space of Building Under Construction (10000 sq. m)		5240.98	16646.14	21287.10
竣工房屋面积　（万平方米）	Floor Space of Building Completed (10000 sq. m)		3307.93	8739.38	12329.65

Continued

Aggregate Data		速度指标 Indicies and Growth Rate								
2005	2006	2006年比下列各年增长(%) Index (2006 as percentage of the following years)					年平均增长(%) Average Annual Growth Rate			
		1978	1990	1995	2000	2005	1979 ~ 2006	1991 ~ 2006	1996 ~ 2006	2001 ~ 2006
100.3	100.8	279.5	80.1	-0.1	0.4	0.8	4.9	3.7	0.0	0.1
102.1	101.6	378.4	124.5	19.1	9.1	1.6	5.7	5.2	1.6	1.5
102.6	101.5		74.5	-0.8	9.7	1.5		3.5	-0.1	1.5
457.22	465.42		18961.7	258.8	338.6	1.8		38.8	12.3	27.9
131.80	174.31		12253.6	264.6	171.4	32.3		35.1	12.5	18.1
1058.28	981.37	-51.7	-42.8	-36.3	-33.7	-7.3	-2.6	-3.4	-4.0	-6.6
2576.98	2707.06	437.4	170.6	70.8	28.6	4.9	6.2	6.4	5.0	4.3
2834.59	3041.44	26.7	-6.8	-7.5	-2.1	7.3	0.8	-0.4	-0.7	-0.4
32.27	38.14	-19.8	-17.8	-32.1	21.3	18.2	-0.8	-1.2	-3.5	3.3
215.99	218.18	482.7	94.1	36.8	-3.3	1.0	6.5	4.2	2.9	-0.6
22.23	20.62	199.7	-7.4	-11.8	-27.0	-7.2	4.0	-0.5	-1.1	-5.1
10.59	12.28	366.9	2.3	-34.0	36.3	16.0	5.7	0.1	-3.7	5.3
242.12	242.10		52.9	11.1	6.5	0.0		2.7	1.0	1.0
388.66	405.04	918.7	242.5	84.6	31.2	4.2	8.6	8.0	5.7	4.6
9334.70	11110.24	4182.0	922.6	309.9	139.8	16.6	14.4	15.6	13.7	15.7
3284.86	4202.31	7609.2	2109.6	1066.0	580.9	27.9	16.8	21.3	25.0	37.7
4328.32	5816.26	9543.9	2765.0	638.2	314.9	34.4	17.7	23.3	19.9	26.8
1789.53	2216.40	1653.2	448.0	216.4	143.6	23.9	10.8	11.2	11.0	16.0
2817.56	3047.53	78.5	26.6	15.0	22.9	8.2	2.1	1.5	1.3	3.5
284.63	254.66	252.8	74.5	32.7	32.4	-10.5	4.6	3.5	2.6	4.8
30.26	36.05	632.7	699.3	196.0	109.2	19.1	7.4	13.9	10.4	13.1
9579.15	10880.77	2350.1	609.8	174.3	136.6	13.6	12.1	13.0	9.6	15.4
458.49	665.14	31423.2	1531.8	550.8	248.3	45.1	22.8	19.1	18.6	23.1
403.81	248.25	827400	577.5	2068.1	94.5	-38.5	38.0	12.7	32.3	11.7
318.46	408.80		391.5	63.1	43.4	28.4		10.5	4.5	6.2
342.24	379.77		205.5	63.0	71.5	11.0		7.2	4.5	9.4
4368.95	5424.85		3584.6	443.5	250.9	24.2		25.3	16.6	23.3
52242.23	63140.49		1104.7	279.3	196.6	20.9		16.8	12.9	19.9
25391.86	28715.39		768.1	228.6	132.9	13.1		14.5	11.4	15.1

2-3 续表 2

指 标	Item	总量指标 1978	1990	1995	2000
交通运输	**Transportation**				
货运量 （万吨）	Freight Traffic (10000 tons)	14626	49399	81830	90436
#铁路	Railways	3224	4235	4143	4077
公路	Highways	4488	27904	49578	59056
水运	Waterways	6557	15908	27161	25902
客运量 （万人）	Passenger Traffic (10000 persons)	25621	48339	84803	107244
#铁路	Railways	2752	4788	5185	4891
公路	Highways	18694	41850	78947	101713
水运	Waterways	4175	1701	623	514
港口货物吞吐量 （万吨）	Volume of Freight Handled at Seaports (10000 tons)	10183	17002	20177	39200
邮电通信	**Postal and Telecommunications Services**				
邮电业务总量 （亿元）	Total Business Revenue (100 million yuan)	1.83	9.98	72.24	323.45
函件 （亿件）	Number of Letters Delivered (100 million pieces)	1.63	3.30	5.31	5.74
年末固定电话用户 （万户）	Year End Number of Eited Telephone subseribers (10000 househalds)			330.17	1138.06
城市	Urban			226.54	535.43
农村	Rural			103.63	602.63
年末移动电话用户 （万户）	Year End Number of Mobnle Telephone subseribers (10000 househalds)			23.19	619.50
国内商业	**Domestic Trade**				
社会消费品零售总额 （亿元）	Total Retail Sales of Consumer Goods (100 million yuan)	84.79	515.43	1741.92	2908.46
对外经济贸易和旅游	**Foreign Trade and Tourism**				
进出口总额 （亿美元）	Total Imports and Exports (USD 100 million)	4.27	41.39	162.78	456.38
进口	Imports	0.09	11.95	64.96	198.69
出口	Exports	4.18	29.44	97.82	257.70
接待海外旅游人数 （万人）	Number of International Tourists Received (10000 persons)	11.33	72.48	76.77	160.94
金融保险 （亿元）	**Banking and Insurance (100 million yuan)**				
金融机构存款	Deposits of Banking System	60.72	860.33	3500.49	8400.75
金融机构贷款	Loans of Banking System	115.29	1013.45	2875.39	5967.66
国内保险保费收入	Domestic Premium		9.31	29.01	132.03
教育、科技、文化	**Education, Science and Technology and Culture**				
教育	**Education**				
高等学校本专科在校学生 （万人）	Students Enrollment in Institutions of Higher Education (10000 persons)	6.05	14.69	20.86	45.19
中等专业学校在校学生 （万人）	Students Enrollment in Specialized Secondary Schools (10000 persons)	3.84	13.99	31.87	43.62
普通中学在校学生 （万人）	Students Enrollment in Regular Secondary Schools (10000 persons)	385.85	281.97	316.75	373.64
小学在校学生 （万人）	Students Enrollment in Primary Schools (10000 persons)	868.90	612.29	644.77	718.55
科技	**Science and Technology**				
县以上科研机构数 （个）	Number of Scientific & Technological Research Institutions of County Level and Above (unit)		326	337	313
各类专业技术人员 （万人）	Scientific and Technical Personnel (10000 persons)	22.18	158.86	184.97	194.24

Continued

Aggregate Data		速度指标 Indicies and Growth Rate								
2005	2006	2006年比下列各年增长(%) Index (2006 as percentage of the following years)					年平均增长(%) Average Annual Growth Rate			
		1978	1990	1995	2000	2005	1979 ~ 2006	1991 ~ 2006	1996 ~ 2006	2001 ~ 2006
112909	125114	755.4	153.3	52.9	38.3	10.8	8.0	6.0	3.9	5.6
5090	5169	60.3	22.1	24.8	26.8	1.5	1.7	1.3	2.0	4.0
76301	84319	1778.8	202.2	70.1	42.8	10.5	11.0	7.2	4.9	6.1
29277	32862	401.2	106.6	21.0	26.9	12.2	5.9	4.6	1.7	4.0
145204	161425	530.0	233.9	90.4	50.5	11.2	6.8	7.8	6.0	7.1
6658	7292	165.0	52.3	40.6	49.1	9.5	3.5	2.7	3.1	6.9
138287	153825	722.9	267.6	94.8	51.2	11.2	7.8	8.5	6.3	7.1
37	27	-99.4	-98.4	-95.7	-94.7	-27.0	-16.5	-22.8	-24.8	-38.8
75517	86359	748.1	407.9	328.0	120.3	14.4	7.9	10.7	14.1	14.1
728.08	997.26	54395.1	9892.6	1280.5	208.3	37.0	25.2	33.3	27.0	20.6
4.21	3.94	141.7	19.4	-25.8	-31.4	-6.4	3.2	1.1	-2.7	-6.1
3059.35	3224.32			876.6	183.3	5.4			23.0	19.0
2089.54	2225.95			882.6	315.7	6.5			23.1	26.8
969.81	998.37			863.4	65.7	2.9			22.9	8.8
2550.00	2873.40			12290.7	363.8	12.7			55.0	29.1
5699.89	6623.18	7711.3	1185.0	280.2	127.7	16.2	16.8	17.3	12.9	14.7
2279.41	2839.95	66333.1	6761.3	1644.7	522.3	24.6	26.1	30.2	29.7	35.6
1049.59	1235.76	1368405	10238.7	1802.2	522.0	17.7	40.5	33.6	30.7	35.6
1229.82	1604.19	38235.6	5349.3	1540.0	522.5	30.4	23.7	28.4	29.0	35.6
378.30	445.19	3829.3	514.2	479.9	176.6	17.7	14.0	12.0	17.3	18.5
22001.44	25860.47	42489.7	2905.9	638.8	207.8	17.5	24.1	23.7	19.9	20.6
15396.59	18485.02	15933.5	1724.0	542.9	209.8	20.1	19.9	19.9	18.4	20.7
437.34	502.83		5301.0	1633.3	280.8	15.0		28.3	29.6	25.0
115.98	130.62	2059.0	789.2	526.2	189.0	12.6	11.6	14.6	18.1	19.4
66.10	73.29	1808.6	423.9	130.0	68.0	10.9	11.1	10.9	7.9	9.0
491.56	471.27	22.1	67.1	48.8	26.1	-4.1	0.7	3.3	3.7	3.9
485.53	455.75	-47.5	-25.6	-29.3	-36.6	-6.1	-2.3	-1.8	-3.1	-7.3
146	144		-55.8	-57.3	-54.0	-1.4		-5.0	-7.4	-12.1
148.67	142.20	541.1	-10.5	-23.1	-26.8	-4.4	6.9	-0.7	-2.4	-5.1

2-3 续表 3

指标	Item	总量指标 1978	1990	1995	2000
#工程技术人员	Engineering Personnel	7.83	31.84	28.38	44.84
文化	**Culture**				
图书出版量 （亿册）	Books Published (100 million copies)	1.94	3.44	4.05	3.47
杂志出版量 （万册）	Magazines Issued (10000 copies)	535	4107	7005	11008
报纸出版量 （亿份）	Newspapers Issued (100 million copies)	2.45	8.27	15.95	23.34
家庭、生活、环境	**Family, People's Livelihood and Environment**				
家庭	**Family**				
总户数 （万户）	Total Househalds (10000 househalds)	1423.11	1806.78	2066.09	2220.38
城镇居民平均每户家庭人口 （人）	Average Household Size in Urban Areas (person)		3.34	3.19	3.07
农村居民平均每户家庭人口 （人）	Average Household Size in Rural Areas (person)		4.10	4.01	3.74
居住	**Housing**				
城镇居民人均住房建筑面积 （平方米）	Per Capita Net Floor Space of Urban Residents (sq. m)	5.7	17.29	21.69	25.54
农村居民人均住房面积 （平方米）	Per Capita Net Floor Space of Rural Residents (sq. m)	9.7	25.20	25.71	33.70
生活	**People's Livelihood**				
城镇居民人均可支配收入 （元）	Per Capita Annual Disposable Income of Urban Residents (yuan)	288	1464	4634	6800
农村居民人均纯收入 （元）	Per Capita Net Income of Rural Residents (yuan)	155	884	2457	3595
居民储蓄存款余额 （亿元）	Outstanding Amount of Saving Deposits (100 million yuan)	12.40	470.86	1922.33	4456.83
工资	**Wages and Welfare**				
工资总额 （亿元）	Total Wages of Staff and Workers (100 million yuan)	29.05	184.60	541.62	705.36
职工平均工资 （元）	Average Wage of Staff and Workers (yuan)	513	2129	5943	10299
卫生	**Health Care**				
卫生机构数 （个）	Number of Health Care Organizations (unit)	9277	12366	12039	12813
#医院卫生院	Hospital and Commune Hospitals	2428	2491	2534	2511
床位数 （万张）	Number of Hospital Beds (10000 units)	12.29	16.45	17.46	17.31
#医院卫生院	Hospital and Commune Hospitals	11.07	14.54	15.48	16.18
卫生技术人员数 （万人）	Number of Medical Technical Personnels (10000 persons)	14.00	21.35	24.55	25.36
#医生	Doctors	5.70	9.94	11.22	11.44
市政建设	**Urban Civil Construction**				
自来水供水量 （亿吨）	Volume of Tap Water Supply (100 million tons)	3.51	25.67	38.23	35.34
排水管道长度 （公里）	Length of Sewer Pipelines (km)	1503	4099	8262	11097
年末实有道路长度 （公里）	Year-end Length of Paved Roads (km)	1893	5812	8163	11011
环境	**Environment**				
污染治理项目本年完成投资 （亿元）	Investment for the pollution Treatment Projeets Completed in this year (100 million yuan)		2.48	5.42	13.11
本年施工污染治理项目数 （个）	Number of Pollution Treatment Itemes Under Construction in 2005 (unit)		1382	919	2412
工业废水排放量 （亿吨）	Volume of Industrial Waste Water Discharged (100 million tons)		24.24	22.02	20.19
工业粉尘去除量 （万吨）	Volume of Industrial Dust Removed (10000 tons)		81	112	210

Continued

Aggregate Data		速度指标 Indicies and Growth Rate								
2005	2006	2006年比下列各年增长(%) Index (2006 as percentage of the following years)					年平均增长(%) Average Annual Growth Rate			
		1978	1990	1995	2000	2005	1979 ~ 2006	1991 ~ 2006	1996 ~ 2006	2001 ~ 2006
20.96	20.54	162.3	-35.5	-27.6	-54.2	-2.0	3.5	-2.7	-2.9	-12.2
4.26	4.73	143.8	37.5	16.8	36.3	11.0	3.2	2.0	1.4	5.3
8743	9069	1595.1	120.8	29.5	-17.6	3.7	10.6	5.1	2.4	-3.2
26.80	26.73	991.0	223.2	67.6	14.5	-0.3	8.9	7.6	4.8	2.3
2426.67	2451.14	72.2	35.7	18.6	10.4	1.0	2.0	1.9	1.6	1.7
2.92	2.88		-13.8	-9.7	-6.2	-1.4		-0.9	-0.9	-1.1
3.74	3.71		-9.5	-7.5	-0.8	-0.8		-0.6	-0.7	-0.1
28.76	29.68	420.7	71.7	36.8	16.2	3.2	6.1	3.4	2.9	2.5
38.59	40.80	320.6	61.9	58.7	21.1	5.7	5.3	3.1	4.3	3.2
12319	14084	4790.3	862.0	203.9	107.1	14.3	14.9	15.2	10.6	12.9
5276	5813	3650.3	557.6	136.6	61.7	10.2	13.8	12.5	8.1	8.3
10581.27	12183.47	98153.8	2487.5	533.8	173.4	15.1	27.9	22.5	18.3	18.2
1252.06	1520.39	5133.7	723.6	180.7	115.5	21.4	15.2	14.1	9.8	13.7
20957	23782	4535.9	1017.1	300.2	130.9	13.5	14.7	16.3	13.4	15.0
15324	17143	84.8	38.6	42.4	33.8	11.9	2.2	2.1	3.3	5.0
2486	2468	1.6	-0.9	-2.6	-1.7	-0.7	0.1	-0.1	-0.2	-0.3
19.75	21.16	72.2	28.6	21.2	22.3	7.2	2.0	1.6	1.8	3.4
18.59	19.58	76.9	34.7	26.5	21.0	5.3	2.1	1.9	2.2	3.2
25.71	27.54	96.7	29.0	12.2	8.6	7.1	2.4	1.6	1.0	1.4
10.87	11.46	101.0	15.3	2.1	0.2	5.4	2.5	0.9	0.2	0.0
39.05	34.36	878.8	33.8	-10.1	-2.8	-12.0	8.5	1.8	-1.0	-0.5
28568	31215	1976.8	661.5	277.8	181.3	9.3	11.4	13.5	12.8	18.8
28674	27058	1329.4	365.6	231.5	145.7	-5.6	10.0	10.1	11.5	16.2
38.95	28.00		1029.0	416.6	113.6	-28.1		16.4	16.1	13.5
782	642		-53.5	-30.1	-73.4	-17.9		-4.7	-3.2	-19.8
29.63	28.72		18.5	30.4	42.2	-3.1		1.1	2.4	6.0
388.73	354.36		337.5	216.4	68.4	-8.8		9.7	11.0	9.1

2-4 国民经济和社会发展结构指标
STRUCTURAL INDCATORS ON NATIONAL ECONOMIC AND SOCIAL DEVELOPMENT

指标	Item	1978	1995	2000	2005	2006
人口与就业	**Population and Employment**					
人口	**Population**					
城乡结构	Urban and Rural Structure					
城镇	Urban	13.7	27.3	41.5	50.5	51.9
乡村	Rural	86.3	72.7	58.5	49.5	48.1
性别结构	Sexual Structure					
男	Male	50.6	50.8	50.6	50.0	50.0
女	Female	49.4	49.2	49.4	50.0	50.0
就业	**Employment**					
产业结构	Industrial Structure					
第一产业	Primary Industry	69.7	46.9	42.8	31.5	29.8
第二产业	Secondary Industry	19.6	32.1	30.2	34.3	34.8
第三产业	Tertiary Industry	10.7	21.0	27.0	34.2	35.4
经济类型结构	Structures by Ownership					
城镇单位从业人员	Staff and Workers Employed in Urban Units	20.9	21.1	15.7	13.9	14.9
国有单位	State-Owned	13.2	13.3	9.5	6.3	6.1
城镇集体单位	Collective-Owned	7.7	6.3	2.7	0.9	0.8
其他单位	Others		1.5	3.5	6.8	8.0
城镇私营企业和个体从业人员	Urban Private Enterprises and Self-employed Workers	0.1	1.5	4.0	13.0	15.8
其他	Others	79.0	77.4	80.3	73.1	69.3
宏观经济	**Macro Economy**					
国民核算	**National Accounting**					
地区生产总值产业结构	Industrial Structures					
第一产业	Primary Industry	27.6	16.8	12.2	8.0	7.1
第二产业	Secondary Industry	52.6	52.7	51.9	56.6	56.6
第三产业	Tertiary Industry	19.8	30.5	35.9	35.4	36.3
地区生产总值支出结构	Domestic Expenditures					
最终消费	Total Consumption	52.4	43.7	43.4	41.2	41.6
居民消费	Resident Consumption	46.2	35.0	32.9	29.2	28.8
政府消费	Government Consumption Expenditure	6.2	8.6	10.5	12.0	12.8
资本形成总额	Gross Capital Formation	31.3	48.1	47.3	50.9	49.3
固定资本	Fixed Capital Formation	16.2	34.1	37.7	47.7	46.3
存货增加	Changes in Stock	15.1	14.0	9.6	3.1	3.0
净出口	Net Exports	16.3	8.2	9.3	7.9	9.1
投资	**Investment**					
经济类型结构	Structure by Ownership					
国有经济	State-Owned	95.2	35.9	40.1	23.8	21.3
集体经济	Collective-Owned	4.8	29.2	15.2	5.1	4.4

2-4 续表3 Continued

指 标	Item	1978	1995	2000	2005	2006
卫生技术人员	Health Care	30.5	8.4	11.9	15.8	15.0
教学人员	Teaching	22.5	27.4	34.1	46.6	48.7
生活、环境	**People's Livelihood and Environment**					
生 活	**People's Livelihood**					
城镇居民消费结构	Consumption Structure of Urban Residents					
食品	Food	55.1	51.9	41.1	37.2	36.0
衣着	Clothing	13.8	12.8	9.2	9.3	9.2
居住	Residence		7.3	8.2	9.2	10.4
其他	Others		28.0	41.5	44.3	44.4
农村居民消费结构	Consumption Structure of Rural Residents					
食品	Food	62.1	54.8	43.5	44.0	41.8
衣着	Clothing	12.1	6.5	5.4	5.4	5.4
居住	Residence	13.6	17.8	18.9	14.4	15.5
其他	Others	12.1	20.9	32.2	36.2	37.3
卫 生	**Health Care**					
卫生机构构成	Structure of Health Care Institutions					
#医院卫生院	Hospitals and Commune Hospitals	26.2	21.0	19.6	16.2	14.4
门诊部	Clinics			0.8	2.4	2.3
妇幼保健院	Maternity and Child Care Institutions	0.9	1.0	0.9	0.7	0.6
疾病预防控制中心	Disease Protection and Controlling Centers	1.2	1.2	1.1	1.0	0.9
卫生技术人员构成	Structure of Medical Technical Personnels					
#医生	Doctors	40.7	45.7	45.1	42.3	41.6
护师、护士	Registered Nurses	12.8	26.2	29.1	31.3	31.2
卫生机构床位数构成	Hospital Beds by Structures					
医院卫生院	Hospitals	90.1	88.7	93.5	94.1	92.5
疗养院、所	Sanatoriums (Stations)	1.1	4.1	3.2	2.5	1.7
其他卫生机构	Other Sanatation Organization	8.9	7.3	3.2	3.4	5.8
环境	**Environment**					
污染治理项目投资结构	Uses of Funds in Pollution Treatment					
治理废水	Waste Water Treatment		61.6	49.8	54.3	54.0
治理废气	Waste Gas Treatment		24.7	41.9	32.9	34.7
治理固体废物	Solid Wastes Treatment		8.5	6.0	3.5	2.6
治理噪声	Noise Abatement		3.5	1.1	3.5	3.1
其他	Others		1.7	1.2	5.9	5.5

2-5 江苏的一天
ONE DAY IN JIANGSU

指标	Item	1978	1995	2000	2005	2006
每天创造的财富	**Daily Production**					
地区生产总值 (亿元)	Gross Domestic Product (100 million yuan)	0.68	14.12	23.43	50.15	59.30
第一产业	Primary Industry	0.19	2.37	2.87	4.00	4.23
第二产业	Secondary Industry	0.36	7.44	12.15	28.37	33.56
工业	Industry	0.32	6.76	10.54	25.57	30.44
建筑业	Construction	0.04	0.68	1.61	2.80	3.12
第三产业	Tertiary Industry	0.14	4.31	8.41	17.78	21.50
#房地产业	Real Estate	0.02	0.37	0.82	2.00	2.51
财政收入 (亿元)	Government Revenue (100 million yuan)	0.17	0.96	2.37	8.56	10.78
粮食 (万吨)	Grain (10000 tons)	6.58	9.00	8.51	7.77	8.33
猪牛羊肉 (吨)	Meat (ton)		5968	6230	6633	6633
水产品 (吨)	Aquatic Products (ton)	1089	6013	8460	10648	11097
粗钢 (万吨)	Steel (10000 tons)	0.15	0.99	1.69	9.00	11.51
钢材 (万吨)	Rolled-Steel (10000 tons)	0.17	2.16	3.84	11.86	15.93
发电量 (亿千瓦小时)	Electricity (100 million kWh)	0.35	1.92	2.49	4.90	6.07
原煤 (万吨)	Coal (10000 tons)	4.68	7.26	6.79	7.72	8.35
水泥 (万吨)	Cement (10000 tons)	1.22	10.87	12.60	26.24	29.81
布 (万米)	Cloth (1000 m)	385	1340	924	1479	1779
每天消费量	**Daily Consumption**					
最终消费 (亿元)	Final Consumption (100 million yuan)	0.36	6.17	10.17	20.65	24.67
居民消费 (亿元)	Resident Consumption	0.32	4.95	7.71	14.63	17.09
城镇居民每人消费性支出 (元)	Per Capita Living Expenditure of Urban Residents (yuan)	0.76	10.34	14.58	23.62	26.37
#食品消费	Food Consumption	0.42	5.36	6.00	8.78	9.49
农村居民每人生活消费支出 (元)	Per Capita Living Expenditure of Rural Residents (yuan)	0.38	5.31	6.40	9.77	11.33
#食品消费	Food Consumption	0.24	2.91	2.79	4.30	4.74
政府消费 (亿元)	Government Consumption Expenditure (100 million yuan)	0.04	1.22	2.45	6.02	7.59
社会消费品零售总额 (亿元)	Total Retail Sales of Consumer Goods (100 million yuan)	0.23	4.77	7.97	15.62	18.15
每天其他经济活动	**Other Daily Economic Activities**					
货物运输量 (万吨)	Freight Traffic (10000 tons)	40.07	224.19	247.77	309.34	342.78
旅客运输量 (万人)	Passenger Traffic (10000 persons)	70.19	232.34	293.82	397.82	442.26
竣工房屋面积 (万平方米)	Floor Space of Housing Completed (sq。m))		45.61	58.32	69.57	78.67
出版报纸 (万份)	Newspaper Published (10000 copies)	67.12	436.99	639.45	734.25	732.33
邮寄函件 (万件)	Letters Delivered (10000 pieces)	44.66	145.48	157.26	115.34	107.95
进出口总额 (万美元)	Total of Imports and Exports (10000 USD)	117	4460	12504	62450	77807
#出口	Export	115	2680	7060	33694	43950
实际外商直接投资 (万美元)	Actual Foreign Direct Investment (10000 USD)		1310	1760	3611	4776
每天人口变动和婚姻	**Daily Population Changes and Marriages**					
出生人数 (人)	Births (person)	2483	2377	1808	1886	1926
死亡人数 (人)	Deaths (person)	968	1266	1299	1436	1457
结婚对数 (对)	Marriages (couple)		1576	1365	1293	1623
离婚对数 (对)	Divorces (couple)		120	153	339	378

2-6 全省人均国民经济主要指标
MAJOR PER CAPITA INDICATORS OF JIANGSU NATIONAL ECONOMY

指　　标	Item	1978	1995	2000	2005	2006
地区生产总值 （元）	Gross Domestic Product (yuan)	430	7319	11765	24560	28814
第一产业	Primary Industry	118	1230	1442	1961	2057
第二产业	Secondary Industry	226	3855	6101	13893	16308
工　业	Industry	202	3504	5294	12524	14790
建筑业	Construction	24	352	808	1369	1518
第三产业	Tertiary Industry	85	2234	4222	8706	10449
#房地产业	Real Estate	9	192	410	981	1218
财政收入 （元）	Government Revenue (yuan)	105	497	1190	4192	5239
地方财政支出 （元）	Government Expenditures (yuan)	49	360	888	2973	3630
全社会固定资产投资额 （元）	Total Investment in Fixed Assets (yuan)	38	2385	4120	11726	13407
#房地产开发	Real Estate Development		342	531	2073	2538
社会消费品零售额 （元）	Total Retail Sales of Consumer Goods (yuan)	146	2473	4001	7647	8817
进出口总额 （美元）	Total Imports and Exports (USD)	7	231	628	3058	3781
#出　口	Total Exports	7	139	354	1650	2136
农村居民纯收入 （元）	Net Income of Rural Residents (yuan)	155	2457	3595	5276	5813
城镇居民可支配收入 （元）	Disposable Income of Urban Residents (yuan)	288	4634	6800	12319	14084
居民储蓄存款 （元）	Outstanding Amount of Saving Deposits of Urban and Rural Residents (yuan)	21	2721	6083	14156	16138
在校大学生数 （人/万人）	Number of Students Enrollment in Institution of Higher Education (person/10000 persons)	10	31	65	166	174
医院病床数 （张/万人）	Hospital Beds (bed/10000 persons)	19	22	22	26	26
卫生技术人员数 （人/万人）	Medical Technical Personnel (person/10000 persons)	24	35	35	34	37
#医　生	Doctors	10	16	16	15	15
主要工农业产品产量 （千克）	Output of Major Industrial and Agricultural Products (kg)					
粮　食	Grain	414	467	427	380	405
棉　花	Cotton	8	8	4	4	5
油　料	Oil - Bearing Crops	6	23	31	29	29
粗　钢	Steel	9	51	85	441	559
原　煤	Coal	294	376	341	378	406
发电量 （千瓦小时）	Electricity (kWh)	218	994	1251	2401	2950

2－7 主要年份总产出

TOTAL OUTPUT OF THE MAJOR YEARS

本表按当年价格计算 (At current price)

年份 Year	总产出（亿元） Total Output (100 million yuan)	第一产业 Primary Industry	第二产业 Secondary Industry	#工业 Industry	第三产业 Tertiary Industry
1952	81.54	31.87	27.19	25.53	22.48
1955	100.53	36.22	35.77	32.82	28.54
1957	114.15	36.81	44.63	41.01	32.71
1962	133.12	40.15	56.38	53.36	36.59
1965	192.52	57.27	97.49	88.08	37.76
1970	273.85	71.33	149.65	135.47	52.87
1975	412.28	91.66	260.23	235.28	60.39
1976	438.59	100.71	271.19	247.59	66.69
1977	487.98	89.16	326.37	297.12	72.45
1978	566.85	105.87	378.99	337.65	81.99
1979	661.26	145.25	427.36	386.05	88.65
1980	750.12	138.45	515.71	467.82	95.96
1981	816.27	153.62	557.41	504.94	105.24
1982	897.85	188.11	593.52	534.87	116.22
1983	1014.55	206.86	679.67	600.70	128.02
1984	1239.44	253.82	836.02	745.36	149.60
1985	1642.70	288.55	1157.52	1036.67	196.63
1986	1960.44	332.66	1380.16	1235.38	247.62
1987	2472.22	380.25	1771.85	1590.31	320.12
1988	3409.56	497.95	2370.81	2152.93	540.80
1989	3839.67	522.25	2713.50	2507.42	603.92
1990	4208.23	580.53	2978.51	2764.10	649.19
1991	4820.22	580.93	3416.59	3161.60	822.70
1992	6862.87	673.82	5089.59	4673.57	1099.46
1993	10245.27	875.37	7757.28	7096.46	1612.62
1994	14163.89	1358.50	10601.01	9826.50	2204.38
1995	17699.96	1721.35	13053.11	11995.30	2925.50
1996	20304.53	1953.13	14764.02	13425.15	3587.38
1997	22314.78	2096.40	16342.27	14703.65	3876.11
1998	23433.26	2129.05	16967.90	15163.56	4336.31
1999	24578.40	2108.71	17714.22	15779.09	4755.47
2000	27034.80	2115.39	19714.71	17653.76	5204.71
2001	29832.61	2174.81	21753.49	19595.68	5904.31
2002	32550.33	1953.50	23884.16	21386.23	6712.67
2003	38729.25	2115.88	28971.95	25882.11	7641.42
2004	46972.13	2417.63	35900.90	32068.53	8653.60
2005	55884.99	2576.98	42602.71	38651.40	10705.30
2006	67587.99	2707.07	51929.85	47381.19	12951.07

2-8 主要年份总产出指数
INDICES OF TOTAL OUTPUT OF THE MAJOR YEARS

按可比价格计算,1952=100　　　　(At comparable price, 1952=100)

年份 Year	总产出 Total Output	第一产业 Primary Industry	第二产业 Secondary Industry	#工业 Industry	第三产业 Tertiary Industry
1952	100.0	100.0	100.0	100.0	100.0
1955	120.0	113.0	134.3	129.7	123.6
1957	127.0	109.1	169.4	165.9	132.1
1962	121.8	93.4	200.8	208.5	121.4
1965	181.6	139.7	372.6	365.0	129.2
1970	263.7	166.3	653.9	651.2	179.4
1975	390.0	204.4	1164.8	1165.2	207.2
1976	420.8	212.3	1267.0	1285.1	232.1
1977	463.9	191.0	1524.5	1543.0	249.8
1978	544.0	232.1	1776.6	1755.8	285.4
1979	598.9	257.4	1983.5	2000.3	291.2
1980	671.6	243.2	2380.5	2417.9	304.9
1981	732.4	262.4	2589.9	2618.8	342.2
1982	802.5	301.5	2796.8	2820.2	376.6
1983	908.5	319.4	3242.2	3211.5	415.6
1984	1090.8	371.9	3955.8	3959.1	477.5
1985	1379.6	383.5	5250.3	5280.7	599.0
1986	1595.5	407.5	6115.4	6161.6	731.7
1987	1912.0	420.2	7474.4	7631.1	906.9
1988	2399.8	448.1	9385.3	9590.3	1288.2
1989	2492.6	449.6	9671.7	10036.5	1422.0
1990	2697.8	460.9	10591.2	11042.5	1502.8
1991	3046.2	455.7	12110.4	12642.3	1807.0
1992	4267.8	515.0	18038.4	18864.6	2272.0
1993	5746.6	573.1	25197.1	26795.1	2887.9
1994	7334.3	642.4	33172.0	35831.4	3354.0
1995	8708.7	730.4	39686.3	42818.5	3903.8
1996	10008.5	803.0	45823.2	49213.2	4471.4
1997	11314.1	856.4	52098.2	55704.5	5035.8
1998	12441.1	885.7	57347.6	61113.7	5676.1
1999	13612.6	925.5	62773.5	66941.5	6330.8
2000	14939.2	959.6	68961.7	73797.1	7079.4
2001	16383.3	988.4	75650.7	81472.0	7946.8
2002	18049.8	1013.1	83613.8	89782.1	8878.3
2003	20560.9	1005.0	96748.4	103967.7	9976.2
2004	23692.0	1065.3	112553.6	121434.3	11356.7
2005	27008.3	1098.4	129038.5	140742.3	13010.7
2006	31275.6	1145.8	150368.6	164358.9	15049.5

2－13 地区生产总值项目结构（2006年）

STRUCTURE OF GROSS DOMESTIC PRODUCT (2006)

单位:亿元 (100 million yuan)

行业	Sector	增加值 Value Added	劳动者报酬 Payment for Laborers	生产税净额 Taxes on Production	固定资产折旧 Depreciation of Fixed Assets	营业盈余 Operating Surplus
地区生产总值	**Gross Domestic Product**	**21645.08**	**8805.23**	**3328.41**	**3232.53**	**6278.91**
第一产业	Primary Industry	1545.01	1361.52	4.72	67.83	110.94
农、林、牧、渔业	Farming, Forestry, Animal Husbandry and Fishery	1545.01	1361.52	4.72	67.83	110.94
第二产业	Secondary Industry	12250.84	4369.89	2340.72	1879.10	3661.13
工业	Industry	11110.24	3689.54	2214.54	1834.05	3372.11
采矿业	Mining and Quarrying	204.16	79.30	47.49	24.71	52.66
制造业	Manufacturing	10350.36	3512.42	2029.50	1595.68	3212.76
电力、燃气及水的生产和供应业	Power, Gas and Water Production and Supply	555.72	97.82	137.55	213.66	106.69
建筑业	Construction	1140.60	680.35	126.18	45.05	289.02
第三产业	Tertiary Industry	7849.23	3073.82	982.97	1285.60	2506.84
交通运输、仓储和邮政业	Transportation, Storage and Post	928.41	266.35	82.86	153.53	425.67
信息传输、计算机服务和软件业	Information Transmmision, Computer Service and Software	383.47	91.69	23.61	140.08	128.09
批发和零售业	Wholesale and Retail Sales	2028.80	650.71	561.60	99.66	716.83
住宿和餐饮业	Hotel and Catering Service	362.14	184.67	31.78	39.23	106.46
金融业	Banking	723.79	170.69	83.18	36.17	433.75
房地产业	Real Estate	914.78	73.50	129.87	509.96	201.45
租赁和商务服务业	Leasing and Commercial Services	284.22	87.96	21.98	56.85	117.43
科学研究、技术服务和地质勘查业	Scientific Research, Polytechnical Service and Geological Prospecting	133.36	77.73	10.18	12.69	32.76
水利、环境和公共设施管理业	Water Coservancy, Environment and Public Facility Management	100.90	49.55	2.57	25.53	23.25
居民服务和其他服务业	Resident Services and Others	352.22	134.28	15.47	19.81	182.66
教育	Education	583.89	466.17	1.65	60.44	55.63
卫生、社会保障和社会福利业	Health Care, Social Security and Social Welfare	255.54	196.32	2.00	24.35	32.87
文化、体育和娱乐业	Culture, Sports and Recreation	145.71	58.98	12.31	24.43	49.99
公共管理和社会组织	Public Management and Social Organizations	652.00	565.22	3.91	82.87	0.00

2－14 三次产业贡献率
CONTRIBUTING RATE OF THE THREE INDUSTRIES

本表按可比价格计算，单位：%　　(At comparable price，%)

年 份 Year	地 区 生产总值 Gross Domestic Product	第一产业 Primary Industry	第二产业 Secondary Industry	#工 业 Industry	第三产业 Tertiary Industry
1990	100.0	3.7	59.0	59.3	37.3
1991	100.0	-11.8	53.2	48.1	58.6
1992	100.0	9.2	62.0	54.9	28.8
1993	100.0	2.6	61.5	55.6	35.9
1994	100.0	5.3	74.2	69.2	20.5
1995	100.0	13.3	59.4	51.4	27.3
1996	100.0	9.4	57.6	46.0	33.0
1997	100.0	5.9	60.3	48.2	33.8
1998	100.0	2.6	63.2	49.7	34.2
1999	100.0	5.6	64.9	57.2	29.5
2000	100.0	4.3	64.3	59.1	31.4
2001	100.0	3.6	55.9	51.0	40.5
2002	100.0	2.7	61.2	54.3	36.1
2003	100.0	-0.1	67.2	60.7	32.9
2004	100.0	3.8	63.6	58.1	32.6
2005	100.0	1.7	61.8	57.0	36.5
2006	100.0	2.7	60.5	56.5	36.8

注：产业贡献率指各产业增加值增量与 GDP 增量之比。

Note：Industrial contributing rate refers to the proportion of the increment of every industrial value added to the increment of GDP.

2－15 三次产业拉动率
PULLING RATE OF THE THREE INDUSTRIES

本表按可比价格计算，单位：%　　(At comparable price，%)

年 份 Year	地 区 生产总值 Gross Domestic Product	第一产业 Primary Industry	第二产业 Secondary Industry	#工 业 Industry	第三产业 Tertiary Industry
1990	5.0	0.2	2.9	3.0	1.9
1991	8.3	-1.0	4.4	4.0	4.9
1992	25.6	2.4	15.8	14.1	7.4
1993	19.8	0.5	12.2	11.0	7.1
1994	16.5	0.9	12.2	11.4	3.4
1995	15.4	2.1	9.1	7.9	4.2
1996	12.2	1.2	7.0	5.6	4.0
1997	12.0	0.7	7.2	5.8	4.1
1998	11.0	0.3	6.9	5.5	3.8
1999	10.1	0.6	6.5	5.8	3.0
2000	10.6	0.5	6.8	6.3	3.3
2001	10.2	0.4	5.7	5.2	4.1
2002	11.7	0.3	7.2	6.3	4.2
2003	13.6	0.0	9.1	8.3	4.5
2004	14.8	0.6	9.4	8.6	4.8
2005	14.5	0.2	9.0	8.3	5.3
2006	14.9	0.4	9.0	8.4	5.5

注：产业拉动率指 GDP 增长速度与各产业贡献率之乘积。

Note：The industrial pulling rate to GDP growth refers to the growth rate of GDP multiplying the industrial contributing rate.

2-16 按支出法计算的地区生产总值
GROSS DOMESTIC PRODUCT BY EXPENDITURE APPROACH

本表按当年价格计算 (At current price)

年份 Year	地区生产总值(亿元) Gross Domestic Product (100 million yuan)	最终消费 Final Consumption Expenditure	居民消费 Resident Consumption Expenditure	政府消费 Government Consumption Expenditure	资本形成总额 Gross Capital Formation	固定资本形成 Fixed Capital Formation	存货增加 Changes in Inventories	货物和服务净出口 Net Export of Goods and Services
1978	249.24	130.55	115.15	15.40	77.98	40.40	37.58	40.71
1980	319.80	175.47	154.72	20.75	97.44	58.25	39.19	46.89
1985	651.82	353.72	300.86	52.86	271.42	193.25	78.17	26.68
1989	1321.85	662.01	557.60	104.41	528.44	336.24	192.20	131.40
1990	1416.50	717.36	608.29	109.07	588.44	374.12	214.32	110.70
1991	1601.38	835.07	656.99	178.08	694.80	461.98	232.82	71.51
1992	2136.02	960.21	735.62	224.59	1069.20	747.29	321.91	106.61
1993	2998.16	1251.08	984.44	266.64	1589.93	1201.41	388.52	157.15
1994	4057.39	1721.45	1350.89	370.56	2018.95	1434.95	584.00	316.99
1995	5155.25	2250.66	1806.43	444.23	2479.30	1756.88	722.42	425.29
1996	6004.21	2721.84	2218.68	503.16	2798.62	2062.17	736.45	483.75
1997	6680.34	3020.94	2417.77	603.17	2925.28	2295.97	629.31	734.12
1998	7199.95	3161.88	2513.52	648.36	3321.44	2642.29	679.15	716.63
1999	7697.82	3339.79	2594.18	745.61	3554.26	2842.65	711.61	803.77
2000	8553.69	3710.72	2815.51	895.21	4044.78	3225.42	819.36	798.19
2001	9456.84	4141.92	3027.67	1114.25	4393.21	3543.16	850.05	921.71
2002	10606.85	4801.91	3475.13	1326.78	4808.67	3994.23	814.44	996.27
2003	12442.87	5484.04	3909.55	1574.49	6182.38	5480.80	701.58	776.45
2004	15003.60	6227.21	4429.02	1798.19	7957.76	6972.68	985.08	818.63
2005	18305.66	7538.04	5339.09	2198.95	9313.16	8739.71	573.45	1454.46
2006	21645.08	9005.61	6236.42	2769.19	10673.86	10021.43	652.43	1965.61

2-17 按支出法计算的地区生产总值指数
INDICES OF GROSS DOMESTIC PRODUCTS BY EXPENDITURES APPROACH

按可比价格计算,1952=100 (At comparable price, 1952=100)

年份 Year	地区生产总值 Gross Domestic Product	最终消费 Final Consumption Expenditure	居民消费 Resident Consumption Expenditure	政府消费 Government Consumption Expenditure	资本形成总额 Gross Capital Formation	固定资本形成 Fixed Capital Formation	存货增加 Changes in Inventories
1952	100.0	100.0	100.0	100.0	100.0	100.0	100.0
1978	371.3	367.6	352.3	545.3	695.7	593.2	847.1
1980	436.0	468.4	448.7	696.3	809.3	811.3	806.4
1985	809.2	824.0	757.4	1595.0	2156.6	2573.0	1541.6
1989	1241.7	1000.3	885.3	2331.2	3610.7	3998.6	3037.7
1990	1303.9	1063.7	949.6	2383.2	4161.1	4791.5	3229.8
1991	1412.1	1162.8	992.5	3246.0	4472.4	5230.2	3389.1
1992	1773.4	1493.5	1253.9	4462.1	5534.2	7583.6	3054.8
1993	2124.4	1787.9	1518.0	5103.7	6603.7	9239.5	3450.0
1994	2474.3	2095.2	1772.7	6068.9	7772.3	10860.6	4074.8
1995	2855.3	2422.4	2027.1	7331.8	9053.4	12381.0	5022.8
1996	3204.5	2670.9	2261.5	7711.4	10229.2	14289.6	5367.3
1997	3587.6	2944.6	2444.1	9193.2	11375.3	16021.8	5834.1
1998	3982.8	3250.8	2677.4	10441.6	12662.2	18662.4	5645.7
1999	4384.8	3593.4	2889.2	12530.4	13870.1	20698.5	5922.1
2000	4848.4	3970.6	3107.9	15034.2	15272.9	22421.1	6900.9
2001	5340.5	4420.0	3371.3	18080.3	16765.7	24392.9	7841.6
2002	5963.5	4993.8	3714.3	21867.4	18721.5	28445.5	7294.1
2003	6775.9	5667.9	4176.3	25417.8	21744.0	35873.5	5035.9
2004	7775.4	6452.9	4780.6	28542.9	25319.8	41206.1	6550.7
2005	8901.2	7391.4	5459.3	32947.9	28664.5	50217.2	3093.4
2006	10227.5	8581.4	6212.7	40097.6	32047.0	56193.1	3449.2

2－18 按产业分资本形成总额
TOTAL CAPITAL BY TYPE OF INDUSTRY

本表按当年价格计算 (At current prices)

年份 Year	资本形成总额(亿元) Gross Capital Formation (100 million yuan)	固定资本形成 Fixed Capital Formation	存货增加 Changes in Inventories	第一产业 Primary Industry 资本形成总额 Gross Capital Formation	固定资本形成 Fixed Capital Formation	存货增加 Changes in Inventories
1978	77.98	40.40	37.58	6.36	2.23	4.13
1980	97.44	58.25	39.19	6.95	2.44	4.51
1985	271.42	193.25	78.17	12.86	4.50	8.36
1989	528.44	336.24	192.20	19.60	10.76	8.84
1990	588.44	374.12	214.32	26.32	11.97	14.35
1991	694.80	461.98	232.82	27.37	12.94	14.43
1992	1069.20	747.29	321.91	36.29	15.69	20.60
1993	1589.93	1201.41	388.52	45.58	21.87	23.71
1994	2018.95	1434.95	584.00	86.38	48.26	38.12
1995	2479.30	1756.88	722.42	113.74	41.94	71.80
1996	2798.62	2062.17	736.45	149.17	45.41	103.76
1997	2925.28	2295.97	629.31	184.87	59.73	125.14
1998	3321.44	2642.29	679.15	201.22	68.37	132.85
1999	3554.26	2842.65	711.61	215.70	69.56	146.14
2000	4044.78	3225.42	819.36	215.35	70.63	144.72
2001	4393.21	3543.16	850.05	221.67	75.12	146.55
2002	4808.67	3994.23	814.44	221.62	76.90	144.72
2003	6182.38	5480.80	701.58	137.30	34.09	103.21
2004	7957.76	6972.68	985.08	117.82	37.70	80.12
2005	9313.16	8739.71	573.45	126.87	45.42	81.45
2006	10673.86	10021.43	652.43	125.43	65.43	60.00

2－18 续表 Continued

年份 Year	第二产业 Secondary Industry 资本形成总额 Gross Capital Formation	固定资本形成 Fixed Capital Formation	存货增加 Changes in Inventories	第三产业 Tertiary Industry 资本形成总额 Gross Capital Formation	固定资本形成 Fixed Capital Formation	存货增加 Changes in Inventories
1978	53.94	27.26	26.68	17.68	10.91	6.77
1980	67.72	39.70	28.02	22.77	16.11	6.66
1985	145.25	89.82	55.43	113.31	98.93	14.38
1989	256.83	125.75	131.08	252.01	199.73	52.28
1990	286.30	139.92	146.38	275.82	222.23	53.59
1991	336.72	196.80	139.92	330.71	252.24	78.47
1992	593.59	399.80	193.79	439.32	331.80	107.52
1993	923.38	669.43	253.95	620.97	510.11	110.86
1994	1073.66	736.45	337.21	858.91	650.24	208.67
1995	1262.85	829.54	433.31	1102.71	885.40	217.31
1996	1356.02	931.49	424.53	1293.43	1085.27	208.16
1997	1370.20	1037.52	332.68	1370.21	1198.72	171.49
1998	1495.48	1133.67	361.81	1624.74	1440.25	184.49
1999	1565.19	1183.18	382.01	1773.37	1589.91	183.46
2000	1926.06	1476.74	449.32	1903.37	1678.05	225.32
2001	2039.67	1572.69	466.98	2131.87	1895.35	236.52
2002	2397.27	1971.56	425.71	2189.78	1945.77	244.01
2003	3358.51	2909.76	448.75	2686.57	2536.95	149.62
2004	4477.75	3713.32	764.43	3362.19	3221.66	140.53
2005	5255.73	4872.11	383.62	3930.56	3822.18	108.38
2006	5919.84	5423.21	496.63	4628.59	4532.79	95.80

主要统计指标解释

可比价格　指计算各种总量指标所采用的扣除了价格变动因素的价格，可进行不同时期总量指标的对比。按可比价格计算总量指标有两种方法：一种是直接用产品产量乘某一年的不变价格计算；另一种是用价格指数进行缩减。

不变价格　指以同类产品某年的平均价格作为固定价格，用于计算各年的产品价值。按不变价格计算的产品价值消除了价格变动因素，不同时期对比可以反映生产的发展速度。新中国成立后，随着工农业产品价格水平的变化，国家统计局先后五次制定了全国统一的工业产品不变价格和农业产品不变价格。从1952年到1957年使用1952年工（农）业产品不变价格，从1957年到1970年使用1957年不变价格，从1971年到1980年使用1970年不变价格，从1981年到1990年使用1980年不变价格，从1991年开始使用1990年不变价格。

平均增长速度　我国计算平均增长速度有两种方法：一种是习惯上经常使用的"水平法"，又称几何平均法，是以间隔期最后一年的水平同基期水平对比来计算平均每年增长（或下降）速度；另一种是"累计法"，又称代数平均法或方程法，是以间隔期内各年水平的总和同基期水平对比来计算平均每年增长（或下降）速度。在一般正常情况下，两种方法计算的平均每年增长速度比较接近；但在经济发展不平衡、出现大起大落时，两种方法计算的结果差别较大。

企业（单位）登记注册类型　是以在工商行政管理机关登记注册的各类企业为划分对象，以工商行政管理部门对企业登记注册的类型为依据，将企业登记注册类型分为内资企业、港澳台商投资企业和外商投资企业三大类。内资企业包括国有企业、集体企业、股份合作企业、联营企业、有限责任公司、股份有限公司、私营公司和其他企业；港澳台商投资企业和外商投资企业分别包括合资经营企业、合作经营企业、独资经营企业和股份有限公司。对不在工商行政管理部门进行登记注册的行政机关、事业单位和社会团体，主要按其经费来源和管理方式进行划分。

国内生产总值（GDP）　指一个国家所有常住单位在一定时期内生产活动的最终成果。国内生产总值有三种表现形态，即价值形态、收入形态和产品形态。从价值形态看，它是所有常住单位在一定时期内生产的全部货物和服务价值超过同期中间投入的全部非固定资产货物和服务价值的差额，即所有常住单位的增加值之和；从收入形态看，它是所有常住单位在一定时期内创造并分配给常住单位和非常住单位的初次收入分配之和；从产品形态看，它是所有常住单位在一定时期内最终使用的货物和服务价值与货物和服务净出口价值之和。在实际核算中，国内生产总值有三种计算方法，即生产法、收入法和支出法。三种方法分别从不同的方面反映国内生产总值及其构成。对于地区，GDP中文名称为"地区生产总值"。

支出法国内生产总值　指一个国家所有常住单位在一定时期内用于最终消费、资本形成总额，以及货物和服务的净出口总额，它反映本期生产总值的使用及构成。对于地区，名称为"支出法地区生产总值"。

最终消费　指常住单位在一定时期内对于货物和服务的全部最终消费支出，也就是常住单位为满足物质、文化和精神生活的需要，从本国经济领土和国外购买的货物和服务的支出；不包括非常住单位在本国经济领土内的消费支出。最终消费分为居民消费和政府消费。

居民消费　指常住住户对货物和服务的全部最终消费支出。居民消费按市场价格计算，即按居民支付的购买者价格计算。购买者价格是购买者取得货物所支付的价格，包括购买者支付的运输和商业费用。居民消费除了直接以货币形式购买货物和服务的消费之外，还包括以其他方式获得的货物和服务的消费支出，即所谓的虚拟消费支出。居民虚拟消费支出包括以下几种类型：单位以实物报酬及实物转移的形式提供给劳动者的货物和服务；住户生产并由本住户消费了的货物和服务，其中的服务仅指住户的自有住房服务；金融机构提供的金融媒介服务；保险公司提供的保险服务。

政府消费　指政府部门为全社会提供公共服务的消费支出和免费或以较低价格向住户提供的货物和服务的净支出。前者等于政府服务的产出价值减去政府单位所获得的经营收入的价值，政府服务的产出价值等于它的经常性业务支出加上固定资产折旧；后者等于政府部门免费或以较低价格向住户提供的货物和服务的市场价值减去向住户收取的价值。

资本形成总额　指常住单位在一定时期内获得的减去处置的固定资产加存货的变动，包括固定资本形成总额和存货增加。

固定资本形成总额　指常住单位购置、转入和自产自用的固定资产，扣除固定资产的销售和转出后的价值，分有形固定资产形成总额和无形固定资产形成总额。有形固定资产形成总额包括一定时期内完成的建筑工程、安装工程和设备工器具购置（减处置）价值，以及土地改良、新增役、种、奶、毛、娱乐用牲畜和新增经济林木价值。无形固定资产形成总额包括矿藏的勘探、计算机软件、娱乐和文学艺术品原件等获得减处置。

存货增加　指常住单位存货实物量变动的市场价值，即期末价值减期初价值的差额。存货增加可以是正值，也可以是负值；正值表示存货上升，负值表示存货下降。它包括生产单位购进的原材料、燃料和储备物资等存货，以及生产单位生产的产成品、在制品等存货等。

货物和服务净出口　指货物和服务出口减货物和服务进口的差额。出口包括常住单位向非常住单位出售或无偿转让的各种货物和服务的价值;进口包括常住单位从非常住单位购买或无偿得到的各种货物和服务的价值。由于服务活动的提供与使用同时发生,因此服务的进出口业务并不发生出入境现象,一般把常住单位从国外得到的服务作为进口,非常住单位从本国得到的服务作为出口。货物的出口和进口都按离岸价格计算。

Explanatory Notes on Main Statistical Indicators

Comparable Prices refer to prices that are used to remove the factors of price change in calculating economic aggregates, so as to facilitate comparison of aggregates over time. Two methods are used for calculating economic aggregates at comparable prices: 1. Multiplying the output of products by their constant prices of certain year; 2. Deflation of data at current prices by relevant price index.

Constant Price refers to the average price of a given product in certain year, which is used for comparison of output value over time. As the output value at constant prices removes the factor of price changes, it reflects the trend of production development over time. Since 1 949, with the changes in general price level, National Bureau of Statistics has issued nationally unified constant prices five times: the 1952 constant prices for 1949 – 1957; the 1957 constant prices for 1957 – 1971; the 1970 constant prices for 1971 – 1981; the 1980 constant prices for 1981 – 1990; and the 1990 constant prices have been used since 1991.

Average Annual Growth Rate Two methods for calculating average annual growth rate are applied in China, one is often called level approach, or the method of calculating geometric average, which is derived by comparing the level of the last year of the interval with that of the beginning year; the other is called accumulative approach or algebraic average or equation method, which is derived by the summation of the actual figure of each year in the interval divided by the figure in the base year. Usually the results calculated by the two methods are fairly close, but they differed sharply when uneven economic development occurred with striking fluctuations in growth.

Registration Status of Enterprises Enterprises are classified into 3 categories, namely domestic-funded enterprises, enterprises with investment from Hong Kong, Macao and Taiwan, and enterprises with foreign investment, in the light of the registration status of an enterprise in industrial and commercial administration agencies. Domestic-funded enterprises include state-owned enterprises, collective-owned enterprises, cooperative enterprises, joint ownership enterprises, limited liability corporations, share-holding corporations Ltd., private enterprises and other enterprises. Included in the enterprises with investment from Hong Kong, Macau and Taiwan and enterprises with foreign investment are joint-venture enterprises, cooperative enterprises, sole investment enterprises and share-holding corporations Ltd. For government agencies, institutions and social organizations which are not requested to be registered in industrial and commercial administration agencies, they are classified mainly by their sources of funds and way of management.

Gross Domestic Product (GDP) refers to the final products of all resident units in a country during a certain period of time. Gross domestic product is expressed in three different forms, i. e. value, income, and products respectively. The form of value refers to the total value of all products and services produced by all resident units during a certain period of time minus total value of intimidate input of materials and services of the nature of non-fixed assets or the summation of the value-added of all resident units; the form of income includes all the income created by all resident units and distributed primarily to all resident and non-resident units; the form of products refers to the value of all final goods and services for final use by all resident units plus the value of net exports of goods and services during a given period of time. In the practice of national accounting, gross domestic product is calculated with three approaches, i. e. production approach, income approach, and expenditure approach, which reflect gross domestic product and its composition from different aspects. The Chinese meaning of "GDP" is "Gross Regional Product" as to the certain region.

GDP Calculated with Expenditure Approach refers to total expenditure on final consumption, total capital formation and net export of goods and services by resident units of a country in a certain period of time. It reflects the composition of GDP by its use.

Final Consumption refers to the total expenditure of resident units on final consumption of goods and services in a certain period, namely the expenditure of the resident units for purchases of goods and services from domestic economic territory and abroad to meet the requirements of material, cultural and spiritual life. It excludes the expenditure of non-resident units on consumption in the economic territory of the country. The final consumption is classified into household consumption and government consumption.

Households Consumption refers to the total expenditure of resident households on the final consumption of goods and services. The households consumption is calculated at market prices, namely the purchasers prices which the households pay; the purchasers prices of goods are the prices the households pay when they obtain the goods, including the transport and commercial expenses paid by the households. In addition to the consumption of goods and services bought by the households directly with money, the expenditure on goods and services obtained by the households in other ways, i. e. the so-called imputed expenditure on consumption, is also included in the households consumption. The imputation expenditure of the households on consumption includes the following types: (a) the goods and services provided to the households by the units in the form of payment in kind and transfer in kind; (b) the goods and services produced and consumed by the households themselves, in which the services refer only to the services provided by the residential buildings owned by the households; (c) the services of financial intermediary provided by the financial institutions; (d) the insurance services provided by the insurance companies.

Government Consumption refers to the expenditure on the consumption of the public services provided by the government to the whole society and the net expenditure on the goods and services provided by the government to the households at free charge or lower prices. The former equals to the output value of the government services minus the value of operating income obtained by the government departments. (The output value of the government services equals to its current operating expenditure plus depreciation of fixed assets). The latter equals to the market value of the goods and services provided by the government free of charge or at low prices to the households minus the value received by the government from the households.

Total Capital Formation refers to the fixed assets acquired minus those disposed and the change in inventory, including the total fixed assets formation and the increase in inventory.

Total Fixed Capital Formation refers to the value of fixed assets purchased, transferred in by the resident units and those produced and used by themselves deducting the value of fixed assets sold and transferred out. It can be classified into total tangible assets formation and total intangible assets formation. The total tangible assets formation include the value of the construction projects, installation projects completed and the equipment, apparatus and instruments purchased as well as the value of land improved, the value of draught animals, breeding stock, milk, wool and recreational animals and the newly increased economic forest in a certain period. The total intangible assets formation includes the prospecting of minerals, the acquisition of computer software, the originals of recreational works and works of literature and arts minus the disposal of them. Increase in Inventory refers to the market value of the change in inventory, i. e. the difference of value between the beginning and the end of the period. The increase in inventory can be positive or negative. A positive value indicates the increase in inventory while a negative value indicates the decrease in stock. The inventory includes the raw materials, fuels and reserve materials purchased by the production units as well as the inventory of finished products, semi-finished products, work in progress. etc.

Increase in Inventory refers to the market value of the change in inventory, i. e. The difference of value between the beginning and the end of the period. The increase in inventory can be positive or negative. A positive value indicates the increase in inventory while a negative value indicates the decrease in stock. The inventory includes the materials, fuels and reserve materials purchased by the production units as well as the inventory of finished products, semi-finished products, work-in-progress, ect.

Net Export of Goods and Services refers to the difference of the exports of goods and services minus the imports of goods and services. The imports include the value of various goods and services sold or gratuitously transferred by the resident units to the non-resident units. The imports include the value of various goods and services purchased or gratuitously acquired by the resident units from the non-resident units. Because the provision of services and the use of them happen simultaneously, the import and export of services do not appear to have the phenomena of crossing the border of the country. The acquisition of services by the resident units from abroad is usually treated as import while the acquisition of services by non-resident units in this country is usually treated as export. The export and import of goods are calculated at FOB.

第 3 篇

人口、就业

POPULATION AND EMPLOYMENT

3－1 全省人口数、户数(常住)
POPULATION AND HOUSEHOLDS(PERMANENT)

年份 Year	总户数(万户) Households (10000)	总人口(万人) Total (10000 persons)	按性别分 Grouped by Sex 男 Male 人口数 Population	 男 Male 比重(%) Proportion	 女 Female 人口数 Population	 女 Female 比重(%) Proportion	平均每户人数(人/户) Average Person Per Household (person)	年平均人口(万人) Average Person Per Year (10000 persons)	人口密度(人/平方公里) Density of Population (person/sq. km)
1990	1806.78	6766.90	3443.68	50.9	3323.22	49.1	3.75		660
1991	1859.70	6843.70	3451.96	50.4	3391.74	49.6	3.68	6805.30	667
1992	1957.85	6911.20	3483.24	50.4	3427.96	49.6	3.53	6877.45	674
1993	1893.28	6967.27	3513.59	50.4	3453.68	49.6	3.68	6939.24	679
1994	1923.44	7020.54	3534.09	50.3	3486.45	49.7	3.65	6993.91	684
1995	2066.09	7066.02	3589.56	50.8	3476.46	49.2	3.42	7043.28	689
1996	2014.21	7110.16	3610.72	50.8	3499.44	49.2	3.53	7088.09	693
1997	2133.69	7147.86	3628.08	50.8	3519.78	49.2	3.35	7129.01	697
1998	2087.92	7182.46	3643.21	50.7	3539.26	49.3	3.44	7165.16	700
1999	2121.51	7213.13	3656.05	50.7	3557.08	49.3	3.40	7197.80	703
2000	2220.38	7327.24	3710.28	50.6	3616.96	49.4	3.30	7270.19	714
2001	2312.87	7354.92	3722.99	50.6	3631.93	49.4	3.18	7341.08	717
2002	2343.17	7380.97	3739.60	50.7	3641.37	49.3	3.15	7367.95	719
2003	2328.87	7405.82	3749.00	50.6	3656.82	49.4	3.18	7393.40	722
2004	2359.52	7432.50	3766.04	50.7	3666.46	49.3	3.15	7419.16	724
2005	2426.67	7474.50	3738.74	50.0	3735.76	50.0	3.08	7453.50	729
2006	2451.14	7549.50	3776.37	50.0	3773.13	50.0	3.08	7512.00	736

3－2 全省市、镇、乡村人口数及其构成
CITY, TOWN, COUNTRY POPULATION AND IT'S COMPOSITION

单位:万人 (10000 persons)

年份 Year	总人口数 Total Population	#城镇人口 City and Town 人口数 Population	 占总人口% Proportion	市 City 人口数 Population	 占总人口% Proportion	镇 Town 人口数 Population	 占总人口% Proportion	乡村 Country 人口数 Population	 占总人口% Proportion
1978	5834.32	800.77	13.7	570.14	9.8	230.63	3.9	5033.55	86.3
1980	5938.19	901.78	15.2	636.41	10.7	265.37	4.5	5036.41	84.8
1985	6213.48	1099.79	17.7					5113.69	82.3
1990	6766.90	1458.94	21.6	1043.45	15.4	415.49	6.1	5307.96	78.5
1991	6843.70	1587.74	23.2	1163.43	17.0	424.31	6.2	5255.96	76.8
1992	6911.20	1643.72	23.8	1182.59	17.1	461.13	6.7	5267.48	76.2
1993	6967.27	1673.58	24.0	1199.26	17.2	474.32	6.8	5293.69	76.0
1994	7020.54	1733.01	24.7	1255.58	17.9	477.43	6.8	5287.53	75.3
1995	7066.02	1929.09	27.3	1331.30	18.8	597.79	8.5	5136.93	72.7
1996	7110.16	1942.50	27.3	1328.18	18.7	614.32	8.6	5167.66	72.7
1997	7147.86	2133.64	29.9	1465.31	20.5	668.33	9.4	5014.22	70.1
1998	7182.46	2262.47	31.5	1537.05	21.4	725.42	10.1	4919.99	68.5
1999	7213.13	2520.09	34.9	1685.84	23.4	834.25	11.6	4693.04	65.1
2000	7327.24	3040.81	41.5	1868.45	25.5	1172.36	16.0	4286.43	58.5
2001	7354.92	3133.20	42.6	1925.22	26.2	1207.98	16.4	4221.72	57.4
2002	7380.97	3299.29	44.7	2021.48	27.4	1277.81	17.3	4081.68	55.3
2003	7405.82	3463.70	46.8	2122.55	28.7	1341.15	18.1	3942.12	53.2
2004	7432.50	3580.98	48.2	2148.59	28.9	1432.39	19.3	3851.52	51.8
2005	7474.50	3774.62	50.5	2273.21	30.4	1501.42	20.1	3699.88	49.5
2006	7549.50	3918.19	51.9	2359.67	31.3	1558.52	20.6	3631.31	48.1

3-3 全省人口自然变动
NATURAL CHANGE OF POPULATION

单位:万人 (10000 persons)

年份 Year	出生 Birth 人数 Population	出生率(‰) Birth Rate	死亡 Death 人数 Population	死亡率(‰) Death Rate	自然增长 Natural Growth 人数 Population	自然增长率(‰) Natural Growth Rate
1978	90.62	15.63	35.32	6.09	55.30	9.54
1979	85.79	14.63	34.31	5.85	51.48	8.78
1980	86.90	14.69	38.87	6.57	48.03	8.12
1981	100.58	16.83	37.18	6.22	63.40	10.61
1982	99.42	16.43	34.77	5.75	64.65	10.68
1983	73.17	11.97	36.39	5.95	36.78	6.02
1984	64.09	10.42	36.32	5.90	27.77	4.52
1985	67.11	10.84	36.35	5.87	30.76	4.97
1986	82.38	13.20	36.19	5.80	46.19	7.40
1987	97.27	15.42	36.50	5.79	60.77	9.63
1988	102.46	16.03	37.65	5.89	64.81	10.14
1989	111.27	17.15	36.31	5.60	74.96	11.55
1990	137.96	20.54	43.86	6.53	94.10	14.01
1991	116.03	17.05	44.23	6.50	71.80	10.55
1992	108.04	15.71	46.49	6.76	61.55	8.95
1993	96.94	13.97	45.87	6.61	51.07	7.36
1994	96.38	13.78	47.98	6.86	48.40	6.92
1995	86.77	12.32	46.20	6.56	40.57	5.76
1996	85.84	12.11	46.64	6.58	39.20	5.53
1997	81.47	11.43	48.76	6.84	32.71	4.59
1998	78.60	10.97	49.01	6.84	29.59	4.13
1999	75.58	10.50	49.95	6.94	25.63	3.56
2000	66.01	9.08	47.40	6.52	18.61	2.56
2001	66.28	9.03	48.60	6.62	17.68	2.41
2002	67.56	9.17	51.50	6.99	16.06	2.18
2003	66.83	9.04	51.98	7.03	14.85	2.01
2004	70.11	9.45	53.42	7.20	16.69	2.25
2005	68.84	9.24	52.40	7.03	16.44	2.21
2006	70.31	9.36	53.18	7.08	17.13	2.28

3-4 全省人口数、户数(户籍)
POPULATION AND HOUSEHOLDS(REGISTERED)

单位:万人 (10000 persons)

年份 Year	总户数(万户) Households (10000)	总人口(万人) Total (10000 persons)	按性别分 Grouped by Sex 男 Male 人口数 Population	比重(%) Proportion	女 Female 人口数 Population	比重(%) Proportion	平均每户人数(人/户) Average Person Per Household (person)	年平均人口(万人) Average Person Per Year (10000 persons)	人口密度(人/平方公里) Density of Population (person/sq. km)
1949	838.00	3512.00	1778.80	50.6	1733.20	49.4	4.19		342
1952	888.00	3739.00	1891.60	50.6	1847.40	49.4	4.21	3697.50	364
1957	985.51	4182.71	2087.06	49.9	2095.65	50.1	4.24	4136.05	408
1962	1089.51	4333.74	2155.01	49.7	2178.73	50.3	3.98	4288.57	422
1965	1110.13	4623.74	2319.92	50.2	2303.82	49.8	4.17	4567.75	451
1970	1215.28	5252.09	2635.02	50.2	2617.07	49.8	4.32	5185.36	512
1975	1315.55	5636.12	2842.86	50.4	2793.26	49.6	4.28	5600.91	549
1976	1348.24	5700.76	2878.79	50.5	2821.97	49.5	4.23	5668.44	556
1977	1385.48	5765.28	2913.01	50.5	2852.27	49.5	4.16	5733.02	562
1978	1423.11	5834.33	2950.45	50.6	2883.88	49.4	4.10	5799.81	569
1979	1443.62	5892.55	2981.05	50.6	2911.50	49.4	4.08	5863.44	574
1980	1471.76	5938.19	3003.75	50.6	2934.44	49.4	4.03	5915.37	579
1981	1518.91	6010.24	3047.66	50.7	2962.58	49.3	3.96	5974.22	586
1982	1554.78	6088.94	3093.60	50.8	2995.34	49.2	3.92	6049.59	593
1983	1574.46	6134.99	3122.06	50.9	3012.93	49.1	3.90	6111.97	598
1984	1597.81	6171.43	3143.01	50.9	3028.42	49.1	3.86	6153.21	602
1985	1633.62	6213.48	3168.25	51.0	3045.23	49.0	3.80	6192.46	606
1986	1681.10	6269.90	3199.18	51.0	3070.72	49.0	3.73	6241.69	611
1987	1736.98	6348.00	3241.71	51.1	3106.29	48.9	3.65	6308.95	619
1988	1834.32	6438.27	3289.49	51.1	3148.78	48.9	3.51	6393.14	628
1989	1903.71	6535.85	3339.10	51.1	3196.75	48.9	3.43	6487.06	637
1990	1956.89	6671.73	3406.33	51.1	3265.40	48.9	3.41	6618.80	650
1991	1987.55	6733.87	3439.29	51.1	3294.58	48.9	3.39	6702.80	656
1992	2015.17	6767.49	3457.77	51.1	3309.72	48.9	3.36	6750.68	660
1993	2034.87	6800.69	3476.26	51.1	3324.43	48.9	3.34	6784.09	663
1994	2055.96	6831.28	3491.72	51.1	3339.56	48.9	3.32	6815.99	666
1995	2085.96	6868.42	3509.59	51.1	3358.83	48.9	3.29	6849.85	669
1996	2113.07	6908.13	3528.95	51.1	3379.19	48.9	3.27	6888.28	673
1997	2146.87	6948.36	3537.04	50.9	3411.32	49.1	3.24	6928.25	677
1998	2186.70	6983.09	3565.55	51.1	3417.54	48.9	3.19	6965.73	681
1999	2221.70	7009.09	3577.71	51.0	3431.37	49.0	3.15	6996.09	683
2000	2268.56	7069.28	3602.92	51.0	3466.36	49.0	3.12	7039.19	689
2001	2300.83	7097.00	3616.16	51.0	3480.84	49.0	3.08	7083.14	692
2002	2323.06	7127.33	3631.10	50.9	3496.23	49.1	3.07	7112.17	695
2003	2344.84	7163.93	3646.60	50.9	3517.33	49.1	3.06	7145.63	698
2004	2359.61	7206.05	3663.62	50.8	3542.43	49.2	3.05	7184.99	702
2005	2382.21	7252.88	3686.09	50.8	3566.79	49.2	3.04	7229.47	707
2006	2390.18	7317.72	3715.24	50.8	3602.48	49.2	3.06	7285.30	713

3-5 全省历次人口普查主要数据
MAJOR DATA OF ALL PREVIOUS PROVINCIAL POPULATION CENSUS

指标	Item	1953	1964	1982	1990	2000	2005
总人口（万人）	Total Population (10000 persons)	3767.29	4452.21	6052.11	6705.68	7304.36	7468
男	Male	1888.95	2242.71	3076.75	3412.32	3698.20	3735
女	Femal	1878.34	2209.50	2975.36	3293.36	3606.16	3733
性别比（女性为100）	Sex Ratio (Femal = 100)	100.6	101.5	103.4	103.6	102.6	100.1
家庭户规模（人/户）	Scale of Family (person/household)	4.19	4.09	3.91	3.66	3.25	3.04
各年龄组人口（万人）	Population by Age Group (10000 persons)						
0-14岁	Aged 0-14	1414.86	1772.66	1753.75	1592.47	1434.20	1155.97
15-64岁	Aged 15-64	2183.21	2514.48	3962.69	4657.93	5224.32	5500.56
65岁以上	Aged 65 and Over	169.22	165.07	335.67	455.28	645.84	810.97
民族人口（万人）	Nationality Population (10000 persons)						
汉族	Han Nationality	3760.92	4443.9	6041.08	6690.37	7278.37	7433.65
占总人口比重（%）	Proportion (%)	99.8	99.8	99.8	99.8	99.6	99.5
少数民族	Minority Nationalites	6.37	8.31	11.03	15.28	25.99	34.35
占总人口比重（%）	Proportion (%)	0.2	0.2	0.2	0.2	0.4	0.5
每十万人拥有的各种受教育程度人口（人）	Educated Population Per 100 Thousand Persons (person)						
大专及以上	Higher Education and Above		386	639	1474	3919	6454
高中和中专	Senior Middle Schools and Secondary Specialized Schools		1470	6981	8670	13079	13980
初中	Junior Middle Schools		5236	20049	26426	36365	37413
小学	Primary Schools		26588	32613	34791	32882	27303
城乡人口（万人）	Urban and Rural Population (10000 persons)						
城镇人口	Urban Population	556.81	660.26	957.22	1446.85	4218.12	3742.21
乡村人口	Rural Population	3210.48	3791.95	5094.89	5258.83	3086.24	3725.79
平均预期寿命（岁）	Average Life Expectancy (age)			69.49	71.62	74.13	75.32
男	Male			67.35	69.46	71.88	72.86
女	Femal			71.56	73.82	76.47	77.85

注:2005年数据为全国1%人口抽样调查(2005年11月1日零时)推算数。

Note: The data of 2005 were estimated according to the sampling investigation of 1% national population (0 o'clock November 1, 2005)

3-6 按地区分的常住人口
POPULATION BY REGION

单位:万人 (10000 persons)

地区		2000年 总人口 Total	2000年 城镇人口 Population of City and Town	2000年 城镇人口比重(%) Proportion	2006年 总人口 Total	2006年 城镇人口 Population of City and Town	2006年 城镇人口比重(%) Proportion
全 省	Province	7304.36	3086.24	42.3	7549.50	3918.19	51.9
苏 南	South Jiangsu	2462.62	1466.74	59.6	2838.34	1903.14	67.1
苏 中	Middle Jiangsu	1688.72	636.49	37.7	1634.29	773.03	47.3
苏 北	North Jiangsu	3153.02	983.01	31.2	3076.87	1242.02	40.4
南京市	Nanjing City	612.62	435.53	71.1	719.06	549.22	76.4
无锡市	Wuxi City	508.66	296.30	58.3	584.17	391.98	67.1
徐州市	Xuzhou City	891.40	298.18	33.5	876.48	392.66	44.8
常州市	Changzhou City	377.63	203.73	53.9	425.69	257.54	60.5
苏州市	Suzhou City	679.22	387.73	57.1	809.86	527.06	65.1
南通市	Nantong City	751.29	251.98	33.5	724.93	339.99	46.9
连云港市	Lianyungang City	456.99	128.03	28.0	450.52	175.70	39.0
淮安市	Huaian City	503.82	144.85	28.8	492.43	188.85	38.4
盐城市	Yancheng City	794.65	282.98	35.6	768.73	326.71	42.5
扬州市	Yangzhou City	458.85	195.90	42.7	445.91	219.39	49.2
镇江市	Zhenjiang City	284.49	143.45	50.4	299.56	177.34	59.2
泰州市	Taizhou City	478.58	188.61	39.4	463.45	213.65	46.1
宿迁市	Suqian City	506.16	128.97	25.5	488.71	158.10	32.4

注:2000年数据为2000年11月1日零时(第五次全国人口普查)登记常住人口数据;2006年数据是根据2006年人口变动情况抽样调查数据推算的年末常住人口数据。

Note: The data of 2000 were the figures of registered permanent population according to the 5th national census in 0 o'clock November 1, 2000; while the data of 2006 were the figures of the year end permanent population, estimated by the change of population in 2006 according to sampling investigation.

3-7 全省人口年龄构成情况(2006年11月1日零时)

COMPOSITION OF POPULATION GROUPED BY AGE (0 o'clock November 1,2006)

本表是2006年人口变动情况抽样调查样本数据,抽样比为5.048‰。
Data in the table are the data of change of population by 5.048‰ sampling survey in 2006

单位:人 (person)

年龄组(岁) Age Group	总人口 Total	#女 Female	市镇 City and Town	市 city	镇 Town	乡村 Country
合 计(total)	**381104**	**193785**	**215944**	**123438**	**92506**	**165160**
0—4	16722	7505	9209	5314	3895	7513
5—9	15981	7114	8836	4889	3947	7145
10—14	23229	10428	11940	6023	5917	11289
15—19	30672	14450	16065	8261	7804	14607
20—24	21355	11716	13184	8209	4975	8171
25—29	25600	13822	17241	11184	6057	8359
30—34	27585	14681	17824	11143	6681	9761
35—39	38043	20407	22730	13047	9683	15313
40—44	37937	19980	22248	12831	9417	15689
45—49	25681	13142	14717	8556	6161	10964
50—54	33416	16875	17736	9720	8016	15680
55—59	25251	12526	13376	7434	5942	11875
60—64	17859	8668	9169	4916	4253	8690
65—69	14459	7134	7616	4255	3361	6843
70—74	11868	6201	6169	3340	2829	5699
75—79	8142	4550	4144	2295	1849	3998
80—84	4712	2841	2401	1313	1088	2311
85—89	2034	1342	1051	564	487	983
90岁及以上 (90 and Above)	558	403	288	144	144	270

3－8　全省人口受教育程度情况（2006 年 11 月 1 日零时）
EDUCATED SITUATION OF POPULATION（0 o'clock November 1,2006）

2006 年人口变动情况抽样调查资料　　　　单位:人
Data in the table are the data of change of population by sampling survey in 2006　　　　(person)

项　目	Item	6 岁及以上人口合计 Aged 6 and over	不识字或识字很少 Illiterate or Near Illiterate	小　学 Primary Shool	初　中 Junior Secondary Shool	高　中 Senior and Specialized Secondary Shool	大　学及以上 Higher Education and Above
合　计	**Province**	**361327**	**31643**	**103446**	**144438**	**55477**	**26323**
男	Male	176442	6833	46914	75902	31621	15172
女	Female	184885	24810	56532	68536	23856	11151
按城乡分	Grouped by City and Country						
城　镇	City	204990	12993	48286	79074	40673	23964
男	Male	100804	2656	21872	40437	22081	13758
女	Eemale	104186	10337	26414	38637	18592	10206
乡　村	Country	156337	18650	55160	65364	14804	2359
男	Male	75638	4177	25042	35465	9540	1414
女	Eemale	80699	14473	30118	29899	5264	945

3－9　全省 15 岁及以上人口的婚姻状况（2006 年 11 月 1 日零时）
MARRIAGE STATUS OF POPULATION AGED 15 AND OVER（0 o'clock November 1,2006）

本表是 2006 年人口变动情况抽样调查样本数据，抽样比为 5.048‰。　　　　单位:人
Data in the table are the data of change of population by 5.048‰ sampling survey in 2006　　　　(person)

年龄组 Age Group	未　婚 Unmarried	初婚有配偶 First Marriages with Spouse	再婚有配偶 Remarriages with Spouse	离　婚 Divorce	丧　偶 Bereft of One's Spouse
合计　(Total)	**50878**	**245319**	**5276**	**2924**	**20774**
15—19	30159	477	27	7	1
20—24	12812	8462	37	36	8
25—29	3844	21387	173	168	28
30—34	917	25847	419	330	72
35—39	667	35834	781	581	180
40—44	473	35632	854	597	381
45—49	366	23763	647	386	519
50—54	484	30646	694	340	1252
55—59	407	22487	543	218	1596
60—64	333	15077	352	96	2001
65 岁及以上(65 and over)	416	25707	749	165	14736

3－10 全省分年龄育龄妇女生育情况
(2005年11月1日至2006年10月31日)
WOMEN IN CHILD－BEARING AGE BY AGE AND THE NUMBER OF CHILDREN (Nov. 1,2005－Oct.31,2006)

本表是2006年人口变动情况抽样调查样本数据,抽样比为5.048‰。 单位:人(Person)
Data in the table are the data of change of population by 5.048‰ sampling survey in 2006

年龄组 Age Group	平均育龄妇女人数 Average Number of Women in Child－Bearing Age	出生人数 Number of Birth Population	生育率(‰) Birth Rate (‰)	一孩 One Child (‰)	二孩 Two Children (‰)	三孩及以上 Three Children and Above (‰)
合计 (Total)	**108198**	**3593**	**33.20**	**26.43**	**6.40**	**0.36**
15－19	14450	30	2.08	1.94	0.11	0.00
20－24	11716	1572	134.18	125.06	8.86	0.26
25－29	13822	1517	109.75	84.89	24.29	0.58
30－34	14681	259	17.64	7.22	9.74	0.68
35－39	20407	135	6.62	2.25	3.82	0.54
40－44	19980	56	2.80	1.40	1.15	0.25
45－49	13142	24	1.83	1.12	0.53	0.15

3－11 全省16岁及以上人口经济活动情况(2006年11月1日零时)
CONDITION OF ECONOMIC ACTIVITIES OF AGE 16 AND ABOVE POPULATION OF WHOLE PROVINCE(0 o'clock November 1,2006)

本表是2006年人口变动情况抽样调查样本数据,抽样比为5.048‰。 单位:人 (person)
Data in the table are the data of change of population by 5.048‰ sampling survey in 2006

年龄组 Age Group	16岁及以上人口 16 age and Above population			经济活动人口 Economic Activities Population			非经济活动人口 Non-economic Activities Population		
	小计 Total	男 Male	女 Female	小计 Total	男 Male	女 Female	小计 Total	男 Male	女 Female
合计 (Total)	**319434**	**153356**	**166078**	**229991**	**118217**	**111774**	**89443**	**35139**	**54304**
16—19	24934	13144	11790	6758	3247	3511	18176	9897	8279
20—24	21355	9639	11716	16012	7494	8518	5343	2145	3198
25—29	25600	11778	13822	23029	11244	11785	2571	534	2037
30—34	27585	12904	14681	25461	12489	12972	2124	415	1709
35—39	38043	17636	20407	35519	17044	18475	2524	592	1932
40—44	37937	17957	19980	35209	17250	17959	2728	707	2021
45—49	25681	12539	13142	22564	11853	10711	3117	686	2431
50—54	33416	16541	16875	26666	15111	11555	6750	1430	5320
55—59	25251	12725	12526	17646	10322	7324	7605	2403	5202
60—64	17859	9191	8668	9936	5700	4236	7923	3491	4432
65岁及以上 65 and Over	41773	19302	22471	11191	6463	4728	30582	12839	17743

3-12 就业基本情况
EMPLOYMENT

指标	Item	1995	2000	2005	2006
从业人员合计 （万人）	Total Number of Employed Persons (10000 persons)	4385.17	4418.14	4510.12	4564.76
第一产业	Primary Industry	2057.08	1890.96	1420.69	1360.30
第二产业	Secondary Industry	1407.64	1335.16	1546.97	1588.54
第三产业	Tertiary Industry	920.45	1192.02	1542.46	1615.92
从业人员构成 （%）	Composition of Employed Persons (%)				
第一产业	Primary Industry	46.9	42.8	31.5	29.8
第二产业	Secondary Industry	32.1	30.2	34.3	34.8
第三产业	Tertiary Industry	21.0	27.0	34.2	35.4
城镇从业人员 （万人）	Urban Employed Persons (10000 persons)	1119.33	1655.00	2101.61	2229.60
城镇单位从业人员	Urban Units Employed Persons	926.48	693.09	628.82	679.37
国有单位	State-owned Units	581.88	421.75	283.75	279.35
城镇集体单位	Urban Collective Owned Units	277.71	117.94	38.70	35.52
其他单位	Others	66.89	153.41	306.37	364.50
内资经济	Inner Funded	29.63	102.03	176.27	206.10
股份合作单位	Share Holding Cooperalive Units		17.84	8.31	7.45
联营单位	Joint Owned Units	11.92	5.45	1.78	1.27
有限责任公司	Limited Liability Corporations		47.07	88.09	91.85
股份有限公司	Share-holding Corporations Ltd.		30.66	52.88	52.98
其他	Others		0.99	25.21	52.55
港澳台商投资单位	Units Funded by Entrepreneurs from Hong Kong, Macao & Taiwan	19.27	20.00	50.38	50.20
外商投资单位	Foreign Funded Units	17.99	31.38	79.72	108.20
私营企业	Private Enterprises	65.89	96.57	397.20	514.50
个体	Self-employed Workers		81.18	189.20	207.80
职工人数 （万人）	Number of Staff and Workers (10000 persons)	915.98	673.25	602.93	645.71
国有单位	State-owned Units	576.24	411.40	273.43	268.41
城镇集体单位	Urban Collective Owned Units	273.96	114.85	36.84	33.58
其他单位	Units of Other Types of Ownership	65.78	147.00	292.67	343.72
城镇单位女性从业人员 （万人）	Numbe of Female Employment in Urban Units (10000 persons)	375.50	270.20	264.94	292.49
年末城镇登记失业人数 （万人）	Number of Registered Unemployed Persons in Urban Areas (year end) (10000 persons)	20.13	30.36	41.63	40.40
年末城镇登记失业率 （%）	Registered Unemployment Rate in Urban Areas (year end)(%)	2.0	3.2	3.6	3.4

3－13 从　业　人　数
NUMBER OF EMPLOYED PERSONS

单位:万人　　(10000 persons)

年　份 Year	从业人数 Total Number of Employed Persons	#城镇单位职工人数 Number of Staff and Workers	国有单位 State-Owned Units	城镇集体单位 Urban Collective-Owned Units	其他单位 Other Uunis	#城镇单位其他从业人员 Others	#城镇私营及个体从业人员 Employed Persons in Urban Private Enterprises and Individual Units
1978	2777.72	581.50	366.37	215.13			1.62
1980	2821.03	644.15	401.98	242.17			2.75
1985	3262.97	782.44	468.80	305.39	8.25		11.86
1989	3519.83	867.55	525.24	324.73	17.58		19.10
1990	4225.02	879.85	536.88	323.34	19.63		23.57
1991	4272.97	899.27	551.52	324.91	22.84		21.92
1992	4315.12	904.09	562.69	313.81	27.59		23.63
1993	4339.81	914.73	574.02	293.57	47.14	12.81	37.11
1994	4362.76	909.83	571.39	277.27	60.67	11.04	52.99
1995	4385.17	915.98	576.24	273.96	65.78	10.50	65.89
1996	4386.97	905.52	575.48	256.91	73.13	10.79	72.80
1997	4388.79	893.74	577.54	239.61	76.59	11.29	90.12
1998	4389.92	752.76	471.52	161.85	119.39	16.41	129.89
1999	4390.71	717.12	445.27	139.03	132.82	18.99	150.34
2000	4418.14	673.25	411.40	114.85	147.00	19.84	177.75
2001	4434.28	625.83	377.40	90.34	158.09	22.35	232.79
2002	4458.02	590.32	329.96	67.11	193.25	25.33	240.61
2003	4468.67	579.10	304.98	52.58	221.54	29.41	352.60
2004	4482.52	575.08	281.03	41.11	252.94	31.77	446.86
2005	4510.12	602.93	273.43	36.83	292.67	25.89	586.40
2006	4564.76	645.71	268.41	33.58	343.72	33.66	722.30

注:1. 从1990年开始从业人数为推算数。
2. 1998年以前的职工人数包括在岗职工人数和下岗职工人数。
3. 1998年开始的职工人数为在岗职工人数,不包括离开本单位仍保留劳动关系的职工人数(下同)。

Note: 1. Since 1990, the number of employed persons was the estimated figure. (The same as in the following tables)
2. Before 1998, the number of staff and workers included employed and laid off personnels.
3. Since 1998, the number of staff and workers included employed personnels, excluded staff and workers who had left self units, but still remained the labour relationship. (The same as in the following tables)

3－14 分三次产业的从业人数
NUMBER OF EMPLOYED PERSONS BY THREE TYPES OF INDUSTRIES

单位:万人 (10000 persons)

年份 Year	从业人数 Total Number of Employed Persons				构成(%) Composition(%)		
		第一产业 Primary Industry	第二产业 Secondary Industry	第三产业 Tertiary Industry	第一产业 Primary Industry	第二产业 Secondary Industry	第三产业 Tertiary Industry
1978	2777.72	1937.06	544.57	296.09	69.7	19.6	10.7
1980	2821.03	1987.28	546.48	287.27	70.4	19.4	10.2
1985	3262.97	1738.09	1065.75	459.13	53.2	32.7	14.1
1989	3519.83	1714.69	1215.40	589.74	48.7	34.5	16.8
1990	4225.02	2389.25	1212.58	623.19	56.6	28.7	14.7
1991	4272.97	2405.68	1226.34	640.95	56.3	28.7	15.0
1992	4315.12	2337.93	1270.80	706.39	54.2	29.4	16.4
1993	4339.81	2228.06	1325.38	786.37	51.4	30.5	18.1
1994	4362.76	2131.65	1375.14	855.97	48.9	31.5	19.6
1995	4385.17	2057.08	1407.64	920.45	46.9	32.1	21.0
1996	4386.97	2014.06	1397.25	975.66	45.9	31.9	22.2
1997	4388.79	1981.54	1382.03	1025.22	45.1	31.5	23.4
1998	4389.92	1946.49	1341.12	1102.31	44.3	30.6	25.1
1999	4390.71	1908.64	1330.39	1151.68	43.5	30.3	26.2
2000	4418.14	1890.96	1335.16	1192.02	42.8	30.2	27.0
2001	4434.28	1813.62	1356.89	1263.77	40.9	30.6	28.5
2002	4458.02	1734.17	1381.99	1341.86	38.9	31.0	30.1
2003	4468.67	1608.72	1452.32	1407.63	36.0	32.5	31.5
2004	4482.52	1506.13	1533.02	1443.37	33.6	34.2	32.2
2005	4510.12	1420.69	1546.97	1542.46	31.5	34.3	34.2
2006	4564.76	1360.30	1588.54	1615.92	29.8	34.8	35.4

3-15 城镇单位（不含私营、个体）从业人员（2006年）
EMPLOYED PERSONS IN URBAN UNITS (2006) (Excluded Privates and Individuals)

单位：万人 (10000 persons)

项目	Item	从业人员年末人数 Employment at the Year-end	在岗职工 Employed	其他从业人员 Others	离开本单位仍保留劳动关系的职工 Workers Left Self Units but Still Remained Labor Relation
总计	**Total**	**679.37**	**645.71**	**33.66**	**53.93**
按登记注册类型分	Grouped by Type of Registration				
国有单位	State-owned Units	279.35	268.41	10.94	23.15
城镇集体单位	Urban Collective-owned Units	35.52	33.58	1.94	8.60
其他单位	Other Units	364.50	343.72	20.79	22.18
内资	Inner Funded	206.10	193.24	12.85	20.67
股份合作单位	Share Holding Cooperative Units	7.45	7.15	0.31	1.02
联营单位	Joint Ownership Units	1.27	1.24	0.03	0.11
有限责任公司	Responsibility Co. Ltd.	91.85	87.29	4.55	11.93
股份有限公司	Share Holding Co. Ltd.	52.98	48.33	4.65	4.01
其他	Others	52.55	49.24	3.31	3.59
港、澳、台投资	Hong Kong Macao and Taiwan Funded	50.20	48.48	1.73	0.82
外商投资	Foreign Funded	108.20	102.00	6.20	0.69
按企业、事业、机关分	Grouped by Character of the Units				
企业	Enterprises	478.06	450.79	27.27	49.22
事业	Institutions	152.23	147.10	5.13	3.58
机关	Government Agencies	49.08	47.82	1.26	1.13
按国民经济行业分	Grouped by Sector				
农、林、牧、渔业	Farming, Forestry, Animal Husbandry and Fishery	14.63	14.36	0.27	1.32
采矿业	Mining and Quarrying	14.70	14.48	0.22	3.68
制造业	Manufacturing	290.85	281.22	9.62	21.83
电力、燃气及水的生产和供应业	Power, Gas and Water Production and Supply	13.02	12.93	0.08	0.48
建筑业	Construction	37.23	32.72	4.52	3.19
交通运输、仓储和邮政业	Transportation, Storage and Post	32.74	30.73	2.01	5.70
信息传输、计算机服务和软件业	Informaiton Transmmision, Computer Service and Software	6.79	5.73	1.06	0.34
批发和零售业	Wholesale and Retail Sales	27.30	26.00	1.30	9.72
住宿和餐饮业	Hotel and Catering	8.77	7.94	0.83	0.80
金融业	Banking	22.90	16.86	6.04	1.14
房地产业	Real Estate	5.88	5.46	0.41	0.32
租赁和商务服务业	Leasing and Commercial Services	8.92	8.52	0.40	1.75
科学研究、技术服务和地质勘查业	Scientific Research, Polytechnical Service and Geological Prospecting	9.22	8.55	0.66	0.30
水利、环境和公共设施管理业	Water Coservancy, Environment and Public Facility Management	10.21	9.58	0.64	0.35
居民服务和其他服务业	Resident Services and Others	1.16	0.94	0.23	0.18
教育	Education	83.36	81.48	1.88	0.91
卫生、社会保障和社会福利业	Health Care, Social Security and Social Welfare	30.59	28.98	1.61	0.42
文化、体育和娱乐业	Culture, Sports and Recreation	5.00	4.76	0.25	0.21
公共管理和社会组织	Public Management and Social Organizations	56.09	54.47	1.62	1.27

3-16 分细行业在岗职工人数(2006年)
NUMBER OF EMPLOYED STAFF AND WORKERS BY SECTOR IN DETAIL (2006)

单位:万人 (10000 persons)

项目	Item	在岗职工人数 Number of Employed Staff and Workers	国有单位 State-Owned Units	城镇集体单位 Urban Collective-Owned Units	其他单位 Other Units
总计	**Total**	**645.71**	**268.41**	**33.58**	**343.72**
按企业、事业、机关分	Grouped by Character of the Units				
企业	Enterprises	450.79	84.57	23.92	342.29
事业	Institutions	147.10	136.22	9.46	1.42
机关	Government Agencies	47.82	47.62	0.20	
按国民经济行业分	**Grouped by Sector**				
农、林、牧、渔业	Farming, Forestry, Animal Husbandry and Fishery	14.36	13.19	0.57	0.60
农业	Farming	10.87	10.50	0.26	0.12
林业	Forestry	0.86	0.86		
畜牧业	Animal Husbandry	0.40	0.25	0.04	0.11
渔业	Fishery	0.32	0.19	0.04	0.08
农、林、牧、渔业服务业	Services(FFAF)	1.91	1.39	0.23	0.29
采矿业	Mining and Quarrying	14.48	9.65	0.85	3.98
制造业	Manufacturing	281.22	16.75	8.25	256.22
电力、燃气及水的生产和供应业	Electric Power, Gas and Water Production and Supply	12.93	7.58	0.32	5.03
电力、热力的生产和供应业	Electric Power, Steam and Hot Water Production and Supply	9.44	5.61	0.14	3.69
燃气生产和供应业	Gas Production and Supply	0.90	0.12		0.77
水的生产和供应业	Tap Water Production and Supply	2.59	1.85	0.18	0.57
建筑业	Construction	32.72	5.04	4.63	23.04
房屋和土木工程建筑业	Civil Engineering	26.84	3.29	4.13	19.42
建筑安装业	Construction and Installation	4.68	1.63	0.43	2.62
建筑装饰业	Building Fitting up and Decoration	0.79	0.06	0.07	0.66
其他建筑业	Other Construction	0.42	0.07		0.34
交通运输、仓储和邮政业	Transportation, Storage and Post	30.73	18.00	1.64	11.09
铁路运输业	Railway Transportation	5.99	5.59	0.27	0.13
道路运输业	Highway Transportation	8.01	3.53	0.75	3.73
城市公共交通业	Urban Public Transit	3.91	2.08	0.04	1.80
水上运输业	Waterway Transportation	6.80	2.47	0.38	3.95
航空运输业	Air Transportation	0.79	0.42		0.37
管道运输业	Pipeline Transportation	0.71	0.70		0.01
装卸搬运和其他运输服务业	Load and Unload, Carry and Other Transportation	1.38	0.59	0.12	0.68
仓储业	Storage	0.81	0.40	0.03	0.38
邮政业	Post	2.33	2.24	0.05	0.04
信息传输、计算机服务和软件业	Information Transmmision, Computer Service and Software	5.73	2.54	0.14	3.04
电信和其他信息传输服务业	Telecommunication and Other Information Transmmision Service	5.01	2.45	0.13	2.43
计算机服务业	Computer Service	0.24	0.09	0.02	0.13
软件业	Software	0.48	0.01		0.48
批发和零售业	Wholesale and Retail Trade	26.00	5.79	3.56	16.64
批发业	Wholesale Trade	12.39	3.55	1.52	7.32
零售业	Retail Trade	13.60	2.24	2.04	9.32

3－16 续表 Continued

单位:万人 (10000 persons)

项目	Item	合计 Total	国有单位 State-Owned Units	城镇集体单位 Urban Collective-Owned Units	其他单位 Other Units
住宿和餐饮业	Hotel and Catering Services	7.94	2.17	0.47	5.29
住宿业	Hotel	5.47	2.00	0.35	3.12
餐饮业	Catering Services	2.47	0.17	0.12	2.17
金融业	Finance	16.86	7.32	2.34	7.19
银行业	Banking	13.42	6.39	2.30	4.72
证券业	Securities	0.33	0.03		0.31
保险业	Insurance	2.75	0.66		2.09
其他金融活动	Other Financial Activities	0.35	0.24	0.04	0.08
房地产业	Real Estate Trade	5.46	1.98	0.30	3.18
房地产开发经营	Real Estate Management	3.29	0.88	0.12	2.29
租赁和商务服务业	Leasing and Commercial Services	8.52	3.53	1.50	3.49
租赁业	Leasing Services	0.20	0.02	0.01	0.17
商务服务业	Commercial Services	8.32	3.51	1.49	3.32
科学研究、技术服务和地质勘查业	Scientific Research, Polytechnical Services and Geological Prospecitng	8.55	6.74	0.12	1.70
研究与试验发展	Scientific Research and Experimental Development	2.60	2.26		0.33
专业技术服务业	Specilized Technoloty Service	4.50	3.14	0.08	1.27
科技交流和推广服务业	Science & Technology Exchange & Popularizaiton	0.75	0.62	0.03	0.09
地质勘查业	Gedogical Prospecting	0.71	0.71		
水利、环境和公共设施管理业	Water Conservance, Environment and Public Facility Management	9.58	7.60	1.35	0.62
水利管理业	Water Conservancy Manegement	2.83	2.75	0.04	0.04
环境管理业	Environment Management	3.86	2.59	1.15	0.13
公共设施管理业	Public Facility Management	2.88	2.26	0.17	0.45
居民服务和其他服务业	Resident Services and Others	0.94	0.59	0.13	0.22
居民服务业	Resident Services	0.62	0.41	0.08	0.13
其他服务业	Others	0.31	0.18	0.04	0.09
教育	Education	81.48	80.15	0.59	0.75
卫生、社会保障和社会福利业	Health Care, Social Security and Social Welfare	28.98	21.27	6.42	1.30
卫生	Health Care	27.40	19.78	6.34	1.28
社会保障业	Social Security	0.94	0.90	0.04	
社会福利业	Social Welfare	0.64	0.58	0.04	0.02
文化、体育和娱乐业	Culture, Sports and Recreation	4.76	4.11	0.32	0.33
新闻出版业	News Publication	0.80	0.70		0.10
广播、电视、电影和音像业	Radio, Television, Film and Stereo	1.89	1.75	0.09	0.04
文化艺术业	Culture and Arts	1.53	1.29	0.22	0.03
体育	Sports	0.30	0.26		0.03
娱乐业	Recreation	0.24	0.10	0.01	0.12
公共管理和社会组织	Public Management and Social Organizations	54.47	54.39	0.08	
#中国共产党机关	Party Agencies	1.42	1.42		
国家机构	Government Agencies	50.97	50.90	0.07	
人民政协和民主党派	People's Political Consultative Conference and Democratic Parties	0.25	0.25		
群众团体、社会团体和宗教组织	Mass Organization and Religious Organization	0.70	0.69	0.01	

3－17　制造业在岗职工人数（2006 年）
NUMBER OF STAFF AND WORKERS EMPLOYED IN MANUFACTURING INDUSTRY（2006）

单位:万人　　　　　　　　　　　　　　　　　　　　　　　　　　　　（10000 persons）

项　目	Item	在岗职工人数 Number of Employed Staff and Workers	国有单位 State-Owned Units	城镇集体单位 Urban Collective-Owned Units	其他单位 Other Units
制造业总计	**Manufacturing Total**	**281.22**	**16.75**	**8.25**	**256.22**
农副食品加工业	Food Processing	4.72	0.36	0.09	4.28
食品制造业	Food Producting	3.10	0.32	0.05	2.74
饮料制造业	Beverage Producting	4.30	0.25	0.04	4.01
烟草加工业	Tobacco Processing	0.75	0.75		
纺织业	Textile Industry	34.46	1.39	0.90	32.17
纺织服装、鞋、帽制造业	Textile, Garments, Shoes and Hats	24.68	0.38	0.90	23.40
皮革、毛皮、羽毛(绒)及其制品业	Leather, Furs, Down and Related Products	5.78	0.08	0.07	5.62
木材加工及木、竹、藤、棕、草制造业	Timber Processing and Wood, Bamboo, Rattan, Palm and Straw Works	1.84		0.02	1.81
家具制造业	Furniture Manufacturing	1.11	0.08	0.03	0.99
造纸及纸制品业	Papermaking and Paper Products	4.03	0.16	0.17	3.69
印刷业和记录媒介的复制	Printing and Record Processing	2.23	0.36	0.26	1.61
文教体育用品制造业	Stationery, Education and Sports Goods	5.35		0.11	5.24
石油加工、炼焦及核燃料加工业	Petroleum Processing, Coking Products and Nuclear Fuel Processing	1.75	0.11	0.11	1.53
化学原料及化学制品制造业	Raw Chemical Material and Chemical Products	17.83	1.35	0.60	15.88
医药制造业	Medical and Pharmaceutical Products	5.70	0.14	0.21	5.35
化学纤维制造业	Chemical Fibers	2.83		0.13	2.70
橡胶制品业	Rubber Products	2.61	0.05	0.09	2.48
塑料制品业	Plastic Products	5.09	0.10	0.39	4.60
非金属矿物制品业	Nonmetal Mineral Products	9.63	1.29	0.39	7.95
黑色金属冶炼及压延加工业	Smelting and Processing of Ferrous Metals	8.12	0.19	0.08	7.84
有色金属冶炼及压延加工业	Smelting and Processing of Nonferrous Metals	2.90	0.91	0.17	1.82
金属制品业	Metal Products	8.48	0.82	0.44	7.22
通用设备制造业	Ordinarty Machinery Manufacturing	22.55	2.81	0.54	19.21
专用设备制造业	Special Purpose Equipment Manufacturing	11.67	0.47	0.29	10.91
交通运输设备制造业	Transportation Equipment Manufacturing	15.57	2.91	0.63	12.04
电气机械及器材制造业	Electric Equipment and Machinery	16.31	0.60	0.85	14.86
通信设备、计算机及其他电子设备制造业	Telecommunication Equipments, Computer and Other Electronic Equipments Manafacturing	47.83	0.44	0.31	47.08
仪器仪表及文化、办公用机械制造业	Instruments, Meters, Cultural and Official Machinery	7.13	0.41	0.14	6.57
工艺品及其他制造业	Handicraft Artical and Other Manufacturing	2.80	0.02	0.23	2.55
废弃资源和废旧材料回收加工业	Waste Recources and Junk Material Recycled	0.10	0.01		0.09

3-18　分行业女性从业人数(2006年)

NUMBER OF FEMALE EMPLOYED BY SECTOR (2006)

单位:万人　(10000 persons)

行业	Item	女性从业人数 Total	国有单位 State-Owned Units	城镇集体单位 Urban Collective-Owned Units	其他单位 Other Units
总计	**Total**	**292.49**	**106.85**	**14.79**	**170.85**
农、林、牧、渔业	Farming, Forestry, Animal Husbandry and Fishery	6.36	6.02	0.13	0.21
采矿业	Mining and Quarrying	5.43	3.29	0.52	1.62
制造业	Manufacturing	145.45	5.57	3.96	135.91
电力、燃气及水的生产和供应业	Power, Gas and Water Production and Supply	3.58	2.05	0.11	1.42
建筑业	Construction	5.55	1.01	0.80	3.74
交通运输、仓储和邮政业	Transportation, Storage and Post	9.25	5.77	0.58	2.90
信息传输、计算机服务和软件业	Information Transmmision, Computer Service and Software	2.60	0.88	0.05	1.67
批发和零售业	Wholesale and Retail Sales	13.00	2.48	1.43	9.10
住宿和餐饮业	Hotel and Catering Service	4.73	1.16	0.30	3.27
金融业	Banking	11.20	4.20	1.01	6.00
房地产业	Real Estate	2.15	0.71	0.16	1.28
租赁和商务服务业	Leasing and Commercial Services	2.96	1.07	0.40	1.48
科学研究、技术服务和地质勘查业	Scientific Research, Polytechnical Service and Geological Prospecting	2.86	2.29	0.04	0.53
水利、环境和公共设施管理业	Water Coservancy, Environment and Public Facility Management	4.02	2.94	0.84	0.24
居民服务和其他服务业	Resident Services and Others	0.46	0.30	0.06	0.10
教育	Education	40.10	39.19	0.48	0.43
卫生、社会保障和社会福利业	Health Care, Social Security and Social Welfare	17.61	13.03	3.78	0.80
文化、体育和娱乐业	Culture, Sports and Recreation	1.87	1.61	0.12	0.14
公共管理和社会组织	Public Management and Social Organizations	13.31	13.28	0.03	

3-19　城镇失业人数及失业率

NUMBER OF URBAN UNEMPLOYED PERSONS AND UNEMPLOYED RATE

单位:万人　(10000 persons)

年份 Year	下岗失业人员就业、再就业人数 Unemployed-Reemployees	年末尚有登记失业人数 Year End Unemployment Registered	年末城镇登记失业率(%) Year End Unemployment Registered Rate
1979	54.70	34.30	5.4
1980	32.78	20.29	3.1
1985	15.25	7.15	0.9
1990	28.06	22.52	2.4
1991	23.33	18.68	2.0
1992	21.43	18.81	2.0
1993	20.64	19.43	2.0
1994	22.19	19.58	2.0
1995	21.49	20.13	2.0
1996	20.78	22.34	2.2
1997	21.40	23.80	2.4
1998	21.61	24.26	2.6
1999	21.57	26.57	2.9
2000	27.01	30.36	3.4
2001	34.94	36.14	3.6
2002	39.96	42.17	4.2
2003	54.46	41.84	4.1
2004	60.22	42.90	3.9
2005	62.92	41.63	3.6
2006	68.65	40.40	3.4

主要统计指标解释

人口数 指一定时点、一定地区范围内的有生命的个人的总和。

年度统计的年末人口数指每年12月31日24时的人口数。年度统计的全国人口总数内未包括台湾省和港澳同胞以及海外华侨人数。

城镇人口和乡村人口

1952－1989年城镇人口是指市辖区内和县辖镇的全部人口；乡村人口是指县辖乡人口。1990－1999年城镇人口是指设区的市的区人口和不设区的市所辖的街道人口以及不设区的市所辖镇的居民委员会人口和县辖镇的居民委员会人口；乡村人口是除上述两种人口以外的全部人口。2000年人口普查和2000年以后城镇人口：市人口是指设区市的人口密度在1500人/平方公里以上的市区人口和人口密度不足1500人的区政府驻地和区辖其他街道人口，以及政府驻地的城市建设延伸到的周边乡镇人口；不设区市的市政府驻地和市辖其他街道人口，以及政府驻地的城市建设延伸到的乡镇人口。镇人口是指镇政府驻地和镇辖其他居委会人口，以及镇政府驻地的城区建设延伸到周边村民委员会人口。

乡村人口是指除上述人口以外的全部人口。

出生率（又称粗出生率） 指在一定时期内（通常为一年）一定地区的出生人数与同期内平均人数（或期中人数）之比。一般用千分率表示。本资料中的出生率指年出生率，其计算公式为：

出生率＝年出生人数/年平均人数×1000

式中：出生人数指活产婴儿，即胎儿脱离母体时（不管怀孕月数），有过呼吸或其他生命现象。年平均人数指年初、年底人口数的平均数，也可用年中人口数代替。

死亡率（又称粗死亡率） 指在一定时期内（通常为一年）一定地区的死亡人数与同期内平均人数（或期中人数）之比，一般用千分率表示。本资料中的死亡率指年死亡率，其计算公式为：

死亡率＝年死亡人数/年平均人数×1000

人口自然增长率 指在一定时期内（通常为一年）人口自然增加数（出生人数减死亡人数）与该时期内平均人数（或期中人数）之比，一般用千分率表示。计算公式为：

人口自然增长率＝（本年出生人数－本年死亡人数）/年平均人数×100

老年人口及人口老龄化 60岁以上（含60岁）或65岁以上（含65岁）人口为老年人口。人口老龄化，是指一定的地区范围内老年人口在总人口中所占比重随时间推移而不断上升的动态变化过程，是随着人口寿命延长和生育水平下降而出现的人口年龄结构的变动趋势，它不是一种绝对数量的描述，而是一种比例关系。它的指标是老年人口系数，即一个地区60岁以上（含60岁）或65岁以上（含65岁）人口的数量在该地区人口总数中所占的百分数。老年人口系数越大，说明其人口老龄化的程度就越高。联合国对人口年龄类型的划分提出了一套标准，作为判断一个国家或地区是否进入老年社会的一个重要依据。它规定65岁及以上的人口超过7%的国家或地区就称之为人口老年型国家或老年型社会，4%～7%为成年型社会，4%以下为年轻型社会。按照国际上通用的标准，60岁及以上人口占总人口的比重达到10%以上，或者65岁及以上人口比重达到7%以上，人口年龄结构进入老年型。

就业人员 指从事一定社会劳动并取得劳动报酬或经营收入的人员，包括在岗职工、再就业的离退休人员、私营业主、个体户主、私营和个体就业人员、乡镇企业就业人员、农村就业人员、其他就业人员（包括民办教师、宗教职业者、现役军人等）。这一指标反映了一定时期内全部劳动力资源的实际利用情况，是研究我国基本国情国力的重要指标。

各单位的就业人员 指在各级国家机关、政党机关、社会团体及企业、事业单位中工作，取得工资或其他形式的劳动报酬的全部人员。包括在岗职工、再就业的离退休人员、民办教师以及在各单位中工作的外方人员和港澳台方人员、兼职人员、借用的外单位人员和第二职业者。不包括离开本单位仍保留劳动关系的职工。各单位的就业人员反映了各单位实际参加生产或工作的全部劳动力。

城镇私营和个体就业人员 城镇私营就业人员指在工商管理部门注册登记，其经营地址设在县城关镇（含城关镇）以上的私营企业就业人员；包括私营企业投资者和雇工。城镇个体就业人员指在工商管理部门注册登记，并持有城镇户口或在城镇长期居住，经批准从事个体工商经营的就业人员；包括个体经营者和在个体工商户劳动的家庭帮工和雇工。

城镇登记失业人员 指有非农业人口，在劳动年龄（16周岁至退休年龄）内，有劳动能力无业而要求就业，并在当地就业服括返聘的离退休人员、民办教师、在国有经济单位工作的外方人员和港、澳、台人员（1998年以后的数据均为在岗职工数据，其他相关指标如职工工资总额，职工平均工资等指标也从1998年按此口径进行了相应调整）。

国有单位职工 指在国有经济单位及其附属机构工作，并由其支付工资的各类人员。

城镇集体单位职工 指在城镇集体经济单位及其管理部门工作，并由其支付工资的各类人员。

其他单位职工 指在联营经济、股份制经济、外商投资经济、港、澳、台投资经济单位工作，并由其支付工资的各类人员。

Explanatory Notes on Main Statistical Indicators

Total Population refers to the total number of people alive at a certain point of time within a given area.

The annual statistics on total population is taken at midnight, the 31st of December, not including residents in Taiwan province, Chinese compatriots in Hong Kong and Macao and overseas Chinese.

Urban Population and Rural Population

Urban population: including the population of urban region with the population density at 1500 persons/sq · km (if there are districls set up by the city); the population of urban distric with the population density at less than 1500 persons/sq · km where the government of district is stationed; the population of other subdistrist under the district as well as the population of township where is the extending area of urban construction. In addition, if there are no districts set up by the city, the population is involved in the region where the city government is stationed; the population of subdistricts under the city as well as the population of township, where is the extending area of urban construction. Town population refers to the population of the place where the town government is stationed and the population of village committee as well as the population of neighbourhood committee where is the extending area of urban construction at the station of town governwent.

Rural population: refers to the total population except the above population.

Birth Rate or (Crude Birth Rate) refers to the ratio of the number of births to the average population (or mid-period population) during a certain period of time (usually a year) which is often expressed in ‰. Birth rate in the chapter refers to annual birth rate. The following formula is used: Birth Rate = Number of Births/Average Number of Population × 1000‰

Number of births refers to live births i. e. the births when babies had showed any vital phenomena regardless of the length of pregnancy.

Annual Average Number of Population is the average of the number of population at the beginning of the year and that at the end of the year. Sometimes it is substituted for with the mid year population.

Death Rate (or Crude Death Rate) refers to the ratio of the number of deaths to the average population (or mid-period population) during a certain period of time (usually a year) which is often expressed in ‰. Death rate in the chapter refers to annual death rate. The following formula is used:

Death Rate = Number of Deaths/Annual Average Number of Population × 1000‰

Natural Growth Rate of Population refers to the ratio of natural increase in population (number of births minus number of deaths) in a certain period of time (usually a year) to the average population (or mid-period population) of the same period which is often expressed in ‰. The following formulas are applied:

Natural Growth of Population = (Number of Births − Number of Deaths)/Average Number of Population × 1000‰

Natural Growth Rate of Population = Birth Rate-Death Rate

Old Age population and Aging Population 60 age and above (including 60 age) or 65 age and above (including 65 age) population is called old age population. Aging population refers that in a certain country or region, among the total population, the proportion of old aged population has a course of movement of increasing ascent with the lapse of time, which indicates an alteration tendency of structure in the age of population followed by the prolonging of population's life and the decreasing of birth level. It is only a ratio relationship, not a description of absolute quantity. The target refers to the coeffieient of old aged population, that is a percentage of population of 60 age and above (including 60 age) or of 65 age and above (including 65 age) among the total population of a certain country or a region. The larger is the coefficient of the old aged population, the higher is the grade of an aging. The United Nation had put forward a set of standard for dividing the type of population's age, as an important basis to determine whether a country or a region had entered the old aged society. The proportion of population of 65 age and above had exceeded more than 7%, than the eountry or region is called old typed country or society; the proportion reaches 4%−7%, it is called adult typed society; and 4% below is called young typed society. According to the international general standard, the proportion of population of 60 age and above had reached more than 10%, and of 65 age and above had reached 7%, the structure of population's age had entered an old aged pattern.

Employed Persons refer to the persons who are engaged in social working and receive remuneration payment or earn business income, including total staff and workers, re-employed retirees, employers of private enterprises, self-employed workers, employees in private enterprises and individual economy, employees in township enterprises, employed persons in the rural areas, and other employed persons (including teachers in the schools run by the local people, people engaged in religious profession and the servicemen, etc.). This indicator reflects the actual utilization of total labour force during a certain period of time and is often used for the research on China's economic situation and national power.

Persons Employed in Various Units refer to all the persons working in government agencies of various levels, political and party organization, social organizations, enterprises and institutions, and receiving wages or other forms of payment. They include fully-employed staff and workers, re-employed retirees, teachers in schools run by the local people, foreigners and Chinese compatriots from Hong Kong, Macao, and Taiwan working in various units, part-time employees, employees of other units working temporarily at current posts, and employees holding the second job, but exclude staff and workers who have left their working units while keeping their labour contract (employment relation) unchanged. This indicator reflects the total number of laborers actually engaged in production or other operations in various units.

Persons Employed in Private Enterprises and Self-Employed Individuals in Urban Areas Persons employed in private enterprises refer to the persons employed in the private enterprises which have been registered at the departments of industrial and commercial administration and are situated at a county town (i. e. a town' where the county government is located) for business operation or at urban areas with the level higher than a county town. The self-employed individuals in urban areas refer to persons who hold the certificates of residence in urban areas or have resided in the urban areas for a long time and have been registered at the departments of industrial and commercial administration and approved to be engaged in individual industrial or commercial business, including self-employed persons as well as helpers and hired labourers who work in the individual households engaged in industrial or commercial business.

Registered Urban Unemployed Persons The registered unemployed persons in urban areas refer to the persons who are registered as permanent residents in the urban areas engaged in non-agricultural activities, aged within the range of working age, capable to labour, unemployed but desirous to be employed and have been registered at the local employment service agencies to apply for a job.

Registered Urban Unemployment Rate Registered unemployment rate in urban areas refers to the ratio of the number of the registered unemployed persons to the sum of the number of persons employed in various units and in private enterprises in urban areas, urban self-employed individuals and the registered urban unemployed persons. The formula is as follows:

Registered urban unemployment rate = number of registered urban unemployed persons ÷ (number of persons employed in urban units + number of persons employed in urban private enterprises + and self-employed individuals in urban Areas + number of reg-istered urban unemployed persons) × 100%.

Staff and Workers refer to the persons who work in (and receive payment therefrom) enterprises and institutions of state ownership, collective ownership, joint ownership, share holding, foreign ownership, and ownership by entrepreneurs from Hong Kong, Macao, and Taiwan, and other types of ownership and their affiliated units, excluding the retired persons invited to work in the units again, teachers in the schools run by the local people and foreigners and persons coming from Hong Kong, Macao and Taiwan and working in the state-owned economic units. (Number of staff and workers in this yearbook include only fully employed staff and workers, excluding those who have left their working units while keeping their labour contract/employment relation unchanged).

Staff and Workers in State-owned Economic Units refer to the persons who work in the state-owned economic units or their attached units and are listed in their payrolls.

Staff and Workers of Collective Owned Units in Urban Areas refer to the persons who work in collective owned units in urban areas and their administration departments and receive payment therefrom.

Staff and Workers in Units of Other types of Ownership refer to those who work in (and receive payment therefrom) enterprises and institutions of joint ownership, share holding, foreign ownership, and ownership by entrepreneurs from Hong Kong, Macao, and Taiwan.

第 4 篇

人民生活

PEOPLE' S LIVELIHOOD

4-1 人民生活水平情况
PEOPLE'S LIVING STANDARD

指标		1990	1995	2000	2005	2006
就业	**Employment**					
农村居民家庭每户整半劳动力（人）	Average Full-time and Half-time Laborers Per Rural Household (person)	2.78	2.79	2.62	2.66	2.67
每一农村劳动力负担人数（人）	Average Persons Supported by a Rural Laborer (person)	1.49	1.44	1.43	1.41	1.39
城镇居民家庭每户就业人口（人）	Average Number of Employees Per Urban Household (person)	2	1.85	1.65	1.42	1.42
每一城镇就业者负担人数（人）	Average Persons Supported by an Urban Employee (person)	1.67	1.72	1.86	2.06	2.03
城镇登记失业率（%）	The Rate of Urban Registered Unemployment (%)	2.4	2.0	3.2	3.6	3.4
收入与支出	**Income**					
城镇居民人均可支配收入（元）	Per Capita Disposable Income of Urban Residents (yuan)	1464	4634	6800	12319	14084
城镇居民生活消费支出（元）	Per Capita Living Expanditure of Urban Residents (yuan)	1339	3772	5323	8622	9629
农村居民人均纯收入（元）	Per Capita Net Income of Rural Residents (yuan)	884	2457	3595	5276	5813
农村居民生活消费支出（元）	Per Capita Living Expenditure of Rural Residents (yuan)	787	1938	2337	3567	4135
职工年平均工资（元）	Annual Average Wage of Workers and Staff (yuan)	2129	5943	10299	20957	23782
人均储蓄存款余额（元）	Per Capita Balance of Saving Deposit (yuan)	696	2721	6083	14156	16138
生活质量	**The Quality of Living**					
居民家庭恩格尔系数（%）	Engle Coefficient of Resident's Household					
城镇居民	Urban Residents	55.5	51.9	41.1	37.2	36.0
农村居民	Rural Residents	52.3	54.8	43.5	44.0	41.8
人均住房面积（平方米）	Per Capita Floor Space of Residential Building (sq. m)					
城市人均建筑面积	Per Capita Construction Space in Urban Areas	17.29	21.69	25.54	28.76	29.68
农村人均住房面积	Per Capita Living Floor Space in Rural Areas	25.20	25.71	33.70	38.59	40.8
交通状况	**Traffic**					
城市每万人拥有公共汽（电）车（辆）	Number of Buses Per 10000 Persons (unit)	3.6	7.1	10.6	9.1	10.4
城市人均拥有道路面积（万平方米）	Per Capita Areas of Paved Road of Urban Residents (10000 sq. m)	6.3	8.3	10.6	16.3	18.7
城市每百户拥有家用汽车（辆）	Number of Motor Vehicels Per 100 Households in Urban Areas (unit)				4.29	5.46
农村每百户拥有摩托车（辆）	Number of Motor cycles Per 100 Households in Rural Areas (unit)	1.50	8.65	28.50	52.74	57.7

4-2 城乡居民家庭人均收入及恩格尔系数

PER CAPITA ANNUAL INCOME AND ENGLE COEFFICIENT OF URBAN AND RURAL HOUSEHOLDS

年 份 Year	城镇居民家庭人均可支配收入 Per Capita Disposal Income of Urban Households		农村居民家庭人均纯收入 Per Capita Net Income of Rural Houselds		城镇居民家庭恩格尔系数(%) Engle Coefficient of Urban Households	农村居民家庭恩格尔系数(%) Engle Coefficient of Rural Households
	绝对数(元) Value (yuan)	实际增长指数(1978=100) Index	绝对数(元) Value (yuan)	实际增长指数(1978=100) Index		
1978	288	100.0	155	100.0	55.1	62.3
1979			200	127.5		59.9
1980	433	141.4	218	150.1	55.1	58.0
1981	448	142.8	258	176.1	55.9	56.9
1982	484	152.9	309	208.9	58.2	55.5
1983	498	156.2	357	241.1	58.6	55.3
1984	626	188.5	448	291.7	56.3	53.0
1985	766	210.4	493	293.2	52.5	52.1
1986	910	235.1	561	312.8	51.2	49.5
1987	1005	234.8	627	324.4	52.0	48.4
1988	1218	232.2	797	340.0	50.8	46.1
1989	1372	225.5	876	315.1	53.9	50.2
1990	1464	232.6	884	335.0	55.5	52.3
1991	1623	239.5	921	315.6	55.7	56.1
1992	2138	290.0	1061	348.1	53.9	54.7
1993	2774	316.9	1267	358.5	49.4	50.2
1994	3779	344.7	1832	380.0	50.1	54.8
1995	4634	363.7	2457	416.1	51.9	54.8
1996	5186	367.3	3029	468.6	51.0	51.2
1997	5765	403.1	3270	489.2	47.7	48.9
1998	6018	420.8	3377	511.2	45.1	47.8
1999	6538	463.7	3495	538.3	44.1	44.7
2000	6800	482.3	3595	557.1	41.1	43.5
2001	7375	522.5	3785	579.4	39.7	42.6
2002	8178	588.8	3996	613.6	40.4	40.0
2003	9263	661.0	4239	645.5	38.3	41.4
2004	10482	721.3	4754	692.0	40.0	44.2
2005	12319	831.1	5276	750.1	37.2	44.0
2006	14084	935.2	5813	813.1	36.0	41.8

4-3 职工工资总额及指数
TOTAL WAGES OF STAFF AND WORKERS AND RELATED INDEX

年份 Year	绝对数（亿元） Absolute Figure (100 million yuan)				指数（以上年为100） Index (preceding year = 100)			
	全部职工 Total	国有单位 State-Owned Units	城镇集体单位 Urban Collective-Owned Units	其他单位 Units of Other Types of Ownership	全部职工 Total	国有单位 State-Owned Units	城镇集体单位 Urban Collective-Owned Units	其他单位 Units of Other Types of Ownership
1978	29.05	19.84	9.21		110.7	110.8	110.6	
1979	33.10	22.46	10.64		113.9	113.2	115.5	
1980	41.63	27.99	13.64		125.8	124.6	128.2	
1981	44.13	29.60	14.53		106.0	105.8	106.5	
1982	48.14	32.35	15.79		109.1	109.3	108.7	
1983	50.78	34.41	16.37		105.5	106.4	103.7	
1984	67.28	43.34	23.25	0.69	132.5	126.0	142.0	
1985	86.17	55.10	30.09	0.98	128.1	127.1	129.4	142.0
1986	105.56	67.93	36.28	1.35	122.5	123.3	120.6	137.8
1987	121.26	78.09	41.30	1.87	114.9	115.0	113.8	138.5
1988	152.53	99.17	50.60	2.76	125.8	127.0	122.5	147.6
1989	165.38	108.56	53.05	3.77	108.4	109.5	104.8	136.6
1990	184.60	123.25	56.70	4.65	111.6	113.5	106.9	123.3
1991	204.43	136.26	62.05	6.12	110.7	110.6	109.4	131.6
1992	251.51	170.85	71.64	9.02	123.0	125.4	115.4	147.4
1993	328.21	221.91	85.85	20.45	130.5	129.9	119.8	226.7
1994	450.44	312.56	103.32	34.56	137.2	140.8	120.3	169.0
1995	541.62	369.10	126.57	45.95	120.2	118.1	122.5	132.9
1996	595.72	411.30	128.61	55.81	110.0	111.4	101.6	121.5
1997	635.44	446.95	124.86	63.63	106.7	108.7	97.1	114.0
1998	628.49	422.35	99.49	106.65	103.0	101.8	92.9	131.3
1999	666.28	443.41	91.90	130.97	106.0	105.0	92.4	122.8
2000	705.36	463.63	82.98	158.75	105.9	104.6	90.3	121.2
2001	758.55	498.61	71.42	188.52	107.5	107.5	86.1	118.8
2002	813.09	506.06	60.42	246.61	107.2	101.5	84.6	130.8
2003	917.33	540.59	53.51	323.23	112.8	106.8	88.6	131.1
2004	1050.35	591.38	48.20	410.77	114.5	109.4	90.1	127.1
2005	1252.06	672.70	48.80	530.56	119.2	113.8	101.2	129.2
2006	1520.39	768.86	52.55	698.97	121.4	114.3	107.7	131.7

注：1998年起职工工资为在岗职工工资，不包括离开本单位仍保留劳动关系的职工的生活补助费（下同）。

Note: Since 1998, the wage bills of staff and workers were for employed personnels, excluded living expense subsidies of the personnels who had left self units, but still remained labour relationship (The same as in the following tables).

4－4 城镇单位(不含私营个体)从业人员劳动报酬(2006年)
LABOUR REWARD OF URBAN UNITS EMPLOYMENT (2006) (EXCLUDED PRIVATE AND INDIVIDUAL UNITS)

单位:亿元 (100million yuan)

项目	Item	从业人员全年劳动报酬 Annual Labour Remuneration of Employment	在岗职工工资总额 Annual Wage of Staff and Workers Employed	其他从业人员劳动报酬 Labour Remuneration of Other Employment	离开本单位仍保留劳动关系职工生活费 Living Income of Workers Left Self Unit Still Remain Labour Relation
总计	**Total**	**1590.91**	**1520.39**	**70.52**	**35.60**
按登记注册类型分	**Grouped by Type of Registreration**				
国有单位	State-owned Units	783.83	768.86	14.97	17.97
城镇集体单位	Urban Collective-owned Units	54.58	52.55	2.03	2.53
其他单位	Other Units	752.50	698.97	53.53	15.10
内资	Inner Funded	419.60	397.28	22.31	14.00
股份合作单位	Share Holding Cooperative Units	12.29	11.82	0.46	0.34
联营单位	Joint－Owned Co. Ltd.	2.21	2.16	0.05	0.06
有限责任公司	Responsibility Co. Ltd.	187.18	180.75	6.43	8.12
股份有限公司	Share Holding Co. Ltd.	134.99	126.00	8.99	3.39
其他	Others	82.92	76.54	6.38	2.09
港、澳、台投资	Foreign Funded	88.90	83.52	5.38	0.53
外商投资	Hong Kong Macao and Taiwan Funded	244.01	218.17	25.84	0.57
按企业、事业、机关分	**Grouped by Character of the Units**				
企业	Enterprises	1019.81	957.67	62.14	30.26
事业	Institutions	393.89	386.93	6.96	3.28
机关	Government Agencies	177.21	175.78	1.43	2.06
按国民经济行业分	**Grouped by Sector**				
农、林、牧、渔业	Farming, Forestry, Animal Husbandry and Fishery	15.00	14.76	0.25	0.53
采矿业	Mining and Quarrying	38.90	38.63	0.27	2.62
制造业	Manufacturing	561.15	528.02	33.13	12.78
电力、燃气及水的生产和供应业	Electric Power, Gas and Water Production and Supply	51.24	51.07	0.17	0.67
建筑业	Construction	67.24	60.00	7.23	2.35
交通运输、仓储和邮政业	Transportation, Storage and Post	81.37	78.30	3.07	4.37
信息传输、计算机服务和软件业	Information Transmission, Computer Service and Software	26.75	24.69	2.05	0.55
批发和零售业	Wholesale and Retail Trade	53.20	51.26	1.94	3.25
住宿和餐饮业	Hotel and Catering Industry	14.43	13.33	1.10	0.39
金融业	Banking	84.01	73.69	10.31	2.15
房地产业	Real Estate	16.28	15.36	0.91	0.24
租赁和商务服务业	Leasing and Commercial Services	18.97	18.38	0.59	0.80
科学研究、技术服务和地质勘查业	Scientific Research, Technical Services and Geological Prospecting	33.11	31.56	1.55	0.25
水利、环境和公共设施管理业	Water Conservancy, Environment and Public Facilcty Service	20.55	19.97	0.58	0.41
居民服务和其他服务业	Resident's Service and Other Services	2.41	2.19	0.22	0.09
教育	Education	210.70	208.31	2.39	1.29
卫生、社会保障和社会福利业	Health Care, Social Security and Service Welfare	86.87	84.30	2.56	0.42
文化、体育和娱乐业	Culture, Sports and Recreation	15.81	15.45	0.35	0.20
公共管理和社会组织	Public Management and Socail Organi－zations	192.93	191.10	1.83	2.24

4-5　城镇单位(不含私营个体)在岗职工工资总额(2006年)
TOTAL WAGES OF STAFF AND WORKERS EMPLOYED IN URBAN UNITS (2006)
(Excluding Private and Individual)

单位:亿元　　(100 million yuan)

项目	Item	在岗职工工资总额 Total Wage of Staff and Workers Employed	国有单位 State-Owned Units	城镇集体单位 Urban Collective-Owned Uints	其他单位 Units of Other Types of Ownership
总计	**Total**	**1520.39**	**768.86**	**52.55**	**698.97**
按企业、事业、机关分	**Grouped by Character of the Units**				
企业	Enterprises	957.67	228.19	33.57	695.91
事业	Institutions	386.93	365.45	18.42	3.06
机关	Government Agencies	175.78	175.22	0.56	
按国民经济行业分	**Grouped by Sector**				
农、林、牧、渔业	Farming, Forestry, Animal Husbandry and Fishery	14.76	13.45	0.58	0.72
采矿业	Mining and Quarrying	38.63	27.75	1.11	9.76
制造业	Manufacturing	528.02	43.76	9.91	474.36
电力、燃气及水的生产和供应业	Electric Power, Gas and Water Production and Supply	51.07	31.32	0.64	19.11
建筑业	Construction	60.00	14.25	6.00	39.75
交通运输、仓储和邮政业	Transportation, Storage and Post	78.30	49.40	2.16	26.73
信息传输、计算机服务和软件业	Information Transmission, Computer Service and Software	24.69	9.45	0.33	14.91
批发和零售业	Wholesale and Retail Trade	51.26	12.43	3.84	34.99
住宿和餐饮业	Hotel and Catering Industry	13.33	3.55	0.67	9.11
金融业	Banking	73.69	28.13	5.95	39.62
房地产业	Real Estate	15.36	5.66	0.64	9.06
租赁和商务服务业	Leasing and Commercial Services	18.38	8.82	2.73	6.83
科学研究、技术服务和地质勘查业	Scientific Research, Technical Services and Geological Prospecting	31.56	24.23	0.29	7.04
水利、环境和公共设施管理业	Water Conservancy, Environment and Public Facility Service	19.97	16.71	1.83	1.43
居民服务和其他服务业	Resident's Service and Other Services	2.19	1.51	0.27	0.41
教育	Education	208.31	205.47	1.12	1.72
卫生、社会保障和社会福利业	Health Care, Social Security and Social Welfare	84.30	68.12	13.75	2.43
文化、体育和娱乐业	Culture, Sports and Recreation	15.45	13.94	0.55	0.97
公共管理和社会组织	Public Management and Socail Organizations	191.10	190.91	0.18	

4-6 制造业在岗职工工资总额（2006年）
TOTAL WAGES OF STAFF AND WORKERS EMPLOYED IN MANUFACTURING INDUSTRY (2006)

单位:亿元 (100 million yuan)

行业		工资总额 Total Wage of Staff and Workers Employed	国有单位 State-Owned Units	城镇集体单位 Urban Collective-Owned Uints	其他单位 Units of Other Types of Ownership
制造业总计	**Manufacturing Total**	**528.02**	**43.76**	**9.91**	**474.36**
农副食品加工业	Food Processing	6.28	0.43	0.09	5.76
食品制造业	Food Producting	5.04	0.38	0.03	4.64
饮料制造业	Beverage Producting	7.10	0.24	0.02	6.83
烟草加工业	Tobacco Processing	4.78	4.78		
纺织业	Textile Industry	47.09	2.73	1.02	43.35
纺织服装、鞋、帽制造业	Textile Garments, Shoes and Hats	33.60	0.78	0.87	31.95
皮革、毛皮、羽毛(绒)及其制品业	Leather, Furs, Down and Related Products	8.26	0.12	0.07	8.07
木材加工及木、竹、藤、棕、草制造业	Timber Processing and Wood, Bamboo, Rattan, Palm and Straw Works	2.06	0.00	0.02	2.04
家具制造业	Furniture Manufacturing	1.75	0.14	0.04	1.57
造纸及纸制品业	Papermaking and Paper Products	9.08	0.40	0.14	8.53
印刷业和记录媒介的复制	Printing and Record Processing	3.77	0.71	0.31	2.75
文教体育用品制造业	Stationery, Education and Sports Goods	7.38	0.00	0.18	7.20
石油加工、炼焦及核燃料加工业	Petroleum Processing, Coking Products and Nuclear Fuel Processing	6.82	0.35	0.34	6.13
化学原料及化学制品制造业	Raw Chemical Material and Chemical Products	39.05	2.81	0.85	35.39
医药制造业	Medical and Pharmaceutical Products	11.62	0.21	0.27	11.14
化学纤维制造业	Chemical Fibers	6.81		0.15	6.66
橡胶制品业	Rubber Products	4.57	0.07	0.11	4.39
塑料制品业	Plastic Products	8.84	0.23	0.54	8.07
非金属矿物制品业	Nonmetal Mineral Products	16.94	4.40	0.44	12.10
黑色金属冶炼及压延加工业	Smelting and Processing of Ferrous Metals	19.35	0.34	0.14	18.87
有色金属冶炼及压延加工业	Smelting and Processing of Nonferrous Metals	4.91	1.47	0.20	3.24
金属制品业	Metal Products	15.05	1.96	0.50	12.58
通用设备制造业	Ordinarly Machinery Manufacturing	47.61	8.76	0.71	38.14
专用设备制造业	Special Purpose Equipment Manufacturing	24.44	0.97	0.33	23.13
交通运输设备制造业	Transportation Equipment Manufacturing	36.41	7.89	0.77	27.74
电气机械及器材制造业	Electric Machinery and Equipment	31.34	1.69	0.90	28.75
通信设备、计算机及其他电子设备制造业	Telecommunication Equipments, Computer and Other Electronic Equipment	99.20	1.05	0.39	97.76
仪器仪表及文化、办公用机械制造业	Instruments, Meters, Cultural and Official Machinery	14.94	0.80	0.18	13.95
工艺品及其他制造业	Handicraft Articale and Other Manufacturing	3.73	0.03	0.30	3.40
废弃资源和废旧材料回收加工业	Waste Resources and Junk Material Recycled	0.22	0.02	0.01	0.20

4-7 职工平均工资及指数
AVERAGE WAGE OF STAFF AND WORKERS AND RELATED INDICES

年份 Year	绝对数（元） Absolute Figure (yuan)				指数（以上年为100） Index (preceding year = 100)			
	全部职工 Total	国有单位 State-Owned Units	城镇集体单位 Urban Collective-Owned Units	其他单位 Units of Other Types of Ownership	全部职工 Total	国有单位 State-Owned Units	城镇集体单位 Urban Collective-Owned Units	其他单位 Units of Other Types of Ownership
1978	513	563	432		108.2	108.9	107.5	
1979	565	618	478		110.3	109.8	110.9	
1980	667	721	578		117.8	116.7	120.7	
1981	672	718	594		100.7	99.6	102.8	
1982	703	748	626		104.6	104.2	105.4	
1983	723	768	643		102.8	102.7	102.7	
1984	931	1003	820	1012	128.8	130.6	127.5	
1985	1135	1211	1015	1237	121.9	120.7	123.8	122.2
1986	1327	1430	1166	1468	116.9	118.1	114.9	118.7
1987	1471	1581	1295	1639	110.9	110.6	111.1	111.6
1988	1796	1936	1564	2059	122.1	122.5	120.8	125.6
1989	1918	2082	1639	2185	106.8	107.5	104.8	106.1
1990	2129	2331	1776	2444	111.0	111.9	108.4	111.9
1991	2302	2501	1932	2773	108.1	107.3	108.8	113.5
1992	2800	3057	2292	3370	121.6	122.2	118.6	121.5
1993	3615	3896	2937	4434	129.1	127.4	128.1	131.6
1994	4974	5491	3728	5827	137.6	140.9	126.9	131.4
1995	5943	6441	4621	7137	119.5	117.3	124.0	122.5
1996	6603	7186	4990	7740	111.1	111.6	108.0	108.4
1997	7108	7745	5183	8376	107.6	107.8	103.9	108.2
1998	8256	8872	6033	8867	105.7	106.3	101.3	102.5
1999	9171	9855	6452	9763	111.1	111.1	106.9	110.1
2000	10299	11109	6962	10698	112.3	112.7	107.9	109.6
2001	11842	12917	7543	11790	115.0	116.3	108.3	110.2
2002	13509	15030	8638	12633	114.1	116.4	114.5	107.2
2003	15712	17502	9836	14656	116.3	116.4	113.9	116.0
2004	18202	20876	11350	16346	115.8	119.3	115.4	111.5
2005	20957	24659	13064	18468	115.1	118.1	115.1	113.0
2006	23782	28722	15550	20691	113.5	116.5	119.0	112.0

4-8 职工平均工资指数 （1978=100）
AVERAGE WAGE INDICES OF STAFF AND WORKERS

年份 Year	全部职工 Total 平均货币工资指数 Index of Average Money Wage	全部职工 Total 平均实际工资指数 Index of Average Real Wage	国有单位 State-Owned Units 平均货币工资指数 Index of Average Money Wage	国有单位 State-Owned Units 平均实际工资指数 Index of Average Real Wage	城镇集体单位 Urban Collective-Owned Units 平均货币工资指数 Index of Average Money Wage	城镇集体单位 Urban Collective-Owned Units 平均实际工资指数 Index of Average Real Wage	其他单位 Units of Other Types of Ownership 平均货币工资指数 Index of Average Money Wage	其他单位 Units of Other Types of Ownership 平均实际工资指数 Index of Average Real Wage
1978	100.0	100.0	100.0	100.0	100.0	100.0		
1979	110.3	109.5	109.8	109.0	110.9	110.1		
1980	130.0	121.7	128.1	119.9	133.8	125.3		
1981	130.0	118.3	128.1	116.6	133.8	121.7		
1982	137.0	122.3	132.9	118.7	144.9	129.4		
1983	140.9	132.7	136.4	128.4	148.8	140.1		
1984	181.5	154.9	178.2	152.0	189.8	161.9	100.0	100.0
1985	221.2	174.9	215.1	170.0	235.0	185.8	122.2	111.5
1986	258.7	189.2	254.0	185.8	269.9	197.4	145.1	124.4
1987	286.7	189.7	280.8	185.8	299.8	198.4	162.0	125.7
1988	350.1	189.0	343.9	185.7	362.0	195.5	203.5	128.8
1989	373.9	174.1	369.8	172.2	379.4	176.6	215.9	117.8
1990	415.0	189.8	414.0	189.3	411.1	188.0	241.5	127.4
1991	448.7	190.5	444.2	188.6	447.2	189.9	274.0	134.2
1992	545.8	213.2	543.0	212.1	530.6	207.3	333.0	149.9
1993	704.7	231.9	692.0	227.7	679.9	223.7	438.1	166.1
1994	969.6	254.6	675.3	256.1	863.0	226.6	575.8	174.2
1995	1158.5	261.7	1144.0	258.5	1069.7	241.7	705.2	183.6
1996	1287.1	262.5	1276.4	260.3	1155.1	235.5	764.8	179.7
1997	1385.6	278.9	1375.7	276.9	1199.8	241.5	827.7	192.0
1998	1609.4	324.1	1575.8	317.3	1396.5	281.2	876.2	203.4
1999	1787.7	365.1	1750.4	357.5	1493.5	305.0	964.7	227.1
2000	2007.6	410.1	1973.2	403.0	1611.6	329.2	1057.1	215.9
2001	2308.4	471.0	2294.3	468.1	1746.1	356.3	1165.0	237.7
2002	2545.6	525.2	2669.6	550.8	1999.5	412.5	1248.3	257.5
2003	3062.8	629.6	3108.7	639.0	2276.9	468.0	1448.2	297.7
2004	3548.2	703.3	3708.0	735.0	2627.3	520.8	1615.2	320.2
2005	4085.2	793.1	4379.9	850.3	3024.1	587.1	1824.9	354.3
2006	4635.9	885.8	5101.6	974.8	3599.5	687.8	2044.6	390.7

4-9 城镇单位(不含私营个体)从业人员平均劳动报酬(2006年)
AVERAGE LABOUR REMUNERATION OF EMPLOYED PERSONS IN URBAN UNITS (2006) (Excluding Private and Individual)

单位:元 (yuan)

项目	Item	从业人员年均劳动报酬 Annual Average Labour Remuneration of Employment	在岗职工平均工资 Annual Average Wage of Staff and Workers Employed	其他从业人年均劳动报酬 Labour Remuneration of Other Employment	离开本单位仍保留劳动关系职工年均生活费 Living Expenses of Workers Left Self Unit Still Remain Labour Relation
总计	**Total**	**23657**	**23782**	**21256**	**6518**
按登记注册类型分	**Grouped by Type of Registreration**				
国有单位	State-owned Units	28143	28722	13817	7758
城镇集体单位	Urban Collective-owned Units	15279	15550	10534	3018
其他单位	Other Units	21006	20691	26215	6548
内资	Inner Funded	20436	20640	17382	6514
股份合作单位	Share Holding Cooperative Units	16199	16363	12904	3244
联营单位	Joint - Owned Co. Ltd.	17302	17308	17051	4612
有限责任公司	Responsibility Co. Ltd.	20453	20773	14280	6501
股份有限公司	Share Holding Co. Ltd.	25487	26071	19394	8387
其他	Others	15954	15729	19271	5520
港、澳、台投资	Hong Kong Macao and Taiwan Funded	18200	17691	32906	6038
外商投资	Foreign Funded	23446	22233	43441	8217
按企业、事业、机关分	**Grouped by Character of the Units**				
企业	Enterprises	21587	21492	23166	5998
事业	Institutions	26030	26462	13643	10748
机关	Government Agencies	36355	37015	11386	18354
按国民经济行业分	**Grouped by Sector**				
农、林、牧、渔业	Farming, Forestry, Animal Husbandry and Fishery	10181	10198	9251	3920
采矿业	Mining and Quarrying	26385	26599	12342	6929
制造业	Manufacturing	19647	19117	35213	5684
电力、燃气及水的生产和供应业	Electric Power, Gas and Water Production and Supply	39066	39186	20465	13705
建筑业	Construction	18260	18563	16083	6828
交通运输、仓储和邮政业	Transportation, Storage and Post	24811	25351	16072	8200
信息传输、计算机服务和软件业	Information Transmission, Computer Service and Software	40801	44202	21198	15829
批发和零售业	Wholesale and Retail Trade	19163	19462	13626	3392
住宿和餐饮业	Hotel and Catering Industry	16577	16984	12848	4697
金融业	Banking	36760	43495	17454	18832
房地产业	Real Estate	27991	28444	22085	7201
租赁和商务服务业	Leasing and Commercial Services	21928	22288	14597	4547
科学研究、技术服务和地质勘查业	Scientific Research, Technical Services and Geological Prospecting	36220	37155	23932	8035
水利、环境和公共设施管理业	Water Conservancy, Environment and publie Facilcty service	20234	20947	9329	11431
居民服务和其他服务业	Resident's Service and Other Services	20691	23323	9779	4943
教育	Education	25352	25647	12676	14161
卫生、社会保障和社会福利业	Health Care, Social Security and Social Welfare	28718	29394	16359	9546
文化、体育和娱乐业	Culture, Sports and Recreation	31667	32572	14285	9630
公共管理和社会组织	Public Management and Socail Organizations	34765	35469	11328	16689

4-10 分细行业在岗职工平均工资(2006年)

AVERAGE WAGE OF STAFF AND WORKERS BY SECTOR IN DETAIL (2006)

单位:元 (yuan)

项目	Item	在岗职工平均工资 Annual Average Wage of Staff and Workers Employed	国有单位 State-Owned Units	城镇集体单位 Urban Collective-Owned Uints	其他单位 Units of Other Types of Ownership
总计	**Total**	**23782**	**28722**	**15550**	**20691**
按企业、事业、机关分	**Grouped by Character of the Units**				
企业	Enterprises	21492	26864	13856	20686
事业	Institutions	26462	26979	19671	21900
机关	Government Agencies	37015	37056	27429	
按国民经济行业分	**Grouped by Sector**				
农、林、牧、渔业	Farming, Forestry, Animal Husbandry and Fishery	10198	10086	11417	11609
农业	Farming	9110	9043	8408	16188
林业	Forestry	9705	9698	18500	12167
畜牧业	Animal Husbandry	10997	10427	10180	12690
渔业	Fishery	10023	9905	4434	12832
农、林、牧、渔业服务业	Farming, Forestry, Animal Husbandry, Fishery Service	16485	18279	15453	9058
采矿业	Mining and Quarrying	26599	28732	13073	24333
制造业	Manufacturing	19117	26222	11817	18888
电力、燃气及水的生产和供应业	Electric Power, Gas and Water Production and Supply	39186	40869	19920	37859
电力、热力的生产和供应业	Electric Power, Steam Hotwater Production and Supply	43650	45993	21823	40892
燃气生产和供应业	Gas Production and Supply	30479	27770	13613	30997
水的生产和供应业	Water Production and Supply	25570	25916	18565	26687
建筑业	Construction	18563	26471	12814	17861
房屋和土木工程建筑业	Housing and Civil Engineering	17241	24776	12750	16790
建筑安装业	Construction Installation	25395	30842	13430	23916
建筑装饰业	Building Fitting up and Decoration	17167	19470	12249	17467
其他建筑业	Other Decoration	29497	18077	22500	32095
交通运输、仓储和邮政业	Transportation, Storage and Postal	25351	27401	13016	23880
铁路运输业	Railway Transportation	24292	24575	14086	32758
道路运输业	Highway Transportation	20649	22619	12272	20442
城市公共交通业	Urban Public Transportation	23438	23356	17501	23673
水上运输业	Waterway Transportation	27113	37523	12760	22136
航空运输业	Aviation Transportation	57429	44047		73071
管道运输业	Pipeline Transportation	39512	39229		65143
装卸搬运和其他运输服务业	Load and unload, Carrying and Other Transportation Services	26208	31700	12214	23933
仓储业	Storage	22908	19630	14556	27124
邮政业	Post	27852	28154	17238	24941
信息传输、计算机服务和软件业	Information Transmission, Computer Service and Software	44202	37596	23203	50891
电信和其他信息传输服务业	Telecommunication and Other Information Transmission Services	44715	37275	23920	53516
计算机服务业	Computer Service	40191	47229	17777	38496
软件业	Software	40728	31519		40834
批发和零售业	Wholesale and Retail Trade	19462	21253	10422	20819
批发业	Wholesale Trade	23088	23267	11307	25524
零售业	Retail Trade	16096	18042	9741	17043

4－10 续 表 Continued

单位:元 (yuan)

项目	Item	在岗职工平均工资 Annual Average Wage of Staff and Workers Employed	国有单位 State-Owned Units	城镇集体单位 Urban Collective-Owned Uints	其他单位 Units of Other Types of Ownership
住宿和餐饮业	Hotel and Catering Services	16984	16465	14752	17390
住宿业	Hotel	17731	17047	15285	18424
餐饮业	Catering Services	15317	10078	13322	15876
金融业	Finance	43495	38539	25441	54234
银行业	Banking	45211	39934	25432	62106
证券业	Securities	63553	37575		65837
保险业	Insurance	34037	28190		35741
其他金融活动	Other Financial Activities	37120	29271	25986	66434
房地产业	Real Estate Trade	28444	28651	21654	28956
房地产开发经营	Real Estate development and Management	31689	31682	24309	32058
租赁和商务服务业	Leasing and Commercial Services	22288	25692	18419	20499
租赁业	Leasing Services	22183	23800	15753	22301
商务服务业	Commercial Services	22290	25701	18433	20405
科学研究、技术服务和地质勘查业	Scientific Research, Polytechnical Services and Geological Prospecitng	37155	36093	23138	42499
研究与试验发展	Scientific Research and Experimental Development	45997	47117	16528	38810
专业技术服务业	Specilized Technology Service	36223	33679	24350	43437
科技交流和推广服务业	Science & Technology Exchange and Popularizaiton	26701	24585	21151	43643
地质勘查业	Goological Prospecting	22084	22097		17263
水利、环境和公共设施管理业	Water Conservance, Environment andPublic Facility Management	20947	22078	13528	23329
水利管理业	Water Conservancy Manegement	21818	21805	17840	26530
环境管理业	Environment Management	16715	18030	12727	26034
公共设施管理业	Public Facility Management	25688	26936	17944	22234
居民服务和其他服务业	Resident Services and Others	23323	25660	21156	18368
居民服务业	Resident Services	23103	26320	16535	17267
其他服务业	Others	23759	24153	29712	19981
教育	Education	25647	25707	19231	24096
卫生、社会保障和社会福利业	Health Care, Social Security and Social Welfare	29394	32433	21489	19009
卫生	Health Care	29072	32176	21482	18971
社会保障业	Social Security	38131	38680	26261	
社会福利业	Social Welfare	30524	31660	17795	21661
文化、体育和娱乐业	Culture, Sports and Recreation	32572	33955	16977	30475
新闻出版业	News Publication	47291	47022		49180
广播、电视、电影和音像业	Radio, Television, Film and Stereo	32941	34348	13781	16702
文化艺术业	Culture and Arts	25367	26578	18382	24090
体育	Sports	31483	31371	12375	33622
娱乐业	Recreation	27416	36160	15960	21241
公共管理和社会组织	Public Management and Social Organizations	35469	35487	22463	
#中国共产党机关	Party Agencies	37159	37159		
国家机构	Government Agencies	35621	35641	21553	
人民政协和民主党派	People's Political Consultative Conference and Democratic Parties	44072	44072		
群众团体、社会团体和宗教组织	Mass Organization and Religion Organizations	38742	38776	30095	

4－11　制造业在岗职工平均工资　（2006 年）

ANNUAL AVERAGE WAGE OF STAFF AND WORKERS EMPLOYED IN UNITS OF MANUFACTURING INDUSTRY (2006)

单位:元　　　　　　　　　　　　　　　　　　　　　　　　　　(yuan)

行业		制造业在岗职工年平均工资 Annual Average Wage	国有单位 State-Owned Units	城镇集体单位 Urban Collective-Owned Uints	其他单位 Units of Other Types of Ownership
制造业总计	**Manufacturing Total**	**19117**	**26222**	**11817**	**18888**
农副食品加工业	Food Processing	13386	11603	10284	13606
食品制造业	Food Producting	16353	11931	5853	17055
饮料制造业	Beverage Producting	16781	9247	5405	17400
烟草加工业	Tobacco Processing	62677	62677		
纺织业	Textile Industry	13712	18943	10979	13556
纺织服装、鞋、帽制造业	Textile Garments, Shoes and Hats	14123	20424	9202	14224
皮革、毛皮、羽毛(绒)及其制品业	Leather, Furs, Down and Related Products	14692	14812	9910	14754
木材加工及木、竹、藤、棕、草制造业	Timber Processing and Wood, Bamboo, Rattan, Palm and Straw Works	11337	7892	8282	11377
家具制造业	Furniture Manufacturing	16104	16462	9557	16329
造纸及纸制品业	Papermaking and Paper Products	23184	24567	7700	23909
印刷业和记录媒介的复制	Printing and Record Processing	17222	19508	11567	17647
文教体育用品制造业	Stationery, Education and Sports Goods	13838	12286	15854	13796
石油加工、炼焦及核燃料加工业	Petroleum Processing, Coking Products and Nuclear Fuel Processing	38444	33074	29196	39497
化学原料及化学制品制造业	Raw Chemical Material and Chemical Products	21955	20056	14306	22410
医药制造业	Medical and Pharmaceutical Products	20599	15042	14671	20951
化学纤维制造业	Chemical Fibers	22612		10988	23156
橡胶制品业	Rubber Products	17945	14307	13568	18171
塑料制品业	Plastic Products	17645	22051	13396	17923
非金属矿物制品业	Nonmetal Mineral Products	17798	33691	11128	15483
黑色金属冶炼及压延加工业	Smelting and Processing of Ferrous Metals	23822	16479	18023	24072
有色金属冶炼及压延加工业	Smelting and Processing of Nonferrous Metals	18097	19755	11586	18040
金属制品业	Metal Products	18387	29976	11830	17713
通用设备制造业	Ordinarly Machinery Manufacturing	20607	31005	12278	19359
专用设备制造业	Special Purpose Equipment Manufacturing	21682	20067	11911	22016
交通运输设备制造业	Transportation Equipment Manufacturing	23818	27066	12208	23639
电气机械及器材制造业	Electric Machinery and Equipment	19778	27573	10440	20008
通信设备、计算机及其他电子设备制造业	Telecommunication Equipments, Computer and Other Electronic Equipment	21623	22498	12093	21682
仪器仪表及文化、办公用机械制造业	Instruments, Meters, Cultural and Official Machinery	22017	19024	12629	22437
工艺品及其他制造业	Handicraft Articale and Other Manufacturing	13434	16479	12670	13484
废弃资源和废旧材料回收加工业	Waste Resources and Junk Material Recycled	21750	14895	15265	22836

4-12 城镇居民家庭基本情况
BASIC CONDITIONS OF URBAN HOUSEHOLDS

指标	Item	1995	2000	2005	2006
基本情况	**Basic Conditions**				
调查户数 （户）	Number of Households Surveyed (household)	2020	2600	5000	5000
平均每户家庭人口 （人）	Average Number of Household Size (person)	3.19	3.07	2.92	2.88
平均每户就业人口 （人）	Average Number of Employees Per Household (person)	1.85	1.65	1.42	1.42
平均每一就业人口负担人数 （人）	Average Persons Supported By a Laborer (person)	1.72	1.86	2.06	2.03
平均每户就业面 （%）	Percentage of Employed Persons Per Household (%)	58.00	53.70	48.63	49.31
平均每人建筑面积（平方米）	Average Construction Floor Space Per Capita (sq. m)	21.69	25.54	28.76	29.68
平均每人使用面积（平方米）	Average Living Floor Space Per Capita (sq. m)	16.30	19.20	21.69	22.40
人均家庭总收入 （元）	**Per Capita Annual Income (yuan)**			**13329.95**	**15248.66**
人均可支配收入	Disposable Income	4634.42	6800.23	12318.57	14084.26
最低收入户	Lowest Income	2495.82	2771.10	3354.90	3802.31
低收入户	Low Income	3001.30	3843.77	5179.42	5967.87
中等偏下户	Medium-Low Income	3684.44	4929.73	7259.61	8377.37
中等收入户	Medium Income	4498.77	6349.98	10294.59	11864.25
中等偏上户	Medium-High Income	5307.41	8229.57	14400.98	16396.50
高收入户	High Income	6394.91	10790.69	19983.54	22745.82
最高收入户	Highest Income	8388.24	14949.09	33699.29	38526.86
人均家庭总支出 （元）	**Per Capita Annual Expenditures (yuan)**			**11897.97**	**13793.04**
人均消费性支出	Living Expenditure	3772.28	5323.18	8621.82	9628.59
#食　品	Food	1957.25	2189.80	3205.79	3462.66
衣　着	Clothing	483.28	492.10	804.23	886.82
家庭设备用品及服务	Facilities, Artical and Services	362.80	570.37	586.84	647.52
医疗保健	Medicine and Medical Services	73.56	294.39	579.32	600.69
交通通讯	Transportation and Communications	176.31	392.38	1050.88	1203.45
娱乐教育文化服务	Recreation, Education and Cultural Services	294.76	670.56	1287.90	1467.36
居　住	Residence	275.23	436.26	794.94	997.53
借贷支出	Debit and Credit Expenditures	1029.61	1347.39	3798.04	5019.74
#存入储蓄款	Deposit Money in Bank	810.72	1020.84	3083.44	4396.90
购买有价证券	Buy Valuable Nogotiable Securities	38.72	31.86	25.32	25.45

单位:元

指 标 Item		全省调查户平均水平 Total Average	最低收入户占10% Lowest Income Make up 10%	#更低收入户占5% Lower Income Make up 5%
水产品类	Aquatic Products	285.58	127.37	111.46
蔬菜类	Vegetables	320.25	208.58	192.75
调味品	Flavorings	42.72	29.49	25.83
糖　类	Sugar	32.32	14.30	11.85
烟草类	Tobacco	215.53	61.17	52.16
酒　类	Liquor	93.02	33.33	26.40
饮　料	Drink	59.26	18.26	13.91
干鲜瓜果类	Dried and Fresh Melons and Fruits	224.55	87.80	68.77
#坚果及果仁	Nuts and Grains	43.42	20.56	16.13
糕点	Cakes	61.03	25.41	20.59
奶及奶制品	Milk and Dairy Products	173.07	61.71	48.83
其他食品	Other Foods	111.64	30.77	28.25
衣　着	Clothing	886.82	241.60	212.94
#服　装	Garments	640.90	160.99	141.74
衣着材料	Clothing Materials	9.68	3.03	2.31
鞋　类	Shoes	192.51	62.91	55.81
其他衣着用品	Other Clothing	35.52	12.87	11.38
家庭设备用品及服务	Facilities, Artical and Service	647.52	131.81	105.91
耐用消费品	Durable Consumer Goods	306.64	38.43	21.91
室内装饰品	Interior Decorations	15.27	0.28	0.21
床上用品	Bed Articles	53.77	11.14	6.30
家庭日用杂品	Daily Use Articles	209.95	75.98	72.53
家具材料	Furniture Materials	3.76	0.16	0.01
家庭服务	Household Services	58.13	5.82	4.94
医疗保健	Medicine and Medical Services	600.69	218.39	211.42
交通和通讯	Transportation and Communications	1203.45	231.80	201.75
#交通费	Transportation	156.93	35.70	34.81
电信费	Telecommunications	335.37	127.73	112.76
教育文化娱乐服务	Recreation, Education and Cultural Services	1467.36	481.63	394.70
文化娱乐用品	Cultural Recreation Articales	404.61	75.52	65.27
文化娱乐服务	Cultural Recreation Services	341.02	37.43	39.00
教　育	Education	721.73	368.68	290.43
居　住	Residence	997.53	341.44	284.64
#租赁房房租	Rent	22.44	25.92	20.45
水	Water	62.44	32.26	29.99
电	Electricity	256.69	130.04	110.07
杂项商品和服务	Miscellaneous Commodities and Services	362.56	81.50	77.81

Continued

(yuan)

按收入水平分组 Grouped by Level of Income					
低收入户 占10% Low Income Make up 10%	中等偏下户 占20% Medium-Low Income Make up 20%	中等收入户 占20% Medium Income Make up 20%	中等偏上户 占20% Medium-High Income Make up 20%	高收入户 占10% High Income Make up 10%	最高收入户 占10% Highest Income Make up 10%
168.37	234.06	312.73	367.18	394.21	383.12
239.96	285.21	340.70	385.46	398.74	364.26
32.14	39.12	45.77	51.55	49.92	46.55
17.44	23.43	32.75	36.48	42.15	69.58
100.90	164.18	243.58	266.49	292.63	393.62
49.16	68.80	98.00	114.78	130.26	171.65
29.10	41.66	64.95	71.08	88.35	113.46
124.38	165.98	226.68	285.71	338.13	380.96
25.23	32.27	44.81	54.42	60.30	72.57
36.10	46.21	62.67	77.08	86.53	100.98
102.36	130.12	184.05	219.64	244.59	285.43
53.84	73.42	106.61	150.09	185.36	212.37
404.98	582.74	763.92	1097.98	1434.54	2106.84
275.93	410.96	541.10	787.53	1056.29	1593.71
6.35	7.03	9.48	13.25	13.18	16.48
97.63	134.37	173.39	242.39	291.84	413.43
20.89	26.06	32.26	44.23	59.06	64.31
256.62	390.13	579.68	765.75	1104.45	1677.96
114.85	183.44	265.85	347.58	515.96	885.04
1.82	2.68	10.91	13.30	29.97	72.67
20.38	30.50	52.56	63.37	87.50	139.67
108.11	152.16	205.73	265.80	346.19	365.13
0.18	0.25	2.22	4.43	7.51	17.58
11.29	21.10	42.40	71.27	117.32	197.87
275.49	423.58	643.37	720.61	1032.54	1032.34
368.95	664.07	923.52	1155.60	2077.51	4198.69
46.96	86.54	136.99	193.11	277.67	419.85
1178.81	271.46	325.60	410.53	499.15	593.30
724.77	871.20	1158.53	1569.08	2482.44	4129.89
140.72	200.10	340.76	470.10	712.87	1210.85
61.57	133.40	214.41	367.26	670.23	1328.45
522.48	537.71	603.36	731.73	1099.34	1590.58
450.02	646.06	748.38	1070.73	1781.13	2706.98
21.52	20.36	24.43	19.87	20.18	27.25
39.72	52.64	63.03	73.37	84.20	98.83
165.64	204.16	265.69	299.66	358.48	411.43
141.87	198.13	306.96	412.32	621.41	1042.19

4-14 城镇居民家庭人均购买主要商品数量 （2006 年）

单位:千克 (kg)

项目		全省调查户平均水平 Total Average	最低收入户占10% Lowest Income Make up 10%	#更低收入户占5% Lower Income Make up 5%
淀粉及薯类	Starches and Tubers	10.46	10.13	9.59
大豆	Soybeans	0.24	0.11	0.12
食用植物油	Edible Vegetable Oil	9.14	8.62	8.13
食用动物油	Edible Animal Oil	0.13	0.14	0.18
猪肉	Pork	20.55	14.78	13.98
牛肉	Beef	1.68	1.44	1.29
羊肉	Mutton	0.62	0.33	0.30
禽类	Poultry	11.27	5.85	5.23
鲜蛋	Fresh Eggs	10.87	9.78	9.04
鱼	Fish	12.87	9.75	8.90
虾	Shrimp	2.92	1.29	1.06
鲜菜	Fresh Vegetables	109.29	93.05	89.28
食糖	Sugar	1.67	1.44	1.37
糖果	Candy	0.58	0.25	0.15
卷烟 （盒）	Cigarettes (pack)	222.91	12.52	12.96
白酒	White Spirit	1.84	1.53	1.31
啤酒	Beer	3.89	2.36	2.24
茶叶	Tea	0.17	0.06	0.04
鲜果	Fresh Fruits	29.00	15.77	12.65
鲜瓜	Fresh Melon	26.58	13.61	10.98
糕点	Cake	3.87	2.31	1.92
鲜乳品	Fresh Dairy Products	20.30	8.22	6.84
奶粉	Milk Powder	0.31	0.17	0.13
酸奶	Sour Milk	3.39	0.91	0.48
男士服装 （件）	Men's Clothing (piece)	2.77	1.35	1.26
女士服装 （件）	Women's Clothing (piece)	3.21	1.27	1.06
童装 （件）	Children's Clothing (piece)	0.82	0.34	0.31

PER CAPITA ANNUAL PURCHASES OF MAJOR COMMODITIES IN URBAN HOUSEHOLDS BY LEVEL OF INCOME (2006)

(kg)

按收入水平分组 Grouped by Level of Income					
低收入户 占10% Low Income Make up 10%	中等偏下户 占20% Medium-Low Income Make up 20%	中等收入户 占20% Medium Income Make up 20%	中等偏上户 占20% Medium-High Income Make up 20%	高收入户 占10% High Income Make up 10%	最高收入户 占10% Highest Income Make up 10%
10.15	10.58	10.37	11.13	10.73	9.52
0.12	0.20	0.25	0.35	0.28	0.32
8.33	9.61	9.65	9.89	8.91	7.29
0.14	0.14	0.13	0.13	0.13	0.06
18.10	20.20	22.56	23.75	21.88	18.75
1.64	1.82	1.75	1.81	1.75	1.20
0.46	0.61	0.71	0.74	0.76	0.54
7.87	10.03	12.85	13.93	14.80	11.84
10.04	10.70	11.16	12.10	11.35	9.91
10.65	12.10	13.90	14.81	14.83	12.63
1.74	2.57	3.20	3.76	3.95	3.58
97.89	104.27	113.57	123.92	119.41	103.71
1.42	1.65	1.82	1.93	1.76	1.34
0.34	0.40	0.59	0.64	0.67	1.43
17.91	21.23	28.27	25.48	24.65	25.84
1.96	2.05	2.04	1.82	1.65	1.37
2.85	3.78	4.90	4.45	3.77	3.90
00.09	0.12	0.23	0.23	0.20	0.21
19.92	23.83	29.30	35.12	39.56	42.18
17.88	22.99	27.66	33.10	36.06	34.37
2.79	3.18	4.14	4.64	4.89	5.20
12.03	16.19	21.49	24.94	28.68	32.15
0.25	0.23	0.34	0.42	0.41	0.36
1.65	2.24	3.56	4.59	5.44	5.94
1.95	2.38	2.72	3.29	3.58	4.39
2.02	2.60	3.11	3.99	4.40	5.58
0.47	0.70	0.81	1.04	1.07	1.39

4－15　城镇居民家庭平均每百户年末耐用品拥有量(2006年)

项　　目				全　省 调查户 平均水平 Total Average	最低收入户 占10% Lowest Income Make up 10%	#更低收入户 占5% Lower Income Make up 5%
成套家具	(套)	Combined Furniture	(unit)	81.13	60.76	57.00
自行车	(辆)	Bicycles	(unit)	155.52	168.38	163.71
助力车	(辆)	Auxiliary Driving Bikes	(unit)	41.12	16.36	13.80
家用汽车	(辆)	Cars for Household Use	(unit)	5.46	0.73	1.00
洗衣机	(台)	Washing Machines	(unit)	100.30	94.09	91.74
电风扇	(台)	Electric Fans	(unit)	208.15	190.38	185.49
电冰箱	(台)	Refrigerators	(unit)	92.92	64.42	57.24
冰柜	(台)	Freezers	(unit)	4.47	3.58	3.37
彩色电视机	(台)	Color TV Sets	(unit)	157.98	119.75	115.94
影碟机	(台)	VCD	(unit)	65.64	46.55	43.00
录音机	(台)	Recorders	(unit)	34.39	21.31	17.53
录放像机	(台)	Videorecorders	(unit)	17.44	4.62	2.50
家用电脑	(台)	Computers	(unit)	52.48	15.69	15.64
组合音响	(套)	Hi-Fi Systems	(unit)	28.86	12.45	11.56
摄像机	(台)	TV Cameras	(unit)	5.76	0.73	0.68
照相机	(架)	Cameras	(unit)	47.60	10.15	6.40
钢琴	(架)	Pianoes	(unit)	2.66	0.74	1.11
其他中高档乐器	(件)	Medium and High-Grade Musical Instruments	(unit)	4.43	1.30	0.96
微波炉	(台)	Microwave Stove	(unit)	78.84	39.67	38.34
空调器	(台)	Air Conditioners	(unit)	132.06	45.56	38.35
取暖器	(台)	Warm Appliances	(unit)	54.33	20.93	17.98
电炊具	(个)	Electric Cooking Tools	(unit)	128.31	90.45	79.55
淋浴热水器	(台)	Showers	(unit)	84.07	47.34	45.52
排油烟机	(台)	Range Hoods	(unit)	80.82	50.56	44.18
消毒碗柜	(台)	Sterilized Cupboards	(unit)	7.31	0.96	0.68
洗碗机	(台)	Bowl Washing Machines	(unit)	0.63	0.77	0.00
饮水机	(台)	Drinking Machines	(unit)	51.50	44.67	43.13
吸尘器	(台)	Vacuum Cleaners	(unit)	18.72	3.65	4.61
健身器材	(件)	Health Care Instruments	(unit)	5.82	0.85	0.68
普通电话	(部)	Telephones	(set)	131.52	107.72	106.18
移动电话	(部)	Mobile Telephones	(set)	132.01	65.62	57.34
传真机	(台)	Fax Machines	(unit)	2.39	0.36	0.73

NUMBER OF DURABLE CONSUMER GOODS OWNED PER 100 URBAN HOUSEHOLDS AT THE YEAR – END BY INCOME LEVEL (2006)

收入水平分组 Grouped by Level of Income					
低收入户 占 10 % Low Income Make up 10%	中等偏下户 占 20 % Medium-Low Income Make up 20%	中等收入户 占 20 % Medium Income Make up 20%	中等偏上户 占 20 % Medium-High Income Make up 20%	高收入户 占 10 % High Income Make up 10%	最高收入户 占 10 % Highest Income Make up 10%
73.88	78.36	78.28	82.35	94.09	100.76
188.13	166.72	154.98	144.52	139.45	131.82
30.99	40.31	46.49	45.47	48.89	47.48
0.24	2.20	1.93	4.70	9.90	23.76
97.71	96.94	98.88	102.85	104.25	108.21
202.52	207.74	210.89	209.62	216.76	213.23
83.04	90.27	95.27	99.22	102.51	105.83
6.84	3.81	4.89	3.70	3.96	5.46
132.67	141.11	155.13	172.56	181.28	200.03
60.65	60.09	63.16	70.65	74.93	82.98
24.41	29.67	36.39	33.61	46.20	49.67
10.54	12.75	16.46	21.23	25.35	30.35
27.30	36.49	50.11	63.44	76.99	96.24
17.98	23.90	26.14	33.58	41.03	46.34
2.11	2.00	3.57	5.65	9.61	20.71
20.61	28.00	44.51	58.82	78.33	95.10
0.85	0.87	1.53	3.11	4.66	8.53
1.87	2.63	4.36	5.10	6.95	9.13
59.37	70.65	82.69	90.97	95.63	99.10
76.67	95.56	128.88	157.47	185.33	230.03
35.36	43.15	54.80	67.95	77.42	72.16
109.75	120.32	131.04	137.62	140.66	157.77
64.85	75.53	84.86	93.56	102.84	111.30
63.18	76.13	81.99	90.80	93.04	98.74
2.24	2.68	4.58	8.04	11.61	25.22
0.05	0.11	0.40	0.78	0.84	1.93
48.65	50.88	50.65	51.41	53.12	61.17
6.12	10.52	15.32	23.89	30.61	43.15
1.87	1.94	4.34	6.50	8.22	19.84
123.71	130.83	132.55	135.25	137.97	145.16
92.89	113.97	133.49	149.23	165.76	189.87
0.52	1.69	2.09	1.97	4.48	6.38

4-16 城镇居民家庭平均每人购买主要商品数量
PER CAPITA ANNUAL PURCHASES OF MAJOR COMMDITIES IN URBAN HOUSEHOLDS

单位：千克　　(kg)

项目	Item	1990	1995	2000	2005	2006
粮食	Grain	119.00	96.31	75.81	72.61	73.41
植物油	Edible Vegetable Oil	6.98	7.31	8.60	8.62	9.14
鲜菜	Fresh Vegetables	117.73	112.30	105.01	104.70	109.29
猪肉	Pork	18.49	19.86	19.71	20.98	20.55
牛羊肉	Beef and Mutton	2.38	1.40	1.77	2.37	2.30
蛋类	Eggs	7.54	10.89	12.78	11.70	11.93
鱼虾	Fish and Shrimp	10.76	14.31	15.89	15.30	15.79
卷烟（盒）	Cigarettes (pack)	33.62	26.10	22.96	21.91	22.91
鲜瓜果及制品	Fresh Melon and Fruits	45.32	48.87	52.81	52.30	56.02
糖果	Candy	0.62	0.66	0.55	0.52	0.58
糕点	Cake	3.94	3.11	3.01	3.73	3.87
鲜酸奶	Fresh Dairy	3.72	4.19	12.04	22.00	23.69
服装（件）	Clothing (piece)	2.45	4.82	5.81	6.95	6.81

4-17 城镇居民家庭平均每百户年末耐用品拥有量
NUMBER OF MAJOR DURABLE CONSUMER GOODS OWNED PER 100 URBAN HOUSEHOLDS AT YEAR-END

项目	Item	1990	1995	2000	2005	2006
自行车（辆）	Bicycles (unit)	217.04	237.46	206.08	152.85	155.52
洗衣机（台）	Washing Machines (unit)	85.81	95.35	96.15	99.38	100.30
电冰箱（台）	Refrigerators (unit)	49.09	69.42	85.64	91.89	92.92
冰柜（台）	Freezers (unit)		1.93	4.42	4.58	4.47
摩托车（辆）	Motorcycles (unit)	1.90	6.77	27.28	27.42	26.77
彩色电视机（台）	Color TV Sets (unit)	51.46	85.22	124.45	153.19	157.98
录放像机（台）	Videorecorders (unit)	2.45	20.57	22.56	17.53	17.44
空调器（台）	Air Conditioners (unit)	0.07	10.53	45.90	123.92	132.06
家用电脑（台）	Computers (unit)			10.65	46.35	52.48
固定电话（部）	Fixed Telephones (set)				130.79	131.52
移动电话（部）	Mobile Telephones (set)			25.47	120.61	132.01

4-18 农民家庭基本情况
BASIC INDICATORS OF RURAL HOUSEHOLDS

指　　标	Item	1995	2000	2005	2006
调查户数　（户）	**Households Surveyed (household)**	**3400**	**3400**	**3400**	**3400**
调查户人口　（人）	**Residents Surveyed (person)**				
常住人口	Permanent Residents	13644	12711	12712	12628
平均每户常住人口	Average Permanent Residents Per Household	4.01	3.74	3.74	3.71
平均每户整、半劳动力	Average Full-Time and Part-Time Laborers Per Household	2.79	2.62	2.66	2.67
平均每个劳动力负担人口（包括劳动力本人）	Average Persons Suported by Each Laborer (including the laborer-self)	1.44	1.43	1.41	1.39
平均每人全年收入　（元）	**Average Per Capita Annual Income (yuan)**				
总收入	Total Revenue	3290.9	4542.0	6682.3	7267.3
纯收入	Net Income	2456.9	3595.1	5276.3	5813.2
现金收入	Cash Income	2323.1	3673.6	6035.3	6544.1
按人均纯收入水平分组的户数占调查总户数的比重　（%）	**Percentage of Households by Per Capita Annual Net Income (%)**				
1000 元以下	Below 1000 yuan	7.6	2.9	1.6	0.9
1000-2000 元	1000-2000 yuan	34.7	17.1	6.6	5.2
2000-3000 元	2000-3000 yuan	27.8	26.8	14.1	12.6
3000-4000 元	3000-4000 yuan	14.4	21.0	18.0	15.2
4000-5000 元	4000-5000 yuan	7.2	12.2	14.7	14.4
5000-6000 元	5000-6000 yuan	8.3	20.0	11.5	12.2
6000-8000 元	6000-8000 yuan			15.4	16.7
8000-10000 元	8000-10000 yuan			8.8	9.9
10000 元以上	10000 yuan and Over			9.3	12.9
平均每人全年支出　（元）	**Average Per Capita Annual Expenditures (yuan)**				
总支出	Total Expenditures	2861.6	3434.3	5281.3	5842.3
#家庭经营性费用支出	Household Business Expenditures	675.2	678.0	1185.1	1193.6
购置生产性固定资产支出	Productive Fixed Assets Expenditures	51.5	28.8	141.4	101.4
生活消费支出	Living Expenditures	1938.0	2337.5	3567.1	4135.2
财产性支出	Property Expenditures	62.3	14.7	6.1	8.9
转移性支出	Transfer Expenditures	16.8	272.0	346.9	379.9
现金支出	Cash Expenditures	2466.1	2970.2	4776.1	5305.7
#生产费用	Productive Costs	579.9	667.2	1261.1	1243.9
税费支出	Tax Expenditures	83.9	97.0	33.3	22.6
生活消费支出	Consumptive Expenditures	1285.8	1922.1	3137.9	3658.2

4－19 农民家庭平均每人总收入和纯收入
ANNUAL PER CAPITA REVENUE AND NET INCOME OF RURAL HOUSEHOLDS

单位:元 (yuan)

指　　标	Item	1995	2000	2005	2006
总收入	**Total Revenue**	**3290.9**	**4542.0**	**6682.3**	**7267.3**
工资性收入	Money Wage	821.9	1663.1	2786.1	3076.4
在非企业组织中劳动的收入	Non-enterprise Units	81.8	283.9	353.7	383.9
在本乡地域内劳动得到的收入	Income From Labour in Native Land		902.7	1474.1	1659.1
#在本地企业劳动得到的收入	Local Enterprises	715.4	740.2	1251.2	1406.9
外出从业得到的收入	Non-enterprise Units		476.5	958.3	1033.5
家庭经营收入	House Business Revenue	2368.0	2636.1	3470.6	3654.7
财产性收入	Property Income	25.5	48.1	150.4	178.5
转移性收入	Transfer Income	75.5	194.7	275.2	357.7
纯收入	**Net Income**	**2456.9**	**3595.1**	**5276.3**	**5813.2**
工资性收入	Money Wage	821.9	1663.1	2786.1	3076.4
家庭经营收入	Household Business	1544.4	1771.0	2125.0	2299.6
农业收入	Farming			946.4	1000.7
林业收入	Forestry			39.6	38.1
牧业收入	Animal Husbandry			256.5	233.4
渔业收入	Fishery			135.6	146.5
工业收入	Industry			147.5	196.7
建筑业收入	Construction			104.0	104.5
交通运输邮电业收入	Transport and Post			188.8	175.7
批零贸易餐饮业收入	Wholesale and Retail Trade and Catering Services			205.3	285.7
社会服务业收入	Other Social Services			61.9	58.0
文教卫生业收入	Education, Culture and Health Care			3.2	5.1
其他家庭经营收入	Other House Business Revenue			36.2	55.3
财产性收入	Property Income	25.6	48.1	150.4	178.5
转移性收入	Transfer Income	65.0	112.9	214.8	258.6

4－20　农民家庭平均每人生活消费支出
PER CAPITA RURAL HOUSEHOLD LIVING EXPENDITURES

单位:元　　(yuan)

指　标	Item	1995	2000	2005	2006
生活消费支出	**Total Living Expenditures**	**1938.0**	**2337.5**	**3567.1**	**4135.2**
食　品	Food	1061.4	1017.6	1569.3	1729.0
主　食	Grain	412.3	259.7	307.2	322.8
副食及其他食品	Non-Staple Food and Others	622.4	670.2	1031.2	1112.6
在外饮食	Travelling Catering Service	26.7	87.7	230.9	293.6
衣　着	Clothing	126.8	126.7	191.1	223.3
居　住	Residence	344.6	441.6	512.5	641.1
#住房装饰	Housing Decoration		53.6	99.5	124.6
家庭设备、用品及服务	Household Facilities, Articales and Services	133.0	115.0	168.0	199.5
交通和通讯	Transportation and Communications	52.3	155.5	363.8	465.2
文化教育娱乐用品及服务	Cultural, Educational and Recreational Article and Services	139.2	269.0	478.9	544.1
医疗保健	Medicine and Medical Services	49.1	129.5	198.5	232.3
其他商品和服务	Other Commodity and Services	31.6	82.6	85.0	100.7

4－21　农民家庭房屋情况
RURAL HOUSEHOLD HOUSING CONDITIONS

指　标	Item	1995	2000	2005	2006
平均每人住房	**Per Capita Housing Conditions**				
人均住房价值　(元)	Value of Per Capita Living Space　(yuan)	4185.7	9397.9	15462.7	16820.9
人均住房面积　(平方米)	Per Capita Living Space　(sq. m)	25.7	33.7	38.6	40.8
按住房类型分	Grouped by Types of House				
#楼房面积	Per Capita Floor Space of Multi-floor Buildings		19.7	25.5	27.1
砖瓦平房面积	Per Capita Floor Space of Brick and Tile-roofed Single-story House		13.5	12.7	13.4
按住房结构分	Grouped by House Structure				
#钢筋混凝土结构	Reinforced Concrete Structures	4.8	8.4	21.6	24.5
砖木结构	Brick and Wood Structures	19.5	24.8	16.6	16.1
平均每人本年新建房屋	**Rooms Newly Built Per Capita**				
新建住房每平方米价值　(元)	Value of Per Square of the Rooms Newly Built　(yuan)	308.5	352.6	563.1	416.9
人均新建(购)住房面积　(平方米)	Per Capita Space of the Rooms Newly Built　(sq. m)	1.29	1.14	0.85	0.68
#钢筋混凝土结构	Reinforced Concrete Structures	0.53	0.43	0.66	0.58
砖木结构	Brick and Wood Structures	0.76	0.69	0.19	0.10
#楼　房	Multi-Floor Houses	0.56	0.75	0.69	0.54

4－22　不同收入组农民家庭基本情况（2006年）
BASIC CONDITION OF RURAL HOUSEHOLD GROUPED BY INCOME (2006)

指　　标	Item	低收入户 Low Income	中低收入户 Medium-Low Income	中等收入户 Medium Income	中高收入户 Medium-High Income	高收入户 High Income
平均每户常住人口　（人）	Average Number of Permanent Residents Per Household (person)	4.12	3.93	3.83	3.51	3.19
平均每户整、半劳动力（人）	Average Full-time and Half-time Laborer Per Household (person)	2.76	2.77	2.75	2.59	2.46
平均每个劳动力负担人口（人）	Average Persons Supported by a Rural labarer (person)	1.49	1.42	1.39	1.35	1.30
平均每人总收入　（元）	Per Capita Total Income (yuan)	3299.4	4964.4	6303.8	8484.9	15041.8
#现金收入	Cash Income	2745.6	4242.1	5519.2	7674.5	14268.3
平均每人总支出　（元）	Per Capita Total Expenditure (yuan)	3497.5	4499.8	5314.8	6631.3	10287.4
#现金支出	Cash Expenditure	3054.1	3979.5	4731.4	6033.1	9734.3
平均每人纯收入　（元）	Per Capita Net Income (yuan)	2235.1	3740.2	5121.9	7059.3	12443.8
工资性收入	Wages Income	1182.5	2082.2	2911.5	3908.4	6028.9
家庭经营收入	Household Business Income	931.7	1467.6	1912.3	2638.3	5182.2
财产性收入	Property Income	24.0	59.2	101.1	190.4	604.6
转移性收入	Transfer Income	97.0	131.1	197.0	322.2	628.1

4－23　不同收入组农民平均每人生活消费支出（2006年）
PER CAPITA LIVING EXPENDITURE OF RURAL HOUSEHOLD GROUPED BY INCOME (2006)

单位：元　　　　(yuan)

指　　标	Item	低收入户 Low Income	中低收入户 Medium-Low Income	中等收入户 Medium Income	中高收入户 Medium-High Income	高收入户 High Income
生活消费支出	**Total Living Expenditures**	**2415.7**	**3144.7**	**3936.6**	**4836.3**	**7042.1**
食　品	Food	1155.8	1410.9	1671.1	1997.1	2635.3
衣　着	Clothing	119.3	160.7	211.0	274.2	393.1
居　住	Residence	297.3	477.2	628.4	708.2	1227.9
家庭设备用品及服务	Household Facilities, Articales and Services	97.8	130.7	186.9	254.6	370.0
交通和通讯	Traffic and Communications	260.3	307.9	405.1	585.6	862.9
文化教育娱乐用品及服务	Cultural, Educational and Recreational Artical and Services	302.8	420.6	530.9	631.5	927.7
医疗保健	Medicine and Medical Services	133.2	168.4	213.6	258.8	432.2
其他商品和服务	Other Commodity and Services	49.3	68.2	89.6	126.2	193.0
生活消费现金支出	**Total Living Cash Expenditures**	**2017.1**	**2684.9**	**3422.8**	**4298.7**	**6553.3**
食　品	Food	776.6	973.7	1194.5	1490.9	2196.1
衣　着	Clothing	118.3	159.8	210.6	273.5	392.9
居　住	Residence	278.9	455.6	591.6	677.5	1178.4
家庭设备用品及服务	Household Facilities, Articales and Services	97.8	130.7	186.9	254.6	370.0
交通和通讯	Traffic and Communications	260.3	307.9	405.1	585.6	862.9
文化教育娱乐用品服务	Cultural, Educational and Recreational Artical and Services	302.8	420.6	530.9	631.5	927.7
医疗保健	Medicine and Medical Services	133.2	168.4	213.6	258.8	432.2
其他商品和服务	Other Commodity and Services	49.3	68.2	89.6	126.2	193.0

4-24 农民家庭平均每人主要消费品消费量
RURAL HOUSEHOLD PER CAPITA CONSUMPTION ON MAJOR CONSUMER GOODS

单位:千克 (kg)

指标	Item	1995	2000	2005	2006
粮 食(原粮)	Grain (Unprocessed Grains)	264.0	288.1	208.6	218.9
#稻 谷	Paddy	184.4	188.2	147.1	152.5
小 麦	Wheat	64.6	72.5	45.4	49.7
蔬菜及其制品	Fresh Vegetables and processed products	120.2	115.7	108.9	113.3
植物油	Edible Vegetable Oil	7.6	8.9	7.8	8.5
动物油	Edible Animal Oil	0.6	0.7	0.3	0.4
肉类及其制品	Meat and Processed Products	14.4	17.8	23.0	23.0
#猪 肉	Pork	10.0	11.5	12.8	12.8
牛羊肉	Beef and Mutton	0.5	0.8	1.3	1.3
家 禽	Poultry	3.2	4.4	5.6	5.5
蛋类及其制品	Eggs	7.6	8.2	6.4	6.9
水产品及其制品	Aquatic Products	7.3	7.7	10.0	10.5
#鱼 类	Fishes	6.5	6.8	8.2	8.7
虾、贝、蟹类	Shrimp, Sheefish and Erab	0.3	0.5	1.2	1.2
水果(含果用瓜)	Fruit(including melon fruits)	21.8	21.1	18.0	20.4
食 糖	Sugar	1.7	1.5	1.2	1.2
卷 烟 (盒)	Cigarettes (pack)	27.8	24.6	27.7	26.8
酒	Liquor	8.2	7.4	11.2	12.1

4-25 农民家庭年末平均每百户耐用消费品拥有量
RURAL HOUSEHOLD YEAR-END POSSESSION OF DURABLE CONSUMER GOODS PER 100 HOUSEHOLDS

指标	Item	1995	2000	2005	2006
电视机 (台)	TV Sets (unit)	96.6	115.9	136.1	139.7
#彩色电视机	Color TV Sets	21.9	53.9	104.7	115.2
影碟机 (台)	VCD (unit)		11.2	30.1	34.9
收录机 (台)	Recorders (unit)	32.7	20.5	11.8	11.9
电话机 (部)	Telephones (set)		51.4	89.4	93.0
移动电话 (部)	Mobile Telephones (set)		9.1	78.0	92.7
洗衣机 (台)	Washing Machines (unit)	29.8	46.1	67.9	73.6
电风扇 (台)	Electric Fans (unit)	167.6	201.4	241.5	246.4
电冰箱 (台)	Refrigerators (unit)	9.1	19.9	36.0	39.1
抽油烟机 (台)	Range Hoods (unit)		5.1	12.6	15.4
自行车 (辆)	Bicycles (unit)	183.4	175.4	162.1	159.7
摩托车 (辆)	Motorcycles (unit)	8.6	28.5	52.7	57.7
空调机 (台)	Air Conditioners (unit)		5.4	22.2	26.3
照相机 (架)	Cameras (unit)	2.3	4.0	6.7	7.3
热水器 (台)	Showers (unit)		11.1	32.1	38.3

4－26 按纯收入分组农民家庭购买商品数量（2006年）
ANNUAL PURCHASES OF COMMODITIES IN RURAL HOUSEHOLDS BY LEVEL OF NET INCOME（2006）

单位：千克 (kg)

项　目	Item	全省平均 Total Average	低收入户 Low Income	中低收入户 Medium Low Income
平均每人购买	Per Capita Perchases of Commodities			
粮食（原粮）	Grain（Unprocessed Grain）	30.51	21.29	24.72
食用植物油	Edible Vegetable Oil	4.20	3.52	3.76
动物油	Animal Oil	0.38	0.38	0.50
蔬菜	Vegetables	22.27	16.53	18.26
豆制品（元）	Beans and Bean Products（yuan）	16.33	14.70	14.33
猪肉	Pork	11.52	7.91	9.39
牛羊肉	Beef and Mutton	1.15	0.90	1.05
家禽	Poulty	4.21	2.19	3.15
鲜蛋	Fresh Eggs	3.57	2.84	3.51
水产品	Aquatic products	9.65	6.88	8.13
食糖	Sugar	1.21	0.98	1.15
卷烟（盒）	Cigarettes（pack）	26.83	17.89	21.95
酒	Liquor	12.13	8.81	10.95
茶叶	Tea	0.10	0.06	0.07
水果（含果用瓜）	Fruits（including melon fruits）	18.13	11.87	15.48
服装（件）	Garments（piece）	3.05	1.92	2.45
鞋（双）	Shoes（pair）	1.86	1.40	1.74
平均每户购买	Per Household Perchases of Commodities			
水泥	Cement	468.97	319.87	368.28
木材（立方米）	Timber（cu. m）	0.07	0.03	0.03
钢材	Rolled Steel	20.42	10.47	25.29
水泥预制件（件）	Cement Prefabricated Components（piece）	1.75	0.59	0.77
砖瓦（块）	Brisks and Tiles（piece）	689.50	536.88	404.82
化肥	Chemical Fertilizers	655.05	721.97	804.59
饼肥	Cake Fertilizers	2.30	0.60	1.98
农药（元）	Chemical Insecticide（yuan）	248.01	218.72	253.84
农用薄膜	Plastic Film for Agricultural Use	3.23	1.40	2.05
平均每百户购买	Per 100 Households Perchases of Commodities			
彩色电视机（台）	Color TV（unit）	6.35	3.24	6.47
收录机（台）	Videorecorders（unit）	0.53	0.29	0.59
照相机（架）	Cameras（unit）	0.12		
洗衣机（台）	Washing Machines（unit）	3.29	3.24	3.97
电风扇（台）	Electric Fans（unit）	9.51	7.82	7.79
电冰箱（台）	Refrigerators（unit）	3.88	1.62	1.03
空调机（台）	Air Conditioners（unit）	3.53	0.88	1.62
油烟机（台）	Range Hoods（unit）	0.97	0.29	0.29
热水器（台）	Showers（unit）	4.49	2.35	3.09
微波炉（台）	Microwave Stoves（unit）	3.03	1.62	1.76
自行车（辆）	Bicycles（unit）	7.12	6.47	5.88
电动自行车（辆）	Power-driven Bicycles（unit）	10.50	7.94	9.56
摩托车（辆）	Motorcycles（unit）	4.38	1.76	3.53
电话（部）	Telephones（set）	6.44	4.26	5.29

单位:千克 (kg)

项 目	Item	中等收入户 Medium Income	中高收入户 Medium High Income	高收入户 High Income
平均每人购买	Per Capita Perchases of Commodities			
粮食(原粮)	Grain(Unprocessed Grain)	30.67	34.36	45.15
食用植物油	Edible Vegetable Oil	4.03	4.34	5.68
动物油	Animal Oil	0.29	0.46	0.26
蔬菜	Vegetables	20.42	25.76	33.02
豆制品 (元)	Beans and Bean Products (yuan)	17.04	17.86	18.35
猪肉	Pork	11.18	13.47	17.06
牛羊肉	Beef and Mutton	1.04	1.29	1.60
家禽	Poulty	3.98	5.37	7.12
鲜蛋	Fresh Eggs	3.19	3.82	4.75
水产品	Aquatic products	9.05	10.93	14.38
食糖	Sugar	1.10	1.37	1.55
卷烟 (盒)	Cigarettes (pack)	27.14	31.56	38.83
酒	Liquor	11.03	13.85	17.28
茶叶	Tea	0.09	0.12	0.18
水果(含果用瓜)	Fruits(including melon fruits)	16.97	20.20	28.62
服装 (件)	Garments (piece)	2.95	3.66	4.70
鞋 (双)	Shoes (pair)	1.85	2.08	2.38
平均每户购买	Per Household Perchases of Commodities			
水泥	Cement	596.88	539.16	520.64
木材 (立方米)	Timber (cu. m)	0.07	0.12	0.10
钢材	Rolled Steel	30.04	12.81	23.48
水泥预制件 (件)	Cement Prefabricated Components (piece)	3.75	0.89	2.76
砖瓦 (块)	Brisks and Tiles (piece)	681.07	707.17	1117.54
化肥	Chemical Fertilizers	694.98	605.23	448.51
饼肥	Cake Fertilizers	2.80	2.94	3.20
农药 (元)	Chemical Insecticide (yuan)	275.30	261.80	230.39
农用薄膜	Plastic Film for Agricultural Use	2.14	5.26	5.28
平均每百户购买	Per 100 Households Perchases of Commodities			
彩色电视机 (台)	Color TV (unit)	6.03	7.94	8.09
收录机 (台)	Videorecorders (unit)	0.44	0.88	0.44
照相机 (架)	Cameras (unit)		0.29	0.29
洗衣机 (台)	Washing Machines (unit)	2.06	3.24	3.97
电风扇 (台)	Electric Fans (unit)	8.82	10.44	12.65
电冰箱 (台)	Refrigerators (unit)	4.56	6.18	6.03
空调机 (台)	Air Conditioners (unit)	4.12	4.12	6.91
油烟机 (台)	Range Hoods (unit)	0.74	1.03	2.50
热水器 (台)	Showers (unit)	7.28	4.71	5.00
微波炉 (台)	Microwave Stoves (unit)	2.35	4.12	5.29
自行车 (辆)	Bicycles (unit)	9.12	7.35	6.76
电动自行车 (辆)	Power driven Bicycles (unit)	10.44	11.76	12.79
摩托车 (辆)	Motorcycles (unit)	4.56	6.32	5.74
电话 (部)	Telephones (set)	7.65	7.50	7.50

主要统计指标解释

职工工资总额 指各单位在一定时期内直接支付给本单位全部职工的劳动报酬总额。工资总额的计算原则应以直接支付给职工的全部劳动报酬为根据。各单位支付给职工的劳动报酬以及其他根据有关规定支付的工资,不论是计入成本的还是不计入成本的,不论是按国家规定列入计征奖金税项目的,还是未列入计征奖金税项目的,不论是以货币形式支付的还是以实物形式支付的,均包括在工资总额内。

职工平均工资 指企业、事业、机关单位的职工在一定时期内平均每人所得的货币工资额。它表明一定时期职工工资收入的高低程度,是反映职工工资水平的主要指标。计算公式为:

职工平均工资 = 报告期实际支付的全部职工工资总额/报告期全部职工平均人数

职工平均工资指数 指报告期职工平均工资与基期职工平均工资的比率,是反映不同时期职工货币工资水平变动情况的相对数。计算公式为:

职工平均工资指数 = 报告期平均工资/基期职工平均工资 × 100%

职工平均实际工资指数 职工平均实际工资指扣除物价变动因素后的职工平均工资。职工平均实际工资指数是反映实际工资变动情况的相对数,表明职工实际工资水平提高或降低的程度。计算公式为:

职工平均实际工资指数 = 报告期平均工资指数/报告期城镇居民消费价格指数 × 100%。

家庭总收入 指调查户中生活在一起的所有家庭成员在调查期得到的工薪收入、经营净收入、财产性收入、转移性收入的总和,不包括借贷收入。收入的统计标准以实际发生的数额为准,无论收入是补发还是预发,只要是调查期得到的都应如实计算,不作分摊。

可支配收入 指调查户可用于最终消费支出和其它非义务性支出以及储蓄的总和,即居民家庭可以用来自由支配的收入。它是家庭总收入扣除交纳的个人所得税、个人交纳的社会保障费以及调查户的记账补贴后的收入。计算公式为:

可支配收入 = 家庭总收入 - 交纳的个人所得税 - 个人交纳的社会保障支出 - 记账补贴

消费支出 指调查户用于本家庭日常生活的全部支出,包括食品、衣着、家庭设备用品及服务、医疗保健、交通和通讯、娱乐教育文化服务、居住、杂项商品和服务八大类等。

农村居民家庭纯收入 指农村常住居民家庭总收入中,扣除从事生产和非生产经营费用支出、缴纳税款和上交承包集体任务金额以后剩余的,可直接用于进行生产性、非生产性建设投资、生活消费和积蓄的那一部分收入。农村居民家庭纯收入包括从事生产性和非生产性的经营收入,在外人口寄回带回和国家财政救济、各种补贴等非经营性收入;既包括货币收入,又包括自产自用的实物收入。但不包括向银行、信用社和向亲友借款等属于借贷性的收入。

农村居民家庭生活消费支出 指农村常住居民家庭用于日常生活的全部开支,是反映和研究农民家庭实际生活消费水平高低的重要指标。

城乡居民储蓄存款余额 指某一时点城乡居民存入银行及农村信用社的储蓄金额,包括城镇居民储蓄存款和农民个人储蓄存款,不包括居民的手存现金和工矿企业、部队、机关、团体等单位存款。

Explanatory Notes on Main Statistical Indicators

Total Wages of Staff and Workers refer to the total remuneration payment to staff and workers in various units during a certain period of time. The calculation of total wages is based on the total remuneration payment to the staff and workers. Therefore, all the wages and salaries and other payments to staff and workers are included in the total wages regardless of their sources, category, and forms (in kind or cash). (Total wages of staff and workers in this yearbook include only total wages of fully employed staff and workers, excluding the living allowances distributed to those who have left their working units while keeping their labour contract/employment relation unchanged).

Average Wage of Staff and Workers refers to the average wage in money terms per person during a certain period of time for staff and workers in enterprises, institutions, and government agencies, which reflects the general level of wage income during a certain period of time and is calculated as follows:

Average Wage of Staff and Workers = Total Wages of Staff and Workers at the Report Period/Average Number of Staff and Workers at the Report Period.

Average Wage Indices of Staff and Workers refers to the ratio of average wage of staff and workers in the report period to that in the base period, which reflects the change of wage of staff and workers at the different period. It is calculated as follows:

Average Wage Indices of Staff and Workers = Average Wage of Staff and Workers at the Report Period/Average Wage of Staff and Workers at the Base Period ×100%

Average Real Wage Indices of Staff and Workers average real wage of staff and workers refers to the average wage of staff and workers after removing the effects of the price changes and average real wage indices of staff and workers refers to the change of real wage, which reflects the relative increasing or decreasing level of real wage of staff and workers, which is calculated as follows:

Average Real Wage Indices of Staff and Workers = Average Wage Indices of Staff and Workers at the Report Period/Urban Consumer Price Indices at the Report Period ×100%

Total Income of Households refers to the sum of incomes of all members living in a same family. The total incomes include wage income, net income of operation, property income, transfered income; exclude debit and credit incomes. The calculating of total incomes is based on the value actually occured during the period of investigation. So long as the incomes are obtained during the period of in vestigation, all the incomes are included in the total incomes, regardless the incomes are re-issued or issued in advance. and don't to be shared.

Disposable Income refers to the sum of final consumption expenditure, non-obligation expenditure and saving deposits of the sample households. They are the incomes which can be freely allocated by household after some deductings. The deductings include the payment of individual taxes, payment of individual social security costs and subsidies of keeping account offered to sample households.

The formula is:

Disposable income = Total income of household-individual taxes payment-individual social security costs payment-subsidies of keeping account.

Consumption Expenditure refers to all of the daily expenditures of sample households, include food, clothing, home equip-ments and articales and services, medicine and health care, means of transportation and telecommunications, recreation, education, culture and services, residence, and miscellaneous goods and services ect. eight categories.

Net Income of Rural Households refers to the total income of the permanent residents of the rural households during a year after the deduction of the expenses for productive and non-productive business operation, the payment for taxes and the payment for collective units for their contracted tasks, which can then be spent for investments in productive and non-productive construction, for consumption in daily life and for savings deposit. It is a comprehensive indicator to show the actual level of the income of the peasants household. The net income of the rural households includes not only the income from the productive and non-productive business operation, but also includes the income from the non-business operation, such as the money remitted or brought back by the members of the household who are in other places, the government relief payment and various subsidies. It includes not only the money income, but also the income in kind. But the income borrowing from banks, friends and relatives is excluded.

Expenditure of Rural Households for Consumption refers to total expenses of rural households on daily life, including expenses on food, clothing, housing, fuel, articles for daily use, and expenses on cultural life and services. This indicator is used to show the actual consumption level of peasants.

The Savings Deposits of Urban and Rural Residents refers to the total value of savings deposits of urban and rural households in banks and rural credit cooperatives at a given point of time, including the savings deposit of urban residents and the savings deposit of rural residents. The cash in hand by residents and the deposits of organizations such as enterprises, military units, government agencies, institutions, etc. are not included.

JIANGSU STATISTICAL YEARBOOK

第 5 篇

固定资产投资

INVESTMENT IN FIXED ASSETS

5－1 全社会固定资产投资主要指标
MAJOR INDICATORS OF TOTAL INVESTMENT IN FIXED ASSETS

指标	Item	1990	1995	2000	2005	2006
投资总额 （亿元）	**Total Investment （100 million yuan）**	**356.30**	**1680.17**	**2995.43**	**8739.71**	**10071.42**
按经济类型分	Grouped by Ownership					
国有经济	State Owned Units	134.86	602.70	1200.01	2077.97	2144.93
集体经济	Collective Owned Units	74.87	491.08	455.86	445.16	441.57
#农村	Rural Area	54.08	362.17	314.27	271.06	199.06
私营个体经济	Individuals			326.08	2623.60	3049.30
#农村	Rural Area			204.87	1405.13	1330.71
联营经济	Joint-Ownership Economic Units		28.26	14.12	7.39	9.45
股份制经济	Share Holding Co. Ltd.		28.63	94.19	395.59	405.52
有限责任公司	Limited Liability Corporations		10.51	93.54	1457.32	1905.11
港澳台投资经济	Economic Units Funded by Entrepreneurs from Hong Kong, Macao and Taiwan		86.51	125.59	589.17	589.62
外商投资经济	Foreign Funded Enterprise Units		213.71	237.63	979.46	1167.21
其他经济	Others	146.57	218.77	448.41	164.05	358.71
按资金来源分	Grouped by Sources of Finance					
国家预算内投资	State Appropriation	15.02	25.83	73.42	67.60	66.59
国内贷款	Domestic Loans	45.47	270.16	489.04	1264.49	1445.16
利用外资	Foreign Investment	15.92	228.89	281.17	836.19	874.82
自筹投资	Fund Raising	106.47	880.02	1827.79	5826.89	6800.90
其他资金来源	Others	173.42	275.27	324.01	1205.90	1590.15
按构成分	Grouped by Use of Funds					
建筑安装工程	Construction Installation	284.24	983.24	1817.08	4879.72	5624.16
设备工器具购置	Purchase of Equipments and Instruments	53.70	536.48	867.74	2544.36	2944.50
其他费用	Others	18.36	160.45	310.61	1315.63	1502.76
按产业分	Grouped by Industry					
#住宅	Residential Housing	156.49	366.67	580.13	1298.75	1697.64
第一产业	Primary Industry	13.15	40.94	116.20	45.42	65.44
第二产业	Secondary Industry	140.38	819.54	1358.56	4872.12	5423.21
第三产业	Tertiary Industry	202.77	819.69	1520.67	3822.17	4582.77
房屋建筑面积 （万平方米）	**Floor Space of Building （10000 sq. m）**					
施工面积	Floor Space Under Construction	12821.31	16234.74	17417.62	35712.52	39169.41
#住宅	Residential Housing	10679.54	10530.29	11273.48	16594.76	18140.97
竣工面积	Floor Space Completed	11732.39	12452.44	13471.88	17838.93	17045.22
#住宅	Residential Housing	10209.36	9036.00	9323.98	7860.33	7121.32
商品房销售面积	Floor Space of Selling House	250.02	798.31	1740.93	5135.55	6101.15

注：1. 由于口径变化全社会投资2006年与2005年数据不可比（下同）。
2. 自筹投资中含发行债券部分（下同）。
3. 2003年开始，资金来源为可用于投资的资金到位数（下同）。
4. 从2004年开始，水利业投资从第一产业调到第三产业（下同）。

Note: 1. The figure of total investment of 2005 and 2006 was incomparable, because of the change of statistical bore(so did as follows).
2. Fund raising included bond publishing (so did as follows).
3. Since 2003, the sources of finance was available for investment (so did as follows).
4. Since 2004, the investment for water conservancy was transferred from primary industry to tertiary industry(so did as follows).

5－2 全社会固定资产投资额

TOTAL INVESTMENT IN FIXED ASSETS

单位:亿元 (100 million yuan)

年份 Items	投资额 Investment	#房地产开发 Real Estate Davelop-ment	#国有经济 State Owned Units	#集体经济 Collective Owned Units	#私营个体 Indivi-Dual
1978	21.75		20.70	1.05	
1979	26.75		25.52	1.23	
1980	34.73		34.73	3.08	
"六五"时期 the Period of the Six-Year Plan	**564.89**		**242.73**	**156.57**	
1981	60.50		26.09	17.81	
1982	76.21		35.58	20.85	
1983	105.27		46.79	21.41	
1984	130.98		53.84	37.44	
1985	191.93		80.43	59.06	
"七五"时期 the Period of the Seven-Year Plan	**1606.75**		**642.46**	**377.21**	
1986	241.23		100.97	61.28	
1987	317.12		128.43	80.35	
1988	371.87		154.04	93.45	
1989	320.23		124.16	67.26	
1990	356.30	11.71	134.86	74.87	
"八五"时期 the Period of the Eignt-Year Plan	**5307.18**	**554.92**	**1944.32**	**1788.50**	
1991	439.98	17.22	172.09	109.87	
1992	711.70	30.42	288.00	276.16	
1993	1144.20	114.01	403.67	493.12	
1994	1331.13	152.42	477.86	418.27	
1995	1680.17	240.85	602.70	491.08	
"九五"时期 the Period of the Nine-Year Plan	**12426.20**	**1463.68**	**4912.01**	**2288.90**	
1996	1949.53	232.62	708.60	465.21	
1997	2203.09	241.55	826.60	447.94	
1998	2535.50	300.24	1031.96	457.36	
1999	2742.65	330.55	1144.84	462.53	148.23
2000	2995.43	358.72	1200.01	455.86	326.08
"十五"时期 the Period of the Ten-Year Plan	**28055.30**	**4583.38**	**8790.13**	**2018.49**	**6453.90**
2001	3302.96	414.36	1285.71	400.36	528.38
2002	3849.24	544.13	1422.06	297.56	769.90
2003	5335.80	809.96	1998.19	456.98	932.11
2004	6827.59	1269.78	2006.20	418.43	1599.91
2005	8739.71	1545.15	2077.97	445.16	2623.60
"十一五"时期 the Period of the Eve-Year Plan					
2006	10071.42	1906.71	2144.93	441.57	3049.30

注:房地产开发投资统计制度从1990年开始建立,城乡私营个体投资统计制度从1999年开始建立。

Notes:The statitistical system of real estate development investment was established in 1990, while that of the urban and rural private and individual investment was established in 1999.

5-3 按登记注册类型分全社会固定资产投资
TOTAL INVESTMENT IN FIXED ASSETS BY TYPE OF REGISTRATION

单位:亿元 (100 million yuan)

登记注册类型	Type of Registration	2005 投资额 Investment	2005 #城镇投资 Urban	2006 投资额 Investment	2006 #城镇投资 Urban
总计	**Total**	**8739.71**	**6230.54**	**10071.42**	**7481.80**
内资企业	Inner Enterprises	7155.37	4959.19	8294.35	5979.39
国有企业	State-Owned Enterprises	1992.81	1958.50	2017.93	1975.89
集体企业	Collective-Owned Enterprises	372.73	136.03	384.91	201.86
股份合作企业	Share Holding Cooperative Enterprises	66.18	35.29	54.56	39.10
联营企业	Joint-Owned Enterprises	30.09	24.89	15.26	12.25
国有联营	State Joint Ownership	16.45	16.39	3.71	3.55
集体联营	Collective Joint Ownership	6.25	2.78	2.10	1.55
国有与集体联营	State-Collective Ownership Joint	3.91	3.39	3.36	1.59
其他联营企业	Other Joint-Owned Enterprises	3.48	2.33	6.09	5.56
有限责任公司	Responsibility Co., Ltd.	1526.03	1245.18	2028.40	1667.76
国有独资公司	State Solely Funded Co.	68.71	68.71	123.29	120.32
其他有限责任公司	Other Responsibility Co., Ltd.	1457.32	1176.47	1905.11	1547.44
股份有限公司	Share Holding Co., Ltd.	395.59	302.59	405.52	310.95
私营企业	Private Enterprises	2607.89	1212.26	3029.06	1705.88
其他企业	Others	164.05	44.45	358.71	65.70
港、澳、台商投资企业	Hong Kong, Macao and Taiwan Funded	589.17	458.31	589.62	477.91
合资经营企业	Joint Funded Enterprises	255.65	207.73	247.85	200.63
合作经营企业	Cooperative Operation Enterprises	12.70	12.15	17.00	13.93
股份有限公司	Share Holding Co. Ltd.	310.52	230.90	309.80	254.13
独资经营企业	Solely Funded Enterprises	10.30	7.53	14.97	9.22
外商投资企业	Foreign Invested Enterprises	979.46	806.83	1167.21	1011.79
合资经营企业	Joint Funded Enterprises	358.92	300.18	402.56	346.06
合作经营企业	Cooperative Operation Enterprises	16.41	12.74	21.12	16.11
独资经营企业	Solely Funded Enterprises	598.20	491.35	733.97	641.07
股份有限公司	Share Holding Co. Ltd.	5.93	2.56	9.56	8.55
个体经营	Individual Investment	15.71	6.21	20.24	12.71
个体户	Individual Self-employed	14.25	5.64	19.20	12.15
个人合伙	Individual Parttennership	1.46	0.57	1.04	0.56

5－4　投资金来源和构成分全社会固定资产投资
TOTAL INVESTMENT IN FIXED ASSETS BY SOURCES OF FINANCE AND USE OF FUNDS

年　份 Year	按资金来源分 Grouped by Sources of Finance			
	国家预算内资金 State Budgetary Appropriation	国内贷款 Domestic Loans	利用外资 Utilization of Foreign Capital	自筹资金 Fund－raising
投资额(亿元) Investment　(100 million yuan)				
1985	17.25	36.79	3.98	64.45
1986	18.74	43.52	12.71	73.27
1987	21.46	63.15	19.15	85.66
1988	17.23	69.94	27.77	106.30
1989	16.80	41.74	19.91	91.66
1990	15.02	45.47	15.92	106.47
1991	16.38	84.77	20.41	290.13
1992	24.73	189.49	40.56	378.30
1993	17.85	253.80	89.48	649.95
1994	17.54	242.93	151.96	744.20
1995	25.83	270.16	228.89	880.02
1996	24.01	282.88	335.16	1001.29
1997	29.63	293.66	390.59	1199.29
1998	49.46	331.83	413.66	1406.39
1999	62.91	399.36	309.02	1639.01
2000	73.42	489.04	281.17	1827.79
2001	69.97	524.51	326.22	1977.97
2002	54.48	735.30	421.21	2237.73
2003	92.61	1141.99	579.51	2999.19
2004	81.30	1233.07	641.66	4201.29
2005	67.60	1264.49	836.19	5826.89
2006	66.59	1445.16	874.82	6800.90
构成(％)　Composition(％)				
1985	9.0	19.1	2.1	33.6
1990	4.2	12.8	4.5	29.9
1995	1.5	16.1	13.6	52.4
1996	1.2	14.5	17.2	51.4
1997	1.3	13.3	17.7	54.5
1998	1.9	13.1	16.3	55.5
1999	2.3	14.6	11.3	59.7
2000	2.5	16.3	9.4	61.0
2001	2.1	15.9	9.9	59.9
2002	1.4	19.1	11.0	58.1
2003	1.7	21.2	10.7	55.5
2004	1.1	17.4	9.1	59.3
2005	0.7	13.8	9.1	63.3
2006	0.6	13.4	8.1	63.1

5-4 续表

Continued

年份 Year	其他资金来源 Others	按构成分 Grouped by Use of Funds 建筑安装工程 Construction Installation	设备工器具购置 Purchases of Equipments and Instruments	其他费用 Others
投资额(亿元) Investment (100 million yuan)				
1985	69.46	149.40	34.41	8.12
1986	92.99	187.33	43.82	10.08
1987	127.71	240.92	60.61	15.60
1988	150.63	281.34	73.71	16.82
1989	150.12	256.23	52.25	11.75
1990	173.42	284.24	53.70	18.36
1991	28.29	347.72	71.33	20.93
1992	78.62	408.59	257.45	45.66
1993	133.12	651.17	395.34	97.69
1994	174.50	775.84	437.87	117.42
1995	275.27	983.24	536.48	160.45
1996	306.19	1151.16	600.59	197.78
1997	289.92	1307.24	688.66	207.19
1998	334.16	1503.62	755.02	276.86
1999	332.35	1682.72	746.75	313.18
2000	324.01	1817.08	867.74	310.61
2001	404.29	1901.68	967.21	434.07
2002	400.52	2091.15	1160.08	598.01
2003	587.42	2906.59	1510.59	918.62
2004	928.38	3886.52	1928.66	1012.41
2005	1205.90	4879.72	2544.36	1315.63
2006	1590.15	5624.16	2944.50	1502.76
构成(%) Composition(%)				
1985	36.2	77.9	17.9	4.2
1990	48.6	80.0	15.1	4.9
1995	16.4	58.5	31.9	9.6
1996	15.7	59.0	30.8	10.2
1997	13.2	59.3	31.3	9.4
1998	13.2	59.3	29.8	10.9
1999	12.1	61.4	27.2	11.4
2000	10.8	60.6	29.0	10.4
2001	12.2	57.6	29.3	13.1
2002	10.4	54.3	30.1	15.6
2003	10.9	54.5	28.3	17.2
2004	13.1	56.9	28.3	14.8
2005	13.1	55.8	29.1	15.1
2006	14.8	55.9	29.2	14.9

5－5　按构成分城镇固定资产投资(2006年)
URBAN INVESTMENT IN FIXED ASSETS BY USE OF FUNDS (2006)

单位:亿元　　(100 million yuan)

行业	Sector	投资额 Invest-ment	建筑工程 Constru－ction	安装工程 Install－ation	设备工器具购置 Tools Purchase	其他 Others
总　计	**Total**	**7481.80**	**3958.59**	**406.32**	**1858.90**	**1257.99**
农、林、牧、渔业	Farming, Forestry, Animal Husbandry and Fishery	14.69	11.64	0.45	1.37	1.22
农　业	Farming	2.13	1.88	0.05	0.04	0.16
林　业	Forestry	1.45	1.02	0.01	0.26	0.16
畜牧业	Animal Husbandry	1.02	0.57	0.06	0.25	0.14
渔　业	Fishery	0.46	0.17	0.02	0.19	0.08
农、林、牧、渔服务业	Farming, Forestry, Animal Husbandry and Fishery Services	9.63	8.00	0.31	0.63	0.69
采矿业	Mining and Quarrying	32.06	17.34	1.96	8.34	4.43
制造业	Manufacturing	2913.93	1038.35	147.04	1490.69	237.85
农副食品加工业	Food Processing	52.29	18.93	4.05	25.19	4.12
食品制造业	Food Production	37.88	13.97	2.52	16.99	4.40
饮料制造业	Beverage Production	25.54	8.53	2.56	12.78	1.67
烟草制品业	Tobacco Processing	4.95	1.34	0.10	3.02	0.50
纺织业	Textile Industry	220.85	79.75	9.23	116.12	15.75
纺织服装、鞋、帽制造业	Textile Garments, Shoes and Hats Products	83.23	38.42	3.99	33.00	7.81
皮革、毛皮、羽毛(绒)及其制品业	Leather, Furs, Down and Related Products	20.26	9.08	0.99	8.37	1.82
木材加工及木、竹、藤、棕、草制品业	Timber Processing and Wood, Bamboo, Rattan, Palm and Straw Works	33.12	14.72	2.16	13.57	2.67
家具制造业	Furniture Manufacturing	18.52	10.79	0.79	5.59	1.34
造纸及纸制品业	Papermaking and Paper Products	60.99	12.72	2.64	42.87	2.76
印刷业和记录媒介的复制	Printing and Record Processing	20.36	6.45	1.54	10.92	1.45
文教体育用品制造业	Stationery, Education and Sports Goods	14.22	6.28	0.71	5.79	1.44
石油加工、炼焦及核燃料加工业	Petroleum Processing, Coking Products and Nuclear Fuel Processing	18.22	5.44	3.66	8.32	0.79
化学原料及化学制品制造业	Raw Chemical Material and Chemical Products	293.61	91.46	29.98	147.27	24.90
医药制造业	Medical and Pharmaceutical Products	58.10	22.11	2.48	21.79	11.72
化学纤维制造业	Chemical Fibers	52.90	9.37	3.85	38.10	1.58
橡胶制品业	Rubber Products	38.63	11.33	1.60	24.34	1.36
塑料制品业	Plastic Products	70.55	27.52	2.67	33.99	6.36
非金属矿物制品业	Nonmetal Mineral Products	92.42	33.72	3.96	45.38	9.35
黑色金属冶炼及压延加工业	Smelting and Processing of Ferrous Metals	138.04	39.91	10.30	73.02	14.81
有色金属冶炼及压延加工业	Smelting and Processing of Nonferrous Metals	31.77	11.48	1.08	17.14	2.07
金属制品业	Metal Products	140.34	58.66	8.39	62.24	11.06
通用设备制造业	Ordinarly Machinery Manufacturing	248.91	111.45	9.97	107.84	19.65
专用设备制造业	Special Purpose Equipment Manufacturing	145.75	65.43	5.49	63.85	10.99
交通运输设备制造业	Transportation Equipment Manufacturing	195.35	70.85	6.60	90.31	27.58
电气机械及器材制造业	Electric Machinery and Equipment	178.19	71.84	8.01	83.66	14.68
通信设备、计算机及其他电子设备	Telecommunication Equipments, Computer and Other Electronic Equipment Manufaturing	472.53	94.95	13.79	344.42	19.37
仪器仪表及文化、办公用机械制造	Instruments, Meters, Cultural and Official Machinery	42.18	16.61	1.15	21.15	3.26
工艺品及其他制造业	Handicraft Artical and Other Manufacturing	100.91	73.33	2.61	12.63	12.34
废弃资源和废旧材料回收加工业	Waste Resouces and Junk Material Recycled	3.33	1.90	0.16	1.04	0.24
电力、燃气及水的生产和供应业	Electric Power, Gas and Water Production and Supply	455.18	129.47	69.56	180.21	75.94

5-5 续表 Continued

单位:亿元 (100 million yuan)

行业	Sector	投资额 Invest-ment	建筑工程 Constru-ction	安装工程 Installa-tion	设备工器具购置 Tools Purchase	其他 Others
电力、热力的生产和供应业	Electric Power, Steam and Hot Water Production and Supply	383.36	96.80	49.84	168.09	68.63
燃气生产和供应业	Gas Production and Supply	15.07	6.75	4.86	2.82	0.65
水的生产和供应业	Tap Water Production and Supply	56.74	25.92	14.86	9.30	6.67
建筑业	Construction	43.26	32.21	2.50	4.79	3.76
交通运输、仓储和邮政业	Transportation, Storage and Post	564.65	425.48	6.93	47.98	84.26
铁路运输业	Railway Transportation	3.69	3.18	0.05	0.19	0.27
道路运输业	Road Transportation	382.68	324.23	1.19	4.47	52.79
城市公共交通业	Urban Public Transit	32.28	13.16	0.14	3.06	15.93
水上运输业	Waterway Transportation	109.63	62.79	2.08	36.64	8.13
管道运输业	Pipeline Transportation	1.29	1.29			
装卸搬运和其他运输服务业	Load and Unload, Carry and Other Transportion	5.32	2.70	0.03	1.83	0.76
仓储业	Storage	25.60	16.34	3.33	1.67	4.25
邮政业	Post	1.67	0.58	0.04	1.05	
信息传输、计算机服务和软件业	Information Transmmision, Computer Service and Software	83.74	19.46	31.45	31.03	1.79
电信和其他信息传输服务业	Telecommunication and Other Information Transmmision Service	76.87	13.48	31.38	30.30	1.71
计算机服务业	Computer Service	0.40	0.10	0.01	0.22	0.08
软件业	Software	6.46	5.89	0.06	0.52	
批发和零售业	Wholesale and Retail Trade	190.57	120.12	14.71	17.97	37.77
住宿和餐饮业	Hotel and Catering Services	78.96	45.68	8.47	9.77	15.04
金融业	Finance	1.39	1.06	0.09	0.21	0.03
银行业	Banking	1.34	1.01	0.09	0.21	0.03
其他金融活动	Other Financial Activities	0.05	0.05			
房地产业	Real Estate Trade	2031.24	1356.06	87.52	21.25	566.42
租赁和商务服务业	Leasing and Commercial Services	56.10	38.52	4.10	2.87	10.61
租赁业	Leasing Services	2.04	0.55	0.19	0.95	0.35
商务服务业	Commercial Services	54.05	37.97	3.91	1.91	10.26
科学研究、技术服务和地质勘查业	Scientific Research, Polytechnical Services and Geological Prospecitng	20.65	12.82	3.90	2.48	1.45
水利、环境和公共设施管理业	Water Conservance, Environment and Public Facility Management	657.16	473.72	7.59	11.10	164.75
水利管理业	Water Conservancy Manegement	41.26	35.97	1.33	0.99	2.97
环境管理业	Environment Management	26.96	17.42	0.64	2.51	6.39
公共设施管理业	Public Facility Management	588.94	420.34	5.62	7.60	155.39
居民服务和其他服务业	Resident Services and Others	11.16	6.85	0.68	1.19	2.44
教育	Education	138.81	115.50	3.63	6.39	13.29
卫生、社会保障和社会福利业	Health Care, Social Security and Social Welfare	56.13	30.97	5.65	9.59	9.92
卫生	Health Care	54.46	29.56	5.55	9.47	9.88
社会保障业	Social Security	0.17	0.11	0.03	0.03	
社会福利业	Social Welfare	1.50	1.30	0.07	0.08	0.05
文化、体育和娱乐业	Culture, Sports and Recreation	49.98	31.10	6.15	6.44	6.28
新闻出版业	News Publication	1.79	1.25	0.29	0.20	0.05
广播、电视、电影和音像业	Radio, Television, Film and Stereo	3.73	2.82	0.17	0.19	0.55
文化艺术业	Culture and Arts	16.95	10.27	3.17	0.77	2.74
体育	Sports	9.78	6.26	0.96	1.96	0.59
娱乐业	Recreation	17.72	10.50	1.56	3.32	2.34
公共管理和社会组织	Public Management and Social Organizations	82.15	52.24	3.95	5.23	20.73

5-6 按建设性质分城镇固定资产投资(2006年)
URBAN INVESTMENT IN FIXED ASSETS BY TYPE OF CONSTRUCTION

单位:亿元 (100 million yuan)

行业	Sector	投资额 Investment	#新建 New Construction	#扩建 Expansion	#改建 Replacement
总计	**Total**	**7481.80**	**2969.61**	**1574.55**	**805.86**
农、林、牧、渔业	Farming, Forestry, Animal Husbandry and Fishery	14.69	5.98	5.15	3.49
农业	Farming	2.13	0.92	0.39	0.82
林业	Forestry	1.45	1.24	0.21	
畜牧业	Animal Husbandry	1.02	0.65	0.37	
渔业	Fishery	0.46	0.29	0.18	
农、林、牧、渔服务业	Farming, Forestry, Animal Husbandry and Fishery Services	9.63	2.88	4.01	2.67
采矿业	Mining and Quarrying	32.06	5.74	18.05	7.95
制造业	Manufacturing	2913.93	1547.69	698.85	500.14
农副食品加工业	Food Processing	52.29	34.96	12.87	3.99
食品制造业	Food Production	37.88	24.12	8.93	3.14
饮料制造业	Beverage Production	25.54	18.02	2.19	5.17
烟草制品业	Tobacco Processing	4.95	1.80	3.15	
纺织业	Textile Industry	220.85	120.49	55.64	24.09
纺织服装、鞋、帽制造业	Textile Garments, Shoes and Hats Production	83.23	53.13	17.38	9.47
皮革、毛皮、羽毛(绒)及其制品业	Leather, Furs, Down and Related Products	20.26	13.45	3.89	2.76
木材加工及木、竹、藤、棕、草制品业	Timber Processing and Wood, Bamboo, Rattan, Palm and Straw Works	33.12	24.51	3.53	4.08
家具制造业	Furniture Manufacturing	18.52	14.32	2.17	0.46
造纸及纸制品业	Papermaking and Paper Products	1.20	1.17	0.03	
印刷业和记录媒介的复制	Printing and Record Processing	20.36	14.06	2.51	2.25
文教体育用品制造业	Stationery, Education and Sports Goods	14.22	7.53	3.76	2.63
石油加工、炼焦及核燃料加工业	Petroleum Processing, Coking Products and Nuclear Fuel Processing	18.22	7.29	0.39	10.38
化学原料及化学制品制造业	Raw Chemical Material and Chemical Products	293.61	154.46	94.38	40.61
医药制造业	Medical and Pharmaceutical Products	58.10	31.75	19.16	5.81
化学纤维制造业	Chemical Fibers	52.90	21.67	29.09	1.70
橡胶制品业	Rubber Products	38.63	18.48	17.97	1.13
塑料制品业	Plastic Products	70.55	41.73	14.14	7.25
非金属矿物制品业	Nonmetal Mineral Products	92.42	55.25	23.08	11.66
黑色金属冶炼及压延加工业	Smelting and Processing of Ferrous Metals	138.04	36.05	45.24	46.73
有色金属冶炼及压延加工业	Smelting and Processing of Nonferrous Metals	31.77	16.58	6.54	4.94
金属制品业	Metal Products	140.34	87.38	25.01	22.61
通用设备制造业	Ordinarly Machinery Manufacturing	248.91	140.37	55.64	39.95
专用设备制造业	Special Purpose Equipment Manufacturing	145.75	89.75	30.87	17.00
交通运输设备制造业	Transportation Equipment Manufacturing	195.35	87.54	67.01	27.33
电气机械及器材制造业	Electric Machinery and Equipment	178.19	105.70	36.14	23.44
通信设备、计算机及其他电子设备	Telecommunication Equipments, Computer and Other Electronic Equipment Manufaturing	472.53	199.55	83.47	144.63
仪器仪表及文化、办公用机械制造	Instruments, Meters, Cultural and Official Machinery	42.18	26.54	5.15	4.34
工艺品及其他制造业	Handicraft Artical and Other Manufacturing	100.91	71.56	21.94	7.01
废弃资源和废旧材料回收加工业	Waste Resouces and Junk Material Recycled	3.33	2.93	0.08	0.33

5－6 续表 Continued

单位:亿元 (100 million yuan)

行业	Sector	投资额 Invest－ment	#新建 New Construc－tion	#扩建 Expan－sion	#改建 Replace－ment
电力、燃气及水的生产和供应业	Electric Power, Gas and Water Production and Supply	455.18	216.49	211.14	27.40
电力、热力的生产和供应业	Electric Power, Steam and Hot Water Production and Supply	383.36	176.60	186.84	19.83
燃气生产和供应业	Gas Production and Supply	15.07	9.07	4.32	1.69
水的生产和供应业	Tap Water Production and Supply	56.74	30.82	19.99	5.88
建筑业	Construction	43.26	21.57	11.64	8.33
交通运输、仓储和邮政业	Transportation, Storage and Post	564.65	278.63	173.12	83.37
铁路运输业	Railway Transportation	3.69	3.69		
道路运输业	Road Transportation	382.68	192.35	126.81	60.16
城市公共交通业	Urban Public Transit	32.28	21.52	5.34	3.19
水上运输业	Waterway Transportation	109.63	37.17	33.32	15.60
管道运输业	Pipeline Transportation	1.29	1.29		
装卸搬运和其他运输服务业	Load and Unload, Carry and Other Transportion	5.32	4.55	0.68	0.08
仓储业	Storage	25.60	16.41	6.84	2.03
邮政业	Post	1.67	1.55	0.12	0.00
信息传输、计算机服务和软件业	Information Transmmision, Computer Service and Software	83.74	13.39	51.84	17.72
电信和其他信息传输服务业	Telecommunication and Other Information Transmmision Service	76.87	7.38	51.22	17.72
计算机服务业	Computer Service	0.40	0.09	0.15	0.00
软件业	Software	6.46	5.93	0.47	0.00
批发和零售业	Wholesale and Retail Trade	190.57	133.11	45.07	10.78
住宿和餐饮业	Hotel and Catering Services	78.96	56.06	13.28	8.56
金融业	Finance	1.39	1.14	0.13	
银行业	Banking	1.34	1.09	0.13	
其他金融活动	Other Financial Activities	0.05	0.05		
房地产业	Real Estate Trade	2031.24	107.76	11.46	4.77
租赁和商务服务业	Leasing and Commercial Services	56.10	47.23	6.34	2.48
租赁业	Leasing Services	2.04	0.79	1.05	0.15
商务服务业	Commercial Services	54.05	46.44	5.29	2.33
科学研究、技术服务和地质勘查业	Scientific Research, Polytechnical Services and Geological Prospecitng	20.65	9.23	11.35	0.07
水利、环境和公共设施管理业	Water Conservancy, Environment and Public Facility Management	657.16	327.29	211.63	114.76
水利管理业	Water Conservancy Manegement	41.26	14.78	14.36	11.62
环境管理业	Environment Management	26.96	8.79	11.85	6.32
公共设施管理业	Public Facility Management	588.94	303.71	185.42	96.82
居民服务和其他服务业	Resident Services and Others	11.16	6.65	3.14	1.33
教育	Education	138.81	74.53	53.02	2.55
卫生、社会保障和社会福利业	Health Care, Social Security and Social Welfare	56.13	28.00	17.99	3.99
卫生	Health Care	54.46	26.86	17.65	3.91
社会保障业	Social Security	0.17	0.08	0.09	
社会福利业	Social Welfare	1.50	1.05	0.25	0.08
文化、体育和娱乐业	Culture, Sports and Recreation	49.98	35.59	9.52	4.00
新闻出版业	News Publication	1.79	0.78	0.60	0.21
广播、电视、电影和音像业	Radio, Television, Film and Stereo	3.73	1.65	1.49	0.59
文化艺术业	Culture and Arts	16.95	13.34	3.38	0.24
体育	Sports	9.78	8.08	1.58	0.13
娱乐业	Recreation	17.72	11.75	2.47	2.83
公共管理和社会组织	Public Management and Social Organizations	82.15	53.55	21.83	4.18

5-7 按控股情况分城镇固定资产投资(2006年)
URBAN INVESTMENT IN FIXED ASSETS BY THE CONDITION OF SHARE HOLDING (2006)

单位:亿元 (100 million yuan)

行业	Sector	投资额 Investment	国有控股 State Share Holding	集体控股 Collective Share Holding
总计	**Total**	**7481.80**	**2447.82**	**412.79**
农、林、牧、渔业	Farming, Forestry, Animal Husbandry and Fishery	14.69	11.51	0.79
农业	Farming	2.13	1.23	0.52
林业	Forestry	1.45	1.45	
畜牧业	Animal Husbandry	1.02		
渔业	Fishery	0.46		0.19
农、林、牧、渔服务业	Farming, Forestry, Animal Husbandry and Fishery Services	9.63	8.83	0.08
采矿业	Mining and Quarrying	32.06	24.94	0.47
制造业	Manufacturing	2913.93	291.62	121.68
农副食品加工业	Food Processing	52.29	1.16	0.81
食品制造业	Food Production	37.88	4.03	0.10
饮料制造业	Beverage Production	25.54	0.65	1.14
烟草制品业	Tobacco Processing	4.95	4.95	
纺织业	Textile Industry	220.85	7.07	12.64
纺织服装、鞋、帽制造业	Textile Garments, Shoes and Hats Production	83.23	0.14	3.01
皮革、毛皮、羽毛(绒)及其制品业	Leather, Furs, Down and Related Products	20.26		0.29
木材加工及木、竹、藤、棕、草制	Timber Processing and Wood, Bamboo, Rattan, Palm and Straw Works	33.12		0.93
家具制造业	Furniture Manufacturing	18.52		0.13
造纸及纸制品业	Papermaking and Paper Products	60.99	0.02	0.26
印刷业和记录媒介的复制	Printing and Record Processing	20.36	0.79	0.50
文教体育用品制造业	Stationery, Education and Sports Goods	14.22		0.30
石油加工、炼焦及核燃料加工业	Petroleum Processing, Coking Products and Nuclear Fuel Processing	18.22	11.42	0.15
化学原料及化学制品制造业	Raw Chemical Material and Chemical Products	293.61	80.97	5.80
医药制造业	Medical and Pharmaceutical Products	58.10	8.67	2.96
化学纤维制造业	Chemical Fibers	52.90	9.83	0.18
橡胶制品业	Rubber Products	38.63	0.04	0.14
塑料制品业	Plastic Products	70.55		0.89
非金属矿物制品业	Nonmetal Mineral Products	92.42	4.36	1.66
黑色金属冶炼及压延加工业	Smelting and Processing of Ferrous Metals	138.04	28.54	9.52
有色金属冶炼及压延加工业	Smelting and Processing of Nonferrous Metals	31.77	4.46	1.52
金属制品业	Metal Products	140.34	1.35	5.27
通用设备制造业	Ordinarly Machinery Manufacturing	248.91	9.23	16.57
专用设备制造业	Special Purpose Equipment Manufacturing	145.75	8.19	8.02
交通运输设备制造业	Transportation Equipment Manufacturing	195.35	40.69	4.00
电气机械及器材制造业	Electric Machinery and Equipment	178.19	5.00	10.70
通信设备、计算机及其他电子设备	Telecommunication Equipments, Computer and Other Electronic Equipment Manufaturing	472.53	23.40	4.35
仪器仪表及文化、办公用机械制造	Instruments, Meters, Cultural and Official Machinery	42.18	5.53	1.34
工艺品及其他制造业	Handicraft Artical and Other Manufacturing	100.91	30.99	28.35
废弃资源和废旧材料回收加工业	Waste Resouces and Waste or Juunk Recycled	3.33	0.12	0.16

5－7　续 表 1　Continued 1

单位:亿元　　(100 million yuan)

行　业	Sector	投资额 Invest-ment	国有控股 State Share Holding	集体控股 Collective Share Holding
电力、燃气及水的生产和供应业	Electric Power, Gas and Water Production and Supply	455.18	344.65	17.79
电力、热力的生产和供应业	Electric Power, Steam and Hot Water Production and Supply	383.36	297.45	10.71
燃气生产和供应业	Gas Production and Supply	15.07	8.03	0.60
水的生产和供应业	Tap Water Production and Supply	56.74	39.17	6.48
建筑业	Construction	43.26	22.96	4.89
交通运输、仓储和邮政业	Transportation, Storage and Post	564.65	491.21	16.46
铁路运输业	Railway Transportation	3.69	2.82	
道路运输业	Road Transportation	382.68	370.76	2.97
城市公共交通业	Urban Public Transit	32.28	28.35	1.85
水上运输业	Waterway Transportation	109.63	80.15	10.68
管道运输业	Waterway Transportation	1.29		
装卸搬运和其他运输服务业	Load and Unload, Carry and Other Transportion	5.32		
仓储业	Storage	25.60	5.09	0.85
邮政业	Post	1.67	1.67	
信息传输、计算机服务和软件业	Information Transmmision, Computer Service and Software	83.74	65.81	0.54
电信和其他信息传输服务业	Telecommunication and Other Information Transmmision Service	76.87	60.93	0.54
计算机服务业	Computer Service	0.40		
软件业	Software	6.46	4.87	
批发和零售业	Wholesale and Retail Trade	190.57	12.13	19.32
住宿和餐饮业	Hotel and Catering Services	78.96	6.62	4.95
金融业	Finance	1.39	0.47	0.81
银行业	Banking	1.34	0.47	0.81
其他金融活动	Other Financial Activities	0.05		
房地产业	Real Estate Trade	2031.24	293.03	160.22
租赁和商务服务业	Leasing and Commercial Services	56.10	17.88	10.44
租赁业	Leasing Services	2.04	0.91	
商务服务业	Commercial Services	54.05	16.97	10.44
科学研究、技术服务和地质勘查业	Scientific Research, Polytechnical Services and Geological Prospecitng	20.65	14.60	1.22
水利、环境和公共设施管理业	Water Conservancy, Environment and Public Facility Management	657.16	579.70	33.42
水利管理业	Water Conservancy Manegement	41.26	40.19	0.41
环境管理业	Environment Management	26.96	19.49	1.38
公共设施管理业	Public Facility Management	588.94	520.02	31.62
居民服务和其他服务业	Resident Services and Others	11.16	3.84	1.45
教育	Education	138.81	117.49	8.64
卫生、社会保障和社会福利业	Health Care, Social Security and Social Welfare	56.13	42.70	2.38
卫生	Health Care	54.46	41.66	1.75
社会保障业	Social Security	0.17	0.17	
社会福利业	Social Welfare	1.50	0.87	0.63
文化、体育和娱乐业	Culture, Sports and Recreation	49.98	31.60	2.43
新闻出版业	Radio, Television, Film and Stereo	1.79	1.58	
广播、电视、电影和音像业	Radio, Television, Film and Stereo	3.73	2.77	0.07
文化艺术业	Culture and Arts	16.95	16.37	0.30
体育	Sports	9.78	8.78	0.95
娱乐业	Recreation	17.72	2.09	1.11
公共管理和社会组织	Public Management and Social Organizations	82.15	75.06	4.90

5－7 续表2 Continued 2

单位:亿元 (100 million yuan)

行业	Sector	私人控股 Private Share Holding	港澳台商控股 Hong Kong, Macao and Taiwan Share Holding	外商控股 Foreign Share Holding
总计	**Total**	**3216.38**	**424.08**	**980.73**
农、林、牧、渔业	Farming, Forestry, Animal Husbandry and Fishery	2.34		0.06
农业	Farming	0.37		0.01
林业	Forestry			
畜牧业	Animal Husbandry	0.96		0.06
渔业	Fishery	0.27		
农、林、牧、渔服务业	Farming, Forestry, Animal Husbandry and Fishery Services	0.73		
采矿业	Mining and Quarrying	6.64		0.01
制造业	Manufacturing	1439.72	246.40	814.51
农副食品加工业	Food Processing	40.12	1.21	8.99
食品制造业	Food Production	29.39	1.50	2.86
饮料制造业	Beverage Production	21.07	0.45	2.23
烟草制品业	Tobacco Processing			
纺织业	Textile Industry	155.62	25.53	19.99
纺织服装、鞋、帽制造业	Textile Garments, Shoes and Hats Production	64.20	6.49	9.39
皮革、毛皮、羽毛(绒)及其制品业	Leather, Furs, Down and Related Products	13.05	3.36	3.56
木材加工及木、竹、藤、棕、草制	Timber Processing and Wood, Bamboo, Rattan, Palm and Straw Works	28.71	1.39	2.09
家具制造业	Furniture Manufacturing	15.24	1.63	1.52
造纸及纸制品业	Papermaking and Paper Products	20.53	6.70	33.48
印刷业和记录媒介的复制	Printing and Record Processing	15.99	0.45	2.63
文教体育用品制造业	Stationery, Education and Sports Goods	9.94	2.18	1.80
石油加工、炼焦及核燃料加工业	Petroleum Processing, Coking Products and Nuclear Fuel Processing	3.52	3.13	
化学原料及化学制品制造业	Raw Chemical Material and Chemical Products	111.98	18.66	76.20
医药制造业	Medical and Pharmaceutical Products	34.28	2.57	9.62
化学纤维制造业	Chemical Fibers	23.58	10.10	9.21
橡胶制品业	Rubber Products	11.49	7.25	19.71
塑料制品业	Plastic Products	52.67	8.63	8.36
非金属矿物制品业	Nonmetal Mineral Products	67.36	3.98	15.06
黑色金属冶炼及压延加工业	Smelting and Processing of Ferrous Metals	37.58	34.36	28.04
有色金属冶炼及压延加工业	Smelting and Processing of Nonferrous Metals	18.64	3.96	3.19
金属制品业	Metal Products	96.21	11.08	26.43
通用设备制造业	Ordinarly Machinery Manufacturing	170.64	9.29	43.18
专用设备制造业	Special Purpose Equipment Manufacturing	98.09	5.00	26.45
交通运输设备制造业	Transportation Equipment Manufacturing	77.85	7.57	65.24
电气机械及器材制造业	Electric Machinery and Equipment	107.96	8.84	45.69
通信设备、计算机及其他电子设备	Telecommunication Equipments, Computer and Other Electronic Equipment Manufaturing	58.76	57.13	328.89
仪器仪表及文化、办公用机械制造	Instruments, Meters, Cultural and Official Machinery	19.81	1.57	13.93
工艺品及其他制造业	Handicraft Artical and Other Manufacturing	33.24	2.38	5.95
废弃资源和废旧材料回收加工业	Waste Resouces and Junk Material Recycled	2.20		0.85

5－7　续表3　Continued 3

单位:亿元　　(100 million yuan)

行　业	Sector	私人控股 Private Share Holding	港澳台商控股 Hong Kong, Macao and Taiwan Share Holding	外商控股 Foreign Share Holding
电力、燃气及水的生产和供应业	Electric Power, Gas and Water Production and Supply	62.34	18.95	11.45
电力、热力的生产和供应业	Electric Power, Steam and Hot Water Production and Supply	50.18	14.86	10.16
燃气生产和供应业	Gas Production and Supply	3.79	2.36	0.29
水的生产和供应业	Tap Water Production and Supply	8.38	1.72	0.99
建筑业	Construction	14.07		1.35
交通运输、仓储和邮政业	Transportation, Storage and Post	36.79	14.20	5.99
铁路运输业	Railway Transportation	0.87		
道路运输业	Road Transportation	8.61		0.34
城市公共交通业	Urban Public Transit	2.08		
水上运输业	Waterway Transportation	7.31	8.06	3.43
管道运输业	Waterway Transportation	1.29		
装卸搬运和其他运输服务业	Load and Unload, Carry and Other Transportion	4.57	0.75	
仓储业	Storage	12.06	5.38	2.22
邮政业	Post			
信息传输、计算机服务和软件业	Information Transmmision, Computer Service and Software	3.48	3.75	10.16
电信和其他信息传输服务业	Telecommunication and Other Information Transmmision Service	1.48	3.75	10.17
计算机服务业	Computer Service	0.40		
软件业	Software	1.59		
批发和零售业	Wholesale and Retail Trade	137.26	8.51	13.35
住宿和餐饮业	Hotel and Catering Services	62.71	0.41	4.27
金融业	Finance	0.05		0.06
银行业	Banking			0.06
其他金融活动	Other Financial Activities	0.05		
房地产业	Real Estate Trade	1346.65	124.87	106.47
租赁和商务服务业	Leasing and Commercial Services	24.41	0.24	3.13
租赁业	Leasing Services	1.14		
商务服务业	Commercial Services	23.27	0.24	3.13
科学研究、技术服务和地质勘查业	Scientific Research, Polytechnical Services and Geological Prospecitng	3.48		1.35
水利、环境和公共设施管理业	Water Conservancy, Environment and Public Facility Management	37.57	5.21	1.26
水利管理业	Water Conservancy Manegement	0.66		
环境管理业	Environment Management	5.88	0.20	0.01
公共设施管理业	Public Facility Management	31.03	5.00	1.27
居民服务和其他服务业	Resident Services and Others	5.86		0.01
教育	Education	12.17		0.51
卫生、社会保障和社会福利业	Health Care, Social Security and Social Welfare	5.85		5.20
卫生	Health Care	5.85		5.20
社会保障业	Social Security			
社会福利业	Social Welfare			
文化、体育和娱乐业	Culture, Sports and Recreation	13.93	0.40	1.62
新闻出版业	News Publication	0.21		
广播、电视、电影和音像业	Radio, Television, Film and Stereo	0.89		
文化艺术业	Culture and Arts	0.15		0.13
体育	Sports	0.05		
娱乐业	Recreation	12.63	0.40	1.49
公共管理和社会组织	Public Management and Social Organizations	1.04	1.15	

5-8 按行业分城镇施工投产项目个数(2006年)
NUMBER OF URBAN PROJECTS UNDER CONSTRUCTION AND PUT INTO USE BY SECTOR (2006)

行业	Sector	施工项目(个) Project under Construction (unit)	#新开工 New Starting This Year	全部建成投产项目(个) Fully Completed Project Turn Over for Production (unit)	项目建成投产率(%) Rate of Projects Completed & Put into Use (%)
总计	**Total**	**13671**	**9238**	**7912**	**57.9**
农、林、牧、渔业	Farming, Forestry, Animal Husbandry and Fishery	83	53	57	68.7
农业	Farming	16	8	10	62.5
林业	Forestry	9	4	8	88.9
畜牧业	Animal Husbandry	7	6	4	57.1
渔业	Fishery	4	4	4	100.0
农、林、牧、渔服务业	Farming, Forestry, Animal Husbandry and Fishery Services	47	31	31	66.0
采矿业	Mining and Quarrying	37	27	23	62.2
制造业	Manufacturing	8907	6205	5289	59.4
农副食品加工业	Food Processing	254	193	161	63.4
食品制造业	Food Production	165	108	86	52.1
饮料制造业	Beverage Production	71	46	39	54.9
烟草制品业	Tobacco Processing	2	1	1	50.0
纺织业	Textile Industry	840	562	510	60.7
纺织服装、鞋、帽制造业	Textile Garments, Shoes and Hats Production	481	331	297	61.7
皮革、毛皮、羽毛(绒)及其制品业	Leather, Furs, Down and Related Products	77	49	49	63.6
木材加工及木、竹、藤、棕、草制	Timber Processing and Wood, Bamboo, Rattan, Palm and Straw Works	180	133	105	58.3
家具制造业	Furniture Manufacturing	69	51	37	53.6
造纸及纸制品业	Papermaking and Paper Products	123	82	74	60.2
印刷业和记录媒介的复制	Printing and Record Processing	111	74	78	70.3
文教体育用品制造业	Stationery, Education and Sports Goods	77	48	47	61.0
石油加工、炼焦及核燃料加工业	Petroleum Processing, Coking Products and Nuclear Fuel Processing	30	20	17	56.7
化学原料及化学制品制造业	Raw Chemical Material and Chemical Products	681	448	376	55.2
医药制造业	Medical and Pharmaceutical Products	187	117	96	51.3
化学纤维制造业	Chemical Fibers	71	44	42	59.2
橡胶制品业	Rubber Products	85	58	46	54.1
塑料制品业	Plastic Products	319	234	188	58.9
非金属矿物制品业	Nonmetal Mineral Products	427	309	267	62.5
黑色金属冶炼及压延加工业	Smelting and Processing of Ferrous Metals	130	74	84	64.6
有色金属冶炼及压延加工业	Smelting and Processing of Nonferrous Metals	109	76	62	56.9
金属制品业	Metal Products	604	453	379	62.7
通用设备制造业	Ordinarly Machinery Manufacturing	1124	817	695	61.8
专用设备制造业	Special Purpose Equipment Manufacturing	618	452	377	61.0
交通运输设备制造业	Transportation Equipment Manufacturing	446	304	248	55.6
电气机械及器材制造业	Electric Machinery and Equipment	665	486	410	61.7
通信设备、计算机及其他电子设备	Telecommunication Equipments, Computer and Other Electronic Equipment Manufaturing	517	314	289	55.9
仪器仪表及文化、办公用机械制造	Instruments, Meters, Cultural and Official Machinery	129	96	66	51.2
工艺品及其他制造业	Handicraft Artical and Other Manufacturing	301	212	157	52.2
废弃资源和废旧材料回收加工业	Waste Resouces and Junk Material Recycled	14	13	6	42.9

5－8 续表 Continued

行业 Sector		施工项目(个) Project under Construction (unit)	#新开工 New Starting This Year	全部建成投产项目(个) Fully Completed Project Turn Over for Production (unit)	项目建成投产率(%) Rate of Projects Completed & Put into Use (%)
电力、燃气及水的生产和供应业	Electric Power, Gas and Water Production and Supply	406	208	213	52.5
电力、热力的生产和供应业	Electric Power, Steam and Hot Water Production and Supply	244	124	150	61.5
燃气生产和供应业	Gas Production and Supply	46	26	22	47.8
水的生产和供应业	Tap Water Production and Supply	116	58	41	35.3
建筑业	Construction	150	111	73	48.7
交通运输、仓储和邮政业	Transportation, Storage and Post	665	379	332	49.9
铁路运输业	Railway Transportation	4	3	2	50.0
道路运输业	Road Transportation	443	254	222	50.1
城市公共交通业	Urban Public Transit	41	18	33	80.5
水上运输业	Waterway Transportation	79	33	30	38.0
管道运输业	Pipeline Transportation	1		1	100.0
装卸搬运和其他运输服务业	Load and Unload, Carry and Other Transportion	15	9	8	53.3
仓储业	Storage	77	60	36	46.8
邮政业	Post	2			0.0
信息传输、计算机服务和软件业	Information Transmmision, Computer Service and Software	116	86	80	69.0
电信和其他信息传输服务业	Telecommunication and Other Information Transmmision Service	110	82	78	70.9
计算机服务业	Computer Service	2	2	1	50.0
软件业	Software	4	2	1	25.0
批发和零售业	Wholesale and Retail Trade	453	338	303	66.9
住宿和餐饮业	Hotel and Catering Services	283	228	199	70.3
金融业	Finance	12	4	8	66.7
银行业	Banking	11	4	7	63.6
其他金融活动	Other Financial Activities	1		1	100.0
房地产业	Real Estate Trade	199	126	85	42.7
租赁和商务服务业	Leasing and Commercial Services	130	89	72	55.4
租赁业	Commercial Services	9	5	7	77.8
商务服务业	Commercial Services	121	84	65	53.7
科学研究、技术服务和地质勘查业	Scientific Research, Polytechnical Services and Geological Prospecitng	46	29	20	43.5
水利、环境和公共设施管理业	Water Conservancy, Environment and Public Facility Management	1166	721	652	55.9
水利管理业	Water Conservancy Manegement	144	98	85	59.0
环境管理业	Environment Management	56	30	25	44.6
公共设施管理业	Public Facility Management	966	593	542	56.1
居民服务和其他服务业	Resident Services and Others	66	52	43	65.2
教育	Education	349	211	186	53.3
卫生、社会保障和社会福利业	Health Care, Social Security and Social Welfare	147	67	58	39.5
卫生	Health Care	135	63	47	34.8
社会保障业	Social Security	2	1	2	100.0
社会福利业	Social Welfare	10	3	9	90.0
文化、体育和娱乐业	Culture, Sports and Recreation	122	70	66	54.1
新闻出版业	News Publication	7	4	1	14.3
广播、电视、电影和音像业	Radio, Television, Film and Stereo	12	6	4	33.3
文化艺术业	Culture and Arts	33	14	12	36.4
体育	Sports	14	5	11	78.6
娱乐业	Recreation	56	41	38	67.9
公共管理和社会组织	Public Management and Social Organizations	334	234	153	45.8

5-9 国有单位固定资产投资

INVEATMENT OF STATE-OWNED UNITS IN CAPITAL CONSTRUCTION

指 标	Item	2005 投资额 Investment	2005 #房地产开发 Real Estate Development	2006 投资额 Investment	2006 #房地产开发 Real Estate Development
建设项目	**Number of Construction Projects**				
施工项目 (个)	Projects Under Construction (unit)	3467		3184	
全部建成投产项目 (个)	Total Projects Completed Put Into Operation (unit)	1872		1614	
建成项目投产率 (%)	Rate of projects Completed put into Production	54.0		50.7	
建设周期 (年)	Construction cycle	1.85		1.97	
资金来源 (亿元)	**Sources of Funds (100 million yuan)**				
国家预算内投资	State Appropriation	65.48		65.54	
国内贷款	Domestic Loans	475.60	41.96	507.44	52.06
利用外资	Foreign Investment	8.01	0.87	9.51	
自筹资金	Fund Raising	1348.29	38.21	1354.0	47.33
其他资金	Others	130.97	68.82	162.59	106.27
投资总额 (亿元)	**Total Investment (100 million yuan)**	**2077.97**	**132.53**	**2144.93**	**159.25**
按构成分	Grouped by Use of Funds				
#建筑工程	Construction	1302.05	94.64	1329.38	94.24
安装工程	Installation	116.27	1.91	107.59	2.8
设备工具器具购置	Purchase of Equipment, Tools and Instruments	270.83	0.21	263.46	0.78
按产业分	Grouped by Industry				
第一产业	Primary Industry	12.24		16.31	
第二产业	Secondary Industry	529.01		507.33	
第三产业	Tertiary Industry	1536.72	132.53	1621.29	159.25
#住 宅	Residential Housing	138.82	99.38	159.13	128.03
按建设性质分	Grouped by Type of Construction				
#新 建	New Construction	1096.19		934.2	
扩 建	Expension	624.40		721.86	
改 建	Replacement	199.60		280.78	
房屋建筑面积 (万平方米)	**Floor Space of Building (10000 sq. m)**				
施工面积	Floor Space Under Construction	4261.43	1420.81	4756.18	1791.77
#住 宅	Residential Housing	1819.41	1241.04	2043.52	1549.43
竣工面积	Floor Space Completed	1859.18	599.24	1823.61	625.21
#住 宅	Residential Housing	774.44	518.34	775.92	528.61

注:建设周期按项目个数计算。

Note: Construction cycle was calculated by the number of construction projects.

5-10 房地产开发投资主要指标
MAJOR INDICAOTRS OF REAL ESTATE INVESTMENT

指标	Item	1990	1995	2000	2005	2006
企业个数 (个)	**Number of Enterprises (unit)**		**1641**	**1930**	**3810**	**4137**
内资	Domestic Funded		1257	1636	3384	3655
#国有	State-owned Enterprises		618	585	248	246
集体	Collective Enterprises		488	482	192	177
港澳台投资	Funded by Entrepreneurs from Hong Kong, Macao and Taiwan		189	197	277	289
外商投资	Foreign Funded		195	97	149	193
投资完成额 (亿元)	**Investment Completed This Year (100 million yuan)**	**11.71**	**240.85**	**358.72**	**1545.15**	**1906.71**
按构成分	Grouped by Use of Funds					
#建筑安装工程	Construction and Installation Projects	9.97	172.75	255.81	1091.29	1334.08
设备工器具购置	Purchase of Equipment, Tools and Instruments	0.01	5.96	3.34	12.53	21.12
按工程用途分	Grouped by Use of Project					
#住宅	Residential Buildings	9.76	139.24	260.79	1133.06	1425.98
#经济适用房屋	Economical Houses		8.74	36.77	138.42	64.23
按资金来源分	Grouped by Sources of Finance					
#国内贷款	Domestic Loans	2.18	54.23	88.01	392.73	532.51
利用外资	Foreign Investment		27.66	5.82	33.16	33.42
自筹投资	Fund Raising	6.34	77.85	101.34	614.76	702.87
其他投资	Others	5.86	108.69	195.48	998.18	1394.10
房屋建筑面积 (万平方米)	**Floor Space of Building (10000 sq. m)**					
施工面积	Floor Space Under Construction	555.45	3510.13	4268.45	15619.26	19108.25
#住宅	Residential Buildings	481.80	2502.75	3348.36	12385.98	14919.05
竣工面积	Floor Space Completed	293.94	1630.06	2143.22	5500.12	5933.51
#住宅	Residential Buildings	257.12	1339.47	1774.80	4497.68	4745.50
土地开发及购置 (万平方米)	**Land Development and Purchase (10000 sq. m)**					
本年土地开发面积	Area of Land Development This Year		1329.00	886.59	1827.36	2158.04
本年土地购置面积	Area of Land Purchase This Year		744.00	1395.98	2848.80	2983.95
商品房销售情况	**Selling of Commercial Houses**					
房屋销售面积 (万平方米)	Floor Space of Selling House (10000 sq. m)	250.02	798.31	1740.93	5135.55	6101.15
#住宅	Residential Buildings		708.89	1555.97	4523.14	5317.20
#经济适用房	Economical Houses		42.80	313.98	187.04	227.48

注:本表资金来源均为资金到位数。

Note: The funds sources of this table were all available for investment

5-11 按登记注册类型分房地产开发投资(2006年)

项目		总计 Total	内资 Inner Funded	国有 State-Owned	集体 Collective-Owned
企业个数 (个)	**Number of Enterprises (unit)**	**4137**	**3655**	**218**	**131**
#亏损企业个数	Loss-Making Enterprises	1806	1594	102	56
本年完成投资	**Investment Completed This Year (100 million yuan)**	**1906.71**	**1644.64**	**140.38**	**19.91**
#商品房建设投资	Investment for Commercial Housing Construction	1369.83	1179.02	109.90	15.35
#土地开发投资	Investment for Land Development	116.20	107.55	3.88	0.75
按构成分	Grouped by Use of Funds				
建筑工程	Construction Projects	1249.16	1083.77	82.01	16.00
安装工程	Installation Projects	84.92	70.54	2.39	0.85
设备工器具购置	Purchase of Equipment, Tools and Instruments	21.12	16.54	0.79	0.14
其他费用	Other Funds	551.51	473.79	55.19	2.91
#土地购置费	Purchase of Land	403.20	344.56	35.34	2.25
按构成用途分	Grouped by Use of Project				
住宅	Residential Buildings	1425.98	1240.20	113.54	14.96
#经济适用房	Economical Houses	64.23	64.01	28.23	0.40
别墅、高档公寓	Villa, Top Grade Flat	151.22	120.33	2.00	1.32
办公楼	Office Buidings	57.07	48.74	2.94	1.37
商业营业用房	Business Buidings	272.40	231.35	7.39	3.07
其他	Others	151.28	124.35	16.51	0.51
本年新增固定资产 (亿元)	**Newly Increased Fixed Assets This Year (100 million yuan)**	**1173.71**	**1023.56**	**83.90**	**18.76**
资金来源 (亿元)	**Finance Sources (100 million yuan)**	**2662.89**	**2275.46**	**170.56**	**26.89**
国内贷款	Domestic Loans	532.51	468.99	46.21	1.18
利用外资	Foreign Investment	33.42	4.97		
自筹资金	Fund Raising	702.87	613.07	42.47	18.21
#自有资金	Self-owned	456.08	391.79	20.58	12.61
其他资金来源	Others	1394.10	1188.43	81.88	7.51
#定金及预收款	Funds ordered and Pre-received	860.96	742.25	35.51	3.10
土地开发 (万平方米)	**Land Development (10000 sq. m)**				
本年完成开发土地面积	Area of Land Development This Year	2158.04	2002.24	111.63	19.42
待开发土地面积	Area of Land to be Developed	4794.53	4267.41	192.47	18.66
本年购置土地面积	Area of Land Purchased This Year	2983.95	2651.54	260.51	24.85
本年土地成交价款	Value of Land Transaction	382.35	299.83	38.56	1.82

INVESTMENT IN REAL ESTATE DEVELOPMENT BY TYPE OF REGISTRATION (2006)

股份合作 Share Holding Cooperation	联　营 Joint-Owned	国有独资公司 State Solely Funded co.	其它有限责任公司 Responsibily Co., Ltd.	股份有限公司 Share Holding Co., Ltd.	私　营 Private	其它 Other
44	**11**	**24**	**1212**	**170**	**1827**	**18**
23	4	6	488	62	843	10
7.91	**4.63**	**17.73**	**679.95**	**61.14**	**704.88**	**8.11**
5.94	3.39	15.56	488.17	43.70	491.21	5.80
0.42			45.71	10.33	46.29	0.16
5.42	1.69	11.49	448.31	44.35	469.29	5.20
0.18	0.19	0.41	31.70	2.41	32.42	0.01
0.18			7.20	0.43	7.79	
2.13	2.75	5.84	192.74	13.95	195.38	2.91
0.74	2.35	3.30	140.78	10.72	146.17	2.91
6.29	4.21	13.75	516.20	49.54	515.67	6.05
		2.24	23.25	0.63	9.26	
0.39		0.45	58.03	4.25	52.95	0.96
0.25		0.12	18.69	2.51	22.34	0.51
0.29		1.26	91.39	6.78	119.85	1.33
1.09	0.42	2.60	53.67	2.31	47.02	0.22
4.61	**1.16**	**30.40**	**425.58**	**41.70**	**414.71**	**2.76**
11.60	**11.80**	**32.41**	**973.25**	**93.74**	**946.74**	**8.48**
2.30	5.65	4.65	217.92	16.28	173.72	1.08
			4.34		0.63	
3.56	1.13	4.48	234.40	29.60	273.93	5.29
2.80	0.38	3.03	149.75	21.69	177.17	3.77
5.73	5.02	23.27	516.59	47.85	498.46	2.11
3.88	2.48	17.06	318.91	29.23	330.65	1.44
15.27			701.91	80.46	1073.56	
24.07		33.81	1610.30	149.43	2225.20	13.47
26.33		7.54	964.70	125.35	1222.28	20.00
2.75		0.40	117.11	8.54	128.34	2.31

5-11 续表

指标	Item	港澳台商投资 Hong Kong, Macao and Taiwan Funded	合资经营 Joinr-Venture Cperation	合作经营 Cooperative Cperation
企业个数 （个）	**Number of Enterprises (unit)**	**289**	**164**	**24**
#亏损企业个数	Loss-Making Enterprises	124	72	8
本年完成投资	**Investment Completed This Year (100 million yuan)**	**148.89**	**77.16**	**5.19**
#商品房建设投资	Investment for Commercial Housing Construction	114.32	58.61	3.55
#土地开发投资	Investment for Land Development	6.14	4.35	0.05
按构成分	Grouped by Use of Funds			
建筑工程	Construction Projects	96.21	53.74	2.99
安装工程	Installation Projects	9.01	4.65	0.73
设备工器具购置	Purchase of Equipment, Tools and Instruments	2.24	0.83	0.29
其他费用	Other Funds	41.42	17.94	1.19
#土地购置费	Purchase of Land	33.97	14.58	0.71
按构成用途分	Grouped by Use of Project			
住宅	Residential Buildings	106.69	57.78	3.74
#经济适用房	Economical Houses			
别墅、高档公寓	Villa, Top Grade Flat	18.65	9.11	1.78
办公楼	Office Buidings	6.29	2.33	0.36
商业营业用房	Business Buidings	28.72	11.78	0.78
其他	Others	7.19	5.28	0.32
本年新增固定资产 （亿元）	**Newly Increased Fixed Assets This Year (100 million yuan)**	**81.70**	**48.39**	**2.90**
资金来源 （亿元）	**Finance Sources (100 million yuan)**	**219.88**	**107.53**	**10.62**
国内贷款	Domestic Loans	37.95	23.62	0.92
利用外资	Foreign Investment	11.43	2.59	0.11
自筹资金	Fund Raising	47.21	25.09	2.76
#自有资金	Self-owned	35.42	18.98	1.34
其他资金来源	Others	123.29	56.23	6.83
#定金及预收款	Funds Ordered and Pre-received	73.57	39.68	4.94
土地开发 （万平方米）	**Land Development (10000 sq. m)**			
本年完成开发土地面积	Area of Land Development This Year	98.36	57.45	
待开发土地面积	Area of Land to be Developed	355.89	203.73	14.97
本年购置土地面积	Area of Land Purchased This Year	212.29	64.07	3.97
本年土地成交价款	Value of Land Transaction	47.28	11.25	0.30

Continued

独资 Solely Furds	股份有限 Share Holding Co. Ltd.	外商投资 Foreign Inveslment	合资经营 Joinr – Venture Cperation	合作经营 Cooperative Cperation	独资 Solely Furds	股份有限 Share Holding Co. Ltd.
98	**3**	**193**	**99**	**19**	**71**	**4**
44		88	50	7	30	1
66.13	**0.41**	**113.19**	**58.02**	**6.92**	**44.34**	**3.91**
51.77	0.38	76.49	36.91	4.77	30.91	3.91
1.74		2.51	1.57		0.94	
39.09	0.40	69.18	39.37	2.65	23.82	3.34
3.63	0.01	5.37	2.99	0.11	1.87	0.40
1.12		2.34	1.78	0.01	0.53	0.02
22.28		36.30	13.89	4.14	18.11	0.16
18.68		24.68	6.66	3.00	15.03	
45.05	0.13	79.09	39.06	6.62	30.19	3.22
		0.22	0.22			
7.63	0.13	12.23	6.24	1.18	4.82	
3.60		2.04	1.56	0.07	0.41	
15.88	0.28	12.33	9.21	0.21	2.22	0.69
1.60		19.74	8.20	0.01	11.52	
28.80	**1.61**	**68.46**	**41.04**	**1.05**	**25.91**	**0.46**
101.29	**0.44**	**167.55**	**87.85**	**9.49**	**66.16**	**4.06**
13.41		25.57	14.68	0.80	9.14	0.95
8.54	0.19	17.02	2.91	2.77	11.34	
19.32	0.05	42.59	20.80	3.74	16.45	1.60
15.11		28.87	13.74	3.07	10.46	1.60
60.03	0.20	82.38	49.46	2.17	29.23	1.52
28.94		45.15	22.70	1.49	20.23	0.72
40.92		57.44	36.25		21.19	
137.20		171.23	71.16	26.86	73.21	
144.25		120.12	61.51	16.29	42.32	
35.73		35.24	6.09	4.40	24.75	

主要统计指标解释

全社会固定资产投资 即固定资产投资额是以货币表现的建造和购置固定资产活动的工作量，它是反映固定资产投资规模、速度、比例关系和使用方向的综合性指标。全社会固定资产投资按登记注册类型可分为国有、集体、个体、联营、股份制、外商、港澳台商、其他等。全社会固定资产投资总额分为城镇项目投资、农村建设项目投资和房地产开发投资三个部分。

城镇和农村建设项目投资 指城镇和农村各种登记注册类型的企业、事业、行政单位及个体户进行的计划总投资500万元及500万元以上的建设项目。

房地产开发投资 指房地产开发公司、商品房建设公司及其他房地产开发法人单位和附属于其他法人单位实际从事房地产开发或经营的活动单位统一开发的包括统代建、拆迁还建的住宅、厂房、仓库、饭店、宾馆、度假村、写字楼、办公楼等房屋建筑物和配套的服务设施，土地开发工程（如道路、给水、排水、供电、供热、通讯、平整场地等基础设施工程）的投资；不包括单纯的土地交易活动。

固定资产投资的资金来源 根据固定资产投资的资金来源不同，分为国家预算内资金、国内贷款、利用外资、自筹资金和其他资金来源。

（1）国家预算内资金：指中央财政和地方财政中由国家统筹安排的基本建设拨款和更新改造拨款，以及中央财政安排的专项拨款中用于基本建设的资金和基本建设拨款改贷款的资金等。

（2）国内贷款：指报告期内企、事业单位向银行及非银行金融机构借入的用于固定资产投资的各种国内借款。包括银行利用自有资金及吸收的存款发放的贷款、上级主管部门拨入的国内贷款、国家专项贷款（包括煤代油贷款、劳改煤矿专项贷款等）、地方财政专项资金安排的贷款、国内储备贷款、周转贷款等。

（3）利用外资：指报告期内收到的用于固定资产投资的国外资金，包括统借统还、自借自还的国外贷款，中外合资项目中的外资，以及对外发行债券和股票等。国家统借统还的外资指由我国政府出面同外国政府、团体或金融组织签订贷款协议、并负责偿还本息的国外贷款。

（4）自筹资金：指建设单位报告期内收到的，用于进行固定资产投资的上级主管部门、地方和企、事业单位自筹资金。

（5）其他资金来源：指报告期内收到的除以上各种拨款、借款、自筹资金以外其他用于固定资产投资的资金。

固定资产投资按国民经济行业分 建设项目归哪个行业，按其建成投产后的主要产品或主要用途及社会经济活动性质来确定。基本建设按建设项目划分国民经济行业，更新改造、国有单位其他固定资产投资及城镇集体投资根据整个企业、事业单位所属的行业来划分。一般情况下，一个建设项目或一个企业、事业单位只能属于一种国民经济行业。

固定资产投资按建设性质分 建设项目的性质一般分为新建、扩建、改建、迁建、恢复。基本建设按建设项目划分建设性质，更新改造、国有单位其他固定资产投资、城镇集体投资及农村投资等按整个企业、事业单位的建设情况确定建设性质，城镇工矿区私人建房等投资不划分建设性质。

（1）新建：一般是指从无到有、"平地起家"新开始建设的单位。有的单位原有的基础很小，经过建设后其新增加的固定资产价值超过原有固定资产价值（原值）三倍以上的也算新建。

（2）扩建：一般是指为扩大原有产品的生产能力，在厂内或其他地点增建主要生产车间（或主要工程）、独立的生产线或分厂的企业；事业单位和行政单位在原单位增建业务用房（如学校增建教学用房、医院增建门诊部或病床用房、行政机关增建办公楼等）也作为扩建。

（3）改建：一般是指现有企业、事业单位为了技术进步，提高产品质量，增加花色品种，促进产品升级换代，降低消耗和成本，加强资源综合利用和三废治理、劳保安全等，采用新技术、新工艺、新设备、新材料等对现有设施、工艺条件进行技术改造或更新（包括相应配套的辅助性生产、生活福利设施）。有的企业为充分发挥现有生产能力，进行填平补齐而增建不增加本单位主要产品生产能力的车间等，也属于改建。

固定资产投资按构成分 固定资产投资活动按其工作内容和实现方式分为建筑安装工程，设备、工具、器具购置，其他费用三个部分。

（1）建筑安装工程（建筑安装工作量）：指各种房屋、建筑物的建造工程和各种设备、装置的安装工程。包括各种房屋建造工程，各种用途设备基础和各种工业窑炉的砌筑工程；为施工而进行的各种准备工作和临时工程以及完工后的清理工作等；铁路、道路的铺设，矿井的开凿及石油管道的架设等；水利工程；防空地下建筑等特殊工程；以及各种机械设备的安装工程；为测定安装工程质量，对设备进行的试运工作。在安装工程中，不包括被安装设备本身的价值。

（2）设备、工具、器具购置：指购置或自制达到固定资产标准的设备、工具、器具的价值，固定资产的标准按财务部门规定。新建单位、扩建单位的新建车间按照设计和计划要求购置或自制的全部设备、工具、器具，不论是否达到固定资产标准均计入"设备、工具、器具购置"中。

(3)其他费用:指在固定资产建造和购置过程中发生的,除建筑安装工程和设备、工具、器具购置以外的各种应摊入固定资产的费用。

施工项目　指报告期内曾进行建筑或安装工程施工活动的建设项目,包括报告期内新开工项目、报告期以前开工跨入报告期继续施工的项目以及报告期施过工并在报告期内全部建成投产或停缓建的项目。

全部建成投产项目　工业项目是指设计文件规定形成生产能力的主体工程及其相应配套的辅助设施全部建成,经负荷试运转,证明具备生产设计规定合格产品的条件,并经过验收鉴定合格或达到竣工验收标准,与生产性工程配套的生活福利设施可以满足近期正常生产的需要,正式移交生产的建设项目。非工业项目是指设计文件规定的主体工程和相应的配套工程全部建成,能够发挥设计规定的全部效益,经验收鉴定合格或达到竣工验收标准,正式移交使用的建设项目。

房屋建筑面积　指从房屋外墙线算起的各层平面面积的总和,包括可供使用的有效面积和房屋结构(如柱、墙)占用的面积。多层建筑按各层(包括地下室)面积总和计算。

住宅建筑面积　指施工和竣工房屋建筑面积中供居住用的施工和竣工房屋建筑面积。

施工面积　指报告期内施工的全部房屋建筑面积。包括本期新开工的面积、上期跨入本期继续施工的房屋面积、上期停缓建在本期恢复施工的房屋面积、本期竣工的房屋面积及本期施工后又停缓建的房屋面积。

竣工面积　指在报告期内房屋建筑按照设计要求已全部完工,达到住人和使用条件,经验收鉴定合格,正式移交使用单位的建筑面积。

房屋建筑面积竣工率　指一定时期内房屋竣工面积占同期房屋施工面积的比率。它是从房屋建筑施工速度的角度反映投资效果和建筑业经济效益的指标。

新增固定资产　指通过投资活动所形成的新的固定资产价值,包括已经建成投入生产或交付使用的工程价值和达到固定资产标准的设备、工具、器具的价值及有关应摊入的费用。它是以价值形式表示的固定资产投资成果的综合性指标,可以综合反映不同时期、不同部门、不同地区的固定资产投资成果。

建设项目投产率　指一定时期内全部建成投入生产项目个数与同期正式施工项目个数的比率。它是从项目建设速度的角度反映投资效果的指标。

建设周期　是指报告期(年)所有正式施工项目全部建成平均需要的时间,它是从宏观角度反映建设速度的指标。建设周期的计算方法有两种:

(1)按建设项目计算:建设周期=报告期正式施工项目个数/报告期全部建成投产项目个数

(2)按投资额计算:建设周期=报告期正式施工项目计划总投资之和/报告期正式施工项目完成投资之和。

Explanatory Notes on Main Statistical Indicators

Total Investment in Fixed Assets in the Whole Country　Total investment in fixed assets refers to the volume of activities in construction and purchases of fixed assets in monetary terms. It is a comprehensive indicator which shows the size, pace, proportional relations and use orientation of the investment in fixed assets. Total investment in fixed assets in the whole country includes, by regis-tration type of ownership, the investment by the state-owned units, collective units, individuals, joint ownership units, share-holding units, as well as investment by businessmen from foreign countries and from Hong Kong, Macau and Taiwan, and by other units. According to China's current management system, the investment in fixed assets in the whole country is classified into the following three parts: investment in capital construction and innovation; urban and rural investment in construction projects as well as investment in real estate development.

Urban and Rual Investiment in construction Projects　regers to total planned investment in construction projects by varxious types of registered urban and rural enterprises, institutions, administrative units and individuals, each with a total of 5 million yuan and above investment.

Investment in Real Estate Development　It includes the investment by the real estate development companies, commercial buildings construction companies and other real estate development units of various types of ownership in the construction of house buildings, such as residential buildings, factory buildings, warehouses, hotels, guesthouses, holiday villages, office buildings, and the complementary service facilities and land development projects, such as roads, water supply, water drainage, power supply, heating, telecommunications, land leveling and other projects of infrastructure. It excludes the activities in simple land transactions.

Sources of Funds for Investment in Fixed Assets　state budgetary appropriation, domestic loans, foreign investment, self-raised funds, and others.

(1) State budgetary appropriation refers to appropriation in the budget of the central and local governments earmarked for capital

construction and for innovation projects, and the special appropriation from the budget of the central government for capital construction and for the transfer fund to banks to be issued as loans for capital construction projects

(2) Domestic loans refer to various funds borrowed by enterprises and institutions from banks and non-bank financial institutions during the reference period for the purpose of investment in fixed assets, including loans issued by banks from their self-owned funds and deposit, loans appropriated by higher responsible authorities, special loans by government (including loan for replacing petroleum with coal, special loan for reform-through-labour coal mines), loans arranged by local government from special funds, domestic reserve loan, and working loan, etc.

(3) Foreign Investment refers to foreign funds received during the reference period for the purpose of investment in fixed assets, including foreign funds borrowed and managed by the government, by individual units, foreign fund in joint venture program, and issue of bonds and stocks at the international financial markets. The foreign funds borrowed and managed by the government refer to foreign loans borrowed by the government from foreign governments, organizations, or financial institutions under official agreements signed by both parties, under which government is responsible for the repayment of both the principal and interests of the foreign loans.

(4) Self-raised funds refer to funds received by construction enterprises from their higher responsible authorities, local governments, or raised by enterprises or institutions themselves for the purpose of investment in fixed assets during the reference period.

(5) Others refer to funds received during the reference period which are not included in the above-mentioned sources.

Investment in Fixed Assets by Sector The classification of construction projects by sector is determined by the major products or the purpose of the projects when they are put into production or use, and by the nature of their social economic activities. The investment in capital construction is classified by construction projects, while investment in innovation, other investment by state-owned units and urban collective units are classified according to the sector which the whole enterprise or institution belongs to. In general, one project or one enterprise or institution can only belong to one sector.

Investment in Fixed Assets by Type of Construction The construction projects in general can be classified by the type of construction into new construction, expansion, reconstruction, moving away and resumption. In capital construction, the type of construction is determined by the condition of the project. In investment in innovation, in other investment by state-owned units, invest—ment by urban collective-owned units and investment in rural areas. The type of construction is determined by the condition of the whole enterprise or institutions. Investment by type of construction is not applied to investment in housing by individuals in industrial and mining areas of cities and towns.

(1) New construction in general refers to newly constructed units. In the case in which the value of the original fixed assets is quite small, and the value of newly added fixed assets exceeds the original ones by three times, the expansion construction is considered as new construction.

(2) Expansion refers to construction of new major production workshop or independent production line within a factory or in other locations, or construction of a branch factory so as to increase the production capacity of the original products. Newly constructed business houses in institutions and administrative organizations (such as the newly constructed teaching buildings in schools, clinics or bed building in hospitals, and office buildings in administrative agencies, etc.) are also classified as expansion.

(3) Reconstruction refers to technical innovation and transformation of the existing equipment and technical conditions undertaken by enterprises and institutions for the purposes of technological advancement, improvement in product quality, enlarging variety of products, promoting new generation of products, reducing production consumption and cost, promoting comprehensive utilization of resources, strengthening treatment of waste gas, waste water and solid wastes, and safety in production, etc. through application of new technologies and techniques, use of new equipment and new materials (including accessory facilities for production or for living and welfare purposes). Construction of new workshops for improving existing production capacity rather than increasing production capacity is also considered as reconstruction.

Investment in Fixed Assets by Structure refers to the three major parts of investment activities, i. e. construction and installation, purchase of equipment and instrument, and other expenses.

(1) Construction and installation (work volume of construction and installation) refers to the construction of various houses and buildings and installation of various kinds of equipment and instruments, including construction of various houses, equipment foundations and industrial kilns and stoves, preparation works for project construction, and clearing up works post project construction, pavement of railways and roads, drilling of mines and putting up of oil pipes, construction of projects of water conservancy, construction of underground air-raid shelters and construction of other special projects, installation of various machinery equipment, testing operation for pretesting the quality of installation projects. The value of equipment installed is not included in the value of installation projects.

(2) Purchase of equipment and instruments refers to the total value of equipment, tools, and vessels purchased or self-produced which come up to standards for fixed assets. Equipment, tools and vessels purchased or self-produced for new workshops by newly established or expanded units are categorized as" purchase of equipment and instruments" no matter whether they come up to the standards for fixed assets or not.

(3) Other expenses refer to expenses occurring during the construction or purchase of fixed assets other than construction, installation or purchase of equipment and instruments.

Projects under Construction refer to projects having construction and installation activities undertaken in the reference period, including projects started in the reference period, or continued from the previous peoind, or completed and put into production or suspended in the reference period.

Projects Completed and Put into Use Industrial projects refer to the major projects and accessory facilities completed which result in forming production capacity and have been checked and accepted while the living and welfare facilities have been completed and can ensure normal production and formally put into production. Non-industrial projects refer to the major projects and accessory facilities completed which possess the designed capacity and have been checked, accepted and formally put into production.

Floor Space of Buildings under Construction refers to total floor space in each story of buildings calculated from the outside line of building walls, including both usable space and the space occupied by constructions like pillars or walls. The floor space of multistory buildings includes the total floor space of each story (including basement).

Floor Space under Construction refers to total floor space of all buildlings under construction during the reference period, including floor space of newly started buildings during the reference period, floor space of construction extended from the previous period to the current period, floor space of construction suspended during the previous period and resumed in the current period, floor space of construction completed in the current period, and floor space of construction started and then suspended in the current period.

Floor Space of Buildings Completed refers to the floor space of buildings completed in the reference period, which have come up to the designed standards and have been put into use.

Completion Rate of Floor Space of Buildings refers to the ratio of the floor space of buildings completed in certain period of time to the floor space of buildings under construction in the same period which reflects the investment result and economic efficiency of the construction industry from the angle of the speed of project construction.

Newly Increased Fixed Assets refer to the newly increased value of fixed assets through investment, including the value of projects completed and put into production, the value of equipment, tools, and vessels considered as fixed assets, as well as the relevant expenses as investment in fixed assets. This is a comprehensive indicator of investment in fixed assets, reflecting the achievements of investment in fixed assets in different periods, different sectors, and different regions.

Rate of Construction Projects Completed and Put into Use refers to the ratio of the number of construction projects completed and put into use in certain period of time to the number of projects under construction in the same period. This reflects the investment efficiency from the angle of the speed of projects construction.

Construction cycle refers to how longtime it wil be taken in average that all the projects formally under construction can be completed in reference year. This indicator reflect the speed of construction in view of macrocosm.

There are tow formula in calculating the construction cycle:

(1) By the number of construction projects

Construction cycle = number of projects formally under construction in reference period (year)

/number of all the projects are completed and put in production in reference period (year)

(2) By the value of investment

Construction cycle = total investment plan for the projects formally under construction in reference period (year)/total fulfihnent of investment on the projects formally under construction in reference period (year).

JIANGSU STATISTICAL YEARBOOK

第6篇

物价

PRICE

6-1 各种物价总指数
GENERAL PRICE INDICES

上年 = 100　　　　　　　　(preceding year = 100)

年份 Year	商品零售价格指数 General Retail Price Index	居民消费价格指数 General Consumer Price Index	城市 Urban	农村 Rural	工业品出厂价格指数 Ex-Factory Price Indices of Industrial Products	原材料、燃料、动力购进价格指数 Raw Material Fuel and Power Purchading Price Indices	固定资产投资价格指数 Price Indices of Investment in Fixed Assets
1979	101.3	101.0	100.7	101.3			
1980	105.8	105.6	105.7	105.6			
1981	101.4	101.5	102.3	100.9			
1982	100.9	100.9	100.9	101.0			
1983	100.1	100.4	100.8	100.0			
1984	102.5	103.0	104.1	102.1			
1985	109.5	109.5	109.6	109.4			
1986	107.1	107.1	106.4	107.7			
1987	109.3	109.2	110.5	107.7			
1988	122.3	121.9	122.6	121.4			
1989	116.8	117.1	116.0	118.5			
1990	102.3	103.2	103.4	103.0			
1991	104.8	104.9	107.7	101.9	103.2	107.0	104.5
1992	105.1	106.6	108.8	104.4	103.8	110.2	112.1
1993	115.9	118.2	118.7	117.3	118.5	125.7	138.8
1994	123.6	123.2	125.3	121.7	121.4	120.1	114.6
1995	114.3	115.8	116.2	115.3	114.2	117.3	107.4
1996	106.8	109.3	110.8	107.1	100.6	103.9	103.2
1997	99.3	101.7	101.3	102.0	97.9	97.9	99.2
1998	98.2	99.4	100.0	99.0	94.5	91.4	98.8
1999	96.9	98.7	98.6	98.8	96.1	94.4	98.3
2000	98.6	100.1	100.0	100.1	101.1	107.1	101.2
2001	98.9	100.8	100.1	101.5	99.1	99.5	100.8
2002	98.4	99.2	98.4	100.2	97.6	98.6	101.3
2003	99.8	101.0	100.9	101.2	102.3	106.5	104.3
2004	102.2	104.1	103.7	104.6	106.5	116.3	109.3
2005	100.3	102.1	102.0	102.4	102.6	107.6	100.9
2006	100.8	101.6	101.6	101.7	101.5	106.4	101.2

6-2 各种物价总指数
GENERAL PRICE INDICES

1978年=100 (1978=100)

年份 Year	商品零售价格指数 General Retail Price Index	居民消费价格指数 General Consumer Price Index	城市 Urban	农村 Rural	工业品出厂价格指数 Ex-Factory Price Indices of Industrial Products	原材料、燃料、动力购进价格指数 Raw Material Fuel and Power Purchading Price Indices	固定资产投资价格指数 Price Indices of Investment in Fixed Assets
1978	100.0	100.0	100.0	100.0			
1979	101.3	101.0	100.7	101.3			
1980	107.7	106.7	106.4	107.0			
1981	108.7	108.3	108.9	107.9			
1982	109.7	109.2	109.9	109.0			
1983	109.8	109.7	110.7	109.0			
1984	112.5	113.0	115.3	111.3			
1985	123.2	123.7	126.4	121.8			
1986	131.9	132.5	134.4	131.1			
1987	144.2	144.7	148.6	141.2			
1988	176.4	176.3	182.1	171.5			
1989	206.0	206.5	211.3	203.2			
1990	210.7	213.1	218.5	209.3	100.0	100.0	100.0
1991	220.9	223.5	235.3	213.3	103.2	107.0	104.5
1992	232.1	238.3	256.0	222.6	107.1	117.9	117.1
1993	269.0	281.7	303.9	261.2	126.9	148.2	162.6
1994	332.5	347.0	380.7	317.8	154.1	178.0	186.3
1995	380.1	401.8	442.4	366.5	176.0	208.8	200.1
1996	405.9	439.2	490.2	392.5	177.0	216.9	206.5
1997	403.1	446.7	496.6	400.3	173.3	212.4	204.9
1998	395.8	444.0	496.6	396.3	163.8	194.1	202.4
1999	383.5	438.2	489.6	391.6	157.4	183.3	199.0
2000	378.1	438.7	489.6	392.0	159.1	196.3	201.4
2001	373.9	442.2	490.1	397.8	157.7	195.3	203.0
2002	368.0	438.6	482.2	398.6	153.9	192.6	205.6
2003	367.3	443.0	486.5	403.4	157.4	205.2	214.4
2004	375.4	461.2	504.5	422.0	167.6	238.6	234.3
2005	376.5	470.9	514.6	432.1	171.9	256.8	236.4
2006	379.5	478.4	522.8	439.5	174.5	273.2	239.2

6-3 商品零售价格分类指数(2006年)
RETAIL PRICE INDICES BY CATEGORY OF COMMODITIES (2006)

上年=100 (preceding year=100)

类别	Item	全省 Provincial Indices	城市 Urban Indices	农村 Rural Indices
商品零售价格指数	**General Retail Price Index**	**100.8**	**100.5**	**101.3**
食品	Food	103.1	103.4	102.6
饮料烟酒	Beverages, Tobacco and Liquor	100.0	100.1	99.8
服装鞋帽	Garments, Shoes, Hats	100.7	100.9	100.0
纺织品	Textiles	100.2	100.1	100.5
中西药品	Chinese Traditional Medicine, Western Medicines	97.3	97.4	97.0
化妆品	Cosmetics	100.1	99.8	100.7
书报杂志	Books, Newspaper, Magazines	99.4	99.8	98.8
文化体育用品	Sports and Recreational Articals	96.9	96.3	98.7
日用品	Daily Use Sundry Articals	100.6	100.7	100.6
家用电器	Household Electric Appliance and Stereo	95.6	94.0	99.5
首饰	Gold, Silver and Pearls Jewelery	120.8	122.4	116.5
燃料	Fuels	112.2	111.8	113.3
建筑装璜材料	Building and Docrative Materials	104.5	105.4	103.5
机电产品	Mechanical and Electrical Products	108.0	108.5	107.1
农业生产资料类	**Means of Agricultural Production General Price Index**	101.7		
小农具	Small Farm Tools	102.4		
饲料	Forage Grass	97.3		
幼禽家畜	Young Livestock and Fowls	90.3		
半机械化农具	Semi-mechanized Farm Tools	130.4		
机械化农具	Mechanized Farm Machinery	100.9		
化学肥料	Chemical Fertilizer	99.7		
农药及农药械	Pesticide and Its Appliances	101.9		
化学农药	Chemical Pesticide	101.9		
农药械	Pasticide Appliances	101.1		
农机用油	Oil for Farm Machinery	114.3		
其他	Others	107.3		

6－4 居民消费价格分类指数（2006 年）
CONSUMER PRICE INDICES BY CATEGORY（2006）

上年＝100 （preceding year＝100）

类别	Item	全省 Provincial Indices	城市 Urban Indices	农村 Rural Indices
居民消费价格总指数	**General Consumer Price Index**	101.6	101.6	101.7
食品	Foods	102.6	102.7	102.6
粮食	Grain	103.5	103.7	103.1
淀粉及薯类	Starches and Tubers	100.7	97.1	105.3
干豆类及豆制品	Bean and Its Products	101.2	101.2	101.1
油脂	Oil or Fat	98.1	98.6	97.5
肉禽及其制品	Meat, Poultry Cheir Processing Products and	96.3	96.4	96.1
蛋	Eggs	95.2	94.1	96.8
水产品	Aquatic Products	103.8	103.5	104.3
菜	Vegetables	106.1	104.8	108.8
#鲜菜	Fresh Vegetables	106.0	104.6	108.7
调味品	Flavoring	100.9	101.0	100.8
糖	Sugar	116.2	113.1	119.7
茶及饮料	Tea and Beverages	100.6	100.8	100.4
干鲜瓜果	Dried and Fresh Fruits and Melons	119.6	117.0	124.6
#鲜果	Freshes Fruits	126.5	122.2	134.5
糕点饼干面包	Cake, Biscuit and Bread	101.0	100.9	101.1
奶及奶制品	Milk and Its Products	102.2	102.4	101.4
在外用膳食品	Out Ward Dinner	103.6	104.6	100.9
其它食品及食品加工服务	Others Foods, Foods Processing and Services	100.9	101.2	100.3
烟酒及用品	Tobacco, Liquor and Articals	99.9	99.7	100.1
烟草	Tobacco	99.3	99.3	99.3
酒	Liquor	100.8	100.4	101.2
吸烟饮酒用品	Smoking and Drinking Articals	100.6	100.9	99.9

6-4 续表 Continued

上年=100 (preceding year=100)

类别	Item	全省 Provincial Indices	城市 Urban Indices	农村 Rural Indices
衣着	Clothing	100.9	101.1	100.4
服装	Garments	100.6	100.6	100.5
衣着材料	Clothing Material	100.6	100.7	100.5
鞋袜帽	Shoes, Socks and Caps	101.3	102.0	99.9
衣着加工服务	Clothing Making Services	105.8	109.6	101.6
家庭设备用品及维修服务	Household Facilities and Articles	101.4	101.6	101.1
耐用消费品	Durable Consumer Goods	101.5	101.5	101.6
室内装饰品	Interior Decorations	101.1	101.0	101.4
床上用品	Bed Articles	99.9	100.0	99.7
家庭日用杂品	Daily Use Household Articles	100.8	101.0	100.4
家庭服务及加工维修服务	Household Services, Processing and Repairing Services	103.7	104.4	101.4
医疗保健和个人用品	Medicine and Medical Articles	101.5	101.2	102.0
医疗保健	Medicine and Healthcare	100.3	99.8	101.2
个人用品及服务	Individual Articals and Services	104.1	104.3	103.6
交通和通讯	Transportation and Communication	99.6	98.7	101.6
交通	Transportation	102.9	102.4	104.1
通信	Communication	96.1	94.2	99.4
娱乐教育文化用品及服务	Recreation, Education and Culture Articles and Services	99.3	99.6	98.8
文娱用耐用消费品及服务	Durable Consumer Goods for Recreational Use and Services	90.4	88.0	95.6
教育	Education	100.7	102.1	98.7
文化娱乐用品	Cultural and Recreational Articals	102.1	102.7	100.9
旅游及外出	Tour and External Business	103.1	103.3	102.5
居住	Housing Condition	104.5	104.7	104.1
建房及装修材料	Building and Docorative Material	105.3	106.7	103.8
租房	Rent	101.6	101.2	102.3
自有住房	Housing	102.3	102.2	102.4
水、电、燃料	Water, Electricity and Fuels	104.6	104.3	105.2

6－5 工业品出厂价格指数
EX－FACTORY PRICE INDICES OF INDUSTRIAL PRODUCTS

上年＝100 (preceding year＝100)

分组名称	Group Name	1995	2000	2004	2005	2006
工业品出厂价格总指数	**General Ex-Factory Price Indices of Industrial Products**	**114.2**	**101.1**	**106.5**	**102.6**	**101.5**
轻工业	Light Industry	117.4	97.9	102.5	100.3	100.4
以农产品为原料	Using Farm Products as Raw Materials	118.5	97.1	105.7	100.9	101.5
以非农产品为原料	Using Non-Farm Products as Raw Materials	115.6	99.5	100.9	100.1	99.7
重工业	Heavy Industry	110.7	102.8	111.7	105.4	102.7
采　掘	Mining and Quarrying	109.8	102.2	136.9	121.6	101.8
原　料	Raw Materials	113.2	110.9	115.6	109.7	103.2
加　工	Manufacturing	108.9	96.7	108.2	102.1	102.5
生产资料	Means of Production	113.1	103.0	107.9	103.2	101.7
采　掘	Mining and Quarrying	109.7	101.9	139.0	121.9	101.0
原　料	Raw Materials	116.3	110.8	114.6	108.9	102.9
加　工	Manufacturing	110.6	97.3	105.0	100.9	101.4
生活资料	Consumer Goods	115.4	96.6	102.0	100.5	100.5
食　品	Food	126.2	89.6	104.3	99.9	101.0
衣　着	Clothing	115.7	100.9	102.0	102.9	101.3
一般日用品	Daily-Use Articles	112.4	98.5	102.1	101.2	100.6
耐用消费品	Durable Consumer Goods	100.6	95.6	98.3	98.2	99.1

6－6 分行业工业品出厂价格指数
EX－FACTORY PRICE INDICES OF INDUSTRIAL PRODUCTS BY SECTOR

上年＝100 (preceding year＝100)

部门名称	Group Name	1995	2000	2004	2005	2006
冶金工业	Metallurgical Industry	100.3	104.1	119.9	103.5	101.8
电力工业	Power Industry	111.6	106.1	103.8	106.0	99.7
煤炭及炼焦工业	Coal Industry	111.2	94.0	138.9	116.1	95.1
石油工业	Petroleum Industry	119.1	144.4	114.9	119.6	118.1
化学工业	Chemical Industry	124.0	105.2	110.4	105.8	101.7
机械工业	Machine Building Industry	104.9	95.8	99.6	100.0	100.8
建筑材料工业	Building Materials Industry	107.2	99.2	106.4	95.4	101.2
森林工业	Timber Industry	99.6	97.1	103.1	103.0	102.1
食品工业	Food Industry	126.2	89.4	107.6	99.6	100.7
纺织工业	Textile Industry	119.2	101.8	106.1	101.5	102.0
缝纫工业	Tailoring Industry	103.4	102.0	102.0	103.3	101.3
皮革工业	Leather Industry	120.0	102.5	101.9	101.5	100.6
造纸工业	Paper Industry	137.7	104.9	101.4	101.8	101.7
文教艺术用品工业	Cultural, Educational and Handicrafts Articles	111.0	103.4	102.1	102.2	101.3
其他工业	Others	140.1	102.6	101.9	100.8	100.7

6-7 原材料、燃料、动力购进价格指数
RAW MATERIAL, FUEL, POWER PURCHASING PRICE INDICES

上年=100 (preceding year=100)

分组名称	Group Name	1995	2000	2004	2005	2006
总指数	**General Index**	**117.3**	**107.1**	**116.3**	**107.6**	**106.4**
燃料动力类	Fuels Power	107.7	112.4	114.4	113.2	111.1
黑色金属材料类	Ferrous Metal	96.0	105.4	121.5	106.7	95.9
有色金属材料和电线类	Non-Ferrous Metal and Wire	124.5	109.9	132.0	120.4	133.2
化工原料类	Chemical Materials	131.7	121.1	118.2	109.8	102.5
木材及纸浆类	Timber and Pulp	124.8	98.6	102.0	103.3	103.8
建筑材料及非金属矿类	Construction Materials and Non-Metal Mining Industry	110.8	97.9	110.0	94.2	96.3
其他工业原材料、半成品类	Other Industrial Raw Materials and Semi-Finished Products		102.1	109.1	105.4	103.3
农副产品类	Farm and Sideline Products	131.9	98.0	121.9	97.4	102.8
纺织原料类	Textile Raw Materials	125.7	100.8	106.3	102.4	105.7

6-8 固定资产投资价格指数
PRICE INDICES OF INVESTMENT IN FIXED ASSETS

上年=100 (preceding year=100)

项目	Item	1995	2000	2004	2005	2006
固定资产投资	**Fixed Assets Investment**	**107.4**	**101.2**	**109.3**	**100.9**	**101.2**
建筑安装工程	Construction and Installation	107.1	102.4	113.9	99.6	100.8
设备、器具	Equipments Tools and Instruments	105.3	97.8	100.5	100.5	100.8
其他费用	Others	113.8	102.6	107.8	106.5	103.5

主要统计指标解释

商品零售价格指数 是反映城乡商品零售价格变动趋势的一种经济指数。零售物价的调整变动直接影响到城乡居民的生活支出和国家的财政收入，影响居民购买力和市场供需平衡，影响消费与积累的比例。因此，计算零售价格指数，可以从一个侧面对上述经济活动进行观察和分析。

居民消费价格指数 是反映一定时期内城乡居民所购买的生活消费品价格和服务项目价格变动趋势和程度的相对数，是对城市居民消费价格指数和农村居民消费价格指数进行综合汇总计算的结果。利用居民消费价格指数，可以观察和分析消费品的零售价格和服务价格变动对城乡居民实际生活费支出的影响程度。

城市居民消费价格指数 是反映城市居民家庭所购买的生活消费品价格和服务项目价格变动趋势和程度的相对数。城市居民消费价格指数可以观察和分析消费品的零售价格和服务项目价格变动对职工货币工资的影响，作为研究职工生活和确定工资政策的依据。

农村居民消费价格指数 是反映农村居民家庭所购买的生活消费品价格和服务项目价格变动趋势和程度的相对数。农村居民消费价格指数可以观察农村消费品的零售价格和服务项目价格变动对农村居民生活消费支出的影响，直接反映农民生活水平的实际变化情况，为分析和研究农村居民生活问题提供依据。

工业品出厂价格指数 是反映全部工业产品出厂价格总水平的变动趋势和程度的相对数，包括工业企业售给本企业以外所有单位的各种产品和直接售给居民用于生活消费的产品。通过工业品出厂价格指数能观察出厂价格变动对工业总产值的影响程度。

固定资产投资价格指数 是反映固定资产投资价格变动趋势和程度的相对数。固定资产投资额是由建筑安装工程投资完成额、设备、工器具购置投资完成额和其他费用投资完成额三部分组成的。编制固定资产投资价格指数应首先分别编制上述三部分投资的价格指数，然后采用加权算术平均法求出固定资产投资价格总指数。

编制固定资产投资价格指数可以准确地反映固定资产投资中涉及的各类商品和取费项目价格变动趋势和变动幅度，消除按现价计算的固定资产投资指标中的价格变动因素，真实地反映固定资产投资的规模、速度、结构和效益，为国家科学地制定、检查固定资产投资计划并提高宏观调控水平，为完善国民经济核算体系提供科学的、可靠的依据。

Explanatory Notes on Main Statistical Indicators

Retail Price Index reflects the general change in retail prices of commodities. The change and adjustment in retail prices directly affect the living expenditure of urban and rural residents, government revenue, purchasing power of residents and the equilibrium of market supply and demand, and the ratio of consumption to accumulation. Therefore, the calculation of retail price index is useful to analyze the changes of the above economic activities.

Consumer Price Index reflects the trend and(degree of changes in prices of consumer goods and services purchased by urban and rural residents, and is a composite index derived from the urban consumer price index and the rural consumler price index. Consumer price index can be used to analyze the impact of consumer price change on actual expenditure for living cost of urban and rural residents.

Urban Consumer Price Index reflects the trend and degree of changes in prices of consumer goods and services purchased by urban households. It can be used to observe and analyze the impact of price changes in consumer goods and services on money wages ot staff and workers, and provide basis for policy making concerning the living cost and wages of staff and workers.

Rural Consumer Price Index reflects the trend and degree of changes in prices of consumer goods and services purchased by rural households. It can be used to observe the impact of change in retail prices of consumer goods and service prices in rural areas on living expenditure of rural households, and to show the changes in the living standard of peasants. It provides basis for analysis and research on condition of life in rural areas.

Ex-factory Price Index of Industrial Products reflects the trend and degree of changes in general ex-factory prices of all industrial products, including sales of industrial products by an industrial enterprise to all units outside the enterprise, as well as sales of consumer goods to residents. It can be used to analyze the impact of ex-factory prices on gross industrial output value.

Price Index of Investment in Fixed Assets reflects the trend and degree of changes in prices of investment in fixed assets. The investment in fixed assets consists of three components. namely the investment in construction and installation, the investment in purchases of equipment and instrument, and the investment in other items. Price index of investment in fixed assets is calculated as the weighted arithmetic mean of the price indices of the three components of investment in fixed assets, Removing the factor of price change in the aggregates of investment at current prices, this indicator shows the changes in the prices of commodities and fees involved in the investment of fixed assets, and can be used to observe the actual size, growth, structure, and efficiency of investment in fixed assets and provides reliable and scientific data for government planning, management, decision making, and further improving the current national accounting system.

JIANGSU STATISTICAL YEARBOOK

第7篇

农 业

AGRICULTURE

7-1 农村基层组织和农业基本情况
BASIC CONDITIONS OF RURAL GRASSROOT UNITS AND AGRICULTURE

指标	Item	1990	1995	2000	2005	2006
农村组织情况 （个）	**Rural Units (unit)**					
乡个数	Township	1452	1046	280	114	110
镇个数	Town	598	936	1202	1036	1007
村委会个数	Village Committees	36130	35982	33259	18282	17605
村民小组个数	Villager Group	340198	341984	331120	265730	263120
乡村户数、人口	**Households, Rural Population**					
乡村户数 （万户）	Households (10000 units)	1508.15	1516.85	1496.27	1505.88	1495.50
乡村人口 （万人）	Population (10000 persons)	5361.80	5321.01	5150.59	5063.25	5014.97
乡村劳动力合计 （万人）	**Rural Laborers (10000 persons)**	**2786.86**	**2773.04**	**2688.03**	**2662.50**	**2656.80**
按性别分	Grouped by Sex					
男	Male	1440.65	1424.43	1382.49	1384.61	1383.51
女	Female	1346.21	1348.61	1305.54	1277.89	1273.29
按行业分	Grouped by Sector					
农林牧渔业	Farming, Forestry, Animal Husbandry, Fishery	1714.49	1541.33	1480.22	1058.28	981.37
#农业	Farming	1536.12	1326.54	1270.58	885.40	829.36
工业	Industry	520.73	531.78	436.81	598.52	648.30
建筑业	Construction	196.25	227.39	252.02	316.38	332.73
交通运输、仓储业和邮电通讯业	Transportation, Storage, Post and Telecommunication	70.90	92.33	89.06	107.76	111.56

7－1　续表　Continued

指　　标	Item	1990	1995	2000	2005	2006
批发、零售贸易业、餐饮业	Wholesale, Retail Sales, Food Service	50.49	73.04	104.81	156.12	168.44
金融、保险业	Banking and Insurance	1.69	2.11	2.50	5.88	6.18
房地产、社会服务业	Real Estate, Social Services	11.08	15.61	22.78	37.24	37.87
卫生、体育、社会福利业	Healthcare, Sports, Social Welfare	10.21	9.69	10.24	11.19	11.46
教育、文化、艺术和广播电视事业	Education, Culture, Arts and Radio, Film, Television	18.40	15.50	14.13	14.43	14.87
科学研究和综合技术服务事业	Scientific Research and Ploytechnical Services	1.73	2.00	2.07	3.04	2.31
乡经济组织管理	Rural Economic Management	12.49	17.37	15.87	12.46	11.82
其他	Others	178.40	244.89	257.52	341.20	329.89
年末实有耕地面积（千公顷）	Cultivated Areas (Year-end) (1000 hectares)	4557.86	4448.31	5008.39	4780.37	4743.00
农业机械总动力（万千瓦）	Total Agricultural Machinery Power (10000 kW)	2004.77	2226.95	2925.29	3135.33	3278.53
化肥施用量（万吨）	Consumption of Chemical Fertilizers (10000 tons)	221.79	292.77	335.45	340.81	342.01
农村用电量（亿千瓦小时）	Electricity Consumed in Rural Areas (100 million kWh)	105.26	238.16	314.60	825.10	1011.79
农作物总播种面积（千公顷）	Total Sown Area (1000 hectares)	8259.18	7909.01	7944.87	7641.20	7608.80
#粮　食	Grain Crops	6363.02	5755.15	5304.31	4909.48	4985.08
主要农产品产量（万吨）	Volume of Major Agricultural Products (10000 tons)					
粮　食	Grain Crops	3264.15	3286.30	3106.63	2834.59	3041.44
棉　花	Cotton Crops	46.42	56.16	31.45	32.27	38.14
油　料	Oil-Bearing Crops	112.39	159.46	225.65	215.99	218.18
肉类产量	Output of Meat	179.02	231.85	328.87	352.34	351.38
水产品产量	Output of Aquatic Products	118.25	219.47	308.79	388.66	405.05

7－2 主要年份耕地面积
AREAS UNDER CULTIVATION OF THE MAJOR

单位:千公顷 (1000 hectares)

年份 Year	年末实有耕地面积 Cultivated Areas (year end)	水田 Paddy Fields	旱地 Dry Fields	年内减少 Decrease in Cultivated Area in the year	#国家基建占地 Capital Construction	人均占有耕地(平方米) Percapita Cultivated(sq. m) 按乡村人口计算 By Rural Population	按农林牧渔业劳动力计算 By Farming, Forestry, Animal Hus-bandry, Fishery Laborers
1949	5523.40	2199.60	3323.80			1846.68	
1952	5808.47	2273.47	3535.00			1820.00	3580.12
1957	5825.20	2545.13	3280.07			1633.34	3960.02
1962	5016.20	2161.33	2854.87			1360.01	3473.35
1965	4947.47	2225.93	2721.54			1246.67	3073.35
1970	4820.63	2509.13	2311.50			1033.34	2480.01
1975	4705.53	2484.83	2220.70	23.00	13.39	946.67	2340.01
1976	4689.37	2831.34	1858.03	24.53	17.53	933.34	2293.34
1977	4672.79	2797.36	1875.43	21.81	15.05	920.00	2313.34
1978	4660.79	2743.14	1917.65	20.20	14.60	913.34	2293.34
1979	4650.40	2781.79	1868.61	18.67	13.20	920.00	2360.01
1980	4641.38	2788.62	1852.76	15.27	10.73	913.34	2380.01
1981	4637.01	2775.35	1861.66	11.67	5.67	900.00	2340.01
1982	4631.21	2755.59	1875.62	14.12	4.80	893.34	2326.68
1983	4630.05	2769.02	1861.03	7.67	5.24	893.34	2306.68
1984	4621.09	2837.99	1783.10	15.80	7.13	886.67	2353.35
1985	4604.03	2804.58	1799.45	21.40	5.87	886.67	2700.01
1986	4590.79	2780.11	1810.68	18.59	7.31	893.34	2793.35
1987	4579.81	2770.17	1809.64	18.19	6.21	886.67	2826.68
1988	4568.84	2767.73	1801.11	12.73	5.91	886.67	2820.01
1989	4562.32	2775.97	1786.35	10.43	4.64	886.67	2713.35
1990	4557.86	2804.13	1753.73	8.78	4.63	853.34	2660.01
1991	4549.97	2840.85	1709.12	11.15	4.80	846.67	2613.35
1992	4521.77	2836.81	1684.96	30.96	13.02	840.00	2673.35
1993	4495.66	2711.40	1784.26	28.83	8.71	840.00	2766.68
1994	4464.00	2658.08	1805.92	33.02	11.98	833.34	2806.68
1995	4448.31	2669.68	1778.63	23.69	11.74	833.34	2886.68
1996	5061.70	3065.60	1996.10	16.21	10.58	954.13	3307.87
1997	5055.67	3110.80	1944.87	16.58	9.41	954.42	3298.93
1998	5036.54	3138.96	1897.58	27.08	17.62	960.22	3288.72
1999	5024.22	3164.01	1860.21	18.26	10.26	967.19	3338.33
2000	5008.39	3145.97	1862.42	21.15	7.10	972.39	3383.54
2001	4974.12	3151.79	1822.33	39.87	16.66	966.91	3424.99
2002	4905.02	3098.00	1807.02	78.77	25.95	957.01	3622.19
2003	4858.34	3060.80	1797.54	66.31	25.71	954.70	3948.04
2004	4795.19	2980.60	1814.59	85.67	27.15	944.35	4225.39
2005	4780.37	2981.12	1799.25	32.67	16.18	944.13	4517.11
2006	4743.00	2957.81	1785.19	63.24	26.90	945.77	4833.04

注:1996年及以后为农业普查接轨数(下同)。

Note: Since 1996, the relative targers were in line with the data of agricultural gereral survey (the same as the following tables).

7－3 农村社会总产值
GROSS OUTPUT VALUE OF RURAL AREAS

单位:亿元 (100 million yuan)

年份 Year	农村社会总产值 Gross Output of Rural Areas	农林牧渔业 Farming, Forestry, Animal Husbandry, Firshery	工业 Industry	建筑业 Construction	运输业 Transportation	批发、零售贸易业、餐饮业 Wholesale, Retail Sale and Catering Services
1978	183.97	105.87	62.43	5.81	2.56	7.30
1980	274.13	138.45	109.33	14.55	3.09	8.71
1985	775.71	288.55	385.54	60.75	19.45	21.42
1989	1872.41	522.25	1113.84	136.05	46.82	53.45
1990	2072.69	580.53	1251.95	133.99	48.27	57.95
1991	2312.06	580.93	1467.37	149.99	50.45	63.32
1992	3516.37	673.82	2463.26	203.63	69.42	106.24
1993	5650.77	875.37	4192.94	300.79	103.49	178.18
1994	8277.73	1335.23	6099.06	382.14	160.28	301.02
1995	10567.60	1686.78	7703.25	498.77	229.84	448.96
1996	10283.46	1693.76	7182.91	554.88	280.74	571.17
1997	11174.08	1816.37	7856.85	560.12	291.97	648.77
1998	11888.17	1849.20	8438.69	571.95	315.60	712.73
1999	12932.64	1837.43	9352.90	622.96	346.84	772.51
2000	14196.79	1869.73	10437.50	667.72	375.89	845.95
2001	15430.92	1956.10	11387.67	730.43	417.35	939.37
2002	17607.05	1779.07	13374.63	828.82	457.88	1166.65
2003	20911.01	1952.20	15910.74	1050.97	541.31	1455.79
2004	25969.12	2417.63	19938.54	1210.63	615.03	1787.29
2005	32223.24	2576.98	25118.33	1497.00	753.81	2277.12
2006	39916.69	2707.06	31668.73	1779.59	884.20	2877.11

7－4 农村社会总产值指数
RELATED INDICES OF GROSS OUTPUT VALUE OF RURAL AREAS

按可比价格计算,1978 = 100 (At comparable price 1978 = 100)

年份 Year	农村社会总产值 Gross Output of Rural Areas	农林牧渔业 Farming, Forestry, Animal Husbandry, Firshery	工业 Industry	建筑业 Construction	运输业 Transportation	批发、零售贸易业、餐饮业 Wholesale, Retail Sale and Catering Services
1978	100.0	100.0	100.0	100.0	100.0	100.0
1980	127.8	104.8	174.0	214.8	103.5	102.4
1985	317.6	165.3	604.8	787.7	571.7	221.0
1989	662.6	193.7	1498.1	1441.8	1124.8	450.8
1990	682.4	198.6	1683.9	1397.4	1141.2	480.9
1991	780.9	196.4	2011.0	1578.4	1205.3	531.0
1992	1212.8	221.9	3476.9	2191.4	1693.6	909.8
1993	1837.3	247.0	5650.0	3051.4	2380.2	1438.4
1994	2537.5	276.8	8065.8	3655.5	3475.8	2291.5
1995	3081.3	314.6	9774.8	4538.2	4740.9	3250.8
1996	3663.7	337.9	11868.0	4884.2	5602.1	4000.9
1997	4172.0	363.8	13660.1	5157.0	6095.1	4753.1
1998	4641.6	378.3	15285.7	5597.9	7003.8	5551.9
1999	5286.4	397.8	17275.2	6398.9	8006.0	6215.9
2000	5746.9	417.8	18893.6	6790.8	8590.7	6739.4
2001	6290.3	436.8	20737.1	7481.5	9606.2	7536.9
2002	7328.8	453.4	24395.9	8559.6	10626.4	9437.9
2003	8520.5	458.1	28453.7	10628.1	12301.3	11532.0
2004	9895.1	494.0	33480.5	11445.1	13066.1	13235.5
2005	11965.0	512.3	41109.5	13791.4	15605.9	16432.8
2006	14938.3	537.5	51880.2	16519.7	18585.5	20920.8

7-5 主要年份农林牧渔业总产值(当年价格)

GROSS OUTPUT VALUE OF FARMING, FORESTRY, ANIMAL HUSBANDRY AND FISHERY

当年价格:亿元 (At current price, 100 million yuan)

年份 Year	农林牧渔业总产值 Gross Outprt Value of FFAF	农业 Farming	林业 Foresty	畜牧业 Animal Husbandry	渔业 Fishery	农林牧渔服务业 Service Industry for Farming, Forestry, Animal Husbandry and Fishery
1949	22.59	19.41	…	3.02	0.16	
1952	31.87	26.14	0.03	5.00	0.70	
1957	36.81	30.10	0.22	5.25	1.24	
1962	40.15	34.19	0.32	4.48	1.16	
1965	57.27	47.02	0.63	8.25	1.37	
1970	71.33	57.08	0.85	11.76	1.64	
1975	91.66	72.17	1.47	15.55	2.47	
1976	100.71	82.53	1.31	14.86	2.01	
1977	89.16	73.05	1.25	12.90	1.96	
1978	105.87	85.17	1.48	16.78	2.44	
1979	145.25	114.26	2.03	25.77	3.19	
1980	138.45	105.98	1.94	26.65	3.88	
1981	153.62	119.90	2.00	27.11	4.61	
1982	188.11	145.69	1.96	35.80	4.66	
1983	206.86	160.38	3.30	36.66	6.52	
1984	253.82	193.28	4.33	47.17	9.04	
1985	288.55	201.85	4.63	66.54	15.53	
1986	332.66	235.07	5.15	69.83	22.61	
1987	380.25	257.90	6.02	87.95	28.38	
1988	497.95	310.20	7.29	140.49	39.97	
1989	522.25	325.02	7.02	148.13	42.08	
1990	580.53	362.46	7.94	160.78	49.35	
1991	580.93	354.42	7.55	168.30	50.66	
1992	673.82	411.33	9.93	188.64	63.92	
1993	875.37	518.55	14.61	236.81	105.40	
1994	1335.23	777.94	18.38	390.70	148.21	
1995	1686.78	986.15	21.42	475.67	203.54	
1996	1693.76	1062.39	23.48	368.54	239.35	
1997	1816.37	1085.26	22.56	430.57	277.98	
1998	1849.20	1096.88	24.16	435.51	292.65	
1999	1837.43	1095.13	26.13	413.95	302.22	
2000	1869.73	1096.02	30.17	430.53	313.01	
2001	1956.10	1142.66	30.76	448.51	334.17	
2002	2011.48	1165.49	36.29	456.02	353.68	
2003	1952.20	981.25	31.49	458.87	371.56	109.03
2004	2417.63	1242.41	40.16	563.44	449.47	122.15
2005	2576.98	1291.06	45.27	599.14	511.86	129.65
2006	2707.06	1389.61	54.25	571.43	552.21	139.57

注:从2003年开始农林牧渔业总产值执行新的国民经济行业分类标准,调出农业产值中的农民家庭兼营商品性工业产值,调入农林牧渔服务业产值,且现行价格正式使用生产价格调查数据,故2003年农林牧渔业总产值数据有所下降,如都按新口径计算2003年农林牧渔业现价总产值则比上年增长9.7%。

Nate: Sine 2003, the total output value of farming, forestry, animal husbandry and fishery is counted with new classified standard of the national economy. The output value of commercialized handicraft products, as the farmer's household sideline, is transferred out from the output value of agriculture and put into the output value of service industry serving for farming, forestry, animal husbandry and fishery. Moreover, the current price is formery used by the production price of investigated data, the current total output value of agricuture of 2003 is some what decreased. But if the data are all counted with new bore, the total output value of agriculture of 2003 (current priee) has an increase of 9.7% over the previous year.

7-6 主要年份农林牧渔业总产值指数

INDICES OF GROSS OUTPUT VALUE OF FARMING, FORESTRY, ANIMAL HUSBANDRY AND FISHERY

按可比价格计算，1949＝100 (At comparable price 1949 = 100)

年份 Year	农林牧渔业总产值 Total	农业 Farming	林业 Forestry	畜牧业 Animal Husbandry	渔业 Fishery	农林牧渔服务业 Farming, Forestry, Animal Husbandry, Fishery and Service Industry
1949	100.0	100.0		100.0	100.0	
1952	144.2	135.7	100.0	166.5	612.2	
1957	157.4	151.4	900.0	159.0	563.4	
1962	134.7	134.1	1387.5	106.8	407.3	
1965	201.4	190.7	2162.5	224.6	534.1	
1970	239.7	232.5	1487.5	255.0	575.6	
1975	294.7	281.6	2487.5	322.3	819.5	
1976	306.2	296.1	3012.5	301.1	773.2	
1977	275.4	264.9	2987.0	280.1	787.8	
1978	334.6	326.8	2525.0	323.9	778.0	
1979	371.1	354.7	2650.0	426.8	858.5	
1980	350.7	326.0	2637.5	435.8	1014.6	
1981	378.4	357.7	2512.5	432.6	1170.7	
1982	434.8	404.2	2662.5	535.6	1231.7	
1983	460.6	433.3	2950.0	525.9	1226.8	
1984	536.3	460.6	3475.0	621.5	1522.0	
1985	553.1	456.1	3750.0	727.9	1922.0	
1986	587.7	486.4	3650.0	732.5	2592.7	
1987	605.9	502.4	3825.0	741.1	2802.4	
1988	646.1	526.3	3587.5	847.5	3051.2	
1989	648.3	529.4	3387.5	843.1	3102.4	
1990	664.6	535.2	3300.5	899.3	3346.3	
1991	657.1	513.3	2971.7	946.3	3385.3	
1992	742.5	583.6	3538.2	1045.7	3913.7	
1993	826.4	619.6	4391.5	1191.6	5275.3	
1994	926.3	668.9	4936.8	1400.2	6278.5	
1995	1052.7	755.4	5774.3	1551.0	7785.4	
1996	1130.6	821.0	6204.0	1599.2	8707.8	
1997	1217.1	873.5	5746.0	1773.5	9532.8	
1998	1265.6	899.4	6313.9	1847.5	10219.7	
1999	1331.1	952.4	6312.3	1911.5	10883.6	
2000	1397.9	981.6	7566.8	2055.1	11688.1	
2001	1461.5	1030.6	7500.2	2103.9	12474.9	
2002	1516.9	1053.8	8681.6	2186.3	13475.4	100.0
2003	1532.8	994.0	10415.4	2248.1	14369.5	130.0
2004	1653.0	1131.5	11389.9	2196.7	15768.3	139.1
2005	1714.2	1143.9	12245.5	2275.4	17448.0	144.6
2006	1798.2	1205.6	14168.0	2302.7	18634.5	153.3

注：2005年起，农林牧渔业及分农、林、牧、渔四业产值的增长速度计算方法由按90不变价计算改为按价格指数缩减法计算。

Note: Since 2005, the calculating method of growth rate for gross output value of fovrming, faestry, animal husbandry and fishery (FFAF) and output value of above four industries (FFAF detailed respectively) was changed from comparable price of 1990 to retrenching price indicies of 2005.

7-7 农林牧渔业分项产值

GROSS OUTPUT VALUE OF FARMING, FORESTRY, ANIMAL HUSBANDRY AND FISHERY BY BRANCH

单位:亿元 (100 million yuan)

指标	Item	总产值(当年价) Gross Output Value (current price)		总产值(1990年不变价) Gross Output Value (1990 fixed price)	
		2005	2006	2005	2006
农林牧渔业总产值	**Total**	**2576.98**	**2707.06**	**1142.55**	**1183.85**
农业产值	Farming	1291.06	1389.61	492.13	514.91
谷物及其他作物	Planting	722.50	764.45	282.05	299.47
#谷 物	Cereal	495.04	522.52	181.90	195.57
薯 类	Tubers	28.41	30.61	2.82	2.75
豆 类	Beans	24.16	22.56	9.16	9.80
棉 花	Cotton	57.31	66.41	23.29	27.90
油 料	Oil-Bearing Crops	64.06	68.62	32.02	32.45
蔬菜园艺作物	Vegetables, Gardening Crops	454.17	499.15	156.86	159.55
#蔬菜(含菜用瓜)	Vegetable(include mealons)	391.98	433.48	121.03	122.81
水果、坚果、饮料和香料作物	Fresh Fruits, Nuts, Beverage and Perfume Crops	100.04	111.27	43.03	45.22
#水果、坚果(含果用瓜)	Fresh Fruits, Nuts (include melons)	87.70	96.51	42.27	44.37
中药材	Chinese Herbal Midicine	14.35	14.75	10.19	10.66
林业产值	Forestry	45.27	54.25	19.45	22.05
林木的培育和种植	Afforestation	29.68	34.25	8.17	9.09
竹木采运	Cutting and Transportation of Bamboos and Timber	6.66	10.67	4.15	5.56
林产品	Forest Products	8.93	9.32	7.13	7.40
牧业产值	Animal Husbandry	599.14	571.43	304.53	306.33
牲畜饲养	Animal Raising	54.43	59.43	19.38	19.40
#牛	Cattle and Buffaloes	7.13	7.53	2.15	2.04
羊	Sheep and Goats	29.24	32.62	8.65	8.70
猪的饲养	Hogs Raising	240.53	200.94	104.55	104.66
家禽饲养	Poultry Raising	239.50	235.53	145.39	145.92
#肉 禽	Live Animal and Poultry Products	116.18	115.41	58.93	58.06
禽 蛋	Poultry and Eggs	121.73	118.10	84.47	85.61
狩猎和捕捉动物	Hunting	1.87	2.14	1.52	1.65
其他畜牧业	Other Animal Husbandry	62.81	73.38	33.69	34.70
渔业产值	Fishery	511.86	552.21	268.10	278.74
海水产品	Seawater Aquatic Products	123.76	140.19	56.53	59.57
内陆水域水产品	Freshwater Aquatic Products	388.10	412.01	211.57	219.17
农林牧渔服务业产值	Output Value of Service Industry Serving for Farming, Forestry, Animal Husbandry, and Fishery	129.65	139.57	58.34	61.82

7－8 农作物播种面积
TOTAL SOWN AREAS OF FARM CROPS

单位：千公顷 (1000 hectares)

年份 Year	总播种面积 Total Sown Areas	粮食作物 Grain Crops	#小麦 Wheat	#稻谷 Rice	#薯类 Tubers	#玉米 Corn	#大豆 Soybeans
1978	8582.74	6310.93	1412.82	2661.18	478.29	445.01	345.36
1980	8248.93	6090.25	1519.47	2676.15	332.02	386.21	236.47
1985	8557.84	6432.44	2170.39	2431.11	282.45	659.62	317.93
1989	8384.33	6454.51	2353.54	2419.67	248.16	501.15	309.39
1990	8259.18	6363.02	2399.19	2454.44	221.65	461.01	244.67
1991	8091.70	6202.77	2364.93	2351.40	214.51	426.44	177.81
1992	8234.63	6180.77	2366.23	2447.27	192.59	421.14	192.28
1993	8032.29	6029.66	2281.66	2278.44	201.00	472.37	270.67
1994	7861.76	5748.78	2114.26	2168.36	179.46	458.95	255.41
1995	7909.01	5755.15	2150.35	2250.31	166.71	461.98	201.32
1996	7914.10	5877.42	2216.26	2335.91	180.59	467.83	179.49
1997	7966.78	5994.43	2341.37	2377.62	169.61	439.00	217.44
1998	8058.28	5946.26	2314.95	2369.70	162.67	473.49	220.83
1999	8023.43	5828.52	2251.70	2398.45	156.89	454.31	210.41
2000	7944.87	5304.31	1954.60	2203.46	158.26	423.16	249.19
2001	7777.42	4886.66	1712.81	2010.25	146.01	429.81	244.37
2002	7797.40	4882.58	1715.85	1982.05	143.75	436.53	243.44
2003	7681.49	4659.47	1620.45	1840.93	134.20	451.90	241.68
2004	7668.98	4774.59	1601.17	2112.90	114.17	389.11	216.42
2005	7641.20	4909.48	1684.44	2209.33	100.16	370.24	214.80
2006	7608.80	4985.08	1734.87	2234.35	90.03	378.74	214.27

7－8 续表 Continued

单位：千公顷 (1000 hectares)

年份 Year	经济作物 Economic Crops	#棉花 Cotton	#油菜籽 Rape-seeds	#花生 Peanuts	#芝麻 Sesame	#黄红麻 Jute and Ambary	#甘蔗 Sugar-cane	#甜菜 Beet-roots	#烤烟 Flue-Cured Tobacco	其他作物 Others
1978	905.84	589.99	156.46	65.49	10.60	20.71	0.75	6.91	7.05	1365.97
1980	957.04	631.00	169.58	83.79	4.61	11.51	0.35	5.78	2.17	1201.64
1985	1302.77	592.24	442.64	134.11	12.85	24.78	4.11	4.39	3.47	822.63
1989	1194.62	535.19	459.12	116.39	6.29	5.14	3.92	2.09	9.47	735.20
1990	1188.41	572.13	440.81	108.71	5.85	5.16	3.35	2.23	5.63	707.75
1991	1202.48	550.61	482.80	102.95	4.79	4.57	3.18	0.73	5.16	686.45
1992	1350.29	673.43	483.78	107.36	7.14	3.99	3.83	0.70	7.39	703.57
1993	1143.39	517.65	458.30	125.42	8.65	5.20	5.50	1.31	2.02	859.24
1994	1225.86	534.57	516.59	146.52	6.65	2.15	4.57	0.70	0.87	887.12
1995	1268.75	564.90	530.66	148.66	7.54	1.31	3.95	0.17	1.17	885.11
1996	1132.24	485.91	498.00	123.55	9.19	0.89	3.66	0.87	1.44	904.44
1997	1063.10	438.74	473.93	117.25	13.66	0.79	3.46	1.51	2.61	909.25
1998	1063.32	416.16	468.94	141.39	16.23	0.54	3.25	0.52	0.09	1048.70
1999	1006.41	261.99	518.83	177.25	20.62	0.41	4.20	0.15	0.01	1188.50
2000	1227.97	295.27	650.50	227.90	18.20	0.20	5.16	0.07	0.02	1412.59
2001	1347.53	383.99	681.04	230.21	15.53	0.36	5.75	0.40	…	1543.23
2002	1255.19	311.35	668.08	223.63	15.00	0.32	6.08	0.38	…	1659.63
2003	1315.37	369.50	683.03	214.52	12.70	0.31	5.98	0.29	…	1706.65
2004	1356.65	409.62	689.86	218.59	11.91	0.16	4.89	0.12	…	1537.74
2005	1237.36	368.27	660.50	174.29	11.92	0.18	4.10	0.02		1494.36
2006	1187.47	354.85	608.57	191.73	11.38	0.04	3.64	0.02		1436.25

7－9 主要农作物播种面积和产量(2006 年)

TOTAL SOWN AREAS OF FARM CROPS AND OUTPUT (2006)

指标	Item	播种面积（千公顷）Sown Areas (1000 hectares)	单位面积产量（千克/公顷）Per hectare Output (kg)	总产量（吨）Total Output (ton)
农作物总播种面积	**Total Swon Areas of Farm Crops**	**7608.80**		
粮食大豆总计	**Total Grain and Soybeans**	**4985.08**	**6101**	**30414400**
夏　粮	Summer Grain	2046.05	4590	9391370
小　麦	Wheat	1734.87	4714	8178151
元　麦	Hull-less Barley	6.62	3704	24522
大　麦	Barley	198.99	4498	895057
蚕豌豆	Broad and Dea Bean	105.57	2781	293640
秋　粮	Autumn Grain	2939.03	7153	21023030
稻　谷	Rice	2234.35	8023	17927174
#中　稻	Early Rice	1662.57	7925	13175530
单季晚稻	Single late Rice	568.24	8309	4721609
双季后作稻	Late Double-crop Rice	3.54	8484	30035
籼稻	Among Rice:Long-grained Nonglutinous Rice	326.77	7505	2452519
薯　类	Tubers	90.03	5927	533639
玉　米	Corn	378.74	5207	1972034
高　粱	Sorghum	0.10	2460	246
谷　子	Millet	0.06	1433	86
其他秋粮	Others	21.48	2464	52927
大　豆	Soybeans	214.27	2506	536924
经济作物	**Economic Crops**	**1187.47**		
棉　花	Cotton	354.85	1075	381375
油　料	Oil-Bearing Crops	812.31	2686	2181805
#花　生	Peanuts	191.73	3485	668179
油菜籽	Rapeseed	608.57	2455	1494039
芝　麻	Sesame	11.38	1596	18165
麻　类	Hemp Grops	1.41	3190	4498
#黄　麻	Jute	0.04	3000	120
苎　麻	Ramie	1.36	3204	4357
糖　类	Sugar Crops	3.66	56348	206233
#甘　蔗	Sugarcane	3.64	56602	206033
甜　菜	Beetroots	0.02	10000	200
烟　叶	Tobacco Crops	0.65	2191	1424
药　材	Crude drugs	12.54		
其他经济作物	Others	2.05	184	378
#薄　荷	Mint	2.05	184	378
其他农作物	**Others**	**1436.25**		
#蔬　菜	Vegetable	1161.17	31500	36576808
瓜果类	Melon and Fruits Crops	125.57	32953	4137965
绿　肥	Organic Fertilizer	21.72		

7－10 主要农产品产量
OUTPUT OF MAJOR FARM CROPS

单位：万吨　　　　(10000 tons)

年份 Year	粮食 Grain	夏粮 Summer Grain	秋粮 Autumn Grain	棉花 Cotton Crops	油料 Oil-Bearing Crops	#花生 Peanuts	#油菜籽 Rape-Seeds
1949	748.50	217.00	531.50	2.81	15.94	11.82	3.60
1952	997.55	277.85	719.70	9.28	21.68	14.38	6.00
1957	1063.60	274.85	788.75	15.01	25.07	19.81	4.93
1962	965.35	280.65	684.70	8.21	10.27	6.38	3.52
1965	1442.75	379.85	1062.90	26.44	21.68	13.87	7.41
1970	1705.15	415.50	1289.65	32.82	21.67	10.31	10.87
1975	2056.85	524.40	1532.45	45.48	29.64	11.73	17.63
1978	2400.65	677.30	1723.35	47.54	37.44	13.60	23.06
1980	2417.95	873.60	1544.35	41.81	38.64	14.50	23.93
1985	3126.52	1064.46	2062.06	47.91	108.78	34.13	73.11
1989	3282.80	1033.00	2249.80	48.47	99.91	31.25	67.72
1990	3264.15	1143.46	2120.69	46.42	112.39	30.12	81.41
1991	3035.51	1032.43	2003.08	55.71	114.06	28.12	85.32
1992	3320.55	1251.19	2069.36	52.74	127.33	30.51	95.88
1993	3279.70	1152.60	2127.10	42.90	125.71	37.66	87.04
1994	3124.05	1105.29	2018.76	45.71	133.59	44.80	87.77
1995	3286.30	1073.46	2212.84	56.16	159.46	48.43	109.54
1996	3476.35	1200.95	2275.40	53.75	147.50	39.65	106.34
1997	3563.79	1226.91	2336.88	50.75	141.93	39.53	100.53
1998	3415.12	864.22	2550.90	46.19	115.63	48.90	64.26
1999	3559.03	1195.96	2363.07	24.60	184.04	63.25	117.89
2000	3106.63	899.75	2206.88	31.45	225.65	79.75	142.99
2001	2942.05	821.44	2120.61	46.05	232.53	84.09	145.81
2002	2907.05	758.18	2148.87	36.28	217.03	83.71	130.81
2003	2471.85	729.29	1742.56	29.10	199.45	51.57	145.74
2004	2829.06	807.24	2021.82	50.28	238.38	69.12	167.32
2005	2834.59	844.42	1990.17	32.27	215.99	55.46	158.67
2006	3041.44	939.14	2102.30	38.14	218.18	66.82	149.40

7－11 人均占有主要农产品产量
PER CAPITA OUTPUT OF MAJOR FARM PRODUCTS

单位：千克/人　　　　(kg/person)

年份 Year	粮食产量 Grain	棉花产量 Cotton	油料产量 Oil-Bearing Grops	生猪饲养量(头/人) Output of Raising Hogs (head/person)	猪、牛、羊肉产量 Output of Pork, Beef and Mutton	水产品产量 Output of Aquatic Products
1952	270.0	2.5	5.9	0.24		4.6
1957	257.0	3.7	6.1	0.34		6.9
1962	225.0	1.9	2.4	0.22		4.5
1965	316.0	5.8	4.8	0.46		5.5
1970	329.0	6.4	4.2	0.50		5.2
1975	367.0	8.1	5.3	0.60		6.5
1978	414.0	8.2	6.5	0.60		6.9
1980	408.5	7.1	6.6	0.70	18.1	7.2
1985	505.0	7.8	17.6	0.64	22.4	10.9
1989	506.1	7.5	15.4	0.60	23.3	17.0
1990	486.0	6.9	16.7	0.59	23.6	17.6
1991	446.1	8.2	16.8	0.59	24.0	17.3
1992	482.8	7.7	18.5	0.61	25.1	19.6
1993	472.6	6.2	18.1	0.62	25.8	22.7
1994	446.7	6.5	19.1	0.65	28.5	25.8
1995	466.6	8.0	22.6	0.69	30.9	31.2
1996	490.4	7.6	20.8	0.51	24.7	34.7
1997	499.9	7.1	19.9	0.57	26.2	37.3
1998	476.6	6.4	16.1	0.63	29.2	39.4
1999	494.5	3.4	25.6	0.63	29.9	41.2
2000	427.3	4.3	31.0	0.66	31.3	42.5
2001	400.8	6.3	31.7	0.67	32.2	43.7
2002	394.6	4.9	29.5	0.67	32.6	45.4
2003	334.4	3.9	27.0	0.68	33.1	46.4
2004	381.3	6.8	32.1	0.66	32.7	49.3
2005	380.3	4.3	29.0	0.66	32.5	52.1
2006	404.9	5.1	29.0	0.68	32.2	53.9

注：从1996年开始，牧业有关数据与农业普查接轨，故小于上年数。

Note: Relative targets of animal husbandry were in line with the data of agricultural general survey since 1996, so they were less than last year.

7－12 蚕、茶、果生产情况
STATISTICS ON SILKWORM COCOONS, TEA AND FRUITS

单位:万吨 (10000 tons)

指标	Item	1990	1995	2000	2005	2006
蚕茧产量	Silkworm Cocoons	12.00	18.62	9.01	10.59	12.28
茶叶产量	Tea	1.41	1.06	1.20	1.21	1.33
红毛茶	Red Tea	0.43	0.13	0.18	0.14	0.17
绿毛茶	Green Tea	0.94	0.91	0.90	1.01	1.12
其他茶	Others	0.04	0.02	0.12	0.06	0.04
水果产量	Fruits	49.33	101.35	176.44	202.18	214.66
#苹　果	Apples	10.63	32.16	69.53	55.28	57.26
柑　桔	Citrus	3.13	4.57	4.27	5.20	4.79
梨	Pears	15.01	24.30	39.01	55.62	61.43
葡　萄	Grapes	2.42	5.79	8.77	15.30	20.83
桃　子	Peaches	11.27	17.74		31.87	35.00
枇　杷	Loquats	0.20	0.74		0.64	0.77
红　枣	Dates	0.19	0.18	0.25	1.00	0.98
柿　子	Persimmons	2.96	7.11	19.41	12.10	15.28
桑园面积　(千公顷)	Area of Mulberry Plantations (1000 hectares)	116.33	228.49	88.12	88.37	88.54
茶园面积　(千公顷)	Area of Tea Plantations (1000 hectares)	13.17	19.29	19.93	24.56	26.82
#当年采摘面积	Pick Area	11.04	10.37	15.47	20.17	21.27
果园　(千公顷)	Area of Orchards (1000 hectares)	104.86	157.75	153.33	191.85	190.44
#苹果园	Apples	46.30	84.46	49.57	38.44	36.52
柑桔园	Citrus	3.50	2.01	3.25	3.88	5.44
梨　园	Pears	14.98	22.89	38.60	47.26	40.20
葡萄园	Grapes	2.59	3.93	5.93	11.44	13.03

7-13 林业生产情况
STATISTICS ON FORESTRY

单位:千公顷 (1000 hectares)

指标	Item	1990	1995	2000	2005	2006
造林面积	Build Forestry Areas	19.63	27.20	51.25	54.67	66.45
用材林	Material Forest	11.42	12.44	40.83	14.20	14.96
经济林	Economic Forest	2.10	11.30	7.28	7.69	9.77
防护林	Windbreak Forest	5.80	3.36	2.95	32.77	41.71
其他林	Others	0.31	0.10	0.19	0.01	0.01
林产品产量 (吨)	Output of Forestery Products (ton)					
油桐籽	Tung-Oil Seed	41	12	38	0	0
油茶籽	Tea-Oil Seed	27	18	38	170	187
竹笋干	Bamboo Shoots	856	1254	1279	686	755
板　栗	Chestnut	2733	7156	13514	20535	22588
白　果	Ginkgo	4037	5303	8729	12000	12500
迹地更新面积	Slash Updateing Areas	0.68	1.13	3.23	2.64	3.74
育苗面积	Raise Seedlings Areas	7.31	8.89	16.56	79.34	91.34
幼林抚育作业面积 (千公顷次)	Young Growth Works Areas (1000 hectares - T)	95.03	125.36	103.57	244.42	251.90
成林抚育实际面积	Adult Growth Actual Areas	58.44	89.87	117.43	251.21	256.54
林木种子采集量 (吨)	Output of Forestry Seeds Pick (ton)	90	203	177	320	340
木材采伐量 (万立方米)	Output of Timber Cut (10000 cu. m)	85.68	153.02	136.16	57.90	89.69
竹材采伐量 (万根)	Bamboo Cut (10000 units)	403.07	732.38	646.60	555.00	613.00
四旁植树 (万株)	Planting (10000 units)	14901	14633	12435	13445	11356
林木种子园个数 (个)	Forest Seeds Fields (unit)	11	16	16	16	18
林木种子园面积 (公顷)	Forest Seeds Field Areas (hectare)	101	108	138	60	57

7－14　畜牧业生产情况
STATISTICS ON LIVESTOCK

指　标	Item	1990	1995	2000	2005	2006
牲畜年末头数　（万头）	**Livestock (Year-end)(10000 units)**					
大牲畜	Large Animals	92.50	123.27	74.51	73.88	71.33
牛	Cattle and Buffalo	71.48	99.06	59.14	64.61	64.30
#良种及改良乳牛	Fine improved Variety Cows	3.49	2.93	6.75	16.11	16.35
马	Horses	2.11	2.48	1.40	1.35	0.64
驴	Donkeys	16.55	18.79	12.57	6.39	5.48
骡	Mules	2.36	2.94	1.40	1.53	91.00
猪	Hogs	1851.10	2118.97	2015.42	1927.20	1826.96
羊	Sheep and Goats	850.80	1273.89	1022.97	1174.99	1186.50
山　羊	Goats	797.45	1211.16	994.39	1155.17	1167.49
绵　羊	Sheep	53.35	62.73	28.58	19.82	19.01
畜产品产量	**Livestock Products**					
猪牛羊出栏头数　（万头）	Hogs,Sheep and Goats　(10000 units)					
当年肉猪出栏头数	Hogs	2116.62	2754.90	2787.35	2974.88	2977.32
当年出售和自宰的肉用牛	Ox by Sold and Killed	12.85	35.62	27.43	30.71	29.20
当年出售和自宰的肉用羊　（万只）	Sheep and Goats by Sold and Killed　(10000 units)	831.81	1724.38	1372.40	1569.06	1578.26
肉类产量　（万吨）	Output of Meat　(10000 tons)	194.03	316.95	328.87	352.34	345.81
猪　肉	Pork	149.24	195.82	206.54	218.54	218.71
牛　肉	Beef	1.86	5.43	5.12	5.71	5.42
羊　肉	Mutton	7.28	16.54	15.75	17.88	17.97
禽　肉	Poultry	34.90	84.33	96.51	104.60	103.71
其他禽产品产量　（吨）	Others　(ton)					
牛奶产量	Cow Milk	86860	99948	255223	566204	583550
绵羊毛产量	Sheep's Wool	1853	2305	1104	640	907
山羊毛产量	Goat's Wool	74	71	17	32	41
蜂　蜜	Cashmere	12186	7275	7116	7079	7352
禽　蛋　（万吨）	Poultry Eggs　(10000 tons)	89.72	175.32	181.38	182.01	185.54

7－15　水产品产量
OUTPUT OF AQUATIC PRODUCTS

单位：万吨　　　　(10000 tons)

指　　标	Item	1990	1995	2000	2005	2006
水产品产量	**Output of Aquatic Products**	**118.25**	**219.47**	**308.79**	**388.66**	**405.04**
海水产品	Seawater Aquatic	33.85	65.08	90.87	113.43	119.08
按生产性质分	Group by Nature					
天然生产	Naturally Grown	30.68	56.70	66.00	58.28	58.44
人工养殖	Artificially Cultured	3.17	8.38	24.87	55.15	60.64
按类别分	Group by Category					
鱼　类	Fish	22.38	37.71	47.33	45.04	36.02
甲壳类	Shrimp, Prawn and Crab	6.02	10.74	12.92	15.44	18.63
贝　类	Shell-fish	5.24	16.23	29.78	51.08	55.91
藻　类	Algae	0.21	0.40	0.84	1.87	1.92
按主要品种分	**Among Seawater Aquatic**					
大黄鱼	Big Yellow Croaker	0.02	0.04	0.31	0.09	0.20
小黄鱼	Small Yellow Croaker	0.54	4.06	4.35	4.29	4.28
带　鱼	Hairtail	5.71	14.30	8.51	9.99	10.42
墨　鱼	Cuttlefish	0.17	0.31	0.20	0.14	0.18
淡水产品	Freshwater Aquatic	84.40	154.39	217.92	275.23	285.97
按生产性质分	Group by Nature					
天然生产	Naturally Grown	16.42	25.47	29.68	32.91	32.69
人工养殖	Artificially Cultured	67.98	128.92	188.24	242.32	253.28
按类别分	Group by Category					
鱼　类	Fish	79.58	139.34	183.06	211.90	215.58
甲壳类	Shirmp, Prawn and Crab	2.64	9.73	31.50	54.48	57.74
贝　类	Shell fish	2.18	5.32	3.36	8.85	8.71
水产养殖面积　（千公顷）	**Aquatic Raise Areas (1000 hectares)**	**448.14**	**555.23**	**705.99**	**813.59**	**821.33**
淡水养殖面积	Freshwater Raise Areas	381.27	467.29	561.81	640.64	640.65
海水养殖面积	Seawater Raise	66.87	87.94	144.18	172.95	180.68

7－16 农业现代化情况
STATISTICS ON AGRICULTURAL MODERNIZATION

单位：千公顷 (1000 hectares)

指标	Item	1990	1995	2000	2005	2006
农业机械化情况	**Statistics on Agricultural Machinery**					
机耕面积	Area Ploughed by Tractors	3632.49	3639.43	4096.55	3923.66	3895.35
机播面积	Seeded Area by Tractors	1046.41	1730.23	1822.72	2123.44	2433.84
#机播三麦面积	Wheats Area by Tractors	1010.26	1661.56	1611.65	1700.87	1894.25
机械植保面积	Plant Protection Area by Tractors	1727.52	2730.54	4573.06	4653.00	4868.00
机械收获面积	Harvest Area by Tractors	531.93	1194.21	2971.78	3787.42	4473.74
农村电气化情况	**Electrification of Rural Area**					
农村用电量（亿千瓦小时）	Electricity Consumed in Rural Area (100 million kWh)	105.26	238.16	314.60	825.10	1011.79
农用物资使用情况	**Used Agricultural Product Material**					
化肥施用量（折纯量）（万吨）	Consumption of Chemical Fertilizers (pure) (10000 tons)	221.79	292.77	335.45	340.81	342.01
每亩耕地施用化肥（折纯量）（千克）	Per Mu Consumption of Chemical Fertilizers (pure) (kg)	32.40	43.80	44.57	47.46	48.07
农用塑料薄膜使用量（万吨）	Used Plastic Film (10000 tons)		5.35	6.51	7.20	7.51
农用柴油使用量（万吨）	Used Diesel Oil (10000 tons)	3.12	59.17	75.98	78.76	81.25
农药使用量（万吨）	Used Agricultural Chemical Insecticides (10000 tons)	7.98	8.87	9.15	10.33	9.86
农田水利情况	**Irrigation and Water Conservancy**					
有效灌溉面积	Effective Irrigation Area	3970.92	3832.78	3900.85	3817.67	3837.72
#机电排灌面积	Electrical Irrigation Area	3518.06	3803.50	3727.55	3543.06	3500.11
占有效灌溉面积的比重（%）	Electrical Irrigation Area Rate in Effective Irrigation Area (%)	88.6	99.2	95.6	92.8	91.2
机电井数（万眼）	Electrical Well (10000)	4.89	4.75	4.62	4.09	3.73
#已配套	Form a Complete Set	3.20	3.11	3.46	2.99	2.62

7－17　主要农业机械和农产品加工机械年底拥有量
AGRICULTURAL MACHINERY AND MACHINERY FOR PROCESSING FARM PRODUCTS AT MAJOR YEAR－END

年　份 Year	农业机械总动力（万千瓦） Total Power of Agricultural Machinery (10000 kW)	农用大中型拖拉机（万台） Large and Medium Agricultural Tractors (10000 units)	农用小型及手扶拖拉机（万台） Mini and Walking Agricultural Tractors (10000 units)	农用排灌动力机械（万千瓦） Machinery for Agricultural Drainage and Irrigation (10000 kW)	农用水泵（万台） Agricultural Water Pump (10000 units)	喷灌机械（万套） Machinery for Sprinkling (10000 units)
1978	855.16	1.18	19.25	363.73	29.20	0.83
1980	1113.05	1.62	25.61	442.48	36.18	2.49
1985	1675.06	1.89	49.16	450.27	37.75	2.08
1989	2212.37	1.88	70.02	475.95	40.29	1.12
1990	2004.77	1.95	71.65	490.83	39.63	0.94
1991	1966.61	2.00	72.64	492.88	40.73	1.07
1992	2016.07	2.07	72.41	494.57	41.55	1.16
1993	2081.75	2.13	73.52	501.35	41.59	1.20
1994	2161.40	2.15	74.98	507.66	42.63	1.31
1995	2226.95	2.32	75.04	508.91	43.36	1.50
1996	2297.43	3.05	76.53	515.99	44.84	1.60
1997	2499.69	3.59	83.32	538.66	50.63	2.99
1998	2594.83	3.98	83.87	553.73	52.20	3.76
1999	2767.89	4.35	86.78	577.99	54.07	3.99
2000	2925.29	5.30	88.89	576.25	65.62	3.71
2001	2957.93	6.16	89.42	618.72	58.09	3.03
2002	2983.89	7.46	89.75	604.04	59.74	3.30
2003	3029.10	8.30	87.46	567.79	58.81	3.22
2004	3052.51	9.51	86.71	599.71	56.88	3.32
2005	3135.33	9.97	90.11	609.08	61.93	3.52
2006	3278.53	11.58	91.37	606.00	62.00	3.43

7－17　续表　Continued

年　份 Year	联合收割机（台） Combine Harvesters (units)	机动脱粒机（万台） Motorized Huller (10000 units)	机动喷雾（粉）器（万部） Motorized Duster (10000 units)	饲料粉碎机（万部） Fodder Grinder (10000 units)	大中型拖拉机配套农具（万件） Large and Medium Tractor Towing Farm Machinery (10000 units)	小型拖拉机配套农具（万件） Mini-Tractor Towing Farm Machinery (10000 units)
1978	295	32.96	2.01	10.18	2.45	33.99
1980	478	40.99	4.33	11.88	3.23	53.58
1985	687	68.51	5.51	7.30	3.38	111.15
1989	1821	86.36	7.08	6.50	3.29	112.49
1990	2411	89.42	9.49	6.51	3.42	118.26
1991	3583	92.29	11.35	6.55	3.91	122.40
1992	5964	93.37	12.37	6.29	4.16	122.33
1993	7279	94.80	12.63	6.06	4.30	124.66
1994	8604	98.32	13.28	5.92	4.37	125.50
1995	12063	105.22	17.08	5.27	4.69	127.74
1996	20074	105.01	19.64	6.32	5.68	129.22
1997	27656	121.42	26.55	7.17	7.00	138.63
1998	33343	123.80	29.10	7.64	7.69	143.08
1999	42266	124.52	31.59	8.02	8.51	148.41
2000	48821	129.69	33.26	8.50	8.62	152.45
2001	52025	120.16	35.17	8.64	8.39	151.48
2002	56151	111.45	34.54	8.74	8.17	145.02
2003	58645	93.56	34.99	8.73	7.84	145.70
2004	61115	91.45	34.88	8.68	7.52	144.45
2005	69569	73.95	37.41	9.97	8.08	143.64
2006	77100	75.00	39.50	9.82	8.37	144.68

7－18　农村居民家庭平均每户生产性固定资产原值(年底数)
ORIGINAL VALUE OF PRODUCTIVE FIXED ASSETS PER RURAL HOUSEHOLD (Year End)

单位:元　　　　(yuan)

年份 Year	合计 Total	役畜和产品畜 Draught and Commodity Animals	大中型铁木农具 Large and Medium-sized Wooden and Iron Farm Tools	农林牧渔业机械 Machinery of Farm, Forestry, Animal Husbandry and Fishery	工业机械 Industrial Machinery	交通运输、仓储及邮政业 Transportation, Storage, Post and Telecommunication	生产用房 Building for Productive Purpose
1985	424.0	67.1	21.6	46.6	9.2	66.8	182.2
1989	816.9	84.8	26.3	146.8	37.4	177.7	295.8
1990	840.7	89.4	33.2	168.7	27.6	159.7	307.2
1991	1107.9	102.0	42.0	224.8	39.5	169.5	478.2
1992	1284.5	114.1	73.6	232.0	53.4	200.3	555.1
1993	1482.0	123.9	101.2	317.1	42.8	232.0	664.5
1994	1658.2	200.3	115.1	405.0	54.3	221.8	592.2
1995	1845.6	221.3	132.5	469.9	85.0	285.8	595.2
1996	2828.9	230.6	93.3	794.1	200.4	409.9	1014.6
1997	3265.5	194.8	100.3	930.5	138.2	677.4	1133.5
1998	3158.9	168.2	116.0	923.6	153.4	526.0	1133.2
1999	3034.9	160.0	81.4	969.9	138.8	594.6	1011.3
2000	4293.8	139.3	291.0	1088.0	430.3	800.4	1544.7
2001	4810.2	137.4	211.7	1143.2	297.6	883.0	1658.6
2002	5044.8	143.8	231.5	1313.2	466.8	906.8	1554.3
2003	5623.8	174.8	239.7	1283.0	444.2	990.5	1876.9
2004	5975.6	188.3	216.5	1353.8	580.6	946.1	2054.6
2005	7134.6	161.3	172.8	1176.6	848.5	1701.7	2017.8
2006	7734.2	152.2	186.9	1349.1	840.3	1642.1	2331.7

注:2000 年以前交通运输、仓储及邮政业只包括运输业;2000－2002 年的只包括交通运输及邮电业。

7－19　农村居民家庭平均每百户拥有主要生产性固定资产数量(年底数)
NUMBER OF MAJOR PRODUCTIVE FIXED ASSETS POSSESSED PER 100 RURAL HOUSEHOLD (Year End)

年份 Year	汽车(辆) Trucks (unit)	大中型拖拉机(台) Large and Medium Agricultural Tractors (set)	小型及手扶拖拉机(台) Mini and Walking Agricultural Tractors (set)	机动脱粒机(台) Motorized Huller (set)	农用水泵(台) Agricultural Water Pump (set)	役畜(头) Draught Animals (head)	产品畜(头) Commodity Animals (head)
1985	0.03	0.01	3.21	2.96	0.70	8.42	18.46
1989	0.10	0.18	6.21	5.45	1.18	8.85	13.41
1990	0.04	0.12	6.37	6.10	1.32	9.07	10.73
1991	0.04	0.07	7.77	9.40	1.41	8.11	19.26
1992	0.06	0.06	8.40	12.51	3.10	6.65	21.26
1993	0.01	0.09	8.63	27.52	6.12	9.07	21.38
1994	0.03	0.27	9.27	14.43	3.33	9.32	20.12
1995	0.09	0.29	10.31	14.05	2.53	10.17	20.38
1996	0.44	0.41	12.04	18.98	7.95	8.73	26.68
1997	0.55	0.26	13.65	21.05	8.32	5.84	18.56
1998	0.75	0.33	15.14	24.08	8.46	4.81	21.94
1999	0.99	1.43	15.85	22.84	8.59	6.22	18.79
2000	1.03	0.49	18.11	24.20	13.23	6.60	26.85
2001	1.03	0.48	19.64	26.59	15.21	4.44	23.09
2002	1.07	0.60	19.38	26.89	16.09	4.68	21.59
2003	1.32	0.85	19.60	25.95	16.94	4.89	22.56
2004	1.26	1.12	17.41	24.90	17.68	3.16	17.94
2005	2.02	0.97	16.99	12.29	17.36	3.66	16.59
2006	2.04	1.21	17.74	13.85	17.84	2.71	17.85

7－20　农业主要经济效益指标

MAIN INDICATOR ON ECONOMIC BENEFIT OF AGRICULTURE

指　标	Item	1990	1995	2000	2005	2006
每个农村劳动力创造的	Per Rural Laborer					
农村社会总产值（元）	Gross Output Value of Rural Area （yuan）	7437.37	38108.36	52605.79	120973.33	150082.49
每个农林牧渔业劳动力创造的	Per Farming, Forestry, Animal Husbandry and Fishery Laborer					
农林牧渔业总产值（元）	Gross Output Value of Farming, Forestry, Animal Husbandry and Fishery （yuan）	3386.02	10943.67	12526.54	23500.48	26544.23
农林牧渔业净产值（元）	Net Output Value of Farming, Forestry, Animal Husbandry and Fishery （yuan）	2017.86	5626.96	6380.30	13631.10	15149.70
粮食产量（公斤）	Output of Grain （kg）	1903.86	2131.12	2081.33	2584.97	2982.30
棉花产量（公斤）	Output of Cotton （kg）	27.08	36.44	21.07	29.42	37.40
油料产量（公斤）	Output of Oil-Bearing Crops （kg）	65.55	103.46	151.18	196.97	213.94
肉类产量（公斤）	Output of Meat （kg）	113.18	198.46	220.88	321.31	344.55
水产品产量（公斤）	Output of Aquatic Products （kg）	68.97	142.39	206.88	354.43	397.17

注：产值均为现行价格。

Notes: Gross output value at current price.

7－21　农村自然灾害情况

BASIC SIATISTICS ON RURAL NATURAL DISASTER

单位：千公顷　　　　(1000 hectares)

指　标	Item	1995	2000	2002	2003	2004	2005	2006
受灾面积	Area Covered	2660.00	3411.68	2288.46	3305.00	836.58	2139.50	1324.00
#旱　灾	Drought	1128.00	1196.87	571.40	33.33	46.93	225.94	115.69
水　灾	Flood	329.60	175.59	681.74	2676.53	111.39	781.97	1075.81
成灾面积	Area Affected	918.50	1630.59	1202.77	1955.58	432.55		
#旱　灾	Drought	454.00	559.05	329.23	5.16	29.25		
水　灾	Flood	109.10	109.16	415.11	1595.27	71.67		

7－22　乡镇企业基本情况（2006 年）

单位:亿元

指　　标	Item	企业个数（个）Number of Enterprises (unit)	从业人员（万人）Employees (10000 persons)	总产值 Total Output Value	增加值 Value Added
总　计	**Total**	**1268904**	**1317.90**	**40505.84**	**9074.57**
按登记注册类型分组	**Grouped by Type of Registration**				
内资企业	Inner Funded	1257965	1199.36	33970.10	7617.20
集体企业	Collective-owned	3218	27.58	1646.93	373.18
股份合作企业	Share Holding Cooperative	8602	16.97	921.08	157.98
联营企业	State-owned and Collective Joint	233	1.07	53.93	12.76
有限责任公司	Responsibility Co. Ltd.	38778	125.49	5342.72	1142.88
股份有限公司	Share Holding Co. Ltd.	2129	27.86	1888.30	368.17
私营企业	Private	243578	558.77	16054.70	3738.04
其他企业	Others	961427	441.63	8062.44	1824.20
港、澳、台商投资企业	Funded from Hong Kong, Macao and Taiwan	5205	58.49	2779.84	634.09
外资投资企业	Foreign Funded	5734	60.05	3755.90	823.28
按国民经济行业分组	**Grouped by Sector**				
农林牧渔业	Farming, Forestry, Animal Husbandry, Fishery	5484	7.18	66.14	14.82
工　业	Industry	591104	1012.88	34620.98	7524.44
建筑业	Construction	24183	86.74	1042.92	266.85
交通运输、仓储和邮政业	Transportation, Storage and Postal	135462	31.92	520.20	144.99
批发和零售	Wholesale and Retail Sales	295914	82.99	2678.91	715.71
住宿和餐饮	Accommodation and eatering industry	73681	35.99	403.91	120.36
社会服务业	Social Services	83064	34.59	447.02	109.95
其他	Others	60012	25.61	725.77	177.46
按经济成份分组	**Grouped by Ecomonic Ownership**				
集体及集体控股企业	Collective and Collective Share Holding	7801	46.36	2990.39	723.47
私营及私营控股企业	Private and Private Share Holding	281969	838.45	29467.58	6626.93
个体企业	Individual	979134	433.08	8047.87	1724.17

BASIC STATISTICS ON TOWNSHIP AND VILLAGE COLLECTIVE ENTERPRISES (2006)

(100 million yuan)

营业收入 Operating Revenue	利润总额 Total Profits	净利润 Net Profits	上交税金 Taxes Turn Over	劳动者报酬 Reward of Laborers	年末固定资产原值 Original Value of Fixed Assets (year end)
40485.64	**1814.62**	**1524.00**	**1186.56**	**1945.18**	**10235.28**
33906.69	1495.74	1234.78	1013.00	1653.51	8036.80
1760.94	85.04	67.73	46.43	56.96	499.43
711.67	34.27	23.78	25.94	24.87	144.89
51.22	1.32	1.56	2.05	2.41	9.66
5333.40	200.28	172.36	167.70	226.44	1265.00
1766.11	98.17	80.77	52.72	49.40	507.58
16377.30	691.27	537.30	519.34	747.55	4029.93
7906.05	385.39	351.29	198.82	545.87	1580.30
2785.82	131.07	118.31	72.71	121.88	893.95
3793.14	187.82	170.91	100.86	169.79	1304.54
69.90	3.09	3.65	0.91	10.65	18.26
33802.11	1430.67	1208.38	980.31	1412.56	8677.99
972.34	61.90	43.90	27.98	119.48	235.08
506.06	36.53	39.25	22.49	66.64	171.08
3576.62	164.34	119.39	78.37	170.49	360.78
447.95	46.53	40.27	22.92	51.48	138.55
448.00	30.78	26.98	14.32	56.62	181.72
662.66	40.78	42.17	39.27	57.25	451.81
3137.15	154.98	123.36	95.02	96.07	951.84
29249.19	1265.47	1063.66	892.87	1313.85	7709.22
8099.30	394.17	336.97	198.68	535.26	1574.22

注：增加值、总产值均为现行价格。

Note: Value added, total gross output value at current price.

主要统计指标解释

农林牧渔业总产值 指以货币表现的农、林、牧、渔业全部产品和对农业生产进行各种支持性服务活动的总量,它反映一定时期内农业生产总规模和总成果。从2003年开始农林牧渔业总产值执行新的国民经济行业分类标准,包括农业、林业、牧业、渔业、农林牧渔服务业,不再包括农民兼营商品性工业。农林牧渔业总产值中的农、林、牧、渔四业的计算方法通常是按农、林、牧、渔业产品及其副产品的产量分别乘以各自单位产品价格求得,现行价格从2003年开始使用生产价格调查的价格;少数生产周期较长,当年没有产品或产品产量不易统计的,则采用间接方法匡算其产值;然后将四业产品产值与农林牧渔服务业相加即为农林牧渔业总产值。1957年以前的农林牧渔业总产值中包括了厩肥和农民自给性手工业(如农民自制衣服、鞋、袜,自己从事粮食初步加工等)。1958年及以后,林业中增加了村及村以下竹木采伐产值;牧业中取消了厩肥产值;副业中取消了农民自给性手工业产值,增加了村及村以下办的工业产值;渔业中增加了海洋捕捞水产品产值。1980年及以后,在副业中增加了农民家庭兼营工业商品部分的产值。从1984年起村及村以下工业产值划归工业。从1993年起取消副业,将野生动物的捕猎划入牧业、野生植物采集和农民家庭兼营商品性工业划归农业,从2003年起不再包括农民家庭兼营商品性工业产值。1996年第一次农业普查以后,由于畜牧业产品年报数据与普查数据之间存在一定的差距,国家统计局农调总队对畜牧业年报数据与普查数据进行衔接,相应的畜牧业产值进行调整。

粮食产量 指全社会的产量。包括国有经济经营的、集体统一经营的和农民家庭经营的粮食产量,还包括工矿企业办的农场和其他生产单位的产量。粮食除包括稻谷、小麦、玉米、高粱、谷子及其他杂粮外,还包括薯类和豆类。其产量计算方法,豆类按去豆荚后的干豆计算;薯类(包括甘薯和马铃薯,不包括芋头和木薯)1963年以前按每4公斤鲜薯折1公斤粮食计算,从1964年开始改为按5公斤鲜薯折1公斤粮食计算。城市郊区作为蔬菜的薯类(如马铃薯等)按鲜品计算,并且不作粮食统计。其他粮食一律按脱粒后的原粮计算。

棉花产量 指全社会的产量。包括春播棉和夏播棉。产量按皮棉计算。

油料产量 指全部油料作物的生产量。包括花生、油菜籽、芝麻、向日葵籽、胡麻籽(亚麻籽)和其他油料。不包括大豆、木本油料和野生油料。花生以带壳干花生计算。

水产品产量 指人工养殖的水产品和天然生长的水产品的捕捞量。包括海水的鱼类、虾蟹类、贝类和藻类以及内陆水域的鱼类、虾蟹类和贝类,不包括淡水水生植物。

猪、牛、羊肉产量 指当年出栏并已屠宰、除去头蹄下水后带骨肉(即胴体重)的重量。

期初(末)畜禽存栏头(只)数 指报告期初(末)农村各种合作经济组织和国营农场、农民个人、机关、团体、学校、工矿企业、部队等单位以及城镇居民饲养的大牲畜、猪、羊、家禽等畜禽的存栏数。

耕地面积 是指年初可用来种植农作物并经常进行耕种、能够正常收获的土地。包括当年实际耕种的熟地、当年新开荒地、休闲不满三年随时可以复耕的地和当年休闲地以及以种植农作物为主并附带种植桑树、茶树、果树和其他林木的土地、沿海、沿湖地区已围垦利用的"海涂"、"湖田"等面积。不包括临时种植农作物的坡度在25度以上的陡坡地、在河套、湖畔、库区临时开发的成片或零星土地,属于专业性的桑园、茶园、果园、果木苗圃、林地、芦苇地、天然或人工草地面积、也不包括已列为国家和省(区、市)退耕计划但临时耕种的土地。

农作物播种面积 指实际播种或移植有农作物的面积。凡是实际种植有农作物的面积,不论种植在耕地上还是种植在非耕地上,均包括在农作物播种面积中。在播种季节基本结束后,因遭灾而重新改种和补种的农作物面积,也包括在内。

有效灌溉面积 指具有一定的水源,地块比较平整,灌溉工程或设备已经配套,在一般年景下当年能够进行正常灌溉的耕地面积。在一般情况下,有效灌溉面积应等于灌溉工程或设备已经配备,能够进行正常灌溉的水田和水浇地面积之和。

农用化肥施用量 指本年内实际用于农业生产的化肥数量,包括氮肥、磷肥、钾肥和复合肥。化肥施用量要求按折纯量计算数量。折纯量是指把氮肥、磷肥、钾肥分别按含氮、含五氧化二磷、含氧化钾的百分之一百成份进行折算后的数量。复合肥按其所含主要成分折算。

农业机械总动力 指主要用于农、林、牧、渔业的各种动力机械的动力总和。包括耕作机械、排灌机械、收获机械、农用运输机械、植物保护机械、牧业机械、林业机械、渔业机械和其他农业机械[内燃机按引擎马力折成瓦(特)计算、电动机按功率折成瓦(特)计算]。不包括专门用于乡、镇、村、组办工业、基本建设、非农业运输、科学试验和教学等非农业生产方面用的动力机械与作业机械。

农林牧渔业劳动力 指全社会直接参加农林牧渔业生产活动的劳动力。

Explanatory Notes on Main Statistical Indicators

Gross Output Value of Farming, Forestry, Animal Husbandry and Fishery refers to the total value of products of farming, forestry, animal husbandry and fishery and various supporting service activities for agricultural production, which reflects the total scale and result of agricultural production during a given period. Since 2003, the total output value of farming, forestry, animal husbandry and fishery is counted with new classified standard of the national economy, including the service industry serving for agricultural production, while excluding the output value of commercialized handicraft products, which is originally managed as a part of farmer's household sideline occupation. Gross output value of farming, forestry, animal husbandry, fishery and the value of service industry is obtained by first multiplying the output of each product with its price, resulting in the output value of each single item. Since 2003, the current price is used by the investigated production price. For a small number of products, annual output of which is not available or difficult to get due to the long production growing process involved, the output value is estimated through an indirect approach. The sum(of output value of all products of farming, forestry, animal husbandry, fishery and service activities for them is then equal to the gross output value of agriculture. Prior to 1957, Chinas gross agricultural output value included barnyard manure and handicraft products for self consumption(clothes, shoes, stockings, and initial grain processing undertaken by peasants). Since 1958, cutting and felling of bamboo and trees by villages and other cooperative organizations under villages have been included in forestry; value of barnyard manure has been excluded from animal husbandry; self consumed handicrafts has been excluded from sideline occupations, while the output value of industries run by villages and cooperative organizations under village had been included in sideline occupations and the output value of fish catches by motor fishing boats has been added to fishery. Since 1980, the value of handicraft products made for sale by individuals in households had been added to sideline occupations. Since 1984, industries run by villages and under villages have been included in the sector of industry. Since 1993, the subdivision of sideline occupations has been canceled, and the hunting of wild animals has been classified into animal husbandry, and the gathering of wild plants and commodity industryrun by rural household have been included infarming. Since 2003, the output value of commercialized handicraft products, as the farmer's household sideline occupation, don't include in farming anymore. The first agriculture census of China in 1996 revealed some discrepancy between the production of animal products from the annual reports and that from the census. Efforts were made by the Rural Socio – economic Survey Organization of NBS to adjust the output value of animal husbandry to make the figures from the annual reports consistent with the census data.

Grain Output refers to the grain production in the whole country including grains produced by state farms, collective units, industrial enterprises and mines. Grain includes rice, wheat, corn, sorghum, millet and other miscellaneous grains as well as tubers and beans. Output of beans refers to dry beans without pods. The output of tubers (sweet potatoes and potatoes, not including taros and cassava) was converted into that of grain at the ratio 4: 1, e. 4 kilograms of fresh tubers was equivalent to 1 kilogram of grain up to 1963. Since 1964 the ratio for conversion has been 5: 1. Tubers supplied as vegetables(such as potatoes) in cities and suburbs are calculated as fresh vegetables and their output is not included in the output of grain. Output of all other grains refers to husked grain.

Cotton Output refers to the cotton production in the whole country including cotton sown in spring and in autumn. Output is measured as the weight of ginned cotton.

Output of Oil-bearing Crops refers to the total production of oil bearing crops of various kinds, including peanuts, (dry, in shell) rapeseeds, sesame, sunflower seeds, flax seeds, and other oil bearing crops. Soybeans, oil-bearing woody plants, and wild oil-bearing crops are not included.

Output of Aquatic Products refers to catches of both artificially cultured and naturally grown aquatic products, including fish, shrimps, crabs and shellfish in sea and inland water as well as seaweed. Freshwater plants are not included.

Output of Pork, Beef, and Mutton refers to the meat of slaughtered hogs, cattle, sheep and goats with head, feet, and offal taken away.

Number of Livestock or Poultry in Stock at Beginning(or End) refers to the total number of large animals, pigs, sheep, fowls, etc. raised by rural cooperative organizations, state farms, rural individuals, government agencies, schools, industrial and mining enterprises, army, and urban residents at the beginning(or end) of the reference period.

Regularly Cultivated Land refers to farmland among the total land resources which is exclusively used for farming and is under regular cultivation with harvest in normal years. Included are currently cultivated land, land that has been abandoned or put in idle for less than 3 years and could be re-used for cultivation at any time, and new-claimed land that has been put into cultivation for more than 3 years. Excluded under this category are steep slope land over 25 degrees under temporary cultivation, land(large or small plots) that is claimed along river bends, lake sides or banks of reservoirs, as well as land that has been designated under the "Green for Grain" programmes of the state and provincial governments but is still temporarily under cultivation.

Sown Area of Crops refers to area of land sown or transplanted with crops regardless of being in cultivated area or non cultivated area. Area of land re-sown due to natural disasters is also included.

Irrigated Area refers to areas that are effectively irrigated, i. e. level land which has water source and complete sets of irrigation facilities to lift and move adequate water for irrigation purpose under normal conditions. Under normal conditions, irrigated area is the sum of watered fields and irrigated fields where irrigation systems or equipment have been installed for regular irrigation purpose.

Consumption of Chemical Fertilizers in Agriculture refers to the quantity of chemical fertilizers applied in agriculture in the year, including nitrogenous fertilizer, phosphate fertilizer, potash fertilizer, and compound fertilizer. The consumption of chemical fertilizers is required in calculation to convert the gross weight into weight containing 100% effective component (e. g. 100% nitrogen content in nitrogenous fertilizer, 100% phosphorous pentoxide contents in phosphate fertilizer, 100% potassium oxide contents in potash fertilizer). Compound fertilizer is converted with its major component.

Total Power of Farm Machinery refers to total mechanical power of machinery used in farming, forestry, animal husbandry, and fishery, including ploughing, irrigation and drainage, harvesting, transport, plant protection, stock breeding, forestry and fishery. The power of internal combustion engines is required to convert horsepower into watts and the power of electric motors is required to beconverted into watts. Machinery employed for non agricultural purposes, such as the machines used in township run and village—run industry, construction, non agricultural transport, scientific experiments and teaching, is excluded.

Labour Force Engaged in Farming, Forestry, Animal Husbandry and Fishery refers to the total laborers who are directly engaged in production of farming, forestry, animal husbandry and fishery.

第 8 篇

工业、能源

INDUSTRY AND ENERGY

8-1 规模以上工业企业单位数和产销总值(2006年)
NUMBER OF INDUSTRIAL ENTERPRISES ABOVE DESIGNATED SIZE AND THEIR TOTAL VALUE OF GROSS OUTPUT AND SALES (2006)

单位:亿元 (100 million yuan)

项目	Item	企业单位数(个) Number of Enterprises (unit)	工业总产值(现价) Total Output Value (current price)	#新产品产值 Output Value of New Products	工业销售产值(现价) Value of Industrial Products Sales (current price)	#出口交货值 Delivery Value for Export
总计	**Total**	**36319**	**41410.40**	**3025.28**	**40802.21**	**10007.28**
按登记注册类型分	**Grouped by Type of Registration**					
内资企业	Inner Funded Enterprises	27824	24398.89	1830.85	24017.26	2239.98
国有企业	State-Owned Enterprises	440	2681.52	287.62	2663.99	173.07
集体企业	Collective-Owned Enterprises	1449	1749.34	158.94	1716.40	123.38
股份合作企业	Share Holding Cooperative Enterprises	875	602.22	25.34	589.37	45.19
联营企业	Joint-Ownership Enterprises	54	43.05	2.90	43.07	2.93
有限责任公司	Responsibility Co. Ltd.	3098	5667.02	817.25	5635.30	504.04
#国有独资	State Solely Funded	54	630.65	67.74	623.04	34.17
股份有限公司	Share Holding Co. Ltd.	476	2417.16	269.02	2388.65	269.94
私营企业	Private Entreprises	21345	11201.54	269.25	10943.95	1116.16
其他企业	Other Enterprises	87	37.04	0.52	36.54	5.27
港、澳、台商投资企业	Hong Kong, Macao and Taiwan Funded Enterprises	3521	4722.37	400.87	4645.28	1592.37
外商投资企业	Foreign Funded Enterprises	4974	12289.14	793.56	12139.67	6174.93
按轻重工业分	**Grouped by Light and Heavy Industry**					
轻工业	Light Industry	15645	12531.67	731.63	12331.98	3157.45
重工业	Heavy Industry	20674	28878.73	2293.65	28470.23	6849.83
按企业规模分	**Grouped by Scale of Enterprise**					
大型企业	Large	315	13105.18	1681.97	13021.28	4176.70
中型企业	Medium	3372	12855.71	1098.52	12654.57	3826.74
小型企业	Small	32632	15449.51	244.79	15126.37	2003.84

单位:亿元 (100 million yuan)

项 目	Item	企业单位数(个) Number of Enterprises (unit)	工业总产值(现价) Total Output Value (current price)	#新产品产值 Output Value of New Products	工业销售产值(现价) Value of Industrial Products Sales (current price)	#出口交货值 Delivery Value for Export
按行业分	**Grouped by Sector**					
采矿业	**Mining and Quarrying**	**181**	**334.67**	**11.74**	**332.06**	**1.01**
煤炭开采和洗选业	Coal Mining and Processing	15	151.14	11.50	150.49	0.72
石油和天然气开采业	Petroleum and Natural Gas Extraction	2	67.96	0.00	67.65	0.00
黑色金属矿采选业	Ferrous Metals Mining and Processing	19	32.82	0.08	32.84	0.00
有色金属矿采选业	Nonferrous Metals Mining and Processing	4	8.20	0.00	8.14	0.00
非金属矿采选业	Nonmetal Minerals Mining and Processing	140	72.90	0.15	71.32	0.29
其他矿采选业	Nonmetal Minerals Mining and Processing	1	1.65	0.00	1.63	0.00
制造业	**Manufacturing**	**35819**	**39153.82**	**3009.72**	**38553.18**	**10006.26**
农副食品加工业	Food Processing	1108	851.06	2.28	841.42	57.52
食品制造业	Food Production	317	217.36	1.01	215.43	20.08
饮料制造业	Beverage Production	215	282.14	12.53	277.32	3.71
烟草加工业	Tobacco Processing	5	213.91	0.00	214.08	0.14
纺织业	Textile Industry	5510	3665.57	132.02	3606.59	766.27
纺织服装、鞋、帽制造业	Textile, Garments, Shoes and Hats	2293	1419.04	66.49	1396.58	527.08
皮革、毛皮、羽毛(绒)及其制品业	Leather, Furs, Down and Related Products	452	294.24	41.64	289.19	132.72
木材加工及木、竹、藤、棕、草制造业	Timber Processing, Wood, Bamboo, Cane, Palm Fiber and Straw Products	803	402.70	14.18	392.70	96.98
家具制造业	Furniture Manufacturing	162	118.26	0.18	116.11	73.44
造纸及纸制品业	Papermaking and Paper Products	584	573.72	4.46	565.79	82.41
印刷业和记录媒介的复制	Printing and Record Pressing	337	127.18	1.04	124.93	13.96
文教体育用品制造业	Stationery, Education and Sports Goods	587	276.16	10.86	273.50	146.21
石油加工、炼焦及核燃料加工业	Petroleum Processing, Coking Products and Nuclear Fuel Processing	140	771.98	38.06	765.39	8.73
化学原料及化学制品制造业	Raw Chemical Materials and Chemical Products	3164	3946.45	143.69	3889.02	506.32

8－1 续表 2 Continued 2

单位：亿元 (100 million yuan)

项目 Item		企业单位数（个）Number of Enterprises (unit)	工业总产值（现价）Total Output Value (current price)	#新产品产值 Output Value of New Products	工业销售产值（现价）Value of Industrial Products Sales (current price)	#出口交货值 Delivery Value for Export
医药制造业	Medical and Pharmaceutical Products	456	524.53	71.63	509.79	62.53
化学纤维制造业	Chemical Fibers	485	999.44	13.70	990.25	77.84
橡胶制品业	Rubber Products	386	350.14	54.92	342.09	99.12
塑料制品业	Plastic Products	1372	807.73	32.83	793.38	168.10
非金属矿物制品业	Nonmetal Mineral Products	1701	1016.86	31.03	1000.79	108.76
黑色金属冶炼及压延加工业	Smelting and Pressing of Ferrous Metals	998	3806.99	333.64	3802.41	236.35
有色金属冶炼及压延加工业	Smelting and Pressing of Nonferrous Metals	793	1408.03	34.24	1384.17	105.63
金属制品业	Metal Products	2157	1524.63	76.99	1490.08	339.29
通用设备制造业	Ordinary Machinery Manufacturing	3793	2484.31	236.80	2439.61	414.34
专用设备制造业	Special Purposes Equipment Manufacturing	1809	1123.44	94.21	1093.63	189.01
交通运输设备制造业	Transportation Equipment Manufacturing	1495	1762.76	300.40	1725.51	424.98
电气机械及器材制造业	Electric Equipment and Machinery	2316	2947.53	464.34	2877.67	522.49
通信设备、计算机及其他电子设备制造业	Telecommunications Equipment, Computer and Other Electronic Equipments	1499	6390.43	766.58	6304.88	4419.24
仪器仪表及文化、办公用机械制造业	Instruments, Meters, Cultural and Official Machinery	471	644.02	24.91	636.66	343.31
工艺品及其他制造业	Handicraft Artical and Other Manufacturing	366	167.75	5.04	163.52	59.66
废弃资源和废旧材料回收加工业	Waste Resouces and Junk Material Recycled	45	35.46	0.00	30.69	0.06
电力、燃气及水的生产和供应业	**Electric Power, Gas and Water Production and Supply**	**319**	**1921.90**	**3.83**	**1916.98**	**0.00**
电力、热力的生产和供应业	Electric Power, Steam and Hot Water Production and Supply	187	1806.14	3.83	1802.42	0.00
燃气生产和供应	Gas Production and Supply	31	69.81	0.00	70.35	0.00
水的生产和供应业	Tap Water Production and Supply	101	45.95	0.00	44.21	0.00

注：本表口径为全部国有及年主营业务收入500万元以上非国有企业(下同)。

Note: Data in this table covers all state-owned enterprises and non-state-owned industrial enterprises with an annual sales income of over 5 million yuan (the same as in the following tables).

8－2 规模以上工业企业主要经济指标（2006年）

单位：亿元

项目	Item	企业单位数（个）Number of Enterprises (unit)	增加值 Added Value	资产总计 Total Assets	流动资产 Circulating Funds
总计	**Total**	**36319**	**10309.22**	**30500.98**	**16238.01**
按登记注册类型分	**Grouped by Type of Registration**				
内资企业	Inner Funded Enterprises	27824	6179.16	17606.22	9097.94
国有企业	State-Owned Enterprises	440	858.91	2714.82	950.26
集体企业	Collective-Owned Enterprises	1449	407.13	1071.89	651.23
股份合作企业	Share Holding Cooperative Enterprises	875	148.03	329.73	224.85
联营企业	Joint-Ownership Enterprises	54	11.65	30.18	16.95
有限责任公司	Responsibility Co. Ltd.	3098	1468.04	5539.29	2580.20
#国有独资	State Solely Funded	54	211.19	987.34	368.15
股份有限公司	Share Holding Co. Ltd.	476	464.17	1715.60	906.52
私营企业	Private Entreprises	21345	2810.93	6175.28	3753.88
其他企业	Other Enterprises	87	10.31	29.43	14.05
港、澳、台商投资企业	Hong Kong,Macao and Taiwan Funded Enterprises	3521	1179.28	4082.89	2296.48
外商投资企业	Foreign Funded Enterprises	4974	2950.77	8811.86	4843.59
按轻重工业分	**Grouped by Light and Heavy Industry**				
轻工业	Light Industry	15645	3361.88	8841.44	4849.12
重工业	Heavy Industry	20674	6947.33	21659.54	11388.89
按企业规模分	**Grouped by Scale of Enterprise**				
大型企业	Large	315	2997.93	9955.29	4648.75
中型企业	Medium	3372	3392.15	11207.05	6005.05
小型企业	Small	32632	3919.13	9338.64	5584.22
按行业分	**Grouped by Sector**				
采矿业	**Mining and Quarrying**	**181**	**190.54**	**448.98**	**144.26**
煤炭开采和洗选业	Coal Mining and Processing	15	86.93	255.61	85.29
石油和天然气开采业	Petroleum and Natural Gas Extraction	2	62.27	90.24	13.20
黑色金属矿采选业	Ferrous Metals Mining and Processing	19	13.54	27.93	14.84
有色金属矿采选业	Nonferrous Metals Mining and Processing	4	2.40	6.58	4.03
非金属矿采选业	Nonmetal Minerals Mining and Processing	140	24.70	67.58	26.29
其他矿采选业	Nonmetal Minerals Mining and Processing	1	0.69	1.04	0.60
制造业	**Manufacturing**	**35819**	**9560.17**	**27042.03**	**15495.62**
农副食品加工业	Food Processing	1108	206.77	378.27	230.48
食品制造业	Food Production	317	63.14	228.08	142.03
饮料制造业	Beverage Production	215	86.87	184.73	89.70
烟草加工业	Tobacco Processing	5	186.32	106.13	68.40
纺织业	Textile Industry	5510	924.59	2562.28	1404.33

MAIN ECONOMIC INDICATORS OF ABOVE DESIGNATED SIZE INDUSTRIAL ENTERPRISES (2006)

(100 million yuan)

应收账款 Accounts Receivable	存货 Stock	#产成品 Finished Products	流动资产年平均余额 Annual Average Balance of Circulating Funds	固定资产原价 Original Value of Fixed Assets	固定资产年平均余额 Annual Average Balance of Fixed Assets	无形资产 Invisible Assets
4954.52	**4280.54**	**1527.95**	**15136.91**	**16280.94**	**10571.79**	**813.52**
2254.48	2403.37	939.68	8590.23	9355.28	5930.36	528.80
131.50	246.76	62.00	934.63	2270.79	1368.34	46.54
179.04	179.06	65.16	617.86	446.73	292.43	24.03
84.21	54.52	28.35	214.27	126.15	75.45	8.51
7.44	3.67	1.63	16.39	14.90	8.34	0.94
545.44	681.60	258.81	2423.58	3066.20	1965.19	218.51
44.88	80.80	24.25	356.04	633.24	369.99	44.07
160.92	290.48	98.59	874.01	943.41	504.19	50.98
1141.25	944.06	423.26	3495.70	2472.97	1706.81	177.58
4.68	3.23	1.88	13.79	14.14	9.62	1.71
754.34	580.80	198.55	2104.99	2088.31	1380.23	87.31
1945.70	1296.36	389.72	4441.69	4837.34	3261.19	197.40
1291.94	1378.93	532.68	4606.33	4474.97	2971.58	267.42
3662.58	2901.61	995.27	10530.58	11805.96	7600.21	546.10
1191.44	1281.69	389.25	4373.53	6112.07	3739.06	245.02
1860.87	1579.50	549.25	5578.41	5955.26	3902.30	305.22
1902.21	1419.35	589.44	5184.96	4213.60	2930.42	263.27
19.32	**23.90**	**8.82**	**135.00**	**368.86**	**209.44**	**26.73**
6.36	11.41	4.08	78.50	167.29	103.37	20.08
3.16	4.16	0.22	13.19	133.37	67.04	0.86
2.39	2.07	0.78	14.31	15.81	7.71	2.36
0.23	0.91	0.58	3.74	2.66	1.29	0.14
7.07	5.28	3.09	24.77	49.10	29.64	3.27
0.10	0.07	0.07	0.49	0.63	0.39	0.01
4832.05	**4227.57**	**1518.35**	**14420.09**	**12871.53**	**8385.88**	**759.98**
40.22	78.37	27.38	218.48	155.76	115.32	12.03
27.26	32.98	10.58	127.22	95.06	61.22	7.06
11.73	31.13	7.92	84.01	103.98	66.01	8.33
8.26	60.34	2.91	122.15	55.94	28.64	0.35
323.65	452.07	189.72	1323.65	1336.24	858.36	86.52

8-2 续表 1

单位:亿元

项目	Item	企业单位数(个) Number of Enterprises (unit)	增加值 Added Value	资产总计 Total Assets	流动资产 Circulating Funds
纺织服装、鞋、帽制造业	Textile, Garments, Shoes and Hats	2293	399.35	794.23	497.00
皮革、毛皮、羽毛(绒)及其制品业	Leather, Furs, Down and Related Products	452	75.91	169.12	113.62
木材加工及木、竹、藤、棕、草制造业	Timber Processing, Wood, Bamboo, Cane, Palm Fiber and Straw Products	803	109.91	227.83	123.50
家具制造业	Furniture Manufacturing	162	28.62	129.13	57.18
造纸及纸制品业	Papermaking and Paper Products	584	158.31	723.24	274.23
印刷业和记录媒介的复制	Printing and Record Pressing	337	40.71	136.36	73.05
文教体育用品制造业	Stationery, Education and Sports Goods	587	73.39	132.84	83.48
石油加工、炼焦及核燃料加工业	Petroleum Processing, Coking Products and Nuclear Fuel Processing	140	77.41	263.59	131.10
化学原料及化学制品制造业	Raw Chemical Materials and Chemical Products	3164	927.44	2871.58	1440.91
医药制造业	Medical and Pharmaceutical Products	456	184.78	438.23	237.03
化学纤维制造业	Chemical Fibers	485	220.51	675.45	288.96
橡胶制品业	Rubber Products	386	93.98	322.82	144.58
塑料制品业	Plastic Products	1372	200.51	624.08	336.40
非金属矿物制品业	Nonmetal Mineral Products	1701	279.54	977.24	469.81
黑色金属冶炼及压延加工业	Smelting and Pressing of Ferrous Metals	998	827.02	2611.25	1289.80
有色金属冶炼及压延加工业	Smelting and Pressing of Nonferrous Metals	793	295.72	481.75	337.86
金属制品业	Metal Products	2157	392.93	1027.40	660.57
通用设备制造业	Ordinary Machinery Manufacturing	3793	637.63	1777.72	1135.71
专用设备制造业	Special Purposes Equipment Manufacturing	1809	295.92	919.15	598.74
交通运输设备制造业	Transportation Equipment Manufacturing	1495	428.33	1691.07	1021.43
电气机械及器材制造业	Electric Equipment and Machinery	2316	738.86	2069.57	1417.80
通信设备、计算机及其他电子设备制造业	Telecommunications Equipment, Computer and Other Electronic Equipments	1499	1392.62	3999.25	2489.11
仪器仪表及文化、办公用机械制造业	Instruments, Meters, Cultural and Official Machinery	471	156.06	394.65	260.74
工艺品及其他制造业	Handicraft Artical and Other Manufacturing	366	47.09	102.53	58.87
废弃资源和废旧材料回收加工业	Waste Resouces and Junk Material Recycled	45	9.91	22.46	19.19
电力、燃气及水的生产和供应业	**Electric Power, Gas and Water Production and Supply**	**319**	**558.51**	**3009.97**	**598.13**
电力、热力的生产和供应业	Electric Power, Steam and Hot Water Production and Supply	187	521.60	2585.39	477.33
燃气生产和供应	Gas Production and Supply	31	14.32	110.60	43.04
水的生产和供应业	Tap Water Production and Supply	101	22.59	313.98	77.76

Continued 1

(100 million yuan)

应收账款 Accounts Receivable	存货 Stock	#产成品 Finished Products	流动资产年平均余额 Annual Average Balance of Circulating Funds	固定资产原价 Original Value of Fixed Assets	固定资产年平均余额 Annual Average Balance of Fixed Assets	无形资产 Invisible Assets
100.92	138.25	62.40	459.36	278.96	191.34	23.10
30.18	40.62	15.70	104.62	51.50	35.12	7.64
23.49	38.44	18.97	117.68	110.82	77.97	8.41
14.21	16.25	4.74	53.44	66.93	55.46	10.12
90.35	63.67	23.26	259.68	527.39	391.25	16.05
27.88	12.46	5.43	68.87	83.09	51.62	3.07
27.68	24.10	6.81	78.15	55.18	38.34	3.69
23.51	57.41	14.15	111.84	185.59	102.29	5.53
383.54	369.54	150.75	1321.50	1675.73	1055.43	88.80
72.50	46.45	22.35	226.80	213.12	135.20	20.93
43.60	72.59	27.35	285.31	459.70	278.04	14.06
54.98	42.34	19.31	133.24	198.29	141.48	7.96
132.25	77.98	32.99	321.38	332.66	221.19	16.63
151.33	109.45	47.17	444.59	582.71	388.55	30.09
172.23	436.58	148.50	1223.55	1354.18	864.91	66.98
107.32	89.96	35.62	304.57	157.72	107.41	11.13
213.57	171.23	69.72	613.47	385.81	260.94	29.16
364.34	330.64	118.35	1072.98	686.24	442.13	69.68
198.56	171.41	63.07	553.29	340.48	226.70	30.95
253.62	276.05	83.71	930.91	672.12	431.27	57.25
590.15	306.11	119.98	1271.59	645.56	417.95	54.72
1225.52	590.35	156.08	2267.52	1866.72	1212.14	58.01
93.11	67.57	20.90	246.54	142.13	94.07	8.61
17.16	16.30	6.44	54.13	48.40	32.73	2.93
8.92	6.93	6.10	19.58	3.55	2.79	0.18
103.16	**29.07**	**0.78**	**581.82**	**3040.54**	**1976.46**	**26.81**
92.88	22.44	0.44	470.62	2725.93	1741.21	19.73
4.33	4.17	0.19	36.09	60.28	45.15	2.58
5.94	2.46	0.16	75.10	254.34	190.11	4.50

8-2 续表 2

单位:亿元

项　　　目	Item	负债合计 Total Liabilitise	所有者权益 Creditor's Equity	#实收资本 Total Capital Hold	主营业务收入 Major Business Revenue
总　计	**Total**	**18477.92**	**12021.04**	**7313.93**	**41015.28**
按登记注册类型分	**Grouped by Type of Registration**				
内资企业	Inner Funded Enterprises	11046.06	6558.14	3262.21	24082.19
国有企业	State-Owned Enterprises	1584.75	1128.06	458.72	2661.53
集体企业	Collective-Owned Enterprises	635.10	436.79	139.94	1712.79
股份合作企业	Share Holding Cooperative Enterprises	198.62	131.11	51.25	580.67
联营企业	Joint-Ownership Enterprises	17.96	12.22	6.95	42.84
有限责任公司	Responsibility Co. Ltd.	3536.42	2002.87	1050.35	5693.16
#国有独资	State Solely Funded	599.20	388.14	223.16	649.47
股份有限公司	Share Holding Co. Ltd.	927.92	787.68	320.79	2441.72
私营企业	Private Entreprises	4126.61	2048.66	1227.10	10912.76
其他企业	Other Enterprises	18.67	10.76	7.09	36.72
港、澳、台商投资企业	Hong Kong, Macao and Taiwan Funded Enterprises	2397.77	1685.12	1214.03	4689.29
外商投资企业	Foreign Funded Enterprises	5034.09	3777.77	2837.69	12243.80
按轻重工业分	**Grouped by Light and Heavy Industry**				
轻工业	Light Industry	5256.98	3584.47	2279.54	12359.38
重工业	Heavy Industry	13220.95	8436.57	5034.39	28655.90
按企业规模分	**Grouped by Scale of Enterprise**				
大型企业	Large	5970.01	3985.09	1798.86	13123.60
中型企业	Medium	6829.03	4376.20	2866.59	12810.05
小型企业	Small	5678.89	3659.75	2648.48	15081.63
按行业分	**Grouped by Sector**				
采矿业	**Mining and Quarrying**	**242.79**	**206.19**	**105.77**	**326.98**
煤炭开采和洗选业	Coal Mining and Processing	155.19	100.43	39.81	149.13
石油和天然气开采业	Petroleum and Natural Gas Extraction	26.82	63.43	45.77	67.99
黑色金属矿采选业	Ferrous Metals Mining and Processing	16.97	10.95	4.23	31.14
有色金属矿采选业	Nonferrous Metals Mining and Processing	3.94	2.64	1.52	7.42
非金属矿采选业	Nonmetal Minerals Mining and Processing	38.91	28.68	14.37	70.08
其他矿采选业	Nonmetal Minerals Mining and Processing	0.97	0.07	0.07	1.22
制造业	**Manufacturing**	**16363.32**	**10676.69**	**6598.77**	**38773.02**
农副食品加工业	Food Processing	244.66	133.61	92.12	855.58
食品制造业	Food Production	130.47	97.60	55.29	212.35
饮料制造业	Beverage Production	104.36	80.37	71.69	273.89
烟草加工业	Tobacco Processing	27.81	78.32	31.21	201.13
纺织业	Textile Industry	1659.18	903.10	574.45	3628.93

Continued 2

(100 million yuan)

主营业务成本 Cost of Major Business	主营业务税金及附加 Tax and Extra of Major Business	营业利润 Operating Profits	利润总额 Total Profits	利税总额 Total Pre-Tax Profits	应交增值税 Value-Added Tax Payable	全部从业人员年平均人数(万人) Annual Average of All Employees (10000 Persons)
36358.55	**242.48**	**1833.52**	**1906.91**	**3168.41**	**1019.03**	**774.50**
21355.10	223.25	948.63	1015.61	1977.03	738.17	482.30
2195.53	110.47	153.49	158.59	416.64	147.57	30.61
1566.90	7.18	60.89	75.33	127.03	44.52	25.54
526.86	2.50	20.31	25.81	46.96	18.64	12.12
38.09	0.15	1.90	2.11	3.43	1.18	1.14
4889.03	32.85	256.46	286.20	518.11	199.05	103.07
528.37	9.77	32.07	35.29	76.20	31.14	18.12
2178.40	22.71	87.29	103.83	176.84	50.30	31.80
9928.88	47.16	366.68	362.08	684.94	275.70	276.81
31.40	0.23	1.61	1.64	3.08	1.21	1.20
4151.16	4.90	258.28	259.22	364.40	100.28	105.60
10852.29	14.33	626.60	632.08	826.99	180.58	186.60
10767.36	135.60	507.30	522.29	970.53	312.65	332.00
25591.19	106.88	1326.22	1384.62	2197.88	706.38	442.50
11757.61	111.16	555.19	595.08	990.38	284.14	159.76
11080.43	76.20	690.51	709.55	1122.41	336.66	248.16
13520.52	55.12	587.82	602.28	1055.63	398.23	366.58
214.06	**11.46**	**46.26**	**47.15**	**85.71**	**27.10**	**17.74**
108.41	2.38	7.72	8.81	23.28	12.08	10.94
21.15	7.42	30.17	29.99	45.50	8.09	1.98
24.53	0.34	1.93	1.92	4.45	2.19	1.12
5.63	0.05	0.88	0.97	1.40	0.38	0.16
53.32	1.26	5.53	5.42	11.00	4.32	3.54
1.03	0.02	0.03	0.03	0.09	0.05	0.01
34468.65	**221.03**	**1684.98**	**1754.03**	**2842.13**	**867.06**	**743.74**
789.83	2.31	22.54	22.94	36.05	10.81	11.14
171.15	0.88	8.77	9.93	18.67	7.87	5.58
215.68	12.35	16.16	16.09	38.99	10.54	6.81
51.99	89.81	46.88	46.80	162.83	26.22	0.77
3339.02	10.95	98.06	104.62	197.98	82.42	114.98

单位:亿元

项目	Item	负债合计 Total Liabilitise	所有者权益 Creditor's Equity	#实收资本 Total Capital Hold	主营业务收入 Major Business Revenue
纺织服装、鞋、帽制造业	Textile, Garments, Shoes and Hats	446.45	347.79	179.74	1392.48
皮革、毛皮、羽毛(绒)及其制品业	Leather, Furs, Down and Related Products	102.78	66.34	37.53	285.85
木材加工及木、竹、藤、棕、草制造业	Timber Processing, Wood, Bamboo, Cane, Palm Fiber and Straw Products	134.51	93.32	50.69	390.40
家具制造业	Furniture Manufacturing	69.59	59.55	27.31	115.60
造纸及纸制品业	Papermaking and Paper Products	463.85	259.38	253.51	563.11
印刷业和记录媒介的复制	Printing and Record Pressing	78.90	57.45	34.56	126.55
文教体育用品制造业	Stationery, Education and Sports Goods	78.07	54.77	38.00	272.05
石油加工、炼焦及核燃料加工业	Petroleum Processing, Coking Products and Nuclear Fuel Processing	176.06	87.52	59.70	774.21
化学原料及化学制品制造业	Raw Chemical Materials and Chemical Products	1573.76	1297.81	720.96	3987.76
医药制造业	Medical and Pharmaceutical Products	198.95	239.28	121.65	518.75
化学纤维制造业	Chemical Fibers	378.24	297.20	206.76	989.04
橡胶制品业	Rubber Products	178.76	144.06	113.35	346.15
塑料制品业	Plastic Products	353.02	271.06	190.06	798.02
非金属矿物制品业	Nonmetal Mineral Products	575.15	402.09	278.37	993.68
黑色金属冶炼及压延加工业	Smelting and Pressing of Ferrous Metals	1667.30	943.95	461.40	3825.00
有色金属冶炼及压延加工业	Smelting and Pressing of Nonferrous Metals	298.49	183.26	112.84	1391.19
金属制品业	Metal Products	626.48	400.92	230.13	1482.64
通用设备制造业	Ordinary Machinery Manufacturing	1089.10	686.80	402.73	2446.58
专用设备制造业	Special Purposes Equipment Manufacturing	533.72	385.43	238.55	1092.66
交通运输设备制造业	Transportation Equipment Manufacturing	1109.98	580.89	400.42	1707.38
电气机械及器材制造业	Electric Equipment and Machinery	1244.94	824.63	481.82	2890.28
通信设备、计算机及其他电子设备制造业	Telecommunications Equipment, Computer and Other Electronic Equipments	2518.33	1480.92	1001.95	6374.92
仪器仪表及文化、办公用机械制造业	Instruments, Meters, Cultural and Official Machinery	223.71	170.94	101.58	642.10
工艺品及其他制造业	Handicraft Artical and Other Manufacturing	57.44	45.09	28.34	163.12
废弃资源和废旧材料回收加工业	Waste Resouces and Junk Material Recycled	19.24	3.21	2.06	31.64
电力、燃气及水的生产和供应业	**Electric Power, Gas and Water Production and Supply**	**1871.81**	**1138.16**	**609.39**	**1915.27**
电力、热力的生产和供应业	Electric Power, Steam and Hot Water Production and Supply	1632.41	952.98	507.74	1800.83
燃气生产和供应	Gas Production and Supply	68.38	42.22	29.75	71.10
水的生产和供应业	Tap Water Production and Supply	171.01	142.96	71.90	43.34

Continued 3

(100 million yuan)

主营业务成本 Cost of Major Business	主营业务税金及附加 Tax and Extra of Major Business	营业利润 Operating Profits	利润总额 Total Profits	利税总额 Total Pre-Tax Profits	应交增值税 Value-Added Tax Payable	全部从业人员年平均人数(万人) Annual Average of All Employees (10000 Persons)
1217.88	4.29	67.59	68.67	106.21	33.26	64.14
250.75	0.72	11.93	11.65	19.84	7.46	13.25
349.83	1.55	14.19	15.16	28.62	11.91	12.77
102.04	0.41	4.13	4.02	5.62	1.19	4.30
478.46	1.17	29.59	31.99	51.92	18.77	9.74
102.68	0.55	10.88	11.17	16.80	5.09	4.91
240.87	0.72	8.90	8.53	15.26	6.01	13.18
755.79	14.79	-13.70	-5.90	23.71	14.83	2.30
3516.92	15.98	209.98	221.63	336.66	99.06	43.34
315.43	2.40	41.46	42.35	76.87	32.11	10.37
931.03	1.38	27.18	29.00	46.42	16.03	10.38
299.23	1.37	14.55	14.15	23.43	7.91	8.80
707.85	1.83	34.75	34.95	53.35	16.56	21.02
857.90	5.14	43.92	49.15	92.35	38.06	28.47
3510.87	8.91	183.02	183.67	289.03	96.46	25.30
1321.71	3.09	36.56	41.12	71.61	27.41	8.71
1298.98	5.20	87.42	81.56	123.53	36.77	34.23
2096.05	8.83	138.83	140.94	220.31	70.54	59.75
919.03	3.70	68.57	70.20	104.62	30.72	28.69
1478.92	11.67	67.67	73.33	125.76	40.77	35.57
2508.32	6.97	132.77	141.39	209.09	60.74	47.56
5900.22	2.41	230.99	242.46	287.93	43.07	99.74
565.97	0.92	34.09	35.18	45.15	9.05	11.02
144.50	0.61	6.75	6.85	12.11	4.65	6.71
29.77	0.13	0.54	0.46	1.38	0.79	0.21
1675.84	**9.98**	**102.28**	**105.73**	**240.57**	**124.86**	**13.03**
1585.42	9.54	98.48	101.19	230.59	119.86	9.73
63.57	0.17	4.00	4.39	7.06	2.50	0.95
26.85	0.27	-0.19	0.16	2.92	2.49	2.35

8－3　国有控股工业企业主要经济指标（2006 年）

单位：亿元

项　目	Item	企业单位数（个）Number of Enterprises (unit)	增加值 Added Value	资产总计 Total Assets
总　计	**Total**	**916**	**1601.48**	**6338.42**
按登记注册类型分	**Grouped by Type of Registration**			
内资企业	Inner Funded Enterprises	817	1421.58	5627.45
国有企业	State-owned Enterprises	440	858.91	2714.82
股份合作企业	Share Holding cooperative Enterprises			
联营企业	Joint-ownership Enterprises	15	2.08	5.93
有限责任公司	Responsibility Co. Ltd.	308	449.75	2263.95
#国有独资	State solely Funded	54	211.19	987.34
股份有限公司	Share Holding Co。Ltd.	53	110.44	642.22
其他企业	Other Enterprises	1	0.39	0.53
港、澳、台商投资企业	Hong Kong, Macao and Taiwan Funded Enterprises	33	43.03	190.91
外商投资企业	Foreign Funded Enterprises	66	136.86	520.06
按轻重工业分	**Grouped by Light and Heavy Industry**			
轻工业	Light Industry	356	359.18	1026.69
重工业	Heavy Industry	560	1242.30	5311.73
按企业规模分	**Grouped by Scale of Enterprise**			
大型企业	Large	65	936.81	3621.89
中型企业	Medium	292	572.44	2266.23
小型企业	Small	559	92.23	450.30
按行业分	**Grouped by Sector**			
采矿业	**Mining and Quarrying**	**32**	**162.21**	**391.46**
煤炭开采和洗选业	Coal Mining and Processing	9	85.57	254.20
石油和天然气开采业	Petroleum and Natural Gas Extraction	2	62.27	90.24
黑色金属矿采选业	Ferrous Metals Mining and Processing	3	8.29	19.80
有色金属矿采选业	Nonferrous Metals Mining and Processing	1	0.44	1.50
非金属矿采选业	Nonmetal Minerals Mining and Processing	17	5.65	25.72
其他矿采选业	Nonmetal Minerals Mining and Processing			
制造业	**Manufacturing**	**752**	**1010.85**	**3703.79**
农副食品加工业	Food Processing	48	4.88	10.65
食品制造业	Food Production	24	4.79	32.00
饮料制造业	Beverage Production	20	15.28	29.72
烟草加工业	Tobacco Processing	5	186.32	106.13
纺织业	Textile Industry	62	36.18	189.33
纺织服装、鞋、帽制造业	Textile, Garments, Shoes and Hats	20	2.85	13.09
皮革、毛皮、羽毛(绒)及其制品业	Leather, Furs, Down and Related Products	4	0.16	0.76
木材加工及木、竹、藤、棕、草制造业	Timber Processing, Wood, Bamboo, Cane, Palm, Fiber and Straw Products	2	18.36	80.04

MAIN ECONOMIC INDICATORS OF STATE SHREHOLOING INDUSTRIAL ENTERPRISES (2006)

(100 million yuan)

应收帐款 Accounts Receivable	存货 Finished Products	流动资产年平均余额 Annual Average Balance of Circulating Funds	固定资产原价 Original Value of Fixed Assets	固定资产净值年平均余额 Annual Average Balance of Net Value of Fixed Assets
385.39	**618.40**	**2318.42**	**4897.71**	**2966.71**
329.17	562.60	2106.12	4230.66	2519.62
131.50	246.76	934.63	2270.79	1368.34
1.07	1.60	3.25	3.49	1.90
154.84	198.15	880.85	1438.95	917.53
44.88	80.80	356.04	633.24	369.99
41.61	115.98	287.04	517.36	231.81
0.14	0.11	0.35	0.08	0.04
9.96	17.68	72.18	239.82	117.03
46.25	38.12	140.12	427.22	330.07
56.48	158.40	485.76	718.57	437.19
328.90	460.00	1832.66	4179.14	2529.52
145.90	343.32	1276.05	2914.89	1640.19
195.56	228.34	861.28	1692.71	1119.12
43.93	46.74	181.09	290.11	207.40
12.53	**18.53**	**109.45**	**335.90**	**189.40**
6.23	11.28	77.68	166.54	102.70
3.16	4.16	13.19	133.37	67.04
1.31	1.32	9.30	12.66	6.00
0.01	0.06	0.74	0.70	0.53
1.82	1.71	8.54	22.63	13.12
314.96	**585.26**	**1820.46**	**2223.95**	**1263.82**
1.18	1.69	5.13	6.70	4.23
1.91	11.17	20.57	9.94	5.91
1.60	8.13	17.36	12.20	6.88
8.26	60.34	122.15	55.94	28.64
11.83	28.48	81.33	128.30	73.26
1.36	2.24	7.83	7.29	4.44
0.12	0.19	0.42	0.76	0.29
9.11	10.53	38.16	36.84	23.97

单位:亿元

项目	Item	企业单位数(个) Number of Enterprises (unit)	增加值 Added Value	资产总计 Total Assets
家具制造业	Furniture Manufacturing	1	0.17	1.16
造纸及纸制品业	Papermaking and Paper Products	7	3.63	11.81
印刷业和记录媒介的复制业	Printing and Record Pressing	28	6.37	22.23
文教体育用品制造业	Stationery, Education and Sports Goods	2	0.18	0.52
石油加工、炼焦及核燃料加工业	Petroleum Processing, Coking Products and Nuclear Fuel Processing	10	35.02	151.91
化学原料及化学制品制造业	Raw Chemical Materials and Chemical Products	71	213.18	894.92
医药制造业	Medical and Pharmaceutical Products	24	15.04	56.39
化学纤维制造业	Chemical Fibers	9	34.48	156.80
橡胶制品业	Rubber Products	3	1.12	4.73
塑料制品业	Plastic Products	11	5.64	20.08
非金属矿物制品业	Nonmetal Mineral Products	42	24.77	93.36
黑色金属冶炼及压延加工业	Smelting and Pressing of Ferrous Metals	15	62.40	229.18
有色金属冶炼及压延加工业	Smelting and Pressing of Nonferrous Metals	6	3.60	12.22
金属制品业	Metal Products	26	39.06	109.95
通用设备制造业	Ordinary Machinery Manufacturing	80	71.55	255.03
专用设备制造业	Special Purposes Equipment Manufacturing	42	16.85	83.25
交通运输设备制造业	Transportation Equipment Manufacturing	78	107.79	604.46
电气机械及器材制造业	Electric Equipment and Machinery	44	55.71	248.67
通信设备、计算机及其他电子设备制造业	Telecommunications Equipment, Computer and Other Electronic Equipments	42	35.12	228.61
仪器仪表及文化、办公用机械制造业	Instruments, Meters, Cultural and Official Machinery	20	8.96	50.68
工艺品及其他制造业	Handicraft Artical and Other Manufacturing	5	1.22	5.50
废弃资源和废旧材料回收加工业	Waste Resources and Junk Material Recycled	1	0.15	0.60
电力、燃气及水的生产和供应业	**Electric Power, Gas and Water Production and Supply**	**132**	**428.42**	**2243.18**
电力、热力的生产和供应业	Electric Power, Steam and Hot Water Production and Supply	54	405.53	1925.34
燃气生产和供应	Gas Production and Supply	9	4.91	63.60
水的生产和供应业	Tap Water Production and Supply	69	17.97	254.23

Continued 1

(100 million yuan)

应收帐款 Accounts Receivable	存货 Finished Products	流动资产年平均余额 Annual Average Balance of Circulating Funds	固定资产原价 Original Value of Fixed Assets	固定资产净值年平均余额 Annual Average Balance of Net Value of Fixed Assets
0.07	**0.33**	**0.50**	**0.87**	**0.46**
0.44	1.41	4.95	11.94	5.36
2.03	1.85	10.83	14.95	8.23
0.05	0.12	0.23	0.29	0.21
9.48	42.95	58.18	139.45	73.51
43.51	88.86	305.73	752.31	424.46
6.27	6.86	29.63	26.65	17.36
4.38	17.05	57.93	173.62	84.82
0.94	0.84	2.58	2.20	1.13
1.42	2.89	9.33	11.58	8.22
8.24	9.90	36.82	65.39	44.94
10.41	24.11	92.42	192.45	102.81
1.82	1.99	7.15	5.64	3.12
13.31	16.83	61.29	49.62	33.50
26.14	68.16	158.97	81.69	44.03
13.48	18.58	54.90	31.51	20.35
55.28	85.11	312.25	252.71	151.03
49.43	36.89	139.74	69.43	47.03
25.34	29.32	151.42	65.16	34.39
6.96	7.24	29.20	15.19	9.19
0.58	1.20	2.92	3.33	2.09
0.00	0.00	0.55	0.00	0.00
57.89	**14.61**	**388.51**	**2337.85**	**1513.49**
52.19	11.48	310.24	2091.01	1328.16
0.66	1.59	19.30	35.79	28.20
5.05	1.54	58.97	211.05	157.13

单位:亿元

项目	Item	负债合计 Total Liabilities	主营业务收入 Major Business Revenue	主营业务成本 Cost of Major Business
总计	**Total**	**3649.97**	**5994.26**	**5096.93**
按登记注册类型分	**Grouped by Type of Registration**			
内资企业	Inner Funded Enterprises	3333.15	5325.96	4528.89
国有企业	State-owned Enterprises	1584.75	2661.53	2195.53
股份合作企业	Share Holding Cooperative Enterprises			
联营企业	Joint-ownership Enterprises	3.77	7.43	6.40
有限责任公司	Responsibility Co. Ltd.	1442.80	1509.69	1249.58
#国有独资	State Solely Owned	599.20	649.47	528.37
股份有限公司	Share Holding Co, Ltd.	301.36	1145.64	1075.88
其他企业	Other Enterprises	0.47	1.67	1.50
港、澳、台商投资企业	Hong Kong, Macao and Taiwan Funded Enterprises	65.97	237.27	218.96
外商投资企业	Foreign Funded Enterprises	250.86	431.03	349.08
按轻重工业分	**Grouped by Light and Heavy Industry**			
轻工业	Light Industry	472.70	878.43	626.54
重工业	Heavy Industry	3177.27	5115.82	4470.38
按企业规模分	**Grouped by Scale of Enterprise**			
大型企业	Large	2005.55	3965.26	3463.09
中型企业	Medium	1358.84	1679.17	1335.24
小型企业	Small	285.58	349.83	298.59
按行业分	**Grouped by Sector**			
采矿业	**Mining and Quarrying**	**211.84**	**242.14**	**144.82**
煤炭开采和洗选业	Coal Mining and Processing	154.37	143.72	103.58
石油和天然气开采业	Petroleum and Natural Gas Extraction	26.82	67.99	21.15
黑色金属矿采选业	Ferrous Metals Mining and Processing	11.75	14.82	11.05
有色金属矿采选业	Nonferrous Metals Mining and Processing	1.09	0.83	0.35
非金属矿采选业	Nonmetal Minerals Mining and Processing	17.81	14.79	8.70
其他矿采选业	Nonmetal Minerals Mining and Processing			
制造业	**Manufacturing**	**2071.89**	**4194.16**	**3561.43**
农副食品加工业	Food Processing	8.67	22.41	21.31
食品制造业	Food Production	21.22	16.25	12.25
饮料制造业	Beverage Production	20.01	34.52	18.91
烟草加工业	Tobacco Processing	27.81	201.13	51.99
纺织业	Textile Industry	108.85	157.16	142.53
纺织服装、鞋、帽制造业	Textile, Garments, Shoes and Hats	6.40	12.40	10.77
皮革、毛皮、羽毛(绒)及其制品业	Leather, Furs, Down and Related Products	0.61	0.77	0.74
木材加工及木、竹、藤、棕、草制造业	Timber Processing, Wood, Bamboo, Cane, Palm, Fiber and Straw Products	59.49	63.05	52.39

Continued 2

(100 million yuan)

主营业务税金及附加 Tax and Extra of Major Business	利润总额 Total Profits	利税总额 Total Pre-Tax Profits	应交增值税 Value-Added Tax Payable	全部从业人员年平均人数(万人) Annual Average of All Employees (10000 Persons)
145.08	**322.62**	**727.28**	**259.58**	**74.38**
144.34	262.03	638.86	232.49	69.15
110.47	158.59	416.64	147.57	30.61
0.03	0.21	0.41	0.17	0.24
16.40	80.48	165.68	68.80	32.53
9.77	35.29	76.20	31.14	18.12
17.44	22.73	56.09	15.92	5.76
0.00	0.01	0.04	0.03	0.00
0.37	9.59	18.23	8.27	2.07
0.37	51.01	70.19	18.81	3.16
97.74	75.94	221.71	48.03	17.65
47.33	246.68	505.56	211.55	56.73
94.14	168.73	412.28	149.40	40.89
49.05	138.80	284.73	96.88	25.64
1.88	15.09	30.27	13.30	7.86
10.31	**40.63**	**73.74**	**22.80**	**14.91**
2.28	8.63	22.90	11.99	10.79
7.42	29.99	45.50	8.09	1.98
0.16	1.01	2.34	1.17	0.80
0.01	0.13	0.22	0.09	0.07
0.44	0.87	2.78	1.47	1.28
126.02	**222.12**	**487.55**	**139.40**	**49.41**
0.03	0.02	0.16	0.11	0.51
0.18	1.09	2.06	0.79	0.55
5.51	3.23	11.17	2.43	1.16
89.81	46.80	162.83	26.22	0.77
0.72	3.69	8.82	4.42	6.14
0.04	0.29	0.60	0.27	0.96
0.00	−0.03	0.00	0.02	0.07
0.16	1.40	3.66	2.10	0.94

8－3 续表 3

单位:亿元

项　目	Item	负债合计 Total Liabilities	主营业务收入 Major Business Revenue	主营业务成本 Cost of Major Business
家具制造业	Furniture Manufacturing	0.66	0.82	0.77
造纸及纸制品业	Papermaking and Paper Products	4.77	6.58	5.24
印刷业和记录媒介的复制业	Printing and Record Pressing	13.56	17.55	13.94
文教体育用品制造业	Stationery, Education and Sports Goods	0.38	0.50	0.42
石油加工、炼焦及核燃料加工业	Petroleum Processing, Coking Products and Nuclear Fuel Processing	111.72	579.97	573.44
化学原料及化学制品制造业	Raw Chemical Materials and Chemical Products	412.18	1089.41	955.51
医药制造业	Medical and Pharmaceutical Products	21.63	42.82	26.85
化学纤维制造业	Chemical Fibers	36.61	207.39	192.91
橡胶制品业	Rubber Products	3.03	3.51	2.68
塑料制品业	Plastic Products	13.23	23.08	21.31
非金属矿物制品业	Nonmetal Mineral Products	59.79	79.92	66.76
黑色金属冶炼及压延加工业	Smelting and Pressing of Ferrous Metals	89.68	215.71	185.04
有色金属冶炼及压延加工业	Smelting and Pressing of Nonferrous Metals	8.33	26.45	25.46
金属制品业	Metal Products	66.33	164.28	145.67
通用设备制造业	Ordinary Machinery Manufacturing	179.12	322.48	277.27
专用设备制造业	Special Purposes Equipment Manufacturing	52.62	70.89	58.85
交通运输设备制造业	Transportation Equipment Manufacturing	408.50	449.30	379.98
电气机械及器材制造业	Electric Equipment and Machinery	137.80	233.36	196.31
通信设备、计算机及其他电子设备制造业	Telecommunications Equipment, Computer and Other Electronic Equipments	167.16	124.21	102.30
仪器仪表及文化、办公用机械制造业	Instruments, Meters, Cultural and Official Machinery	28.56	24.24	17.08
工艺品及其他制造业	Handicraft Artical and Other Manufacturing	2.71	3.41	2.39
废弃资源和废旧材料回收加工业	Waste Resources and Junk Material Recycled	0.46	0.59	0.37
电力、燃气及水的生产和供应业	**Electric Power, Gas and Water Production and Supply**	**1366.24**	**1557.96**	**1390.68**
电力、热力的生产和供应业	Electric Power, Steam and Hot Water Production and Supply	1197.99	1495.56	1344.65
燃气生产和供应	Gas Production and Supply	40.99	28.79	25.32
水的生产和供应业	Tap Water Production and Supply	127.26	33.61	20.71

Continued 3

(100 million yuan)

主营业务税金及附加 Tax and Extra of Major Business	利润总额 Total Profits	利税总额 Total Profits	应交增值税 Value-Added Tax Payable	全部从业人员年平均人数(万人) Annual Average of All Employees (10000 Persons)
0.01	**-0.10**	**-0.10**	**0.00**	**0.07**
0.05	0.19	0.63	0.39	0.20
0.07	1.45	2.50	0.98	0.56
0.00	0.05	0.08	0.03	0.03
13.85	-13.59	12.04	11.79	1.07
7.08	76.49	113.27	29.70	7.36
0.34	5.21	8.42	2.87	1.19
0.36	7.44	13.03	5.22	1.64
0.02	0.11	0.31	0.17	0.18
0.02	0.46	0.97	0.49	0.27
0.51	4.49	8.75	3.75	1.38
1.11	17.29	30.24	11.84	1.72
0.10	0.33	0.94	0.51	0.20
0.45	7.44	12.60	4.70	1.47
0.85	15.60	25.75	9.31	5.13
0.27	2.33	4.73	2.13	1.60
3.26	17.48	30.92	10.18	7.85
0.66	13.65	19.62	5.31	1.99
0.38	6.38	9.29	2.52	3.29
0.11	2.60	3.72	1.01	0.95
0.02	0.24	0.39	0.13	0.16
0.06	0.10	0.16	0.00	0.00
8.74	**59.86**	**165.99**	**97.38**	**10.06**
8.46	58.73	160.86	93.68	7.54
0.09	1.56	3.44	1.78	0.57
0.19	-0.42	1.69	1.92	1.95

8－4 “三资”工业企业主要经济指标（2006 年）

单位：亿元

项　　　目	Item	企业单位数（个）Number of Enterprises (unit)	增加值 Added Value	资产总计 Total Assets
总　　计	**Total**	**8495**	**4130.05**	**12894.76**
按轻重工业分	**Grouped by Light and Heavy Industry**			
轻工业	Light Industry	4026	1253.15	3702.52
重工业	Heavy Industry	4469	2876.90	9192.24
按企业规模分	**Grouped by Scale of Enterprise**			
大型企业	Large	145	1104.67	3147.86
中型企业	Medium	1610	1740.27	5991.34
小型企业	Small	6740	1285.12	3755.55
按行业分	**Grouped by Sector**			
采矿业	**Mining and Quarrying**	**11**	**4.18**	**12.97**
非金属矿采选业	Nonmetal Minerals Mining and Processing	11	4.18	12.97
制造业	**Manufacturing**	**8390**	**3993.85**	**12181.49**
农副食品加工业	Food Processing	175	89.32	186.57
食品制造业	Food Production	91	32.19	125.25
饮料制造业	Beverage Production	41	27.03	61.78
纺织业	Textile Industry	1021	207.40	628.58
纺织服装、鞋、帽制造业	Textile, Garments, Shoes and Hats	868	157.49	280.44
皮革、毛皮、羽毛(绒)及其制品业	Leather, Furs, Down and Related Products	176	38.63	94.67
木材加工及木、竹、藤、棕、草制造业	Timber Processing, Wood, Bamboo, Cane, Palm, Fiber and Straw Products	78	18.56	49.83
家具制造业	Furniture Manufacturing	79	20.98	54.46
造纸及纸制品业	Papermaking and Paper Products	127	107.40	593.21
印刷业和记录媒介的复制	Printing and Record Pressing	61	17.12	49.61
文教体育用品制造业	Stationery, Education and Sports Goods	249	44.53	93.50
石油加工、炼焦及核燃料加工业	Petroleum Processing, Coking Products and Nuclear Fuel Processing	17	14.36	44.31

MAIN ECONOMIC INDICATORS OF FOREIGN – FUNDED INDUSTRIAL ENTEPRISES (2006)

(100 million yuan)

应收帐款 Accounts Receivable	存货 Finished Products	流动资产年平均余额 Annual Average Balance of Circulating Funds	固定资产原价 Original Value of Fixed Assets	固定资产净值年平均余额 Annual Average Balance of Net Value of Fixed Assets
2700.04	**1877.16**	**6546.68**	**6925.65**	**4641.43**
629.57	558.82	1928.86	1997.52	1324.86
2070.48	1318.35	4617.82	4928.13	3316.56
789.41	429.94	1615.48	1768.60	1159.99
1172.40	856.84	2914.92	3313.65	2210.25
738.24	590.39	2016.28	1843.41	1271.19
1.58	**0.69**	**4.04**	**11.79**	**6.69**
1.58	0.69	4.04	11.79	6.69
2655.62	**1862.04**	**6372.84**	**6202.88**	**4199.47**
17.22	45.77	117.77	72.98	56.16
16.43	11.66	70.88	51.41	31.71
4.69	9.36	25.64	51.97	29.07
85.03	105.92	322.76	346.20	221.26
40.06	42.71	169.80	107.72	73.59
17.25	24.73	60.42	32.09	22.29
4.47	9.75	29.57	22.63	13.95
11.69	13.30	32.44	22.35	15.34
64.25	46.98	189.39	458.05	346.22
12.52	4.87	26.83	27.76	18.30
19.03	17.74	54.70	38.33	26.47
7.14	6.21	19.78	20.73	12.88

8－4 续表 1

单位：亿元

项目	Item	企业单位数（个） Number of Enterprises (unit)	增加值 Added Value	资产总计 Total Assets
化学原料及化学制品制造业	Raw Chemical Materials and Chemical Products	637	337.74	1165.64
医药制造业	Medical and Pharmaceutical Products	116	59.15	161.52
化学纤维制造业	Chemical Fibers	47	63.28	278.19
橡胶制品业	Rubber Products	121	64.37	247.18
塑料制品业	Plastic Products	414	91.16	339.78
非金属矿物制品业	Nonmetal Mineral Products	313	84.60	371.15
黑色金属冶炼及压延加工业	Smelting and Pressing of Ferrous Metals	120	161.35	518.67
有色金属冶炼及压延加工业	Smelting and Pressing of Nonferrous Metals	150	99.52	195.46
金属制品业	Metal Products	398	125.08	385.78
通用设备制造业	Ordinary Machinery Manufacturing	564	191.68	607.69
专用设备制造业	Special Purposes Equipment Manufacturing	397	109.30	386.54
交通运输设备制造业	Transportation Equipment Manufacturing	368	169.90	663.45
电气机械及器材制造业	Electric Equipment and Machinery	562	254.96	776.41
通信设备、计算机及其他电子设备制造业	Telecommunications Equipment, Computer and Other Electronic Equipments	890	1280.70	3523.17
仪器仪表及文化、办公用机械制造业	Instruments, Meters, Cultural and Official Machinery	164	102.97	235.41
工艺品及其他制造业	Handicraft Artical and Other Manufacturing	134	15.47	44.81
废弃资源和废旧材料回收加工业	Waste Resouces and Junk Material Recycled	12	7.62	18.43
电力、燃气及水的生产和供应业	**Electric Power, Gas and Water Production and Supply**	**94**	**132.02**	**700.29**
电力、热力的生产和供应业	Electric Power, Steam and Hot Water Production and Supply	72	120.24	617.81
燃气生产和供应	Gas Production and Supply	17	10.81	66.14
水的生产和供应业	Tap Water Production and Supply	5	0.98	16.34

Continued 1

(100 million yuan)

应收帐款 Accounts Receivable	存货 Finished Products	流动资产年平均余额 Annual Average Balance of Circulating Funds	固定资产原价 Original Value of Fixed Assets	固定资产净值年平均余额 Annual Average Balance of Net Value of Fixed Assets
182.25	144.56	475.99	711.28	534.27
27.73	18.62	90.25	87.46	49.66
17.45	29.04	112.27	238.65	134.25
40.22	32.34	94.33	164.47	118.80
73.70	40.67	170.66	208.06	137.88
61.29	38.59	155.90	254.83	168.77
47.10	99.65	259.36	229.51	164.84
42.13	37.04	112.34	81.11	55.91
87.50	62.74	213.84	164.88	112.26
127.50	112.30	370.09	243.39	166.47
80.56	76.80	219.86	158.64	110.19
120.76	113.19	345.20	283.24	192.23
226.99	128.78	469.02	294.66	185.91
1142.54	531.54	1977.20	1712.18	1119.10
62.55	44.32	146.99	93.23	64.60
7.25	6.42	22.05	23.59	16.01
8.34	6.47	17.50	1.48	1.10
42.84	**14.43**	**169.80**	**710.99**	**435.26**
39.55	11.01	149.51	657.24	391.74
3.01	3.23	17.67	39.57	30.16
0.27	0.19	2.62	14.18	13.37

8－4 续表 2

单位:亿元

项 目 Item		负债合计 Total Liabilities	主营业务收入 Major Business Revenue	主营业务成本 Cost of Major Business
总 计	**Total**	**7431.86**	**16933.08**	**15003.46**
按轻重工业分	**Grouped by Light and Heavy Industry**			
轻工业	Light Industry	2104.10	4866.63	4225.79
重工业	Heavy Industry	5327.76	12066.45	10777.67
按企业规模分	**Grouped by Scale of Enterprise**			
大型企业	Large	1952.91	5090.63	4670.25
中型企业	Medium	3459.52	6994.96	6103.96
小型企业	Small	2019.43	4847.50	4229.25
按行业分	**Grouped by Sector**			
采矿业	**Mining and Quarrying**	**7.36**	**13.06**	**9.04**
非色金属矿采选业	Nonmetal Minerals Mining and Processing	7.36	13.06	9.04
制造业	**Manufacturing**	**6992.09**	**16579.63**	**14725.59**
农副食品加工业	Food Processing	116.12	363.90	334.32
食品制造业	Food Production	63.95	100.83	75.90
饮料制造业	Beverage Production	38.29	68.07	52.66
纺织业	Textile Industry	359.83	786.64	712.48
纺织服装、鞋、帽制造业	Textile, Garments, Shoes and Hats	155.30	515.70	442.04
皮革、毛皮、羽毛(绒)及其制品业	Leather, Furs, Down and Related Products	54.38	146.27	129.71
木材加工及木、竹、藤、棕、草制造业	Timber Processing, Wood, Bamboo, Cane, Palm, Fiber and Straw Products	26.97	61.70	54.98
家具制造业	Furniture Manufacturing	27.80	87.57	78.48
造纸及纸制品业	Papermaking and Paper Products	375.50	373.07	306.21
印刷业和记录媒介的复制	Printing and Record Pressing	25.99	44.30	32.60
文教体育用品制造业	Stationery, Education and Sports Goods	52.93	165.44	144.60
石油加工、炼焦及核燃料加工业	Petroleum Processing, Coking Products and Nuclear Fuel Processing	23.99	60.55	55.19

Continued 2

(100 million yuan)

主营业务税金及附加 Tax and Extra of Major Business	利润总额 Total Profits	利税总额 Total Pre-Tax Profits	应交增值税 Value Added Tax Payable	全部从业人员年平均人数(万人) Annual Average of All Employees (10000 persons)
19.23	**891.30**	**1191.38**	**280.86**	**292.20**
8.01	222.36	333.61	103.24	117.63
11.22	668.94	857.78	177.62	174.57
6.26	200.74	240.32	33.32	69.27
7.11	421.56	564.61	135.94	123.62
5.86	268.99	386.45	111.60	99.32
0.15	**1.65**	**2.69**	**0.89**	**0.22**
0.15	1.65	2.69	0.89	0.22
18.64	**838.40**	**1107.96**	**250.92**	**289.62**
0.41	11.23	15.13	3.49	2.87
0.15	6.32	10.99	4.52	2.22
2.59	2.99	8.68	3.10	1.02
0.87	25.46	41.80	15.47	25.49
0.78	26.65	40.95	13.52	27.91
0.20	7.03	10.56	3.33	7.21
0.11	2.60	4.22	1.51	1.83
0.04	3.36	3.96	0.56	3.08
0.16	26.99	39.88	12.72	4.33
0.06	6.96	8.67	1.65	1.46
0.28	5.58	8.56	2.71	8.15
0.11	2.30	3.55	1.14	0.24

单位:亿元

项目	Item	负债合计 Total Liabilities	主营业务收入 Major Business Revenue	主营业务成本(个) Number of Enterprises (unit)
化学原料及化学制品制造业	Raw Chemical Materials and Chemical Products	593.24	1288.59	1100.47
医药制造业	Medical and Pharmaceutical Products	67.63	165.89	97.07
化学纤维制造业	Chemical Fibers	120.05	325.35	302.49
橡胶制品业	Rubber Products	130.65	231.89	199.05
塑料制品业	Plastic Products	172.27	353.59	305.61
非金属矿物制品业	Nonmetal Mineral Products	184.54	282.50	235.25
黑色金属冶炼及压延加工业	Smelting and Pressing of Ferrous Metals	338.97	836.06	769.84
有色金属冶炼及压延加工业	Smelting and Pressing of Nonferrous Metals	108.57	485.59	455.13
金属制品业	Metal Products	204.66	464.40	392.94
通用设备制造业	Ordinary Machinery Manufacturing	318.47	735.62	603.05
专用设备制造业	Special Purposes Equipment Manufacturing	201.97	425.53	351.89
交通运输设备制造业	Transportation Equipment Manufacturing	398.87	678.21	583.55
电气机械及器材制造业	Electric Equipment and Machinery	468.97	1058.61	905.31
通信设备、计算机及其他电子设备制造业	Telecommunications Equipment, Computer and Other Electronic Equipments	2191.10	5932.67	5516.91
仪器仪表及文化、办公用机械制造业	Instruments, Meters, Cultural and Official Machinery	130.20	466.25	421.09
工艺品及其他制造业	Handicraft Artical and Other Manufacturing	24.07	52.93	46.15
废弃资源和废旧材料回收加工业	Waste Resouces and Junk Material Recycled	16.82	21.88	20.62
电力、燃气及水的生产和供应业	**Electric Power, Gas and Water Production and Supply**	**432.40**	**340.39**	**268.82**
电力、热力的生产和供应业	Electric Power, Steam and Hot Water Production and Supply	383.83	287.31	221.94
燃气生产和供应	Gas Production and Supply	36.81	50.71	45.60
水的生产和供应业	Tap Water Production and Supply	11.77	2.37	1.28

Continued 3

(100 million yuan)

主营业务税金及附加 Tax and Extra of Major Business	利润总额 Total Profits	利税总额 Total Pre-Tax Profits	应交增值税 Value Added Tax Payable	全部从业人员年平均人数(万人) Annual Average of All Employees (10000 persons)
1.93	100.44	136.79	34.42	8.81
0.24	17.60	30.80	12.96	3.26
0.37	10.56	17.81	6.88	2.52
0.68	9.35	14.36	4.33	5.29
0.22	18.17	24.34	5.94	10.60
0.63	17.48	28.12	10.02	7.18
0.28	39.02	52.96	13.67	3.74
0.30	19.82	25.83	5.71	2.77
0.37	40.37	49.59	8.86	9.94
0.76	65.13	80.62	14.73	13.13
0.35	35.21	44.81	9.25	9.27
5.16	38.75	55.81	11.90	12.12
0.50	49.80	62.73	12.43	19.79
0.82	223.80	256.14	31.52	86.44
0.13	22.59	25.73	3.01	6.34
0.08	2.53	3.85	1.24	2.56
0.06	0.30	0.70	0.34	0.06
0.43	**51.25**	**80.73**	**29.05**	**2.36**
0.33	47.44	74.82	27.05	1.60
0.09	3.62	5.57	1.85	0.66
0.01	0.19	0.34	0.15	0.11

8－5 私营工业企业主要经济指标（2006 年）

单位：亿元

行业	Item	企业单位数（个）Number of Enterprises (unit)	增加值 Added Value	资产总计 Total Assets
总计	**Total**	**21345**	**2810.93**	**6175.28**
按登记注册类型分	Private Solely Funds Enterprises			
私营独资企业	Private Solely Funds Enterprises	4621	404.84	688.22
私营合伙企业	Private Partnership Enterprises	652	74.77	110.76
私营有限责任公司	Private Responsibility Co., Ltd.	15504	2244.07	5154.68
私营股份有限公司	Private Share Holding Co., Ltd.	568	87.25	221.61
按轻重工业分	**Grouped by Light and Heavy Industry**			
轻工业	Light Industry	9294	1098.72	2347.63
重工业	Heavy Industry	12051	1712.22	3827.65
按企业规模分	**Grouped by Scale of Enterprise**			
大型企业	Large	40	250.65	733.57
中型企业	Medium	907	638.65	1734.70
小型企业	Small	20398	1921.64	3707.01
按行业分	**Grouped by Sector**			
采矿业	Mining and Quarrying	**86**	**14.84**	**23.15**
煤炭开采和洗选业	Ferrous Metals Mining and Processing	4	1.20	0.89
黑色金属矿采选业	Ferrous Metals Mining and Processing	10	4.31	7.45
有色金属矿采选业	Nonferrous Metals Mining and Processing	2	0.35	1.70
非金属矿采选业	Nonmetal Minerals Mining and Processing	70	8.98	13.11
制造业	**Manufacturing**	**21231**	**2788.40**	**6106.86**
农副食品加工业	Food Processing	733	87.32	137.74
食品制造业	Food Production	147	16.57	38.58
饮料制造业	Beverage Production	118	14.18	27.75
纺织业	Textile Industry	3802	444.01	1097.98
纺织服装、鞋、帽制造业	Textile, Garments, Shoes and Hats	1225	125.35	174.14
皮革、毛皮、羽毛（绒）及其制品业	Leather, Furs, Down and Related Products	223	22.19	36.00
木材加工及木、竹、藤、棕、草制造业	Timber Processing, Wood, Bamboo, Cane, Palm, Fiber and Straw Products	663	63.11	84.42
家具制造业	Furniture Manufacturing	64	5.13	15.55
造纸及纸制品业	Papermaking and Paper Products	342	31.80	76.43

MAIN ECONOMIC INDICATORS OF PRIVATE INDUSTRIAL ENTERPRISES (2006)

(100 million yuan)

应收帐款 Accounts Receivable	存货 Finished Products	流动资产年平均余额 Annual Average Balance of Circulating Funds	固定资产原价 Original Value of Fixed Assets	固定资产净值年平均余额 Annual Average Balance of Net Value of Fixed Assets
1141.25	**944.06**	**3495.70**	**2472.97**	**1706.81**
154.88	103.67	397.78	288.29	205.84
25.13	16.85	62.53	54.63	37.97
930.61	788.86	2913.38	2038.43	1398.99
30.62	34.67	122.01	91.63	64.00
357.91	382.11	1243.59	1075.48	743.80
783.34	561.94	2252.10	1397.50	963.01
79.13	92.73	343.35	334.42	220.97
262.27	270.04	982.72	664.09	438.17
799.85	581.28	2169.62	1474.46	1047.67
3.01	**2.54**	**12.41**	**10.58**	**6.89**
0.06	0.09	0.35	0.58	0.51
0.97	0.56	4.50	2.92	1.56
0.12	0.00	0.67	0.02	0.02
1.87	1.89	6.88	7.06	4.81
1134.53	**940.75**	**3467.18**	**2429.40**	**1674.54**
14.63	22.21	71.49	57.52	42.46
4.48	6.13	18.71	16.53	13.76
2.02	5.31	11.70	12.95	10.31
160.89	190.33	590.87	525.89	355.56
29.60	32.86	98.58	64.63	47.77
7.06	8.30	19.37	9.26	6.43
8.69	15.78	43.98	43.25	33.32
1.72	2.15	7.94	5.23	3.75
16.30	10.37	41.91	35.77	26.46

8-5 续 表 1

单位:亿元

项 目	Item	企业单位数(个) Number of Enterprises (units)	增加值 Added Value	资产总计 Total Assets
印刷业和记录媒介的复制	Printing and Record Pressing	178	11.98	42.52
文教体育用品制造业	Stationery, Education and Sports Goods	294	25.83	33.80
石油加工、炼焦及核燃料加工业	Petroleum Processing, Coking Products and Nuclear Fuel Processing	82	16.12	35.79
化学原料及化学制品制造业	Raw Chemical Materials and Chemical Products	1758	237.98	509.15
医药制造业	Medical and Pharmaceutical Products	205	28.61	60.77
化学纤维制造业	Chemical Fibers	373	114.76	259.27
橡胶制品业	Rubber Products	199	20.65	50.22
塑料制品业	Plastic Products	755	67.22	154.77
非金属矿物制品业	Nonmetal Mineral Products	1046	114.37	302.47
黑色金属冶炼及压延加工业	Smelting and Pressing of Ferrous Metals	733	258.05	583.07
有色金属冶炼及压延加工业	Smelting and Pressing of Nonferrous Metals	471	104.11	161.46
金属制品业	Metal Products	1386	165.79	387.30
通用设备制造业	Ordinary Machinery Manufacturing	2484	265.07	585.63
专用设备制造业	Special Purposes Equipment Manufacturing	1068	109.71	267.43
交通运输设备制造业	Transportation Equipment Manufacturing	786	111.36	293.03
电气机械及器材制造业	Electric Equipment and Machinery	1262	221.57	454.28
通信设备、计算机及其他电子设备制造业	Telecommunications Equipment, Computer and Other Electronic Equipments	428	53.23	136.57
仪器仪表及文化、办公用机械制造业	Instruments, Meters, Cultural and Official Machinery	191	26.52	63.99
工艺品及其他制造业	Handicraft Artical and Other Manufacturing	191	24.12	34.38
废弃资源和废旧材料回收加工业	Waste Resouces and Junk Material Recycled	24	1.69	2.37
电力、燃气及水的生产和供应业	**Electric Power, Gas and Water Production and Supply**	**28**	**7.68**	**45.27**
电力、热力的生产和供应业	Electric Power, Steam and Hot Water Production and Supply	22	7.07	39.46
燃气生产和供应	Gas Production and Supply	4	0.49	3.51
水的生产和供应业	Tap Water Production and Supply	2	0.12	2.30

Continued 1

(100 million yuan)

应收帐款 Accounts Receivable	存货 Finished Products	流动资产年平均余额 Annual Average Balance of Circulating Funds	固定资产原价 Original Value of Fixed Assets	固定资产净值年平均余额 Annual Average Balance of Net Value of Fixed Assets
9.03	3.98	20.87	25.29	16.97
7.76	5.42	20.15	13.72	9.97
5.27	4.92	18.60	13.20	8.75
97.39	75.36	305.92	180.74	120.86
8.90	9.82	31.07	29.37	19.60
18.02	27.99	105.79	146.70	101.05
9.35	6.20	24.85	22.24	15.48
36.02	21.32	86.85	66.03	45.36
52.39	38.75	153.67	152.32	105.14
78.02	85.72	332.16	198.04	144.24
35.73	28.51	111.25	43.68	29.01
80.46	64.56	244.14	128.21	87.35
141.40	96.08	345.45	233.80	157.94
63.98	44.02	163.58	90.23	60.93
52.00	41.34	167.80	100.14	67.23
137.34	61.49	287.84	132.67	90.95
35.95	16.86	81.38	47.80	31.18
13.60	8.98	41.03	18.20	11.56
6.19	5.67	18.83	15.04	10.37
0.36	0.32	1.40	0.92	0.81
3.71	**0.76**	**16.11**	**33.00**	**25.37**
2.99	0.68	12.02	30.84	24.21
0.70	0.09	2.73	0.62	0.28
0.02	0.00	1.36	1.54	0.88

单位:亿元

项 目	Item	负债合计 Total Liabilities	主营业务收入 Major Business Revenue	主营业务成本 Cost of Major Business
总 计	**Total**	**4126.61**	**10912.76**	**9928.88**
按登记注册类型分	Private Solely Funds Enterprises			
私营独资企业	Private Solely Funds Enterprises	455.51	1544.84	1402.59
私营合伙企业	Private Partnership Enterprises	66.87	288.27	261.85
私营有限责任公司	Private Responsibility Co., Ltd.	3467.04	8750.29	7971.28
私营股份有限公司	Private Share Holding Co., Ltd.	137.20	329.37	293.16
按轻重工业分	**Grouped by Light and Heavy Industry**			
轻工业	Light Industry	1616.66	4254.00	3906.76
重工业	Heavy Industry	2509.96	6658.77	6022.12
按企业规模分	**Grouped by Scale of Enterprise**			
大型企业	Large	482.51	1074.53	988.50
中型企业	Medium	1183.14	2439.25	2189.45
小型企业	Small	2460.97	7398.98	6750.93
按行业分	**Grouped by Sector**			
采矿业	Mining and Quarrying	**14.52**	**46.29**	**39.95**
煤炭开采和洗选业	Ferrous Metals Mining and Processing	0.45	4.85	4.32
黑色金属矿采选业	Ferrous Metals Mining and Processing	4.84	13.81	11.28
有色金属矿采选业	Nonferrous Metals Mining and Processing	1.50	1.66	1.52
非金属矿采选业	Nonmetal Minerals Mining and Processing	7.73	25.97	22.83
制造业	**Manufacturing**	**4078.01**	**10838.74**	**9864.73**
农副食品加工业	Food Processing	88.57	355.53	328.33
食品制造业	Food Production	25.91	61.87	54.14
饮料制造业	Beverage Production	15.84	47.35	40.17
纺织业	Textile Industry	784.57	1750.55	1624.31
纺织服装、鞋、帽制造业	Textile, Garments, Shoes and Hats	112.74	449.45	410.35
皮革、毛皮、羽毛(绒)及其制品业	Leather, Furs, Down and Related Products	25.96	79.11	71.87
木材加工及木、竹、藤、棕、草制造业	Timber Processing, Wood, Bamboo, Cane, Palm, Fiber and Straw Products	41.27	231.50	210.60
家具制造业	Furniture Manufacturing	10.54	17.97	16.00
造纸及纸制品业	Papermaking and Paper Products	56.54	123.83	113.41

Continued 2

(100 million yuan)

主营业务税金及附加 Tax and Extra of Major Business	利润总额 Operating Profits	利税总额 Total Profits	应交增值税 Value-Added Tax Payable	全部从业人员年平均人数(万人) Annual Average of All Employees (10000 Persons)
47.16	**362.08**	**684.94**	**275.70**	**276.81**
8.64	52.52	106.91	45.74	45.80
1.47	9.57	19.54	8.50	7.57
35.20	285.89	533.56	212.46	214.50
1.84	14.10	24.93	8.99	8.94
18.54	120.85	237.11	97.71	135.89
28.61	241.23	447.83	177.99	140.93
2.28	46.57	70.31	21.46	13.70
10.12	92.08	161.38	59.18	57.83
34.76	223.43	453.25	195.06	205.28
0.57	**1.97**	**4.53**	**1.99**	**1.41**
0.09	0.15	0.31	0.07	0.03
0.15	0.71	1.71	0.86	0.29
0.00	0.08	0.10	0.02	0.01
0.34	1.02	2.41	1.05	1.09
46.40	**359.95**	**678.48**	**272.13**	**274.91**
1.38	9.80	16.85	5.67	6.25
0.41	1.62	3.75	1.72	1.84
2.30	1.94	6.50	2.26	1.41
6.21	46.24	93.51	41.07	58.80
2.09	13.84	27.06	11.13	24.22
0.37	2.19	4.82	2.27	3.85
1.16	10.04	18.34	7.13	8.84
0.08	0.49	1.04	0.47	0.83
0.70	2.71	7.03	3.62	3.58

8-5 续 表 3

单位:亿元

项 目 Item		负债合计 Total Liabilities	主营业务收入 Major Business Revenue	主营业务成本 Cost of Major Business
印刷业和记录媒介的复制	Printing and Record Pressing	29.21	44.77	39.04
文教体育用品制造业	Stationery, Education and Sports Goods	21.78	95.28	86.08
石油加工、炼焦及核燃料加工业	Petroleum Processing, Coking Products and Nuclear Fuel Processing	23.81	73.21	69.83
化学原料及化学制品制造业	Raw Chemical Materials and Chemical Products	335.66	954.17	864.55
医药制造业	Medical and Pharmaceutical Products	38.83	96.04	80.44
化学纤维制造业	Chemical Fibers	175.35	496.63	470.33
橡胶制品业	Rubber Products	33.85	83.39	74.59
塑料制品业	Plastic Products	100.70	266.91	242.86
非金属矿物制品业	Nonmetal Mineral Products	193.62	411.48	365.74
黑色金属冶炼及压延加工业	Smelting and Pressing of Ferrous Metals	418.16	1092.59	1030.31
有色金属冶炼及压延加工业	Smelting and Pressing of Nonferrous Metals	103.49	468.67	443.80
金属制品业	Metal Products	258.43	624.89	556.38
通用设备制造业	Ordinary Machinery Manufacturing	382.56	983.91	871.35
专用设备制造业	Special Purposes Equipment Manufacturing	172.32	382.20	330.75
交通运输设备制造业	Transportation Equipment Manufacturing	202.10	412.10	365.79
电气机械及器材制造业	Electric Equipment and Machinery	284.08	850.42	764.90
通信设备、计算机及其他电子设备制造业	Telecommunications Equipment, Computer and Other Electronic Equipments	83.17	200.04	176.87
仪器仪表及文化、办公用机械制造业	Instruments, Meters, Cultural and Official Machinery	36.81	92.39	77.49
工艺品及其他制造业	Handicraft Artical and Other Manufacturing	20.49	84.87	77.24
废弃资源和废旧材料回收加工业	Waste Resouces and Junk Material Recycled	1.64	7.60	7.21
电力、燃气及水的生产和供应业	**Electric Power, Gas and Water Production and Supply**	**34.09**	**27.74**	**24.20**
电力、热力的生产和供应业	Electric Power, Steam and Hot Water Production and Supply	28.93	25.13	21.88
燃气生产和供应	Gas Production and Supply	2.91	2.13	1.98
水的生产和供应业	Tap Water Production and Supply	2.25	0.48	0.33

Continued 3

(100 million yuan)

主营业务税金及附加 Tax and Extra of Major Business	利润总额 Total Profits	利税总额 Total Pre-Tax Profits	应交增值税 Value-Added Tax Payable	全部从业人员年平均人数(万人) Annual Average of All Employees (10000 Persons)
0.29	1.40	3.45	1.77	2.01
0.40	2.57	5.89	2.93	4.18
0.30	0.51	1.92	1.11	0.52
3.64	32.06	58.37	22.68	15.64
0.38	3.96	7.05	2.72	2.75
0.63	14.89	20.71	5.19	5.04
0.49	3.22	5.83	2.12	2.19
1.15	8.10	15.94	6.69	7.48
2.66	16.00	34.35	15.69	13.75
3.48	28.72	54.89	22.69	10.60
1.21	10.82	20.09	8.06	3.95
3.20	23.71	42.83	15.92	17.17
5.19	39.67	75.99	31.13	29.29
2.10	16.75	31.44	12.59	11.92
2.00	16.79	30.58	11.80	11.03
3.06	33.51	58.50	21.92	16.16
0.72	8.26	14.85	5.87	6.27
0.40	7.04	10.60	3.17	2.25
0.39	3.01	5.90	2.50	3.02
0.04	0.09	0.40	0.27	0.09
0.18	**0.17**	**1.93**	**1.58**	**0.49**
0.17	0.18	1.88	1.52	0.43
0.00	-0.03	0.00	0.03	0.02
0.00	0.01	0.05	0.03	0.04

8-6 规模以上工业企业主要经济效益指标（2006 年）

单位：%

项 目	Item	企业亏损面 Loss Making Rate of Enterprises	产值利税率 Rate Between Pre-Tax Profit and Output Value	销售利税率 Rate Between Pre-Tax Profit and Sales
总 计	**Total**	**11.84**	**7.65**	**7.72**
按登记注册类型分	**Grouped by Type of Registration**			
内资企业	Inner Funded Enterprise	9.71	8.10	8.21
国有企业	State-Owned Enterprise	27.50	15.54	15.65
集体企业	Collective-Owned Enterprise	11.87	7.26	7.42
股份合作企业	Share Holding Cooperative Enterprises	8.57	7.80	8.09
联营企业	Joint-Ownership Enterprises	11.11	7.97	8.01
有限责任公司	Responsibility Co. Ltd.	15.07	9.14	9.10
#国有独资	State Solely Funded	25.93	12.08	11.73
股份有限公司	Share Holding Co. Ltd.	13.66	7.32	7.24
私营企业	Private Entreprises	8.37	6.11	6.28
其他企业	Other Enterprises	11.49	8.32	8.39
港、澳、台商投资企业	Hongkong, Macao and Taiwan Funded Enterprise	18.86	7.72	7.77
外商投资企业	Foreign Funded Enterprise	18.74	6.73	6.75
按轻重工业分	**Grouped by Light and Heavy Industry**			
轻工业	Light Industry	13.27	7.74	7.85
重工业	Heavy Industry	10.75	7.61	7.67
按企业规模分	**Grouped by Scale of Enterprise**			
大型企业	Large	6.67	7.56	7.55
中型企业	Medium	14.92	8.73	8.76
小型企业	Small	11.57	6.83	7.00
按行业分	**Grouped by Sector**			
采矿业	**Mining and Quarrying**	**4.97**	**25.61**	**26.21**
煤炭开采和洗选业	Coal Mining and Processing	0.00	15.40	15.61
石油和天然气开采业	Petroleum and Natural Gas Extraction	0.00	66.95	66.93
黑色金属矿采选业	Ferrous Metals Mining and Processing	5.26	13.55	14.28
有色金属矿采选业	Nonferrous Metals Mining and Processing	0.00	17.02	18.81
非金属矿采选业	Nonmetal Minerals Mining and Processing	5.71	15.09	15.69
其他矿采选业	Nonmetal Minerals Mining and Processing	0.00	5.76	7.76
制造业	**Manufacturing**	**11.74**	**7.26**	**7.33**
农副食品加工业	Food Processing	9.84	4.24	4.21
食品制造业	Food Production	15.14	8.59	8.79
饮料制造业	Beverage Production	12.09	13.82	14.24
烟草加工业	Tobacco Processing	0.00	76.12	80.96
纺织业	Textile Industry	13.01	5.40	5.46

MAIN INDICATORS ON ECONOMIC BENEFIT OF ABOVE DESIGNATED SIZE INDUSTRIAL ENTERPRISES (2006)

(%)

资金利税率 Rate between Pre - Tax Prafit and Assets	资产负债率 Assets Liability Ratio	流动资产周转次数(次/年) Turnover of Total Circulating Funds (times/year)	成本费用利润率 Ratio of Profits to Industrial Cost	全员劳动生产率(现价产值计算)(元/人) Total Labor Productivity (current price) (yuan/person)	产品销售率 Proportion of Products Sold
12.32	**60.58**	**2.71**	**4.88**	**133108**	**98.53**
13.62	62.74	2.80	4.42	128118	98.44
18.09	58.37	2.85	6.59	280597	99.35
13.95	59.25	2.77	4.57	159382	98.12
16.21	60.24	2.71	4.62	122138	97.87
13.87	59.52	2.61	5.13	102419	100.04
11.81	63.84	2.35	5.27	142431	99.44
10.50	60.69	1.82	5.78	116528	98.79
12.83	54.09	2.79	4.44	145946	98.82
13.17	66.82	3.12	3.44	101546	97.70
13.16	63.45	2.66	4.66	85726	98.66
10.46	58.73	2.23	5.82	111671	98.37
10.74	57.13	2.76	5.42	158137	98.78
12.81	59.46	2.68	4.44	101261	98.41
12.12	61.04	2.72	5.07	157002	98.59
12.21	59.97	3.00	4.76	187650	99.36
11.84	60.94	2.30	5.86	136692	98.44
13.01	60.81	2.91	4.16	106911	97.91
24.88	**54.08**	**2.42**	**17.53**	**107413**	**99.22**
12.80	60.71	1.90	6.30	79462	99.57
56.71	29.72	5.15	103.17	314313	99.53
20.19	60.77	2.18	6.68	120900	100.08
27.73	59.88	1.98	14.99	154393	99.25
20.21	57.57	2.83	8.53	69871	97.83
10.83	93.12	2.51	2.25	1018029	98.79
12.46	**60.51**	**2.69**	**4.74**	**128542**	**98.47**
10.80	64.68	3.92	2.76	185669	98.87
9.91	57.21	1.67	4.89	113123	99.11
25.99	56.49	3.26	6.53	127536	98.29
107.99	26.20	1.65	72.59	2434655	100.08
9.07	64.75	2.74	2.96	80411	98.39

8-6 续 表

单位:%

项 目 Item		企业亏损面 Loss Making Rate of Enterprises	产值利税率 Rate Between Pre-Tax Profit and Output Value	销售利税率 Rate Between Pre-Tax Profit and Sales
纺织服装、鞋、帽制造业	Textile, Garments, Shoes and Hats	11.86	7.48	7.63
皮革、毛皮、羽毛(绒)及其制品业	Leather, Furs, Down and Related Products	12.83	6.74	6.94
木材加工及木、竹、藤、棕、草制造业	Timber Processing, Wood, Bamboo, Cane, Palm Fiber and Straw Products	4.36	7.11	7.33
家具制造业	Furniture Manufacturing	20.99	4.76	4.87
造纸及纸制品业	Papermaking and Paper Products	15.24	9.05	9.22
印刷业和记录媒介的复制	Printing and Record Pressing	17.51	13.21	13.28
文教体育用品制造业	Stationery, Education and Sports Goods	10.73	5.52	5.61
石油加工、炼焦及核燃料加工业	Petroleum Processing, Coking Products and Nuclear Fuel Processing	17.14	3.07	3.06
化学原料及化学制品制造业	Raw Chemical Materials and Chemical Products	9.42	8.53	8.44
医药制造业	Medical and Pharmaceutical Products	17.76	14.65	14.82
化学纤维制造业	Chemical Fibers	16.91	4.64	4.69
橡胶制品业	Rubber Products	14.51	6.69	6.77
塑料制品业	Plastic Products	13.99	6.60	6.69
非金属矿物制品业	Nonmetal Mineral Products	13.40	9.08	9.29
黑色金属冶炼及压延加工业	Smelting and Pressing of Ferrous Metals	12.42	7.59	7.56
有色金属冶炼及压延加工业	Smelting and Pressing of Nonferrous Metals	11.48	5.09	5.15
金属制品业	Metal Products	10.29	8.10	8.33
通用设备制造业	Ordinary Machinery Manufacturing	7.67	8.87	9.00
专用设备制造业	Special Purposes Equipment Manufacturing	9.23	9.31	9.57
交通运输设备制造业	Transportation Equipment Manufacturing	13.31	7.13	7.37
电气机械及器材制造业	Electric Equipment and Machinery	11.01	7.09	7.23
通信设备、计算机及其他电子设备制造业	Telecommunications Equipment, Computer and Other Electronic Equipments	18.08	4.51	4.52
仪器仪表及文化、办公用机械制造业	Instruments, Meters, Cultural and Official Machinery	12.95	7.01	7.03
工艺品及其他制造业	Handicraft Artical and Other Manufacturing	13.11	7.22	7.42
废弃资源和废旧材料回收加工业	Waste Resouces and Junk Material Recycled	13.33	3.90	4.37
电力、燃气及水的生产和供应业	**Electric Power, Gas and Water Production and Supply**	**26.33**	**12.52**	**12.56**
电力、热力的生产和供应业	Electric Power, Steam and Hot Water Production and Supply	20.86	12.77	12.80
燃气生产和供应	Gas Production and Supply	22.58	10.11	9.93
水的生产和供应业	Tap Water Production and Supply	37.62	6.36	6.74

Continued

(%)

资金利税率 Rate between Pre - Tax Prafit and Assets	资产负债率 Assets Liability Ratio	流动资产周转次数(次/年) Turnover of Total Circulating Funds (times/year)	成本费用利润率 Ratio of Profits to Industrial Cost	全员劳动生产率(现价产值计算)(元/人) Total Labor (current price) Productivity (yuan/person)	产品销售率 Proportion of Products Sold
16.32	56.21	3.03	5.19	62261	98.42
14.19	60.77	2.73	4.26	57290	98.28
14.63	59.04	3.32	4.04	86051	97.52
5.16	53.89	2.16	3.61	66624	98.18
7.98	64.14	2.17	5.98	162484	98.62
13.95	57.87	1.84	9.65	82839	98.23
13.10	58.77	3.48	3.25	55676	99.04
11.07	66.80	6.92	-0.76	337293	99.15
14.16	54.80	3.02	5.87	213975	98.54
21.23	45.40	2.29	8.89	178187	97.19
8.24	56.00	3.47	3.01	212489	99.08
8.53	55.37	2.60	4.27	106794	97.70
9.83	56.57	2.48	4.57	95408	98.22
11.08	58.85	2.24	5.19	98181	98.42
13.84	63.85	3.13	5.03	326907	99.88
17.38	61.96	4.57	3.03	339614	98.31
14.13	60.98	2.42	5.84	114787	97.73
14.54	61.26	2.28	6.10	106719	98.20
13.41	58.07	1.97	6.85	103132	97.35
9.23	65.64	1.83	4.47	120420	97.89
12.38	60.15	2.27	5.12	155342	97.63
8.27	62.97	2.81	3.93	139631	98.66
13.25	56.68	2.60	5.77	141612	98.86
13.94	56.02	3.01	4.39	70235	97.48
6.18	85.68	1.62	1.49	466429	86.57
9.40	**62.19**	**3.29**	**5.83**	**428787**	**99.74**
10.43	63.14	3.83	5.96	536118	99.79
8.69	61.83	1.97	6.29	150909	100.76
1.10	54.47	0.58	0.35	96238	96.21

8－7 国有控股工业企业主要经济效益指标（2006年）

单位：%

行业	Item	企业亏损面 Loss Making Rate of Enterprises	产值利税率 Rate Between Pre-Tax Profit and Output Value	销售利税率 Rate Between Pre-Tax Profit and Sales
总计	**Total**	**23.91**	**12.26**	**12.13**
按登记注册类型分	Grouped by Type of Registration			
内资企业	Inner Funded Enterprises	23.99	12.13	12.00
国有企业	State-owned Enterprises	27.50	15.54	15.65
股份合作企业	Share Holding Cooperative Enterprises			
联营企业	Joint-ownershinp Enterprises	13.33	5.30	5.54
有限责任公司	Responsibility Co. Ltd.	20.45	11.15	10.97
#国有独资	State Solely Ownded	25.93	12.08	11.73
股份有限公司	Share Holding Co, Ltd.	18.87	5.14	4.90
其他企业	Other Enterprises		3.14	2.64
港、澳、台商投资企业	Hong Kong, Macao and Taiwan Funded Enterprises	15.15	7.83	7.68
外商投资企业	Foreign Funded Enterprises	27.27	16.29	16.28
按轻重工业分	Grouped by Light and Heavy Industry			
轻工业	Light Industry	30.34	25.67	25.24
重工业	Heavy Industry	19.82	9.98	9.88
按企业规模分	**Grouped by Scale of Enterprise**			
大型企业	Large	9.23	10.50	10.40
中型企业	Medium	19.18	17.23	16.96
小型企业	Small	28.09	8.56	8.65
按行业分	**Grouped by Sector**			
采矿业	**Mining and Quarrying**	**15.63**	**30.15**	**30.45**
煤炭开采和洗选业	Coal Mining and Processing		15.74	15.93
石油和天然气开采业	Petroleum and Natural Gas Extraction		66.95	66.93
黑色金属矿采选业	Ferrous Metals Mining and Processing	33.33	14.72	15.76
有色金属矿采选业	Nonferrous Metals Mining and Processing		26.82	26.95
非金属矿采选业	Nonmetal Minerals Mining and Processing	23.53	19.20	18.81
其他矿采选业	Nonmetal Minerals Mining and Processing			
制造业	**Manufacturing**	**22.61**	**11.81**	**11.62**
农副食品加工业	Food Processing	22.92	0.66	0.70
食品制造业	Food Production	12.50	12.72	12.67
饮料制造业	Beverage Production	10.00	34.82	32.36
烟草加工业	Tobacco Processing		76.12	80.96
纺织业	Textile Industry	45.16	6.21	5.61
纺织服装、鞋、帽制造业	Textile, Garments, Shoes and Hats	15.00	5.07	4.88
皮革、毛皮、羽毛（绒）及其制品业	Leather, Furs, Down and Related Products	50.00	0.25	0.25

MAIN INDICATORS ON ECONOMIC BENEFIT OF STATE - SHARE HOLDING INDUSTRIAL ENTERPRISES (2006)

(%)

资金利税率 Rate between Pre - Tax Prafit and Assets	资产负债率 Assets Liability Ratio	流动资产周转次数(次/年) Turnover of Total Circulating Funds (times/year)	成本费用利润率 Ratio of Profits to Industrial Cost	全员劳动生产率(现价产值计算)(元/人) Total Labor (current price) Productivity (yuan/person)	产品销售率 Proportion of Products Sold
13.76	**57.58**	**2.59**	**5.78**	**215301**	**99.59**
13.81	59.23	2.53	5.28	205570	99.52
18.09	58.37	2.85	6.59	280597	99.35
8.00	63.56	2.29	2.93	86302	95.45
9.21	63.73	1.71	5.62	138238	99.30
10.50	60.69	1.82	5.78	116528	98.79
10.81	46.93	3.99	2.03	191589	100.29
11.20	88.65	4.72	0.72		100.00
9.63	34.55	3.29	4.20	207724	100.07
14.93	48.24	3.08	13.27	433338	100.12
24.02	46.04	1.81	10.66	203469	99.59
11.59	59.82	2.79	5.07	218983	99.59
14.14	55.37	3.11	4.52	229111	99.54
14.38	59.96	1.95	9.20	223284	99.81
7.79	63.42	1.93	4.48	117387	99.09
24.67	**54.12**	**2.21**	**21.17**	**108763**	**99.69**
12.69	60.73	1.85	6.40	79309	99.79
56.71	29.72	5.15	103.17	314313	99.53
15.26	59.36	1.59	7.34	103197	100.25
17.71	72.80	1.13	18.58	67714	95.50
12.84	69.23	1.73	6.44	44268	99.05
15.81	**55.94**	**2.30**	**5.71**	**204592**	**99.46**
1.66	81.33	4.37	0.10	95706	98.87
7.77	66.33	0.79	7.06	86801	98.65
46.09	67.35	1.99	12.70	131441	99.25
107.99	26.20	1.65	72.59	2434655	100.08
5.71	57.49	1.93	2.37	58957	100.63
4.93	48.85	1.58	2.37	29671	99.17
0.27	81.11	1.85	-3.25	20842	97.89

8-7 续 表

单位:%

行业	Item	企业亏损面 Loss Making Rate of Enterprises	产值利税率 Rate Between Pre-Tax Profit and Output Value	销售利税率 Rate Between Pre-Tax Profit and Sales
木材加工及木、竹、藤、棕、草制造业	Timber Processing, Wood, Bamboo, Cane, Palm, Fiber and Straw Products		5.73	5.81
		100.00	-11.71	-11.82
造纸及纸制品业	Papermaking and Paper Products	42.86	8.89	9.54
印刷业和记录媒介的复制业	Printing and Record Pressing	32.14	14.60	14.23
文教体育用品制造业	Stationery, Education and Sports Goods		15.44	15.46
石油加工、炼焦及核燃料加工业	Petroleum Processing, Coking Products and Nuclear Fuel Processing	40.00	2.09	2.08
化学原料及化学制品制造业	Raw Chemical Materials and Chemical Products	14.08	10.99	10.40
医药制造业	Medical and Pharmaceutical Products	29.17	23.73	19.67
化学纤维制造业	Chemical Fibers	22.22	6.38	6.28
橡胶制品业	Rubber Products		9.41	8.76
塑料制品业	Plastic Products		4.06	4.22
非金属矿物制品业	Nonmetal Mineral Products	23.81	10.80	10.95
黑色金属冶炼及压延加工业	Smelting and Pressing of Ferrous Metals	20.00	14.20	14.02
有色金属冶炼及压延加工业	Smelting and Pressing of Nonferrous Metals	16.67	3.29	3.54
金属制品业	Metal Products	23.08	7.63	7.67
通用设备制造业	Ordinary Machinery Manufacturing	18.75	8.06	7.99
专用设备制造业	Special Purposes Equipment Manufacturing	16.67	6.66	6.67
交通运输设备制造业	Transportation Equipment Manufacturing	29.49	6.55	6.88
电气机械及器材制造业	Electric Equipment and Machinery	13.64	8.48	8.41
通信设备、计算机及其他电子设备制造业	Telecommunications Equipment, Computer and Other Electronic Equipments	23.81	8.00	7.48
仪器仪表及文化、办公用机械制造业	Instruments, Meters, Cultural and Official Machinery	20.00	15.34	15.37
工艺品及其他制造业	Handicraft Artical and Other Manufacturing		10.90	11.50
废弃资源和废旧材料回收加工业	Waste Resources and Junk Material Recycled		26.94	26.94
电力、燃气及水的生产和供应业	**Electric Power, Gas and Water Production and Supply**	**33.33**	**10.65**	**10.65**
电力、热力的生产和供应业	Electric Power, Steam and Hot Water Production and Supply	16.67	10.74	10.76
燃气生产和供应	Gas Production and Supply	33.33	12.78	11.94
水的生产和供应业	Tap Water Production and Supply	46.38	4.92	5.03

Continued

(%)

资金利税率 Rate between Pre - Tax Prafit and Assets	资产负债率 Assets Liability Ratio	流动资产周转次数(次/年) Turnover of Total Circulating Funds (times/year)	成本费用利润率 Ratio of Profits to Industrial Cost	全员劳动生产率(现价产值计算)(元/人) Total Labor (current price) Productivity (yuan/person)	产品销售率 Proportion of Products Sold
5.89	74.33	1.65	2.25	195594	99.43
-10.10	56.62	1.65	-11.18	23729	98.82
6.10	40.37	1.33	3.01	186124	98.70
13.10	60.99	1.62	8.92	113191	102.93
17.40	73.05	2.18	10.18	62481	99.96
9.15	73.54	9.97	-2.33	326222	100.05
15.51	46.06	3.56	7.53	289590	99.43
17.93	38.36	1.45	13.55	126432	96.46
9.13	23.35	3.58	3.73	210328	99.28
8.31	64.08	1.36	3.26	61198	99.84
5.55	65.89	2.47	2.03	205391	96.14
10.70	64.04	2.17	5.88	180003	102.51
15.49	39.13	2.33	8.73	362423	99.75
9.11	68.21	3.70	1.24	179936	94.98
13.29	60.33	2.68	4.75	265475	99.42
12.69	70.23	2.03	5.05	139521	99.53
6.29	63.21	1.29	3.37	105495	96.93
6.67	67.58	1.44	4.00	137358	98.57
10.50	55.42	1.67	6.15	280284	98.15
5.00	73.12	0.82	5.17	106759	102.64
9.70	56.35	0.83	11.76	94743	97.73
7.83	49.25	1.17	7.78	76541	97.29
28.89	76.27	1.08	23.75	429389	100.00
8.73	**60.91**	**4.01**	**4.00**	**425815**	**99.91**
9.82	62.22	4.82	4.10	537752	99.92
7.24	64.44	1.49	5.38	86171	101.88
0.78	50.06	0.57	-1.19	92186	97.88

8-8 “三资”工业企业主要经济效益指标（2006年）

单位：%

项目	Item	企业亏损面 Loss Making Rate of Enterprises	产值利税率 Rate Between Pre-Tax Profit and Output Value	销售利税率 Rate Between Pre-Tax Profit and Sales
总计	**Total**	**18.79**	**7.00**	**7.04**
按轻重工业分	**Grouped by Light and Heavy Industry**			
轻工业	Light Industry	19.23	6.81	6.86
重工业	Heavy Industry	18.39	7.08	7.11
按企业规模分	**Grouped by Scale of Enterprise**			
大型企业	Large	8.97	4.69	4.72
中型企业	Medium	17.83	8.08	8.07
小型企业	Small	19.23	7.89	7.97
按行业分	**Grouped by Sector**			
采矿业	**Mining and Quarrying**		**20.93**	**20.63**
非金属矿采选业	Nonmetals Mining and Processing		20.93	20.63
制造业	**Manufacturing**	**18.88**	**6.65**	**6.68**
农副食品加工业	Food Processing	20.57	4.30	4.16
食品制造业	Food Production	17.58	10.78	10.90
饮料制造业	Beverage Production	21.95	11.74	12.75
纺织业	Textile Industry	18.32	5.25	5.31
纺织服装、鞋、帽制造业	Textile, Garments, Shoes and Hats	14.86	7.86	7.94
皮革、毛皮、羽毛（绒）及其制品业	Leather, Furs, Down and Related Products	15.91	7.19	7.22
木材加工及木、竹、藤、棕、草制造业	Timber Processing, Wood, Bamboo, Cane, Palm, Fiber and Straw Products	20.51	6.50	6.85
家具制造业	Furniture Manufacturing	29.11	4.49	4.52
造纸及纸制品业	Papermaking and Paper Products	25.20	10.58	10.69
印刷业和记录媒介的复制	Printing and Record Pressing	31.15	19.39	19.57

MAIN INDICATORS ON ECONOMIC BENEFIT OF FOREIGN – FUNDED INDUSTRIAL ENTERPRISES (2006)

(%)

资金利税率 Rate between Pre – Tax Prafit and Assets	资产负债率 Assets Liability Ratio	流动资产周转次数(次/年) Turnover of Total Circu-lating Funds (times/year)	成本费用利润率 Ratio of Profits to Industrial Cost	全员劳动生产率(现价产值 计算)(元/人) Total Labor (current price) Productivity (yuan/person)	产品销售率 Proportion of Products Sold
10.65	**57.63**	**2.59**	**5.53**	**141344**	**98.67**
10.25	56.83	2.52	4.78	106536	98.68
10.81	57.96	2.61	5.84	164798	98.66
8.66	62.04	3.15	4.09	159482	98.86
11.02	57.74	2.40	6.38	140778	98.76
11.76	53.77	2.40	5.86	129397	98.34
25.10	**56.76**	**3.23**	**14.73**	**190910**	**97.73**
25.10	56.76	3.23	14.73	190910	97.73
10.48	**57.40**	**2.60**	**5.31**	**137900**	**98.65**
8.70	62.24	3.09	3.18	311406	99.93
10.71	51.05	1.42	6.64	145199	100.30
15.87	61.98	2.65	4.76	265103	98.59
7.68	57.25	2.44	3.33	81354	98.01
16.83	55.38	3.04	5.45	56427	99.19
12.76	57.44	2.42	5.05	53601	98.21
9.71	54.13	2.09	4.41	101253	96.14
8.29	51.05	2.70	3.99	68142	98.34
7.45	63.30	1.97	7.70	248065	99.00
19.21	52.39	1.65	18.60	117644	98.19

8－8 续 表

单位：%

行业	Item	企业亏损面 Loss Making Rate of Enterprises	产值利税率 Rate Between Pre-Tax Profit and Output Value	销售利税率 Rate Between Pre-Tax Profit and Sales
文教体育用品制造业	Stationery, Education and Sports Goods	17.67	5.17	5.18
石油加工、炼焦及核燃料加工业	Petroleum Processing, Coking Products and Nuclear Fuel Processing	17.65	5.80	5.87
化学原料及化学制品制造业	Raw Chemical Materials and Chemical Products	15.54	10.76	10.62
医药制造业	Medical and Pharmaceutical Products	21.55	17.95	18.57
化学纤维制造业	Chemical Fibers	25.53	5.50	5.48
橡胶制品业	Rubber Products	23.97	6.08	6.19
塑料制品业	Plastic Products	23.19	6.83	6.88
非金属矿物制品业	Nonmetal Mineral Products	23.32	9.87	9.96
黑色金属冶炼及压延加工业	Smelting and Pressing of Ferrous Metals	24.17	6.33	6.33
有色金属冶炼及压延加工业	Smelting and Pressing of Nonferrous Metals	18.00	5.31	5.32
金属制品业	Metal Products	19.10	10.60	10.68
通用设备制造业	Ordinary Machinery Manufacturing	**12.77**	**10.92**	**10.96**
专用设备制造业	Special Purposes Equipment Manufacturing	15.37	10.44	10.53
交通运输设备制造业	Transportation Equipment Manufacturing	21.47	8.06	8.23
电气机械及器材制造业	Electric Equipment and Machinery	19.57	5.83	5.93
通信设备、计算机及其他电子设备制造业	Telecommunications Equipment, Computer and Other Electronic Equipments	21.57	4.31	4.32
仪器仪表及文化、办公用机械制造业	Instruments, Meters, Cultural and Official Machinery	17.07	5.53	5.52
工艺品及其他制造业	Handicraft Artical and Other Manufacturing	23.88	7.16	7.27
废弃资源和废旧材料回收加工业	Waste Resouces and Junk Material Recycled	16.67	2.76	3.20
电力、燃气及水的生产和供应业	**Electric Power, Gas and Water Production and Supply**	12.77	23.60	23.72
电力、热力的生产和供应业	Electric Power, Steam and Hot Water Production and Supply	11.11	25.86	26.04
燃气生产和供应	Gas Production and Supply	17.65	11.07	10.98
水的生产和供应业	Tap Water Production and Supply	20.00	14.23	14.39

Continued

(%)

资金利税率 Rate between Pre - Tax Prafit and Assets	资产负债率 Assets Liability Ratio	流动资产周转次数(次/年) Turnover of Total Circu-lating Funds (times/year)	成本费用利润率 Ratio of Profits to Industrial Cost	全员劳动生产率(现价产值计算)(元/人) Total Labor (current price) Productivity (yuan/person)	产品销售率 Proportion of Products Sold
10.55	56.61	3.02	3.49	54647	99.75
10.89	54.13	3.06	3.95	609323	96.24
13.54	50.89	2.71	8.43	383213	99.23
22.02	41.87	1.84	11.83	181461	97.21
7.23	43.15	2.90	3.36	250899	99.90
6.74	52.86	2.46	4.21	121696	98.04
7.89	50.70	2.07	5.40	86023	98.76
8.66	49.72	1.81	6.60	117825	99.26
12.49	65.35	3.22	4.88	431280	98.92
15.35	55.55	4.32	4.24	359200	98.68
15.21	53.05	2.17	9.45	125826	98.89
15.03	52.41	1.99	9.67	146027	98.89
13.58	52.25	1.94	8.93	117896	98.34
10.39	60.12	1.96	6.02	140128	98.10
9.58	60.40	2.26	4.92	128839	97.76
8.27	62.19	3.00	3.90	148159	98.64
12.16	55.31	3.17	5.08	162527	99.17
10.11	53.71	2.40	5.01	60363	98.00
3.76	91.29	1.25	1.40	1253161	82.07
13.34	**61.75**	**2.00**	**17.37**	**559400**	**99.57**
13.82	62.13	1.92	19.51	753810	99.33
11.64	55.65	2.87	7.32	164463	101.19
2.13	72.03	0.90	8.00	90595	95.31

8－9 私营工业企业主要经济效益指标（2006 年）

单位：%

项 目	Item	企业亏损面 Loss Making Rate of Enterprises	产值利税率 Rate Between Pre-Tax Profit and Output Value	销售利税率 Rate Between Pre-Tax Profit and Sales
总 计	**Total**	**8.37**	**6.11**	**6.28**
按登记注册类型分	**Grouped by Light and Heavy Industry**			
私营独资企业		4.98	6.68	6.92
私营合伙企业		5.21	6.56	6.78
私营有限责任公司		9.46	5.95	6.10
私营股份有限公司		9.86	7.44	7.57
按轻重工业分	**Grouped by Light and Heavy Industry**			
轻工业	Light Industry	9.59	5.45	5.57
重工业	Heavy Industry	7.44	6.54	6.73
按企业规模分	**Grouped by Scale of Enterprise**			
大型企业	Large	5.00	6.53	6.54
中型企业	Medium	11.03	6.48	6.62
小型企业	Small	8.26	5.94	6.13
按行业分	**Grouped by Sector**			
采矿业	**Mining and Quarrying**	**1.16**	**9.16**	**9.78**
煤炭开采和洗选业	Coal Mining and Processing		6.04	6.37
黑色金属矿采选业	Petroleum and Natural Gas Extraction			
有色金属矿采选业	Ferrous Metals Mining and Processing		12.12	12.41
非金属矿采选业	Nonmetals Mining and Processing		5.98	5.98
制造业	**Manufacturing**	**1.43**	**8.44**	**9.27**
农副食品加工业	Food Processing			
食品制造业	Food Production	8.37	6.10	6.26
饮料制造业	Beverage Production	5.18	4.68	4.74
纺织业	Textile Industry	14.97	5.67	6.06
纺织服装、鞋、帽制造业	Textile, Garments, Shoes and Hats	10.17	13.12	13.72
皮革、毛皮、羽毛（绒）及其制品业	Leather, Furs, Down and Related Products			
木材加工及木、竹、藤、棕、草制造业	Timber Processing, Wood, Bamboo, Cane, Palm, Fiber and Straw Products	10.52	5.26	5.34
家具制造业	Furniture Manufacturing	8.73	5.84	6.02
造纸及纸制品业	Papermaking and Paper Products	10.31	5.83	6.09
印刷业和记录媒介的复制	Printing and Record Pressing	2.11	7.68	7.92

MAIN INDICATORS ON ECONOMIC BENEFIT OF
– PRIVATE INDUSTRIAL ENTERPRISES (2006)

(%)

资金利税率 Rate between Pre – Tax Prafit and Assets	资产负债率 Assets Liability Ratio	流动资产周转次数(次/年) Turnover of Total Circulating Funds (times/year)	成本费用利润率 Ratio of Profits to Industrial Cost	全员劳动生产率(现价产值计算)(元/人) Total Labor (current price) Productivity (yuan/person)	产品销售率 Proportion of Products Sold
13.17	**66.82**	**3.12**	**3.44**	**101546**	**97.70**
17.71	66.19	3.88	3.54	88392	97.40
19.44	60.38	4.61	3.47	98791	97.42
12.37	67.26	3.00	3.38	104617	97.78
13.40	61.91	2.70	4.48	97576	97.27
11.93	68.86	3.42	2.93	80856	98.00
13.93	65.57	2.96	3.77	121495	97.51
12.46	65.78	3.13	4.52	182956	98.88
11.36	68.20	2.48	3.93	110426	97.45
14.09	66.39	3.41	3.12	93611	97.62
23.47	**62.71**	**3.73**	**4.52**	**105054**	**96.99**
35.89	50.68	13.75	3.33	382777	94.87
28.28	65.03	3.07	5.57	149042	100.48
14.33	88.04	2.46	5.10	659264	100.00
20.60	**58.92**	**3.77**	**4.17**	**82610**	**95.46**
13.20	66.78	3.13	3.44	101428	97.70
14.79	64.31	4.97	2.84	139755	98.13
11.55	67.18	3.31	2.71	90283	97.25
29.52	57.09	4.05	4.49	100366	98.25
9.88	71.46	2.96	2.72	75509	98.32
18.49	64.74	4.56	3.19	51749	97.47
18.68	72.13	4.08	2.86	57700	98.04
23.73	48.88	5.26	4.54	71434	97.33

8－9 续 表

单位:%

行业	Item	企业亏损面 Loss Making Rate of Enterprises	产值利税率 Rate Between Pre-Tax Profit and Output Value	销售利税率 Rate Between Pre-Tax Profit and Sales
文教体育用品制造业	Stationery, Education and Sports Goods	12.50	5.38	5.79
石油加工、炼焦及核燃料加工业	Petroleum Processing, Coking Products and Nuclear Fuel Processing	10.82	5.49	5.68
化学原料及化学制品制造业	Raw Chemical Materials and Chemical Products	11.80	7.72	7.71
医药制造业	Medical and Pharmaceutical Products	5.78	5.96	6.19
化学纤维制造业	Chemical Fibers	12.20	2.58	2.62
橡胶制品业	Rubber Products	7.00	5.97	6.12
塑料制品业	Plastic Products	11.71	7.03	7.35
非金属矿物制品业	Nonmetal Mineral Products	15.28	4.08	4.17
黑色金属冶炼及压延加工业	Smelting and Pressing of Ferrous Metals	8.04	6.99	6.99
有色金属冶炼及压延加工业	Smelting and Pressing of Nonferrous Metals	9.27	5.87	5.97
金属制品业	Metal Products	9.85	8.04	8.35
通用设备制造业	Ordinary Machinery Manufacturing	11.60	4.93	5.02
专用设备制造业	Special Purposes Equipment Manufacturing	9.55	4.22	4.29
交通运输设备制造业	Transportation Equipment Manufacturing	8.15	6.55	6.85
电气机械及器材制造业	Electric Equipment and Machinery	5.23	7.48	7.72
通信设备、计算机及其他电子设备制造业	Telecommunications Equipment, Computer and Other Electronic Equipments	7.21	7.81	8.22
仪器仪表及文化、办公用机械制造业	Instruments, Meters, Cultural and Official Machinery	7.51	7.21	7.42
工艺品及其他制造业	Handicraft Artical and Other Manufacturing	6.97	6.71	6.88
废弃资源和废旧材料回收加工业	Waste Resouces and Junk Material Recycled	10.28	7.22	7.43
电力、燃气及水的生产和供应业	**Electric Power, Gas and Water Production and Supply**	**9.95**	**11.27**	**11.47**
电力、热力的生产和供应业	Electric Power, Steam and Hot Water Production and Supply	6.28	6.70	6.95
燃气生产和供应	Gas Production and Supply	12.50	5.10	5.24
水的生产和供应业	Tap Water Production and Supply	32.14	7.12	6.95

Continued

(%)

资金利税率 Rate between Pre－Tax Prafit and Assets	资产负债率 Assets Liability Ratio	流动资产周转次数(次/年) Turnover of Total Circulating Funds (times/year)	成本费用利润率 Ratio of Profits to Industrial Cost	全员劳动生产率(现价产值计算)(元/人) Total Labor (current price) Productivity (yuan/person)	产品销售率 Proportion of Products Sold
8.90	67.74	2.26	2.82	61872	97.16
10.28	73.97	2.95	2.25	88709	97.81
9.13	68.70	2.15	3.26	59725	97.36
19.57	64.45	4.73	2.78	61772	97.97
7.01	66.53	3.94	0.71	309185	94.33
13.68	65.93	3.12	3.48	152193	97.79
13.92	63.90	3.09	4.31	104190	96.93
10.01	67.63	4.69	3.08	227915	98.27
14.46	67.40	3.36	4.03	94281	96.73
12.05	65.06	3.07	3.14	89877	97.68
13.27	64.01	2.68	4.04	83193	97.16
11.52	71.72	3.29	2.70	243445	98.02
14.32	64.09	4.21	2.37	263353	97.89
12.92	66.73	2.56	3.98	96560	96.88
15.10	65.32	2.85	4.22	90485	97.29
14.00	64.44	2.34	4.61	92054	96.74
13.01	68.97	2.46	4.25	100932	97.23
15.44	62.53	2.95	4.11	137139	97.88
13.20	60.90	2.46	4.32	84843	98.07
20.16	**57.52**	**2.25**	**8.22**	**118054**	**98.56**
20.21	59.60	4.51	3.69	79808	97.09
18.01	68.87	5.41	1.20	195399	98.27
4.64	75.31	1.72	0.61	157734	98.52

8－10　规模以上工业企业主要产品生产、销售、库存（2006年）
PRODUCTION,SALE AND STOCK OF MAJOR PRODUCTS OF ABOVE DESIGNATED SIZE INDUSTRIAL ENTERPRISES(2006)

单位:万吨　　　　(10000 tons)

产品名称		Item		年初库存 Year－Begin－ning Stock	本年生产 Production	本年销售 Sales	年末库存 Year－End Stock
原煤		Coal		49.41	3047.53	2656.82	38.55
天然原油		Crude Oil		1.38	188.49	179.46	1.39
原盐		Salt		52.63	527.30	495.72	62.36
精制食用植物油		Refined Edible Plant Oil		6.06	254.68	245.60	15.01
配混合饲料		Mixed Forage		3.35	276.07	270.63	7.72
乳制品		Dairy Products		0.13	43.73	43.36	0.40
罐头		Canned Food		0.59	6.25	6.30	0.50
卷烟	(亿支)	Cigaretes	(100 million pieces)	24.56	845.41	868.69	0.96
化学纤维		Chemical Fibers		16.41	665.14	647.85	22.10
纱		Yarn		16.10	350.56	343.00	15.81
布	(亿米)	Cloth	(100 million m)	3.18	64.95	64.85	3.25
#棉布		Pure Cotton Cloth		1.94	39.08	39.05	1.95
棉混纺布(混纺交织布)		Blend Cloth		0.74	14.29	14.21	0.82
绒线(毛线)		Knitting Wool		0.55	11.16	11.21	0.50
毛机织物(呢绒)	(亿米)	Woollen Goods	(100 million m)	0.20	2.70	2.66	0.22
丝	(吨)	Silk	(ton)	0.08	2.68	2.59	0.11
丝织品	(亿米)	Knitting Silk	(100 million m)	1.37	25.92	25.82	1.47
人造板	(万立方米)	Manmade Board	(10000 cu. m)	26.76	1362.09	1360.85	27.99
汽油		Gasoline		2.98	200.58	194.59	3.83
煤油		Kerosene		2.74	99.45	98.85	3.00
燃料油		Fuel Oil		2.38	181.38	156.65	1.45
焦炭		Coke		11.08	952.80	551.41	8.24
硫酸	(折100%)	Sulphuric Acid (100%)		8.53	403.21	316.57	5.50
浓硝酸	(折100%)	Concentrated Nitric Acid(100%)		0.13	9.74	0.86	0.06
氢氧化钠(烧碱)	(折100%)	Caustic Ash (Sodium Hydroxide) (100%)		0.69	205.23	179.68	7.98
碳酸钠(纯碱)		Soda Ash (Sodium Carbonate)		5.45	247.23	246.47	5.78
农用化学肥料(折纯)		Chemical Fertilizers (100%)		10.88	254.66	253.86	9.56
#氮肥(折含N 100%)		Nitrogen(N100%)		5.87	211.66	212.57	5.07
磷肥(折合P2O5 100%)		Phosphate(P2O5 100%)		5.01	43.00	41.29	4.49
化学农药原药(折有效成分100%)		Chemical Pesticide (100% effectiveness)		2.50	36.05	34.34	2.60
乙烯		Ethylene		0.70	140.17	9.81	0.52
染料		Dye		0.86	18.86	18.61	1.01
合成洗涤剂		Synthetic Detergents		0.15	16.95	16.78	0.31
化学药品原药(化学原料药)		Chemical Raw Material of Medicines		0.24	7.66	7.14	0.48

8－10 续表 Continued

单位：万吨 (10000 tons)

产品名称		Item		年初库存 Year－Begin－ning Stock	本年生产 Production	本年销售 Sales	年末库存 Year－End Stock
橡胶轮胎外胎(轮胎外胎)	(万条)	External Tyre	(10000 Turige)	416.67	11788.58	11830.71	373.45
水泥		Cement		217.79	10880.77	10891.63	202.27
平板玻璃	(万重量箱)	Plate Glass	(10000 wtcases)	250.01	5512.52	5502.91	260.55
生铁		Pig Iron		27.19	3346.53	981.50	16.29
粗钢		Raw Steel		82.91	4202.31	1769.87	92.03
钢材		Rolled Steel		138.76	5816.26	5805.49	171.98
铁合金		Iron Alloy		0.25	15.00	14.77	0.33
十种有色金属		Ten Kinds of Nonferrous Metal		0.65	31.89	31.33	0.88
工业锅炉	(万蒸发量吨)	Industrial Boiler	(10000 steam ton)	0.21	3.48	3.46	0.24
内燃机	(万千瓦)	Internal-combustion Engine		337.10	7739.63	7219.62	398.60
金属切削机床	(万台)	Metal-cutting Machines	(10000 units)	0.63	7.07	6.99	0.71
#数控机床		Digital Machine Tools		0.20	1.40	1.36	0.24
缝纫机	(万架)	Sewing Machines	(10000 units)	4.29	25.45	26.90	2.84
大中型拖拉机	(万台)	Large and Medium Tractors	(1000 units)	0.12	4.06	3.97	0.21
汽车	(万辆)	Motor Vechicales	(10000 units)	1.60	27.48	28.00	1.08
#载货汽车		Trucks		0.21	6.86	6.85	0.22
轿车		Sedan		0.37	14.60	14.63	0.34
摩托车	(万辆)	Motoreycle	(10000 units)	6.39	179.05	176.41	8.99
两轮自行车(自行车)	(万辆)	Bicycle	(10000 units)	55.89	1238.16	1244.16	49.88
家用洗衣机	(万台)	Household Washing Machines	(10000 units)	16.57	587.26	588.23	15.31
家用吸尘器	(万台)	Dust Catcher	(10000 units)	24.25	1696.07	1684.80	35.51
家用电冰箱	(万台)	Household Refrigerators	(10000 units)	5.66	513.61	509.94	9.30
家用电风扇	(万台)	Electric Fan	(10000 units)	25.86	138.99	148.11	12.13
房间空气调节器	(万台)	Airconditioner	(10000 units)	10.41	474.31	460.07	24.65
吸排油烟机	(万台)	Range Hoods	(10000 units)	4.37	32.39	34.69	2.06
程控交换机	(万线)	Program Controlling Switchboard	(10000 lines)	0.00	11.94	11.94	0.00
#数字程控交换机		Digital Program Controlling Switch-board		0.00	9.50	9.50	0.00
微型电子计算机	(万台)	Mini Electronic Computer	(100 million units)	29.40	4374.64	4380.47	23.57
#笔记本计算机		Note Book computer		27.85	2762.16	2766.99	23.02
打印机	(万台)	Stamp Machine	(10000 units)	43.77	150.57	193.26	1.08
集成电路	(亿块)	Integrated Circuit	(10000 piece)	3.08	118.27	119.78	1.36
#大规模集成电路		Large Scale Integrated Circuit		0.56	42.13	41.75	0.92
彩色电视机	(万台)	Color TV Sets	(10000 units)	25.30	248.25	240.89	32.28
照相机	(万台)	Cameras	(10000 units)	14.96	2084.12	1887.03	212.05
#数码照相机		Digital Cameras		7.40	1997.23	1794.73	209.89

8－11 综合能源平衡表
AGGREGATE BALANCE SHEET OF ENERGY

单位:万吨标准煤　　10000tons standardized coal

项目	Item	2000	2003	2004	2005
可供消费的能源总量	**Total Energy Avaiable for Consumption**				
一次能源生产量	Primary Energy Output	1996.86	2223.44	2231.58	2267.63
回收能	Retrieved	136.24	94.38	160.74	356.07
进口量	Imported	708.45	1128.00	1409.08	14517.62
出口量	Exported	48.20	107.76	64.40	186.52
年初年末库存差额	Stock Changes in the Year	13.21	51.62	－142.53	－19.73
能源消费总量	**Total Energy consumption**	**8612.43**	**11060.68**	**13651.69**	**16895.39**
在总量中:	of This Total:				
农、林、牧、渔、水利业	Farming forestry, Animal Husbandry, Fishery and water conservancy	400.39	363.53	369.43	321.57
工业	Industry	6743.95	8702.57	11041.13	13748.43
建筑业	constlructlion	41.34	77.08	93.24	204.68
交通运输、仓储及邮电通讯业	Transportation, Storage, post and Telecommunication	358.52	718.83	878.06	899.43
批发和零售贸易餐饮业	Wholesale and Retail and catering Trade	169.94	157.95	191.66	249.84
其他	others	209.38	237.57	255.92	373.21
生活消费	Residential consumption	688.91	803.15	822.25	1098.23
在总量中:	of This Total:				
终端消费	Final consumption	8220.49	10379.78	12901.81	16039.17
#工业	Industry	6352.00	8021.68	10291.26	12892.22
损失量	Loss	269.36	479.60	567.62	653.43

8-12 规模以上工业企业主要能源消费量
MAJOR ENERGY CONSUMPTION OF ABOVE DESIGNATED INDUSTRIAL ENTERPRISES

单位:万吨 (10000 tons)

名称	Item	1995	2000	2004	2005	2006
煤炭	Coal	5980.45	8243.97	14260.59	16490.60	17750.78
焦炭	Coke	252.27	311.11	1057.33	1562.66	1908.74
原油	Crude Oil	1027.52	1383.59	1865.04	2250.86	2293.19
汽油	Gasoline	17.93	26.94	33.41	32.07	35.29
煤油	Kerasene	1.27	26.01	7.78	3.75	3.43
柴油	Diesel Oil	29.97	62.90	134.35	117.88	103.58
燃料油	Fuel Oil	122.27	165.03	302.03	212.52	186.43
液化石油气	LPG	29.26	35.20	46.40	53.40	44.63

8-13 规模以上工业企业平均每天主要能源消费量
AVERAGE DAILY ENERGY CONSUMPTION OF ABOVE DESIGNATED INDUSTRIAL ENTERPRISES

单位:万吨 (10000 tons)

名称	Item	1995	2000	2004	2005	2006
煤炭	Coal	163848	225862	390701	451797	486323
焦炭	Coke	6912	8524	28968	42813	52294
原油	Crude Oil	28151	37907	51097	61667	62827
汽油	Gasoline	491	738	915	879	967
煤油	Kerasene	35	713	213	103	94
柴油	Diesel Oil	821	1723	3681	3230	2838
燃料油	Fuel Oil	3350	4521	8275	5822	5108
液化石油气	LPG	802	964	1271	1463	1223

8－14　全社会用电情况
BASIC SITUATION OF TOTAL ELECTRICITY CONSUMPTION

单位:亿千瓦时　　(100 million kWh)

项　目	Item	2000	2004	2005	2006
全社会用电量	**Total**	**971.34**	**1820.09**	**2193.45**	**2569.75**
按产业分	Grouped by Type of Industry				
第一产业	Primary Industry	48.83	38.34	29.12	24.92
第二产业	Secondary Industry	717.84	1473.56	1793.34	2110.55
第三产业	Tertiary Industry	79.06	137.17	170.27	200.00
按行业分	Grouped by Sector				
农林牧渔水利业	Farming, Forestry, Animal Husbandry, Fishery and Water Conservancy	48.83	38.34	29.12	24.92
#排灌	Irrigation	30.60		12.05	8.97
工业	Industry	709.76	1451.80	1771.28	2088.68
#轻工业	Light Industry	220.55	502.84	519.99	578.06
重工业	Heavy Industry	489.21	948.96	1251.29	1510.62
#制造业	Manufacturing	545.03	1148.49	1745.07	1645.82
#纺织业	Textile Industry	80.36	183.16	228.39	269.24
化学原料及化学制品制造业	Chemical Raw Materials and Chemical Products	112.07	181.67	210.26	241.77
非金属矿物制品业	Non-Ferrous metal Mining and Processing	54.41	101.26	118.77	133.43
黑色金属冶炼及压延加工业	Smelting and Pressing of Ferrous Metals	71.34	173.23	224.90	279.92
通用及专用设备制造业	Ordinary and Special Purpose Equipment	32.83	76.42	67.39	81.07
建筑业	Construction	8.08	21.76	22.06	21.87
交通运输、仓储和邮政业	Transportation, Post and Telecommunication	7.26	11.18	16.45	16.90
信息传输、计算机服务和软件业	Information Transmission, Computer Service and Software	3.75	7.30	9.01	10.99
商业、住宿和餐饮业	Commerce, Hotel and Catering Industry	25.34	53.06	55.52	64.57
金融、房地产、商务及居民服务业	Banking, Real Estate, Commercial and Residents' Service	8.59	16.74	27.72	35.88
公共事业及管理组织	Public undertaking and Management Organizations	34.11	48.89	61.58	71.66
城乡居民生活用电	Electricity Consumption by Urban and Rural Residents	125.62	171.02	200.72	234.29
城镇居民	Urban Area	52.08	84.55	102.18	118.51
乡村居民	Rural Area	73.54	86.46	98.54	115.77

8－15 主要发电厂发电情况

厂 名	Item	2005 装机容量（万千瓦）Installed Capacity (10000 kW)	2005 发电量（亿千瓦时）Electricity Production (100 million kWh)	2006 装机容量（万千瓦）Installed Capacity (10000 kW)	2006 发电量（亿千瓦时）Electricity Production (100 million kWh)
全省总计	**Total**	**4213.3**	**2098.69**	**5273.0**	**2525.49**
#统调发电厂	Unified Planning Power Plant	3750.6	1830.83	4728.7	2207.21
非统调发电厂	Non-Unified Planning Power Plant	462.7	267.86	544.3	318.28
电网公司保留电厂	Electricity Network co. to be Retained Plant	130.0	88.24	130.0	71.95
徐州发电有限公司	Xuzhou Power Co. Ltd.	130.0	88.24	130.0	71.95
中国国电集团公司	China Guodian Group Co.	429.5	236.58	551.0	262.57
#国电谏壁发电有限公司	Guodian Jianbi Power Co. Ltd.	160.0	106.35	160.0	94.34
天生港发电有限公司	Tianshenggang Power Co. Ltd.	121.0	55.54	121.0	60.18
国电江阴苏龙发电有限公司	Guodian Jiangyin Sulong Power Co. Ltd.	121.5	63.02	121.5	67.92
国电常州发电有限公司	Guodian Changzhou Power Co. Ltd.			120.0	27.63
国电宿迁热电有限公司	Guodian Suqian Thermal Power Co. Ltd.	27.0	11.67	27.0	12.46
中国华能集团公司	China Huaneng Group Co.	379.3	225.85	616.3	282.54
#华能南通发电有限公司	Nantong Power Plant of Huaneng Group	140.4	84.03	140.4	76.60
华能太仓发电有限公司	Taicang Power Plant of Huaneng Group	64.0	40.10	184.0	98.39
华能淮阴发电有限公司	Huaiyin Power Plant of Huaneng Group	110.0	61.58	176.0	69.58
华能南京发电有限公司	Nanjing Power Plant of Huaneng Group	64.0	39.36	64.0	34.51
华能金陵燃机	Huanang Jinling Internal－Combustion Engine Plant			39.0	0.81
中国电力投资集团公司	China Power Investment Group Co.	177.0	107.86	179.7	91.25
#中电投常熟发电有限公司	Changshu Power Co. Ltd.	123.0	75.14	123.0	65.66
中电投贾汪发电有限公司	Jiawang Power Co. Ltd.	54.0	30.77	54.0	23.87
中国大唐集团公司	China Datang Group Co.	145.0	62.88	151.0	76.37
大唐徐塘发电有限公司	Datang Xutang Power Co. Ltd.	120.0	46.88	126.0	63.06
大唐下关发电有限公司	Datang Xiaguan Power Co. Ltd.	25.0	16.00	25.0	13.32
中国华电集团公司	China Huadian Group Co.	432.0	137.04	433.0	171.79
华电戚墅堰发电有限公司	Qishuyan Power Co. Ltd.	44.0	27.98	44.0	27.37
华电戚墅堰燃机	Qishuyan Internal－Combustion Engine Plant	78.0	3.27	78.0	21.35
华电扬州发电有限公司	Yangzhou Power Co. Ltd.	110.0	49.39	110.0	59.70
华电望亭发电有限公司	Wanting Power Co. Ltd.	200.0	56.40	123.0	41.89

ELECTRICITY PRODUCTION OF MAJOR POWER PLANTS

厂　名	Item	2005 装机容量（万千瓦）Installed Capacity (10000 kW)	2005 发电量（亿千瓦时）Electricity Production (100 million kWh)	2006 装机容量（万千瓦）Installed Capacity (10000 kW)	2006 发电量（亿千瓦时）Electricity Production (100 million kWh)
华电望亭燃机	Wanting Internal - Combustion Engine Plant			78.0	21.48
辅业集团公司	Fuye Group Co.	175.0	105.03	241.0	101.81
扬州第二发电有限公司	Yangzhou No. 2 Power Co. Ltd.	120.0	72.03	186.0	75.21
射阳港发电有限公司	Sheyanggang Power Co. Ltd.	55.0	33.00	55.0	26.59
江苏省国信集团公司	Jiangsu Province Guoxin Group Co.	155.5	71.81	166.5	88.97
#新海发电有限公司	Xinhai Power Co. Ltd.	115.0	53.01	115.0	60.68
盐城发电有限公司	Yancheng Power Co. Ltd.	40.5	18.80	40.5	21.37
华润集团公司	Huarun Group Co.	612.0	238.20	682.5	357.63
#华润电力(常熟)有限公司	Huarun(Changsu)Power Co. Ltd.	190.0	67.35	195.0	103.68
江苏镇江发电有限公司	Jiangsu Zhenjiang Power Co. Ltd.	176.0	56.59	181.5	92.40
徐州华润发电有限公司	Xuzhou Huarun Power Co. Ltd.	120.0	73.36	124.0	64.95
华润南京发电有限公司	Huarun Nanjing Power Co. Ltd.	93.0	29.14	93.0	48.43
徐州华鑫发电有限公司	Xuzhou Huaxing Power Co. Ltd.	33.0	11.76	66.0	32.27
其他公司投资电厂	Other Plant Invested by Other Co.	561.8	276.55	1012.5	403.66
太仓港环保发电有限公司	Taicang Environmental Protection Power Co. Ltd.	147.0	96.99	153.0	83.98
利港发电有限公司	Ligang Power Co. Ltd.	140.0	85.10	264.0	86.11
国华太仓发电有限公司	Guohua Taicang Power Co. Ltd.	60.0	8.41	120.0	64.14
张家港华兴电力有限公司	Zhangjiagang Huaxing Power Co. Ltd.	39.8	3.50	78.0	21.30
国电江苏谏壁发电有限公司	Guodian Jiangsu Jianbi Power Co. Ltd.	66.0	31.35	66.0	34.64
苏州蓝天燃机热电有限公司	Suzhou Lantian Internal-combustion Thermal Power Co. Ltd.	36.0	3.25	36.0	17.42
江苏南热发电有限公司	Jiangsu Nanjing Thermal Power Co. Ltd.	35.5	23.86	35.5	20.42
张家港华宇发电有限公司	Zhangjiagang Huayu Power Co. Ltd.	25.0	16.45	27.5	13.79
盐城市热电公司	Yancheng Thermal Power Co. Ltd.	12.5	7.64	12.5	4.28
张家港沙洲电力有限公司	Zhangjiagang Shazhou Power Co. Ltd.			120.0	43.55
连云港田湾核电	Lianyungang Tianwan Nuclear Power Co. Ltd.			100.0	14.04
地方电厂	Local Power Plant	666.2	345.36	655.5	345.51
自备电厂	Self-provided Power Plant	350.1	203.29	454.0	271.44

注：本表统计口径为6000千瓦及以上机组。

Note: The statistical scope of this table was 6000KW and above power generation.

主要统计指标解释

工业 指从事自然资源的开采,对采掘品和农产品进行加工和再加工的物质生产部门。具体包括:(1)对自然资源的开采,如采矿、晒盐、森林采伐等(但不包括禽兽捕猎和水产捕捞);(2)对农副产品的加工、再加工,如粮油加工、食品加工、缫丝、纺织、制革等;(3)对采掘品的加工、再加工,如炼铁、炼钢、化工生产、石油加工、机器制造、木材加工等,以及电力、自来水、煤气的生产和供应等;(4)对工业品的修理、翻新,如机器设备的修理、交通运输工具(包括小卧车)的修理等。

1984 年以前农村的村及村以下办工业归属农业,1984 年以后划归工业。

国有及国有控股企业 指国有企业加上国有控股企业。国有企业是指企业全部资产归国家所有,并按《中华人民共和国企业法人登记管理条例》规定登记注册的非公司制的经济组织。1957 年以前的公私合营和私营工业,后均改造为国营工业,1992 年改为国有工业,这部分工业的资料不单独分列时,均包括在国有企业内。国有控股企业是对混合所有制经济的企业进行的"国有控股"分类。它是指这些企业的全部资产中国有资产(股份)相对其他所有者中的任何一个所有者占资(股)最多的企业。该分组反映了国有经济控股情况。

集体企业 指企业资产归集体所有,并按《中华人民共和国企业法人登记管理条例》规定登记注册的经济组织。是社会主义公有制经济的组成部分。包括城乡所有使用集体投资举办的企业,以及部分个人通过集资自愿放弃所有权并依法经工商行政管理机关认定为集体所有制的企业。

股份合作企业 指以合作制为基础,由企业职工共同出资入股,吸收一定比例的社会资产投资组建,实行自主经营,自负盈亏,共同劳动,民主管理,按劳分配与按股分红相结合的一种集体经济组织。

联营企业 指两个及两个以上相同或不同所有制性质的企业法人或事业单位法人,按自愿、平等、互利的原则,共同投资组成的经济组织。联营企业包括:国有联营企业指国有企业与国有企业间的联营;集体联营企业指集体企业与集体企业间的联营;国有与集体联营企业指国有企业与集体企业间的联营。

有限责任公司 指根据《中华人民共和国公司登记管理条例》规定登记注册,由两个以上,五十个以下的股东共同出资,每个股东以其所认缴的出资额对公司承担有限责任,公司以其全部资产对其债务承担责任的经济组织。

有限责任公司包括国有独资公司以及其他有限责任公司。

股份有限公司 指根据《中华人民共和国企业法人登记管理条例》规定登记注册,其全部注册资本由等额股份构成并通过发行股票筹集资本,股东以其认购的股份对公司承担有限责任,公司以其全部资产对其债务承担责任的经济组织。

私营企业 指由自然人投资设立或由自然人控股,以雇佣劳动为基础的营利性经济组织。包括按照《公司法》、《合伙企业法》、《私营企业暂行条例》规定登记注册的私营有限责任公司、私营股份有限公司、私营合伙企业和私营独资企业。

港、澳、台商投资企业 指企业注册登记类型中的港、澳、台资合资、合作、独资经营企业和股份有限公司之和。

外商投资企业 指企业注册登记类型中的中外合资、合作经营企业、外资企业和外商投资股份有限公司之和。

"三资"企业 系指港、澳、台商投资企业和外资企业的简称。

轻工业 指主要提供生活消费品和制作手工工具的工业。按其所使用的原料不同,可分为两大类:(1)以农产品为原料的轻工业,是指直接或间接以农产品为基本原料的轻工业。主要包括食品制造、饮料制造、烟草加工、纺织、缝纫、皮革和毛皮制作、造纸以及印刷等工业;(2)以非农产品为原料的轻工业,是指以工业品为原料的轻工业。主要包括文教体育用品、化学药品制造、合成纤维制造、日用化学制品、日用玻璃制品、日用金属制品、手工工具制造、医疗器械制造、文化和办公用机械制造等工业。

重工业 是指为国民经济各部门提供物质技术基础的主要生产资料的工业。按其生产性质和产品用途,可以分为下列三类:(1)采掘(伐)工业,是指对自然资源的开采,包括石油开采、煤炭开采、金属矿开采、非金属矿开采和木材采伐等工业;(2)原材料工业,指向国民经济各部门提供基本材料、动力和燃料的工业。包括金属冶炼及加工、炼焦及焦炭、化学、化工原料、水泥、人造板以及电力、石油和煤炭加工等工业;(3)加工工业,是指对工业原材料进行再加工制造的工业。包括装备国民经济各部门的机械设备制造工业、金属结构、水泥制品等工业,以及为农业提供的生产资料如化肥、农药等工业。

根据上述划分原则,修理业中以重工业产品为修理作业对象的划为重工业,反之划为轻工业。

工业总产值 是以货币表现的工业企业在一定时期内生产的已出售或可供出售工业产品总量,它反映一定时间内工业生产的总规模和总水平。它包括:在本企业内不再进行加工,经检验、包装入库(规定不需包装的产品除外)的成品价值,对外加工费收入,自制半成品、在产品期末初差额价值。工业总产值采用"工厂法"计算,即以工业企业作为一个整体,按企业工业生产活动的最终成果来计算,企业内部不允许重复计算,不能把企业内部各个车间(分厂)生产的成果相加。但在企业之间、行业之间、地区之间存在着重复计算。

轻重工业总产值的划分是按"工厂法"计算的,即一个工业企业生产的主要产品性质属于轻工业,则该企业的全部总产值作为轻工业总产值;如它的主要产品性质属于重工业,则该企业的全部总产值作为重工业总产值。

工业增加值 是指工业行业在报告期内以货币表现的工业生产活动的最终成果。

实收资本 指企业实际收到的投资人投入的资本。按投资主体可分为国家资本、集体资本、法人资本、个人资本、港澳台资本和外商资本等。

资产总计 指企业拥有或控制的能以货币计量的经济资源。包括各种财产、债权和其他权利。资产按其流动性划分为流动资产、长期投资、固定资产、无形及递延资产和其他资产。

(1)流动资产 指企业可以在一年内或者超过一年的一个生产周期内变现或耗用的资产合计。包括现金及各种存款、短期投资、应收及预付款项、存货等。

(2)固定资产 指企业固定资产净值、固定资产清理、在建工程、待处理固定资产损失所占用的资金合计。

(3)无形资产 指企业长期使用而没有实物形态的资产。包括专利权、非专利技术、商标权、著作权、土地使用权、商誉等。

负债合计 指企业承担的能以货币计量,将以资产或劳务偿付的债务。负债一般按偿还期长短分为流动负债和长期负债、递延税项等。

(1)流动负债 指企业在一年内或者超过一年的一个营业周期内需要偿还的债务合计,其中包括短期借款、应付及预收款项、应付工资、应交税金和应交利润等。

(2)长期负债 指企业在一年以上或者超过一年的一个营业周期以上需要偿还的债务合计,其中包括长期借款、应付债务、长期应付款项等。

所有者权益 指企业投资人对企业净资产的所有权。企业净资产等于企业全部资产减去全部负债后的余额,其中包括投资者对企业的最初投入,以及资本公积金、盈余公积金和未分配利润,对股份制企业即为股东权益。

固定资产原价 指企业在建造、购置、安装、改建、扩建、技术改造某项固定资产时所支出的全部货币总额。它一般包括买价、包装费、运杂费和安装费等。

固定资产净值 是指固定资产原价减去历年已提折旧额后的净额。

流动资产 是指可以在一年或者超过一年的一个营业周期内变现或者耗用的资产,包括现金及各种存款、短期投资、应收及预付货款、存货等。

主营业务收入 指企业销售商品、提供劳务及让渡资产信用权等日常活动中所产生的收入。

主营业务成本 指企业销售商品、提供劳及让渡资产信用权等日常活动而发生的实际成本。

主营业务税金及附加 企业日常活动应负担的税金及附加,包括营业税、消费税、城市维护建设税、资源税、土地增值税和教育费附加等。

利润总额 指企业实现的利润。

应交增值税 指企业在报告期内应交纳的增值税额。

资产负债率 该指标既反映企业经营风险的大小,也反映企业利用债权人提供的资金从事经营活动的能力。计算公式为:

资产负债率 = 负债总额/资产总额 × 100%

工业成本费用利润率 指在一定时期内实现的利润与成本费用之比,是反映工业生产成本及费用投入的经济效益指标,同时也是反映降低成本的经济效益的指标。计算公式为:

工业成本费用利润率(%) = 利润总额/成本及费用总额 × 100%

工业增加值率 指在一定时期内工业增加值占同期工业总产值的比重,反映降低中间消耗的经济效益。计算公式为:

工业增加值率(%) = 工业增加值(现价)/(工业总产生 + 本年应交销项税) × 100%

流动资产周转次数 指在一定时期内流动资产完成的周转次数,反映流动资产的周转速度。计算公式为:

流动资产周转次数 = 产品销售收入/全部流动资产平均余额

产品销售率 指报告期工业销售产值与同期全部工业总产值之比,是反映工业产品已实现销售的程度,分析工业产销衔接情况,研究工业产品满足社会需求程度的指标。计算公式为:

产品销售率(%) = 工业销售产值/工业总产值(现价) × 100%

全员劳动生产率 指根据产品的价值量指标计算的平均每一个就业人员在单位时间内的产品生产量。是考核企业经济活动的重要指标,是企业生产技术水平、经营管理水平、职工技术熟练程度和劳动积极性的综合表现。目前我国的全员劳动生产率是将工业企业的工业增加值除以同一时期全部就业人员的平均人数来计算的。计算公式为:

全员劳动生产率(%) = 工业增加值/全部就业人员平均人数 × 100%

Explanatory Notes on Main Statistical Indicators

Industry refers to the material production sector which is engaged in extraction of natural resources and processing and reprocessing of minerals and agricultural products, including(1) extraction of natural resources, such as mining, salt production, logging(but not including hunting and fishing); (2) processing and reprocessing of farm and sideline produces, such as rice husking, flour milling, wine making, oil pressing, cotton ginning, silk reeling, spinning and weaving, and leather making; (3) manufacture of industrial products, such as steel making, iron smelting, chemicals manufacturing, petroleum processing, machine building, timber processing; water and gas production and electricity generation and supply; (4) repairing of industrial products such as the repairing of machinery and means of transport(including cars).

Prior to 1984, the rural industry run by villages and cooperative organizations under village was classified into agriculture. Since 1984, it has been grouped into industry.

(1) **State-owned and State-share holding Enterprises** State-owned enterprises refer to industrial enterprises where the means of production are all owned by the state. Joint state-private industries and private industries, which existed before 1957, have been transformed into state run industries. Statistics on these enterprises has been included in the state-owned industries since 1992 when separation of data was no longer necessary. State-share holding Enterprises refers to classification of "state-share holding" to the mixed-owned enterprises, which indicate that among the total assets of enterprises, the state assets(share) occupying the most part (share) than any other enterprises. Such group reflects the condition of share-holding of the state-owned economy.

(2) **Collective-owned Enterprises** refer to industrial enterprises where the means of production are owned collectively, including urban and rural enterprises invested by collectives and some enterprises which were formerly owned privately but have been registered in industrial and commercial administration agency as collective units through raising fund from the public.

(3) **Share-holding Cooperative Enterprises** refer to economic units set up on cooperative basis, with funding partly from members of the enterprise and partly from outside investment, where the operation and management is decided by the members who also participate in the production, and the distribution of income is based both on work(labour input) and on shares(capital input).

(4) **Joint – operation enterprises** refer to economic units that are established by joint investment by two or more corporate enterprises or institutions of the same or different types of ownership on voluntary, equal and mutual-beneficial basis. They include:

a) state-owned joint-operation enterprises(joint operation between state-owned enterprises);

b) collective joint-operation enterprises(joint operation between collective enterprises; and

c) state-collective joint-operation enterprises(joint operation between state and collective enterprises).

(5) **Limited Liability Corporations** refer to economic units registered in accordance with the Regulation of the People's Republic of China on the Management of Registration of Corporations, with capitals from 2 to 49 investors, each investor bears limited liability to the corporation depending on his/her holding of shares, and the corporation bears liability to its debt to the maximum of its total assets.

(6) **Share-holding Corporations Ltd.** refer to economic units registered in accordance with the Regulation of the People's Republic of China on the Management of Registration of Corporate Enterprises, with total registered capitals divided into equal shares and raised through issuing stocks. Each investor bears limited liability to the corporation depending on the holding of shares, and the corporation bears liability to its debt to the maximum of its total assets.

(7) **Private Enterprises** refer to economic units invested or controlled(by holding the majority of the shares) by natural persons who hire labours for profit-making activities. Included in this category are private limited liability corporations, private share-holding corporations Ltd., private partnership enterprises and private sole investment enterprises registered in accordance with the Corporation Law, Partnership Enterprise Law and Tentative Regulation on Private Enterprises.

(8) **Enterprises with Funds form Hong Kong, Macao and Taiwan** refers to all industrial enterprises registered as the joint-venture, cooperative, sole(exclusive) investment industrial enterprises and limited liability corporations with funds from Hong Kong, Macao and Taiwan.

(9) **Foreign Funded Enterprises** refers to all industrial enterprises registered as the joint-venture, cooperative, sole(exclusive) investment industrial enterprises and limited liability corporations with foreign funds.

Light Industry refers to the industry that produces consumer goods and hand tools. It consists of two categories, depending on the materials used:

(1) Industries using farm products as raw materials. These are branches of light industry which directly or indirectly use farm products as basic raw materials, including the manufacture of food and beverages, tobacco processing, textile, clothing, fur and leather manufacturing, paper making, printing, etc.

(2) Industries using non farm products as raw materials. These are branches of light industry which use manufactured goods as raw-materials, including the manufacture of cultural, educational articles and sports goods, chemicals, synthetic fiber, chemical products for daily use, glass products for daily use, metal products for daily use, hand tools, medical apparatus and instruments, and the manufacture of cultural and clerical machinery.

Heavy Industry refers to the industry which produces capital goods, and provides various sectors of the national economy with necessary material and technical basis. It consists of the following three branches according to the purpose of production or the use of products:

(1) Mining, quarrying and logging industry refers to the industry that extracts natural resources. including extraction of petroleum, coal, metal and non – metal ores and logging.

(2) Raw materials industry refers to the industry that provides various sectors of the national economy with raw materials. fuels and power. It includes smelting and processing of metals, coking and coke chemistry, chemical materials and building materials such as cement, plywood, and power, petroleum refining and coal dressing.

(3) Manufacturing industry refers to the industry that processes raw materials. It includes machine building industry which equips sectors of the national economy, industries of metal structure and cement products, industries producing means of agricultural production, such as chemical fertilizers and pesticides. According to the above principle of classification, the repairing trades which are engaged primarily in repairing products of heavy industry are classified into heavy industry while these engaged in repairing products of light in – dustry are classified into light industry.

Gross Industrial Output Value is the total volume of industrial products sold or available for sale in value terms which reflects the total achievements and overall scale of industrial production during a given period. It includes the value of the finished products, which are not to be further processed in the enterprises and have been inspected, packed and put in storage, the value of industrial services rendered to other units, and the changes in the value of the semi – finished products and products in process between the be – ginning and closing of the period. The gross industrial output value is calculated with "factory method". No double calculations are to be made within the same enterprise. However, double counting does occur among different enterprises.

Output value of light and heavy industries is based on the "factory" method. If the major products of an industrial enterprise are classified as light industry products, the entire gross output value of that enterprise is classified into the light industry; the same principle applies to heavy industry.

Value – added of Industry refers to the final results of industrial production of the industrial trade in money terms during the reference period.

Acctually Received Capital refer main management capital actually received by enterprises used for long – term circulation, including state capital, legal pe ~ on capital, collective capital, individual capital, Hong Kong Macao Taiwan capital and foreign capital.

Total Assets refer to all economic resources, owned or controlled by enterprises, that could be measured in monetary terms, including properties, creditors equity and other economic rights of all forms. Classified by the degree of equitability, total assets include circulating assets, long term investment, fixed assets, intangible assets and deferred assets, and other assets.

(1) Circulating assets (working capital) refer to assets which can be cashed in or spent or consumed in an operating cycle of one year or over one year, including cash, aII kinds of deposits, short term investment, receivables, advance payment, stock, etc.

(2) Fixed assets refer to the net value of fixed assets, elearance of fixed assets, project under construction, fixed assets losses in suspense. These are corporations' fund holdings.

(3) Intangible assets refer to the assets without material form used by enterprises over a long time, such as patents, non – patent technologies, trade marks, copyright, land use right, business reputation, etc.

Total Liabilities refer to the debts, measured in monetary terms, that enterprises are responsible for repayment in the form of cash, assets or labour. Classified by terms of repayment, liability include liquid liabilities and long-term liabilities.

(1) Liquid liabilities (also called quick liabilities or immediate liabilities) refer to enterprises' total debt payable within an operating cycle of one year or over one year, including short term loans, payable and advance payments, wages payable, taxes payable and profit payable, etc.

(2) Long term liabilities refers to total debt payable within an operating cycle of one year or over one year, including long-term

loans, payable liabilities, long-term payable, etc.

Creditors' Equity refers to investors ownership of net assets of the enterprise. It is equal to the total assets of the enterprise minus its total liabilities, including the primary input from investors, capital accumulation fund, surplus accumulation fund and undistributed profit. It is the shareholder's equity in share-holdting companies.

Original Value of Fixed Assets refers to the original value of all fixed assets owned by industrial enterprises, calculated at the cost paid at the time of purchase, installation, reconstruction, expansion, and technical innovation and transformation of the said assets, which includes expenses on purchase, package, transportation, and installation, etc.

Net Value of Fixed Assets is obtained by deducting depreciation over years from the original value of fixed assets.

Working Capital(Circulating Assets) refers to assets which can be cashed in or spent or consumed in an operating cycle of one year or over one year, which includes cash, various deposits, short term investment, and receivable payments, and advance payments, stock, etc.

Major Business Revenue refer to the revenue from the sales of products, service provided and transferring the usage right of assets ect. daily activities.

Cost of Major Business refers to the actual cost of products of industrial enterprises, service provided and transferring the usage right of assets ect. daily activities.

Tax and extra of Major Business refers to the tax and extra, including city maintenance and construction tax, operation tax, consumption tax, resources tax, extra charges for education and tax on land value added, which should be born by the enterprises.

Total Profits refer to the profits gained by the enterprises.

Value-added Tax Payable refers to the amount of the value added tax which should be paid by the enterprises in the reporting period.

Ratio of Debts to Assets reflect both the operation risk and the capability of the enterprise in making use of the capital from the creditors. It is calculated as follows:

Ratio of debts to assets(%) = (Total debts/total assets) × 100%

Ratio of Profits to Total Industrial Costs refers to the ratio of profits realized in a given period to the total costs in the same period, which reflects the economic efficiency of input cost and is calculated as follows:

Ratio of Profits to Total Industrial Cost(%) = (Total Profits/Total Costs) × 100%

Value - added Rate of Industry refers to the ratio of value added of industry in a given period to the gross output value in the same period, which reflects the economic efficiency of cutting down the intermediate input and is calculated as follows:

Value-added Rate of Industry(%) = [Value - added of Industry (at current prices)]/[Gross Output Value(at Current Prices) + taxes payable this year] × 100%

Turnover of Working Capital refers to the number of times of turnover of working capital in a given period of time, which reflects the speed of the turnover of working capital and is calculated as follows:

Turnover of Working Capital(%) = (Sales Revenue of Products)/(Average Balance of Total Working Capital) × 100%

Ratio of Sales to Gross Output Value refers to the sales of industrial products to the gross industrial output value during the reference period, and is important in reflecting the linkage between production and sales and the extent of the needs of the society that has been met by the supply of industrial products. It is calculated as follows:

Ratio of Sales to Gross Output Value = [Industrial sales/Gross industrial output value(at current prices)] × 100%

Overall Labour Productivity of Industrial Enterprises refers to the average output per employed person in industrial enterprises in value terms. At present, the value added and the average number of staff and workers of an industrial enterprises in a given period are used to calculate the overall labour productivity. The formula used is:

Overall Labour Productivity = (Value Added of Industry)/(Average Number of Staff and Workers)

第 9 篇

建筑业

CONSTRUCTION

9-1 建筑施工企业概况

BASIC STATISTICS ON CONSTRUCTION ENTERPRISES

年份 Year	总计 Total	国有经济 State-Owned	地方 Local-Owned	部属 Central-Owned	城镇集体经济 Urban Collective-Owned	乡镇企业及其它经济 Rural and Township Industry and Others
企业单位个数（个） Number of Enterprises（unit）						
1985	2360	114	86	28	148	2098
1989	2408	175	144	31	204	2029
1990	2284	162	138	24	201	1921
1991	2316	173	147	26	209	1934
1992	2417	203	176	27	251	1963
1993	2810	308	273	35	429	2073
1994	3348	389	353	36	513	2446
1995	3426	406	370	36	505	2515
1996	3528	589	554	35	868	2071
1997	3546	564	525	39	884	2098
1998	3587	573	535	38	881	2133
1999	3994	550	514	36	980	2464
2000	3948	529	485	44	903	2516
2001	3872	469	424	45	631	2772
2002	4084	489	438	51	440	3155
2003	4267	358	322	36	326	3583
2004	5241	318	279	39	266	4657
2005	5909	556	524	32	220	5133
2006	6371	444	439	5	206	5721
全部职工平均人数（万人） Average Staff and Workers（10000 persons）						
1985	124.09	17.60	13.82	3.78	14.05	92.44
1989	128.55	22.08	15.10	6.98	20.30	86.17
1990	124.31	21.53	15.24	6.29	23.94	78.44
1991	126.44	22.06	15.83	6.23	25.46	78.92
1992	143.44	24.67	17.66	7.01	30.07	88.70
1993	175.06	34.58	27.50	7.08	34.00	106.48
1994	212.17	44.60	31.60	13.00	34.37	133.20
1995	232.94	45.42	38.58	6.84	51.56	135.96

9－1　续表 1　Continued 1

年　　份 Year	总　计 Total	国有经济 State-Owned	地　方 Local-Owned	部　属 Central-Owned	城镇集体经济 Urban Collective-Owned	乡镇企业及其它经济 Ruraland Township Industry andOthers
1996	220.71	59.55	52.14	7.41	55.26	105.90
1997	215.69	51.20	44.57	6.63	61.70	102.78
1998	232.32	50.52	42.22	8.30	83.97	97.83
1999	222.80	46.30	38.85	7.45	63.59	112.91
2000	221.48	43.85	36.41	7.44	59.73	117.9
2001	239.52	41.74	35.33	6.41	44.11	153.67
2002	251.36	45.96	39.26	6.70	30.27	175.13
2003	277.91	30.37	23.85	6.52	23.62	223.92
2004	305.64	30.06	23.31	6.75	15.84	259.74
2005	342.24	60.77	53.98	6.79	13.50	267.97
2006	379.77	50.24	48.44	1.80	17.49	312.04
建筑业总产值　（亿元） **Gross Out put Value of Construction Enterprise** (100 **million yuan**)						
1985	82.63	14.32	10.92	3.39	10.80	57.52
1989	142.05	30.94	9.52	11.42	23.97	87.14
1990	147.23	32.00	21.49	10.51	29.76	85.47
1991	176.21	37.84	26.04	11.80	34.35	104.02
1992	265.80	58.20	40.07	18.12	55.99	151.62
1993	449.99	104.73	82.40	22.33	86.87	258.40
1994	738.60	171.60	131.04	40.56	178.46	388.53
1995	998.11	257.36	207.39	49.97	259.76	480.98
1996	1049.42	377.92	318.79	59.13	253.63	417.88
1997	1102.12	352.86	294.21	58.65	308.08	441.18
1998	1224.42	335.16	272.55	62.61	387.29	501.97
1999	1338.46	343.12	282.03	61.09	346.97	648.37
2000	1546.17	376.59	308.3	68.29	377.31	792.27
2001	1859.41	414.58	339.7	74.88	284.90	1159.93
2002	2199.52	492.90	414.84	78.06	222.35	1484.27
2003	2794.94	345.39	258.10	87.29	194.75	2254.80
2004	3656.66	436.40	299.08	137.32	134.09	3086.17
2005	4368.95	865.07	727.50	137.57	154.46	3349.42
2006	5424.85	812.35	770.02	42.33	190.51	4421.99

9-1 续表 2 Continued 2

年份 Year	总计 Total	国有经济 State-Owned	地方 Local-Owned	部属 Central-Owned	城镇集体经济 Urban Collective-Owned	乡镇企业及其它经济 Ruraland Township Industry andOthers
施工房屋面积 （万平方米） Floor Space of Buildings Under Construction (10000sq. m)						
1985	5570.32	619.94	536.58	83.36	690.92	4259.46
1989	5447.40	672.60	547.40	125.20	927.70	3847.10
1990	5240.98	699.10	580.30	118.80	1070.40	3471.48
1991	5711.13	778.71	660.44	118.27	1143.12	3789.30
1992	7780.32	1049.90	901.00	148.90	1688.30	5042.12
1993	10229.96	1801.32	1573.13	228.19	2045.54	6383.10
1994	13201.21	2356.00	2062.20	293.90	3269.60	7575.61
1995	16646.14	3470.96	3135.28	335.68	4621.48	8553.70
1996	15672.95	5032.00	4663.09	368.91	3723.69	6917.26
1997	16191.85	4407.38	4031.04	376.34	4344.53	7439.94
1998	17803.33	3831.67	3593.61	238.06	5887.35	8084.31
1999	18748.25	3830.22	3633.96	196.26	4710.61	10207.42
2000	21287.10	4096.75	3871.42	225.33	4982.85	12207.50
2001	24319.01	3706.55	3380.84	325.71	4060.51	16551.95
2002	27753.39	3669.91	3301.01	368.90	3113.95	20969.53
2003	33949.95	1893.32	1503.56	389.76	2369.63	29687.00
2004	43170.57	2815.09	2273.46	541.63	1655.20	38700.28
2005	52242.23	7706.17	7383.99	322.18	1966.09	42569.97
2006	63140.49	6553.90	6329.13	224.77	2248.13	54338.46
竣工房屋面积 （万平方米） Floor Space of Buildings Completed (10000sq. m)						
1985	3527.20	272.55	245.03	27.52	382.94	2871.71
1989	3446.50	284.50	246.40	38.10	502.10	2659.90
1990	3307.93	354.40	302.20	52.20	617.00	2336.53
1991	3422.75	361.35	322.27	39.08	618.49	2442.91
1992	4387.99	446.60	395.90	50.70	837.40	3103.99
1993	5767.78	772.59	705.11	67.48	1077.09	3918.10
1994	9336.28	903.20	838.60	64.60	1620.00	6813.08
1995	8739.38	1304.03	1243.04	60.99	2056.55	5378.80
1996	8252.13	1946.38	1872.36	74.02	2141.69	4164.06

9－1　续表 3　Continued 3

年　份 Year	总　计 Total	国有经济 State-Owned	地　方 Local-Owned	部　属 Central-Owned	城镇集体经济 Urban Collective-Owned	乡镇企业及其它经济 Ruraland Township Industry andOthers
1997	8787.36	1678.84	1601.39	77.46	2600.34	4508.18
1998	9958.90	1748.46	1686.40	62.05	3497.35	4713.10
1999	10558.22	1692.42	1636.92	55.50	2751.61	6114.19
2000	12329.65	1961.86	1896.93	64.93	2986.11	7381.68
2001	14268.89	1822.02	1718.15	103.87	2622.17	9824.70
2002	15478.58	1877.94	1773.00	104.94	1867.91	11732.73
2003	17730.02	879.14	786.81	92.33	1490.80	15360.08
2004	21756.82	1246.57	1084.82	161.75	1040.82	19469.43
2005	25391.86	3696.89	3526.71	170.18	1113.19	20581.78
2006	28715.39	2517.69	2448.11	69.58	1244.15	24953.55
房屋建筑面积竣工率　(%) Rate of Floor Space of Buildings Completed　(%)						
1985	66.2	44.0	45.7	33.0	55.4	67.4
1989	63.3	42.3	45.0	30.4	54.1	69.1
1990	63.1	50.7	52.1	43.9	57.6	67.3
1991	59.9	46.4	48.8	33.0	54.1	64.5
1992	56.4	42.5	43.9	34.0	49.6	61.6
1993	56.4	42.9	44.8	29.6	52.7	61.4
1994	70.7	38.3	40.7	22.0	49.5	89.9
1995	52.5	34.9	39.6	18.2	44.5	62.9
1996	52.7	38.7	40.2	20.1	57.5	60.2
1997	54.3	38.1	39.7	20.6	59.9	60.6
1998	55.9	45.6	46.9	26.1	59.4	58.3
1999	56.3	44.2	45.0	28.3	58.4	59.9
2000	57.9	47.9	49.0	28.8	59.9	60.5
2001	58.7	49.2	50.8	31.9	64.6	59.4
2002	55.8	51.2	53.7	28.4	60.0	56.0
2003	52.2	46.4	52.3	23.7	62.9	51.7
2004	50.4	44.3	47.7	29.9	62.9	50.3
2005	48.6	48.0	47.8	52.8	56.6	48.3
2006	45.5	38.4	38.7	31.0	55.3	45.9

注:本表资料包括施工总承包和专业承包企业,不含劳务分包企业(下同)。

Note:In this table,the data including general contract and specilized contract enterprises under construction, excluding labor divided contract(the same as in the following tables).

9-2 按行业分建筑业主要经济指标(2006年)
MAJOR ECONOMIC INDICATORS OF CONSTRUCTION ENTERPRISES BY SECTOR(2006)

指标	Item	房屋和土木工程建筑业 Housing and Civil Engineering Construction	房屋工程 Housing Construciton	土木工程	建筑安装业 Construction and Installation	建筑装饰业 Building Decorative Construction
施工企业个数 (个)	Number of Construction Enterprises (unit)	3297	2090	1207	1011	1411
建筑业总产值 (亿元)	Construction Enterprises Gross Output Value (100 million yuan)	4767.67	3869.19	898.48	361.21	206.18
#建筑工程	Construction	4655.72	3791.08	864.64	47.10	196.03
安装工程	Construction and Installation	88.49	59.79	28.70	311.82	6.42
固定资产折旧	Depreciation on Fixed Assets	39.14	22.39	16.75	4.20	2.01
本年应付工资总额	Wages Payable of This Year	654.09	573.90	80.19	43.13	25.98
本年应付福利费总额	Welfare Costs Payable of This Year	76.80	67.24	9.56	5.40	2.52
工程结算税金及附加	Taxes and Added Taxes of Settle Accounts	133.76	104.66	29.09	10.66	6.17
竣工产值 (亿元)	Buildings Completed Output Value (100 million yuan)	3679.53	2986.20	693.33	325.99	178.05
房屋建筑施工面积 (万平方米)	Floor Space of Buildings Under Construction (10000 sq. m)	62522.04	62064.99	457.05	468.28	
#本年新开工	Beginning Projects in this Year	37309.72	37008.83	300.89	256.04	
投标承包面积	Floor Space of Biding System	55522.52	55172.33	350.19	305.00	
房屋建筑竣工面积 (万平方米)	Floor Space of Buildings Completed (10000 sq. m)	28453.83	28225.76	228.07	202.28	
自有机械设备总台数 (万台)	Number of Machinery and Equipment Owned (10000 sets)	86.42	70.94	15.48	9.91	6.62
自有机械设备总功率 (万千瓦)	Total Power of Machinery and Equipment Owned (10000 kW)	1407.68	928.25	479.43	99.64	51.58
自有机械设备净值 (亿元)	Net Value of Machinery and Equipment Owned (100million yuan)	247.39	151.69	95.70	23.26	8.31
职工平均人数 (万人)	Annual Average Number of Staff and Workers (10000 persons)	338.70	289.83	48.87	20.73	13.88
全员劳动生产率 (元/人)	Overall Labor Productivity (yuan/person)	140763	133497	183854	174285	148501
技术装备率 (元/人)	Value of Machines Per Laborer (yuan/person)	7331	5192	21129	11871	5625
动力装备率 (千瓦/人)	Motive Power Per Laborer (kW/person)	4.17	3.18	10.59	5.09	3.49
利润总额 (亿元)	Total Profits(100 million yuan)	132.19	90.58	41.61	20.86	7.67

注:装修装饰业从事装修装饰工程的从1999年起免填单位工程施工个数。

Note: Since 1999, The number of single projects under constructions was free from report for the fitting up and docorating industry engaged in the projects of fitting up and docorating.

9－3 按登记注册类型分建筑业主要经济指标(2006年)

指标	Item	合计 Total	内资企业 Domestic Funded	国有 State-Owned
施工企业个数（个）	Number of Construction Enterprises (unit)	6371	6255	295
建筑业总产值（亿元）	Construction Enterprises Gross OutputValue (100 million yuan)	5424.85	5374.78	352.90
#建筑工程	Construction	4977.80	4942.15	303.68
安装工程	Construction and Installation	411.36	397.73	47.19
固定资产折旧	Depreciation on Fixed Assets	47.71	47.05	5.19
本年应付工资总额	Wages Payable of This Year	732.77	728.54	37.49
本年应付福利费总额	Welfare Costs Payable of This Year	85.82	85.18	4.14
工程结算税金及附加	Taxes and Added Taxes of Settle Accounts	153.17	151.85	10.52
竣工产值（亿元）	Buildings Completed Output Value (100millionyuan)	4252.85	4205.59	275.32
房屋建筑施工面积（万平方米）	Floor Space of Buildings Under Construction (10000sq. m)	63140.49	62866.60	1391.76
#本年新开工	Beginning Projects in this Year	37663.56	37557.36	825.30
#投标承包面积	Floor Space of Biding System	55908.05	55671.51	1307.99
房屋建筑竣工面积（万平方米）	Floor Space of Buildings Completed (10000sq. m)	28715.39	28556.78	773.84
自有机械设备总台数（万台）	Number of Machinery and Equipment Owned (10000 sets)	104.98	104.24	7.60
自有机械设备总功率（万千瓦）	Total Power of Machinery and Equipment Owned (10000kW)	1617.33	1603.46	199.52
自有机械设备净值（亿元）	Net Value of Machinery and Equipment Owned (100millionyuan)	294.23	290.96	33.79
职工平均人数（万人）	Annual Average Number of Staff and Workers (10000persons)	379.77	377.13	21.73
全员劳动生产率（元/人）	Overall Labor Productivity (yuan/person)	142847	142517	162395
技术装备率（元/人）	Value of Machines Per Laborer (yuan/person)	7779	7744	17856
动力装备率（千瓦/人）	Motive Power Per Laborer (kW/person)	4.28	4.27	10.54
利润总额（亿元）	Total Profits (100 million yuan)	164.31	160.74	7.35

MAJOR ECONOMIC INDICATORS OF CONSTRUCTION ENTERPRISES BY REGISTRATION STATUS(2006)

集　体 Collective-Owned	股份合作 ShareHolding Cooperative Enterprises	联　营 Joint-Owned Enterprises	有限责任 Limited Liability Enterprises	股份有限 Limited ShareHolding Enterprises	私　营 Private Enterprises	其　他 Others	港、澳、台商投资企业 Funded by Entrepreneurs from Hong Kong, Macao and Taiwan	外商投资企　业 Foreign Funded Enterprises
301	272	32	2061	290	2981	23	50	66
279.02	149.94	29.62	2469.90	600.85	1484.64	7.90	16.68	33.39
268.65	137.22	28.46	2252.62	578.48	1365.75	7.31	14.02	21.63
9.16	12.19	1.17	199.17	21.68	106.65	0.53	2.50	11.13
2.02	1.67	1.01	21.51	3.06	12.49	0.10	0.29	0.38
41.61	19.39	1.65	329.59	92.65	205.35	0.80	1.39	2.84
4.51	2.48	0.18	39.38	12.23	22.09	0.17	0.14	0.50
6.66	4.80	1.02	69.40	16.58	42.56	0.30	0.42	0.90
247.71	119.29	13.90	1880.97	468.04	1193.32	7.04	14.60	32.66
3611.51	1855.05	24.38	28983.22	8488.01	18456.96	55.70	27.35	246.54
2475.92	1221.88	15.74	17334.21	4197.22	11456.53	30.58	22.14	84.05
3200.07	1619.08	18.56	26956.29	7020.33	15498.95	50.23	22.40	214.15
2023.25	956.29	10.78	12816.80	3347.07	8611.73	17.02	0.00	158.61
6.40	3.56	0.28	50.17	6.31	29.76	0.16	0.38	0.36
89.95	54.95	5.13	673.40	153.37	422.27	4.86	7.41	6.46
15.60	10.24	1.30	127.53	20.46	81.17	0.88	1.58	1.68
26.17	12.43	1.23	164.84	37.98	112.12	0.62	0.89	1.74
106616	120621	240388	149835	158181	132415	126990	186970	191718
6314	7866	12516	7833	5431	6940	15017	18629	10119
3.64	4.22	4.94	4.14	4.07	3.61	8.27	8.72	3.88
6.71	5.05	0.78	81.02	12.11	47.54	0.19	1.34	2.24

9－4 按登记注册类型分建筑业财务状况(2006年)

单位:亿元

指标	Item	合计 Total	内资企业 Domestic Funded	国有 State-Owned
资本金合计	Total Capital Assets	825.16	806.47	67.30
流动资产合计	Circulating Funds	3129.30	3074.78	266.08
#存货	Stock	1022.63	1013.22	70.45
固定资产合计	Total Fixed Asstes	570.20	561.38	58.21
固定资产原价合计	Total Original Value of Fixed Assets	763.50	752.64	86.78
#生产经营用	Used by Production	595.67	587.19	68.84
累计折旧	Total Depreciation Drawn Accumulated	264.11	260.70	35.35
#本年折旧	Depreciation Draw This Year	47.71	47.05	5.19
在建工程	Project Under Construction	49.37	48.32	3.66
资产总计	Total Assets	3907.01	3841.82	343.94
流动负债合计	Total Circulating Liability	2463.88	2424.13	242.06
长期负债合计	Total Long-term Liability	59.11	58.50	5.24
所有者权益合计	Creditors Equity	1384.03	1359.19	96.64
工程结算收入	Project Settlement Revenue	4356.28	4310.05	342.47
工程结算成本	Cost of Project Settlement Accounts	3836.29	3797.77	303.11
工程结算税金及附加	Taxes and Extra Charges on Project Settlement Accounts	153.17	151.85	10.52
工程结算利润	Profits of Project Settlement Accounts	337.34	331.62	27.66
其他业务利润	Other Profit	16.75	15.79	1.91
经营费用	Management Expenses	29.48	28.82	1.17
管理费用	Management Expenses	178.39	175.31	20.74
#税金	Taxes	7.16	7.00	0.52
利润总额	Total Profit	164.31	160.74	7.35
应交所得税	Payable Income Taxes	45.16	44.70	2.05
应付利润	Payable Profit	47.95	46.86	1.54
本年应付工资总额	Payable Total Wages This Year	732.77	728.54	37.49
本年应付福利费	PayableTotalWelfareThisYear	85.82	85.18	4.14
亏损企业个数 (个)	Number of Loss-Making Enterprises (unit)	818	795	43

FINANCIAL INDICATORS OF CONSTRUCTION BY REGISTRATION STATUS(2006)

(100 million yuan)

集　体 Collective-Owned	股份合作 ShareHolding Cooperative Enterprises	联　营 Joint-Owned Enterprises	有限责任 Limited Liability Enterprises	股份有限 Limited ShareHolding Enterprises	私　营 Private Enterprises	其　他 Others	港、澳、台商投资企业 Funded by Entrepreneurs from Hong Kong, Macao and Taiwan	外商投资企业 Foreign Funded Enterprises
32.65	28.84	3.60	345.26	57.80	268.37	2.65	8.56	10.14
112.43	83.11	16.28	1365.22	223.88	996.57	11.20	20.51	34.01
44.91	33.94	5.07	449.35	70.13	335.66	3.71	4.56	4.85
26.05	20.76	3.63	251.88	34.02	163.40	3.43	3.46	5.36
35.94	26.56	5.69	335.68	46.76	213.38	1.85	5.27	5.60
27.98	20.81	5.00	253.81	38.12	171.23	1.39	3.83	4.64
13.44	9.54	2.10	114.93	16.23	68.28	0.85	2.02	1.38
2.02	1.67	1.01	21.51	3.06	12.49	0.10	0.29	0.38
2.01	3.01	0.00	22.29	2.46	13.06	1.84	0.20	0.85
143.96	109.76	20.14	1708.19	277.70	1222.12	16.01	25.06	40.13
90.19	60.37	12.10	1062.70	179.37	766.80	10.54	13.58	26.16
2.34	0.95	0.67	29.93	3.37	13.99	2.02	0.48	0.12
51.43	48.44	7.37	615.57	94.96	441.34	3.45	11.00	13.84
177.47	122.99	27.20	1952.30	467.82	1211.44	8.36	15.09	31.14
155.09	107.93	24.37	1719.97	423.38	1056.61	7.31	12.42	26.10
6.66	4.80	1.02	69.40	16.58	42.56	0.30	0.42	0.90
14.50	9.41	1.76	152.72	26.26	98.68	0.63	2.01	3.72
0.25	0.21	0.02	8.69	1.75	2.87	0.09	0.44	0.52
1.22	0.85	0.05	10.21	1.59	13.59	0.12	0.24	0.42
7.62	4.29	0.83	77.62	14.68	49.08	0.45	1.19	1.89
0.30	0.25	0.05	3.50	0.38	1.98	0.01	0.08	0.07
6.71	5.05	0.78	81.02	12.11	47.54	0.19	1.34	2.24
1.65	1.31	0.17	22.41	3.59	13.46	0.05	0.22	0.24
2.12	1.77	0.28	20.28	4.58	16.18	0.10	0.35	0.74
41.61	19.39	1.65	329.59	92.65	205.35	0.80	1.39	2.84
4.51	2.48	0.18	39.38	12.23	22.09	0.17	0.14	0.50
19	28	9	215	23	455	3	11	12

9－5　按行业分建筑业财务状况(2006 年)
FINANCIAL INDICATORS OF CONSTRUCTION BY SECTOR(2006)

单位:万元　　(10000 yuan)

指标	Item	房屋和土木工程建筑业 Housing and Civil Engineering Construction	房屋工程 Housing Construciton	土木工程	建筑安装业 Construction and Installation	建筑装饰业 Building Decorative Construction
资本金合计	Total Capital Assets	646.84	462.22	184.62	92.30	53.28
流动资产合计	Circulating Funds	2558.33	1779.61	778.71	343.47	147.75
#存货	Stock	846.84	653.50	193.34	112.46	44.35
固定资产合计	Total Fixed Asstes	458.70	269.07	189.63	60.85	25.85
固定资产原价合计	Total Original Value of Fixed Assets	627.28	368.42	258.86	71.14	30.90
#生产经营用	Used by Production	493.48	279.28	214.20	52.17	22.35
累计折旧	Total Depreciation Drawn Accumulated	221.76	126.81	94.95	21.96	9.26
#本年折旧	Depreciation Draw This Year	39.14	22.39	16.75	4.20	2.01
在建工程	Project Under Construction	35.19	16.15	19.05	10.17	2.67
资产总计	Total Assets	3181.24	2155.02	1026.22	431.09	182.53
流动负债合计	Total Circulating Liability	2022.02	1437.99	584.02	277.94	100.26
长期负债合计	Total Long-term Liability	51.73	30.30	21.43	4.26	1.57
所有者权益合计	Creditors Equity	1107.49	686.73	420.76	148.88	80.70
工程结算收入	Project Settlement Revenue	3745.03	2856.32	888.71	342.08	182.71
工程结算成本	Costof Project Settlement Accounts	3322.14	2552.86	769.28	286.40	153.95
工程结算税金及附加	Taxes and Extra Chargeson ProjectSettlement Accounts	133.76	104.66	29.09	10.66	6.17
工程结算利润	Profits of Project Settlement Accounts	268.08	183.76	84.32	41.41	19.47
其他业务利润	Other Profit	12.03	9.77	2.26	3.08	0.99
经营费用	Operating Expenses	21.06	15.04	6.02	3.61	3.12
管理费用	Management Expenses	134.68	92.35	42.33	26.38	11.75
#税金	Taxes	5.53	3.82	1.71	0.76	0.61
利润总额	Total Profit	132.19	90.58	41.61	20.86	7.67
应交所得税	PayableIncome Taxes	36.83	25.14	11.69	4.87	2.25
应付利润	Payable Profit	34.61	21.97	12.64	8.97	2.84
本年应付工资总额	Payable Total Wages This Year	654.09	573.90	80.19	43.13	25.98
本年应付福利费	Payable Total Welfare This Year	76.80	67.24	9.56	5.40	2.52
亏损企业个数　(个)	Number of Loss-Making Enterprises (unit)	326	181	145	141	239

主要统计指标解释

建筑业统计单位 指从事房屋、构筑物建造、装饰装修、设备安装活动和工程准备、提供施工设备服务等其他建筑活动的法人企业。建筑业法人企业应同时具备的条件是:①依法成立,有自己的名称、组织机构和场所,能够承担民事责任;②独立拥有和使用资产,承担负债,有权与其他单位签订合同;③独立核算盈亏,能够编制资产负债表。

建筑业总产值(即自行完成施工产值) 是以货币表现的建筑业企业在一定时期内生产的建筑业产品和服务的总和。建筑业总产值包括:

(1)建筑工程产值:指列入建筑工程预算内的各种工程价值。

(2)安装工程产值:指设备安装工程价值,不包括被安装设备本身价值。

(3)其他产值:指建筑业总产值中除建筑工程、安装工程以外的产值。包括房屋、构筑物修理所完成的产值(不包括被修理的房屋、构筑物本身的价值)、非标准设备制造产值、总包企业向分包企业收取的管理费和不能明确划分的施工活动所完成的产值。

房屋建筑施工面积 指在报告期内施过工的全部房屋建筑面积,包括本期新开工的房屋面积、上期跨入本期继续施工的房屋面积、上期停缓建在本期恢复施工的房屋面积、本期竣工的房屋面积及本期施工后又停缓建的房屋面积。

房屋建筑竣工面积 指在报告期内房屋建筑按照设计要求全部完工,达到了住人和使用条件,经检查验收鉴定合格的房屋建筑面积。

自有机械设备年末总台数 指归本企业(或单位)所有,属于本企业(或单位)固定资产的生产性机械设备年末总台数。包括施工机械、生产设备、运输设备以及其他设备。

自有机械设备年末总功率 指本企业(或单位)自有施工机械、生产设备、运输设备以及其他设备等列为固定资产的生产性机械设备年末总功率,按设定能力或查定能力计算。包括机械本身的动力和为该机械服务的单独动力设备,如电动机等。计算单位用千瓦,动力换算可按1马力=0.735千瓦折合成千瓦数。电焊机、变压器、锅炉不计算动力。

工程结算收入 指企业承包工程实现的工程价款结算收入,以及向发包单位收取的除工程价款以外按规定列作营业收入的各种款项,如临时设施费、劳动保险费、施工机械调迁费等以及向发包单位收取的各种索赔款。

工程结算利润 指已结算工程实现的利润,如亏损以"-"号表示。计算公式为:

工程结算利润=工程结算收入-工程结算成本-工程结算税金及附加-经营费用

企业总收入 指与企业生产经营直接有关的各项收入,包括工程结算收入和其他业务收入。计算公式为:

企业总收入=工程结算收入+其他业务收入

计算建筑业劳动生产率的平均人数 指建筑业企业(或单位)报告期实际拥有的、与建筑施工活动有关的人员的平均人数,包括参加本企业(或单位)建筑施工活动的非本企业(或单位)人员,但不包括企业内部社会服务性机构的人员以及由本企业支付工资但所从事的工作与本企业生产基本无关的人员。

Explanatory Notes on Main Statistical Indicators

Statistical Unit in Construction refers to corporate enterprise engaged in the construction of buildings and structures and in the installation of equipment. A corporate constrnction enterprise should meet the following 3 requirements: ①being set up in line with relevant legal basis, having its full name, organization and location, and capable of taking civil liabilities; ②independently possessing and using its assets and assuming its liabilities, and entitled to sign contracts with other institutions; and ③making independent accounts of its profits and losses, and capable of compiling its own balance sheet.

Gross Output Value of Construction (Output Value of Projects Under Construction) refers to total of construction products and services expressed in money terms, completed by construction enterprises during a given period of time. It includes:

(1) Output: value of construction projects, that is the value of projects covered by the project budgets;

(2) Output value of installation projects, that is the value of the installation of equipment, (excluding the value of the equipment to be installed);

(3) Other Output Value refers to the total output of construction industry except the output value of constrution projects, output value of installation projects. It covered the output value of buildings and strucutres repairing (excluding the value of buildings and structures being repaired); output value of manufactured non-standard equipment; management expenses collected by general contracted enterprises from branch contracted enterprises, and the output value of const ruction activities which can't to be divided definitely.

Floor Space of Buildings Under Construction refers to floor space of buildings under construction during the reference period, including newly started buildings, buildings started earlier and continued during the reference period, and buildings suspended earlier but restarted during the reference period, buildings completed during the reference period, and buildings under construction and then suspended during the reference period.

Floor Space of Buildings Completed refers to the floor space of buildings that are completed in the reference period in accordance with the requirements of the design, up to the standard for putting them into use, and have been checked and accepted by concerned departments as qualified ones.

Total Number of Machinery and Equipment Owned by the End of Year refers to the number of machines and equipment owned by the enterprises, and listed as the fixed assets of the enterprises by the end of the year, including machinery and equipment for construction, production and transportation.

Total Power of Machinery and Equipment Owned by the End of Year refers to the total power of machinery and equipment owned by the enterprises, and listed as the fixed assets of the enterprises by the end of the year, including machinery and equipment for construction, production and transportation. The power of the machinery is calculated on basis of the designed or verified capacity, covering the power of the machinery/equipment and the separate power equipment serving the machinery/equipment (such as electric motors), but excluding welders, transformers and boilers. The unit used for the calculation of power is kilowatt, with horsepower converted to kilowatt by 1 horsepower = 0.735 kilowatt.

Income from Settlement of Projects refers to the income received by the construction enterprise from the contracted project through settlement procedures, and other charges to the contractoree as operational costs in addition to the value of the project, such as temporary facility fee, labour insurance premium, moving cost of construction equipment, as well as various types of claims to the contractee.

Profit from Settlement of Projects refers to profit realized through settled projects. It is calculated with the following formula:

Profit from Settlement of Projects = Income from Settlement of Projects – Settled Cost – Settled Taxes and Other Cost – cost of Operation

Total Revenue of Enterprises refers to the sum of income from production and operation of enterprises, including income from settlement of projects and other operational income, namely:

Total Revenue of Enterprises = Income from Settlement of Projects + Other Operational Income

Number of Average Personnels of Labor Productivity refers to the average personnels actually held by construction enterprises (units) and related to construction activities in the reference period, including the personnels of other enterprises, who took part in the construction activities of these enterprises, but excluding the personnels of the inner social service institutions, and the personnels their wages were paid by the enterprises but did not take part in the construction activities basically.

JIANGSU STATISTICAL YEARBOOK

第10篇

交通运输、邮电

TRANSPORTATION,POSTAL AND TELECOMMUNICATIONS SERVICES

10－1 交通运输业基本情况
TRANSPORTATION

指　　标	Item	1990	1995	2000	2005	2006
运输线路长度　（公里）	**Length of Transportation Routes　(km)**					
铁路营业里程	Total Railway's Length in Operation	748	742	752	1599	1603
铁路正线延展长度	Mainline Railway's Length Completed	1250	1290	1439	2301	2301
公路通车里程	Total Highway in Operation	24772	25970	58013	82739	126972
#等级公路里程	Length of Expressway and Class Ⅰ to Ⅳ Highway	23582		47718	74957	108642
#高速公路	Expressway			1105	2886	3355
一级公路	Class Ⅰ Highway			2863	4214	5188
二级公路	Class Ⅱ Highway			10184	13998	16839
内河航道里程	Navigable Inland Waterways	23665	23803	24335	24800	24796
输油管道里程	Petroleum Pipelines	334	334	334	760	760
公路桥梁　（座）	Highway Bridges　(unit)	8886	9793	20678	25239	39740
（米）	(m)	283948	337978	840649	1321763	1918343
客运量　（万人）	**Total passenger Traffic　(10000 persons)**	**48339**	**84803**	**107244**	**145204**	**161425**
铁　路	Railway	4788	5185	4891	6658	7292
公　路	Highway	41850	78947	101713	138287	153825
水　运	Waterway	1701	623	514	37	27
民用航空	Civil Aviation		48	126	222	280
旅客周转量（亿人公里）	**Turnover volume of passonger Traffic (100 million person-km)**	**324.94**	**630.56**	**776.26**	**1222.03**	**1366.95**
货物运输量　（万吨）	**Total Freight Traffic　(10000 tons)**	**49399**	**81830**	**90436**	**112909**	**125114**
铁　路	Railway	4235	4143	4077	5090	5169
公　路	Highway	27904	49578	59056	76301	84319
水　运	Waterway	15908	27161	25902	29277	32862
输油管道	Petroleum Pipelines	1352	946	1395	2236	2759
货物周转量（亿吨公里）	**Turnover Volume of Freight Traffic (100 million ton-km)**	**730.22**	**1376.88**	**1505.57**	**3068.88**	**3644.79**
民用车辆拥有量（万辆）	**Civil Motor Vehicles　(10000 coaches)**			588.73	969.66	1032.41
#民用汽车拥有量	Civil Vehicles	27.68	51.19	74.51	192.25	240.80
#载客汽车	Passenger Vehicles	9.55	21.99	41.16	144.63	190.73
载货汽车	Trucks	16.97	27.83	31.46	43.35	44.89
#营运汽车	Motor Vehicle in Operation			28.64	37.89	41.02
#私人汽车	Private Vehicle	1.40	5.22	18.94	109.43	148.37
民用运输船舶拥有量（万艘）	**Civil Transport Vessels　(10000 units)**	16.58	14.09	7.27	5.13	4.33
机动船	Motor Vessels			5.39	3.45	2.97
驳船	Barges			1.88	1.68	1.36
港口货物吞吐量（万吨）	**Cargo Handled At Ports　(10000 tons)**	17002	20177	41364	75548	86359

10－2 客 运 量
PASSENGER TRAFFIC

单位：万人 (10000 persons)

年 份 Year	总 计 Total	铁 路 Railway	公 路 Highway	水 运 Waterway	民用航空 Civil Aviation
1978	25621	2752	18694	4175	
1980	34002	3364	26463	4175	
1985	53935	4819	45751	3365	
1989	52073	5421	44439	2213	
1990	48339	4788	41850	1701	
1991	50264	4932	43764	1568	
1992	55400	5035	48748	1617	
1993	59666	5533	53331	797	5
1994	61104	5471	54930	677	26
1995	84803	5185	78947	623	48
1996	91870	4502	86801	499	68
1997	93684	4433	88826	341	84
1998	97033	4451	92215	273	94
1999	101000	4824	95564	504	108
2000	107244	4891	101713	514	126
2001	110713	5029	105105	430	149
2002	115889	5297	110138	284	170
2003	123462	5104	118046	147	165
2004	128516	5997	122218	91	210
2005	145204	6658	138287	37	222
2006	161425	7293	153824	27	280

注：民用航空客运量从 1993 年起仅指省内航空公司完成数，不包括航空港的旅客发送量。

Note: Since 1993, the passenger traffic by civil aviation only referred to the fulfillment in our province, the number of passengers sent out by air harbour was excluded.

10－3 旅 客 周 转 量
TURNOVER VOLUME OF PASSENGER TRAFFIC

单位：亿人公里 (100 million person-km)

年 份 Year	总 计 Total	铁 路 Railway	公 路 Highway	水 运 Waterway	民用航空 Civil Aviation
1978	105.29	46.35	49.93	9.01	
1980	140.15	61.60	68.25	10.30	
1985	273.76	107.46	156.30	10.00	
1989	346.43	138.51	200.90	7.02	
1990	324.94	124.13	195.24	5.57	
1991	342.12	132.57	204.11	5.44	
1992	515.08	147.53	361.28	6.27	
1993	520.86	161.36	355.50	3.42	0.58
1994	641.09	166.94	367.98	3.28	2.89
1995	630.56	163.69	459.08	3.42	4.37
1996	647.73	143.85	459.70	2.51	5.67
1997	657.93	144.68	504.05	1.64	7.56
1998	680.02	141.15	527.62	1.12	10.13
1999	725.66	157.65	554.04	1.40	12.57
2000	776.25	165.87	594.48	1.45	14.45
2001	874.63	173.40	682.25	1.06	17.93
2002	924.31	183.80	719.08	0.70	20.71
2003	978.03	182.88	774.11	0.50	20.53
2004	1109.19	226.73	855.41	0.27	26.78
2005	1222.03	245.37	948.10	0.11	28.45
2006	1366.95	267.99	1062.61	0.10	36.25

10-4 货 运 量
FREIGHT TRAFFIC

单位:万吨 (10000 tons)

年份 Year	总计 Total	铁路 Railway	公路 Highway	水运 Waterway	内河 Inland Waterway	海运 Seashipping	输油管道 Petroleum Pipeline
1978	14626	3224	4488	6557	6557		357
1980	16527	3420	4427	6482	6452	30	2198
1985	46842	4037	23255	18117	18067	50	1433
1989	55086	4489	30599	18665	18578	87	1333
1990	49399	4235	27904	15908	15809	99	1352
1991	49298	4078	27948	16064	15884	180	1208
1992	56953	4343	30730	20751	20533	218	1129
1993	66339	4344	35060	25915	25610	305	1020
1994	69470	4318	36899	27279	26920	359	974
1995	81830	4143	49578	27161	26728	433	948
1996	84666	4361	50571	28819	28429	390	915
1997	82290	4131	52441	24826	24424	402	892
1998	80429	3793	54328	21363	21059	304	945
1999	81529	3941	54803	21596	20045	1551	1188
2000	90436	4077	59056	25902	24275	1627	1395
2001	87505	4239	59058	22583	21030	1553	1622
2002	88588	4407	60299	22411	20681	1730	1468
2003	93511	4462	64321	23320	20845	2475	1405
2004	100093	4665	69058	24812	21239	3573	1554
2005	112909	5090	76301	29277	25061	4216	2236
2006	125114	5169	84319	32862	25779	7083	2759

10-5 货 物 周 转 量
TURNOVER VOLUME OF FREIGHT TRAFFIC

单位:亿吨公里 (100 million ton-km)

年份 Year	总计 Total	铁路 Railway	公路 Highway	水运 Waterway	内河 Inland Waterway	海运 Seashipping	输油管道 Petroleum Pipeline
1978	283.85	172.72	11.24	87.97	87.97		11.92
1980	382.77	186.31	11.45	93.56	91.51	2.05	91.45
1985	575.58	240.48	81.30	205.90	194.83	11.07	47.90
1989	776.51	292.40	174.92	264.70	238.73	25.97	44.49
1990	730.22	297.44	154.01	233.65	209.53	24.12	45.12
1991	788.41	301.73	166.21	280.59	240.23	40.36	39.88
1992	963.94	333.85	179.92	400.78	361.87	38.91	49.39
1993	1193.87	346.49	235.07	578.01	520.51	57.50	34.30
1994	1246.12	372.13	243.33	598.02	523.21	74.81	32.64
1995	1376.88	393.51	281.04	670.75	585.84	84.91	31.58
1996	1412.56	380.09	289.44	712.33	635.20	77.13	30.70
1997	1370.63	355.73	303.40	681.42	617.18	64.24	30.08
1998	1353.23	343.41	316.14	661.85	579.51	82.34	31.71
1999	1400.55	342.65	319.75	704.01	436.89	267.12	33.91
2000	1505.57	371.32	340.72	746.39	463.17	283.22	46.84
2001	1524.96	371.97	340.73	757.58	489.01	268.57	54.37
2002	1549.12	377.17	351.95	770.03	395.05	374.98	49.63
2003	1817.44	408.69	365.01	995.34	444.98	550.36	47.97
2004	2398.64	434.72	386.91	1523.63	468.13	1055.50	52.87
2005	3068.88	480.49	459.18	2056.90	631.98	1424.92	71.73
2006	3644.79	497.42	542.09	2515.09	583.94	1931.15	89.54

10-6 全社会港口码头泊位和通过能力（2006年）
NUMBER OF BERTHS AND TRANSVERSING CAPACITY IN ALL PORTS (2006)

指标	Item	合计 Total	沿海港口 Coastal Ports	内河港口 Ports of Inland Rivers
生产用码头泊位	Number of Berths of Ports			
泊位个数 （个）	Number of Berths (unit)	9076	105	8971
泊位长度 （米）	Length of Ports Line (m)	362548	10404	352144
泊位年通过能力	Comprehensive Transversing Capacity			
货物 （万吨）	Freight (10000 tons)	80582	4582	76000
集装箱 （万TEU）	Container (10000 TEU)	427	76	351
旅客 （万人）	Passenger (10000 persons)	648		648
汽车 （万辆）	Truck (10000 unit)	610		610
非生产用码头泊位	Ports for Nonproductive Use			
泊位个数 （个）	Number of Berths (unit)	39		
泊位长度 （米）	Length of Ports Line (10000 m)	2053		

10-7 主要港口吞吐量(2006年)
VOLUME OF FREIGHT AND PASSENGER HANDLED AT MAJOR PORTS (2006)

港口	Ports	旅客吞吐量（万人） Passenger (10000 persons)	#离港 Departure	货物吞吐量（万吨） Freight (10000 tons)	#外贸 Foreign Trade
总计	Total	10.52	5.17	86358.75	13421.80
沿海港口	Coastal Ports	6.49	3.21	7682.95	4526.42
#连云港	Liangyuangang	6.49	3.21	7232.20	4480.63
内河港口	Ports of Inland Rivers	4.03	1.96	78675.80	8895.38
#长江干流水系	Yangtze River Maintream System	4.03	1.96	53873.91	8870.33
#长江支流水系	Yangtze River Tributary System			7065.26	20.93
京杭运河水系	Jing-Hang Canal System			17441.37	4.12
淮河水系	Huaihe River System			274.26	

10－8　全省民用车辆拥有量(2006年)
NUMBER OF CIVIL MOTOR VEHICLES OWNED BY WHOLE PROVINCE (2006)

单位:辆　　(coach)

指标	Item	总计 Total	营运 Working	非营运 Non-working	#进口 Import
合　计	**Total**	**10324094**	**609420**	**9714674**	**172175**
汽　车	Civil Vehicles	2776039	586304	2189735	75653
载客汽车	Passenger Vehicles	1907262	113884	1793378	69717
#大　型	Large Scale	50828	39295	11533	589
中　型	Medium Scale	104450	18645	85805	4720
小　型	Small Scale	1578008	51663	1526345	64350
#轿　车	Cars	1226744	50855	1175889	50081
载货汽车	Trucks	448951	274458	174493	4483
#重　型	Heavy Scale	58520	47733	10787	447
中　型	Medium Scale	176156	111103	65053	424
轻　型	Light Scale	203211	110574	92637	3609
#普通载货	Ordinary Trucks	304848	175148	129700	4009
其他汽车	Other Vehicles	419826	197962	221864	1453
#三轮汽车	Tricycle Motors	281883	128374	153509	
低速汽车	Lowspeed Vehicles	86112	47721	38391	
摩托车	Motor	7520758		7520758	96467
#普　通	Ordinary Motor	6752062		6752062	87868
轻　便	Light Motors	768696		768696	8599
挂　车	Freight Trailers	27241	23116	4125	55
其他类型车	Other Motor Vehicles	56		56	

10－9　私人车辆拥有量
NUMBER OF PRIVATE－OWNED VEHICLES

单位:辆　　(coach)

指标	Item	2000	2003	2004	2005	2006
民用汽车	Civil Vehicles	189356	587180	781961	1094252	1483746
载客汽车	Passenger Vehicles	122944	458104	639579	942143	1320186
#大　型	Large Scale	925	903	911	905	1132
轿　车	Cars	92734	263120	406271	607462	901122
载货汽车	Ordinary Trucks	65608	125907	137241	146146	155936
#重　型	Large Scale		10209	14649	17523	19966
其他汽车	Other	804	3169	5141	5963	7624
摩托车	Motors	4347810	5927415	6566640	7045361	7470998
挂车	Freight Trailers	1207	4477	5234	4756	5305

10－10　全省公路运输汽车拥有量

NUMBER OF TRANSPORT MOTOR VEHICLES OWNED BY WHOLE PROVINCE

单位：辆　　(coach)

指标	Item	2000	2003	2004	2005	2006
合计	**Total**	**543888**	**901307**	**1442805**	**1728571**	**2246767**
载客汽车	Passenger Vehicles					
辆数	Number	273013	565448	985657	1248238	1788873
客位　(万客位)	Seats　(10000 seats)	266.66	486.71	731.82	956.60	1314.76
载货汽车	Trucks					
辆数	Number	270875	335859	457148	480333	457894
#普通载货汽车	Ordinary Trucks	265011	319859	437322	459171	442936
吨位　(万吨)	Tonnages　(10000 tons)	95.51	123.04	180.49	204.14	217.75
#普通载货汽车	Ordinary Trucks	90.53	110.60	162.66	183.24	200.18

10－11　全社会运输船舶拥有量

NUMBER OF TRANSPORT VESSELS OWNED BY WHOLE PROVINCE

指标	Item	2005			2006		
		艘 Number (unit)	载客量(客位) Passenger Capacity (seat)	净载重量(万吨位) Dead Weight Tonnage (10000)	艘 Number (unit)	载客量(客位) Passenger Capacity (seat)	净载重量(万吨位) Dead Weight Tonnage (10000)
总计	**Total**	**51241**	**43198**	**1357.15**	**43293**	**62514**	**1415.65**
内河船舶	Inland Waterways Vessels	50614	42708	1087.57	42844	62514	1064.37
沿海船舶	Coastal Vessels	558	490	113.36	367		142.69
远洋船舶	Oceanic Vessels	69		156.22	82		208.59
总计中：	Among Which						
机动船	Motor Vessels	34464	41284	894.35	29688	59996	1010.10
客船	Passenger Ships	578	38684	1.48	787	46785	1.33
客货船	Passenger Ships	33	2600	0.67	40	13211	0.73
货船	Cargo Ships	31717		892.20	26976		1008.04
拖轮	Tugboats	2136			1885		
驳船	Cargo Barges	16777	1914	462.80	13605	2518	405.55

10－12　邮电业务基本情况
BASIC CONDITIONS OF POST AND TELECOMMUNICATION SERVICES

指标		Item	1995	2000	2005	2006
邮电业务总量	**（亿元）**	**Total Volume of Post & Telecommunication Services (100 million yuan)**	**72.24**	**323.45**	**728.08**	**997.26**
邮政业务总量		Postal Services		20.13	52.95	62.53
电信业务总量		Telecommunicatoin Services		303.32	675.13	934.73
邮电业务收入	**（亿元）**	Revenue from Post and Telecommunication Services (100 million yuan)			459.58	524.48
电政业务收入		Postal Revenue			44.50	49.35
电信业务收入		Telecommunication Revenue			415.08	475.13
函件	（亿件）	Letters (100 million pcs)	5.31	5.74	4.21	3.94
包件	（万件）	Parcels (10000 pcs)	1619.00	534.00	610.14	604.37
特快专递	（万件）	Special Express (10000 pcs)	870.00	938.57	1719.24	2085.28
报刊期发数	（万份）	Newspapers and Magazines Circulation (10000 pcs)	1655.00	1730.00	1294.38	1218.40
长途电话通话量	（亿次）	Long-distance Calls (100 million pages)	8.59	11.82	58.94	73.29
移动短信业务量	（亿条）	Short－distance Mobile calls (100 million pages)			312.95	415.49
年末固定电话用户	（万户）	Urban Telephone Subscribers at Year-end (10000 subscribers)	330.17	1138.06	3059.35	3224.32
城市		City	226.54	535.43	2089.54	2225.95
乡村		Countryside	103.63	602.63	969.81	998.37
#住宅电话		Residential Telephone Subscribers			2325.33	2357.56
城市		City	176.47	424.43	1457.62	1474.98
乡村		Countryside			867.71	882.58
年末移动电话用户	（万户）	Mobile Telephone Subscribers at Year-end (10000 subscribers)	23.19	619.50	2550.00	2873.40
国际互联网用户	（万户）	International Exchange Network Users (10000 subscribers)	0.01	183.31	449.46	577.95
邮政局所		Post Office (unit)			2866	2779
邮路及农村投递路线总长度	（万公里）	Length of Postal Routes and Rural Delivery Routes (10000 km)	30.26	35.92	37.85	37.73
#汽车邮路		Highway Routes	4.38	5.94	8.05	8.16
铁路邮路		Railway Routes	0.42	0.48	0.48	0.48
长话电路业务电路	（万路）	Long Distance Telephone Lines (10000 lines)	6.41	15.32	182.92	290.79
邮电通信工具拥有量		**Telecommunications Facilities**				
局用电话交换机容量	（万门）	City Switchboard Capacity (10000 units)			2134.04	2271.21
移动电话交换机容量	（万门）	Mobile Telephone Switchboard Capacity (10000 units)			3397.00	4239.48
长途电话交换机容量	（路端）	Long Distance Telephone Switchborad Capacity (circuit)			921507	940132
长途光缆线路长度	（公里）	Length of Long Distance Optical Cable (km)			25699.15	26634.75

10 - 13　邮电通信水平
LEVEL OF POST AND TELECOMMUNICATION SERVICES

指　　标	Item	2000	2004	2005	2006
邮电通信水平	**Level of Postal and Telecommunication**				
每局所服务面积（平方公里）	Per Bureau (Office) Service Area (sq. m)		20.71	35.80	36.92
每百人平均函件量（件/百人）	Number of Letters Mailed Per 100 Persons (unit/100 persons)	783.38	594.79	563.25	521.89
每百人平均订阅报刊量（份/百人）	Number of Newspaper and Magazine Subscribed Per 100 Persons (unit/100 persons)	23.61	18.68	17.32	16.14
每百人平均包件（件/百人）	Number of Parcels Per 100 Persons (unit/100 persons)	7.29	8.57	8.16	8.01
每百人长途电话量（次/百人）	Number of Long Distance Telephone Calls Per 100 Persons (unit/100 persons)	1613.16	6820.00	7885.48	9707.93
每百人移动短信量（条/人）	Number of Short Distance Mobile Telephone Calls Per 100 Persons (unit/100 persons)			418.69	550.36
电话普及率（部/百人）	Rate of Popularization of Telephones (unit/100 persons)	23.99	64.60	75.05	80.77
固定电话普及率（部/百人）	Rate of Popularization of Fixed Telephones (units/100 persons)	15.53	34.75	40.93	42.71
移动电话普及率（部/百人）	Rate of Popularization of Mobile Telephones (unit/100 persons)	8.45	29.85	34.12	38.06
人均邮电业务量（元/人）	Per Capital Business Volume of Post (yuan/person)	441.43	749.89	974.09	1320.96
开通移动电话的市县（个）	Number of Cities and Counties with Mobile Telephone Communication (unit)	77	72	65	65
设有局所的乡（镇）比重（%）	Percentage of Townships (Towns) with Post and Telecommunications Offices (%)	98.7	99.9	100.0	100.0
通邮路的乡（镇）比重（%）	Percentage of Townships (Towns) with Postal Routes (%)	98.9	100.0	100.0	100.0
开办特快专递业务市县（个）	Number of Cities and Counties with Special Express Mail (unit)	77	72	65	65

主要统计指标解释

铁路营业里程　又称营业长度(包括正式营业和临时营业里程),指办理客货运输业务的铁路正线总长度。凡是全线或部分建成双线及以上的线路,以第一线的实际长度计算;复线、站线、段管线、岔线和特殊用途线以及不计算运费的联络线都不计算营业里程。铁路营业里程是反映铁路运输业基础设施发展水平的重要指标,也是计算客货周转量、运输密度和机车车辆运用效率等指标的基础资料。

铁路正线延展里程　指正线第一线、第二线、第三线和其他正线建筑里程之和,不包括站线、段管线、岔线及特殊用途线的延展里程。它是作为计算铁路线上钢轨、枕木及路基砂石需要量的主要依据。

公路里程　指在一定时期内实际达到《公路工程技术标准 JTJ01－88》规定的等级公路,并经公路主管部门正式验收交付使用的公路里程数。包括大中城市的郊区公路以及通过小城镇街道部分的公路里程和桥梁、渡口的长度,不包括大中城市的街道、厂矿、林区生产用道和农业生产用道的里程。两条或多条公路共同经由同一路段,只计算一次,不得重复计算里程长度。它是反映公路建设发展规模的重要指标,也是计算运输网密度等指标的基础资料。

内河航道里程　也称内河通航里程,指在一定时期内,能通航运输船舶及排筏的天然河流、湖泊水库、运河及通航渠道的长度。包括全年季节性通航累计三个月以上的航道,不包括仅供零散流放竹、木排的河道。它是反映内河水运网规模、水平和发展情况的主要指标。

输油(气)管道长度　也称输油(气)里程,指油品(或天然气)的实际输送距离,一般按输油(气)管道的单线长度计算。若包括复线和备用线长度则称为输油(气)管道延展长度,是指管道铺设的实际长度。我们通常使用的是不包括复线的“输油(气)管道里程”,它是反映管道运输发展规模和水平的主要指标。

货(客)运量　指在一定时期内,各种运输工具实际运送的货物(旅客)数量。它是反映运输业为国民经济和人民生活服务的数量指标,也是制定和检查运输生产计划、研究运输发展规模和速度的重要指标。货运按吨计算,客运按人计算。货物不论运输距离长短、货物类别,均按实际重量统计。旅客不论行程远近或票价多少,均按一人一次客运量统计;半价票、小孩票也按一人统计。

货物(旅客)周转量　指在一定时期内,由各种运输工具运送的货物(旅客)数量与其相应运输距离的乘积之总和。它是反映运输业生产总成果的重要指标,也是编制和检查运输生产计划,计算运输效率、劳动生产率以及核算运输单位成本的主要基础资料。计算货物周转量通常按发出站与到达站之间的最短距离,也就是计费距离计算。计算公式为:

货物(旅客)周转量 = $\sum$货物(旅客)运输量 × 运输距离

沿海主要港口货物吞吐量　指经水运进出沿海主要港区范围,并经过装卸的货物数量,包括邮件及办理托运手续的行李、包裹以及补给运输船舶的燃、物料和淡水。货物吞吐量按货物流向分为进口、出口吞吐量,按货物交流性质分为外贸货物吞吐量和国内贸易货物吞吐量。货物吞吐量的货类构成及其流向,是衡量港口生产能力大小的重要指标。

邮电业务总量　指以价值量形式表现的邮电通信企业为社会提供各类邮电通信服务的总数量。邮电业务量按专业分类包括函件、包件、汇票、报刊发行、邮政快件、特快专递、邮政储蓄、集邮、公众电报、用户电报、传真、长途电话、出租电路、无线寻呼、移动电话、分组交换数据通信、出租代维等。计算方法为各类产品乘以相应的平均单价(不变价)之和,再加上出租电路和设备、代用户维护电话交换机和线路等的服务收入。它综合反映了一定时期邮电业务发展的总成果,是研究邮电业务量构成和发展趋势的重要指标。计算公式为:

邮电业务总量 = $\sum$(各类邮电业务量 × 不变单价) + 出租代维及其他业务收入

无线寻呼用户　无线寻呼是指电话用户通过无线寻呼中心,在规定范围内向携带小型寻呼机的用户发出声音、数字或文字显示信息。在寻呼台办理登记手续携带小型寻呼机的用户,称为无线寻呼用户。

移动电话用户　是指通过移动电话交换机进入移动电话网、占用移动电话号码的电话用户。用户数量以报告期末在移动电话营业部门实际办理登记手续进入移动电话网的户数进行计算,一部移动电话统计为一户。

电话用户　指接入国家公众固定电话网,并按固定电话业务进行经营管理的电话用户。1997 年以前,电话用户分为市内电话用户和农村电话用户。“市内电话用户”是指接入县城及县以上城市的电话网上的电话用户;“农村电话用户”是指接入县邮电局农话台及县以下农村电话交换点,以县城为中心(除市话用户外)联通县、乡(镇)、行政村、村民小组的用户。从 1997 年起,电话用户数分组调整为以用户所在区域划分为“城市电话用户”和“乡村电话用户”,与过去的按市内电话和农村电话划分方法不同。而电话用户总数、电话机总部数统计范围不变。

城市电话用户　指直辖市、省辖市、地级市、县级市的市区、市郊区及县城(包括县人民政府所在地的县城关区或行政建制相当于县人民政府所在地的镇)范围内接入局用交换机的电话用户数,包括分布在农村地区的独立工矿区、林区、驻军等接入局用交换机的电话用户数。

乡村电话用户 指县城关区以下的集镇和农村接入局用交换机的电话用户数。

住宅电话用户 是指安装在居民住宅或农民家里并按照住宅电话用户登记注册和收费的电话用户。包括私人付费、单位付费和按规定免费安装的住宅电话用户。

局用交换机容量 是指安装在本地电信运营商内用于接续本地固定电话的电话交换机容量，有倍增设备按倍增后的数量计数。包括现用和备用的人工或自动交换机的全部容量。

Explanatory Notes on Main Statistical Indicators

Length of Railways in Operation refers to the total length of the trunk line under passenger and freight transportation(including both full operation and temporary operation). The calculation is based on the actual length of the first line even if this linc has a full or partial double track or more tracks, excluding double tracks, station sidings, tracks under the charge of stations, branch lines, special-purpose lines and the non-payable connecting lines. The length of railways in operation is an important indicator to show the development of the infrastructure for the railway transport, and also the essential data to calculate volume of passenger freight transport, traffic density and utilization efficiency of the locomotives and carriages.

Extenuation Length of Trunk Lines refers to the sum of the first, the second, the third lines and other constructed length of the trunk railways, excluding the extenuation length of the station lines, lines under the jurisdiction depots, siding and lines for special purpose. It provides important information for the calculation of the needs for rails, sleepers, sand and stone for the construction ot railways.

Length of Highways refers to the length of highways which are built in conformity with the grades specified by the highway engineering standard formulated by the Ministry of Communications, and have been formally checked and accepted by the departments of highways and put into use. The length of highways includes that of the suburb highways at large and medium-sized cities, highways passing through streets at small cities and towns, and also the length of bridges and ferries. It does not include the length of streets in big and medium-sized cities and highways built for the production purpose at factories, mines, forest areas and agricultural areas. If two or more highways go the same section of the way, the length of the section is only calculated for once and no duplication is allowed. The length of highways is an important indicator to show the development of the highway construction and to provide essential information to calculate the transport network density.

Length of Navigable Inland Waterways an indicator reflecting the size and development of inland water network, it refers to the length of the natural rivers, lakes, reservoirs, canals, and ditches open to navigation during a given period, which enables the transport by ships and rafts. It includes the channels open to navigation for over an accumulative 3 months in a year, yet this does not include the river courses which are only used to float odd logs and bamboo rafts.

Length of Oil(Gas) Pipelines used as an indicator to show the development, scale and level of the pipeline transportation, it refers to the actual transport distance of oil (or gas) products, and is in general calculated in the length of single pipe line. If the length of the double pipelines and alternate pipeline are included, it is called the extension length of the oil (gas) pipelines, which indicates the actual length of the pipelines built, excluding double pipelines.

Freight(Passenger) Traffic refers to the volume of freight (passenger) transported with various means. Freight transport is calculated in tons and passenger traffic is calculated in the number of persons. Despite the type of freight and travelling distance, the freight transport is calculated in the actual weight of the goods; and despite the travelling distance and ticket price, the passenger traffic is calculated by the principle that one person can be counted only once in one travel. The passenger who travel with a half price ticket or a child ticket is also calculated as one person. The freight(passenger) traffic provides a quantitative measure to show how the transport industry serves the national economy and people, and is also an important indicator for planning the transport industry and for studying the development scale and speed of the transport industry.

Freight Ton-kilometers (Passenger-kilometers) refer to the sum of the products of the volume of transported cargo (passengers) multiplying by the transport distance, usually using ton-kilometer and passenger-kilometer as units for measurement. Normally, the shortest distance between the departure station and the destination station(i. e., the payable distance) is the basis to calculate the freight ton-kilometers. This is an important indicator to show the total results of the transport industry, to prepare and examine the transport plan and to measure the efficiency, the labour productivity and the unit cost of transport.

The formula is as follows:

Freight Ton-kilometers(Passenger-kilometers) = {fFreight(Passenger) Traffic × Distance of Transportation}

Measuring unit: ton-kilometer(person-kilometer)

Volume of Freight Handled in Major Coastal Ports refers to the volume of cargo passing in and out the harbor area of the major coastal ports and having been loaded and unloaded. The volume includes that of the postal matters, registered luggage and fuels, materials and fresh water as supplies of the ships. The volume of freight handled may be classified by direction of flow as freight for import and freight for export, or by nature of cargo as freight for domestic trade and freight for foreign trade. As an important indicator, the volume of freight handled by type of cargo and by main flow direction reflects the production capacity of ports.

Business Volume of Post and Telecommunications refers to the total amount of post and telecommunications services, expressed in value terms, provided by the post and telecommunications departments for the society. Post and telecommunication services can be classified as letters, parcels, remittance, issue of newspapers and magazines, fast mail service, express mail service, savings deposits, stamps for collection, public and individual telegraph service, facsimiles, long-distance telephone service, leasing of telephone lines, urban paging service, mobile telephone service, data transfer and transmission, etc. The accounting approach is to multiply the service products of all types with their average unit price (constant price) to get sum of business value, plus income from other services such as leasing of telephone lines and equipment, maintenance of telephone switchboards and lines on behalf of customers. This indicator reflects the overall results of post and telecommunications service during a given period, and is important to study the composition of business service and the development of post and telecommunications service.

The formula is as follows:

Business Volume of Post and Telecommunications = $\sum$ (Transaction of Post and Telecommunication Service × Constant Price) + Income from Leasing, Maintenance and other Services.

Subscribers of Wireless Paging Services Wireless paging service refers the service by which telephone users send audio, digital or character signals to persons carrying small-size pagers within the designated areas through wireless paging centers. The page carriers who have registered in paging centers are counted as paging subscribers.

Mobile Telephone Subscribers refer to the persons who own mobile telephone numbers and are connected with the mobile telephone communication network through the mobile telephone switchboards. The number of subscribers is calculated by the subscribers who have completed registration at mobile communication business centers and entered into the mobile telephone network. One mobile telephone is taken as a subscriber.

Telephone Subscribers refer to subscribers that are connected to the public line telephone network provided with telephone services. Before 1997, telephone subscribers were classified as city subscribers and village subscribers. City subscribers referred to those connected to city telephone networks in county towns and cities, while village subscribers referred to those connected to village telephone stations at and below counties. Since 1997, the classification of telephone subscribers was modified on the basis of physical location of the subscribers as rban telephone subscribers and ural telephone subscribers, which is different from the previous classification of catgorizing local telephones and ural telephones, while the definition of total subscribers and total number of telephones remain unchanged.

Urban Telephone Subscribers refer to subscribers telephone subscribers, located at municipalities, cities under the jurisdiction of province, cities at prefectural level, downtown and suburb of city at county level town and county towns (including country towns where county government located, and towns of county level according to the administrative organizational system), that are connected to the public line telephone network, including rural mineral area, forest area, military area.

Rural Telephone Subscribers refer to telephone subscribers, located at towns under county town and country, that are connected to the public line telephone network.

Household Telephone Subscribers refer to telephone sets installed in the dwelling units of urban or rural residents, and registered as residence subscribers for payment, including 3 types of payment for the service: private payment, public payment and free service.

Capacity of Office Telephone Exchanges refers to the capacity (measured in gate) of telephone exchanges installed in the offices of local telecommunication service providers for communication between fixed telephones. It includes the capacity of both manual and automatic exchanges in use and for stand-by purpose. Equipment with expansion function is to be counted by the expanded capacity.

JIANGSU STATISTICAL YEARBOOK

第 11 篇

国内贸易

DOMESTIC TRADE

11－1 按地区分社会消费品零售总额
TOTAL RETAIL SALES OF CONSEUMER GOODS BY REGION

单位：亿元 (100 million yuan)

年份 Year	社会消费品零售总额 Total Retail Sales of Consumer Goods	市 City	县 County	县以下 Below County Level
1978	84.79	27.65	16.68	40.46
1979	99.16	32.57	19.27	47.32
1980	122.56	41.21	23.28	58.07
1981	134.79	47.12	24.74	62.93
1982	150.01	50.91	27.29	71.81
1983	169.12	58.61	29.55	80.96
1984	205.05	74.45	36.42	94.18
1985	262.57	99.96	45.32	117.29
1986	304.58	111.92	51.13	141.53
1987	360.74	134.65	60.23	165.86
1988	471.83	198.46	66.28	207.09
1989	509.56	221.01	68.33	220.22
1990	515.43	231.26	67.05	217.12
1991	578.12	281.69	67.37	229.06
1992	704.52	364.47	74.59	265.46
1993	967.77	540.19	86.09	341.49
1994	1359.61	790.70	96.21	472.71
1995	1741.92	1015.29	131.13	595.51
1996	2080.44	1246.34	141.15	692.95
1997	2300.61	1383.27	158.99	758.36
1998	2453.84	1483.96	171.23	798.65
1999	2649.56	1610.27	190.08	849.21
2000	2908.46	1784.83	208.90	914.73
2001	3233.35	2140.08	223.87	869.40
2002	3656.57	2525.45	230.67	900.44
2003	4194.50	2959.44	256.18	978.88
2004	4892.18	3517.10	295.74	1079.34
2005	5699.89	4117.22	346.25	1236.42
2006	6623.18	4822.93	413.50	1386.75

注：1. 1996 年及以后社会消费品零售总额及各分组指标中不含售给城乡居民生活用住房的零售额。
2. 2004 年为经普数据，2005 年为按经普口径统计数据，1993－2003 年原则根据原各年环比发展速度和 2004 年经济普查数据调整。

Note：1. Since 1996, the residential house was excluded in the total retail sales of consumer goods and all the targets by groups.
2. The data of 2004 were the figures of general survey of economy, That of the 2006 were the figures of statistics according to the bore of general survey of economy, and that of the 1993－2003 were reajusted in principle according to the development velocity of link relative and general survey of economy.

11-2 按行业分社会消费品零售总额
TOTAL RETAIL SALES OF CONSEUMER GOODS BY SECTOR

单位:亿元 (100 million yuan)

年份 Year	批发和零售业 Wholesale and Retail Sales Trade	住宿业 Hotel	餐饮业 Catering Trade	其他行业 Others
1978	79.18		3.24	2.37
1979	91.61		3.90	3.65
1980	114.35		4.72	3.49
1981	125.16		5.17	4.46
1982	138.87		5.49	5.65
1983	156.28		6.14	6.70
1984	188.80		7.61	8.64
1985	240.69		10.45	11.43
1986	279.25		12.53	12.80
1987	329.31		15.84	15.59
1988	432.06		20.33	19.44
1989	467.11		22.47	19.98
1990	472.72		24.17	18.54
1991	529.94		27.86	20.32
1992	644.61		33.64	26.27
1993	888.24		44.74	34.79
1994	1238.30		71.44	49.87
1995	1573.01		95.21	73.70
1996	1901.47		135.64	43.33
1997	2082.71		167.92	49.99
1998	2208.24		192.52	53.08
1999	2367.59		227.58	54.39
2000	2583.19		269.59	55.69
2001	2845.89		326.71	60.76
2002	3179.23		410.83	66.52
2003	3613.67		510.94	69.88
2004	4333.18	41.67	496.10	21.22
2005	5016.09	49.81	583.09	50.91
2006	5815.78	67.68	678.83	60.89

注:1. 批发和零售业中包括原制造业和其他行业中原农民对非农业居民的零售额。

2. 2003 年前住宿业包括餐饮业和在其他行业中。

Note: 1. Wholesale and retail sales trade including the retail sales of mannufacturing industry and retail sales of the farmers to nonagricultural residents which was included in the original other industry.

2. Before 2003, the retail sales of hotel industry was involved in other industries.

11－3 按类别分社会消费品零售总额分类

TOTAL RETAIL SALES OF CONSEUMER GOODS BY CATEGORY

单位：亿元 (100 million yuan)

年份 Year	社会消费品零售总额 Total Retail Sales of Consumer Goods	食品类 Foods	衣着类 Clothing	日用品类 Daily Use Goods
1978	84.79	43.25	20.00	7.60
1979	99.16	50.37	23.01	8.77
1980	122.56	62.04	28.76	10.14
1981	134.79	68.63	31.68	11.76
1982	150.01	77.71	32.28	12.73
1983	169.12	87.19	36.32	14.02
1984	205.05	104.23	45.41	17.03
1985	262.57	135.03	56.52	21.55
1986	304.58	156.87	59.45	25.52
1987	360.74	189.35	71.46	29.20
1988	471.83	246.23	89.09	45.81
1989	509.56	266.71	99.87	42.19
1990	515.43	285.13	91.53	38.12
1991	578.12	315.11	102.33	47.41
1992	704.52	360.71	126.11	76.09
1993	967.77	492.59	167.43	105.58
1994	1359.61	692.04	229.78	165.70
1995	1741.92	888.38	292.64	210.77
1996	2080.44	1081.83	349.11	264.22
1997	2300.61	1170.55	372.01	308.97
1998	2453.84	1257.59	342.56	329.55
1999	2649.56	1351.81	361.13	359.81
2000	2908.46	1438.24	408.35	361.52
2001	3233.35	1585.63	470.77	445.23
2002	3656.57	1805.68	511.75	494.49
2003	4194.50	2015.04	589.33	630.02
2004	4892.18	2464.17	662.40	747.73
2005	5699.89	2793.17	839.29	874.33
2006	6623.18	3168.19	970.22	1114.10

11－3 续表 Continued

单位:亿元 (100 million yuan)

年份 Year	文化娱乐用品类 Goods of Culture and Entertainment	书报杂志类 Newspaper and Magazines	药和医疗用品类 Medicine and Medical Goods	房屋及建筑材料类 Houses and Building Material	燃料类 Fuel
1978	3.25	0.71	3.89	2.99	3.10
1979	4.36	0.97	3.98	4.41	3.29
1980	5.66	1.49	4.30	6.00	4.17
1981	5.75	1.52	4.41	6.59	4.45
1982	6.84	1.72	5.32	8.73	4.68
1983	7.54	2.01	6.10	10.96	4.98
1984	10.03	2.51	6.41	13.62	5.81
1985	16.39	3.28	6.91	16.13	6.76
1986	20.62	3.78	8.67	20.97	8.70
1987	23.46	3.86	10.17	24.31	8.93
1988	34.64	4.28	12.75	27.09	11.94
1989	36.42	5.94	15.04	30.54	12.85
1990	34.47	6.68	18.55	26.88	14.07
1991	35.26	8.24	22.73	32.95	14.09
1992	42.98	11.41	30.51	39.45	17.26
1993	64.84	15.26	45.49	55.16	21.42
1994	82.94	21.76	58.47	84.30	24.63
1995	104.52	27.87	73.16	114.97	29.61
1996	126.90	37.89	97.77	84.86	37.87
1997	160.58	45.78	123.08	80.07	39.57
1998	183.06	60.12	146.00	91.28	43.68
1999	200.31	63.59	173.82	88.23	50.87
2000	221.34	78.53	235.59	101.21	63.69
2001	223.10	84.06	267.08	83.76	73.72
2002	296.53	91.99	286.24	100.48	69.41
2003	325.49	98.99	363.66	84.73	87.24
2004	336.74	102.84	396.37	79.01	102.93
2005	430.58	106.29	437.33	84.78	134.12
2006	511.93	115.23	484.66	92.81	166.04

11－4 限额以上批发和零售业基本情况（2006年）
BASIC CONDITIONS OF ENTERPRISES ABOVE DESIGNATED SIZE IN WHOLESALE AND RETAIL SALES TRADE（2006）

项 目	Item	法人企业（个）Number of Corporations（unit）	产业活动单位数（个）Number of Activities units（unit）	零售营业面积（平方米）Floor Space of Retail Business（sq. m）	从业人员（人）Persons Engaged（person）
总　计	**Total**	3720	8783	12963550	417696
#国有及国有控股	State-Owned and State Share Holding	496	1362	3311396	111652
批发业	**Wholesale Trade**	**1800**	**2688**	**2701317**	**145762**
#国有及国有控股	State-Owned and State Share Holding	283	449	1829333	74203
按登记注册类型分	**Grouped by Type of Registration**				
内资企业	Inner Enterprises	1783	2634	2508504	138435
国有企业	State-Owned Enterprises	157	229	36770	31514
集体企业	Collective-Owned Enterprises	50	263	143092	3977
股份合作企业	Share Holding Cooperative Enterprises	10	18	14100	1030
联营企业	Joint-Owned Enterprises	12	23	43015	786
国有联营企业	State Joint Ownership Enterprises	4	4	15000	511
集体联营企业	Collective Joint Ownership Enterprises	2	4	531	63
国有与集体联营企业	State-collective Joint Enterprises	6	15	27484	212
有限责任公司	Responsibility Co. Ltd.	512	820	340772	33091
国有独资公司	State-funded Enterprises	15	60	54660	1496
其他有限责任公司	Other Limited Liability Corporations	497	760	286112	31595
股份有限公司	Share Holding Co. Ltd.	61	84	1691827	36773
私营企业	Private Enterprises	970	1183	236768	30921
私营独资企业	Private-funded Enterprises	23	52	5929	596
私营合伙企业	Private Partnership Enterpises	8	19	1650	188
私营有限责任公司	Private Limited Liability Corporations	907	1079	222020	28308
私营股份有限公司	Private Share-holding Corporations Ltd.	32	33	7169	1829
其他企业	Other Enterprises	11	14	2160	343
港、澳、台商投资企业	Hong Kong, Macao and Taiwan Funded	7	36	189173	1335
合资经营企业	Joint-venture Enterprises	4	32	17060	482
独资经营企业	Solely Funded Enterprises	3	4	172113	853
外商投资企业	Foreign－Invested Enterprises	10	18	3640	5992
合资经营企业	Joint-venture Enterprises	3	7	640	3527
合作经营企业	Gooperative Enterprises	0	1	0	25
独资经营企业	Solely Funded Enterprises	6	9	3000	2434
外商投资股份有限公司	Foreign Funded Share Holding Co. Ltd.	1	1	0	6
按行业分	**Grouped by Sector**				
农畜产品批发	Wholesale of Agricultural and Animal products	95	159	20285	4756

11－4 续表1 Continued 1

项目	Item	法人企业(个) Number of Corporations (unit)	产业活动单位数(个) Number of Activities units(unit)	零售营业面积(平方米) Floor Space of Retail Business(sq. m)	从业人员(人) Persons Engaged (person)
食品、饮料及烟草制品批发	Wholesale of Foods, Beverage and Tobacco	160	281	273519	20555
纺织、服装及日用品批发	Wholesale of Textile Products, Garments and Daily Sundry Articals	337	358	70647	24237
文化、体育用品及器材批发	Wholesale of Cultural and Sports Goods and Equipments	33	42	6863	2163
医药及医疗器材批发	Wholesale of Medicines and Medical Applians	68	111	61612	9513
矿产品、建材及化工产品批发	Wholesale of Mineral Products, Building Materials and Chemical Products	735	1171	2100183	60895
机械设备、五金交电及电子产品批发	Wholesale of Machinery Equipment, Hardware, Transport and Electronic Products	315	376	133353	21086
贸易经纪与代理	Trade Broker and Agent	1	1	0	8
其他批发	Others	56	189	34855	2549
零售业	**Retail Sales Trade**	**1920**	**6095**	**10262233**	**271934**
#国有及国有控股	State－Owned and State Share Holding	213	913	1482063	37449
按登记注册类型分	**Grouped by Type of Registration**				
内资企业	Inner Enterprises	1864	5380	8333765	227039
国有企业	State-Owned Enterprises	137	481	580536	18328
集体企业	Collective-Owned Enterprises	55	217	130004	5830
股份合作企业	Share Holding Cooperative Enterprises	24	84	40831	1796
联营企业	Joint-Owned Enterprises	11	34	37721	1238
国有联营企业	State Joint Ownership Enterprises	4	4	12971	486
集体联营企业	Collective Joint Ownership Enterprise	5	5	20058	404
国有与集体联营企业	State-collective Joint Enterprises	1	2	4592	74
其他联营企业	Other Joint Ownership Enterprises	1	23	100	274
有限责任公司	Responsibility Co. Ltd.	584	2330	3632222	98520
国有独资公司	State solely funded Enterprises	6	26	104399	1056
其他有限责任公司	Other Limited Liability Corporations	578	2304	3527823	97464
股份有限公司	Share Holding Co. Ltd.	72	303	1141923	30141
私营企业	Private Enterprises	969	1911	2729360	69415
私营独资企业	Private-funded Enterprises	81	144	96829	4747
私营合伙企业	Private Partnership Co., Ltd.	17	20	29806	887
私营有限责任公司	Private Limited Liability Corporations	824	1677	2409746	59857
私营股份有限公司	Private Share-holding Corporations Ltd.	47	70	192979	3924
其他企业	Other Enterprises	12	20	41168	1771
港、澳、台商投资企业	Hong Kong, Macao and Taiwan Funded	21	176	367586	18293
合资经营企业	Joint-venture Enterprises	8	116	199699	5527

11-4 续表2 Continued 2

项 目 Item		法人企业(个) Number of Corporations (unit)	产业活动单位数(个) Number of Activities units(unit)	零售营业面积(平方米) Floor Space of Retail Business(sq. m)	从业人员(人) Persons Engaged (person)
合作经营企业	Cooperative Enterprises	2	2	20300	601
独资经营企业	Solely Funded Enterprises	11	57	147087	12105
股份有限公司	Share Holding Co. Ltd.	0	1	500	60
外商投资企业	Foreign Invested Enterprises	35	539	1560882	26602
合资经营企业	Joint-venture Enterprises	15	504	1323523	20607
合作经营企业	Cooperative Enterprises	4	14	59915	1348
独资经营企业	Solely Funded Enterprises	16	20	168544	4258
外商投资股份有限公司	Foreign Funded Share Holding Co. Ltd.	0	1	8900	389
按行业分	**Grouped by Sectors**				
综合零售	Retail Sale of Department	501	2041	5929790	158069
食品、饮料及烟草制品专门零售	Monopoly Retail of Foods, Beverage and Tabaccos	96	525	115001	10529
纺织、服装及日用品专门零售	Monopoly Retail of Textile Products, Garments and Daily Sundry Articals	76	148	170680	7850
文化、体育用品及器材专门零售	Monopoly Retail of Cultural, Sports Goods and Equipments	165	475	338246	11387
医药及医疗器材专门零售	Monopoly Retail of Medicine and Medical Appliance	122	1604	340095	18711
汽车、摩托车、燃料及零配件专门零售	Monopoly of Retail of Motor Vehicle, Motorcycle, Fual and Parts	598	751	1863441	30838
家用电器及电子产品专门零售	Monopoly Retail of Home Electric Appliance and Electronic Products	247	417	1017716	27833
五金、家具及室内装修材料专门]零售	Monopoly Retail of Hardwares, Furniture and Interior Decoration Materials	54	64	391907	3842
无店铺及其他零售	Retail of Storeless and Others	61	70	95357	2875
按经营方式分	**Grouped by Management Forms**				
独立商店	Independent - stores	1582	2311	6543252	157420
连锁商店总店	Chain - Stores General	131	156	2276576	22203
连锁商店分店	Chain - stores Branch	132	3344	1175720	81344
其 他	Others	75	284	266685	10967
按零售业态分	**Grouped by Operating Situation**				
百货商店	Department Stores	220	308	2606151	68145
超级市场	Supermarkets	324	1696	3510643	94341
专业店	Special Store	881	2964	2948853	75607
专卖店	Monopoly Store	233	424	704020	15459
其 他	Others	262	703	492566	18382

注：产业活动单位和从业人员包括本省和外省各行业法人在本省的批发和零售业产业活动单位数和从业人数，不包括本省法人在外省的批发和零售业产业活动单位数和从业人数(下同)。

Note: The number of activities units and employees included the wholesale and retail activities units and employees of corporation of Jiangsu and other province established in Jiangsu, but excluded the wholesale and retail activities units and employees of corporation of Jiangsu established in other province(the same as the following tables).

11－5 限额以上住宿和餐饮业基本情况(2006年)

BASIC CONDITIONS OF ENTERPRISES ABOVE DESIGNATED SIZE IN HOTEL AND CATERING TRADE(2006)

项目	Item	法人企业数(个) Number of Corporations (unit)	产业活动单位数(个) Number of Activities units(unit)	餐饮营业面积(平方米) Floor space of Catering Business(sq. m)	从业人员数(人) Persons Engaged (person)
总计	Total	1624	2192	2852986	213256
#国有及国有控股	State-Owned and State Share Holding	272	300	411934	41758
住宿业	**Hotel**	**628**	**686**	**907223**	**92545**
#国有及国有控股	State-Owned and State Share Holding	212	225	312391	34001
按登记注册类型分组	**Grouped by Type of Registration**				
内资企业	Inner Enterprises	584	633	808967	79182
国有企业	State-owned Enterprises	162	174	225189	23343
集体企业	Collective-owned Enterprises	42	46	33375	3355
股份合作企业	Share Holding cooperative Enterprises	7	7	5180	509
联营企业	Joinr-Owned Enterprises	7	7	4459	901
国有联营企业	State-Joint ownership Enterprises	4	4	2900	632
集体联营企业	Collective-Joint ownership Enterprises	1	1	450	60
国有与集体联营企业	State-Collective Joint Enterprises	1	1	859	82
其他联营企业	Other Joint ownership Enterprises	1	1	250	127
有限责任公司	Responsibility Co. Ltd.	141	153	245295	25628
国有独资公司	State-Funded Enterprises	7	7	10059	1631
其他有限责任公司	Other Limited Liability Corperation	134	146	235236	23997
股份有限公司	Share Holding Co. Ltd.	13	18	20400	2917
私营企业	Private Enterprises	203	217	267530	21674
私营独资企业	Private-funded Enterprises	49	54	58785	4302
私营合伙企业	Private Partnership Co. Ltd.	6	6	13400	832
私营有限责任公司	Private limited Liability Corporations	138	144	179025	15416
私营股份有限公司	Private Share-holding Co. Ltd.	10	13	16320	1124
其他企业	Other Enterprises	9	11	7539	855
港、澳、台商投资企业	Hong Kong Macao and Taiwan Funded	20	28	53029	5795
合资经营企业	Joint-Venture Enterprises	11	19	42096	4359
合作经营企业	Cooperative Enterprises	3	3	4285	584
独资经营企业	Solely Funded Enterprises	5	5	3048	542
股份有限公司	Share Holding Co. Ltd.	1	1	3600	310
外商投资企业	Foreign Invested Enterprises	24	25	45227	7568
合资经营企业	Joint-Venture Enterprises	11	11	25255	3808
合作经营企业	Cooperative Enterprises	2	2	1800	422
独资经营企业	Solely Funded Enterprises	10	11	15346	2915
外商投资股份有限公司	Foreign Funded Share Holding Co. Ltd.	1	1	2826	423
按行业分组	**Grouped by sector**				
旅游饭店	Tourist Hotel	547	587	843833	85661
一般旅馆	Regular Hotel	76	92	61040	6636
其他住宿服务	Other Accommodation Service	5	7	2350	248
按星级等级分组	**Grouped by star Class**				
五星	Five Stars Class	27	30	91399	11829
四星	Four Stars Class	85	90	225099	21831

11－5 续表 Continued

项 目	Item	法人企业数（个） Number of Corporation (unit)	产业活动单位数（个） Number of Activities units(unit)	餐饮营业面积（平方米） Floor space of Catering Business(sq. m)	从业人员数（人） Persons Engaged (person)
三星	Three Stars Class	243	250	341423	32143
二星	Two Stars Class	170	187	139191	12873
一星	One Star Class	6	15	7264	1217
其他	Others	97	114	102847	12652
餐饮业	**Catering Trade**	**996**	**1506**	**1945763**	**120711**
#国有及国有控股	State-Owned and State Share Holding	60	75	99543	7757
按登记注册类型分组	**Grouped by Type of Regislration**				
内资企业	Inner Enterprises	933	1206	1679254	94613
国有企业	State-Owned Enterprises	42	56	71956	5077
集体企业	Collective-Owned Enterprises	26	28	28316	2145
股份合作企业	Share Holding Cooperative Enterprises	11	11	18400	1082
联营企业	Joinr-Owned Enterprises	3	3	6280	155
国有联营企业	State-Joint Ownership Enterprises	1	1	5100	69
集体联营企业	Collective Ownership Enterprises	1	1	280	48
国有与集体联营企业	State-Collective Joint Enterprises	1	1	900	38
有限责任公司	Responsibility Co. Ltd.	142	184	281975	18393
国有独资公司	State-Funded Enterprises	6	6	2660	477
其他有限责任公司	Other Limited Liability Corperation	136	178	279315	17916
股份有限公司	Share Holding Co Ltd.	14	19	25909	1247
私营企业	Private Enterprises	673	882	1222323	65165
私营独资企业	Private-Funded Enterprises	205	317	336633	16876
私营合伙企业	Private Partnership Co. Ltd.	16	20	21310	1138
私营有限责任公司	Private Limited Liability Corporations	416	507	809946	44456
私营股份有限公司	Private Share-holding Co. Ltd.	36	38	54434	2695
其他企业	Other Enterprises	22	23	24095	1349
港、澳、台商投资企业	Hong Kong, Macao and Taiwan Funded	30	36	69596	3635
合资经营企业	Joint-Venture Enterprises	13	16	30616	1593
合作经营企业	Cooperative Enterprises	3	4	3660	241
独资经营企业	Solely Funded Enterprises	14	16	35320	1801
外商投资企业	Foreign Invested Enterprises	33	264	196913	22463
合资经营企业	Joint -Venture Enterprices	12	96	85711	9765
合作经营企业	Cooperative Enterprices	4	7	4541	450
独资经营企业	Solely Funded Enterprises	17	161	106661	12248
按行业分组	**Grouped by sector**				
正餐服务	Dinner	923	1122	1723356	97264
快餐服务	Fast Food	43	307	194594	20294
饮料及冷饮服务	Beverage and Cold Drink Services	7	9	5353	320
其他餐饮服务	Other	23	68	22460	2833
按经营方式分组	**Grouped by Management Forms**				
独立商店	Independent-stores	911	1094	1686998	93905
连锁商店总店	Chain-stores-General	24	23	171462	3082
连锁商店分店	Chain-stores-Branch	13	323	22390	18924
其他	Others	48	66	64913	4800

11－6 批发和零售业商品购销存总额（2006年）

TOTAL VALUE OF COMMODITY PURCHASING, SALES AND INVENTORY OF ENTERPRISES ABOVE DESIGNATED SIZE IN WHOLESALE AND RETAIL SALE TRADE (2006)

单位：亿元 (100 million yuan)

项目	Item	商品购进总额 Total Purchas-ing Value	商品销售总额 Total Sales	批发 Whole-sale Trade	零售 Retail Sale Trade	商品库存总额 Total Value of Inventory
总计	**Total**		**18920.05**	**13104.27**	**5815.78**	
限额以上企业和单位	**Aloove Designated Size Enterprises and Units**	**6928.18**	**7762.72**	**5559.76**	**2202.95**	**470.86**
#国有及国有控股	State-owned and State Share Holding	2439.57	2745.99	2301.43	444.56	163.52
批发业	**Wholesale Trade**	**5125.35**	**5669.17**	**5363.12**	**306.05**	**313.33**
#国有及国有控股	State -owned and State Share Holding	2192.19	2466.45	2259.63	206.82	140.93
按登记注册类型分组	**Grouped by Type of Registration**					
内资企业	Inner Enterprises	5003.80	5517.26	5234.18	283.08	296.57
国有企业	State-Owned Enterprises	813.13	1079.86	1067.41	12.46	76.21
集体企业	Collective-Owned Enterprises	70.75	74.51	68.11	6.39	10.42
股份合作企业	Share Holding Cooperative Enterprises	30.14	35.60	34.71	0.89	1.70
联营企业	Joint-Owned Enterprises	50.18	49.71	41.96	7.75	1.84
国有联营企业	State Joint Ownership Enterprises	35.97	35.75	29.16	6.59	0.86
集体联营企业	Collective Joint Ownership Enterprises	1.82	1.94	1.89	0.05	0.01
国有与集体联营企业	State-Collective Joint Enterprises	12.39	12.03	10.91	1.11	0.97
有限责任公司	Responsibility Co. Ltd.	1201.28	1353.77	1312.06	41.71	71.52
国有独资公司	State Solely Funded Corporations	48.31	64.97	64.92	0.04	4.45
其他有限责任公司	Other Limilted Liability Corporations	1152.97	1288.80	1247.13	41.67	67.07
股份有限公司	Share Holding Co. Ltd.	1141.39	1107.69	921.58	186.12	42.41
私营企业	Private Enterprises	1686.73	1803.08	1775.59	27.49	91.91
私营独资企业	Private-Funded Enterprises	12.95	19.31	18.97	0.34	1.14
私营合伙企业	Private Partnership Enterprises	3.69	3.82	3.57	0.25	0.27
私营有限责任公司	Private Limited Liability Corporations	1405.59	1549.10	1523.03	26.07	64.65
私营股份有限公司	Private Share Holding Co., Ltd.	264.50	230.84	230.02	0.83	25.83
其他企业	Other	10.21	13.03	12.77	0.26	0.56
港、澳、台商投资企业	Hong Kong, Macao and Taiwan Funded	76.06	81.76	59.55	22.21	8.44
合资经营企业	Joint Venture Enterprises	4.25	8.05	7.15	0.90	0.08
独资经营企业	Solely Funded Enterprises	71.80	73.72	52.40	21.31	8.36
外商投资企业	Foreign Invested Enterprises	45.49	70.15	69.38	0.76	8.32
合资经营企业	Joint Venture Enterprises	4.09	5.09	4.50	0.59	0.24
合作经营企业	Cooperative Enlerprises	1.84	1.98	1.98	0.00	0.02
独资经营企业	Solely Funded Enterprises	38.52	61.82	61.65	0.17	8.05
外商投资股份有限公司	Foreign Funded Share Holding Co. Ltd.	1.03	1.26	1.26	0.00	0.01

单位：亿元 (100 million yuan)

项目	Item	商品购进总额 Total Purchasing Value	商品销售总额 Total Sales	批发 Whole-sale Trade	零售 Retail Sale Trade	商品库存总额 Total Value of Inventory
按行业分	**Grouped by Sector**					
农畜产品批发	Wholesale of Agricultural and Animal Products	72.00	74.64	72.98	1.67	16.72
食品、饮料及烟草制品批发	Wholesale of Foods, Beverage and Tabaccos	528.53	667.97	633.98	33.99	46.87
纺织、服装及日用品批发	Wholesale of Textile Products, Garments and Daily Sundry Articals	735.74	1019.08	1015.52	3.55	46.29
文化、体育用品及器材批发	Wholesale of Cultural, Sports Goods and Equipments	84.88	77.08	74.62	2.45	4.73
医药及医疗器材批发	Wholesale of Medicine and Medical Appliance	118.39	142.14	110.01	32.13	9.21
矿产品、建材及化工产品批发	Wholesale of Ore Products, Building Material and Chemical Products	2667.60	2716.01	2512.31	203.70	103.81
机械设备、五金交电及电子产品批发	Wholesale of Hardware, Electric Appliance and Electronic Products	840.53	880.09	852.24	27.85	83.03
贸易经纪与代理	Trade Broker and Agency Services	0.49	0.58	0.58	0.00	0.00
其他批发	Other Wholesale	77.18	91.58	90.88	0.71	2.66
零售业	**Retail Sales Trade**	**1802.83**	**2093.55**	**196.65**	**1896.90**	**157.52**
#国有及国有控股	State-Owned and State Share Holding	247.38	279.54	41.79	237.75	22.59
按登记注册类型分组	**Grouped by Type of Registration**					
内资企业	Inner Enterprises	1561.80	1801.91	160.80	1641.12	138.43
国有企业	State-Owned Enterprises	95.83	100.38	10.00	90.38	10.70
集体企业	Collective-Owned Enterprises	18.76	23.97	2.86	21.11	1.79
股份合作企业	Share Holding Cooperative Enterprises	5.78	6.22	0.52	5.70	0.43
联营企业	Joint-Owned Enterprises	8.40	8.56	1.93	6.63	1.25
国有联营企业	State Joint Ownership Enterprises	3.26	2.96	0.31	2.65	0.82
集体联营企业	Collective Joint Ownership Enterprises	4.39	4.77	1.56	3.21	0.35
国有与集体联营企业	State-collective Joint Enterprises	0.47	0.46	0.00	0.46	0.03
其他联营企业	Other Joint Ownership Enterprises	0.28	0.37	0.07	0.31	0.05
有限责任公司	Responsibility Co. Ltd.	594.22	731.01	55.19	675.82	59.87
国有独资公司	State-funded Enterprises	9.16	13.93	4.21	9.72	0.60
其他有限责任公司	Other Limited Liability Corporations	585.05	717.08	50.97	666.10	59.27
股份有限公司	Share Holding Co. Ltd.	264.70	301.67	51.75	249.92	14.00
私营企业	Private Enterprises	566.95	622.54	38.45	584.09	49.69
私营独资企业	Private-funded Enterprises	15.55	18.08	1.05	17.03	2.00
私营合伙企业	Private Partnership Enterpises	3.74	3.86	0.04	3.83	0.50
私营有限责任公司	Private Limited Liability Corporations	482.93	533.46	30.58	502.88	42.34
私营股份有限公司	Private Share-holding Corporations Ltd.	64.73	67.14	6.79	60.36	4.85

11－6 续表2 Continued

单位:亿元 (100 million yuan)

项 目	Item	商品购进总额 Total Purchas-ing Value	商品销售总额 Total Sales	批发 Whole-sale Trade	零售 Retail Sale Trade	商品库存总额 Total Value of Inventory
其他企业	Other Enterprises	7.16	7.56	0.10	7.46	0.69
港、澳、台商投资企业	Hong Kong, Macao and Taiwan Funded	35.64	48.70	0.71	47.99	3.12
合资经营企业	Joint Venture Enterprises	17.83	27.43	0.06	27.37	1.81
合作经营企业	Cooperatime Enterprises	4.14	4.64	0.00	4.64	0.27
独资经营企业	Hongkong, Solely Funded Enterprises	13.32	15.72	0.66	15.06	0.93
股份有限公司	Share Holding Co. Ltd.	0.36	0.92	0.00	0.92	0.11
外商投资企业	Foreign Invested Enterprises	205.40	242.94	35.14	207.80	15.98
合资经营企业	Joint Venture Enterprises	146.28	173.68	35.07	138.61	12.35
合作经营企业	Cooperalive Enterprises	25.11	29.06	0.00	29.06	1.44
独资经营企业	Solely Funded Enterprises	31.02	37.21	0.06	37.15	2.20
外商投资股份有限公司	Foreign Funded Share Holding Co. Ltd.	2.98	2.98	0.00	2.98	0.00
按行业分	**Grouped by Sector**					
综合零售	Retail Sale of Department	695.68	828.22	47.62	780.60	67.69
食品、饮料及烟草制品专门零售	Monopoly Retail of Foods, Beverage and Tobaccos	32.98	42.55	4.31	38.24	2.93
纺织、服装及日用品专门零售	Monopoly Retail of Textile Products, Garments and Daily Sundry Articals	26.37	32.07	0.57	31.50	2.25
文化、体育用品及器材专门零售	Monopoly Retail of Cultural, Sports Goods and Equipments	67.14	63.77	4.61	59.16	12.21
医药及医疗器材专门零售	Monopoly Retail of Medicine and Medical Appliance	124.72	131.02	30.23	100.79	11.74
汽车、摩托车、燃料及零配件 专门零售	Monopoly of Retail of Motor Vehicle, Motorcycle, Fual and Parts	556.26	623.84	60.14	563.70	37.07
家用电器及电子产品专门零售	Monopoly Retail of Home Electric Appliance and Electronic Products	262.06	327.07	44.97	282.10	20.23
五金、家具及室内装修材料专门零售	Monopoly Retail of Hardwares, Furniture and Interior Decoration Materials	20.95	25.89	1.53	24.36	2.27
无店铺及其他零售	Retail of Storeless and Others	16.68	19.13	2.68	16.45	1.13
按经营方式分	**Grouped by Management Forms**					
独立商店	Independent－stores	1208.38	1388.83	111.92	1276.92	105.47
连锁商店总店	Chain－Stores General	350.58	418.97	68.29	350.68	31.23
连锁商店分店	Chain－stores Branch	180.35	210.07	5.13	204.94	16.25
其 他	Others	63.52	75.67	11.31	64.36	4.58
按零售业态分	**Grouped by Operating Situation**					
百货商店	Department Stores	344.55	423.17	14.99	408.18	32.82
超级市场	Supermarkets	373.30	430.91	33.41	397.49	37.08
专业店	Special Store	689.26	802.65	101.89	700.77	61.10
专卖店	Monopoly Store	280.21	290.98	23.70	267.28	18.33
其 他	Others	115.51	145.85	22.67	123.18	8.19
限额以下企业(单位)和个体	**Enterprises (units) Below Designated Size and Individuals**		**11157.33**	**7544.51**	**3612.83**	

11－7　限额以上住宿和餐饮业经营情况(2006年)

MANAGEMENT CONDITIONS OF ENTERPRISES ABOVE DESIGNATED SIZE IN HOTEL AND CATERING INDUSTRY(2006)

金额单位:亿元　　(100 million yuan)

项目	Item	营业额 Business Value	客房收入 Revenue of Gust Room	餐费收入 Catering Service Revenue
总计	**Total**	**247.88**	**61.60**	**166.95**
#国有及国有控股	State-Owned and State Share Holding	45.59	18.32	20.57
住宿业	**Hotel**	**105.22**	**49.21**	**44.07**
#国有及国有控股	State-Owned and State Share Holding	37.70	15.81	15.78
按登记注册类型分组	**Grouped by Type of Registration**			
内资企业	Inner Enterprises	83.65	37.02	36.26
国有企业	State-owned Enterprises	21.51	9.41	9.51
集体企业	Collective-owned Enterprises	3.15	1.43	1.37
股份合作企业	Share Holding cooperative Enterprises	0.45	0.25	0.15
联营企业	Joinr-Owned Enterprises	1.06	0.55	0.40
国有联营企业	State-Joint ownership Enterprises	0.76	0.34	0.33
集体联营企业	Collective-Joint ownership Enterprises	0.17	0.12	0.03
国有与集体联营企业	State-Collective Joint Enterprises	0.05	0.04	0.01
其他联营企业	Other Joint ownership Enterprises	0.09	0.06	0.03
有限责任公司	Responsibility Co. Ltd.	29.42	13.20	13.01
国有独资公司	State-Funded Enterprises	2.03	0.93	0.80
其他有限责任公司	Other Limited Liability Corperation	27.39	12.26	12.21
股份有限公司	Share Holding Co. Ltd.	6.19	1.99	1.80
私营企业	Private Enterprises	21.16	9.83	9.76
私营独资企业	Private-funded Enterprises	3.52	1.45	1.86
私营合伙企业	Private Partnership Co. Ltd.	0.78	0.16	0.54
私营有限责任公司	Private limited Liability Corporations	15.66	7.72	6.79
私营股份有限公司	Private Share-holding Co. Ltd.	1.20	0.49	0.58
其他企业	Other Enterprises	0.71	0.38	0.26
港、澳、台商投资企业	Hong Kong Macao and Taiwan Funded	9.15	5.05	3.39
合资经营企业	Joint-Venture Enterprises	7.23	3.77	2.88
合作经营企业	Cooperative Enterprises	0.79	0.49	0.24
独资经营企业	Solely Funded Enterprises	0.81	0.60	0.14
股份有限公司	Share Holding Co. Ltd.	0.33	0.19	0.13
外商投资企业	Foreign Invested Enterprises	12.42	7.14	4.42
合资经营企业	Joint-Venture Enterprises	4.65	2.45	1.76
合作经营企业	Cooperative Enterprises	0.67	0.33	0.30
独资经营企业	Solely Funded Enterprises	6.29	4.03	1.93
外商投资股份有限公司	Foreign Funded Share Holding Co. Ltd.	0.81	0.34	0.43
按行业分组	**Grouped by sector**			
旅游饭店	Tourist Hotel	99.18	45.83	41.94
一般旅馆	Regular Hotel	5.82	3.23	2.07
其他住宿服务	Other Accommodation Service	0.22	0.15	0.06
按星级等级分组	**Grouped by star Class**			
五星	Five Stars Class	21.37	10.02	8.15
四星	Four Stars Class	28.81	12.96	12.50

11－7 续表 1 Continued

项　　目	Item	营业额 Business Value	客房收入 Revenue of Gust Room	餐费收入 Catering Service Revenue
三星	Three Stars Class	30.27	13.25	13.83
二星	Two Stars Class	10.18	4.80	4.28
一星	One Star Class	0.75	0.59	0.12
其他	Others	13.85	7.59	5.20
餐饮业	**Catering Trade**	**142.66**	**12.39**	**122.87**
#国有及国有控股	State-Owned and State Share Holding	7.90	2.50	4.79
按登记注册类型分组	**Grouped by Type of Regislration**			
内资企业	Inner Enterprises	107.26	11.29	89.19
国有企业	State-Owned Enterprises	4.96	1.52	3.10
集体企业	Collective-Owned Enterprises	2.26	0.47	1.44
股份合作企业	Share Holding Corperative Enterprises	1.04	0.14	0.85
联营企业	Joinr-Owned Enterprises	0.27	0.09	0.17
国有联营企业	State-Joint Ownership Enterprises	0.20	0.07	0.13
集体联营企业	Collective Joint Ownership Enterprises	0.04	0.02	0.03
国有与集体联营企业	State-Collective Joint Enterprises	0.02	0.00	0.02
有限责任公司	Responsibility Co. Ltd.	20.31	2.98	15.71
国有独资公司	State-Funded Enterprises	0.46	0.06	0.36
其他有限责任公司	Other Limited Liability Corperation	19.85	2.92	15.35
股份有限公司	Share Holding Co Ltd.	1.48	0.11	1.27
私营企业	Private Enterprises	74.90	5.97	64.71
私营独资企业	Private-Funded Enterprises	18.48	1.19	16.16
私营合伙企业	Private Partnership Co. Ltd.	1.04	0.08	0.91
私营有限责任公司	Private Limited Liability Corporations	52.58	4.42	45.29
私营股份有限公司	Private Share-holding Co. Ltd.	2.80	0.28	2.35
其他企业	Other Enterprises	2.04	0.00	1.94
港、澳、台商投资企业	Hong Kong, Macao and Taiwan Funded	4.56	0.24	4.02
合资经营企业	Joint-Venture Enterprises	2.28	0.17	1.95
合作经营企业	Cooperative Enterprises	0.37	0.00	0.32
独资经营企业	Solely Funded Enterprises	1.92	0.07	1.75
外商投资企业	Foreign Invested Enterprises	30.83	0.86	29.66
合资经营企业	Joint-Venture Enterprices	17.29	0.74	16.33
合作经营企业	Cooperative Enterprices	0.45	0.05	0.37
独资经营企业	Solely Funded Enterprises	13.08	0.07	12.96
按行业分组	**Grouped by sector**			
正餐服务	Dinner	109.39	12.26	89.87
快餐服务	Fast Food	30.46	0.03	30.38
饮料及冷饮服务	Beverage and Cold Drink Services	0.37	0.01	0.33
其他餐饮服务	Other	2.44	0.09	2.30
按经营方式分组	**Grouped by Management Forms**			
独立商店	Independent-stores	106.55	11.63	88.23
连锁商店总店	Chain-stores-General	27.58	0.01	27.44
连锁商店分店	Chain-stores-Branch	3.16	0.06	3.07
其他	Others	5.37	0.69	4.13

11－7　续表2　Continued

项　　目	Item	商品销售收入 Sales Revenue of Commodity	其他收入 Other Revenue	年末拥有床位数（个） Year End Number of Beds(unit)	年末拥有餐位数（位） Year End Number of Seats(unit)
总计	**Total**	**8.29**	**11.03**	**191174**	**941765**
#国有及国有控股	State-Owned and State Share Holding	3.12	3.58	59304	145444
住宿业	**Hotel**	**4.36**	**7.58**	**140597**	**308687**
#国有及国有控股	State-Owned and State Share Holding	2.87	3.24	50321	109420
按登记注册类型分组	**Grouped by Type of Registration**				
内资企业	Inner Enterprises	4.17	6.20	122189	276146
国有企业	State-owned Enterprises	0.74	1.85	36228	75615
集体企业	Collective-owned Enterprises	0.11	0.25	5997	12788
股份合作企业	Share Holding cooperative Enterprises	0.01	0.04	870	2120
联营企业	Joinr-Owned Enterprises	0.04	0.07	1639	2705
国有联营企业	State-Joint ownership Enterprises	0.03	0.06	963	1900
集体联营企业	Collective-Joint ownership Enterprises	0.01	0.00	80	105
国有与集体联营企业	State-Collective Joint Enterprises	0.00	0.00	386	400
其他联营企业	Other Joint ownership Enterprises	0.00	0.00	210	300
有限责任公司	Responsibility Co. Ltd.	0.85	2.37	36198	78939
国有独资公司	State-Funded Enterprises	0.09	0.21	1989	5094
其他有限责任公司	Other Limited Liability Corperation	0.76	2.16	34209	73845
股份有限公司	Share Holding Co. Ltd.	1.89	0.51	3565	8593
私营企业	Private Enterprises	0.48	1.10	36131	92676
私营独资企业	Private-funded Enterprises	0.03	0.18	6828	20429
私营合伙企业	Private Partnership Co. Ltd.	0.03	0.05	784	7838
私营有限责任公司	Private limited Liability Corporations	0.37	0.79	26441	59609
私营股份有限公司	Private Share-holding Co. Ltd.	0.05	0.08	2078	4800
其他企业	Other Enterprises	0.06	0.02	1561	2710
港、澳、台商投资企业	Hong Kong Macao and Taiwan Funded	0.03	0.69	9523	16178
合资经营企业	Joint-Venture Enterprises	0.03	0.55	6488	13717
合作经营企业	Cooperative Enterprises	0.01	0.06	1547	1090
独资经营企业	Solely Funded Enterprises	0.00	0.07	1260	651
股份有限公司	Share Holding Co. Ltd.	0.00	0.00	228	720
外商投资企业	Foreign Invested Enterprises	0.16	0.69	8885	16363
合资经营企业	Joint-Venture Enterprises	0.11	0.32	4050	8955
合作经营企业	Cooperative Enterprises	0.00	0.04	741	1100
独资经营企业	Solely Funded Enterprises	0.04	0.30	3584	4708
外商投资股份有限公司	Foreign Funded Share Holding Co. Ltd.	0.01	0.03	510	1600
按行业分组	**Grouped by sector**				
旅游饭店	Tourist Hotel	4.24	7.17	125929	286973
一般旅馆	Regular Hotel	0.12	0.40	14045	20604
其他住宿服务	Other Accommodation Service	0.00	0.00	623	1110
按星级等级分组	**Grouped by star Class**				
五星	Five Stars Class	1.95	1.25	14125	27199
四星	Four Stars Class	0.74	2.61	28908	69011

11－7　续表3　Continued

项　　目　　Item		商品销售收入 Sales Revenue of Commodity	其他收入 Other Revenue	年末拥有床位数（个） Year End Number of Beds(unit)	年末拥有餐位数（位） Year End Number of Seats(unit)
三星	Three Stars Class	1.05	2.13	49811	124967
二星	Two Stars Class	0.34	0.77	23504	50854
一星	One Star Class	0.00	0.05	2213	2077
其他	Others	0.29	0.77	22036	34579
餐饮业	**Catering Trade**	**3.93**	**3.46**	**50577**	**633078**
#国有及国有控股	State-Owned and State Share Holding	0.26	0.34	8983	36024
按登记注册类型分组	**Grouped by Type of Regislration**				
内资企业	Inner Enterprises	3.68	3.10	46907	541692
国有企业	State-Owned Enterprises	0.15	0.18	6062	26782
集体企业	Collective-Owned Enterprises	0.12	0.22	2134	11119
股份合作企业	Share Holding Cooperative Enterprises	0.01	0.04	699	5737
联营企业	Joinr-Owned Enterprises	0.00	0.00	362	1230
国有联营企业	State-Joint Ownership Enterprises	0.00	0.00	175	600
集体联营企业	Collective-Joint Ownership Enterprises	0.00	0.00	187	400
国有与集体联营企业	State-Collective Joint Enterprises	0.00	0.00	0	230
有限责任公司	Responsibility Co. Ltd.	0.81	0.81	10799	89613
国有独资公司	State-Funded Enterprises	0.01	0.03	256	1465
其他有限责任公司	Other Limited Liability Cooperation	0.80	0.78	10543	88148
股份有限公司	Share Holding Co. Ltd.	0.10	0.01	748	8765
私营企业	Private Enterprises	2.40	1.82	26103	387849
私营独资企业	Private-Funded Enterprises	1.00	0.12	6120	117783
私营合伙企业	Private Partnership Co. Ltd.	0.03	0.01	749	5945
私营有限责任公司	Private Limited Liability Corporations	1.33	1.54	17109	245885
私营股份有限公司	Private Share-holding Co. Ltd.	0.04	0.14	2125	18236
其他企业	Other Enterprises	0.08	0.01	0	10597
港、澳、台商投资企业	Hong Kong, Macao and Taiwan Funded	0.11	0.19	1428	21355
合资经营企业	Joint-Venture Enterprises	0.00	0.15	648	10425
合作经营企业	Cooperative Enterprises	0.03	0.01	0	862
独资经营企业	Solely Funded Enterprises	0.07	0.03	780	10068
外商投资企业	Foreign Invested Enterprises	0.14	0.17	2242	70031
合资经营企业	Joint-Venture Enterprices	0.07	0.16	1830	29241
合作经营企业	Cooperative Enterprices	0.02	0.01	90	1924
独资经营企业	Solely Funded Enterprises	0.05	0.00	322	38866
按行业分组	**Grouped by sector**				
正餐服务	Dinner	3.83	3.42	50133	546897
快餐服务	Fast Food	0.05	0.01	76	75710
饮料及冷饮服务	Beverage and Cold Drink Services	0.01	0.02	130	1288
其他餐饮服务	Other	0.04	0.01	238	9183
按经营方式分组	**Grouped by Management Forms**				
独立商店	Independent-stores	3.41	3.28	47658	537606
连锁商店总店	Chain-stores-General	0.11	0.02	15	63764
连锁商店分店	Chain-stores-Branch	0.02	0.01	200	8270
其他	Others	0.40	0.15	2704	23438

11－8　限额以上批发和零售业企业财务状况(2006 年)

单位:亿元

项　　目	Item	资产总计 Total Assets	#流动资产 Cirlcula－ting Funds	#固定资产 Fixed Assets	负债合计 Total Liabilities
总计	**Total**	**2633.89**	**1912.37**	**370.18**	**1875.80**
#国有及国有控股	State-Owned and State Share Holding	1007.50	705.60	163.78	616.85
批发业	**Hotel**	**1790.61**	**1385.63**	**191.95**	**1264.65**
#国有及国有控股	State-Owned and State Share Holding	911.60	648.82	134.25	541.76
按登记注册类型分组	**Grouped by Type of Registration**				
内资企业	Inner Enterprises	1750.68	1351.23	189.37	1230.08
国有企业	State-owned Enterprises	523.87	403.34	57.96	270.50
集体企业	Collective-owned Enterprises	35.34	28.64	2.64	32.06
股份合作企业	Share Holding cooperative Enterprises	7.80	5.97	0.53	6.90
联营企业	Joint-Owned Enterprises	12.86	11.55	0.80	9.51
国有联营企业	State-Joint ownership Enterprises	7.75	6.99	0.57	5.20
集体联营企业	Collective-Joint ownership Enterprises	2.78	2.72	0.04	2.69
国有与集体联营企业	State-Collective Joint Enterprises	2.33	1.84	0.19	1.62
有限责任公司	Responsibility Co. Ltd.	437.69	353.28	39.21	353.50
国有独资公司	State-Funded Enterprises	24.65	18.18	4.53	13.35
其他有限责任公司	Other Limited Liability Corperation	413.04	335.10	34.68	340.15
股份有限公司	Share Holding Co. Ltd.	264.39	144.08	61.77	168.95
私营企业	Private Enterprises	464.69	402.36	26.00	385.23
私营独资企业	Private-funded Enterprises	3.48	2.79	0.23	2.99
私营合伙企业	Private Partnership Co. Ltd.	1.06	0.93	0.12	0.88
私营有限责任公司	Private limited Liability Corporations	415.58	358.54	24.03	339.92
私营股份有限公司	Private Share-holding Co. Ltd.	44.58	40.10	1.63	41.44
其他企业	Other Enterprises	4.02	2.01	0.46	3.43
港、澳、台商投资企业	Hong Kong Macao and Taiwan Funded	21.89	17.46	1.88	18.24
合资经营企业	Joint-Venture Enterprises	1.42	1.08	0.07	0.97
独资经营企业	Solely Funded Enterprises	20.47	16.38	1.81	17.28
外商投资企业	Foreign－Invested Enterprises	18.03	16.93	0.71	16.32
合资经营企业	Joint-Venture Enterprises	1.03	0.75	0.18	0.32
独资经营企业	Solely Funded Enterprises	16.99	16.17	0.53	16.01
外商投资股份有限公司	Share Holding Co. Ltd.	0.01	0.01	0.00	－0.01
按行业分	**Grouped by sector**				
农畜产品批发	Wholesale of Agricultural and Animal products	66.25	50.75	7.57	59.76
食品、饮料及烟草制品批发	Wholesale of Foods, Beverage and Tobacco	300.90	243.06	35.95	98.74
纺织、服装及日用品批发	Wholesale of Textile, Garments and Daily Sundry Articals	367.74	282.78	26.75	277.88
文化、体育用品及器材批发	Wholesale of Cultural and Sports Goods and Equipments	32.36	19.87	5.90	19.48
医药及医疗器材批发	Wholesale of Medicines and Medical Aplians	58.58	45.01	5.39	44.07
矿产品、建材及化工产品批发	Wholesale of Mineral Products, Building Material and Chemical Products	658.95	476.19	95.17	500.40
机械设备、五金交电及电子产品批发	Wholesale of Machinery Equipments, Hardware, Transport and Electronic Products	258.32	235.07	11.51	225.77
贸易经纪与代理	Trade Broker and Agent	0.06	0.06	0.00	0.02
其他批发	Others	47.44	32.83	3.72	38.53
零售业	**Retail Sales Trade**	**843.28**	**526.74**	**178.23**	**611.14**
#国有及国有控股	State-Owned and State Share Holding	95.90	56.77	29.52	75.09
按登记注册类型分组	**Grouped by Type of Registration**				
内资企业	Inner Enterprises	725.40	444.06	155.62	534.22

FINANCIAL INDICATORS OF ENTERPRISES ABOVE DESIGNATED SIZE IN WHOLESALE AND RETAIL TRADE (2006)

(100 million yuan)

所有者权益合计 Creditors' Equity	主营业务收入 Revenue of Major Business	主营业务成本 Cost of Major Business	主营业务利润 Profits of Major Business	其他业务利润 Profit of Other Business	利润总额 Total Profits
758.09	**6807.99**	**6260.86**	**470.25**	**44.11**	**173.19**
390.65	2494.72	2251.00	222.09	7.37	117.16
525.95	**5135.45**	**4765.61**	**325.34**	**14.11**	**137.81**
369.85	2317.41	2095.15	203.78	4.72	116.11
520.60	4999.66	4652.60	307.44	11.26	134.95
253.38	1035.51	899.64	126.85	2.84	86.91
3.28	68.34	64.62	2.38	0.29	0.31
0.90	32.04	30.47	1.16	0.11	0.32
3.35	44.03	42.82	0.67	0.10	0.16
2.54	31.68	30.92	0.26	0.08	0.05
0.10	2.01	1.95	0.04	0.00	0.00
0.71	10.34	9.95	0.37	0.02	0.11
84.19	1219.98	1147.54	57.26	4.62	11.89
11.30	52.78	46.39	5.94	0.12	3.30
72.89	1167.20	1101.15	51.32	4.50	8.59
95.44	1008.34	945.01	61.63	1.28	23.98
79.46	1579.68	1511.35	57.18	2.02	11.06
0.49	16.85	15.72	0.68	0.01	0.16
0.18	3.50	3.32	0.15	0.00	0.03
75.66	1377.12	1313.12	53.65	1.91	10.12
3.14	182.22	179.19	2.70	0.10	0.74
0.60	11.73	11.15	0.31	0.00	0.31
3.64	80.38	74.59	0.97	2.66	1.95
0.45	6.32	5.39	0.83	-0.01	0.01
3.19	74.05	69.20	0.14	2.67	1.94
1.71	55.41	38.43	16.93	0.18	0.92
0.70	2.05	1.54	0.51	0.01	-0.04
0.99	52.28	35.86	16.38	0.18	0.96
0.02	1.08	1.03	0.04	0.00	0.00
6.49	70.18	66.53	3.11	0.70	0.24
202.16	570.39	459.72	98.00	3.95	81.04
89.86	982.10	921.63	55.52	2.23	12.04
12.87	66.90	60.79	5.15	0.13	1.42
14.51	125.33	115.11	8.71	0.28	1.74
158.55	2481.87	2361.16	109.09	3.48	32.73
32.55	755.92	701.14	43.44	2.80	7.65
0.05	0.50	0.49	0.00	0.00	0.00
8.91	82.26	79.03	2.32	0.52	0.96
232.14	1672.55	1495.24	144.91	30.01	35.38
20.80	**177.31**	**155.85**	**18.31**	**2.65**	**1.05**
191.18	1462.31	1311.38	120.99	20.72	28.64

11－8 续表

单位:亿元

项目	Item	资产总计 Total Assets	#流动资产 Cirlculating Funds	#固定资产 Fixed Assets	负债合计 Total Liabilities
国有企业	State-owned Enterprises	46.16	25.52	15.43	34.23
集体企业	Collective-owned Enterprises	7.91	4.68	1.86	6.14
股份合作企业	Share Holding corperative Enterprises	2.02	1.11	0.46	1.50
联营企业	Joinr-Owned Enterprises	3.20	2.82	0.25	2.79
国有联营企业	State-Joint ownership Enterprises	2.12	1.87	0.16	2.05
集体联营企业	Collective-Joint ownership Enterprises	0.85	0.78	0.05	0.66
国有与集体联营企业	State-Collective Joint Enterprises	0.14	0.09	0.05	0.05
其他联营企业	Other Joint Ownership Enterprises	0.09	0.09	0.00	0.03
有限责任公司	Responsibility Co. Ltd.	271.14	163.94	65.53	212.71
国有独资公司	State-Funded Enterprises	1.45	0.79	0.50	1.08
其他有限责任公司	Other Limited Liability Corperation	269.69	163.15	65.03	211.63
股份有限公司	Share Holding Co. Ltd.	158.51	84.20	31.60	93.03
私营企业	Private Enterprises	231.04	160.11	36.99	178.56
私营独资企业	Private-funded Enterprises	6.24	5.07	0.66	4.33
私营合伙企业	Private Partnership Co. Ltd.	1.06	0.82	0.22	0.75
私营有限责任公司	Private limited Liability Corporations	195.02	135.39	30.76	150.93
私营股份有限公司	Private Share-holding Co. Ltd.	28.72	18.84	5.35	22.54
其他企业	Other Enterprises	5.42	1.67	3.50	5.27
港、澳、台商投资企业	Hong Kong Macao and Taiwan Funded	20.47	13.21	5.08	14.15
合资经营企业	Joint-Venture Enterprises	12.23	6.55	4.01	7.77
合作经营企业	Gooperative Enterprises	1.87	1.66	0.19	1.78
独资经营企业	Solely Funded Enterprises	6.37	5.01	0.88	4.60
外商投资企业	Foreign Invested Enterprises	97.41	69.46	17.53	62.77
合资经营企业	Joint-venture Enterprises	73.58	55.45	11.39	51.65
合作经营企业	Cooperative Enterprises	2.73	2.11	0.51	2.63
独资经营企业	Solely Funded Enterprises	21.09	11.91	5.63	8.49
按行业分	**Grouped by sector**				
综合零售	Retail Sale of Department	378.10	201.68	106.48	288.30
食品、饮料及烟草制品专门零售	Monopoly Retail of Foods,Beverage and Tobaccos	14.86	9.90	2.77	11.16
纺织、服装及日用品专门零售	Monopoly Retail of Textile Products, Garments and Daily Sundry Articals	19.74	8.67	9.80	13.76
文化、体育用品及器材专门零售	Monopoly Retail of Cultural, Sports Goods and Equipments	41.04	26.32	10.41	24.75
医药及医疗器材专门零售	Monopoly Retail of Medicine and Medical Appliance	62.60	47.33	7.32	51.26
汽车、摩托车、燃料及零配件专门零售	Monopoly of Retail of Motor Vehicle, Motorcycle, Fual and Parts	178.60	128.41	27.22	133.32
家用电器及电子产品专门零售	Monopoly Retail of Home Electric Appliance and Electronic Products	129.63	93.86	8.70	75.68
五金、家具及室内装修材料专门零售	Monopoly Retail of Hardwares, Furniture and Interior Decoration Materials	12.30	6.34	3.95	8.32
无店铺及其他零售	Retail of Storeless and Others	6.42	4.23	1.58	4.60
按经营方式分	**Grouped by Management Forms**				
独立商店	Independent－stores	577.18	344.09	139.68	423.15
连锁商店总店	Chain－Stores General	185.49	131.25	25.02	125.62
连锁商店分店	Chain－stores Branch	49.99	31.71	9.24	39.56
其他	Others	30.62	19.69	4.29	22.81
按零售业态分	**Grouped by Operating Situation**				
百货商店	Department Stores	265.02	123.18	86.18	190.85
超级市场	Supermarkets	136.62	88.03	30.70	114.23
专业店	Special Store	316.06	222.86	42.94	213.50
专卖店	Monopoly Store	78.36	61.01	10.42	59.28
其他	Others	47.23	31.66	7.98	33.29

Continued

(100 million yuan)

所有者权益合计 Creditors' Equity	主营业务收入 Revenue of Major Business	主营业务成本 Cost of Major Business	主营业务利润 Profits of Major Business	其他业务利润 Profit of Other Business	利润总额 Total Profits
11.93	68.24	55.39	10.96	0.98	1.78
1.77	21.33	19.47	1.14	0.10	0.11
0.52	5.23	4.85	0.30	0.01	0.02
0.40	7.52	6.91	0.55	0.07	0.05
0.07	2.70	2.51	0.17	0.01	-0.02
0.20	4.10	3.74	0.33	0.04	0.05
0.08	0.39	0.38	0.01	0.02	0.01
0.06	0.32	0.28	0.03	0.00	0.01
58.43	591.35	532.75	49.05	10.24	7.17
0.37	2.84	2.38	0.45	0.18	-0.07
58.07	588.50	530.36	48.60	10.05	7.24
65.48	220.83	188.10	23.34	4.56	16.39
52.48	542.09	499.11	35.14	4.69	3.17
1.91	15.63	14.04	1.07	0.04	0.04
0.31	3.32	3.03	0.20	0.01	-0.02
44.09	465.64	430.37	28.88	4.14	2.16
6.17	57.51	51.67	4.99	0.50	0.99
0.16	5.73	4.80	0.51	0.08	-0.05
6.32	37.79	32.41	4.18	1.52	0.67
4.46	20.64	17.27	3.19	0.81	0.99
0.09	4.01	3.59	0.41	0.17	-0.10
1.77	13.14	11.55	0.58	0.53	-0.21
34.64	172.45	151.45	19.74	7.77	6.06
21.93	139.50	125.04	14.06	6.50	2.83
0.11	6.59	4.92	1.26	0.16	0.31
12.60	26.36	21.50	4.42	1.10	2.93
89.80	667.11	577.35	78.13	18.97	15.10
3.71	30.55	26.49	3.52	0.48	0.71
5.97	21.56	17.66	3.01	0.40	0.73
16.29	54.02	40.89	10.78	0.59	2.18
11.34	112.84	103.35	7.80	0.43	0.12
45.28	479.88	454.91	19.38	1.38	3.07
53.95	269.66	242.19	18.59	7.18	12.64
3.98	20.98	17.68	2.62	0.49	0.83
1.82	15.96	14.73	1.07	0.08	-0.01
154.03	1116.52	1001.51	97.56	13.71	19.33
59.87	362.39	319.20	32.44	10.98	13.47
10.43	143.78	128.63	11.48	4.99	2.32
7.81	49.86	45.90	3.43	0.34	0.26
74.17	362.69	305.48	50.98	7.26	14.24
22.39	327.65	291.80	30.02	12.44	1.94
102.56	661.24	597.80	46.58	8.92	16.07
19.08	212.44	199.89	10.40	0.73	2.31
13.94	108.53	100.27	6.92	0.66	0.83

11－9 限额以上住宿和餐饮业企业财务状况(2006年)

FINANCIAL INDICATORS OF ENTERPRISES ABOVE DESIGNATED SIZE IN HOTEL AND CATERING INDUSTRY (2006)

单位:亿元

项目	Item	资产总计 Total Assets	#流动资产 Cirlcula－ting Funds	#固定资产 Fixed Assets	负债合计 Total Liabilities
总计	**Total**	**441.32**	**115.54**	**212.38**	**295.11**
#国有及国有控股	State-Owned and State Share Holding	135.42	29.29	68.39	64.08
住宿业	**Hotel**	**288.89**	**59.81**	**150.46**	**186.35**
#国有及国有控股	State-Owned and State Share Holding	119.64	26.24	59.24	53.71
按登记注册类型分组	**Grouped by Type of Registration**				
内资企业	Inner Enterprises	232.78	52.49	115.11	137.89
国有企业	State-owned Enterprises	67.04	12.51	41.95	35.59
集体企业	Collective-owned Enterprises	5.86	1.58	3.45	4.01
股份合作企业	Share Holding corperative Enterprises	0.61	0.13	0.37	0.51
联营企业	Joinr-Owned Enterprises	1.70	0.55	0.91	0.96
国有联营企业	State-Joint ownership Enterprises	1.43	0.51	0.86	0.64
集体联营企业	Collective-Joint ownership Enterprises	0.09	0.01	0.03	0.01
国有与集体联营企业	State-Collective Joint Enterprises	0.02	0.00	0.01	0.04
其他联营企业	Other Joint ownership Enterprises	0.15	0.02	0.01	0.27
有限责任公司	Responsibility Co. Ltd.	93.37	20.42	38.96	50.77
国有独资公司	State-Funded Enterprises	5.28	1.61	3.00	1.73
其他有限责任公司	Other Limited Liability Corperation	88.09	18.81	35.96	49.04
股份有限公司	Share Holding Co. Ltd.	9.62	2.57	5.57	4.29
私营企业	Private Enterprises	53.74	14.52	23.74	41.12
私营独资企业	Private-funded Enterprises	8.34	2.73	4.19	5.12
私营合伙企业	Private Partnership Co. Ltd.	0.98	0.27	0.23	0.68
私营有限责任公司	Private limited Liability Corporations	41.88	10.66	18.01	34.06
私营股份有限公司	Private Share-holding Co. Ltd.	2.55	0.85	1.30	1.27
其他企业	Other Enterprises	0.84	0.21	0.17	0.64
港、澳、台商投资企业	Hong Kong Macao and Taiwan Funded	22.30	3.33	13.07	24.08
合资经营企业	Joint-Venture Enterprises	13.65	1.97	8.22	17.44
合作经营企业	Cooperative Enterprises	4.85	0.62	2.58	3.66
独资经营企业	Solely Funded Enterprises	2.68	0.73	1.58	1.72
股份有限公司	Share Holding Co. Ltd.	1.12	0.02	0.69	1.26
外商投资企业	Foreign Invested Enterprises	33.81	3.99	22.28	24.39
合资经营企业	Joint-Venture Enterprises	14.86	1.19	11.06	13.10
合作经营企业	Cooperative Enterprises	2.20	0.13	1.59	1.40
独资经营企业	Solely Funded Enterprises	13.62	2.37	8.09	7.75
外商投资股份有限公司	Foreign Funded Share Holding Co. Ltd.	3.13	0.29	1.54	2.14
按行业分组	**Grouped by sector**				
旅游饭店	Tourist Hotel	274.13	56.06	142.84	177.03
一般旅馆	Regular Hotel	14.26	3.59	7.34	8.96
其他住宿服务	Other Accommodation Service	0.50	0.15	0.27	0.36
按星级等级分组	**Grouped by star Class**				
五星	Five Stars Class	79.90	13.76	36.11	49.06
四星	Four Stars Class	81.46	14.25	48.41	51.25
三星	Three Stars Class	72.04	19.17	35.70	49.65
二星	Two Stars Class	20.95	5.44	11.18	14.33

FINANCIAL INDICATORS OF ENTERPRISES ABOVE DESIGNATED SIZE IN WHOLESALE AND RETAIL TRADE (2006)

(100 million yuan)

所有者权益合计 Creditors' Equity	主营业务收入 Revenue of Major Business	主营业务成本 Cost of Major Business	主营业务利润 Profits of Major Business	其他业务利润 Profir of Other Business	利润总额 Total Profits
146.21	**228.57**	**99.39**	**93.81**	**1.65**	**-0.89**
71.35	44.28	16.21	21.96	0.74	-1.75
102.54	**97.80**	**33.71**	**51.04**	**1.21**	**-3.80**
65.94	36.53	13.12	18.62	0.61	-1.43
94.89	80.57	29.57	39.67	1.18	-2.74
31.45	20.38	7.10	9.76	0.39	-1.79
1.85	2.99	1.39	1.03	0.08	0.03
0.10	0.44	0.15	0.24	0.00	0.03
0.73	1.06	0.38	0.51	0.02	0.00
0.79	0.76	0.22	0.42	0.01	0.01
0.08	0.17	0.10	0.01	0.01	0.02
-0.02	0.05	0.03	0.02	0.00	-0.02
-0.11	0.09	0.02	0.06	0.00	-0.01
42.60	28.65	9.87	15.37	0.51	-0.90
3.55	2.03	0.62	1.30	0.04	0.03
39.05	26.62	9.25	14.06	0.47	-0.93
5.33	5.72	2.67	2.77	0.01	0.70
12.62	20.71	7.74	9.75	0.17	-0.78
3.22	3.42	1.59	1.41	0.00	-0.02
0.30	0.78	0.40	0.20	0.00	0.00
7.82	15.48	5.28	7.65	0.17	-0.78
1.28	1.04	0.48	0.49	0.00	0.02
0.21	0.61	0.28	0.24	0.00	-0.02
-1.78	5.99	1.53	3.79	0.01	-1.24
-3.79	4.06	1.16	2.42	0.01	-0.79
1.19	0.79	0.20	0.55	0.01	-0.28
0.96	0.81	0.12	0.56	0.00	-0.04
-0.13	0.33	0.05	0.26	0.00	-0.14
9.42	11.25	2.61	7.57	0.01	0.18
1.76	4.65	1.32	3.06	0.00	-0.17
0.80	0.65	0.14	0.34	0.01	0.03
5.87	5.14	0.97	3.59	0.00	0.30
0.99	0.81	0.18	0.58	0.00	0.02
97.10	93.01	31.50	49.10	1.17	-3.36
5.30	4.57	2.14	1.83	0.04	-0.35
0.14	0.22	0.07	0.10	0.00	-0.09
30.83	18.69	5.47	11.71	0.27	-0.36
30.21	27.56	8.91	15.58	0.24	-0.45
22.38	29.43	11.23	13.56	0.38	-1.50
6.61	9.33	4.09	3.88	0.22	-0.33

11－9　续表

单位:亿元

项　　目	Item	资产总计 Total Assets	#流动资产 Calcula－ting Funds	#固定资产 Fixed Assets	负债合计 Total Liabilities
一星	One Star Class	1.73	0.26	1.13	0.56
其他	Others	32.81	6.93	17.92	21.50
餐饮业	**Catering Trade**	**152.43**	**55.74**	**61.92**	**108.76**
#国有及国有控股	State-Owned and State Share Holding	15.78	3.05	9.15	10.37
按登记注册类型分组	**Grouped by Type of Regislration**				
内资企业	Inner Enterprises	121.98	44.08	50.07	90.69
国有企业	State-Owned Enterprises	9.92	2.38	5.16	6.81
集体企业	Collective-Owned Enterprises	7.04	2.24	4.59	5.38
股份合作企业	Share Holding Cooperative Enterprises	2.97	0.73	2.00	2.79
联营企业	Joinr-Owned Enterprises	0.73	0.12	0.58	0.74
国有联营企业	State-Joint Ownership Enterprises	0.61	0.05	0.56	0.64
集体联营企业	Collective-Joint Ownership Enterprises	0.06	0.03	0.02	0.06
国有与集体联营企业	State-Collective Joint Enterprises	0.05	0.05	0.00	0.04
其他联营企业	Other Joint Ownership Enterprises	0.00	0.00	0.00	0.00
有限责任公司	Responsibility Co. Ltd.	28.41	9.03	11.53	21.61
国有独资公司	State-Funded Enterprises	0.21	0.10	0.08	0.16
其他有限责任公司	Other Limited Liability Corperation	28.20	8.93	11.45	21.44
股份有限公司	Share Holding Co Ltd.	0.97	0.31	0.53	0.72
私营企业	Private Enterprises	70.69	28.61	25.11	52.05
私营独资企业	Private-Funded Enterprises	10.49	3.69	4.69	5.76
私营合伙企业	Private Partnership Co. Ltd.	0.65	0.44	0.09	0.23
私营有限责任公司	Private Limited Liability Corporations	53.08	23.25	18.20	41.44
私营股份有限公司	Private Share-holding Co. Ltd.	6.47	1.23	2.13	4.61
其他企业	Other Enterprises	1.25	0.66	0.55	0.61
港、澳、台商投资企业	Hong Kong, Macao and Taiwan Funded	6.59	2.07	1.99	2.66
合资经营企业	Joint-Venture Enterprises	2.71	0.44	1.25	1.59
合作经营企业	Cooperative Enterprises	0.69	0.31	0.35	0.09
独资经营企业	Solely Funded Enterprises	3.19	1.32	0.39	0.98
股份有限公司	Share Holding Co. Ltd.				
外商投资企业	Foreign Invested Enterprises	23.86	9.58	9.86	15.41
合资经营企业	Joint Funded Enterprices	14.65	6.28	6.06	10.14
合作经营企业	Cooperative Enterprices	0.26	0.17	0.07	0.21
独资经营企业	Solely Funded Enterprises	8.95	3.13	3.73	5.05
外商投资股份有限公司	Foreign Funded Share Holding Co. Ltd.				
按行业分组	**Grouped by sector**				
正餐服务	Dinner	136.48	50.46	54.50	99.08
快餐服务	Fast Food	11.61	3.78	6.61	7.41
饮料及冷饮服务	Beverage and Cold Drink Services	0.20	0.11	0.02	0.04
其他餐饮服务	Other	4.14	1.38	0.79	2.23
按经营方式分组	**Grouped by Management Forms**				
独立商店	Independent-stores	130.04	47.60	51.78	94.70
连锁商店总店	Chain-stores-General	13.27	4.47	6.46	7.95
连锁商店分店	Chain-stores-Branch	1.01	0.49	0.41	0.73
其他	Others	8.11	3.18	3.27	5.38

Continued

(100 million yuan)

所有者权益合计 Creditors' Equity	主营业务收入 Revenue of Major Business	主营业务成本 Cost of Major Business	主营业务利润 Profits of Major Business	其他业务利润 Profit of Other Business	利润总额 Total Profits
1.17	0.32	0.22	-0.10	0.00	-0.13
11.32	12.46	3.80	6.40	0.10	-1.04
43.67	130.77	65.68	42.78	0.44	2.91
5.41	7.75	3.09	3.35	0.13	-0.32
31.28	100.00	53.92	32.76	0.57	-0.02
3.11	4.83	2.05	1.65	0.10	-0.20
1.66	2.14	1.30	0.48	0.00	-0.09
0.18	1.04	0.53	0.32	0.00	-0.05
-0.01	0.27	0.10	0.14	0.00	0.00
-0.03	0.20	0.07	0.12	0.00	0.00
0.01	0.04	0.02	0.02	0.00	0.00
0.01	0.02	0.02	0.00	0.00	0.00
0.00	0.00	0.00	0.00	0.00	0.00
6.80	19.53	9.30	8.16	0.10	-0.31
0.05	0.45	0.23	0.19	0.01	-0.03
6.75	19.08	9.07	7.97	0.09	-0.28
0.25	0.92	0.60	0.17	0.05	-0.04
18.64	69.29	38.84	21.20	0.29	0.42
4.73	14.34	9.08	3.66	0.05	0.57
0.43	0.96	0.52	0.32	0.00	0.02
11.63	51.18	27.69	16.22	0.21	-0.09
1.86	2.80	1.56	1.00	0.02	-0.07
0.64	1.98	1.19	0.63	0.03	0.24
3.93	4.10	2.02	1.26	0.01	-0.21
1.12	2.12	1.02	0.75	0.00	-0.10
0.60	0.33	0.15	0.16	0.01	-0.06
2.22	1.65	0.85	0.35	0.00	-0.05
8.46	26.67	9.74	8.76	-0.14	3.15
4.51	13.10	4.54	5.87	-0.09	1.95
0.05	0.37	0.18	0.15	0.00	0.00
3.89	13.19	5.01	2.73	-0.06	1.20
0.00	0.00	0.00	0.00	0.00	0.00
37.40	100.98	53.86	33.69	0.55	-0.40
4.20	27.24	10.49	8.47	-0.13	3.24
0.16	0.27	0.08	0.04	0.00	0.01
1.91	2.28	1.24	0.59	0.02	0.06
35.35	98.21	52.51	32.37	0.55	-0.36
5.32	25.96	9.66	7.88	-0.13	3.14
0.28	1.49	0.72	0.63	0.01	0.14
2.73	5.10	2.78	1.90	0.01	0.00

11－10　批发和零售业、住宿和餐饮业连锁总店经营情况（2006 年）

项　　目　Item		连　锁 总店数 （个） Number of General Stores (unit)	连　锁 门店数 （个） Number of Sales Room (unit)	#在省外 门　店 Outside the Province	商品销售总　额 （或营业总收入） （亿元） Total Sales (or Business Revenue) (100 million yuan)
总　　计	**Total**	**142**	**12743**	**1169**	**2376.57**
批发和零售业	**Retail Sale Trade**	**122**	**11489**	**1051**	**2345.54**
#国有及国有控股	State-Owned and State Share Holding	9	1811	239	373.62
按零售业态分	Grouped by Operating Situation				
百货商店	Depatiment Stores	3	778	7	155.76
超级市场	Super Markets	43	3078	237	362.72
专业店	Special Stores	61	6952	743	1731.38
专卖店	Monopoly Stores	5	253	64	7.56
便利店	Convenient Stores	8	343		4.55
其　他	Others	1	3		3.46
餐饮业	**Catering Trade**	**20**	**1254**	**118**	**31.02**
#外商及港澳台投资	Foreign, Hong Kong, Macao and Taiwan Entrepreneuts Funded	5	274	33	21.83
按行业分	Grouped by Sector				
正　餐	Fast Food	3	12		0.38
快　餐	Fast Food	15	1207	116	30.26
其　他	Others	2	35	2	0.39

MANAGEMENT CONDITIONS OF GENERAL CHAIN STORES OF WHOLESALE AND RETAIL SALE TRADE, HOTEL AND CATERING TRADE SERVICE (2006)

#商 品零售额 Retail Sales	零售或餐饮营业面积(平方米) Floor Space of Retail and Catering service Business (sq. m)	从业人员(人) Employees (person)	利润总额(亿元) Total Profits (100 million yuan)	资产总计(亿元) Total Assets (100 million yuan)	负债总计(亿元) Total Liabilities (100 million yuan)
1497.03	**8644875**	**279613**	**48.71**	**446.10**	**283.34**
1466.01	**8467058**	**252806**	**45.51**	**433.58**	**275.67**
314.18	2033398	68106	6.45	86.99	50.95
124.39	614791	17739	5.50	34.92	16.34
300.85	2440897	81016	2.44	61.90	49.36
991.72	5021230	143826	34.90	284.08	177.24
3.40	16229	1677	0.18	2.55	1.73
4.46	22038	1631	-0.10	0.97	1.02
3.46	15000	440	0.16	6.05	5.74
31.02	**177817**	**26807**	**3.20**	**12.52**	**7.67**
21.83	104603	18526	2.91	8.76	5.55
0.38	8350	310	0.00	0.08	0.04
30.26	165792	25706	3.18	12.40	7.63
0.39	3675	791	0.01	0.04	0.00

11－11 省外批发和零售业、住宿和餐饮业连锁总店在江苏分店经营情况（2006 年）
MANAGEMENT CONDITIONS OF BRANCH STORES OF WHOLESALE AND RETAIL SALE TRADE HOTEL AND CATERING TRADE OF GENERAL CHAIN STORES OF OTHER PROVINCE IN JIANGSU (2006)

项目	Item	连锁门店数（个） Number of Sales Rooms of Chain Stores (unit)	商品销售总额（或营业总收入）（亿元） Total Sales (or Business Revenue) (100 million yuan)	#商品零售额 Retail Sales	零售或餐饮营业面积（平方米） Floor Space of Business (sq. m)	从业人员（人） Employees (person)
总　计	**Total**	**144**	**229.80**	**192.70**	**1626506**	**30742**
批发和零售业	**Wholesale and Retail Sales Trade**	**128**	**228.06**	**191.29**	**1595006**	**29463**
#外商及港澳台投资	Foreign, Hong Kong, Macao and Taiwan Entrepreneuts Funded	15	45.77	45.68	181612	5172
按零售业态分	Grouped by Operating Situation					
百货商店	Departiment Stores	4	10.57	10.57	71738	1666
超级市场	Super Markets	106	162.53	161.08	957204	24795
专业店	Special Stores	12	49.80	14.62	544051	2016
专卖店	Monopoly Stores	1	0.15	0.01	200	17
便利店	Convenient Stores	3	1.35	1.35	6100	635
仓储会员店	Storage Member Stores	1	2.27	2.27	6713	221
家居建材店	Residential Building Material Stores	1	1.38	1.38	9000	113
住宿业	**Hotel**	**2**	**0.34**	**0.01**	**22340**	**212**
餐饮业	**Catering Trade**	**14**	**1.40**	**1.40**	**9160**	**1067**
#外商及港澳台投资	Foreign, Hong Kong, Macao and Taiwan Entrepreneuts Funded	11	1.12	1.12	5060	869
按行业分	Grouped by Sector					
正　餐	Dinner	6	0.53	0.53	5384	376
快　餐	Fast Food	6	0.78	0.78	3228	604
其　他	Others	2	0.10	0.10	548	87
#茶馆	Tea House	1	0.06	0.06	449	65

11－12 商品交易市场情况
TRANSACTION MARKETS

项目	Item	1990	1995	2000	2003	2004	2005	2006
商品交易市场数(个)	Number of Transaction Markets (unit)	4720	5111	6268	5706	5487	4934	4339
按地区分	Grouped by Area							
城　市	City	574	1293	2027	2529	2439	2279	2157
农　村	Countryside	4146	3818	4241	3177	3048	2655	2182
按市场类型分	Grouped by Type of Market							
消费品市场	Consumer Goods Market		4711	5548	4940	4753	4293	3825
生产资料市场	Means of production Market		400	720	766	734	641	514

11－13　亿元以上商品交易市场基本情况（2006年）

BASIC CONDITIONS OF TRANSACTION MARKETS WHOSE TRANSACTION VALUE EACH REACHED MORE THAN 100 MILLION YUAN (2006)

项　　目	Item	市场个数（个）Number of Markets (unit)	年末摊位数（个）Year-end Number of Stands (unit)	年末已出租摊位（个）Year-end Number of Rented stands (unit)	#出租给个体 Rented to Individual
合　计	**Total**	**477**	**274271**	**259954**	**246514**
按经营环境分	**Grouped by Form of Operation Environment**				
露天式	Open Air	43	12358	11974	11824
封闭式	Seal Off	355	222719	211086	200730
其　他	Others	79	39194	36894	33960
按经营方式分	**Grouped by Form of Operation**				
批　发	Whole Sale	229	150135	141000	132002
零　售	Retail Sale	248	124136	118954	114512
按市场类别分	**Grouped by Catergary of Market**				
综合市场	Integrated Market	191	118731	111745	108718
工业品综合市场	Industrial Products	41	44504	42108	41555
农副产品综合市场	Farm and Side-line Products	150	74227	69637	67163
专业市场	Special Market	260	141526	134376	126928
纺织品服装鞋帽市场	Textile Products, Garments, Shoes and Hats	36	55988	54407	53300
食品饮料烟酒市场	Foods, Beverage and Tabacco	14	4128	3589	3567
家具市场	Furnitures	13	5332	5296	5231
小商品市场	Small Commodities	9	6611	6601	6430
文化音像书报杂志市场	Culture, Stereo, TV, Books, Newspaper and Magzines	2	296	296	208
旧货市场	Secondhand Goods	5	1901	1876	1752
机动车市场	Motor Driven Vehicles	10	1575	1356	1055
金属材料市场	Matel Material	21	6195	5815	3966
煤炭市场	Coal	1	30	30	18
木材市场	Timber	14	5158	5049	4501
建材装饰材料市场	Building and Decorate Material	62	26379	23560	22532
粮油市场	Grain and Oil	7	991	966	944
干鲜果品市场	Dried and Flesh Fruits	10	5266	5139	5139
水产品市场	Aquatic Products	16	3518	3324	3282
蔬菜市场	Vegetables	11	4492	4350	4334
肉食禽蛋市场	Meat, Poulty and Eggs	9	1936	1876	1859
土畜产品市场	Local and Animal Products	2	556	486	472
农业生产资料市场	Means of Agricultural Production	1	550	491	456
计算机市场	Computers	6	1386	1377	924
花卉市场	Flowers	3	2220	2134	2089
五金电料市场	Hardware and Electrical Materials	8	7018	6358	4869
其他市场	Other Market	26	14014	13833	10868

项　　目　Item		商品成交额（亿元）Transaction Value (100 million yuan)	营业面积（万平方米）Floor Space of Business (10000 sq. m)	交易业主从业人员（人）Transaction Proprietor Engaged (person)
合　计	**Total**	**5817.13**	**1893.07**	**663537**
按经营环境分	**Grouped by Form of Operation Environment**			
露天式	Open Air	208.62	205.88	37018
封闭式	Seal Off	4755.14	1219.06	537916
其　他	Others	853.37	468.14	88603
按经营方式分	**Grouped by Form of Operation**			
批　发	Whole Sale	4970.28	1463.48	439580
零　售	Retail Sale	846.85	429.59	223957
按市场类别分	**Grouped by Catergary of Market**			
综合市场	Integrated Market	897.00	490.58	230495
工业品综合市场	Industrial Products	313.48	307.97	112181
农副产品综合市场	Farm and Side-line Products	583.52	182.61	118314
专业市场	Special Market	4285.31	1274.61	385467
纺织品服装鞋帽市场	Textile Products, Garments, Shoes and Hats	1273.24	186.37	130347
食品饮料烟酒市场	Foods, Beverage and Tabacco	106.45	34.42	13044
家具市场	Furnitures	76.93	113.40	32887
小商品市场	Small Commodities	66.36	19.22	17054
文化音像书报杂志市场	Culture, Stereo, TV, Books, Newspaper and Magzines	6.22	1.49	1300
旧货市场	Secondhand Goods	18.25	32.02	8598
机动车市场	Motor Driven Vehicles	213.92	42.43	2873
金属材料市场	Matel Material	1314.02	90.63	23587
煤炭市场	Coal	8.71	20.00	280
木材市场	Timber	102.91	89.29	12917
建材装饰材料市场	Building and Decorate Material	398.93	383.58	73458
粮油市场	Grain and Oil	70.11	28.57	3885
干鲜果品市场	Dried and Flesh Fruits	67.45	51.70	4653
水产品市场	Aquatic Products	136.22	23.31	13500
蔬菜市场	Vegetables	92.34	31.20	11792
肉食禽蛋市场	Meat, Poulty and Eggs	95.46	15.33	5670
土畜产品市场	Local and Animal Products	4.20	5.26	793
农业生产资料市场	Means of Agricultural Production	5.18	4.59	975
计算机市场	Computers	42.92	5.09	5120
花卉市场	Flowers	28.26	49.41	7250
五金电料市场	Hardware and and Electrical Materials	157.21	47.32	15484
其他市场	Other Market	634.82	127.88	47575

11－14 个体工商业基本情况（2006 年）
SELF－EMPLOYMENT BUSINESS（2006）

单位：亿元 （100 million yuan）

行业	Sector	户数（万户）Households (10000 units)	就业人数（万人）Employed Persons (10000 persons)	资金数额 Capital	总产值 Total Output Value	销售总额或营业收入 Total Sales Value or Rusiness Revenue
总计	**Total**	**187.01**	**301.30**	**719.26**	**1517.13**	**2459.52**
按行业分	Grouped by Sector					
#农林牧渔业	Farming, Forestry, Animal Husbandry and Fishery	3.03	3.96	26.34	63.73	41.61
制造业	Manufacturing	19.09	42.83	118.09	1344.71	
建筑业	Construction	0.57	1.23	5.11	70.44	
交通运输、仓储和邮政业	Transportation, storage and post	7.55	8.90	53.74		96.94
批发和零售业	Wholesale, Retail Sales	120.45	181.20	355.99		1606.55
住宿和餐饮业	Hotel and Catering Trade	11.09	24.30	59.10		368.82
居民服务和其他服务业	Resident's Service and Other Services	19.35	29.67	66.50		138.72

11－15 私营企业情况（2006 年）
PRIVATE ENTERPRISES（2006）

单位：亿元 （100 million yuan）

行业	Sector	户数（万户）Households (10000 units)	雇工人数（万人）Employed Persons (10000 persons)	投资者人数（万人）Owners (10000 persons)	注册资金 Registered Capital	总产值 Total Output Valuve	销售总额 Total Sales Value
总计	**Total**	**60.01**	**788.63**	**129.29**	**9717.07**	**4719.85**	**4981.53**
按行业分	Grouped by Sector						
#农林牧渔业	Farming, Forestry, Animal Husbandry and Fishery	1.25	9.66	2.07	156.33	96.94	39.26
制造业	Manufacturing	26.03	497.06	51.54	4032.60	4069.12	
建筑业	Construction	2.90	73.75	8.07	866.35	372.01	
交通运输、仓储和邮政业	Transportation, storage and post	1.08	11.39	2.94	165.89		372.04
批发和零售业	Wholesale, Retail Sales	18.01	112.22	38.40	2031.45		2676.78
住宿和餐饮业	Hotel and Catering Trade	0.60	10.38	1.23	74.99		181.80
居民服务和其他服务业	Resident's Service and Other Services	2.03	17.11	4.44	168.14		169.05

主要统计指标解释

社会消费品零售总额　指各种经济类型的批发和零售业、住宿和餐饮业及其他行业对城乡居民和社会集团的消费品零售额总和。这个指标反映通过各种商品流通渠道向居民和社会集团供应的生活消费品来满足他们的生活需要，是研究人民生活、社会消费品购买力、货币流通等问题的重要指标。对居民的消费品零售额：指售给城乡居民用于生活消费的商品。对社会集团的消费品零售额：指售给机关、团体、部队、学校、企业、事业单位和城市街道居民委员会、农村村民委员会用公款购买的用作非生产、非经营使用的消费品。

社会消费品零售额包括：(1)售给城乡居民作为生活用的商品及修建房屋用的建筑材料；(2)售给机关、团体、学校、部队、企业、事业单位的职工食堂和旅店(招待所)附设专门供本店旅客食用，不对外营业的食堂的各种食品、燃料；企业、单位和国营农场直接售给本单位职工和职工食堂的自己生产的产品；(3)售给部队干部、战士生活用的粮食、副食品、衣着品、日用品、燃料；(4)售给来华的外国人、华侨、港澳台同胞的消费品(包括友谊商店、在海关前后设立的免税商店、外轮供应公司等)；(5)居民自费购买的中、西药品，中药材及医疗用品；(6)报社，出版社直接售给居民和社会集团的报纸、图书、杂志，集邮公司(包括邮局集邮专柜)出售的新、旧(盖销的)纪念邮票。特种邮票、首日封、集邮册、集邮Ⅰ具等；(7)旧货寄售商店(信托商店)自购、自销部分的商品零售额；(8)煤气公司、液化石油气站售给居民和社会集团的的煤气灶具和灌装液化石油气；(9)售给社会集团的办公用品、纸张、帐册、文印用品、计算工具、书报杂志和奖品；公共用品和纺织品、针织品；学校用的教学用具；文体用品；非专用的劳动保护用品，如工作服，套袖、围裙、手套、毛巾、肥皂等；日用百货和杂品，包括职工食堂用的餐具、炊具、设备和清洁卫生工具等；家具、设备、日用电器、电讯设备、电影器材和照相器材等；取暖用的设备和燃料，防暑、降温的饮料；非生产经营用的交通工具如小轿车、面包车、工具车、卡车和油料；零星修理用的各种零配件、材料、工具，建筑材料等；举办各种招待会、茶话会、宴会用的烟酒茶和各种食品及馈赠的礼品；从公费医疗经费中开支的中、西药品、中药材和医疗器材以及其他非生产性设备和用品。

社会消费品零售额不包括：(1)农民之间相互买卖的商品；(2)城市居民通过市场或其他形式在城市居民中相互转让出售旧的生活用品；(3)售给农民或村办的生产单位各种生产工具、原材料和辅助材料；(4)售给国有农场、国有拖拉机站、排灌站、农村集体、农业生产单位和农民的各种农业生产资料和燃料；(5)售给工业(包括科研单位附属的工厂、学校办工厂)、交通运输业、建筑安装企业和建筑单位用的各种生产资料和建筑材料；(6)售给饮食业加工用的粮食、副食品、调味品、燃料等；(7)售给批发和零售业、住宿和餐饮业、居民服务业(旅行社、理发店、旅馆、照相馆、日用品修理业等)、公共事业等单位直接用于业务经营活动方面的设备、工具、器材、原料、材料、燃料和印制各种票证用的纸张等；(8)售给各种经济类型的批发和零售业、餐饮业作为转卖或加工后专卖的商品；(9)旧货寄售商店(信托商店)受居民委托寄售卖出的商品；(10)公用事业的营业收入(如市内公共汽车、电车、轮渡的车船票收入、公园门票收入等)、服务业的营业收入(如旅店的房租收入、理发店的理发收入、日用品修理行业的修理费收入等)、文化艺术事业收入(如电影、戏剧票收入、博物馆门票收入等)；(11)邮电局出售邮票(包括普通邮票、纪念邮票、特种邮票)、汇款单、电报稿纸的收入；(12)自来水、电力、煤气热力生产(供应)单位的产品通过管道、输电线路供应给居民和社会集团的水、电、煤气、暖气的收入；(13)售给对外营业影剧院的设备和器材；(14)售给自然科学研究单位直接用于科学研究的各种仪器仪表、化学试剂。元器件，工具和其它有关设备；(15)售给消防队、清洁队、出租汽车公司等单位用于业务活动的设备、车辆和燃料；(16)售给企业单位生产上专用的劳动保护用品，包括绝缘、防毒、耐酸、耐油，防烧、隔热以及高空、水下作业用的专用防护设备和用品；(17)售给民政部门救灾用的商品，售给人防工程的设备和材料。

市的零售额　指设立在直辖市、省辖市的市区和郊区以及县级市的市区的各行业消费品零售额。不包括省辖市的市属县、县级市的市区以外的消费品零售额。

县的零售额　指设立在县城关区(镇)的各行业消费品零售额。

县以下的零售额　指设立在县城关区(镇)以及县级市的市区以外的集镇和农村的各行业消费品零售额。但不包括分布在农村的独立工矿、林区的消费品零售额。这部分零售额，按管辖这些工矿、林区的单位级别分别列入市或县的零售额。

批发和零售业商品购、销、存总额　指各种登记注册类型的批发和零售企业、产业活动单位、个体经营者以本单位为总体的商品购进、销售、库存总额。

商品购进总额　指从本单位以外的单位和个人购进(包括从境外直接进口)作为转卖或加工后转卖的商品总额。

商品销售总额　指对本单位以外的单位和个人出售(包括对境外直接出口)本单位经营的商品总额(含增值税)。

商品批发额　指商品零售额以外的一切商品销售额。包括售给生产经营单位用于生产或经营用的商品销售额；售给批发零售贸易业、餐饮业用于转卖或加工后转卖的商品销售额；直接向国(境)外出口和委托外贸部门代理出口的商品销售额。

商品零售额　指售给城乡居民用于生活消费、售给社会集团用公款购买用作非生产、非经营使用的商品销售额。

商品库存总额　指报告期末各种登记注册类型的批发和零售业企业、产业活动单位、个体经营者已取得所有权的商品。

商品交易市场　指有固定场所、设施，有若干经营者入场实行集中、公开交易各类实物商品的市场。

商品交易市场成交额　指商品交易市场内所有经营者所实现的商品销售金额。商品交易市场包括消费品市场和生产资料市场。

Explanatory Notes on Main Statistical Indicators

Total Retail Sales of Consumer Goods refers to the sum of consumer goods sold by various economic ownerships of wholesale, retail sales, hotel and catering trade and other sectors to urban and rural residents and social groups. This indicator is used to show the supply of consumer goods through various channels to residents and social groups. It is a very important indicator for the study on problem of people's livelihood, social consumer goods purchasing power and currency circulation ect.. Retail sales of consumer goods sold to res-idents, refers to the commodities sold to urban and rural residents for their daily use. Retail sales of consumer goods sold to social groups, refers to the commodities sold to agencies, social groups, military units, schools, enterprises, institutions, urban subdistrict committee and village committee for non-production and non-operation use, and purchased by public money of these units.

The Retail Sales of Consumer Goods Include: (1) commodities sold to urban and rural residents for their daily use, and building materials sold to them for the construction and repair of houses. (2) food and fuel sold to conteens of hotels and hostels that only serve their guests not the outside customers; commmodities produced by enterprises, institutions or state farms and sold directly to their employees or their conteens; (3) grain and non-staple food, clothing, daily articles and fuels sold to caders and soldiers of military units; (4) consumer goods sold to foreigners, overseas Chinese, and Chinese compatriots from Hong Kong, Macao and Taiwan (include friendship stores, tax-free shops), shops established in front of or behined the costoms houses, foreign shipping supply companies; (5) Chinese and western medicines, herbs and medical facilities purchased by residents; (6) newspapers, books and magazines directly sold to residents and social groups by publishers, new and old commemorative stamps, special stamps, first-day covers, stamp albums and other stamp-collection articles sold by stamp companies (include stamp collection special cupboard of the post office); (7) consumer goods purchased and then sold by second-hand shops; (8) stoves and other heating facilties and liquefied gas sold to residents and social group by gas companies and liquefied gas stations; (9) Consumer goods sold to social groups and purchased by public money of these units including: office applians and supplies, paper, account books, printers, counters, books, newspapers, magazines and awards, articales for common use, textile goods, knitting goods, teaching tools, stationery and sports goods, non-special use labor protection articales, such as working coat, oversleeves, aprons, gloves, towels and soaps, daily use articales and miscellanous goods, include table ware, cook utensils, equipments, cleaning and hygiene tools of canteens, furnitures, equipments, electric appliances, dispatch equipment, film and photo equipments; equipments and fuels for warm oneself, beverage for heatstrok prevention and temperature lowering; nonproduction transport tools, such as cars, mini-buses, tool vehicals, trunks and petroleum; spar parts and fitting, materials, tools and construction materials for old repairing usr; tabacco, liquor, tea and foods of all kinds for reception, tea party, banquet, presentation of gifts; Chinese and western medicines, herb and medical facilities, and other non-production equipments and articales paid by expenditure for free medical services.

The Retail Sales of Consumer Goods Exclude: (1) Sales of commodities among the farmers; (2) daily use articales transfered and sold from each other through market or other types; (3) various production tools, raw materials and subsidiary materials sold to farmers or production units run by village; (4) various means of agricultural production and fuels sold to state-owned farms, state-owned tractor stations, irrigation and drainage stations, rural collective units and farmers and agricultural production units; (5) various meas of production and building materials sold to factories (include attached factories of scientific research institutions, and factories run by schools), transportation industry, construction installation enterprises, construction units and residents; (6) grain non-staples foods, flavorings, fuels sold to catering trade for processing; (7) equipments, tools, facilities, raw materials, materials, fuels, paper for printing various cards, notes, certificates, and tickets, sold to wholesale and retail sales trade, hatel and catering trade, services (travel service, barber shops, hotels, photo studioes, daily use articales repairing industries ect.), public services for the use of direct operational activities, (8) commodities sold to wholesale and retail sales trade, hotel and catering trade for the purpose of re-selling or re-selling after further processing; (9) commodities sold by second-hand cominision shops (trust shops) trusted by residents; (10) operational revenue of public services (revenue by sold tickets of urban buses, trolley buses, furry; entrance tickets of parkes), operational revenue of services (such as rent of hotels, hair-cutting of babershops, repairing of daily use articales); revenue of art and cultural industries (such as revenue by sold the tickets of films and dramas, and the entrance tickets of museums); (11) stamps (include ordinary stamps, commemorative stamps, special stamps), money orders, telegram papers sold by post and telecommunication offices; (12) revenue from tap water, electricity, gas, central heating sold to residents and social groups through pipe line, and transmission line by tap water, electricity, gas, gasheating production (supply) units; (13) revenue from equipments and facilities sold to operational theaters; (14) revenue from instruments, meters, chemical reagent, components, tools and other relative equipments sold to natural scientific research institutions for the use of direct scientific research; (15) revenue from equipments, vehicles and fuels sold to fire brigades, cleaning squards, taxi-companies for their business activities; (16) revenue from special labor protection articals (include special protection equipments and articale of insulation, gas defence, acid proof, oil-resisting, burning prevention, heat insulation, high altitude works and under water works) sold to production units; (17) revenue from disaster relief commodities sold to civil administration department; equipmenta and materials sold to civil defence projects.

Retail Sales of the Cities refers to the retail sales of consumer gppds sold by various sectors, which are set up at the urban and suburb districts of the cities under the direct jurisdiction of the central government and provincial government, and urban districts of the county level cities. Excluded the retail sales of consumer goods of the counties under the cities jurisdicted by the provincial government, outside the urban districts of the county level cities.

Retail Sales of the Counties refers to the retail sales of consumer goods sold by various sectors which are set up at the urban districts (town) of the counties.

Retail Sales Below the County Level refers to the retail sales of consumer goods sold by various sectors which are set up at the market towns or rural areas outside the urban districts (towns) of the counties and county level cities. Excluded the retail sales of consumer goods sold by the units which are distributed at independent industrial and mineral and forestry areas in rural districts. This part of retail sales are listed in the cities and counties according to the jurisdictional relationship of the units respectively.

Purchase, Sales and Stock of Commodities by Wholesale and Retail Trade refers to the purchase, sales and stock of commodities by wholesale and retail enterprises, industrial activity units and individual sellers of different status of registration.

Total Purchases of Commodities refers to the total value of purchases of commodities by the establishments from other establishments or individuals (including direct import from abroad) for the purpose of re-selling.

Total Sales of Commodities refers to the total value (included added tax) of commodities sold by the establishments to other establishments and individuals (including direct export).

Wholesale of Commodities refers to all the total sales of commodities except the retail sales of consumer goods. Included the sales of commodities to production or operation units for the purpose of production and operation; the sales of commodities to wholesale and retail sale trade and catering industry for the purpose of re-selling or re-selling after further processing; the sales of commodities for direct export to abroad or export on a commission basis by entrusted the foreign trade department.

Retail Sale of Commodities refers to the commodities sold to urban and rural residents for their daily use, to social groups for the use of non-production and non-operation and purchased by public money of the social groups.

Total Value of Commodity Stock refers to the total commodities owned by wholesale and retail sale enterprises, economic active units and individual sellers of various types of registeration status at the end of the reference period.

Commodity Transaction Markets refers to the markets provided with fixed place and equipments, and there are some operators who engaged in transaction of various substancial commodities in the markets by public and concentrating transaction.

Value of Transaction at Transaction Markets refers to the total sales value of commodities realized by the operators in the transaction market. Commodity transaction markets include consumer good markets and means of production markets.

JIANGSU STATISTICAL YEARBOOK

第 12 篇

对外经济贸易和旅游

FOREIGN ECONOMY, TRADE AND TOURISM

12－1 对外经济主要指标
MAJOR INDICATORS OF FOREIGN TRADE AND ECONOMIC COOPERATION

单位:亿美元 (USD 100 million)

指标	Item	1995	2000	2005	2006
进出口总额	**Total Imports and Exports**	**162.78**	**456.38**	**2279.41**	**2839.95**
进口总额	Total Imports	64.96	198.68	1049.59	1235.77
初级产品	Primary Goods		24.33	97.08	113.89
工业制成品	Manufactured Goods		174.35	952.51	1121.88
出口总额	Total Exports	97.82	257.70	1229.82	1604.19
初级产品	Primary Goods		8.40	15.77	21.05
工业制成品	Manufactured Goods		249.30	1214.05	1583.13
合同外商直接投资项目（个）	**Contracted project of Foreign Direct Investment (unit)**	**4056**	**2645**	**7126**	**7016**
合同外商直接投资金额	**Contracted Value of Foreign Direct Investment**	**129.70**	**106.11**	**457.22**	**465.42**
实际外商直接投资金额	**Actual Value of Foreign Direct Investment**	**47.81**	**64.23**	**131.80**	**174.31**
外商投资企业基本情况	**Registered Foreign-funded Enterprises**				
年底登记户数（户）	Number of Registered Enterprises (unit)	24099	18192	33321	36463
投资总额	Total Investment	571.54	774.80	2657.28	3242.61
注册资本	Registered Capital	346.09	419.64	1321.32	1653.60
对外经济合作	**Economic and Technical Cooperation with Foreign Countries**				
合同金额	Contracted Value	2.81	9.80	33.10	46.81
#对外承包工程	Contracted Projects	1.95	5.85	29.01	42.68
对外劳务合作	Labor Services	0.86	3.94	4.05	4.12
完成营业额	Value of Business Fulfilled	2.59	8.01	31.97	43.54
#对外承包工程	Contracted Projects	1.98	4.97	25.11	37.65
对外劳务合作	Labor Services	0.61	3.03	6.81	5.88
接待海外旅游者（万人次）	**Total Number of Overseas Tourists Rlceieved (10000 person-times)**	**76.77**	**160.94**	**378.30**	**445.19**
外国人	Foreigners	50.33	98.15	262.15	314.89
香港同胞	Compatriots from Hong Kong	14.66	24.90	41.34	47.41
澳门同胞	Compatriots from Macao		2.16	3.65	4.30
台湾同胞	Compatriots from Taiwan	11.78	35.73	71.16	78.59
旅游外汇收入	**Foreign Exchange Income from Tourism**	**2.60**	**7.24**	**22.60**	**27.87**

12－2　人民币对主要外币年平均汇价(中间价)
AVERAGE EXCHANGE RATE OF RMB YUAN AGAINST MAIN CONVERTIBLE CURRENCIES　(MIDDLE PRICE)

单位:人民币元　(RMB yuan)

年　份 Year	100 美元 100 US Dollars	100 日元 100 Japanese Yen	100 港元 100 Hong Kong Dollars
1985	293.66	1.2457	37.57
1986	345.28	2.0694	44.22
1987	372.21	2.5799	47.74
1988	372.21	2.9082	47.70
1989	376.51	2.7360	48.28
1990	478.32	3.3233	61.39
1991	532.33	3.9602	68.45
1992	551.46	4.3608	71.24
1993	576.20	5.2020	74.41
1994	861.87	8.4370	111.53
1995	835.10	8.9225	107.96
1996	831.42	7.6352	107.51
1997	828.98	6.8600	107.09
1998	827.91	6.3488	106.88
1999	827.83	7.2932	106.66
2000	827.84	7.6864	106.18
2001	827.70	6.8075	106.08
2002	827.70	6.6237	106.07
2003	827.70	7.1466	106.24
2004	827.68	7.6552	106.23
2005	819.17	7.4484	105.30
2006	797.18	6.8570	102.62

12－3　对外贸易进出口总额
TOTAL IMPORTS AND EXPORTS

单位:亿美元　(USD 100 million)

年　份 Year	海关进出口总额(经营单位) Total Import and Export Value by Customs (Running Unit)			海关进出口总额(目源地) Total Import and Export Value by Customs (Goods Destination or Original Place)		
	合　计 Total	进　口 Imports	出　口 Exports	合　计 Total	进　口 Imports	出　口 Exports
1985	19.87	4.01	15.86			
1986	24.12	5.42	18.70			
1987	28.73	7.56	21.17			
1988	34.58	10.41	24.17			
1989	38.43	13.07	25.36			
1990	41.39	11.95	29.44			
1991	53.10	18.85	34.25			
1992	69.62	29.60	40.02			
1993	91.29	44.77	46.52	107.75	59.81	47.94
1994	117.59	50.73	66.86	122.47	52.86	69.61
1995	162.78	64.96	97.82	180.05	79.42	100.63
1996	206.88	90.87	116.01	222.17	102.92	119.25
1997	236.21	95.32	140.89	252.93	108.82	144.11
1998	264.26	107.75	156.51	281.66	122.09	159.57
1999	312.61	129.52	183.09	328.62	142.80	185.82
2000	456.38	198.68	257.70	491.98	228.17	263.81
2001	513.55	224.77	288.78	544.84	250.91	293.93
2002	703.05	318.25	384.80	745.09	354.80	390.29
2003	1136.70	545.30	591.40	1213.37	617.26	596.11
2004	1708.57	833.60	874.97	1794.72	913.67	881.05
2005	2279.41	1049.59	1229.82	2384.86	1138.75	1246.11
2006	2839.95	1235.77	1604.19	2990.58	1360.67	1629.91

12－4 进出口总额超十亿美元企业(2006年)

单位:万美元 (USD 10000)

名称		进出口总额	进口	出口
名硕电脑(苏州)有限公司	Minshou Computer (Suzhou) Co. Ltd.	1627463	661181	966282
三星电子(苏州)半导体有限公司	Sanxing Electric(Suzhou) Semiconductor Co. Ltd.	815861	404154	411707
友达光电(苏州)有限公司	Yuanda Photoelectricty(Suzhou) Co. Ltd.	651534	417362	234172
仁宝资讯工业(昆山)有限公司	Renbao Communication Industrial(Kunsan) Co. Ltd.	553487	93331	460156
希捷国际科技(无锡)有限公司	Xijie International Science & Technology (Wuxi) Co. Ltd.	441606	210148	231457
苏州三星电子液晶显示器有限公司	Suzhou Sanxing Electronic Liquid Crystal Display Utensil Co. Ltd.	344857	174554	170302
昆山飞力仓储服务有限公司	Kunshan Feili Storage Service Co. Ltd.	330407	330407	
乐金飞利浦液晶显示(南京)有限公司	Lejing Philip Liquid Crystal Display(Nanjing) Co. Ltd.	309799	209209	100590
明基电通信息技术有限公司	Miji Telecommunication IT Co. Ltd.	294636	76822	217814
华宝通讯(南京)有限公司	Huabao Communication(Nanjing) Co. Ltd.	292790	133197	159592
无锡夏普电子元器件有限公司	Wuxi Sharp Electronic Component Co. Ltd.	264145	113114	151031
飞索半导体(苏州)有限公司	Feishu Semiconductor(Suzhou) Co. Ltd.	252031	89207	162824
仁宝信息技术(昆山)有限公司	Renbao Information Technology(Suzhou) Co. Ltd.	247354	30835	216519
迈拓科技(苏州)有限公司	Manto Science & Technology(Suzhou) Co. Ltd.	218144	72560	145584
海力士－意法半导体有限公司	Hailishi－Italy & France Semiconductor Co. Ltd.	200789	177831	22958
纬新资通(昆山)有限公司	Weixin Communication(Kunshan) Co. Ltd.	194453	30482	163971
华映视讯(吴江)有限公司	Huaying Video Communication(Wujiang) Co. Ltd.	171238	112961	58277
亚旭电子科技(江苏)有限公司	Yaxu Electronic Science & Technology (Jiangsu) Co. Ltd.	156430	67115	89315
江苏舜天国际集团有限公司	Jiangsu shentian International Group Co. Ltd.	153519	35831	117689
江苏苏美达集团公司	Jiangsu Sumeida Group Co. Ltd.	153209	72593	80616
仁宝电子科技(昆山)有限公司	Renbao Electronic Science & Technology (Kunshan) Co. Ltd.	147144	43245	103899
苏州飞利浦消费电子有限公司	Suzhou Philip Consumptive Electronic Co. Ltd.	144955	46189	98766

ENTERPRISES WITH A TOTAL OF IMPORT AND EXPORT VALUE EXCEEDING ONE BILLION USD (2006)

单位:万美元　　　　(USD 10000)

名称		进出口总额	进口	出口
旭电(苏州)科技有限公司	Xudian(Suzhou)Science & Technology Co. Ltd.	137476	81372	56104
南京瀚宇彩欣科技有限责任公司	Nanjing Hanyu Caixin Science & Technology Responsibility Co. Ltd.	137451	96412	41040
江苏国泰国际集团有限公司	Jiangsu Guotai International Group Co. Ltd.	135115	16020	119095
苏州三星电子电脑有限公司	Suzhou Sanxin Electronic Computer Co. Ltd.	135047	47790	87258
纬智资通(昆山)有限公司	Weizhi Communication(Kunshan) Co. Ltd.	134586	13767	120819
纬创资通(昆山)有限公司	Weicuang Communication(Kunshan) Co. Ltd.	131509	68185	63324
日立显示器件(苏州)有限公司	HATACHI Showing Utensil(Suzhou)Co. Ltd.	125401	65586	59815
江苏汇鸿国际集团有限公司	Jiangsu Huihong International Group Co. Ltd.	121947	13234	108714
江苏开元国际集团有限公司	Jiangsu Kaiyuan International Group Co. Ltd.	121218	40130	81088
英飞凌科技模组(苏州)有限公司	Yingfeiling Science & Technology Mould Component(Suzhou) Co. Ltd.	120164	32339	87825
索尼数字产品(无锡)有限公司	Sony Digital Products(Wuxi)Co. Ltd.	119675	33285	86390
江苏三房巷集团有限公司	Jiangsu Sanfangxiang Group Co. Ltd.	118984	84090	34894
南京LG同创彩色显示系统有限责任公司	Nanjing LG Ton Chuang Color Showing System Responsibility Co. Ltd.	118965	44983	73981
神迅电脑(昆山)有限公司	Shenxun Computer(Kunshan)Co. Ltd.	117058	48496	68562
苏州进出口(集团)有限公司	Suzhou Import and Export Group Co. Ltd.	117055	11618	105437
微盟电子(昆山)有限公司	Weimeng Electronic(Kunshan)Co. Ltd.	115321	51015	64306
昆达电脑科技(昆山)有限公司	Kunda Computer Science & Technology (Kunshan)Co. Ltd.	110188	47829	62359
佳能(苏州)有限公司	Jianeng(Suzhou)Co. Ltd.	106847	28680	78167
南京夏普电子有限公司	Ninjing Sharp Electronic Co. Ltd.	106460	55498	50962
志合电脑(苏州工业园区)有限公司	Zhihe Computer (Suzhou Industrial Park Zone)Co. Ltd.	106007	39947	66060
统宝光电(南京)有限公司	Tongbao Photoelectricity Co. Ltd.	105878	61323	44555
英飞凌科技(苏州)有限公司	Yingfeiling Science & Technology(Suzhou) Co. Ltd.	103712	67738	35974
天弘(苏州)科技有限公司	Tianhong(Suzhou)Science & Techonology Co. Ltd.	102664	54893	47770

12－5 按贸易方式和经济类型分的进出口总额
TOTAL IMPORTS AND EXPORTS BY TYPE OF TRADE AND OWNERSHIP

单位:万美元 (USD 10000)

项目	Item	1995		2000		2003	
		进口 Imports	出口 Exports	进口 Imports	出口 Exports	进口 Imports	出口 Exports
总计	**Total**	**649637**	**978166**	**1986857**	**2576979**	**5453078**	**5913965**
按贸易方式分	**Grouped by Type of Trade**						
一般贸易	General Trade	111328	591604	805495	1211041	1685708	2247981
来料加工装配贸易	Processing and Assembling Trade Provided with Raw Material	59356	62605	177242	230389	535835	616224
进料加工贸易	Raw Material Input Processing Trade	275754	322281	760323	1134768	2369003	3042645
来料加工装配进口的设备	Processing and Assembling Import Equipment Provided with Material	920		3250		7412	
外商作为投资进口的设备	Goods as Invested for Import Equipments	194066		205002		621062	
出料加工贸易	Raw Material Output Processing Trade	6	61	245	208	132	88
易货贸易	Replace Goods with Goods Trade	273	226	14			
保税仓库进出境货物	Import and Export Goods of Protcetive Tariff Storage	6454	282	19877	178	98602	1428
保税区仓储转口货物	Transit Goods of Storage in Protcetive Tariff Area			13505	175	108477	4520
按经济类型分	**Grouped by Ownership**						
#国有企业	State-owned Enterprises	156154	658499	341580	978705	616303	1218592
集体企业	Collective-owned Enterprises	6571	26014	69063	142478	170964	341308
外商投资企业	Foreign-funded Enterprises	485810	293481	1572744	1445478	4489180	4113516
#中外合作	Sino-Foreign Cooperative	21967	8481	19324	22813	21803	29638
中外合资	Sino-Foreign Joint Funded	342411	200544	688667	577231	1187650	1062970
外商独资	Foreign Funded	121432	84456	864753	845434	3279727	3020908

12－5 续表 Continued

单位:万美元 (USD 10000)

项目	Item	2004		2005		2006	
		进口 Imports	出口 Exports	进口 Imports	出口 Exports	进口 Imports	出口 Exports
总计	**Total**	**8335995**	**8749665**	**10495916**	**12298215**	**12357660**	**16041885**
按贸易方式分	**Grouped by Type of Trade**						
一般贸易	General Trade	2330934	3048526	2567227	4063266	2826514	5315091
来料加工装配贸易	Processing and Assembling Trade Provided with Raw Material	1284383	1032481	2206083	2136794	2606088	2823576
进料加工贸易	Raw Material Input Processing Trade	3481590	4663719	4281335	6068317	4795488	7789884
来料加工装配进口的设备	Processing and Assembling Import Equipment Provided with Material	12206		16598		25603	
外商作为投资进口的设备	Goods as Invested for Import Equipments	813164		713437		808564	
出料加工贸易	Raw Material Output Processing Trade	323	256	323	212	365	343
易货贸易	Replace Goods with Goods Trade		2				
保税仓库进出境货物	Import and Export Goods of Pro－tective Tariff Storage	167432	4048	480551	18072	809748	72862
保税区仓储转口货物	Transit Goods of Storage in Protec－tive Tariff Area	188153	5423	149628	6584	213943	12295
按经济类型分	**Grouped by Ownership**						
#国有企业	State-owned Enterprises	747453	1284597	724622	1437264	668662	1579037
集体企业	Collective-owned Enterprises	217800	379995	295997	424385	267035	446692
外商投资企业	Foreign-funded Enterprises	7031995	6522432	9051633	9422831	10739914	12361846
#中外合作	Sino-Foreign Cooperative	33172	37426	46125	50670	97208	94802
中外合资	Sino-Foreign Joint Funded	1658827	1543897	1988967	2004875	2392255	2398139
外商独资	Foreign Funded	5339996	4941109	7016541	7367286	8250451	9868906

12－6 进口商品分类总额
TOTAL VALUE OF IMPORTS BY CATEGORY OF COMMODITIES

单位:万美元 (USD 10000)

项目	Item	2000	2004	2005	2006
总额	**Total**	**1986857**	**8335995**	**10495916**	**12357660**
初级产品	**Primary Goods**	**243306**	**773154**	**970816**	**1138881**
#食品及活动物	Food and Living Animal	6992	20225	28847	32247
饮料及烟类	Beverages and Tobacco	24	105	44	180
非食用原料	Non-Edible Raw Materials	199534	603463	808066	904846
矿物燃料、润滑油及有关原料	Mineral Fuels, Lubricants and Related Raw Materials	32777	106324	107273	138831
动植物油、脂及蜡	Animal and Vegetable Oils,Fats and Waxes	3979	43037	26586	62777
工业制成品	**Manufactured Goods**	**1743551**	**7562841**	**9525099**	**11218779**
#化学成品及有关产品	Chemicals and Related Products	305997	1058072	1326580	1504635
按原料分类的制成品	Manufactured Goods Grouped by Raw Materials	361815	812478	971346	1110503
机械及运输设备	Machinery and Transport Equipment	968560	4072513	5290062	6515826
杂项制品	Miscellaneous Products	106909	1619779	1933346	2082266

12－7 出口商品分类总额
TOTAL VALUE OF EXPORTS BY CATEGORY OF COMMODITIES

单位:万美元 (USD 10000)

项目	Item	2000	2004	2005	2006
总额	**Total**	**2576979**	**8749665**	**12298215**	**16041885**
初级产品	**Primary Goods**	**83977**	**138574**	**157683**	**210543**
#食品及活动物	Food and Living Animal	44048	61932	72218	94228
饮料及烟类	Beverages and Tobacco	109	999	814	718
非食用原料	Non-Edible Raw Materials	25181	40378	52379	71289
矿物燃料、润滑油及有关原料	Mineral Fuels, Lubricants and Related Raw Materials	14026	33972	29711	38236
动植物油、脂及蜡	Animal and Vegetable Oils,Fats and Waxes	613	1292	2561	6072
工业制成品	**Manufactured Goods**	**2493002**	**8611091**	**12140532**	**15831342**
#化学成品及有关产品	Chemicals and Related Products	193596	456874	657343	817431
按原料分类的制成品	Manufactured Goods Grouped by Raw Materials	490649	1311139	1805190	2450890
机械及运输设备	Machinery and Transport Equipment	969493	4831114	7014182	9486590
杂项制品	Miscellaneous Products	839264	2011964	2661011	3072220

12－8 进出口商品细分类总额（2006 年）
VALUE OF IMPORTS AND EXPORTS BY CATEGORY OF COMMODITIES (2006)

单位：万美元　　(USD 10000)

项　目	Item	进出口总额 Total Improts and Exports Value	进　口 Imports	出　口 Exports
总　计	**Total**	**28399545**	**12357660**	**16041885**
初级产品	**Primary Goods**	**1349424**	**1138881**	**210543**
食品及活动物	**Food and Living Animal**	**126475**	**32247**	**94228**
活动物	Alive Animals	439	325	114
肉及肉制品	Meat and Related Products	9071	4709	4362
乳品及蛋品	Dairy Products and Eggs	1033	962	71
鱼、甲壳及软体类动物及制品	Fish, Shellfish and Molluscs	17069	1233	15836
谷物及其制品	Cereals and Related Products	7901	530	7371
蔬菜及水果	Vegetables and Fruits	55281	13952	41329
糖、糖制品及蜂蜜	Sugar, Sugar Products and Natural Honey	2597	232	2365
咖啡、茶、可可、调味料及制品	Coffee, Tea, Cocoa, Flouring and Related Products	9594	4043	5551
饲料	Forage	10271	4748	5523
杂项食品	Miscellaneous Food	13220	1514	11706
饮料及烟类	**Beverages and Tobacco**	**898**	**180**	**718**
#饮料	Beverages	884	167	717
非食用原料	**Non-Edible Materials**	**976135**	**904846**	**71289**
生皮及生毛皮	Raw Hides and Raw Furs	11340	11328	12
油籽及含油果实	Oil Seeds and Oil-bearing Fruits	138101	137692	409
生橡胶	Raw Rubber	69761	66078	3683
软木及木材	Cork and Wood	46307	39713	6594
纸浆及废纸	Paper Pulp and Paper Waste	157166	156872	294
纺织纤维及废料	Textile Fiber and Waste	202633	170130	32503
天然肥料及矿物	Natural Fertilizers and Minerals	31179	28631	2548
金属矿砂及金属废料	Metallic Ore and Metallic Waste	290218	287563	2655
其他动、植物原料	Other Raw Materials of Animals and Plants	29430	6840	22590
矿物燃料、润滑油及有关原料	**Mineral Fuels, Lubricants and Related Materials**	**177067**	**138831**	**38236**
#煤、焦炭及煤砖	Coal, Coke and Coal Brick	31485	15683	15802
石油、石油产品及有关原料	Petroleum, Petroleum Products and Related Materials	120148	97731	22417
天燃气及人造气	Natural Gas and Man-Made Gas	25435	25417	18
动植物油、脂及蜡	**Animal and Vegetable Oils and Wax**	**68849**	**62777**	**6072**
动物油、脂	Animal Oil, Fat	2268	859	1409
植物油、脂	Vegetable Oil, Fat	52389	48024	4365
已加工的动植物油、脂及蜡	Processed Animal and Vegetable Oils, Fats and Wax	14191	13893	298

12－8 续表 Continued

单位:万美元 (USD 10000)

指 标	Item	进出口总额 Total Improts and Exports Value	进 口 Imports	出 口 Exports
工业制成品	**Manufactured Goods**	**27050121**	**11218779**	**15831342**
化学成品及有关产品	**Chemicals and Related Products**	**2322066**	**1504635**	**817431**
有机化学品	Organic Chemicals	1141152	807136	334016
无机化学品	Inorganic Chemicals	124123	51980	72143
染料、鞣料及着色料	Dye, Tanning Material and Colouring Materials	98129	43863	54266
医药品	Medical and Pharmaceutical Products	70173	16244	53929
精油、香料及盥洗、光洁制品	Essential Oils, Perfumed Materials and Cosmetics	36575	15617	20958
制成肥料	Finished Fertilizers	4438	2249	2189
初级形状的塑料	Primary Shaped Plastics	406636	281718	124918
非初级形状的塑料	Non-Primary Shaped Plastics	181849	133589	48260
其他化学原料及产品	Other Chemical Materials and Related Products	258991	152239	106752
按原料分类的制成品	**Manufactured Goods Grouped by Materials**	**3561393**	**1110503**	**2450890**
皮革、皮革制品及已鞣毛皮	Leather and Related Products and Tanned Furs	49169	28600	20569
橡胶制品	Rubber and Related Products	140282	29768	110514
软木及木制品	Cork and Wooden Products	136517	4494	132023
纸及纸板;纸浆、纸及纸板制品	Paper, Paperboard and Related Products and Paper Pulp	158896	49412	109484
纺纱、织物、制成品及有关产品	Textile Fabrics, Textile Materials and Related Pro－ducts	1125176	205778	919398
非金属矿物制品	Non-Metallic Mineral Products	192867	69390	123477
钢铁	Iron and Steel	740333	314367	425966
有色金属	Nonferrous Metal	406885	269015	137870
金属制品	Metallic Products	611268	139680	471588
机械及运输设备	**Machinery and Transport Equipment**	**16002416**	**6515826**	**9486590**
动力机械及设备	Power-Driven Machinery and Related Equipment	268731	114951	153780
特种工业专用机械	Special Industrial Machinery of Particular Use	801773	618755	183018
金工机械	Metalworking Machinery	302738	250151	52587
通用工业机械设备及零件	Equipment and Accessories for General Industrial Machinery	826980	399113	427867
办公用机械及自动数据处理设备	Machinery for Office Use and Automatic Data－Pro－cessing Equipment	4827190	695900	4131290
电信及声音的录制及重放装置设备	Telecommunication and Recorders	2287446	334208	1953238
电力机械、器具及其电气零件	Electronic Machinery, Equipment and Accessories	6052589	4031507	2021082
陆路车辆	Overland Vehicles	484536	67413	417123
其他运输设备	Other Transport Equipment	150433	3828	146605
杂项制品	**Miscellaneous Products**	**5154486**	**2082266**	**3072220**
活动房屋;卫生、水道、供热及照明装置	Movable Houses, Public Health, Waterway, Heat Supply and Lighting Installation	43766	2164	41602
家具及其零件;褥垫及类似填充制品	Furniture and Accessories, Beddings and Filler Products and Similar Products for Stuffing	214184	4190	209994
旅行用品、手提包及类似品	Travel Articles, Handbag and Similar Articles	69400	855	68545
服装及衣着附件	Garments and Clothing Accessories	1286299	9030	1277269
鞋靴	Parts of Footwear	105799	5733	100066
专业、科学及控制用仪器和装置	Instruments and Equipment for Professional, Scien－tific and Control Use	2502218	1601160	901058
摄影器材、光学物品及钟表	Photographic and Optical Equipment and Clocks	356331	272159	84172
杂项制品	Miscellaneous Products	576490	186975	389515

12－9 按国家和地区分进出口额
IMPORTS AND EXPORTS VALUE BY COUNTRIES AND REGIONS

单位：万美元 (USD 10000)

国别（地区）	Countries (Districts)	2005 进出口 Imports and Exports	2005 进口 Imports	2005 出口 Exports	2006 进出口 Imports and Exports	2006 进口 Imports	2006 出口 Exports
亚洲	**Asia**	**13986654**	**8405469**	**5581185**	**16777394**	**9798286**	**6979108**
#巴林	Bahrain	3071	1222	1849	3283	710	2573
孟加拉国	Bangladesh	70192	670	69522	81565	990	80575
缅甸	Myanmar	7537	422	7115	10762	198	10565
柬埔寨	Cambodia	16205	187	16018	21533	191	21342
塞浦路斯	Cyprus	2214	7	2207	2687	1	2686
香港	Hong Kong	1512606	151670	1360936	1681799	124688	1557111
印度	India	223605	79883	143722	310936	87648	223288
印度尼西亚	Indonesia	211495	101777	109718	288856	149734	139122
伊朗	Iran	42046	6564	35482	56811	11704	45107
以色列	Israel	38779	10373	28406	50474	15098	35376
日本	Japan	3546745	1947085	1599660	4119492	2313090	1806402
科威特	Kuwait	12129	5611	6518	25009	13577	11432
澳门	Macao	4450	145	4305	5900	142	5758
马来西亚	Malaysia	656955	393724	263231	821696	441318	380378
巴基斯坦	Pakistan	29598	2177	27421	42262	4539	37723
菲律宾	Philippines	384405	313937	70468	487509	404871	82637
卡塔尔	Qatar	7458	4484	2973	13094	4847	8247
沙特阿拉伯	Saudi Arabia	103824	63558	40266	139962	64815	75148
新加坡	Singapore	581173	269416	311757	825183	335553	489630
韩国	Korea, Rep.	2705227	2168721	536506	2984843	2234568	750275
斯里兰卡	Sri Lanka	14169	190	13979	15504	392	15112
叙利亚	Syrian	10168	0	10168	16768	170	16598
泰国	Thailand	359857	238522	121335	530435	367943	162492
土耳其	Turkey	87156	4451	82705	126469	6599	119870
阿拉伯联合酋长国	United Arab Emirates	121551	14331	107220	184314	12234	172080
越南	Viet Nam	74911	11530	63381	103562	17654	85909
台湾省	Taiwan Province	2600973	2114357	486616	3059671	2498313	561358
非洲	**Africa**	**230389**	**48054**	**182335**	**317197**	**48140**	**269057**
#喀麦隆	Kameroon	1598	726	871	4733	3205	1529
埃及	Egypt	24857	2551	22306	32649	1040	31609
加蓬	Gabon	5421	5260	161	3708	3085	623
摩洛哥	Morocco	14233	2171	12063	16283	3003	13280
尼日利亚	Nigeria	30273	53	30220	39012	93	38919
南非	South Africa	81929	25367	56563	98792	22318	76474
欧洲	**Europe**	**3968102**	**915418**	**3052684**	**5184528**	**1110515**	**4074013**
#比利时	Belgium	160397	42581	117816	203300	48048	155252
丹麦	Denmark	44862	11007	33855	56425	11294	45131
英国	United Kindom	373133	53048	320085	468429	71906	396523

12－9 续表 Continued

单位:万美元 (USD 10000)

国别(地区)	Countries (Districts)	2005 进出口 Imports and Exports	2005 进口 Imports	2005 出口 Exports	2006 进出口 Imports and Exports	2006 进口 Imports	2006 出口 Exports
德国	Germany	1063231	324632	738599	1358301	420678	937624
法国	France	255889	62152	193737	309723	73737	235985
爱尔兰	Ireland	97548	4187	93362	140941	5684	135257
意大利	Italy	240675	78148	162527	320702	102595	218108
荷兰	Netherlands	721953	38523	683430	980307	70260	910047
希腊	Greece	26944	829	26115	32184	812	31372
葡萄牙	Portugal	15837	5818	10019	30423	3647	26776
西班牙	Spain	117886	17415	100471	202788	19473	183315
奥地利	Austria	35701	22003	13698	47171	29115	18056
芬兰	Finland	142155	38469	103686	134212	33247	100965
匈牙利	Hungary	57407	3754	53653	87063	5310	81753
挪威	Norway	23278	6220	17058	30707	7861	22847
波兰	Poland	68858	10397	58461	106174	7908	98266
罗马尼亚	Romania	13566	872	12693	19462	1409	18053
瑞典	Sweden	128990	83175	45814	144423	81479	62944
瑞士	Switzerland	55362	34348	21014	77116	42665	34451
俄罗斯联邦	Russia Fed.	123082	46546	76536	149127	34787	114339
乌克兰	Ukraine	39530	7470	32059	52964	7883	45082
捷克	Czech Rep.	51387	6075	45312	81279	8495	72785
拉丁美洲	**Latin America**	**579335**	**250918**	**328417**	**827139**	**292826**	**534314**
#阿根廷	Argentina	46801	29944	16857	64404	38130	26274
巴西	Brazil	194375	128136	66240	254513	151866	102647
智利	Chile	55907	32859	23048	63502	26998	36504
哥伦比亚	Colombia	12965	430	12535	20031	312	19719
危地马拉	Guatemala	9329	43	9286	13999	42	13957
墨西哥	Mexico	128974	28517	100457	211445	29062	182383
巴拿马	Panama	26190	17	26173	44811	10	44801
秘鲁	Peru	18184	10662	7522	23033	8578	14456
乌拉圭	Uruguay	5033	1494	3538	10870	5718	5152
委内瑞拉	Venezuela	13022	4816	8206	17931	1287	16644
北美洲	**North America**	**3618110**	**685589**	**2932521**	**4813803**	**901098**	**3912705**
#加拿大	Canada	296555	90460	206094	385320	10844	274476
美国	United States	3321120	595086	2726035	4428417	790254	3638163
大洋洲	**Oceania**	**411300**	**190227**	**221073**	**479246**	**206558**	**272688**
#澳大利亚	Australia	358082	164619	193464	400522	177812	222711
新西兰	New Zealand	38160	14886	23275	44417	16583	27834
巴布亚新几内亚	Papua New Guinea	10284	9483	801	10408	9795	613
附:东南亚国家联盟	Association of Southeast－Asia Nations	2293107	1329574	963533	3090734	1717619	1373114
欧洲联盟	European Union	3688524	811855	2876670	4820736	1008983	3811753
亚太经济合作组织	Asia-Pacific Economic Cooperation	17263615	9129778	8133836	21016148	10703301	10312848

12-10 主要商品进口数量和金额
MAJOR IMPORT COMMODITIES IN VOLUME AND VALUE

单位：数量：万吨 (10000 tons)
金额：万美元 (USD 10000)

商品名称	Item	2005 数量 Volume	2005 金额 Value	2006 数量 Volume	2006 金额 Value
谷物及谷物粉	Grain and Grain Powder	3	595	2	327
大豆	Soybean	474	137867	496	132211
食用植物油	Edible Vegetable Oil	48	19906	92	42018
其他植物油	Other Edible Vegetable Oil	7	4277	11	6006
天然橡胶	Natural Rubber	11	14298	16	30607
合成橡胶 （吨）	Synthetic Rubber (ton)	186020	29994	202121	35157
原木 （万立方米）	Log (10000 cu. m)	178	31450	185	31341
锯材 （立方米）	Wood Sawn (cu. m)	167823	5963	185777	7170
纸浆	Paper Pulp	195	97188	233	125475
羊毛 （吨）	Wool (ton)	110308	61863	122323	64050
纺织用合成纤维	Synthetic Fibre for Textile	19	35159	15	30290
纺织用人造纤维 （吨）	Man-made Fibre for Textile (ton)	12310	2043	5306	1143
铁矿砂及其精矿	Iron Ores	1849	151393	2443	171334
成品油	Petroleum Products Refined	49	27414	52	39937
苯乙烯	Styrene	157	167750	139	158128
乙二醇	Glycol	132	116247	129	109749
对苯二甲酸	Telephthalic Acid	196	156731	203	176276
医药品 （吨）	Medical and Pharmaceutical Products (ton)	1134	13158	1660	16286
合成有机染料 （吨）	Synthetic Organic Dyeing (ton)	5181	3228	5625	3903
钛白粉 （吨）	Titanium Dioxide (ton)	13162	2656	13274	2743
初级形状的塑料）	Primary Shaped Plastic	126	220640	144	270387
农药 （吨）	Chemical Pesticide (ton)	5107	3755	7235	4689
牛皮革及马皮革 （吨）	Cattle Leather and Horse Leather (ton)	34573	22773	35404	24906
纸及纸板	Paper and Paperboard	28	31304	35	44513
合成纤维纱线 （吨）	Synthetic Fabric (ton)	63069	20483	61643	19777
丝织物 （万米）	Silk and Satins (10000 m)	229	1212	195	1181
棉机织物 （万米）	Cotton Textiles (10000 m)	8241	28573	8151	27398
合成纤维长丝机织物 （万米）	Synthetic Fibre Filament Textiles (10000 m)	18320	41437	18503	41377
合成短纤与棉混纺机织物 （万米）	Synthetic Fiber and Blend Fabric of Cotton (10000 m)	1877	4801	1782	4691
涂覆或浸渍塑料的织物 （吨）	Coated Textiles for Industrial Use (ton)	6788	6725	8558	8712
针织或钩编织物 （吨）	Knitwear and Crocheted Fabrics (ton)	20184	19608	23599	22329
鞋靴零件;护腿及类似品	Parts of Footwear, Shinguard and Similar Articles	0	1193		1128
制电灯泡及类似品用玻璃外壳 （吨）	Glassware of Producing Electric bulbs and Similar Articles (ton)	4682	1676	1176	2481
废钢	Waste Steel	248	67473	134	36230
钢坯及粗锻件	Steel Base and Related Crude Forgings	27	17375	13	17368
钢材	Rolled Steel	271	331449	229	284110
未锻造的铜及铜材 （吨）	Unforging Copper and Copper Material (ton)	162856	85815	157654	134019
#铜材）	Copper	94132	61306	120015	109359
未锻造的铝及铝材 （吨）	Unforging Aluminium and Aluminium	119080	44864	130271	59634
#铝材	Aluminium	86747	39058	86663	48739
钢铁或铝制结构体及其部件 （吨）	Iron and Steel and Aluminium Units and Accessories (ton)	12409	4803	12959	5605

12－10 续表 Continued

单位：数量：万吨 (10000 tons)
　　　金额：万美元 (USD 10000)

商品名称	Item	2005 数量 Volume	2005 金额 Value	2006 数量 Volume	2006 金额 Value
活塞式内燃机的零件 (吨)	Parts of Piston Internal-combustion Engine (ton)	9141	12423	8149	14537
液泵及液体提升机 (万台)	Hydraulic Pumps and Lifters (10000 sets)	1200.40	19750	446.16	19761
制冷设备用压缩机 (万台)	Compressors for Refrigerating Equipment (10000 sets)	156	13659	148	12033
空气调节器 (台)	Air Conditioners (unit)	22136	2630	31282	2812
冷冻机和制冷设备	Refrigerating Equipment		11891		11283
机械提升搬运装卸设备及零件	Machine Lifting, Transporting and Loading and Unloading Equipment and Accessories		33898		48792
建筑及采矿用机械及零件	Construction and Mining Machinery and Spare Parts		21154		30073
食品加工机械及零件	Food Processing Machinery and Spare Parts		3307		1832
制造纸及纸制品用机械及零件	Paper and Related Articles Production Machinery		17709		17686
印刷、装订机械及零件	Printing and Bookbinding Machinery		17513		18667
纺织机械及零件	Textile Machinery		66794		118602
工业用缝纫机 (台)	Industrial Use Sewing Machine (unit)	14991	2784	8065	1870
金属加工机床 (台)	Machine Tools (unit)	23655	122831	25451	193116
金属冶炼铸造设备及零件	Metal Smelting and Forging Machines and Accessories		9093		14688
金属轧机及零件	Metal Rolling Machine and Accessories		3026		9304
玻璃热加工机械及零件	Glass Hot-working Machinery		4800		6331
橡胶或塑料加工机械及零件	Rubber and Plastic Processing Machinery		55795		62160
型模及金属铸造用型箱 (吨)	Metal Forging Molds (ton)	2368	29651	2514	28919
阀门 (万套)	Valves (10000 sets)	3671	23368	2568	29888
自动数据处理设备及其部件 (万台)	Automatic Data Processing Machines and Accessories (10000 units)	4474	190018	5266	219697
自动数据处理设备的零件 (吨)	Accessories of Automatic Data Processing Machines (ton)	52770	344769	41240	438005
电动机及发电机 (万台)	Electric Motors and Generators (10000 sets)	11417	28583	14893	33678
旋转式电力设备的零件 (吨)	Parts of Turning Electric Equipments (ton)	13335	7862	15718	9709
变压、整流、电感器及零件	Transformer, Recitifier, Inductance and Accessories		89423		114823
焊接机器及零件	Parts of Welding Machines		12063		15349
有线电话或电报交换机 (台)	Wired Telephone of Telegraphic Switchoard	172	140	400	121
有线电话电报设备的零附件 (吨)	Spare Parts of Line Telephonic and Telegraphic Equipments (ton)	1704	36099	1478	23053
未录的磁带及类似品	Unrecorded Tape and the Kinds		60445		89720
录放音、像机及唱机的零附件 (吨)	Accessories of Videorecorder, Camera and Gramophone (ton)	3461	31295	2133	23864
电视、收音机及无线电讯设备的零附件 (吨)	TV Sets, Radio and Spare Parts of Wireless Dispatch Equip－ments (tons)	19740	210630	23618	208827
电容器及其零件 (吨)	Condenser and Accessories (ton)	7124	84342	8089	106101
印刷电路	Printing Electric Appliance	402	179138	397	226528
通断及保护电路装置及零件	Electrical Apparatus and Spare Parts for Switching or Protec－ting Electrical Circuits		184564		232885
电视显像管 (万只)	Cathode－ray TV Picture Tube (10000 sets)	85	3362	48	1307
彩色数据/图形显示管 (万只)	Color Data/Picture Shower (10000 sets)	198	10064	40	2016
二极管、晶体管及类似半导体器件 (亿个)	Diodes, Transistors and Similar Semi Conductors (100 million units)	298	151925	328	176837
集成电路及微电子组件 (亿个)	Integrated Circuit and Micro－electronic Sets (100 million units)	130	2212634	163	2697333
电线和电缆 (吨)	Insulated Wire or Cable (ton)	32836	37692	36020	50509
汽车和汽车底盘 (辆)	Motor Vehicles and Chassis (unit)	1990	7926	4010	11537
汽车零件	Parts of Motor Vehicles		33490		44975
医疗仪器及器械	Medical Instruments and Appliances		13679		12917
计量检测分析自控仪器及器具	Automatic Instruments of Measuring, Examining and Analy－sing and Related Apparatus		148089		197046
塑料制品 (吨)	Plastic Products (ton)	47866	46872		57496
机电产品 (含以上列名商品)	**Mechanical and Electrical Products (Including the Listed Commodities above)**		**7247537**		**8645076**
高新技术产品 (含以上列名商品)	**High and New Tech Products (Including the Listed Commodities above)**		**4034263**		**5054563**

12－11 主要商品出口数量和金额
MAJOR EXPORT COMMODITIES IN VOLUME AND VALUE

单位：数量：万吨　金额：万美元　　(10000 tons)　(USD 10000)

商品名称	Item	2005 数量 Volume	2005 金额 Value	2006 数量 Volume	2006 金额 Value
冻鸡 (吨)	Frozen Chicken (ton)	2040	226	192	21
水海产品	Aquatic and Sea Products	4	6589	4	7671
谷物及谷物粉	Grain and Grain Power	1	310	3	709
蔬菜	Vegetables	36	21278	43	29918
干豆	Dry Beans	1	447	2	696
鲜、干水果及坚果	Flesh, Dried Fruits and Nuts		454		1720
食用油籽	Edible Oil Seeds	1	697	1	404
食用植物油 (吨)	Edible Vegetable Oil (ton)	10798	826	66910	4269
天然蜂蜜 (吨)	Natural Honey (ton)	10273	918	2879	344
茶叶 (吨)	Tea (ton)	4923	856	7740	1230
猪肉罐头 (吨)	Pork Can (ton)	1045	162	1227	169
蘑菇罐头 (吨)	Canned Mushroom (ton)	2967	225	5083	544
植物榨油后的剩余物	Surplus after Oil Pressing	17	4159	7	1586
猪鬃 (吨)	Bristle (ton)	2585	2083	237	1876
肠衣 (吨)	Casings (ton)	18245	9392	22487	11599
填充用羽毛、羽绒 (吨)	Feathers and Dawn (ton)	3987	4715	4183	4533
药材 (吨)	Crude Druges (ton)	3700	428	2312	407
生丝 (吨)	Raw Silk (ton)	943	2211	665	2015
兔毛 (吨)	Rabbit Hair (ton)	735	1312	884	1500
煤	Coal	190	13929	206	14209
合成有机染料 (吨)	Synthetic Organic Dye (ton)	37427	17945	3797	17366
医药品 (吨)	Medical and Pharmaceutical Products (ton)	60688	48267	64327	53935
新的充气橡胶轮胎 (万条)	Rubber Tyres (10000 units)	3714	60157	4238	82598
家用或装饰用木制品 (吨)	Wooden Products for Household and Decorated Use (ton)	18350	3315	18681	3847
纸及纸板	Paper and Paperboard	85	64257	121	89155
纺织纱线、织物及制品	Textile Yarn Thread, Woven Goods and Related Products		785162		920958
水泥	Cement	195	6538	499	17679
平板玻璃 (万平方米)	Plate Glass (10000 sq. m)	2501	7830	2882	8814
玻璃制品	Glass Products		19744		23338
家用陶瓷器皿 (吨)	Porcelain and Pottery Ware for Household Use (ton)	79194	7723	99777	10583
装饰用陶瓷制品 (吨)	Porcelain and Pottery Ware for Decoration (ton)	47388	2508	55822	3244
生铁及镜铁	Pig Iron and Spiegeleise	48	14219	26	7862
钢材	Rolled Steel	241	171088	575	389375
未锻造的铜及铜材 (吨)	Unforging Copper and Copper Material (ton)	93036	41510	101368	65596
未锻造的铝及铝材 (吨)	Unforging Aluminium and Aluminium Material (ton)	60689	19178	123366	40024
钢铁或铜制标准紧固件 (吨)	Iron and Steel, Copper Nails and Bolts (ton)	217106	27360	267782	35263
手用或机用工具 (吨)	Hand Tools and Tools for Machines (ton)	179047	58660	188454	68003
锁 (吨)	Locks (ton)	42273	14994	41312	17967
纺织机械及零件	Textile Machinery		18445		22435
普通缝纫机 (万台)	Ordinary Sewing Machines (10000 sets)	99	3829	131	55340
金属加工机床 (万台)	Machine Tools (10000 sets)	210	18748	189	26049

12－11 续表 Continued

单位：数量：万吨 (10000 tons)
金额：万美元 (USD 10000)

商品名称	Item	2005 数量 Volume	2005 金额 Value	2006 数量 Volume	2006 金额 Value
自动数据处理设备及其部件（万台）	Automatic Data Processing Equipment and Accessories (10000 units)	22457	2371411	27167	3033716
自动数据处理设备的零件（吨）	Spare Parts of Automatic Data Processing Equipment (tons)	148836	773607	173116	902076
轴承（万套）	Bearings (10000 units)	32324	15335	40648	18640
电动机及发电机（万台）	Electric Motors and Generators (10000 sets)	15729	34444	2121	53770
静止式变流器（万个）	Static Converters (10000 units)	19936	72025	33103	92821
原电池（万个）	Primary Cells and Batterices (10000 units)	35310	2860	35600	2923
手持或车载无线电话（万台）	Hand or Car Cordless Phones (10000 units)	2894	119781	6586	248806
扬声器（万个）	Loudspeakers (10000 units)	17469	18220	16910	20886
录音机及收录(放)音组合机（万台）	Sound Recording Apparatus (10000 sets)	160	9862	124	9842
电视机（万台）	TV sets (10000 sets)	962	210520	1113	304231
电视、收音机及无线电讯设备的零附件（吨）	TV Sets, Radio and Spare Parts of Wireless Dispatch Equipments (ton)	81175	516125	116286	680097
电容器（吨）	Electrical Capacitors (ton)	11521	35007	13798	44705
印刷电路	Printing Electric Appliance	156.33	125654	245.00	173618
通断及保护电路装置及零件	Eletrical Apparatus and Spare Parts for Switching or Protecting Electrical Circuits		62759		91073
二极管及类似半导体器件（亿个）	Diodes, Transistors and Similar Semi Conductors (100 million units)	318	78145	408	143910
集成电路及微电子组件（万个）	Integrated Circulate and Micro－Electronic Compositions (10000 units)	659329	415343	815061	649266
电线和电缆（吨）	Insulated Wire or Cable (ton)	94891	57928	138581	99125
集装箱（个）	Containers (unit)	203034	75433	381606	108685
汽车和汽车底盘（辆）	Motor Vechicles and Chassis (unit)	75083	13868	90506	32597
汽车零件	Parts of Motor Vehicles		93461		134060
自行车（万辆）	Bicycles (10000 units)	956	43285	890	43113
摩托车及自行车的零件	Motorbicycles and Parts of Bicycles		27871		34869
船舶（艘）	Ships (unit)	4771	63669	2479	139893
照相机（万架）	Cameras (10000 sets)	29	599	29	576
复印机（台）	Photocopier (unit)	745469	54205	2017693	125708
医疗仪器及器械	Medical Instruments and Appliances		26883		39010
家具及零件	Furniture and spore parts		115457		139306
床垫、寝具及类似品	Beddings and Similar Products		54315		70688
灯具、照明装置及类似品	Lamps and Lanterns, Lighting Installation and Similar Products		30268		34440
旅行用品及箱包	Travel Articles, Suitcases and Handbags and Similar Articles		57081		67638
服装及衣着附件	Garments and Clothing Accessories		1096489		1277956
鞋类	Parts of Footwear		88365		100066
塑料制品	Plastic Products	49	93512	58	117446
玩具	Toys		63637		71171
足球、篮球、排球（万个）	Footballs, Basketballs and Volleyballs (10000 units)	2731	3653	3434	5213
贵金属或包贵金属的首饰	Metal and Related Jewelry		2833		3366
柳编结品（吨）	Wickerwork (ton)	6239	1525	3810	801
鬃刷（万把）	Bristle Brushes (10000 doz.)	16948	2949	19832	3582
人造花（吨）	Man Made Flowers (ton)	2423	928	477	1366
热水瓶（万个）	Vacuum Flasks (10000 units)	586	2749	739	2815
机电产品（含以上列名商品）	**Mechanical and Electrical Products (Including the Listed Commodities above)**		**8402327**		**11137955**
高新技术产品（含以上列名商品）	**High and New Tech Products (Including the Listed Commodities above)**		**5247169**		**6996483**

12-12 合同外商直接投资项目

NUMBER OF CONTRACTED PROJECTS OF FOREIGN DIRECT INVESTMENT

单位:个 (unit)

指标	Item	2006年止累计 2006 Year end Accumu-lated	1990	1995	2000	2005	2006
合计	**Total**	**78757**	**395**	**4056**	**2645**	**7126**	**7016**
合资经营企业	Joint Venture	42535	358	2827	1119	1749	1883
合作经营企业	Cooperative Operation	2828	8	265	116	112	91
独资经营企业	Foreign Solely Funded	33369	29	964	1410	5259	5039
外商投资股份制企业	Share Holding with Foreign Investment	25				6	3

12-13 合同外商直接投资金额

VALUE OF CONTRACTED PROJECTS OF FOREIGN DIRECT INVESTMENT

单位:万美元 (USD 10000)

指标	Item	2006年止累计 2006 Year end Accumu-lated	1990	1995	2000	2005	2006
合计	**Total**	**28017339**	**24416**	**1296951**	**1061059**	**4643882**	**4654157**
合资经营企业	Joint Venture	7330220	14478	662155	348861	602054	586157
合作经营企业	Cooperative Operation	1129217	6640	67518	55431	73794	67634
独资经营企业	Foreign Solely Funded	19501513	3298	567278	656767	3949724	3997153
外商投资股份制企业	Share Holding with Foreign Investment	56389				18310	3213

12－14　实际外商直接投资金额
ACTUAL VALUE OF FOREIGN DIRECT INVESTMENT

单位：万美元　　　　(USD 10000)

指　　标	Item	1985～2006	1990	1995	2000	2001
外商直接投资	**Foreign Direct Investment**	**12039598**	**14110**	**478058**	**642358**	**712201**
合资经营企业	Joint Venture	4169236	13787	332166	227369	227166
合作经营企业	Cooperative Operation	490628	249	27684	35755	26180
独资经营企业	Foreign Solely Funded	7337641	74	118208	378946	457620
外商投资股份制企业	Share Holding with Foreign Investment	42093			288	1235

12－14　续表　Continued

单位：万美元　　　　(USD 10000)

指　　标	Item	2002	2003	2004	2005	2006
外商直接投资	**Foreign Direct Investments**	**1036615**	**1580214**	**1213783**	**1318339**	**1743140**
合资经营企业	Joint Venture	260969	334151	266231	248652	364883
合作经营企业	Cooperative Operation	29241	38229	29823	19130	21722
独资经营企业	Foreign Solely Funded	740698	1206690	903836	1041074	1356017
外商投资股份制企业	Share Holding with Foreign Investment	5707	1144	13893	9483	518

12－15　按行业分外商直接投资(2006年)
FOREIGN DIRECT INVESTMENT GROUPED BY SECTOR(2006)

单位:万美元　　　　　　　　　　　　　　　　　　　　　　　　　　　　　　　　　(USD 10000)

行　　业	Item	项　目(个) Number of Projects(unit)	合同外资 Contracted Foreign Capital	实际外资 Actual Investment
总计	**Total**	**7016**	**4654157**	**1743140**
农、林、牧、渔业	Farming, Forestry, Animal Husbandry and Fishery	120	66241	10818
采矿业	Mining and Quarrying	7	5509	3303
制造业	Manufacturing	5469	3491356	1371264
农副食品加工业	Food Processing	79	31850	15339
食品制造业	Food Production	80	36100	15511
饮料制造业	Beverage Production	25	23498	8038
纺织业	Textile Industry	333	154092	80839
纺织服装、鞋、帽制造业	Textile Garments, Shoes and Hats Products	649	219745	57809
皮革、毛皮、羽毛(绒)及其制品业	Leather, Furs, Down and Related Products	62	22736	6401
木材加工及木、竹、藤、棕、草制品业	Timber Processing and Wood, Bamboo, Rattan, Palm and Straw Works	61	37232	7052
家具制造业	Furniture Manufacturing	65	45220	9190
造纸及纸制品业	Papermaking and Paper Products	66	41735	43556
印刷业和记录媒介的复制	Printing and Record Processing	27	10195	5462
文教体育用品制造业	Stationery, Education and Sports Goods	93	36972	9424
石油加工、炼焦及核燃料加工业	Petroleum Processing, Coking Products and Nuclear Fuel Processing	8	11780	8793
化学原料及化学制品制造业	Raw Chemical Material and Chemical Products	243	178805	97802
医药制造业	Medical and Pharmaceutical Products	77	64347	15945
化学纤维制造业	Chemical Fibers	21	32421	20418
橡胶制品业	Rubber Products	38	28747	19979
塑料制品业	Plastic Products	221	74313	35099
非金属矿物制品业	Nonmetal Mineral Products	187	101243	49766
黑色金属冶炼及压延加工业	Smelting and Processing of Ferrous Metals	8	5897	22873
有色金属冶炼及压延加工业	Smelting and Processing of Nonferrous Metals	77	64856	26342
金属制品业	Metal Products	289	176549	69916

12－15 续 表 Continued

单位:万美元 (USD 10000)

行 业	Item	项 目(个) Number of Projects(unit)	合同外资 Contracted Foreign Capital	实际外资 Actual Investment
通用设备制造业	Ordinarly Machinery Manufacturing	541	309726	91119
专用设备制造业	Special Purpose Equipment Manufacturing	622	380322	80838
交通运输设备制造业	Transportation Equipment Manufacturing	281	216122	82737
电气机械及器材制造业	Electric Machinery and Equipment	518	405211	117843
通信设备、计算机及其他电子设备制造业	Telecommunication Equipments, Computer and Other Electronic Equipment Manufaturing	606	690411	343362
仪器仪表及文化、办公用机械制造业	Instruments, Meters, Cultural and Official Machinery	111	56850	20842
工艺品及其他制造业	Handicraft Artical and Other Manufacturing	77	33456	8062
废弃资源和废旧材料回收加工业	Waste Resouces and Junk Material Recycled	4	925	927
电力、燃气及水的生产和供应业	Electric Power, Gas and Water Production and Supply	55	56071	47716
建筑业	Construction	61	61284	18041
交通运输、仓储和邮政业	Transportation, Storage and Post	71	85624	28868
信息传输、计算机服务和软件业	Information Transmmision, Computer Service and Software	103	24042	3982
批发和零售业	Wholesale and Retail Trade	203	70674	39659
住宿和餐饮业	Hotel and Catering Services	112	48132	11814
金融业	Finance	1	1400	1000
房地产业	Real Estate Trade	474	580242	163304
租赁和商务服务业	Leasing and Commercial Services	208	82002	16848
科学研究、技术服务和地质勘查业	Scientific Research, Polytechnical Services and Geological Prospecitng	55	21791	3114
水利、环境和公共设施管理业	Water Conservance, Environment and Public Facility Management	15	13990	11296
居民服务和其他服务业	Resident Services and Others	26	16915	6174
教育	Education	1	291	105
卫生、社会保障和社会福利业	Health Care, Social Security and Social Welfare	2	439	1026
文化、体育和娱乐业	Culture, Sports and Recreation	33	28154	4808

12－16 按国家或地区分外商直接投资

FOREIGN DIRECT INVESTMENT BY COUNTRIES OR DISTRICTS

单位:万美元 (USD 10000)

国家和地区 Countries and Districts		2006年止累计 Aconmulated at the end of 2006			2000		
		项目(个) Number of Projects (unit)	合同外资 Contracted Foreign Capital	实际投资 Actual Investment	项目(个) Number of Projects (unit)	合同外资 Contracted Foreign Capital	实际投资 Actual Investment
合计	**Total**	**78757**	**28017339**	**12039598**	**2645**	**1061059**	**642358**
亚洲	**Asia**				**1751**	**500061**	**392755**
#香港	Hong Kong	27077	7801368	2954512	595	204658	153648
澳门	Macao	638	141397	45588	19	2073	2061
台湾	Taiwan Province	14261	3337168	1030207	584	131101	58096
印度尼西亚	Indonesia	262	127512	42669	7	1426	1495
日本	Japan	6122	2063353	1265920	252	73320	63311
马来西亚	Malaysia	575	322390	117239	16	17763	2035
菲律宾	Philippines	238	86379	23743	14	1254	372
新加坡	Singapore	2751	1708677	1079708	82	38291	76055
韩国	Korea, Rep.	3162	1109583	553930	143	21004	21746
泰国	Thailand	529	157219	45624	11	2566	2661
非洲	**Africa**				**26**	**13292**	**5654**
欧洲	**Europe**				**183**	**229324**	**97738**
#比利时	Belgium	97	39455	39760	5	2996	3682
丹麦	Denmark	86	41509	26025	5	2439	1578
英国	United Kindom	854	455227	226806	39	28359	20789
德国	Germany	1000	485616	287876	47	134191	11299
法国	France	497	198566	125208	17	10804	14408
爱尔兰	Ireland	20	4485	1173			
意大利	Italy	497	169137	104244	18	23894	11727
卢森堡	Luxembourg	35	38860	12330	1	517	580
荷兰	Netherlands	273	274217	192944	7	13372	22210
希腊	Greece	8	414	139			
葡萄牙	Portugal	17	1958	1007	2	343	
西班牙	Spain	215	77381	29372	4	220	270
芬兰	Finland	49	31950	9943	2	3938	860
瑞士	Switzerland	127	67568	36297	3	1402	2482
拉丁美洲	**Latin America**				**176**	**172081**	**70850**
北美洲	**North America**				**419**	**109750**	**62955**
#加拿大	Canada	1540	376779	95600	62	9460	4189
美国	United States	8566	2432007	938202	352	93696	56973
大洋洲	**Oceania**				**89**	**35819**	**10706**
#澳大利亚	Australia	1461	375543	98998	54	8247	4049

12－16 续 表 Continued

单位:万美元 (USD 10000)

国家和地区 Countries and Districts		2005			2006		
		项目(个) Number of Projects (unit)	合同外资 Contracted Foreign Capital	实际投资 Actual Investment	项目(个) Number of Projects (unit)	合同外资 Contracted Foreign Capital	实际投资 Actual Investment
合计	**Total**	**7126**	**4643882**	**1318339**	**7016**	**4654157**	**1743140**
亚洲	**Asia**	**4653**	**2749773**	**715551**	**4806**	**2981661**	**921409**
#香港	Hong Kong	1988	1301538	295406	2302	1626456	431682
澳门	Macao	37	12026	3745	38	24786	6747
台湾	Taiwan Province	1105	512826	60802	1061	545951	80969
印度尼西亚	Indonesia	22	21779	2320	22	21704	8837
日本	Japan	528	328382	170088	432	252706	141389
马来西亚	Malaysia	69	44243	15555	67	52216	16653
菲律宾	Philippines	13	9630	4187	17	8560	2469
新加坡	Singapore	252	175204	70505	260	175278	81950
韩国	Korea, Rep.	447	254894	80475	432	207020	130687
泰国	Thailand	43	37735	2190	16	10026	4035
非洲	**Africa**	**149**	**101808**	**30123**	**129**	**113440**	**52681**
欧洲	**Europe**	**629**	**334925**	**119772**	**543**	**217325**	**165425**
#比利时	Belgium	13	6058	2189	8	4561	4914
丹麦	Denmark	11	6948	1571	8	6463	6003
英国	United Kindom	116	54032	13564	94	34865	20327
德国	Germany	129	50687	36479	109	19398	33028
法国	France	62	29522	16971	54	20705	10222
爱尔兰	Ireland	4	3105	649	2	439	452
意大利	Italy	72	41808	5853	80	25258	7214
卢森堡	Luxemboury	7	7418	4473	7	7088	4281
荷兰	Netherlands	44	51993	13632	36	54152	38892
希腊	Greece	1	20	22	1	7	0
葡萄牙	Portugal			161	3	291	90
西班牙	Spain	38	20118	7131	41	11775	8775
芬兰	Finland	7	2225	282	6	2773	2119
瑞士	Switzerland	23	12032	6747	15	4497	8361
拉丁美洲	**Latin America**	**545**	**595994**	**258338**	**474**	**623192**	**350161**
北美洲	**North America**	**881**	**478601**	**83693**	**794**	**339373**	**123036**
#加拿大	Canada	170	63601	8556	199	66031	15000
美国	United States	701	389834	70904	593	265108	91353
大洋洲	**Oceania**	**406**	**290006**	**66932**	**389**	**271492**	**87415**
#澳大利亚	Australia	138	70698	8003	119	58081	20951

12－17　年末登记外商投资企业行业分布情况(2006 年)
SECTOR DISTRIBUTION REGISTERED OF FOREIGN　FUNDED ENTERPRISES AT THE YEAR－END(2006)

行　业	Item	企业数(个) Number of Registered Enterprises (unit)	投资总额(万美元) Total Investment (USD 10000)	注册资本(万美元) Registered Capital (USD 10000)	#外方 Capital Invested by Foreign Partner
总计	**Total**	**36463**	**32426088**	**16536042**	**14087208**
农、林、牧、渔业	Farming, Forestry, Animal Husbandry and Fishery	498	720085	132605	119025
采矿业	Mining and Quarrying	20	46267	26546	17456
制造业	Manufacturing	30519	25992292	13337846	11452559
电力、燃气及水的生产和供应业	Electric Power, Gas and Water Production and supply	252	869381	329041	196392
建筑业	Construction	337	308522	199398	168608
交通运输、仓储和邮政业	Transportation, Storage and Post service	264	495404	252494	172431
信息传输、计算机服务和软件业	Information Transmmision, Computer Service and Software	405	222548	108478	105346
批发和零售业	Wholesale and Retail Trade	464	204529	116226	94352
住宿和餐饮业	Hotel and Catering Services	414	230723	130591	109294
金融业	Finance	11	19173	11784	11770
房地产业	Real Estate Trade	1588	2177413	1265553	1099505
租赁和商务服务业	Leasing and Commercial Services	728	346450	223560	203731
科学研究、技术服务和地质勘查业	Scientific Research, Polytechnical Services and Geological Prospecitng	315	346957	157423	143913
水利、环境和公共设施管理业	Water Conservancy, Environment and Public Facility Management	72	122871	63979	44880
居民服务和其他服务业	Resident Services and Others Services	324	123697	67817	59643
教育	Education	12	4239	2236	1541
卫生、社会保障和社会福利业	Health Care, Social Security and Social Welfare	18	43595	18067	12952
文化、体育和娱乐业	Culture, Sports and Recreation	188	126632	79469	66772
其他	Other	34	25310	12929	7038

12－18　对外承包工程和劳务合作

CONTRACTED PROJECTS AND LABOR SERVICES CO－OPERATION WITH FOREIGN COUNTRIES

年　份 Year	合　同　数(份) Number of Contracts (unit)	合同金额 (万美元) Contracted Value (USD 10000)	实际完成营业额 (万美元) Value of Business Fulfilled (USD 10000)	年末在外人数(人) Number of Persons Abroad at the year-end(person)
总　计　Total				
1985	88	2966		
1990	77	4046	4046	1271
1995	309	28113	25928	8206
1996	312	36379	29048	12372
1997	427	47621	38465	15046
1998	652	62476	52166	23223
1999	805	81531	61263	32425
2000	1066	97983	80083	43051
2001	1454	125790	113206	65369
2002	1245	171692	155902	73683
2003	1253	208649	197512	79053
2004	3748	245052	248113	91086
2005	2318	330973	319738	100280
2006	5445	468098	435416	112421
对外承包工程 Contracted Projects				
1985	13	262		
1990	32	3571	3521	881
1995	101	19495	19774	2946
1996	148	24040	22725	3298
1997	239	34599	31011	5997
1998	224	38224	34878	5784
1999	273	52110	34636	7403
2000	306	58544	49722	8616
2001	513	71200	62747	8320
2002	587	133743	105403	10992
2003	642	174201	142671	13449
2004	3317	213267	188958	21073
2005	1853	290079	251095	30211
2006	4975	426788	376509	38432
对外劳务合作 Labor Cooperation				
1985	75	2704		
1990	45	475	525	390
1995	205	8591	6120	5260
1996	163	12253	6287	9068
1997	188	13022	7454	9049
1998	427	24250	17271	17439
1999	523	29286	26538	25012
2000	754	39394	30293	34426
2001	911	48689	45316	56852
2002	622	37401	49989	62670
2003	597	33444	53984	65576
2004	421	31322	56974	69984
2005	464	40451	68056	70049
2006	467	41243	58843	73984
对外设计咨询 Design consulting				
2002	36	548	510	21
2003	14	1004	857	28
2004	10	463	2181	29
2005	1	443	587	20
2006	3	67	64	5

12－19 接待海外旅游者人数和收入
NUMBER OF OUERSEAS TOURISTS RECEIVED AND EARNINGS

指标	Item	1990	1995	2000	2005	2006
接待人数（人次）	**Number of Received Tourists (person-times)**	**724826**	**767692**	**1609439**	**3783023**	**4451921**
外国人	Foreigners	235720	503278	981486	2621472	3148877
亚洲	Asia			630705	1597371	1828925
日本	Japan	82559	175849	299176	635260	828797
菲律宾	Philippines	1577	2591	4436	21791	17235
新加坡	Singapore	9057	37170	58513	133521	155240
泰国	Thailand	5197	6494	19623	63427	62695
印度尼西亚	Indonesia	1390	8308	14548	36298	33868
马来西亚	Malaysia		21893	115748	232236	223920
韩国	Korea		23560	96849	353345	404588
其他	Others			21812	121493	102582
美洲	America			131620	388015	495158
美国	United States	17681	40815	108455	303362	391297
加拿大	Canada	3726	7402	17388	65294	80198
其他	Others			5777	19359	23663
欧洲	Europe			168221	496143	657814
英国	United Kingdom	6081	19590	28567	77726	125216
法国	France	6397	22091	32960	77917	106479
德国	Germany	9158	27052	30394	119195	167115
意大利	Italy	4448	16103	19239	51965	56988
瑞士	Switzerland			4842	14938	17540
瑞典	Sweden			5652	21332	25995
俄罗斯	Russia Fed.	1568	1668	7024	21867	33508
西班牙	Spain		8112	7162	29474	28919
其他	Others			32381	81729	96054
大洋洲	Oceania			24537	100238	118294
澳大利亚	Australia	3016	6533	20522	73928	92665
其他	Others			4015	26310	25629
非洲及其他	Africa and Others			26403	39705	48686
香港同胞	Hong Kong Chinese	82481 (Hong Kong and Macao)	146636 (Hong Kong and Macao)	248958	413467	474148
澳门同胞	Macao Chinese			21653	36501	43017
台湾同胞	Taiwan Chinese	406625	117778	357342	711583	785879
接待人天数（人天）	**Number of Received (Person-days)**	**1090121**	**1734032**	**6103764**	**14369090**	**17681940**
外国人	Foreigners	399150	1193235	3669436	10071313	12435508
香港同胞	Hong Kong Chinese	142527 (Hong Kong and Macao)	281358 (Hong Kong and Macao)	557459	1387882	1707261
澳门同胞	Macao Chinese			65491	121217	208943
台湾同胞	Taiwan Chinese	548444	259439	1811378	2788678	3330228
旅游外汇收入（万美元）	**Foreign Exchange Earnings From Touricm (10000 USD)**	**7064**	**25988**	**72384**	**225974**	**278664**

12－20　分市接待海外旅游者人数
NUMBER OF OVERSEAS TOURISTS RECEIVED BY CITIES

指　　标	Item	1990	1995	2000	2005	2006
接待人数	**Number of Received Tourists**	**724826**	**767692**	**1609439**	**3783023**	**4451921**
（人次）	**（person-times）**					
南京市	Nanjing City	263345	231704	419006	876279	1009166
无锡市	Wuxi City	142873	150553	283739	616786	713052
徐州市	Xuzhou City	4325	4988	17825	73010	100488
常州市	Changzhou City	6570	19474	33067	181966	218593
苏州市	Suzhou City	261601	245700	566672	1185892	1379723
南通市	Nantong City	9594	29556	58257	151305	180616
连云港市	Lianyungang City	2400	4488	11518	53758	68891
淮安市	Huaian City	797	2513	6307	21634	24918
盐城市	Yancheng City	1206	3017	10903	40710	45807
扬州市	Yangzhou City	15701	38177	85477	238649	300711
镇江市	Zhenjiang City	16414	37522	104906	306482	363806
泰州市	Taizhou City			9082	29249	34847
宿迁市	Suqian City			2680	7303	11303
接待天数	**Number of Receptive Days**	**1090121**	**1734032**	**6103764**	**14369090**	**17681940**
（人天）	**（person-days）**					
南京市	Nanjing City	462279	554895	1843992	3727063	4216399
无锡市	Wuxi City	187801	324836	699695	1494466	1819363
徐州市	Xuzhou City	10318	19749	320888	521027	677756
常州市	Changzhou City	17506	80119	283173	894506	1136846
苏州市	Suzhou City	319285	475323	1159069	3562266	4327083
南通市	Nantong City	33093	100342	413186	931749	1124839
连云港市	Lianyungang City	11746	18290	130841	353333	481352
淮安市	Huaian City	1938	6262	112055	198218	265771
盐城市	Yancheng City	3555	11667	180299	245070	321047
扬州市	Yangzhou City	22190	82199	325179	969662	1321754
镇江市	Zhenjiang City	20410	60350	404583	1062850	1457154
泰州市	Taizhou City			161615	305715	391755
宿迁市	Suqian City			69189	103165	140821

注：1990、1995年扬州包括泰州，淮安包括宿迁。

Note：In 1990 and 1995，Taizhou was included in Yangzhou，Suqian was included in Huaian.

12－21 国内旅游人数和收入
TOTAL NUMBER OF DOMESTIC TOURISTS AND EARNINGS FORM DOMESTIC TOURISM

项　　目	Item	1995	2000	2003	2005	2006
接待人数（万人次）	**Number of Received Tourists (person-times)**	**4403.40**	**7191.53**	**11423.82**	**17234.26**	**19935.79**
南京市	Nanjing City	764.66	1272.70	2223.92	3189.66	3700.01
无锡市	Wuxi City	841.08	1127.77	1765.16	2637.50	3032.89
徐州市	Xuzhou City	177.84	360.09	583.58	993.59	1148.50
常州市	Changzhou City	331.30	428.33	817.10	1282.78	1502.00
苏州市	Suzhou City	821.06	1496.05	2350.17	3656.87	4135.34
南通市	Nantong City	228.44	319.88	514.97	743.08	882.87
连云港市	Lianyungang City	120.12	308.49	501.58	700.28	802.51
淮安市	Huaian City	299.85	280.89	406.10	549.85	635.15
盐城市	Yancheng City	258.18	328.80	415.09	529.91	610.86
扬州市	Yangzhou City	301.20	436.66	685.33	1113.05	1316.10
镇江市	Zhenjiang City	259.67	442.75	670.23	1166.97	1380.60
泰州市	Taizhou City		286.02	349.87	488.28	567.10
宿迁市	Suqian City		103.10	140.72	182.44	221.86
国内旅游收入（亿元）	**Earnings from Domestic Tourism (100 million yuan)**	**261.07**	**587.52**	**975.00**	**1625.62**	**2012.15**
南京市	Nanjing City	51.55	101.08	209.88	328.20	405.48
无锡市	Wuxi City	48.85	101.75	167.33	280.07	351.49
徐州市	Xuzhou City	8.18	23.87	42.68	76.81	96.87
常州市	Changzhou City	22.12	36.10	70.13	114.42	140.01
苏州市	Suzhou City	44.42	125.22	211.87	380.28	465.46
南通市	Nantong City	16.29	28.24	40.24	65.13	79.96
连云港市	Lianyungang City	7.97	24.21	41.23	61.06	75.79
淮安市	Huaian City	12.81	12.48	21.34	34.55	44.15
盐城市	Yancheng City	18.70	29.46	30.44	38.04	46.47
扬州市	Yangzhou City	19.14	37.26	50.99	92.36	115.10
镇江市	Zhenjiang City	11.04	41.93	54.02	103.48	127.61
泰州市	Taizhou City		20.46	27.40	41.01	50.47
宿迁市	Suqian City		5.46	7.45	10.21	13.27

注：1995 年扬州包括泰州，淮安包括宿迁。

Note: In 1995, Taizhou was included in Yangzhou, Suqian was included in Huaian.

12－22 开发区基本情况（2006 年）
BASIC CONDITIONS OF DEVELOPMENT ZONES（2006）

名称	Name	业务总收入（亿元）Total Business Income（100 million yuan）	地方一般预算收入（万元）Local General Budgetary Revenue（10000 yuan）
全省开发区总计	**Total**	**33724.51**	**4955928**
国家级	**State Level**		
南通经济技术开发区	Nantong Economic Technology Development Zone	483.00	97573
连云港经济技术开发区	Lianyungang Economic Technology Development Zone	325.00	58517
昆山经济技术开发区	Kunshan Economic Technology Development Zone	2407.28	210000
苏州工业园区	Suzhou Industrial Park Zone	2561.15	525860
南京经济技术开发区	Nanjing Economic Technology Development Zone	1358.02	101371
张家港保税区	Zhangjiagang Bonded Zone	1271.29	60006
南京高新技术产业开发区	Nanjing High－new Tech Industrial Development Zone	708.11	77072
常州高新技术产业开发区	Changzhou High－new Tech Industry Development Zone	982.81	204431
苏州高新技术产业开发区	Suzhou High－new Tech Industry Development Zone	2000.02	303674
无锡高新技术产业开发区	Wuxi High－new Tech Industry Development Zone	2236.14	352900
宜兴环保科技工业园	Yixing Environment and Tech Industrial Park Zone	125.60	25712
苏州太湖国家旅游度假区	Suzhou Taihu Lake National Tour and Holiday Zone	75.33	17317
无锡太湖国家旅游度假区	Wuxi Taihu Lake National Tour and Holiday Development Zone	120.52	19600
省级	**Provincial Level**		
镇江经济开发区	Zhenjiang Economic Development Zone	522.60	64504
扬州经济开发区	Yangzhou Economic Development Zone	514.40	101500
淮安经济开发区	Huaian Economic Development Zone	139.50	30161
徐州经济开发区	Xuzhou Economic Development Zone	301.00	34790
盐城经济开发区	Yancheng Economic Development Zone	201.58	37898
泰州经济开发区	Taizhou Economic Development Zone	211.12	22129
宿迁经济开发区	Suqian Economic Development Zone	32.99	15666
江宁经济开发区	Jiangning Economic Development Zone	710.36	147512
南京化学工业园区	Nanjing Chemical Industrial Park Zone	687.80	14184
六合经济开发区	Liuhe Economic Development Zone	120.15	40816
南京浦口经济开发区	Nanjing Pukou Economic Development Zone	135.05	34195
溧水经济开发区	Lishui Economic Development Zone	121.97	19531
江苏高淳经济开发区	Jiangsu Gaochun Economic Development Zone	90.58	12011

12－22 续表1 Continued 1

名　　称	Name	业务总收入（亿元）Total Business Income (100 million yuan)	地方一般预算收入（万元）Local General Budgetary Revenue (10000 yuan)
江阴经济开发区	Jiangyin Economic Development zone	1510.38	96932
锡山经济开发区	Xishan Economic Development Zone	550.04	72000
江苏无锡蠡园高新技术产业园区	Jiangsu Wuxi Liyuan High－New Tech Iudustrial Park Zone	164.70	26291
江苏无锡惠山经济开发区	Jiangsu Wuxi Huishan Economic Development Zone	247.21	29308
江苏宜兴陶瓷产业园区	Jiangsu Yixing Pottery and Porcelain Industrial Park Zone	36.02	7592
常熟经济开发区	Changshu Economic Development Zone	980.37	120212
江苏常熟东南经济开发区	Changshu Southeask Economic Development Zone	111.59	25750
江苏太仓港经济开发区	Jiangsu Taicang Port Economic Development Zone	512.44	135818
苏州吴中经济开发区	Suzhou Wuzhong Economic Development Zone	381.24	91081
吴江经济开发区	Wujiang Economic Development Zone	870.08	77122
江苏吴江汾湖经济开发区	Jiangsu Wujiang Fenhu Lake Economic Development Zone	238.04	45720
张家港经济开发区	Zhangjiagang Economic Development Zone	460.57	66988
苏州浒墅关经济开发区	Suzhou Xushiguan Economic Development Zone	80.53	35865
苏州相城经济开发区	Suzhou Xiangcheng Economic Development Zone	43.89	13053
江苏常州天宁经济开发区	Changzhou Tianning Economic Development Zone	223.01	28795
常州外向型农业综合开发区	Changzhou outside-Oriented Agricultural Comprehensive Development Zone	160.58	37880
江苏武进高新技术产业园区	Jiangsu Wujin High－new Tech Industrial Park Zone	402.83	75105
常州戚墅堰经济开发区	Changzhou Qishuyan Economic Development Zone	85.26	22158
溧阳经济开发区	Liyang Economic Development Zone	249.19	45218
金坛经济开发区	Jintan Economic Development Zone	156.38	31698
常州钟楼经济开发区	Changzhou Zhonglou Economic Development Zone	130.19	35252
江苏武进经济开发区	Jiangsu Wujin Economic Development Zone	20.04	5500
丹阳经济开发区	Danyang Economic Development Zone	292.12	22100
扬中经济开发区	Yangzhong Economic Development Zone	0.01	7586
句容经济开发区	Jurong Economic Development Zone	95.68	11274
丹徒经济开发区	Dantu Economic Development Zone	77.36	3820
江苏南通崇川经济开发区	Jiangsu Nantong Chongchuan Economic Development Zone	159.14	24800
通州经济开发区	Tongzhou Economic Development Zone	260.09	38264
如东经济开发区	Rudong Economic Development Zone	174.02	22000
海门经济开发区	Haimen Economic Development Zone	260.29	46330
如皋经济开发区	Rugao Economic Development Zone	169.50	23000
南通港闸经济开发区	Nantong Gangzha Economic Development Zone	218.84	34920
启东经济开发区	Qidong Economic Development Zone	161.36	21657
江苏海安经济开发区	Jiangsu Haian Economic Development Zone	205.91	29290
靖江经济开发区	Jingjiang Economic Development Zone	229.97	34030

12－22 续表 2 Continued 2

名称	Name	业务总收入（亿元）Total Business Income（100 million yuan）	地方一般预算收入（万元）Local General Budgetary Revenue（10000 yuan）
泰兴经济开发区	Taixing Economic Development Zone	135.09	32560
姜堰经济开发区	Jiangyan Economic Development Zone	112.90	13023
兴化经济开发区	Xinghua Economic Development Zone	67.55	4173
仪征经济开发区	Yizheng Economic Development Zone	110.84	22648
高邮经济开发区	Gaoyou Economic Development Zone	60.89	8869
宝应经济开发区	Baoying Economic Development Zone	67.52	11969
江都经济开发区	Jiangdu Economic Development Zone	187.14	25405
江苏淮安工业园区	Jiangsu Huaian Economic Development Zone	42.92	4290
射阳经济开发区	Sheyang Economic Development Zone	110.03	7000
阜宁经济开发区	Funing Economic Development Zone	103.50	7800
江苏大丰经济开发区	Jiangsu Dafeng Economic Development Zone	38.00	5500
江苏响水经济开发区	Jiangsu Xiangshui Economic Development Zone	30.66	3300
铜山经济开发区	Tongshan Economic Development Zone	98.31	17520
江苏丰县经济开发区	Jiangsu Fengxian Economic Development Zone	45.55	5800
江苏东海经济开发区	Jiangsu Donhai Economic Development Zone	38.36	5057
赣榆经济开发区	Ganyu Economic Development Zone	70.87	12200
南京珍珠泉旅游度假区	Nanjing Peal Spring Tourism Holiday Zone	0.43	
溧阳天目湖旅游度假区	Liyang Tianmuhu Lake Tourism	37.25	12897
昆山旅游度假区	Kunshan Tourism Holiday Zone		
（淀山湖旅游度假中心）	(Dianshanhu Lake Tourism Holiday Center)	9.56	2066
（阳澄湖旅游度假中心）	(Yangchenghu Lake Tourism Holiday Center)	9.32	6656
无锡太湖山水城旅游度假区	Wuxi Taihu Lake Mountain, Water and City Tourism Holiday Zone	103.24	17601
南通外向型农业综合开发区	Nantong Outside－oriented Agricultural Comprehensive Development Zone	113.96	13528
射阳外向型农业综合开发区	Sheyang Outside－oriented Agricultural Comprehensive Development Zone	17.58	1826
赣榆海洋经济开发区	Ganyu ocean Economic Developmonl zone	9.80	880
大丰海洋经济开发区	Dafeng ocean Economic Developmonl zone	59.63	7000
吕四海洋经济开发区	Lushi ocean Economic Developmonl zone	65.28	8670
南京栖霞经济开发区	Nanjing Qixia Economic Developmonl zone	26.18	10026
南京雨花经济开发区	Nanjing Yuhua Economic Development Zone	30.05	9823
南京江宁滨江经济开发区	Nanjing Jiangning Riverside Economic Development Zone	45.23	5386
南京白下高新技术产业园区	Nanjing Baixia High－New Tech Industrial Park Zone	38.59	12875
江苏无锡经济开发区	Jiangsu Wuxi Economic Development Zone	117.53	12950
江苏无锡硕放工业园区	Jiangsu Wuxi Shuofang Industrial Park Zone	80.38	18200
江苏宜兴经济开发区	Jiangsu Yixing Economic Development Zone	98.66	12875
江苏江阴临港经济开发区	Jiangsu jiangyin Linggang Economic Development Zone	869.45	80000
江苏昆山高新技术产业园区	Jiangsu Kunshan High－New Tech Industrial Park Zone	940.58	189600

12－22 续表3 Continued 3

名 称 Name		业务总收入（亿元）Total Business Income (100 million yuan)	地方一般预算收入（万元）Local General Budgetary Revenue (10000 yuan)
江苏昆山花桥经济开发区	Jiangsu Kunshan Huaqiao Economic Development Zone	91.13	22368
江苏常州新北工业园区	Jiangsu Changzhou New North Industrial Park Zone		
江苏镇江京口工业园区	Jiangsu Zhengjiang Jingkou Industrial Park Zone	30.52	1452
江苏镇江润州工业园区	Jiangsu Zhengjiang Runzhou Industrial Park Zone	20.55	2511
江苏海门工业园区	Jiangsu Haimen Industrial Park Zone	29.11	4513
江苏泰州海陵工业园区	Jiangsu Taizhou Hailing Industrial Park Zone	31.04	22345
江苏泰州高港高新技术产业园区	Jiangsu Taizhou Gaogang High－New Tech Industrial Park Zone	0.00	4600
江苏江阴－靖江工业园区	Jiangsu Jiangyin－Jingjiang Industrial Park Zone	57.51	4008
江苏扬州维扬经济开发区	Jiangsu Yangzhou Weiyang Economic Development Zone	61.16	11326
江苏扬州邗江经济开发区	Jiangsu Yangzhou Hanjiang Economic Development Zone	67.97	18500
江苏扬州化学工业园区	Jiangsu Yangzhou Chemical Industrial Park Zone	45.36	6500
江苏楚州经济开发区	Jiangsu Chuzhou Economic Development Zone	26.71	4123
江苏淮阴经济开发区	Jiangsu Huaiying Economic Development Zone	43.08	5080
江苏金湖经济开发区	Jiangsu Jinhu Economic Development Zone	21.98	8432
江苏盱眙经济开发区	Jiangsu Xuyi Economic Development Zone	55.90	7000
江苏洪泽经济开发区	Jiangsu Hongze Economic Development Zone	30.89	4435
江苏涟水经济开发区	Jiangsu Lianshui Economic Development Zone	48.21	3028
江苏亭湖经济开发区	Jiangsu Tinghu Economic Development Zone	86.71	7802
江苏盐都经济开发区	Jiangsu Yandu Economic Development Zone	120.40	10600
江苏东台经济开发区	Jiangsu Dongtai Economic Development Zone	42.36	4945
江苏滨海经济开发区	Jiangsu Binhai Economic Development Zone	18.60	3860
江苏建湖经济开发区	Jiangsu Jianhu Economic Development Zone	65.02	8016
江苏徐州工业园区	Jiangsu Xuzhou Industrial Park Zone	6.32	685
江苏新沂经济开发区	Jiangsu Xinyi Economic Development Zone	34.21	12000
江苏睢宁经济开发区	Jiangsu Shuining Economic Development Zone	17.00	1739
江苏沛县经济开发区	Jiangsu Peixian Economic Development Zone	35.63	4786
江苏邳州经济开发区	Jiangsu Pizhou Economic Development Zone	54.33	20560
江苏连云经济开发区	Jiangsu Lianyun Economic Development Zone	26.00	8707
江苏海州经济开发区	Jiangsu Haizhou Economic Development Zone	20.12	4080
江苏灌云经济开发区	Jiangsu guanyun Economic Development Zone	4.21	1484
江苏连云港化学工业园区	Jiangsu Lianyungang Chemical Industrial Park Zone	19.65	4650
江苏宿城经济开发区	Jiangsu Sucheng Economic Development Zone	22.98	9840
江苏沭阳经济开发区	Jiangsu Shuyang Economic Development Zone	37.68	9096
江苏泗洪经济开发区	Jiangsu Sihong Economic Development Zone	31.00	11500
江苏宿豫经济开发区	Jiangsu Suyu Economic Development Zone	32.27	8081
江苏泗阳经济开发区	Jiangsu Siyang Economic Development Zone	33.86	9964

12－22 续表4 Continued 4

名 称 Name		进出口总额（万美元）Total Value of Import and Export (10000 USD)	#出口额 Export Value	实际外商直接投资额（万美元）Actual Value of Foreign Direct Investment (10000 USD)
全省开发区总计	**Total**	**21021353**	**11403417**	**1397584**
国家级	**State Level**			
南通经济技术开发区	Nantong Economic Technology Development Zone	169471	106210	30458
连云港经济技术开发区	Lianyungang Economic Technology Development Zone	124425	51675	17005
昆山经济技术开发区	Kunshan Economic Technology Development Zone	3499512	2088795	74529
苏州工业园区	Suzhou Industrial Park Zone	4990541	2504101	159847
南京经济技术开发区	Nanjing Economic Technology Development Zone	904379	337307	16900
张家港保税区	Zhangjiagang Bonded Zone	345475	57061	18961
南京高新技术产业开发区	Nanjing High－new Tech Industrial Development Zone	106836	44168	6630
常州高新技术产业开发区	Changzhou High－new Tech Industry Development Zone	306344	191541	37245
苏州高新技术产业开发区	Suzhou High－new Tech Industry Development Zone	3484875	2041011	84726
无锡高新技术产业开发区	Wuxi High－new Tech Industry Development Zone	1860828	1039237	158085
宜兴环保科技工业园	Yixing Environment and Tech Industrial Park Zone	20721	17845	7267
苏州太湖国家旅游度假区	Suzhou Taihu Lake National Tour and Holiday Zone	5607	3267	869
无锡太湖国家旅游度假区	Wuxi Taihu Lake National Tour and Holiday Development Zone	6513	3178	2703
省级	**Provincial Level**			
镇江经济开发区	Zhenjiang Economic Development Zone	205226	61340	27322
扬州经济开发区	Yangzhou Economic Development Zone	200826	146781	22376
淮安经济开发区	Huaian Economic Development Zone	51466	30976	3443
徐州经济开发区	Xuzhou Economic Development Zone	100883	58287	8745
盐城经济开发区	Yancheng Economic Development Zone	48142	1847	11263
泰州经济开发区	Taizhou Economic Development Zone	66979	51804	10875
宿迁经济开发区	Suqian Economic Development Zone	4323	1986	1645
江宁经济开发区	Jiangning Economic Development Zone	517128	260800	34722
南京化学工业园区	Nanjing Chemical Industrial Park Zone	1328	588	11467
六合经济开发区	Liuhe Economic Development Zone	33602	30053	7265
南京浦口经济开发区	Nanjing Pukou Economic Development Zone	9927	8482	6434
溧水经济开发区	Lishui Economic Development Zone	7391	6109	1777
江苏高淳经济开发区	Jiangsu Gaochun Economic Development Zone	8842	7598	1439

12－22 续表5 Continued 5

名　　称　Name		进出口总额(万美元) Total Value of Import and Export (10000 USD)	#出口额 Export Value	实际外商直接投资额(万美元) ActualValue of Foreign Direct Investment (10000 USD)
江阴经济开发区	Jiangyin Economic Development Zone	207471	116947	31013
锡山经济开发区	Xishan Economic Development Zone	159832	80310	26384
江苏无锡蠡园高新技术产业园区	Jiangsu Wuxi Liyuan High－New Tech Iudustrial Park Zone	22887	15732	3078
江苏无锡惠山经济开发区	Jiangsu Wuxi Huishan Economic Development Zone	16089	9015	5178
江苏宜兴陶瓷产业园区	Jiangsu Yixing Pottery and Porcelain Industrial Park Zone	3407	3235	58
常熟经济开发区	Changshu Economic Development Zone	342074	209101	37968
江苏常熟东南经济开发区	Changshu Southeask Economic Development Zone	63106	41226	17830
江苏太仓港经济开发区	Jiangsu Taicang Port Harbour Area Development Zone	92115	35239	31116
苏州吴中经济开发区	Suzhou Wuzhong Economic Development Zone	187615	104423	27199
吴江经济开发区	Wujiang Economic Development Zone	1177012	576054	29433
江苏吴江汾湖经济开发区	Jiangsu Wujiang Fenhu Lake Economic Development Zone	48577	31342	5400
张家港经济开发区	Zhangjiagang Economic Development Zone	258654	122040	22150
苏州浒墅关经济开发区	Suzhou Xushiguan Economic Development Zone	50		6519
苏州相城经济开发区	Suzhou Xiangcheng Economic Development Zone	35130	22811	8817
江苏常州天宁经济开发区	Changzhou Tianning Economic Development Zone	19819	17464	3290
常州外向型农业综合开发区	Changzhou outside－Oriented Agricultural Comprehensive Development Zone	16821	14240	4324
江苏武进高新技术产业园区	Jiangsu Wujin High－new Tech Industrial Development Zone	120408	82633	12105
常州戚墅堰经济开发区	Changzhou Qishuyan Economic Development Zone	7420	7162	5386
溧阳经济开发区	Liyang Economic Development Zone	18699	16453	5358
金坛经济开发区	Jintan Economic Development Zone	30275	24747	9354
常州钟楼经济开发区	Changzhou Zhonglou Economic Development Zone	15245	10319	7060
江苏武进经济开发区	Jiangsu Wujin Economic Development Zone	1558	1446	3193
丹阳经济开发区	Danyang Economic Development Zone	31620	24727	6438
扬中经济开发区	Yangzhong Economic Development Zone	8775	4518	505
句容经济开发区	Jurong Economic Development Zone	18480	11896	5837
丹徒经济开发区	Dantu Economic Development Zone	2201	913	938
江苏南通崇川经济开发区	Jiangsu Nantong Chongchuan Economic Development Zone	73333	43098	9417
通州经济开发区	Tongzhou Economic Development Zone	51776	43012	14666
如东经济开发区	Rudong Economic Development Zone	19627	16172	21395
海门经济开发区	Hanmen Economic Development Zone	31612	25258	28325
如皋经济开发区	Rugao Economic Development Zone	14636	12123	15012
南通港闸经济开发区	Nantong Gangzha Economic Development Zone	92555	70263	7177
启东经济开发区	Qidong Economic Development Zone	14398	11839	31463
江苏海安经济开发区	Jiangsu Haian Economic Development Zone	24397	19742	20347
靖江经济开发区	Jingjiang Economic Development Zone	37063	30963	9206

12－22 续表6 Continued 6

名 称 Name		进出口总额（万美元）Total Value of Import and Export (10000 USD)	#出口额 Export Value	实际外商直接投资额（万美元）Actual Value of Foreign Direct Investment (10000 USD)
泰兴经济开发区	Taixing Economic Development Zone	16976	9124	13172
姜堰经济开发区	Jiangyan Economic Development Zone	11920	8147	7944
兴化经济开发区	Xinghua Economic Development Zone	2130	1731	910
仪征经济开发区	Yizheng Economic Development Zone	6685	4533	9216
高邮经济开发区	Gaoyou Economic Development Zone	2986	2869	2063
宝应经济开发区	Baoying Economic Development Zone	10097	6533	1291
江都经济开发区	Jiangdu Economic Development Zone	17169	13464	9004
江苏淮安工业园区	Jiangsu Huaian Economic Development Zone	6043	4335	1201
射阳经济开发区	Sheyang Economic Development Zone	3192	2070	187
阜宁经济开发区	Funing Economic Development Zone	2361	2130	2152
江苏大丰经济开发区	Jiangsu Dafeng Economic Development Zone	3397	3348	1631
江苏响水经济开发区	Jiangsu Xiangshui Economic Development Zone	609	608	
铜山经济开发区	Tongshan Economic Development Zone	5180	4651	1789
江苏丰县经济开发区	Jiangsu Fengxian Economic Development Zone	1477	978	519
江苏东海经济开发区	Jiangsu Donhai Economic Development Zone	5038	3635	4913
赣榆经济开发区	Ganyu Economic Development Zone	1287	1180	3597
南京珍珠泉旅游度假区	Nanjing Peal Spring Tourism Holiday Zone			240
溧阳天目湖旅游度假区	Liyang Tianmuhu Lake Tourism	863	863	6333
昆山旅游度假区	Kunshan Tourism Holiday Zone			
（淀山湖旅游度假中心）	(Dianshanhu Lake Tourism Holiday Center)	2577	2358	
（阳澄湖旅游度假中心）	(Yangchenghu Lake Tourism Holiday Center)	847	621	117
无锡太湖山水城旅游度假区	Wuxi Taihu Lake Mountain, Water and City Tourism Holiday Zone	8135	7139	1275
南通外向型农业综合开发区	Nantong Outside－oriented Agricultural Comprehensive Development Zone	4125	3220	7554
射阳外向型农业综合开发区	Sheyang Outside－oriented Agricultural Comprehensive Development Zone	92	92	154
赣榆海洋经济开发区	Ganyu ocean Economic Developmonl zone	434	365	174
大丰海洋经济开发区	Dafeng ocean Economic Developmonl zone	3186	3141	1711
吕四海洋经济开发区	Lushi ocean Economic Developmonl zone	3001	2938	2980
南京栖霞经济开发区	Nanjing Qixia Economic Developmonl zone	6269	4965	1651
南京雨花经济开发区	Nanjing Yuhua Economic Development Zone	1647	1355	1229
南京江宁滨江经济开发区	Nanjing Jiangning Riverside Economic Development Zone	3392	2425	3973
南京白下高新技术产业园区	Nanjing Baixia High－New Tech Industrial Park Zone	30929	25816	
江苏无锡经济开发区	Jiangsu Wuxi Economic Development Zone	17008	10756	
江苏无锡硕放工业园区	Jiangsu Wuxi Shuofang Industrial Park Zone	5864	1639	1820
江苏宜兴经济开发区	Jiangsu Yixing Economic Development Zone	11576	10521	8259
江苏江阴临港经济开发区	Jiangsu jiangyin Linggang Economic Development Zone	88196	41560	1311
江苏昆山高新技术产业园区	Jiangsu Kunshan High－New Tech Industrial Park Zone	257901	112166	18470

名 称 Name		进出口总额（万美元）Total Value of Import and Export (10000 USD)	#出口额 Export Value	实际外商直接投资额（万美元）Actual Value of Foreign Direct Investment (10000 USD)
江苏昆山花桥经济开发区	Jiangsu Kunshan Huaqiao Economic Development Zone	15006	9549	
江苏常州新北工业园区	Jiangsu Changzhou New North Industrial Park Zone			
江苏镇江京口工业园区	Jiangsu Zhengjiang Jingkou Industrial Park Zone	3991	3990	2252
江苏镇江润州工业园区	Jiangsu Zhengjiang Runzhou Industrial Park Zone	1403	1382	929
江苏海门工业园区	Jiangsu Haimen Industrial Park Zone			
江苏泰州海陵工业园区	Jiangsu Taizhou Hailing Industrial Park Zone	5578	4788	4285
江苏泰州高港高新技术产业园区	Jiangsu Taizhou Gaogang High－New Tech Industrial Park Zone	23221	18623	6336
江苏江阴－靖江工业园区	Jiangsu Jiangyin－Jingjiang Industrial Park Zone			
江苏扬州维扬经济开发区	Jiangsu Yangzhou Weiyang Economic Development Zone	7685	6963	3476
江苏扬州邗江经济开发区	Jiangsu Yangzhou Hanjiang Economic Development Zone	6969	5706	3115
江苏扬州化学工业园区	Jiangsu Yangzhou Chemical Industrial Park Zone	12239	1451	2270
江苏楚州经济开发区	Jiangsu Chuzhou Economic Development Zone	1398	1313	67
江苏淮阴经济开发区	Jiangsu Huaiying Economic Development Zone	3670	3062	381
江苏金湖经济开发区	Jiangsu Jinhu Economic Development Zone	4352	4138	739
江苏盱眙经济开发区	Jiangsu Xuyi Economic Development Zone	240	171	774
江苏洪泽经济开发区	Jiangsu Hongze Economic Development Zone	207	166	154
江苏涟水经济开发区	Jiangsu Lianshui Economic Development Zone	2912	2780	723
江苏亭湖经济开发区	Jiangsu Tinghu Economic Development Zone			960
江苏盐都经济开发区	Jiangsu Yandu Economic Development Zone	4081	1098	2913
江苏东台经济开发区	Jiangsu Dongtai Economic Development Zone	462	306	795
江苏滨海经济开发区	Jiangsu Binhai Economic Development Zone	72	1	53
江苏建湖经济开发区	Jiangsu Jianhu Economic Development Zone	321	299	175
江苏徐州工业园区	Jiangsu Xuzhou Industrial Park Zone	227	227	453
江苏新沂经济开发区	Jiangsu Xinyi Economic Development Zone	7645	3264	1073
江苏睢宁经济开发区	Jiangsu Shuining Economic Development Zone	6212	1531	266
江苏沛县经济开发区	Jiangsu Peixian Economic Development Zone	493	48	1273
江苏邳州经济开发区	Jiangsu Pizhou Economic Development Zone	7253	7007	2670
江苏连云经济开发区	Jiangsu Lianyun Economic Development Zone	3014	3010	3152
江苏海州经济开发区	Jiangsu Haizhou Economic Development Zone	4456	3663	258
江苏灌云经济开发区	Jiangsu guanyun Economic Development Zone	0	0	0
江苏连云港化学工业园区	Jiangsu Lianyungang Chemical Industrial Park Zone	114	102	1907
江苏宿城经济开发区	Jiangsu Sucheng Economic Development Zone	1092	1006	293
江苏沭阳经济开发区	Jiangsu Shuyang Economic Development Zone	1124	1123	606
江苏泗洪经济开发区	Jiangsu Sihong Economic Development Zone	970	968	524
江苏宿豫经济开发区	Jiangsu Suyu Economic Development Zone	4305	4322	435
江苏泗阳经济开发区	Jiangsu Siyang Economic Development Zone	1725	1574	500

主要统计指标解释

进出口总额 海关进出口总额指实际进出我国国境的货物总金额。包括对外贸易实际进出口货物,来料加工装配进出口货物,国家间、联合国及国际组织无偿援助物资和赠送品,华侨、港澳台同胞和外籍华人捐赠品,租赁期满归承租人所有的租赁货物,进料加工进出口货物,边境地方贸易及边境地区小额贸易进出口货物(边民互市贸易除外),中外合资企业、中外合作经营企业、外商独资经营企业进出口货物和公用物品,到、离岸价格在规定限额以上的进出口货样和广告品(无商业价值、无使用价值和免费提供出口的除外),从保税仓库提取在中国境内销售的进口货物,以及其他进出口货物。进出口总额用以观察一个国家在对外贸易方面的总规模。我国规定出口货物按离岸价格统计,进口货物按到岸价格统计。

商品经营单位所在地进、出口额 指所在地海关注册登记的有进出口经营权的企业实际进、出口额。

商品目的地进口额和商品货源地出口额 目的地进口额指进口货物的消费、使用或最终抵运地的实际进口额,货源地出口额是指出口货物的产地或原始发货地的实际出口额。

外商直接投资 指外国企业和经济组织或个人(包括华侨、港澳台胞以及我国在境外注册的企业)按我国有关政策、法规,用现汇、实物、技术等在我国境内开办外商独资企业、与我国境内的企业或经济组织共同举办中外合资经营企业、合作经营企业或合作开发资源的投资(包括外商投资收益的再投资)。2005 年外商直接投资为经过商务部确认数。

对外承包工程 指各对外承包公司以招标议标承包方式承揽的下列业务:(1)承包国外工程建设项目,(2)承包我国对外经援项目,(3)承包我国驻外机构的工程建设项目,(4)承包我国境内利用外资进行建设的工程项目,(5)与外国承包公司合营或联合承包工程项目时我国公司分包部分,(6)对外承包兼营的房屋开发业务。对外承包工程的营业额是以货币表现的本期内完成的对外承包工程的工作量,包括以前年度签订的合同和本年度新签订的合同在报告期内完成的工作量。

对外劳务合作 指以收取工资的形式向业主或承包商提供技术和劳动服务的活动。我国对外承包公司在境外开办的合营企业,中国公司同时又提供劳务的,其劳务部分也纳入劳务合作统计。劳务合作营业额按报告期内向雇主提交的结算数(包括工资、加班费和奖金等)统计。

旅游者人数

(1)入境国际旅游者人数:指来中国参观、访问、旅行、探亲、访友、休养、考察、参加会议和从事经济、科技、文化、教育、宗教等活动的外国人、华侨、港澳同胞和台湾同胞的人数。不包括外国在我国的常驻机构,如使领馆、通讯社、企业办事处的工作人员;来我国常住的外国专家、留学生以及在岸逗留不过夜人员。

(2)出境居民人数:指大陆居民因公务活动或私人事务短期出境的人数。公务活动出境居民人数包括在国际交通工具上的中国服务员工,因私出境居民人数不包括在国际交通工具上的中国服务员工。

(3)国内旅游者人数:指我国大陆居民和在我国常住 1 年以上的外国人、华侨、港澳台同胞离开常住地在境内其他地方的旅游设施内至少停留一夜,最长不超过 6 个月的人数。

国际旅游(外汇)收入 指入境旅游的外国人、华侨、港澳同胞和台湾同胞在中国大陆旅游过程中发生的一切旅游支出,对于国家来说就是国际旅游(外汇)收入。

Explanatory Notes on Main Statistical Indicators

Total Imports and Exports at Customs refer to the value of commodities imported into and exported from the boundary of China. They include the actual imports and exports through foreign trade, imported and exported goods under the processing and assembling trades and materials, supplies and gifts as aid given gratis between governments and by the United Nations and other international organizations, and contributions donated by overseas Chinese, compatriots in Hong Kong and Macao and Chinese with foreign citizenship, leasing commodities owned by tenant at the expiration of leasing period, the imported and exported commodities processed with imported materials, commodities trading in border areas (excluding mutual exchange goods), the imported and exported commodities and articles for public use of the Sino-foreign joint ventures, cooperative enterprises and ventures exclusively with foreign own investment. Also included are import or export of samples and advertising goods for whose CIF or FOB value are beyond the permitted ceiling (excluding goods of no trading or use value and free commodities for export), imported goods sold in China from bonded warehouses and other imported or exported goods. The indicator of the total imports and exports at customs can be used to observe the total size of external trade in a country. In accordance with the stipulation of the Chinese government, imports are calculated at CIF, while exports are calculated at FOB.

Import Export Value by Location of Chinas Foreign Trade Managing Units refers to actual value of imports and exports carried out by corporations which have been registered by the local customhouse and are vested with fight to run import export business.

Import Value of Commodities by the Places of their Destination and Export Value of Commodities by the Places of their Origin in China: The former indicator refers to the value of import commodities of the places of their consumption, utilization or the places of their final destination. The latter indicator refers to the value of export commodities of the places of their origin or the places of the commodities dispatched. Foreign direct innestment of 2005 was the volume affirmed by the commercial department.

Direct Investment by Foreign Entrepreneurs refers to the investments inside China by foreign enterprises and economic organizations or individuals (including overseas Chinese, compatriots from Hong Kong and Macao, and Chinese enterprises registered abroad), following the relevant policies and laws of China, for the establishment of ventures exclusively with foreign own investment, Sino-foreign joint ventures and cooperative enterprises or for co-operative exploration of resources with enterprises or economic organizations in China. It includes the re investment of the foreign entrepreneurs with the profits gained from the investment. Foreign direct investment of 2005 was the volume affirmed by the Commercial Department.

Contracted Projects with Foreign Countries refer to projects undertaken by Chinese contractors (project contracting companies) through bidding process. They include: (1) overseas civil engineering construction projects financed by foreign investors; (2) overseas projects financed by the Chinese government through its foreign aid programs; (3) construction projects of Chinese diplomatic missions, trade offices and other institutions stationed abroad; (4) construction projects in China financed by foreign investment; (5) sub-contracted projects to be taken by Chinese contractors through a joint umbrella project with foreign contractor(s); (6) housing development projects. The business income from international contracted projects is the work volume of contracted projects completed during the reference period, expressed in monetary terms, including completed work on projects signed in previous years.

Service Cooperation with Foreign Countries refers to the activities of providing technology and labour services to employers or contractors in the forms of receiving salaries and wages. Labour services providing by contractual joint ventures of Chinese international contracting corporations should be included in the statistics of service co-operation with foreign countries. The business income of labour service co operation is the income in the form of wages and salaries, overtime pay, bonuses and other remuneration received from the employers during the reference period.

Number of Tourists

(1) International tourists refer to foreigners, overseas Chinese, Chinese compatriots from Hong Kong, Macao and Taiwan coming to China for sight-seeing, visits, tours, family reunions, vacations, study tours, conferences and other activities of a business, scientific and technological, cultural, educational and religious nature. It does not include representatives and employees of resident institutions of foreign countries in China such as embassies, consulates, news agencies and offices of foreign companies and organizations, nor does it include long-term foreign experts or students residing in China, or persons in transition without spending a night in China.

(2) Chinese residents going abroad refer to Chinese residents going abroad for short terms for either public business or private purposes. Chinese employees working on international transport carriers are included in those going abroad for public business purpose, not in those for private purpose.

(3) Domestic tourists refer to residents of the mainland of China who stay for one night at least but no more than 6 months at tourist facilities in other places than their permanent residence within the territory of the mainland China, including foreigners, overseas Chinese and Chinese compatriots from Hong Kong, Macao and Taiwan who have resided in China for over one year.

Foreign Exchange Earnings from International Tourism refer to the total expenditures of foreigners, overseas Chinese, Chinese compatriots from Hong Kong, Macao and Taiwan during their stay in the mainland of China, which are earnings of foreign exchange from international tourism from the point of view from China.

JIANGSU STATISTICAL YEARBOOK

第13篇

财政、金融、保险

GOVERNMENT FINANCE,BANKING AND INSURANCE

13－1 历年财政收支

FINANCIAL REVENUE AND EXPENDITURE OVER THE YEARS

年 份 Year	财政总收入 Total Financial Revenue	#地方财政收入 Local Financial Revenue	#地方一般预算收入 General Budgetary Revenue	#各项税收 Government Taxes Revenue	地方财政支出 Local Financial Expenditure	#地方一般预算支出 Local General Budgetary Expenditure
1950	3.95	3.95	3.95	3.89	0.76	0.76
1951	5.32	5.32	5.32	5.10	0.98	0.98
1952	6.80	6.80	6.80	6.30	2.11	2.11
1953	7.78	7.78	7.78	7.18	2.50	2.50
1954	8.67	8.67	8.67	7.93	2.88	2.88
1955	8.47	8.47	8.47	7.76	2.88	2.88
1956	9.66	9.66	9.66	8.49	4.08	4.08
1957	10.10	10.10	10.10	8.56	4.80	4.80
1958	17.82	17.82	17.82	10.97	11.27	11.27
1959	24.94	24.94	24.94	12.53	14.36	14.36
1960	26.19	26.19	26.19	12.52	17.52	17.52
1961	17.45	17.45	17.45	9.68	8.66	8.66
1962	13.31	13.31	13.31	9.76	6.23	6.23
1963	13.70	13.70	13.70	9.11	6.64	6.64
1964	17.24	17.24	17.24	10.44	9.54	9.54
1965	19.40	19.40	19.40	11.79	8.07	8.07
1966	22.89	22.89	22.89	12.97	9.05	9.05
1967	17.02	17.02	17.02	11.38	7.93	7.93
1968	16.20	16.20	16.20	11.07	6.14	6.14
1969	21.75	21.75	21.75	13.85	8.58	8.58
1970	28.66	28.66	28.66	17.34	11.33	11.33
1971	34.12	34.12	34.12	19.50	12.51	12.51
1972	37.84	37.84	37.84	21.95	14.97	14.97
1973	42.22	42.22	42.22	23.42	16.31	16.31
1974	39.51	39.51	39.51	23.63	17.89	17.89
1975	43.41	43.41	43.41	26.26	17.70	17.70
1976	44.02	44.02	44.02	28.35	18.71	18.71
1977	51.65	51.65	51.65	32.20	19.96	19.96
1978	61.09	61.09	61.09	35.93	28.38	28.38
1979	59.28	59.28	59.28	38.33	32.06	32.06
1980	62.45	62.45	62.45	41.36	28.95	28.95
1981	63.04	63.04	63.04	44.64	23.79	23.79
1982	66.61	66.61	66.61	49.84	24.63	24.63
1983	73.63	73.63	73.63	54.57	32.29	32.29
1984	76.28	76.28	76.28	61.79	39.15	39.15
1985	89.00	89.00	89.00	80.32	50.53	50.53
1986	98.73	98.73	98.73	87.29	66.16	66.16
1987	107.17	107.17	107.17	94.96	68.00	68.00
1988	117.96	117.96	117.96	107.74	81.45	81.45
1989	126.39	126.39	126.39	122.82	92.25	92.25
1990	136.20	136.20	136.20	130.96	100.97	100.97
1991	143.29	143.29	143.29	125.91	128.18	128.18
1992	152.31	152.31	152.31	145.49	125.86	125.86
1993	221.30	221.30	221.30	220.05	163.87	163.87
1994	293.41	136.62	136.62	121.05	200.17	200.17
1995	350.08	172.64	172.64	146.39	253.49	253.49
1996	427.99	223.17	223.17	184.65	310.94	310.94
1997	512.93	273.20	255.59	210.56	379.51	364.36
1998	579.90	308.20	296.58	244.20	434.17	424.90
1999	680.23	384.78	343.36	314.26	528.56	484.65
2000	865.00	501.33	448.31	409.14	645.57	591.28
2001	1064.99	620.40	572.15	523.84	782.64	729.64
2002	1483.68	834.64	643.70	565.30	1049.31	860.25
2003	1968.92	1164.29	798.11	690.53	1402.04	1047.68
2004	2216.41	1398.83	980.43	833.64	1719.32	1312.04
2005	3124.83	1868.26	1322.68	1107.27	2216.21	1673.40
2006	3935.87	2388.58	1656.68	1389.13	2726.77	2013.25

注：我省财政总收入为地方一般预算收入、基金预算收入、上划中央四税之和，地方财政收入为地方一般预算收入、基金预算收入之和，地方财政支出为地方一般预算支出、基金预算支出之和。

Notes: Total financial revenue is the sum of local general budgetary revenue, funds budgetary revenue and four taxes trunover to central government; local. financial revenue is the sum of general budgetary revenue, funds budgetary revenue; local financial expenditure is the sum of local budgetary expenditure and funds budgetary expenditure.

13－2　财 政 收 支
FINANCIAL REVENUE AND EXPENDITURE

单位:亿元　　　　(100 million yuan)

指标	Item	1995	2000	2005	2006
一般预算收入	**General Budgetary Revenue**	**172.64**	**448.31**	**1322.68**	**1656.68**
#各项税收	Government Taxes Revenue	166.97	409.14	1107.27	1389.13
#增值税	Taxes on Value Added	52.61	108.64	265.57	329.43
营业税	Run Taxes	42.31	96.00	342.82	431.81
企业所得税	Enterprise Income Taxes	20.57	88.65	177.70	220.87
个人所得税	Individual Income Taxes	5.07	33.28	66.20	81.73
城市维护建设税	Taxes on City Maintenance and Construction	13.79	26.62	70.66	84.92
房产税	Real Estate Taxes	4.30	11.83	40.13	48.87
耕地占用税	Tax on Use of Cultivated Land	4.78	3.03	12.16	17.75
基金预算收入	**Funds Revenue**		**53.02**	**545.58**	**731.90**
上划中央收入	**Turn Over Revenue to the Central Government**	**177.44**	**363.80**	**1256.57**	**1547.29**
消费税	General Tax on Consumption	19.61	37.88	98.80	988.30
增值税	Tax on Added Value	157.83	325.92	796.71	114.72
企业所得税	Enterprise Income Taxes			261.77	321.67
个人所得税	Individual Income Taxes			99.29	122.60
一般预算支出	**General Budgetary Expenditure**	**253.49**	**591.28**	**1673.40**	**2013.25**
#基本建设支出	Capital Construction	18.69	45.80	153.71	181.89
企业挖潜改造资金	Expenditure for Innovation of Enterprise	14.62	52.39	63.33	71.72
科技三项费用	Science and Technology Promotion Funds	2.33	7.92	27.13	39.30
农业水气象支出	Agriculture Expenditure	21.49	46.77	97.57	122.50
科教文卫支出	Science, Education, Culture and Health Care	82.69	171.67	384.17	447.48
抚恤和社会福利支出	Pensions and social welfare	7.13	13.55	43.11	48.56
社会保障补助支出	Social security		11.60	63.71	83.85
行政管理费	Adiministration	26.88	55.71	182.11	231.89
城市维护费	City Maintenance	17.29	47.04	156.52	173.91
政策性补贴支出	Expenditure for Price Subsidies	11.15	12.30	14.21	45.19
专项支出	Special Expenditure	8.08	15.34	43.61	56.01
基金预算支出	**Funds Expenditure**		**54.29**	**542.82**	**713.52**

13－3 用于文教、卫生、科学部门的财政支出
EXPENDITURE FOR CULTURE, EDUCATION, HEALTH CARE AND SCIENTIFIC RESEARCH

单位：亿元 (100 million yuan)

年份 Year	合计 Total	文体广播事业费 Expenditure for Operating Expenses of Culture Sport and Broadcasting	#文化事业 Expenditure for Operating Expenses of Culture	#广播电影电视事业费 Expenditure for Operating Expenses of Broadcasting, Film and Television	教育支出 Expenditure for Operating Expenses of Education	科学支出 Operating Expenses for Science	医疗卫生支出 Expenditure for Health Care	#卫生事业费 Operating Expenses for Health Care	#行政事业单位医疗 Expenditure for Free Medical Services
1978	4.98	0.50	0.20		3.07	0.06	1.35	1.15	0.21
1980	6.79	0.64	0.26		4.31	0.07	1.77	1.48	0.29
1985	14.70	1.74	0.43	0.36	9.24	0.24	3.48	2.67	0.81
1989	26.16	3.09	0.71	0.56	15.95	0.79	6.33	3.75	2.28
1990	29.65	3.35	0.77	0.68	18.24	0.94	7.12	4.13	2.69
1991	32.83	3.81	0.91	0.76	19.52	1.06	8.44	4.72	3.37
1992	38.28	4.39	1.04	0.85	23.31	1.22	9.37	5.17	3.79
1993	49.62	5.67	1.32	1.14	30.33	1.43	12.18	6.27	5.47
1994	72.78	6.95	1.79	1.26	47.58	2.03	16.22	8.95	6.61
1995	82.69	8.54	2.25	1.41	52.91	2.26	18.98	9.62	8.57
1996	103.19	10.41	2.83	1.71	66.68	2.86	23.25	11.69	10.65
1997	118.96	12.96	3.17	1.88	75.59	3.53	26.88	13.19	12.62
1998	136.75	14.38	3.82	1.88	89.73	4.01	28.63	13.55	13.92
1999	154.35	16.38	4.20	2.21	102.46	4.45	31.06	14.48	15.20
2000	171.67	17.05	4.35	1.95	117.42	4.63	32.57	15.07	15.98
2001	206.00	18.93	4.56	2.00	144.61	5.06	37.40	17.57	17.92
2002	231.59	22.19	5.20	2.34	162.41	5.10	41.89	19.07	20.25
2003	265.84	25.67	6.38	2.39	179.08	5.52	55.57	28.68	23.57
2004	315.33	32.11	8.10	2.47	214.37	6.46	62.39	32.87	26.99
2005	384.17	42.92	9.77	3.58	258.24	7.95	75.06	42.14	30.40
2006	447.48	49.13	13.02	51.25	298.23	10.60	89.52	53.54	32.66

注：本表仅指直接对应科目的支出，不含基本建设支出等其他科目中用于文教、卫生、科学部门的支出。
Note: In this table, expenditure only refers to the direct corresponding subjests exdudes expenditure for other subjests as education, culture, healthcare and scientific department ect. in capital construction.

13－4 财政收入占地区生产总值的比重 FINANCIAL REVENUE AS PERCENTAGE TO GROSS DOMESTIC PRODUCT

单位:亿元 (100 million yuan)

年份 Year	财政总收入 Total Revenue	地方一般预算收入 Local Financial General Budgetary Revenue	地区生产总值 Gross Domestic Product	财政总收入占地区生产总值的比重(%) Percentage of FinancialRevenue to GDP(%)	地方一般预算收入占地区生产总值的比重(%) Percentage of Local Financial Revenue to GDP(%)
1978	61.09	61.09	249.24	24.5	24.5
1979	59.28	59.28	298.55	19.9	19.9
1980	62.45	62.45	319.80	19.5	19.5
1981	63.04	63.04	350.02	18.0	18.0
1982	66.61	66.61	390.17	17.1	17.1
1983	73.63	73.63	437.65	16.8	16.8
1984	76.28	76.28	518.85	14.7	14.7
1985	89.00	89.00	651.82	13.7	13.7
1986	98.73	98.73	744.94	13.3	13.3
1987	107.17	107.17	922.33	11.6	11.6
1988	117.96	117.96	1208.85	9.8	9.8
1989	126.39	126.39	1321.85	9.6	9.6
1990	136.20	136.20	1416.50	9.6	9.6
1991	143.29	143.29	1601.38	8.9	8.9
1992	152.31	152.31	2136.02	7.1	7.1
1993	221.30	221.30	2998.16	7.4	7.4
1994	293.41	136.62	4057.39	7.2	3.4
1995	350.08	172.64	5155.25	6.8	3.3
1996	427.99	223.17	6004.21	7.1	3.7
1997	512.93	255.59	6680.34	7.7	3.8
1998	579.90	296.58	7199.95	8.1	4.1
1999	680.23	343.36	7697.82	8.8	4.5
2000	865.00	448.31	8553.69	10.1	5.2
2001	1064.99	572.15	9456.84	11.3	6.1
2002	1483.68	643.70	10606.85	14.0	6.1
2003	1968.92	798.11	12442.87	15.8	6.4
2004	2216.41	980.43	15003.60	14.8	6.5
2005	3124.83	1322.68	18305.66	17.1	7.2
2006	3935.87	1656.68	21645.08	18.2	7.7

13-5 金融机构人民币存款年末余额
DEPOSITS BALANCE OF BANKING INSTITUTIONS (YEAR-END)

单位:亿元 (100 million yuan)

指标	Item	1995	2000	2004	2005	2006
各项存款	**Deposits**	**3500.49**	**8400.75**	**18211.02**	**22001.44**	**25860.47**
企业存款	Deposits of Enterprises	1164.92	3207.93	6749.58	7531.73	9011.29
活期存款	Demand		2200.89	4363.58	4440.76	5511.97
定期储蓄	Time		1007.04	2386.00	3090.97	3499.32
财政存款	Treasury Deposits	49.97	61.07	240.47	203.39	305.55
机关团体存款	Deposits of Government Agency and Organizations		54.45	426.56	811.01	1059.02
城乡居民储蓄存款	Urban and Rural Savings Deposits	1922.33	4456.83	8863.10	10581.27	12183.47
活期存款	Demand		893.42	2401.35	2864.13	3429.51
定期储蓄	Time		3563.41	6461.75	7717.14	8753.96
农业存款	Agricultural Deposits	86.19	261.65	599.45	658.66	790.62
信托存款	Trusted Deposits	242.48	15.79	0.73	99.40	0.40
委托存款	Entrusted Deposits		60.71	65.01	84.61	55.14
其他存款	Others	34.60	282.32	1266.12	2031.37	2454.98

13-6 金融机构人民币贷款年末余额
LOANS BALANCE OF BANKING INSTITUTIONS (YEAR-END)

单位:亿元 (100 million yuan)

指标	Item	1995	2000	2004	2005	2006
各项贷款	**Loans**	**2875.39**	**5967.66**	**13480.98**	**15396.59**	**18485.02**
#短期贷款	Short-term Loans	2178.78	4558.17	7337.82	7809.97	9281.57
工业贷款	Industrial Loans	704.78	1190.94	2118.55	2265.98	3330.94
商业贷款	Commercial Loans	739.70	945.73	959.53	993.42	1117.73
建筑业贷款	Construction Loans	36.08	129.46	278.01	282.46	318.26
农业贷款	Agricultural Loans	89.09	232.51	574.58	672.58	745.92
乡镇企业贷款	Loans to Township Enterprises	355.09	621.00	1129.01	1254.10	1160.33
三资企业贷款	Loans to Sino-foreign Joint Venture, Cooperative Enterprises and Foreign-funded Enterprises	82.58	365.88	312.35	306.15	263.62
私营企业及个体贷款	Loans to Private Enterprises and Individuals	2.74	27.52	155.08	160.19	214.79
其他短期贷款	Other Short-term Loans	168.72	1045.13	1810.71	1875.09	2129.98
#个人短期消费贷款	Individual Short-term Consumptive Loans		82.86	142.00	131.55	159.89
中长期贷款	Medium-term and Long-term Loans	410.79	1007.28	4743.21	5689.27	7395.33
基本建设贷款	Loans for Capital Construction		516.70	2525.54	2887.94	3668.26
技术改造贷款	Loans for Technical Transformations		242.44	144.88	136.65	111.49
其他中长期贷款	Other Medium and Long-term Loans		248.14	2072.79	2664.68	3615.58
#个人中长期消费贷款	Individual Medium and Long-term Consumptive Loans			1199.14	1488.92	1728.63
融资租赁	Loans for Accommodation and Rent		1.80	5.68	7.58	8.73
委托贷款	Entrusted Loans		76.86	62.30	74.22	23.34
票据融资	Bill Financing			1082.58	1738.47	1763.61
#贴现	Discount			1082.56	1738.45	1763.61
各项垫款	Money Advanced Payment for Others			20.73	13.78	12.44

13-7 金融机构外币存款年末余额
DEPOSITS BALANCE OF BANKING INSTITUTIONS (YEAR-END)

单位:亿美元 (USD 100 million)

指标	Item	2000	2001	2002	2003	2004	2005	2006
各项存款	**Deposits**	**75.73**	**83.21**	**93.81**	**94.73**	**96.88**	**101.63**	**110.42**
单位存款	Deposits of Enterprises	30.99	33.03	36.12	39.41	47.45	57.04	66.54
活期	Demand	9.44	13.19	20.05	26.25	35.09	43.65	49.09
定期	Time	21.55	19.84	16.07	13.16	12.36	13.39	17.45
储蓄存款	Savings Deposits	39.78	45.48	51.32	49.26	40.41	34.60	34.75
活期	Demand	0.93	1.83	3.52	5.16	6.03	6.77	9.17
定期	Time	38.85	43.65	47.80	44.10	34.38	27.83	25.58
其他存款	Others	4.96	4.70	6.37	6.06	9.02	9.99	9.13

13-8 金融机构外币存贷款年末余额
LOANS BALANCE OF BANKING INSTITUTIONS (YEAR-END)

单位:亿美元 (USD 100 million)

指标	Item	2000	2001	2002	2003	2004	2005	2006
各项贷款	**Loans**	**27.13**	**33.08**	**47.47**	**87.65**	**92.55**	**109.70**	**115.08**
#短期贷款	Short-term Loans	11.87	14.04	24.88	49.01	40.63	50.18	40.57
#境内短期贷款	Short-term Loans	11.87	14.04	24.88	49.01	40.63	50.18	40.57
中长期贷款	Medium-term and Long-term Loans	7.51	7.77	8.49	18.88	29.17	31.56	40.92
#境内中长期贷款	Medium-term and Long-term Loans Within the Boundaries	7.51	7.77	8.49	18.88	29.17	31.50	40.92
进出口贸易融资	Import and Export Trade Financing	2.30	2.32	4.87	10.10	13.14	18.86	24.34
票据融资	Bill Financing	0.02	0.08	0.15	0.12	0.17	0.30	0.26
各项垫款	Money Advanced Payment for Others		3.03	3.35	3.12	1.98	2.13	2.25
境外筹资转贷款	Fund Raising Transfered to Loans Outside the Boundaries		4.97	5.62	6.38	7.45	6.75	6.74

13-9 国有独资商业银行人民币存款年末余额
DEPOSITS BALANCE OF STATE - OWNED AND STATE FUNDED COMMERCIAL BANK (YEAR - END)

单位:亿元 (100 million yuan)

指标	Item	1995	2000	2004	2005	2006
各项存款	**Deposits**	**2129.33**	**5139.18**	**10075.12**	**11885.18**	**13878.32**
企业存款	Deposits of Enterprises	835.79	2037.37	3980.73	4215.34	4915.32
活期存款	Demand	709.51	1496.44	2849.76	2713.95	3371.10
定期储蓄	Time	126.28	540.93	1130.97	1501.39	1544.22
机关团体存款				200.31	560.68	756.82
城乡居民储蓄存款	Urban and Rural Savings Deposits	1248.69	2872.80	5489.56	6422.94	7307.93
活期存款	Demand		581.65	1549.67	1813.24	2131.25
定期储蓄	Time		2291.15	3939.89	4609.70	5176.68
农业存款	Agricultural Deposits	13.28	22.41	24.59	23.67	2.48
其他存款	Others		206.60	379.93	662.55	895.77

13-10 国有独资商业银行人民币贷款年末余额
LOANS BALANCE OF STATE - OWNED AND STATE FUNDED COMMERCIAL BANK (YEAR - END)

单位:亿元 (100 million yuan)

指标	Item	1995	2000	2004	2005	2006
各项贷款	**Loans**	**1695.07**	**3626.81**	**7402.98**	**8062.55**	**9682.11**
#短期贷款	Short-term Loans	1317.99	2695.94	3307.84	3163.09	3762.77
工业贷款	Industrial Loans	536.78	978.96	1443.25	1464.48	2378.58
商业贷款	commercial Loans	430.83	530.24	358.47	316.00	321.88
建筑业贷款	Construction Loans	36.08	110.52	191.87	185.41	126.14
农业贷款	Agricultural Loans	43.09	63.21	56.64	51.03	21.94
乡镇企业贷款	Loans to Township Enterprises	86.22	149.63	295.62	298.83	
三资企业贷款	Loans to Sino-foreign Joint Venture, Cooperative Enterprises and Foreign-funded Enterprises	63.01	287.32	213.75	228.58	157.73
私营企业及个体贷款	Loans to Private Enterprises and Individuals	0.36	19.26	68.10	65.40	67.58
其他短期贷款	Other Short-term Loans	121.62	489.47	745.87	630.78	674.38
中长期贷款	Medium-term and Long-term Loans	364.09	794.37	3226.37	3791.79	4854.05
#基本建设贷款	Loans for Capital Construction	265.10	372.37	1750.76	1975.82	2539.41
技术改造贷款	Loans for Technical Transformations	64.86	235.67	116.24	103.06	87.73
贴　现	Discount		67.33	699.63	1100.83	1059.28

13－11 各类金融机构人民币存款年末余额
DEPOSITS BALANCE OF VARIOUS BANKING INSTITUTIONS (YEAR－END)

单位:亿元 (100 million yuan)

项目	Item	2000	2004	2005	2006
金融机构合计	**Total**	**8400.75**	**18211.02**	**22001.44**	**25860.47**
国有独资银行	State-owned Funds	5139.18	10075.12	11885.18	13878.32
工商银行	Industrial and Commercial Bank of China	1616.20	2913.99	3277.39	3686.54
农业银行	Agricultural Bank of China	1473.98	3006.23	3612.87	4271.37
中国银行	Bank of China	741.11	1923.66	2377.02	2752.85
建设银行	Construction Bank of China	1307.92	2231.23	2617.89	3167.56
政策性银行	Bank of Budgetary Subsidies	22.65	57.81	92.29	106.69
国家开发银行	National Development Bank	13.63	38.42	63.16	53.84
中国进出口银行	National Development Bank	–	0.94	1.97	11.48
农业发展银行	Agricultural Development Bank of China	9.02	18.45	27.16	41.37
其他商业银行	Other Commercial Bank	1091.48	3295.87	4199.1	5039.89
交通银行	Bank of Communications	482.28	1045.46	1282.54	1517.78
中信实业银行	CITIC Industrial Bank	166.79	432.85	537.6	669.92
光大银行	China Everbright Bank	56.42	207.85	264.63	326.62
华夏银行	China Huxia Bank	106.87	301.96	393.76	458.9
广东发展银行	Guangdong Development Bank	42.83	232.19	265.13	268.05
深圳发展银行	Shenzhen Development Bank		97.42	121.5	134.55
招商银行	China Merchant Bank	91.11	305.96	423.1	509.7
上海浦东发展银行	Shanghai Pudong Development Bank	124.60	371.40	477.37	580.68
兴业银行	Fujian Industrial Bank		137.91	178.79	209.23
民生银行	China Minsheng Bank Co. Ltd.	20.58	162.87	254.71	324.75
恒丰银行	Evergrowing Bank Co. Ltd.				39.71
城市商业银行	Urban Commercial Bank	359.07	1154.19	1441.94	1763.39
农村合作银行	Rural Cooperative Bank			59.09	271.69
农村商业银行	Rural Commercial Bank		495.46	1157.47	1412.02
城市信用社	Urban Credit Cooperative	54.96	6.30	7.62	9.26
农村信用社	Rural Credit Cooperative	1170.47	1884.59	1582.92	1652.05
财务公司	Financial Companies	16.97	21.60	47.13	31.63
信托投资公司	Trusted Investment Agencies	117.49	64.70	161.27	6.35
租赁公司	Rent Companies	1.28	0.65	0.73	1.05
邮政储汇局	Saving Deposits Agency of Postal Offices	402.76	947.12	1203.74	1407.92

13－12 各类金融机构人民币贷款年末余额
LOANS BALANCE OF VARIOUS BANKING INSTITUTIONS (YEAR－END)

单位:亿元 (100 million yuan)

项　　目	Item	2000	2004	2005	2006
金融机构合计	**Total**	**5967.66**	**13480.98**	**15396.59**	**18485.02**
国有独资银行	State-owned Funds	3626.81	7402.98	8062.55	9682.11
工商银行	Industrial and Commercial Bank of China	1238.96	2262.15	2325.18	2730.49
农业银行	Agricultural Bank of China	1000.39	2041.75	2333.20	2738.50
中国银行	Bank of China	526.08	1478.17	1570.30	1870.24
建设银行	Construction Bank of China	861.35	1620.91	1833.88	2342.90
政策性银行	Bank of Budgetary Subsidies	455.33	1060.47	1266.85	1473.02
国家开发银行	National Development Bank	125.62	651.00	784.22	868.90
中国进出口银行	National Development Bank		75.53	88.14	113.43
农业发展银行	Agricultural Development Bank of China	329.71	333.94	394.49	490.69
其他商业银行	Other Commercial Bank	741.07	2533.42	3041.29	3868.74
交通银行	Bank of Communications	343.02	770.22	879.43	1039.94
中信实业银行	CITIC Industrial Bank	109.55	356.31	458.29	572.24
光大银行	China Everbright Bank	34.22	160.67	211.43	284.13
华夏银行	China Huxia Bank	64.96	209.36	261.49	331.14
广东发展银行	Guangdong Development Bank	32.65	175.79	194.30	186.92
深圳发展银行	Shenzhen Development Bank		93.73	92.32	108.52
招商银行	China Merchant Bank	59.28	239.81	247.91	389.26
上海浦东发展银行	Shanghai Pudong Development Bank	86.93	300.28	367.47	477.73
兴业银行	Fujian Industrial Bank		100.18	119.43	159.26
民生银行	China Minsheng Bank Co. Ltd.	10.46	127.07	209.27	286.65
恒丰银行	Evergrowing Bank Co. Ltd.				32.95
城市商业银行	Urban Commercial Bank	237.14	749.14	942.09	1103.64
农村合作银行	Rural Cooperative Bank			45.06	200.86
农村商业银行	Rural Commercial Bank		306.83	736.50	905.79
城市信用社	Urban Credit Cooperative	38.91	4.09	5.42	6.10
农村信用社	Rural Credit Cooperative	745.68	1318.46	1110.95	1165.05
财务公司	Financial Companies	19.98	23.44	38.04	34.68
信托投资公司	Trusted Investment Agencies	100.49	76.42	138.69	23.92
租赁公司	Rent Companies	2.22	5.75	7.52	8.44

13－13 货币供应量(年末)
MONEY SUPPLY AT THE YEAR END

单位:亿元 (100 million yuan)

指标	Item	2000	2004	2005	2006
货币和准货币(M_2)	Money and Quasi－Money (M_2)	9773.97	20525.62	24640.67	29024.09
货币(M_1)	Money (M_1)	4060.37	8077.92	9057.14	11018.20
流通中现金(M_0)	Currency in Circulation (M_0)	1519.81	2642.12	3035.12	3501.85
活期存款	Demand	2540.56	5435.80	6022.02	7516.35
准货币	Quasi－Money	5713.60	12447.70	15583.53	18005.89
定期存款	Time	1007.04	2386.00	3156.97	3552.15
储蓄存款	Saving Deposits	4456.83	8863.10	10581.27	12183.36
其他存款	Others	249.73	1198.60	1845.29	2270.38

13－14 金融机构现金收入
CASH INCOME OF BANKING INSTITUTIONS

单位:亿元 (100 million yuan)

指标	Item	2000	2004	2005	2006
收入总计	**Total**	**19076.03**	**46291.68**	**53640.10**	**62174.98**
#商品销售收入	Commodity Sales	3478.19	7236.59	8161.66	8963.24
服务事业收入	Service Trade	1010.24	2026.22	2182.98	2241.44
税款收入	Taxes	119.67	259.28	288.65	308.33
城乡个体经营收入	Urban and Rural Individual Business	835.18	1790.24	2188.13	2378.07
储蓄存款收入	Saving Deposits	11111.6	29739.86	34823.69	40908.77
其他金融机构收入	Other Banking Institutions	237.77	191.12	177.22	176.01
汇兑收入	Remittances	360.49	441.98	419.31	421.82
有价证券收入	Valuable Securities	106.83	77.95	73.86	58.91

13－15 金融机构现金支出
CASH EXPENDITURES OF BANKING INSTITUTIONS

单位:亿元 (100 million yuan)

指 标	Item	2000	2004	2005	2006
支出总计	**Total**	**19283.38**	**46673.62**	**54033.12**	**62641.72**
#工资性支出	Wages and Other Payments to Individuals	1778.23	4368.13	4957.02	5741.86
农副产品采购支出	Purchases of Agricultural and Sideline Products	645.71	1365.72	1639.75	1839.22
行政企业管理费支出	Government, Institutions and Enterprises Overhead	1591.13	2893.20	3074.55	3112.49
个体经营支出	Individual Business	1119.95	2298.42	2748.78	3019.75
储蓄存款支出	Saving Deposists	11345.14	29362.66	34242.54	40276.10
其他金融机构支出	Other Banking Institutions	132.00	147.49	172.64	163.34
汇兑支出	Remittances	184.43	231.96	237.05	215.25
有价证券支出	Valuable Securities	94.49	59.14	55.93	90.70

13－16 银行现金收入与支出
CASH REVENUE AND EXPENDITURES OF BANKING SYSTEM

单位:亿元 (100 million yuan)

指 标	Item	2000	2004	2005	2006
收入总计	**Total**	**15084.72**	**38886.16**	**46257.11**	**53916.35**
#商品销售收入	Commodity Sales	2717.14	5976.15	7267.11	8137.08
服务事业收入	Service Trade	774.10	1715.12	1906.31	1991.35
税款收入	Taxes	68.92	180.67	216.91	246.89
城乡个体经营收入	Urban and Rural Individual Business	455.32	1432.82	1854.93	2024.65
储蓄存款收入	Savings Deposits	9168.72	25959.37	30869.33	36246.43
支出总计	**Total**	**14892.47**	**38214.89**	**45806.11**	**53451.91**
#工资性支出	Wages and Other Payments to Individuals	1335.28	3466.94	4239.46	5113.04
农副产品采购支出	Purchases of Agricultural and Sideline Products	325.14	829.45	1173.94	1462.78
行政企事业管理费支出	Government, Institutions and Enterprises Overhead	1304.58	2439.24	2715.83	2771.84
个体经营支出	Individual Business	570.19	1710.74	2226.55	2504.99
储蓄存款支出	Savings Deposits	9402.53	25547.23	30345.86	35597.17

13－17 农村信用社存贷款年末余额
RURAL CREDIT ASSOCIATION DEPOSITS AND LOANS BALANCE (YEAR－END)

单位：亿元 (100 million yuan)

指　　标	Item	1995	2000	2004	2005	2006
各项存款	**Deposits**	**522.30**	**1170.47**	**1884.59**	**1582.92**	**1652.05**
#农业存款	Agricultural Deposits		239.02	434.58	288.77	318.69
企业存款	Enterprises Deposits		59.72	149.18	107.8	105.48
农民个人储蓄存款	Saving Deposits	434.37	856.22	1241.11	1106.61	1129.26
各项贷款	**Loans**	**403.62**	**745.68**	**1318.46**	**1110.95**	**1165.05**
#农业贷款	Agricultural Loans	44.86	168.70	482.39	511.52	536.56
企业贷款	Enterprises Loans	281.31	458.43	623.24	461.03	481.06

13－18 农村信用社现金收支
CASH REVENUE AND EXPENDITURES OF RURAL CREDIT ASSOCIATION

单位：亿元 (100 million yuan)

指　　标	Item	2000	2004	2005	2006
收入合计	**Cash Revenue**	**3680.25**	**7387.72**	**7356.11**	**8253.01**
#商品销售收入	Commodity Sales	658.36	1252.29	886.55	819.00
税款收入	Taxes	47.62	78.61	71.70	61.43
服务业收入	Service Trade	214.52	310.86	276.17	249.47
城乡个体经营收入	Urban and Rural Individual Business	350.65	357.33	332.82	353.42
储蓄存款收入	Savings Deposits	1818.64	3772.37	3939.10	4649.84
有价证券收入	Income for Securities	1.61	5.71	0.91	2.46
支出合计	**Cash Expenditure**	**4079.46**	**8441.31**	**8196.51**	**9162.91**
#工资性支出	Wages	414.67	900.01	714.66	626.80
农副产品采购支出	Purchases of Agricultural and Sideline Products	304.81	536.15	465.59	376.36
工矿及其他产品采购收入	Expenditure for Purchases of Industrial and Mineral Products	138.74	380.99	235.57	316.42
城乡个体经营支出	Urban and Rural Individual Business	511.24	587.09	521.50	514.75
行政企事业管理费支出	Government, Institutions and Enterprises Overhead	253.16	450.18	353.74	336.47
储蓄存款支出	Savings Deposits	1815.19	3807.00	3881.15	4665.40
有价证券支出	Expenditure for Securities	2.32	0.88	1.19	0.10

13－19　金融机构机构、人员情况表

NUMBER OF INSTITUTIONS AND STAFF AND WORKERS OF BANKING ORGANIZATIONS

项　目	Item	机构数（家）Number of Institutions（unit）		职工人数（人）Number of Staff and Workers（person）	
		2005	2006	2005	2006
合　计	**Total**	**9662**	**9093**	**147533**	**151031**
人民银行		69	69	4335	4326
国有独资银行	State-owned Funds	5124	4692	84802	85804
工商银行	Industrial and Commercial Bank of China	1236	1061	19331	19042
农业银行	Agricultural Bank of China	1832	1618	27001	26987
中国银行	Bank of China	965	940	16548	17701
建设银行	Construction Bank of China	1091	1073	21922	22074
政策性银行	Bank of Budgetary Subsidies	91	94	2096	2191
国家开发银行	National Development Bank	1	1	131	123
进出口银行	Banking of Imports and Exports	1	1	47	52
农业发展银行	Agricultural Development Bank of China	89	92	1918	2016
其他商业银行	Other Commercial Bank	607	609	14096	15435
交通银行	Bank of Communications	353	350	6438	6621
中信实业银行	CITIC Industrial Bank	75	74	2010	2203
光大银行	China Everbright Bank	18	19	649	771
华夏银行	China Huxia Bank	32	32	913	1013
广东发展银行	Guangdong Development Bank	20	20	625	628
深圳发展银行	Shenzhen Development Bank	10	10	372	456
招商银行	China Merchant Bank	28	32	1065	1255
上海浦东发展银行	Shanghai Pudong Development Bank	39	41	1116	1231
兴业银行	Fujian Industrial Bank	19	16	364	518
民生银行	China Minsheng Bank Co. Ltd.	13	14	544	670
恒生银行	Evergrowing Bank Co. Ltd.	0	1		69
城市商业银行	Urban Commercial Bank	474	477	8614	8683
农村合作银行	Rural Cooperative Bank		333		3804
农村商业银行	Rural Commercial Bank	705	694	6761	6913
城市信用社	Urban Credit Cooperative	2	2	32	45
农村信用社	Rural Credit Cooperative	2474	2115	25413	23617
财务公司	Financial Companies	3	3	48	50
信托投资公司	Trusted Investment Agencies	5	4	181	127
租赁公司	Rent Companies	3	1	37	36

13－20 保险业务主要指标
MAJOR INDICATORS OF INSURANCE BUSINESS

单位:亿元 (100 million yuan)

指　　标	Item	2000	2004	2005	2006
保费收入	Premium	131.93	418.95	437.34	502.83
财产险	Property Insurance	40.45	84.52	93.64	120.42
#机动车辆保险	Machine Driving Cars Insurance	22.53	56.39	64.40	87.71
人身意外伤害险	Accident Insurance	4.20	9.42	10.89	12.55
健康险	Healthy Insurance	4.00	20.88	24.37	32.03
寿险	Personal Insurance	83.29	304.12	308.43	337.83
各项赔款和给付	Claim and Payment	34.29	113.20	118.83	159.17
财产险	Property Insurance	20.37	44.16	53.30	78.70
#机动车辆保险	Machine Driving Cars Insurance	12.37	34.81	40.76	62.40
人身意外伤害险	Accident Insurance	1.39	2.87	3.29	3.70
健康险	Healthy Insurance	1.27	6.63	9.04	12.42
寿险	Personal Insurance	11.26	59.55	53.21	64.36
保险公司数 (家)	Number of Insurance Co. (unit)	9	23	29	39
保险公司分支机构(家)	Branches of Insurance Co. (unit)	755	5159	4033	4636
从业人员数 (万人)	Number of Employee (10000 persons)	6.00	15.75	14.72	15.47

13－21 各保险公司保费收入、赔款情况
PREMIUM AND CLAIM AND PAYMENT OF VARIOUS INSURANCE COMPANIES

单位:亿元 (100 million yuan)

指　　标	Item	保费收入 Premium		各项赔款和给付 Claim and Payment	
		2005	2006	2005	2006
总　　计	**Total**	**437.34**	**502.83**	**118.83**	**159.17**
财产保险公司合计	**Property Insurance Co. Ltd.**	**97.50**	**125.76**	**54.43**	**80.65**
#中国人民保险公司	PICC	40.75	45.22	26.26	36.96
中华联合财产保险股份有限公司	CUIC (property, Stock Ltd.)	15.03	17.76	6.86	12.19
中国太平洋财产保险股份有限公司	CPIC (Property, Stock Ltd.)	13.87	17.51	7.46	9.27
中国平安保险股份有限公司(产险)	PAICC (Property, Stock Ltd.)	7.64	11.54	3.72	6.12
天安保险股份有限公司	TAIC (Stock Ltd.)	7.03	7.75	4.34	5.93
永安财产保险股份有限公司	HTIC (Stock Ltd.)	3.23	5.20	1.57	1.88
人寿保险公司合计	**Life Insurance Co. Ltd.**	**339.84**	**377.07**	**64.40**	**78.53**
#中国人寿保险公司	CLIC (Life)	192.98	211.72	35.33	43.78
中国太平洋人寿保险股分有限公司	CPIC (Life, Stock Ltd.)	59.21	51.20	21.79	27.18
中国平安保险股份有限公司(寿险)	PAICC (Life, Stock Ltd.)	45.85	55.93	6.05	5.87
新华人寿保险股份有限公司	XHIC (Life, Stock Ltd.)	16.39	18.72	0.29	0.41
泰康人寿保险股份有限公司	TKIC (Life, Stock Ltd.)	9.69	11.24	0.74	0.58
太平人寿保险股份有限公司	TPIC (Life Stock Ltd.)	5.64	11.52	0.13	0.45

13－22　江苏辖区证券市场基本情况
BASIC SITUATION OF SECURITIES MARKETS UNDER JIANGSU PROVINCE

项　　目	Item	2000	2003	2004	2005	2006
上市公司数（家）	Number of Listed Companies (unit)	58	81	87	90	99
#A 股	A Shares	56	79	82	88	97
B 股	B Shares	5	5	5	2	5
辅导企业数	Number of Guidance Enterprises (unit)	60	111	98	104	96
证券公司数（家）	Number of Securities Companies (unit)	6	7	7	7	6
证券营业部数（家）	No. of Securities Business Department (unit)	147	182	194	202	208
证券交易服务部数（家）	No. of Securities Trading Service (unit)	0	55	56	57	57
期货经纪公司（家）	No. of Futures Broker Companies (unit)	12	12	12	12	12
期货经纪公司营业部（个）	No. of Trading Offices of Futures Broker Co. (unit)		15	20	23	25
证券投资咨询机构数（家）	No. of Securities Investment Consultative Institutions (unit)	4	4	3	3	3
证券从业人员数（人）	No. of Personnels Engaged in Securities (person)	3366	4111	4098	3925	4200
期货从业人员数（人）	No. of Personnels Engaged in Futures (person)	309	422	508	570	576
证券投资者开户数（万户）	No. of Opening Accoount of Securities Investors (10000 households)	241	303	322	330	329
期货投资者开户数（户）	No. of Opening Account of Futuers (household)	2306	9110	11619	15606	21041
上市公司募集资金总额（亿元）	Total Capital Volume Collected by Listed Co. (100 million yuan)	88.61	48.66	22.22	16.68	54.35
发行	Issuing	55.32	42.87	16.44	8.82	28.68
配股	Share Right Issued	21.07	1.79	2.87		
增发	Adding the Share Issue	12.22		2.93	7.86	21.37
可转债	Transferable Loans		4.00			4.30
上市公司总资产（亿元）	Total Assets of Listed Co.	1098.82	1762.00	2170.09	2407.00	2770
上市公司净资产（亿元）	Net Assets of Listed Co. (100 million yuan)	691.61	912.36	1023.00	1075.00	1114
上市公司总股本（亿股）	Total Capital Shares of Listed Co. (100 million shares)	251.67	319.38	345.83	362.47	406.64
市价总值（亿元）	Total Market Value (100 million yuan)	2532.66	2490.75	1943.80	1729.44	4137.69
上市公司净利润（亿元）	Net Profits of Listed co. (100 million yuan)	59.36	68.96	97.54	72.44	20.96
上市公司每股收益（元）	Per Share Income of Listed Co. (yuan)	0.27	0.22	0.25	0.19	0.05
证券经营机构证券交易量（亿元）	Trading Volume of Securities Managerial Institutions (100 million yuan)	8412	4507	5998	3902	14448.97
期货经营机构代理交易量（亿元）	Trading Volume of Agency by Futures Managerial Institutions (100 million yuan)	786	8157	11368	9825	17053.62

主要统计指标解释

财政收入　指国家财政参与社会产品分配所取得的收入，是实现国家职能的财力保证。财政收入所包括的内容几经变化，目前主要包括：

(1)各项税收：包括增值税、营业税、消费税、土地增值税、城市维护建设税、资源税、城市土地使用税、印花税、个人所得税、企业所得税、关税、农牧业税和耕地占用税等。

(2)专项收入：包括征收排污费收入、征收城市水资源费收入、教育费附加收入等。

(3)其他收入：包括基本建设贷款归还收入、基本建设收入、捐赠收入等。

(4)国有企业亏损补贴：这项为负收入，冲减财政收入。

财政支出　国家财政将筹集起来的资金进行分配使用，以满足经济建设和各项事业的需要，主要包括：

(1)基本建设支出：指按国家有关规定，属于基本建设范围内的基本建设有偿使用、拨款、资本金支出以及经国家批准对专项和政策性基建投资贷款，在部门的基建投资额中统筹支付的贴息支出。

(2)企业挖潜改造资金：指国家预算内拨给的用于企业挖潜、革新和改造方面的资金。包括各部门企业挖潜改造资金和企业挖潜改造贷款资金，为农业服务的县办"五小"企业技术改造补助，挖潜改造贷款利息支出。

(3)地质勘探费用：指国家预算用于地质勘探单位的勘探工作费用，包括地质勘探管理机构及其事业单位经费、地质勘探经费。

(4)科技三项费用：指国家预算用于科技支出的费用，包括新产品试制费、中间试验费、重要科学研究补助费。

(5)支援农村生产支出：指国家财政支援农村集体(户)各项生产的支出。包括对农村举办的小型农田水利和打井、喷灌等的补助费，对农村水土保持措施的补助费，对农村举办的小水电站的补助费，特大抗旱的补助费，农村开荒补助费，扶持乡镇企业资金，农村农技推广和植保补助费，农村草场和畜禽保护补助费，农村造林和林木保护补助费，农村水产补助费，发展粮食生产专项资金。

(6)农林水利气象等部门的事业费用：指国家财政用于农垦、农场、农业、畜牧、农机、林业、森工、水利、水产、气象、乡镇企业的技术推广、良种推广(示范)、动植物(畜禽、森林)保护、水质监测、勘探设计、资源调查、干部训练等项费用，园艺特产场补助费，中等专业学校经费，飞播牧草试验补助费，营林机构、气象机构经费，渔政费以及农业管理事业费等。

(7)工业交通商业等部门的事业费：指国家预算支付给工交商各部门用于事业发展的经费，包括勘探设计费、中等专业学校经费、技术学校经费、干部训练费。

(8)文教科学卫生事业费：指国家预算用于文化、出版、文物、教育、卫生、中医、公费医疗、体育、档案、地震、海洋、通讯、电影电视、计划生育、党政群干部训练、自然科学、社会科学、科协等项事业的经费支出和高技术研究专项经费。主要包括工资、补助工资、福利费、离退休费、助学金、公务费、设备购置费、修缮费、业务费、差额补助费。

(9)抚恤和社会福利救济费：指国家预算用于抚恤和社会福利救济事业的经费。包括由民政部门开支的烈士家属和牺牲病残人员家属的一次性、定期抚恤金，革命伤残人员的抚恤金，各种伤残补助费，烈军属、复员退伍军人生活补助费，退伍军人安置费，优抚事业单位经费，烈士纪念建筑物管理、维修费，自然灾害救济事业费和特大自然灾害灾后重建补助费等。

(10)国防支出：指国家预算用于国防建设和保卫国家安全的支出，包括国防费、国防科研事业费、民兵建设以及专项工程支出等。

(11)行政管理费：包括行政管理支出，党派团体补助支出，外交支出，公安安全支出，司法支出，法院支出，检察院支出和公检法办案费用补助。

(12)价格补贴支出：指经国家批准，由国家财政拨给的政策性补贴支出。主要包括粮食加价款，粮、棉、油差价补贴，棉花收购价外奖励款，副食品风险基金，市镇居民的肉食价格补贴，平抑市价肉食、蔬菜价差补贴等以及经国家批准的教材课本、报刊新闻纸等价格补贴。

中央财政收入和地方财政收入　指按财政体制划分的中央本级收入和地方本级收入。1994 年分税制财政体制以后，属于中央财政的收入包括关税、海关代征消费税和增值税，消费税，中央企业所得税，地方银行和外资银行及非银行金融企业所得税，铁道、银行总行、保险总公司等集中缴纳的营业税、所得税、利润和城市维护建设税，增值税的 75% 部分，证券交易税(印花税)50% 部分和海洋石油资源税。属于地方财政的收入包括营业税，地方企业所得税，个人所得税，城镇土地使用税，固定资产投资方向调节税，城镇维护建设税，房产税，车船使用税，印花税，屠宰税，农牧业税，农业特产税，耕地占用税，契税，增值税 25% 部分，证券交易税(印花税)50% 部分和除海洋石油资源税以外的其他资源税。

存款　指企业、机关、团体或居民根据资金必须收回的原则，把货币资金存入银行或其他信用机构保管并取得一定利息的一种信用活动形式。根据存款对象的不同可划分为企业存款、财政存款、机关团体存款、基本建设存款、城镇储蓄存款、农村存款等科目。它是银行信贷资金的主要来源。

贷款 指银行或其他信用机构根据资金必须归还的原则，按一定利率，为企业、个人等提供资金的一种信用活动形式。我国银行贷款分为流动资金贷款、固定资产贷款、城乡个体工商户贷款以及农业贷款等科目。

保险公司 在中国境内的、经过保险监督部门批准设立，并依法登记注册的各类商业保险公司。

保险金额 指保险人承担赔偿或者给付保险金责任的最高限额。

保费 指投保人为取得保险人在约定范围内所承担赔偿责任而支付给保险人的费用。

赔款 指保险人根据保险合同的规定，向被保险人支付的赔偿保险责任损失的金额。

给付 包括死伤医疗给付和满期给付。死伤医疗给付是指保险人根据人寿保险及长期健康保险合同的规定，因被保险人在保险期内发生保险责任范围内的保险事故支付给被保险人（或受益人）的金额。满期给付是指被保险人生存期满，保险人按人寿保险合同规定支付给被保险人的满期保险金额。

Explanatory Notes on Main Statistical Indicators

Government Revenue refers to the revenue of the government finance by means of participating in the distribution of the social products,which is the financial resources for ensuring the government to function. The contents of government revenue have been changed several times. Now it includes the following main items:

(1) Various tax revenues,including value added tax,business tax,consumption tax,land value added tax,tax on city maintenance and construction,resources tax,tax on use of urban land,stamp tax,personal income tax,enterprise income tax,tariff,tax on agriculture and animal husbandry and tax on occupancy of cultivated land,etc.

(2) Special revenues,including revenue collected from imposing fee on sewage treatment,revenue collected from imposing foe on urban water resources,and extra-charges for education,etc.

(3) Other revenues,including revenue from the repayment of capital construction loan,revenue from capital construction projects, and donations and grants.

(4) Planned subsidies for the losses of the state-owned enterprises. This is an item of negative revenue,used to eat up part of the government revenue.

Government Expenditure refers to the distribution and use of the funds the government finance has raised,so as to meet the needs of economic construction and various causes. It includes the following main items:

(1) Expenditure for capital construction:It refers to the non-gratuitous use and appropriation of funds for capital construction in the range of capital construction,outlay of capital as well as the loans on capital construction approved by the government for special purpose or policy purpose and the expenditure with discount paid in an overall way within the amount of the funds appropriated to the departments for capital construction.

(2) Innovation funds of the enterprises:They refer to the funds appropriated from the government budget for the enterprises to tap the latent power,upgrade the technology and carry out innovation,including the innovation fund of the departments,loan of the enterprises for innovation,subsidies on the innovation of the small fertilizer plant,small cement plant,small coal mines,small machinery plant and small steel plant,the expenditure of interest for the loan for innovation.

(3) Geological prospecting expenses:They refer to the expenses appropriated from the government budget to the geological prospecting units for the expenditure of the prospecting work,including the expenditures of the administrative agencies for geological prospecting and their institutional units as well as the geological prospecting expenditure.

(4) expenditures for science and technology promotion:They refer to the expenses appropriated from the government budget for the scientific and technological expenditure,including new products development expenditure,expenditure for intermediate trial and subsidies on important scientific researches.

(5) Expenditure for supporting rural production:It refers to the expenditures appropriated from the government budget for supporting the various expenditures of the rural collective units or households for production,including the subsidies to the small water conservancy projects and well drilling,sprinkling irrigation projects run by the villages;subsidies on the rural water and soil conserving measures;subsidies to the small power stations run by the villages;subsidies to the expenditure for fighting against particularly severe draughts;subsidies on the rural waste land exclamation;fund for supporting the township enterprises;subsidies to the expenditure for popularization of the agricultural technologies and plant protection in the rural areas;subsidies to the expenditure for the protection of grasslands and cattle and fowls;subsidies on afforestation and forest protection in rural areas;subsidies on the rural aquatic products in-

dustry;special fund for developing grain production.

(6)Operating expenses of the departments of farming,forestry,water conservancy and meteorology etc,They refer to the expenses appropriated from the government budget for the expenditures of agricultural exclamation,farms,agriculture,animal husbandry,agricultural machinery,forestry,timber industry,water conservancy,aquatic products industry,meteorology,technology popularization in township enterprises,popularization (demonstration) of improved varieties,plant (cattle and fowls,forest) protection,water quality monitoring,prospecting and designing,resources investigation,cadres training,subsidies to horticulture gardens,expenditure of specialized secondary schools,subsidies on the experiments of sowing herbage seeds by flights,expenditures of afforestation agencies and meteorology agencies,expenses for fishery administration and operating expenses for agricultural administration,etc.

(7)Operating expenses of the departments of industry,transport and commerce:They refer to the expenses appropriated from the government budget to the departments of industry,transport and commerce for the expenditure of business development,including expenses for prospecting and designing,expenditures of specialized secondary schools,expenditures of the technical training schools and expenditures for cadres training,etc.

(8)Operating expenses of the departments of culture,education,science and public health:They refer to the expenses appropriated from the government budget for the expenditures of the causes of culture,publication,cultural relics,education,public health,traditional Chinese medical science,free medical services,sports,archives,earthquake,ocean,communications,broadcasting,film and television,family planning;expenditure for training of cadres of government,party and mass organization;expenditures for natural sciences,social sciences,associations for science and technology and the special expenditure for the high-tech researches. They include mainly wages,extra wages,welfare funds,pension for the retirees,stipend,expenses for official business,expenses for equipment purchases,expenses for repairs,business expenses and subsidies to the units which are unable to support their expenditures by their own earnings.

(9)Pension for the disabled or for the families of the bereaved and relief funds for social welfare:They refer to the funds appropfiated from the government budget for the expenditures of pension for the disabled or for the families of the bereaved and relief funds for social welfare,including the lump-sum or regular pension paid by the departments of civil affairs to the members of martyrs families and families of those who died for the public interest,pension to the revolutionary disabled,subsidies for permanent disability of various kinds,subsidies to the military martyrs dependents and the demobilized servicemen,expenditure for settling down the demobilized servicemen,operating expenses of the consoling institutions,expenses for management and repair of the commemorative buildings for the martyrs,the expenses managed by the departments of civil affairs for the retirees and those who have quitted their work,expenses for social relief in rural and urban areas,operating expenses for providing relief to the areas of natural calamity and subsidies on the reconstruction after the particularly severe natural calamities,etc.

(10)Expenditures for national defence:They refer to the funds appropriated from the government budget for the expenditures for building up national defence and safeguarding national security,including expenses of national defence,expenses of scientific researches on national defence,expenses for building up peoples militia and expenditure for special projects,ete.

(11)Administrative expenses:They include expenditure for administration,subsidies to the parties and mass organizations,diplomatic expenditure,expenditure for public security,judicial expenditure,law court expenditure,procuratorial expenditure and subsidies to the expenses for treating the cases by the public security departments,procuratorial organs and law courts.

(12)Expenditure for price subsidies:It refers to the expenditure appropriated,with the approval of the government,from the government budget for the policy subsidies to) price adjustment,including the fund for the increase of grain prices,the subsidies to the difference between the selling prices and purchasing prices of grains,cotton and edible oil,awards in addition to the purchasing prices of cotton,risk fund for non-staple food,subsidies on the prices of meat and meat products,subsidies on the price difference for curbing the high market prices of meat,meat pruducts and vegetables and the subsidies approved by the government on the prices of textbooks and newsprint of newspapers and periodicals.

Revenue of the central government and revenue of the local governments:In accordance with the classification of the structure of the government finance in 1994 on the basis of the classification of channels for collection of tax revenues,the revenue of the central government and the revenue of the local governments have different coverage. The revenue of the central government includes tariff,consumption tax and value added tax levied by the customs,consumption tax,income tax of the enterprises subordinate to the central government,income taxes of the local banks,foreign-funded banks and non-bank financial institutions,business tax,income tax and profits of railways,head offices of banks,head office of insurance company,which are handed over to the government in a centralized way,tax on city maintenance and construction,75% of the value added tax,tax on ocean petroleum resources,50% of the tax on stock dealing(stamp tax). The revenue of the local governments includes business tax,income tax of the enterprises subordinate to the local government, personal income tax, tax on the use of urban land, tax on the adjustment of the investment in fixed assets, tax on town maintenance and construction, tax on real estates, tax on the use of vehicles and ships, stamp tax, slaughter tax, tax on agriculture and animal husbandry, tax on special agricultural products, tax on the occupancy of cultivated land, contract tax, 25% of the value added tax, 50% of the tax on stock dealing (stamp tax) and tax on resources other than the ocean petroleum resources.

Deposit is a form of credit by which enterprises, institutions, organizations or residents can put money into banks and other credit institutions for safekeeping and interest earning under the principle of freedrawal. According to different depositors, deposits are divided into enterprise deposits, treasury deposits, deposits of government agencies and organizations, capital construction deposits, urban saving deposits, rural deposits and other deposits. Deposits are major sources of credit funds of banks.

Loan is a form of credit by which banks and other credit institutions provide funds at certain interest rate to enterprises and individual in the light of the principle of unconditional repayment. Loans from Chinese banks include circulation capital loans, fixed asset loans, loans to urban and rural individuals engaged in industrial and commercial business and agricutural loans.

Insurance Companies refer to commercial insurance companies of various forms registered by law and established in China with the approval ol insurance regulatory agencies.

Amount Insured refers to maximum that the insurant will get for the claim of the case insured.

Premium is the free paid by the insurant to the insurer to obtain the obligation of compensation from the insurance with the agreed terms.

Settled Claim is the compensation paid by the insurer t( ) the insurant in accordance with the insurance contact.

Payment includes payment for death, injury or medical treatment and mature payment. Payment for death injury or medical treatment refers to money paid to insurant (or the benificiary) in accordance with the life or health insurance contract when the insurant encounters accidents within the insured period covered in the contract. Mature payment refers to the mature payment to the insurant in accordance with the life insurance contract at the end of the insured period.

JIANGSU STATISTICAL YEARBOOK

第14篇

科技、教育

SCIENCE, TECHNOLOGY AND EDUCATION

14－1　科技活动基本情况
BASIC STATISTICS ON SCIENTIFIC AND TECHNICAL ACTIVITIES

单位：亿元　　　　(100 million yuan)

指　　标	Item	2000	2003	2004	2005	2006
科技机构数（个）	**Number of Scientific and Technical Research Institutions (unit)**	**1784**	**2726**	**3765**	**3751**	**3620**
#科研单位	Research Institutions	355	257	315	159	281
大中型工业企业	Large and Medium-sized Industrial Enterprises	968	960	1373	1193	1259
高等院校	Institutions of Higher Education	461	445	401	541	377
其他	Others		1064	1676	1858	1703
科技活动人员数（万人）	**Persons Engaged in Scientific and Technical Activities (1000 persons)**	**19.42**	**33.18**	**33.55**	**38.17**	**38.11**
#科学家工程师	Scientists and Engineers	11.03	20.89	19.87	23.08	23.89
科技活动经费筹集总额	**Funding for Scientific and Technical Research**	**134.57**	**372.81**	**515.47**	**613.55**	**713.79**
上级拨款	Apropriations	19.05	54.77	62.14	89.97	93.90
自筹资金	Self Raising	96.75	243.78	384.00	435.52	522.90
金融机构贷款	Loans from Banking Institution	12.00	37.73	43.70	57.05	74.33
事业单位资金	Institutional Funds		11.61	8.16	8.17	8.31
国外资金	Foreign Funds		1.48	1.95	1.69	2.33
其他收入	Others	6.77	23.43	15.52	21.15	12.01
科技活动经费支出总额	**Expenditures of Scientific and Technical Research Funds**	**125.14**	**373.61**	**518.50**	**621.48**	**726.98**
#内部支出	Internal Expenses	114.84	338.02	481.67	572.96	691.24
#劳务费	Service Fees	29.44	72.90	106.02	111.34	125.41
固定资产购建支出	Purchasing Fixed Assets		93.20	149.65	199.74	251.06
研究与发展经费内部支出	Internal Expenses of Research and Development	50.83	150.46	213.98	270.30	346.05
研究与发展经费支出占地区生产总值比重（%）	Ratio of Internal Expenses of Research and Development to GDP (%)	0.59	1.21	1.38	1.48	1.60

14－2　研究与发展课题情况
RESEARCH AND DEVELOPMENT PROJECTS

单位：项　　　　(units)

指　　标	Item	2000	2003	2004	2005	2006
研究与发展课题	Research and Development Projects	12962	20579	28187	29610	31929
#科研单位	Research Institutions	2477	2220	2236	1946	2797
高等院校	Institutes of Higher Education	7857	11637	17543	13503	14628
大中型工业企业	Large and Medium-sized Industrial Enterprises	2628	3177	3822	9241	9935
其他	Others		3545	4586	4920	4569
#基础研究	Basic Research	2214	3719	6390	5152	5427
应用研究	Practical Research	5538	7793	9467	8034	9102
实验发展	Experiment Development	5210	9067	12330	16424	17400

14－3 县级以上政府部门所属研究与开发机构(2006 年)

STATE-OWNED RESEARCH AND DEVELOPMENT INSTITUTIONS ABOVE COUNTY LEVEL(2006)

项目	Item	机构数(个) Institutions (unit)	从业人员总数(人) Employees (Person)
总计	**Total**	**144**	**14610**
按隶属关系分	By Administrative Relationship		
地方部门属	Local Departments	128	10271
省级部门属	Provincial Departments	54	7991
计划单列市部门属	Departments of City Speccfically Designated in the State plan	9	416
地市级部门属	Departments of City and Region Under Province	65	1864
中央部门属	Central Departments	16	4339
#中国科学院	Academy of Science of China	4	829
按国民经济行业分	By Sector		
农、林、牧、渔业	Farming, Forestry, Animal Husbandry and Fishery	39	3703
农业	Farming	23	2605
林业	Forestry	4	369
畜牧业	Animal Husbandry	2	200
渔业	Fishery	7	445
农、林、牧、渔服务业	Service far FFAF	3	84
制造业	Manufacturing	16	1905
纺织服装、鞋、帽制造业	Textile, Garments, Shoes and Hats	1	69
印刷业和记录媒介的复制	Printing and Record Pressing	1	23
医药制造业	Medical and Pharmaceutial Products Manufacturing	6	665
非金属矿物制品业	Nonmetal Mineral Products	1	11
通用设备制造业	Ordinary Machinery Manufacturing	3	275
电气机械及器材制造业	Electric Equipment and Machinery	1	12
通信设备、计算机及其他电子设备制造业	Telecommunications Equipment, Computer and Other Electronic Equipments	3	850
电力、燃气及水的生产和供应业	Electric Power, Gas and Tap Water Production and Supply	2	56
电力、热力的生产和供应业	Electric Power, Steam and Hot Water Production and Supply	2	56
建筑业	Construction	3	206
房屋和土木工程建筑业	Housing an Civil Engineering Construction	3	206
交通运输、仓储和邮政业	Transportation, Storage and Postal Service	1	183
道路运输业	Route Fronsportation	1	183
信息传输、计算机服务和软件业	Information Transmission, Comperter Service and Software	1	12
计算机服务业		1	12
科学研究、技术服务和地质勘查业	Scientific Research, Polytechnical Services and Geological Prospecting	42	3842
研究与试验发展	Research and Experimental Development	23	1733
专业技术服务业	Professional Technology Service	12	1175
科技交流和推广服务业	Science & Technology, Exchang and Popularization Service	3	183
地质勘查业	Gealogical Prospecting	4	751
水利、环境和公共设施管理业	Water Conservancy, Environment and Public Facility Management	16	1979
水利管理业	Water Conservancy Management	6	1395
环境管理业	Environmental Manegement	9	541
公共设施管理业	Public Facility Management	1	43
教育	Education	3	100
教育	Education	3	100
卫生、社会保障和社会福利业	Health Care, Social Security and Social Welfare	18	2525
卫生	Health Care	18	2525
文化、体育和娱乐业	Culture, Sports and Recreation	3	99
文化艺术业	Cultural and Artistic Industry	2	59
体育	Sports	1	40

STATE-OWNED RESEARCH AND DEVELOPMENT INSTITUTIONS ABOVE COUNTY LEVEL(2006)

#单位在职科技活动人员 Personnels at Post Engaged in Scientific and Technical Activities	#科学家、工程师 Scientists and Engineers	经费收入总额(万元) Total Funds Revenue (10000 yuan)	#政府资金 Government Appropriated	经费支出总额(万元) Total Funds Expenditure (10000 yuan)	#科技经费支出 Expenditure for Science & Technology
10929	**7457**	**324550**	**164780**	**321767**	**208096**
7441	4870	205244	104103	211108	122865
5689	3785	172472	91638	182249	99636
279	195	7852	4438	6781	5479
1473	890	24920	8026	22079	17749
3488	2587	119306	60677	110659	85231
656	538	29452	25858	29797	28930
2193	1549	54040	39040	52285	43120
1457	1111	34333	26999	33260	30834
237	128	5180	4056	5190	4179
123	60	2842	1894	2587	1454
317	204	7194	4943	7232	5532
59	46	4490	1147	4018	1121
1653	934	50169	18377	44709	23254
69	51	1894	1652	1973	1973
23	13	308	180	307	183
560	352	18825	4302	17168	5114
11	3	69	10	69	34
217	130	8064	5763	6184	5924
9	7	20	4	20	15
764	378	20991	6466	18988	10013
36	20	344	17	353	135
36	20	344	17	353	135
160	135	5808	16	4451	4365
160	135	5808	16	4451	4365
175	120	6624	1423	4384	3884
175	120	6624	1423	4384	3884
11	4	30	14	34	34
11	4	30	14	34	34
3161	2220	92705	69108	90631	76690
1425	1098	47094	36554	46100	41419
988	660	24830	16087	24206	20323
169	29	3632	2013	3332	3081
579	433	17149	14453	16993	11867
1477	1151	53264	19246	42438	36399
1055	888	37466	14555	31014	29512
388	233	15560	4529	11186	6793
34	30	239	162	239	95
89	6	2882	1414	2650	2403
89	6	2882	1414	2650	2403
1893	1264	56740	14325	78388	16488
1893	1264	56740	14325	78388	16488
81	54	1944	1800	1443	1323
43	21	787	681	857	738
38	33	1157	1118	586	586

14－4 县级以上政府部门所属研究与开发机构基本情况
BASIC STATISTICS ON STATE－OWNED RESEARCH AND DEVELOPMENT INSTITUTIONS ABOVE COUNTY LEVEL

指 标		Item		1995	2000	2004	2005	2006
机构数	（个）	Number of Institutions	（unit）	337	313	263	146	144
职工总数	（人）	Employees	（person）	53090	44071	26569	13482	14610
#科学家工程师		Scientists and Engineers		24428	21122	11604	7099	7457
其他科技人员		Others		10796	7498	5382	1315	
经费收入总额	（亿元）	Funds Revenue	（100 million yuan）	28.56	56.09	62.45	20.09	32.45
#政府拨款		Government Appropriations		6.88	24.88	11.91	13.67	16.48
经费支出总额	（亿元）	Expenditures	（100 million yuan）	28.57	51.53	54.55	17.16	32.18
#基本建设支出		Expenditures for Capital Construction		2.44	4.14	1.91	3.28	

14－5 县级以上政府部门所属研究与开发机构成果
ACHIEVEMENTS OF STATE-OWNED RESEARCH AND DEVELOPMENT INSTITUTIONS ABOVE COUNTY LEVEL

年 份 year	科学著作（万字） Scientific Works （10000 words）	科学论文（篇） Papers （piece）
1978	2138	2532
1989	1717	3263
1990	2540	3728
1991	2454	3392
1992	2086	3962
1993	2273	4629
1994	2783	4049
1995	4196	4662
1996	107（部）	4378
1997	93（种）	4906
1998	92（种）	4798
1999	139（种）	4782
2000	113（种）	4774
2001	139（种）	4872
2002	129（种）	5502
2003	116（种）	5463
2004	106（种）	5214
2005	110（种）	4306
2006	153（种）	4920

14－6 县级以上政府部门所属研究与开发机构课题情况(2006 年)

PROJECTS OF STATE-OWNED RESEARCH AND DEVELOPMENT INSTITUTIONS ABOVE COUNTY LEVEL(2006)

指标	Item	课题数(个) Number of Projects (unit)	#R&D 课题 R&D Projects	课题经费内部支出(万元) Expenditure for Projects (10000 yuan)	#政府资金 Government Appropriation	#R&D 课题经费 Fumds for R&D Projects
总　计	**Total**	**3829**	**2487**	**77077**	**47721**	**44554**
中央政府部门下达课题	Projects Assigned by Central Governmental Departmentss	1091	913	32190	26843	24208
自然科学基金课题	Natural Scientific Foundation	250	249	3438	3258	3437
863 计划课题	863 Plan	55	54	2560	2446	2559
八五攻关计划课题	8th Five year Plan Key Tackling Plan Itcms	40	28	1082	869	701
国家星火计划课题	National Spark Plan	1	1	3	3	3
国家攀登计划课题	National Scale New Heights Plan	51	51	1243	837	1243
国家社会科学基金课题	National Sacial Scientific Fundation	7	7	67	67	67
其它课题	Other Projects	687	523	23797	19363	16197
地方政府部门下达课题	Projects Assigned by Local Governmental Depurtments	1366	769	25179	17757	10386
地方自然科学基金课题	Local Natural Scientific Fundation	110	103	687	568	652
地方攻关计划课题	Local Key Tackling Plan Items	131	96	2054	1530	1407
地方星火计划课题	Local Spark Plan	8	0	105	105	0
地方社会科学基金课题	Local Social Scientific Fundation	38	21	589	162	425
其它课题	Other Projects	1079	549	21744	15392	7903
企业委托课题	Projects Entrusted by Enterprises	598	207	13093	196	5312
自选课题	Self-Selected	468	395	2932	2070	2222
国际合作课题	Intermational Coorperate	73	56	897	292	706
其它课题	Others	233	147	2786	564	1721

指标	Item	课题投入人员(人) Project Personnels Input (person)	#科学家、工程师 Scientists and Engineers	#R&D 人员 R&D Persdonnels	#外聘的流动研究人员 Floating Research Personnels Invited from Outside	#在读研究生 Postgraduates (studying)
总　计	**Total**	**6460**	**4878**	**3708**	**384**	**609**
中央政府部门下达课题	Projects Assigned by Central Governmental Departmentss	2609	2064	1752	195	247
自然科学基金课题	Natural Scientific Foundation	322	285	318	45	79
863 计划课题	863 Plan	93	77	93	7	12
八五攻关计划课题	8th Five Year Plan Key Tackling Plan Items	113	93	71	5	17
国家星火计划课题	National Spark Pean	0	0	0	0	0
国家攀登计划课题	National Scale New Heights Plan	61	55	61	17	5
国家社会科学基金课题	National Sacial Scientific Fundation	28	28	28	6	0
其它课题	Other Projects	1992	1526	1182	115	133
地方政府部门下达课题	Projects Assigned by Local Governmental Depurtments	2394	1653	1109	80	175
地方自然科学基金课题	Local Natural Scientific Fundation	167	133	156	6	27
地方攻关计划课题	Local Key Tackling Plan Items	257	169	160	12	26
地方星火计划课题	Local Spark Plan	19	10	0	1	1
地方社会科学基金课题	Local Social Scientific Fundation	121	65	45	3	2
其它课题	Other Projects	1830	1276	748	58	119
企业委托课题	Projects Entrusted by Enterprises	578	419	202	21	20
自选课题	Self-Selected	522	456	415	74	131
国际合作课题	International Coorperate	112	94	69	12	11
其它课题	Others	245	192	161	3	25

14－7 大中型工业企业科技情况
BASIC STATISTICS ON SCIENTIFIC AND TECHNICAL ACTIVITIES OF LARGE AND MEDIUM-SIZED INDUSTRIAL ENTERPRISES

单位:亿元 (100 million yuan)

指标	Item	1995	2000	2004	2005	2006
企业数 (个)	Number of Enterprise	2329	2091	3157	3374	3672
#有科技机构的企业数	Enterprises Having Technical Development Institutions	1068	779	1569	1695	1831
企业办科技机构数 (个)	Science and Technilogy Institutions of Enterprises (unit)	1599	968	1373	1193	1259
从事科技的人员数 (万人)	Science and Technology Personnel (10000 persons)	11.48	14.71	16.95	20.25	20.50
#有高、中级职称或大学本科及以上学历的人员	Personnel with Senior, Medium, Professional Titles or University and over Education	3.67	7.13	9.11	11.54	12.19
#科技机构中的人员	Personnel in Science and Technology Institutions	3.66	4.46	7.45	6.20	6.77
#有高中级职称或大学本科及以上学历的人员	Personnel with Senior, Medium, Junior profes-sional or over University Record	1.78	2.65	3.37	3.89	
科技经费筹集额	Funds of Science and Technology	45.80	95.39	309.48	389.79	480.39
#上级拨款	Appropriations from Higher Authorities	1.76	3.58	4.88	8.00	11.25
金融机构贷款	Loans from Banking Institutions	7.49	10.51	25.53	43.09	60.05
本企业自筹	Enterprise Self-Raising	35.14	77.36	271.17	324.39	401.90
科技经费支出总额	Total Expenditures of Science and Technology	42.25	90.83	312.03	400.08	497.87
内部支出中	Internal Expenses					
#科技人员劳务费	Expenses for Science and Technology Personnel	6.81	19.50	60.93	65.74	78.87
原材料费	Services and Raw Materials	13.86	27.32	88.71	112.79	150.64
固定资产购建费	Purchasing of Fixed Assets			90.61	133.12	179.51
用于开发新产品经费	New Product Development Expenditures	20.78	47.46	115.90	227.78	326.17
外部支出经费	External Funds	2.36	9.40	29.75	41.20	28.61
技术改造支出总额	Total Technical Updating Expenditures	92.21	100.52	266.66	279.57	274.18
技术引进支出总额	Total Technical Introduced	23.37	20.97	54.97	41.55	34.28
#引进设计、图纸、工艺、专利用款	Design, Blueprint, Technology and Patent Expenditures	1.85	15.11			
用于消化吸收的经费	Digesting and Absorbing Expenditures	1.17	0.99	6.37	6.06	9.16
购买国内技术用款	Purchasing Domestic Technology	1.36	3.39	9.03	9.62	9.22
科技活动产出	Science and Technology Output					
新产品销售收入	New Product Sales Revenue	329.10	973.30	2414.03	2679.67	3270.33
新产品销售利润	Profit of New Products Sales	37.45				
企业专利申请数 (件)	Total Patent Application (unit)	405	1183	3878	5226	6267
#发明专利数	Number of Invention Patents			972	1408	1762
企业拥有发明专利数 (件)	Total Number of Invention Patents (unit)			1639	2868	4213

14-8 大中型工业企业研究与发展经费内部支出
BASIC STATISTICS ON INTRAMURAL R&D EXPENDITURE OF LARGE AND MEDIUM-SIZED INDUSTRIAL ENTERPRISES

单位:亿元 (100 million yuan)

项 目	Item	2000	2004	2005	2006
总计	**Total**	**33.15**	**123.99**	**175.84**	**238.77**
按登记注册类型分	**Grouped by Type of Registration**				
内资企业	Inner Funded Enterprises	29.26	91.19	123.04	160.35
国有企业	State-Owned Enterprises	11.37	10.51	14.29	19.21
集体企业	Collective-Owned Enterprises	4.63	4.42	6.19	4.95
股份合作企业	Share Holding Cooperative Enterprises	0.99	1.27	1.32	1.62
联营企业	Joint-Ownership Enterprises	0.3	0.04	0.12	0.09
有限责任公司	Responsibility Co. Ltd.	7.06	39.26	51.03	64.66
#国有独资	State Solely Funded	3.52	10.88	15.88	11.07
股份有限公司	Share Holding Co. Ltd.	4.65	24.09	30.45	38.65
私营企业	Private Entreprises	0.25	11.53	19.56	31.14
其他企业	Other Enterprises	0	0.01	0.08	0.04
港、澳、台商投资企业	Hong Kong, Macao and Taiwan Funded Enterprises	1.42	8.05	16.63	23.42
外商投资企业	Foreign Funded Enterprises	2.48	24.75	36.17	55.00
按企业规模分	**Grouped by Scale of Enterprise**				
大型企业	Large	22.16	58.32	85.90	120.77
中型企业	Medium	10.99	65.67	89.94	118.00
按行业分	**Grouped by Sector**				
采矿业	**Mining and Quarrying**	**0.75**	**2.84**	**2.65**	**2.83**
煤炭开采和洗选业	Coal Mining and Processing	0.43	2.29	1.85	2.05
石油和天然气开采业	Petroleum and Natural Gas Extraction	0.21	0.44	0.61	0.66
黑色金属矿采选业	Ferrous Metals Mining and Processing	0.05	0.02	0.01	0.03
有色金属矿采选业	Nonferrous Metals Mining and Processing	0.01	0.02	0.02	0.01
非金属矿采选业	Nonmetal Minerals Mining and Processing	0.05	0.06	0.14	0.08
其他矿采选业	Nonmetal Minerals Mining and Processing				
制造业	**Manufacturing**	**31.88**	**120.50**	**172.26**	**235.28**
农副食品加工业	Food Processing	0.13	0.17	0.27	0.45
食品制造业	Food Production	0.05	0.71	0.83	0.54
饮料制造业	Beverage Production	0.69	0.19	0.49	0.74
烟草加工业	Tobacco Processing	0.09	0.10	0.15	0.14
纺织业	Textile Industry	2.7	7.45	6.85	8.51
纺织服装、鞋、帽制造业	Textile, Garments, Shoes and Hats	0.23	2.86	4.44	4.85
皮革、毛皮、羽毛(绒)及其制品业	Leather, Furs, Down and Related Products	0.04	0.11	0.25	0.29

14－8 续表 Continued

单位:亿元 (100 million yuan)

项目	Item	2000	2004	2005	2006
木材加工及木、竹、藤、棕、草制造业	Timber Processing, Wood, Bamboo, Cane, Palm Fiber and Straw Products	0.01	1.40	2.94	1.69
家具制造业	Furniture Manufacturing	0	0.01	0.02	0.11
造纸及纸制品业	Papermaking and Paper Products	0.33	2.09	1.22	3.36
印刷业和记录媒介的复制	Printing and Record Pressing	0.05	0.25	0.17	0.18
文教体育用品制造业	Stationery, Education and Sports Goods	0	0.07	0.27	0.69
石油加工、炼焦及核燃料加工业	Petroleum Processing, Coking Products and Nuclear Fuel Processing	0.43	0.53	0.57	0.47
化学原料及化学制品制造业	Raw Chemical Materials and Chemical Products	5.07	17.42	29.01	36.22
医药制造业	Medical and Pharmaceutical Products	1.34	5.09	6.38	7.86
化学纤维制造业	Chemical Fibers	1.36	2.07	4.33	7.10
橡胶制品业	Rubber Products	0.17	0.62	0.60	1.03
塑料制品业	Plastic Products	0.33	1.62	2.26	2.94
非金属矿物制品业	Nonmetal Mineral Products	0.53	1.33	1.98	2.94
黑色金属冶炼及压延加工业	Smelting and Pressing of Ferrous Metals	1.03	8.39	12.39	22.54
有色金属冶炼及压延加工业	Smelting and Pressing of Nonferrous Metals	0.35	1.53	1.15	2.37
金属制品业	Metal Products	0.65	3.06	3.75	7.19
通用设备制造业	Ordinary Machinery Manufacturing	3.8	12.90	18.58	20.48
专用设备制造业	Special Purposes Equipment Manufacturing	1.42	5.09	6.12	11.00
交通运输设备制造业	Transportation Equipment Manufacturing	3.24	11.56	14.89	19.01
电气机械及器材制造业	Electric Equipment and Machinery	2.77	14.03	20.50	29.52
通信设备、计算机及其他电子设备制造业	Telecommunications Equipment, Computer and Other Electronic Equipments	4.16	17.80	28.59	38.67
仪器仪表及文化、办公用机械制造业	Instruments, Meters, Cultural and Official Machinery	0.67	1.54	2.83	3.93
工艺品及其他制造业	Handicraft Artical and Other Manufacturing		0.49	0.42	0.48
废弃资源和废旧材料回收加工业	Waste Resouces and Junk Material Recycled				
电力、燃气及水的生产和供应业	**Electric Power, Gas and Water Production and Supply**	**0.52**	**0.66**	**0.93**	**0.67**
电力、热力的生产和供应业	Electric Power, Steam and Hot Water Production and Supply	0.47	0.52	0.92	0.56
燃气生产和供应	Gas Production and Supply	0.01	0.00	0.00	0.00
水的生产和供应业	Tap Water Production and Supply	0.04	0.11	0.01	0.11

14－9　高等学校科技活动情况
BASIC STATISTICS ON SCIENTIFIC AND TECHNICAL ACTIVITIES OF INSTITUTIONS OF HIGHER EDUCATION

指　标	Item	1995	2000	2004	2005	2006
参加科技统计的高校　（所）	Institutions of Higher Education in Statistics (unit)	47	48	38	39	49
从事科技活动人数　（人）	Personnel in Scientific and Technical Activities (person)	57787	59252	37110	39003	41657
教　师	Teachers	28270	30497	21848	22999	25989
其他技术人员	Other Technical Persons	27073	26174	15262	15315	15668
辅助人员	Assistants	2444	2581	1336	689	682
从事研究与发展活动人员（人）	Perssonnel in Research and Development (person)	20295	18919	21848	22999	25989
#正教授	Professors	1908	1832	3500	3741	3931
副教授	Associate Professors	4507	4100	6273	6590	7236
讲　师	Lecturers	4849	6761	6846	7486	9088
助　教	Assistants	1563	1380	4389	4616	5359
研究与发展机构　（个）	Institution of Research and Development (unit)	408	469	339	361	335
机构中研究与发展人员（人）	Personnel (person)	5496	5901	6415	7265	7530
当年研究与开发经费收入（万元）	Funds Revenue of Research and Development (10000 yuan)	50695	142685	354513	390441	434139
#科技事业费	Scientific and Technical Funds	4958	8915	30804	31608	35410
主管部门专项费	Speical Funds of Responsible Department for the Work	7398	14835	28578	47648	42061
国务院各部门专项费	Speical Funds of State Council Department	2728	10807	66567	59097	60435
省专项费	Provincial Special Foundation	3215	11405	26287	25956	36269
企事业单位委托经费	Entrusting Funds of Enterprises and Institutions	24705	70874	161059	181625	204118
国家自然科学基金	State Natural Sciences Foundation	1654	6640	17646	23256	24864
各种收入转入科研经费	Funds from Other Revenues	1179	4101	15254	18045	26978
研究与发展课题　（项）	Projects of Research and Development (unit)	9810	8412	12344	13503	14682
#基础研究	Fundamental Research	1710	2007	3919	4723	4912
应用研究	Applied Research	6177	5084	6591	6861	7463
实验发展	Experimental Development	11923	1321	1834	1919	2307
研究与发展成果	Achievements of Research and Development					
出版科学专著　（部）	Publishing Scientific Works (book)	558	449	224	153	169
发表学术论文　（篇）	Publishing Papers (piece)	19153	24303	34408	39868	46383
#国外发表	Abroad	2277	2710	4376	5436	8054
全国性学术刊物发表	National Journals	11199	15763			
地方性学术刊物发表	Local Journals	5727	5830			
科技成果转让　（项）	Scientific Achievements Transfered (unit)	660	660	1526	558	651
获奖成果数　（项）	Prized Achievements (unit)	743	262	219	360	346
#国家级	National Level	35	11	19	36	19
部省级	Provincial Level	383	251	200	170	176

14－10 各类专业技术人员数
NUMBER OF SCIENTIFIC AND TECHNICAL PERSONNELS

单位:万人 （10000 persons）

年　份 Year	各类专业技术人员总计 Total	#工程技术人员 Engineering	#农业技术人员 Agriculture	#科学研究人员 Scientific Research and Experiment	#卫生技术人员 Health Care	#教学人员 Teaching
1980	43.87	9.63	1.13	1.47	9.02	17.13
1985	83.41	20.70	1.76	1.59	13.35	35.90
1989	150.56	34.08	2.37	1.86	17.42	49.88
1990	158.86	31.84	2.35	1.84	13.87	44.50
1991	166.02	25.86	2.39	0.67	13.54	44.57
1992	174.70	27.36	2.53	0.73	14.17	44.98
1993	172.71	41.72	2.50	2.19	19.90	50.83
1994	179.94	27.88	2.21	0.60	14.99	47.57
1995	184.97	28.38	2.65	0.60	15.48	50.72
1996	189.49	44.82	3.68	1.90	21.75	59.15
1997	193.46	44.51	3.90	1.94	22.13	62.46
1998	202.15	47.53	4.45	1.74	22.72	63.83
1999	198.20	45.67	4.51	1.48	22.86	64.94
2000	194.24	44.84	4.61	1.81	23.04	66.15
2001	186.05	40.11	4.18	1.75	23.19	66.95
2002	175.79	35.79	3.74	1.56	22.96	67.56
2003	163.20	29.19	3.74	1.82	22.07	68.01
2004	147.23	22.16	3.25	1.77	20.86	69.25
2005	148.67	20.96	3.18	1.83	23.45	69.33
2006	142.20	20.54	3.11	1.69	21.35	69.27

14－11 地方国有经济单位各类专业技术人员基本情况
BASIC STATISTICS ON SCIENTIFIC AND TECHNICAL PERSONNEL IN LOCAL STATE-OWNED ECONOMIC UNITS

单位:万人 （10000 persons）

指　标	Item	1990	1995	2000	2004	2005	2006
总　计	**Total**	**112.20**	**130.07**	**154.57**	**123.53**	**124.97**	**114.39**
#高级职称	Senior Professional	3.49	5.77	9.84	9.04	10.10	10.91
中级职称	Medium Titles	25.29	34.64	48.38	45.12	47.18	45.83
初级职称	Junior Titles	68.46	78.92	81.18	59.48	58.08	49.59
工程技术人员	Engineering	24.10	28.38	32.27	14.38	13.18	11.82
农业技术人员	Agriculture	2.32	2.65	4.04	3.24	3.16	3.02
科学研究人员	Scientific Research and Experiment	0.79	0.60	1.63	0.69	0.75	0.78
卫生技术人员	Health Care	12.74	15.48	17.76	19.92	25.51	17.05
教学人员	Teaching	41.70	50.72	65.44	67.16	67.24	67.46
其他人员	Others	30.55	32.24	33.43	18.14	15.13	14.26

14－12　三种专利申请受理量
THREE TYPES OF PATENT APPLICATIONS EXAMINED

单位:件　　(unit)

指　　标	Item	1990	1995	2000	2004	2005	2006
申请受理量合计	**Total Applications Examined**	**2706**	**4078**	**8210**	**23532**	**34811**	**53267**
#发　明	Creations and Inventions	384	538	1159	4423	6582	10214
实用新型	Utility Models	2085	2708	4590	9405	11071	13386
外观设计	Designs	237	832	2461	9704	17158	29667
#非职务	Non-service	1620	2665	4530	13737	20693	30486
职　务	Service	886	1413	3680	9795	14118	22781
大专院校	Universities and Colleges	135	164	212	1342	2529	2498
科研单位	Scientific Resarch Institutions	112	104	129	290	382	352
工矿企业	Industrial and Mineral Enterprises	522	887	3296	8115	11157	19778
机关团体	Government Agencies and Organizations	117	258	43	48	50	153

14－13　三种专利授权量
THREE KINDS OF PATENTS GRANTED

单位:件　　(unit)

指　　标	Item	1990	1995	2000	2004	2005	2006
申请授权量合计	**Total**	**1455**	**2413**	**6432**	**11330**	**13580**	**19352**
#发　明	Creations and Inventions	69	72	341	1026	1241	1631
实用新型	Utility Models	1236	1884	4095	5474	6483	8849
外观设计	Designs	150	457	1996	4830	5856	8872
#非职务	Non-service	916	1506	3125	5827	7021	9876
职务	Service	539	907	3307	5503	6559	9476
大专院校	Universities and Colleges	104	112	139	461	896	1367
科研单位	Scientific Resarch Institutions	78	73	106	142	182	233
工矿企业	Industrial and Mineral Enterprises	297	447	3022	4836	5436	7835
机关团体	Government Agencies and Organizations	60	275	40	64	45	41

14－14 全省产品质量监督检查情况（2006年）
RESULTS OF SAMPLING CHECK ON THE QUALITY OF PRODUCTS UNDER PROVINCIAL SUPERVISION (2006)

产品名称	Item	监督检查企业数(家) Number of Enterprises Supervised & Checked(unit)	查出不合格产品企业数(家) Number of Enterprises With Products Ungualified (unit)	不合格产品企业所占比例(%) Proportion of Enterprises With Products Unqualified (%)
合　计	**Total**	**12676**	**1318**	**10.4**
农用产品	**Products for Agricultural Production**	**1199**	**77**	**6.4**
拖拉机	Tractors	29	3	10.3
农用化肥	Chemical Fertilizers	510	25	4.9
化学农药	Chemical Pesticides	394	19	4.8
饲　料	Forages	206	23	11.2
其　它	Others	60	7	11.7
加工食品和饮料	**Food and Beverage**	**2694**	**469**	**17.4**
小麦粉、大米	Wheat Flour, Rice	741	120	16.2
肉制品	Meat Products	129	10	7.8
食用盐	Edible Salt	16	0	0.0
调味品	Flavouring	34	2	5.9
白　酒	White Spirit	361	83	23.0
啤　酒	Beer	22	0	0.0
黄酒,果酒	Yellow Rice Wine, Fruit Wine	20	4	20.0
食用植物油	Edible Vegertable Oil	114	10	8.9
罐　头	Canned Food	5	0	0.0
糕点,糖果	Cake and Candy	179	18	10.1
非酒精液体饮料	Non－Spirit Beverage	95	45	47.4
冷冻饮品	Frozen Beverage	683	158	23.1
乳制品	Dairy Products	44	7	15.9
其　它	Other	251	12	4.8
家用电器	**Household Electric Appliances**	**79**	**4**	**5.1**
电视机、录像机	TV sets and videocorder	2	0	0.0
吸油烟器	Range Hoods	4	0	0.0
空调器	Air Conditioners	16	0	0.0
电热器具	Electric Heating Appliances	10	0	0.0
其它	Others	47	4	8.5
轻工产品	**Light Industrial Products**	**2098**	**167**	**8.0**
纸	Paper	13	3	13.1
纸制品	Paper Products	264	18	6.8
家具	Furniture	310	28	9.0
眼镜(架,片)	Spectacles (Glass & Frame)	911	41	4.5
镇流器	Ballast	18	1	5.6
燃气灶具	Gas Kitchen Range	8	0	0.0

14－14 续 表 1 Continued

产 品 名 称	Item	监督检查企业数(家) Number of Enterprises Supervised & Checked(unit)	查出不合格产品企业数(家) Number of Enterprises With Products Ungualified (unit)	不合格产品企业所占比例(%) Proportion of Enterprises With Products Unqualified (%)
化妆品	Cosmetic	150	9	6.0
橡胶,塑料制品	Rubber and Plastic Products	19	3	15.8
其它	Others	405	64	15.8
纺织,鞋类产品	**Textile and Shoes**	**420**	**66**	**15.7**
布、印染色织坯布	Cloth, Printing and Dyeing Color Grey	65	7	10.8
毛织品	Wool Fabrics	37	5	13.5
针织品	Knit Goods	22	2	9.1
鞋	Shoes	69	18	26.1
其它	Others	227	34	15.0
化工产品	**Chemical Products**	**1033**	**69**	**6.7**
涂料,油漆	Paint	368	50	13.6
化学试剂	Chemical Reagent	177	4	2.3
其它	Others	488	15	3.1
建材产品	**Building Raw Materials**	**1058**	**131**	**12.4**
水泥	Cement	257	8	3.1
水泥预制构件	Cement Prefabricated Components	139	2	1.4
水暖管件	Waterpipe	235	58	24.7
人造板	Man－Made Board	25	5	20.0
其它	Others	402	58	14.4
机电产品	**Mechanical and Electrical Products**	**2392**	**216**	**9.0**
轴承	Bearings	39	8	20.5
阀类,泵	Valves	205	20	9.8
电线,电缆	Electric Wire, Electric Cable	614	49	8.0
电动工具	Electric Tools	69	10	14.5
低压电器及元件	Low-voltage Electric Elements	106	2	1.9
消防器材	Fire-fighting Equipment & Materials	106	6	5.6
电动机,柴油机	Motors & Diesel Engines	296	30	10.1
其它	Others	957	91	9.5
冶金产品,金属产品	**Metallurgical and Metal Products**	**1059**	**61**	**5.8**
线材	Wire Rod	83	10	12.1
型材	Section Steel	271	14	5.2
其它	Others	705	37	5.3
能源产品	**Energy Products**	**26**	**0**	**0.0**
汽油,柴油	Gasolin, Diesel Oil	16	0	0.0
其它	Coke	10	0	0.0
其它	**Energy Products**	**618**	**58**	**9.4**

14－14　续表 2　Continued

产品名称	Item	检查批次（批次）Number of Batch-times Supervised & Checked (unit)	合格批次（批次）Proportion of Batch-times Products Qualified (unit)	批次合格率（%）Rate of Batch-times Qualified (%)
合　计	**Total**	**12676**	**11358**	**89.6**
农用产品	**Products for Agricultural Production**	**1199**	**1122**	**93.6**
拖拉机	Tractors	29	26	89.7
农机配件	Farm Machinery Fittings	510	485	95.1
化学农药	Chemical Pesticides	394	375	95.2
饲　料	Forages	206	183	88.8
其　它	Others	60	53	88.3
加工食品和饮料	**Food and Beverage**	**2694**	**2225**	**82.6**
小麦粉、大米	Wheat Flour, Rice	741	621	83.8
肉制品	Meat Products	129	119	92.2
食用盐	Edible Salt	16	16	100.0
调味品	Flavouring	34	32	94.1
白　酒	White Spirit	361	278	77.0
啤　酒	Beer	22	22	100.0
黄酒，果酒	Yellow Rice Wine, Fruit Wine	20	16	80.0
食用植物油	Edible Vegertable Oil	114	104	91.2
罐　头	Canned Food	5	5	100.0
糕点，糖果	Cake and Candy	179	161	89.9
非酒精液体饮料	Non－Spirit Beverage	95	50	52.6
冷冻饮品	Frozen Beverage	683	525	76.9
乳制品	Dairy Products	44	37	84.1
其　它	Other	251	239	95.2
家用电器	**Household Electric Appliances**	**79**	**75**	**94.9**
电视机、录像机	TV sets and videocorder	2	2	100.0
吸油烟器	Range Hoods	4	4	100.0
空调器	Air Conditioners	16	16	100.0
电热器具	Electric Heating Appliances	10	10	100.0
其它	Others	47	43	91.5
轻工产品	**Light Industrial Products**	**2098**	**1931**	**92.0**
纸	Paper	13	10	76.9
纸制品	Paper Products	264	246	93.2
家具	Furniture	310	282	91.0
眼镜（架，片）	Spectacles (Glass & Frame)	911	870	95.5
镇流器	Ballast	18	17	94.4
燃气灶具	Gas Kitchen Range	8	8	100.0

14－14　续 表 3　Continued

产 品 名 称	Item	检查批次（批次）Number of Batch-times Supervised & Checked (unit)	合格批次（批次）Proportion of Batch-times Products Qualified (unit)	批次合格率（%）Rate of Batch-times Qualified (%)
化妆品	Cosmetic	150	141	94.0
橡胶,塑料制品	Rubber and Plastic Products	19	16	84.2
其它	Others	405	341	84.2
纺织,鞋类产品	**Textile and Shoes**	**420**	**354**	**84.3**
布、印染色织坯布	Cloth, Printing and Dyeing Color Grey	65	58	89.2
毛织品	Wool Fabrics	37	32	86.5
针织品	Knit Goods	22	20	90.9
鞋	Shoes	69	51	73.9
其它	Others	227	193	85.0
化工产品	**Chemical Products**	**1033**	**964**	**93.3**
涂料,油漆	Paint	368	318	86.4
化学试剂	Chemical Reagent	177	173	97.7
其它	Others	488	473	96.9
建材产品	**Building Raw Materials**	**1058**	**927**	**87.6**
水泥	Cement	257	249	96.9
水泥预制构件	Cement Prefabricated Components	139	137	98.6
水暖管件	Waterpipe	235	177	75.3
人造板	Man－Made Board	25	20	80.0
其它	Others	402	344	85.6
机电产品	**Mechanical and Electrical Products**	**2392**	**2176**	**91.0**
轴承	Bearings	39	31	79.5
阀类,泵	Valves	205	185	90.2
电线,电缆	Electric Wire, Electric Cable	614	565	92.0
电动工具	Electric Tools	69	59	85.5
低压电器及元件	Low-voltage Electric Elements	106	104	98.1
消防器材	Fire-fighting Equipment & Materials	106	100	94.3
电动机,柴油机	Motors & Diesel Engines	296	266	89.9
其它	Others	957	866	90.5
冶金产品,金属产品	**Metallurgical and Metal Products**	**1059**	**998**	**94.2**
线材	Wire Rod	83	73	88.0
型材	Section Steel	271	257	94.8
其它	Others	705	668	94.8
能源产品	**Energy Products**	**26**	**26**	**100.0**
汽油,柴油	Gasolin, Diesel Oil	16	16	100.0
其它	Coke	10	10	100.0
其它	**Energy Products**	**618**	**560**	**90.6**

14－15 教育事业基本情况
BASIC STATISTICS ON EDUCATION

单位:万人　　(10000 persons)

项　　目	Item	1990	1995	2000	2005	2006
学校数　（所）	**Number of Schools　(unit)**					
普通高等学校	Regular Institutions of Higher Eduction	70	67	71	115	119
普通中等学校	Secondary Schools	6377	5093	4222	3530	3498
中等专业学校	Specialized Schools	195	213	185	150	157
普通中学	Regular Secondary Schools	5808	4439	3675	3141	3098
#高　中	Senior Secondary Shools	1017	963	859	849	838
职业高中	Vocational Senior Secondary Schools	374	441	362	239	243
小　学	Primary Schools	30557	27062	19110	6261	5940
特殊教育	Special Schools	95	132	123	109	107
专任教师　（万人）	**Number of Fulltime Teachers (10000 persons)**					
普通高等学校	Regular Institutions of Higher Eduction	2.76	2.73	3.31	6.73	7.84
普通中等学校	Secondary Schools	19.63	22.16	25.02	31.13	31.92
中等专业学校	Specialized Schools	1.20	1.30	1.37	1.42	1.62
普通中学	Regular Secondary Schools	17.25	18.91	21.59	27.98	28.42
#高　中	Senior Secondary Shools	3.27	3.59	5.46	8.88	9.39
职业高中	Vocational Senior Secondary Schools	1.18	1.95	2.06	1.73	1.88
小　学	Primary Schools	26.95	27.35	28.90	26.16	26.05
特殊教育	Special Schools	0.17	0.27	0.27	0.25	0.27
招生数　（万人）	**New Student Enrollment (10000 persons)**					
普通高等教育	Regular Higher Eduction	4.56	7.13	18.22	39.02	39.09
研究生	Postgraduates	0.23	0.38	0.97	2.87	3.18
本专科生	University and College Students	4.33	6.75	17.25	36.15	35.91
普通中等学校	Secondary Schools	109.51	136.80	157.94	197.19	195.43
中等专业学校	Specialized Secondary Schools	4.28	12.27	10.64	24.45	26.12
普通中学	Regular Secondary Schools	99.08	114.03	141.44	157.55	152.75
#高　中	Senior Secondary Shools	13.95	18.47	29.93	52.25	53.69
职业高中	Vocational Senior Secondary Schools	6.15	10.50	5.86	15.19	16.56
小　学	Primary Schools	90.12	130.42	95.53	61.93	63.75
特殊教育	Special Schools	0.24	0.71	0.39	0.40	0.39
在校学生　（万人）	**Students Enrollment (10000 persons)**					
普通高等教育	Regular Higher Eduction	15.38	21.95	47.48	123.77	139.53
研究生	Postgraduates	0.69	1.09	2.29	7.79	8.91
本专科生	University and College Students	14.69	20.86	45.19	115.98	130.62
普通中等学校	Secondary Schools	311.50	374.86	433.97	592.97	585.17
中等专业学校	Specialized Secondary Schools	13.99	31.87	43.62	66.10	73.29
普通中学	Regular Secondary Schools	281.97	316.75	373.64	491.56	471.27
#高　中	Senior Secondary Shools	40.76	47.71	80.18	145.34	152.57
职业高中	Vocational Senior Secondary Schools	15.54	26.24	16.71	35.31	40.61
小　学	Primary Schools	612.29	644.77	718.55	485.53	455.75
特殊教育	Special Schools	1.02	3.98	3.59	3.07	3.00
毕业生数　（万人）	**Graduate (10000 persons)**					
普通高等教育	Regular Higher Eduction	4.61	6.17	8.01	24.46	27.66
研究生	Postgraduates	0.27	0.22	0.44	1.49	1.93
本专科生	University and College Students	4.34	5.95	7.57	22.97	25.73
普通中等学校	Secondary Schools	85.27	105.40	117.74	180.99	188.44
中等专业学校	Specialized Secondary Schools	3.84	5.17	14.49	10.90	12.99
普通中学	Regular Secondary Schools	76.45	92.62	96.00	162.98	166.32
#高　中	Senior Secondary Shools	13.77	13.65	22.99	42.65	44.97
职业高中	Vocational senior Secondary Schools	4.98	7.61	7.25	7.11	9.13
小　学	Primary Schools	103.78	99.03	114.78	105.52	97.82
特殊教育	Special Schools	0.05	0.22	0.36	0.43	0.43

注:2000 年以前职业高中为职业中学数据。

Note: Before 2000, the figure of voctional senior seeondary schools was vocational secondary schools.

14－16 各级各类教育事业(2006年)
BASIC STATISTICS ON EDUCATION BY LEVEL AND TYPE (2006)

单位:万人 (10000 persons)

指标	Item	学校数(所) Number of Schools (unit)	毕业生数 Graduates	招生数 New Student Enrollment	在校学生数 Students Enrollment in schools	教职工数 Teachers and Staff	#专任教师 Full-time Teachers
普通高等教育	Regular Higher Education	119	27.66	39.09	139.53	13.22	7.84
研究生	Postgraduates	44	1.93	3.18	8.91		
本专科学生	Undergraduate and Students of College for Prefessional Training	35	25.73	35.91	130.62		
普通中等专业学校	Regular Specialized Secondary Schools	157	12.99	26.12	73.29	2.30	1.62
普通中学	Regular Secondary Schools	3098	166.32	152.75	471.27	34.09	28.42
高　中	Senior Secondary Schools	838	44.97	53.69	152.57	2.35	9.39
初　中	Junior Secondary Schools	2260	121.35	99.06	318.71	28.84	19.03
职业高中	Vocational Senior Middle Schools	243	9.13	16.56	40.61	2.35	1.88
技工学校	Technical Schools	139	6.00	10.64	28.88	1.39	0.97
小　学	Primary Schools	5940	97.82	63.75	455.75	28.84	26.05
特殊教育学校	Special Schools	107	0.43	0.39	3.00	0.34	0.26
幼儿园	Kindergartens	6503	56.47	66.06	150.15	7.98	5.61
工读学校 (人)	Missed Children Schools (person)	3	177	101	222	98	72
成人高等教育	Adult Higher Education	23	4.28	11.45	32.45	0.99	0.65
#广播电视大学	Radio and TV Universities	2	1.47	0.00	4.91	0.67	0.45
职工高等学校	Schools of Higher Education for Staff	2	299	398	1498	654	390
教育学院	Pedagogical College	4	0.45	0.34	1.51	0.14	0.09
成人中等专业学校	Specialized Secondary Schools for Adults	122	1.70	2.52	5.46	0.68	0.40
成人中学	Secondary Schools for Adults	361	9.13		3.24	0.24	0.14
成人技术培训学校	Technical Training Schools for Adults	5994	360.20		271.33	1.04	0.57
成人初等学校	Primary Schools for Adults	587	1.90		3.25	0.14	0.08
网络教育	Network Education	4	0.60	0.72	1.60		
学历文凭考试机构	Schooling and Diploma Examing	11	0.14		0.16	0.03	0.01

14－17 全 省 研 究 生 数
NUMBER OF POSTGRADUATES

单位:人 (person)

指 标	Item	1990	1995	2000	2005	2006
高等学校	**Institutions of Higher Education**					
招生数	New Student Enrollment	2214	3730	21705	28306	31393
在读人数	Student Enrollment	6718	10700	52875	76783	87900
#女 性	Female	1175	2384	19409	31608	36655
毕业生数	Graduates	2626	2202	8918	14699	19036
研究所(院)	**Research Institutions (Academies)**					
招生数	New Student Enrollment	62	65	318	379	400
在读人数	Student Enrollment	191	191	758	1101	1209
#女 性	Female	20	27	187	309	356
毕业生数	Graduates	91	45	117	184	277

14－18 各级各类学校女在校学生和女专任教师数
NUMBER OF FEMALE STUDENTS ENROLLMENT AND TEACHERS BY LEVEL AND TYPE OF SCHOOLS

单位:万人 (10000 persons)

指 标	Item	1990	1995	2000	2005	2006
女在校学生数 (万人)	Number of Female Students in Schools (10000 persons)					
普通高等教育本、专科	Regular Institutions of Higher Education	4.30	6.79	16.32	53.99	62.20
普通中等专业学校	Regular Specialized Secondary Schools	6.04	16.19	23.17	35.78	38.75
普通中学	Regular Secondary Schools	117.64	139.72	166.00	224.09	214.36
职业高中	Professional Senior Secondary Schools	6.69	12.30	7.23	16.51	19.17
小 学	Primary Schools	288.49	306.29	338.08	222.77	208.34
女在校学生占在校学生总数 (%)	**Percentage of Female Students in Schools to Total Students (%)**					
普通高等教育本、专科	Regular Institutions of Higher Education	29.3	32.6	38.1	46.6	44.6
普通中等专业学校	Regular Specialized Secondary Schools	43.1	50.8	53.1	54.1	52.9
普通中学	Regular Secondary Schools	41.7	44.1	44.4	45.6	45.5
职业高中	Professional Senior Secondary Schools	43.1	46.9	43.3	46.8	47.2
小 学	Primary Schools	47.1	47.5	47.1	45.9	45.7
女专任教师数 (万人)	Number of Full Time Female Teachers (10000 persons)					
普通高等学校	Regular Institutions of Higher Education	0.71	0.76	1.14	2.77	3.05
普通中等专业学校	Regular Specialized Secondary Schools	0.42	0.52	0.58	0.69	0.8
普通中学	Regular Secondary Schools	4.28	5.58	7.69	11.86	12.31
职业高中	Professional Senior Secondary Schools	0.28	0.63	0.81	0.75	0.85
小 学	Primary Schools	10.34	11.64	13.93	14.08	14.27
女专任教师占专任教师总数 (%)	Percentage of Full Time Female Teachers to Total Teachers (%)					
普通高等学校	Regular Institutions of Higher Education	25.8	27.8	34.5	41.2	61.9
普通中等专业学校	Regular Specialized Secondary Schools	35.2	39.9	42.0	48.6	49.3
普通中学	Regular Secondary Schools	24.8	29.5	35.6	42.4	43.3
职业高中	Professional Senior Secondary Schools	24.7	32.4	39.4	43.6	45.3
小 学	Primary Schools	38.4	42.5	48.2	53.8	54.8

注:2000 年以前职业高中为职业中学数据。

Note:Before 2000,the figure of vocational senior secondary schools was vocational secorndary school.

14－19　普通高等教育分科在校学生数
STUDENT ENROLLMENT IN REGULAR HIGHER EDUCATION BY FIELD OF STUDY

单位:人　　　　(person)

项　目	Item	2005 合　计 Total	2005 本　科 Regular College Course	2005 专　科 Specialized Subject	2006 合　计 Total	2006 本　科 Regular College Course	2006 专　科 Specialized Subject
合　计	**Total**	**1159795**	**640335**	**519460**	**1306181**	**709884**	**596297**
哲　学	Philosophy	309	309		298	298	
经济学	Economics	59887	35346	24541	65552	40022	25530
法　学	Law	33180	22664	10516	33254	23196	10058
教育学	Education	48825	15745	33080	47884	16786	31098
文　学	Literature	86917	86917	66805	181679	100800	80879
历史学	History	2215	2215		2226	2226	
理　学	Science	69956	69390	566	73816	73186	630
工　学	Engineering	515896	249706	266190	587968	278522	309446
农　学	Agriculture	20839	9043	11796	20897	9636	11261
医　学	Medicine	56072	44993	11079	64450	48874	15576
管理学	Management	198894	104007	94887	228157	116338	111819

14－20　普通高等教育分科招生数
NEW STUDENT ENROLLMENT IN REGULAR HIGHER EDUCATION BY FIELD OF STUDY

单位:人　　　　(person)

项　目	Item	2005 合　计 Total	2005 本　科 Regular College Course	2005 专　科 Specialized Subject	2006 合　计 Total	2006 本　科 Regular College Course	2006 专　科 Specialized Subject
合　计	**Total**	**361479**	**182726**	**178753**	**359065**	**190628**	**168437**
哲　学	Philosophy	89	89		104	104	
经济学	Economics	17779	9836	7943	17782	11124	6658
法　学	Law	9532	6151	3381	8549	5325	3224
教育学	Education	9698	4157	5541	8984	4295	4689
文　学	Literature	49244	26305	22939	50940	28490	22450
历史学	History	587	587		506	506	
理　学	Science	19480	19346	134	18989	18747	242
工　学	Engineering	168804	72122	96682	166984	75836	91148
农　学	Agriculture	6121	2532	3589	5619	2683	2936
医　学	Medicine	14378	11081	3297	15204	11041	4163
管理学	Management	65767	30520	35247	65404	32477	32927

14－21　普通高等教育分科毕业生数
GRADUATES OF REGULAR HIGHER EDUCATION BY FIELD OF STUDY

单位：人　　　　(person)

项　目	Item	2005 合计 Total	2005 本科 Regular College Course	2005 专科 Specialized Subject	2006 合计 Total	2006 本科 Regular College Course	2006 专科 Specialized Subject
合　计	**Total**	**229679**	**119375**	**110304**	**257296**	**126203**	**131093**
哲　学	Philosophy	35	35		75	75	
经济学	Economics	10989	6276	4713	12176	6984	5192
法　学	Law	8133	4760	3373	8144	5069	3075
教育学	Education	14943	3386	11557	16697	3482	13215
文　学	Literature	30108	16263	13845	34527	17269	17258
历史学	History	656	656		513	513	
理　学	Science	13816	13757	59	15480	15318	162
工　学	Engineering	100193	47256	52937	111606	48258	63348
农　学	Agriculture	5816	2179	3637	5572	1960	3612
医　学	Medicine	9501	6637	2864	10217	7149	3068
管理学	Management	35489	18170	17319	42289	20126	22163

14－22　普通高等学校分科专任教师数（2006年）
NUMBER OF FULL－TIME TEACHERS BY FIELD OF STUDY IN REGULAR HIGHER EDUCATIONAL INSTITUTIONS (2006)

单位：人　　　　(person)

项　目	Item	合　计 Total	正高级 Senior	副高级 Deputy	中级 Secondary	初　级 Primary	无职称 Non－title
合　计	**Total**	**78353**	**7459**	**21029**	**16452**	**18766**	**4647**
哲　学	Philosophy	2379	243	753	834	439	110
经济学	Economics	3960	343	1059	1445	880	233
法　学	Law	2563	202	669	922	627	143
教育学	Education	5910	274	1581	2079	1573	403
文　学	Literature	15971	959	3500	5255	5097	1160
历史学	History	663	129	214	229	69	22
理　学	Science	9474	1277	2995	3023	1773	406
工　学	Engineering	26306	2708	7372	8803	5913	1510
农　学	Agriculture	2243	359	545	720	479	140
医　学	Medicine	3850	573	1084	1319	729	145
管理学	Management	5034	392	1257	1823	1187	375

14－23 每万人口在校学生数和中小学升学情况
NUMBER OF STUDENTS PER 10000 POPULATION AND ENROLLMENT RATE OF SECONDARY AND PRIMARY SCHOOLS

年份 Year	平均每万人口中 Number of Students per 10000 Population			小学学龄儿童入学率（%） Percentage of School-Age Children Enrolled（%）	小学毕业生升学率（%） Percentage of Graduates of Primary Schools Entering Junior Secondary Schools（%）	初中毕业生升学率（%） Percentage of Graduates of Junior Secondary Schools Entering Senior Secondary Schools（%）
	大学生（人） University and College Students（person）	中学生（人） Secondary School Students（person）	小学生（人） Primary School Students（person）			
1978	10.4	667.9	1489.3	96.7	90.3	42.3
1980	14.2	553.8	1409.4	97.1	81.3	28.4
1985	19.2	492.3	1091.1	99.5	74.2	29.5
1989	23.0	426.4	980.9	98.8	79.8	38.2
1990	21.7	460.3	904.8	99.9	82.0	39.6
1991	21.1	467.4	869.1	99.3	84.2	40.0
1992	22.1	476.6	846.5	99.5	85.9	41.8
1993	25.9	481.3	853.9	99.4	88.0	45.4
1994	28.7	503.8	877.7	99.4	93.5	51.1
1995	29.5	530.5	912.5	99.8	96.6	56.8
1996	31.0	549.1	967.4	99.8	96.6	61.2
1997	33.4	547.9	1024.6	99.8	97.1	63.8
1998	38.0	550.3	1046.8	99.8	97.5	62.4
1999	49.8	565.8	1027.6	99.8	97.2	65.1
2000	61.7	592.3	980.7	99.8	97.2	68.5
2001	79.6	643.1	933.4	98.7	97.9	73.9
2002	94.9	710.7	860.6	99.6	98.2	78.6
2003	116.1	761.3	782.3	99.6	98.7	83.2
2004	133.8	795.3	710.7	99.7	98.8	84.8
2005	155.2	793.3	649.6	99.8	99.8	89.6
2006	173.0	775.1	603.7	99.9	100.0	93.5

14－24 各级学校教师负担学生数
STUDENT－TEACHER RATIO BY LEVEL OF SCHOOL

年份 Year	普通高等学校 Institutions of Regular Higher Education		普通中等学校 Regular Secondary Schools		小学 Primary Schools	
	教师数（万人） Number of Teachers（10000 persons）	平均每个教师负担学生数（人） Student-Teacher Ratio（person）	教师数（万人） Number of Teachers（10000 persons）	平均每个教师负担学生数（人） Student-Teacher Ratio（person）	教师数（万人） Number of Teachers（10000 persons）	平均每个教师负担学生数（人） Student-Teacher Ratio（person）
1978	1.34	4.5	16.75	23.3	27.07	32.1
1980	1.59	5.3	16.83	19.5	27.97	29.9
1985	2.30	5.2	16.53	18.5	25.91	26.2
1989	2.79	5.3	19.00	16.0	26.74	23.6
1990	2.76	5.3	19.63	15.9	26.95	22.7
1991	2.76	5.2	20.06	15.9	27.00	22.0
1992	2.70	5.7	20.32	16.2	26.66	21.9
1993	2.70	6.7	20.71	16.2	25.59	23.2
1994	2.73	7.4	21.28	16.6	26.95	22.9
1995	2.73	7.6	22.16	16.9	27.35	23.6
1996	2.74	8.1	22.82	17.1	27.96	24.6
1997	2.79	8.6	23.26	16.8	28.32	25.9
1998	2.86	9.6	23.57	16.8	28.20	26.7
1999	3.04	11.8	24.10	16.9	28.41	26.1
2000	3.31	13.7	25.02	17.3	28.90	24.9
2001	3.80	15.4	25.96	18.2	28.84	23.8
2002	4.43	15.8	27.38	19.2	27.95	22.7
2003	4.98	18.3	28.74	19.6	26.84	21.6
2004	5.90	18.0	30.19	19.6	29.22	19.9
2005	6.73	18.4	31.14	19.0	26.16	18.6
2006	7.84	17.8	31.92	18.3	26.05	17.5

主要统计指标解释

科技活动 指在自然科学、农业科学、医药科学、工程与技术科学、人文与社会科学领域(简称科学技术领域)中,与科技知识的产生、发展、传播和应用密切相关的有组织的活动。可分为研究与试验发展(R&D)、研究与试验发展成果应用及相关的科技服务三类活动。

科技活动人员 指直接从事科技活动、以及专门从事科技活动管理和为科技活动提供直接服务的人员。累计从事科技活动的实际工作时间占全年制度工作时间10%及以上的人员。(1)直接从事科技活动的人员包括:在独立核算的科学研究与技术开发机构、高等学校、各类企业及其他事业单位内设的研究室、实验室、技术开发中心及中试车间(基地)等机构中从事科技活动的研究人员、工程技术人员、技术工人及其它人员;虽不在上述机构工作,但编入科技活动项目(课题)组的人员;科技信息与文献机构中的专业技术人员;从事论文设计的研究生等。(2)专门从事科技活动管理和为科技活动提供直接服务的人员包括:独立核算的科学研究与技术开发机构、科技信息与文献机构、高等学校、各类企业及其他事业单位主管科技工作的负责人,专门从事科技活动的计划、行政、人事、财务、物资供应、设备维护、图书资料管理等工作的各类人员,但不包括保卫、医疗保健人员、司机、食堂人员、茶炉工、水暖工、清洁工等为科技活动提供间接服务的人员。

科学家与工程师 指科技活动人员中具有高、中级技术职称(职务)的人员和不具有高、中级技术职称(职务)的大学本科及以上学历人员。

研究与试验发展(R&D) 指在科学技术领域,为增加知识总量、以及运用这些知识去创造新的应用而进行的系统的创造性的活动,包括基础研究、应用研究、试验发展三类活动。

基础研究 指为了获得关于现象和可观察事实的基本原理的新知识(揭示客观事物的本质、运动规律,获得新发现、新学说)而进行的实验性或理论性研究,它不以任何专门或特定的应用或使用为目的。其成果以科学论文和科学著作为主要形式。

应用研究 指为获得新知识而进行的创造性研究,主要针对某一特定的目的或目标。应用研究是为了确定基础研究成果可能的用途,或是为达到预定的目标探索应采取的新方法(原理性)或新途径。其成果形式以科学论文、专著、原理性模型或发明专利为主。

试验发展 指利用从基础研究、应用研究和实际经验所获得的现有知识,为产生新的产品、材料和装置,建立新的工艺、系统和服务,以及对已产生和建立的上述各项作实质性的改进而进行的系统性工作。其成果形式主要是专利、专有技术、具有新产品基本特征的产品原型或具有新装置基本特征的原始样机等。在社会科学领域,试验发展是指把通过基础研究、应用研究获得的知识转变成可以实施的计划(包括为进行检验和评估实施示范项目)的过程。人文科学领域没有对应的试验发展活动。

研究与试验发展人员 指参与研究与试验发展项目研究、管理和辅助工作的人员,包括项目(课题)组人员,企业科技行政管理人员和直接为项目(课题)活动提供服务的辅助人员。

研究与试验发展人员全时当量 指全时人员数加非全时人员按工作量折算为全时人员数的总和。例如:有两个全时人员和三个非全时人员(工作时间分别为20%、30%和70%),则全时当量为2+0.2+0.3+0.7=3.2人年。

专业技术人员 指从事专业技术工作和专业技术管理工作的人员,即企事业单位中已经聘任专业技术职务从事专业技术工作和专业技术管理工作的人员,以及未聘任专业技术职务,现在专业技术岗位上工作的人员。包括工程技术人员,农业技术人员,科学研究人员,卫生技术人员,教学人员,经济人员,会计人员,统计人员,翻译人员,图书资料、档案、文博人员,新闻出版人员,律师、公证人员,广播电视播音人员,工艺美术人员,体育人员,艺术人员及企业政治思想工作人员,共十七个专业技术职务类别。

科技活动经费筹集 指从各种渠道筹集到的计划用于科技活动的经费,包括政府资金、企业资金、事业单位资金、金融机构贷款、国外资金和其他资金等。

政府资金 指从各级政府部门获得的计划用于科技活动的经费,包括科学事业费、科技三项费、科研基建费、科学基金、教育等部门事业费中计划用于科技活动的经费以及政府部门预算外资金中计划用于科技活动的经费等。

企业资金 指从自有资金中提取或接受其他企业委托的、科研院所和高校等事业单位接受企业委托获得的,计划用于科研和技术开发的经费。不包括来自政府、金融机构及国外的计划用于科技活动的资金。

金融机构贷款 指从各类金融机构获得的用于科技活动的贷款。

科技活动经费内部支出 指报告年内用于科技活动的实际支出包括劳务费、科研业务费、科研管理费,非基建投资购建的固定资产、科研基建支出以及其他用于科技活动的支出。不包括生产性活动支出、归还贷款支出及转拨外单位支出。

劳务费 指以货币或实物形式直接或间接支付给从事科技活动人员的劳动报酬及各种费用。包括各种形式的工资、津贴、奖金、福利、离退休人员费用、人民助学金等。

固定资产购建费　指报告年内使用非基建投资购建的固定资产和用于科研基建投资的实际支出额，即固定资产实际支出和科研基建投资实际完成额之和。固定资产是指长期使用而不改变原有实物形态的主要物资设备、图书资料、实验材料和标本以及其他设备和家具、房屋、建筑物。

新产品　指采用新技术原理、新设计构思研制、生产的全新产品，或在结构、材质、工艺等某一方面比原有产品有明显改进，从而显著提高了产品性能或扩大了使用功能的产品。既包括政府有关部门认定并在有效期内的新产品，也包括企业自行研制开发，未经政府有关部门认定，从投产之日起一年之内的新产品。

专利　是专利权的简称，是对发明人的发明创造经审查合格后，由专利局依据专利法授予发明人和设计人对该项发明创造享有的专有权。包括发明、实用新型和外观设计。

发明　指对产品、方法或者其改进所提出的新的技术方案。

实用新型　指对产品的形状、构造或者其结合所提出的适于实用的新的技术方案。

外观设计　指对产品的形状、图案、色彩或者其结合所作出的富有美感并适于工业上应用的新设计。

普通高等学校　指按照国家规定的设置标准和审批程序批准举办，通过国家统一招生考试，招收高中毕业生为主要培养对象，实施高等学历教育的全日制大学、独立设置的学院和高等专科学校、高等职业学校和其他机构。

成人高等学校　指按照国家规定的设置标准和审批程序批准举办的，通过全国成人高等教育统一招生考试，招收具有高中毕业或同等学历的人员为主要培养对象，利用脱产、业余或函授等多种形式对其实施高等学历教育的学校。包括广播电视大学、职工高等学校、农民高等学校、管理干部学院、教育学院、独立函授学院、其他机构。

小学学龄儿童入学率　指调查范围内已入小学学习的学龄儿童占校内外学龄儿童总数（包括弱智儿童，不包括盲聋哑儿童）的比重。计算公式为：

小学学龄儿童入学率 = 已入学的小学学龄儿童数/校内外小学学龄儿童总数 × 100%

Explanatory Notes on Main Statistical Indicators

Scientific and Technological Activities(S&T Activities)　refer to organized activities which are closely related with the creation, development, dissemination and application of the scientific and technical knowledge in the fields of natural sciences, agricultural science, medical science, engineering and technological science, humanities and social sciences (referred to as scientific and technological fields). S&T activities can be classified in to 3 categories: research and development(R&D) activities, application of R&D results, and related S&T services.

Personnel Engaged in S&T Activities　refer to personnel directly engaged in S&T activities, in the management of S&T activ—ities, and in providing direct service to S&T activities, who spend over 10% of the total working hours in a year in S&T activities. (1) Personnel directly engaged in S&T activities include researchers, engineers, technicians and other related personnel engaged in S&T activities in independent—accounting R&D institutions, institutions of higher learning, and in research institutes, laboratories, technology development centers and central experiment workshops under enterprises and institutions. Also included are people working in S&T research project teams, professional and technical personnel working in S&T information archiving institutes, and graduate students working on the design of their thesis. (2) Personnel engaged in the management of S&T activities and in providing direct service to S&T activities include senior management people responsible for S&T activities in independent-accounting R&D institutions, S&T infor-mation archiving institutes, institutions of higher learning, and in enterprises and institutions where S&T activities are undertaken. Also included are people responsible for the planning, administration, personnel management, financial management, logistics supply, equipment maintenance, information and library management that are related with S&T activities. People providing indirect services are excluded, such as security, medical service, drivers, plumbers, cleaners and those providing catering and related service.

Scientists and Engineers　refer to persons engaged in S&T activities who have obtained titles of senior and middle level professional positions, and those without such position but have completed university or higher education.

Research and Development(R&D)　refers to systematic and creative activities in the field of science and technology aiming at increasing the knowledge and using the knowledge for new application. R&D includes 3 categories of activities: basic research, applied research and experiments and development.

Basic Research　refers to empirical or theoretical research aiming at obtaining new knowledge on the fundamental principles of phenomena of observable facts to reveal the nature and law of movement of objects and to acquire new discoveries or new theories. Basic research takes no specific or designated application as the aim of the research. Results of basic research are mainly released or disseminated in the form of scientific papers or monographs.

Applied research refers to creative research aiming at obtaining new knowledge on a specific objective or target. Purpose of the applied research is to identify the possible use of results from basic research, or to explore new (fundamental) methods or new approaches. Results of applied research are expressed in the form of scientific papers, monographs, fundamental models or invention patents

Experiments and Development refer to systematic activities aiming at using the knowledge from basic and applied researches or from practical experience to develop new products, materials and equipment, to establish new production process, systems and services, or to make substantial improvement on the existing products, process or services. Results of experiment and development activities are embodied in patents, exclusive technology, monotype of new products or equipment. In social sciences, experiment and development activities refer to the process of converting the knowledge from basic or applied researches into feasible programmes (including conduct of demonstration projects for assessment and evaluation). There is no experiment and development activities in the science of humani-ties. R&D Personnel refer to persons engaged in research, management and supporting activities of R&D, including persons in the project teams, persons engaged in the management of S&T activities of enterprises and supporting staff providing direct service to the research projects.

R&D Personnel refer to persons engaged in reasearch, menagement and supporting activities of R&D, including persons in project teams, persons engaged in management of S&T activities of enterprises and supporting staff providing direct service to the research projects.

Full-time Equivalent of R&D Personnel refers to the sum of the full-time persons and the full-time equivalent of part-time persons converted by workload. For instance, if there are 2 full-time persons and 3 part-time workers (20%, 30% and 70% of working hours respectively on R&D activities), the full-time equivalent is 2 + 0.2 + 0.3 + 0.7 = 3.2 person-years.

Professional and Technical Personnel refer to person engaged in professional and technical work or in the management of professional and technical activities, i. e., people with professional or technical positions who are engaged in professional and technical work or in the management of professional and technical activities, and people without professional or technical positions but are working on professional or technical posts. They include professionals and technicians working in 17 categories of technical occupations including engineering, agriculture, scientific researches, medical service, teaching, economic research and application, accounting, statistics, translation, libraries, archives, cultural and museum service, journalism and publication, lawyers, notarization service, radio and television broadcasting, handicraft and fine arts, sports, performing art, and political workers in enterprises.

Funding for S&T Activities refers to funds obtained from various sources for S&T activities, including government funds, self-raised funds by enterprises, self-raised funds by institutions, loans from financial institutions, foreign funds and other funds.

Government Funds refer to funds obtained from government agencies at all levels to be used for S&T activities, including fund for scientific undertakings, 3 kinds of fund for S&T activities, fund for capital construction for scientific researches, science fund, funds from education expenditures by education departments for S&T activities, and extra-budget fund from government agencies for S&T activities.

Self-raised Funds by Enterprises refers to self-raised funds by enterprises from their own expenditure or from other enterprises and funds received by universities or research institutions from enterprises for scientific research or technical development projects. Excluded in this category are funds from government agencies, financial institutions or from foreign institutions. Loans from Financial Institutions refer to loans from various financial institutions for S&T activities.

Loans from Financial Institutions refer to loans from various financial institutions for S&T activities.

Service Fees refer to direct or indirect payment, in cash or in kind, made to personnel engaged in S&T activities as remuneration and other fees. They include, in various forms, salaries, subsidies, bonus, benefits, retirement pension, stipend, etc.

Purchase or Construction of Fixed Assets refers to the fixed assets purchased or constructed using funds other than the investment in capital construction, and the actual expenditure on capital construction for scientific researches. In other words, it is the sum of the actual expenditure on fixed assets and the accomplished investment in capital construction for scientific researches. Fixed assets refer to main materials and equipment, literatures and documents in libraries, materials for experiments, specimen, instruments, furniture, buildings and constructions that can be used for a long time without changing the form and shape of those articles or constructions.

New Products refer to new products produced with new technology and new design, or products that represent noticeable improvement in terms of structure, material, or production process so as to improve significantly the character or function of the older versions. They include new products certified by relevant government agencies within the period of certification, as well as new products designed and produced by enterprises within a year without certification by government agencies.

Patent is an abbreviation for the patent right and refers to the exclusive right of ownership by the inventors or designers for the creation or inventions, given from the patent offices after due process of assessment and approval in accordance with the Patent Law.

Patents are granted for inventions, utility models and designs.

Inventions refer to the new technical proposals to the products or methods or their modifications.

Utility Models refer to the practical and new technical proposals on the shape and structure of the product or the combination of both.

Designs refer to the aesthetics and industrially applicable new designs for the shape, pattern and color of the product, or their combinations.

Regular Institutions of Higher Learning refer to educational establishments set up according to the government evaluation and approval procedures, enrolling graduates from senior secondary schools and providing higher education courses and training for senior professionals. They include full-time universities, colleges, high professional schools, high vocatoinal universities and other institutions.

Institutions of Higher Learning for Adults refer to educational establishments, set up in line with the government evalution and approval procedures, enrolling personnels with senior secondary school or equivalent education as main training objects, and providing higher education courses in many forms of full time, spare time, or correspondence for adults. Institutions of higher learning for adults include Radio and TV universities, schools of high education for staff and workers and peasants, colleges for management cadres, pedagogical colleges, independent correspondence colleges and other institutions.

Enrollment Rate of Primary School Age Children refers to the proportion of school age children enrolled at schools to the total number of school age children both in and outside schools (including retarded children, but excluding blind, deaf and mute children). The formula is:

Enrollment Rate of Primary School-age Children = (Total Primary School—age Children at Schools) (Total Primary School age Children Both at and outside Schools) 100%

JIANGSU STATISTICAL YEARBOOK

第 15 篇

文化、体育、卫生、环保

CULTURE,SPORTS,PUBLIC HEALTH AND ENVIRONMENT PROTECTION

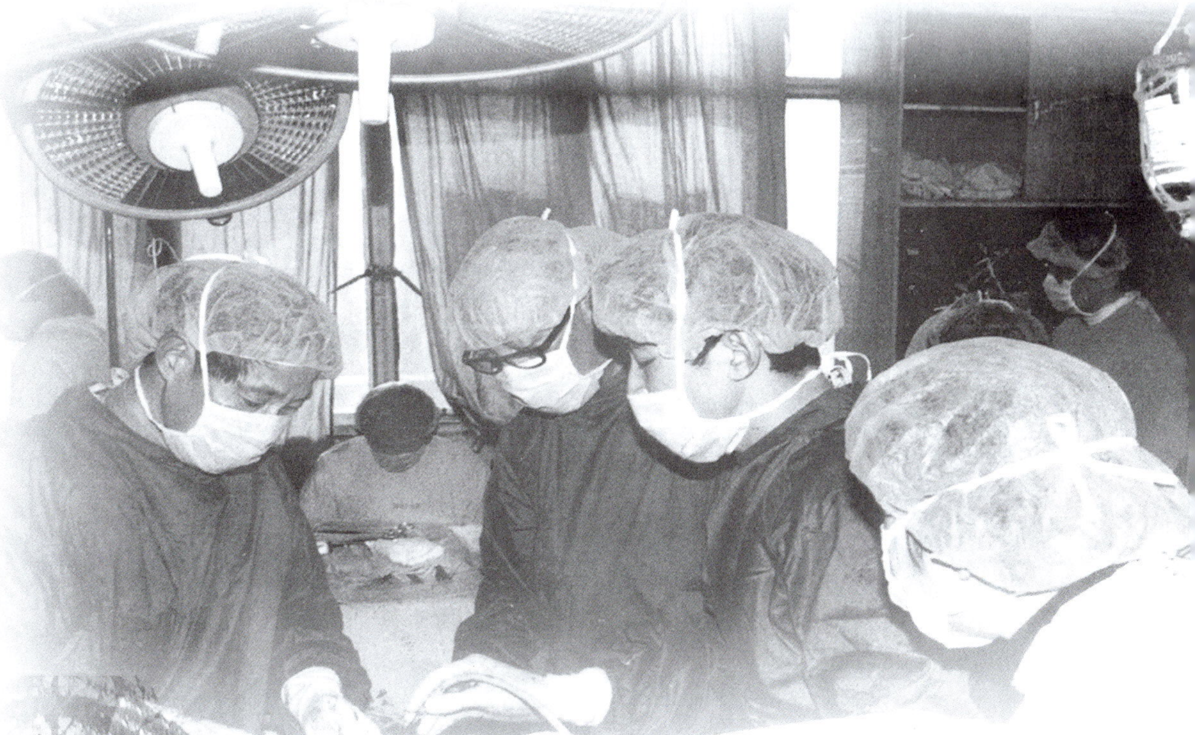

15 - 1 文化艺术和文物事业机构、人员情况

NUMBER OF CULTURAL INSTITUTION AND PERSONNEL

项目	Item	机构数(个) Institution (unit)		从业人员(人) Personnel (person)	
		2005	2006	2005	2006
合计	**Total**	**22968**	**23389**	**97426**	**103573**
艺术业	Art	289	276	7946	7754
#艺术表演团体	Art Performance Troupes	129	127	5250	5220
话剧、儿童剧、滑稽剧团	Drama, Children Plays and Comedy Troupes	6	6	253	252
歌剧、舞剧、歌舞剧团	Opera, Dance Drama, Song and Dance Drama Troupes	1	1	141	139
歌舞团、轻音乐团	Song and Dance Troupes, Light Music Troupes	17	14	995	858
乐　团	Philharmonic and Chorus Troupes	3	3	123	139
戏曲剧团	Local Opera Troupes	80	79	3072	2977
曲、杂、木、皮团	Acrobatics and Circus, Puppet Play, Shadow Play and Recitation and ballad Troupes	21	19	499	506
综合性剧团	Comprehensive Art Centers	1	5	167	349
#艺术表演场馆	Art Centers	87	81	2085	1877
#剧场、影剧院	Theaters and Music Halls	78	67	1935	1348
图书馆业	Libraries	103	104	2363	2429
#少儿图书馆	Children's Libraries	5	6	45	49
群众文化服务业	Mass Culture	1534	1477	5542	5324
群众艺术馆、文化馆	Mass Art Centers	117	115	1955	1963
文化站	Cultural Stations	1417	1362	3587	3361
#乡镇文化站	Township Cultural Stations	1197	1145	3003	2845
艺术教育业	Art Education	17	18	500	753
中等专业学校	Secondary Art Schools	7	8	386	637
文化干部学校	Cultural Cardre Schools	1	1	4	5
其他教育机构	Others	9	9	110	111
文化市场经营单位	Operative Institutions of cultural market	20611	21100	76002	82099
文艺科研	Art Research Institutions	8	7	58	82
其他文化产业	Others	205	273	2108	2126
艺术创作机构	Art Creating Institutions	70	65	392	379
艺术展览机构	Art Exhibition Agency	9	10	169	177
其　他	Others	126	198	1547	1570
非文化产业	Non-cultural Industry	27	24	436	479
文物业	Cultural Relic Industry	174	176	2471	2906
文物保护管理机构	Institutions of Historical Relics Preservation	64	65	292	314
文物科研及其他文物机构	Institutions of Cultural Relics Scientific Research	2	2	17	15
博物馆	Museums	99	100	1862	2265
综合类	Synthesized	49	50	1131	1442
历史类	Histories	39	39	584	658
艺术类	Arts	10	10	134	152
其　他	Other	1	1	13	13
文物商店	Cultural Relics Shops	19	9	300	307

15－2　群众艺术馆、文化馆(站)业务活动及经费情况 (2006 年)
BASIC STATISTICS ON ACTIVITIES AND EXPENDITURES OF MASS ART CENTERS AND CULTURAL CENTERS (2006)

项　目	Item	总　计 Total	群众艺术馆 Mass Art Centers	文化站 Cultural Stations
单位数　(个)	Number of Units　(unit)	1477	115	1362
举办展览　(个)	Number of Exhibitions　(unit)	7869	812	7057
组织文艺活动　(次)	Art Performances and Story－telling Sessions　(times)	23997	4668	19329
举办训练班班次　(次)	Training Courses Number of Class　(times)	9093	3373	5720
举办训练班结业人次　(万人次)	Number of Persons Completing Courses　(10000 person－times)	35.1	12.5	22.6
群众艺术馆、文化馆负责指导单位　(个)	Units Responsible for Guiding Mass Art Center and Cultural Centers　(unit)			
馆办文艺团体	Art Group Run by cultural staling	256	256	
基层文化示范点	Cultural Excmplary spots of Grass－roots	522	522	
农村集镇文化中心	Cultural Centers in Rural Towns	1265	1265	
文化户　(户)	Households Specializing in Cultural Activecties　(household)	5812	5812	
群众业余文艺团队	Part－time Art Groups	3501	3501	
总支出　(万元)	Total Expenditures　(10000 yuan)	31166.8	15846.8	15320.0
#公用支出	Expanditure for Public use	10310.0	5542.8	4767.2
维修费	Maintenance Expenses	1112.4	368.7	743.7

注：本表仅为文化部门系统内。

Note: The data in this table only refer to those under the administration of the cultural departments.

15－3　公共图书馆业务活动及经费情况 (2006 年)
FACILITIES, SERVICES AND EXPENDITURES OF PUBLIC LIBRARIES (2006)

项　目	Item	总　计 Total	#省级公共图书馆 Public Libraries of Provincial Level	#县级公共图书馆 Public Libraries of County Level
总藏量　(万册、件)	Total Collections　(10000 volumes)	3410.2	828.7	1427.2
书架单层总长度　(万米)	Total Length of Bookshelves　(10000 m)	86.3	11.9	25.1
累计发放有效借书证数　(万个)	Number of Library Cards Distributed Accumulately　(10000 units)	82.3	2.1	46.4
书刊文献外借册次　(万册次)	Total Number of Circulation　(10000 person－times)	1094.0	58.7	628.7
书刊文献外借册次　(万册次)	Number of Books Borrowed by the Readers　(10000 volume－times)	1642.2	50.4	1006.2
为读者服务举办各种活动次数　(次)	Number of Activities Serve for Readers　(times)	2932	256	1451
举办各种活动参加人数　(万人次)	Number of Readers Involved　(10000 person－times)	215.3	2.8	106.5
总支出　(万元)	Total Expenditures　(10000 yuan)	23976	5826	10000
#藏量购置费	Purchase Expenses	5072	2157	1449
本年新购藏量　(万册、件)	Number of Books Purchased During the year　(10000 volumes)	168.2	21.4	99.8
公用房屋建筑面积　(万平方米)	Floor Space of Public Buildings　(10000 sq. m)	49.1	3.2	29.9
#书库	Stock Rooms	12.2	2.6	4.9
阅览室座席　(万个)	Seating Capacity of Reading Rooms　(10000 seats)	2.6	0.1	1.7

15－4 报纸、期刊出版情况（2006年）
BASIC STATISTICS ON NEWSPAPER AND PERIODICALS PUBLISHED (2006)

项 目	Item	种 数（种）Number of Publications (kind)	总印数（万册、万份）Printed Copies (10000)	总印张（万印张）Printed Sheets (10000)
报 纸	**Newspaper**	**143**	**267261**	**1018267**
期 刊	**Periodicals**	**439**	**9069**	**36663**
#综 合	Comprehensiveness	20	489	3247
哲学、社会科学	Philosophy and Social Sciences	78	1685	8023
自然科学、技术	Natural Sciences and Technology	260	2027	7871
文化、教育	Culture and Education	49	4015	12732
文学、艺术	Literature and Art	26	475	3839
画 刊	Pictorials	1	5	19
少年儿童读物	**Children's Reading Material**	**5**	**372**	**931**

15－5 图书出版情况（2006年）
BASIC STATISTICS ON BOOKS PUBLISHED (2006)

项 目	Item	出版图书种数（种）Number of Publications (kind)	#租型图书 Books for Lending	总印数（万册、万份）Printed Copies (10000)	总印张（万印张）Printed Sheets (10000)
总 计	**Total**	**9550**	**934**	**47277**	**303581**
马列主义、毛泽东思想	Marxism-Leninism, Mao Zedong Thought	15		29	436
哲 学	Philosophy	174	1	87	1370
社会科学总论	General Social Sciences	66		34	490
政治、法律	Politics and Law	201		262	4314
军 事	Military Affairs	7		32	469
经 济	Economics	262		145	1933
文化、科学、教育、体育	Culture, Science, Education and Sports	5865	929	44212	260533
语言、文字	Languages	271		327	4523
文 学	Literature	435	2	503	6003
艺 术	Arts	499	1	473	2455
历史、地理	History and Geography	261		149	2385
自然科学总论	General Natural Sciences	13	1	10	81
数理科学、化学	Mathematics and Chemistry	242		266	6685
天文学、地理科学	Astronomy and Geology	27		12	124
生物科学	Biology	27		25	486
医药、卫生	Medicine and Health Care	291		253	4217
农业科学	Agricultural Science	122		58	411
工业技术	Industrial Technology	697		362	6020
交通运输	Transportation	21		9	178
环境科学	Environmental Science	1		0	7
航空、航天	Aeronautics and Aerospace	23		13	136
综合性图书	General Books	30		15	324

注：该表为使用中国标准书号部分。

Note: In this table, the data were used according to the standard serial number of China.

15－6 广播、电视事业发展情况
BASIC STATISTICS ON BROADCASTING AND TELEVISION STATIONS

项目	Item	1995	2000	2004	2005	2006
职工人数（人）	Number of Staff and Workers (person)	21505	28208	32225	33551	35378
广播电台（座）	Number of Broadcasting Stations (set)	61	14	14	14	14
中短波发射台及转播台（座）	Number of Broadcasting Transmission Stations and Relaying Stations (set)	21	21	21	21	21
中短波发射机功率（千瓦）	Broadcast Power of Transmitters (kW)	458	505	490	542	565
广播人口覆盖率（%）	Listener Rating (%)	86.9	99.6	99.7	99.7	99.9
电视台（座）	Number of Television Stations (set)	52	14	14	14	14
电视发射及转播台（座）	Television Transmission Stations and Relaying Stations (set)	153	147	147	111	112
发射机功率（千瓦）	Power of Transmitters (kW)	419	429	463	463	475
电视人口覆盖率（%）	Viewer Rating (%)	93.5	99.5	99.5	99.5	99.9

15－7 广播、电视节目制作时间
PRODUCTION OF BROADCASTING AND TV PROGRAMS

单位：小时 (hour)

项目	Item	1995	2000	2004	2005	2006
广播节目制作	**Production of Broadcasting Programs**	**197793**	**335483**	**544258**	**491458**	**500707**
#新　闻	News Programs	24574	42722	68085	69994	81237
专　题	Special Subject Programs	40465	61658	205692	148229	140609
教　育	Educational Programs	6168	16515			
文艺(综艺)	Programs of Entertainment	90838	129893	140614	148248	130242
广　告	Advertisment		31440	60750	57666	63218
服务信息	Service Programs	35746	53255			
电视节目制作	**Production of TV Programs**	**28738**	**42404**	**156774**	**212222**	**216089**
#新　闻	News Programs	4659	9460	31648	49939	34761
专　题	Special Subject Programs	3854	8111	31139	36679	42204
教　育	Educational Programs	7450	248			
文艺(综艺)	Programs of Entertainment	544	10311	19915	14131	17088
广　告	Advertisment		7739	25216	33596	50488
服务信息	Service Programs	12231	6535			

15－8 体委系统职工人数（2006 年）
NUMBER OF STAFF AND WORKERS IN SPORTS COMMISSIONS（2006）

单位：人 （person）

项　目	Items	总　计 Total	#体　育 行政机关 Sports Adminis-tration	#优　秀 运动队 Excellent Sports Teams	#体育运 动学校 Physical Education and Sports Schools	#业　余 体　校 Popular Sparetime Sports Schools	#体育场 （馆） Public Stadiums and Gym-nasiums	#其　他 Others
总　计	**Total**	**7679**	**1033**	**2421**	**781**	**1652**	**923**	**869**
公务员	Orderly	860	860					
教练员	Coaches	1433		300	267	732	132	2
运动员	Athletes	1346		1346				
科研人员	Scientific and Tech－nical Personnel	102		26	6	10		60
医务人员	Medical Personnel	80		58	9	8	3	2
文化教师	Teachers	766		124	253	372	17	
管理人员	Administrative Staff	1753	110	339	139	341	401	423
其他人员	Others	1339	63	228	107	189	370	382

15－9 等级运动员、裁判员发展人数
NUMBER OF ATHLETES AND REFEREES IN GRADES

单位：人 （person）

项　目	Item	1990	1995	2000	2005	2006
等级运动员发展人数	**Number of Athletes in Grades**					
运动健将	Master of Sports	40	54	76	104	137
一级	First Grade	54	88	200	212	420
二级	Second Grade	318	441	1028	1992	1705
等级裁判员发展人数	**Number of Referees in Grades**					
国家（际）级	National（International）Referees	7	16	30	48	38
一级	First Grade	86	157	194	242	396
二级	Second Grade	384	408	779	1780	1880
全省各级体委举办运动会情况	**Number of Sports Meets Held by Sports Commissions at All Levels in the Province**					
运动会次数 （次）	Number of Sports Meets （times）	1771	1008	964	87	66

15－10 运动员在各级比赛中获奖牌情况（2006 年）
AWARDS FOR ATHLETES IN COMPETITIONS OF ALL LEVELS（2006）

单位：个 （unit）

项　录	Item	冠　军 Champion	亚　军 Second Place	季　军 Third Place
世界最高比赛	World Highest Competition	11	4	11
亚洲最高比赛	Asian Highest Competition	35	11	13
全国最高比赛	National Highest Competition	33	29	41

15－11 卫生事业基本情况（2006年）
BASIC STATISTICS ON HEALTH CARE (2006)

项目	Item	机构数（个）Institutions (unit)	床位数（张）Hospital Beds (beds)	卫生工作人员（人）Personnel (persons)	#卫生技术人员 Medical Technical Personnel	#医生 Doctors
总计	**Total**	**17143**	**211626**	**334508**	**275368**	**114590**
医院	Total Hospitals	1061	142735	181563	144261	56237
综合医院	Comprehensive Hospitals	716	97354	126099	100888	39320
中医院	Hospitals of Chinese Medicines	87	16656	25476	20762	8686
中西结合医院	Hospitals of Chinese Medicines Combined with Western Medicines	11	2036	2693	2166	878
专科医院	Specialized Hospitals	243	25993	27009	20274	7306
#传染病院	Infections Diseases Hospitals	14	3642	4344	3314	1029
精神病院	Mental Hospitals	44	9785	6951	4837	1661
结核病院	Tuberculosis Hospitals	3	371	255	194	57
妇产(科)医院	Hospitals for Maternity and Child Care	15	1777	3145	2437	790
儿科医院	Children's Hospitals	8	1613	2747	2147	677
职业病院	Vocational Hospitals	3	300	119	94	41
肿瘤医院	Tumor Hospitals	9	1834	1983	1556	545
护理院	Nursing Hospitals	4	696	286	171	47
疗养院	Sanatoriums	25	3580	1321	548	172
社区卫生服务中心	Centers of Communities Sanitary Services	188	6680	10078	8463	3837
卫生院	Rural Township Hospitals	1407	53055	74574	63108	27393
门诊部	Clinics	395	127	4305	3495	1735
急救中心(站)	Emergency Treatment Centers (Stations)	18	0	602	239	148
采供血机构	Blood Collection and Supply Institutions	32	1	1389	850	96
妇幼保健院(所、站)	Maternity and Child Care Centers	107	1771	5054	4093	1979
专科疾病防治院(所、站)	Special Disease Protectoin and Treatment Hospitals (Stations)	48	954	1091	836	419
疾病预防控制中心(防疫站)	Disease Protection and Controlling Centers (Antiepidemic Stations)	153	666	8198	6274	3795
卫生监督所	Sanitation Supervision Agenicies	103	15	3820	3034	1493
卫生监督检验(监测、检测)所(站)	Sanitation Supervision and Test Labs (Stations)	1	0	7	5	0
医学科学研究机构	Institutions of Medical Sciences Research	10	411	919	549	243
医学在职培训机构	In－service Training of Medical Science	32	0	1571	263	129
其他卫生机构	Other Health Care Institutions	202	1631	2195	1529	826
县(区)诊所、卫生所、医务室、卫生服务站	County (District) Chinics, Sanitation Offices and Medical Matter Centers Sanitation Service Station	13361	0	37821	37821	16088

15－12 卫 生 机 构 数
NUMBER OF HEALTH CARE INSTITUTIONS

单位:个　(unit)

年　份 Year	总　计 Total	医　院 Hospitals	卫生院 Commune Hospitals	疗养院 Sanatoriums	门诊部 Clinics
1978	9277	2428			7
1980	9943	2457			11
1985	11515	2460			32
1989	12325	4463			34
1990	12366	2491			35
1991	12377	2495			36
1992	12277	2493			36
1993	12074	2483			36
1994	12067	2559			36
1995	12039	2534			35
1996	14944	2617			35
1997	13386	2620			33
1998	14572	2610			30
1999	13699	2641			30
2000	12813	634	1877	29	106
2001	13208	662	1771	29	119
2002	12368	891	1625	28	293
2003	12733	920	1602	21	313
2004	14447	995	1493	24	371
2005	15324	1014	1472	26	372
2006	17143	1061	1407	25	395

15－12　续 表　Continued

单位:个　(unit)

年　份 Year	妇幼保健院(所、站) Maternity and Child Care Institutions	专科疾病防治院(所、站) Special Disease Protection and Treatment Hospitals	疾病预防控制中心(防疫站) Disease Protecting and Controlling Centers	医学科学研究机构 Institutions of Medical Sciences Research
1978	84	9	107	12
1980	99	17	119	11
1985	105	84	127	16
1989	114	95	135	16
1990	114	108	135	16
1991	114	112	137	14
1992	115	114	135	14
1993	117	120	141	18
1994	117	121	141	17
1995	117	122	141	17
1996	115	121	142	18
1997	114	121	143	18
1998	114	120	144	18
1999	116	122	147	18
2000	112	118	142	17
2001	112	113	147	17
2002	111	80	145	14
2003	106	59	136	13
2004	107	45	143	12
2005	107	49	154	12
2006	107	48	153	10

15－13　卫生机构人员数
NUMBER OF PERSONS ENGAGED IN HEALTH CARE INSTITUTIONS

单位:万人　　　　(10000 persons)

年　　份 Year	卫生工作人　　员 Medical Working Personnel	卫生技术人　　员 Medical Technical Personnel	#医　生 Doctors	#护师、护士 Registered Nurses	每万人拥有医生(人) Number of Doctors per 10000 Population (person)
1978	17.45	14.00	5.70	1.79	9.7
1980	19.03	15.04	6.10	2.08	10.2
1985	23.68	18.28	7.65	3.61	12.3
1989	26.82	20.75	9.67	5.06	14.7
1990	27.58	21.35	9.94	5.34	14.6
1991	28.63	22.22	10.20	5.61	14.9
1992	29.39	22.89	10.43	5.76	15.1
1993	30.20	23.44	10.63	5.99	15.3
1994	30.85	24.05	10.94	6.28	15.6
1995	31.57	24.55	11.22	6.44	15.9
1996	31.90	25.02	11.34	6.69	16.0
1997	32.42	25.48	11.58	6.95	16.2
1998	32.61	25.67	11.61	7.13	16.2
1999	32.64	25.60	11.59	7.26	16.1
2000	32.18	25.36	11.44	7.39	15.6
2001	32.08	25.36	11.46	7.54	16.2
2002	30.08	24.00	10.22	7.25	14.3
2003	30.37	24.37	10.40	7.37	14.5
2004	30.95	25.01	10.60	7.70	14.7
2005	31.61	25.71	10.87	8.05	15.0
2006	33.45	27.54	11.46	8.59	15.7

注：从2002年起,医生系执业(助理)医师数,护师(士)系注册护士数。

Note: Since 2002, the number of doctors refers to the practitioner (assistant) doctors, and the number nurses of refers to the registered nurses.

15－14　卫生机构床位数
NUMBER OF BEDS IN HEALTH CARE INSTITUTIONS

单位:万张　　　　(10000 beds)

年　　份 Year	总　计 Total	医　院 Hospitals	卫生院 Commune Hospitals	疗 养 院 Sanatoriums	专科疾病防治院(所、站) Special Disease Protection and Treatment Hospitals	每万人拥有医院、卫生院床位数(张) Number of Hospital Beds per 10000 Population (bed)
1978	12.29	11.70		0.13		19.0
1980	12.75	11.62		0.23		19.6
1985	14.29	12.65		0.55		20.4
1989	16.08	14.22		0.64	0.01	21.7
1990	16.45	14.54		0.67		21.5
1991	16.77	14.85		0.74		21.7
1992	17.02	15.07		0.73		21.8
1993	17.33	15.29		0.73		21.9
1994	17.45	15.42		0.72		22.0
1995	17.46	15.48		0.71		21.9
1996	17.03	15.78		0.69		22.2
1997	17.03	15.90		0.62		22.2
1998	17.01	15.91		0.59		22.2
1999	17.25	16.17		0.55		22.4
2000	17.31	10.01	6.18	0.56	0.13	22.1
2001	17.32	10.14	6.13	0.55	0.09	22.9
2002	17.45	11.38	5.58	0.44	0.10	23.8
2003	17.99	11.54	5.63	0.37	0.08	24.0
2004	18.90	12.31	5.42	0.39	0.14	24.6
2005	19.75	13.18	5.41	0.49	0.10	25.6
2006	21.16	14.27	5.31	0.36	0.10	26.8

15－15 医疗机构门诊情况（2006年）
SITUATION OF HOSPITAL OUT PATIENT SERVICE OF HEALTH INSTITUTIONS（2006）

指标	Item	诊疗人次（万人次）Total Number of Patients Treated (10000 person-times)	门诊 Out-patients Sevvice	急诊 Emergency Patients
合计	**Total**	**17784**	**16042**	**1263**
医院	Hospitals	10506	9381	875
#综合医院	Comprehensive Hospitals	7441	6577	690
中医医院	Hospitals of Chinese Medicines	1725	1565	111
专科医院	Specialized Hospitals	1182	1105	54
疗养院	Sanatoriums	21	15	0
社区卫生服务中心	Sanitation Service Centers of Communities	1052	919	81
卫生院	Commune Hospitals	5433	5027	288
#乡镇卫生院	Township Hospitals	5375	4975	283
门诊部	Clinics	323	313	3
妇幼保健院(所、站)	Maternity and Child Care Centers	350	302	15
专科疾病防治院(所、站)	Specialized Stations	99	85	1

15－16 医疗机构住院服务、病床使用情况（2006年）
SITUATION OF HOSPITALIZATION SERVICE AND BEDS UTILIZATION OF HEALTH INSTITUTIONS （2006）

指标	Item	病床使用率（%）Utilization Rate of Beds (%)			入院人数（万人）Hospital Admissions (10000 person)			每百门急诊人次的入院人数（人）Hospital Admissions per 100 Patient－times (person)
		合计 Total	非营利 Unprofitable	营利 Profitable	合计 Total	非营利 Unprofitable	营利 Profitable	
合计	**Total**	**71.9**	**73.0**	**52.2**	**480**	**451.98**	**17.09**	**2.77**
医院	Hospitals	84.3	86.5	52.7	346	328.85	16.89	3.37
#综合医院	Comprehensive Hospitals	84.3	86.2	51.6	256	245.47	10.88	3.53
中医医院	Hospitals of Chinese Medicines	84.7	85.2	55.1	47	46.32	0.54	2.80
专科医院	Specialized Hospitals	84.1	88.2	51.0	37	33.51	3.73	3.21
疗养院	Sanatoriums	23.1	26.1	0.0	1.6	1.59	0	10.58
社区卫生服务中心	Sanitation Service Centers of Communities	44.3	44.4	35.7	10.4	10.34	0.11	1.04
卫生院	Commune Hospitals	43.4	42.1	25.1	116	104.92	0.08	2.18
#乡镇卫生院	Township Hospitals	43.4	42.1	25.1	115	104.11	0.08	2.19
门诊部	Clinics	28.9	29.8	12.3	0.04	0.03	0	0.01
妇幼保健院(所、站)	Maternity and Child Care Centers	78.7	78.7	0.0	5.89	5.89	0	1.86
专科疾病防治院(所、站)	Specialized Prevention & Treatment Stations or Centers	64.0	64.8	0.0	0.37	0.35	0	0.43

15－17　法定报告传染病发病及死亡情况（2006年）
LEGAL REPORT ON INFECTIONS DISEASE INCIDENCE AND DEATH（2006）

病名		发病率（1/10万）Incidence（1/100 thousand）	死亡率（1/10万）Rate of Death（1/100 thousand）	病死率（%）Rate of Death from Illness（%）
霍乱	Cholera	0.02	0.001	6.67
病毒性肝炎	Viral Hepatitis	42.07	0.040	0.10
痢疾	Dysentery	21.92	0.004	0.02
伤寒副伤寒	Typhoid and Paralyphoid	0.90	0.001	0.15
艾滋病	Aids	0.12	0.040	36.05
淋病	Gonorhea	23.73	0	0
梅毒	Syphilis	16.60	0.001	0.01
麻疹	Measles	6.10	0.004	0.07
百日咳	Pertussis	0.08	0.002	3.39
流脑	Epidemic Encephalitis	0.09	0.010	12.50
猩红热	Scarlet Fever	1.18	0	0
出血热	Hemorrhage Fever	0.37	0.010	1.44
狂犬病	Hydrophobia	0.14	0.140	99.06
钩端螺旋体病	Leplospirosis	0.01	0	0
乙脑	Encephalitis B	0.11	0.010	6.02
疟疾	Malaria	0.86	0	0
新生儿破伤风	Newborn Baby Tetanus	5.89	0.560	9.43
肺结核	Pulmonary Tuberculosis	65.99	0.280	0.42

15－18　孕产妇及婴儿死亡率
DEATH RATE OF PREGNANT WOMAN AND BABY

指标	Item	2000	2004	2005	2006
孕产妇死亡率　（1/10万）	Death Rate of Pregnant Woman（1/100 thousand）	28.51	20.74	18.56	11.47
婴儿死亡率　（‰）	Death Rate of Baby（‰）	11.20	8.03	6.69	5.95
5岁以下儿童死亡率（‰）	Death Rate of Child of Aged 5 and Below（‰）	14.61	10.14	8.56	7.62

15－19 环境保护基本情况
BASIC STATISTICS ON ENVIRONMENTAL PROTECITION

项　　目	Item	1995	2000	2004	2005	2006
环保系统建设情况	**Construction of Environmental Agencies**					
机构数	Number of Agencies	501	873	575	587	572
#科研所	Scientific Reasearch Center	8	10	12	13	12
监测站	Monitoring Station	11	122	106	100	107
监理所	Supervising Administrative Center	12	272	169	173	150
人员数	Number of Staff and Workers	5672	7433	8463	8631	9239
#科技人员	Scientific and Technical Personnel	3698	341	237	234	223
监测人员	Monitoring Personnel	727	2574	3117	3098	3355
监理人员	Supervising Administrative Personnel	225	1714	2442	2435	2719
污染排放与处理情况	**Discharge and Treatment of Pollution**					
废　水	Waster Water					
工业废水排放量（亿吨）	Industrial Waste Water Emission (100 million tons)	22.02	20.19	26.35	29.63	28.72
#符合排放标准的	According to Standard	14.41	18.57	25.62	28.89	28.05
城镇生活污水排放量（亿吨）	Volume of Urban Domestic Sewage Emission (100 million tons)		14.74	20.26	22.31	22.84
工业废水排放达标量（亿吨）	Volume of Industrial Waste Water Emission Standiardized (100million toun)	14.41	18.57	25.62	28.89	28.05
工业废水排放的污染物（公斤）	Filth of Industrial Waste Water Discharged (kg)					
汞及其无机化合物	Mercury and Inorganic Compound	75	10	20	50	2.9
砷及其无机化合物	Arsenic and Inorganic Compound	166274	52040	3990	4170	3183
铅及其无机化合物	Aluminium and Inorganic Compound	9021	13330	33170	20750	10368
酚	Phenol	462699	114230	74250	88020	77078

15－19 续表1 Continued

项目	Item	1995	2000	2004	2005	2006
氰化物	Cyanide	97199	48420	57940	36800	18658
废 气	Waste Gas					
工业废气排放量（亿标立米）	Volume of Industrial Waste Gas Emission (100 million standardized cu. m)	7872.11	9078.20	17818.42	20196.58	24880.86
#生产工艺排放的	Waste Gas in the Process of Production	1888.00	2556.56	6789.17	7448.51	9561.40
#净化处理的	Gas Purified	1547.87	2218.03			
二氧化硫排放量（万吨）	Volume of Sulphur Dioxide Emission (10000 tons)		89.05	123.99	137.34	130.38
#工 业	Industry	104.47	84.33	118.32	131.24	124.14
生 活	Daily Life		4.72	5.67	6.10	6.24
烟尘排放量（万吨）	Volume of Soot Emission (10000 tons)		39.60	41.51	45.25	42.97
#工 业	Industry	54.00	37.47	39.76	42.64	40.17
生 活	Daily Life		2.13	1.75	2.61	2.80
工业粉尘排放量（万吨）	Volume of Industrial Soot Emission (10000 tons)	27.00	25.68	35.27	35.45	30.20
二氧化硫去除量（万吨）	Volume of Sulphur Dioxide Removed (10000 tons)	12.72	18.72	47.93	73.29	103.68
工业烟尘去除量（万吨）	Volume of Industrial Soot Removed (10000 tons)	772.14	725.41	1227.54	1771.51	2329.19
工业粉尘去除量（万吨）	Volume of Industrial Dust Removed (10000 tons)	112.00	210.48	387.85	388.73	354.36
建成城市烟尘控制区数（个）	Number of Zones of Urban Soot Controlling Established (unit)	236	138	253	142	183
烟尘控制区面积（万平方公里）	Areas of Soot Controlling (10000 sq. km)	0.12	0.15	0.31	0.30	0.37
固体废物	**Solid Waste Residue**					
工业固体废物产生量（万吨）	Industrial Solid Waste Residue Produced (10000 tons)	2883.00	3038.19	4672.53	5757.37	7195.04
#危险废物	Dangerous Residue		76.51	85.81	83.90	98.58

15－19　续表2　Continued

项　　目	Item	1995	2000	2004	2005	2006
工业固体废物综合利用率（%）	Rate of Industrial Solid Waste Utilized in a Conprehensive Way (%)	77.5	85.5	92.3	94.9	94.1
工业固体废物综合利用量（万吨）	Volume of Industrial Solid Waste Utilized in a Comprehensive Way (10000 tons)	2295.34	2598.40	4596.36	5986.51	6966.17
工业固体废物排放量（万吨）	Volume of Industrial Solid Waste Dischaged (10000 tons)	25.61	4.50	0.06	0.01	0.03
“三废”综合利用产品产值（亿元）	Output Value of Products Made from comprehensive Utilization of waste Water, waste Gas and Solid wastes (100 million yuan)		21.87	56.67	93.20	144.05
噪　声	**Noice**					
建成城市环境噪声达标区数（个）	Number of Urban Environmental Noice Zones Standardized and Established (unit)	168	143	290	207	200
环境噪声达标面积（万平方公里）	Areas of Environmental Noice Standardized and Established (10000 sq. km)	0.06	0.1	0.23	0.24	0.3
工业污染治理项目及投资情况	**Investment in Anti-Industrial Pollution Projects**					
本年施工污染治理项目数（个）	Number of Anti-Pollution Projects Under Construction in This Year (unit)	919	2412	814	782	642
废水治理项目	Waste Water	357	966	382	425	347
废气治理项目	Waste Gas	359	1216	324	257	223
固体废物治理项目	Solid Wastes	38	68	22	27	17
噪声治理项目	Noice Abatement	127	98	37	27	20
其他	Others	38	64	49	46	35
污染治理项目本年完成投资（亿元）	Investment in Anti-Pollution Projects Completed in This Year (100 million yuan)	5.42	13.11	22.10	38.95	28.00
废水治理项目	Waste Water	3.34	6.53	8.25	8.16	9.34
废气治理项目	Waste Gas	1.34	5.49	11.99	28.46	17.15
固体废物治理项目	Solid Wastes	0.46	0.79	0.53	0.20	0.23
噪声治理项目	Noice Abatement	0.19	0.14	0.16	0.22	0.13
其他	Others	0.09	0.16	1.17	1.91	1.16
生态环境保护情况	**Ecological and Environmental Protection**					
自然保护区面积（万公顷）	Areas of Natural Reserves (10000 hactares)	49.90	59.55	75.42	85.15	86.18
自然保护区个数（个）	Number of Natural Reserves (unit)	10	23	26	40	38
保护区面积占辖区面积（%）	Ratio of the Area of Reserves to the Area Under Jurisdiction (%)	4.8	5.8	6.0	6.8	6.9
生态示范区个数（个）	Number of Ecological Model Zones (unit)		28	76	59	58
已批准国家级生态示范区（个）	Number of State Level Ecological Model Zones Permitted (unit)		28	76	59	58

15-20 工业"三废"排放及处理情况（2006 年）

行业名称	Branch	工业企业数（个）Number of Industrial Enterprises (unit)	工业废水排放总量（万吨）Total Volume of Industrial Waste Water Discharged (10000 tons)	#直接排入海的 Discharged Directly to the Sea
总计	**Total**	**5926**	**258428.38**	**695.20**
采矿业	**Mining and Quarrying**	**52**	**2405.92**	
煤炭开采和洗选业	Coal Mining and Processing	25	1554.26	
石油和天然气开采业	Petroleum and Natural Gas Extraction	3	4.53	
黑色金属矿采选业	Ferrous Metals Mining and Processing	4	203.95	
有色金属矿采选业	Nonferrous Metals Mining and Processing	9	279.49	
非色金属矿采选业	Nonmetal Minerals Mining and Processing	9	302.97	
其他采矿业	Others	2	60.72	
制造业	**Manufacturing**	**5551**	**210959.75**	**695.20**
农副食品加工业	Food Processing	178	2254.62	28.92
食品制造业	Food Production	95	3261.88	20.08
饮料制造业	Beverage Production	87	3601.72	68.50
烟草加工业	Tobacco Processing	3	92.11	
纺织业	Textile Industry	1095	48436.23	
纺织服装、鞋、帽制造业	Textile Garments, Shoes and Hats	92	2031.79	
皮革、毛皮、羽毛(绒)及其制造业	Leather, Furs, Down and Related Products	47	732.41	
木材加工及木、竹、藤、棕、草制造业	Timber Processing, Wood, Bamboo, Cane, Palm Fiber and Straw Products	27	95.61	
家具制造业	Furniture Manufacturing	11	35.00	
造纸及纸制品业	Papermaking and Paper Products	144	18537.36	72.00
印刷业和记录媒介的复制	Printing and Record Pressing	18	92.56	
文教体育用品制造业	Stationery, Education and Sports Goods	12	27.41	
石油加工、炼焦及核燃料加工业	Petroleum Processing and Coking Products	40	10065.77	
化学原料及化学制品制造业	Raw Chemical Materials and Chemical Products	1135	61779.72	495.75

DISCHARGE AND TREATMENT OF INDUSTRIAL WASTE WATER, WASTE GAS AND SOLID WASTES (2006)

工业废水排放达标量（万吨）Volume of Treated Industrial Waste Water up to the Discharge Standardtzed (10000 tons)	工业废气排放总量（亿标立方米）Total Volume of Industrial Waste Gas Emission (100 million cu. m)	燃料燃烧过程中废气排放总量（亿标立方米）Total Volume of Waste Gas in the Process of Fuel Burning (100 million cu. m)	工业烟尘去除量（吨）Volume of Soot Removed (ton)	工业粉尘排放量（吨）Volume of Industrial Dust Emission (ton)
252609.79	**24880.86**	**15319.46**	**23291914**	**273099**
2385.06	**29.85**	**24.79**	**7667**	**1648**
1533.43	10.15	10.15	1711	
4.50	2.02	1.98	191	
203.95	2.78	0.64	277	345
279.49	1.29	0.74	216	5
302.97	13.40	11.07	5162	331
60.72	0.21	0.21	110	967
205651.13	**14473.08**	**4951.33**	**2471591**	**267507**
2080.80	74.61	34.95	10376	321
3081.12	39.45	27.89	17175	89
3514.41	38.95	37.79	10393	61
92.11	8.43	2.98	126	1
47646.25	427.75	420.97	172706	79
1970.40	38.95	38.90	49418	12
724.33	3.49	3.49	999	
95.58	53.95	26.60	2605	387
33.20	1.47	1.47	279	2
18325.20	388.83	381.36	107157	
89.84	3.63	1.77	180	26
25.91	0.31	0.31	105	
9949.72	641.91	573.55	566795	580
59488.61	1530.64	963.33	583008	4405

15－20 续表 1

行 业 名 称	Branch	工业企业数（个）Number of Industrial Enterprises (unit)	工业废水排放总量（万吨）Total Volume of Industrial Waste Water Discharged (10000 tons)	#直接排入海的 Discharged Directly to the Sea
医药制造业	Medical and Pharmaceutical Products	162	6959.27	
化学纤维制造业	Chemical Fibers	58	6437.94	
橡胶制品业	Rubber Products	53	405.78	
塑料制品业	Plastic Products	51	239.51	
非金属矿物制品业	Nonmetal Mineral Products	596	2897.91	
#水泥制造	Cement Manufaturing	222	1356.74	
黑色金属冶炼及压延加工业	Smelting and Pressing of Ferrous Metals	188	24518.40	0.05
有色金属冶炼及压延加工业	Smelting and Pressing of Nonferrous Metals	85	881.24	
金属制品业	Metal Products	588	3285.95	1.60
通用设备制造业	Ordinary Machinery Manufacturing	201	1748.35	
专用设备制造业	Special Purposes Equipment Manufacturing	101	702.57	
交通运输设备制造业	Transportation Equipment Manufacturing	108	1579.31	8.30
电气机械及器材制造业	Electric Equipment and Machinery	101	1249.46	
通信设备、计算机及其他电子设备制造业	Telecommunication Equipment, Computer and Other Electric Equipment	152	5695.50	
仪器仪表及文化、办公用机械制造业	Instruments, Meters, Cultural and Official Machinery	79	2869.20	
工艺品及其他制造业	Handicraft Artical and Other Manufacturing	20	147.47	
废弃资源和废旧材料回收加工业	Waste Resources and Junk Materials Recycled	24	297.74	
电力、燃气及水的生产和供应业	**Electric Power, Gas and Water Production and Supply**	**248**	**39872.01**	
电力、热力的生产和供应业	Electric Power and Hot Water Production and Supply	218	31339.47	
#火力发电业	Thermal Power Production and Supply	206	30825.66	
燃气生产和供应	Gas Production and Supply	5	358.39	
水的生产和供应业	Tap Water Production and Supply	25	8174.15	

Continued

工业废水排放达标量（万吨）Volume of Treated Industrial Waste Water up to the Discharge Standardtzed (10000 tons)	工业废气排放总量（亿标立方米）Total Volume of Industrial Waste Gas Emission (100 million cu. m)	燃料燃烧过程中废气排放总量（亿标立方米）Total Volume of Waste Gas in the Process of Fuel Burning (100 million cu. m)	工业烟尘去除量（吨）Volume of Soot Removed (ton)	工业粉尘排放量（吨）Volume of Industrial Dust Emission (ton)
6936.24	27.91	24.20	5139	13
6380.44	474.60	326.92	358727	101
391.39	100.93	42.81	17201	19
231.88	47.24	35.01	1184	1
2875.64	3193.13	617.78	45654	215484
1337.38	2819.50	413.59	33604	203250
24054.11	5631.78	1053.01	492977	42629
880.01	120.55	25.57	3907	346
3131.66	333.82	226.50	11083	915
1717.46	72.63	21.45	6616	1078
681.38	34.15	5.88	1198	160
1566.32	313.60	11.34	3603	240
1218.50	93.60	18.19	860	132
5202.50	584.57	18.84	1159	336
2821.87	185.69	5.08	334	52
146.49	0.27	0.27	2	
297.73	6.26	3.13	624	40
39421.14	**10353.87**	**10319.74**	**20810218**	**1788**
30888.60	10288.54	10288.54	20810022	1102
30374.89	10251.97	10251.97	20790197	
358.39	64.79	30.66	52	686
8174.15	0.54	0.54	144	

行业名称	Branch	工业粉尘去除量（吨）Volume of Industrial Dust Removed (ton)	工业固体废物产生量（万吨）Volume of Industrial Solid Wastes Produced (10000 tons)	工业固体废物综合利用量（万吨）Volume of Industrial Solid Wastes Utilizd in a Comprehensive Way (10000 tons)
总　计	**Total**	**3543557**	**6672.71**	**6460.12**
采矿业	**Mining and Quarrying**	**5876**	**353.21**	**278.11**
煤炭开采和洗选业	Coal Mining and Processing		195.17	227.55
石油和天然气开采业	Petroleum and Natural Gas Extraction		0.22	0.11
黑色金属矿采选业	Ferrous Metals Mining and Processing	2100	88.80	18.39
有色金属矿采选业	Nonferrous Metals Mining and Processing	41	16.68	16.68
非色金属矿采选业	Nonmetal Minerals Mining and Processing	2516	28.33	15.37
其他采矿业	Others	1220	24.01	0.01
制造业	**Manufacturing**	**3530834**	**3707.32**	**3471.26**
农副食品加工业	Food Processing	2720	28.28	27.85
食品制造业	Food Production	8413	48.02	47.64
饮料制造业	Beverage Production	20	50.94	50.49
烟草加工业	Tobacco Processing	3412	0.19	0.19
纺织业	Textile Industry	568	156.01	139.66
纺织服装、鞋、帽制造业	Textile Garments, Shoes and Hats	25	12.17	11.36
皮革、毛皮、羽毛(绒)及其制造业	Leather, Furs, Down and Related Products		3.81	1.57
木材加工及木、竹、藤、棕、草制造业	Timber Processing, Wood, Bamboo, Cane, Palm Fiber and Straw Products	28273	4.00	3.82
家具制造业	Furniture Manufacturing	18	0.35	0.27
造纸及纸制品业	Papermaking and Paper Products		229.83	146.18
印刷业和记录媒介的复制	Printing and Record Pressing	225	0.96	0.88
文教体育用品制造业	Stationery, Education and Sports Goods		0.11	0.11
石油加工、炼焦及核燃料加工业	Petroleum Processing and Coking Products	1607	77.63	96.02
化学原料及化学制品制造业	Raw Chemical Materials and Chemical Products	28213	629.46	594.88

Continued

工业固体废物贮存量（万吨）Volume of Industrial Solid Wastes Accumulated (1000 tons)	工业固体废物处置量（万吨）Volume of Industrial Solid Wastes Treated (10000 tons)	三废综合利用产品产值（万元）Output Value of Products Made from Comprehensive Utilization of Waste Gas, Waste Water and Solid Wastes (10000 yuan)	生产工艺过程废气排放总量（亿标立方）Total Volume of Waste Gas from the Process of Production (100 million cu. m)	工业二氧化硫排放量（吨）Volume of Sulphur Dioxide Emission (ton)	#生产工艺过程中排放的 Industrial Sulphur Dioxide from the Process of Production
189.17	**233.78**	**1440509**	**9561.40**	**1148448**	**82652**
55.06	**59.45**	**3564**	**5.06**	**2404**	**231**
7.03	0.00	476		638	
0.07	0.04		0.05	17	1
35.00	35.41	94	2.14	254	109
0.00	0.01	942	0.55	107	
12.96		1861	2.33	1376	120
	24.00	190		12	
110.77	**157.21**	**1373043**	**9521.75**	**442434**	**82007**
0.01	0.42	2239	39.66	3827	
0.00	0.38	6930	11.56	2993	
0.00	0.46	5664	1.16	5629	
	0.00		5.45	64	
0.04	16.31	11612	6.78	50780	
	0.81	58	0.05	4908	
0.00	2.24	2046		464	
0.00	0.18	10353	27.35	2076	
	0.08	5		172	
	83.64	6903	7.47	15231	
0.05	0.03	83	1.86	198	0
0.00	0.00	2		79	
	3.07	92756	68.35	33391	3842
20.26	24.79	265313	567.31	94910	14386

行　业　名　称	Branch	工业粉尘去除量（吨）Volume of Industrial Dust Removed (ton)	工业固体废物产生量（万吨）Volume of Industrial Solid Wastes Produced (10000 tons)	工业固体废物综合利用量（万吨）Volume of Industrial Solid Wastes Utilizd in a Comprehensive Way (10000 tons)
医药制造业	Medical and Pharmaceutical Products	40	14.37	13.90
化学纤维制造业	Chemical Fibers	1485	67.13	66.44
橡胶制品业	Rubber Products	455	8.61	7.99
塑料制品业	Plastic Products		1.80	1.70
非金属矿物制品业	Nonmetal Mineral Products	2813191	354.48	352.86
#水泥制造	Cement Manufaturing	2715165	324.58	324.52
黑色金属冶炼及压延加工业	Smelting and Pressing of Ferrous Metals	621583	1900.96	1805.16
有色金属冶炼及压延加工业	Smelting and Pressing of Nonferrous Metals	987	14.85	14.59
金属制品业	Metal Products	3484	25.54	21.99
通用设备制造业	Ordinary Machinery Manufacturing	8412	19.34	16.34
专用设备制造业	Special Purposes Equipment Manufacturing	914	3.02	2.79
交通运输设备制造业	Transportation Equipment Manufacturing	2408	10.37	7.79
电气机械及器材制造业	Electric Equipment and Machinery	223	4.12	3.30
通信设备、计算机及其他电子设备制造业	Telecommunication Equipment, Computer and Other Electric Equipment	2810	19.13	15.38
仪器仪表及文化、办公用机械制造业	Instruments, Meters, Cultural and Official Machinery	368	8.39	6.67
工艺品及其他制造业	Handicraft Artical and Other Manufacturing		0.06	0.06
废弃资源和废旧材料回收加工业	Waste Resources and Junk Materials Recycled	980	13.40	13.38
电力、燃气及水的生产和供应业	**Electric Power, Gas and Water Production and Supply**	**5016**	**2604.37**	**2703.01**
电力、热力的生产和供应业	Electric Power and Hot Water Production and Supply	5016	2600.21	2700.20
#火力发电业	Thermal Power Production and Supply		2579.25	2679.23
燃气生产和供应	Gas Production and Supply		0.21	0.21
水的生产和供应业	Tap Water Production and Supply		3.95	2.61

Continued

工业固体废物贮存量(万吨) Volume of Industrial Solid Wastes Accumulated (1000 tons)	工业固体废物处置量(万吨) Volume of Industrial Solid Wastes Treated (10000 tons)	三废综合利用产品产值(万元) Output Value of Products Made from Comprehensive Utilization of Waste Gas, Waste Water and Solid Wastes (10000 yuan)	生产工艺过程废气排放总量(亿标立方) Total Volume of Waste Gas from the Process of Production (100 million cu. m)	工业二氧化硫排放量(吨) Volume of Sulphur Dioxide Emission (ton)	#生产工艺过程中排放的 Industrial Sulphur Dioxide from the Process of Production
0.01	0.47	23000	3.71	3092	4
0.06	0.63	8848	147.69	27531	2
	0.61	591	58.12	3053	13
0.00	0.10	9288	12.23	812	18
	1.62	542633	2575.35	73771	30129
	0.07	518501	2405.91	48850	29030
90.24	5.56	291171	4578.78	104584	33185
0.00	0.26	42445	94.98	2347	106
0.08	3.46	8874	107.32	5559	0
0.00	2.99	5367	51.18	2537	66
0.00	0.23	2118	28.27	575	
0.01	2.58	3729	302.25	1367	66
	0.81	1574	75.42	739	40
0.00	3.75	19252	565.73	1014	149
0.00	1.72	5536	180.61	587	0
0.00	0.00			24	
0.00	0.02	4653	3.13	125	
23.32	**17.06**	**63465**	**34.13**	**695271**	**415**
23.32	15.72	63463		694602	
23.32	15.72	63087		691424	
		2	34.13	606	415
	1.34			62	

行业名称 Branch		工业二氧化硫去除总量（吨）Total Volume of Sulphur Dioxide Removed (ton)	#生产工艺过程去除的 Removed in the Process of Production	工业烟尘排放量（吨）Volume of Soot Emission (ton)
总　计	**Total**	**1036810**	**368525**	**367064**
采矿业	**Mining and Quarrying**	**249**	**23**	**883**
煤炭开采和洗选业	Coal Mining and Processing	83		177
石油和天然气开采业	Petroleum and Natural Gas Extraction			15
黑色金属矿采选业	Ferrous Metals Mining and Processing	50		81
有色金属矿采选业	Nonferrous Metals Mining and Processing	20		79
非色金属矿采选业	Nonmetal Minerals Mining and Processing	94	23	501
其他采矿业	Others	2		31
制造业	**Manufacturing**	**454101**	**368486**	**176313**
农副食品加工业	Food Processing	191		1867
食品制造业	Food Production	941		1882
饮料制造业	Beverage Production	405		2551
烟草加工业	Tobacco Processing	47		5
纺织业	Textile Industry	8805	6	23829
纺织服装、鞋、帽制造业	Textile Garments, Shoes and Hats	194		1151
皮革、毛皮、羽毛(绒)及其制造业	Leather, Furs, Down and Related Products	52		270
木材加工及木、竹、藤、棕、草制造业	Timber Processing, Wood, Bamboo, Cane, Palm Fiber and Straw Products	252	45	1113
家具制造业	Furniture Manufacturing	70		66
造纸及纸制品业	Papermaking and Paper Products	23161		5315
印刷业和记录媒介的复制	Printing and Record Pressing			135
文教体育用品制造业	Stationery, Education and Sports Goods			49
石油加工、炼焦及核燃料加工业	Petroleum Processing and Coking Products	305622	305370	14007
化学原料及化学制品制造业	Raw Chemical Materials and Chemical Products	75614	44647	34978

Continued

工业锅炉 Industrial Boiler		#烟尘排放达标的 Soot Discharge Standardized		工业窑炉数（座） Number of Industrial Kiln Stove (unit)	#烟尘排放达标的 Soot Discharge Standardized
（台） (unit)	（蒸吨） (steam tons)	（台） (unit)	（蒸吨） (steam tons)		
5782	**178775**	**5605**	**175936**	**3248**	**3027**
107	**554**	**103**	**540**	**18**	**10**
66	383	62	369	10	5
15	38	15	38		
3	9	3	9	2	2
12	33	12	33		
8	90	8	90	6	3
3	1	3	1		
5006	**39734**	**4838**	**38631**	**3198**	**2985**
213	937	207	924	4	3
88	539	87	539	6	4
82	717	80	715	2	2
7	41	7	41		
1345	7840	1329	7782	169	168
83	519	80	512	10	10
43	116	43	116		
33	198	29	187	3	3
7	22	7	22		
163	3838	160	3820	6	6
11	23	10	23	2	2
5	5	5	5	1	1
55	3388	53	2799	165	161
1454	8719	1393	8506	332	318

15－20 续表 5

行业名称	Branch	工业二氧化硫去除总量（吨）Total Volume of Sulphur Dioxide Removed (ton)	#生产工艺过程去除的 Removed in the Process of Production	工业烟尘排放量（吨）Volume of Soot Emission (ton)
医药制造业	Medical and Pharmaceutical Products	356		1115
化学纤维制造业	Chemical Fibers	5079	0	9459
橡胶制品业	Rubber Products	1401	0	1179
塑料制品业	Plastic Products	86		340
非金属矿物制品业	Nonmetal Mineral Products	19403	17266	42583
#水泥制造	Cement Manufaturing	16745	16666	8797
黑色金属冶炼及压延加工业	Smelting and Pressing of Ferrous Metals	5372	1148	27398
有色金属冶炼及压延加工业	Smelting and Pressing of Nonferrous Metals	425		713
金属制品业	Metal Products	400		2840
通用设备制造业	Ordinary Machinery Manufacturing	21		1454
专用设备制造业	Special Purposes Equipment Manufacturing	54		307
交通运输设备制造业	Transportation Equipment Manufacturing	107	4	652
电气机械及器材制造业	Electric Equipment and Machinery	46		332
通信设备、计算机及其他电子设备制造业	Telecommunication Equipment, Computer and Other Electric Equipment	5979		508
仪器仪表及文化、办公用机械制造业	Instruments, Meters, Cultural and Official Machinery	4		144
工艺品及其他制造业	Handicraft Artical and Other Manufacturing			14
废弃资源和废旧材料回收加工业	Waste Resources and Junk Materials Recycled	15		56
电力、燃气及水的生产和供应业	**Electric Power, Gas and Water Production and Supply**	**581948**	**16**	**186024**
电力、热力的生产和供应业	Electric Power and Hot Water Production and Supply	581948	16	184520
#火力发电业	Thermal Power Production and Supply	579326		182615
燃气生产和供应	Gas Production and Supply			1416
水的生产和供应业	Tap Water Production and Supply			89

Continued

工业锅炉 Industrial Boiler		#烟尘排放达标的 Soot Discharge Standardized		工业窑炉数（座）Number of Industrial Kiln Stove (unit)	#烟尘排放达标的 Soot Discharge Standardized
（台）(unit)	（蒸吨）(steam tons)	（台）(unit)	（蒸吨）(steam tons)		
147	563	135	538	5	5
92	2717	92	2717	60	60
82	982	79	970	7	7
38	121	38	121	5	5
108	663	105	655	958	849
20	270	19	270	300	277
161	4932	157	4809	644	627
44	105	40	100	112	102
243	451	227	445	310	272
114	232	104	229	175	167
42	87	40	85	49	46
103	454	91	453	80	78
37	58	36	54	40	40
131	1305	129	1301	26	24
55	133	55	133	17	15
10	19	10	19		
10	14	10	14	10	10
600	**138257**	**599**	**136555**	**9**	**9**
594	138233	593	136531		
563	137417	562	135715		
4	14	4	14	9	9
2	10	2	10		

主要统计指标解释

供水综合生产能力 指按供水设施取水、净化、送水、出厂输水干管等环节实际测定计算的综合生产能力。

供水管道长度 指从送水泵到用户水表之间所有管道的长度。在同一条街道埋设两条或两条以上管道时，应按每条管道的长度计算。

供水总量 指报告期供水企业(单位)供出的全部水量。包括有效供水量及损失水量。

生活用水量 指居民日常生活与公共福利设施的用水量，包括居民、饮食店、旅馆、医院、理发店、浴池、洗衣店、游泳池、商店、学校、机关、部队等单位的用水量。

城市人口用水普及率 指城市用水人口数与城市人口总数之比。计算公式为：

用水普及率 = 城市用水人口数/城市人口总数 × 100%

燃气综合生产能力 指报告期末燃气生产厂制气、净化、输送等环节的综合生产能力，不包括备用设备能力。一般按设计能力计算，如果实际生产能力大于设计能力时，应按实际测定的生产能力计算。测定时应以制气、净化、输送三个环节中最薄弱的环节为主。

燃气供气管道长度 指报告期末从气源厂压缩机的出口或门站出口到各类用户引入管之间的全部已经通气投入使用的管道长度。不包括煤气生产厂、输配站、液化气储存站、灌瓶站、储配站、气化站、混气站、供应站等厂(站)内的管道。按不同的材质、压力级别、管径分别统计。

燃气供应总量 指报告期燃气企业(单位)向用户供应的燃气数量。包括销售量及损失量。

燃气普及率 指报告期末使用燃气的城市人口数与城市人口总数的比率。计算公式为：

燃气普及率 = 用气人口数/城市人口总数 × 100%

道路长度 指道路长度和与道路相通的桥梁、隧道的长度，按车行道中心线计算。

排水管道长度 指所有排水总管、干管、支管、检查井及连接井进出口等长度之和。

计算时应按单管计算，即在同一条街道上如有两条或两条以上并排的排水管道时，应按每条排水管道的长度相加计算。

城市污水处理能力 指污水处理厂(或处理装置)每昼夜处理污水量的设计能力。

营运车数 指报告期末公交企业(单位)用于运营业务的全部车辆数。以企业(单位)固定资产台帐中已投入运营的车辆数为准；新购、新制和调入的运营车辆，自投入之日起开始计算；调出、报废和调作他用的运营车辆，自上级主管机关批准之日起不再计入。

园林绿地面积 指报告期末用于园林和绿化的各种绿地面积。包括公共绿地、居住区绿地、单位附属绿地、防护绿地、生产绿地、道路绿地和风景林地面积。不包括：

1. 屋顶绿化、垂直绿化、阳台绿化和室内绿化。
2. 以物质生产为主的林地、耕地、牧草地、果园和竹园等。
3. 城市总体规划中不列入绿地的水域。

公共绿地指向公众开放的市级、区级、居住区级各类公园、街旁游园，包括其范围内的水域。其中居住区级公园应不小于1万平方米，街旁游园的宽度不小于8米，面积不小于400平方米。

Explanatory Notes on Main Statistical Indicators

Comprehensive Production Capacity of Tap Water refers to the actual comprehensive production capacity of the waterworks, taking the capacity of the main links such as waterflow, purification, conveyance and outflow of the trunk pilelines into account.

Length of Water Pipelines refers to the total length of all the pipelines between the water pumps and the user's water meters. If there are two or more than two pipelies buried in a same street, the length of every pipeline should be taken into account.

Volume of Water Supply refers to the total volume of water supply by the water supply enterprises (units) during the reference period, including both the effective water supply and loss.

Consumption of Water for Residential Use refers to the water consumption of households for daily life and the water consumption of public welfare facilities, including the consumption of restaurants, hotels, hospitals, barber shops, public bathhouses, laundries, swimming pools, shops, schools, institutions, army units and other units.

Percentage of Urban Population with Access to Tap Water refers to the ratio of the urban population with access to tap water to the total urban population. The formula is:

Percentage of Population with Access to Tap Water = (Urban Population with Access to Tap Water)/(Urban Population) × 100%

Comprehensive Production Capacity of Burning Gas refers to the comprehensive production capacity of the burning gas—works in burning gas generation, purification and delivering, excluding the reserve capacity of the equipment. In general, the capacity is counted in accordance with the designed requirement. If the actual production capacity is larger than designed requirement, it should be counted according to the actual capacity through determination. In determination, the most weak link should be determined as the main one among the three links of burning gas generation, purification and delivering.

Length of Burning Gas Pipelines refers to the total length of pipelines between the outlet of the compressor, blower or burning gas tank of the source factory and the burning gas meters of users, which are all put in use, excluding the pipelines in burning gas—works(stations) and the pipelines of transportation and distribution station, liquefied petroluem gas storage station, pipeline and bottle station, storage and distribution station, gasification station, gas mixed station, supply station. They are counted respectively according to the different quality of materials, level of preasure and the size of bores.

Volume of Burning Gas Supply refers to the volume of burning gas supplied by the burning gas enterprises, including both the sales volume and loss.

Percentage of Urban Population with Access to Burning Gas refers to the ratio of the urban population with access to burning gas to the urban population at the reference period. The formula is:

Percentage of Urban Population with Access to Burning Gas = (Urban Population with Access to Burning Gas)/Urban Population) × 100%

Length of Roads refers to the length of roads, as well as the length of bridges and tunnels, the same as the roads, and taking the middle line of traffic lane into account.

Length of Sewage Pipes refers to the total length of general drainage, trunks, branch and blind drainages, inspection wells, connection wells, inlets and outlets, ete., taking the single pipe into account. Namely if there are two or more than two pipes standing side by side in a street, the length of every pipe should put into account.

Daily Disposal Capacity of Urban Sewage refers to the designed 24 hour capacity of sewage disposal at the sewage treatment works.

Number of Vehicles(Public Transit) in Working refers to the total of operatoinal vehicles(buses and trolley buses) available at the end of the reference period, taking them as the fixed assets registered in account book of the enterprises and put in operation as the accounting standard. Vehicles, newly bought, newly manufactured and transfered in from other units, should be put into account since the day of putting into operation, while the vehicles, transfered to other units, being scrapped and turned to other use, should not be put into account since the day of permission made by higher responsible department.

Area of Gardens and Green Areas refers to the various green land used for gardening and afforestation at the end of reference period, including public green land, residential area green land, subsidiary green land of the units, protection green land, production green land, roadside green land and scenic forest land, excluding:

1. Roof, perpendicular, balcony and indoor green area.
2. Areas taking the material production as the main aim, such as forest land, cultivated land, pasture, orchard and bamboo forest.
3. Water areas which are not listed in the urban general plan.

Public Green Land refers to various level gardens and streetside pleasure gardens of the city, district and residential quarter, they are opened to public, including water area. Among the gardens, the area of residential quarter garden is no less than 1 0000 square meters; the width of streetside garden is no less than 8 meters, and its area is no less than 400 square meters.

第16篇

档案、司法、社会福利、其他

ARCHIVES,JUDGEMENT,SOCIAL WELFARE AND OTHERS

16－1　档案事业机构人员数（2006年）
NUMBER OF PERSONS AND INSTITUTIONS OF ARCHIVES（2006）

项　　目	Item	机构数（个）Number of Institutions (unit)	专职人员数（人）Full-Time Persons (person)	#女　性 Female	#大专以上文化程度 University College and Higher Level
总　计	**Total**	**1941**	**4196**	**2680**	**3669**
档案行政管理部门	Administrative Department of Archives	120	925	355	831
档案馆	Archives	169	1355	768	1174
档案室(处、科)	Archives Offices（Sections）	1652	1916	1557	1664

16－2　档案馆档案资料馆藏和利用情况
CONDITIONS OF FILES STORED AND USED IN ARCHIVES

指　　标	Item	1995	2000	2005	2006
馆藏档案	**Archives Stored**				
全　宗　（个）	Whole Volume（unit）	13018	13756	15363	15803
案　卷　（万卷/万件）	Files（10000 volumes）	569.60	769.02	913.74	1050
录音录像影片档案　（盘）	Records, Films of Videotape Files（copy）	10002	20270	52498	57694
照片档案　（万张）	Picture Files（10000 pieces）	37.05	51.08	38.42	48.22
馆藏资料　（万册）	**Number of Material Stored（10000 volumes）**	**128.00**	**120.00**	**122.04**	**124.00**
档案馆面积　（平方米）	**Areas of Archives（sq. m）**	**159532**	**213419**	**209148**	**244146**
#库房面积	Areas of Storerooms	918532	111336	114737	125949
档案资料利用	**Use of Material**				
利用档案人次　（万人次）	Number of Person-times Using Files Material（10000 person-times）	9.28	12.61	12.14	16.00
利用档案卷次　（万券/万件次）	Number of Archives Used（10000 volume-times）	42.52	46.40	37.48	51.00
利用资料　（万册/万件次）	Number of Data Used（10000 volumes-times）	12.54	3.70	4.14	4.50
复制档案、资料　（万页）	Copies of Files and Material（10000 pages）	75.20	52.22	40.20	67.15
开放档案	**Opening archives**				
全　宗　（个）	Whole Volume（unit）	6716	7852.00	9523	9486
案　卷　（万卷/件）	Files（10000 volumes）	97.61	183.67	163.33	173

16－3　律师、公证及调解工作基本情况
BASIC STATISTICS ON LAWYERS, NOTARIZATION AND MEDIATION

项　　目	Item	1995	2000	2005	2006
律师工作	**Lawyers**				
律师事务所（个）	Number of Lawyer Offices (unit)	414	579	709	775
律师所工作人员（人）	Number of Lawyers (person)	3150	6766	9829	10664
担任法律顾问（家）	Number of Units with Legal Advisors (unit)	22054	23355	30796	35642
民事案件诉讼代理（件）	Agent of Civil Cases (cases)	9236	46023	85107	96473
刑事诉讼辩护及代理（件）	Defender and Agent of Criminal Cases (cases)	13254	17117	20301	21302
经济案件诉讼代理（件）	Agent of Economic Cases (cases)	25822	41854	32202	35487
非诉讼法律事务（件）	Agent of Non-Litigious Legal Affairs (cases)	52002	26746	41451	45869
解答法律咨询（人次）	Agent of Legal Advisory Services (person-times)	272809	214560	326291	310161
代写法律事务文书（件）	Agent of Legal Document Written on Behalf of Clients (cases)	39390	52386	59474	46952
公证工作	**Notarization**				
公证处（个）	Number of Notary Offices (unit)	110	118	112	112
公证人员（人）	Notarial Personnel (person)	654	784	1023	1009
#公证员	Notaries	526	595	550	547
助理公证员	Assistant Notaries	43	73	256	244
办理国内公证文书（件）	Number of Domestic Notarized Documents (cases)	302248	362896	542289	542899
#经济公证	Notarized Business	156650	214708	364424	360980
人民调解工作	**People's Mediation**				
人民调解委员会（个）	Number of People's Mediation Committees (unit)	57607	50509	33327	31903
调解人员（人）	Number of Mediators (person)	1003238	786300	374810	310002
调解民事纠纷（件）	Number of Civil Disputes Mediated (cases)	303718	327622	255647	256204

16－4　涉外公证文书分类
FOREIGN-RELATED NOTARIAL DOCUMENTS BY TYPE

单位:件　　　　(case)

指　　标	Item	2000	2003	2004	2005	2006
合　　计	**Total**	**107747**	**108428**	**117601**	**124690**	**140574**
出　　生	Births	15292	13120	15907	16414	17748
学　　历	Schooling	13901	12578	12884	13745	15303
经　　历	Personal Histories	6315	3350	6748	3967	3372
生存、居住	Survial and Residence	238	275	760	514	924
死　　亡	Deaths	257	588	220	477	378
收　　养	Children Adoption	635	179	2098	494	90
亲属关系	Kinship	9673	9712	9398	10145	10609
婚姻状况	Marital Status	9928	6442	7280	5816	6343
继 承 权	Rights of Inheritance	335	158	21	2	8
遗　　嘱	Testaments	45	41	4	6	14
委 托 书	Trust Deeds	735	1793	1250	1886	1369
声 明 书	Declarations	699	1790	2302	2545	2863
受、未受刑事处分	Criminal Records & Uncriminal Records	13420	15785	13838	16237	18010
文本相符	Confirmation of Copies and Photo-Offset Copies to Originals	10287	11120	14747	19045	22189
其　　他	Others	25987	31497	30144	33397	21277

16－5　调解民事纠纷分类
CIVIL DISPUTES MEDIATED BY TYPE

单位:件　　　　(case)

项　　目	Item	1990	1995	2000	2006
合　　计	**Total**	**320426**	**303718**	**327622**	**256204**
婚　　姻	Marriages	49328	54167	64539	58231
继　　承	Rights of Inheritance	10034	13006	13304	9954
赡、抚、扶养	Family Fostering	24298	29195	52500	8675
其他婚姻家庭	Other Marriage Family	46855	38268	22813	3596
房屋、宅基地	Housing and Housing Sites	46197	52350	32022	18661
邻　　里	Neighbor Disputes	21920	26137	50547	30078
债　　务	Debts	22893	29325	27082	44220
生产经营	Business	24154	22345	22879	27653
损害赔偿	Compensation for Damages	25749	23160	20755	14051
其　　他	Others	48998	15765	21181	36419

16－6　国内公证文书分类
DOMESTIC NOTARIAL DOCUMENTS BY TYPE

单位:件　　(case)

项　目	Item	2000	2004	2005	2006
总　计	**Total**	**362896**	**577656**	**542289**	**542899**
经济公证	**Notarized Documents on Economic Affairs**	**214708**	**393995**	**364424**	**360980**
购　销	Purchases and Sales of Products	15637	1876	1760	1439
联　营	Joint Business	1076	439	66	473
拍　卖	Auctions	2624	1363	4762	1991
贷　款	Loans	56836	231522	222922	232387
担　保	Guarantees	1850	2758	5924	2896
招标、投标	Bidding	6128	16147	11397	10013
科技协作	Coordination of Science and Technology	94	60	159	32
供用电	Supply and Use of Electric Power	1089	91	113	218
劳务合同	Labor Contracts	11251	3037	1875	2255
建筑工程承包	Construction Project Contracts	1832	628	301	370
工商服务业承包	Industrial and Commercial Service Contracts	4352	1219	647	210
农林牧副渔业承包	Farming, Forestry, Animal Husbandry, Sideline Production and Fishery Contracts	7070	1168	766	566
财产租赁	Property Leases	6597	3604	500	350
企业租赁	Enterprise Leases	1403	290	272	128
资产经营责任制	System of Assets Business Responsibility	581	177	114	271
其他经济合同	Other Business Contracts	15347	75624	15614	11492
法人(代表人)资格	Legal Person (agent) Identification	1282	1331	863	735
法人委托书	Legal Person Trust Deeds	3310	7215	9007	11822
公司章程	Corporation Constitutions	706	120	107	268
执行许可证明	Operating Permits	236	721	1153	864
其　他	Others	75407	44605	86102	42440
民事公证	**Notarized Documents on Civil Relations**	**148188**	**183661**	**177865**	**181919**
收　养	Child Adoption	842	489	205	504
解除收养	Adoption Renouncements	174	319	11	22
继承权	Rights of Inheritance	6627	14557	17044	18865
遗　嘱	Testaments	4494	5279	5651	5468
产　权	Property Rights	1638	2325	1508	2937
亲属关系	Kinship Confirmation	3255	3456	2579	2732
死　亡	Death Certificates	93	175	42	85
房屋买卖	Purchases and Sales of Houses	4870	8676	13339	10233
房屋租赁	House Leases	2548	717	757	495
留学协议	Foreign Study Contracts	709	1769	763	1366
遗赠扶养协议	Donations and Family Fostering	670	517	517	603
其他民事协议	Other Civil Agreements	31211	25869	24778	20450
委托书	Trust Deeds	4236	24815	25626	35294
赠与书	Presentaton Documents	5464	9740	9084	7443
声明书	Declarations	6227	13010	13407	18761
现场监督	Field Supervision	10325	10781	6250	4088
文本相符	Confirmation of Copies and Photo-Offset Copies to Originals	729	2430	2993	5322
宅基地使用权	Rights to Housing Site	551	209	30	74
证据保全	Evidence Preservation	2366	7211	8257	9108
计划生育协议	Birth Control Contracts	9555	1041	698	383
其　他	Others	51604	50276	44326	20253

16－7 民政事业费支出情况
OPERATING EXPENSES FOR CIVIL ADMINISTRATION

单位:万元 (10000 yuan)

年 份 Year	民政事业费实际支出合计 Actual Operating Expenses for Civil Administration	#抚恤事业费 Commiserate	#社会救济福利事业费 Subsidies of Social Welfare	#自然灾害救济费 Subsidies of Natural Calamity	#由集体单位供给的 Collletive Funds
1980	15208	5138	7188	2882	6176
1985	24095	11115	10976	2004	11922
1989	27647	9098	7396	4203	11477
1990	46657	20676	20333	5648	21595
1991	69567	20530	27005	22032	27730
1992	60808	22548	23267	14993	23433
1993	60972	25920	27448	7605	27022
1994	72276	31933	34078	6265	32392
1995	87470	38966	39544	8961	38558
1996	104278	48874	46470	8935	47955
1997	119396	57247	52304	9846	54823
1998	141192	67183	63207	10803	64214
1999	157082	78084	69053	9945	64430
2000	175738	86088	78046	11604	68995
2001	187786	89952	87732	10102	70716
2002	205763	54223	72244	8918	59355
2003	255690	58221	91748	27724	49075
2004	309196	72157	117935	13954	43909
2005	419996	103882	178157	14999	51442
2006	502744	118955	229594	17130	

16－8 社会救济人员情况
PERSONS RECEIVING SUBSIDIES OR RELIEF FUNDS

单位:万人 (10000 persons)

指标	Item	2001	2004	2005	2006
社会救济总人数	Number of Persons Receiving Social Relief Funds	155.96	120	129.5	148.1
城镇居民最低生活保障人数	Number of Persons Receiving Lowest Cost-of-living in Urban Area	22.71	38.2	42.3	43.1
农村居民最低生活保障和传统救济总人数	Number of Persons Receiving Lowest Cost-of-living and Tranditional Relief in Rural Area	133.25	81.9	87.2	105

16－9　社会福利企业单位机构和工作人员数

NUMBER OF SOCIAL WELFARE ENTERPRISES AND PERSONS ENGAGED

指　　标	Item	2005 机　构（个）Institutions (unit)	2005 工作人员（人）Staff (person)	2006 机　构（个）Institutions (unit)	2006 工作人员（人）Staff (person)
总　　计	**Total**	**4535**	**276100**	**4537**	**256123**
#国有社会福利企业	Run by State-owned Social Welfare Enterprises	20	2107		
集体社会福利企业	Run by Collective Social Welfare Enterprises	4351	269484		
民办社会福利企业	Run by Civilian Social Welfare Enterprises	164	4509		
#福利工厂	Social Welfare Factories	4457	269286	4476	253785
假肢厂	Artificial Limb Factories	1	97	1	94
其它福利企业	Others	76	6532	59	2076

16－10　收养类单位基本情况（2006 年）

BASIC STATISTICS ON ADOPTIVE HOMES (2006)

项　　目	Item	院数（个）Homes (unit)	工作人员（人）Staff (person)	床位（张）Beds (unit)	年末收养人员（人）Persons Housed (year-end)
总计	**Total**	**1953**	**17654**	**140822**	**103219**
#工商登记	State Run	30	196	1245	940
编制部门登记	Collective Run	404	6973	37750	25236
民政部门登记	Civilian Run	1189	8694	83192	63226
未登记	NO Run	330	1791	18635	13817
#优抚类收养性单位	Special Care Adoptive Homes	20	792	1602	1365
福利类收养性单位	Welfare Homes	1933	16862	139220	101854
社会福利院	Social Welfare Homes	70	1806	10618	7676
儿童福利院	Baby Welfare Homes	8	587	1741	1636
社会福利医院	Psychopathy Welfare Homes	11	1681	3913	3304
城镇收养性老年福利机构	Urban Elderly Welfare Units	1051	9135	80098	53346
农村收养性老年福利机构	Rural Elderly Welfare Units	789	3620	42715	35804
其它收养性福利机构	Other Adoptive Welfare Units	4	33	135	88

16－11 工会、妇联基本情况
BASIC STATISTICS ON LABOUR UNION AND WOMEN'S FEDERATION

单位：个 (unit)

项目	Item	1995	2000	2004	2005	2006
工会基本情况	**Basic Condition of Labour Union**					
基层工会组织数	Number of Basic Level Labour Union Organizations	36215	37160	213686	224605	251980
职工人数 （万人）	Number of Staff and Workers (10000 persons)	714.26	691.97	937.32	1017.65	1160.69
#女职工人数	Women Workers	305.53	288.81	398.53	424.14	491.62
会员人数 （万人）	Number of Members (10000 persons)	645.48	626.67	924.18	1002.25	1148.06
#女会员人数	Women Members	275.81	262.26	386.42	411.46	478.01
女职工工作委员会	Number of Women Workers Working Committees	22843	24743	32660	42342	53028
建立工会经费审查组织	Number of Units Established with Funds Examing by Labour Union			31783	38390	46620
建立职工代表大会制度的单位	Number of Units Established with Workers Delegating Congress System	23194	17684	23063	30075	34997
实行厂务公开的单位	Number of Units Carried Out the Factory Business to Public			19724	23355	27897
建立工会劳动保护监督检查委员会	Number of Units Established with Labour Protection, Supervisting and Examing Committees			16337	21018	26556
建立工会劳动法律监督组织	Number of Organizations Established with Law of Labour Supervising Committees by Labour Union			14850	18641	20569
建立劳动争议调解委员会的单位	Number of Units Established with Mediating Committee of Labour Disputes	18292	13418	17793	21687	26345
建有职工技协组织	Number of Organizations Established with Technical Association of Staff and Workers			1470	1818	1856
妇联基本情况	**Basic Condition of Women's Federation**					
基层妇代会数	Number of Basic Level Units of Women Dlegating Congress			33933	32520	34744
乡以上妇女组织	Township Above Women's Organizations			1663	1577	
参加技术培训人数 （万人）	Number of Perosns Taking Part in Technical Training (10000 persons)	337.19	496.39	17.30		
妇联干部数 （人）	Number of Cadres of Women's Federation (person)	3265	3231	2428	2532	2515
按年龄分	Grouped by Age					
35岁以下	Aged 35 and Below	881		698	1045	941
36－45岁	Aged 36－45	1553		1094	888	1053
46－55岁	Aged 46－55	790		627	542	490
56岁以上	Aged 56 and Above	41		9	57	31
按文化程度分	Grouped by Educational Attainment					
研究生	Postgraduates	12		19	66	75
大学本科、大专学历	University or College	1824		2053	2215	2201
高中、中专及以下	Senior Middle School, Specialized Secondary School and Below	1429		356	251	239

16－12 公安机关立案的刑事案件情况

CRIMINAL CASES REGISTERED IN PUBLIC SECURITY ORGANS

案件类别	Category of Cases	立案（起） Number of Cases Registered(case)		构成（%） Composition	
		2005	2006	2005	2006
合计	**Total**	**424166**	**418231**	**100.0**	**100.0**
杀人	Homicide	766	735	0.2	0.2
伤害	Injury	4802	4747	1.1	1.1
抢劫	Robbery	5279	5173	1.2	1.2
强奸	Rape	1893	1859	0.4	0.4
拐卖人口	Kidnapping and Selling People	42	18	0.0	0.0
盗窃	Larceny	329056	333057	77.6	79.6
诈骗	Fraud	16636	16763	3.9	4.0
持有使用伪造货币	Forging and Fabricating Bills	112	94	0.026	0.022
其他	Others	65580	55785	15.5	13.3

16－13 公安机关受理、查处治安案件情况

OFFENSE CASES AGAINST PUBLIC ORDER HANDLED BY PUBLIC SECURITY ORGANS

案件类别	Category of Cases	2006	
		受理 Number of Cases Accepted to be Treated	查处 Number ofCases Investigated and Treated
合计（起）	**Total（case）**	**1032975**	**1024048**
扰乱公共场所秩序	Disturbing Work or Public Order	5979	5979
寻衅滋事	Gang Fighting or Picking Quarrels and Making Troubles	14824	14627
非法携带枪支、弹药、管制刀具	Unlawful Carring Firearms Amanition and Controlled Cutting Tools	5791	5787
违反危险物品管理规定	Violating Regulation on Mangement of Dangerous Articals	2364	2361
欧打他人	Beating Other Body	263817	262093
偷窃	Robbing Other People of Their Valuables	392924	388080
骗取、抢夺、敲榨勒索	Defrauding, Snatching or Extorting and Racketeering Valuables	26712	26341
伪造、变造、倒卖有价票证、凭证	Forging and Fraudulently Selling Valuable Bills and Certifications	328	328
利用迷信活动危害社会	Endangering the Public Interest by Making use of Superstition	1034	1034
卖淫、嫖娼	Prostitution or Going Whoring	16227	16214
赌博	Gambling	38748	38717
其他	Others	264227	262487

16－14　交通事故情况(2006 年)
BASIC STATISTICS ON TRAFFIC ACCIDENTS (2006)

类　别	Item	发生数(起) Number of Traffic Accidents (case)	死亡人数(人) Number of Deaths (person)	受伤人数(人) Number of Injuries (person)	损失折款(万元) Losses Coverted into Cash (10000 yuan)
总计	**Total**	**23854**	**6891**	**23461**	**9179.3**
#一次死亡 3 人以上事故	Accident with More than three Persons' Death at one Time	69	256	110	317.4
机动车	Motor-driven Vehicles	21794	6427	21565	8913.1
#汽车	Automobiles	12961	4031	12261	7572.5
摩托车	Motorcycles	6504	1475	7384	899.6
非机动车	Non-motor-driven Vehicles	2060	464	1869	266.3
#自行车	Bicycles	574	129	517	53.4
行人乘车人	Pedestrians and Passengers	369	145	258	117.8

16－15　火灾事故情况(2006 年)
BASIC STATISTICS ON FIRE ACCIDENTS (2006)

项　目	Item	合计 Total	按事故发生程度分 By Degree of Fires	
			重大 Extraordinary	一般 Ordinary
发生 (起)	Fires (case)	18060	5	18055
死亡 (人)	Deaths (person)	91	10	81
受伤 (人)	Injuries (person)	60	2	58
损失折款 (万元)	Losses Converted into Cash (10000 yuan)	3973.7	174.8	3798.9
平均每起事故损失 (万元)	Average Loss per Fire (10000 yuan)	0.22	34.96	0.21

16－16 检察机关直接立案侦查案件情况（2006 年）
CASES UNDER DIRECT INVESTIGATION BY PROCURATOR'S OFFICES(2006)

案件分类 Case Item		受案（件）Cases Accepted (case)	立案件数（件）Number of Cases Registered (case)	立案人数（人）Person of Cases Registered (person)	#要案 Key Case	结案件数（件）Number of Cases Settled (case)	结案人数（人）Person of Cases Settled (person)
合计	Total	3458	1756	1831	126	1707	1767
贪污贿赂案件	Sub-total of Cases on Corruption and Bribery	2764	1534	1593	120	1495	1543
贪污	Corruption	882	373	411	19	373	405
贿赂	Bribery	1678	1018	1029	95	975	982
挪用公款	Misappropriation of Public Funds	171	135	142	4	135	141
集体私分	Collective Illegal Possession of Public Funds	22	8	11	2	12	15
巨额财产 来源不明	Unstated Source of Large Properities	11					
其他	Others						
渎职案件	Sub-total of Cases on Abuse and Dereliction of Duty	694	222	238	6	212	224
滥用职权	Abuse of Power	207	72	78	3	71	77
玩忽职守	Dereliction of Duty	206	79	80	2	76	78
徇私舞弊	Fraudulent Practice	189	46	55	1	42	46
其他	Others	92	25	25	0	23	23

注：结案中含上年旧存（以下各表同）。

Note: Data of cases settled include cases turned over from previous year. (The same as in the following tables).

16－17 检察机关审查批准、决定逮捕犯罪嫌疑人和提起公诉被告人情况（2006 年）
ARRESTS OF CRIMINAL SUSPECTS AND DEFENDANTS UNDER PUBLIC PROSECUTION APPROVED BY PROCURATOR'S OFFICES(2006)

案件分类 Item		批捕、决定逮捕合计 Total of Arrests		决定起诉合计 Total of Public Prosecutions	
		件 (case)	人 (person)	件 (case)	人 (person)
合计	**Total**	**35111**	**52940**	**45735**	**71724**
公安、安全、监狱机关提请	**Sub-total of Requests by Departments of State and Public Security and Prisons**	**34179**	**51985**	**44502**	**70397**
危害国家安全案	Offences Against State Security	3	3	2	2
危害公共安全案	Offences Against Public Security	2830	3032	6086	6381
破坏社会主义市场经济秩序案	Offences Against socialist Economic Order	952	1316	1412	2258
侵犯公民人身、民主权利案	Offences Against Citizens' Personal and Democratic Rights	4760	5916	6448	8265
侵犯财产案	Offences Against Properties	19612	30915	22992	37650
妨害社会管理秩序案	Offences Against Social Management of Order	6010	10786	7554	15827
危害国防利益案	Offences Against National Defense	12	17	8	14
检察机关直接立案侦查案件	**Sub-total of Cases Handled by Procuratorates**	**932**	**955**	**1233**	**1327**
贪污贿赂案	Offences on Corruption and Bribery	879	896	1139	1227
渎职案	Offences on Abuse and Dereliction of Duty	53	59	94	100

16－18　检察机关处理申诉案件情况（2006年）
APPEALS HANDLED BY PROCURATOR'S OFFICES(2006)

案件分类	Cases	受案（件）Cases Accepted (case)	立案复查（件）Cases Registered for Reinvestigation (case)	结案（件）Cases Settled (case)	#改变原决定 Original Decision Changed
合计	**Total**	**413**	**129**	**116**	**24**
不服检察机关处理决定	Appeals against Decision of Procurator's Offices	131	51	47	15
不服不批捕	Appeals against Rejection of Arrest	26	13	8	0
不服不起诉	Appeals against Rejection of Prosecuting	24	16	12	2
不服撤案	Appeals against Withdrawal of the Case	0	0	1	1
不服原免予起诉	Appeals against Original Exemption of Lawsuit	9	5	5	2
其他	Others	72	17	21	10
不服法院刑事判决裁定	Appeals against Judgment of Criminal Case	282	78	69	9
刑罚执行中被害人申诉	Appeals of the Victim at the Punishment	45	11	10	0
刑罚执行中被告人申诉	Appeals of the Defendant at the Punishment	166	51	44	9
刑罚执行完毕后被害人申诉	Appeals of the Victim after the Punishment	7	3	3	0
刑罚执行完毕后被告人申诉	Appeals of the Defendant after the Punishment	64	13	12	0

16－19　人民法院审理刑事一审案件收结案情况（2006年）
FIRST TRIAL CRIMINAL CASES ACCEPTED AND SETTLED BY COURTS (2006)

单位:件　　(case)

项目	Item	收案 Cases Accepted	结案 Cases Settled
合计	**Total**	**46649**	**46680**
危害公共安全罪	Offences Against Public Security	6029	6018
破坏社会主义市场经济秩序罪	Offences Against Socialist Economic Order	1396	1415
侵犯公民人身权利民主权利罪	Offences Against Citizens's Personal and Democratic Rights	7959	8026
侵犯财产罪	Offences Against Properties	22534	22524
妨害社会管理秩序罪	Offences Against Social Management of Order	7482	7473
危害国防利益罪	Offences Against National Defense	12	12
贪污贿赂罪	Offences on Corruption and Bribery	1164	1139
渎职罪	Offences on Dereliction of Duty	70	70
其他	Others	3	3
合计中含自诉案件	Private Prosecution of Total	1640	1690

注:结案含上年旧存(下同)。
Note: Data of cases Settled include cases turned over from previous year. The same as the following tables.

16-20 人民法院审理婚姻家庭、继承一审案件收结案情况（2006年）
FIRST TRIAL CIVIL CASES OF MARRIAGES, FAMILY AFFAIRS AND INHERITANCE ACCEPTED AND SETTLED BY COURTS(2006)

单位：件 (case)

项目	Item	收案 Cases Accepted	结案 Cases Settled	调解 Mediation	判决 Judgement	驳回 Reject	撤诉 With-drawal	其他 Other
合计	**Total**	**71857**	**71846**	**31950**	**27766**	**339**	**11303**	**488**
婚姻家庭	Marriages and Family Affairs	70715	70707	31519	27319	328	11071	470
离婚	Divorce	60233	60148	26752	23972	278	8786	360
赡养纠纷	Support Disputes	2031	2037	713	685	3	606	30
抚养、扶养关系纠纷	Upbringing Disputes	2523	2520	1442	620	11	428	19
抚育费纠纷	Upbringing Fee Disputes	1841	1872	806	664	12	372	18
其他	Others	4087	4130	1806	1378	24	879	43
继承	Inheritance	1142	1139	431	447	11	232	18
法定继承	Legal Inheritance	581	584	233	215	2	125	9
遗嘱继承	Testament Inheritance	81	76	30	37		7	2
其他	Others	480	479	168	195	9	100	7

16-21 人民法院审理合同纠纷一审案件收结案情况（2006年）
FIRST TRIAL CASES OF CONTRACTS DISPUTES ACCEPTED AND SETTLED BY COURTS (2006)

单位：件 (case)

项目	Item	收案 Cases Accepted	结案 Cases Settled	调解 Mediation	判决 Judgement	驳回 Reject	撤诉 With-drawal	其他 Other
合计	**Total**	**151688**	**150201**	**45876**	**60673**	**2228**	**38724**	**2700**
借款合同	Loan Contracts	43858	43661	13141	21025	293	8718	484
买卖合同	Trade Contracts	43772	43821	13949	16048	455	12402	967
电信合同	Telecom Contracts	3095	3121	711	565	6	1837	2
租赁合同	Lease Contracts	8819	8683	2521	3352	119	2572	119
劳动争议	Work Disputes	7102	6885	1737	3229	471	1327	121
房地产合同	Real Estate Contracts	4413	4437	1154	1878	120	1229	56
供用动力合同	Labor Contracts	355	356	85	92	3	140	36
建设工程合同	Construction Contracts	5408	5257	1477	2195	126	1329	130
农村承包合同	Rural Contracts	1946	1944	487	758	113	563	23
承揽合同	Contracts for Work	9855	9791	2672	3307	135	3356	321
其他	Others	23065	22245	7942	8224	387	5251	441

16-22 人民法院审理权属、侵权纠纷及其他民事一审收结案情况（2006年）
FIRST TRIAL CASES OF DISPUTES OF RIGHT, INFRINGEMENT OF RIGHT AND OTHER CIVIL AFFAIRS ACCEPTED AND SETTLED BY COURTS(2006)

单位：件 (case)

项目	Item	收案 Cases Accepted	结案 Cases Settled	调解 Mediation	判决 Judgement	驳回 Reject	撤诉 With-drawal	其他 Other
合计	**Total**	**91090**	**92155**	**29867**	**42293**	**933**	**12666**	**6396**
人身损害赔偿	Compensate for Personal Harm	60501	61337	24521	30533	219	5826	238
所有权及其相关权利	Ownership and Related Rights	14805	14913	3857	6014	436	4404	202
特别程序	Special Proceedings	8850	9034	18	2853	76	292	5795
人身权纠纷	Personal Rights	362	364	78	175	9	95	7
特殊侵权纠纷	Disputes of Special Infringement of Right	1958	1962	570	839	28	499	26
不当得利	Unjustified Enrichment	784	781	151	291	65	259	15
票据、证券、股票纠纷	Disputes of Bill, Securities and Stocks	1108	957	142	403	29	336	47
知识产权案件	Intellectual Rights	842	878	93	264	24	478	19
其他	Others	1880	1929	437	921	47	477	47

16-23 人民法院行政一审案件收结案情况（2006年）
FIRST TRIAL ADMINISTRATIVE CASES ACCEPTED AND SETTLED BY COURTS(2006)

单位：件 (case)

项目	Item	收案 Cases Accepted	结案 Cases Settled	维持 Affirmation of Original Judgement	撤销 Cancel	驳回 Reject	撤诉 With-drawal	单独赔偿 Separate Compen-sation	其他 Other
合计	**Total**	**4412**	**4416**	**553**	**272**	**1292**	**1775**	**240**	**524**
土地等资源	Land	588	601	43	40	205	209	33	104
公安	Public Security	361	363	78	2	130	133	36	20
城建	City Construction	1683	1672	165	124	483	722	66	178
交通运输	Traffic and Transport	103	105	16	2	30	52	7	5
工商	Industry and Commerce	136	139	13	2	43	73	7	8
环保	Environment Protection	26	28	3	1	3	14	1	7
计划生育	Family Planning	36	39	4		9	21	4	5
税务	Tax	20	15	2		4	8		1
卫生	Health	31	33	3	1	10	18	1	1
乡政府	Townships Government	135	139	1	5	46	65	17	22
劳动和社会保障	Labour and Social Security	555	549	140	58	137	189	15	25
其他	Other	738	733	85	37	192	271	53	148

主要统计指标解释

民政事业费支出 指报告期内本辖区各项民政事业费实际支出的总数额。包括抚恤事业费、军队移交地方安置的离退休人员费用、社会救济福利事业费、救灾支出以及其它民政事业费。

城镇居民最低生活保障人数 指在报告期末家庭平均收入在当地规定的最低生活保障线以下的城镇居民数。包括"三无"对象、失业人员和在职、下岗、退休人员等。

农村居民最低生活保障人数 指报告期末在建立农村最低生活保障制度的地区,得到当地政府或集体给予最低生活保障的农业人口数。

农村传统救济人数 指未开展最低生活保障制度的农村地区,仍沿用传统救济制度救济贫困人口数。

收养性福利单位 指荣誉军人康复医院、复员军人疗养院、复退军人精神病院、光荣院、社会福利院、儿童福利院、精神病福利院、城镇老年福利机构、农村老年福利机构以及其它收养性单位的总称。

社会福利企业 指以集中安置有一定劳动能力的残疾人就业为目的(残疾职工占生产人员10%以上)、带有社会福利性质的特殊企业的总称。

律师 指受聘参加法律顾问处工作,担任法律顾问、刑(民)事代理人、刑事辩护人,办理非诉讼事件、解答法律询问,代写法律事务文书等主要从事律师业务的专职法律工作者和兼职律师。

公证人员 指在国家公证机关依法办理公证事务的司法人员,包括公证员、助理公证员和在公证处工作的其他人员。

办理公证文书 指公证处在一定时期内办结的公证文书件数。公证文书按司法部规定或批准的格式制作,包括国内公证和涉外公证两部分。国内公证分为经济合同公证和民事法律关系公证两大类。

调解人员 指在人民调解委员会担负调解民间一般民事纠纷和轻微违法行为引起纠纷的工作人员,包括调解委员会的委员和调解小组的调解员。

调解民间纠纷 指调解委员会依照法律规定,根据自愿原则,用说服教育的方法调解民间发生的有关民事权利和义务的争执,促成当事双方达到协议和谅解,解决纠纷。包括婚姻家庭纠纷,财产权益纠纷等,不包括法院受理调解的民事案件数。

受理劳动争议案件数 指劳动争议仲裁委员会根据国家有关规定,对劳动争议当事人的申请予以审查,符合受理条件而正式立案、准备处理的劳动争议案件数。

决定逮捕 指检察机关对直接受理、自行侦查的案件,认为需要逮捕犯罪嫌疑人时,依据法律作出的逮捕决定。

批准逮捕 指检察机关对公安机关、国家安全机关、监狱管理机关提出逮捕的犯罪嫌疑人进行审查,根据事实,依法作出逮捕决定。

决定起诉 指检察机关对公安机关、国家安全机关、监狱管理机关和检察机关内设机构反贪污贿赂部门移送起诉的刑事犯罪嫌疑人进行审查,根据事实,依法向人民法院提起公诉。

Explanatory Notes on Main Statistical Indicators

Operation Expenses for Civil Adiministration refer to the total actual expenditures for all the operating expenses of civil administration in this jurisdiction district at reference period, including pensions, settlement allowance for the retirees who are transfered from P. L. A. units to the local government to be settled down, social welfare, disaster relief and other civil administration expenses.

Number of Persons Receiving Lowest-Lost-Living in Urban Area refer to the number of urban residents their family average income is below the lowest living standard insurance line at the year end, according to the local regulation; including "three proverty-striken people", unemployment, employees, laid off and retired personnels.

Number of Persons Receiving Lowest-Cost-Living in Rural Area refer the number of rural population in rural area with the system of lowest living standard insurance has been established, they are being insured by the local government and collective units.

Number of Traditional Relief Persons in Rural Areas refer to the rural areas which has not been established the system of lowest living standard insurance, the poor people are still succoured according to the traditional relief system.

Adopting Social Welfare Institutions refer to the all names of social welfare homes and adopting social welfare institutions, including homes for disabled soldiers, convalescent homes for demobilized soldiers, psychopathy welfare homes for demobilized soldiers, homes for disabled veterancs, social welfare homes, children welfare homes, urban eldery welfare units, rural elderly welfare units.

Social Welfare Enterprises refer the all names of special enterprises with the social welfare character, for the aim of employment of the disabled persons who still provide certain labor capacity, and are settled down concentratively (10% above are disabled staff and workers).

Lawyers are legal workers who are employed full time by legal counseling firms to act as a legal adivisers, agents in criminal civil lawsuits or defenders in criminal lawsuits, or to handle non-liligious legal affairs, to advise on matters of law or to write legal papers for others. Both full time and part time lawyers are included.

Notary Personnel refer to judicial workers of the state notary offices handling notarization work according to law. They include notaries and other people working for notary offices.

Notarized Documents refer to documents settled by notary offices in a year. The notary documents are drawn up in accordance with the regulations of the Ministry of Justice, including domestic documents and foreign-related documents. Domestic documents are divided into two major categories, documents on economic contracts and documents on civil legal relation.

Mediators refer to workers on peoples mediation committees responsible for mediating in civil disputes and cases of slight infraction of the law. They include members of the mediation committees and mediators of mediation groups.

Mediatoin of Civil Disputes refers to mediation committees work in mediating in civil disputes concerning civil rights and duties through persuasion and education in accordance with the provisions of law on a voluntary basis, so as to solve disputes by helping the parties involved come to an agreement and understanding. These disputes include divora cases and disputes over property ownership, but exclude the civil cases to be handled by the court.

Number of Labour Dispute Cases Accepted refer to the number of cases of labour dispute submitted that, after being reviewed by the labour dispute arbitraction committees in line with relevant state regulations, are accepted and registered for treatment.

Decision on Arrest refers to decision made by procurators office, in accordance:e with laws, to arrest the suspect(s) in the cases that are accepted and to be investigated by procurators office.

Approval for Arrest refers to the decision made b procurators office, in accordance with laws and relevant facts, to approve the arrest of the suspect(s) that is proposed by the public security departments or authority of prisons.

Decision on Prosecution refers to the decision made by procurators office, in accordance with laws and relevent facts, to institute proeedings to the people court against the suspect(s) of criminal cases handed by the public security departments, state security departments or authority of prisons, or by the anti-corruption departments within the procurators office.

JIANGSU STATISTICAL YEARBOOK

第17篇

城市经济与建设

URBAN ECONOMY AND CONSTRUCTION

17－1　主要城市土地面积、人口情况（2006年）
LAND AREA AND POPULATION OF MAJOR MUNICIPALITIES (2006)

城　市 Municipality		土地面积（平方公里）Land Area (sq. km)	年末总人口（万人）Total Populations (year-end) (10000 persons)	#女 Female	当年出生人口（万人）Births (10000 persons)	当年死亡人口（万人）Deaths (10000 persons)	人口密度（人/平方公里）Population Density (person/sq. km)
南京市区	Nanjing	4723	524.64	256.98	3.71	2.67	1111
无锡市区	Wuxi	1623	232.30	116.48	1.49	1.49	1432
徐州市区	Xuzhou	1160	181.60	87.49	1.24	0.54	1566
常州市区	Changzhou	1864	222.48	111.10	1.74	1.49	1194
苏州市区	Suzhou	1650	230.15	116.07	1.78	1.28	1395
南通市区	Nantong	355	86.64	43.75	0.61	0.53	2441
连云港市区	Lianyungang	943	70.96	34.83	0.63	0.28	752
淮安市区	Huaian	3171	276.48	134.30	3.34	1.05	872
盐城市区	Yancheng	1720	152.64	74.22	1.54	0.67	887
扬州市区	Yangzhou	980	116.82	58.21	0.79	0.71	1192
镇江市区	Zhenjiang	1082	102.72	50.57	0.73	0.54	950
泰州市区	Taizhou	444	64.25	32.01	0.66	0.51	1446
宿迁市区	Suqian	2108	155.35	75.74	1.37	0.55	737

17－2　主要城市就业情况（2006年）
EMPLOYMENT OF MAJOR MUNICIPALITIES (2006)

单位:万人　　(10000 persons)

城　市 Municipality		年末从业人员数 Employment (year-end)	#在岗职工人数 Staff and Workers Employed	#城镇私营和个体人数 Employment in Private Enterprises and Self-employed Individuals of Urban Areas	从业人员按三次产业分 Employment Grouped by Type of Industry: 第一产业 Primary Industry	第二产业 Secondary Industry	第三产业 Tertiary Industry
南京市区	Nanjing	280.79	87.68	83.66	24.74	116.10	139.95
无锡市区	Wuxi	170.88	34.78	68.65	6.99	101.23	62.66
徐州市区	Xuzhou	99.74	30.18	26.55	12.48	34.42	52.84
常州市区	Changzhou	176.78	25.55	71.22	14.92	98.44	63.42
苏州市区	Suzhou	146.97	53.87	34.50	10.88	86.25	49.84
南通市区	Nantong	46.69	18.92	8.57	3.69	21.30	21.70
连云港市区	Lianyungang	46.02	14.12	8.99	5.59	17.35	23.08
淮安市区	Huaian	137.97	18.10	16.87	49.32	36.73	51.91
盐城市区	Yancheng	66.95	14.44	10.92	17.69	22.39	26.87
扬州市区	Yangzhou	66.31	16.05	15.82	5.85	32.59	27.87
镇江市区	Zhenjiang	55.94	17.26	11.43	8.83	25.79	21.32
泰州市区	Taizhou	37.29	9.21	8.82	4.35	18.65	14.29
宿迁市区	Suqian	86.55	5.95	10.98	27.93	31.52	27.10

17－3　主要城市地区生产总值及指数（2006年）
GROSS DOMESTIC PRODUCT OF MAJOR MUNICIPALITIES（2006）

单位：亿元　　　　(100 million yuan)

城　市 Municipality		地区生产总值 Gross Domestic Product	第一产业 Primary Industry	第二产业 Secondary Industry	第三产业 Tertiary Industry	人均地区生产总值（元） Per Capita GDP (yuan)	地区生产总值指数（上年=100） GDP Index (2005=100)	人均地区生产总值指数（上年=100） Per Capita Index (2005=100)
南京市区	Nanjing	2559.00	56.12	1242.63	1260.25	41054	114.7	110.2
无锡市区	Wuxi	1892.20	17.01	1065.09	810.10	62434	115.4	110.1
徐州市区	Xuzhou	747.71	10.13	431.24	306.34	39927	115.6	112.6
常州市区	Changzhou	1185.17	28.24	735.14	421.79	40574	115.3	111.1
苏州市区	Suzhou	1946.55	19.66	1195.57	731.32	67032	116.5	109.9
南通市区	Nantong	455.36	4.87	272.76	177.73	42577	115.2	114.7
连云港市区	Lianyungang	237.87	13.25	126.74	97.88	29649	114.1	112.7
淮安市区	Huaian	407.26	56.59	203.46	147.21	15370	114.9	114.3
盐城市区	Yancheng	323.31	37.02	165.10	121.18	20782	125.7	116.8
扬州市区	Yangzhou	506.38	13.20	298.22	194.96	38310	115.6	113.3
镇江市区	Zhenjiang	455.77	9.44	279.51	166.82	40083	114.8	113.7
泰州市区	Taizhou	270.12	5.44	189.00	75.68	41990	115.7	115.1
宿迁市区	Suqian	172.26	26.07	97.23	48.96	11933	118.3	119.8

17－4　主要城市固定资产投资（2006年）
INVESTMENT IN FIXED ASSETS OF MAJOR MUNICIPALITIES（2006）

单位：亿元　　　　(100 million yuan)

城　市 Municipality		城镇固定资产投资 Urban Investment in Fixed Assers	房地产开发投资 Investment in Real Estate Development	#住宅 Resdential Building	新增固定资产 Newly Increased Fixed Assets	商品房屋销售建筑面积（万平方米） Construction Floor Space of Commercial House Sold (10000 sq. m)	#住宅 Resdential Building
南京市区	Nanjing	1169.26	338.00	243.82	660.45	961.40	895.88
无锡市区	Wuxi	788.84	202.08	135.75	626.13	419.45	350.45
徐州市区	Xuzhou	336.40	45.16	37.95	175.25	135.29	116.94
常州市区	Changzhou	501.96	140.39	97.98	311.64	377.65	317.83
苏州市区	Suzhou	714.90	249.51	204.44	729.98	626.87	558.29
南通市区	Nantong	197.35	53.87	43.95	128.24	231.88	208.92
连云港市区	Lianyungang	170.08	39.77	30.04	104.94	94.46	81.42
淮安市区	Huaian	202.02	50.76	38.97	119.07	125.13	100.51
盐城市区	Yancheng	169.89	36.31	27.23	79.14	134.29	127.27
扬州市区	Yangzhou	201.89	43.58	29.25	110.14	203.84	163.61
镇江市区	Zhenjiang	224.72	40.45	33.23	208.63	125.94	115.13
泰州市区	Taizhou	132.20	26.37	20.69	93.06	95.44	82.61
宿迁市区	Suqian	79.26	24.70	18.24	49.21	104.84	77.89

17－5 主要城市工业基本情况（2006年）
BASIC STATISTICS ON INDUSTRY OF MAJOR MUNICIPALITIES (2006)

单位:亿元 (100 million yuan)

城市 Municipality		工业企业单位数(个) Number of Industrial Enterprises (unit)	#大中型企业 Enterprises of Large and Medium Size	工业增加值 Value Added of Industry	资产总计 Total Assets	负债合计 Total Liabilities	主营业务收入 Major Business Income	利税总额 Total Pre-tax Profits
南京市区	Nanjing	1605	252	899.31	3380.64	1879.47	4427.38	389.17
无锡市区	Wuxi	2963	335	808.28	2631.39	1599.14	3501.70	234.23
徐州市区	Xuzhou	576	47	336.82	756.83	481.55	883.66	140.87
常州市区	Changzhou	3421	240	604.25	2018.35	1278.77	2642.81	168.78
苏州市区	Suzhou	2084	451	991.86	3214.48	1809.48	3989.93	266.30
南通市区	Nantong	939	81	207.93	698.78	390.31	733.24	70.57
连云港市区	Lianyungang	270	39	86.07	269.11	150.95	276.21	30.67
淮安市区	Huaian	716	36	150.67	388.76	235.27	551.75	67.22
盐城市区	Yancheng	573	45	117.03	323.44	216.73	471.34	34.70
扬州市区	Yangzhou	793	84	250.04	631.74	373.49	779.09	100.34
镇江市区	Zhenjiang	595	65	218.10	755.76	511.66	734.13	69.03
泰州市区	Taizhou	414	43	174.79	386.40	215.26	577.70	46.93
宿迁市区	Suqian	279	19	36.62	94.80	57.70	118.71	12.26

17－6 主要城市工业总产值（2006年）
GROSS OUTPUT VALUE OF INDUSTRY OF MAJOR MUNICIPALITIES (2006)

单位:亿元 (100 million yuan)

城市 Municipality		工业总产值 Tatal Output Value of Industry	内资企业 Inner Funded Enterprises	外商港澳台投资企业 Foreign, Hong Kong, Macao and Taiwan Funded Enterprises	#国有控股企业 State-owned Share Holding Enterprises	#大中型企业 Large and Medium-sized Enterprises	#制造业 Manufacturing
南京市区	Nanjing	4389.05	2581.51	1807.53	1845.79	3443.87	4269.02
无锡市区	Wuxi	3490.78	1696.66	1794.13	270.79	2095.32	3458.00
徐州市区	Xuzhou	906.90	810.28	96.62	533.87	610.60	668.27
常州市区	Changzhou	2648.25	1806.87	841.29	183.57	1181.71	2607.45
苏州市区	Suzhou	3966.35	584.15	3382.21	105.03	3006.63	3927.55
南通市区	Nantong	740.00	285.65	454.34	193.47	371.64	687.88
连云港市区	Lianyungang	283.33	123.24	160.09	63.66	210.63	256.68
淮安市区	Huaian	518.01	455.39	62.61	142.26	252.09	487.15
盐城市区	Yancheng	481.43	310.97	170.46	38.29	256.24	455.27
扬州市区	Yangzhou	812.15	602.77	209.38	197.79	478.29	700.94
镇江市区	Zhenjiang	731.82	378.65	353.17	149.28	444.62	646.45
泰州市区	Taizhou	579.26	486.30	92.96	153.82	417.79	577.36
宿迁市区	Suqian	122.81	107.71	15.11	22.02	54.40	116.82

17－7 主要城市财政收支（2006年）
GOVERNMENT REVENUE AND EXPENDITURES OF MAJOR MUNICIPALITIES (2006)

单位：亿元 (100 million yuan)

城市 Municipality		地方财政一般预算收入 Local Financial General Budgetary Revenue	#各项税收 Taxes	地方财政一般预算支出 Local Financial General Budgetary Expenditure	#文教科卫事业费 Expenditure for Culture Education, Science & Technology And Healthcare	#社会保障补助支出 Subsidies Expenditure for Social Security	#城市维护费 Expenditure for City Maintenance
南京市区	Nanjing	235.97	208.27	247.42	44.70	6.87	48.55
无锡市区	Wuxi	138.75	123.35	136.30	25.37	3.93	11.60
徐州市区	Xuzhou	43.47	35.07	47.69	10.55	5.40	3.82
常州市区	Changzhou	98.45	85.53	94.57	16.52	2.87	15.19
苏州市区	Suzhou	168.02	156.56	175.61	25.53	10.06	22.66
南通市区	Nantong	42.50	36.69	41.58	6.79	1.73	2.68
连云港市区	Lianyungang	21.01	17.53	24.88	4.33	0.48	1.34
淮安市区	Huaian	28.21	21.22	39.61	9.78	1.31	3.64
盐城市区	Yancheng	18.81	15.58	26.37	7.07	1.07	0.91
扬州市区	Yangzhou	36.53	28.78	38.68	6.71	1.08	1.28
镇江市区	Zhenjiang	35.48	27.28	36.93	7.85	0.98	1.62
泰州市区	Taizhou	24.90	19.52	28.85	4.16	1.58	1.23
宿迁市区	Suqian	9.75	7.35	20.29	4.50	0.63	0.62

17－8 主要城市金融机构存贷款余额（2006年）
DEPOSITS AND LOANS BALANCE OF BANKING INSTITUTIONS OF MAJOR MUNICIPALITIES (2006)

单位：亿元 (100 million yuan)

城市 Municipality		存款余额 Deposits Balance	#企业存款 Deposits of Enterprises	#居民储蓄存款 Savings Deposits from Residents	贷款余款 Loans Balance	#工业贷款 Industrial Loans	#商业贷款 Commercial Loans	#中长期贷款 Long and Middle Term Loans
南京市区	Nanjing	5698.05	2747.61	1768.03	5035.06	457.61	283.14	2804.65
无锡市区	Wuxi	2494.03	962.51	1047.56	1600.00	374.57	103.76	504.37
徐州市区	Xuzhou	686.47	227.99	334.74	313.38	71.82	21.59	99.74
常州市区	Changzhou	1644.73	499.68	790.38	1164.62	311.99	60.00	378.49
苏州市区	Suzhou	2603.75	1122.74	993.07	2136.04	228.87	54.87	1234.15
南通市区	Nantong	785.16	333.51	333.45	572.22	124.87	64.60	200.65
连云港市区	Lianyungang	309.93	115.28	140.34	224.56	37.13	20.63	76.83
淮安市区	Huaian	349.34	109.24	178.85	233.74	26.71	23.42	78.50
盐城市区	Yancheng	337.25	111.72	180.15	227.43	48.28	24.46	61.51
扬州市区	Yangzhou	538.51	204.47	270.25	369.78	74.46	24.60	150.14
镇江市区	Zhenjiang	483.37	180.52	236.30	378.07	70.10	16.36	142.96
泰州市区	Taizhou	312.16	117.80	136.21	211.27	56.47	4.83	74.14
宿迁市区	Suqian	111.64	31.68	58.02	92.09	15.32	12.84	40.38

17－9　主要城市贸易、外经(2006年)

DOMESTIC TRADE AND FOREIGN ECONOMY OF MAJOR MUNICIPALITY(2006)

单位:亿美元　(USD 100 million)

城市 Municipality		社会消费品零售总额(亿元) Total Retail Sales of Consumer Goods (100 million yuan)	进出口总额 Total Imports and Exports	出口 Exports	进口 Imports	合同外商直接投资 Contract of Foreign Direct Investment	实际外商直接投资 Actial Foreign Direct Investment
南京市区	Nanjing	1095.30	312.60	171.21	141.39	28.90	16.39
无锡市区	Wuxi	614.50	295.11	158.85	136.26	51.21	20.67
徐州市区	Xuzhou	249.22	13.23	8.47	4.76	4.38	1.34
常州市区	Changzhou	382.54	95.27	70.89	24.39	23.72	10.11
苏州市区	Suzhou	492.30	937.02	510.91	426.10	76.82	28.41
南通市区	Nantong	140.83	65.48	42.09	23.39	17.47	4.51
连云港市区	Lianyungang	86.14	25.03	12.76	12.26	5.89	1.89
淮安市区	Huaian	146.49	9.16	5.57	3.59	3.99	0.95
盐城市区	Yancheng	119.20	10.80	5.25	5.55	3.57	1.65
扬州市区	Yangzhou	164.04	24.46	18.16	6.30	16.40	4.49
镇江市区	Zhenjiang	134.13	34.61	16.37	18.24	9.33	4.00
泰州市区	Taizhou	76.16	12.08	9.25	2.83	4.24	2.90
宿迁市区	Suqian	52.14	1.77	1.46	0.31	1.18	0.30

17－10　主要城市邮电、电力(2006年)

POST AND TELECOMMUNICATIONS SERVICES AND POWER CONSUMPTION OF MAJOR MUNICIPALITIES (2006)

城市 Municipality		邮电业务收入(亿元) Revenue From Posts and Telecommunication Services (100 million yuan)	本地电话用户(万户) Telephones (10000 Subscribers)	年末移动电话用户(万户) Mobile Telephones (10000 Subscribers)	国际互联网用户(万户) Internet Service (10000 Subscribers)	全年用电量(亿千瓦小时) Power Consumption (100 million kWh)	#城乡居民生活用电 Urban and Rural Residents Power Consumption
南京市区	Nanjing	72.47	312.61	458.84	65.96	260.23	179.95
无锡市区	Wuxi	40.80	181.80	265.91	38.25	189.31	152.97
徐州市区	Xuzhou	16.04	116.17	86.84	20.42	71.54	56.69
常州市区	Changzhou	30.96	152.97	199.46	23.99	165.41	135.19
苏州市区	Suzhou	47.38	193.37	307.89	34.37	181.11	135.27
南通市区	Nantong	13.29	49.45	81.99	8.25	61.05	48.99
连云港市区	Lianyungang	7.33	46.16	47.49	7.99	23.98	16.30
淮安市区	Huaian	9.22	92.70	56.38	8.42	43.75	33.90
盐城市区	Yancheng	8.48	56.41	68.25	6.20	22.32	14.77
扬州市区	Yangzhou	11.51	64.49	74.82	20.67	36.63	24.03
镇江市区	Zhenjiang	9.03	65.89	68.90	10.64	62.68	52.35
泰州市区	Taizhou	5.33	32.78	39.02	4.11	27.62	21.99
宿迁市区	Suqian	4.20	34.41	34.14	1.75	13.82	9.46

17－11　主要城市环境保护（2006年）
ENVIRONMENTAL PROTECTION OF MAJOR MUNICIPALITIES (2006)

城　市 Municipality		工业废水排放达标量（亿吨）Industrial Waste Water Discharged (100 million tons)	工业二氧化硫排放量（亿吨）Industrial Sulphur Dioxide Emission (100 million tons)	工业废气排放量（亿标米）Volume of Industrial Waste Gas Emission (100 million standardized cu. m)	工业烟尘排放量（万吨）Volume of Industrial Soot Removed (10000 tons)	"三废"综合利用产品产值（亿元）Output Value of Products Made from Comprehensive Utilization of Waster Gas, Waste Water and Solid Wasted (100 million yuan)	环境噪声达标面积（平方公里）Areas of Environmental Noice Standardized and Established (10000 sq. km)
南京市区	Nanjing	3.97	14.10	3873.3	4.03	16.59	435.5
无锡市区	Wuxi	2.48	3.23	1026.5	1.41	2.27	301.9
徐州市区	Xuzhou	0.38	2.03	751.7	0.78	1.64	133.0
常州市区	Changzhou	2.14	5.72	679.1	2.19	19.46	107.6
苏州市区	Suzhou	2.23	8.60	1237.4	2.25	2.38	270.6
南通市区	Nantong	0.60	7.54	979.2	2.51	3.51	72.0
连云港市区	Lianyungang	0.18	3.50	299.6	1.33	0.69	70.7
淮安市区	Huaian	0.19	4.51	791.6	1.90	1.52	68.4
盐城市区	Yancheng	0.11	1.84	128.6	0.19	0.24	25.5
扬州市区	Yangzhou	0.58	6.27	646.9	0.57	1.72	94.0
镇江市区	Zhenjiang	0.72	7.68	1451.3	2.90	2.29	86.3
泰州市区	Taizhou	0.11	0.87	354.1	0.22	1.64	40.4
宿迁市区	Suqian	0.12	1.57	19.4	0.46	0.12	56.0

17－12　主要城市居民收支情况（2006年）
INCOME AND EXPENDITURE OF MAJOR MUNICIPALITY HOUSEHOLDS (2006)

单位:元　　(yuan)

城　市 Municipality		在岗职工平均工资 Average Wage of Employed Staff and Workers	城镇居民人均可支配收入 Per Capita Disposable Income of Urban Residents	城镇居民人均消费支出 Per Capita Living Expenditure of Urban Residents	#食　品 Food	#衣着用品 Clothing Articles	#家庭设备、用品及服务 Household Facilities, Articles and Services
南京市区	Nanjing	32951	17538	12234	4145	989	888
无锡市区	Wuxi	30723	18189	11372	4360	930	846
徐州市区	Xuzhou	29194	12837	8621	2928	909	458
常州市区	Changzhou	28502	16650	12503	4467	1072	911
苏州市区	Suzhou	30388	18532	12472	4502	970	810
南通市区	Nantong	25974	14058	9332	3425	925	719
连云港市区	Lianyungang	22014	11475	8324	2884	704	590
淮安市区	Huaian	18255	10447	7077	2822	713	464
盐城市区	Yancheng	19314	12052	7378	2789	836	468
扬州市区	Yangzhou	24727	12945	8273	3352	892	502
镇江市区	Zhenjiang	25910	14291	9196	3664	730	590
泰州市区	Taizhou	19587	12682	8184	3436	933	437
宿迁市区	Suqian	18084	8172	4976	2216	518	275

17 - 13 主要城市居民消费支出、物价（2006 年）
LIVING EXPENDITURE AND PRICE OF MAJOR MUNICIPALITY HOUSEHOLDS (2006)

单位:元 (yuan)

城市 Municipality		城镇居民人均消费支出 Per Capita Living Expenditures for Consumption of Urban Residents				人均住房建筑面积（平方米）Per Capita Construction Floor Space of Residential Building (sq. m)	居民消费价格指数（上年=100）Consumer Price Index (preceding year = 100)
		#医疗保健 Medicine and Medical Services	#交通和通讯 Transportation and Telecommunication	#娱乐、教育、文化服务 Recreation, Education and Cultural Services	#居住 Residence		
南京市区	Nanjing	875	1469	2158	1278	25.2	101.7
无锡市区	Wuxi	830	1312	1568	991	27.1	101.7
徐州市区	Xuzhou	550	1206	1226	963	23.9	101.5
常州市区	Changzhou	782	1616	1637	1541	28.7	101.8
苏州市区	Suzhou	634	1985	1927	1184	29.8	101.6
南通市区	Nantong	689	1015	1304	881	29.4	101.7
连云港市区	Lianyungang	755	933	1060	1105	31.4	101.4
淮安市区	Huaian	503	744	976	604	28.7	101.4
盐城市区	Yancheng	373	785	1072	731	25.3	101.0
扬州市区	Yangzhou	515	718	1291	696	32.4	101.5
镇江市区	Zhenjiang	478	1191	1438	780	28.1	101.7
泰州市区	Taizhou	385	926	1002	615	32.4	101.3
宿迁市区	Suqian	249	444	615	495	36.8	101.6

17 - 14 主要城市文教、科技、卫生（2006 年）
CULTURE, EDUCATION, SCIENCE AND TECHNOLOGY AND PUBLIC HEALTH OF MAJOR MUNICIPALITYIES (2006)

城市 Municipality		高等学校在校学生数（万人）Number of Students Enrollement in Regular Institutions of High Education (10000 persons)	各类专业技术人员数（万人）Number of Scientific and Technical Personnel (10000 persons)	公共图书馆图书藏量（万册）Total Volume of Collections of Public Libraries (10000 volumes)	卫生机构数（个）Number of Health care Institutions (units)	卫生机构床位数（万张）Number of Beds in Health care Institutions (10000 units)	执业（助理）医师（万人）Practitioner Doctors (Assistant) (10000 persons)
南京市区	Nanjing	62.08	57.00	1146	1913	2.52	1.42
无锡市区	Wuxi	7.76	20.95	170	1204	1.35	0.67
徐州市区	Xuzhou	10.41	11.12	77	672	1.15	0.47
常州市区	Changzhou	9.24	19.38	167	763	0.96	0.48
苏州市区	Suzhou	9.47	14.40	196	793	1.21	0.61
南通市区	Nantong	6.54	6.91	102	533	0.64	0.31
连云港市区	Lianyungang	2.81	7.97	61	492	0.45	0.25
淮安市区	Huaian	5.09	8.68	74	394	0.76	0.36
盐城市区	Yancheng	3.34	7.82	59	489	0.47	0.27
扬州市区	Yangzhou	6.98	6.71	122	642	0.62	0.28
镇江市区	Zhenjiang	7.29	6.43	95	437	0.49	0.27
泰州市区	Taizhou	2.56	8.17	42	107	0.25	0.13
宿迁市区	Suqian	0.20	2.83	19	371	0.31	0.14

17－15 城市公用事业基本情况
BASIC STATISICS ON URBAN PUBLIC UTILITIES

指标	Item	1990	1995	2000	2005	2006
城市基本情况	**Basic condition of Municipality**					
建成区面积（平方公里）	Developed Areas (sq. km)		1109	1382	2379	2583
城市人口密度（人/平方公里）	Population Density of Urban Districts (person/sq. km)		1743	2260	1321	1953
供水、供气	**Water Supply and Gas Supply**					
自来水年供水量（亿吨）	Annual Supply of Tap Water (100million tons)	25.67	38.23	35.34	39.05	34.36
#生活用水量	Residential Consumption	6.24	10.52	14.57	18.59	15.73
平均每人日生活用水（升）	Per Capita Day (litre)	176.4	225.6	265.6	211.5	204.55
用水普及率（%）	Population with Access to Tap Water(%)	91.3	98.9	99.2	96.3	99.24
人工煤气供气量（亿立方米）	Coal Gas Supply (100 million cu. m)	14.27	28.22	36.26	129.08	142.00
#家庭用量	Residential Use	1.59	3.09	3.91	2.78	1.81
煤气管道长度（公里）	Length of Gas Pipelines (km)	1118	2041	4277	5320	3836
液化气家庭用量（万吨）	Residential Consumption of Liquefied Gas (10000 tons)	12.27	43.61	49.24	64.99	59.14
用气普及率（%）	Population with Access to Gas (%)	36.8	81.8	95.8	93.3	97.06
市政工程	**Municipal Engineering**					
年末实有道路长度（公里）	Length of Road (year end) (km)	5812	8163	11011	28674	27058
平均每万人拥有（公里）	Per 10000 Population (km)	6.5	8.3	8.7	11.5	12.2
年末实有道路面积（万平方米）	Area of Road(year end) (10000 sq. m)	5672	8669	13357	40830	41623
平均每万人拥有（万平方米）	Per 10000 Population (10000 sq. m)	6.3	8.3	10.6	16.3	18.7
排水管道长度（公里）	Length of Sewer Pipelines (km)	4099	8262	11097	28568	31215
排水管道密度（公里/平方公里）	Density of Drainage Pipelines (km/sq. km)	5.7	7.5	8.0	12.0	2.74
公共交通	**Public Traffic**					
公共汽(电)车总数（辆）	Operating Public Transportation Vehicles (unit)	2827	8101	14838	22197	22002
平均每万人拥有（辆）	Per 10000 Population (unit)	3.6	7.1	10.6	9.1	10.42
出租汽车（万辆）	Taxi (10000 units)	0.6	1.8	3.7	4.1	42032
城市绿化	**Landscaping in Cities**					
公共绿地面积（公顷）	Public Green Areas (hectare)	3447	7402	10248	25687	25868
人均公共绿地面积（公顷）	Public Green Areas Per Capita (sq. m)	3.8	6.9	8.1	10.3	11.62
公园面积（公顷）	Area of of Parks (hectare)	2991	5648	5159	9924	10608
环境卫生	**Sanitation and Hygiene**					
清运垃圾（万吨）	Garbage Disposal (10000 tons)	288	398	515	835	851.3
清运粪便（万吨）	Disposal of Night Soil (10000 tons)	221	209	309	388	126.9
每万人拥有公厕（座）	Public Restrooms Per 10000 Population (unit)	9.0	7.0	5.9	4.2	4.1

17－16 城市自来水情况
BASIC STATISTICS ON TAP WATER SUPPLY IN CITIES

年份 Year 城市 Municipality	综合生产能力（万吨/日）General Production Capacity (10000 tons/day)	全年供水总量（万吨）Total Aunual Supply of Tap Water (10000 tons)	#生产用水量 Productive Use	#生活用水量 Residential Use	用水人口（万人）Residents With Access to Tap Water (10000 persons)	人均日生活用水量（升）Daily Per Capita Residential Tap Water Comsuption (liter)	城市人口用水普及率（%）Population With Access to Tap Water (%)
1978	112.3	35056	20073	12013	347.2	94.8	83.6
1980	142.6	45221	26005	16323	463.0	89.0	92.2
1985	218.9	76609	40908	29280	585.4	137.0	89.0
1989	856.3	233848	167472	54326	896.6	166.0	88.3
1990	941.7	256664	181543	62369	968.0	176.4	91.3
1991	1056.1	282691	201088	68287	1049.2	178.3	93.8
1992	1191.4	317812	224575	77010	1158.6	182.1	96.0
1993	1299.5	342780	239520	83041	1238.6	183.7	97.1
1994	1368.9	358696	243332	93030	1212.3	210.2	98.7
1995	1388.7	382325	190471	105192	1277.5	225.6	98.9
1996	1424.4	349423	192948	135429	1300.7	285.3	99.0
1997	1457.1	343106	189889	131650	1346.1	267.9	99.3
1998	1543.6	358999	199055	137663	1388.0	271.8	99.2
1999	1585.5	339066	173487	138264	1425.4	265.8	99.1
2000	1641.6	353366	172552	145707	1503.1	265.6	99.2
2001	1698.5	332155	156019	156717	1745.2	246.0	91.0
2002	1803.7	380991	182591	168929	2048.7	225.9	89.0
2003	1835.0	380395	174834	171830	2167.7	217.2	91.9
2004	1871.4	392462	179602	179068	2273.7	215.8	94.0
2005	1977.6	390460	161320	185906	2408.5	211.5	96.3
2006	2298.1	501852	235322	180290	2617.4	204.6	99.2
南京市区 Nanjing	579.4	117603	57908	37778	431.3	240.0	100.0
无锡市区 Wuxi	155.4	30080	13329	15967	230.0	190.2	99.0
徐州市区 Xuzhou	58.4	15699	2863	6646	122.2	149.0	99.1
常州市区 Changzhou	130.5	30763	15417	17017	120.2	205.0	100.0
苏州市区 Suzhou	177.8	37635	12125	17940	184.0	267.1	100.0
南通市区 Nantong	80.0	14848	6369	6072	86.6	192.0	100.0
连云港市区 Lianyungang	31.5	6603	1977	2874	70.7	111.4	99.6
淮安市区 Huaian	30.5	7502	1880	4219	88.7	130.3	98.6
盐城市区 Yancheng	37.3	9830	4835	3439	62.4	151.0	100.0
扬州市区 Yangzhou	51.0	11315	3754	3491	63.8	150.0	100.0
镇江市区 Zhenjiang	62.2	14137	6035	5934	83.9	193.8	98.2
泰州市区 Taizhou	31.0	5213	1729	2175	57.2	104.3	100.0
宿迁市区 Suqian	15.0	2928	804	1582	37.75	114.8	92.1

17－17 城市煤气、液化石油气情况

BASIC STATISTICS ON SUPPLY OF GAS AND LIQUEFIED PETROLEUM GAS IN CITIES

年 份 Year 城 市 Municipality	全年供气总量 Total Gas Supply		家庭用气量 Residential Use		用气人口(万人) Population with Access to Gas (10000 persons)		城市气化率(%) Percentage of Population Using Gas for Household Use (%)
	人工煤气(万立方米) Coal Gas (10000 cu. m)	液化石油气(吨) Liquefied Petroleum Gas (ton)	人工煤气(万立方米) Coal Gas (10000 cu. m)	液化石油气(吨) Liquefied Petroleum Gas (ton)	人工煤气 Coal Gas	液化石油气 Liquefied Petroleum Ges	
1978	11756	23666	1592	22043	15.7	48.4	15.7
1980	11401	32591	2215	31350	20.0	69.6	17.8
1985	13155	42495	3851	38834	39.9	76.2	17.9
1989	140497	190471	13429	105671	93.0	186.1	32.5
1990	142681	216936	15902	122691	101.2	219.3	36.8
1991	142665	252342	17750	137780	116.3	261.2	41.9
1992	147625	337456	20943	190861	131.0	373.1	53.3
1993	153994	442089	23774	258003	150.6	498.0	63.5
1994	184552	574191	26281	337126	180.3	558.8	74.1
1995	282227	436131	30877	361990	213.4	637.3	81.8
1996	271852	543989	35837	468838	243.3	701.2	86.6
1997	274853	468106	34055	392574	244.1	746.2	87.8
1998	331580	620344	34797	430131	271.1	798.3	93.0
1999	350299	667556	41206	427971	323.9	814.1	94.9
2000	362606	705010	39141	492377	324.7	882.9	95.8
2001	376025	780527	44685	523600	373.2	1200.3	82.0
2002	788537	1252001	38761	632199	361.1	1600.0	85.2
2003	802430	1357710	47369	687358	405.8	1673.5	88.6
2004	1027886	1226675	40926	708033	333.8	1712.1	92.0
2005	1290834	1110300	27831	649936	234.1	1720.0	93.3
2006	1420015	1042278	18120	591415	177.1	1408.8	97.1
南京市区 Nanjing	1398020	168276	2765	78962	5.9	259.9	100.0
无锡市区 Wuxi	1789	19330	1532	12291	10.6	98.2	96.1
徐州市区 Xuzhou	5699	33860	4050	28690	49.0	68.0	94.9
常州市区 Changzhou		42115		30553		60.5	100.0
苏州市区 Suzhou	35	242230	4580	49174	46.0	80.0	100.0
南通市区 Nantong	15	36000	2991	26600	32.8	53.7	99.9
连云港市区 Lianyungang		10169		9790		37.5	84.1
淮安市区 Huaian		37637		34023		73.7	97.4
盐城市区 Yancheng		10160		888		52.0	99.4
扬州市区 Yangzhou	11	31708	2017	25208	31.0	32.0	98.8
镇江市区 Zhenjiang		45335		15029		35.8	93.4
泰州市区 Taizhou		20025		17850		54.1	94.6
宿迁市区 Suqian		6240		5076		34.8	84.9

17－18 城市市政工程情况
BASIC STATISTICS ON MUNICIPAL ENGINEERING IN CITIES

年份 Year 城市 Municipality	年末实有道路长度（公里） Length of Roads (year-end) (km)	年末实有道路面积（万平方米） Area of Roads (10000 sq. m)	排水管道长度（公里） Length of Drainage Pipelines (km)	城市污水日处理能力（万吨） Day Capacity of Sewerage Disposal (10000 tons)	城市路灯盏数（千盏） Number of Street Light (1000 units)	人均拥有道路面积（平方米/人） Per Capita of Road Areas (sq. m person)	排水管道密度（公里/平方公里） Density of Drainage Pipelines (kmsq. km)	污水处理率（%） Rate of Sewerage Disposal (%)
1978	1893	1154	1503					
1980	1881	1160	1650	0.1	48	2.3		0.2
1985	2437	1623	2277	1.8	71	2.5	5.3	0.6
1989	5272	6607	3782	91.3	122	7.7	5.7	23.0
1990	5812	5672	4099	103.5	129	6.3	5.7	16.4
1991	5658	5216	4872	133.2	144	5.8	5.4	13.4
1992	6781	6587	5721	155.5	165	7.0	5.6	16.7
1993	7090	7581	6653	160.7	194	7.4	4.7	22.9
1994	6150	7094	7019	236.7	194	7.1	6.0	31.8
1995	8163	8669	8262	273.5	215	8.3	7.5	38.7
1996	8552	9711	8860	390.3	256	8.9	7.5	42.7
1997	9440	10438	8812	434.3	290	9.3	7.1	47.5
1998	9618	11336	9574	589.3	328	9.8	7.6	49.3
1999	10066	12283	10382	632.9	381	10.2	8.0	58.1
2000	11011	13357	11097	712.9	437	10.6	8.0	61.8
2001	16702	20309	13974	736.7	549	10.6	9.0	65.3
2002	22656	26987	16744	800.4	753	11.7	8.6	66.0
2003	25541	31859	20343	906.6	971	13.5	9.6	69.9
2004	26598	35596	25537	1017.8	1169	14.7	11.3	76.1
2005	28674	40830	28568	1084.7	1296	16.3	12.0	77.7
2006	27058	41623	31215	1224.9	1501	18.7	2.7	81.8
南京市区 Nanjing	5244	7392	3274	431.3	144	17.1	1.4	83.2
无锡市区 Wuxi	4382	4906	5354	165.4	164	21.1	3.3	82.7
徐州市区 Xuzhou	1200	1569	957	31.5	55	12.7	2.7	84.0
常州市区 Changzhou	1349	2158	2366	85.7	79	18.0	6.9	87.7
苏州市区 Suzhou	2621	4982	3977	57.3	200	27.1	5.9	90.2
南通市区 Nantong	604	1282	1326	45.4	83	14.8	3.7	80.3
连云港市区 Lianyungang	877	1304	980	10.1	49	18.4	2.3	66.7
淮安市区 Huaian	789	1229	953	16.5	48	13.7	1.9	80.4
盐城市区 Yancheng	311	842	292	5.0	47	13.5	0.6	72.3
扬州市区 Yangzhou	868	1025	626	26.1	93	16.1	2.5	81.1
镇江市区 Zhenjiang	876	1385	1182	33.5	46	16.2	2.1	83.4
泰州市区 Taizhou	734	1107	685	9.2	50	19.4	2.1	85.7
宿迁市区 Suqian	498	998	428	3.2	26	24.3	2.0	49.6

17－19 城市园林绿化情况

BASIC STATISTICS ON PARKS, GARDENS AND GREEN AREAS IN CITIES

年份 Year 城市 Municipality	园林绿地面积(公顷) Total Area of Parks, Gardens and Green Areas in Cities (hectare)	#公共绿地 Public Green Areas	建成区绿化覆盖面积(公顷) Coverage Space of Green Areas Developed (hectare)	公园 Park 个数(个) Number (unit)	公园 Park 面积(公顷) Area (hectare)	人均公共绿地面积(平方米) Per Capita Public Green Areas (sq. m)	建成区绿化覆盖率(%) Coverage Rate of Green Area Developed (%)
1978	7303			59	786		
1980	6582	1341		72	944	2.7	19.3
1985	7998	1450		83	1030	2.3	20.6
1989	18148	3214	12804	172	2725	3.7	19.2
1990	20337	3447	14112	184	2991	3.8	19.5
1991	19096	3841	16423	201	3071	4.3	18.4
1992	20898	4283	21726	217	2958	4.5	21.4
1993	30174	5882	31133	242	5179	5.8	22.1
1994	33089	6124	34728	241	5396	6.1	29.6
1995	48564	7226	34093	264	5648	6.9	30.8
1996	50558	7528	35964	283	5263	6.9	30.3
1997	52349	8175	38356	287	4831	7.3	30.9
1998	54756	8891	40513	295	4920	7.7	32.3
1999	57386	9581	43725	303	5027	8.0	33.7
2000	60064	10248	45925	313	5159	8.1	33.2
2001	94175	12724	49456	374	5549	6.6	31.9
2002	137702	16252	68413	403	6374	7.1	35.3
2003	145956	18743	74929	446	7317	7.9	35.4
2004	172563	21617	85367	489	9098	8.9	37.9
2005	189070	25687	94778	539	9924	10.3	39.8
2006	152885	25868	107752	492	10608	11.6	41.7
南京市区 Nanjing	74276	5694	26156	59	2606	13.2	45.5
无锡市区 Wuxi	7972	2555	8137	38	1290	11.0	41.2
徐州市区 Xuzhou	4760	1142	5466	34	742	9.3	37.9
常州市区 Changzhou	4037	1333	4368	21	404	11.1	40.6
苏州市区 Suzhou	7985	2757	9215	138	1492	15.0	43.0
南通市区 Nantong	2153	806	2468	8	72	9.3	41.6
连云港市区 Lianyungang	2759	597	3183	10	184	8.4	37.2
淮安市区 Huaian	3124	819	3409	9	289	9.1	38.3
盐城市区 Yancheng	2313	508	2708	12	119	8.1	37.8
扬州市区 Yangzhou	2625	1123	2829	8	247	17.6	40.4
镇江市区 Zhenjiang	3293	1119	3566	17	598	13.1	39.6
泰州市区 Taizhou	1846	469	2097	10	248	8.2	41.9
宿迁市区 Suqian	6410	402	1895	4	141	9.8	39.8

17－20　城市环境卫生情况

BASIC STATISTICS ON URBAN ENVIRONMENTAL SANITATION

年份 Year 城市 Municipality	清扫面积（万平方米）Sweeping Areas (10000 sq. m)	生活垃圾清运量（万吨）Residential Garbages Disposal Cleared (10000 tons)	粪便清运量（万吨）Night Soil Disposal Cleared (10000 tons)	无害化处理厂日处理能力（吨）Day Disposal Capacities of No Harmful Disposal Factory (ton)	垃圾粪便年处理量（万吨）Annual Garbages and Night Soil Disposal Cleared (10000 tons)	环卫机械（辆）Machines of Environment Sanitation (unit)	公共厕所（座）Public Toilet (unit)
1978	503	79	229			223	3545
1980	601	158	232			296	3712
1985	1078	159	147	20		734	4700
1989	2136	262	260	162		1735	7910
1990	2445	288	221	385		1322	8072
1991	3068	341	271	1588	357.3	1604	9974
1992	3432	409	419	7622	531.7	1785	9265
1993	4095	408	441	14014	654.1	1998	9162
1994	4240	360	388	16442	658.8	1736	7095
1995	5429	398	209	13810	532.5	2072	7263
1996	6252	426	198	13125	523.9	2144	6932
1997	7085	479	196	15813	606.0	2351	7675
1998	7589	486	302	18570	721.4	2407	7486
1999	8221	505	310	43419	756.0	2458	7337
2000	8773	515	309	17392	762.9	2569	7393
2001	10971	634	338	17324	868.1	3800	9532
2002	16101	723	400	19997	985.9	4573	11016
2003	20874	775	406	20728	1060.9	4456	10660
2004	22505	808	389	23569	1106.6	4494	10260
2005	27101	835	388	24000	1030.5	5094	10591
2006	29409	851	126.9	24545	813.7	5447	9165
南京市区 Nanjing	7015	162	12.4	5500	155.3	780	1315
无锡市区 Wuxi	1950	89	33.7	3200	112.8	580	706
徐州市区 Xuzhou	907	56	0.2	1500	48.0	179	507
常州市区 Changzhou	1374	32	4.6	850	36.4	292	765
苏州市区 Suzhou	6292	94	11.4	2550	95.7	1441	1088
南通市区 Nantong	765	22	1.6	804	30.9	128	311
连云港市区 Lianyungang	726	31	3.4	795	38.0	112	282
淮安市区 Huaian	670	20	5.3	1100	25.3	111	523
盐城市区 Yancheng	581	19	9.2	400	14.6	143	161
扬州市区 Yangzhou	836	20	1.5	500	20.0	153	290
镇江市区 Zhenjiang	699	24	2.1	500	26.2	170	215
泰州市区 Taizhou	507	16	0.6	600	16.4	77	298
宿迁市区 Suqian	483	16	0.9	350	17.0	34	384

17－21　城市公共汽(电)车、出租汽车情况
BASIC STATISTICS ON BUSES (TROLLEY BUSES) AND TAXIS IN CITIES

年　份　Year 城　市　Municipality	年末实有公共汽(电)车营运车数(辆) Operating Public Transit Vehicles (year-end) (unit)	实有公共汽(电)车营运标准车台(标台) Operating Standard Public Transit Vehicles (Standardized) (unit)	公共汽(电)车营运线路长度(公里) Length of Public Transit Route (km)	公共汽(电)车客运总量(万人次) Passengers Carried by Transit (10000 person-times)	每万人拥有公共交通车辆(标台) Public Transit Vehicales Per 10000 Population (Standardized) (unit)	出租汽车营运车数(辆) Operating Taxis (unit)
1978	1407		1772			
1980	1605		1920	100671		150
1985	2237		2904	143146		605
1989	2826	3167	4603	135947	3.7	4555
1990	2827	3210	3991	130641	3.6	5775
1991	2968	3727	4229	124409	4.1	5005
1992	4578	4855	6939	120282	5.1	8133
1993	6384	5954	7570	109248	5.8	9838
1994	7367	6808	10127	110921	6.8	12307
1995	8019	7215	13642	95362	7.1	18073
1996	7962	7144	3544	104583	6.6	25403
1997	9665	7916	5684	124805	7.0	32493
1998	12411	10080	5198	157600	8.9	34661
1999	14136	11625	5858	191831	9.7	36613
2000	14838	13341	6896	246314	10.6	36603
2001	16244	14871	7296	224582	7.8	41480
2002	16902	15874	12397	245227	6.9	41933
2003	17822	17015	14696	233586	7.2	40073
2004	19079	19098	15888	263088	7.9	40746
2005	22197	22484	18077	283760	9.1	41476
2006	22002	22898	12121	304669	10.4	42032
南京市区 Nanjing	5126	5893	2553	95029	14.4	9262
无锡市区 Wuxi	2826	3312	690	30907	14.3	3840
徐州市区 Xuzhou	1708	1577	731	23962	12.8	3357
常州市区 Changzhou	1608	1611	819	18940	13.4	1842
苏州市区 Suzhou	2056	1988	283	39110	10.8	3203
南通市区 Nantong	761	892	460	7860	10.3	1277
连云港市区 Lianyungang	249	228	459	11670	3.2	1595
淮安市区 Huaian	588	916	676	10404	10.2	903
盐城市区 Yancheng	292	303	250	2939	4.9	810
扬州市区 Yangzhou	742	822	563	13055	12.9	1842
镇江市区 Zhenjiang	733	788	268	8766	9.2	1254
泰州市区 Taizhou	238	210	405	2200	3.7	306
宿迁市区 Suqian	328	260	200	2480	6.3	900

主要统计指标解释

供水综合生产能力 指按供水设施取水、净化、送水、出厂输水干管等环节实际测定计算的综合生产能力。

供水管道长度 指从送水泵到用户水表之间所有管道的长度。在同一条街道埋设两条或两条以上管道时，应按每条管道的长度计算。

供水总量 指报告期供水企业(单位)供出的全部水量。包括有效供水量及损失水量。

生活用水量 指居民日常生活与公共福利设施的用水量，包括居民、饮食店、旅馆、医院、理发店、浴池、洗衣店、游泳池、商店、学校、机关、部队等单位的用水量。

城市人口用水普及率 指城市用水人口数与城市人口总数之比。计算公式为：

用水普及率 = 城市用水人口数/城市人口总数 × 100%

燃气综合生产能力 指报告期末燃气生产厂制气、净化、输送等环节的综合生产能力，不包括备用设备能力。一般按设计能力计算，如果实际生产能力大于设计能力时，应按实际测定的生产能力计算。测定时应以制气、净化、输送三个环节中最薄弱的环节为主。

燃气供气管道长度 指报告期末从气源厂压缩机的出口或门站出口到各类用户引入管之间的全部已经通气投入使用的管道长度。不包括煤气生产厂、输配站、液化气储存站、灌瓶站、储配站、气化站、混气站、供应站等厂(站)内的管道。按不同的材质、压力级别、管径分别统计。

燃气供应总量 指报告期燃气企业(单位)向用户供应的燃气数量。包括销售量及损失量。

燃气普及率 指报告期末使用燃气的城市人口数与城市人口总数的比率。计算公式为：

燃气普及率 = 用气人口数/城市人口总数 × 100%

道路长度 指道路长度和与道路相通的桥梁、隧道的长度，按车行道中心线计算。

排水管道长度 指所有排水总管、干管、支管、检查井及连接井进出口等长度之和。

计算时应按单管计算，即在同一条街道上如有两条或两条以上并排的排水管道时，应按每条排水管道的长度相加计算。

城市污水处理能力 指污水处理厂(或处理装置)每昼夜处理污水量的设计能力。

营运车数 指报告期末公交企业(单位)用于运营业务的全部车辆数。以企业(单位)固定资产台帐中已投入运营的车辆数为准；新购、新制和调入的运营车辆，自投入之日起开始计算；调出、报废和调作他用的运营车辆，自上级主管机关批准之日起不再计入。

园林绿地面积 指报告期末用于园林和绿化的各种绿地面积。包括公共绿地、居住区绿地、单位附属绿地、防护绿地、生产绿地、道路绿地和风景林地面积。不包括：

1. 屋顶绿化、垂直绿化、阳台绿化和室内绿化。
2. 以物质生产为主的林地、耕地、牧草地、果园和竹园等。
3. 城市总体规划中不列入绿地的水域。

公共绿地指向公众开放的市级、区级、居住区级各类公园、街旁游园，包括其范围内的水域。其中居住区级公园应不小于1万平方米，街旁游园的宽度不小于8米，面积不小于400平方米。

Explanatory Notes on Main Statistical Indicators

Comprehensive Production Capacity of Tap Water refers to the actual comprehensive production capacity of the waterworks, taking the capacity of the main links such as waterflow, purification, conveyance and outflow of the trunk pilelines into account.

Length of Water Pipelines refers to the total length of all the pipelines between the water pumps and the user' s water meters. If there are two or more than two pipelies buried in a same street, the length of every pipeline should be taken into account.

Volume of Water Supply refers to the total volume of water supply by the water supply enterprises(units) during the reference period, including both the effective water supply and loss.

Consumption of Water for Residential Use refers to the water consumption of households for daily life and the water consumption of public welfare facilities, including the consumption of restaurants, hotels, hospitals, barber shops, public bathhouses, laundries, swimming pools, shops, schools, institutions, army units and other units.

Percentage of Urban Population with Access to Tap Water refers to the ratio of the urban population with access to tap water to the total urban population. The formula is:

Percentage of Population with Access to Tap Water = (Urban Population with Access to Tap Water)/(Urban Population) ×100%

Comprehensive Production Capacity of Burning Gas refers to the comprehensive production capacity of the burning gas—works in burning gas generation, purification and delivering, excluding the reserve capacity of the equipment. In general, the capacity is counted in accordance with the designed requirement. If the actual production capacity is larger than designed requirement, it should be counted according to the actual capacity through determination. In determination, the most weak link should be determined as the main one among the three links of burning gas generation, purification and delivering.

Length of Burning Gas Pipelines refers to the total length of pipelines between the outlet of the compressor, blower or burning gas tank of the source factory and the burning gas meters of users, which are all put in use, excluding the pipelines in burning gas—works(stations) and the pipelines of transportation and distribution station, liquefied petroluem gas storage station, pipeline and bottle station, storage and distribution station, gasification station, gas mixed station, supply station. They are counted respectively according to the different quality of materials, level of preasure and the size of bores.

Volume of Burning Gas Supply refers to the volume of burning gas supplied by the burning gas enterprises, including both the sales volume and loss.

Percentage of Urban Population with Access to Burning Gas refers to the ratio of the urban population with access to burning gas to the urban population at the reference period. The formula is:

Percentage of Urban Population with Access to Burning Gas = (Urban Population with Access to Burning Gas)/Urban Population) ×100%

Length of Roads refers to the length of roads, as well as the length of bridges and tunnels, the same as the roads, and taking the middle line of traffic lane into account.

Length of Sewage Pipes refers to the total length of general drainage, trunks, branch and blind drainages, inspection wells, connection wells, inlets and outlets, ete. , taking the single pipe into account. Namely if there are two or more than two pipes standing side by side in a street, the length of every pipe should put into account.

Daily Disposal Capacity of Urban Sewage refers to the designed 24 hour capacity of sewage disposal at the sewage treatment works.

Number of Vehicles(Public Transit) in Working refers to the total of operatoinal vehicles(buses and trolley buses) available at the end of the reference period, taking them as the fixed assets registered in account book of the enterprises and put in operation as the accounting standard. Vehicles, newly bought, newly manufactured and transfered in from other units, should be put into account since the day of putting into operation, while the vehicles, transfered to other units, being scrapped and turned to other use, should not be put into account since the day of permission made by higher responsible department.

Area of Gardens and Green Areas refers to the various green land used for gardening and afforestation at the end of reference period, including public green land, residential area green land, subsidiary green land of the units, protection green land, production green land, roadside green land and scenic forest land, excluding:

1. Roof, perpendicular, balcony and indoor green area.
2. Areas taking the material production as the main aim, such as forest land, cultivated land, pasture, orchard and bamboo forest.
3. Water areas which are not listed in the urban general plan.

Public Green Land refers to various level gardens and streetside pleasure gardens of the city, district and residential quarter, they are opened to public, including water area. Among the gardens, the area of residential quarter garden is no less than 1 0000 square meters; the width of streetside garden is no less than 8 meters, and its area is no less than 400 square meters.

JIANGSU STATISTICAL YEARBOOK

第18篇

部分区经济社会基本情况

BASIC SITUATION OF ECONOMY AND SOCIETY OF PART DISTRICTS

18－1 人口、面积(2006 年)
POPULATION AND LAND AREA (2006)

市辖区	District Under the Jurisdiction of Municipality	年末总人口(万人) Year End Total Population (10000 persons)	出生人口(人) Births (Person)	死亡人口(人) Deaths (person)	年末总户数(万户) Year End Total Households (10000 household)	土地面积(平方公里) Land Area (sq. m)	人口密度(人/平方公里) Population Density (person/sq. m)
南京市浦口区	Nanjing Pukou District	50.44	3857	2936	16.17	912	553
南京市栖霞区	Nanjing Qixia District	41.43	2540	1934	12.59	376	1102
南京市雨花区	Nanjing Yuhua District	20.72	1634	1017	7.20	135	1539
南京市江宁区	Nanjing Jiangning District	84.55	7620	4447	29.01	1573	538
南京市六合区	Nanjing Luhe District	87.22	7328	4736	28.61	1467	594
无锡市锡山区	Wuxi Xishan District	39.43	2782	2745	12.07	396	996
无锡市惠山区	Wuxi Huishan District	39.52	2492	2717	12.51	327	1208
无锡市滨湖区	Wuxi Binghu District	46.87	2956	2489	15.42	609	770
徐州市贾汪区	Xuzhou Jiawang District	48.64	2466	1124	14.63	690	705
常州市新北区	Changzhou Xinbei District	42.21	4240	2862	13.09		
常州市武进区	Changzhou Wujin District	96.29	7807	7822	34.45	1247	772
苏州市虎丘区	Suzhou Huqui District	31.00	2638	1496	9.27	258	1202
苏州市吴中区	Suzhou Wuzhong District	56.98	4770	3232	18.06	742	768
苏州市相城区	Suzhou Xiangcheng District	35.50	2559	2245	12.15	416	853
南通市崇川区	Nantong Chongchuan District	54.89	4080	2895	17.74	100	5489
南通市港闸区	Nantong Gangzha District	18.23	1090	1541	7.22	134	1358
连云港市连云区	Lianyungang Lianyun District	20.02	1752	1031	6.78	535	374
淮安市楚州区	Huaian Chuzhou District	121.11	15837	3130	35.21	1522	796
淮安市淮阴区	Huaian Huaiyin District	89.15	10612	4793	26.80	1264	705
盐城市盐都区	Yancheng Yandu District	70.78	7242	4142	26.09	1024	691
扬州市邗江区	Yangzhou Hanjiang District	49.82	3250	3737	16.03	749	665
扬州市维扬区	Yangzhou Weiyang District	36.51	2333	1627	11.78	74	4934
镇江市丹徒区	Zhenjiang Dantu District	27.50	2278	1862	10.14	749	367
泰州市海陵区	Taizhou Hailing District	42.99	3971	2785	16.01	223	1925
泰州市高港区	Taizhou Gaogang District	21.26	2657	2344	6.90	221	962
宿迁市宿豫区	Suqian Suyu District	68.98	3667	2288	18.58	1254	550

18－2 从业人员(2006 年)
EMPLOYMENT (2006)

市辖区	District Under the Jurisdiction of Municipality	从业人员 Employment	第一产业 Primary Industry	第二产业 Secondary Industry	第三产业 Tertiary Industry	在岗职工人数 Staff and Workers Employed	私营企业和个体从业人员 Employment in Private Enterprises and Self-employed Individuals
南京市浦口区	Nanjing Pukou District	22.22	3.59	12.45	6.18	4.44	7.37
南京市栖霞区	Nanjing Qixia District	16.69	2.06	12.15	2.48	3.80	6.62
南京市雨花区	Nanjing Yuhua District	12.40	0.41	10.30	1.69	1.03	4.62
南京市江宁区	Nanjing Jiangning District	49.69	9.17	29.63	10.89	9.01	14.57
南京市六合区	Nanjing Luhe District	37.37	8.59	17.15	11.63	6.05	12.14
无锡市锡山区	Wuxi Xishan District	37.52	3.13	24.49	9.90	3.43	14.57
无锡市惠山区	Wuxi Huishan District	42.19	2.22	30.58	9.39	2.03	20.39
无锡市滨湖区	Wuxi Binghu District	28.58	1.02	15.32	12.24	6.75	11.24
徐州市贾汪区	Xuzhou Jiawang District	16.57	7.25	5.13	4.18	1.35	5.44
常州市新北区	Changzhou Xinbei District	32.66	3.47	18.23	10.96	1.93	11.76
常州市武进区	Changzhou Wujin District	87.05	11.05	54.06	21.94	5.47	34.89
苏州市虎丘区	Suzhou Huqui District	23.46	1.19	16.43	5.84	12.92	7.25
苏州市吴中区	Suzhou Wuzhong District	43.11	6.19	24.83	12.09	7.28	23.16
苏州市相城区	Suzhou Xiangcheng District	22.22	2.90	14.51	4.81	3.65	16.90
南通市崇川区	Nantong Chongchuan District						2.65
南通市港闸区	Nantong Gangzha District						1.42
连云港市连云区	Lianyungang Lianyun District	2.62	0.58	0.85	1.25	0.89	1.04
淮安市楚州区	Huaian Chuzhou District	59.20	26.64	14.49	18.08	5.47	8.66
淮安市淮阴区	Huaian Huaiyin District	44.18	16.59	12.34	15.25	2.93	6.42
盐城市盐都区	Yancheng Yandu District	30.30	12.55	8.65	9.10	3.56	8.21
扬州市邗江区	Yangzhou Hanjiang District	32.34	3.97	15.88	12.49	2.14	12.64
扬州市维扬区	Yangzhou Weiyang District	7.22	0.59	3.57	3.06	1.37	2.28
镇江市丹徒区	Zhenjiang Dantu District	20.17	4.96	9.53	5.68	2.86	5.33
泰州市海陵区	Taizhou Hailing District	13.57	1.63	5.94	6.00	2.04	8.77
泰州市高港区	Taizhou Gaogang District	12.16	1.86	6.37	3.93	1.48	3.75
宿迁市宿豫区	Suqian Suyu District	39.54	12.80	13.36	13.37	2.22	8.01

18－3 地区生产总值(2006年)
GROSS DOMESTIC PRODUCT (2006)

市辖区 District Under the Jurisdiction of Municipality		地区生产总值(亿元)	第一产业 Primary Industry	第二产业 Secondary Industry	#工业 Industry	第三产业 Tertiary Industry	地区生产总值指数(上年=100) GDP Index (2005=100)
南京市浦口区	Nanjing Pukou District	132.52	12.43	64.09	50.39	56.00	120.5
南京市栖霞区	Nanjing Qixia District	110.78	4.10	67.20	50.44	39.48	118.7
南京市雨花区	Nanjing Yuhua District	88.01	0.83	56.84	47.36	30.34	119.0
南京市江宁区	Nanjing Jiangning District	278.14	18.15	172.60	134.30	87.39	119.8
南京市六合区	Nanjing Luhe District	179.29	19.18	99.36	83.79	60.74	120.5
无锡市锡山区	Wuxi Xishan District	212.44	5.70	137.27	126.88	69.47	115.4
无锡市惠山区	Wuxi Huishan District	267.33	5.87	193.46	179.23	68.00	114.1
无锡市滨湖区	Wuxi Binghu District	281.06	3.40	160.86	146.16	116.80	114.2
徐州市贾汪区	Xuzhou Jiawang District	65.89	6.94	36.26	34.38	22.69	115.9
常州市新北区	Changzhou Xinbei District	203.50	5.75	148.35	138.90	49.40	
常州市武进区	Changzhou Wujin District	571.96	21.58	405.96	385.41	144.42	121.2
苏州市虎丘区	Suzhou Huqui District	470.57	1.29	395.43	384.78	73.85	116.4
苏州市吴中区	Suzhou Wuzhong District	322.30	10.02	200.83	184.86	114.45	119.8
苏州市相城区	Suzhou Xiangcheng District	194.47	6.04	114.51	107.39	73.93	117.7
南通市崇川区	Nantong Chongchuan District	200.90	1.01	99.87	81.90	100.02	115.2
南通市港闸区	Nantong Gangzha District	100.08	1.89	78.69	70.64	19.50	115.0
连云港市连云区	Lianyungang Lianyun District	27.37	3.91	10.21	8.92	13.25	117.2
淮安市楚州区	Huaian Chuzhou District	101.67	22.60	45.50	33.50	33.57	115.4
淮安市淮阴区	Huaian Huaiyin District	89.40	23.61	44.88	38.71	20.91	115.1
盐城市盐都区	Yancheng Yandu District	120.05	22.96	62.80	56.32	34.29	115.5
扬州市邗江区	Yangzhou Hanjiang District	166.68	10.25	102.78	94.76	53.65	115.7
扬州市维扬区	Yangzhou Weiyang District	32.17	1.13	20.47	18.53	10.57	115.6
镇江市丹徒区	Zhenjiang Dantu District	89.71	5.99	53.64	48.99	30.08	115.0
泰州市海陵区	Taizhou Hailing District	59.66	1.68	31.28	26.36	26.70	116.2
泰州市高港区	Taizhou Gaogang District	43.38	3.09	25.81	21.68	14.48	116.5
宿迁市宿豫区	Suqian Suyu District	66.11	14.56	36.46	31.03	15.09	115.0

18-4 投资、财政收支(2006年)

INVESTMENT, GOVERNMENT REVENUE AND EXPENDI TURE (2006)

市辖区 District Under the Jurisdiction of Municipality		城镇固定资产投资 Urban Investment in Fixed Assers	房地产开发投资 Investment in Real Estate Development	#住宅 Resdential Building	地方财政一般预算收入 Local Financial General Budgetary Revenue	#各项税收 Taxes	地方财政一般预算支出 Local Financial General Budgetary Expenditure
南京市浦口区	Nanjing Pukou District	72.00	29.93	26.30	15.18	13.73	16.85
南京市栖霞区	Nanjing Qixia District	83.17	36.08	30.82	10.76	10.64	9.44
南京市雨花区	Nanjing Yuhua District	49.73	20.27	18.94	9.22	8.89	8.07
南京市江宁区	Nanjing Jiangning District	211.29	39.77	33.53	29.01	27.62	28.38
南京市六合区	Nanjing Luhe District	64.76	10.68	9.86	14.00	11.43	17.75
无锡市锡山区	Wuxi Xishan District	87.39	24.31	15.07	15.26	13.56	14.04
无锡市惠山区	Wuxi Huishan District	116.21	35.94	27.85	19.83	16.81	18.24
无锡市滨湖区	Wuxi Binghu District	99.07	46.23	37.43	21.01	19.59	14.88
徐州市贾汪区	Xuzhou Jiawang District	49.55	0.88	0.65	2.48	2.04	4.02
常州市新北区	Changzhou Xinbei District	84.60	25.01	18.73	20.44	19.52	14.16
常州市武进区	Changzhou Wujin District	133.89	42.28	35.09	33.38	27.63	30.30
苏州市虎丘区	Suzhou Huqui District	153.91	30.24	22.96	30.37	29.79	20.92
苏州市吴中区	Suzhou Wuzhong District	74.39	38.30	30.95	27.51	25.93	24.66
苏州市相城区	Suzhou Xiangcheng District	47.82	24.90	16.93	14.52	13.67	12.10
南通市崇川区	Nantong Chongchuan District	80.75	41.87	34.13	19.09	18.41	5.39
南通市港闸区	Nantong Gangzha District	39.48	4.49	2.78	7.26	7.01	3.50
连云港市连云区	Lianyungang Lianyun District	18.77	15.72	10.71	3.78	3.62	2.61
淮安市楚州区	Huaian Chuzhou District	28.07	8.21	5.05	3.24	2.42	8.11
淮安市淮阴区	Huaian Huaiyin District	40.80	6.13	4.52	3.30	2.74	6.62
盐城市盐都区	Yancheng Yandu District	43.81	9.41	7.09	4.92	4.01	8.01
扬州市邗江区	Yangzhou Hanjiang District	59.21	15.41	11.12	8.01	6.87	8.43
扬州市维扬区	Yangzhou Weiyang District	30.96	10.63	5.40	5.49	5.21	2.84
镇江市丹徒区	Zhenjiang Dantu District	29.91	6.79	6.07	6.14	5.38	5.47
泰州市海陵区	Taizhou Hailing District	28.64	8.06	6.59	4.65	4.26	4.72
泰州市高港区	Taizhou Gaogang District	20.78	3.44	2.97	3.70	3.27	3.76
宿迁市宿豫区	Suqian Suyu District	27.22	5.99	5.55	2.09	1.54	5.63

18－5　规模以上工业产值(2006年)

GROSS OUTPUT VALUE OF ABOVEDESIGNATED SIZE INDUSTRYAO (2006)

市辖区 District Under the Jurisdiction of Municipality		规模以上工业企业个数(个) Number of Industrial Enterprises (unit)	工业总产值(亿元) Tatal Output Value of Industry (100 million yuan)	内资企业 Inner Funded Enterprises	外商港澳台商投资企业 Foreign, Hong Kong, Macao and Taiwan Funded Enterprises	外商港澳台商投资企业 Foreign, Hong Kong, Macao and Taiwan Funded Enterprises
南京市浦口区	Nanjing Pukou District	181	196.26	131.78	50.72	13.77
南京市栖霞区	Nanjing Qixia District	191	211.33	138.54	17.45	55.34
南京市雨花区	Nanjing Yuhua District	157	191.90	167.08	5.28	19.54
南京市江宁区	Nanjing Jiangning District	399	459.29	177.87	67.39	214.02
南京市六合区	Nanjing Luhe District	259	282.13	191.37	31.76	59.00
无锡市锡山区	Wuxi Xishan District	589	586.42	345.10	118.16	123.17
无锡市惠山区	Wuxi Huishan District	800	630.38	460.65	84.42	85.31
无锡市滨湖区	Wuxi Binghu District	585	381.40	291.59	32.65	57.15
徐州市贾汪区	Xuzhou Jiawang District	133	114.45	107.28	0.00	7.17
常州市新北区	Changzhou Xinbei District	537	442.32	217.96	95.13	129.22
常州市武进区	Changzhou Wujin District	1734	1361.03	986.04	238.65	136.33
苏州市虎丘区	Suzhou Huqui District	377	1348.76	99.98	115.45	1133.34
苏州市吴中区	Suzhou Wuzhong District	655	551.09	153.05	133.94	264.10
苏州市相城区	Suzhou Xiangcheng District	437	303.85	167.88	60.85	75.12
南通市崇川区	Nantong Chongchuan District	291	254.90	107.09	31.70	116.11
南通市港闸区	Nantong Gangzha District	386	238.92	100.12	10.22	128.58
连云港市连云区	Lianyungang Lianyun District	53	15.47	10.53	0.62	4.32
淮安市楚州区	Huaian Chuzhou District	208	92.27	89.12	2.15	0.99
淮安市淮阴区	Huaian Huaiyin District	201	121.83	118.68	2.36	0.79
盐城市盐都区	Yancheng Yandu District	298	167.77	149.65	9.85	8.27
扬州市邗江区	Yangzhou Hanjiang District	390	353.13	296.62	22.90	33.61
扬州市维扬区	Yangzhou Weiyang District	109	65.64	45.51	10.73	9.40
镇江市丹徒区	Zhenjiang Dantu District	200	165.66	114.19	24.10	27.37
泰州市海陵区	Taizhou Hailing District	169	91.86	74.29	9.60	7.97
泰州市高港区	Taizhou Gaogang District	145	83.20	66.49	12.45	4.26
宿迁市宿豫区	Suqian Suyu District	135	57.44	55.84	0.54	1.06

18-6 规模以上工业效益(2006年)
ECONOMIC RESULT OF ABOVE DESIGNATED SIZE INDUSTRYL (2006)

市辖区 District Under the Jurisdiction of Municipality		主营业务收入(亿元) Major Business Income (100 million yuan)	利润总额(亿元) Total Profits (100 million yuan)	利税总额(亿元) Total Pre-tax Profits (100 million yuan)	本年应交增值税(亿元) Added Value Payable (100 million yuan)	从业人员年平均人数(万人) Annual Average Persons Employed (10000 persons)
南京市浦口区	Nanjing Pukou District	193.14	7.18	15.70	7.73	4.25
南京市栖霞区	Nanjing Qixia District	205.80	6.35	13.65	6.63	4.24
南京市雨花区	Nanjing Yuhua District	183.69	5.26	14.46	8.25	4.40
南京市江宁区	Nanjing Jiangning District	452.28	36.39	51.70	13.61	10.91
南京市六合区	Nanjing Luhe District	273.16	12.58	23.00	9.14	6.61
无锡市锡山区	Wuxi Xishan District	590.74	23.85	34.41	8.97	11.40
无锡市惠山区	Wuxi Huishan District	631.24	21.80	37.92	14.43	12.08
无锡市滨湖区	Wuxi Binghu District	382.37	17.80	30.94	11.37	8.18
徐州市贾汪区	Xuzhou Jiawang District	112.71	2.95	7.88	4.01	2.42
常州市新北区	Changzhou Xinbei District	440.36	22.11	31.68	8.58	8.14
常州市武进区	Changzhou Wujin District	1250.58	51.93	79.84	24.54	23.41
苏州市虎丘区	Suzhou Huqui District	1325.54	49.62	64.62	14.23	22.22
苏州市吴中区	Suzhou Wuzhong District	534.89	21.06	33.27	11.31	19.12
苏州市相城区	Suzhou Xiangcheng District	310.64	13.40	20.70	6.77	10.75
南通市崇川区	Nantong Chongchuan District	254.87	20.52	26.87	5.86	5.85
南通市港闸区	Nantong Gangzha District	237.74	16.96	26.00	8.49	5.22
连云港市连云区	Lianyungang Lianyun District	14.90	7.52	7.92	0.35	0.43
淮安市楚州区	Huaian Chuzhou District	89.99	2.66	6.42	3.29	3.39
淮安市淮阴区	Huaian Huaiyin District	119.11	8.16	12.72	3.76	1.98
盐城市盐都区	Yancheng Yandu District	162.71	5.91	12.84	5.49	4.55
扬州市邗江区	Yangzhou Hanjiang District	334.80	13.50	28.22	12.66	8.17
扬州市维扬区	Yangzhou Weiyang District	61.70	1.03	2.40	1.24	1.95
镇江市丹徒区	Zhenjiang Dantu District	163.68	7.55	15.18	6.77	3.46
泰州市海陵区	Taizhou Hailing District	87.16	1.57	3.38	1.59	2.82
泰州市高港区	Taizhou Gaogang District	80.17	2.67	6.62	3.19	2.23
宿迁市宿豫区	Suqian Suyu District	56.95	1.65	3.57	1.72	2.38

18－7 贸易、外资(2006年)
TRADE AND FOREIGN ECONOMY (2006)

市辖区 District Under the Jurisdiction of Municipality		社会消费品零售总额(亿元) Total Retail Sales of Consumer Goods (100 million yuan)	出口总额(万美元) Total Imports and Exports (USD 1000)	合同外商直接投资(万美元) Contract of Foreign Direct Investment (USD 1000)	实际外商直接投资(万美元) Actial Foreign Direct Investment (USD 1000)	星级饭店个数(个) Star Class Hotel (unit)
南京市浦口区	Nanjing Pukou District	46.69	19134	20099	11243	7
南京市栖霞区	Nanjing Qixia District	37.65	17603	13025	5814	3
南京市雨花区	Nanjing Yuhua District	49.60	13216	9370	4823	3
南京市江宁区	Nanjing Jiangning District	77.11	295782	92880	43535	7
南京市六合区	Nanjing Luhe District	74.89	18132	28288	12218	5
无锡市锡山区	Wuxi Xishan District	60.62	122963	91666	27762	2
无锡市惠山区	Wuxi Huishan District	47.39	65195	64562	16448	2
无锡市滨湖区	Wuxi Binghu District	76.99	62922	39692	14327	15
徐州市贾汪区	Xuzhou Jiawang District	16.16	1358	2448	520	
常州市新北区	Changzhou Xinbei District	68.38	193543	85130	38033	3
常州市武进区	Changzhou Wujin District	127.34	250687	85860	38033	9
苏州市虎丘区	Suzhou Huqui District	39.22	2070777	200654	78973	4
苏州市吴中区	Suzhou Wuzhong District	99.71	245684	110457	44500	12
苏州市相城区	Suzhou Xiangcheng District	59.06	107438	64806	21629	2
南通市崇川区	Nantong Chongchuan District	109.88	183723	27625	11887	
南通市港闸区	Nantong Gangzha District	30.95	94391	30942	9745	
连云港市连云区	Lianyungang Lianyun District	16.23	10311	8007	3681	11
淮安市楚州区	Huaian Chuzhou District	34.06	1348	4407	1192	4
淮安市淮阴区	Huaian Huaiyin District	23.16	1502	3633	1106	4
盐城市盐都区	Yancheng Yandu District	29.46	7784	10673	3000	1
扬州市邗江区	Yangzhou Hanjiang District	38.83	33508	39333	10030	3
扬州市维扬区	Yangzhou Weiyang District	25.05	18410	17188	5827	
镇江市丹徒区	Zhenjiang Dantu District	17.66	7329	12147	3540	
泰州市海陵区	Taizhou Hailing District	62.53	13978	9010	6023	7
泰州市高港区	Taizhou Gaogang District	9.67	19975	15001	8571	1
宿迁市宿豫区	Suqian Suyu District	14.78	6498	1391	481	1

18－8　教育、卫生(2006 年)

EDUCATION AND PUBLIC HEALTH (2006)

市辖区 District Under the Jurisdiction of Municipality		普通中学在校学生(万人) Regular Secondary School Students Enrollment (1000 person)	小学在校学生(万人) Primary School Student Enrollment (1000 persons)	医院卫生院数(个) Number of Hospitals and commune Hospitals (units)	医院卫生院床位数(张) Number of Beds in Hospitals and Commune Hospitals (unit)	执业(助理)医师(人) Practitioner (Assistant) Doctors (persons)	在岗职工平均工资(元) Average Wages of Employed Workers (yuan)
南京市浦口区	Nanjing Pukou District	2.68	2.87	10	972	726	22719
南京市栖霞区	Nanjing Qixia District	1.51	1.85	13	865	904	25677
南京市雨花区	Nanjing Yuhua District	0.98	1.04	5	481	500	26001
南京市江宁区	Nanjing Jiangning District	4.89	4.45	15	1145	1283	22354
南京市六合区	Nanjing Luhe District	5.07	4.40	7	1397	1441	23714
无锡市锡山区	Wuxi Xishan District	2.45	3.07	1	400	801	28261
无锡市惠山区	Wuxi Huishan District	2.49	3.22	1	160	633	27275
无锡市滨湖区	Wuxi Binghu District	1.59	2.65	14	4272	1737	30966
徐州市贾汪区	Xuzhou Jiawang District	3.37	3.07	10	944	506	16952
常州市新北区	Changzhou Xinbei District	2.16	2.42			354	22250
常州市武进区	Changzhou Wujin District	6.49	7.82	6	1312	1253	25151
苏州市虎丘区	Suzhou Huqui District	1.56	1.60	4	295	542	25085
苏州市吴中区	Suzhou Wuzhong District	3.09	2.93	8	977	1082	28603
苏州市相城区	Suzhou Xiangcheng District	2.06	2.07	3	286	474	28556
南通市崇川区	Nantong Chongchuan District	1.11	3.76	7	492	176	
南通市港闸区	Nantong Gangzha District	0.45	0.92	6	1252	47	
连云港市连云区	Lianyungang Lianyun District	0.57	1.05	7	640	536	16434
淮安市楚州区	Huaian Chuzhou District	8.07	8.84	6	948	1112	11670
淮安市淮阴区	Huaian Huaiyin District	5.90	6.38	2	598	538	13873
盐城市盐都区	Yancheng Yandu District	4.11	3.15	2	586	841	14308
扬州市邗江区	Yangzhou Hanjiang District	3.29	2.65	4	376	670	17103
扬州市维扬区	Yangzhou Weiyang District	0.35	0.97	9	1055	605	17114
镇江市丹徒区	Zhenjiang Dantu District	1.63	1.35	4	413	498	20161
泰州市海陵区	Taizhou Hailing District	1.85	1.96	6	1526	953	16753
泰州市高港区	Taizhou Gaogang District	1.05	1.07	1	140	232	18094
宿迁市宿豫区	Suqian Suyu District	5.53	5.61	22	905	456	14028

第19篇

区域经济

REGIONAL ECONOMY

19－1 三大区域主要经济指标（2006年）
MAJOR ECONOMIC INDICATORS OF THREE REGIONS（2006）

指标	Item	苏南 Southern Jiangsu	苏中 Mid Jiangsu	苏北 Northern Jiangsu
年末总人口（万人）	Population（Year-end）（10000 persons）	2304.57	1732.03	3281.12
土地面积（平方公里）	Land Area（sq. km）	28080	20432	54357
耕地面积（千公顷）	Cultivated Land（1000 hectares）	950.35	929.72	1762.73
地区生产总值（亿元）	Gross Domestic Product（100 million yuan）	13485.61	3860.78	4235.70
第一产业	Primary Industry	328.36	357.58	753.60
第二产业	Secondary Industry	8046.78	2191.19	2028.00
#工业	Industry	7445.80	1862.25	1686.67
第三产业	Tertiary Industry	5110.47	1312.01	1454.10
人均地区生产总值（元）	Per Capita GDP（yuan）	48559	23501	13699
地区生产总值指数（上年＝100）	Indices of GDP（preceding year＝100）	115.3	115.4	115.0
粮食产量（万吨）	Grain（10000 tons）	640.61	631.89	1242.97
油料产量（万吨）	Oil-bearing Crops（10000 tons）	33.04	41.21	91.67
棉花产量（万吨）	Cotton（10000 tons）	3.68	17.31	12.28
规模以上工业利税总额（亿元）	Total Pre-tax Profits（over scal）（100 million yuan）	2094.18	535.50	464.09
城镇固定资产投资额（亿元）	Urban Completed Investment in Fixed Assets（100 million yuan）	4614.11	1129.88	1737.81
社会消费品零售总额（亿元）	Total Retail Sale of Consumer Goods（100 million yuan）	3977.66	1249.12	1396.40
进出口总额（亿美元）	Total Imports and Exports（USD 100 million）	2602.09	161.53	76.34
#出口	Exports	1440.45	117.50	46.24
实际外商直接投资（亿美元）	Actual Foreign Direct Invesment（USD 100 million）	123.58	39.94	10.79
地方财政一般预算收入（亿元）	Local Financial Budgetary Revenue	1046.56	216.62	210.82
地方财政一般预算支出（亿元）	Local Financial Budgetary Expenditure（100 million yuan）	1044.84	266.08	362.21
金融机构存款余额（亿元）	Deposits Balance of Banking Institution（100 million yuan）	18274.43	4153.08	3432.92
#居民储蓄存款	Saving Deposits by Residents	7447.60	2617.87	2117.99
金融机构贷款余额（亿元）	Loans Balance of Banking Institution（100 million yuan）	14177.18	2354.54	1953.37
城镇居民人均可支配收入（元）	Per Capita Disposable Income of Urban Households（yuan）	17391	13263	11799
农村居民人均纯收入（元）	Per Capita Net Income of Rural Households（yuan）	8221	5915	4733
居民人均储蓄存款（元）	Per Capita Saving Deposits of Residents（yuan）	32317	15114	6455

19－2　三大区域经济社会基本情况（2006年）

指标	Item	苏南合计 Southern Jiangsu Total	南京 Nanjing Municipality	无锡 Wuxi Municipality	常州 Changzhou Municipality	苏州 Suzhou Municipality
人口、就业	**Population and Employment**					
土地面积（平方公里）	Land Area (sq. km)	28080	6582	4788	4375	8488
年末户籍人口（万人）	Population (Registered) (Year-end) (10000 persons)	2304.57	607.23	457.80	354.67	616.08
男	Male	1156.58	310.41	229.11	178.63	304.51
女	Female	1147.99	296.82	228.69	176.04	311.57
年均户籍人口（万人）	Yearly Average Population (Registered) (10000 persons)	2289.89	601.51	455.32	353.16	611.70
年末常住人口（万人）	Population (Permanent) (10000 persons)	2838.34	719.06	584.17	425.69	809.86
城镇化率（%）	Rate of Urbanization (%)	67.1	76.4	67.1	60.5	65.1
年末总户数（万户）	Total Households (Year-end)	777.80	196.29	151.93	122.32	207.24
#乡村户数	Rural Households	303.89	61.51	83.67	77.96	111.51
出生人口（万人）	Births (10000 persons)	17.00	4.41	3.05	2.82	4.63
死亡人口（万人）	Deaths (10000 persons)	13.98	3.10	3.17	2.15	3.91
人口自然增长率（‰）	Natural Growth Rate of Population (‰)	1.32	2.18	-0.27	1.90	1.18
人口密度（人/平方公里）	Density of Population (person/sq. km)	1011	1092	1220	973	954
从业人员（万人）	Employed Persons (10000 persons)	1476.08	327.41	307.90	256.39	431.20
第一产业	Primary Industry	167.10	37.38	30.20	31.00	35.94
第二产业	Secondary Industry	789.55	138.75	171.80	140.34	263.70
#工业	Industry	676.28	97.17	157.38	117.75	242.19
第三产业	Tertiary Industry	519.42	151.28	105.90	85.05	131.56
单位从业人员（万人）	Number of Employed Persons (10000 persons)	338.41	96.44	58.67	36.50	114.09
国有经济	State-owned Units	114.19	45.25	18.89	13.63	21.69
城镇集体经济	Collective Owned Units in Urban Areas	13.36	4.48	2.58	1.51	2.56
其他单位合计	Others	210.86	46.70	37.20	21.37	89.85
内资	Domestic-funded Units	92.70	30.02	17.35	13.86	21.67
港澳台商投资	Economic Units Funded by Entrepreneurs from Hong Kong, Macao and Taiwan	34.01	5.97	5.25	3.23	16.34
外商投资单位	Foreign-funded Economic Units	84.15	10.71	14.60	4.27	51.84
在岗职工人数（万人）	Number of Fully Employed Workers and Staff (10000 persons)	320.93	91.85	50.81	35.47	111.39
#国有单位	State-owned Units	109.71	43.37	17.85	13.21	21.14
城镇集体单位	Collective Owned Units in Urban Areas	12.74	4.30	2.36	1.47	2.43
港澳台商投资单位	Economic Units Funded by Entrepreneurs from Hong Kong, Macao and Taiwan	32.56	5.81	4.39	3.15	16.04

BACIS SITUATION OF ECONOMY AND SOCIETY OF THREE REGIONS (2006)

镇江 Zhenjiang Municipality	苏中合计 Mid Jiangsu Total	南通 Nantong Municipality	扬州 Yangzhou Municipality	泰州 Taizhou Municipality	苏北合计 Northern Jiangsu Total	徐州 Xuzhou Municipality	连云港 Lianyungang Municipality	淮安 Huaian Municipality	盐城 Yancheng Municipality	宿迁 Suqian Municipality
3847	20432	8001	6634	5797	54357	11258	7500	10072	16972	8555
268.79	1732.03	769.79	458.64	503.60	3281.12	934.73	479.42	532.76	804.73	529.47
133.92	870.26	382.47	231.12	256.67	1688.65	481.46	248.34	273.44	413.22	272.18
134.87	861.77	387.32	227.52	246.93	1592.47	453.27	231.08	259.32	391.51	257.29
268.20	1730.64	770.33	457.48	502.83	3264.80	930.02	475.80	530.27	801.70	527.01
299.56	1634.29	724.93	445.91	463.45	3076.87	876.48	450.52	492.43	768.73	488.71
59.2	47.3	46.9	49.2	46.1	40.4	44.8	39.0	38.4	42.5	32.4
100.02	606.86	278.77	156.06	172.04	1005.51	284.25	137.25	160.10	276.98	146.94
60.16	280.18	214.40	98.03	120.56	553.88	182.57	90.50	98.01	185.96	104.91
2.10	12.50	4.89	3.16	4.45	35.74	8.13	5.71	6.01	9.44	6.46
1.65	11.59	5.51	2.54	3.54	14.35	3.42	2.39	2.13	4.32	2.09
1.65	0.53	-0.81	1.37	1.81	6.55	5.06	6.98	7.32	6.39	8.29
779	800	906	672	799	566	779	601	489	453	571
153.18	949.22	449.45	243.89	255.88	1600.20	469.15	241.74	281.68	318.95	288.68
32.58	220.23	108.22	47.42	64.59	598.94	177.20	95.24	101.01	115.48	110.01
74.96	408.37	190.99	112.49	104.89	464.16	144.99	71.70	68.31	88.52	90.64
61.79	266.03	119.15	80.28	66.60	310.56	102.41	41.97	42.57	59.20	64.41
45.63	320.62	150.24	83.98	86.40	537.10	146.96	74.80	112.36	114.95	88.03
32.71	125.37	57.21	35.40	32.76	190.30	60.14	30.41	32.49	48.82	18.45
14.73	52.91	20.08	18.19	14.64	111.13	41.57	16.21	17.03	24.31	12.00
2.23	9.82	3.15	2.74	3.93	12.33	3.82	2.87	2.53	2.24	0.87
15.75	62.64	33.98	14.47	14.19	66.84	14.74	11.33	12.92	22.27	5.58
9.80	36.47	16.35	9.86	10.27	52.76	12.58	7.70	10.29	16.92	5.29
3.22	9.47	5.69	2.01	1.77	6.72	1.35	1.20	1.42	2.56	0.18
2.73	16.70	11.93	2.60	2.16	7.36	0.81	2.44	1.21	2.79	0.11
31.41	119.73	54.97	34.73	30.03	182.04	56.91	28.91	31.50	46.42	18.31
14.13	50.57	19.41	17.72	13.45	107.00	39.87	15.82	16.82	22.61	11.88
2.18	9.16	3.03	2.71	3.42	11.68	3.57	2.52	2.52	2.21	0.87
3.17	9.37	5.63	2.00	1.75	6.54	1.21	1.20	1.42	2.53	0.18

19－2 续表 1

指标	Item	苏南合计 Southern Jiangsu Total	南京 Nanjing Municipality	无锡 Wuxi Municipality	常州 Changzhou Municipality	苏州 Suzhou Municipality
外商投资单位	Foreign-funded Economic Units	78.57	9.89	10.98	4.22	50.76
私营企业从业人员 （万人）	Number of Employed Persons in Private Enterprises （10000 persons）	483.92	92.29	95.67	80.01	182.70
个体从业人员 （万人）	Number of Self-employed Individuals （10000 persons）	131.85	27.92	23.70	22.48	42.63
年末城镇登记失业人员 （万人）	Year End Registered Unemployed Persons in Urban Areas （10000 persons）	20.54	6.01	4.21	3.26	5.48
年末城镇登记失业率 （%）	Year End Registered Unemployed Persons in Urban Areas （%）	3.27	3.33	3.18	3.44	3.22
国民核算	**National Accounting**					
地区生产总值 （亿元）	Gross Domestic Product （100 million yuan）	13485.61	2773.78	3300.59	1569.46	4820.26
第一产业	Primary Industry	328.36	82.02	51.34	59.45	94.01
第二产业	Secondary Industry	8046.78	1359.94	1968.75	947.42	3152.03
#工业	Industry	7445.80	1181.94	1849.85	868.44	2978.55
第三产业	Tertiary Industry	5110.47	1331.82	1280.50	562.59	1574.22
人均地区生产总值 （按常住人口计算，元）	Per Capita GDP（Permanent） （yuan）	48559	39376	57719	37435	61500
人均地区生产总值 （按户籍人口计算，元）	Per Capita GDP（Registered） （yuan）	58892	46114	72489	44440	78801
地区生产总值指数 （上年＝100）	Indices of GDP （preceding year＝100）	115.3	115.1	115.3	115.2	115.5
第一产业	Primary Industry	104.1	104.0	106.3	105.0	103.4
第二产业	Secondary Industry	115.7	115.4	115.4	115.8	115.7
#工业	Industry	116.2	115.9	115.9	116.2	116.3
第三产业	Tertiary Industry	115.5	115.5	115.5	115.5	115.8
地区生产总值构成 （%）	GDP. structure （%）	100.0	100.0	100.0	100.0	100.0
第一产业	Primary Industry	2.4	3.0	1.6	3.8	2.0
第二产业	secondary	59.7	49.0	59.6	60.4	65.4
#工业	Industry	55.2	42.6	56.0	55.3	61.8
第三产业	Tertiary Industry	37.9	48.0	38.8	35.8	32.7
固定资产投资	**Investment in Fixed Assets**					
城镇固定资产投资额 （亿元）	Urban Investment in Fixed Assets （100 million yuan）	4614.11	1228.31	1015.02	607.85	1462.90
房地产投资	Investment in Real Estate Development	1337.20	351.17	276.81	171.04	470.75
#住宅	Residence	987.46	253.64	192.48	123.38	361.78
固定资产投资本年资金来源构成 （%）	Grouped by Source of Finance （%）	100.0	100.0	100.0	100.0	100.0

Continued

镇 江 Zhenjiang Municipality	苏中合计 Mid Jiangsu Total	南 通 Nantong Municipality	扬 州 Yangzhou Municipality	泰 州 Taizhou Municipality	苏北合计 Northern Jiangsu Total	徐 州 Xuzhou Municipality	连云港 Lianyungang Municipality	淮 安 Huaian Municipality	盐 城 Yancheng Municipality	宿 迁 Suqian Municipality
2.72	16.27	11.56	2.59	2.12	7.16	0.81	2.41	1.12	2.72	0.11
33.24	209.99	111.70	53.89	44.40	203.22	46.91	25.21	36.10	61.66	33.32
15.13	67.62	28.52	16.77	22.33	82.63	24.03	10.08	19.29	20.85	8.37
1.58	7.94	3.36	2.46	2.12	11.91	3.26	1.84	2.51	2.92	1.39
3.18	3.21	3.20	3.10	3.33	3.46	3.03	3.61	3.82	3.12	3.71
1021.52	3860.78	1758.34	1100.16	1002.28	4235.70	1428.80	527.38	651.06	1174.26	454.20
41.54	357.58	168.06	94.52	95.00	753.60	180.82	96.26	123.78	245.65	107.09
618.64	2191.19	985.04	620.59	585.56	2028.00	741.36	241.55	305.23	536.18	203.68
567.02	1862.25	815.06	545.90	501.29	1686.67	632.84	188.36	252.61	456.98	155.88
361.34	1312.01	605.24	385.05	321.72	1454.10	506.62	189.57	222.05	392.43	143.43
34293	23501	24133	24543	21509	13699	16257	11656	13155	15177	9232
38088	22308	22826	24048	19933	12974	15363	11084	12278	14647	8618
115.2	115.4	115.7	115.2	115.3	115.0	115.1	115.2	115.0	115.0	115.0
107.3	104.7	104.2	104.8	104.6	105.7	106.8	106.3	105.0	105.2	104.3
115.6	117.4	117.8	117.0	117.1	118.7	116.9	119.1	119.2	119.6	121.3
117.3	118.5	119.2	118.1	118.3	118.2	116.9	119.7	118.1	119.1	120.5
115.4	115.5	115.8	115.3	115.5	115.3	115.7	115.3	115.5	115.6	115.5
100.0	100.0	100.0	100.0	100.0	100.0	100.0	100.0	100.0	100.0	100.0
4.1	9.3	9.6	8.6	9.5	17.8	12.7	18.3	19.0	20.9	23.6
60.6	56.8	56.0	56.4	58.4	47.9	51.9	45.8	46.9	45.7	44.8
55.5	48.2	46.4	49.6	50.0	39.8	44.3	35.7	38.8	38.9	34.3
35.4	34.0	34.4	35.0	32.1	34.3	35.5	35.9	34.1	33.4	31.6
300.03	1129.88	487.57	357.83	284.47	1737.81	598.52	300.12	305.56	347.75	185.86
67.42	254.77	107.93	83.43	63.41	314.75	70.80	55.07	66.35	65.51	57.02
56.19	194.51	88.89	58.80	46.82	244.00	59.17	39.89	51.06	49.63	44.25
100.0	100.0	100.0	100.0	100.0	100.0	100.0	100.0	100.0	100.0	100.0

19-2 续表 2

指标	Item	苏南合计 Southern Jiangsu Total	南京 Nanjing Municipality	无锡 Wuxi Municipality	常州 Changzhou Municipality	苏州 Suzhou Municipality
国家预算内资金	State Appropriation	0.4	1.3	0.1	0.3	0.0
国内贷款	Domestic Loans	19.9	21.0	13.0	17.0	25.6
利用外资	Foreign Inventment	11.0	7.0	18.0	3.6	13.3
自筹资金	Fund Raising	47.0	51.5	52.2	54.5	34.8
其他资金	Others	21.6	19.3	16.7	24.7	26.2
新增固定资产（亿元）	Newly Increased Investment in Fixed Assets (100 million yuan)	3618.05	701.56	808.12	381.94	1485.98
商品房销售建筑面积（万平方米）	Floor Space of Selling Commercial Houses (10000 sq. m)	3774.93	1010.50	648.58	479.12	1391.38
#住宅	Residencial Buildings	3321.03	940.99	553.40	407.89	1193.52
商品房空置面积（万平方米）	Total Sales of Commercial Houses (10000 sq. m)	799.01	73.68	102.57	51.26	524.98
#住宅	Residencial Buildings	515.71	45.34	72.30	17.82	351.32
财政、金融、保险	**Finance, Banking and Insurance**					
财政总收入（亿元）	Local Financial Budgetary Revenue (100 million yuan)	2467.89	603.91	517.35	277.27	918.10
地方财政一般预算收入（亿元）	Local Financial Budgetary Revenue (100 million yuan)	1046.56	246.44	220.89	118.88	400.23
#各项税收	Taxes of All Types	914.95	216.49	190.15	102.48	358.97
#增值税	Value-added Tax	238.81	45.58	54.97	25.18	99.10
营业税	Operation Tax	264.89	72.83	49.47	28.38	101.56
企业所得税	Income Tax of Enterprises	135.99	30.87	29.33	13.56	56.65
个人所得税	Induvidual Income Tax	50.34	12.19	10.98	5.40	19.88
地方财政一般预算支出（亿元）	Local Financial Budgetary Expenditure (100 million yuan)	1044.84	262.46	213.40	117.70	386.20
#基本建设支出	Expenditure for Capital Construction	108.31	18.32	24.93	8.84	54.57
企业挖潜改造资金	Expenditure for Innovation Enterprise	49.91	20.58	15.56	3.26	7.64
科技三项费用	Expenditure for S & T Promotion	21.66	3.47	4.51	2.78	9.82
农林水气象支出	Agricalture, Forestry, water conservansy and Metoorology	58.17	12.31	10.86	7.52	23.02
文教科卫事业费	Expenditure for Culture, Education, Science and Health Care	191.43	48.18	40.91	23.28	64.16
抚恤和社会福利救济费	Relief Expenditure for Pension and Social Welfare	23.30	8.36	4.50	2.70	6.26
社会保障补助支出	Subsidy Expenditure for Social Security	42.59	7.07	8.95	3.05	22.19
城市维护费	City Maintenance Expenditure	147.06	49.47	19.16	16.24	57.70
金融机构存款余额（亿元）	Deposits Balance of Banking Institutions (100 million yuan)	18274.43	5802.21	3772.06	1974.01	5797.95
#企业存款	Deposits of Enterprises	7137.89	2768.79	1327.59	563.78	2198.28

Continued

镇 江 Zhenjiang Municipality	苏中合计 Mid Jiangsu Total	南 通 Nantong Municipality	扬 州 Yangzhou Municipality	泰 州 Taizhou Municipality	苏北合计 Northern Jiangsu Total	徐 州 Xuzhou Municipality	连云港 Lianyungang Municipality	淮 安 Huaian Municipality	盐 城 Yancheng Municipality	宿 迁 Suqian Municipality
0.1	2.5	5.2	0.4	0.1	0.5	0.3	0.0	1.0	1.0	0.6
14.3	12.7	13.2	11.2	13.5	7.7	6.0	17.9	6.0	2.8	6.0
8.3	8.9	12.0	6.7	6.0	1.6	0.3	2.0	4.6	1.3	0.8
60.5	61.0	54.9	64.8	67.2	81.2	92.5	60.3	76.4	89.7	77.8
16.9	15.0	14.6	16.8	13.2	9.0	0.9	19.8	12.1	5.2	14.8
240.45	733.74	295.38	216.25	222.11	972.41	302.49	190.16	172.11	190.26	117.39
245.35	1127.42	471.75	391.93	263.74	1200.64	288.46	194.54	204.87	265.72	247.05
225.23	959.92	409.02	324.17	226.73	1037.72	252.21	159.56	174.59	245.66	205.70
46.52	175.74	65.55	75.86	34.33	132.95	20.82	13.44	3.64	23.57	71.48
28.93	91.48	44.43	37.10	9.95	76.47	10.56	4.57	0.57	12.33	48.43
151.26	529.67	217.57	158.03	154.07	501.14	180.85	78.34	92.90	110.97	38.07
60.12	216.62	92.53	63.02	61.07	210.82	71.03	33.96	36.94	48.84	20.05
46.87	177.29	78.82	50.35	48.12	164.13	56.57	26.91	28.23	38.07	14.36
13.99	49.43	21.10	13.57	14.76	40.67	15.83	5.64	7.68	9.09	2.43
12.65	49.49	23.54	14.78	11.18	52.37	16.10	10.33	7.66	12.45	5.83
5.59	20.78	9.76	4.84	6.19	15.97	6.14	3.04	2.44	3.27	1.08
1.90	8.17	3.94	2.01	2.22	6.55	2.04	1.15	1.07	1.71	0.58
65.08	266.08	112.62	75.64	77.82	362.21	107.31	57.64	62.16	85.89	49.20
1.64	16.34	6.16	5.26	4.93	16.31	3.23	3.85	3.31	2.58	3.34
2.88	8.41	2.63	1.75	4.03	7.61	0.95	1.70	2.70	1.71	0.54
1.07	4.91	2.30	1.32	1.29	3.79	1.07	0.43	0.70	1.32	0.29
4.45	20.68	7.74	6.46	6.48	29.04	7.07	4.63	5.28	7.18	4.88
14.90	64.24	26.64	17.75	19.84	104.30	29.74	14.13	16.69	28.39	15.35
1.48	7.95	3.49	2.23	2.23	15.89	4.44	1.99	3.03	3.50	2.93
1.33	11.69	5.62	2.58	3.48	18.34	7.94	1.86	2.26	4.07	2.21
4.48	11.00	5.26	2.41	3.33	15.84	5.79	2.44	4.13	2.03	1.45
928.20	4153.08	2113.95	1085.26	953.87	3432.92	1193.72	506.11	511.37	939.73	281.99
279.45	1051.60	520.57	291.35	239.67	821.71	293.48	142.07	137.01	190.89	58.26

19－2　续表　3

指　　标	Item	苏南合计 Southern Jiangsu Total	南京 Nanjing Municipality	无锡 Wuxi Municipality	常州 Changzhou Municipality	苏州 Suzhou Municipality
居民储蓄存款	Savings Deposits by Residents	7447.60	1834.88	1649.56	1014.00	2427.41
金融机构贷款余额（亿元）	Loans Balance of Banking Institutions (100 million yuan)	14177.18	5098.13	2632.72	1348.60	4429.70
#工业贷款	Industrial Loans	2510.36	465.20	764.00	350.57	772.58
商业贷款	Commercial Loans	665.78	289.81	152.05	67.26	119.26
农业贷款	Agricultural Loans	197.29	41.60	40.18	32.05	48.23
私营个体贷款	Private and Individual	179.93	35.41	64.76	8.46	60.96
#个人消费贷款	Industrial Loans	1514.78	397.62	207.93	146.13	712.54
保费收入（亿元）	Premium (100 million yuan)	304.39	89.96	66.23	42.61	83.93
财产险	Property Insurance	86.24	21.88	18.17	11.22	30.13
人寿险	life Insurance	218.16	68.08	48.07	31.39	53.80
赔款和给付（亿元）	Claim and Payment (100 million yuan)	107.78	28.34	23.42	14.08	34.94
财产险	Proparty Insurance	53.85	13.83	14.01	7.02	15.45
人寿险	life Insurance	53.93	14.51	9.41	7.06	19.49
农业	**Agriculture**					
乡村从业人员（万人）	Rural Employees (10000 persons)	558.24	122.16	148.75	126.49	206.87
#农林牧渔业	Farming, Forestry, Animal Husbandry and Fishery	201.24	36.83	29.51	30.30	34.84
工业	Industry	144.35	30.71	79.73	49.92	111.45
建筑业	Construction	76.45	22.04	9.79	15.83	13.17
耕地面积（千公顷）	Cultivated Area (1000 hectares)	950.35	243.69	145.37	178.43	239.65
农林牧渔业总产值（亿元）	Gross Output Value of Farming, Forestry, Animal Husbandry and Fishery (100 million yuan)	519.60	165.06	101.23	109.08	172.18
农业	Farming	280.66	90.08	46.97	53.27	66.31
林业	Forestry	14.27	2.06	4.30	1.25	7.24
牧业	Animal Husbandry	106.66	33.46	26.69	18.39	21.43
渔业	Fishery	101.89	34.17	17.73	30.97	60.19
农林牧渔服务业	Service Industry of FFAF	16.12	5.29	5.54	5.19	17.02
农业机械总动力（万千瓦）	Total Power of Agricultural Machinery (10000 kW)	641.90	198.50	135.80	257.00	186.30
化肥施用量（万吨）	Consumption of Chemical Fertilizer (10000 tons)	74.94	13.45	8.85	8.72	10.96
农村用电量（亿千瓦小时）	Electricity Consumed in Rural Areas (100 million kWh)	128.25	23.51	236.06	111.12	366.47
有效灌溉面积(千公顷)	Irrigated Area (1000 hectares)	78.45	19.42	14.03	15.48	20.93
农作物总播种面积（千公顷）	Total Sown Area (1000 hectares)	151.23	37.75	18.00	23.66	29.79
#粮食	Grain	100.34	15.37	11.90	14.58	17.57
主要产品产量（万吨）	Total Output of Major Products (10000 tons)					
粮食	Grain	640.61	105.99	77.83	105.81	123.52
油料	Oil-bearing Crops	33.04	19.22	2.92	8.26	6.36
棉花（吨）	Cotton (ton)	36833	5536	0	320	3757

Continued

镇江 Zhenjiang Municipality	苏中合计 Mid Jiangsu Total	南通 Nantong Municipality	扬州 Yangzhou Municipality	泰州 Taizhou Municipality	苏北合计 Northern Jiangsu Total	徐州 Xuzhou Municipality	连云港 Lianyungang Municipality	淮安 Huaian Municipality	盐城 Yancheng Municipality	宿迁 Suqian Municipality
521.75	2617.87	1347.89	675.54	594.44	2117.99	722.89	281.85	288.97	639.49	184.79
668.03	2354.54	1211.74	597.25	545.55	1953.37	565.06	325.90	332.78	534.10	195.53
158.01	523.26	278.07	120.80	124.40	297.32	93.44	41.70	40.70	98.26	23.22
37.40	183.84	93.31	52.24	38.29	268.11	68.14	44.27	47.78	75.48	32.44
35.23	214.05	105.33	46.49	62.23	334.58	77.65	53.33	48.87	103.71	51.01
10.34	22.36	12.26	5.47	4.63	12.51	1.78	3.98	2.77	3.32	0.65
50.55	192.99	83.84	65.11	44.05	175.72	39.47	36.42	28.54	31.77	39.52
21.65	101.45	43.07	30.86	27.52	89.93	27.53	13.14	14.74	26.83	7.70
4.84	19.43	8.54	5.81	5.09	19.06	5.57	2.84	3.20	4.81	2.63
16.81	82.02	34.54	25.06	22.43	70.87	21.96	10.29	11.54	22.02	5.07
6.99	18.20	6.50	5.40	6.29	24.77	5.20	3.38	5.21	8.75	2.24
3.54	13.16	5.40	4.14	3.63	14.90	4.04	1.62	2.54	4.79	1.90
3.46	5.04	1.10	1.26	2.67	9.87	1.15	1.75	2.67	3.95	0.33
96.65	444.59	342.07	166.10	202.30	980.78	352.40	170.02	211.16	285.09	226.94
31.97	144.47	105.41	46.84	61.09	400.29	175.25	94.51	98.69	127.94	108.79
37.84	138.83	72.63	43.28	41.16	177.51	66.42	19.46	19.58	39.79	36.44
9.74	52.96	64.52	30.84	31.54	130.49	38.19	24.40	22.02	29.92	20.70
172.72	929.72	470.11	305.50	317.54	1762.73	596.80	368.86	487.64	778.18	438.53
73.67	644.13	310.14	182.63	171.21	980.16	334.21	187.27	219.79	553.05	192.49
44.34	298.76	135.67	80.43	87.11	505.37	217.51	94.84	134.29	257.78	113.26
1.93	15.96	2.33	5.30	3.36	19.36	7.99	3.50	5.64	11.66	9.01
11.96	153.78	81.82	37.14	42.20	219.17	84.76	37.50	49.63	147.73	31.97
11.84	135.54	77.80	51.76	29.98	193.57	18.85	44.24	26.19	100.71	34.35
3.59	40.09	12.50	7.99	8.57	42.70	5.10	7.19	4.04	35.17	3.89
131.40	613.60	293.20	183.10	214.70	1218.00	464.80	270.00	298.10	422.80	339.70
9.52	65.50	27.16	19.35	21.03	120.15	69.26	31.37	32.71	58.82	31.75
34.05	342.32	68.68	26.37	47.06	274.29	32.93	13.60	8.25	33.65	10.62
13.11	77.83	42.14	25.64	27.85	144.63	47.67	29.25	30.76	61.02	33.71
23.36	155.79	87.26	47.39	56.83	290.20	101.53	55.67	74.18	137.23	67.36
15.93	97.21	54.46	36.79	41.42	199.30	61.32	44.56	59.42	82.46	53.49
99.57	631.89	319.48	245.08	282.25	1242.97	357.98	276.99	381.46	535.33	317.64
7.63	41.21	40.49	11.47	13.76	91.67	14.62	12.37	15.80	35.82	8.87
1726	173127	54846	8372	20893	122836	49175	20546	2354	192348	5021

19－2 续表 4

指标	Item	苏南合计 Southern Jiangsu Total	南京 Nanjing Municipality	无锡 Wuxi Municipality	常州 Changzhou Municipality	苏州 Suzhou Municipality
肉类	Meat	64.34	19.63	14.21	11.25	15.87
#猪肉	Pork	38.94	10.50	9.09	6.37	8.33
牛肉	Beef	1.58	0.32	0.11	0.01	0.00
羊肉	Mutton	3.51	0.83	0.12	0.22	0.23
水产品	Aquatic Products	68.50	19.04	13.11	13.69	30.38
工业（规模以上）	**Industry (Above Designated size)**					
工业企业单位数 （个）	Number of Industrial Enterprises (unit)	20530	1889	4962	4233	7485
#内资企业	Domestic Funded Enterprises	14368	1334	3829	3521	4207
外商港澳台商投资企业	Enterprises Funded by Foreign, Hong Kong, Macao and Taiwan Entrepreneurs	6162	555	1133	712	3278
#国有控股企业	state-owned Share Holding Enterprises	536	207	104	54	85
#大型企业	Large Enterprises	248	35	56	17	129
中型企业	Medium-sized Enterprises	2446	234	527	286	1246
工业总产值 （亿元）	Gross Output Value of Industry (100 million yuan)	29269.17	4692.81	7115.29	3293.77	12538.51
#内资企业	Domestic Funded Enterprises	14941.34	2821.65	4626.60	2245.91	4191.51
外商港澳台商投资企业	Enterprises Funded by Foreign, Hong Kong, Macao and Taiwan Entrepreneurs	14327.82	1871.16	2488.69	1047.86	8347.00
#国有控股企业	state-owned share Holding Enterprlises	3175.07	1895.66	549.28	191.01	301.67
#大中型企业	Large and Medium-sized Enterprises	19793.89	3543.20	4586.77	1508.87	9297.30
#高技术产业企业	High New Tech Industry	8627.04	1938.13	1746.71	504.35	4017.42
#轻工业	light Tndustry	8013.19	700.50	1858.97	908.72	4105.03
#制造业	Manufacturing	28647.54	4568.12	6992.57	3241.86	12314.99
电力、燃气及水的生产和供应业	Electric Power, Gas and water Production and supply	514.62	90.63	84.98	45.11	221.15
工业增加值 （亿元）	Value-added of Industry (100 million yuan)	6932.69	973.60	1661.78	757.93	3078.40
资产合计 （亿元）	Total Industrial Assets (100 million yuan)	22647.12	3560.76	5307.64	2356.62	9996.62
#流动资产平均余额	Average Balance of Circulation Funds	11765.04	1758.41	2876.04	1335.96	5099.21
固定资产净值平均余额	Average Balance of Net Value of Fixed Assets	7356.22	1251.91	1507.60	662.51	3421.57
负债合计 （亿元）	Total Liabilities (100 million yuan)	13811.40	1984.68	3281.91	1508.35	6087.87
主营业务收入 （亿元）	Major Business Revenue (100 million yuan)	29129.34	4714.13	7062.47	3243.79	12533.02
#主营业务税金及附加	Major Business tax and Extra	114.32	64.53	17.94	9.57	17.02
利税总额 （亿元）	Total Pre-tax Profits (100 million yuan)	2094.18	407.98	515.67	228.91	811.41
#利润总额	Total Profits	1369.92	214.88	351.10	142.27	591.43
从业人员平均人数 （万人）	Average Number of Staff and Workers Employed (10000 persons)	508.94	55.86	111.41	65.74	239.12

Continued

镇 江 Zhenjiang Municipality	苏中合计 Mid Jiangsu Total	南 通 Nantong Municipality	扬 州 Yangzhou Municipality	泰 州 Taizhou Municipality	苏北合计 Northern Jiangsu Total	徐 州 Xuzhou Municipality	连云港 Lianyungang Municipality	淮 安 Huaian Municipality	盐 城 Yancheng Municipality	宿 迁 Suqian Municipality
7.21	64.61	37.73	22.39	24.88	126.48	50.38	20.30	22.08	63.56	22.95
4.81	32.91	18.30	14.23	18.64	74.63	27.68	14.03	14.97	37.27	14.67
0.06	0.13	0.02	0.09	0.01	2.94	1.61	1.96	0.49	0.27	1.00
0.54	5.25	3.44	0.42	1.64	9.13	4.64	0.75	0.86	5.31	1.78
7.77	104.08	72.28	36.74	22.03	162.80	17.07	50.41	24.15	85.19	24.69
1961	8659	4217	2252	2190	7143	1586	838	1350	2513	856
1477	6948	3104	1927	1917	6521	1478	678	1266	2283	816
484	1711	1113	325	273	622	108	160	84	230	40
86	146	61	53	32	233	69	47	68	33	16
11	35	11	13	11	32	14	3	4	9	2
153	514	247	143	124	349	77	54	68	122	28
1628.78	6505.95	2949.53	1891.88	1664.54	4556.99	1632.55	463.25	794.07	1378.15	288.97
1055.67	4609.72	1880.08	1380.40	1349.25	3769.53	1460.90	266.77	705.18	1069.27	267.40
573.11	1896.23	1069.45	511.48	315.30	787.46	171.65	196.48	88.89	308.87	21.57
237.44	816.70	195.34	446.49	174.86	861.30	553.71	68.36	154.47	42.71	42.05
857.74	2885.80	1108.64	924.62	852.54	2071.07	879.93	245.94	329.39	543.37	72.43
420.42	1514.37	641.75	408.29	464.32	470.43	121.60	85.09	75.45	176.84	11.46
439.98	2729.57	1411.46	723.11	595.00	1789.42	512.77	228.60	310.40	611.69	125.96
1530.00	6318.59	2887.06	1777.42	1654.10	4169.34	1362.12	431.89	750.43	1342.18	282.72
72.74	123.93	62.47	52.67	8.79	193.81	107.94	21.71	26.90	31.00	6.26
460.97	1766.64	792.99	501.31	472.33	1312.86	536.54	132.72	217.08	345.46	81.06
1425.48	3800.04	1638.38	1141.55	1020.11	2969.74	1094.10	372.07	539.01	795.66	168.89
695.42	1904.66	829.29	518.20	557.18	1310.93	448.29	171.53	219.10	394.70	77.31
512.62	1266.71	539.58	440.61	286.52	1196.29	456.42	146.78	239.59	281.23	72.28
948.59	2210.73	940.79	650.16	619.78	1803.80	674.14	205.75	318.65	511.34	93.91
575.94	6315.14	2919.56	1806.02	1589.57	4490.77	1586.71	450.34	822.74	1344.05	286.93
5.26	30.30	7.94	13.27	9.08	92.02	46.34	3.28	24.23	12.67	5.50
130.21	535.50	241.32	154.75	139.43	464.09	203.29	43.39	89.48	100.95	26.98
70.24	314.65	157.05	84.44	73.15	204.15	87.04	23.86	35.67	45.74	11.84
36.80	132.92	57.01	43.97	31.93	128.56	42.46	12.30	19.95	40.74	13.10

指 标	Item	苏南合计 Southern Jiangsu Total	南京 Nanjing Municipality	无锡 Wuxi Municipality	常州 Changzhou Municipality	苏州 Suzhou Municipality
建筑业	**Construction**					
建筑企业单位数 （个）	Number of Construction Enterprise (unit)	3382	1146	447	518	962
建筑企业从业人员 （万人）	Number of Persons Engaged in Construction Enterprises (10000 persons)	127.32	36.13	18.13	23.78	38.75
建筑业总产值 （亿元）	Gross Output Value of Construction (100 million yuan)	1999.67	716.17	259.12	353.38	529.87
房屋建筑施工面积 （万平方米）	Floor Space of Building Under Construction (10000 sq. m)	19693.87	5187.06	3123.63	4127.15	6244.73
房屋建筑竣工面积 （万平方米）	Floor Space of Buildings Completed (10000 sq. m)	9142.28	2056.20	1756.82	1889.28	2946.65
交通运输、邮电业	**Transportation, Postal and Telecommunication Sercices**					
公路里程 （公里）	Total Length of Highways (km)	35582	9689	6683	5546	8483
#等级公路	Expressway and Class Ⅰ to Ⅳ Highways	33175	8087	6505	5008	8419
#高速公路	Expressway	1253	359	240	117	432
一级公路	Class Ⅰ Highway	2431	419	288	459	880
公路客运量 （万人）	Passenger Traffic of Highways (10000 persons)	99826	19930	21315	15958	35182
公路货运量 （万吨）	Freight Traffic of Highways (10000 tons)	39628	11249	8845	5692	8891
民用汽车拥有量 （万辆）	Number of Civil Motor Vehicles Owned (10000 units)	157.79	36.32	35.44	20.18	56.76
#私人汽车拥有量	Number of Private-owned Vehicles	99.68	22.71	20.30	11.92	39.50
邮电业务总量 （亿元）	Total Telecommunications Services (100 million yuan)	338.65	93.55	67.46	39.20	113.40
#邮政业务总量	Total Post Services	30.76	7.99	6.52	4.04	9.50
本地电话用户 （万户）	Number of Local Telephone Subscribers (10000 subscribers)	1550.21	344.23	331.25	214.27	516.41
移动电话用户 （万户）	Number of Mobile Telephone Subscribers (10000 subscribers)	2051.40	488.31	431.39	255.00	729.51
国际互联网用户 （万户）	Number of Subscribers of Internet Service (10000 subscriber)	243.42	67.48	56.76	29.19	71.89
全年用电量 （亿千瓦小时）	Total Consumption of Electricity (100 million kWh)	1681.27	270.57	400.99	212.68	686.49
#工业用电	Consumption of Electricity for Industrial Use	1384.62	187.04	343.34	175.00	588.41
居民生活用电	Consumption of Electricity for Living Use by Residents	133.78	34.97	28.40	17.28	42.83

Continued

镇 江 Zhenjiang Municipality	苏中合计 Mid Jiangsu Total	南 通 Nantong Municipality	扬 州 Yangzhou Municipality	泰 州 Taizhou Municipality	苏北合计 Northern Jiangsu Total	徐 州 Xuzhou Municipality	连云港 Lianyungang Municipality	淮 安 Huaian Municipality	盐 城 Yancheng Municipality	宿 迁 Suqian Municipality
309	1883	739	729	415	1530	352	169	334	513	162
10.53	157.26	66.28	34.59	56.38	102.27	25.93	12.01	24.18	29.81	10.34
141.13	2433.55	1228.35	571.42	633.78	1010.25	255.95	135.82	225.33	292.51	100.65
1011.30	31952.09	17203.31	6424.78	8324.00	11940.95	2883.67	1585.00	2359.45	3911.05	1201.78
493.33	13356.70	6182.60	3306.10	3868.00	6569.33	1696.25	827.00	1424.90	1925.87	695.31
5181	30532	14015	9247	7270	60858	14857	9357	9975	16871	9798
5156	27005	12320	7688	6997	48462	11470	8668	7276	13642	7406
105	658	217	240	201	1444	299	281	346	310	208
385	1025	380	173	472	1732	778	173	208	420	153
7441	23428	9978	8595	4855	28263	7712	7059	3822	6858	2812
4951	14717	7594	4902	2221	19257	7494	4286	2335	3393	1749
9.09	36.05	16.93	10.03	9.10	44.25	14.81	6.94	6.79	10.09	5.62
5.26	21.65	10.65	6.14	4.86	27.04	9.75	3.55	3.60	6.34	3.81
25.03	118.71	42.95	26.69	49.06	113.84	39.96	17.39	15.45	28.98	12.06
2.70	16.78	7.40	4.96	4.42	14.98	3.95	1.76	1.99	5.93	1.35
144.05	643.92	269.45	190.93	183.54	965.23	290.73	144.95	162.27	253.40	113.88
147.18	593.61	281.27	162.86	149.47	720.66	219.54	108.54	94.70	206.18	91.70
18.08	67.01	20.97	31.79	14.24	74.34	28.54	13.29	11.84	16.34	4.33
110.54	371.29	163.60	94.22	113.47	376.49	139.99	49.17	65.49	89.78	32.07
90.83	287.85	126.65	69.10	92.10	275.53	109.26	33.18	49.23	63.50	20.35
10.30	45.36	20.07	13.26	12.02	55.15	15.05	7.91	9.46	15.93	6.80

19－2 续表 6

指 标	Item	苏南合计 Southern Jiangsu Total	南京 Nanjing Municipality	无锡 Wuxi Municipality	常州 Changzhou Municipality	苏州 Suzhou Municipality
批发零售贸易、餐饮业	**Wholesale and Retail Trade and Catering Services**					
社会消费品零售总额 （亿元）	Total Retail Sale of Consumer Goods (100 million yuan)	3977.66	1166.85	959.47	515.83	1055.44
#市	City	3380.25	1088.78	805.83	468.07	791.69
县	County	43.77	43.77	0.00	0.00	0.00
#批发和零售业	Wholesale and Retail Trade	3494.72	1026.64	856.78	452.06	918.12
住宿和餐饮业	Catering Services	423.25	126.28	86.15	57.36	117.16
对外经济贸易、旅游	**Foreign Economy, Trade and Tourism**					
进出口总额 （亿美元）	Total Imports and Exports (USD 100 million)	2602.09	315.35	391.93	104.49	1742.58
出口	Exports	1440.45	173.65	214.40	78.96	946.81
进口	Imports	1161.64	141.70	177.53	25.53	795.77
合同外商直接投资 （亿美元）	Contracted Foreign Direct Investment (USD 100 million)	320.13	30.82	80.53	32.96	159.24
实际外商直接投资 （亿美元）	Actual Foreign Direct Investment (USD 100 million)	123.58	15.19	27.52	12.51	61.05
接待海外旅游者人数 （万人次）	Number of Overseas Received Tourists (10000 persons)	368.43	100.92	71.31	21.86	137.97
星级饭店数 （个）	Number of Tourist Hotels (unit)	412	127	66	60	130
旅游外汇收入（亿美元）	Foreign Exchange Earnings from Tourism (USD 100 million)	21.74	6.77	3.17	1.81	7.48
教育	**Education**					
学校总数 （所）	Total Number of Schools (unit)	2903	751	580	468	745
#普通高校	Institutions of Regular Higher Education	83	41	11	9	17
普通中等专业学校	Regular Specialized Secondary Schools	77	29	20	8	13
普通中学	Regular Secondary Schools	976	223	193	172	265
小学	Primary Schools	1531	385	303	252	397

Continued

镇 江 Zhenjiang Municipality	苏中合计 Mid Jiangsu Total	南 通 Nantong Municipality	扬 州 Yangzhou Municipality	泰 州 Taizhou Municipality	苏北合计 Northern Jiangsu Total	徐 州 Xuzhou Municipality	连云港 Lianyungang Municipality	淮 安 Huaian Municipality	盐 城 Yancheng Municipality	宿 迁 Suqian Municipality
280.07	1249.12	621.96	355.83	271.33	1396.40	460.08	211.53	230.15	367.61	127.03
225.88	742.16	298.24	254.06	189.86	696.48	288.39	86.14	146.49	136.46	39.00
0.00	72.78	49.37	23.41	0.00	300.46	53.72	71.22	49.13	79.65	46.74
241.13	1100.02	566.26	304.02	229.74	1237.42	393.83	189.64	199.19	335.22	119.52
36.29	141.07	54.13	47.82	39.13	160.19	63.11	21.37	26.06	32.12	17.53
47.74	161.53	100.21	32.64	28.67	76.34	18.53	27.26	10.22	18.03	2.30
26.63	117.50	71.83	23.61	22.06	46.24	12.53	14.57	6.59	10.61	1.94
21.11	44.02	28.38	9.03	6.61	30.10	6.01	12.69	3.62	7.42	0.36
16.59	105.97	69.39	24.49	12.09	34.55	6.85	9.64	6.41	9.37	2.28
7.30	39.94	25.75	7.61	6.58	10.79	2.44	3.46	1.16	3.25	0.49
36.38	51.62	18.06	30.07	3.48	25.14	10.05	6.89	2.49	4.58	1.13
29	123	48	53	22	230	48	63	41	50	28
2.51	4.20	1.75	2.08	0.37	1.93	0.79	0.61	0.18	0.27	0.08
359	2155	880	598	677	4762	1344	733	784	1035	866
5	14	6	5	3	22	7	3	6	5	1
7	22	7	10	5	58	12	4	14	10	18
123	767	315	207	245	1355	369	214	215	322	235
194	1253	516	346	391	3156	907	490	503	662	594

指　　标　Item		苏南合计 Southern Jiangsu Total	南京 Nanjing Municipality	无锡 Wuxi Municipality	常州 Changzhou Municipality	苏州 Suzhou Municipality
毕业生总数　（万人）	Total Number of Graduates （10000 persons）	102.24	31.40	20.12	15.83	23.52
#普通高校	Institutions of Regular Higher Education	18.50	11.60	1.63	1.86	2.12
普通中等专业学校	Regular Specialized Secondary Schools	5.98	1.67	1.45	0.69	1.55
普通中学	Regular Secondary Schools	45.40	11.23	9.75	7.40	11.53
小学	Primary Schools	26.23	5.93	5.74	4.55	6.81
招生总数　（万人）	Total Number of New Student Enrollment （10000 persons）	106.72	33.41	21.48	16.16	24.42
#普通高校	Institutions of Regular Higher Education	24.63	13.83	2.64	2.58	3.66
普通中等专业学校	Regular Specialized Secondary Schools	10.96	2.76	2.90	1.41	2.83
普通中学	Regular Secondary Schools	41.05	9.64	8.81	7.12	10.55
小学	Primary Schools	20.43	4.73	4.79	3.36	5.46
在校学生数　（万人）	Total Number of Students Enrollment （10000 persons）	417.16	131.97	82.20	64.84	94.13
#普通高校	Institutions of Regular Higher Education	100.74	62.08	9.13	9.42	12.82
普通中等专业学校	Regular Specialized Secondary Schools	33.25	8.76	8.44	4.62	8.27
普通中学	Regular Secondary Schools	127.37	30.56	27.19	21.59	32.47
小学	Primary Schools	135.35	30.25	31.47	23.49	35.15
专任教师总数（万人）	Total Number of Full-time Teachers （10000 persons）	24.82	8.32	4.93	3.28	5.82
#普通高校	Institutions of Regular Higher Education	5.65	3.43	0.53	0.50	0.79
普通中等专业学校	Regular Specialized Secondary Schools	0.78	0.27	0.22	0.07	0.16
普通中学	Regular Secondary Schools	9.05	2.27	2.04	1.32	2.43
小学	Primary Schools	7.88	2.04	1.77	1.14	2.09
幼儿园数　（所）	Kindergartens （unit）	1678	494	392	231	357
在园幼儿数　（万人）	School-age Children Enrolled in Schools （10000 persons）	51.52	11.36	11.88	8.31	14.94
成人高等学校在校学生数　（万人）	Total Number of Adult students in Institutions of Higher Eduedtion （10000 persons）	24.54	15.62	0.75	1.85	3.71

Continued

镇江 Zhenjiang Municipality	苏中合计 Mid Jiangsu Total	南通 Nantong Municipality	扬州 Yangzhou Municipality	泰州 Taizhou Municipality	苏北合计 Northern Jiangsu Total	徐州 Xuzhou Municipality	连云港 Lianyungang Municipality	淮安 Huaian Municipality	盐城 Yancheng Municipality	宿迁 Suqian Municipality
11.36	64.25	28.06	17.60	18.59	152.84	48.47	22.96	24.17	31.86	25.38
1.28	2.97	1.20	1.34	0.43	4.26	1.86	0.65	0.96	0.68	0.11
0.62	2.40	0.98	1.20	0.22	4.61	0.83	0.52	0.85	1.58	0.83
5.49	35.50	15.41	9.05	11.04	85.42	27.93	12.49	12.51	19.43	13.05
3.20	20.53	8.94	5.43	6.16	51.06	16.16	8.14	8.62	8.16	9.98
11.25	60.50	25.51	17.54	17.45	140.36	42.66	21.72	23.65	26.84	25.48
1.92	4.78	1.94	1.92	0.92	6.49	2.96	0.72	1.59	1.14	0.09
1.07	4.85	2.32	2.10	0.42	10.31	2.42	1.70	1.32	1.97	2.90
4.93	32.74	14.04	8.49	10.21	78.96	25.02	12.51	12.49	14.19	14.76
2.10	12.82	5.25	3.72	3.86	30.50	8.41	5.13	5.31	5.85	5.79
44.02	236.24	101.67	67.63	66.95	614.24	227.07	86.66	92.00	105.75	102.76
7.29	16.08	6.54	6.98	2.56	22.70	10.41	2.81	5.48	3.80	0.20
3.16	14.00	6.67	6.04	1.29	26.04	5.96	3.81	4.01	6.06	6.20
15.56	99.52	42.48	25.90	31.14	244.38	77.79	38.42	36.96	46.25	44.96
14.99	92.42	40.15	25.18	27.08	227.98	64.62	38.11	38.44	40.43	46.38
2.46	13.40	5.54	3.87	3.99	28.92	8.78	4.48	4.63	6.40	4.62
0.41	0.89	0.36	0.38	0.14	1.30	0.56	0.17	0.30	0.22	0.05
0.06	0.27	0.09	0.11	0.07	0.58	0.15	0.04	0.09	0.11	0.19
0.99	6.40	2.65	1.71	2.04	12.97	3.88	2.03	1.94	3.08	2.04
0.85	5.20	2.12	1.50	1.58	12.97	3.87	2.05	2.10	2.66	2.29
204	1213	453	333	427	3612	630	867	339	998	778
5.04	30.96	12.36	9.87	8.72	67.67	18.89	12.69	11.29	15.38	9.43
2.60	2.87	1.13	1.66	0.08	5.04	2.90	0.37	0.86	0.86	0.05

指 标	Item	苏南合计 Southern Jiangsu Total	南京 Nanjing Municipality	无锡 Wuxi Municipality	常州 Changzhou Municipality	苏州 Suzhou Municipality
科技、文化、卫生	**Science, Culture and Public Health**					
各类专业技术人员（万人）	Number of Scientific and Technical Personnel (10000 persons)	192.48	62.78	39.41	24.43	53.16
#中级技术职称以上	Personnel with Medium and above Titles	59.48	19.54	14.54	8.09	12.27
公共图书馆（个）	Public Libraries (unit)	48	18	9	4	10
公共图书馆藏书量（千册,件）	Total Collections of Public Libraries (10000 volumes)	22728	11868	2492	2015	4874
卫生机构数（个）	Number of Health Institutions (unit)	8100	2085	2176	586	2285
#医院	Hospitals	395	159	60	34	109
卫生院	Commune Hospitals	363	38	86	74	96
疾病预防控制中心（防疫站）	Sanitation and Antiepidemic Agencies	71	21	11	8	24
妇幼保健院（所、站）	Maternity and Child Care Centers	41	14	5	9	7
卫生机构床位数（万张）	Number of Beds in Health Institutions (10000 units)	9.86	2.70	2.10	1.32	2.89
#医院	Hospital	6.92	2.01	1.33	0.89	2.12
卫生院	Commune Hospitals	1.78	0.09	0.48	0.37	0.58
卫生技术人员（万人）	Number of Medical and Technical Personnel (10000 persons)	13.20	3.69	2.58	1.84	3.70
#医院、卫生院	Hospitals and Commune Hospitals	9.40	2.36	1.81	1.54	2.69
#执业(助理)医师	Practitioner (Assistant) Doctors	5.34	1.52	1.07	0.71	1.49
注册护士	Registered Nurses	4.31	1.26	0.83	0.61	1.18

Continued

镇江 Zhenjiang Municipality	苏中合计 Mid Jiangsu Total	南通 Nantong Municipality	扬州 Yangzhou Municipality	泰州 Taizhou Municipality	苏北合计 Northern Jiangsu Total	徐州 Xuzhou Municipality	连云港 Lianyungang Municipality	淮安 Huaian Municipality	盐城 Yancheng Municipality	宿迁 Suqian Municipality
12.70	63.21	28.16	18.42	16.63	85.60	26.53	15.17	11.95	19.94	12.01
5.04	25.53	8.85	7.04	9.64	28.26	9.65	4.96	3.98	6.24	3.43
7	22	10	7	5	36	7	7	7	9	6
1479	5415	2402	1906	1107	5589	1542	1046	1094	1429	478
968	3947	1931	1352	664	5096	1327	981	645	1339	804
33	148	45	59	44	522	116	60	44	113	189
69	541	271	142	128	613	111	106	137	148	111
7	35	9	20	6	48	14	10	9	10	5
6	20	7	8	5	46	14	8	8	11	5
0.85	4.83	2.27	1.37	1.19	6.64	2.03	0.96	1.14	1.59	0.92
0.58	2.69	1.15	0.86	0.67	4.84	1.50	0.65	0.77	1.02	0.90
0.25	1.95	1.02	0.44	0.49	1.61	0.48	0.25	0.35	0.54	0.00
1.39	5.86	2.57	1.65	1.64	8.64	2.89	1.25	1.40	2.09	1.01
1.01	4.77	2.09	1.27	1.40	7.07	2.51	0.96	1.16	1.60	0.84
0.55	2.68	1.18	0.76	0.74	3.50	1.07	0.55	0.56	0.92	0.41
0.42	1.69	0.74	0.51	0.44	2.63	0.87	0.43	0.46	0.54	0.34

指标	Item	苏南合计 Southern Jiangsu Total	南京 Nanjing Municipality	无锡 Wuxi Municipality	常州 Changzhou Municipality	苏州 Suzhou Municipality
人民生活	**People's Livelihood**					
在岗职工工资总额（亿元）	Total Wages of Fully-Employed Staff and Workers (100 million yuan)	917.01	299.60	151.67	92.84	301.95
在岗职工平均工资（元）	Average Wage of Fully-Employed Staff and Workers (yuan)	28914	32459	29658	26553	28010
#国有单位	State-owned Units	37475	36853	38537	36036	45093
城镇集体单位	Collective Owned Units in Urban Areas	20810	18270	21667	25643	27041
港澳台投资单位	Units Funded by Entrepreneurs from Hong Kong, Macao and Taiwan	19690	17714	24024	17262	20638
外商投资单位	Foreign-funded Economic Units	24201	25946	26284	20631	23766
城镇居民人均可支配收入（元）	Per Capita Disposable Income of Urban Households (yuan)	17391	17538	18189	16650	18532
城镇居民人均消费支出（元）	Per Capita Living Expenditure for Consumption of Urban Households (yuan)	11876	12234	11372	12503	12472
#食品支出	Expenditure for Food	4239	4145	4360	4467	4502
恩格尔系数（城镇）(%)	Engle coefficient (Urban, %)	35.7	33.9	38.3	35.7	36.1
农村居民人均纯收入（元）	Per Capita Net Income of Rural Households (yuan)	8221	7045	8880	8001	9278
农村居民人均生活费支出（元）	Per Capita Living Expenditure for Consumption of Rural Households (yuan)	6233	5530	6515	6518	6811
#食品支出	Expenditure for Food	2314	2135	2309	2460	2473
恩格尔系数（农村）(%)	Engle coeppicient (Rural, %)	37.1	38.6	35.5	37.7	36.3
居民人均储蓄存款（元）	Per Capita Saving Deposits of Residents (yuan)	32317	30217	36032	28590	39401
城镇居民人均住房建筑面积（平方米）	Per Capita Residential Space of Urban Residents (sq. m)	29.5	25.2	27.1	28.7	29.8
农村居民人均住房面积（平方米）	Per Capita Residential Space of Rural Residents (sq. m)	56.1	44.7	58.3	58.3	65.3
居民消费价格指数（上年＝100）	Consumer Price Indices (preceding year＝100)		101.7	101.7	101.8	101.6

Continued

镇 江 Zhenjiang Municipality	苏中合计 Mid Jiangsu Total	南 通 Nantong Municipality	扬 州 Yangzhou Municipality	泰 州 Taizhou Municipality	苏北合计 Northern Jiangsu Total	徐 州 Xuzhou Municipality	连云港 Lianyungang Municipality	淮 安 Huaian Municipality	盐 城 Yancheng Municipality	宿 迁 Suqian Municipality
70.95	241.63	117.40	72.33	51.90	326.23	125.10	51.22	51.78	72.47	25.67
22924	20326	21662	20847	17309	17961	21897	17760	16590	15690	14053
28113	26672	29305	26073	23672	20815	23639	19683	20015	19665	16145
14887	13753	16456	12131	12661	11197	11058	11700	10332	13074	7937
14815	14894	16109	13964	12275	11749	16602	12416	9785	10420	10023
22999	16414	17684	13797	12736	14437	19155	15284	14711	12483	8641
14291	13263	14058	12945	12682	11799	12837	11475	10447	12052	8172
9196	8629	9332	8273	8184	7881	8621	8324	7077	7378	4976
3664	3407	3425	3352	3436	2833	2928	2884	2822	2789	2216
39.8	39.5	36.7	40.5	42.0	35.9	34.0	34.7	39.9	37.8	44.5
6717	5915	6106	5813	5695	4733	4896	4265	4430	5393	4228
5068	4235	4313	4314	4046	3046	3220	2797	2885	3260	2824
2020	1640	1659	1728	1538	1335	1320	1266	1299	1413	1339
39.9	38.7	38.5	40.1	38.0	43.8	41.0	45.3	45.0	43.3	47.4
19411	15114	17510	14729	11804	6455	7734	5879	5424	7947	3490
28.1	33.0	29.4	32.4	32.4	28.5	23.9	31.4	28.7	25.3	36.8
44.6	45.0	50.1	38.8	42.0	30.2	32.2	26.0	30.4	34.0	24.9
101.7		101.7	101.5	101.3		101.5	101.4	101.4	101.0	101.6

19－3 江苏沿江八市主要指标占长江三角洲比重（2006年）
PROPORTION OF MAIN INDICATORS OF EIGHT CITIES ALONG THE RIVER IN YANGTZE RIVER DELTA（2006）

指　标	Item	长江三角洲 Yangtze River Delta	江苏沿江八市 Eight Cities Along the Yangtze River	江苏沿江八市占长江三角洲比重（%） Proportion of Eight Cities in Yangtze River Delta（%）
年末总人口（万人）	Year－end Total Population（10000 persons）	8321.6	4036.6	48.5
土地面积（万平方公里）	Land Area（10000 sq. km）	11.0	4.9	44.2
地区生产总值（亿元）	Gross Domestic Product（100 million yuan）	39531.7	17346.4	43.9
第一产业	Primary Industry	1471.1	685.9	46.6
第二产业	Secondary Industry	21734.8	10238.0	47.1
#工业	Industry	19786.1	9308.1	47.0
第三产业	Tertiary Industry	16325.8	6422.5	39.3
农林牧渔业总产值（亿元）	Gross Output Value of Farming, Forestry Animal Husbandry and Fishery（100 million yuan）	2560.7	1163.7	45.4
粮食产量（万吨）	Output of Grain（10000 tons）	1991.9	1272.5	63.9
水产品产量（万吨）	Output of Aquatic Products（10000 tons）	624.4	172.6	27.6
规模以上工业总产值（亿元）	Gross Industrial Output Value of Over Scale Enterprises（100 million yuan）	77312.8	35775.1	46.3
城镇固定资产投资（亿元）	Urban Investment in Fixed Assets（100 million yuan）	14655.4	5744.0	39.2
#房地产开发投资	Investment in Real Estate Development	4076.5	1592.0	39.1
社会消费品零售总额（亿元）	Total Retail Sales of Consumer Goods（100 million yuan）	12351.8	5226.8	42.3
进出口总额（亿美元）	Total Imports and Exports（USD 100 million）	6257.3	2763.6	44.2
#出口	Exports	3553.7	1558.0	43.8
实际外商直接投资（亿美元）	Actual Foreign Direct Investment（USD 100 million）	315.6	163.5	51.8
地方财政一般预算收入（亿元）	General Budgetary Revenue in Local Finance（100 million yuan）	3758.6	1263.2	33.6
地方财政一般预算支出（亿元）	General Budgetary Expenditure in Local Finance（100 million yuan）	4073.1	1310.9	32.2
金融机构存款余额（亿元）	Deposits Balance of Banking Institutions（100 million yuan）	67797.0	22427.5	33.1
#居民储蓄存款	Saving Deposits of Residents	27117.0	10065.5	37.1
金融机构贷款余额（亿元）	Loans Balance of Banking Institutions（100 million yuan）	50421.4	16531.7	32.8

19－4　沿江开发区域主要指标占全省比重（2006年）
PROPORTION OF MAIN INDICATORS OF DEVELOPMENT ZONES ALONG THE YANGTZE RIVER IN JIANGSU PROVINCE (2006)

指　　标	Item	全　省 Province	沿江开发区域 Development Zones Along the Yangtze River	沿江开发区域占全省比重（%） Proportion of Development Zones Along the Yangtze River in Jiangsu Province（%）
年末总人口（万人）	Year－end Total Population (10000 persons)	7317.72	2485.53	34.0
土地面积（万平方公里）	Land Area (10000 sq. km)	10.26	2.46	24.0
地区生产总值（亿元）	Gross Domestic Product (100 million yuan)	21645.08	10658.89	49.2
第一产业	Primary Industry	1545.01	382.99	24.8
第二产业	Secondary Industry	12250.84	6190.49	50.5
#工业	Industry	11110.24	5609.78	50.5
第三产业	Tertiary Industry	7849.23	4085.41	52.0
农林牧渔业总产值（亿元）	Gross Output Value of Farming, Forestry Animal Husbandry and Fishery (100 million yuan)	2707.06	700.42	25.9
规模以上工业总产值（亿元）	Gross Industrial Output Value of Over Scale Enterprises (100 million yuan)	41410.40	20720.93	50.0
#制造业	Manufacturing	39153.82	20055.89	51.2
城镇固定资产投资额（亿元）	Urban Investment in Fixed Assets (100 million yuan)	7481.80	3433.98	45.9
#房地产开发投资	Real Estate avelopment	1906.71	884.94	46.4
社会消费品零售总额（亿元）	Total Retail Sales of Consumer Goods (100 million yuan)	6623.18	3245.37	49.0
进出口总额（亿美元）	Total Imports and Exports (USD 100 million)	2839.95	919.80	32.4
#出口	Exports	1604.19	538.88	33.6
实际外商直接投资（亿美元）	Actual Foreign Direct Investment (USD 100 million)	173.04	87.48	50.6
地方财政一般预算收入（亿元）	General Budgetary Revenue in Local Finance (100 million yuan)	1656.68	767.00	46.3
地方财政一般预算支出（亿元）	General Budgetary Expenditure in Local Finance (100 million yuan)	2013.25	790.23	39.3
金融机构存款余额（亿元）	Deposits Balance of Banking Institutions (100 million yuan)	25860.47	14226.29	55.0
#居民储蓄存款	Saving Deposits of Residents	12183.47	6260.64	51.4
金融机构贷款余额（亿元）	Loans Balance of Banking Institutions (100 million yuan)	18485.02	10877.17	58.8

注：总人口为户籍人口。

Note: Total population is the household registered population

19－5　沿江开发区域主要指标（2006 年）

MAIN INDICATORS OF DEVELOPMENT ZONES ALONG THE YANGTZE RIVER (2006)

地　　区	Region	年末总人口（万人）Population (year-end) (10000 persons)	土地面积（平方公里）Land Area (sq. km)	人口密度（人/平方公里）Density of Population (person/sq. km)	从业人员（万人）Employed Persons (10000 persons)	#第二产业 Secondary Industry	#第三产业 Tertiary Industry
沿江合计	**Total**	**22485.53**	**24642**	**1009**	**1485.20**	**715.67**	**543.00**
南京市区	Nanjing	524.64	4723	1111	280.79	116.10	139.95
江 阴 市	Jiangyin	119.45	988	1210	77.37	43.89	25.29
常州市区	Changzhou	222.48	1864	1194	176.78	98.44	63.42
常 熟 市	Changshu	105.48	1094	964	79.58	50.35	23.30
张家港市	Zhangjiagang	88.78	772	1150	59.00	35.04	17.33
太 仓 市	Taicang	46.14	620	744	33.35	20.72	7.81
南通市区	Nantong	86.64	355	2441	46.69	21.30	21.70
启 东 市	Qidong	112.44	1208	931	76.62	28.99	25.70
如 皋 市	Rugao	141.85	1492	951	72.68	30.09	23.66
通 州 市	Tongzhou	125.64	1166	1078	74.76	33.09	23.72
海 门 市	Haimen	101.05	939	1076	62.57	27.06	18.75
扬州市区	Yangzhou	116.82	980	1192	66.31	32.59	27.87
仪 征 市	Yizheng	59.70	901	663	35.54	17.69	11.83
江 都 市	Jiangdu	106.85	1330	803	49.74	23.08	16.56
镇江市区	Zhenjiang	102.72	1082	950	55.94	25.79	21.30
丹 阳 市	Danyang	80.61	1047	770	49.71	26.59	12.18
扬 中 市	Yangzhong	27.39	331	828	16.23	9.30	3.89
句 容 市	Jurong	58.07	1387	419	31.30	13.28	8.27
泰州市区	Taizhou	64.25	444	1446	37.29	18.65	14.29
靖 江 市	Jingjiang	66.47	665	1000	35.58	16.19	12.75
泰 兴 市	Taixing	128.05	1254	1021	67.36	27.44	23.44

地　　区	Region	地区生产总值（亿元）Gross Domectic Product (100 million yuan)	第一产业 Primary Industry	第二产业 Seconary Industry	#工　业 Industry	第三产业 Tertiary Industry	人均地区生产总值（元）Per Capita GDP (yuan)
沿江合计	**Total**	**10658.89**	**382.99**	**6190.49**	**5609.78**	**4085.41**	**43054**
南京市区	Nanjing	2559.00	56.12	1242.63	1085.91	1260.25	49305
江 阴 市	Jiangyin	980.17	17.16	620.45	596.45	342.56	82346
常州市区	Changzhou	1185.17	28.24	735.14	686.06	421.79	53475
常 熟 市	Changshu	809.28	17.49	484.26	462.64	307.54	76979
张家港市	Zhangjiagang	841.62	12.48	545.69	529.36	283.45	95271
太 仓 市	Taicang	366.63	15.63	223.05	204.18	127.95	79789
南通市区	Nantong	455.36	4.87	272.76	234.36	177.73	52955
启 东 市	Qidong	238.59	35.06	124.73	97.32	78.80	21178
如 皋 市	Rugao	180.27	24.75	94.13	76.94	61.39	12701
通 州 市	Tongzhou	270.58	24.46	161.17	136.74	84.95	21483
海 门 市	Haimen	261.09	23.65	153.36	128.94	84.08	25797
扬州市区	Yangzhou	506.38	13.20	298.22	272.01	194.96	43563
仪 征 市	Yizheng	130.10	8.55	86.09	75.32	35.46	21862
江 都 市	Jiangdu	230.20	21.28	142.02	122.22	66.90	21577
镇江市区	Zhenjiang	455.77	9.44	279.51	249.69	166.82	44526
丹 阳 市	Danyang	300.24	16.40	176.84	167.38	107.00	37318
扬 中 市	Yangzhong	125.05	3.93	76.32	68.81	44.80	45747
句 容 市	Jurong	124.30	11.76	74.04	69.80	38.50	21413
泰州市区	Taizhou	270.12	5.44	189.00	167.98	75.68	42329
靖 江 市	Jingjiang	161.89	9.07	93.83	82.88	58.99	24407
泰 兴 市	Taixing	207.08	24.01	117.25	94.79	65.82	16167

19－5 续表2 Continued

地区	Region	三次产业占GDP比重(%) Percentage of Three Industries to GDP(%) 第一产业 Primary Industry	第二产业 Seconary Industry	#工业 Industry	第三产业 Tertiary Industry	地方财政一般预算收入占GDP比重(%) Percentage of General Budgetary Revenue in Local Finance to GDP(%)	外贸依存度(%) Interdependent Level to Foreign Trade (%)
沿江合计	**Total**	**3.6**	**58.1**	**52.6**	**38.3**	**7.2**	**68.8**
南京市区	Nanjing	2.2	48.6	42.4	49.2	9.2	97.4
江阴市	Jiangyin	1.8	63.3	60.9	34.9	6.2	68.4
常州市区	Changzhou	2.4	62.0	57.9	35.6	8.3	64.1
常熟市	Changshu	2.2	59.8	57.2	38.0	5.3	61.7
张家港市	Zhangjiagang	1.5	64.8	62.9	33.7	7.3	119.2
太仓市	Taicang	4.3	60.8	55.7	34.9	7.5	102.0
南通市区	Nantong	1.1	59.9	51.5	39.0	9.3	114.6
启东市	Qidong	14.7	52.3	40.8	33.0	3.9	14.3
如皋市	Rugao	13.7	52.2	42.7	34.1	4.2	23.9
通州市	Tongzhou	9.0	59.6	50.5	31.4	3.9	32.1
海门市	Haimen	9.1	58.7	49.4	32.2	3.7	17.7
扬州市区	Yangzhou	2.6	58.9	53.7	38.5	7.2	38.5
仪征市	Yizheng	6.6	66.2	57.9	27.3	6.2	13.4
江都市	Jiangdu	9.2	61.7	53.1	29.1	4.0	9.8
镇江市区	Zhenjiang	2.1	61.3	54.8	36.6	7.8	60.5
丹阳市	Danyang	5.5	58.9	55.7	35.6	4.4	18.1
扬中市	Yangzhong	3.1	61.0	55.0	35.8	4.8	10.4
句容市	Jurong	9.5	59.6	56.2	31.0	4.3	28.5
泰州市区	Taizhou	2.0	70.0	62.2	28.0	9.2	35.7
靖江市	Jingjiang	5.6	58.0	51.2	36.4	6.9	32.4
泰兴市	Taixing	11.6	56.6	45.8	31.8	5.3	19.1

19－5　续表3　Continued

地　　区	Region	规模以上工业企业个数（个）Number of Over Scale Industrial Enterprises (unit)	从业人员平均人数（万人）Average Number of Employees (10000 persons)	工业总产值（亿元）Total Output Value of Industry (100 million yuan)	#制造业 Manufacturing	主营业务收入（亿元）Major Business Revenue (100 million yuan)	利税总额（亿元）Total Pre-tax Profits (100 million yuan)
沿江合计	**Total**	**17335**	**350.76**	**20720.93**	**20055.89**	**20494.93**	**1654.75**
南京市区	Nanjing	1605	50.05	4389.05	4269.02	4427.38	389.17
江阴市	Jiangyin	1065	36.83	2640.98	2582.10	2606.75	209.64
常州市区	Changzhou	3421	51.12	2648.25	2607.45	2642.81	168.78
常熟市	Changshu	1536	31.51	1558.27	1502.44	1520.92	116.81
张家港市	Zhangjiagang	830	29.91	2049.92	2028.30	2069.33	142.98
太仓市	Taicang	746	15.41	696.83	609.68	693.67	59.41
南通市区	Nantong	939	14.63	740.00	687.88	733.24	70.57
启东市	Qidong	531	5.80	304.19	303.06	300.45	24.86
如皋市	Rugao	546	7.18	297.63	297.13	295.69	16.48
通州市	Tongzhou	737	9.81	538.68	536.55	529.57	51.16
海门市	Haimen	462	6.32	487.14	483.62	482.91	42.84
扬州市区	Yangzhou	793	19.47	812.15	700.94	779.09	100.34
仪征市	Yizheng	310	5.61	312.20	310.73	307.20	8.80
江都市	Jiangdu	568	8.83	438.10	437.96	403.78	25.91
镇江市区	Zhenjiang	595	11.44	731.82	646.45	734.13	69.03
丹阳市	Danyang	722	14.26	467.78	466.01	433.74	27.94
扬中市	Yangzhong	330	5.38	204.08	203.52	192.96	18.71
句容市	Jurong	314	5.73	225.11	214.02	215.10	14.53
泰州市区	Taizhou	414	8.32	579.26	577.36	577.70	46.93
靖江市	Jingjiang	441	6.59	307.38	304.71	280.46	24.28
泰兴市	Taixing	430	6.55	292.12	286.96	268.05	25.59

地　区	Region	城镇固定资产投资(亿元) Urban Investment in Fixed Assets (100 million yuan)	#房地产开发 Real Estate Development	社会消费品零售总额(亿元) Total Retail Sales of Consumer Goods (100 million yuan)	进出口总额(亿美元) Total Imports and Exports (USD 100 million)	#出　口 Exports	实际外商直接投资(亿美元) Actual Direct Foreign Investment (USD 100 million)
沿江合计	**Total**	**3433.98**	**884.94**	**3245.37**	**919.80**	**538.88**	**87.48**
南京市区	Nanjing	1169.26	338.00	1095.30	312.60	171.21	16.39
江 阴 市	Jiangyin	143.49	41.20	201.25	84.05	45.71	3.94
常州市区	Changzhou	501.96	140.39	382.54	95.27	70.89	10.11
常 熟 市	Changshu	138.93	41.07	176.72	62.65	42.02	6.43
张家港市	Zhangjiagang	122.30	35.40	112.17	125.89	54.87	4.48
太 仓 市	Taicang	144.26	20.96	55.54	46.90	23.62	4.42
南通市区	Nantong	197.35	53.87	140.83	65.48	42.09	4.51
启 东 市	Qidong	58.42	11.60	84.16	4.28	3.80	4.24
如 皋 市	Rugao	36.41	7.65	83.98	5.41	4.49	3.26
通 州 市	Tongzhou	50.73	8.94	87.21	10.88	9.59	4.50
海 门 市	Haimen	45.82	8.97	87.11	5.79	4.79	4.87
扬州市区	Yangzhou	201.89	43.58	164.04	24.46	18.16	4.49
仪 征 市	Yizheng	49.06	7.87	44.64	2.19	0.85	1.26
江 都 市	Jiangdu	51.16	14.86	67.77	2.82	2.14	1.04
镇江市区	Zhenjiang	224.72	40.45	134.13	34.61	16.37	4.00
丹 阳 市	Danyang	41.08	12.35	75.49	6.81	5.56	1.67
扬 中 市	Yangzhong	13.28	6.41	34.57	1.64	0.99	0.83
句 容 市	Jurong	20.94	8.22	35.88	4.45	3.48	0.80
泰州市区	Taizhou	132.20	26.37	76.16	12.08	9.25	2.90
靖 江 市	Jingjiang	45.31	9.21	47.24	6.58	5.80	2.00
泰 兴 市	Taixing	45.38	7.58	58.65	4.95	3.19	1.33

19－5　续表5　Continued

单位:亿元　(100 million yuan)

地　　区	Region	地方财政一般预算收入 General Budgetary Revenue in Local Finance	#各项税收 Taxes	地方财政一般预算支出 General Budgetary Expenditure in Local Finance	年末金融机构存款余额 Deposits Balance of Banking Institutions (year－end)	#城乡居民储蓄存款 Savings Deposits by Residents	年末金融机构贷款余额 Loans Balance of Banking Institutions (year－end)
沿江合计	**Total**	**767.00**	**645.99**	**790.23**	**14226.29**	**6260.64**	**10877.17**
南京市区	Nanjing	235.97	208.27	247.42	5698.05	1768.03	5035.06
江阴市	Jiangyin	60.48	47.26	55.42	845.06	338.34	739.43
常州市区	Changzhou	98.45	85.53	94.57	1644.73	790.38	1164.62
常熟市	Changshu	43.08	38.15	42.10	776.85	420.74	486.32
张家港市	Zhangjiagang	61.09	48.27	55.61	729.09	316.30	600.70
太仓市	Taicang	27.59	24.54	25.83	324.93	151.69	264.77
南通市区	Nantong	42.50	36.69	41.58	785.16	333.45	572.22
启东市	Qidong	9.24	7.90	12.44	226.46	186.72	106.74
如皋市	Rugao	7.51	6.56	13.09	205.55	153.64	94.63
通州市	Tongzhou	10.57	8.98	13.14	264.88	196.03	131.79
海门市	Haimen	9.62	8.01	11.33	247.46	189.32	119.26
扬州市区	Yangzhou	36.53	28.78	38.68	538.51	270.25	369.78
仪征市	Yizheng	8.11	6.79	8.57	119.04	74.79	64.69
江都市	Jiangdu	9.16	7.20	10.88	233.66	176.90	79.69
镇江市区	Zhenjiang	35.48	27.28	36.93	483.37	236.30	378.07
丹阳市	Danyang	13.29	10.44	14.02	234.18	151.18	168.21
扬中市	Yangzhong	5.99	5.07	6.60	121.38	76.94	70.99
句容市	Jurong	5.36	4.08	7.53	89.27	57.35	50.76
泰州市区	Taizhou	24.90	19.52	28.85	312.16	136.21	211.27
靖江市	Jingjiang	11.20	8.48	11.11	186.66	118.67	89.13
泰兴市	Taixing	10.89	8.19	14.54	159.86	117.43	79.05

19－5　续表 6　Continued

地　区	Region	公路里程（公里）Total Length of Highways (km)	民用汽车拥有量（万辆）Number of Civil Motor Vehicles Owned (10000 units)	公路客运量（万人）Passenger Traffic (10000 persons)	公路货运量（万吨）Freight Traffic (10000 tons)	邮电业务总量（亿元）Total Volume of Post and Telecommunication (100 million yuan)	全社会用电量（亿千瓦时）Total Consumption of Electricity (100 million kWh)
沿江合计	**Total**	**39580**	**119.24**	**70436**	**37448**	**278.76**	**1245.06**
南京市区	Nanjing	7132	35.73	19412	10336	88.99	260.23
江阴市	Jiangyin	1925	8.61	4050	2300	15.20	153.37
常州市区	Changzhou	2713	16.61	10537	3942	31.47	165.41
常熟市	Changshu	1952	7.89	4365	1059	13.91	78.46
张家港市	Zhangjiagang	1285	6.72	3485	1658	12.07	171.27
太仓市	Taicang	963	3.79	1975	848	6.94	47.52
南通市区	Nantong	571	6.15	6063	3845	13.57	61.05
启东市	Qidong	2513	2.11	912	450	4.98	11.38
如皋市	Rugao	2727	1.94	719	1044	5.42	18.98
通州市	Tongzhou	1929	2.27	292	881	5.38	20.24
海门市	Haimen	1974	2.00	781	836	4.77	17.57
扬州市区	Yangzhou	1681	5.73	4297	1980	11.75	36.63
仪征市	Yizheng	1395	1.26	663	784	2.84	12.73
江都市	Jiangdu	1941	1.86	2373	1164	5.69	14.15
镇江市区	Zhenjiang	1281	4.83	4151	2779	12.77	62.68
丹阳市	Danyang	1614	2.74	1585	1127	6.81	30.72
扬中市	Yangzhong	432	1.10	749	301	2.63	5.61
句容市	Jurong	1854	1.17	956	744	2.82	11.52
泰州市区	Taizhou	1013	2.70	1188	478	11.17	27.62
靖江市	Jingjiang	859	1.93	706	364	9.28	20.52
泰兴市	Taixing	1827	2.10	1177	528	10.30	17.38

19－5　续 表 7　Continued

地　区	Region	各类专业技术人员（万人）Number of Scientific and Technical Personnel (10000 persons)	中专以上在校生数（万人）Number of Students Enrolled in Above Secondary Specialized Shools (10000 persons)	公共图书馆图书藏量（千册）Total Volume of Collections of Public Libraries (1000 volumes)	卫生技术人员（万人）Number of Medical and Technical Personnel (10000 persons)	工业废水排放达标量（万吨）Valume of Industrial Was Water Emission Standiardized (10000 tons)	"三废"综合利用产品产值（万元）Output Value of Products Made from Comprehensive Utilization of "three wastes" (100 million yuan)
沿江合计	**Total**	**169.35**	**120.90**	**21715**	**12.23**	**155981**	**78.55**
南京市区	Nanjing	57.00	63.49	11462	3.46	36905	16.59
江 阴 市	Jiangyin	8.65	1.09	534	0.56	23062	1.51
常州市区	Changzhou	19.38	15.09	1670	1.30	20937	19.46
常 熟 市	Changshu	7.51	1.65	1353	0.51	9882	0.57
张家港市	Zhangjiagang	6.95	0.90	477	0.45	15103	27.81
太 仓 市	Taicang	3.36	0.62	246	0.26	4672	0.36
南通市区	Nantong	6.91	10.51	1023	0.73	5960	3.51
启 东 市	Qidong	4.27	0.55	196	0.26	2694	0.02
如 皋 市	Rugao	3.22	0.19	177	0.34	1313	0.12
通 州 市	Tongzhou	4.71	1.07	378	0.36	1089	0.06
海 门 市	Haimen	3.66	0.34	216	0.32	1067	0.49
扬州市区	Yangzhou	6.71	9.99	1221	0.63	5694	1.72
仪 征 市	Yizheng	2.66	0.34	218	0.20	3642	0.18
江 都 市	Jiangdu	3.76	0.77	245	0.41	871	0.00
镇江市区	Zhenjiang	6.43	9.66	952	0.66	6935	2.29
丹 阳 市	Danyang	2.75	0.53	222	0.35	1501	0.84
扬 中 市	Yangzhong	1.38	0.00	218	0.17	186	0.06
句 容 市	Jurong	1.67	0.26	87	0.21	1409	0.01
泰州市区	Taizhou	8.17	3.27	420	0.28	1049	1.64
靖 江 市	Jingjiang	3.87	0.00	250	0.34	3680	0.19
泰 兴 市	Taixing	6.32	0.59	151	0.42	8328	1.14

19-6 沿海地带主要指标（2006年）
MAIN INDCATORS OF THE COASTAL REGIONS(2006)

地 区	Region	年末总人口（万人）Population (year-end) (10000 persons)	土地面积（平方公里）Land Area (sq. km)	人口密度（人/平方公里）Density of Population (person/sq. km)	从业人员（万人）Employed Persons (10000 persons)	#第二产业 Secondary Industry	#第三产业 Tertiary Industry
沿海合计	**Total**	**1723.89**	**28382**	**607**	**866.37**	**300.67**	**291.96**
南通市区	Nantong	86.64	355	2441	46.69	21.30	21.70
海安县	Haian	95.03	1108	858	54.98	23.68	15.79
如东县	Rudong	107.14	1733	618	61.14	26.77	20.92
启东市	Qidong	112.44	1208	931	76.62	28.99	25.70
通州市	Tongzhou	125.64	1166	1078	74.76	33.09	23.72
海门市	Haimen	101.05	939	1076	62.57	27.06	18.75
连云港市区	Lianyungang	70.96	943	752	46.02	17.35	23.08
赣榆县	Ganyu	108.18	1427	758	52.65	20.93	12.41
东海县	Donghai	117.34	2250	521	57.41	15.37	15.44
灌云县	Guanyun	107.50	1852	580	48.09	10.52	13.79
灌南县	Guannan	75.45	1027	735	37.57	7.53	10.08
盐城市区	Yancheng	152.64	1720	887	66.95	22.39	26.87
响水县	Xiangshui	59.55	1461	408	18.66	3.67	9.90
滨海县	Binhai	111.28	1915	581	35.88	6.51	14.04
射阳县	Sheyang	104.79	2997	350	37.92	9.25	12.47
东台市	Dongtai	115.35	3221	358	52.25	15.68	16.66
大丰市	Dafeng	72.92	3059	238	36.21	10.58	10.63

19－6 续表1 Continued

地 区	Region	地区生产总值（亿元）Gross Domectic Product (100 million yuan)	第一产业 Primary Industry	第二产业 Seconary Industry	#工 业 Industry	第三产业 Tertiary Industry	人均地区生产总值（元）Per Capita GDP (yuan)
沿海合计	**Total**	**3062.49**	**438.30**	**1570.09**	**1301.07**	**1054.10**	**17823**
南通市区	Nantong	455.36	4.87	272.76	234.36	177.73	52955
海安县	Haian	177.42	25.17	91.98	73.31	60.27	18640
如东县	Rudong	175.02	30.10	86.88	67.41	58.04	16295
启东市	Qidong	238.59	35.06	124.73	97.32	78.80	21178
通州市	Tongzhou	270.58	24.46	161.17	136.74	84.95	21483
海门市	Haimen	261.09	23.65	153.36	128.94	84.08	25797
连云港市区	Lianyungang	237.87	13.25	126.74	95.15	97.88	33710
赣榆县	Ganyu	91.82	23.95	37.28	31.24	30.59	8507
东海县	Donghai	92.73	26.88	36.08	30.08	29.77	7974
灌云县	Guanyun	55.93	18.30	21.28	15.84	16.35	5263
灌南县	Guannan	49.03	13.88	20.17	16.05	14.98	6561
盐城市区	Yancheng	323.31	37.02	165.10	139.65	121.18	21226
响水县	Xiangshui	54.13	15.40	23.28	19.93	15.45	9229
滨海县	Binhai	93.30	25.32	38.62	32.34	29.36	8469
射阳县	Sheyang	142.13	40.41	57.75	51.94	43.97	13591
东台市	Dongtai	194.73	44.03	88.10	76.65	62.60	16864
大丰市	Dafeng	149.45	36.55	64.80	54.12	48.10	20491

19－6　续表2　Continued

地　　区　Region		三次产业占GDP比重(%) Percentage of Three Industries to GDP (%)				地方财政一般预算收入占GDP的比重 Percentage of General Budgetary Revenue in Local Finance to GDP(%)	外贸依存度(%) Interdependent Level to Foreign Trade (%)
		第一产业 Primary Industry	第二产业 Seconary Industry	#工　业 Industry	第三产业 Tertiary Industry		
沿海合计	**Total**	**14.3**	**51.3**	**42.5**	**34.4**	**5.2**	**36.1**
南通市区	Nantong	1.1	59.9	51.5	39.0	9.3	114.6
海安县	Haian	14.2	51.8	41.3	34.0	3.9	17.2
如东县	Rudong	17.2	49.6	38.5	33.2	3.5	22.5
启东市	Qidong	14.7	52.3	40.8	33.0	3.9	14.3
通州市	Tongzhou	9.0	59.6	50.5	31.4	3.9	32.1
海门市	Haimen	9.1	58.7	49.4	32.2	3.7	17.7
连云港市区	Lianyungang	5.6	53.3	40.0	41.1	8.8	83.9
赣榆县	Ganyu	26.1	40.6	34.0	33.3	4.4	3.1
东海县	Donghai	29.0	38.9	32.4	32.1	4.3	10.2
灌云县	Guanyun	32.7	38.0	28.3	29.2	4.2	3.3
灌南县	Guannan	28.3	41.1	32.7	30.6	5.3	5.2
盐城市区	Yancheng	11.5	51.1	43.2	37.5	5.8	26.6
响水县	Xiangshui	28.4	43.0	36.8	28.5	4.1	9.1
滨海县	Binhai	27.1	41.4	34.7	31.5	3.3	1.8
射阳县	Sheyang	28.4	40.6	36.5	30.9	3.3	3.9
东台市	Dongtai	22.6	45.2	39.4	32.1	3.4	10.0
大丰市	Dafeng	24.5	43.4	36.2	32.2	3.4	8.0

19－6　续表3　Continued

地　区	Region	规模以上工业企业个数（个）Number of Over Scale Industrial Enterprises (unit)	从业人员平均人数（万人）Average Number of Employees (10000 persons)	工业总产值（亿元）Total Output Value of Industry (100 million yuan)	#制造业 Manufacturing	主营业务收入（亿元）Major Business Revenue (100 million yuan)	利税总额（亿元）Total Pre-tax Profits (100 million yuan)
沿海合计	**Total**	**6517**	**93.25**	**4228.11**	**4099.96**	**4159.75**	**351.62**
南通市区	Nantong	939	14.63	740.00	687.88	733.24	70.57
海安县	Haian	498	6.64	307.52	306.36	303.24	16.46
如东县	Rudong	504	6.62	274.36	272.46	274.46	18.95
启东市	Qidong	531	5.80	304.19	303.06	300.45	24.86
通州市	Tongzhou	737	9.81	538.68	536.55	529.57	51.16
海门市	Haimen	462	6.32	487.14	483.62	482.91	42.84
连云港市区	Lianyungang	270	5.62	283.33	256.68	276.21	30.67
赣榆县	Ganyu	175	2.20	54.65	50.77	53.21	3.40
东海县	Donghai	158	1.72	55.19	54.54	53.65	4.22
灌云县	Guanyun	122	1.57	29.20	29.07	28.24	2.21
灌南县	Guannan	113	1.19	40.88	40.83	39.03	2.89
盐城市区	Yancheng	573	11.71	481.43	455.27	471.34	34.70
响水县	Xiangshui	162	2.06	64.75	62.79	58.71	6.08
滨海县	Binhai	186	2.31	80.10	78.58	78.71	6.74
射阳县	Sheyang	258	3.46	153.27	150.47	148.31	9.87
东台市	Dongtai	478	6.32	195.50	194.33	192.13	17.00
大丰市	Dafeng	351	5.25	137.90	136.70	136.34	9.00

19－6 续表4 Continued

地 区	Region	城镇固定资产投资（亿元）Urban Investment in Fixed Assets (100 million yuan)	#房地产开发 Real Estate Development	社会消费品零售总额（亿元）Total Retail Sales of Consumer Goods (100 million yuan)	进出口总额（亿美元）Total Imports and Exports (USD 100 million)	#出 口 Exports	实际外商直接投资（亿美元）Actual Direct Foreign Investment (USD 100 million)
沿海合计	**Total**	**1051.05**	**213.85**	**1047.19**	**138.61**	**91.46**	**30.35**
南通市区	Nantong	197.35	53.87	140.83	65.48	42.09	4.51
海安县	Haian	60.76	11.49	65.29	3.83	3.19	2.85
如东县	Rudong	38.07	5.42	73.39	4.94	4.17	3.21
启东市	Qidong	58.42	11.60	84.16	4.28	3.80	4.24
通州市	Tongzhou	50.73	8.94	87.21	10.88	9.59	4.50
海门市	Haimen	45.82	8.97	87.11	5.79	4.79	4.87
连云港市区	Lianyungang	170.08	39.77	86.14	25.03	12.76	1.89
赣榆县	Ganyu	36.07	4.72	40.49	0.36	0.34	0.57
东海县	Donghai	29.92	4.76	36.96	1.19	0.95	0.45
灌云县	Guanyun	33.20	2.89	29.80	0.23	0.21	0.23
灌南县	Guannan	30.85	2.93	18.15	0.32	0.22	0.32
盐城市区	Yancheng	169.89	36.31	119.20	10.80	5.25	1.65
响水县	Xiangshui	24.49	1.42	13.91	0.62	0.38	0.00
滨海县	Binhai	15.13	3.03	25.29	0.21	0.17	0.06
射阳县	Sheyang	19.46	3.28	41.62	0.69	0.44	0.23
东台市	Dongtai	35.29	9.24	58.75	2.44	1.67	0.32
大丰市	Dafeng	35.53	5.22	38.91	1.51	1.44	0.45

19－6　续 表 5　Continued

单位:亿元　　(100 million yuan)

地　　区	Region	地方财政一般预算收入 General Budgetary Revenue in Locel Finance	#各项税收 Taxes	地方财政一般预算支出 General Budgetary Expenditure in Local Finance	年末金融机构存款余额 Deposits Balance of Banking Institutions (year－end)	#城乡居民储蓄存款 Savings Deposits by Residents	年末金融机构贷款余额 Loans Balance of Banking Institutions (year－end)
沿海合计	**Total**	**159.49**	**130.97**	**225.40**	**3189.35**	**1987.27**	**1889.41**
南通市区	Nantong	42.50	36.69	41.58	785.16	333.45	572.22
海安县	Haian	6.95	5.55	9.64	213.00	159.41	107.77
如东县	Rudong	6.16	5.13	11.40	171.42	129.31	79.33
启东市	Qidong	9.24	7.90	12.44	226.46	186.72	106.74
通州市	Tongzhou	10.57	8.98	13.14	264.88	196.03	131.79
海门市	Haimen	9.62	8.01	11.33	247.46	189.32	119.26
连云港市区	Lianyungang	21.01	17.53	24.88	309.93	140.34	224.56
赣榆县	Ganyu	4.00	2.81	9.95	59.26	43.99	33.01
东海县	Donghai	4.00	2.84	9.59	63.10	44.84	32.39
灌云县	Guanyun	2.33	1.79	6.79	45.75	32.76	23.63
灌南县	Guannan	2.62	1.95	6.43	28.05	19.91	12.30
盐城市区	Yancheng	18.81	15.58	26.37	337.25	180.15	227.43
响水县	Xiangshui	2.24	1.71	5.32	32.68	23.90	20.89
滨海县	Binhai	3.12	2.40	8.64	53.70	39.07	30.02
射阳县	Sheyang	4.67	3.40	9.14	83.31	65.27	53.84
东台市	Dongtai	6.66	5.00	10.46	161.31	123.97	62.97
大丰市	Dafeng	5.01	3.72	8.30	106.62	78.82	51.26

19－6　续表6　Continued

地　区	Region	公路里程（公里）Total Length of Highways (km)	民用汽车拥有量（万辆）Number of Civil Motor Vehicles Owned (10000 units)	公路客运量（万人）Passenger Traffic (10000 persons)	公路货运量（万吨）Freight Traffic (10000 tons)	邮电业务总量（亿元）Total Volume of Postal and Telecommunication (100 million yuan)	全社会用电量（亿千瓦时）Total Consumption of Electricity (100 million kWh)
沿海合计	**Total**	**34478**	**30.32**	**22159**	**15056**	**78.26**	**265.14**
南通市区	Nantong	571	6.15	6063	3845	13.57	61.05
海安县	Haian	2194	1.27	783	742	4.38	16.66
如东县	Rudong	2237	1.47	428	872	4.45	17.71
启东市	Qidong	2513	2.11	912	450	4.98	11.38
通州市	Tongzhou	1929	2.27	292	881	5.38	20.24
海门市	Haimen	1974	2.00	781	836	4.77	17.57
连云港市区	Lianyungang	834	2.96	2824	1185	8.23	23.98
赣榆县	Ganyu	2324	1.10	1429	1106	2.75	7.16
东海县	Donghai	2779	1.23	1378	1078	2.66	9.13
灌云县	Guanyun	2215	0.71	725	481	2.12	4.30
灌南县	Guannan	1204	0.48	703	436	1.62	3.97
盐城市区	Yancheng	1895	3.23	3236	1240	9.23	22.32
响水县	Xiangshui	1520	0.73	654	65	1.63	5.19
滨海县	Binhai	1836	1.40	239	726	2.37	6.28
射阳县	Sheyang	2450	0.90	248	116	3.13	9.60
东台市	Dongtai	3086	1.21	1030	735	3.64	16.29
大丰市	Dafeng	2917	1.08	434	262	3.33	12.30

19－6　续表7　Continued

地　区	Region	各类专业技术人员（万人）Number of Scientific and Technical Personnel (10000 persons)	中专以上在校生数（万人）Number of Students Enrolled in Above Secondary Specialized Schools (10000 persons)	公共图书馆图书藏量（千册）Total Volume of Collections of Public Libraries (1000 volumes)	卫生技术人员（万人）Number of Medical and Technical Personnel (10000 persons)	工业废水排放达标量（万吨）Valume of Industrial Was Water Emission Standiardized (10000 tons)	"三废"综合利用产品产值（万元）Output Value of Products Made from Comprehensive Utilization of "three wastes" (10000 yuan)
沿海合计	**Total**	**57.11**	**30.10**	**4486**	**5.19**	**24682**	**88258**
南通市区	Nantong	6.91	10.51	1023	0.73	5960	35057
海安县	Haian	3.09	0.77	268	0.28	1928	2546
如东县	Rudong	5.40	0.38	144	0.27	1325	3897
启东市	Qidong	4.27	0.55	196	0.26	2694	240
通州市	Tongzhou	4.71	1.07	378	0.36	1089	553
海门市	Haimen	3.66	0.34	216	0.32	1067	4916
连云港市区	Lianyungang	7.97	6.61	608	0.57	1753	6880
赣榆县	Ganyu	1.58		153	0.20	507	
东海县	Donghai	1.43		130	0.19	500	785
灌云县	Guanyun	1.29		67	0.16	938	260
灌南县	Guannan	0.83		89	0.13	81	10
盐城市区	Yancheng	7.82	9.40	590	0.61	1079	2435
响水县	Xiangshui	1.09		31	0.12	1087	210
滨海县	Binhai	1.34		94	0.27	897	
射阳县	Sheyang	1.73	0.46	147	0.21	390	4956
东台市	Dongtai	2.22		197	0.27	1673	17254
大丰市	Dafeng	1.78		156	0.23	1715	8260

19－7 沿东陇海线地区主要指标（2006 年）

MAIN INDICATORS OF THE EAST REGION ALONG THE LONG-HAI RAILWAY(2006)

地 区	Region	年末总人口（万人）Population (year-end) (10000 persons)	土地面积（平方公里）Land Area (sq. km)	人口密度（人/平方公里）Density of Population (person/sq. km)	从业人员（万人）Employed Persons (10000 persons)	#第二产业 Secondary Industry	#第三产业 Tertiary Industry
东陇海合计	**Total**	**755.14**	**9890**	**764**	**387.94**	**129.41**	**139.44**
徐州市区	Xuzhou	181.60	1160	1566	99.74	34.42	52.84
铜山县	Tongshan	120.72	1877	643	54.37	16.35	12.40
新沂市	Xinyi	99.06	1571	631	49.67	16.30	13.28
邳州市	Pizhou	165.46	2088	792	80.73	29.62	22.40
连云港市区	Lianyungang	70.96	943	752	46.02	17.35	23.08
东海县	Donghai	117.34	2250	521	57.41	15.37	15.44

19－7 续表1 Continued

地 区	Region	地区生产总值（亿元）Gross Domectic Product (100 million yuan)	第一产业 Primary Industry	第二产业 Seconary Industry	#工 业 Industry	第三产业 Tertiary Industry	人均地区生产总值（元）Per Capita GDP (yuan)
东陇海合计	**Total**	**1487.94**	**137.51**	**786.12**	**660.03**	**564.31**	**19820**
徐州市区	Xuzhou	747.71	10.13	431.24	370.35	306.34	41369
铜山县	Tongshan	168.66	25.23	91.24	80.27	52.19	14036
新沂市	Xinyi	91.01	22.32	38.26	32.82	30.43	9261
邳州市	Pizhou	149.96	39.70	62.56	51.36	47.70	9104
连云港市区	Lianyungang	237.87	13.25	126.74	95.15	97.88	33710
东海县	Donghai	92.73	26.88	36.08	30.08	29.77	7974

19－7　续表2　Continued

地　区	Region	三次产业占 GDP 比重(%) Percentage of Three Industries to GDP(%)				地方财政一般预算收入占 GDP 比重 Percentage of General Budgetary Revenue in local Finance to GDP(%)	外贸依存度(%) Interdependent Level to Foreign Trade (%)
		第一产业 Primary Industry	第二产业 Seconary Industry	#工　业 Industry	第三产业 Tertiary Industry		
东陇海合计	**Total**	**9.2**	**52.8**	**44.4**	**37.9**	**5.7**	**23.4**
徐州市区	Xuzhou	1.4	57.7	49.5	41.0	5.8	14.1
铜山县	Tongshan	15.0	54.1	47.6	30.9	4.4	3.2
新沂市	Xinyi	24.5	42.0	36.1	33.4	3.7	8.0
邳州市	Pizhou	26.5	41.7	34.2	31.8	4.0	13.7
连云港市区	Lianyungang	5.6	53.3	40.0	41.1	8.8	83.9
东海县	Donghai	29.0	38.9	32.4	32.1	4.3	10.2

19－7　续表3　Continued

地　区	Region	规模以上工业企业个数(个) Number of Over Scale Industrial Enterprises (unit)	从业人员平均人数(万人) Average Number of Employees (10000 persons)	工业总产值(亿元) Total Output Value (100 million yuan)	#制造业 Manufacturing	主营业务收　入(亿元) Major Business Revenue (100 million yuan)	利税总额(亿元) Total Pre-tax Profits (100 million yuan)
东陇海合计	**Total**	**1604**	**44.03**	**1779.23**	**1486.59**	**1731.69**	**225.10**
徐州市区	Xuzhou	576	22.46	906.90	668.27	883.66	140.87
铜山县	Tongshan	239	6.83	303.18	286.44	292.74	32.91
新沂市	Xinyi	107	2.54	90.38	86.66	88.93	6.61
邳州市	Pizhou	254	4.85	140.26	134.00	136.50	9.82
连云港市区	Lianyungang	270	5.62	283.33	256.68	276.21	30.67
东海县	Donghai	158	1.72	55.19	54.54	53.65	4.22

19－7 续表4 Continued

地 区	Region	城镇固定资产投资（亿元）Urban Investment in Fixed Assets (100 million yuan)	#房地产开发 Real Estate Development	社会消费品零售总额（亿元）Total Retail Sales of Consumer Goods (100 million yuan)	进出口总额（亿美元）Total Imports and Exports (USD 100 million)	#出 口 Export	实际外商直接投资（亿美元）Actual Direct Foreign Investment (USD 100 million)
东陇海合计	**Total**	**714.60**	**107.26**	**480.17**	**43.61**	**25.70**	**4.49**
徐州市区	Xuzhou	336.40	45.16	249.22	13.23	8.47	1.34
铜山县	Tongshan	72.56	10.15	37.44	0.67	0.51	0.30
新沂市	Xinyi	58.57	3.07	30.48	0.91	0.47	0.12
邳州市	Pizhou	47.07	4.35	39.93	2.57	2.53	0.39
连云港市区	Lianyungang	170.08	39.77	86.14	25.03	12.76	1.89
东海县	Donghai	29.92	4.76	36.96	1.19	0.95	0.45

19－7 续表5 Continued

单位:亿元 (100 million yuan)

地 区	Region	地方财政一般预算收入 General Budgetary Revenue in Locel Finance	#各项税收 Taxes	地方财政一般预算支出 General Budgetary Expenditure in Local Finance	年末金融机构存款余额 Deposits Balance of Banking Institutions (year－end)	#城乡居民储蓄存款 Savings Deposits by Residents	年末金融机构贷款余额 Loans Balance of Banking Institutions (year－end)
东陇海合计	**Total**	**85.13**	**68.76**	**113.87**	**1341.76**	**728.23**	**734.59**
徐州市区	Xuzhou	43.47	35.07	47.69	686.47	334.74	313.38
铜山县	Tongshan	7.38	5.80	11.83	144.82	103.01	72.15
新沂市	Xinyi	3.34	2.71	8.17	54.21	40.41	35.32
邳州市	Pizhou	5.93	4.82	11.70	83.22	64.89	56.78
连云港市区	Lianyungang	21.01	17.53	24.88	309.93	140.34	224.56
东海县	Donghai	4.00	2.84	9.59	63.10	44.84	32.39

19－7　续 表 6　Continued

地　区 Region		公路里程（公里）Total Length of Highways (km)	民用汽车拥用量（万辆）Namber of Civil Motor Vehicles Owned (10000 units)	公路客运量（万人）Passenger Traffic (10000 persons)	公路货运量（万吨）Freight Traffic (10000 tons)	邮电业务总量（亿元）Total Volume of Postal and Telecom-munication (100 million yuan)	全社会用电量（亿千瓦时）Total Consumption of Electricity (100 million kWh)
东陇海合计	**Total**	**11812**	**15.64**	**10140**	**7479**	**47.34**	**149.85**
徐州市区	Xuzhou	1078	6.55	3238	1919	32.20	71.54
铜山县	Tongshan	2532	2.41	1234	1274	1.45	17.43
新沂市	Xinyi	1836	0.93	463	974	1.14	17.38
邳州市	Pizhou	2753	1.57	1003	1049	1.65	10.39
连云港市区	Lianyungang	834	2.96	2824	1185	8.23	23.98
东海县	Donghai	2779	1.23	1378	1078	2.66	9.13

19－7　续 表 7　Continued

地　区 Region		各类专业技术人员（万人）Number of Scientific and Technical Personnel (10000 persons)	中专以上在校生数（万人）Number of Students Enrolled in Above Secondary Specialized Shools (10000 persons)	公共图书馆图书藏量（千册、件）Total Volume of Collections of Public Libraries (1000 volumes)	卫生技术人　员（万人）Number of Medical and Technical Personnel (10000 persons)	工业废水排放达标量（万吨）Valume of Industrial Was Water Emission Standiardized (10000 tons)	“三废”综合利用产品产值(万元) Output Value of Products From Comprehersive Use of “three wastes” (10000 yuan)
东陇海合计	**Total**	**28.96**	**22.99**	**1885**	**2.95**	**10971**	**139803**
徐州市区	Xuzhou	11.12	16.12	769	1.25	3766	16432
铜山县	Tongshan	2.59		151	0.27	2880	67611
新沂市	Xinyi	2.57		111	0.22	1769	6734
邳州市	Pizhou	3.29	0.26	116	0.47	303	41361
连云港市区	Lianyungang	7.97	6.61	608	0.57	1753	6880
东海县	Donghai	1.43		130	0.19	500	785

JIANGSU STATISTICAL YEARBOOK

第 20 篇

市县社会经济

CITY (COUNTY) SOCIAL ECONOMY

20－1　全省各类法人单位地区分布情况　（2006 年）
REGIONAL DISTRIBUTION O CORPORATION UNITS OF ALL KINDS IN WHOLE PROVINCE (2006)

市　县	City and County	合计 Total	企业法人 Enterprise Corporatc-ions	事业法人 Institution Corporations	机关 Agencico	社会团体 Social Organi-zations	民办非企业 Mass-run Nonen-terprises	其他组织机构 Other Organizat-ions
全　　省	**Total**	**536112**	**446461**	**36291**	**10260**	**9171**	**5955**	**27974**
南 京 市	**Nanjing Municipality**	**51555**	**44028**	**3257**	**1167**	**891**	**494**	**1718**
溧 水 县	Lishui County	2202	1702	267	78	27	8	120
高 淳 县	Gaochun County	2040	1441	245	84	63	20	187
无 锡 市	**Wuxi Municipality**	**74343**	**67776**	**2594**	**665**	**941**	**405**	**1962**
江 阴 市	Jiangyin City	16904	15358	566	131	234	60	555
宜 兴 市	Yixing City	13488	11885	582	139	184	125	573
徐 州 市	**Xuzhou Municipality**	**30744**	**22571**	**3125**	**1047**	**523**	**396**	**3082**
丰　　县	Fengxian County	3104	2055	416	114	107	34	378
沛　　县	Peixian County	3256	2358	311	115	54	16	402
铜 山 县	Tongshan County	3421	2525	371	80	38	65	342
睢 宁 县	Suining County	2534	1511	365	103	16	30	509
新 沂 市	Xinyi City	2908	2046	357	80	92	33	300
邳 州 市	Pizhou City	3964	2821	446	136	26	15	520
常 州 市	**Changzhou Municipality**	**43357**	**37708**	**2437**	**648**	**775**	**278**	**1511**
溧 阳 市	Liyang City	4431	3392	416	114	151	23	335
金 坛 市	Jintan City	4256	3349	430	112	81	74	210
苏 州 市	**Suzhou Municipality**	**106557**	**99069**	**2859**	**911**	**908**	**408**	**2402**
常 熟 市	Changshu City	13569	12654	366	68	87	41	353
张家港市	Zhangjiagang City	15330	14375	386	111	125	39	294
昆 山 市	Kunshan City	17364	16323	463	109	95	41	333
吴 江 市	Wujiang City	11197	10340	294	84	130	13	336
太 仓 市	Taicang City	7023	6336	267	84	90	16	230

市 县	City and County	合计 Total	企业法人 Enterprise Corporatc-ions	事业法人 Institution Corporations	机关 Agencico	社会团体 Social Organi-zations	民办非企业 Mass-run Nonen-terprises	其他组织机构 Other Organizat-ions
南通市	**Nantong Municipality**	**53327**	**44087**	**3794**	**852**	**1019**	**612**	**2963**
海安县	Haian County	6710	5700	483	85	70	85	287
如东县	Rudong County	6471	5295	488	85	110	93	400
启东市	Qidong City	5631	4316	542	120	158	57	438
如皋市	Rugao City	6784	5031	571	126	124	189	743
通州市	Tongzhou City	9009	7493	719	113	148	64	472
海门市	Haimen City	6097	5068	418	110	121	46	334
连云港市	**Lianyungang Municipality**	**17312**	**12333**	**2047**	**700**	**307**	**171**	**1754**
赣榆县	Ganyu County	3856	2779	371	102	87	45	472
东海县	Donghai County	3141	2239	355	115	12	20	400
灌云县	Guanyun County	2547	1656	374	103	30	22	362
灌南县	Guannan County	2152	1397	354	99	30	11	261
淮安市	**Huaian Municipality**	**20942**	**12891**	**2947**	**847**	**479**	**1025**	**2753**
涟水县	Lianshui County	3134	1659	399	113	16	30	917
洪泽县	Hongze County	2081	1251	284	96	59	168	223
盱眙县	Xuyi County	2343	1274	521	100	43	13	392
金湖县	Jinhu County	2213	1548	322	89	66	13	175
盐城市	**Yancheng Municipality**	**36373**	**26820**	**3940**	**1044**	**1031**	**672**	**2866**
响水县	Xiangshui County	2125	1267	295	88	118	83	274
滨海县	Binhai County	3360	2413	436	107	78	12	314
阜宁县	Funing County	3424	2207	436	99	54	289	339
射阳县	Sheyang County	3796	2696	531	99	109	11	350
建湖县	Jianhu County	3371	2472	403	118	86	10	282

20－1 续表2 Continued

市 县 City and County		合计 Total	企业法人 Enterprise Corporatc-ions	事业法人 Institution Corporations	机关 Agencico	社会团体 Social Organi-zations	民办非企业 Mass-run Nonen-terprises	其他组织机构 Other Organizat-ions
东台市	Dongtai City	6290	4977	509	122	92	113	477
大丰市	Dafeng City	4171	3168	466	102	84	61	290
扬州市	**Yangzhou Municipality**	**31325**	**24942**	**2555**	**669**	**734**	**396**	**2029**
宝应县	Baoying County	3625	2442	373	85	96	22	607
仪征市	Yizheng City	3772	2958	400	98	33	51	232
高邮市	Gaoyou City	4187	2981	474	100	103	140	389
江都市	Jiangdu City	6962	5680	530	81	202	55	414
镇江市	**Zhenjiang Municipality**	**27931**	**22864**	**2289**	**608**	**721**	**183**	**1266**
丹阳市	Danyang City	7766	6512	543	125	138	33	415
扬中市	Yangzhong City	3191	2585	277	75	80	23	151
句容市	Jurong City	4378	3526	453	101	57	10	231
泰州市	**Taizhou Municipality**	**30248**	**23803**	**2766**	**520**	**653**	**416**	**2090**
兴化市	Xinghua City	4745	3306	549	95	58	47	690
靖江市	Jingjiang City	5962	4859	477	82	128	111	305
泰兴市	Taixing City	6898	5529	620	85	76	126	462
姜堰市	Jiangyan City	5962	4752	518	78	147	73	394
宿迁市	**Suqian Municipality**	**12098**	**7569**	**1681**	**582**	**189**	**499**	**1578**
沭阳县	Shuyang County	4385	3043	394	142	57	224	525
泗阳县	Siyang County	2023	1175	305	102	41	118	282
泗洪县	Sihong County	1887	1010	369	108	13	69	318

20－2 人　　口（2006年）
POPULATION (2006)

市　县	City and County	年末总人口（万人）Total Population at the Year-end (10000 persons)	#女　性 Female	年平均人口（万人）Average Person Per Year (10000 persons)	出生人口（人）Birth (person)	死亡人口（人）Death (person)	人口自然增长率（‰）Natural Growth Rate (‰)
南京市	**Nanjing Municipality**	**607.23**	**296.82**	**601.51**	**44106**	**30965**	**2.18**
溧水县	Lishui County	40.59	19.71	40.48	3156	1442	4.23
高淳县	Gaochun County	42.00	20.13	42.02	3818	2829	2.35
无锡市	**Wuxi Municipality**	**457.80**	**228.69**	**455.32**	**30491**	**31741**	**-0.27**
江阴市	Jiangyin City	119.45	59.34	119.03	8069	7740	0.28
宜兴市	Yixing City	106.05	52.87	105.89	7560	9121	-1.47
徐州市	**Xuzhou Municipality**	**934.73**	**453.27**	**930.02**	**81255**	**34235**	**5.06**
丰　县	Fengxian County	112.11	54.25	111.57	9832	4930	4.39
沛　县	Peixian County	121.74	59.30	121.11	10070	3563	5.37
铜山县	Tongshan County	120.72	59.10	120.16	11037	4836	5.16
睢宁县	Suining County	134.04	64.75	133.46	9468	3519	4.46
新沂市	Xinyi City	99.06	48.14	98.27	8617	1611	7.13
邳州市	Pizhou City	165.46	80.24	164.71	19879	10408	5.75
常州市	**Changzhou Municipality**	**354.67**	**176.04**	**353.16**	**28166**	**21465**	**1.90**
溧阳市	Liyang City	77.32	37.81	77.04	6323	3114	4.17
金坛市	Jintan City	54.87	27.13	54.49	4446	3409	1.90
苏州市	**Suzhou Municipality**	**616.08**	**311.57**	**611.70**	**46325**	**39111**	**1.18**
常熟市	Changshu City	105.48	53.94	105.13	8521	7672	0.81
张家港市	Zhangjiagang City	88.78	44.79	88.34	6074	5917	0.18
昆山市	Kunshan City	66.68	33.39	66.07	5978	3635	3.55
吴江市	Wujiang City	78.84	39.72	78.58	5486	5542	-0.07
太仓市	Taicang City	46.14	23.66	45.95	2474	3577	-2.40

20－1　续表　Continued

市　县	City and County	年末总人口（万人）Total Population at the Year-end (10000 persons)	#女　性 Female	年平均人口（万人）Average Person Per Year (10000 persons)	出生人口（人）Birth (person)	死亡人口（人）Death (person)	人口自然增长率（‰）Natural Growth Rate (‰)
南 通 市	**Nantong Municipality**	**769.79**	**387.32**	**770.33**	**48886**	**55143**	**－0.81**
海 安 县	Haian County	95.03	47.71	95.18	5285	5796	－0.54
如 东 县	Rudong County	107.14	53.84	107.41	5929	8672	－2.55
启 东 市	Qidong City	112.44	56.99	112.66	7448	7861	－0.37
如 皋 市	Rugao City	141.85	70.67	141.93	9653	10012	－0.25
通 州 市	Tongzhou City	125.64	63.28	125.95	7511	10508	－2.38
海 门 市	Haimen City	101.05	51.08	101.21	6937	6979	－0.04
连云港市	**Lianyungang Municipality**	**479.42**	**231.08**	**475.80**	**57070**	**23852**	**6.98**
赣 榆 县	Ganyu County	108.18	51.83	107.94	12248	7474	4.42
东 海 县	Donghai County	117.34	56.46	116.30	17290	5600	10.05
灌 云 县	Guanyun County	107.50	51.74	106.27	13324	2811	9.89
灌 南 县	Guannan County	75.45	36.23	74.73	7922	5179	3.67
淮 安 市	**Huaian Municipality**	**532.76**	**259.32**	**530.27**	**60083**	**21259**	**7.32**
涟 水 县	Lianshui County	106.40	51.17	105.89	13300	4525	8.29
洪 泽 县	Hongze County	38.71	19.20	38.78	2601	1674	2.39
盱 眙 县	Xuyi County	74.87	36.63	74.61	8301	3168	6.88
金 湖 县	Jinhu County	36.29	18.01	36.15	2461	1437	2.83
盐 城 市	**Yancheng Municipality**	**804.73**	**391.51**	**801.70**	**94377**	**43184**	**6.39**
响 水 县	Xiangshui County	59.55	28.57	58.66	11136	2247	15.15
滨 海 县	Binhai County	111.28	53.39	110.16	15725	5422	9.35
阜 宁 县	Funing County	107.38	51.60	107.02	18074	6298	11.00
射 阳 县	Sheyang County	104.79	51.19	104.58	10387	5483	4.69
建 湖 县	Jianhu County	80.82	39.00	80.56	9330	4097	6.50

20－2　续表2　Continued

市　县 City and County		年末总人口（万人）Total Population at the Year-end (10000 persons)	#女　性 Female	年平均人口（万人）Average Person Per Year (10000 persons)	出生人口（人）Birth (person)	死亡人口（人）Death (person)	人口自然增长率（‰）Natural Growth Rate (‰)
东台市	Dongtai City	115.35	57.30	115.47	7913	7823	0.08
大丰市	Dafeng City	72.92	36.24	72.94	6391	5143	1.71
扬州市	**Yangzhou Municipality**	**458.64**	**227.52**	**457.48**	**31638**	**25367**	**1.37**
宝应县	Baoying County	92.54	45.70	92.32	6541	3740	3.03
仪征市	Yizheng City	59.70	29.28	59.51	4035	2114	3.23
高邮市	Gaoyou City	82.73	41.31	82.72	5853	5286	0.69
江都市	Jiangdu City	106.85	53.02	106.69	7318	7089	0.21
镇江市	**Zhenjiang Municipality**	**268.79**	**134.87**	**268.20**	**20954**	**16527**	**1.65**
丹阳市	Danyang City	80.61	40.39	80.46	6885	5954	1.16
扬中市	Yangzhong City	27.39	13.84	27.34	2804	2084	2.63
句容市	Jurong City	58.07	30.07	58.05	3953	3107	1.46
泰州市	**Taizhou Municipality**	**503.60**	**246.93**	**502.83**	**44469**	**35358**	**1.81**
兴化市	Xinghua City	154.69	74.51	154.50	12973	8016	3.21
靖江市	Jingjiang City	66.47	33.31	66.33	4630	4612	0.03
泰兴市	Taixing City	128.05	62.82	128.09	9963	8184	1.39
姜堰市	Jiangyan City	90.14	44.28	90.09	10275	9417	0.95
宿迁市	**Suqian Municipality**	**529.47**	**257.29**	**527.01**	**64589**	**20926**	**8.29**
沭阳县	Shuyang County	177.05	85.96	176.60	18725	7800	6.19
泗阳县	Siyang County	96.83	46.69	96.08	16350	5125	11.68
泗洪县	Sihong County	100.24	48.90	99.62	15835	2457	13.43

20－3　户数及土地面积（2006年）

NUMBER OF HOUSEHOLDS AND LAND AREA（2006）

市　县	City and County	年末总户数（万户）Number of Households at the Year-end（10000 households）	#乡村户数 Rural Household	人口密度（人/平方公里）Density of Population（person/sq. km）	土地面积（平方公里）Land Area（sq. km）	耕地面积（千公顷）Cultivated Area（1000 hectares）	#水　田 Paddy Fields
南京市	**Nanjing Municipality**	**196.29**	**61.51**	**923**	**6582**	**243.69**	**169.13**
溧水县	Lishui County	13.62	10.13	380	1067	43.47	30.56
高淳县	Gaochun County	14.11	11.15	530	792	36.58	27.85
无锡市	**Wuxi Municipality**	**151.93**	**83.67**	**956**	**4788**	**145.37**	**120.62**
江阴市	Jiangyin City	36.47	28.31	1210	988	40.94	34.80
宜兴市	Yixing City	37.86	27.10	487	2177	64.86	54.67
徐州市	**Xuzhou Municipality**	**284.25**	**182.57**	**830**	**11258**	**596.80**	**214.34**
丰　县	Fengxian County	32.32	25.52	775	1446	75.34	7.33
沛　县	Peixian County	38.48	25.02	902	1349	75.92	34.00
铜山县	Tongshan County	38.60	28.12	643	1877	109.51	54.23
睢宁县	Suining County	37.33	28.18	759	1767	99.84	30.65
新沂市	Xinyi City	33.50	21.05	631	1571	79.02	31.18
邳州市	Pizhou City	47.44	35.30	792	2088	111.31	41.20
常州市	**Changzhou Municipality**	**122.32**	**77.96**	**811**	**4375**	**178.43**	**130.51**
溧阳市	Liyang City	26.19	19.60	504	1535	63.85	51.07
金坛市	Jintan City	21.19	14.70	562	976	39.09	32.94
苏州市	**Suzhou Municipality**	**207.24**	**111.51**	**726**	**8488**	**239.65**	**165.23**
常熟市	Changshu City	33.92	26.18	964	1094	58.05	43.87
张家港市	Zhangjiagang City	34.10	20.04	1150	772	36.37	31.56
昆山市	Kunshan City	22.43	11.49	771	865	20.11	16.74
吴江市	Wujiang City	25.54	16.75	721	1093	38.33	36.54
太仓市	Taicang City	14.95	7.46	744	620	34.86	31.22

市 县 City and County		年末总户数（万户）Number of Households at the Year-end (10000 households)	#乡村户数 Rural Household	人口密度（人/平方公里）Density of Population (person/sq. km)	土地面积（平方公里）Land Area (sq. km)	耕地面积（千公顷）Cultivated Area (1000 hectares)	#水田 Paddy Fields
南通市	**Nantong Municipality**	**278.77**	**214.40**	**962**	**8001**	**470.11**	**281.10**
海安县	Haian County	33.52	25.59	858	1108	54.67	44.30
如东县	Rudong County	38.02	31.63	618	1733	109.44	84.58
启东市	Qidong City	47.38	40.04	931	1208	69.25	0.00
如皋市	Rugao City	44.82	35.82	951	1492	81.61	61.09
通州市	Tongzhou City	46.67	39.72	1078	1166	79.56	74.98
海门市	Haimen City	37.85	30.58	1076	939	60.16	2.49
连云港市	**Lianyungang Municipality**	**137.25**	**90.50**	**639**	**7500**	**368.86**	**177.32**
赣榆县	Ganyu County	33.54	23.56	758	1427	67.80	23.67
东海县	Donghai County	31.11	25.34	521	2250	128.35	63.99
灌云县	Guanyun County	29.13	20.46	580	1852	100.79	45.71
灌南县	Guannan County	21.18	15.62	735	1027	59.11	33.69
淮安市	**Huaian Municipality**	**160.10**	**98.01**	**529**	**10072**	**487.64**	**264.38**
涟水县	Lianshui County	28.57	21.10	637	1670	103.14	44.27
洪泽县	Hongze County	12.58	7.94	278	1394	37.30	28.49
盱眙县	Xuyi County	22.21	14.22	300	2493	112.61	51.08
金湖县	Jinhu County	13.07	7.94	270	1344	49.68	30.03
盐城市	**Yancheng Municipality**	**276.98**	**185.96**	**474**	**16972**	**778.18**	**381.26**
响水县	Xiangshui County	17.00	11.49	408	1461	61.31	24.41
滨海县	Binhai County	33.59	24.21	581	1915	95.28	35.58
阜宁县	Funing County	35.19	21.36	746	1439	86.59	79.81
射阳县	Sheyang County	35.93	25.41	350	2997	142.40	49.19
建湖县	Jianhu County	30.38	19.16	697	1160	64.75	62.72

20－3 续表2 Continued

市 县 City and County		年末总户数（万户）Number of Households at the Year-end (10000 households)	#乡村户数 Rural Household	人口密度（人/平方公里）Density of Population (person/sq. km)	土地面积（平方公里）Land Area (sq. km)	耕地面积（千公顷）Cultivated Area (1000 hectares)	#水 田 Paddy Fields
东台市	Dongtai City	41.75	33.17	358	3221	124.36	35.47
大丰市	Dafeng City	29.48	21.12	238	3059	103.39	22.40
扬州市	**Yangzhou Municipality**	**156.06**	**98.03**	**691**	**6634**	**305.50**	**288.48**
宝应县	Baoying County	30.43	20.55	633	1461	76.50	70.34
仪征市	Yizheng City	20.86	14.16	663	901	49.02	41.37
高邮市	Gaoyou City	27.29	17.79	422	1962	76.87	75.36
江都市	Jiangdu City	38.30	25.40	803	1330	69.19	69.19
镇江市	**Zhenjiang Municipality**	**100.02**	**60.16**	**699**	**3847**	**172.72**	**54.90**
丹阳市	Danyang City	29.22	20.50	770	1047	54.44	47.35
扬中市	Yangzhong City	11.04	7.34	828	331	10.80	9.74
句容市	Jurong City	21.36	15.12	419	1387	66.62	34.52
泰州市	**Taizhou Municipality**	**172.04**	**120.56**	**869**	**5797**	**317.54**	**267.55**
兴化市	Xinghua City	53.18	39.28	646	2394	129.88	122.98
靖江市	Jingjiang City	22.97	15.69	1000	665	29.70	24.19
泰兴市	Taixing City	42.32	32.28	1021	1254	73.49	51.95
姜堰市	Jiangyan City	30.66	22.33	867	1040	63.42	49.87
宿迁市	**Suqian Municipality**	**146.94**	**104.91**	**619**	**8555**	**438.53**	**201.74**
沭阳县	Shuyang County	48.81	36.46	770	2298	141.08	53.68
泗阳县	Siyang County	27.03	18.50	683	1418	70.37	30.35
泗洪县	Sihong County	28.85	19.98	367	2731	133.64	53.78

20－4 年末从业人员（2006年）
NUMBER OF EMPLOYED PERSONS (YEAR－END) (2006)

单位：万人 (10000 persons)

市县	City and County	从业人员 Total Employed Persons	第一产业 Primary Industry	第二产业 Secondary Industry	#工业 Industry	第三产业 Tertiary Industry	#批发和零售业 Wholesale and Retail Trade
南京市	**Nanjing Municipality**	**327.41**	**37.38**	**138.75**	**97.17**	**151.28**	**48.59**
溧水县	Lishui County	22.49	5.24	11.15	6.63	6.10	1.09
高淳县	Gaochun County	24.13	7.40	11.50	5.68	5.23	1.08
无锡市	**Wuxi Municipality**	**307.90**	**30.20**	**171.80**	**157.38**	**105.90**	**33.15**
江阴市	Jiangyin City	77.37	8.19	43.89	38.91	25.29	6.35
宜兴市	Yixing City	59.65	15.02	26.68	21.77	17.95	5.39
徐州市	**Xuzhou Municipality**	**469.15**	**177.20**	**144.99**	**102.41**	**146.96**	**32.48**
丰县	Fengxian County	58.74	37.56	11.50	7.49	9.68	2.32
沛县	Peixian County	57.52	23.87	18.36	10.64	15.29	3.15
铜山县	Tongshan County	54.37	25.62	16.35	10.63	12.40	0.73
睢宁县	Suining County	68.38	28.86	18.44	11.44	21.07	3.75
新沂市	Xinyi City	49.67	20.10	16.30	10.34	13.28	2.93
邳州市	Pizhou City	80.73	28.71	29.62	22.59	22.40	5.70
常州市	**Changzhou Municipality**	**256.39**	**31.00**	**140.34**	**117.75**	**85.05**	**27.98**
溧阳市	Liyang City	46.11	9.85	23.41	14.94	12.85	3.70
金坛市	Jintan City	33.50	6.23	18.49	13.49	8.78	2.58
苏州市	**Suzhou Municipality**	**431.20**	**35.94**	**263.70**	**242.19**	**131.56**	**44.47**
常熟市	Changshu City	79.58	5.92	50.35	45.09	23.30	8.77
张家港市	Zhangjiagang City	59.00	6.64	35.04	32.22	17.33	6.07
昆山市	Kunshan City	59.06	3.30	37.70	34.84	18.06	7.53
吴江市	Wujiang City	53.24	4.37	33.64	31.37	15.22	5.68
太仓市	Taicang City	33.35	4.83	20.72	19.54	7.81	2.39

20－4 续表1 Continued

市 县	City and County	从业人员 Total Employed Persons	第一产业 Primary Industry	第二产业 Secondary Industry	#工 业 Industry	第三产业 Tertiary Industry	#批发和零售业 Wholesale and Retail Trade
南 通 市	**Nantong Municipality**	**449.45**	**108.22**	**190.99**	**119.15**	**150.24**	**39.89**
海 安 县	Haian County	54.98	15.51	23.68	14.73	15.79	3.93
如 东 县	Rudong County	61.14	13.44	26.77	17.15	20.92	4.51
启 东 市	Qidong City	76.62	21.94	28.99	15.86	25.70	7.10
如 皋 市	Rugao City	72.68	18.93	30.09	16.95	23.66	4.69
通 州 市	Tongzhou City	74.76	17.95	33.09	20.03	23.72	7.68
海 门 市	Haimen City	62.57	16.75	27.06	15.26	18.75	6.83
连云港市	**Lianyungang Municipality**	**241.74**	**95.24**	**71.70**	**41.97**	**74.80**	**18.71**
赣 榆 县	Ganyu County	52.65	19.31	20.93	10.53	12.41	3.78
东 海 县	Donghai County	57.41	26.60	15.37	8.20	15.44	3.49
灌 云 县	Guanyun County	48.09	23.71	10.52	6.48	13.79	3.10
灌 南 县	Guannan County	37.57	19.96	7.53	4.88	10.08	1.97
淮 安 市	**Huaian Municipality**	**281.68**	**101.01**	**68.31**	**42.57**	**112.36**	**18.29**
涟 水 县	Lianshui County	58.07	24.38	9.80	5.66	23.89	2.87
洪 泽 县	Hongze County	23.47	8.08	8.14	5.85	7.26	1.45
盱 眙 县	Xuyi County	41.52	12.88	8.71	6.41	19.93	1.79
金 湖 县	Jinhu County	20.66	6.35	4.94	3.83	9.37	1.57
盐 城 市	**Yancheng Municipality**	**318.95**	**115.48**	**88.52**	**59.20**	**114.95**	**25.68**
响 水 县	Xiangshui County	18.66	5.09	3.67	2.54	9.90	1.74
滨 海 县	Binhai County	35.88	15.33	6.51	3.78	14.04	2.34
阜 宁 县	Funing County	35.94	16.21	7.68	4.29	12.05	2.02
射 阳 县	Sheyang County	37.92	16.20	9.25	6.65	12.47	3.00
建 湖 县	Jianhu County	35.14	10.05	12.76	7.30	12.33	2.28

20－4 续表2 Continued

市县	City and County	从业人员 Total Employed Persons	第一产业 Primary Industry	第二产业 Secondary Industry	#工业 Industry	第三产业 Tertiary Industry	#批发和零售业 Wholesale and Retail Trade
东台市	Dongtai City	52.25	19.91	15.68	9.49	16.66	3.90
大丰市	Dafeng City	36.21	15.00	10.58	8.28	10.63	2.55
扬州市	**Yangzhou Municipality**	**243.89**	**47.42**	**112.49**	**80.28**	**83.98**	**21.15**
宝应县	Baoying County	48.36	14.95	18.84	10.14	14.57	3.48
仪征市	Yizheng City	35.54	6.02	17.69	13.16	11.83	2.28
高邮市	Gaoyou City	43.94	10.50	20.29	14.20	13.15	2.85
江都市	Jiangdu City	49.74	10.10	23.08	14.86	16.56	4.11
镇江市	**Zhenjiang Municipality**	**153.18**	**32.58**	**74.96**	**61.79**	**45.63**	**13.46**
丹阳市	Danyang City	49.71	10.94	26.59	22.95	12.18	4.44
扬中市	Yangzhong City	16.23	3.05	9.30	8.35	3.89	0.98
句容市	Jurong City	31.30	9.76	13.28	8.74	8.27	2.05
泰州市	**Taizhou Municipality**	**255.88**	**64.59**	**104.89**	**66.60**	**86.40**	**26.96**
兴化市	Xinghua City	66.45	27.35	17.97	11.89	21.13	6.24
靖江市	Jingjiang City	35.58	6.64	16.19	13.47	12.75	3.55
泰兴市	Taixing City	67.36	16.48	27.44	15.02	23.44	7.39
姜堰市	Jiangyan City	49.20	9.77	24.64	13.11	14.79	5.13
宿迁市	**Suqian Municipality**	**288.68**	**110.01**	**90.64**	**64.41**	**88.03**	**19.20**
沭阳县	Shuyang County	99.96	35.70	30.04	22.81	34.24	5.84
泗阳县	Siyang County	51.31	18.09	18.95	13.30	14.27	3.71
泗洪县	Sihong County	50.86	28.25	10.13	7.32	12.42	2.78

20－5 在岗职工及私营个体从业人员(2006年)

NUMBER OF EMPLOYED STAFF AND WORKERS AND BUSINESSMEN OF PRIVATE UNITS AND INDIVIDUALS (2006)

单位:万人 (10000 persons)

市 县	City and County	在岗职工人数 Employed	#国有单位 State-Owned Units	#城镇集体单位 Urban Collective-Owned Units	#港澳台商投资单位 Units Funded by Entrepreneurs from Hong Kong, Macao & Taiwan	#外商投资单位 Foreign Funded Units	私营企业和个体从业人员 Individuals and Employed Persons in Private Enterprises
南京市	**Nanjing Municipality**	**91.85**	**43.37**	**4.30**	**5.81**	**9.89**	**120.20**
溧水县	Lishui County	2.26	1.20	0.16	0.35	0.14	6.16
高淳县	Gaochun County	1.92	1.18	0.07		0.04	10.84
无锡市	**Wuxi Municipality**	**50.81**	**17.85**	**2.36**	**4.39**	**10.98**	**119.37**
江阴市	Jiangyin City	10.18	4.36	0.70	1.38	0.58	28.92
宜兴市	Yixing City	5.85	2.92	0.38	0.34	0.59	21.80
徐州市	**Xuzhou Municipality**	**56.91**	**39.87**	**3.57**	**1.21**	**0.81**	**70.94**
丰县	Fengxian County	3.25	2.32	0.39	0.07	0.09	3.52
沛县	Peixian County	4.17	3.26	0.54			5.53
铜山县	Tongshan County	5.17	2.98	0.35	0.00	0.04	5.10
睢宁县	Suining County	3.66	2.61	0.36	0.50	0.05	4.84
新沂市	Xinyi City	5.11	2.83	0.44	0.15	0.17	7.50
邳州市	Pizhou City	5.36	3.88	0.47	0.05	0.02	10.04
常州市	**Changzhou Municipality**	**35.47**	**13.21**	**1.47**	**3.15**	**4.22**	**102.49**
溧阳市	Liyang City	5.22	2.34	0.12	0.21	0.43	15.43
金坛市	Jintan City	4.69	1.43	0.22	0.45	1.05	13.81
苏州市	**Suzhou Municipality**	**111.39**	**21.14**	**2.43**	**16.04**	**50.76**	**225.34**
常熟市	Changshu City	10.42	2.63	0.43	1.59	1.31	41.82
张家港市	Zhangjiagang City	11.57	3.66	0.44	1.11	1.26	37.06
昆山市	Kunshan City	16.89	2.54	0.44	3.68	9.20	30.43
吴江市	Wujiang City	8.50	2.08	0.25	0.72	4.72	24.57
太仓市	Taicang City	10.14	1.68	0.21	1.98	4.76	14.61

20－5 续表1 Continued

单位:万人 (10000 persons)

市 县 City and County		在岗职工人数 Employed	#国有单位 State-Owned Units	#城镇集体单位 Urban Collective-Owned Units	#港澳台商投资单位 Units Funded by Entrepreneurs from Hong Kong, Macao & Taiwan	#外商投资单位 Foreign Funded Units	私营企业和个体从业人员 Individuals and Employed Persons in Private Enterprises
南 通 市	**Nantong Municipality**	**54.97**	**19.41**	**3.03**	**5.63**	**11.56**	**140.22**
海 安 县	Haian County	6.03	1.96	0.18	0.43	0.67	19.18
如 东 县	Rudong County	5.54	2.38	0.35	0.91	0.78	17.88
启 东 市	Qidong City	5.85	1.89	0.57	1.03	1.01	18.65
如 皋 市	Rugao City	5.96	2.33	0.18	0.74	1.24	25.22
通 州 市	Tongzhou City	6.74	2.19	0.56	0.89	1.99	20.46
海 门 市	Haimen City	5.94	2.41	0.46	0.82	1.43	17.87
连云港市	**Lianyungang Municipality**	**28.91**	**15.82**	**2.52**	**1.20**	**2.41**	**35.30**
赣 榆 县	Ganyu County	3.49	2.48	0.22	0.13	0.21	8.34
东 海 县	Donghai County	4.25	2.88	0.12	0.32	0.35	7.82
灌 云 县	Guanyun County	4.35	2.93	0.70	0.19	0.10	4.75
灌 南 县	Guannan County	2.71	1.62	0.45	0.09	0.04	3.91
淮 安 市	**Huaian Municipality**	**31.50**	**16.82**	**2.52**	**1.42**	**1.12**	**55.40**
涟 水 县	Lianshui County	4.27	2.48	0.42	0.66		8.30
洪 泽 县	Hongze County	2.38	0.92	0.22	0.19	0.12	4.47
盱 眙 县	Xuyi County	3.85	2.30	0.49			8.81
金 湖 县	Jinhu County	2.91	1.44	0.18	0.28	0.20	6.24
盐 城 市	**Yancheng Municipality**	**46.42**	**22.61**	**2.21**	**2.53**	**2.72**	**82.52**
响 水 县	Xiangshui County	3.29	2.24	0.33	0.10	0.09	6.44
滨 海 县	Binhai County	3.20	2.10	0.10	0.01	0.00	6.65
阜 宁 县	Funing County	4.25	1.89	0.13	0.09	0.48	8.11
射 阳 县	Sheyang County	6.07	2.75	0.22	0.64	0.14	8.95
建 湖 县	Jianhu County	4.81	1.86	0.37	0.03	0.00	10.57

单位:万人　　(10000 persons)

市　县	City and County	在岗职工人数 Employed	#国有单位 State-Owned Units	#城镇集体单位 Urban Collective-Owned Units	#港澳台商投资单位 Units Funded by Entrepreneurs from Hong Kong, Macao & Taiwan	#外商投资单位 Foreign Funded Units	私营企业和个体从业人员 Individuals and Employed Persons in Private Enterprises
东台市	Dongtai City	5.52	2.82	0.39	0.11	0.30	13.41
大丰市	Dafeng City	4.84	2.03	0.19	0.63	0.54	10.81
扬州市	**Yangzhou Municipality**	**34.73**	**17.72**	**2.71**	**2.00**	**2.59**	**70.65**
宝应县	Baoying County	4.74	2.41	0.60	0.21	0.62	7.67
仪征市	Yizheng City	5.24	2.30	0.24	0.14	0.46	11.33
高邮市	Gaoyou City	3.55	1.83	0.56	0.30	0.19	11.33
江都市	Jiangdu City	5.16	2.43	0.89	0.41	0.13	14.82
镇江市	**Zhenjiang Municipality**	**31.41**	**14.13**	**2.18**	**3.17**	**2.72**	**48.37**
丹阳市	Danyang City	6.61	3.57	0.51	0.96	0.44	19.33
扬中市	Yangzhong City	3.00	1.17	0.22	0.11	0.07	4.86
句容市	Jurong City	4.54	2.12	0.58	1.11	0.23	6.36
泰州市	**Taizhou Municipality**	**30.03**	**13.45**	**3.42**	**1.75**	**2.12**	**66.74**
兴化市	Xinghua City	4.72	2.95	0.49	0.33	0.16	13.09
靖江市	Jingjiang City	5.22	2.06	0.43	0.41	0.26	12.73
泰兴市	Taixing City	5.91	2.57	0.83	0.14	0.25	12.82
姜堰市	Jiangyan City	4.98	1.90	0.22	0.31	0.60	12.92
宿迁市	**Suqian Municipality**	**18.31**	**11.88**	**0.87**	**0.18**	**0.11**	**41.70**
沭阳县	Shuyang County	5.70	3.53	0.29	0.10	0.03	9.76
泗阳县	Siyang County	2.70	1.95	0.27			10.02
泗洪县	Sihong County	3.95	2.89	0.18			5.32

20－6 乡村从业人员 （2006 年）
RURAL EMPLOYMENT（2006）

单位：万人 （10000 persons）

市 县	City and County	乡村从业人员 Total Employment	#农林牧渔业 Farming, Forestry, Animal Husbandry and Fishery	#工 业 Industry	#建筑业 Construction	#交通运输、仓储及邮政业 Transportation, Storage, and Postal Services	#批发和零售业 Wholesale and Retail Trade
南 京 市	**Nanjing Municipality**	**122.16**	**36.83**	**30.71**	**22.04**	**6.90**	**6.77**
溧 水 县	Lishui County	17.03	5.04	3.88	3.21	0.98	1.01
高 淳 县	Gaochun County	22.23	7.39	4.53	6.43	1.12	0.96
无 锡 市	**Wuxi Municipality**	**148.75**	**29.51**	**79.73**	**9.79**	**4.99**	**6.80**
江 阴 市	Jiangyin City	51.74	8.00	27.75	3.76	1.80	2.56
宜 兴 市	Yixing City	43.71	14.81	17.28	4.13	1.79	2.04
徐 州 市	**Xuzhou Municipality**	**352.40**	**175.25**	**66.42**	**38.19**	**11.23**	**13.29**
丰 县	Fengxian County	53.48	37.55	6.53	3.66	0.75	1.23
沛 县	Peixian County	50.40	23.20	9.10	7.49	1.42	1.87
铜 山 县	Tongshan County	46.73	24.94	8.06	5.45	2.10	0.19
睢 宁 县	Suining County	62.76	28.84	10.35	6.76	1.40	2.61
新 沂 市	Xinyi City	40.37	20.02	6.04	5.50	1.16	1.54
邳 州 市	Pizhou City	68.76	28.50	18.14	6.63	2.80	3.85
常 州 市	**Changzhou Municipality**	**126.49**	**30.30**	**49.92**	**15.83**	**5.45**	**6.29**
溧 阳 市	Liyang City	30.63	9.68	7.34	7.45	1.75	1.42
金 坛 市	Jintan City	20.96	6.12	6.88	4.38	0.80	0.87
苏 州 市	**Suzhou Municipality**	**206.87**	**34.84**	**111.45**	**13.17**	**6.74**	**11.50**
常 熟 市	Changshu City	48.52	5.85	27.57	3.11	1.81	3.54
张家港市	Zhangjiagang City	30.92	5.97	16.49	1.93	1.02	1.51
昆 山 市	Kunshan City	22.73	3.21	13.94	1.13	0.69	1.18
吴 江 市	Wujiang City	32.36	4.32	18.77	1.88	0.96	2.05
太 仓 市	Taicang City	16.14	4.69	8.58	0.62	0.36	0.42

20－6 续表1 Continued

单位:万人 (10000 persons)

市 县	City and County	乡村从业人员 Total Employment	#农林牧渔业 Farming, Forestry, Animal Husbandry and Fishery	#工业 Industry	#建筑业 Construction	#交通运输、仓储及邮政业 Transportation, Storage, and Postal Services	#批发和零售业 Wholesale and Retail Trade
南通市	**Nantong Municipality**	**342.07**	**105.41**	**72.63**	**64.52**	**16.80**	**25.48**
海安县	Haian County	42.09	14.89	8.08	8.20	2.20	2.46
如东县	Rudong County	50.25	12.64	13.24	9.17	2.69	2.97
启东市	Qidong City	62.29	21.62	10.68	10.80	3.15	5.43
如皋市	Rugao City	61.40	18.82	11.58	12.21	3.22	3.46
通州市	Tongzhou City	58.95	17.87	13.11	12.03	2.60	4.80
海门市	Haimen City	51.29	16.37	9.64	10.71	2.44	5.66
连云港市	**Lianyungang Municipality**	**170.02**	**94.51**	**19.46**	**24.40**	**5.39**	**5.54**
赣榆县	Ganyu County	39.75	19.26	5.15	9.92	1.11	1.57
东海县	Donghai County	48.85	27.11	6.41	6.63	1.52	1.44
灌云县	Guanyun County	38.88	22.68	3.72	3.50	0.97	1.22
灌南县	Guannan County	30.94	19.96	2.18	2.65	1.19	0.71
淮安市	**Huaian Municipality**	**211.16**	**98.69**	**19.58**	**22.02**	**5.83**	**6.96**
涟水县	Lianshui County	48.76	24.23	2.50	3.10	0.89	1.34
洪泽县	Hongze County	18.04	8.07	3.10	2.14	0.68	0.62
盱眙县	Xuyi County	32.68	12.10	2.91	1.72	0.91	0.85
金湖县	Jinhu County	14.48	5.99	1.27	0.96	0.35	0.45
盐城市	**Yancheng Municipality**	**285.09**	**127.94**	**39.79**	**29.92**	**12.51**	**10.94**
响水县	Xiangshui County	19.23	8.03	3.45	0.89	0.55	0.61
滨海县	Binhai County	38.15	18.27	3.26	2.91	2.03	1.32
阜宁县	Funing County	36.15	16.01	3.20	4.60	1.11	1.13
射阳县	Sheyang County	36.16	17.74	3.24	3.39	1.59	1.83
建湖县	Jianhu County	28.96	11.32	6.26	3.39	1.38	1.42

单位：万人 (10000 persons)

市 县	City and County	乡村从业人员 Total Employment	#农林牧渔业 Farming, Forestry, Animal Husbandry and Fishery	#工业 Industry	#建筑业 Construction	#交通运输、仓储及邮政业 Transportation, Storage, and Postal Services	#批发和零售业 Wholesale and Retail Trade
东台市	Dongtai City	46.70	22.09	7.83	5.71	2.15	1.55
大丰市	Dafeng City	31.64	14.48	5.25	2.23	1.20	1.28
扬州市	**Yangzhou Municipality**	**166.10**	**46.84**	**43.28**	**30.84**	**7.06**	**9.38**
宝应县	Baoying County	40.50	14.75	7.19	9.60	1.94	2.31
仪征市	Yizheng City	23.65	5.96	6.58	4.15	0.78	0.94
高邮市	Gaoyou City	32.36	10.48	7.60	5.82	1.43	1.72
江都市	Jiangdu City	36.29	9.85	9.11	7.57	1.51	1.71
镇江市	**Zhenjiang Municipality**	**96.65**	**31.97**	**37.84**	**9.74**	**3.59**	**3.53**
丹阳市	Danyang City	34.69	10.82	16.23	2.91	1.05	1.08
扬中市	Yangzhong City	11.71	3.04	6.13	0.63	0.41	0.44
句容市	Jurong City	23.95	9.41	5.68	4.20	0.93	0.91
泰州市	**Taizhou Municipality**	**202.30**	**61.09**	**41.16**	**31.54**	**12.97**	**13.09**
兴化市	Xinghua City	60.58	25.52	7.41	5.19	4.38	3.66
靖江市	Jingjiang City	25.00	6.18	7.84	1.85	1.80	1.21
泰兴市	Taixing City	56.77	16.21	11.03	10.00	3.14	4.96
姜堰市	Jiangyan City	39.85	9.28	9.38	10.40	2.55	2.16
宿迁市	**Suqian Municipality**	**226.94**	**108.79**	**36.44**	**20.70**	**6.37**	**9.67**
沭阳县	Shuyang County	84.13	35.47	16.07	5.93	2.49	3.53
泗阳县	Siyang County	38.24	17.92	6.17	4.88	0.96	1.71
泗洪县	Sihong County	41.27	27.70	3.70	2.09	0.72	1.23

20－7 地区生产总值(2006年)
GROSS DOMESTIC PRODUCT (2006)

单位:亿元　　　　(100 million yuan)

市县 City and County		地区生产总值 Total Gross Domestic Product	第一产业 Primary Industry	第二产业 Secondary Industry	#工业 Industry	第三产业 Tertiary Industry	人均地区生产总值(元) Per Capita GDP (yuan)
南京市	**Nanjing Municipality**	**2773.78**	**82.02**	**1359.94**	**1181.94**	**1331.82**	**46114**
溧水县	Lishui County	103.75	11.67	58.73	50.03	33.35	25630
高淳县	Gaochun County	111.03	14.23	58.58	46.00	38.22	26423
无锡市	**Wuxi Municipality**	**3300.59**	**51.34**	**1968.75**	**1849.85**	**1280.50**	**72489**
江阴市	Jiangyin City	980.17	17.16	620.45	596.45	342.56	82346
宜兴市	Yixing City	428.03	17.32	256.72	243.78	153.99	40422
徐州市	**Xuzhou Municipality**	**1428.80**	**180.82**	**741.36**	**632.84**	**506.62**	**15363**
丰县	Fengxian County	67.94	20.63	25.77	19.76	21.54	6089
沛县	Peixian County	147.60	30.61	68.01	59.79	48.98	12187
铜山县	Tongshan County	168.66	25.23	91.24	80.27	52.19	14036
睢宁县	Suining County	72.10	21.28	27.64	24.04	23.18	5402
新沂市	Xinyi City	91.01	22.32	38.26	32.82	30.43	9261
邳州市	Pizhou City	149.96	39.70	62.56	51.36	47.70	9104
常州市	**Changzhou Municipality**	**1569.46**	**59.45**	**947.42**	**868.44**	**562.59**	**44440**
溧阳市	Liyang City	217.63	16.57	123.54	106.51	77.52	28249
金坛市	Jintan City	182.00	14.63	97.50	81.50	69.87	33401
苏州市	**Suzhou Municipality**	**4820.26**	**94.01**	**3152.03**	**2978.55**	**1574.22**	**78801**
常熟市	Changshu City	809.28	17.49	484.26	462.64	307.54	76979
张家港市	Zhangjiagang City	841.62	12.48	545.69	529.36	283.45	95271
昆山市	Kunshan City	932.01	10.53	632.41	605.06	289.07	141064
吴江市	Wujiang City	500.80	17.11	321.43	304.40	162.26	63731
太仓市	Taicang City	366.63	15.63	223.05	204.18	127.95	79789

20－7 续表1 Continued

单位：亿元 (100 million yuan)

市 县	City and County	地区生产总值 Total Gross Domestic Product	第一产业 Primary Industry	第二产业 Secondary Industry	#工业 Industry	第三产业 Tertiary Industry	人均地区生产总值(元) Per Capita GDP (yuan)
南通市	**Nantong Municipality**	**1758.34**	**168.06**	**985.04**	**815.06**	**605.24**	**22826**
海安县	Haian County	177.42	25.17	91.98	73.31	60.27	18640
如东县	Rudong County	175.02	30.10	86.88	67.41	58.04	16295
启东市	Qidong City	238.59	35.06	124.73	97.32	78.80	21178
如皋市	Rugao City	180.27	24.75	94.13	76.94	61.39	12701
通州市	Tongzhou City	270.58	24.46	161.17	136.74	84.95	21483
海门市	Haimen City	261.09	23.65	153.36	128.94	84.08	25797
连云港市	**Lianyungang Municipality**	**527.38**	**96.26**	**241.55**	**188.36**	**189.57**	**11084**
赣榆县	Ganyu County	91.82	23.95	37.28	31.24	30.59	8507
东海县	Donghai County	92.73	26.88	36.08	30.08	29.77	7974
灌云县	Guanyun County	55.93	18.30	21.28	15.84	16.35	5263
灌南县	Guannan County	49.03	13.88	20.17	16.05	14.98	6561
淮安市	**Huaian Municipality**	**651.06**	**123.78**	**305.23**	**252.61**	**222.05**	**12278**
涟水县	Lianshui County	74.07	25.56	27.13	21.64	21.38	6995
洪泽县	Hongze County	48.89	11.75	20.44	16.94	16.70	12607
盱眙县	Xuyi County	74.52	18.85	35.08	28.53	20.59	9988
金湖县	Jinhu County	46.32	11.03	19.12	16.82	16.17	12815
盐城市	**Yancheng Municipality**	**1174.26**	**245.65**	**536.18**	**456.98**	**392.43**	**14647**
响水县	Xiangshui County	54.13	15.40	23.28	19.93	15.45	9229
滨海县	Binhai County	93.30	25.32	38.62	32.34	29.36	8469
阜宁县	Funing County	100.03	24.10	45.48	33.88	30.45	9347
射阳县	Sheyang County	142.13	40.41	57.75	51.94	43.97	13591
建湖县	Jianhu County	118.73	22.83	55.27	48.70	40.63	14738

单位:亿元　(100 million yuan)

市　县 City and County		地区生产总值 Total Gross Domestic Product	第一产业 Primary Industry	第二产业 Secondary Industry	#工业 Industry	第三产业 Tertiary Industry	人均地区生产总值(元) Per Capita GDP (yuan)
东台市	Dongtai City	194.73	44.03	88.10	76.65	62.60	16864
大丰市	Dafeng City	149.45	36.55	64.80	54.12	48.10	20491
扬州市	**Yangzhou Municipality**	**1100.16**	**94.52**	**620.59**	**545.90**	**385.05**	**24048**
宝应县	Baoying County	116.02	25.19	54.40	44.79	36.43	12567
仪征市	Yizheng City	130.10	8.55	86.09	75.32	35.46	21862
高邮市	Gaoyou City	123.72	26.20	58.42	49.12	39.10	14956
江都市	Jiangdu City	230.20	21.28	142.02	122.22	66.90	21577
镇江市	**Zhenjiang Municipality**	**1021.52**	**41.54**	**618.64**	**567.02**	**361.34**	**38088**
丹阳市	Danyang City	300.24	16.40	176.84	167.38	107.00	37318
扬中市	Yangzhong City	125.05	3.93	76.32	68.81	44.80	45747
句容市	Jurong City	124.30	11.76	74.04	69.80	38.50	21413
泰州市	**Taizhou Municipality**	**1002.28**	**95.00**	**585.56**	**501.29**	**321.72**	**19933**
兴化市	Xinghua City	178.36	39.15	82.54	68.95	56.67	11544
靖江市	Jingjiang City	161.89	9.07	93.83	82.88	58.99	24407
泰兴市	Taixing City	207.08	24.01	117.25	94.79	65.82	16167
姜堰市	Jiangyan City	161.66	17.33	91.92	75.20	52.41	17944
宿迁市	**Suqian Municipality**	**454.20**	**107.09**	**203.68**	**155.88**	**143.43**	**8618**
沭阳县	Shuyang County	124.12	35.90	51.78	44.20	36.44	7028
泗阳县	Siyang County	81.21	22.15	34.98	28.09	24.08	8452
泗洪县	Sihong County	81.00	26.03	29.72	24.46	25.25	8131

20－8 地区生产总值构成(2006 年)
COMPOSITION AND INDICES OF GROSS DOMESTIC PRODUCT (2006)

市　县	City and County	地区生产总值指数(上年=100) GDP Index (2005=100)	三次产业占 GDP 比重(%) Percentage of Three Industries to GDP 第一产业 Primary Industry	第二产业 Secondary Industry	第三产业 Tertiary Industry	地方财政一般预算收入占 GDP 比重(%) Percentage of General Budetary Revenue in Local Finance to GDP(%)	外贸依存度(%) Interdependent Level to Foreign Trade(%)
南京市	**Nanjing Municipality**	**115.1**	**3.0**	**49.0**	**48.0**	**8.9**	**90.6**
溧水县	Lishui County	123.1	11.2	56.6	32.1	4.4	12.7
高淳县	Gaochun County	117.9	12.8	52.8	34.4	5.3	7.9
无锡市	**Wuxi Municipality**	**115.3**	**1.6**	**59.6**	**38.8**	**6.7**	**94.7**
江阴市	Jiangyin City	122.3	1.8	63.3	34.9	6.2	68.4
宜兴市	Yixing City	116.3	4.0	60.0	36.0	5.1	23.6
徐州市	**Xuzhou Municipality**	**115.1**	**12.7**	**51.9**	**35.5**	**5.0**	**10.3**
丰县	Fengxian County	115.3	30.4	37.9	31.7	3.6	3.3
沛县	Peixian County	116.0	20.7	46.1	33.2	4.1	1.0
铜山县	Tongshan County	116.7	15.0	54.1	30.9	4.4	3.2
睢宁县	Suining County	115.0	29.5	38.3	32.1	3.4	7.5
新沂市	Xinyi City	115.7	24.5	42.0	33.4	3.7	8.0
邳州市	Pizhou City	116.7	26.5	41.7	31.8	4.0	13.7
常州市	**Changzhou Municipality**	**115.2**	**3.8**	**60.4**	**35.8**	**7.6**	**53.1**
溧阳市	Liyang City	118.5	7.6	56.8	35.6	5.4	12.8
金坛市	Jintan City	18.5	8.0	53.6	38.4	4.7	24.8
苏州市	**Suzhou Municipality**	**115.5**	**2.0**	**65.4**	**32.7**	**8.3**	**288.2**
常熟市	Changshu City	118.5	2.2	59.8	38.0	5.3	61.7
张家港市	Zhangjiagang City	118.5	1.5	64.8	33.7	7.3	119.2
昆山市	Kunshan City	124.9	1.1	67.9	31.0	7.0	365.6
吴江市	Wujiang City	120.8	3.4	64.2	32.4	7.0	227.2
太仓市	Taicang City	122.5	4.3	60.8	34.9	7.5	102.0

20－8 续表1 Continued

市 县 City and County		地区生产总值指数（上年＝100）GDP Index（2005＝100）	三次产业占GDP比重（%）Percentage of Three Industries to GDP			地方财政一般预算收入占GDP比重（%）Percentage of General Budetary Revenue in Local Finance to GDP（%）	外贸依存度（%）Interdependent Level to Foreign Trade（%）
			第一产业 Primary Industry	第二产业 Secondary Industry	第三产业 Tertiary Industry		
南通市	**Nantong Municipality**	**115.7**	**9.6**	**56.0**	**34.4**	**5.3**	**45.4**
海安县	Haian County	116.1	14.2	51.8	34.0	3.9	17.2
如东县	Rudong County	115.3	17.2	49.6	33.2	3.5	22.5
启东市	Qidong City	116.0	14.7	52.3	33.0	3.9	14.3
如皋市	Rugao City	116.3	13.7	52.2	34.1	4.2	23.9
通州市	Tongzhou City	116.0	9.0	59.6	31.4	3.9	32.1
海门市	Haimen City	116.1	9.1	58.7	32.2	3.7	17.7
连云港市	**Lianyungang Municipality**	**115.2**	**18.3**	**45.8**	**35.9**	**6.4**	**41.2**
赣榆县	Ganyu County	117.4	26.1	40.6	33.3	4.4	3.1
东海县	Donghai County	117.4	29.0	38.9	32.1	4.3	10.2
灌云县	Guanyun County	117.0	32.7	38.0	29.2	4.2	3.3
灌南县	Guannan County	117.6	28.3	41.1	30.6	5.3	5.2
淮安市	**Huaian Municipality**	**115.0**	**19.0**	**46.9**	**34.1**	**5.7**	**12.5**
涟水县	Lianshui County	115.4	34.5	36.6	28.9	3.0	3.2
洪泽县	Hongze County	115.0	24.0	41.8	34.2	4.2	1.7
盱眙县	Xuyi County	114.8	25.3	47.1	27.6	3.5	0.5
金湖县	Jinhu County	114.9	23.8	41.3	34.9	3.9	10.6
盐城市	**Yancheng Municipality**	**115.0**	**20.9**	**45.7**	**33.4**	**4.2**	**12.2**
响水县	Xiangshui County	114.5	28.4	43.0	28.5	4.1	9.1
滨海县	Binhai County	114.8	27.1	41.4	31.5	3.3	1.8
阜宁县	Funing County	115.7	24.1	45.5	30.4	3.7	5.6
射阳县	Sheyang County	115.1	28.4	40.6	30.9	3.3	3.9
建湖县	Jianhu County	114.7	19.2	46.6	34.2	3.9	7.0

市　县	City and County	地区生产总值指数(上年＝100) GDP Index (2005＝100)	三次产业占GDP比重(%) Percentage of Three Industries to GDP 第一产业 Primary Industry	第二产业 Secondary Industry	第三产业 Tertiary Industry	地方财政一般预算收入占GDP比重(%) Percentage of General Budetary Revenue in Local Finance to GDP(%)	外贸依存度(%) Interdependent Level to Foreign Trade(%)
东台市	Dongtai City	114.5	22.6	45.2	32.1	3.4	10.0
大丰市	Dafeng City	115.6	24.5	43.4	32.2	3.4	8.0
扬州市	**Yangzhou Municipality**	**115.2**	**8.6**	**56.4**	**35.0**	**5.7**	**23.7**
宝应县	Baoying County	115.5	21.7	46.9	31.4	3.9	12.8
仪征市	Yizheng City	115.0	6.6	66.2	27.3	6.2	13.4
高邮市	Gaoyou City	115.5	21.2	47.2	31.6	3.8	8.7
江都市	Jiangdu City	115.8	9.2	61.7	29.1	4.0	9.8
镇江市	**Zhenjiang Municipality**	**115.2**	**4.1**	**60.6**	**35.4**	**5.9**	**37.3**
丹阳市	Danyang City	115.0	5.5	58.9	35.6	4.4	18.1
扬中市	Yangzhong City	114.9	3.1	61.0	35.8	4.8	10.4
句容市	Jurong City	115.3	9.5	59.6	31.0	4.3	28.5
泰州市	**Taizhou Municipality**	**115.3**	**9.5**	**58.4**	**32.1**	**6.1**	**22.8**
兴化市	Xinghua City	114.7	21.9	46.3	31.8	3.7	8.1
靖江市	Jingjiang City	117.1	5.6	58.0	36.4	6.9	32.4
泰兴市	Taixing City	115.5	11.6	56.6	31.8	5.3	19.1
姜堰市	Jiangyan City	116.5	10.7	56.9	32.4	4.9	16.1
宿迁市	**Suqian Municipality**	**115.0**	**23.6**	**44.8**	**31.6**	**4.4**	**4.0**
沭阳县	Shuyang County	115.2	28.9	41.7	29.4	4.0	1.1
泗阳县	Siyang County	115.2	27.3	43.1	29.7	3.1	2.2
泗洪县	Sihong County	115.1	32.1	36.7	31.2	3.4	1.3

20－9 农林牧渔业总产值(2006年)
GROSS OUTPUT VALUE OF FARMING, FORESTRY, ANIMAL HUSBANDRY AND FISHERY (2006)

单位:亿元　　　　(100 million yuan)

市县	City and County	农林牧渔业总产值 Total Output Value of Farming, Forestry, Animal Husbandry and Fishery	农业 Farming	林业 Forestry	畜牧业 Animal Husbandry	渔业 Fishery	农林牧渔服务业 Service for Farming, Forestry, Animal Husbandry, Fishery
南京市	**Nanjing Municipality**	**165.06**	**90.08**	**2.06**	**33.46**	**34.17**	**5.29**
溧水县	Lishui County	23.98	13.95	0.24	4.41	3.70	1.68
高淳县	Gaochun County	28.48	11.77	0.17	4.58	11.53	0.43
无锡市	**Wuxi Municipality**	**101.23**	**46.97**	**4.30**	**26.69**	**17.73**	**5.54**
江阴市	Jiangyin City	32.98	11.88	0.96	12.02	5.07	3.05
宜兴市	Yixing City	36.03	17.86	1.76	6.07	9.35	0.98
徐州市	**Xuzhou Municipality**	**334.21**	**217.51**	**7.99**	**84.76**	**18.85**	**5.10**
丰县	Fengxian County	39.59	30.52	0.54	6.84	0.50	1.18
沛县	Peixian County	59.41	36.69	0.54	17.90	3.57	0.70
铜山县	Tongshan County	50.13	32.21	1.96	12.25	2.82	0.88
睢宁县	Suining County	41.36	26.96	0.80	11.18	2.14	0.28
新沂市	Xinyi City	44.64	26.62	1.66	10.85	4.88	0.63
邳州市	Pizhou City	77.90	53.18	2.01	17.86	4.43	0.42
常州市	**Changzhou Municipality**	**109.08**	**53.27**	**1.25**	**18.39**	**30.97**	**5.19**
溧阳市	Liyang City	30.45	15.14	0.83	4.07	9.93	0.49
金坛市	Jintan City	28.93	13.09	0.27	3.81	10.50	1.26
苏州市	**Suzhou Municipality**	**172.18**	**66.31**	**7.24**	**21.43**	**60.19**	**17.02**
常熟市	Changshu City	31.52	15.28	0.71	3.34	9.78	2.42
张家港市	Zhangjiagang City	22.88	10.30	1.45	3.07	3.01	5.05
昆山市	Kunshan City	22.04	5.80	1.99	1.49	11.47	1.29
吴江市	Wujiang City	30.74	13.06	1.01	3.30	12.42	0.94
太仓市	Taicang City	28.61	13.26	0.71	6.09	6.10	2.44

20－9 续表1 Continued

单位：亿元 (100 million yuan)

市县	City and County	农林牧渔业总产值 Total Output Value of Farming, Forestry, Animal Husbandry and Fishery	农业 Farming	林业 Forestry	畜牧业 Animal Husbandry	渔业 Fishery	农林牧渔服务业 Service for Farming, Forestry, Animal Husbandry, Fishery
南通市	**Nantong Municipality**	**310.14**	**135.67**	**2.33**	**81.82**	**77.80**	**12.50**
海安县	Haian County	51.63	18.47	0.33	27.51	2.92	2.39
如东县	Rudong County	61.86	23.57	0.59	16.14	20.21	1.35
启东市	Qidong City	64.77	23.07	0.16	7.01	33.09	1.44
如皋市	Rugao City	45.13	25.38	0.26	14.87	2.81	1.80
通州市	Tongzhou City	39.25	21.30	0.47	7.32	7.80	2.35
海门市	Haimen City	40.13	19.11	0.37	7.44	10.30	2.91
连云港市	**Lianyungang Municipality**	**187.27**	**94.84**	**3.50**	**37.50**	**44.24**	**7.19**
赣榆县	Ganyu County	50.62	16.14	1.07	7.91	24.88	0.62
东海县	Donghai County	51.44	32.88	0.92	10.17	5.61	1.86
灌云县	Guanyun County	40.17	22.64	0.32	11.22	3.72	2.27
灌南县	Guannan County	25.85	15.55	0.84	5.03	2.51	1.92
淮安市	**Huaian Municipality**	**219.79**	**134.29**	**5.64**	**49.63**	**26.19**	**4.04**
涟水县	Lianshui County	49.10	33.28	1.34	12.18	1.48	0.83
洪泽县	Hongze County	24.50	10.78	1.59	5.75	5.84	0.53
盱眙县	Xuyi County	35.98	23.67	0.64	5.06	6.02	0.61
金湖县	Jinhu County	20.08	10.27	0.98	2.80	5.26	0.77
盐城市	**Yancheng Municipality**	**553.05**	**257.78**	**11.66**	**147.73**	**100.71**	**35.17**
响水县	Xiangshui County	35.06	18.90	0.73	7.87	4.48	3.08
滨海县	Binhai County	52.84	25.23	2.23	12.69	11.44	1.24
阜宁县	Funing County	54.32	19.92	0.73	19.26	8.93	5.48
射阳县	Sheyang County	94.02	40.76	2.09	19.95	23.15	8.06
建湖县	Jianhu County	46.85	19.29	0.50	11.92	11.94	3.20

20－9　续表2　Continued

单位:亿元　　　　(100 million yuan)

市　县	City and County	农林牧渔业总产值 Total Output Value of Farming, Forestry, Animal Husbandry and Fishery	农　业 Farming	林　业 Forestry	畜牧业 Animal Husbandry	渔　业 Fishery	农林牧渔服务业 Service for Farming, Forestry, Animal Husbandry, Fishery
东台市	Dongtai City	98.70	44.75	2.26	33.05	13.41	5.22
大丰市	Dafeng City	91.50	54.50	1.64	13.31	15.46	6.59
扬州市	**Yangzhou Municipality**	**182.63**	**80.43**	**5.30**	**37.14**	**51.76**	**7.99**
宝应县	Baoying County	47.74	16.53	1.29	6.40	21.77	1.75
仪征市	Yizheng City	16.69	9.73	0.82	4.53	0.68	0.94
高邮市	Gaoyou City	50.24	19.50	0.97	9.66	17.91	2.19
江都市	Jiangdu City	38.83	20.30	1.66	9.37	6.66	0.83
镇江市	**Zhenjiang Municipality**	**73.67**	**44.34**	**1.93**	**11.96**	**11.84**	**3.59**
丹阳市	Danyang City	28.58	17.27	0.32	4.09	5.51	1.39
扬中市	Yangzhong City	6.97	3.76	0.38	1.38	0.87	0.59
句容市	Jurong City	20.90	13.65	1.01	3.11	2.40	0.74
泰州市	**Taizhou Municipality**	**171.21**	**87.11**	**3.36**	**42.20**	**29.98**	**8.57**
兴化市	Xinghua City	72.96	35.62	0.99	10.53	21.43	4.40
靖江市	Jingjiang City	16.84	8.44	0.33	4.85	1.85	1.37
泰兴市	Taixing City	40.66	20.52	1.17	15.40	2.38	1.19
姜堰市	Jiangyan City	31.10	17.36	0.56	8.65	3.36	1.16
宿迁市	**Suqian Municipality**	**192.49**	**113.26**	**9.01**	**31.97**	**34.35**	**3.89**
沭阳县	Shuyang County	64.10	47.10	3.04	10.26	3.31	0.39
泗阳县	Siyang County	38.65	21.65	3.42	5.58	6.45	1.55
泗洪县	Sihong County	45.71	21.27	0.68	6.78	16.30	0.69

20－10 农业生产情况(2006年)
BASIC CONDITIONS OF AGRICULTURAL PRODUCTION (2006)

市　县	City and County	农作物总播种面积(千公顷) Total Sown Area (1000 hectares)	#粮食作物 Grain Grops	农业机械总动力(万千瓦) Total Power of Agricultural Machinery (10000 kW)	农用化肥施用量(万吨) Consumption of Chemical Fertilizer (10000 tons)	农村用电量(亿千瓦小时) Electricity Consumed in Rural Area (100 million kWh)	有效灌溉面积(千公顷) Irrigated Area (1000 hectares)
南京市	**Nanjing Municipality**	**377.49**	**153.65**	**198.5**	**13.45**	**23.51**	**19.42**
溧水县	Lishui County	68.99	29.62	28.9	1.31	4.43	2.84
高淳县	Gaochun County	59.48	24.47	48.0	2.82	1.87	3.41
无锡市	**Wuxi Municipality**	**180.01**	**119.02**	**135.8**	**8.85**	**236.06**	**14.03**
江阴市	Jiangyin City	47.32	33.60	32.1	2.17	109.15	4.09
宜兴市	Yixing City	85.68	55.86	59.9	4.10	46.28	6.26
徐州市	**Xuzhou Municipality**	**1015.28**	**613.20**	**464.8**	**69.26**	**32.93**	**47.67**
丰　县	Fengxian County	129.04	81.76	61.7	11.25	1.46	7.53
沛　县	Peixian County	137.11	81.61	78.4	9.20	3.25	7.01
铜山县	Tongshan County	166.26	102.02	70.5	10.14	6.55	9.92
睢宁县	Suining County	167.43	117.88	65.0	9.84	4.29	7.02
新沂市	Xinyi City	132.52	72.09	53.9	8.06	1.70	7.04
邳州市	Pizhou City	213.05	107.29	88.3	14.59	6.83	6.68
常州市	**Changzhou Municipality**	**236.59**	**145.81**	**257.0**	**8.72**	**111.12**	**15.48**
溧阳市	Liyang City	91.64	51.16	46.7	3.23	23.97	6.07
金坛市	Jintan City	56.60	34.97	35.8	2.68	7.13	3.84
苏州市	**Suzhou Municipality**	**297.92**	**175.70**	**186.3**	**10.96**	**366.47**	**20.93**
常熟市	Changshu City	79.60	43.43	31.1	3.08	41.31	5.69
张家港市	Zhangjiagang City	58.68	41.54	32.2	1.26	92.14	3.58
昆山市	Kunshan City	29.36	19.64	23.2	1.27	55.97	2.01
吴江市	Wujiang City	49.06	25.12	46.1	2.15	99.07	3.83
太仓市	Taicang City	50.44	31.11	16.2	1.20	27.99	3.44

市县 City and County		农作物总播种面积（千公顷）Total Sown Area (1000 hectares)	#粮食作物 Grain Grops	农业机械总动力（万千瓦）Total Power of Agricultural Machinery (10000 kW)	农用化肥施用量（万吨）Consumption of Chemical Fertilizer (10000 tons)	农村用电量（亿千瓦小时）Electricity Consumed in Rural Area (100 million kWh)	有效灌溉面积（千公顷）Irrigated Area (1000 hectares)
南通市	**Nantong Municipality**	**872.62**	**544.58**	**293.2**	**27.16**	**68.68**	**42.14**
海安县	Haian County	107.14	81.66	50.7	3.79	8.17	5.47
如东县	Rudong County	172.89	131.25	73.3	6.38	6.78	9.48
启东市	Qidong City	155.24	75.73	40.2	3.51	5.13	5.89
如皋市	Rugao City	160.21	112.01	55.7	4.13	11.00	6.13
通州市	Tongzhou City	136.51	80.30	35.8	3.02	14.66	7.87
海门市	Haimen City	111.09	45.90	26.8	5.24	15.70	6.00
连云港市	**Lianyungang Municipality**	**556.67**	**445.62**	**270.0**	**31.37**	**13.60**	**29.25**
赣榆县	Ganyu County	97.91	71.96	75.2	4.30	4.73	5.35
东海县	Donghai County	197.84	159.71	69.9	8.02	4.78	9.84
灌云县	Guanyun County	140.47	113.83	62.9	10.08	1.82	8.94
灌南县	Guannan County	91.87	78.29	38.0	4.87	0.79	3.93
淮安市	**Huaian Municipality**	**741.78**	**594.23**	**298.1**	**32.71**	**8.25**	**30.76**
涟水县	Lianshui County	151.38	119.80	51.8	5.75	1.22	6.98
洪泽县	Hongze County	59.61	49.41	50.8	3.45	0.52	2.65
盱眙县	Xuyi County	161.78	121.70	54.5	4.21	1.18	6.26
金湖县	Jinhu County	75.90	66.13	39.8	4.02	1.28	3.25
盐城市	**Yancheng Municipality**	**1372.32**	**824.63**	**422.8**	**58.82**	**33.65**	**61.02**
响水县	Xiangshui County	105.33	63.16	31.5	4.25	2.00	4.54
滨海县	Binhai County	165.71	95.42	63.6	5.29	3.00	6.38
阜宁县	Funing County	140.93	114.25	48.9	5.12	3.83	8.58
射阳县	Sheyang County	215.88	126.33	67.4	11.04	5.23	10.21
建湖县	Jianhu County	107.41	90.25	35.9	3.65	4.25	5.88

20－10 续表2 Continued

市 县 City and County		农作物总播种面积（千公顷）Total Sown Area (1000 hectares)	#粮食作物 Grain Grops	农业机械总动力（万千瓦）Total Power of Agricultural Machinery (10000 kW)	农用化肥施用量（万吨）Consumption of Chemical Fertilizer (10000 tons)	农村用电量（亿千瓦小时）Electricity Consumed in Rural Area (100 million kWh)	有效灌溉面积（千公顷）Irrigated Area (1000 hectares)
东台市	Dongtai City	246.89	128.39	69.3	9.31	6.51	8.71
大丰市	Dafeng City	237.66	97.13	46.7	11.57	4.04	8.48
扬州市	**Yangzhou Municipality**	**473.87**	**367.95**	**183.1**	**19.35**	**26.37**	**25.64**
宝应县	Baoying County	118.79	94.49	35.5	3.54	2.89	5.48
仪征市	Yizheng City	62.30	50.61	25.6	1.64	2.36	3.52
高邮市	Gaoyou City	130.35	104.87	39.3	4.80	5.68	6.51
江都市	Jiangdu City	103.19	75.75	50.9	6.73	4.90	6.74
镇江市	**Zhenjiang Municipality**	**233.63**	**159.28**	**131.4**	**9.52**	**34.05**	**13.11**
丹阳市	Danyang City	83.81	66.79	47.6	3.17	20.57	5.20
扬中市	Yangzhong City	18.95	15.10	12.0	0.74	3.11	0.97
句容市	Jurong City	76.51	42.04	42.1	3.23	3.59	3.84
泰州市	**Taizhou Municipality**	**568.31**	**414.22**	**214.7**	**21.03**	**47.06**	**27.85**
兴化市	Xinghua City	228.96	177.34	86.9	8.23	16.19	11.53
靖江市	Jingjiang City	55.61	44.83	26.0	2.54	8.07	2.95
泰兴市	Taixing City	137.98	96.26	50.7	3.27	11.95	6.42
姜堰市	Jiangyan City	114.25	73.74	38.4	5.70	6.80	5.68
宿迁市	**Suqian Municipality**	**673.57**	**534.85**	**339.7**	**31.75**	**10.62**	**33.71**
沭阳县	Shuyang County	236.29	173.84	109.1	13.42	3.69	11.79
泗阳县	Siyang County	105.18	79.26	56.7	3.59	1.18	5.30
泗洪县	Sihong County	183.43	156.79	97.9	7.70	1.56	7.72

20-11 农 产 品 产 量(2006年)
OUTPUT OF AGRICULTURAL PRODUCTS (2006)

单位:万吨 (10000 tons)

市 县	City and County	粮食产量 Grain	油料产量 Oil-Bearing Crops	棉花产量(吨) Cotton (ton)	肉类总产量 Meat	#猪牛羊肉 Pork, Beef and Mutton	水产品产量 Aquatic Products
南京市	**Nanjing Municipality**	**105.99**	**19.22**	**5536**	**19.63**	**11.65**	**19.04**
溧水县	Lishui County	21.24	4.56	650	2.86	1.40	2.47
高淳县	Gaochun County	18.47	4.03	105	3.62	1.81	3.75
无锡市	**Wuxi Municipality**	**77.83**	**2.92**		**14.21**	**9.32**	**13.11**
江阴市	Jiangyin City	21.43	0.41		5.07	3.01	2.29
宜兴市	Yixing City	36.71	2.07		4.36	2.86	7.88
徐州市	**Xuzhou Municipality**	**357.98**	**14.62**	**49175**	**50.38**	**33.92**	**17.07**
丰县	Fengxian County	42.77	0.84	16010	4.29	3.65	0.40
沛县	Peixian County	50.91	0.80	4651	11.36	4.90	2.27
铜山县	Tongshan County	61.58	1.13	8235	7.14	4.74	3.64
睢宁县	Suining County	65.47	2.62	5589	6.43	4.85	2.28
新沂市	Xinyi City	41.98	7.28		7.34	5.02	3.60
邳州市	Pizhou City	64.30	1.58	11925	10.56	6.98	3.65
常州市	**Changzhou Municipality**	**105.81**	**8.26**	**320**	**11.25**	**6.60**	**13.69**
溧阳市	Liyang City	40.97	6.06	203	1.90	1.15	3.50
金坛市	Jintan City	24.53	1.43	117	2.42	1.43	3.90
苏州市	**Suzhou Municipality**	**123.52**	**6.36**	**3757**	**15.87**	**8.56**	**30.38**
常熟市	Changshu City	30.91	1.57	2050	2.35	1.60	4.40
张家港市	Zhangjiagang City	27.62	0.53	909	1.67	0.81	1.86
昆山市	Kunshan City	13.79	0.57	54	1.24	0.79	5.56
吴江市	Wujiang City	18.90	2.03		2.93	2.13	7.89
太仓市	Taicang City	21.29	0.97	744	5.02	1.50	3.04

20－11 续表 1 Continued

单位：万吨 (10000 tons)

市县	City and County	粮食产量 Grain	油料产量 Oil-Bearing Crops	棉花产量（吨）Cotton (ton)	肉类总产量 Meat	#猪牛羊肉 Pork, Beef and Mutton	水产品产量 Aquatic Products
南通市	**Nantong Municipality**	**319.48**	**40.49**	**54846**	**37.73**	**21.75**	**72.28**
海安县	Haian County	60.41	1.77	1183	7.52	4.62	2.72
如东县	Rudong County	80.98	5.01	18373	7.35	3.84	22.01
启东市	Qidong City	28.39	9.68	15554	4.47	1.88	32.73
如皋市	Rugao City	68.87	4.51	639	8.06	5.13	2.26
通州市	Tongzhou City	51.05	8.51	9444	5.36	3.61	4.87
海门市	Haimen City	18.77	9.42	9590	3.91	1.91	7.16
连云港市	**Lianyungang Municipality**	**276.99**	**12.37**	**20546**	**20.30**	**16.74**	**50.41**
赣榆县	Ganyu County	41.92	6.00	1020	4.10	3.39	31.23
东海县	Donghai County	99.29	5.90	136	6.44	5.04	5.89
灌云县	Guanyun County	70.93	0.16	14428	4.84	4.15	3.81
灌南县	Guannan County	49.84	0.29	2355	3.27	2.80	2.85
淮安市	**Huaian Municipality**	**381.46**	**15.80**	**2354**	**22.08**	**16.32**	**24.15**
涟水县	Lianshui County	75.67	3.54	222	5.07	3.71	2.26
洪泽县	Hongze County	33.65	0.46		1.83	1.20	4.84
盱眙县	Xuyi County	77.66	7.59	72	3.46	2.47	5.22
金湖县	Jinhu County	41.65	1.04	2060	1.28	0.88	4.73
盐城市	**Yancheng Municipality**	**535.33**	**35.82**	**192348**	**63.56**	**42.85**	**85.19**
响水县	Xiangshui County	39.09	2.50	13068	3.52	2.92	4.63
滨海县	Binhai County	61.55	8.55	12147	8.55	5.81	7.64
阜宁县	Funing County	77.60	1.83	2689	14.01	10.16	5.64
射阳县	Sheyang County	80.80	4.15	68469	6.88	3.64	15.64
建湖县	Jianhu County	65.50	1.60	4637	4.13	2.32	8.26

20－11 续表2 Continued

单位:万吨 (10000 tons)

市 县 City and County		粮食产量 Grain	油料产量 Oil-Bearing Crops	棉花产量(吨) Cotton (ton)	肉类总产量 Meat	#猪牛羊肉 Pork, Beef and Mutton	水产品产量 Aquatic Products
东台市	Dongtai City	76.64	8.87	24443	9.17	6.39	14.03
大丰市	Dafeng City	58.01	5.81	51638	7.79	4.66	13.34
扬州市	**Yangzhou Municipality**	**245.08**	**11.47**	**8372**	**22.39**	**14.74**	**36.74**
宝应县	Baoying County	65.76	2.22	176	4.11	2.56	13.81
仪征市	Yizheng City	27.69	1.09	195	3.46	2.08	0.59
高邮市	Gaoyou City	73.02	2.91	6102	5.16	3.47	15.26
江都市	Jiangdu City	49.76	4.00	1128	5.73	3.43	3.79
镇江市	**Zhenjiang Municipality**	**99.57**	**7.63**	**1726**	**7.21**	**5.41**	**7.77**
丹阳市	Danyang City	42.17	1.69	92	2.71	2.14	3.30
扬中市	Yangzhong City	9.86	0.13		0.81	0.68	0.62
句容市	Jurong City	26.17	4.09	1457	1.68	1.35	2.02
泰州市	**Taizhou Municipality**	**282.25**	**13.76**	**20893**	**24.88**	**20.29**	**22.03**
兴化市	Xinghua City	122.93	3.34	17996	4.75	3.25	15.24
靖江市	Jingjiang City	30.44	1.02		3.56	3.23	0.90
泰兴市	Taixing City	62.13	4.60		8.45	7.53	1.83
姜堰市	Jiangyan City	52.91	3.96	2809	6.21	4.82	3.30
宿迁市	**Suqian Municipality**	**317.64**	**8.87**	**5021**	**22.95**	**17.45**	**24.69**
沭阳县	Shuyang County	105.51	3.53	1496	8.68	6.65	3.50
泗阳县	Siyang County	48.75	1.83	396	3.70	2.87	5.33
泗洪县	Sihong County	83.04	2.17	1924	4.96	3.68	7.87

20－12 工业企业单位数(2006年)
NUMBER OF INDUSTRIAL ENTERPRISES (2006)

单位:个 (unit)

市县	City and County	工业企业个数 Number of Industrial Enterprises	内资企业 Domestic Funded Enterprises	外商港澳台商投资企业 Foreign, HongKong Macao and Taiwan Invested Enterprises	#国有控股企业 State-owned Share Holding Enterprises	#大中型企业 Large and Medium Scale Enterprises	#轻工业 Light Indestry
南京市	**Nanjing Municipality**	**1889**	**1334**	**555**	**207**	**269**	**630**
溧水县	Lishui County	176	135	41	8	9	68
高淳县	Gaochun County	108	88	20	5	8	55
无锡市	**Wuxi Municipality**	**4962**	**3829**	**1133**	**104**	**583**	**1665**
江阴市	Jiangyin City	1065	832	233	31	166	531
宜兴市	Yixing City	934	764	170	4	82	275
徐州市	**Xuzhou Municipality**	**1586**	**1478**	**108**	**69**	**91**	**536**
丰县	Fengxian County	134	130	4	6	2	48
沛县	Peixian County	184	174	10	5	3	112
铜山县	Tongshan County	239	227	12	3	18	87
睢宁县	Suining County	92	86	6	0	3	37
新沂市	Xinyi City	107	93	14	3	13	39
邳州市	Pizhou City	254	232	22	3	5	50
常州市	**Changzhou Municipality**	**4233**	**3511**	**712**	**54**	**303**	**1556**
溧阳市	Liyang City	367	316	51	6	36	98
金坛市	Jintan City	445	337	108	3	27	196
苏州市	**Suzhou Municipality**	**7485**	**4207**	**3278**	**85**	**1375**	**3701**
常熟市	Changshu City	1536	1260	276	4	162	928
张家港市	Zhangjiagang City	830	641	189	5	155	434
昆山市	Kunshan City	1218	247	971	11	353	448
吴江市	Wujiang City	1071	708	363	8	170	655
太仓市	Taicang City	746	411	335	15	84	457

注:工业统计范围为全部国有及年主营业务收入500万元以上非国有工业企业(下同)。

Note: The statistical scope of industry covers all the state-owned industrial enterprises and the non-stated-owned industrial enterprises with major business reuenue of over 5 million yuan. Similarly in following tables.

20－12 续表1 Continued

单位:个 (unit)

市县	City and County	工业企业个数 Number of Industrial Enterprises	内资企业 Domestic Funded Enterprises	外商港澳台商投资企业 Foreign, HongKong Macao and Taiwan Invested Enterprises	#国有控股企业 State-owned Share Holding Enterprises	#大中型企业 Large and Medium Scale Enterprises	#轻工业 Light Indestry
南通市	**Nantong Municipality**	**4217**	**3104**	**1113**	**61**	**258**	**2465**
海安县	Haian County	498	427	71	1	32	274
如东县	Rudong County	504	385	119	2	27	333
启东市	Qidong City	531	379	152	2	21	279
如皋市	Rugao City	546	466	80	0	20	325
通州市	Tongzhou City	737	516	221	5	44	493
海门市	Haimen City	462	276	186	1	33	238
连云港市	**Lianyungang Municipality**	**838**	**678**	**160**	**47**	**57**	**381**
赣榆县	Ganyu County	175	156	19	2	4	100
东海县	Donghai County	158	123	35	3	9	62
灌云县	Guanyun County	122	112	10	10	2	72
灌南县	Guannan County	113	99	14	2	3	43
淮安市	**Huaian Municipality**	**1350**	**1266**	**84**	**68**	**72**	**660**
涟水县	Lianshui County	133	124	9	5	9	79
洪泽县	Hongze County	121	110	11	6	10	52
盱眙县	Xuyi County	244	240	4	3	11	107
金湖县	Jinhu County	136	128	8	3	6	48
盐城市	**Yancheng Municipality**	**2513**	**2283**	**230**	**33**	**131**	**1195**
响水县	Xiangshui County	162	157	5	3	6	79
滨海县	Binhai County	186	179	7	2	5	74
阜宁县	Funing County	226	193	33	2	11	113
射阳县	Sheyang County	258	241	17	4	10	159
建湖县	Jianhu County	279	270	9	3	16	100

20－12　续表2　Continued

单位：个　　　　　　　　　　　　　　　　　　　　　　　　　　　　　　　(unit)

市　县	City and County	工业企业个数 Number of Industrial Enterprises	内资企业 Domestic Funded Enterprises	外商港澳台商投资企业 Foreign, HongKong Macao and Taiwan Invested Enterprises	#国有控股企业 State-owned Share Holding Enterprises	#大中型企业 Large and Medium Scale Enterprises	#轻工业 Light Industry
东台市	Dongtai City	478	435	43	1	20	249
大丰市	Dafeng City	351	296	55	6	18	214
扬州市	**Yangzhou Municipality**	**2252**	**1927**	**325**	**53**	**156**	**991**
宝应县	Baoying County	228	193	35	5	11	101
仪征市	Yizheng City	310	266	44	15	16	162
高邮市	Gaoyou City	353	325	28	1	16	146
江都市	Jiangdu City	568	535	33	1	29	209
镇江市	**Zhenjiang Municipality**	**1961**	**1477**	**484**	**86**	**164**	**735**
丹阳市	Danyang City	722	575	147	14	52	305
扬中市	Yangzhong City	330	248	82	12	31	76
句容市	Jurong City	314	212	102	19	16	173
泰州市	**Taizhou Municipality**	**2190**	**1917**	**273**	**32**	**135**	**727**
兴化市	Xinghua City	440	413	27	5	15	118
靖江市	Jingjiang City	441	372	69	10	34	97
泰兴市	Taixing City	430	374	56	5	22	153
姜堰市	Jiangyan City	465	413	52	4	21	182
宿迁市	**Suqian Municipality**	**856**	**816**	**40**	**16**	**30**	**407**
沭阳县	Shuyang County	274	263	11	0	4	93
泗阳县	Siyang County	186	180	6	1	2	69
泗洪县	Sihong County	117	115	2	11	5	87

20－13 工 业 总 产 值(2006年)
GROSS OUTPUT VALUE OF INDUSTRY (2006)

单位:亿元 (100 million yuan)

市 县 City and County		工业总产值 Gross Output Value of Industry	内资企业 Domestic Funded Enterprises	外商港澳台商投资企业 Foreign, HongKong Macao and Taiwan Invested Enterprises	#国有控股企业 State-owned Share Holding Enterprises	#大中型企业 Large and Medium Scale Enterprises	#轻工业 Light Industry
南京市	**Nanjing Municipality**	**4692.81**	**2821.65**	**1871.16**	**1895.66**	**3543.20**	**700.50**
溧水县	Lishui County	165.52	117.94	47.58	9.37	40.76	48.67
高淳县	Gaochun County	138.25	122.21	16.04	40.50	58.57	53.27
无锡市	**Wuxi Municipality**	**7115.29**	**4626.60**	**2488.69**	**549.28**	**4586.77**	**1858.97**
江阴市	Jiangyin City	2640.98	2104.90	536.08	277.01	2090.15	991.15
宜兴市	Yixing City	983.53	825.04	158.48	1.48	401.31	170.57
徐州市	**Xuzhou Municipality**	**1632.55**	**1460.90**	**171.65**	**553.71**	**879.93**	**512.77**
丰县	Fengxian County	39.34	34.40	4.94	0.90	3.85	14.74
沛县	Peixian County	98.91	90.77	8.14	3.25	4.41	50.40
铜山县	Tongshan County	303.18	296.94	6.24	4.30	182.60	154.66
睢宁县	Suining County	53.59	33.87	19.72	0.00	16.49	29.61
新沂市	Xinyi City	90.38	75.42	14.96	9.81	52.85	40.38
邳州市	Pizhou City	140.26	119.23	21.03	1.58	9.13	24.36
常州市	**Changzhou Municipality**	**3293.87**	**2245.91**	**1047.86**	**191.01**	**1508.87**	**908.72**
溧阳市	Liyang City	383.54	275.60	107.94	3.62	241.67	48.64
金坛市	Jintan City	262.08	163.44	98.63	3.82	85.50	90.73
苏州市	**Suzhou Municipality**	**12538.51**	**4191.51**	**8347.00**	**301.67**	**9297.30**	**4105.03**
常熟市	Changshu City	1558.27	1041.76	516.51	21.09	937.06	838.61
张家港市	Zhangjiagang City	2049.92	1599.72	450.20	49.69	1631.25	656.57
昆山市	Kunshan City	2798.66	135.46	2663.20	18.06	2300.53	643.37
吴江市	Wujiang City	1468.48	510.55	957.93	32.52	1047.22	541.66
太仓市	Taicang City	696.83	319.86	376.96	75.29	374.62	346.70

20－13 续表1 Continued

单位:亿元 (100 million yuan)

市 县	City and County	工业总产值 Gross Output Value of Industry	内资企业 Domestic Funded Enterprises	外商港澳台商投资企业 Foreign, HongKong Macao and Taiwan Invested Enterprises	#国有控股企业 State-owned Share Holding Enterprises	#大中型企业 Large and Medium Scale Enterprises	#轻工业 Light Industry
南通市	**Nantong Municipality**	**2949.53**	**1880.08**	**1069.45**	**195.34**	**1108.64**	**1411.46**
海安县	Haian County	307.52	258.37	49.15	0.12	112.07	175.02
如东县	Rudong County	274.36	194.76	79.60	0.93	97.54	155.59
启东市	Qidong City	304.19	214.91	89.28	0.17	84.93	137.49
如皋市	Rugao City	297.63	258.54	39.09	0.00	88.72	119.17
通州市	Tongzhou City	538.68	358.62	180.06	0.60	186.53	341.85
海门市	Haimen City	487.14	309.22	177.92	0.07	167.21	224.47
连云港市	**Lianyungang Municipality**	**463.25**	**266.77**	**196.48**	**68.36**	**245.94**	**228.60**
赣榆县	Ganyu County	54.65	48.60	6.05	2.74	5.98	30.20
东海县	Donghai County	55.19	30.06	25.13	0.42	22.31	26.36
灌云县	Guanyun County	29.20	25.83	3.36	1.41	1.51	14.45
灌南县	Guannan County	40.88	39.04	1.85	0.13	5.51	14.55
淮安市	**Huaian Municipality**	**794.07**	**705.18**	**88.89**	**154.47**	**329.39**	**310.40**
涟水县	Lianshui County	76.68	71.58	5.10	7.57	23.31	32.69
洪泽县	Hongze County	59.68	47.84	11.85	1.41	14.60	13.22
盱眙县	Xuyi County	86.28	85.22	1.06	1.17	19.81	28.09
金湖县	Jinhu County	53.43	45.16	8.27	2.06	19.58	27.88
盐城市	**Yancheng Municipality**	**1378.15**	**1069.27**	**308.87**	**42.71**	**543.37**	**611.69**
响水县	Xiangshui County	64.75	48.21	16.54	0.71	21.59	26.18
滨海县	Binhai County	80.10	76.68	3.43	0.18	19.80	38.76
阜宁县	Funing County	119.53	97.81	21.73	0.42	20.23	59.58
射阳县	Sheyang County	153.27	129.83	23.44	1.15	31.85	112.14
建湖县	Jianhu County	145.66	134.57	11.09	0.19	80.83	84.89

20－13 续 表 2 Continued

单位:亿元 (100 million yuan)

市 县 City and County		工业总产值 Gross Output Value of Industry	内资企业 Domestic Funded Enterprises	外商港澳台商投资企业 Foreign, HongKong Macao and Taiwan Invested Enterprises	#国有控股企业 State-owned Share Holding Enterprises	#大中型企业 Large and Medium Scale Enterprises	#轻工业 Light Industry
东台市	Dongtai City	195.50	163.42	32.07	0.03	68.38	91.50
大丰市	Dafeng City	137.90	107.79	30.12	1.73	44.46	84.28
扬州市	**Yangzhou Municipality**	**1891.88**	**1380.40**	**511.48**	**446.49**	**924.62**	**723.11**
宝应县	Baoying County	159.50	129.34	30.16	54.68	68.58	41.00
仪征市	Yizheng City	312.20	88.70	223.49	193.78	205.28	225.80
高邮市	Gaoyou City	169.93	150.15	19.78	0.10	46.12	63.67
江都市	Jiangdu City	438.10	409.43	28.66	0.14	126.35	119.30
镇江市	**Zhenjiang Municipality**	**1628.78**	**1055.67**	**573.11**	**237.44**	**857.74**	**439.98**
丹阳市	Danyang City	467.78	381.24	86.54	76.67	245.21	118.05
扬中市	Yangzhong City	204.08	170.21	33.87	8.25	127.03	23.71
句容市	Jurong City	225.11	125.57	99.54	3.24	40.87	96.85
泰州市	**Taizhou Municipality**	**1664.54**	**1349.25**	**315.30**	**174.86**	**852.54**	**595.00**
兴化市	Xinghua City	210.07	173.84	36.23	3.56	55.73	48.50
靖江市	Jingjiang City	307.38	226.24	81.15	9.64	172.56	56.05
泰兴市	Taixing City	292.12	226.87	65.25	1.92	109.48	101.75
姜堰市	Jiangyan City	275.71	236.00	39.70	5.92	96.97	116.57
宿迁市	**Suqian Municipality**	**288.97**	**267.40**	**21.57**	**42.05**	**72.43**	**125.96**
沭阳县	Shuyang County	68.72	65.09	3.63	0.00	4.78	19.50
泗阳县	Siyang County	51.96	49.61	2.36	0.04	3.18	19.56
泗洪县	Sihong County	45.48	45.00	0.48	19.99	10.06	26.09

20－14　工业企业主要经济指标(2006年)

MAJOR ECONOMIC INDICATORS ON INDUSTRIAL ENTERPRISES (2006)

单位：亿元　　　　(100 million yuan)

市　县	City and County	工业增加值 Value Added of Industry	资产合计 Total Assets	负债合计 Total Liabilities	主营业务收入 Major Business Revenue	利税总额 Total Pre-tax Profits	#利润总额 Total Profits
南京市	**Nanjing Municipality**	**973.60**	**3560.76**	**1984.68**	**4714.13**	**407.98**	**214.88**
溧水县	Lishui County	39.43	98.88	58.98	158.54	11.82	6.51
高淳县	Gaochun County	34.86	81.24	46.23	128.21	7.00	4.53
无锡市	**Wuxi Municipality**	**1661.78**	**5307.64**	**3281.91**	**7062.47**	**515.66**	**351.10**
江阴市	Jiangyin City	623.34	2071.90	1313.46	2606.75	209.64	149.93
宜兴市	Yixing City	230.16	604.36	369.30	954.03	71.80	43.29
徐州市	**Xuzhou Municipality**	**536.54**	**1094.10**	**674.14**	**1586.71**	**203.29**	**87.04**
丰　县	Fengxian County	11.64	26.04	14.27	36.53	2.74	1.18
沛　县	Peixian County	25.78	35.40	21.14	94.64	6.35	3.03
铜山县	Tongshan County	82.05	145.94	79.43	292.74	32.91	17.99
睢宁县	Suining County	15.55	23.75	15.30	53.71	3.99	2.77
新沂市	Xinyi City	27.00	62.07	42.70	88.93	6.61	3.49
邳州市	Pizhou City	37.71	44.07	19.76	136.50	9.82	4.44
常州市	**Changzhou Municipality**	**768.16**	**2356.62**	**1508.35**	**3243.79**	**228.98**	**142.33**
溧阳市	Liyang City	86.53	201.76	142.10	345.98	32.02	15.49
金坛市	Jintan City	67.15	136.51	87.49	255.00	28.11	17.75
苏州市	**Suzhou Municipality**	**3075.13**	**9996.62**	**6087.87**	**12533.02**	**808.13**	**591.43**
常熟市	Changshu City	406.16	1206.01	720.45	1520.92	116.81	79.60
张家港市	Zhangjiagang City	510.71	1629.87	1071.13	2069.33	142.98	92.18
昆山市	Kunshan City	629.42	2002.27	1207.75	2783.58	157.18	129.44
吴江市	Wujiang City	362.39	1231.06	820.57	1475.59	68.73	48.88
太仓市	Taicang City	177.86	712.93	458.50	693.67	59.41	36.21

20－14 续表1 Continued

单位:亿元 (100 million yuan)

市 县 City and County		工 业 增加值 Value Added of Industry	资 产 合 计 Total Assets	负 债 合 计 Total Liabilities	主营业务 收 入 Major Business Revenue	利 税 总 额 Total Pre-tax Profits	#利润总额 Total Profits
南 通 市	**Nantong Municipality**	**792.99**	**1638.38**	**940.79**	**2919.56**	**241.32**	**157.05**
海 安 县	Haian County	84.87	151.53	95.58	303.24	16.46	9.70
如 东 县	Rudong County	73.38	127.85	72.55	274.46	18.95	11.63
启 东 市	Qidong City	82.30	118.28	65.41	300.45	24.86	16.08
如 皋 市	Rugao City	77.79	162.30	101.47	295.69	16.48	9.50
通 州 市	Tongzhou City	140.67	223.54	121.35	529.57	51.16	32.92
海 门 市	Haimen City	126.07	156.10	94.11	482.91	42.84	26.83
连云港市	**Lianyungang Municipality**	**132.72**	**372.07**	**205.75**	**450.34**	**43.39**	**23.86**
赣 榆 县	Ganyu County	13.47	27.56	13.51	53.21	3.40	1.49
东 海 县	Donghai County	14.47	35.87	16.87	53.65	4.22	2.86
灌 云 县	Guanyun County	7.29	18.29	8.99	28.24	2.21	0.89
灌 南 县	Guannan County	11.41	21.24	15.44	39.03	2.89	0.48
淮 安 市	**Huaian Municipality**	**217.08**	**539.01**	**318.65**	**822.74**	**89.48**	**35.67**
涟 水 县	Lianshui County	17.71	31.49	19.38	76.26	5.38	1.55
洪 泽 县	Hongze County	13.43	34.92	19.34	59.09	7.20	4.21
盱 眙 县	Xuyi County	22.49	51.33	23.76	84.59	6.02	2.90
金 湖 县	Jinhu County	12.78	32.50	20.90	51.04	3.67	2.14
盐 城 市	**Yancheng Municipality**	**345.46**	**795.66**	**511.34**	**1344.05**	**100.95**	**45.74**
响 水 县	Xiangshui County	16.51	35.58	20.55	58.71	6.08	3.85
滨 海 县	Binhai County	20.65	53.04	24.47	78.71	6.74	3.51
阜 宁 县	Funing County	28.98	54.78	34.93	118.49	6.32	2.75
射 阳 县	Sheyang County	41.79	68.72	46.38	148.31	9.87	4.80
建 湖 县	Jianhu County	38.13	83.92	52.88	140.02	11.24	5.45

单位：亿元　　　　(100 million yuan)

市　县 City and County		工业增加值 Value Added of Industry	资产合计 Total Assets	负债合计 Total Liabilities	主营业务收入 Major Business Revenue	利税总额 Total Pre-tax Profits	#利润总额 Total Profits
东台市	Dongtai City	48.67	92.90	59.87	192.13	17.00	7.56
大丰市	Dafeng City	33.70	83.28	55.53	136.34	9.00	4.08
扬州市	**Yangzhou Municipality**	**552.04**	**1141.55**	**650.16**	**1806.06**	**154.75**	**84.44**
宝应县	Baoying County	40.00	79.72	46.94	155.39	10.53	6.30
仪征市	Yizheng City	63.45	209.91	87.98	307.20	8.80	1.93
高邮市	Gaoyou City	40.60	81.40	53.54	160.55	9.17	4.00
江都市	Jiangdu City	107.22	138.79	88.20	403.78	25.91	15.35
镇江市	**Zhenjiang Municipality**	**460.97**	**1425.48**	**948.59**	**1575.94**	**130.21**	**70.24**
丹阳市	Danyang City	125.32	375.47	250.04	433.74	27.94	13.97
扬中市	Yangzhong City	55.98	173.80	116.74	192.96	18.71	9.51
句容市	Jurong City	61.57	120.44	70.15	215.10	14.53	6.49
泰州市	**Taizhou Municipality**	**472.33**	**1020.11**	**619.78**	**1589.57**	**139.43**	**73.15**
兴化市	Xinghua City	57.06	106.93	58.13	203.79	19.99	11.54
靖江市	Jingjiang City	82.39	231.00	172.89	280.46	24.28	12.70
泰兴市	Taixing City	84.04	157.96	97.03	268.05	25.59	13.51
姜堰市	Jiangyan City	74.06	137.82	76.48	259.57	22.65	14.53
宿迁市	**Suqian Municipality**	**81.06**	**168.89**	**93.91**	**286.93**	**26.98**	**11.84**
沭阳县	Shuyang County	17.02	23.62	11.91	67.64	5.07	2.71
泗阳县	Siyang County	14.47	22.05	8.73	53.25	3.47	2.15
泗洪县	Sihong County	12.95	28.42	15.57	47.33	6.18	1.56

20－15 交 通 运 输 （2006 年）
TRANSPORTATION（2006）

市　县 City and County		公路里程（公里）Total Length of Highway（km）	#等级公路 Grade Highway	公路客运量（万人）Passenger Traffic of Highways（10000 persons）	公路货运量（万吨）Freight Traffic of Highways（10000 tons）	民用汽车拥有量（万辆）Civil Vehicles Owned（10000 units）	#私人汽车 Private Vehicles
南京市	**Nanjing Municipality**	**9689**	**8087**	**19930**	**11249**	**36.32**	**22.71**
溧水县	Lishui County	1291	1223	345	569	1.17	0.86
高淳县	Gaochun County	1266	1144	242	344	0.67	0.45
无锡市	**Wuxi Municipality**	**6683**	**6505**	**21315**	**8845**	**35.44**	**20.30**
江阴市	Jiangyin City	1925	1912	4050	2300	8.61	4.98
宜兴市	Yixing City	2207	2047	3837	1238	5.18	2.87
徐州市	**Xuzhou Municipality**	**14857**	**11470**	**7712**	**7494**	**14.81**	**9.75**
丰　县	Fengxian County	1689	1489	386	749	0.97	0.67
沛　县	Peixian County	2467	1978	617	705	1.25	0.87
铜山县	Tongshan County	2532	1896	1234	1274	2.41	1.89
睢宁县	Suining County	2502	1889	771	824	1.14	0.86
新沂市	Xinyi City	1836	1342	463	974	0.93	0.63
邳州市	Pizhou City	2753	2140	1003	1049	1.57	1.05
常州市	**Changzhou Municipality**	**5546**	**5008**	**15958**	**5692**	**20.18**	**11.92**
溧阳市	Liyang City	1422	1349	3296	1116	1.91	1.06
金坛市	Jintan City	1411	970	2125	634	2.06	0.64
苏州市	**Suzhou Municipality**	**8483**	**8419**	**35182**	**8891**	**56.76**	**39.50**
常熟市	Changshu City	1952	1950	4365	1059	7.89	5.68
张家港市	Zhangjiagang City	1285	1252	3485	1658	6.72	5.13
昆山市	Kunshan City	1893	1459	5207	933	7.49	4.89
吴江市	Wujiang City	1971	1950	2840	707	4.81	3.80
太仓市	Taicang City	963	961	1975	848	3.79	2.78

20－15 续表1 Continued

市 县	City and County	公路里程（公里） Total Length of Highway (km)	#等级公路 Grade Highway	公路客运量（万人） Passenger Traffic of Highways (10000 persons)	公路货运量（万吨） Freight Traffic of Highways (10000 tons)	民用汽车拥有量（万辆） Civil Vehicles Owned (10000 units)	#私人汽车 Private Vehicles
南通市	**Nantong Municipality**	**14015**	**12320**	**9978**	**7594**	**16.93**	**10.65**
海安县	Haian County	2194	2132	783	742	1.27	0.76
如东县	Rudong County	2237	1568	428	872	1.47	0.92
启东市	Qidong City	2513	2383	912	450	2.11	1.54
如皋市	Rugao City	2727	2122	719	1044	1.94	1.35
通州市	Tongzhou City	1929	1806	292	881	2.27	1.46
海门市	Haimen City	1974	1868	781	836	2.00	1.42
连云港市	**Lianyungang Municipality**	**9357**	**8668**	**7059**	**4286**	**6.94**	**3.55**
赣榆县	Ganyu County	2324	2324	1429	1106	1.10	0.62
东海县	Donghai County	2779	2777	1378	1078	1.23	0.74
灌云县	Guanyun County	2215	1773	725	481	0.71	0.16
灌南县	Guannan County	1204	1073	703	436	0.48	0.31
淮安市	**Huaian Municipality**	**9975**	**7276**	**3822**	**2335**	**6.79**	**3.60**
涟水县	Lianshui County	1954	1399	130	303	0.85	0.53
洪泽县	Hongze County	889	781	193	102	0.44	0.19
盱眙县	Xuyi County	2201	1440	114	0	0.76	0.46
金湖县	Jinhu County	1039	676	205	226	0.43	0.19
盐城市	**Yancheng Municipality**	**16871**	**13642**	**6858**	**3393**	**10.09**	**6.34**
响水县	Xiangshui County	1520	1182	654	65	0.73	0.54
滨海县	Binhai County	1836	1070	239	726	1.40	0.87
阜宁县	Funing County	1614	874	402	115	0.87	0.62
射阳县	Sheyang County	2450	2274	248	116	0.90	0.66
建湖县	Jianhu County	1553	1060	615	134	0.67	0.43

20－15 续表2 Continued

市 县 City and County		公路里程（公里）Total Length of Highway (km)	#等级公路 Grade Highway	公路客运量（万人）Passenger Traffic of Highways (10000 persons)	公路货运量（万吨）Freight Traffic of Highways (10000 tons)	民用汽车拥有量（万辆）Civil Vehicles Owned (10000 units)	#私人汽车 Private Vehicles
东台市	Dongtai City	3086	2928	1030	735	1.21	0.77
大丰市	Dafeng City	2917	2546	434	262	1.08	0.75
扬州市	**Yangzhou Municipality**	**9247**	**7688**	**8595**	**4902**	**10.03**	**6.14**
宝应县	Baoying County	1918	1501	710	546	0.78	0.39
仪征市	Yizheng City	1395	1389	663	784	1.26	0.55
高邮市	Gaoyou City	2312	1723	552	428	0.86	0.43
江都市	Jiangdu City	1941	1570	2373	1164	1.86	1.02
镇江市	**Zhenjiang Municipality**	**5181**	**5156**	**7441**	**4951**	**9.09**	**5.26**
丹阳市	Danyang City	1614	1614	1585	1127	2.74	1.81
扬中市	Yangzhong City	432	432	749	301	1.10	0.72
句容市	Jurong City	1854	1844	956	744	1.17	0.79
泰州市	**Taizhou Municipality**	**7270**	**6997**	**4855**	**2221**	**9.10**	**4.86**
兴化市	Xinghua City	1993	1942	1104	461	1.66	0.73
靖江市	Jingjiang City	859	778	706	364	1.93	0.99
泰兴市	Taixing City	1827	1817	1177	528	2.10	1.23
姜堰市	Jiangyan City	1578	1509	680	390	1.73	1.08
宿迁市	**Suqian Municipality**	**9798**	**7406**	**2812**	**1749**	**5.62**	**3.81**
沭阳县	Shuyang County	3355	2242	2471	1588	1.43	1.03
泗阳县	Siyang County	1332	1163	182	117	0.75	0.54
泗洪县	Sihong County	2290	1923	218	140	0.81	0.51

20－16 邮电、电力（2006年）
POSTAL AND TELECOMMUNICATIONS, POWER SERVICES (2006)

市县	City and County	邮电业务总量（亿元）Post & Telecommunication Services (100 million yuan)	本地电话用户（万户）Telephone Subscribers (10000 subscribers)	移动电话年末用户（万户）Number of Mobile Telephones Subscribers at Year-end (10000 subscribers)	国际互联网用户（万户）International Exchange Network Users (10000 subscribers)	全年用电量（亿千瓦时）Total Consumption of Electricity of the Year (100 million kWh)	#工业用电 Consumption of Electricity for Industrial Use
南京市	**Nanjing Municipality**	**93.55**	**344.23**	**488.31**	**67.48**	**270.57**	**187.04**
溧水县	Lishui County	2.49	16.04	15.16	0.83	6.47	4.80
高淳县	Gaochun County	2.07	15.58	14.32	0.69	3.88	2.29
无锡市	**Wuxi Municipality**	**67.46**	**331.25**	**431.39**	**56.76**	**400.99**	**343.34**
江阴市	Jiangyin City	15.20	82.89	100.83	11.28	153.37	140.58
宜兴市	Yixing City	9.68	66.56	64.65	7.23	58.31	49.78
徐州市	**Xuzhou Municipality**	**39.96**	**290.73**	**219.54**	**28.54**	**139.99**	**109.26**
丰县	Fengxian County	1.02	24.87	11.90	1.09	4.72	2.37
沛县	Peixian County	1.31	28.82	31.00	1.31	10.38	7.94
铜山县	Tongshan County	1.45	27.03	12.80	1.22	17.43	14.30
睢宁县	Suining County	1.19	29.86	12.00	1.14	8.15	5.53
新沂市	Xinyi City	1.14	26.69	28.00	1.53	17.38	15.30
邳州市	Pizhou City	1.65	37.30	37.00	1.82	10.39	7.12
常州市	**Changzhou Municipality**	**39.20**	**214.27**	**255.00**	**29.19**	**212.68**	**175.00**
溧阳市	Liyang City	4.17	31.52	31.28	2.72	31.46	27.51
金坛市	Jintan City	3.57	29.78	24.26	2.48	15.81	12.29
苏州市	**Suzhou Municipality**	**113.40**	**516.41**	**729.51**	**71.89**	**686.49**	**588.41**
常熟市	Changshu City	13.91	80.30	89.94	9.51	78.46	66.64
张家港市	Zhangjiagang City	12.07	67.40	77.49	7.13	171.27	161.56
昆山市	Kunshan City	19.16	79.69	124.94	9.38	102.11	87.84
吴江市	Wujiang City	13.77	61.81	86.79	7.29	105.72	95.18
太仓市	Taicang City	6.94	33.85	42.47	4.22	47.52	41.62

20－16 续表1 Continued

市县 City and County		邮电业务总量(亿元) Post & Telecommunication Services (100 million yuan)	本地电话用户(万户) Telephone Subscribers (10000 subscribers)	移动电话年末用户(万户) Number of Mobile Telephones Subscribers at Year-end (10000 subscribers)	国际互联网用户(万户) International Exchange Network Users (10000 subscribers)	全年用电量(亿千瓦时) Total Consumption of Electricity of the Year (100 million kWh)	#工业用电 Consumption of Electricity for Industrial Use
南通市	**Nantong Municipality**	**42.95**	**269.45**	**281.27**	**20.97**	**163.60**	**126.65**
海安县	Haian County	4.38	32.25	28.73	2.10	16.66	12.77
如东县	Rudong County	4.45	33.21	30.93	1.76	17.71	13.52
启东市	Qidong City	4.98	37.25	32.16	2.09	11.38	7.52
如皋市	Rugao City	5.42	39.22	37.76	2.25	18.98	14.23
通州市	Tongzhou City	5.38	42.33	36.48	2.39	20.24	16.17
海门市	Haimen City	4.77	35.73	33.23	2.15	17.57	13.45
连云港市	**Lianyungang Municipality**	**17.39**	**144.95**	**108.54**	**13.29**	**49.17**	**33.18**
赣榆县	Ganyu County	2.75	29.42	18.71	1.66	7.16	4.41
东海县	Donghai County	2.66	27.77	18.35	1.45	9.13	6.52
灌云县	Guanyun County	2.12	23.53	13.68	1.19	4.30	2.69
灌南县	Guannan County	1.62	18.07	10.31	1.00	3.97	2.63
淮安市	**Huaian Municipality**	**15.45**	**162.27**	**94.70**	**11.84**	**65.49**	**49.23**
涟水县	Lianshui County	1.97	26.83	11.42	0.89	5.61	3.76
洪泽县	Hongze County	1.04	10.53	7.60	0.62	6.31	5.24
盱眙县	Xuyi County	1.65	19.28	10.17	0.85	5.81	3.74
金湖县	Jinhu County	1.32	12.93	9.12	1.07	4.00	2.60
盐城市	**Yancheng Municipality**	**28.98**	**253.40**	**206.18**	**16.34**	**89.78**	**63.50**
响水县	Xiangshui County	1.63	15.50	10.47	0.87	5.19	3.71
滨海县	Binhai County	2.37	23.95	16.93	0.90	6.28	3.94
阜宁县	Funing County	2.85	25.64	19.04	1.18	9.56	7.01
射阳县	Sheyang County	3.13	33.44	24.25	1.64	9.60	6.49
建湖县	Jianhu County	2.80	27.33	20.16	1.48	7.68	5.22

市县	City and County	邮电业务总量（亿元）Post & Telecommunication Services (100 million yuan)	本地电话用户（万户）Telephone Subscribers (10000 subscribers)	移动电话年末用户（万户）Number of Mobile Telephones Subscribers at Year-end (10000 subscribers)	国际互联网用户（万户）International Exchange Network Users (10000 subscribers)	全年用电量（亿千瓦时）Total Consumption of Electricity of the Year (100 million kWh)	#工业用电 Consumption of Electricity for Industrial Use
东台市	Dongtai City	3.64	30.88	25.25	1.95	16.29	12.72
大丰市	Dafeng City	3.33	40.24	21.84	2.13	12.30	9.07
扬州市	**Yangzhou Municipality**	**26.69**	**190.93**	**162.86**	**31.79**	**94.22**	**69.10**
宝应县	Baoying County	3.02	29.46	16.87	2.00	6.87	4.07
仪征市	Yizheng City	2.84	23.41	17.72	2.91	12.73	10.09
高邮市	Gaoyou City	3.40	28.69	21.51	2.14	10.00	7.08
江都市	Jiangdu City	5.69	44.89	31.95	4.06	14.15	9.98
镇江市	**Zhenjiang Municipality**	**25.03**	**144.05**	**147.18**	**18.08**	**110.54**	**90.83**
丹阳市	Danyang City	6.81	39.78	42.88	3.90	30.72	25.67
扬中市	Yangzhong City	2.63	17.87	15.70	2.08	5.61	3.79
句容市	Jurong City	2.82	20.51	19.70	1.46	11.52	9.02
泰州市	**Taizhou Municipality**	**49.06**	**183.54**	**149.47**	**14.24**	**113.47**	**92.10**
兴化市	Xinghua City	10.39	40.46	30.48	2.48	30.01	25.70
靖江市	Jingjiang City	9.28	30.76	27.26	2.76	20.52	16.84
泰兴市	Taixing City	10.30	46.98	29.61	2.83	17.38	12.78
姜堰市	Jiangyan City	7.92	32.55	23.10	2.07	17.94	14.77
宿迁市	**Suqian Municipality**	**12.06**	**113.88**	**91.70**	**4.33**	**32.07**	**20.35**
沭阳县	Shuyang County	3.71	37.18	25.79	1.07	8.29	5.11
泗阳县	Siyang County	2.04	20.76	15.47	0.78	4.81	2.78
泗洪县	Sihong County	2.03	21.52	16.30	0.74	5.15	3.01

20－17 固定资产投资完成额(2006年)
COMPLETED INVESTMENT IN FIXED ASSETS (2006)

单位:亿元 (100 million yuan)

市县	City and County	城镇固定资产投资 Urban Investment in Fixed Assets	房地产开发投资 Investment in Real Estate Development	#住宅 Residential Buildings	新增固定资产 Newly Added Fixed Assets	商品房屋销售建筑面积(万平方米) Constraction Floor Space of the Commercial Houses Sold (10000 sq. m)	#住宅 Rescdential Buildings
南京市	**Nanjing Municipality**	**1228.31**	**351.17**	**253.64**	**701.56**	**1010.50**	**940.99**
溧水县	Lishui County	32.22	4.62	3.92	17.06	29.33	27.92
高淳县	Gaochun County	26.84	8.56	5.90	24.05	19.77	17.19
无锡市	**Wuxi Municipality**	**1015.02**	**276.81**	**192.48**	**808.12**	**648.58**	**553.40**
江阴市	Jiangyin City	143.49	41.20	32.31	129.48	95.82	85.61
宜兴市	Yixing City	82.69	33.53	24.42	52.51	133.31	117.34
徐州市	**Xuzhou Municipality**	**598.52**	**70.80**	**59.17**	**302.49**	**288.46**	**252.21**
丰　县	Fengxian County	25.67	3.21	2.71	23.52	20.26	18.74
沛　县	Peixian County	47.24	3.66	2.05	7.14	13.78	11.14
铜山县	Tongshan County	72.56	10.15	9.13	55.19	57.98	56.03
睢宁县	Suining County	11.00	1.20	0.88	5.95	12.70	11.27
新沂市	Xinyi City	58.57	3.07	3.05	6.78	29.90	24.90
邳州市	Pizhou City	47.07	4.35	3.40	28.66	18.55	13.19
常州市	**Changzhou Municipality**	**607.85**	**171.04**	**123.38**	**381.94**	**479.12**	**407.89**
溧阳市	Liyang City	59.00	15.44	13.00	34.80	49.18	43.38
金坛市	Jintan City	46.89	15.21	12.40	35.50	52.29	46.68
苏州市	**Suzhou Municipality**	**1462.90**	**470.75**	**361.78**	**1485.98**	**1391.38**	**1193.52**
常熟市	Changshu City	138.93	41.07	26.66	127.26	122.66	101.69
张家港市	Zhangjiagang City	122.30	35.40	25.18	120.19	95.03	78.27
昆山市	Kunshan City	204.36	73.64	52.65	264.83	352.29	301.56
吴江市	Wujiang City	138.15	50.16	36.87	105.96	133.07	103.06
太仓市	Taicang City	144.26	20.96	15.98	137.76	61.45	50.65

20－17 续表1 Continued

单位：亿元 (100 million yuan)

市 县	City and County	城镇固定资产投资 Urban Investment in Fixed Assets	房地产开发投资 Investment in Real Estate Development	#住宅 Residential Buildings	新增固定资产 Newly Added Fixed Assets	商品房屋销售建筑面积（万平方米） Constraction Floor Space of the Commercial Houses Sold (10000 sq. m)	#住宅 Rescdential Buildings
南通市	**Nantong Municipality**	**487.57**	**107.93**	**88.89**	**295.38**	**471.75**	**409.02**
海安县	Haian County	60.76	11.49	9.09	28.20	36.10	29.71
如东县	Rudong County	38.07	5.42	4.35	19.16	16.85	14.01
启东市	Qidong City	58.42	11.60	9.38	36.83	84.06	67.32
如皋市	Rugao City	36.41	7.65	6.66	14.68	18.76	16.03
通州市	Tongzhou City	50.73	8.94	7.74	31.22	32.06	30.18
海门市	Haimen City	45.82	8.97	7.72	37.03	52.04	42.85
连云港市	**Lianyungang Municipality**	**300.12**	**55.07**	**39.89**	**190.16**	**194.54**	**159.56**
赣榆县	Ganyu County	36.07	4.72	3.43	40.55	34.42	25.78
东海县	Donghai County	29.92	4.76	2.81	19.04	28.09	21.84
灌云县	Guanyun County	33.20	2.89	1.88	24.66	17.76	15.28
灌南县	Guannan County	30.85	2.93	1.73	0.97	19.81	15.24
淮安市	**Huaian Municipality**	**305.56**	**66.35**	**51.06**	**172.11**	**204.87**	**174.59**
涟水县	Lianshui County	27.42	4.44	4.00	13.72	20.89	20.50
洪泽县	Hongze County	20.57	3.53	2.36	16.90	28.06	24.34
盱眙县	Xuyi County	38.34	4.56	3.16	11.28	10.22	8.92
金湖县	Jinhu County	17.21	3.06	2.58	11.14	20.57	20.32
盐城市	**Yancheng Municipality**	**347.75**	**65.51**	**49.63**	**190.26**	**265.72**	**245.66**
响水县	Xiangshui County	24.49	1.42	0.86	17.66	13.82	11.76
滨海县	Binhai County	15.13	3.03	2.04	11.94	25.30	21.90
阜宁县	Funing County	26.93	3.63	2.64	21.63	12.67	12.04
射阳县	Sheyang County	19.46	3.28	3.21	9.67	24.34	24.34
建湖县	Jianhu County	21.04	3.38	2.23	11.55	16.75	13.86

20－17 续表2 Continued

单位:亿元 (100 million yuan)

市 县	City and County	城镇固定资产投资 Urban Investment in Fixed Assets	房地产开发投资 Investment in Real Estate Development	#住宅 Residential Buildings	新增固定资产 Newly Added Fixed Assets	商品房屋销售建筑面积(万平方米) Constraction Floor Space of the Commercial Houses Sold (10000 sq. m)	#住宅 Rescdential Buildings
东台市	Dongtai City	35.29	9.24	7.13	25.12	30.12	26.99
大丰市	Dafeng City	35.53	5.22	4.30	13.57	8.42	7.49
扬州市	**Yangzhou Municipality**	**357.83**	**83.43**	**58.80**	**216.25**	**391.93**	**324.17**
宝应县	Baoying County	29.45	9.14	6.66	24.28	40.33	34.78
仪征市	Yizheng City	49.06	7.87	6.49	43.39	37.87	34.73
高邮市	Gaoyou City	26.27	7.98	4.77	18.00	46.75	32.34
江都市	Jiangdu City	51.16	14.86	11.63	20.43	63.14	58.71
镇江市	**Zhenjiang Municipality**	**300.03**	**67.42**	**56.19**	**240.45**	**245.35**	**225.23**
丹阳市	Danyang City	41.08	12.35	11.32	17.08	61.74	56.28
扬中市	Yangzhong City	13.28	6.41	5.54	6.25	21.49	20.39
句容市	Jurong City	20.94	8.22	6.11	8.49	36.18	33.43
泰州市	**Taizhou Municipality**	**284.47**	**63.41**	**46.82**	**222.11**	**263.74**	**226.73**
兴化市	Xinghua City	22.40	8.75	4.65	17.45	39.07	32.70
靖江市	Jingjiang City	45.31	9.21	8.85	39.62	37.23	34.85
泰兴市	Taixing City	45.38	7.58	5.97	39.59	30.41	25.52
姜堰市	Jiangyan City	38.86	11.18	6.64	32.38	61.59	51.05
宿迁市	**Suqian Municipality**	**185.86**	**57.02**	**44.25**	**117.39**	**247.05**	**205.70**
沭阳县	Shuyang County	49.47	13.76	11.35	28.26	76.45	68.34
泗阳县	Siyang County	36.70	9.11	5.99	26.20	40.22	36.08
泗洪县	Sihong County	20.43	9.45	8.67	13.72	25.54	23.39

20－18 国内贸易对外经济(2006年)
DOMESTIC AND FOREIGN TRADE AND FOREIGN ECONOMY (2006)

市县	City and County	社会消费品零售总额(亿元) Total Retail of Consumer Goods (100 million Yuan)	进出口总额(亿美元) Total Imports and Exports (USD 100 million)	出口 Exports	进口 Imports	合同外商直接投资(亿美元) Contracted Foreign Direct Investment (USD 100 million)	实际外商直接投资(亿美元) Actual Foreign Direct Investment (USD 100 million)
南京市	**Nanjing Municipality**	**1166.85**	**315.35**	**173.65**	**141.70**	**30.82**	**15.19**
溧水县	Lishui County	33.27	1.65	1.49	0.16	0.43	0.29
高淳县	Gaochun County	38.28	1.10	0.95	0.15	1.49	0.34
无锡市	**Wuxi Municipality**	**959.47**	**391.93**	**214.40**	**177.53**	**80.53**	**27.52**
江阴市	Jiangyin City	201.25	84.05	45.71	38.35	18.94	3.94
宜兴市	Yixing City	143.72	12.68	9.84	2.84	10.38	2.91
徐州市	**Xuzhou Municipality**	**460.08**	**18.53**	**12.53**	**6.01**	**6.85**	**2.44**
丰县	Fengxian County	25.32	0.28	0.23	0.05	0.11	0.07
沛县	Peixian County	46.59	0.18	0.13	0.05	0.56	0.18
铜山县	Tongshan County	37.44	0.67	0.51	0.16	0.78	0.30
睢宁县	Suining County	31.09	0.68	0.18	0.50	0.03	0.04
新沂市	Xinyi City	30.48	0.91	0.47	0.44	0.35	0.12
邳州市	Pizhou City	39.93	2.57	2.53	0.04	0.64	0.39
常州市	**Changzhou Municipality**	**515.83**	**104.49**	**78.96**	**25.53**	**32.96**	**12.51**
溧阳市	Liyang City	75.08	3.50	3.17	0.32	4.17	1.21
金坛市	Jintan City	58.20	5.65	4.85	0.80	5.06	1.20
苏州市	**Suzhou Municipality**	**1055.44**	**1742.58**	**946.81**	**795.77**	**159.24**	**61.05**
常熟市	Changshu City	176.72	62.65	42.02	20.63	15.33	6.43
张家港市	Zhangjiagang City	112.17	125.89	54.87	71.02	16.45	4.48
昆山市	Kunshan City	135.01	427.45	243.66	183.79	25.05	11.72
吴江市	Wujiang City	83.70	142.73	71.76	70.97	13.66	5.58
太仓市	Taicang City	55.54	46.90	23.62	23.28	11.94	4.42

20－18 续表1 Continued

市县 City and County		社会消费品零售总额（亿元）Total Retail of Consumer Goods (100 million Yuan)	进出口总额（亿美元）Total Imports and Exports (USD 100 million)	出口 Exports	进口 Imports	合同外商直接投资（亿美元）Contracted Foreign Direct Investment (USD 100 million)	实际外商直接投资（亿美元）Actual Foreign Direct Investment (USD 100 million)
南通市	**Nantong Municipality**	**621.96**	**100.21**	**71.83**	**28.38**	**69.39**	**25.75**
海安县	Haian County	65.29	3.83	3.19	0.65	4.70	2.85
如东县	Rudong County	73.39	4.94	4.17	0.77	8.98	3.21
启东市	Qidong City	84.16	4.28	3.80	0.48	11.26	4.24
如皋市	Rugao City	83.98	5.41	4.49	0.91	11.42	3.26
通州市	Tongzhou City	87.21	10.88	9.59	1.29	6.09	4.50
海门市	Haimen City	87.11	5.79	4.79	1.00	9.45	4.87
连云港市	**Lianyungang Municipality**	**211.53**	**27.26**	**14.57**	**12.69**	**9.64**	**3.46**
赣榆县	Ganyu County	40.49	0.36	0.34	0.03	1.82	0.57
东海县	Donghai County	36.96	1.19	0.95	0.24	0.95	0.45
灌云县	Guanyun County	29.80	0.23	0.21	0.03	0.37	0.23
灌南县	Guannan County	18.15	0.32	0.22	0.10	0.60	0.32
淮安市	**Huaian Municipality**	**230.15**	**10.22**	**6.59**	**3.62**	**6.41**	**1.16**
涟水县	Lianshui County	21.78	0.30	0.28	0.02	0.68	0.24
洪泽县	Hongze County	20.77	0.10	0.10	0.00	0.66	0.11
盱眙县	Xuyi County	21.58	0.05	0.04	0.00	0.68	0.11
金湖县	Jinhu County	19.52	0.61	0.59	0.03	0.39	0.11
盐城市	**Yancheng Municipality**	**367.61**	**18.03**	**10.61**	**7.42**	**9.37**	**3.25**
响水县	Xiangshui County	13.91	0.62	0.38	0.24	0.10	0.00
滨海县	Binhai County	25.29	0.21	0.17	0.05	0.22	0.06
阜宁县	Funing County	32.19	0.71	0.52	0.19	1.00	0.32
射阳县	Sheyang County	41.62	0.69	0.44	0.25	1.01	0.23
建湖县	Jianhu County	37.74	1.05	0.74	0.31	0.80	0.21

市　县 City and County		社会消费品零售总额（亿元）Total Retail of Consumer Goods（100 million Yuan）	进出口总额（亿美元）Total Imports and Exports（USD 100 million）	出　口 Exports	进口 Imports	合同外商直接投资（亿美元）Contracted Foreign Direct Investment（USD 100 million）	实际外商直接投资（亿美元）Actual Foreign Direct Investment（USD 100 million）
东台市	Dongtai City	58.75	2.44	1.67	0.77	1.12	0.32
大丰市	Dafeng City	38.91	1.51	1.44	0.07	1.56	0.45
扬州市	**Yangzhou Municipality**	**355.83**	**32.64**	**23.61**	**9.03**	**24.49**	**7.61**
宝应县	Baoying County	39.09	1.86	1.30	0.56	0.88	0.42
仪征市	Yizheng City	44.64	2.19	0.85	1.35	3.04	1.26
高邮市	Gaoyou City	40.29	1.35	1.17	0.19	0.76	0.40
江都市	Jiangdu City	67.77	2.82	2.14	0.68	3.42	1.04
镇江市	**Zhenjiang Municipality**	**280.07**	**47.74**	**26.63**	**21.11**	**16.59**	**7.30**
丹阳市	Danyang City	75.49	6.81	5.56	1.25	2.63	1.67
扬中市	Yangzhong City	34.57	1.64	0.99	0.64	1.89	0.83
句容市	Jurong City	35.88	4.45	3.48	0.97	2.74	0.80
泰州市	**Taizhou Municipality**	**271.33**	**28.67**	**22.06**	**6.61**	**12.09**	**6.58**
兴化市	Xinghua City	40.62	1.80	1.16	0.65	0.08	0.22
靖江市	Jingjiang City	47.24	6.58	5.80	0.78	3.02	2.00
泰兴市	Taixing City	58.65	4.95	3.19	1.76	2.35	1.33
姜堰市	Jiangyan City	48.66	3.26	2.67	0.59	2.40	1.21
宿迁市	**Suqian Municipality**	**127.03**	**2.30**	**1.94**	**0.36**	**2.28**	**0.49**
沭阳县	Shuyang County	40.66	0.17	0.17	0.00	0.22	0.07
泗阳县	Siyang County	23.24	0.22	0.20	0.02	0.43	0.06
泗洪县	Sihong County	22.09	0.14	0.11	0.03	0.45	0.06

20－19 财政收支(2006年)

MAJOR INDICATORS OF GOVERNMENT FINANCE (2006)

单位:亿元　　(100 million yuan)

市县	City and County	地方财政一般预算收入 General Budetary Revenue in Local Finance	#各项税收 Taxes	地方财政一般预算支出 General Budetary Expenditure in Local Finance	#基本建设支出 Expenditure for Capital Construction	#社会保障补助支出 Subsidy Expenditure for Social Security	#文教科卫支出 Expenditure for CESH
南京市	**Nanjing Municipality**	**246.44**	**216.49**	**262.46**	**18.32**	**30.87**	**48.18**
溧水县	Lishui County	4.55	3.76	7.08	0.09	0.52	1.97
高淳县	Gaochun County	5.92	4.46	7.96	0.88	0.68	1.51
无锡市	**Wuxi Municipality**	**220.89**	**190.15**	**213.40**	**24.93**	**29.33**	**40.91**
江阴市	Jiangyin City	60.48	47.26	55.42	4.53	8.00	10.48
宜兴市	Yixing City	21.66	19.54	21.68	0.83	2.14	5.06
徐州市	**Xuzhou Municipality**	**71.03**	**56.57**	**107.31**	**3.23**	**6.14**	**29.74**
丰县	Fengxian County	2.44	1.85	8.32	0.37	0.23	2.62
沛县	Peixian County	6.02	4.52	10.86	0.04	0.77	3.09
铜山县	Tongshan County	7.38	5.80	11.83	0.81	0.75	3.38
睢宁县	Suining County	2.46	1.81	8.74	0.18	0.07	3.10
新沂市	Xinyi City	3.34	2.71	8.17	0.31	0.42	2.88
邳州市	Pizhou City	5.93	4.82	11.70	0.15	0.39	4.13
常州市	**Changzhou Municipality**	**118.88**	**102.48**	**117.70**	**8.84**	**13.56**	**23.28**
溧阳市	Liyang City	11.80	9.96	13.57	0.08	1.12	3.82
金坛市	Jintan City	8.63	6.99	9.56	0.14	0.80	2.94
苏州市	**Suzhou Municipality**	**400.23**	**358.97**	**386.20**	**54.57**	**56.65**	**64.16**
常熟市	Changshu City	43.08	38.15	42.10	8.29	5.63	8.66
张家港市	Zhangjiagang City	61.09	48.27	55.61	10.46	8.42	10.29
昆山市	Kunshan City	65.37	59.59	56.23	0.08	9.78	8.33
吴江市	Wujiang City	35.08	31.85	30.83	0.79	4.77	6.82
太仓市	Taicang City	27.59	24.54	25.83	1.39	3.52	4.53

20－19　续表1　Continued

单位：亿元 (100 million yuan)

市　县	City and County	地方财政一般预算收入 General Budetary Revenue in Local Finance	#各项税收 Taxes	地方财政一般预算支出 General Budetary Expenditure in Local Finance	#基本建设支出 Expenditure for Capital Construction	#社会保障补助支出 Subsidy Expenditure for Social Security	#文教科卫支出 Expenditure for CESH
南通市	**Nantong Municipality**	**92.53**	**78.82**	**112.62**	**6.16**	**9.76**	**26.64**
海安县	Haian County	6.95	5.55	9.64	0.13	0.44	3.08
如东县	Rudong County	6.16	5.13	11.40	0.24	0.57	3.01
启东市	Qidong City	9.24	7.90	12.44	0.42	0.91	3.04
如皋市	Rugao City	7.51	6.56	13.09	0.02	0.55	3.38
通州市	Tongzhou City	10.57	8.98	13.14	0.16	0.97	3.98
海门市	Haimen City	9.62	8.01	11.33	0.15	1.12	3.36
连云港市	**Lianyungang Municipality**	**33.96**	**26.91**	**57.64**	**3.85**	**3.04**	**14.13**
赣榆县	Ganyu County	4.00	2.81	9.95	0.23	0.17	3.20
东海县	Donghai County	4.00	2.84	9.59	0.30	0.25	2.82
灌云县	Guanyun County	2.33	1.79	6.79	0.09	0.08	2.07
灌南县	Guannan County	2.62	1.95	6.43	0.07	0.16	1.71
淮安市	**Huaian Municipality**	**36.94**	**28.23**	**62.16**	**3.31**	**2.44**	**16.69**
涟水县	Lianshui County	2.25	1.77	8.15	0.38	0.13	2.97
洪泽县	Hongze County	2.07	1.77	4.21	0.11	0.26	1.19
盱眙县	Xuyi County	2.59	1.90	5.83	0.08	0.18	1.56
金湖县	Jinhu County	1.82	1.57	4.35	0.05	0.19	1.18
盐城市	**Yancheng Municipality**	**48.84**	**38.07**	**85.89**	**2.58**	**3.27**	**28.39**
响水县	Xiangshui County	2.24	1.71	5.32	0.30	0.11	1.65
滨海县	Binhai County	3.12	2.40	8.64	0.11	0.25	3.38
阜宁县	Funing County	3.67	2.87	9.49	0.20	0.15	3.59
射阳县	Sheyang County	4.67	3.40	9.14	0.16	0.26	3.27
建湖县	Jianhu County	4.66	3.40	8.18	0.14	0.23	2.98

单位:亿元 (100 million yuan)

市县	City and County	地方财政一般预算收入 General Budetary Revenue in Local Finance	#各项税收 Taxes	地方财政一般预算支出 General Budetary Expenditure in Local Finance	#基本建设支出 Expenditure for Capital Construction	#社会保障补助支出 Subsidy Expenditure for Social Security	#文教科卫支出 Expenditure for CESH
东台市	Dongtai City	6.66	5.00	10.46	0.24	0.49	3.57
大丰市	Dafeng City	5.01	3.72	8.30	0.06	0.43	2.88
扬州市	**Yangzhou Municipality**	**63.02**	**50.35**	**75.64**	**5.26**	**4.84**	**17.75**
宝应县	Baoying County	4.52	3.55	9.68	0.47	0.55	2.72
仪征市	Yizheng City	8.11	6.79	8.57	0.15	0.36	2.35
高邮市	Gaoyou City	4.70	4.03	7.83	0.28	0.20	2.56
江都市	Jiangdu City	9.16	7.20	10.88	0.75	0.58	3.42
镇江市	**Zhenjiang Municipality**	**60.12**	**46.87**	**65.08**	**1.64**	**5.59**	**14.90**
丹阳市	Danyang City	13.29	10.44	14.02	0.72	1.29	3.33
扬中市	Yangzhong City	5.99	5.07	6.60	0.11	0.57	1.54
句容市	Jurong City	5.36	4.08	7.53	0.07	0.21	2.18
泰州市	**Taizhou Municipality**	**61.07**	**48.12**	**77.82**	**4.93**	**6.19**	**19.84**
兴化市	Xinghua City	6.56	5.46	12.92	0.37	0.44	4.52
靖江市	Jingjiang City	11.20	8.48	11.11	0.71	1.16	2.90
泰兴市	Taixing City	10.89	8.19	14.54	0.17	0.87	4.97
姜堰市	Jiangyan City	7.92	6.48	10.39	0.19	0.98	3.29
宿迁市	**Suqian Municipality**	**20.05**	**14.36**	**49.20**	**3.34**	**1.08**	**15.35**
沭阳县	Shuyang County	5.01	3.15	12.12	0.20	0.17	4.85
泗阳县	Siyang County	2.51	1.78	8.23	0.29	0.06	2.79
泗洪县	Sihong County	2.78	2.08	8.56	0.02	0.06	3.21

20－20 金融、保险主要指标（2006年）
MAJOR INDICATORS OF BANKING AND INSURANCE (2006)

单位：亿元 (100 million yuan)

市县 City and County		年末金融机构存款余额 Deposits Balance of Banking Institutions (Year-end)	#居民储蓄存款 Savings Deposits of Residents	年末金融机构贷款余额 Loans Balance of Banking Institutions (Year-end)	#短期贷款 Short-term Loans	保费收入 Premiums	赔款和给付 Claim and Payment
南京市	**Nanjing Municipality**	**5802.21**	**1834.88**	**5098.13**	**1879.01**	**89.96**	**28.34**
溧水县	Lishui County	55.26	34.19	30.49	16.21		
高淳县	Gaochun County	48.91	32.66	32.58	19.77		
无锡市	**Wuxi Municipality**	**3772.06**	**1649.56**	**2632.72**	**1596.33**	**66.23**	**23.42**
江阴市	Jiangyin City	845.06	338.34	739.43	542.85	16.77	5.23
宜兴市	Yixing City	432.96	263.66	293.29	200.84	9.59	2.89
徐州市	**Xuzhou Municipality**	**1193.72**	**722.89**	**565.06**	**346.61**	**27.53**	**5.20**
丰县	Fengxian County	57.94	47.97	24.51	21.99	1.76	0.32
沛县	Peixian County	102.22	78.63	35.80	26.38	2.57	0.42
铜山县	Tongshan County	144.82	103.01	72.15	54.55	1.45	0.50
睢宁县	Suining County	64.83	53.25	27.14	23.23	1.83	0.32
新沂市	Xinyi City	54.21	40.41	35.32	27.28	1.58	0.47
邳州市	Pizhou City	83.22	64.89	56.78	34.75	3.32	0.59
常州市	**Changzhou Municipality**	**1974.01**	**1014.00**	**1348.60**	**805.81**	**42.61**	**14.08**
溧阳市	Liyang City	190.81	131.06	108.67	75.22	3.58	0.97
金坛市	Jintan City	138.51	92.57	75.31	47.39	3.60	0.89
苏州市	**Suzhou Municipality**	**5797.95**	**2427.41**	**4429.70**	**1913.72**	**83.93**	**34.94**
常熟市	Changshu City	776.85	420.74	486.32	267.25	13.52	5.46
张家港市	Zhangjiagang City	729.09	316.30	600.70	376.07	10.63	4.33
昆山市	Kunshan City	775.13	274.04	507.96	185.03	8.64	3.34
吴江市	Wujiang City	588.23	271.59	433.93	252.06	7.81	3.41
太仓市	Taicang City	324.93	151.69	264.77	104.05	5.59	2.35

20－20　续表1　Continued

单位:亿元　　(100 million yuan)

市　县	City and County	年末金融机构存款余额 Deposits Balance of Banking Institutions (Year-end)	#居民储蓄存款 Savings Deposits of Residents	年末金融机构贷款余额 Loans Balance of Banking Institutions (Year-end)	#短期贷款 Short-term Loans	保费收入 Premiums	赔款和给付 Claim and Payment
南通市	**Nantong Municipality**	**2113.95**	**1347.89**	**1211.74**	**786.43**	**43.07**	**6.50**
海安县	Haian County	213.00	159.41	107.77	85.76	5.26	0.64
如东县	Rudong County	171.42	129.31	79.33	59.62	4.70	0.58
启东市	Qidong City	226.46	186.72	106.74	86.92	3.72	0.61
如皋市	Rugao City	205.55	153.64	94.63	60.00	4.58	0.65
通州市	Tongzhou City	264.88	196.03	131.79	103.61	4.84	0.83
海门市	Haimen City	247.46	189.32	119.26	87.25	3.64	0.83
连云港市	**Lianyungang Municipality**	**506.11**	**281.85**	**325.90**	**193.12**	**13.14**	**3.38**
赣榆县	Ganyu County	59.26	43.99	33.01	24.00	1.43	0.35
东海县	Donghai County	63.10	44.84	32.39	24.55	1.10	0.08
灌云县	Guanyun County	45.75	32.76	23.63	20.58	0.66	0.26
灌南县	Guannan County	28.05	19.91	12.30	9.50	0.86	0.26
淮安市	**Huaian Municipality**	**511.37**	**288.97**	**332.78**	**197.82**	**14.74**	**5.21**
涟水县	Lianshui County	46.08	32.80	25.33	20.90	1.15	0.49
洪泽县	Hongze County	32.33	21.50	21.56	18.04	0.84	0.31
盱眙县	Xuyi County	42.48	28.34	26.11	22.14	0.76	0.14
金湖县	Jinhu County	41.06	27.47	26.02	21.54	0.96	0.37
盐城市	**Yancheng Municipality**	**939.73**	**639.49**	**534.10**	**376.05**	**26.83**	**8.75**
响水县	Xiangshui County	32.68	23.90	20.89	15.72	0.91	0.25
滨海县	Binhai County	53.70	39.07	30.02	25.53	1.50	0.33
阜宁县	Funing County	75.70	60.02	33.66	27.07	2.07	0.32
射阳县	Sheyang County	83.31	65.27	53.84	42.34	2.56	0.52
建湖县	Jianhu County	89.23	68.29	54.03	42.09	2.46	0.53

20－20 续表2 Continued

单位：亿元 (100 million yuan)

市 县	City and County	年末金融机构存款余额 Deposits Balance of Banking Institutions (Year-end)	#居民储蓄存款 Savings Deposits of Residents	年末金融机构贷款余额 Loans Balance of Banking Institutions (Year-end)	#短期贷款 Short-term Loans	保费收入 Premiums	赔款和给付 Claim and Payment
东台市	Dongtai City	161.31	123.97	62.97	50.11	4.04	0.54
大丰市	Dafeng City	106.62	78.82	51.26	41.29	2.97	0.50
扬州市	**Yangzhou Municipality**	**1085.26**	**675.54**	**597.25**	**348.16**	**30.86**	**5.40**
宝应县	Baoying County	88.57	71.60	43.78	32.49	2.81	0.46
仪征市	Yizheng City	119.04	74.79	64.69	36.50	3.19	0.62
高邮市	Gaoyou City	105.50	82.01	39.29	31.40	3.03	0.67
江都市	Jiangdu City	233.66	176.90	79.69	61.68	6.77	1.03
镇江市	**Zhenjiang Municipality**	**928.20**	**521.75**	**668.03**	**370.59**	**21.65**	**6.99**
丹阳市	Danyang City	234.18	151.18	168.21	121.56	6.66	1.77
扬中市	Yangzhong City	121.38	76.94	70.99	45.42	2.98	0.87
句容市	Jurong City	89.27	57.35	50.76	27.36	2.27	0.78
泰州市	**Taizhou Municipality**	**953.87**	**594.44**	**545.55**	**340.43**	**27.52**	**6.29**
兴化市	Xinghua City	141.24	109.77	84.17	65.61	3.52	0.81
靖江市	Jingjiang City	186.66	118.67	89.13	54.65	4.98	0.98
泰兴市	Taixing City	159.86	117.43	79.05	48.60	5.33	1.04
姜堰市	Jiangyan City	153.96	112.36	81.92	64.58	3.81	0.72
宿迁市	**Suqian Municipality**	**281.99**	**184.79**	**195.53**	**127.50**	**7.70**	**2.24**
沭阳县	Shuyang County	69.83	53.08	40.69	32.19	1.76	0.47
泗阳县	Siyang County	48.22	36.69	27.41	20.24	1.47	0.29
泗洪县	Sihong County	52.30	36.99	35.34	24.89	1.16	0.31

20－21 人 民 生 活（2006年）
PEOPLE'S LIVELIHOOD (2006)

市 县	City and County	在岗职工平均工资（元）Average Wages of Fully Employed Staff and Workers (yuan)	农民人均纯收入（元）Per Capita Net Income of Rural Households (yuan)	农民人均生活消费支出（元）Per Capita Living Expenditure of Rural Households (yuan)	#食品 Food	农村居民恩格尔系数（%）Engle Coefficient of Rural Residents (%)	农村居民人均住房面积（平方米）Per Capita Living Space of Housing of Rural Residents (sq. m)
南京市	**Nanjing Municipality**	**32459**	**7068**	**5530**	**2135**	**38.6**	**44.7**
溧水县	Lishui County	21598	6762	5593	2051	36.7	49.2
高淳县	Gaochun County	22493	7048	5218	2065	39.6	45.0
无锡市	**Wuxi Municipality**	**29658**	**8881**	**6515**	**2309**	**35.5**	**58.3**
江阴市	Jiangyin City	28952	9411	6318	2405	38.1	65.4
宜兴市	Yixing City	24424	8005	5492	2165	39.4	44.5
徐州市	**Xuzhou Municipality**	**21897**	**4896**	**3220**	**1320**	**41.0**	**32.2**
丰县	Fengxian County	12530	4537	3117	1340	43.0	31.8
沛县	Peixian County	13688	5142	3666	1285	35.1	31.5
铜山县	Tongshan County	15604	5591	3515	1403	39.9	33.9
睢宁县	Suining County	11984	4314	2932	1424	48.5	34.7
新沂市	Xinyi City	13423	4516	3145	1170	37.2	26.9
邳州市	Pizhou City	13413	5088	3027	1268	41.9	31.3
常州市	**Changzhou Municipality**	**26553**	**8001**	**6518**	**2460**	**37.7**	**58.3**
溧阳市	Liyang City	21778	6998	5576	2152	38.6	42.7
金坛市	Jintan City	21404	7305	6558	2676	40.8	44.0
苏州市	**Suzhou Municipality**	**28010**	**9281**	**6811**	**2473**	**36.3**	**65.3**
常熟市	Changshu City	25411	9293	7051	2514	35.7	69.6
张家港市	Zhangjiagang City	26042	9279	7772	2764	35.6	67.1
昆山市	Kunshan City	25989	9410	7294	2542	34.9	71.5
吴江市	Wujiang City	25911	9237	6018	2245	37.3	52.0
太仓市	Taicang City	25503	9285	5741	1967	34.3	71.8

20－21 续表1 Continued

市 县	City and County	在岗职工平均工资(元) Average Wages of Fully Employed Staff and Workers (yuan)	农民人均纯收入(元) Per Capita Net Income of Rural Households (yuan)	农民人均生活消费支出(元) Per Capita Living Expenditure of Rural Households (yuan)	#食品 Food	农村居民恩格尔系数(%) Engle Coefficient of Rural Residents (%)	农村居民人均住房面积(平方米) Per Capita Living Space of Housing of Rural Residents (sq. m)
南通市	**Nantong Municipality**	**21662**	**6106**	**4313**	**1659**	**38.5**	**50.1**
海安县	Haian County	19825	5900	4523	1682	37.2	47.0
如东县	Rudong County	18436	5420	4038	1605	39.7	55.7
启东市	Qidong City	18011	6730	4185	1737	41.5	49.0
如皋市	Rugao City	17937	5002	3424	1346	39.3	46.8
通州市	Tongzhou City	20735	6680	4849	1686	34.8	55.1
海门市	Haimen City	20833	7190	5164	2027	39.3	45.9
连云港市	**Lianyungang Municipality**	**17760**	**4265**	**2797**	**1266**	**45.3**	**0.0**
赣榆县	Ganyu County	13612	4602	2583	1230	47.6	23.8
东海县	Donghai County	13718	4419	3183	1414	44.4	20.9
灌云县	Guanyun County	13799	3940	2281	1011	44.3	25.1
灌南县	Guannan County	13712	3758	2774	1277	46.0	28.1
淮安市	**Huaian Municipality**	**16590**	**4430**	**2885**	**1299**	**45.0**	**30.4**
涟水县	Lianshui County	12719	4010	3068	1301	42.4	29.2
洪泽县	Hongze County	15959	4805	2798	1263	45.1	30.1
盱眙县	Xuyi County	15027	4463	2725	1141	41.9	31.6
金湖县	Jinhu County	14700	4814	4234	2087	49.3	37.3
盐城市	**Yancheng Municipality**	**15690**	**5393**	**3260**	**1413**	**43.3**	**34.0**
响水县	Xiangshui County	12513	4420	2543	1226	48.2	23.5
滨海县	Binhai County	12949	4695	2831	1495	52.8	21.9
阜宁县	Funing County	13294	4894	3135	1367	43.6	31.8
射阳县	Sheyang County	13291	5483	2964	1218	41.1	30.4
建湖县	Jianhu County	14235	5323	3090	1415	45.8	34.1

市县 City and County		在岗职工平均工资（元）Average Wages of Fully Employed Staff and Workers (yuan)	农民人均纯收入（元）Per Capita Net Income of Rural Households (yuan)	农民人均生活消费支出（元）Per Capita Living Expenditure of Rural Households (yuan)	#食品 Food	农村居民恩格尔系数（%）Engle Coefficient of Rural Residents (%)	农村居民人均住房面积（平方米）Per Capita Living Space of Housing of Rural Residents (sq. m)
东台市	Dongtai City	15873	6217	3656	1364	37.3	51.3
大丰市	Dafeng City	15131	6124	4649	1751	37.7	43.5
扬州市	**Yangzhou Municipality**	**20847**	**5813**	**4314**	**1728**	**40.1**	**38.8**
宝应县	Baoying County	14797	5451	3450	1420	41.2	37.4
仪征市	Yizheng City	20261	5501	4411	1960	44.4	46.1
高邮市	Gaoyou City	17287	5482	4116	1666	40.5	37.7
江都市	Jiangdu City	17260	6131	4411	1603	36.3	37.3
镇江市	**Zhenjiang Municipality**	**22924**	**6717**	**5068**	**2020**	**39.9**	**44.6**
丹阳市	Danyang City	20198	7109	5595	2173	38.8	47.5
扬中市	Yangzhong City	19499	8000	5255	1822	34.7	56.9
句容市	Jurong City	17915	6090	4418	1886	42.7	37.4
泰州市	**Taizhou Municipality**	**17309**	**5695**	**4046**	**1538**	**38.0**	**42.0**
兴化市	Xinghua City	15219	5456	3384	1378	40.7	33.7
靖江市	Jingjiang City	17031	6173	5753	2061	35.8	57.8
泰兴市	Taixing City	16535	5722	3747	1554	41.5	48.3
姜堰市	Jiangyan City	16272	5549	4311	1442	33.4	34.0
宿迁市	**Suqian Municipality**	**14053**	**4228**	**2824**	**1339**	**47.4**	**24.9**
沭阳县	Shuyang County	11947	4278	2749	1285	46.8	24.7
泗阳县	Siyang County	12308	4240	2963	1605	54.2	26.9
泗洪县	Sihong County	12269	4147	2599	1169	45.0	24.2

20－22 科 技 、教 育 (2006年)
SCIENCE, TECHNOLOGY AND EDUCATION (2006)

单位：万人 (10000 persons)

市 县	City and County	各类专业技术人员 Number of Scientific and Technical Personnel	#中级技术职称以上 Personnel with Meduim and above Titles	在校学生总数 Student Enrollment	#普通中等专业学校 Regular and Specialized Secondary Schools	#普通中学 Regular Secondary Schools	#小学 Primary Schools
南京市	**Nanjing Municipality**	**62.78**	**19.54**	**131.97**	**8.76**	**30.56**	**30.25**
溧水县	Lishui County	0.47	0.27	5.69	0.68	2.86	2.13
高淳县	Gaochun County	0.52	0.29	5.16	0.29	2.60	2.26
无锡市	**Wuxi Municipality**	**39.41**	**14.54**	**82.20**	**8.44**	**27.19**	**31.47**
江阴市	Jiangyin City	8.65	3.11	19.71	0.40	8.06	8.75
宜兴市	Yixing City	6.96	2.54	14.80	0.66	6.58	6.48
徐州市	**Xuzhou Municipality**	**26.53**	**9.65**	**227.07**	**5.96**	**77.79**	**64.62**
丰县	Fengxian County	1.83	0.83	33.34		10.17	9.63
沛县	Peixian County	3.30	0.99	28.87		11.34	8.73
铜山县	Tongshan County	2.59	0.84	26.42		10.29	6.89
睢宁县	Suining County	1.83	0.85	32.80		12.21	10.97
新沂市	Xinyi City	2.57	0.68	23.00		8.83	6.21
邳州市	Pizhou City	3.29	1.08	27.05	0.26	13.94	11.21
常州市	**Changzhou Municipality**	**24.43**	**8.09**	**64.84**	**4.62**	**21.59**	**23.49**
溧阳市	Liyang City	4.20	1.43	10.75	0.02	4.69	4.83
金坛市	Jintan City	3.20	0.98	6.94	0.29	3.58	3.05
苏州市	**Suzhou Municipality**	**53.16**	**12.27**	**94.13**	**8.27**	**32.47**	**35.15**
常熟市	Changshu City	7.51	1.69	13.27	0.60	4.90	6.43
张家港市	Zhangjiagang City	6.95	1.84	11.21	0.51	4.79	4.85
昆山市	Kunshan City	12.40	2.48	10.50	0.24	3.79	4.20
吴江市	Wujiang City	7.24	1.30	9.85	0.39	4.76	4.41
太仓市	Taicang City	3.36	0.84	5.58	0.36	2.16	2.77

20－22　续表1　Continued

单位:万人　　(10000 persons)

市　县 City and County		各类专业技术人员 Number of Scientific and Technical Personnel	#中级技术职称以上 Personnel with Meduim and above Titles	在校学生总数 Student Enrollment	#普通中等专业学校 Regular and Specialized Secondary Schools	#普通中学 Regular Secondary Schools	#小学 Primary Schools
南通市	**Nantong Municipality**	**28.16**	**8.85**	**101.67**	**6.67**	**42.48**	**40.15**
海安县	Haian County	3.09	0.66	11.23	0.77	5.20	4.53
如东县	Rudong County	5.40	0.82	12.27	0.38	5.65	5.40
启东市	Qidong City	4.27	0.72	11.75	0.55	5.80	5.29
如皋市	Rugao City	3.22	0.69	17.58	0.19	8.33	7.15
通州市	Tongzhou City	4.71	0.82	14.71	1.07	6.91	6.65
海门市	Haimen City	3.66	0.70	12.10	0.34	5.61	5.73
连云港市	**Lianyungang Municipality**	**15.17**	**4.96**	**86.66**	**3.81**	**38.42**	**38.11**
赣榆县	Ganyu County	1.58	0.71	19.62		9.73	9.24
东海县	Donghai County	1.43	0.60	20.14		10.50	9.11
灌云县	Guanyun County	1.29	0.34	17.52		8.09	9.01
灌南县	Guannan County	0.83	0.34	11.45		5.42	5.41
淮安市	**Huaian Municipality**	**11.95**	**3.98**	**92.00**	**4.01**	**36.96**	**38.44**
涟水县	Lianshui County	1.27	0.46	17.51		8.33	7.95
洪泽县	Hongze County	0.51	0.32	4.82		2.20	2.19
盱眙县	Xuyi County	0.91	0.40	12.96		5.66	5.94
金湖县	Jinhu County	0.57	0.36	4.26		2.10	1.92
盐城市	**Yancheng Municipality**	**19.94**	**6.24**	**105.75**	**6.06**	**46.25**	**40.43**
响水县	Xiangshui County	1.09	0.31	7.20		3.48	3.52
滨海县	Binhai County	1.34	0.47	14.20		6.81	5.80
阜宁县	Funing County	1.91	0.53	12.53		6.27	5.26
射阳县	Sheyang County	1.73	0.61	12.27		5.58	5.32
建湖县	Jianhu County	2.07	0.63	9.47		4.66	3.91

20－22 续表2 Continued

单位:万人 (10000 persons)

市 县 City and County		各类专业技术人员 Number of Scientific and Technical Personnel	#中级技术职称以上 Personnel with Meduim and above Titles	在校学生总数 Student Enrollment	#普通中等专业学校 Regular and Specialized Secondary Schools	#普通中学 Regular Secondary Schools	#小学 Primary Schools
东台市	Dongtai City	2.22	0.71	12.48		6.52	4.98
大丰市	Dafeng City	1.78	0.63	8.01		3.76	3.57
扬州市	**Yangzhou Municipality**	**18.42**	**7.04**	**67.63**	**6.04**	**25.90**	**25.18**
宝应县	Baoying County	2.45	0.87	11.52	0.65	5.46	4.99
仪征市	Yizheng City	2.66	1.01	7.75	0.34	3.66	3.09
高邮市	Gaoyou City	2.85	1.05	10.45	0.68	4.63	4.61
江都市	Jiangdu City	3.76	1.45	12.24	0.77	5.31	5.63
镇江市	**Zhenjiang Municipality**	**12.70**	**5.04**	**44.02**	**3.16**	**15.56**	**14.99**
丹阳市	Danyang City	2.75	0.72	11.78	0.53	5.35	5.01
扬中市	Yangzhong City	1.38	0.44	3.33		1.87	1.46
句容市	Jurong City	1.67	0.46	7.31	0.26	3.32	2.85
泰州市	**Taizhou Municipality**	**16.63**	**9.64**	**66.95**	**1.29**	**31.14**	**27.08**
兴化市	Xinghua City	6.53	3.60	17.26		9.15	7.40
靖江市	Jingjiang City	3.87	2.32	8.28		3.91	3.58
泰兴市	Taixing City	6.32	3.68	18.30	0.59	8.61	7.85
姜堰市	Jiangyan City	4.28	3.15	10.82		5.12	4.70
宿迁市	**Suqian Municipality**	**12.01**	**3.43**	**102.76**	**6.20**	**44.96**	**46.38**
沭阳县	Shuyang County	5.26	0.81	34.91	1.61	15.03	17.40
泗阳县	Siyang County	1.89	0.83	17.32	1.05	8.01	7.26
泗洪县	Sihong County	2.04	0.63	19.17	1.22	8.74	8.18

20－23 文化、卫生（2006年）
CULTURE AND PUBLIC HEALTH (2006)

市县	City and County	公共图书馆（个）Public Libraries (unit)	公共图书馆图书藏量（千册）Total Collections of Public Libraries (1000 volumes)	卫生机构数（个）Number of Health Institutions (unit)	卫生机构床位数（张）Number of Hospital Beds (unit)	卫生技术人员（人）Medical Technical Personnel (person)	#执业（助理）医师 Practitioner (Assistant) Doctors
南京市	**Nanjing Municipality**	**18**	**11868**	**2085**	**26980**	**36935**	**15169**
溧水县	Lishui County	2	276	123	775	1215	444
高淳县	Gaochun County	1	130	49	1051	1094	482
无锡市	**Wuxi Municipality**	**9**	**2492**	**2176**	**20999**	**25783**	**10723**
江阴市	Jiangyin City	1	534	472	4383	5646	2263
宜兴市	Yixing City	1	263	500	3080	4434	1732
徐州市	**Xuzhou Municipality**	**7**	**1542**	**1327**	**20264**	**28914**	**10719**
丰县	Fengxian County	1	106	159	1097	1886	975
沛县	Peixian County	1	186	192	2063	3162	1425
铜山县	Tongshan County	1	151	64	1474	2655	1023
睢宁县	Suining County	1	103	29	1205	1890	667
新沂市	Xinyi City	1	111	62	1365	2180	871
邳州市	Pizhou City	1	116	149	1534	4671	1106
常州市	**Changzhou Municipality**	**4**	**2015**	**1180**	**13247**	**18414**	**7085**
溧阳市	Liyang City	1	193	223	2314	2988	1190
金坛市	Jintan City	1	152	194	1373	2430	1087
苏州市	**Suzhou Municipality**	**10**	**4874**	**2285**	**28872**	**36951**	**14948**
常熟市	Changshu City	1	1353	335	3756	5140	2078
张家港市	Zhangjiagang City	1	477	419	3714	4482	1939
昆山市	Kunshan City	1	480	308	3076	4453	1725
吴江市	Wujiang City	1	355	286	3915	5579	2034
太仓市	Taicang City	1	246	144	2316	2591	1078

市 县	City and County	公共图书馆(个) Public Libraries (unit)	公共图书馆图书藏量(千册) Total Collections of Public Libraries (1000 volumes)	卫生机构数(个) Number of Health Institutions (unit)	卫生机构床位数(张) Number of Hospital Beds (unit)	卫生技术人员(人) Medical Technical Personnel (person)	#执业(助理)医师 Practitioner (Assistant) Doctors
南通市	**Nantong Municipality**	**10**	**2402**	**1931**	**22687**	**25679**	**11763**
海安县	Haian County	1	268	200	2478	2752	1208
如东县	Rudong County	1	144	236	2180	2713	1235
启东市	Qidong City	1	196	212	2189	2643	1327
如皋市	Rugao City	1	177	324	2784	3400	1526
通州市	Tongzhou City	1	378	207	3680	3635	1533
海门市	Haimen City	1	216	219	2974	3239	1803
连云港市	**Lianyungang Municipality**	**7**	**1046**	**982**	**9600**	**12468**	**5455**
赣榆县	Ganyu County	1	153	144	1501	2010	913
东海县	Donghai County	1	130	111	1196	1899	877
灌云县	Guanyun County	1	67	152	1354	1603	702
灌南县	Guannan County	1	89	83	1078	1303	484
淮安市	**Huaian Municipality**	**7**	**1094**	**645**	**11373**	**14003**	**5573**
涟水县	Lianshui County	1	94	75	1501	1966	735
洪泽县	Hongze County	1	110	71	574	954	377
盱眙县	Xuyi County	1	68	54	1125	1437	575
金湖县	Jinhu County	1	87	51	588	820	331
盐城市	**Yancheng Municipality**	**9**	**1429**	**1339**	**15908**	**20925**	**9160**
响水县	Xiangshui County	1	31	53	989	1218	543
滨海县	Binhai County	1	94	318	1224	2682	842
阜宁县	Funing County	1	86	47	1119	1941	1027
射阳县	Sheyang County	1	147	109	1724	2119	908
建湖县	Jianhu County	1	128	91	1766	1836	844

市 县 City and County		公共图书馆(个) Public Libraries (unit)	公共图书馆图书藏量(千册) Total Collections of Public Libraries (1000 volumes)	卫生机构数(个) Number of Health Institutions (unit)	卫生机构床位数(张) Number of Hospital Beds (unit)	卫生技术人员(人) Medical Technical Personnel (person)	#执业(助理)医师 Practitioner (Assistant) Doctors
东台市	Dongtai City	1	197	130	2687	2739	1274
大丰市	Dafeng City	1	156	102	1659	2293	1025
扬州市	**Yangzhou Municipality**	**7**	**1906**	**1351**	**13714**	**16509**	**7571**
宝应县	Baoying County	1	95	230	1515	2037	968
仪征市	Yizheng City	1	218	84	1635	2015	869
高邮市	Gaoyou City	1	127	132	1563	2152	1090
江都市	Jiangdu City	1	245	263	2836	4050	1813
镇江市	**Zhenjiang Municipality**	**7**	**1479**	**968**	**8486**	**13892**	**5506**
丹阳市	Danyang City	2	222	237	1898	3491	1430
扬中市	Yangzhong City	1	218	104	595	1665	644
句容市	Jurong City	1	87	190	1111	2100	726
泰州市	**Taizhou Municipality**	**5**	**1107**	**664**	**11876**	**16368**	**7446**
兴化市	Xinghua City	1	158	108	2566	3176	1467
靖江市	Jingjiang City	1	250	164	2101	3436	1423
泰兴市	Taixing City	1	151	154	2582	4177	1834
姜堰市	Jiangyan City	1	128	131	2158	2758	1374
宿迁市	**Suqian Municipality**	**6**	**478**	**853**	**9235**	**10112**	**4086**
沭阳县	Shuyang County	1	55	143	2587	2970	979
泗阳县	Siyang County	1	159	197	1481	1969	852
泗洪县	Sihong County	1	70	142	2092	2090	820

20-24 环 境 保 护 (2006 年)
ENVIRONMENTAL PROTECTION (2006)

市 县 City and County		工业废水排放达标量(万吨) Volume of Treated Industrial Waste Water up to the Discharged Standards (10000 tons)	工业二氧化硫去除量(万吨) Total Volume of Industrial Sulphur Dioxide Removed (10000 tons)	工业烟尘去除量(万吨) Volume of Industrial Soot Removed (10000 tons)	工业固体废物综合利用率(%) Percentage of Industrial Solid Wastes Used in a Comprehensive Way (%)	"三废"综合利用产品产值(万元) Output Value of Products Made from Comprehensive Use of "there Wastes" (10000 yuan)	环境噪声达标区总面积(平方公里) Total Area of Enviromental Noice zone up to the Standards (sq. m)
南 京 市	**Nanjing Municipality**	**40163**	**34.50**	**277.30**	**88.5**	**171284**	**452**
溧 水 县	Lishui County	743	0.15	0.57	99.5	4063	11
高 淳 县	Gaochun County	2515	0.00	0.50	99.9	1273	6
无 锡 市	**Wuxi Municipality**	**52617**	**8.77**	**203.60**	**97.4**	**47184**	**398**
江 阴 市	Jiangyin City	23062	4.65	110.97	96.9	15066	49
宜 兴 市	Yixing City	5822	1.62	28.80	100.0	9429	47
徐 州 市	**Xuzhou Municipality**	**9613**	**10.09**	**267.16**	**96.8**	**135621**	**245**
丰 县	Fengxian County	215	0.21	0.97	100.0	897	14
沛 县	Peixian County	477	1.09	13.87	97.0	1476	21
铜 山 县	Tongshan County	2880	3.61	159.89	108.7	67611	17
睢 宁 县	Suining County	203		0.07	100.0	1110	13
新 沂 市	Xinyi City	1769	0.20	4.35	27.0	6734	24
邳 州 市	Pizhou City	303	2.01	59.17	100.0	41361	23
常 州 市	**Changzhou Municipality**	**26779**	**2.80**	**55.66**	**98.5**	**488646**	**141**
溧 阳 市	Liyang City	3305		0.67	100.0	290481	18
金 坛 市	Jintan City	2537	0.00	3.68	99.3	3577	16
苏 州 市	**Suzhou Municipality**	**73138**	**26.15**	**326.03**	**98.4**	**383519**	**510**
常 熟 市	Changshu City	9882	5.87	104.96	96.8	5736	80
张家港市	Zhangjiagang City	15103	4.45	33.15	99.4	278150	31
昆 山 市	Kunshan City	9292	2.51	2.95	86.8	29053	88
吴 江 市	Wujiang City	11935	2.12	11.07	99.9	43212	18
太 仓 市	Taicang City	4672	6.23	112.43	99.9	3569	22

20－24　续表1　Continued

市　县	City and County	工业废水排放达标量（万吨） Volume of Treated Industrial Waste Water up to the Discharged Standards (10000 tons)	工业二氧化硫去除量（万吨） Total Volume of Industrial Sulphur Dioxide Removed (10000 tons)	工业烟尘去除量（万吨） Volume of Industrial Soot Removed (10000 tons)	工业固体废物综合利用率（%） Percentage of Industrial Solid Wastes Used in a Comprehensive Way (%)	"三废"综合利用产品产值（万元） Output Value of Products Made from Comprehensive Use of "there Wastes" (10000 yuan)	环境噪声达标区总面积（平方公里） Total Area of Enviromental Noice zone up to the Standards (sq. m)
南通市	**Nantong Municipality**	**15376**	**4.25**	**91.53**	**98.2**	**48403**	**132**
海安县	Haian County	1928	0.01	0.01	97.5	2546	
如东县	Rudong County	1325	0.23	0.71	99.7	3897	9
启东市	Qidong City	2694	0.66	0.59	98.7	240	15
如皋市	Rugao City	1313	0.00	1.47	100.0	1194	18
通州市	Tongzhou City	1089	0.31	0.84	97.7	553	8
海门市	Haimen City	1067	0.07	0.20	98.3	4916	10
连云港市	**Lianyungang Municipality**	**3779**	**2.93**	**83.83**	**91.3**	**7935**	**112**
赣榆县	Ganyu County	0.14	1.07	100.0		10	
东海县	Donghai County	500		0.20	100.0	785	10
灌云县	Guanyun County	938	0.02	0.33	100.0	260	9
灌南县	Guannan County	81	0.00		99.0	10	12
淮安市	**Huaian Municipality**	**6155**	**2.08**	**79.33**	**99.8**	**29139**	**100**
涟水县	Lianshui County	276	0.00	0.21	100.0	437	10
洪泽县	Hongze County	1849	0.29	2.23	99.8	12570	6
盱眙县	Xuyi County	1205	0.01	0.26	99.7	225	8
金湖县	Jinhu County	938	0.01	0.20	100.0	707	7
盐城市	**Yancheng Municipality**	**8961**	**2.61**	**67.37**	**96.9**	**43297**	**43**
响水县	Xiangshui County	1087	0.25	3.12	99.8	210	
滨海县	Binhai County	897	0.20	0.01	100.0		
阜宁县	Funing County	1396	0.04	2.20	100.0	1075	2
射阳县	Sheyang County	390	0.52	28.94	89.9	4956	
建湖县	Jianhu County	726	0.39	0.29	98.5	9108	11

20－24 续表2 Continued

市县 City and County		工业废水排放达标量（万吨）Volume of Treated Industrial Waste Water up to the Discharged Standards (10000 tons)	工业二氧化硫去除量（万吨）Total Volume of Industrial Sulphur Dioxide Removed (10000 tons)	工业烟尘去除量（万吨）Volume of Industrial Soot Removed (10000 tons)	工业固体废物综合利用率（%）Percentage of Industrial Solid Wastes Used in a Comprehensive Way (%)	"三废"综合利用产品产值（万元）Output Value of Products Made from Comprehensive Use of "there Wastes" (10000 yuan)	环境噪声达标区总面积（平方公里）Total Area of Enviromental Noice zone up to the Standards (sq. m)
东台市	Dongtai City	1673	0.05	0.29	100.0	17254	
大丰市	Dafeng City	1715	0.27	0.54	98.5	8260	4
扬州市	**Yangzhou Municipality**	**12327**	**3.70**	**127.98**	**83.2**	**19379**	**199**
宝应县	Baoying County	966	0.11	0.15	100.0	198	22
仪征市	Yizheng City	3642	0.55	32.39	94.3	1783	39
高邮市	Gaoyou City	1154	0.02	0.00	93.8	235	26
江都市	Jiangdu City	871	0.08	0.26	92.9	10	18
镇江市	**Zhenjiang Municipality**	**10032**	**3.52**	**159.69**	**89.0**	**31934**	**129**
丹阳市	Danyang City	1501	0.23	4.28	99.9	8444	25
扬中市	Yangzhong City	186			92.0	550	9
句容市	Jurong City	1409	1.52	0.43	98.6	68	9
泰州市	**Taizhou Municipality**	**18162**	**1.34**	**12.70**	**99.3**	**31381**	**90**
兴化市	Xinghua City	2083	0.10	3.49	98.8	506	9
靖江市	Jingjiang City	3680	0.38	0.53	98.6	1853	12
泰兴市	Taixing City	8328	0.09	1.05	99.3	11375	16
姜堰市	Jiangyan City	3020	0.53	2.61	100.0	1243	12
宿迁市	**Suqian Municipality**	**4062**	**0.94**	**4.93**	**100.0**	**2988**	**97**
沭阳县	Shuyang County	456	0.02	0.38	100.0	199	17
泗阳县	Siyang County	1041	0.03	0.21	100.0	1570	13
泗洪县	Sihong County	1360	0.05	3.81	100.0	1	11

第 21 篇

县(市)社会经济发展序列

COUNTY (CITY) SOCIAL ECONOMIC DEVELOPMENT ALIGNMENT

21-1 年末总人口（2006年）
TOTAL POPULATION AT THE YEAR-END (2006)

位次 No.	县（市）名称 County (City)		绝对数（万人）Absolute Figure (10000 persons)	位次 No.	县（市）名称 County (City)		绝对数（万人）Absolute Figure (10000 persons)
1	沭阳县	Shuyang County	177.05	27	新沂市	Xinyi City	99.06
2	邳州市	Pizhou City	165.46	28	泗阳县	Siyang County	96.83
3	兴化市	Xinghua City	154.69	29	海安县	Haian County	95.03
4	如皋市	Rugao City	141.85	30	宝应县	Baoying County	92.54
5	睢宁县	Suining County	134.04	31	姜堰市	Jiangyan City	90.14
6	泰兴市	Taixing City	128.05	32	张家港市	Zhangjiagang City	88.78
7	通州市	Tongzhou City	125.64	33	高邮市	Gaoyou City	82.73
8	沛县	Peixian County	121.74	34	建湖县	Jianhu County	80.82
9	铜山县	Tongshan County	120.72	35	丹阳市	Danyang City	80.61
10	江阴市	Jiangyin City	119.45	36	吴江市	Wujiang City	78.84
11	东海县	Donghai County	117.34	37	溧阳市	Liyang City	77.32
12	东台市	Dongtai City	115.35	38	灌南县	Guannan County	75.45
13	启东市	Qidong City	112.44	39	盱眙县	Xuyi County	74.87
14	丰县	Fengxian County	112.11	40	大丰市	Dafeng City	72.92
15	滨海县	Binhai County	111.28	41	昆山市	Kunshan City	66.68
16	赣榆县	Ganyu County	108.18	42	靖江市	Jingjiang City	66.47
17	灌云县	Guanyun County	107.50	43	仪征市	Yizheng City	59.70
18	阜宁县	Funing County	107.38	44	响水县	Xiangshui County	59.55
19	如东县	Rudong County	107.14	45	句容市	Jurong City	58.07
20	江都市	Jiangdu City	106.85	46	金坛市	Jintan City	54.87
21	涟水县	Lianshui County	106.40	47	太仓市	Taicang City	46.14
22	宜兴市	Yixing City	106.05	48	高淳县	Gaochun County	42.00
23	常熟市	Changshu City	105.48	49	溧水县	Lishui County	40.59
24	射阳县	Sheyang County	104.79	50	洪泽县	Hongze County	38.71
25	海门市	Haimen City	101.05	51	金湖县	Jinhu County	36.29
26	泗洪县	Sihong County	100.24	52	扬中市	Yangzhong City	27.39

21－2 地区生产总值（2006年）
GROSS DOMESTIC PRODUCT (2006)

位次 No.	县（市）名称 County (City)		绝对数（亿元）Absolute Figure (100 million yuan)	位次 No.	县（市）名称 County (City)		绝对数（亿元）Absolute Figure (100 million yuan)
1	江阴市	Jiangyin City	980.17	27	射阳县	Sheyang County	142.13
2	昆山市	Kunshan City	932.01	28	仪征市	Yizheng City	130.10
3	张家港市	Zhangjiagang City	841.62	29	扬中市	Yangzhong City	125.05
4	常熟市	Changshu City	809.28	30	句容市	Jurong City	124.30
5	吴江市	Wujiang City	500.80	31	沭阳县	Shuyang County	124.12
6	宜兴市	Yixing City	428.03	32	高邮市	Gaoyou City	123.72
7	太仓市	Taicang City	366.63	33	建湖县	Jianhu County	118.73
8	丹阳市	Danyang City	300.24	34	宝应县	Baoying County	116.02
9	通州市	Tongzhou City	270.58	35	高淳县	Gaochun County	111.03
10	海门市	Haimen City	261.09	36	溧水县	Lishui County	103.75
11	启东市	Qidong City	238.59	37	阜宁县	Funing County	100.03
12	江都市	Jiangdu City	230.20	38	滨海县	Binhai County	93.30
13	溧阳市	Liyang City	217.63	39	东海县	Donghai County	92.73
14	泰兴市	Taixing City	207.08	40	赣榆县	Ganyu County	91.82
15	东台市	Dongtai City	194.73	41	新沂市	Xinyi City	91.01
16	金坛市	Jintan City	182.00	42	泗阳县	Siyang County	81.21
17	如皋市	Rugao City	180.27	43	泗洪县	Sihong County	81.00
18	兴化市	Xinghua City	178.36	44	盱眙县	Xuyi County	74.52
19	海安县	Haian County	177.42	45	涟水县	Lianshui County	74.07
20	如东县	Rudong County	175.02	46	睢宁县	Suining County	72.10
21	铜山县	Tongshan County	168.66	47	丰县	Fengxian County	67.94
22	靖江市	Jingjiang City	161.89	48	灌云县	Guanyun County	55.93
23	姜堰市	Jiangyan City	161.66	49	响水县	Xiangshui County	54.13
24	邳州市	Pizhou City	149.96	50	灌南县	Guannan County	49.03
25	大丰市	Dafeng City	149.45	51	洪泽县	Hongze County	48.89
26	沛县	Peixian County	147.60	52	金湖县	Jinhu County	46.32

21－3 第一产业增加值(2006年)
VALUE-ADDED OF THE PRIMARY INDUSTRY (2006)

位次 No.	县(市)名称 County (City)		绝对数(亿元) Absolute Figure (100 million yuan)	位次 No.	县(市)名称 County (City)		绝对数(亿元) Absolute Figure (100 million yuan)
1	东台市	Dongtai City	44.03	27	睢宁县	Suining County	21.28
2	射阳县	Sheyang County	40.41	28	江都市	Jiangdu City	21.28
3	邳州市	Pizhou City	39.70	29	丰县	Fengxian County	20.63
4	兴化市	Xinghua City	39.15	30	盱眙县	Xuyi County	18.85
5	大丰市	Dafeng City	36.55	31	灌云县	Guanyun County	18.30
6	沭阳县	Shuyang County	35.90	32	常熟市	Changshu City	17.49
7	启东市	Qidong City	35.06	33	姜堰市	Jiangyan City	17.33
8	沛县	Peixian County	30.61	34	宜兴市	Yixing City	17.32
9	如东县	Rudong County	30.10	35	江阴市	Jiangyin City	17.16
10	东海县	Donghai County	26.88	36	吴江市	Wujiang City	17.11
11	高邮市	Gaoyou City	26.20	37	溧阳市	Liyang City	16.57
12	泗洪县	Sihong County	26.03	38	丹阳市	Danyang City	16.40
13	涟水县	Lianshui County	25.56	39	太仓市	Taicang City	15.63
14	滨海县	Binhai County	25.32	40	响水县	Xiangshui County	15.40
15	铜山县	Tongshan County	25.23	41	金坛市	Jintan City	14.63
16	宝应县	Baoying County	25.19	42	高淳县	Gaochun County	14.23
17	海安县	Haian County	25.17	43	灌南县	Guannan County	13.88
18	如皋市	Rugao City	24.75	44	张家港市	Zhangjiagang City	12.48
19	通州市	Tongzhou City	24.46	45	句容市	Jurong City	11.76
20	阜宁县	Funing County	24.10	46	洪泽县	Hongze County	11.75
21	泰兴市	Taixing City	24.01	47	溧水县	Lishui County	11.67
22	赣榆县	Ganyu County	23.95	48	金湖县	Jinhu County	11.03
23	海门市	Haimen City	23.65	49	昆山市	Kunshan City	10.53
24	建湖县	Jianhu County	22.83	50	靖江市	Jingjiang City	9.07
25	新沂市	Xinyi City	22.32	51	仪征市	Yizheng City	8.55
26	泗阳县	Siyang County	22.15	52	扬中市	Yangzhong City	3.93

21-4 第二产业增加值(2006年)
VALUE-ADDED OF THE SECONDARY INDUSTRY (2006)

位次 No.	县(市)名称 County (City)		绝对数(亿元) Absolute Figure (100 million yuan)	位次 No.	县(市)名称 County (City)		绝对数(亿元) Absolute Figure (100 million yuan)
1	昆山市	Kunshan City	632.41	27	沛县	Peixian County	68.01
2	江阴市	Jiangyin City	620.45	28	大丰市	Dafeng City	64.80
3	张家港市	Zhangjiagang City	545.69	29	邳州市	Pizhou City	62.56
4	常熟市	Changshu City	484.26	30	溧水县	Lishui County	58.73
5	吴江市	Wujiang City	321.43	31	高淳县	Gaochun County	58.58
6	宜兴市	Yixing City	256.72	32	高邮市	Gaoyou City	58.42
7	太仓市	Taicang City	223.05	33	射阳县	Sheyang County	57.75
8	丹阳市	Danyang City	176.84	34	建湖县	Jianhu County	55.27
9	通州市	Tongzhou City	161.17	35	宝应县	Baoying County	54.40
10	海门市	Haimen City	153.36	36	沭阳县	Shuyang County	51.78
11	江都市	Jiangdu City	142.02	37	阜宁县	Funing County	45.48
12	启东市	Qidong City	124.73	38	滨海县	Binhai County	38.62
13	溧阳市	Liyang City	123.54	39	新沂市	Xinyi City	38.26
14	泰兴市	Taixing City	117.25	40	赣榆县	Ganyu County	37.28
15	金坛市	Jintan City	97.50	41	东海县	Donghai County	36.08
16	如皋市	Rugao City	94.13	42	盱眙县	Xuyi County	35.08
17	靖江市	Jingjiang City	93.83	43	泗阳县	Siyang County	34.98
18	海安县	Haian County	91.98	44	泗洪县	Sihong County	29.72
19	姜堰市	Jiangyan City	91.92	45	睢宁县	Suining County	27.64
20	铜山县	Tongshan County	91.24	46	涟水县	Lianshui County	27.13
21	东台市	Dongtai City	88.10	47	丰县	Fengxian County	25.77
22	如东县	Rudong County	86.88	48	响水县	Xiangshui County	23.28
23	仪征市	Yizheng City	86.09	49	灌云县	Guanyun County	21.28
24	兴化市	Xinghua City	82.54	50	洪泽县	Hongze County	20.44
25	扬中市	Yangzhong City	76.32	51	灌南县	Guannan County	20.17
26	句容市	Jurong City	74.04	52	金湖县	Jinhu County	19.12

21－5 全部工业增加值（2006年）
VALUE-ADDED OF ALL INDUSTRIES (2006)

位次 No.	县（市）名称 County (City)		绝对数（亿元）Absolute Figure (100 million yuan)	位次 No.	县（市）名称 County (City)		绝对数（亿元）Absolute Figure (100 million yuan)
1	昆山市	Kunshan City	605.06	27	沛县	Peixian County	59.79
2	江阴市	Jiangyin City	596.45	28	大丰市	Dafeng City	54.12
3	张家港市	Zhangjiagang City	529.36	29	射阳县	Sheyang County	51.94
4	常熟市	Changshu City	462.64	30	邳州市	Pizhou City	51.36
5	吴江市	Wujiang City	304.40	31	溧水县	Lishui County	50.03
6	宜兴市	Yixing City	243.78	32	高邮市	Gaoyou City	49.12
7	太仓市	Taicang City	204.18	33	建湖县	Jianhu County	48.70
8	丹阳市	Danyang City	167.38	34	高淳县	Gaochun County	46.00
9	通州市	Tongzhou City	136.74	35	宝应县	Baoying County	44.79
10	海门市	Haimen City	128.94	36	沭阳县	Shuyang County	44.20
11	江都市	Jiangdu City	122.22	37	阜宁县	Funing County	33.88
12	溧阳市	Liyang City	106.51	38	新沂市	Xinyi City	32.82
13	启东市	Qidong City	97.32	39	滨海县	Binhai County	32.34
14	泰兴市	Taixing City	94.79	40	赣榆县	Ganyu County	31.24
15	靖江市	Jingjiang City	82.88	41	东海县	Donghai County	30.08
16	金坛市	Jintan City	81.50	42	盱眙县	Xuyi County	28.53
17	铜山县	Tongshan County	80.27	43	泗阳县	Siyang County	28.09
18	如皋市	Rugao City	76.94	44	泗洪县	Sihong County	24.46
19	东台市	Dongtai City	76.65	45	睢宁县	Suining County	24.04
20	仪征市	Yizheng City	75.32	46	涟水县	Lianshui County	21.64
21	姜堰市	Jiangyan City	75.20	47	响水县	Xiangshui County	19.93
22	海安县	Haian County	73.31	48	丰县	Fengxian County	19.76
23	句容市	Jurong City	69.80	49	洪泽县	Hongze County	16.94
24	兴化市	Xinghua City	68.95	50	金湖县	Jinhu County	16.82
25	扬中市	Yangzhong City	68.81	51	灌南县	Guannan County	16.05
26	如东县	Rudong County	67.41	52	灌云县	Guanyun County	15.84

21－6　第三产业增加值（2006年）
VALUE-ADDED OF THE TERTIARY INDUSTRY（2006）

位次 No.	县（市）名称 County（City）		绝对数（亿元）Absolute Figure（100 million yuan）	位次 No.	县（市）名称 County（City）		绝对数（亿元）Absolute Figure（100 million yuan）
1	江阴市	Jiangyin City	342.56	27	扬中市	Yangzhong City	44.80
2	常熟市	Changshu City	307.54	28	射阳县	Sheyang County	43.97
3	昆山市	Kunshan City	289.07	29	建湖县	Jianhu County	40.63
4	张家港市	Zhangjiagang City	283.45	30	高邮市	Gaoyou City	39.10
5	吴江市	Wujiang City	162.26	31	句容市	Jurong City	38.50
6	宜兴市	Yixing City	153.99	32	高淳县	Gaochun County	38.22
7	太仓市	Taicang City	127.95	33	沭阳县	Shuyang County	36.44
8	丹阳市	Danyang City	107.00	34	宝应县	Baoying County	36.43
9	通州市	Tongzhou City	84.95	35	仪征市	Yizheng City	35.46
10	海门市	Haimen City	84.08	36	溧水县	Lishui County	33.35
11	启东市	Qidong City	78.80	37	赣榆县	Ganyu County	30.59
12	溧阳市	Liyang City	77.52	38	阜宁县	Funing County	30.45
13	金坛市	Jintan City	69.87	39	新沂市	Xinyi City	30.43
14	江都市	Jiangdu City	66.90	40	东海县	Donghai County	29.77
15	泰兴市	Taixing City	65.82	41	滨海县	Binhai County	29.36
16	东台市	Dongtai City	62.60	42	泗洪县	Sihong County	25.25
17	如皋市	Rugao City	61.39	43	泗阳县	Siyang County	24.08
18	海安县	Haian County	60.27	44	睢宁县	Suining County	23.18
19	靖江市	Jingjiang City	58.99	45	丰县	Fengxian County	21.54
20	如东县	Rudong County	58.04	46	涟水县	Lianshui County	21.38
21	兴化市	Xinghua City	56.67	47	盱眙县	Xuyi County	20.59
22	姜堰市	Jiangyan City	52.41	48	洪泽县	Hongze County	16.70
23	铜山县	Tongshan County	52.19	49	灌云县	Guanyun County	16.35
24	沛县	Peixian County	48.98	50	金湖县	Jinhu County	16.17
25	大丰市	Dafeng City	48.10	51	响水县	Xiangshui County	15.45
26	邳州市	Pizhou City	47.70	52	灌南县	Guannan County	14.98

21-7 人均地区生产总值(2006年)
PER CAPITA GROSS DOMESTIC PRODUCT (2006)

位次 No.	县(市)名称	County (City)	绝对数(元) Absolute Figure (yuan)	位次 No.	县(市)名称	County (City)	绝对数(元) Absolute Figure (yuan)
1	昆山市	Kunshan City	141064	27	高邮市	Gaoyou City	14956
2	张家港市	Zhangjiangang City	95271	28	建湖县	Jianhu County	14738
3	江阴市	Jiangyin City	82346	29	铜山县	Tongshan County	14036
4	太仓市	Taicang City	79789	30	射阳县	Sheyang County	13591
5	常熟市	Changshu City	76979	31	金湖县	Jinhu County	12815
6	吴江市	Wujiang City	63731	32	如皋市	Rugao City	12701
7	扬中市	Yangzhong City	45747	33	洪泽县	Hongze County	12607
8	宜兴市	Yixing City	40422	34	宝应县	Baoying County	12567
9	丹阳市	Danyang City	37318	35	沛县	Peixian County	12187
10	金坛市	Jintan City	33401	36	兴化市	Xinghua City	11544
11	溧阳市	Liyang City	28249	37	盱眙县	Xuyi County	9988
12	高淳县	Gaochun County	26423	38	阜宁县	Funing County	9347
13	海门市	Haimen City	25797	39	新沂市	Xinyi City	9261
14	溧水县	Lishui County	25630	40	响水县	Xiangshui County	9229
15	靖江市	Jingjiang City	24407	41	邳州市	Pizhou City	9104
16	仪征市	Yizheng City	21862	42	赣榆县	Ganyu County	8507
17	江都市	Jiangdu City	21577	43	滨海县	Binhai County	8469
18	通州市	Tongzhou City	21483	44	泗阳县	Siyang County	8452
19	句容市	Jurong City	21413	45	泗洪县	Sihong County	8131
20	启东市	Qidong City	21178	46	东海县	Donghai County	7974
21	大丰市	Dafeng City	20491	47	沭阳县	Shuyang County	7028
22	海安县	Haian County	18640	48	涟水县	Lianshui County	6995
23	姜堰市	Jiangyuan City	17944	49	灌南县	Guannan County	6561
24	东台市	Dongtai City	16864	50	丰县	Fengxian County	6089
25	如东县	Rudong County	16295	51	睢宁县	Suining County	5402
26	泰兴市	Taixing City	16167	52	灌云县	Guanyun County	5263

21－8 城镇固定资产投资(2006年)

COMPLETED INVESTMENT OF URBAN UNITS IN FIXED ASSETES (2006)

位次 No.	县(市)名称 County (City)		绝对数(亿元) Absolute Figure (100 million yuan)	位次 No.	县(市)名称 County (City)		绝对数(亿元) Absolute Figure (100 million yuan)
1	昆山市	Kunshan City	204.36	27	泗阳县	Siyang County	36.70
2	太仓市	Taicang City	144.26	28	如皋市	Rugao City	36.41
3	江阴市	Jiangyin City	143.49	29	赣榆县	Ganyu County	36.07
4	常熟市	Changshu City	138.93	30	大丰市	Dafeng City	35.53
5	吴江市	Wujiang City	138.15	31	东台市	Dongtai City	35.29
6	张家港市	Zhangjiagang City	122.30	32	灌云县	Guanyun County	33.20
7	宜兴市	Yixing City	82.69	33	溧水县	Lishui County	32.22
8	铜山县	Tongshan County	72.56	34	灌南县	Guannan County	30.85
9	海安县	Haian County	60.76	35	东海县	Donghai County	29.92
10	溧阳市	Liyang City	59.00	36	宝应县	Baoying County	29.45
11	新沂市	Xinyi City	58.57	37	涟水县	Lianshui County	27.42
12	启东市	Qidong City	58.42	38	阜宁县	Funing County	26.93
13	江都市	Jiangdu City	51.16	39	高淳县	Gaochun County	26.84
14	通州市	Tongzhou City	50.73	40	高邮市	Gaoyou City	26.27
15	沭阳县	Shuyang County	49.47	41	丰县	Fengxian County	25.67
16	仪征市	Yizheng City	49.06	42	响水县	Xiangshui County	24.49
17	沛县	Peixian County	47.24	43	兴化市	Xinghua City	22.40
18	邳州市	Pizhou City	47.07	44	建湖县	Jianhu County	21.04
19	金坛市	Jintan City	46.89	45	句容市	Jurong City	20.94
20	海门市	Haimen City	45.82	46	洪泽县	Hongze County	20.57
21	泰兴市	Taixing City	45.38	47	泗洪县	Sihong County	20.43
22	靖江市	Jingjiang City	45.31	48	射阳县	Sheyang County	19.46
23	丹阳市	Danyang City	41.08	49	金湖县	Jinhu County	17.21
24	姜堰市	Jiangyan City	38.86	50	滨海县	Binhai County	15.13
25	盱眙县	Xuyi County	38.34	51	扬中市	Yangzhong City	13.28
26	如东县	Rudong County	38.07	52	睢宁县	Suining County	11.00

21-9 地方财政一般预算收入（2006年）
LOCAL FINANCIAL BUDGETARY REVENUE (2006)

位次 No.	县（市）名称 County (City)		绝对数（亿元）Absolute Figure (100 million yuan)	位次 No.	县（市）名称 County (City)		绝对数（亿元）Absolute Figure (100 million yuan)
1	昆山市	Kunshan City	65.37	27	邳州市	Pizhou City	5.93
2	张家港市	Zhangjiagang City	61.09	28	高淳县	Gaochun County	5.92
3	江阴市	Jiangyin City	60.48	29	句容市	Jurong City	5.36
4	常熟市	Changshu City	43.08	30	沭阳县	Shuyang County	5.01
5	吴江市	Wujiang City	35.08	31	大丰市	Dafeng City	5.01
6	太仓市	Taicang City	27.59	32	高邮市	Gaoyou City	4.70
7	宜兴市	Yixing City	21.66	33	射阳县	Sheyang County	4.67
8	丹阳市	Danyang City	13.29	34	建湖县	Jianhu County	4.66
9	溧阳市	Liyang City	11.80	35	溧水县	Lishui County	4.55
10	靖江市	Jingjiang City	11.20	36	宝应县	Baoying County	4.52
11	泰兴市	Taixing City	10.89	37	赣榆县	Ganyu County	4.00
12	通州市	Tongzhou City	10.57	38	东海县	Donghai County	4.00
13	海门市	Haimen City	9.62	39	阜宁县	Funing County	3.67
14	启东市	Qidong City	9.24	40	新沂市	Xinyi City	3.34
15	江都市	Jiangdu City	9.16	41	滨海县	Binhai County	3.12
16	金坛市	Jintan City	8.63	42	泗洪县	Sihong County	2.78
17	仪征市	Yizheng City	8.11	43	灌南县	Guannan County	2.62
18	姜堰市	Jiangyan City	7.92	44	盱眙县	Xuyi County	2.59
19	如皋市	Rugao City	7.51	45	泗阳县	Siyang County	2.51
20	铜山县	Tongshan County	7.38	46	睢宁县	Suining County	2.46
21	海安县	Haian County	6.95	47	丰县	Fengxian County	2.44
22	东台市	Dongtai City	6.66	48	灌云县	Guanyun County	2.33
23	兴化市	Xinghua City	6.56	49	涟水县	Lianshui County	2.25
24	如东县	Rudong County	6.16	50	响水县	Xiangshui County	2.24
25	沛县	Peixian County	6.02	51	洪泽县	Hongze County	2.07
26	扬中市	Yangzhong City	5.99	52	金湖县	Jinhu County	1.82

21－10　人均地方一般预算收入（2006年）
PER CAPITA LOCAL FINANCIAL BUDGETARY REVENUE (2006)

位次 No.	县（市）名称	County (City)	绝对数（元） Absolute Figure (yuan)	位次 No.	县（市）名称	County (City)	绝对数（元） Absolute Figure (yuan)
1	昆山市	Kunshan City	9894	27	东台市	Dongtai City	577
2	张家港市	Zhangjiagang City	6915	28	如东县	Rudong County	573
3	太仓市	Taicang City	6004	29	高邮市	Gaoyou City	568
4	江阴市	Jiangyin City	5081	30	洪泽县	Hongze County	535
5	吴江市	Wujiang City	4464	31	如皋市	Rugao City	529
6	常熟市	Changshu City	4098	32	金湖县	Jinhu County	503
7	扬中市	Yangzhong City	2190	33	沛县	Peixian County	497
8	宜兴市	Yixing City	2045	34	宝应县	Baoying County	490
9	靖江市	Jingjiang City	1689	35	射阳县	Sheyang County	446
10	丹阳市	Danyang City	1652	36	兴化市	Xinghua City	425
11	金坛市	Jintan City	1584	37	响水县	Xiangshui County	381
12	溧阳市	Liyang City	1532	38	赣榆县	Ganyu County	371
13	高淳县	Gaochun County	1409	39	邳州市	Pizhou City	360
14	仪征市	Yizheng City	1363	40	灌南县	Guannan County	350
15	溧水县	Lishui County	1124	41	盱眙县	Xuyi County	347
16	海门市	Haimen City	950	42	东海县	Donghai County	344
17	句容市	Jurong City	924	43	阜宁县	Funing County	343
18	姜堰市	Jiangyan City	879	44	新沂市	Xinyi City	340
19	江都市	Jiangdu City	859	45	沭阳县	Shuyang County	284
20	泰兴市	Taixing City	850	46	滨海县	Binhai County	283
21	通州市	Tongzhou City	839	47	泗洪县	Sihong County	279
22	启东市	Qidong City	820	48	泗阳县	Siyang County	261
23	海安县	Haian County	730	49	灌云县	Guanyun County	219
24	大丰市	Dafeng City	687	50	丰县	Fengxian County	218
25	铜山县	Tongshan County	614	51	涟水县	Lianshui County	212
26	建湖县	Jianhu County	579	52	睢宁县	Suining County	184

21-11 粮食产量（2006年）
OUTPUT OF GRAIN（2006）

位次 No.	县（市）名称 County（City）		绝对数（万吨）Absolute Figure（10000 tons）	位次 No.	县（市）名称 County（City）		绝对数（万吨）Absolute Figure（10000 tons）
1	兴化市	Xinghua City	122.93	27	江都市	Jiangdu City	49.76
2	沭阳县	Shuyang County	105.51	28	泗阳县	Siyang County	48.75
3	东海县	Donghai County	99.29	29	丰县	Fengxian County	42.77
4	泗洪县	Sihong County	83.04	30	丹阳市	Danyang City	42.17
5	如东县	Rudong County	80.98	31	新沂市	Xinyi City	41.98
6	射阳县	Sheyang County	80.80	32	赣榆县	Ganyu County	41.92
7	盱眙县	Xuyi County	77.66	33	金湖县	Jinhu County	41.65
8	阜宁县	Funing County	77.60	34	溧阳市	Liyang City	40.97
9	东台市	Dongtai City	76.64	35	响水县	Xiangshui County	39.09
10	涟水县	Lianshui County	75.67	36	宜兴市	Yixing City	36.71
11	高邮市	Gaoyou City	73.02	37	洪泽县	Hongze County	33.65
12	灌云县	Guanyun County	70.93	38	常熟市	Changshu City	30.91
13	如皋市	Rugao City	68.87	39	靖江市	Jingjiang City	30.44
14	宝应县	Baoying County	65.76	40	启东市	Qidong City	28.39
15	建湖县	Jianhu County	65.50	41	仪征市	Yizheng City	27.69
16	睢宁县	Suining County	65.47	42	张家港市	Zhangjiagang City	27.62
17	邳州市	Pizhou City	64.30	43	句容市	Jurong City	26.17
18	泰兴市	Taixing City	62.13	44	金坛市	Jintan City	24.53
19	铜山县	Tongshan County	61.58	45	江阴市	Jiangyin City	21.43
20	滨海县	Binhai County	61.55	46	太仓市	Taicang City	21.29
21	海安县	Haian County	60.41	47	溧水县	Lishui County	21.24
22	大丰市	Dafeng City	58.01	48	吴江市	Wujiang City	18.90
23	姜堰市	Jiangyan City	52.91	49	海门市	Haimen City	18.77
24	通州市	Tongzhou City	51.05	50	高淳县	Gaochun County	18.47
25	沛县	Peixian County	50.91	51	昆山市	Kunshan City	13.79
26	灌南县	Guannan County	49.84	52	扬中市	Yangzhong City	9.86

21－12 油料产量（2006年）
OUTPUT OF OIL－BEARING CROPS（2006）

位次 No.	县（市）名称 County（City）	绝对数（万吨）Absolute Figure（10000 tons）	位次 No.	县（市）名称 County（City）	绝对数（万吨）Absolute Figure（10000 tons）
1	启东市 Qidong City	9.68	27	宝应县 Baoying County	2.22
2	海门市 Haimen City	9.42	28	泗洪县 Sihong County	2.17
3	东台市 Dongtai City	8.87	29	宜兴市 Yixing City	2.07
4	滨海县 Binhai County	8.55	30	吴江市 Wujiang City	2.03
5	通州市 Tongzhou City	8.51	31	阜宁县 Funing County	1.83
6	盱眙县 Xuyi County	7.59	32	泗阳县 Siyang County	1.83
7	新沂市 Xinyi City	7.28	33	海安县 Haian County	1.77
8	溧阳市 Liyang City	6.06	34	丹阳市 Danyang City	1.69
9	赣榆县 Ganyu County	6.00	35	建湖县 Jianhu County	1.60
10	东海县 Donghai County	5.90	36	邳州市 Pizhou City	1.58
11	大丰市 Dafeng City	5.81	37	常熟市 Changshu City	1.57
12	如东县 Rudong County	5.01	38	金坛市 Jintan City	1.43
13	泰兴市 Taixing City	4.60	39	铜山县 Tongshan County	1.13
14	溧水县 Lishui County	4.56	40	仪征市 Yizheng City	1.09
15	如皋市 Rugao City	4.51	41	金湖县 Jinhu County	1.04
16	射阳县 Sheyang County	4.15	42	靖江市 Jingjiang City	1.02
17	句容市 Jurong City	4.09	43	太仓市 Taicang City	0.97
18	高淳县 Gaochun County	4.03	44	丰县 Fengxian County	0.84
19	江都市 Jiangdu City	4.00	45	沛县 Peixian County	0.80
20	姜堰市 Jiangyan City	3.96	46	昆山市 Kunshan City	0.57
21	涟水县 Lianshui County	3.54	47	张家港市 Zhangjiagang City	0.53
22	沭阳县 Shuyang County	3.53	48	洪泽县 Hongze County	0.46
23	兴化市 Xinghua City	3.34	49	江阴市 Jiangyin City	0.41
24	高邮市 Gaoyou City	2.91	50	灌南县 Guannan County	0.29
25	睢宁县 Suining County	2.62	51	灌云县 Guanyun County	0.16
26	响水县 Xiangshui County	2.50	52	扬中市 Yangzhong City	0.13

21－13　肉类总产量(2006年)
TOTAL OUTPUT OF MEAT (2006)

位次 No.	县（市）名称 County (City)		绝对数（万吨） Absolute Figure (10000 tons)	位次 No.	县（市）名称 County (City)		绝对数（万吨） Absolute Figure (10000 tons)
1	阜宁县	Funing County	14.01	27	启东市	Qidong City	4.47
2	沛县	Peixian County	11.36	28	宜兴市	Yixing City	4.36
3	邳州市	Pizhou City	10.56	29	丰县	Fengxian County	4.29
4	东台市	Dongtai City	9.17	30	建湖县	Jianhu County	4.13
5	沭阳县	Shuyang County	8.68	31	宝应县	Baoying County	4.11
6	滨海县	Binhai County	8.55	32	赣榆县	Ganyu County	4.10
7	泰兴市	Taixing City	8.45	33	海门市	Haimen City	3.91
8	如皋市	Rugao City	8.06	34	泗阳县	Siyang County	3.70
9	大丰市	Dafeng City	7.79	35	高淳县	Gaochun County	3.62
10	海安县	Haian County	7.52	36	靖江市	Jingjiang City	3.56
11	如东县	Rudong County	7.35	37	响水县	Xiangshui County	3.52
12	新沂市	Xinyi City	7.34	38	仪征市	Yizheng City	3.46
13	铜山县	Tongshan County	7.14	39	盱眙县	Xuyi County	3.46
14	射阳县	Sheyang County	6.88	40	灌南县	Guannan County	3.27
15	东海县	Donghai County	6.44	41	吴江市	Wujiang City	2.93
16	睢宁县	Suining County	6.43	42	溧水县	Lishui County	2.86
17	姜堰市	Jiangyan City	6.21	43	丹阳市	Danyang City	2.71
18	江都市	Jiangdu City	5.73	44	金坛市	Jintan City	2.42
19	通州市	Tongzhou City	5.36	45	常熟市	Changshu City	2.35
20	高邮市	Gaoyou City	5.16	46	溧阳市	Liyang City	1.90
21	涟水县	Lianshui County	5.07	47	洪泽县	Hongze County	1.83
22	江阴市	Jiangyin City	5.07	48	句容市	Jurong City	1.68
23	太仓市	Taicang City	5.02	49	张家港市	Zhangjiagang City	1.67
24	泗洪县	Sihong County	4.96	50	金湖县	Jinhu County	1.28
25	灌云县	Guanyun County	4.84	51	昆山市	Kunshan City	1.24
26	兴化市	Xinghua City	4.75	52	扬中市	Yangzhong City	0.81

21－14 规模以上工业企业利税总额（2006年）

PRE－TAX PROFITS OF ABOVE DESIGNATED SIZE INDUSTRIAL ENTERPRISES（2006）

位次 No.	县（市）名称 County（City）		绝对数（亿元） Absolute Figure（100 million yuan）	位次 No.	县（市）名称 County（City）		绝对数（亿元） Absolute Figure（100 million yuan）
1	江阴市	Jiangyin City	209.64	27	建湖县	Jianhu County	11.24
2	昆山市	Kunshan City	157.18	28	宝应县	Baoying County	10.53
3	张家港市	Zhangjiagang City	142.98	29	射阳县	Sheyang County	9.87
4	常熟市	Changshu City	116.81	30	邳州市	Pizhou City	9.82
5	宜兴市	Yixing City	71.80	31	高邮市	Gaoyou City	9.17
6	吴江市	Wujiang City	68.73	32	大丰市	Dafeng City	9.00
7	太仓市	Taicang City	59.41	33	仪征市	Yizheng City	8.80
8	通州市	Tongzhou City	51.16	34	洪泽县	Hongze County	7.20
9	海门市	Haimen City	42.84	35	高淳县	Gaochun County	7.00
10	铜山县	Tongshan County	32.91	36	滨海县	Binhai County	6.74
11	溧阳市	Liyang City	32.02	37	新沂市	Xinyi City	6.61
12	金坛市	Jintan City	28.11	38	沛县	Peixian County	6.35
13	丹阳市	Danyang City	27.94	39	阜宁县	Funing County	6.32
14	江都市	Jiangdu City	25.91	40	泗洪县	Sihong County	6.18
15	泰兴市	Taixing City	25.59	41	响水县	Xiangshui County	6.08
16	启东市	Qidong City	24.86	42	盱眙县	Xuyi County	6.02
17	靖江市	Jingjiang City	24.28	43	涟水县	Lianshui County	5.38
18	姜堰市	Jiangyan City	22.65	44	沭阳县	Shuyang County	5.07
19	兴化市	Xinghua City	19.99	45	东海县	Donghai County	4.22
20	如东县	Rudong County	18.95	46	睢宁县	Suining County	3.99
21	扬中市	Yangzhong City	18.71	47	金湖县	Jinhu County	3.67
22	东台市	Dongtai City	17.00	48	泗阳县	Siyang County	3.47
23	如皋市	Rugao City	16.48	49	赣榆县	Ganyu County	3.40
24	海安县	Haian County	16.46	50	灌南县	Guannan County	2.89
25	句容市	Jurong City	14.53	51	丰县	Fengxian County	2.74
26	溧水县	Lishui County	11.82	52	灌云县	Guanyun County	2.21

21－15 社会消费品零售总额（2006年）
TOTAL RETAIL SALE OF CONSUMER GOODS (2006)

位 次 No.	县（市）名称 County (City)		绝对数（亿元） Absolute Figure (100 million yuan)	位 次 No.	县（市）名称 County (City)		绝对数（亿元） Absolute Figure (100 million yuan)
1	江 阴 市	Jiangyin City	201.25	27	赣 榆 县	Ganyu County	40.49
2	常 熟 市	Changshu City	176.72	28	高 邮 市	Gaoyou City	40.29
3	宜 兴 市	Yixing City	143.72	29	邳 州 市	Pizhou City	39.93
4	昆 山 市	Kunshan City	135.01	30	宝 应 县	Baoying County	39.09
5	张家港市	Zhangjiagang City	112.17	31	大 丰 市	Dafeng City	38.91
6	通 州 市	Tongzhou City	87.21	32	高 淳 县	Gaochun County	38.28
7	海 门 市	Haimen City	87.11	33	建 湖 县	Jianhu County	37.74
8	启 东 市	Qidong City	84.16	34	铜 山 县	Tongshan County	37.44
9	如 皋 市	Rugao City	83.98	35	东 海 县	Donghai County	36.96
10	吴 江 市	Wujiang City	83.70	36	句 容 市	Jurong City	35.88
11	丹 阳 市	Danyang City	75.49	37	扬 中 市	Yangzhong City	34.57
12	溧 阳 市	Liyang City	75.08	38	溧 水 县	Lishui County	33.27
13	如 东 县	Rudong County	73.39	39	阜 宁 县	Funing County	32.19
14	江 都 市	Jiangdu City	67.77	40	睢 宁 县	Suining County	31.09
15	海 安 县	Haian County	65.29	41	新 沂 市	Xinyi City	30.48
16	东 台 市	Dongtai City	58.75	42	灌 云 县	Guanyun County	29.80
17	泰 兴 市	Taixing City	58.65	43	丰 县	Fengxian County	25.32
18	金 坛 市	Jintan City	58.20	44	滨 海 县	Binhai County	25.29
19	太 仓 市	Taicang City	55.54	45	泗 阳 县	Siyang County	23.24
20	姜 堰 市	Jiangyan City	48.66	46	泗 洪 县	Sihong County	22.09
21	靖 江 市	Jingjiang City	47.24	47	涟 水 县	Lianshui County	21.78
22	沛 县	Peixian County	46.59	48	盱 眙 县	Xuyi County	21.58
23	仪 征 市	Yizheng City	44.64	49	洪 泽 县	Hongze County	20.77
24	射 阳 县	Sheyang County	41.62	50	金 湖 县	Jinhu County	19.52
25	沭 阳 县	Shuyang County	40.66	51	灌 南 县	Guannan County	18.15
26	兴 化 市	Xinghua City	40.62	52	响 水 县	Xiangshui County	13.91

21-16 出口总额（2006年）
TOTAL EXPORTS (2006)

位次 No.	县（市）名称 County (City)		绝对数（万美元）Absolute Figure (USD 10000)	位次 No.	县（市）名称 County (City)		绝对数（万美元）Absolute Figure (USD 10000)
1	昆山市	Kunshan City	2436643	27	高邮市	Gaoyou City	11651
2	吴江市	Wujiang City	717560	28	兴化市	Xinghua City	11581
3	张家港市	Zhangjiagang City	548733	29	扬中市	Yangzhong City	9915
4	江阴市	Jiangyin City	457069	30	东海县	Donghai County	9502
5	常熟市	Changshu City	420239	31	高淳县	Gaochun County	9498
6	太仓市	Taicang City	236191	32	仪征市	Yizheng City	8462
7	宜兴市	Yixing City	98431	33	建湖县	Jianhu County	7398
8	通州市	Tongzhou City	95937	34	金湖县	Jinhu County	5887
9	靖江市	Jingjiang City	57982	35	阜宁县	Funing County	5209
10	丹阳市	Danyang City	55643	36	铜山县	Tongshan County	5084
11	金坛市	Jintan City	48491	37	新沂市	Xinyi City	4680
12	海门市	Haimen City	47907	38	射阳县	Sheyang County	4364
13	如皋市	Rugao City	44906	39	响水县	Xiangshui County	3789
14	如东县	Rudong County	41703	40	赣榆县	Ganyu County	3356
15	启东市	Qidong City	38028	41	涟水县	Lianshui County	2804
16	句容市	Jurong City	34776	42	丰县	Fengxian County	2299
17	泰兴市	Taixing City	31882	43	灌南县	Guannan County	2203
18	海安县	Haian County	31881	44	灌云县	Guanyun County	2096
19	溧阳市	Liyang City	31725	45	泗阳县	Siyang County	1991
20	姜堰市	Jiangyan City	26665	46	睢宁县	Suining County	1837
21	邳州市	Pizhou City	25323	47	沭阳县	Shuyang County	1712
22	江都市	Jiangdu City	21417	48	滨海县	Binhai County	1653
23	东台市	Dongtai City	16716	49	沛县	Peixian County	1298
24	溧水县	Lishui County	14909	50	泗洪县	Sihong County	1096
25	大丰市	Dafeng City	14414	51	洪泽县	Hongze County	1036
26	宝应县	Baoying County	12963	52	盱眙县	Xuyi County	448

21-17 实际外商直接投资(2006年)
ACTUAL FOREIGN DIRECT INVESTMENT (2006)

位次 No.	县(市)名称 County (City)		绝对数(万美元) Absolute Figure (USD 10000)	位次 No.	县(市)名称 County (City)		绝对数(万美元) Absolute Figure (USD 10000)
1	昆山市	Kunshan City	117190	27	宝应县	Baoying County	4222
2	常熟市	Changshu City	64268	28	高邮市	Gaoyou City	3965
3	吴江市	Wujiang City	55827	29	邳州市	Pizhou City	3940
4	海门市	Haimen City	48707	30	高淳县	Gaochun County	3416
5	通州市	Tongzhou City	44987	31	阜宁县	Funing County	3219
6	张家港市	Zhangjiagang City	44843	32	东台市	Dongtai City	3210
7	太仓市	Taicang City	44221	33	灌南县	Guannan County	3167
8	启东市	Qidong City	42441	34	铜山县	Tongshan County	3006
9	江阴市	Jiangyin City	39396	35	溧水县	Lishui County	2851
10	如皋市	Rugao City	32604	36	涟水县	Lianshui County	2410
11	如东县	Rudong County	32079	37	射阳县	Sheyang County	2310
12	宜兴市	Yixing City	29104	38	灌云县	Guanyun County	2301
13	海安县	Haian County	28469	39	兴化市	Xinghua City	2234
14	靖江市	Jingjiang City	20012	40	建湖县	Jianhu County	2092
15	丹阳市	Danyang City	16680	41	沛县	Peixian County	1813
16	泰兴市	Taixing City	13255	42	新沂市	Xinyi City	1197
17	仪征市	Yizheng City	12609	43	盱眙县	Xuyi County	1137
18	姜堰市	Jiangyan City	12062	44	金湖县	Jinhu County	1135
19	溧阳市	Liyang City	12053	45	洪泽县	Hongze County	1111
20	金坛市	Jintan City	12001	46	沭阳县	Shuyang County	688
21	江都市	Jiangdu City	10425	47	丰县	Fengxian County	669
22	扬中市	Yangzhong City	8304	48	滨海县	Binhai County	649
23	句容市	Jurong City	8049	49	泗阳县	Siyang County	602
24	赣榆县	Ganyu County	5716	50	泗洪县	Sihong County	600
25	大丰市	Dafeng City	4517	51	睢宁县	Suining County	385
26	东海县	Donghai County	4469	52	响水县	Xiangshui County	25

21－18 在岗职工平均工资(2006年)
AVERAGE WAGE OF STAFF AND WORKERS EMPLOYED (2006)

位次 No.	县(市)名称 County (City)		绝对数(元) Absolute Figure (yuan)	位次 No.	县(市)名称 County (City)		绝对数(元) Absolute Figure (yuan)
1	江阴市	Jiangyin City	28952	27	洪泽县	Hongze County	15959
2	张家港市	Zhangjiagang City	26042	28	东台市	Dongtai City	15873
3	昆山市	Kunshan City	25989	29	铜山县	Tongshan County	15604
4	吴江市	Wujiang City	25911	30	兴化市	Xinghua City	15219
5	太仓市	Taicang City	25503	31	大丰市	Dafeng City	15131
6	常熟市	Changshu City	25411	32	盱眙县	Xuyi County	15027
7	宜兴市	Yixing City	24424	33	宝应县	Baoying County	14797
8	高淳县	Gaochun County	22493	34	金湖县	Jinhu County	14700
9	溧阳市	Liyang City	21778	35	建湖县	Jianhu County	14235
10	溧水县	Lishui County	21598	36	灌云县	Guanyun County	13799
11	金坛市	Jintan City	21404	37	东海县	Donghai County	13718
12	海门市	Haimen City	20833	38	灌南县	Guannan County	13712
13	通州市	Tongzhou City	20735	39	沛县	Peixian County	13688
14	仪征市	Yizheng City	20261	40	赣榆县	Ganyu County	13612
15	丹阳市	Danyang City	20198	41	新沂市	Xinyi City	13423
16	海安县	Haian County	19825	42	邳州市	Pizhou City	13413
17	扬中市	Yangzhong City	19499	43	阜宁县	Funing County	13294
18	如东县	Rudong County	18436	44	射阳县	Sheyang County	13291
19	启东市	Qidong City	18011	45	滨海县	Binhai County	12949
20	如皋市	Rugao City	17937	46	涟水县	Lianshui County	12719
21	句容市	Jurong City	17915	47	丰县	Fengxian County	12530
22	高邮市	Gaoyou City	17287	48	响水县	Xiangshui County	12513
23	江都市	Jiangdu City	17260	49	泗阳县	Siyang County	12308
24	靖江市	Jingjiang City	17031	50	泗洪县	Sihong County	12269
25	泰兴市	Taixing City	16535	51	睢宁县	Suining County	11984
26	姜堰市	Jiangyan City	16272	52	沭阳县	Shuyang County	11947

21－19 农村居民人均纯收入（2006年）
PER CAPITA NET INCOME OF RURAL HOUSEHOLDS (2006)

位次 No.	县（市）名称 County (City)	绝对数（元） Absolute Figure (yuan)	位次 No.	县（市）名称 County (City)	绝对数（元） Absolute Figure (yuan)
1	江 阴 市 Jiangyin City	9411	27	射 阳 县 Sheyang County	5483
2	昆 山 市 Kunshan City	9410	28	高 邮 市 Gaoyou City	5482
3	常 熟 市 Changshu City	9293	29	兴 化 市 Xinghua City	5456
4	太 仓 市 Taicang City	9285	30	宝 应 县 Baoying County	5451
5	张家港市 Zhangjiagang City	9279	31	如 东 县 Rudong County	5420
6	吴 江 市 Wujiang City	9237	32	建 湖 县 Jianhu County	5323
7	宜 兴 市 Yixing City	8005	33	沛 县 Peixian County	5142
8	扬 中 市 Yangzhong City	8000	34	邳 州 市 Pizhou City	5088
9	金 坛 市 Jintan City	7305	35	如 皋 市 Rugao City	5002
10	海 门 市 Haimen City	7190	36	阜 宁 县 Funing County	4894
11	丹 阳 市 Danyang City	7109	37	金 湖 县 Jinhu County	4814
12	高 淳 县 Gaochun County	7048	38	洪 泽 县 Hongze County	4805
13	溧 阳 市 Liyang City	6998	39	滨 海 县 Binhai County	4695
14	溧 水 县 Lishui County	6762	40	赣 榆 县 Ganyu County	4602
15	启 东 市 Qidong City	6730	41	丰 县 Fengxian County	4537
16	通 州 市 Tongzhou City	6680	42	新 沂 市 Xinyi City	4516
17	东 台 市 Dongtai City	6217	43	盱 眙 县 Xuyi County	4463
18	靖 江 市 Jingjiang City	6173	44	响 水 县 Xiangshui County	4420
19	江 都 市 Jiangdu City	6131	45	东 海 县 Donghai County	4419
20	大 丰 市 Dafeng City	6124	46	睢 宁 县 Suining County	4314
21	句 容 市 Jurong City	6090	47	沭 阳 县 Shuyang County	4278
22	海 安 县 Haian County	5900	48	泗 阳 县 Siyang County	4240
23	泰 兴 市 Taixing City	5722	49	泗 洪 县 Sihong County	4147
24	铜 山 县 Tongshan County	5591	50	涟 水 县 Lianshui County	4010
25	姜 堰 市 Jiangyan City	5549	51	灌 云 县 Guanyun County	3940
26	仪 征 市 Yizheng City	5501	52	灌 南 县 Guannan County	3758

21－20 居民人均储蓄存款(2006年)
PER CAPITA SAVINGS DEPOSIT OF RESIDENTS (2006)

位次 No.	县(市)名称 County (City)		绝对数(元) Absolute Figure (yuan)	位次 No.	县(市)名称 County (City)		绝对数(元) Absolute Figure (yuan)
1	昆山市	Kunshan City	41097	27	铜山县	Tongshan County	8533
2	常熟市	Changshu City	39887	28	建湖县	Jianhu County	8450
3	张家港市	Zhangjiagang City	35627	29	溧水县	Lishui County	8423
4	吴江市	Wujiang City	34446	30	高淳县	Gaochun County	7775
5	太仓市	Taicang City	32872	31	宝应县	Baoying County	7737
6	江阴市	Jiangyin City	28324	32	金湖县	Jinhu County	7569
7	扬中市	Yangzhong City	28090	33	兴化市	Xinghua City	7096
8	宜兴市	Yixing City	24862	34	沛县	Peixian County	6459
9	丹阳市	Danyang City	18754	35	射阳县	Sheyang County	6229
10	海门市	Haimen City	18735	36	阜宁县	Funing County	5590
11	靖江市	Jingjiang City	17853	37	洪泽县	Hongze County	5554
12	溧阳市	Liyang City	16950	38	丰县	Fengxian County	4279
13	金坛市	Jintan City	16871	39	新沂市	Xinyi City	4079
14	海安县	Haian County	16775	40	赣榆县	Ganyu County	4066
15	启东市	Qidong City	16607	41	响水县	Xiangshui County	4013
16	江都市	Jiangdu City	16556	42	睢宁县	Suining County	3973
17	通州市	Tongzhou City	15602	43	邳州市	Pizhou City	3922
18	仪征市	Yizheng City	12527	44	东海县	Donghai County	3821
19	姜堰市	Jiangyan City	12465	45	泗阳县	Siyang County	3789
20	如东县	Rudong County	12069	46	盱眙县	Xuyi County	3785
21	如皋市	Rugao City	10831	47	泗洪县	Sihong County	3690
22	大丰市	Dafeng City	10809	48	滨海县	Binhai County	3511
23	东台市	Dongtai City	10748	49	涟水县	Lianshui County	3083
24	高邮市	Gaoyou City	9913	50	灌云县	Guanyun County	3048
25	句容市	Jurong City	9875	51	沭阳县	Shuyang County	2998
26	泰兴市	Taixing City	9171	52	灌南县	Guannan County	2639

JIANGSU STATISTICAL YEARBOOK

第22篇

乡镇基本情况

BASIC CONDITIONS OF COUNTRY AND TOWN

22-1　乡镇基本情况（2006年）
BASIC CONDITIONS OF COUNTRY AND TOWN

名　称	Name	总人口（人）Total Population (person)	从业人员（人）Employment (person)	土地面积（公顷）Land Area (hectares)	耕地面积（公顷）Cultivated Area (hectares)	财政收入（万元）Financial Revenue (10000 yuan)	粮食产量（吨）Output of Grain (ton)
南京市	**Nanjing City**						
市辖区	**Jurisdictional Area**						
桥林镇	Qiaolin Town	44335	21908	11970	5523	15084	16518
永宁镇	Yongning Town	43945	22589	11550	3854	11192	14955
汤泉镇	Tangquan Town	22187	10022	4500	1491	17230	0
星甸镇	Xingdian Town	38706	16132	13300	5268	12611	14373
石桥镇	Shiqiao Town	25981	14617	6759	3797	9966	10776
乌江镇	Wujiang Town	22171	12766	5700	2112	11193	6976
盘城镇	Pancheng Town	39901	14632	5150	2303	6796	11379
湖熟镇	Hushu Town	81730	37433	14500	5915	12051	60430
横溪镇	Hengxi Town	75745	51080	21500	4739	13400	34320
雄州镇	Xiongzhou Town	114877	70833	7030	1709	15056	12396
冶山镇	Yeshan Town	44669	19823	10400	5288	3687	16509
八百桥镇	Babaiqiao Tow	67977	32409	16236	4570	5157	36646
横梁镇	Hengliang Town	40373	24681	8700	3293	3948	16233
东沟镇	Donggou Town	29189	13236	4200	2000	1222	8602
龙袍镇	Longpao Town	33082	20018	4100	2997	4372	18655
玉带镇	Yudai Town	29713	15570	4900	2020	2836	12298
瓜埠镇	Guabu Town	30178	14665	4300	1411	3889	11910
新集镇	Xinji Town	40698	19667	8400	3956	7257	24774
程桥镇	Chengqiao Town	46541	28456	12200	4586	4403	30233
竹镇镇	Zhuzhen Town	62011	31183	20900	6377	2766	38217
马集镇	Maji Town	33784	20255	9900	3516	3784	24793
马鞍镇	Maan Town	47484	20870	11855	4478	3779	21348
新篁镇	Xinhuang Town	26920	13996	9000	3112	2457	15363
溧水县	**Lishui County**						
永阳镇	Yongyang Town	102424	66933	14300	3769	20766	27527
白马镇	Baima Town	38118	19857	14600	4854	3168	30210
东屏镇	Dongping Town	43149	20887	12900	4463	2737	34568
柘塘镇	Zhetang Town	27838	17310	4600	3226	5322	14025
石湫镇	Shiqiu Town	46276	23071	11900	2825	4435	26601
洪蓝镇	Honglan Town	46138	24858	10900	2776	3008	29006
晶桥镇	Jingqiao Town	38596	22683	13500	2778	7370	29277
和凤镇	Hefeng Town	51132	25600	19100	3189	3168	28943
高淳县	**Gaochun County**						
淳溪镇	Chunxi Town	108239	73628	8357	3292	10904	15645
阳江镇	Yangjiang Town	69588	45131	12503	5521	6081	31306
砖墙镇	Zhuanqiang Town	34299	22173	6900	1573	5371	9857

续 表 1 Continued

名 称 Name		总人口（人）Total Population (person)	从业人员（人）Employment (person)	土地面积（公顷）Land Area (hectares)	耕地面积（公顷）Cultivated Area (hectares)	财政收入（万元）Financial Revenue (10000 yuan)	粮食产量（吨）Output of Grain (ton)
古 柏 镇	Gubo Town	35082	21146	5100	2175	7015	13429
漆 桥 镇	Qiqiao Town	25462	14742	5400	2265	3964	12425
固 城 镇	Gucheng Town	39316	24505	8500	3463	4679	18852
东 坝 镇	Dongba Town	44615	27585	10432	5077	5197	27159
桠 溪 镇	Yaxi Town	60061	33409	14914	6827	4362	54439
无 锡 市	**Wuxi City**						
市 辖 区	**Jurisdictional Area**						
安 镇 镇	Anzhen Town	115585	36663	6853	2375	37143	23249
羊 尖 镇	Yangjian Town	55146	33540	5046	2350	29092	20429
鹅 湖 镇	Ehu Town	63014	37566	5457	1651	19918	15983
东北塘镇	Dongbeitang Town	51280	20544	1830	248	27000	999
锡 北 镇	Xibei Town	54497	44210	6238	2177	22810	18236
东 港 镇	Donggang Town	117941	74824	8431	2405	66691	26481
堰 桥 镇	Yanqiao Town	120890	66105	8032	1006	75565	5455
前 洲 镇	Qianzhou Town	66498	32380	3654	1168	39159	12177
玉 祁 镇	Yuqi Town	70551	45689	3970	1066	58729	8625
洛 社 镇	Luoshe Town	181506	103589	9350	2142	106509	14670
钱 桥 镇	Qianqiao Town	60205	42454	4595	620	84550	1386
阳 山 镇	Yangshan Town	35006	25670	3658	712	12989	4905
硕 放 镇	Shuofang Town	84146	52753	4656	1579	45707	7391
坊 前 镇	Fangqian Town	50554	28268	1464	372	38443	50
梅 村 镇	Meicun Town	26929	18775	2550	944	52240	3854
鸿 山 镇	Hongshan Town	75095	48148	5800	2738	30733	22217
滨 湖 镇	Binhu Town	47411	21153	4500	516	35386	3824
华 庄 镇	Huazhuang Town	74482	38338	3588	1246	46379	3608
太 湖 镇	Taihu Town	56969	32311	2419	340	58793	1165
马 山 镇	Mashan Town	31568	20887	17624	462	116317	2125
胡 埭 镇	Hudai Town	35348	17022	5509	662	25878	3499
江 阴 市	**Jiangyin City**						
澄 江 镇	Chengjiang Town	251725	147879	12657	1686	345950	7651
璜 土 镇	Huangtu Town	54804	30219	4749	1589	24672	14027
利 港 镇	Ligang Town	57744	48748	5942	2162	41468	22025
申 港 镇	Shengang Town	55675	28743	3879	1288	47189	12740
夏 港 镇	Xiagang Town	45747	26836	2640	598	42994	5786
月 城 镇	Yuecheng Town	50739	23708	3853	1310	21166	10705
青 阳 镇	Qingyang Town	95647	41412	6756	2531	40152	19679
霞 客 镇	Xiake Town	143926	73260	11017	2931	60451	30596
南 闸 镇	Nanzha Town	51912	26405	4500	1219	22202	11017
云 亭 镇	Yunting Town	68000	40787	3990	1404	27549	7988
华 士 镇	Huashi Town	121447	80303	7464	2003	97301	11436
周 庄 镇	Zhouzhuang Town	157764	102887	7572	2758	92696	14538

续 表 2 Continued

名 称 Name		总人口（人）Total Population (person)	从业人员（人）Employment (person)	土地面积（公顷）Land Area (hectares)	耕地面积（公顷）Cultivated Area (hectares)	财政收入（万元）Financial Revenue (10000 yuan)	粮食产量（吨）Output of Grain (ton)
新 桥 镇	Xinqiao Town	46039	36403	2000	295	46576	2591
长 泾 镇	Changjing Town	80318	57053	5330	1882	31118	20418
顾 山 镇	Gushan Town	86341	48434	4971	1358	35324	16676
祝 塘 镇	Zhutang Town	114013	66764	5959	2922	38718	19248
宜 兴 市	**Yixing City**						
张 渚 镇	Zhangzhu Town	73159	42860	17561	3771	23705	12920
西 渚 镇	Xizhu Town	27480	15464	6666	3055	5734	12694
太 华 镇	Taihua Town	24646	15069	9157	753	5889	3408
徐 舍 镇	Xushe Town	44665	24352	6276	3767	10209	28570
鲸 塘 镇	Jingtang Town	31950	19058	6287	3254	3805	21316
芳 庄 镇	Fangzhuang Town	23624	12693	4480	2600	5218	16830
官 林 镇	Guanlin Town	71259	51629	10458	3860	46764	34860
杨 巷 镇	Yangxiang Town	47667	24679	8642	4040	8383	24876
新 建 镇	Xinjian Town	26141	13170	4430	2386	11691	11558
和 桥 镇	Heqiao Town	68609	38231	10510	4090	23628	31111
高 塍 镇	Gaocheng Town	42866	25733	8118	2565	28445	20887
万 石 镇	Wanshi Town	26364	12822	4377	2486	8891	26778
周 铁 镇	Zhoutie Town	57347	28876	7300	3928	26315	30402
芳 桥 镇	Fangqiao Town	30135	16118	5500	2842	9466	25042
新 庄 镇	Xinzhuang Town	38243	21006	4979	2814	9322	16581
丁 蜀 镇	Dingshu Town	128143	90800	15024	2945	38296	15322
大 浦 镇	Dapu Town	31302	17438	4545	2196	16140	13043
湖 㳇 镇	Hufu Town	23094	13376	9324	1225	8527	2584
新 街 镇	Xinjie Town	29015	14650	6974	2428	9266	12392
徐 州 市	**Xuzhou City**						
市 辖 区	Jurisdictional Area						
贾 汪 镇	Jiawang Town	65816	20609	7956	2338	702	16752
青山泉镇	Qingshanquan Town	54044	27826	8366	3639	11631	25940
大 吴 镇	Dawu Town	85019	33287	6620	1758	8037	24826
紫 庄 镇	Zizhuang Town	63826	23100	6668	3200	618	30194
塔 山 镇	Tashan Town	67296	25487	9468	5438	1325	37300
汴 塘 镇	Biantang Town	55145	16900	10500	4325	641	27344
江 庄 镇	Jiangzhuang Town	32428	11680	7496	4228	3558	33024
大黄山镇	Dahuangshan Town	43083	18691	4300	1381	1813	18813
大 庙 镇	Damiao Town	69677	26538	7900	2980	7015	37519
丰 县	**Fengxian County**						
凤 城 镇	Fengcheng Town	58010	26676	6197	2875	9090	21858
首 羡 镇	Shouxian Town	85863	40174	12176	8363	3308	26177
顺 河 镇	Shunhe Town	56544	29495	8648	5831	2078	34868
常 店 镇	Changdian Town	62905	42560	7727	4426	2758	31840

续　表　3　Continued

名　称 Name		总人口（人）Total Population (person)	从业人员（人）Employment (person)	土地面积（公顷）Land Area (hectares)	耕地面积（公顷）Cultivated Area (hectares)	财政收入（万元）Financial Revenue (10000 yuan)	粮食产量（吨）Output of Grain (ton)
欢口镇	Huankou Town	95151	43830	10500	6562	4399	82240
师寨镇	Shizhai Town	80185	43144	10450	5933	3506	38056
华山镇	Huashan Town	82190	46383	11300	4131	4903	25023
梁寨镇	Liangzhai Town	59650	30850	8680	4550	2997	22924
范楼镇	Fanlou Town	78530	43768	11610	7331	3071	39024
孙楼镇	Sunlou Town	49102	27480	6608	3406	2925	23428
宋楼镇	Songlou Town	88062	48001	12214	3340	3434	47517
大沙河镇	Dashahe Town	58786	29543	8150	2010	2328	12536
王沟镇	Wanggou Town	94181	47978	12621	8067	3981	40214
赵庄镇	Zhaozhuang Town	67631	37214	9100	5010	2208	23591
沛　县	**Peixian County**						
龙固镇	Longgu Town	58061	29956	5302	2670	2772	26470
杨屯镇	Yangtun Town	56084	24087	4100	2040	3631	29919
大屯镇	Datun Town	82734	35592	7380	3776	7704	40479
沛城镇	Peicheng Town	84512	52689	6600	5161	10182	60306
胡寨镇	Huzhai Town	38059	22733	4594	2727	1822	30784
魏庙镇	Weimiao Town	51636	29230	5200	3709	2060	29323
五段镇	Wuduan Town	45912	21239	4700	2800	2310	52787
张庄镇	Zhangzhuang Town	92380	44855	11200	6806	1914	55807
张寨镇	Zhangzhai Town	82596	37458	10634	6847	762	60471
敬安镇	Jingan Town	64023	31760	9600	4997	2711	29774
河口镇	Hekou Town	55673	29930	8257	5308	1269	9814
栖山镇	Qishan Town	64134	27099	8951	6386	707	23883
鹿楼镇	Lulou Town	72080	35285	12540	5658	2572	46404
朱寨镇	Zhuzhai Town	60116	25985	7900	4482	1557	34260
安国镇	Anguo Town	80934	47629	13329	5634	4810	35088
铜山县	**Tongshan County**						
铜山镇	Tongshan Town	172564	48576	5000	986	26300	10465
何桥镇	Heqiao Town	48626	20729	7400	4115	1366	32624
黄集镇	Huangji Town	53990	24800	8340	4533	1761	35400
马坡镇	Mapo Town	49332	21375	6900	3210	1572	34677
郑集镇	Zhengji Town	49934	19853	6800	3600	1110	45821
柳新镇	Liuxin Town	70088	39390	8500	3753	12190	23129
刘集镇	Liuji Town	62001	26106	8360	3706	2125	32417
大彭镇	Dapeng Town	60825	35160	7600	3526	1913	19922
汉王镇	Hanwang Town	54909	21525	9300	2708	1690	19437
三堡镇	Sanbao Town	44363	42148	7157	3622	2914	30734
棠张镇	Tangzhang Town	56347	25000	8500	4480	2716	29050
张集镇	Zhangji Town	71550	45500	14800	5965	3115	51334
房村镇	Fangcun Town	65305	39828	13600	6902	804	48990
伊庄镇	Yizhuang Town	42800	22900	8560	3259	793	32152

续 表 4 Continued

名 称 Name		总人口（人）Total Population (person)	从业人员（人）Employment (person)	土地面积（公顷）Land Area (hectares)	耕地面积（公顷）Cultivated Area (hectares)	财政收入（万元）Financial Revenue (10000 yuan)	粮食产量（吨）Output of Grain (ton)
单集镇	Shanji Town	64872	27715	13210	7333	1100	60867
徐庄镇	Xuzhuang Town	62856	29460	13259	6003	724	71777
大许镇	Daxu Town	74792	29154	12900	6284	908	58650
茅村镇	Maocun Town	68104	30646	8396	2898	1145	24625
柳泉镇	Liuquan Town	57653	26305	10520	3466	2112	46037
利国镇	Liguo Town	51136	22154	6650	2582	12660	16359
睢宁县	**Suining County**						
睢城镇	Suicheng Town	195176	117058	10760	4000	6099	37447
王集镇	Wangji Town	76125	41515	13355	7261	1228	43604
双沟镇	Shuanggou Town	54121	30238	9527	5067	1605	29659
岚山镇	Lanshan Town	78069	41369	12835	7700	2543	50045
李集镇	Liji Town	53544	24732	6368	3498	1965	29319
桃元镇	Taoyuan Town	83607	37089	10900	6246	1508	46224
官山镇	Guanshan Town	79225	46058	12528	7401	1621	69653
高作镇	Gaozuo Town	55597	35238	6227	3548	2257	28747
沙集镇	Shaji Town	57330	28191	4000	3520	1448	32156
凌城镇	Lingcheng Town	77716	38173	9365	5234	1476	60512
邱集镇	Qiuji Town	106541	52059	14079	8878	1766	77416
古邳镇	Gupi Town	73431	45219	11200	5216	1327	39582
姚集镇	Yaoji Town	95700	44700	16700	6700	1682	51000
魏集镇	Weiji Town	76848	38200	12938	7316	1474	44645
梁集镇	Liangji Town	75437	38680	9889	5779	1573	44130
庆安镇	Qingan Town	75127	40126	11571	6600	2174	60496
新沂市	**Xinyi City**						
新安镇	Xinan Town	225804	105676	8270	3133	9949	29170
草桥镇	Caoqiao Town	65973	41018	10025	3546	2229	42023
港头镇	Gangtou Town	41228	19804	7818	3423	815	37871
合沟镇	Hegou Town	52444	28752	6172	2236	896	35353
窑湾镇	Yaowan Town	64001	26838	11597	4366	1704	41389
棋盘镇	Qipan Town	78689	39083	16735	8057	970	57678
王庄镇	Wangzhuang Town	53546	22921	10333	4981	978	33230
邵店镇	Shaodian Town	37542	17599	5845	1902	1333	40896
高流镇	Gaoliu Town	45052	22623	9186	6142	1378	28100
阿湖镇	Ahu Town	58022	25912	12545	7607	674	3203
北沟镇	Beigou Town	60898	28556	13259	7544	1565	92475
时集镇	Shiji Town	49375	22943	12119	7237	936	49795
瓦窑镇	Wayao Town	33886	18241	6172	3378	1198	24270
双塘镇	Shuangtang Town	32000	13900	6533	3066	971	21653
唐店镇	Tangdian Town	34840	18380	5181	2822	1142	29755
新店镇	Xindian Town	47000	21438	12760	4720	472	44739

名 称 Name		总人口（人）Total Population (person)	从业人员（人）Employment (person)	土地面积（公顷）Land Area (hectares)	耕地面积（公顷）Cultivated Area (hectares)	财政收入（万元）Financial Revenue (10000 yuan)	粮食产量（吨）Output of Grain (ton)
邳州市	**Pizhou City**						
运河镇	Yunhe Town	243488	108910	10806	3956	17007	33689
邳城镇	Picheng Town	71898	31934	9028	5034	959	25329
官湖镇	Guanhu Town	99789	54580	8880	2338	13570	9053
四户镇	Sihu Town	50690	25450	8100	4880	1490	47957
宿羊山镇	Suyangshan Town	74930	36213	6013	4535	2352	19340
八义集镇	Bayiji Town	79841	35103	9112	6467	980	42150
土山镇	Tushan Town	46437	29200	8900	4380	580	22500
碾庄镇	Nianzhuang Town	85776	37460	12100	7125	3410	48643
港上镇	Gangshang Town	57000	32165	6399	3120	1053	14202
邹庄镇	Zouzhuang Town	48795	27462	7366	3987	953	28941
占城镇	Zhancheng Town	53175	31507	6380	3978	860	34178
新河镇	Xinhe Town	56764	28416	9797	4983	2600	52625
八路镇	Balu Town	43936	21184	6730	3662	713	33046
炮车镇	Paoche Town	64814	37942	6695	2804	1344	28536
铁富镇	Tiefu Town	105106	48877	12444	6020	1428	44507
岔河镇	Chahe Town	41106	20738	7030	3369	1200	41260
戴圩镇	Daiwei Town	47812	19880	6150	3152	1837	29331
陈楼镇	Chenlou Town	51037	25455	5347	2197	4220	8891
邢楼镇	Xinglou Town	46750	23500	9650	5516	1718	30965
戴庄镇	Daizhuang Town	45063	21860	7373	3291	986	25358
车辐山镇	Chefushan Town	47311	23800	3400	3130	726	22909
燕子埠镇	Yanzibu Town	33746	15801	7700	4200	491	13719
赵墩镇	Zhaodun Town	84000	48035	12000	6000	1330	47093
议堂镇	Yitang Town	34386	17752	5760	2864	1670	30552
常州市	**Changzhou City**						
市辖区	Jurisdictional Area						
新闸镇	Xinzha Town	32005	16573	1460	127	16037	1119
丁堰镇	Dingyan Town	14044	8521	1167	132	18040	415
潞城镇	Lucheng Town	20876	14431	1550	411	21410	2179
春江镇	Chunjiang Town	119948	61238	14109	4716	61242	44459
孟河镇	Menghe Town	91560	39596	8824	3687	17560	39274
新桥镇	Xinqiao Town	24766	11867	2714	1021	18954	8930
薛家镇	Xuejia Town	37913	16768	3757	979	20795	10889
罗溪镇	Luoxi Town	42584	22154	5351	1795	14039	16846
西夏墅镇	Xixiashu Town	40502	22238	5196	2374	12636	23310
湖塘镇	Hutang Town	239343	95699	8406	465	60000	2463
牛塘镇	Niutang Town	64019	34959	4506	1390	26650	9700
洛阳镇	Luoyang Town	71858	31540	5570	2005	25517	11923

续 表 6 Continued

名 称	Name	总人口（人）Total Population (person)	从业人员（人）Employment (person)	土地面积（公顷）Land Area (hectares)	耕地面积（公顷）Cultivated Area (hectares)	财政收入（万元）Financial Revenue (10000 yuan)	粮食产量（吨）Output of Grain (ton)
遥观镇	Yaoguan Town	58800	36691	4468	913	40883	9642
横林镇	Henglin Town	75672	37581	4668	1045	36206	6477
横山桥镇	Hengshanqiao Town	47525	37989	3703	763	31650	5429
芙蓉镇	Furong Town	23121	13184	2088	634	10301	5538
焦溪镇	Jiaoxi Town	44093	21347	4149	1156	17984	11787
郑陆镇	Zhenglu Town	53728	25872	4754	1603	20528	12792
雪堰镇	Xueyan Town	28275	15580	3396	1153	9051	9150
潘家镇	Panjia Town	30728	16988	4865	1554	11704	14508
漕桥镇	Caoqiao Town	41441	16627	4060	2053	13012	20004
前黄镇	Qianhuang Town	35110	21662	4955	2504	11974	26000
礼嘉镇	Lijia Town	41480	18053	3717	1221	18110	13451
寨桥镇	Zhaiqiao Town	28910	17875	5613	1371	14110	13988
邹区镇	Zouqu Town	50392	29678	4056	1362	24160	9484
卜弋镇	Buyi Town	31391	15358	3970	1844	8816	14376
夏溪镇	Xiaxi Town	38787	22251	4993	2254	6105	5007
嘉泽镇	Jiaze Town	40313	20071	5638	2321	7392	985
湟里镇	Huangli Tow	44854	22188	5398	2090	21493	7822
东安镇	Dongan Town	29271	19026	3317	1230	23300	1000
奔牛镇	Benniu Town	50025	32374	5578	2240	15645	25186
溧阳市	**Liyang City**						
溧城镇	Licheng Town	244341	130669	11399	4246	65221	30595
埭头镇	Daitou Town	28020	17695	4369	2006	19795	13157
上黄镇	Shanghuang Town	25668	13953	4200	1725	8202	12361
戴埠镇	Daibu Town	33912	22709	6130	2708	7741	17786
横涧镇	Hengjian Town	18123	9183	7500	976	2118	4922
天目湖镇	Tianmuhu Town	58710	26582	20450	4905	16129	24224
别桥镇	Bieqiao Town	29828	19160	3543	2713	3865	14035
绸缪镇	Choumiao Town	18740	10893	3570	1715	4547	12728
上兴镇	Shangxing Town	34752	16766	11052	3830	5068	34073
上沛镇	Shangpei Town	38448	21351	11644	4948	5899	37155
竹箦镇	Zhuze Town	36520	17800	11280	4290	6350	28800
后周镇	Houzhou Town	20832	9732	4152	2314	2716	16021
前马镇	Qianma Town	24948	12852	4819	2547	2859	14461
南渡镇	Nandu Town	67803	30332	10800	6065	10021	47235
新昌镇	Xinchang Town	34969	18569	6600	2733	4817	19285
社渚镇	Shezhu Town	49400	25544	12670	5894	5470	60113
周城镇	Zhoucheng Town	24268	13712	7090	2130	10156	19328
金坛市	**Jintan City**						
金城镇	Jincheng Town	138320	103472	10300	4123	40791	23860
河头镇	Hetou Town	16298	9856	2800	1301	7026	10685
建昌镇	Jianchang Town	24758	13795	4843	2337	1437	14986

续 表 7 Continued

名 称 Name		总人口（人） Total Population（person）	从业人员（人） Employment（person）	土地面积（公顷） Land Area（hectares）	耕地面积（公顷） Cultivated Area（hectares）	财政收入（万元） Financial Revenue（10000 yuan）	粮食产量（吨） Output of Grain（ton）
白 塔 镇	Baita Town	19438	10063	3922	2064	2638	12048
直 溪 镇	Zhixi Town	33519	23950	5819	3016	6243	20886
朱 林 镇	Zhulin Town	17655	13368	3585	2023	3042	13325
薛 埠 镇	Xuebu Town	43284	30287	16400	5611	12687	25568
茅 麓 镇	Maolu Town	23983	15864	7100	2611	2705	13834
社 头 镇	Shetou Town	23359	15521	4372	2553	2025	17970
西 岗 镇	Xigang Town	19490	13310	4114	2275	3291	15682
指 前 镇	Zhiqian Town	18039	13378	4800	1134	3900	6394
洮 西 镇	Taoxi Town	25854	17611	5029	2223	2497	19082
水 北 镇	Shuibei Town	27848	15333	5055	2175	3978	18647
儒 林 镇	Rulin Town	33588	16660	10500	1249	3360	14718
尧 塘 镇	Yaotang Town	27367	20142	4825	2669	7558	8823
苏 州 市	**Suzhou City**						
市 辖 区	Jurisdictional Area						
浒墅关镇	Xushuguan Town	49499	20664	4000	1206	16858	3924
通 安 镇	Tongan Town	42344	21692	3783	1179	12420	8205
东 渚 镇	Dongzhu Town	33092	19300	3772	1303	8368	2110
甪 直 镇	Luzhi Town	142221	109850	9799	2145	59168	11779
藏 书 镇	Cangshu Town	33104	18118	4397	736	11565	1935
木 渎 镇	Mudu Town	207549	185697	3823	10	86459	50
胥 口 镇	Xukou Town	46603	29594	10000	582	43110	1340
浦 庄 镇	Puzhuang Town	31120	17480	2875	923	12325	5366
渡 村 镇	Ducun Town	35498	23925	2979	1605	13349	4490
东 山 镇	Dongshan Town	56993	35653	9600	474	11819	644
光 福 镇	Guangfu Town	66131	41948	6912	1568	14640	873
西 山 镇	Xishan Town	48907	25576	8342	786	11864	2882
望 亭 镇	Wangting Town	43895	32458	4406	1814	32190	8719
黄 埭 镇	Huangdai Town	78684	69006	5600	1113	41200	10651
渭 塘 镇	Weitang Town	69367	41620	3669	868	40996	4970
北 桥 镇	Beiqiao Town	57293	24970	4752	2331	26507	7942
阳澄湖镇	Yangchenghu Town	64300	48768	9677	2380	17893	4896
娄 葑 镇	Loufeng Town	255020	187656	7256	1120	284137	1068
唯 亭 镇	Weiting Town	144318	97671	11574	3192	153525	4916
胜 浦 镇	Shengpu Town	53503	42484	1620	40	16394	0
常 熟 市	**Changshu City**						
虞 山 镇	Yushan Town	378392	264340	21476	4779	355101	49954
梅 李 镇	Meili Town	101120	63129	8084	3873	46453	27090
海 虞 镇	Haiyu Town	127749	88099	10866	3914	63336	35353
新 港 镇	Xingang Town	139362	85602	11379	3721	137871	10033
古 里 镇	Guli Town	105374	74751	11666	3304	66882	38077
沙家浜镇	Shajiabang Town	72249	52855	8040	1438	34032	11117

续 表 8 Continued

名 称 Name		总人口（人）Total Population (person)	从业人员（人）Employment (person)	土地面积（公顷）Land Area (hectares)	耕地面积（公顷）Cultivated Area (hectares)	财政收入（万元）Financial Revenue (10000 yuan)	粮食产量（吨）Output of Grain (ton)
支塘镇	Zhitang Town	84861	41066	12896	5557	32808	49194
董浜镇	Dongbang Town	66088	51383	6261	3299	27765	10966
辛庄镇	Xinzhuang Town	75003	56397	10426	3511	44402	27334
尚湖镇	Shanghu Town	98077	63733	11288	4302	38168	44230
张家港市	**Zhangjiagang City**						
杨舍镇	Yangshe Town	264750	203630	15283	6165	266352	40849
塘桥镇	Tangqiao Town	171416	119411	9442	5044	101208	37374
金港镇	Jingang Town	281079	112069	12598	4913	106309	36571
锦丰镇	Jinfeng Town	167527	85001	11410	5290	277706	38832
乐余镇	Leyu Town	95858	54290	8707	4422	36185	36445
凤凰镇	Fenghuang Town	114076	56058	7877	3779	52315	23415
南丰镇	Nanfeng Town	62837	33294	4750	2573	65994	17901
大新镇	Daxin Town	61255	33500	3998	1908	17276	16856
昆山市	**Kunshan City**						
玉山镇	Yushan Town	169185	121160	11800	1451	370445	11914
巴城镇	Bacheng Town	96098	59249	15521	1147	60168	14976
周市镇	Zhoushi Town	125610	68545	8156	573	110251	7670
陆家镇	Lujia Town	98107	60397	3580	707	85487	7649
花桥镇	Huaqiao Town	81333	63162	5000	1362	60312	12756
淀山湖镇	Dianshanhu Town	60007	39894	5600	1064	26559	10487
张浦镇	Zhangpu Town	141681	109068	11627	1872	101428	19698
周庄镇	Zhouzhuang Town	32059	20550	3605	468	26237	4265
千灯镇	Qiandeng Town	130227	81057	8159	1366	60275	16298
锦溪镇	Jinxi Town	71705	44447	9069	1303	18543	13964
吴江市	**Wujiang City**						
松陵镇	Songling Town	221396	154049	20802	2768	286210	16116
同里镇	Tongli Town	47768	24478	10291	4087	35385	10202
平望镇	Pingwang Town	82865	59390	13565	4370	44800	23739
盛泽镇	Shengze Town	161359	125065	14774	5048	193062	24393
横扇镇	Hengshan Town	44074	32893	5758	2914	21882	10017
七都镇	Qidu Town	68465	42864	8620	2167	36639	16010
震泽镇	Zhenze Town	78424	45500	9561	2871	38042	15946
桃源镇	Taoyuan Town	78941	50531	9130	3452	31732	9507
汾湖镇	Fenhu Town	168310	94616	25800	8626	116442	32165
太仓市	**Taicang City**						
城厢镇	Chengxiang Town	256001	144958	13649	5069	233768	26053
沙溪镇	Shaxi Town	136971	89984	13244	6049	42671	53388
浏河镇	Liuhe Town	50497	40328	6883	4347	28081	27732
浮桥镇	Fuqiao Town	128525	97089	14444	6526	163298	52221
璜泾镇	Huangjing Town	79146	51292	8384	4562	29934	36106
双凤镇	Shuangfeng Town	30132	23531	6250	2865	10448	15140

名 称 Name		总人口（人）Total Population (person)	从业人员（人）Employment (person)	土地面积（公顷）Land Area (hectares)	耕地面积（公顷）Cultivated Area (hectares)	财政收入（万元）Financial Revenue (10000 yuan)	粮食产量（吨）Output of Grain (ton)
陆渡镇	Ludu Town	51310	38912	2503	918	23664	7473
南通市	**Nantong City**						
市辖区	**Jurisdictional Area**						
观音山镇	Guanyinshan Town	58606	25472	3117	1360	16489	12446
狼山镇	Langshan Town	36439	12552	1942	241	11336	1808
新开镇	Xinkai Town	30588	12999	1453	481	11157	2432
竹行镇	Zhuhang Town	38568	23482	3198	1713	6701	9661
小海镇	Xiaohai Town	38460	25573	2704	1306	6327	9214
陈桥乡	Chenqiao Country	27598	12113	2909	1552	9389	14848
幸福乡	Xingfu Country	24003	12697	2048	1135	5863	12009
海安县	**Haian County**						
海安镇	Haian Town	189113	118056	11315	3514	76585	45749
城东镇	Chengdong Town	95139	44936	10848	4063	6699	57739
曲塘镇	Qutang Town	101873	52555	11552	6449	9893	76834
李堡镇	Libao Town	83959	44918	9453	4258	3682	53313
老坝港镇	Laobagang Town	21101	10355	3680	1443	1915	12422
角斜镇	Jiaoxie Town	46640	23705	6599	3559	1555	34004
西场镇	Xichang Town	47964	26092	5540	2637	3412	39084
大公镇	Dagong Town	64039	33154	8928	5398	2333	57576
孙庄镇	Sunzhuang Town	35553	19188	5019	1891	2959	23753
雅周镇	Yazhou Town	61896	33778	8330	3683	2655	46079
胡集镇	Huji Town	39329	19540	5100	2366	1830	32771
白甸镇	Baidian Town	33071	19591	5305	2930	1921	35270
南莫镇	Nanmo Town	56690	29061	7420	3761	3090	44725
墩头镇	Duntou Town	71218	41998	11556	6137	3106	69419
如东县	**Rudong County**						
栟茶镇	Bingcha Town	58979	30856	9300	4172	2359	39445
洋口镇	Yangkou Town	75763	39074	12200	6640	3013	79534
苴镇	Juzhen Town	38768	18610	8300	3898	2338	40577
长沙镇	Changsha Town	38991	23449	9200	3581	1792	20504
大豫镇	Dayu Town	41606	25678	9300	4710	2223	15694
掘港镇	Juegang Town	208060	105029	25600	11364	44029	102780
兵房镇	Bingfang Town	65807	35872	9700	6334	2147	19584
马塘镇	Matang Town	84309	33226	13700	8016	10967	99098
丰利镇	Fengli Town	85346	38277	13600	8377	5287	92710
曹埠镇	Caobu Town	49221	18967	9000	4553	2740	60750
岔河镇	Chahe Town	84799	46811	13800	7458	9962	105741
双甸镇	Shuangdian Town	75142	34266	10900	6198	7018	78985
新店镇	Xindian Town	39061	19354	7800	3898	4461	45518
河口镇	Hekou Town	65582	36460	11300	5109	8131	69514
袁庄镇	Yuanzhuang Town	60032	37891	9600	5100	3980	64072

续 表 10 Continued

名 称 Name		总人口（人）Total Population (person)	从业人员（人）Employment (person)	土地面积（公顷）Land Area (hectares)	耕地面积（公顷）Cultivated Area (hectares)	财政收入（万元）Financial Revenue (10000 yuan)	粮食产量（吨）Output of Grain (ton)
启东市	**Qidong City**						
汇龙镇	Huilong Town	174969	41983	9523	3963	35606	18067
大兴镇	Daxing Town	50356	31988	5369	3884	3301	15721
南阳镇	Nanyang Town	64189	39316	7454	4776	4658	20031
惠丰镇	Huifeng Town	28676	19554	3328	2242	4349	7991
民主镇	Minzhu Town	35508	25301	4391	2969	5732	10545
北新镇	Beixin Town	42514	24464	5503	3134	3709	15476
久隆镇	Jiulong Town	54829	32771	6160	3803	3753	19842
王鲍镇	Wangbao Town	43651	29367	5500	3176	2369	13549
合作镇	Hezuo Town	42883	28194	5546	3053	2166	13620
志良镇	Zhiliang Town	36467	22646	4420	2409	1508	9367
吕四港镇	Lusigang Town	98288	43042	6608	2923	9143	11331
天汾镇	Tianfen Town	35642	19699	2308	1595	4946	8930
兆民镇	Zhaomin Town	31726	21754	3980	2027	4572	6436
海复镇	Haifu Town	29187	17588	3310	1968	1789	7710
少直镇	Shaozhi Town	46980	31276	5718	3054	1192	15453
向阳镇	Xiangyang Town	31383	20866	3558	2700	2275	11796
东元镇	Dongyuan Town	29371	17523	3664	2140	2095	8766
近海镇	Jinhai Town	34075	21549	4092	2591	1842	10340
寅阳镇	Yinyang Town	36670	23914	5268	3101	3283	11293
和合镇	Hehe Town	42109	24689	4920	3322	3354	5776
惠萍镇	Huiping Town	42201	28357	4900	3266	3636	10518
新安镇	Xinan Town	39444	24759	4340	2593	2053	8591
东海镇	Donghai Town	33676	21373	4730	2855	5187	12077
启隆乡	Qilong Country	3328	1506	1986	1250	3266	5917
如皋市	**Rugao City**						
如城镇	Rucheng Town	227841	142647	15969	6480	39401	39609
柴湾镇	Chaiwan Town	51399	24998	6604	3635	5361	33772
雪岸镇	Xuean Town	35912	16888	5084	2880	1479	25386
东陈镇	Dongchen Town	47178	22677	6148	3450	4670	35030
丁堰镇	Dingyan Town	54287	27568	7048	4125	7221	46737
白蒲镇	Baipu Town	80804	38126	8540	4856	7574	50801
林梓镇	Linzi Town	45305	21054	5949	3555	4142	39854
下原镇	Xiayuan Town	60619	29984	7076	3819	3867	36914
九华镇	Jiuhua Town	76313	40933	7399	4450	10460	52884
郭园镇	Guoyuan Town	56309	26862	5348	2746	3898	26786
石庄镇	Shizhuang Town	64781	30571	6106	2976	5264	24778
长江镇	Changjiang Town	68985	27914	6423	3862	17406	32358
吴窑镇	Wuyao Town	64561	33429	6436	3237	4157	27895
江安镇	Jiangan Town	91426	43218	8655	4892	7622	35986
高明镇	Gaoming Town	54315	24742	6657	3491	3551	25855

续 表 11 Continued

名 称 Name		总人口（人）Total Population (person)	从业人员（人）Employment (person)	土地面积（公顷）Land Area (hectares)	耕地面积（公顷）Cultivated Area (hectares)	财政收入（万元）Financial Revenue (10000 yuan)	粮食产量（吨）Output of Grain (ton)
常 青 镇	Changqing Town	48003	21563	5900	3391	3003	24199
搬 经 镇	Banjing Town	85127	40185	11509	6217	3674	52949
磨 头 镇	Motou Town	82029	40980	10315	5351	5291	45604
桃 园 镇	Taoyuan Town	44651	22252	5840	3088	4028	30283
袁 桥 镇	Yuanqiao Town	47837	22542	6581	3649	3267	31106
通 州 市	**Tongzhou City**						
金 沙 镇	Jinsha Town	209555	81180	12691	6117	77789	40868
西 亭 镇	Xiting Tow	45862	23642	5692	3161	4762	27101
二 甲 镇	Erjia Town	84012	40159	7593	4038	7663	19639
东 社 镇	Dongshe Town	41275	21888	5005	2954	2706	17244
三 余 镇	Sanyu Town	68534	32440	7882	5007	5430	16604
北兴桥镇	Beixingqiao Town	40362	20728	5848	3538	1677	12197
海 晏 镇	Haiyan Town	41112	22726	6967	4275	1940	13090
十 总 镇	Shizong Town	37825	21111	4780	2942	4894	21743
骑 岸 镇	Qian Town	50331	28468	8080	4349	3534	43899
五 甲 镇	Wujia Town	33332	16735	4184	2352	2991	14664
石 港 镇	Shigang Town	70183	34968	10900	5556	10309	58794
四 安 镇	Sian Town	40390	19051	4621	3046	5555	27243
刘 桥 镇	Liuqiao Town	49421	25525	6279	3110	5027	34549
新 联 镇	Xinlian Town	27537	14869	4229	2299	3906	23011
平 潮 镇	Pingchao Town	78107	31685	6179	2780	18490	27804
平 东 镇	Pingdong Town	43343	23212	4677	2251	5644	23483
五 接 镇	Wujie Town	37562	18926	3780	1880	3179	19083
兴 仁 镇	Xingren Town	43030	20560	3929	1568	14185	13276
兴 东 镇	Xingdong Town	31606	16037	3008	1218	5339	11543
张芝山镇	Zhangzhishan Town	34853	16029	3074	1627	7194	7521
川 港 镇	Chuangang Town	53279	27399	5200	2555	12133	13400
先 锋 镇	Xianfeng Town	34338	16686	2666	1196	7980	6368
姜 灶 镇	Jiangzao Town	60482	31552	5281	2893	11718	13894
海 门 市	**Haimen City**						
海 门 镇	Haimen Town	137859	73758	6100	2314	33953	7480
三 星 镇	Sanxing Town	36264	22038	3600	1536	19097	6244
天 补 镇	Tianbu Town	28897	18991	3173	1548	6449	6266
三 和 镇	Sanhe Town	32301	20532	3638	1991	6331	5192
德 胜 镇	Desheng Town	46513	33199	5462	2820	8088	4193
三 厂 镇	Sanchang Tow	85190	63842	6329	3436	18839	12533
常 乐 镇	Changle Town	49748	31799	6001	2875	6968	14502
麒 麟 镇	Qilin Town	31865	21358	3809	1950	2905	5500
悦 来 镇	Yuelai Town	53979	35029	5426	3313	4321	17097
万 年 镇	Wannian Town	30393	21654	2800	1815	2391	8201
三 阳 镇	Sanyang Town	31303	20252	4500	1864	2129	6504

续 表 12 Continued

名 称 Name		总人口（人） Total Population (person)	从业人员（人） Employment (person)	土地面积（公顷） Land Area (hectares)	耕地面积（公顷） Cultivated Area (hectares)	财政收入（万元） Financial Revenue (10000 yuan)	粮食产量（吨） Output of Grain (ton)
四甲镇	Sijia Town	57906	40388	5990	2746	6005	16890
货隆镇	Huolong Town	32645	15771	3705	2030	2896	4350
余东镇	Yudong Town	31211	18656	3000	1498	1636	6384
正余镇	Zhengyu Town	37033	26466	3580	1617	4114	5169
包场镇	Baochang Town	54730	38016	4358	2377	5956	9774
刘浩镇	Liuhao Town	60980	35404	5430	3545	2558	9250
东灶港镇	Dongzaogang Town	36250	23509	3880	1936	2808	3541
临江镇	Linjiang Town	31056	19900	4166	2453	2192	6302
王浩镇	Wanghao Town	28493	17402	2028	1709	1573	8420
树勋镇	Shuxun Town	35890	23168	3791	1921	2051	7063
海永乡	Haiyong Country	4950	3881	368	333	1435	755
连云港市	**Lianyungang City**						
市辖区	Jurisdictional Area						
朝阳镇	Chaoyang Town	19545	9340	2446	772	8112	5247
宿城乡	Sucheng Country	4360	2460	1800	92	880	262
高公岛乡	Gaogongdao Country	2845	1679	807	0	834	0
南城镇	Nancheng Town	7937	3040	380	35	1080	312
云台乡	Yuntai Country	33029	15203	5812	1429	2266	16218
花果山乡	Huaguoshan Country	15368	8348	3330	936	2602	11351
宁海乡	Ninghai Country	25639	9471	4600	2448	2034	24005
新坝镇	Xinba Town	30424	18350	6946	4504	1354	57856
锦屏镇	Jinping Town	29792	10360	5214	2360	1512	24071
赣榆县	**Ganyu County**						
青口镇	Qingkou Town	167843	76886	9280	3135	15093	26218
柘汪镇	Zhewang Town	51978	23875	7230	2473	5307	13157
石桥镇	Shiqiao Town	60913	25008	7343	3626	2192	17588
金山镇	Jinshan Town	46625	16068	7000	3584	2373	22428
黑林镇	Heilin Town	40455	17598	8798	2615	887	12611
厉庄镇	Lizhuang Town	34749	13345	6130	2918	1704	12044
海头镇	Haitou Town	80606	30776	7900	2955	6052	17287
塔山镇	Tashan Town	58903	25765	8498	4459	873	30860
赣马镇	Ganma Town	81665	34840	8430	5310	2605	42460
班庄镇	Banzhuang Town	54526	32878	9048	4500	900	17087
城头镇	Chengtou Town	47529	19967	6670	3560	1510	23006
门河镇	Menhe Town	35271	14611	4854	3297	733	18274
城西镇	Chengxi Town	44952	19317	4527	3113	1367	23448
欢墩镇	Huandun Town	39058	17609	7900	1766	1206	8934
宋庄镇	Songzhuang Town	26052	11781	3120	1428	886	12808
沙河镇	Shahe Town	115212	43834	13156	7727	4317	63957
墩尚镇	Dunshang Town	37586	16109	4744	2713	1315	23025
罗阳镇	Luoyang Town	35788	15937	3733	2500	1917	26768

续 表 13 Continued

名 称 Name		总人口（人）Total Population (person)	从业人员（人）Employment (person)	土地面积（公顷）Land Area (hectares)	耕地面积（公顷）Cultivated Area (hectares)	财政收入（万元）Financial Revenue (10000 yuan)	粮食产量（吨）Output of Grain (ton)
东 海 县	Donghai County						
牛 山 镇	Niushan Town	135509	75885	9279	2563	7076	36194
白塔埠镇	Baita Town	56915	35600	10329	6052	1282	74807
浦 南 镇	Punan Town	58690	27145	12600	5894	6742	80835
黄 川 镇	Huangchuan Town	59115	29618	9383	4438	1854	53970
石梁河镇	Shilianghe Town	41121	20296	7157	2936	433	27086
青 湖 镇	Qinghu Town	54925	24300	9433	6069	1726	46168
石 榴 镇	Shiliu Town	60540	31230	7040	5344	2142	49626
温 泉 镇	Wenquan Town	14798	6680	3582	1398	2009	7322
双 店 镇	Shuangdian Town	43815	20532	11745	7031	908	21741
桃 林 镇	Taolin Town	69638	30492	16978	9386	1428	47193
洪 庄 镇	Hongzhuang Town	32994	15529	6719	4224	839	22172
安 峰 镇	Anfeng Town	66149	32254	13417	7799	2203	65877
房 山 镇	Fangshan Town	78000	41000	14972	9200	1501	99701
平 明 镇	Pingming Town	71375	33333	15731	10160	3192	130072
驼 峰 乡	Tuofeng Country	60746	32439	10425	7204	1769	71269
南 辰 乡	Nanchen Country	18275	9670	3050	560	998	5195
横 沟 乡	Henggou Country	33022	15064	6689	3069	569	22138
李 埝 乡	Linian Country	32780	11599	7009	3180	751	8009
山左口乡	Shanzuokou Country	40738	16963	8909	5092	2561	26319
石 湖 乡	Shihu Country	30824	15497	7226	4397	1032	29317
曲 阳 乡	Quyang Country	36450	17426	7542	3967	569	30770
张 湾 乡	Zhangwan Country	30512	15595	9500	5793	1284	61066
灌 云 县	Guanyun County						
伊 山 镇	Yishan Town	145767	56004	7675	4611	4473	41483
板 浦 镇	Banpu Town	64691	39273	7999	4987	2495	42310
杨 集 镇	Yangji Town	68688	32922	7673	5579	1471	40886
燕尾港镇	Yanweigang Town	10800	4889	1399	78	712	1010
同 兴 镇	Tongxing Town	38406	14432	5378	3805	1095	19589
四 队 镇	Sidui Town	33769	14360	4153	2794	1013	29881
圩 丰 镇	Weifeng Town	43158	24148	4111	3704	1204	65021
龙 苴 镇	Longju Town	48634	20528	6400	4512	1383	36548
伊 芦 乡	Yilu Country	37435	14934	5129	4886	667	48667
鲁 河 乡	Luhe Country	32798	12595	4673	3195	829	24347
图 河 乡	Tuhe Country	59380	27758	9500	4026	1797	37769
沂 北 乡	Yibei Country	45250	17585	4462	3950	702	29710
下 车 乡	Xiache Country	48537	24772	4785	4531	1198	41071
白 蚬 乡	Baixian Country	38743	18494	5497	3625	1230	39084
东王集乡	Dongwangji Country	62157	29130	9197	5644	1521	55354
侍 庄 乡	Shizhuang Country	43623	17900	6610	3610	1469	37384
小 伊 乡	Xiaoyi Country	53270	27320	7952	5454	1002	50872

名 称	Name	总人口（人）Total Population (person)	从业人员（人）Employment (person)	土地面积（公顷）Land Area (hectares)	耕地面积（公顷）Cultivated Area (hectares)	财政收入（万元）Financial Revenue (10000 yuan)	粮食产量（吨）Output of Grain (ton)
穆圩乡	Muwei Country	31520	14965	6240	4023	672	33026
陡沟乡	Dougou Country	59508	21117	7317	5298	1419	39111
南岗乡	Nangang Country	41667	16100	6055	4380	1076	30000
灌南县	**Guannan County**						
新安镇	Xinan Town	164555	78532	14291	6653	8429	91048
堆沟港镇	Duigougang Town	38635	18729	6293	2874	4264	24072
长茂镇	Changmao Town	37884	19716	5910	2760	1425	31257
北陈集镇	Beichenji Town	36952	19380	5527	3155	1006	28740
张店镇	Zhangdian Town	38046	19602	5917	3539	1611	26943
三口镇	Sankou Town	60003	29722	8656	5147	2100	67330
孟兴庄镇	Mengxingzhuang Town	63255	23896	7756	4064	2365	42309
汤沟镇	Tanggou Town	29298	14887	3291	1657	2719	19203
百禄镇	Bailu Town	63021	31769	10502	4141	1691	48406
五队乡	Wudui Country	42716	21842	7550	3779	1500	38569
田楼乡	Tianlou Country	34790	17372	5206	2725	1403	29823
李集乡	Liji Country	66320	32253	8785	4063	1219	51226
新集乡	Xinji Country	33999	15465	5868	2450	1361	25466
花园乡	Huayuan Country	35426	16085	6628	2713	2190	33338
淮安市	**Huaian City**						
市辖区	Jurisdictional Area						
钵池乡	Bochi Country	6686	10581	655	161	3757	1174
徐杨乡	Xuyang Country	22360	14900	1771	1074	2540	4140
淮城镇	Huaicheng Town	184694	93240	4200	807	8452	6136
平桥镇	Pingqiao Town	40484	19232	4600	2974	354	30552
上河镇	Shanghe Town	29240	13360	3375	2207	364	25025
马甸镇	Madian Town	31139	14720	3400	1968	1950	22056
朱桥镇	Zhuqiao Town	46977	27959	5158	3159	747	42642
溪河镇	Xihe Town	33100	18542	4308	2533	628	24440
施河镇	Shihe Town	45733	16894	5775	3843	1077	35304
车桥镇	Cheqiao Town	63729	30519	6400	3627	434	39813
泾口镇	Jingkou Town	46019	20844	5680	3369	664	40416
流均镇	Liujun Town	64072	26446	8860	2855	1395	41501
博里镇	Boli Town	47534	24741	7191	4011	410	55658
仇桥镇	Quiqiao Town	44245	20446	7447	3538	270	46200
复兴镇	Fuxing Town	39123	19819	6454	3396	274	39607
苏嘴镇	Suzui Town	41746	24210	5987	3190	386	26545
钦工镇	Qingong Town	34290	16067	5040	2679	261	28210
顺河镇	Shunhe Town	43784	20083	7756	3675	1067	48602
季桥镇	Jiqiao Town	35487	18875	5140	2952	548	37868
席桥镇	Xiqiao Town	27030	11274	3000	1973	665	19352
林集镇	Linji Town	22245	9621	3660	1901	615	22981

续 表 15 Continued

名 称	Name	总人口（人）Total Population (person)	从业人员（人）Employment (person)	土地面积（公顷）Land Area (hectares)	耕地面积（公顷）Cultivated Area (hectares)	财政收入（万元）Financial Revenue (10000 yuan)	粮食产量（吨）Output of Grain (ton)
南闸镇	Nanzha Town	32367	18272	3457	2404	373	34015
范集镇	Fanji Town	31553	17019	9192	4023	203	70308
建淮乡	Jianhuai Country	37110	17533	3479	2035	649	18694
茭陵乡	Jiaoling Country	35621	17819	3546	2041	206	21598
宋集乡	Songji Country	34772	16092	5723	2669	477	31209
城东乡	Chengdong Country	46459	20489	3724	1266	860	16669
南马厂乡	Nanmachang Country	13574	7210	1731	885	182	8828
三堡乡	Sanbao Country	33295	14256	3708	1655	532	18195
王营镇	Wangying Town	153372	55518	5052	2026	8827	9148
赵集镇	Zhaoji Town	42898	19287	9825	3062	580	23136
吴城镇	Wucheng Town	32856	15771	5312	3085	937	21438
南陈集镇	Nanchenji Town	61921	36376	13468	5700	791	38525
码头镇	Matou Town	25377	10057	3280	2097	157	15815
王兴镇	Wangxing Town	33793	17061	5800	3952	601	28351
棉花庄镇	Mianhuazhuang Town	42026	22483	6078	3980	622	27083
丁集镇	Dingji Town	32360	11927	4030	2873	1521	16704
五里镇	Wuli Town	29641	14800	5100	3321	830	22996
徐溜镇	Xuliu Town	37816	18560	6430	3600	1221	28360
渔沟镇	Yugou Town	52836	25786	9700	5492	1410	42100
吴集镇	Wuji Town	36426	15593	5700	3833	112	21780
西宋集镇	Xisongji Town	49668	23381	7390	3622	1305	27390
三树镇	Sanshu Town	37038	19125	7968	4023	810	31711
韩桥乡	Hanqiao Country	31655	13664	12070	2529	731	19377
新渡乡	Xindu Country	25803	12098	4650	2681	860	18012
老张集乡	Laozhangji Country	28259	16823	5088	3086	925	25811
凌桥乡	Lingqiao Country	30169	15647	6856	3406	698	28442
袁集乡	Yuanji Country	26854	12198	3940	2592	803	18180
刘老庄乡	Liulaozhuang Country	24280	14150	4120	3279	228	16160
古寨乡	Guzhai Country	20941	9820	4490	2540	536	14925
和平镇	Heping Town	31774	17750	7202	3148	1107	41795
武墩镇	Wudun Town	25401	11501	4558	2463	1100	26552
盐河镇	Yanhe Town	34687	19411	6792	4996	1045	34596
城南乡	Chengnan Country	30617	13460	3245	635	4368	5946
黄码乡	Huangma Country	44507	22122	6018	2938	1231	27481
涟水县	**Lianshui County**						
涟城镇	Liancheng Town	101200	36820	3960	1550	5606	10260
高沟镇	Gaogou Town	69962	37288	5462	3280	1426	21920
唐集镇	Tangji Town	34801	21820	6051	3793	361	44327
保滩镇	Baotan Town	25032	11462	4082	2134	430	15387
大东镇	Dadong Town	27250	15250	3888	3084	260	21850
五港镇	Wugang Town	34988	21100	5932	2853	566	24460

续 表 16 Continued

名称 Name		总人口（人）Total Population (person)	从业人员（人）Employment (person)	土地面积（公顷）Land Area (hectares)	耕地面积（公顷）Cultivated Area (hectares)	财政收入（万元）Financial Revenue (10000 yuan)	粮食产量（吨）Output of Grain (ton)
梁岔镇	Liangcha Town	37021	16634	3757	3647	620	28079
石湖镇	Shihu Town	14028	12080	2300	1097	300	4800
朱码镇	Zhuma Town	36729	16127	2085	1436	1388	12242
岔庙镇	Chamiao Town	46429	25840	6462	4397	393	26840
东胡集镇	Donghuji Town	32005	26295	4654	3592	413	31217
南集镇	Nanji Town	31303	13400	5847	3117	266	21986
义兴镇	Yixing Town	22516	9074	3670	1769	122	12973
成集镇	Chengji Town	22833	13120	2670	2460	203	14230
红窑镇	Hongyao Town	34465	17584	4799	2856	183	33114
陈师镇	Chenshi Town	30256	19620	3706	2506	398	16230
前进镇	Qianjin Town	29417	13914	5087	2535	271	21370
徐集乡	Xuji Country	39680	23125	3779	3778	304	28980
黄营乡	Huangying Country	35332	17450	4033	3740	298	19150
洪泽县	**Hongze County**						
高良涧镇	Gaoliangjian Town	99477	59105	2085	1665	6006	18143
蒋坝镇	Jiangba Town	11464	5917	295	295	1753	3612
仁和镇	Renhe Town	28593	17986	7438	2684	814	33164
岔河镇	Chahe Town	39375	20877	12500	4075	794	49763
西顺河镇	Xishunhe Town	9146	4235	1900	307	3476	3936
老子山镇	Laozishan Town	17834	7093	1750	120	400	1010
三河镇	Sanhe Town	23390	15203	2938	2025	506	21699
朱坝镇	Zhuba Town	29363	13188	3760	2926	977	31505
黄集镇	Huangji Town	42257	24655	9150	4044	1189	48519
万集镇	Wanji Town	26360	12683	5562	2855	988	32715
东双沟镇	Dongshuanggou Town	36041	30016	4300	3664	1389	38523
共和镇	Gonghe Town	25115	15143	3850	2980	1541	31989
盱眙县	**Xuyi County**						
盱城镇	Xucheng Town	118233	58491	9260	2822	4993	18230
马坝镇	Maba Town	67060	36406	18957	7066	4010	63698
官滩镇	Guantan Town	35020	18157	9573	4199	2096	32723
旧铺镇	Jiupu Town	35920	18376	14979	4515	1010	43240
桂五镇	Guiwu Town	34482	17145	17393	3281	1233	36030
管镇镇	Guanzhen Town	31942	16520	4928	2217	993	17710
河桥镇	Heqiao Town	36960	19223	17612	3727	1247	33193
鲍集镇	Baoji Town	49456	26985	11950	4478	1463	27820
黄花塘镇	Huanghuatang Town	31500	16480	13121	4930	1660	52027
明祖陵镇	Mingzuling Town	33230	20389	9098	3325	1100	38845
铁佛镇	Tiefo Town	33910	18834	9881	4498	882	41070
淮河镇	Huaihe Town	28370	15739	10895	2242	1002	12135
仇集镇	Qiuji Town	31350	16080	16776	2662	1074	25150
观音寺镇	Guanyinsi Town	32570	16921	12197	4284	1260	32760

续 表 17 Continued

名 称	Name	总人口（人）Total Population (person)	从业人员（人）Employment (person)	土地面积（公顷）Land Area (hectares)	耕地面积（公顷）Cultivated Area (hectares)	财政收入（万元）Financial Revenue (10000 yuan)	粮食产量（吨）Output of Grain (ton)
维桥乡	Weiqiao Country	22280	11122	7445	2793	808	21816
穆店乡	Mudian Country	26820	12640	10270	3368	1006	31836
王店乡	Wangdian Country	34700	18140	15958	4260	956	38950
古桑乡	Gusang Country	21630	12682	9313	2567	1210	21700
兴隆乡	Xinglong Country	32450	17892	8980	3387	830	28070
金湖县	**Jinhu County**						
黎城镇	Licheng Town	100880	76985	6600	1505	7130	16965
金南镇	Jinnan Town	37145	22251	10201	4326	2128	38840
闵桥镇	Minqiao Town	23757	14677	6791	2579	1724	25419
塔集镇	Taji Town	25723	13400	4221	2608	1495	26541
银集镇	Yinji Town	20678	10734	5109	2578	1089	27799
涂沟镇	Tugou Town	25488	13776	5898	2403	1261	27059
前锋镇	Qianfeng Town	28433	16274	7329	2848	1648	50659
吕良镇	Luliang Town	21474	12538	7480	2262	1158	42808
陈桥镇	Chenqiao Town	25398	11648	5486	3926	2149	43313
金北镇	Jinbei Town	21723	8884	6667	2848	1370	37329
戴楼镇	Dailou Country	21345	12366	7981	2961	2885	35956
盐城市	**Yancheng City**						
市辖区	Jurisdictional Area						
南洋镇	Nanyang Town	40523	24560	6287	5805	4910	14072
青墩镇	Qingdun Town	50580	25689	9560	4969	1512	32863
新兴镇	Xinxing Town	34021	16720	5560	2421	3383	21175
永丰镇	Yongfeng Town	35063	14153	5362	3110	1442	30962
便仓镇	Biancang Town	32680	15243	7197	3649	2034	38868
伍佑镇	Wuyou Town	32410	11630	4460	2150	2714	21394
步凤镇	Bufeng Town	55368	25694	12930	6306	1428	38984
大纵湖镇	Dazonghu Town	30051	12549	7470	2159	1210	21166
北龙港镇	Beilonggang Town	35433	12341	8100	2372	1277	23498
楼王镇	Louwang Town	41620	14877	6930	3249	1700	45245
学富镇	Xuefu Town	29347	11422	4224	2321	1630	31711
义丰镇	Yifeng Town	39535	20245	6320	2827	2853	34684
尚庄镇	Shangzhuang Town	39045	15366	5836	3178	1456	42747
葛武镇	Gewu Town	29803	13038	4500	2141	716	28349
北蒋镇	Beijiang Town	32769	15679	5000	2599	1203	35977
秦南镇	Qinnan Town	86380	32755	11617	7045	3248	93125
龙冈镇	Longgang Town	81203	47815	9339	5275	10844	62242
潘黄镇	Panhuang Town	66978	48078	5965	2550	17864	31688
郭猛镇	Guomeng Town	46595	21785	6242	3546	3540	43745
大冈镇	Dagang Town	73560	26649	13081	6143	4453	64510
响水县	**Xiangshui County**						

续 表 18 Continued

名 称 Name		总人口（人）Total Population (person)	从业人员（人）Employment (person)	土地面积（公顷）Land Area (hectares)	耕地面积（公顷）Cultivated Area (hectares)	财政收入（万元）Financial Revenue (10000 yuan)	粮食产量（吨）Output of Grain (ton)
响水镇	Xiangshui Town	80174	32176	5121	1970	8716	5535
陈家港镇	Chenjiagang Town	62028	23779	8518	3380	9697	32186
小尖镇	Xiaojian Town	63719	22458	10835	5975	2532	43496
黄圩镇	Huangwei Town	31675	15280	6877	3430	1432	25478
大有镇	Dayou Town	30768	13297	5726	2643	2092	23553
双港镇	Shuanggang Town	31974	17952	4842	2789	1583	27124
南河镇	Nanhe Town	56443	22478	11674	7337	1874	49824
运河镇	Yunhe Town	37746	14052	7085	4158	1329	25715
张集乡	Zhangji Country	35814	20285	7980	2686	1518	28016
六套乡	Liutao Country	33965	14967	6045	4005	1015	23416
七套乡	Qitao Country	27424	16023	5886	3537	1392	22931
老舍乡	Laoshe Country	33887	18300	6975	4297	1425	27156
滨海县	**Binhai County**						
东坎镇	Dongkan Town	226634	111050	16957	5211	13715	42255
五汛镇	Wuxun Town	82266	29195	15267	7420	3177	72888
蔡桥镇	Caiqiao Town	55345	21247	9212	4464	1907	41089
正红镇	Zhenghong Town	103407	35459	14500	7675	1844	74282
通榆镇	Tongyu Town	38740	17881	5600	2670	1665	28074
界牌镇	Jiepai Town	72415	28420	12194	5463	2312	36987
八巨镇	Baju Town	49313	18810	6893	3805	2256	23598
八滩镇	Batan Town	80588	31500	11185	4356	2507	47999
滨海港镇	Binhaigang Town	76557	38226	13800	5671	1674	44435
滨淮镇	Binhuai Town	73241	24927	13455	5610	3024	42497
天场乡	Tianchang Country	44548	18789	8150	3313	1652	26058
大套乡	Datao Country	41893	16147	6341	2641	1006	21753
陈涛乡	Chentao Country	64380	27982	11091	4870	1045	44667
振东乡	Zhendong Country	55114	21344	10400	3481	1763	35971
樊集乡	Fanji Country	34239	18127	6677	2582	1016	25349
阜宁县	**Funing County**						
阜城镇	Fucheng Town	194797	89712	5307	2540	7300	22299
沟墩镇	Goudun Town	61348	32947	11166	6932	2215	76743
吴滩镇	Wutan Town	35700	16702	6046	3861	1263	40765
合利镇	Heli Town	24562	10640	3784	2449	754	24616
陈良镇	Chenliang Town	42064	14252	6752	4430	1355	53351
施庄镇	Shizhuang Town	38734	16258	5077	3519	1322	38475
三灶镇	Sanzao Town	52950	20306	9120	5919	778	51847
郭墅镇	Guoshu Town	40133	13824	6307	4014	982	55699
新沟镇	Xingou Town	48301	19931	7742	4725	2254	55107
陈集镇	Chenji Town	54100	23589	8877	5834	1933	53512
羊寨镇	Yangzhai Town	57526	21730	9420	5055	1044	50004
芦蒲镇	Lupu Town	50495	20842	8653	4445	668	31479

续 表 19 Continued

名 称	Name	总人口（人）Total Population (person)	从业人员（人）Employment (person)	土地面积（公顷）Land Area (hectares)	耕地面积（公顷）Cultivated Area (hectares)	财政收入（万元）Financial Revenue (10000 yuan)	粮食产量（吨）Output of Grain (ton)
硕 集 镇	Shuoji Town	32099	13763	4713	3234	911	31284
板 湖 镇	Banhu Town	47634	24300	6906	4581	2679	51968
东 沟 镇	Donggou Town	51723	25330	6548	4210	2475	37543
益 林 镇	Yilin Town	55815	24986	4256	2728	8140	18588
公 兴 镇	Gongxing Town	32496	11801	5777	3351	678	35203
杨 集 镇	Yangji Town	38343	15263	6662	3372	900	38031
古 河 镇	Guhe Town	55866	24208	8979	5889	1015	41458
罗 桥 镇	Luoqiao Town	59126	23014	8810	5507	1015	65839
射 阳 县	**Sheyang County**						
合 德 镇	Hede Town	167376	61079	13132	5725	10484	28276
临 海 镇	Linhai Town	74923	29427	18625	7125	2431	49628
千 秋 镇	Qianqiu Town	59318	24034	15750	6694	592	62501
通 洋 镇	Tongyang Town	41581	17366	9541	4385	703	46191
四 明 镇	Siming Town	38339	16410	7946	4350	456	46434
阜 余 镇	Fuyu Town	45387	18237	11315	5727	615	68381
海 河 镇	Haihe Town	56644	22532	13003	6066	726	59488
陈 洋 镇	Chenyang Town	48331	23000	9464	4626	947	40467
海 通 镇	Haitong Town	35726	15567	7333	3109	3001	19605
兴 桥 镇	Xingqiao Town	52938	21477	12914	4862	1119	41976
新 坍 镇	Xintan Town	52135	18833	9816	4661	801	37791
长 荡 镇	Changdang Town	46290	18407	9591	4267	975	45229
盘 湾 镇	Panwan Town	40618	19718	9504	4209	2005	25247
特 庸 镇	Teyong Town	41445	14849	10295	4602	1003	19126
洋 马 镇	Yangma Town	32610	12236	9860	4100	985	28669
黄 尖 镇	Huangjian Town	30355	13150	7882	3180	1319	23687
盐 东 镇	Yandong Town	56564	26779	14195	5759	4785	29432
黄沙港镇	Huangshagang Town	31259	10860	8648	1471	1622	8933
耦 耕 镇	Ougeng Town	31417	13410	7395	3750	806	17372
建 湖 县	**Jianhu County**						
近 湖 镇	Jinhu Town	188786	83635	8927	3800	23602	42917
建 阳 镇	Jianyang Town	56522	33000	7200	4751	4260	58145
蒋 营 镇	Jiangying Town	34681	16241	7480	3744	2393	30527
恒 济 镇	Hengji Town	32101	17482	8008	2884	4205	31687
颜 单 镇	Yandan Town	33561	16011	8974	2970	2789	32713
沿 河 镇	Yanhe Town	41864	19641	8181	3660	1865	39207
芦 沟 镇	Lugou Town	44821	19414	8586	4423	1772	52609
庆 丰 镇	Qingfeng Town	61839	30389	9400	5420	3612	60856
上 冈 镇	Shanggang Town	80561	36127	8800	4475	3418	51150
冈 东 镇	Gangdong Town	39089	16126	8240	3802	1091	28902
草堰口镇	Caoyankou Town	36269	17200	6087	3375	1222	36867
冈 西 镇	Gangxi Town	34727	17760	6811	4079	1144	48436

续 表 20 Continued

名称 Name		总人口（人）Total Population (person)	从业人员（人）Employment (person)	土地面积（公顷）Land Area (hectares)	耕地面积（公顷）Cultivated Area (hectares)	财政收入（万元）Financial Revenue (10000 yuan)	粮食产量（吨）Output of Grain (ton)
钟庄镇	Zhongzhuang Town	39593	19208	7000	4143	1845	47490
宝塔镇	Baota Town	31095	15601	5078	3133	1032	35244
高作镇	Gaozuo Town	38278	19041	4800	3958	1726	47879
东台市	**Dongtai City**						
秦东镇	Qindong Tow	43460	21474	7574	3943	5254	38104
时堰镇	Shiyan Town	42094	18249	5867	3178	3843	29427
后港镇	Hougang Town	30345	13961	4362	2748	2172	21017
台南镇	Tainan Town	43054	19526	6341	3821	1970	28815
广山镇	Guangshan Town	23749	10238	3645	2444	1045	17846
廉怡镇	Lianyi Town	35033	13280	5356	3348	1839	27591
五烈镇	Wulie Town	32826	17921	4413	2877	1876	23066
梁垛镇	Liangduo Town	43800	22530	6880	3748	6225	32242
安丰镇	Anfeng Town	53609	28610	7121	3453	5608	35236
南沈灶镇	Nanshenzao Town	53871	27720	10324	5555	1720	33019
富安镇	Fuan Town	67845	28080	10574	5840	4658	45245
富东镇	Fudong Town	30842	14856	6425	3192	1229	25921
唐洋镇	Tangyang Town	51144	22101	10748	5665	1426	29500
新街镇	Xinjie Town	43323	21280	10289	4165	1539	19721
许河镇	Xuhe Town	48697	21240	10688	5432	1660	27814
三仓镇	Sancang Town	73703	28445	15708	7267	3161	27964
新曹镇	Xincao Town	18930	8789	6903	3488	1366	16857
曹撇镇	Caopie Town	31711	14774	8366	4018	1099	14858
头灶镇	Touzao Town	47018	23733	12316	5564	3217	25973
四灶镇	Sizao Town	38900	18323	7780	4123	1954	27134
海丰镇	Haifeng Town	25467	11949	6132	2894	1152	20982
弶港镇	Jianggang Town	27509	14904	10588	2553	1658	13564
东台镇	Dongtai Town	221388	44158	16400	5849	13955	48979
大丰市	**Dafeng City**						
大中镇	Dazhong Town	158499	88708	17110	7043	18462	44473
草堰镇	Caoyan Town	40710	18500	9589	4780	1297	39883
白驹镇	Baiju Town	40869	19930	11160	5736	2924	56661
刘庄镇	Liuzhuang Town	43501	21598	9624	5138	2293	45062
西团镇	Xituan Town	33293	18089	9614	5083	4525	36722
小海镇	Xiaohai Town	41057	21036	12114	6507	1236	32033
大桥镇	Daqiao Town	34649	17580	10254	4400	1230	20384
草庙镇	Caomiao Town	28164	16219	12279	4377	2700	25324
万盈镇	Wanying Town	49494	26373	14256	6454	2779	24938
南阳镇	Nanyang Town	37588	17496	9352	4900	4200	20328
裕华镇	Yuhua Town	42045	24834	10943	5428	2207	21051
新丰镇	Xinfeng Town	76792	30602	20178	8944	4644	35552
三龙镇	Sanlong Town	56054	32765	15257	6779	2584	30053
方强镇	Fangqiang Town	31856	15638	7253	3844	1253	15954

续 表 21 Continued

名 称 Name		总人口（人） Total Population (person)	从业人员（人） Employment (person)	土地面积（公顷） Land Area (hectares)	耕地面积（公顷） Cultivated Area (hectares)	财政收入（万元） Financial Revenue (10000 yuan)	粮食产量（吨） Output of Grain (ton)
扬州市	**Yangzhou City**						
市辖区	Jurisdictional Area						
八里镇	Bali Town	22375	13414	2326	665	5386	8217
施桥镇	Shiqiao Town	39817	19386	2306	976	7236	11457
湾头镇	Wantou Town	33142	16431	2756	701	11378	8026
汤汪乡	Tangwang Country	25130	11897	1581	333	7264	0
公道镇	Gongdao Town	35995	17829	6600	2397	7238	26206
方巷镇	Fangxiang Town	46115	22769	7554	3127	5065	32387
槐泗镇	Huaisi Town	47509	22351	6085	2299	8238	23604
瓜洲镇	Guazhou Town	40581	24405	4618	1740	7388	18264
杭集镇	Hangji Town	35733	16329	3464	1059	19986	12145
李典镇	Lidian Town	39393	21288	7100	2231	6532	23483
沙头镇	Shatou Town	42918	26209	6394	2738	10786	26252
头桥镇	Touqiao Town	43568	20655	3840	2299	4760	27921
甘泉镇	Ganquan Town	48559	26626	7680	2903	7946	28682
泰安镇	Taian Town	20983	9889	3243	1317	3096	9058
杨庙镇	Yangmiao Town	24131	15268	3115	1338	3267	11372
西湖镇	Xihu Town	27333	15703	2700	655	7554	6453
平山乡	Pingshan Country	9184	5355	780	230	5480	625
双桥乡	Shuangqiao Country	8632	5307	639	3	12198	0
城北乡	Chengbei Country	22704	14607	2100	384	5010	2842
宝应县	**Baoying County**						
安宜镇	Anyi Town	128000	79360	14135	3817	21764	50179
范水镇	Fanshui Town	84023	43823	16755	6706	5500	87604
夏集镇	Xiaji Town	60281	33859	12200	5698	2473	83388
柳堡镇	Liubao Town	53617	30766	16734	4657	4873	69490
射阳湖镇	Sheyanghu Town	92523	45716	18150	6180	4729	80145
广洋湖镇	Guangyanghu Town	37674	21321	9020	2792	1806	38999
鲁垛镇	Luduo Town	34479	21524	6130	2899	1681	44439
小官庄镇	Xiaoguanzhuang Town	30776	17895	4600	2647	1672	36964
望直港镇	Wangzhigang Town	59486	37003	9000	4234	2528	56254
曹甸镇	Caodian Town	70537	38449	10000	4195	4279	62494
西安丰镇	Xianfeng Town	36675	16646	5839	1824	2738	25222
山阳镇	Shanyang Town	56897	30413	12343	4104	2734	54183
黄塍镇	Huangcheng Town	28138	13317	4200	1810	1395	24610
泾河镇	Jinghe Town	60278	29029	8317	3827	2383	54248
仪征市	**Yizheng City**						
真州镇	Zhenzhou Town	193118	86618	7925	3036	13929	13188
青山镇	Qingshan Town	25894	17365	4934	2530	2133	9084
朴席镇	Puxi Town	33463	16908	4718	2152	2803	23151
新集镇	Xinji Town	42707	23018	6389	3642	4716	30168
新城镇	Xincheng Town	68498	46417	10787	6653	3784	42899

续 表 22 Continued

名 称 Name		总人口（人） Total Population (person)	从业人员（人） Employment (person)	土地面积（公顷） Land Area (hectares)	耕地面积（公顷） Cultivated Area (hectares)	财政收入（万元） Financial Revenue (10000 yuan)	粮食产量（吨） Output of Grain (ton)
马 集 镇	Maji Town	45495	24731	10693	6325	5625	30186
刘 集 镇	Liuji Town	45345	24490	9065	5571	2320	34507
陈 集 镇	Chenji Town	38613	20976	8154	5198	2584	31411
大 仪 镇	Dayi Town	46890	26575	10863	6736	5002	49048
谢 集 乡	Xieji Country	27642	14030	6718	3082	1739	18265
月 塘 乡	Yuetang Country	29411	14071	7645	4093	1658	21005
高 邮 市	**Gaoyou City**						
高 邮 镇	Gaoyou Town	147972	113047	3900	1240	14757	24046
龙 虬 镇	Longqiu Town	43925	23622	8937	2609	4753	40785
马 棚 镇	Mapeng Town	18527	10180	2266	1854	1500	16698
车 逻 镇	Cheluo Town	33040	14029	2844	2604	3865	34985
八 桥 镇	Baqiao Town	22933	11920	4000	2295	2653	27065
汉 留 镇	Hanliu Town	30738	14225	6670	3382	2863	41485
汤 庄 镇	Tangzhuang Town	33820	18901	4633	3577	7097	47034
卸 甲 镇	Xiejia Town	67804	37301	13684	5940	9353	88007
三 垛 镇	Sanduo Town	57260	23129	7537	5075	4465	59272
甘 垛 镇	Ganduo Town	38903	19866	5181	4170	569	36387
司 徒 镇	Situ Town	22031	12775	7416	1910	1454	22966
横 泾 镇	Hengjing Town	23157	12157	6133	2207	914	20668
界 首 镇	Jieshou Town	33111	15771	8580	2462	2379	36824
周 山 镇	Zhoushan Town	28015	12876	6202	3103	930	36579
周 巷 镇	Zhouxiang Town	33427	14714	7950	3551	1772	49005
临 泽 镇	Linze Town	64402	35418	11810	4535	3621	63766
送 桥 镇	Songqiao Town	25848	10365	4750	1810	2674	25252
郭 集 镇	Guoji Town	22272	17667	5300	3082	3861	28680
天 山 镇	Tianshan Town	20062	15500	4558	1335	6832	19166
菱塘回族乡	Lingtang Huizu Country	22049	17198	5100	1378	6409	20602
江 都 市	**Jiangdu City**						
仙 女 镇	Xiannu Town	157421	88156	14158	4047	34102	42862
小 纪 镇	Xiaoji Town	94585	47180	17778	7972	11243	86086
武 坚 镇	Wujian Town	41763	26416	6180	3501	4199	39930
樊 川 镇	Fanchuan Town	70565	44179	10770	5851	6391	62674
真 武 镇	Zhenwu Town	55575	34701	5420	3379	5431	37562
宜 陵 镇	Yiling Town	50976	22439	5986	2540	6600	28358
丁 沟 镇	Dinggou Town	61703	30960	10232	6245	4963	49743
郭 村 镇	Guocun Town	86320	35727	10292	4212	3225	51545
邵 伯 镇	Shaobo Town	76996	52997	11465	3628	9072	39318
丁 伙 镇	Dinghuo Town	47661	31005	8020	3265	6600	29246
大 桥 镇	Daqiao Town	136639	69785	16016	4752	12179	58940
吴 桥 镇	Wuqiao Town	50530	24322	5500	2775	3224	30347
浦 头 镇	Putou Town	45883	19275	4290	1813	3853	21238
镇 江 市	**Zhenjiang City**						

名 称	Name	总人口（人）Total Population (person)	从业人员（人）Employment (person)	土地面积（公顷）Land Area (hectares)	耕地面积（公顷）Cultivated Area (hectares)	财政收入（万元）Financial Revenue (10000 yuan)	粮食产量（吨）Output of Grain (ton)
市辖区	Jurisdictional Area						
象山镇	Xiangshan Town	33430	21044	4348	293	8079	623
谏壁镇	Jianbi Town	34147	19370	3200	598	16111	3650
姚桥镇	Yaoqiao Town	42915	26897	5588	2731	3256	28688
大路镇	Dalu Town	28127	14565	1750	1277	3672	16876
丁岗镇	Dinggang Town	20560	11750	3536	1525	1402	14713
蒋乔镇	Jiangqiao Town	18766	11500	4707	645	21443	4358
高桥镇	Gaoqiao Town	28054	17730	4508	1636	4080	14026
辛丰镇	Xinfeng Town	57562	34939	9090	3359	10665	30405
谷阳镇	Guyang Town	40951	23168	8296	2096	9668	17707
上党镇	Shangdang Town	53554	31205	13560	4065	4586	29513
宝堰镇	Baoyan Town	44747	26163	8069	2991	4578	34609
高资镇	Gaozi Town	42132	22576	10052	1962	10371	18610
世业镇	Shiye Town	14231	8044	4400	1251	1164	12466
丹阳市	**Danyang City**						
司徒镇	Situ Town	61361	41053	12129	6494	15410	39405
延陵镇	Yanling Town	65907	34790	11543	6324	8264	52522
珥陵镇	Erling Town	52530	27962	8371	4635	4726	40361
导墅镇	Daoshu Town	51031	26691	8056	4873	7344	44227
皇塘镇	Huangtang Town	52097	35092	8054	4235	12258	38172
吕城镇	Lucheng Town	52492	29822	6789	4054	12714	35165
陵口镇	Lingkou Town	45648	30300	6445	3814	4479	36287
访仙镇	Fangxian Town	53310	32648	7384	4297	9127	39922
界牌镇	Jiepai Town	40850	24508	2371	973	13724	8193
新桥镇	Xinqiao Town	33347	24299	2618	1227	13076	10906
后巷镇	Houxiang Town	50364	39274	6387	2516	27496	17730
埤城镇	Picheng Town	37413	22680	7322	3261	11738	18181
云阳镇	Yunyang Town	92504	55804	10310	5175	29375	42751
扬中市	**Yangzhong City**						
三茅镇	Sanmao Town	146324	91510	8049	3416	30898	29812
新坝镇	Xinba Town	52595	25468	4920	2125	38019	19371
油坊镇	Youfang Town	46462	27686	4593	2235	12542	20837
八桥镇	Baqiao Town	36939	19410	3458	1672	7323	15382
西来桥镇	Xilaiqiao Town	18423	9429	1950	860	2187	7376
句容市	**Jurong City**						
华阳镇	Huayang Town	42136	22767	11600	3514	12011	24220
黄梅镇	Huangmei Town	44807	24651	12530	3734	8740	30107
下蜀镇	Xiashu Town	40026	18205	12200	2341	11043	17284
白兔镇	Baitu Town	40408	23279	11500	4500	4193	33703
边城镇	Biancheng Town	36212	19892	10900	2898	5371	23718
茅山镇	Maoshan Town	48461	22878	11980	4563	4299	29703
后白镇	Houbai Town	61295	32411	15004	5183	5901	44447

名称 Name		总人口（人） Total Population (person)	从业人员（人） Employment (person)	土地面积（公顷） Land Area (hectares)	耕地面积（公顷） Cultivated Area (hectares)	财政收入（万元） Financial Revenue (10000 yuan)	粮食产量（吨） Output of Grain (ton)
郭庄镇	Guozhuang Town	64075	31981	13496	5568	3400	46663
天王镇	Tianwang Town	67685	35817	19190	5351	4300	41448
宝华镇	Baohua Town	23492	11482	10000	1202	6207	11162
泰州市	**Taizhou City**						
市辖区	Jurisdictional Area						
九龙镇	Jiulong Town	25227	17216	3090	1140	11166	12181
永安洲镇	Yonganzhou Town	26540	14504	5122	1294	7262	14699
白马镇	Baima Town	23043	10900	2500	1330	1748	12488
野徐镇	Yexu Town	20819	9743	1997	932	2200	9902
寺巷镇	Sixiang Town	66576	34304	5029	1396	9857	20100
兴化市	**Xinghua City**						
戴窑镇	Daiyao Town	68415	27170	10045	5670	4220	70479
合陈镇	Hechen Town	55622	22118	9928	5939	2662	56787
永丰镇	Yongfeng Town	50154	21178	7802	4540	2432	55088
新垛镇	Xinduo Town	25931	11942	4903	2885	1515	38104
安丰镇	Anfeng Town	72772	25712	9900	5380	5642	59678
海南镇	Hainan Town	35395	14512	7209	3649	2074	46065
钓鱼镇	Diaoyu Town	44961	18975	7552	4187	2481	48574
大邹镇	Dazou Town	27831	10103	4655	2719	1241	24587
沙沟镇	Shagou Town	27981	11265	7003	2030	2295	14343
中堡镇	Zhongbao Town	32825	13575	8320	2969	1572	33293
李中镇	Lizhong Town	35630	16501	8027	2634	1965	28345
西郊镇	Xijiao Town	28881	14454	7024	3416	1733	29877
临城镇	Lincheng Town	52811	22607	9274	5427	4817	46875
垛田镇	Duotian Town	56584	28274	5955	2132	2564	762
竹泓镇	Zhuhong Town	39850	16366	6445	3760	2185	39188
沈伦镇	Shenlun Town	28598	11821	4959	3019	1562	30523
大垛镇	Daduo Town	42170	18055	7276	3745	3757	49524
荻垛镇	Diduo Town	46157	18915	7241	4438	3003	53648
陶庄镇	Taozhuang Town	45323	20329	6960	4320	2735	52742
昌荣镇	Changrong Town	36844	17114	6180	3500	1559	50468
茅山镇	Maoshan Town	31081	12654	4304	2751	2460	27685
周庄镇	Zhouzhuang Town	56287	21816	9252	5545	5480	63218
陈堡镇	Chenbao Town	45304	19097	8068	4270	3599	53858
戴南镇	Dainan Town	113118	40770	10773	4640	55785	62268
张郭镇	Zhangguo Town	64697	39394	8441	4017	12979	49181
昭阳镇	Zhaoyang Town	151537	73665	5026	1265	11629	13797
大营镇	Daying Town	27833	11864	5067	3300	1418	33562
老圩乡	Laowei Country	26426	9887	5243	3080	1917	29958
下圩镇	Xiawei Town	26071	14962	4912	3141	1701	32563
周奋乡	Zhoufen Country	26330	11873	5786	2524	1109	17570
缸顾乡	Ganggu Country	20772	9628	4633	2040	1618	16791

名 称	Name	总人口（人）Total Population (person)	从业人员（人）Employment (person)	土地面积（公顷）Land Area (hectares)	耕地面积（公顷）Cultivated Area (hectares)	财政收入（万元）Financial Revenue (10000 yuan)	粮食产量（吨）Output of Grain (ton)
城东镇	Chengdong Town	30418	13174	5547	2670	2226	23597
西鲍乡	Xibao Country	28755	14065	5241	2800	1815	38354
林湖乡	Linhu Country	37005	14163	6638	3487	2427	36747
靖江市	**Jingjiang City**						
靖城镇	Jingcheng Town	167200	145854	6706	1986	29099	21349
新桥镇	Xinqiao Town	59177	24762	6135	3062	18100	39703
东兴镇	Dongxing Town	34502	18873	3568	2061	8615	25140
斜桥镇	Xieqiao Town	46406	20156	4398	1710	5782	23670
西来镇	Xilai Town	55138	22153	5137	2819	7403	30729
季市镇	Jishi Town	49524	22406	4163	1991	5247	24386
孤山镇	Gushan Town	40684	19397	4799	2460	6973	29371
红光镇	Hongguang Town	27848	13165	4045	2338	2800	31481
生祠镇	Shengci Town	22774	8943	2974	1628	3288	19425
马桥镇	Maqiao Town	45820	26865	5974	3357	7258	39545
泰兴市	**Taixing City**						
黄桥镇	Huangqiao Town	95038	50370	7029	3560	8580	39650
分界镇	Fenjie Town	59890	30583	7088	3671	1900	42064
古溪镇	Guxi Town	26812	12468	3367	1572	1827	18985
横垛镇	Hengduo Town	34176	17332	3715	1978	1023	20605
元竹镇	Yuanzhu Town	38973	20311	4754	2392	883	26332
珊瑚镇	Shanhu Town	53338	27833	4951	2733	1696	31980
广陵镇	Guangling Town	58392	29820	5866	2892	1358	30804
南沙镇	Nansha Town	31264	17002	3295	1666	863	19142
曲霞镇	Quxia Town	34108	16740	3526	1967	1380	23489
张桥镇	Zhangqiao Town	55117	29588	6177	3209	2803	32714
溪桥镇	Xiqiao Town	32365	16635	3091	1581	1818	15532
刘陈镇	Liuchen Town	33884	17329	4086	2203	883	25871
河失镇	Heshi Town	57764	29013	6456	3206	3135	39239
新街镇	Xinjie Town	60010	31599	4733	3579	1523	39847
姚王镇	Yaowang Town	52843	27791	6688	2678	11984	32676
宣堡镇	Xuanbao Town	51420	27168	5388	2906	3396	32245
胡庄镇	Huzhuang Town	48140	24927	4938	3289	1031	30551
马甸镇	Madian Town	27769	13844	1867	1328	2300	14191
泰兴镇	Taixing City	214504	112360	6408	1866	41667	21150
七圩镇	Qiwei Town	25061	13147	3010	1246	7605	16230
蒋华镇	Jianghua Town	51662	25618	6532	3126	5998	39534
大生镇	Dasheng Town	40739	20191	6205	2470	18244	26493
过船镇	Guochuan Town	24873	12955	3451	1298	3985	13287
根思乡	Gensi Country	51581	25557	5065	3248	599	34044
姜堰市	**Jiangyan City**						
姜堰镇	Jiangyan Town	178115	85609	7831	3111	60190	20929
溱潼镇	Qintong Town	33276	16507	3160	1525	8477	12588

续 表 26 Continued

名 称	Name	总人口（人）Total Population (person)	从业人员（人）Employment (person)	土地面积（公顷）Land Area (hectares)	耕地面积（公顷）Cultivated Area (hectares)	财政收入（万元）Financial Revenue (10000 yuan)	粮食产量（吨）Output of Grain (ton)
蒋垛镇	Jiangduo Town	51839	29500	6600	4069	4518	31255
顾高镇	Gugao Town	28620	16444	3700	2366	3908	18404
大伦镇	Dalun Town	36167	18291	5600	3243	3647	30316
张甸镇	Zhangdian Town	72560	38961	8980	6215	8709	54400
大泗镇	Dasi Town	30116	12737	3000	2134	2385	16285
梁徐镇	Liangxu Town	50365	30126	5970	3950	11052	35463
苏陈镇	Suchen Town	56092	30390	5884	4711	12177	42043
桥头镇	Qiaotou Town	24725	16012	3800	2357	2504	20042
淤溪镇	Yuxi Town	42694	28242	7800	3980	3526	17008
白米镇	Baimi Town	45910	28392	5100	3603	26369	33699
娄庄镇	Louzhuang Town	48488	24662	6800	4530	9510	41788
沈高镇	Shengao Town	37100	21822	5600	3669	5571	30841
兴泰镇	Xingtai Town	24392	14613	3700	2432	3601	23467
俞垛镇	Yuduo Town	50170	28726	8200	5178	8473	40790
华港镇	Huagang Town	41756	23068	7200	3860	7454	27752
罡杨镇	Gangyang Town	21687	14967	3400	2304	7867	20099
宿迁市	**Suqian City**						
市辖区	Jurisdictional Area						
双庄镇	Shuangzhuang Town	35139	17310	4178	1828	2471	11778
耿车镇	Gengche Town	33829	17178	3501	1466	2111	12185
埠子镇	Buzi Town	52984	28004	5242	2665	1544	23544
龙河镇	Longhe Town	50415	29115	5800	2585	1311	21035
洋北镇	Yangbei Town	38581	19189	5956	3048	1437	28309
仓集镇	Cangji Town	48200	25210	5591	3794	957	23732
洋河镇	Yanghe Town	62941	26360	4584	1944	4342	12171
中扬镇	Zhongyang Town	51879	23060	9315	5524	1618	36140
郑楼镇	Zhenglou Town	47133	21363	6086	2677	1157	23546
陈集镇	Chenji Town	44862	15340	6867	3753	1159	26105
罗圩乡	Luowei Country	45418	23247	4903	3122	1159	27169
南蔡乡	Nancai Country	40387	20236	5175	2393	957	16964
屠园乡	Tuyuan Country	34799	18998	6298	4152	762	35029
三棵树乡	Sankeshu Country	31540	15501	3623	1887	1527	21883
顺河镇	Shunhe Town	76385	36626	7117	2056	2808	18352
晓店镇	Xiaodian Town	36374	19147	5147	2319	879	14117
蔡集镇	Caiji Town	42840	21960	4900	2613	1008	15136
王官集镇	Wangguanji Town	50023	24909	6270	3087	1225	30459
皂河镇	Zaohe Town	50952	21243	26409	2152	1367	24144
仰化镇	Yanghua Town	32602	18000	5236	2470	980	25737
大兴镇	Daxing Town	52837	27669	5838	3174	1455	22566
丁嘴镇	Dingzui Town	34198	16120	5300	2358	1053	19695
来龙镇	Lailong Town	38014	19282	7496	4183	1012	45379
黄墩镇	Huangdun Town	26549	10896	5125	2460	707	29925

名 称 Name		总人口（人）Total Population (person)	从业人员（人）Employment (person)	土地面积（公顷）Land Area (hectares)	耕地面积（公顷）Cultivated Area (hectares)	财政收入（万元）Financial Revenue (10000 yuan)	粮食产量（吨）Output of Grain (ton)
陆集镇	Luji Town	33035	17304	5786	3122	1106	23537
关庙镇	Guanmiao Town	39984	21956	7946	4276	986	40255
侍岭镇	Shiling Town	31691	15474	6393	3011	1303	27634
新庄镇	Xinzhuang Town	22293	10180	5368	3058	653	32635
井头乡	Jingtou Country	28243	18380	6816	2234	3120	26400
曹集乡	Caoji Country	30328	15267	4700	2435	955	24647
保安乡	Baoan Country	21288	11982	4460	2725	849	28782
沭阳县	**Shuyang City**						
沭城镇	Shucheng Town	353037	209738	27715	13789	14116	93081
陇集镇	Longji Town	25830	15303	4688	3269	1087	23375
胡集镇	Huji Town	51553	29441	6868	3548	1771	29730
钱集镇	Qianji Town	34182	14905	4949	3043	1080	19313
塘沟镇	Tanggou Town	42049	21981	5795	3496	1227	29087
马厂镇	Machang Town	64951	35802	8412	5684	1976	50163
沂涛镇	Yitao Town	74532	45612	9456	5931	1907	56232
庙头镇	Miaotou Town	42733	22983	5847	3609	1080	23549
韩山镇	Hanshan Town	37689	18700	6557	4092	1300	30745
华冲镇	Huachong Town	44696	21254	5455	3375	1754	32899
桑墟镇	Sangxu Town	49027	25330	5319	2719	3278	26514
悦来镇	Yuelai Town	42997	24741	8803	5772	1325	56981
刘集镇	Liuji Town	38226	18528	7200	4968	1021	44924
李恒镇	Liheng Town	38681	19430	6688	4057	1213	32400
扎下镇	Zhaxia Town	54182	28360	5534	2900	1772	7830
颜集镇	Yanji Town	54078	39393	6921	3760	1792	11856
潼阳镇	Tongyang Town	47637	25335	9968	6539	1311	19930
龙庙镇	Longmiao Town	49801	30943	4860	2785	1787	20684
高墟镇	Gaoxu Town	34721	20310	6115	3929	986	41118
耿圩镇	Gengwei Town	37302	19850	7044	3875	1023	27300
汤涧镇	Tangjian Town	36296	15598	5500	3216	1443	27080
新河镇	Xinhe Town	40447	20700	4860	2650	1128	0
贤官镇	Xianguan	50714	27822	5029	3394	1455	22283
吴集镇	Wuji Town	43036	20429	7305	4067	1199	29273
湖东镇	Hudong Town	40616	24382	6343	4516	1154	52961
青伊湖镇	Qingyihu Town	36524	16530	5000	2760	1221	29846
北丁集乡	Beidingji Country	27784	12955	3880	2021	865	9171
周集乡	Zhouji Country	28630	15261	4387	2673	948	26124
东小店乡	Dongxiaodian Country	32528	16506	5099	3122	1361	20775
张圩乡	Zhangwei Country	26289	16353	3902	2420	931	14978
茆圩乡	Maowei Country	36384	21796	7223	5174	1148	30967
西圩乡	Xiwei Country	30053	16819	4776	3867	807	6588
万匹乡	Wanpi Country	33881	14792	3495	2447	1269	8286
官墩乡	Guandun Country	30471	16431	5603	3605	974	28610

续 表 28 Continued

名 称 Name		总人口（人）Total Population (person)	从业人员（人）Employment (person)	土地面积（公顷）Land Area (hectares)	耕地面积（公顷）Cultivated Area (hectares)	财政收入（万元）Financial Revenue (10000 yuan)	粮食产量（吨）Output of Grain (ton)
泗 阳 县	**Siyang County**						
众 兴 镇	Zhongxing Town	290006	116950	25419	10533	6747	82400
爱 园 镇	Aiyuan Town	53005	26527	6501	3018	698	27452
王 集 镇	Wangji Town	74120	31753	8531	4753	1131	30129
裴 圩 镇	Peiwei Town	61180	29953	7686	4224	1055	24597
新 袁 镇	Xinyuan Town	45836	24643	5359	3227	779	17025
李 口 镇	Likou Town	50941	25092	6585	3492	632	22541
临 河 镇	Linhe Town	43418	21230	5872	2506	572	23837
穿 城 镇	Chuancheng Town	38162	21526	5436	3022	535	31019
张家圩镇	Zhangjiawei Town	38302	22766	5764	3458	532	28431
高 渡 镇	Gaodu Town	34181	16590	5721	2693	634	22698
卢 集 镇	Luji Town	40677	19740	8002	5451	993	33140
庄 圩 乡	Zhuangwei Country	37826	20705	4876	3053	818	24653
里 仁 乡	Liren Country	35222	19620	4482	2554	588	20142
三 庄 乡	Sanzhuang Country	38949	19462	6588	4050	635	27872
南刘集乡	Nanliuji Country	35016	15969	4803	3354	423	17600
八 集 乡	Baji Country	26900	13147	3863	2430	546	12354
泗 洪 县	**Sihong County**						
青 阳 镇	Qingyang Town	206866	132284	25322	12254	7525	109384
双 沟 镇	Shuanggou Town	51681	28209	7428	2782	2877	17891
上 塘 镇	Shangtang Town	53469	28000	13299	6539	1230	46351
魏 营 镇	Weiying Town	35974	17105	10615	4354	1061	39690
临 淮 镇	Linhuai Town	16425	9298	2100	157	589	855
半 城 镇	Bancheng Town	18043	8633	8300	780	597	7759
孙 园 镇	Sunyuan Town	45545	19930	9604	5162	1339	60438
梅 花 镇	Meihua Town	30423	16500	9350	4757	970	24731
归 仁 镇	Guiren Town	62040	24952	11459	6021	1363	56314
金 锁 镇	Jinsuo Town	42686	33578	8073	4423	1306	35515
朱 湖 镇	Zhuhu Town	39403	21008	7370	3595	1125	38069
界 集 镇	Jieji Town	41029	21240	8960	5862	1168	58682
太 平 镇	Taiping Town	34623	17601	7251	3618	996	39070
龙 集 镇	Longji Town	42406	18394	8741	5608	1295	31441
四 河 乡	Sihe Country	33949	13587	6222	2239	830	19514
峰 山 乡	Fengshan Country	26122	13004	5684	1818	649	11552
天岗湖乡	Tianganghu Country	32813	16623	8918	3801	872	26429
车 门 乡	Chemen Country	28586	12841	8436	3485	833	41058
瑶 沟 乡	Yaogou Country	24322	11782	5664	2915	747	33561
石 集 乡	Shiji Country	23075	12136	8940	3213	791	42053
城 头 乡	Chengtou Country	20566	10216	7817	3720	720	50675
陈 圩 乡	Chenwei Country	35296	16314	8821	3605	978	55158
曹 庙 乡	Caomiao Country	35454	15890	9185	4845	941	43147

附录一

APPENDIX I

全国分省主要指标

MAJOR INDICATORS BY REGION

附录1－1　人口与就业（2006年）
POPULATION AND EMPLOYMENT (2006)

单位：万人　　　　(10000 persons)

地　区	Region	年末总人口 Year-end Total Population	职工人数 Staff and Workers	#国有单位 State-Owned	#城镇集体单位 Urban Collective-owned Units	#港澳台商投资单位 Hong Kong Macao and Taiwan Investment	#外商投资单位 Foreign Investment
全　国	**National Total**	**131448**	**11160.6**	**6170.5**	**726.0**	**593.1**	**747.2**
北　京	Beijing	1581	453.1	172.9	16.4	20.9	49.3
天　津	Tianjin	1075	172.0	78.0	7.8	10.3	40.0
河　北	Hebei	6898	488.1	339.6	34.9	9.3	13.7
山　西	Shanxi	3375	357.2	249.1	28.8	5.3	1.7
内蒙古	Inner Mongolia	2397	239.3	158.5	11.3	1.3	2.7
辽　宁	Liaoning	4271	476.0	292.5	37.2	9.2	37.6
吉　林	Jilin	2723	259.9	171.1	19.2	2.6	7.4
黑龙江	Heilongjiang	3823	459.2	284.0	35.9	3.1	4.4
上　海	Shanghai	1815	264.5	116.7	10.1	22.6	50.2
江　苏	**Jiangsu**	**7550**	**645.7**	**268.4**	**33.6**	**48.5**	**102.0**
浙　江	Zhejiang	4980	580.7	177.5	27.5	59.3	71.1
安　徽	Anhui	6110	320.9	193.3	26.7	4.9	7.0
福　建	Fujian	3558	412.2	144.1	17.2	106.2	70.8
江　西	Jiangxi	4339	271.9	191.9	16.0	8.3	5.9
山　东	Shandong	9309	874.3	409.3	59.6	27.1	105.5
河　南	Henan	9392	692.1	391.8	83.9	7.9	8.8
湖　北	Hubei	5693	495.3	285.9	35.6	9.2	14.6
湖　南	Hunan	6342	390.0	249.7	27.6	7.8	7.7
广　东	Guangdong	9304	935.0	374.4	66.4	210.7	118.5
广　西	Guangxi	4719	267.8	186.4	16.0	5.1	6.5
海　南	Hainan	836	73.9	55.8	3.7	1.8	2.2
重　庆	Chongqing	2808	213.0	120.4	12.2	2.3	4.9
四　川	Sichuan	8169	500.9	304.4	40.1	3.7	7.2
贵　州	Guizhou	3757	201.9	137.9	8.9	0.8	1.3
云　南	Yunnan	4483	248.0	171.0	12.6	1.9	2.1
西　藏	Tibet	281	17.0	16.1	0.5	0.0	0.0
陕　西	Shaanxi	3735	323.7	239.6	19.7	1.6	1.2
甘　肃	Gansu	2606	190.2	140.9	8.4	0.5	0.6
青　海	Qinghai	548	41.2	31.2	2.0	0.2	0.0
宁　夏	Ningxia	604	56.7	35.5	1.1	0.0	1.0
新　疆	Xinjiang	2050	238.9	182.9	5.2	0.7	1.1

附录1－2　地区生产总值（2006年）
GROSS DOMESTIC PRODUCT（2006）

地　区	Region	地区生产总值（亿元）Gross Domestic Products (100 million yuan)	第一产业 Primary Industry	第二产业 Secondary Industry	#工　业 Industry	第三产业 Tertiary Industry	人均地区生产总值（元）Per Capita GDP (yuan)
全　国	**National Total**	**209406.8**	**24700.0**	**102004.0**	**90351.5**	**82702.8**	**15973**
北　京	Beijing	7720.3	98.0	2217.2	1848.5	5405.1	49505
天　津	Tianjin	4337.7	119.0	2485.8	2290.8	1732.9	40961
河　北	Hebei	11613.7	1605.4	6071.3	5453.4	3937.0	16894
山　西	Shanxi	4746.5	276.6	2742.5	2482.7	1727.4	14106
内蒙古	Inner Mongolia	4790.0	641.7	2329.5	1978.2	1818.8	20047
辽　宁	Liaoning	9257.1	976.4	4720.8	4167.6	3559.9	21802
吉　林	Jilin	4249.2	686.0	1886.6	1628.5	1676.6	15625
黑龙江	Heilongjiang	6216.8	734.0	3397.4	3081.9	2085.4	16268
上　海	Shanghai	10297.0	93.8	4997.8	4641.6	5205.4	57310
江　苏	**Jiangsu**	**21645.1**	**1545.0**	**12250.8**	**11110.2**	**7849.2**	**28814**
浙　江	Zhejiang	15648.9	923.0	8437.7	7537.9	6288.2	31684
安　徽	Anhui	6141.9	1027.2	2656.0	2200.5	2458.7	10044
福　建	Fujian	7501.6	885.2	3736.1	3306.1	2880.3	21152
江　西	Jiangxi	4618.8	786.3	2319.0	1806.1	1513.5	10679
山　东	Shandong	21846.7	2138.9	12729.0	11556.0	6978.8	23546
河　南	Henan	12464.1	2049.4	6762.4	6070.9	3652.3	13279
湖　北	Hubei	7497.2	1140.4	3363.8	2929.2	2993.0	13150
湖　南	Hunan	7493.2	1331.3	3123.5	2667.8	3038.4	11830
广　东	Guangdong	25968.6	1571.4	13430.6	12500.2	10966.6	28077
广　西	Guangxi	4802.0	1031.9	1882.3	1595.9	1887.8	10240
海　南	Hainan	1052.4	344.2	287.8	217.6	420.4	12650
重　庆	Chongqing	3486.2	428.5	1500.1	1234.1	1557.6	12437
四　川	Sichuan	8637.8	1603.5	3775.2	3144.7	3259.1	10546
贵　州	Guizhou	2267.4	392.9	982.0	857.2	892.5	5750
云　南	Yunnan	4001.9	751.2	1710.2	1407.0	1540.5	8961
西　藏	Tibet	290.1	51.1	80.0	21.6	159.0	10396
陕　西	Shaanxi	4383.9	488.5	2318.2	1970.8	1577.2	11762
甘　肃	Gansu	2275.0	333.2	1048.2	873.1	893.6	8749
青　海	Qinghai	641.1	69.6	330.8	265.0	240.7	11753
宁　夏	Ningxia	707.0	79.2	347.5	288.3	280.3	11784
新　疆	Xinjiang	3019.0	533.2	1437.9	1218.7	1047.9	14871

附录1－3　地区生产总值构成及增速（2006年）
STRUCTURE AND GROWTH RATE OF GROSS DOMESTIC PRODUCT (2006)

地　区 Region		地区生产总值构成（%）Structure of GDP(%)	第一产业 Primary Industry	第二产业 Secondary Industry	#工　业 Industry	第三产业 Tertiary Industry	地区生产总值比上年增长（%）Growth Rate of GDP Over 2005 (%)
全　　国	**National Total**	**100.0**	**11.8**	**48.7**	**43.1**	**39.5**	**10.7**
北　　京	Beijing	100.0	1.3	28.7	23.9	70.0	12.0
天　　津	Tianjin	100.0	2.7	57.3	52.8	40.0	14.4
河　　北	Hebei	100.0	13.8	52.3	47.0	33.9	13.2
山　　西	Shanxi	100.0	5.8	57.8	52.3	36.4	11.8
内蒙古	Inner Mongolia	100.0	13.4	48.6	41.3	38.0	18.0
辽　　宁	Liaoning	100.0	10.5	51.0	45.0	38.5	13.8
吉　　林	Jilin	100.0	16.1	44.4	38.3	39.5	15.0
黑龙江	Heilongjiang	100.0	11.8	54.7	49.6	33.5	12.0
上　　海	Shanghai	100.0	0.9	48.5	45.1	50.6	12.0
江　　苏	**Jiangsu**	**100.0**	**7.1**	**56.6**	**51.3**	**36.3**	**14.9**
浙　　江	Zhejiang	100.0	5.9	53.9	48.2	40.2	13.6
安　　徽	Anhui	100.0	16.7	43.3	35.9	40.0	12.9
福　　建	Fujian	100.0	11.8	49.8	44.1	38.4	13.4
江　　西	Jiangxi	100.0	17.0	50.2	39.1	32.8	12.3
山　　东	Shandong	100.0	9.8	58.3	52.9	31.9	14.7
河　　南	Henan	100.0	16.4	54.3	48.7	29.3	14.1
湖　　北	Hubei	100.0	15.2	44.9	39.1	39.9	12.1
湖　　南	Hunan	100.0	17.8	41.7	35.6	40.5	12.1
广　　东	Guangdong	100.0	6.1	51.7	48.1	42.2	14.1
广　　西	Guangxi	100.0	21.5	39.2	33.2	39.3	13.5
海　　南	Hainan	100.0	32.7	27.4	20.7	39.9	12.5
重　　庆	Chongqing	100.0	12.3	43.0	35.4	44.7	12.2
四　　川	Sichuan	100.0	18.6	43.7	36.4	37.7	13.3
贵　　州	Guizhou	100.0	17.3	43.3	37.8	39.4	11.5
云　　南	Yunnan	100.0	18.8	42.7	35.1	38.5	11.9
西　　藏	Tibet	100.0	17.6	27.6	7.5	54.8	13.4
陕　　西	Shaanxi	100.0	11.1	52.9	45.0	36.0	12.7
甘　　肃	Gansu	100.0	14.6	46.1	38.4	39.3	11.4
青　　海	Qinghai	100.0	10.9	51.6	41.3	37.5	12.2
宁　　夏	Ningxia	100.0	11.2	49.2	40.8	39.6	12.5
新　　疆	Xinjiang	100.0	17.7	47.6	40.4	34.7	11.0

附录1－4 固定资产投资完成额（2006年）
COMPLETED INVESTMENT IN FIXED ASSETS（2006）

地 区	Region	城镇固定资产投资额（亿元）Urban Investment in Fixed Assets（100 million yuan）	#房地产开发 Real Estate Developoment	商品房销售额（亿元）Sales Value of Commercial Housing（100 million yuan）	#住宅 Residence	商品房竣工面积（万平方米）Floor space of commercial Housing completed（10000 sq. m）	商品房住宅销售面积（万平方米）Sales Floor space of commercial Residence（1000 sq. m）
全国总计	**National Total**	**93472.4**	**19382.5**	**20509.7**	**17038.0**	**53019.4**	**60628.1**
北 京	Beijing	3086.3	1719.9	2159.0	1626.3	3193.9	2607.6
天 津	Tianjin	1679.0	402.3	696.3	619.5	1520.2	1458.6
河 北	Hebei	4430.6	480.0	358.6	321.4	1172.7	1707.6
山 西	Shanxi	2059.2	208.6	153.3	130.0	661.1	767.6
内蒙古	Inner Mongolia	3264.8	325.0	257.0	202.3	1301.7	1414.3
辽 宁	Liaoning	4977.2	1142.2	923.9	788.7	2845.1	3006.1
吉 林	Jilin	2366.1	310.5	194.1	169.9	664.8	956.8
黑龙江	Heilongjiang	2040.4	321.3	325.5	264.3	1398.1	1482.7
上 海	Shanghai	3497.5	1275.6	2177.1	1841.0	3274.3	3025.4
江 苏	**Jiangsu**	**7481.8**	**1906.7**	**2191.7**	**1756.2**	**5933.5**	**6101.2**
浙 江	Zhejiang	5428.0	1572.8	1678.4	1357.9	3717.5	3495.1
安 徽	Anhui	3057.9	637.5	535.9	438.6	2067.2	2307.8
福 建	Fujian	2730.1	787.4	807.5	637.3	1408.3	2021.7
江 西	Jiangxi	2377.4	343.6	291.4	250.8	1492.3	1683.2
山 东	Shandong	8714.9	1178.7	988.5	851.1	3383.2	3797.2
河 南	Henan	4843.8	582.0	483.6	401.2	1677.5	2439.9
湖 北	Hubei	3039.9	564.8	521.0	463.9	1817.7	2038.5
湖 南	Hunan	2718.4	556.1	389.9	300.4	1706.2	2021.6
广 东	Guangdong	6552.6	1834.3	2490.6	2135.7	3992.5	5106.4
广 西	Guangxi	1947.3	370.0	329.9	270.7	1130.5	1502.0
海 南	Hainan	396.7	89.3	70.9	66.5	106.6	195.2
重 庆	Chongqing	2252.0	629.6	505.7	418.7	2224.8	2239.5
四 川	Sichuan	3927.6	919.5	896.3	762.3	3023.5	4022.8
贵 州	Guizhou	1048.7	187.6	150.2	122.8	534.8	831.7
云 南	Yunnan	1924.1	314.6	366.3	298.7	856.6	1561.7
西 藏	Tibet	196.4	7.4	7.4	3.2	18.1	34.1
陕 西	Shaanxi	2285.7	394.8	274.7	243.5	792.1	1115.2
甘 肃	Gansu	925.9	97.7	91.7	82.2	420.3	515.5
青 海	Qinghai	384.6	31.2	22.4	19.8	127.7	113.5
宁 夏	Ningxia	448.7	76.9	78.4	63.0	524.2	379.9
新 疆	Xinjiang	1415.1	120.4	156.7	130.0	595.6	849.9

附录1-5　地方财政一般预算收入与支出（2006年）
LOCAL GOVERNMENT BUDGETARY REVENUE AND EXPENDITURE (2006)

单位:亿元　　　　　　　　　　　　　　　　　　　　　　　(100 million yuan)

地　区	Region	地方一般预算收入 Local Government Budgetary Revenue	#增值税 Added Value Taxes	#企　业所得税 Enterprise Income Taxes	#个　人所得税 Individual Income Taxes	地方一般预算支出 Local Government Budgetary Expenditure	#基本建设 Capital Construction	#社会保障补助支出 Subsidy Expenditure for Social Security
地方总计	**National Total**	**18303.6**	**3196.4**	**2182.5**	**981.5**	**30431.3**	**2906.9**	**1882.7**
北　京	Beijing	1117.2	117.8	213.9	102.3	1296.8	99.3	37.4
天　津	Tianjin	417.0	80.7	53.5	21.2	543.1	83.3	51.6
河　北	Hebei	620.5	140.6	66.4	29.4	1180.4	69.0	82.9
山　西	Shanxi	583.4	118.8	52.7	15.7	915.6	54.7	68.0
内蒙古	Inner Mongolia	343.4	59.5	27.3	12.1	812.1	125.3	40.1
辽　宁	Liaoning	817.7	124.4	74.0	35.6	1422.7	137.3	202.4
吉　林	Jilin	245.2	43.0	17.9	11.7	718.4	59.1	81.8
黑龙江	Heilongjiang	386.8	103.2	23.8	16.0	968.5	55.6	134.9
上　海	Shanghai	1576.1	270.2	271.5	131.1	1795.6	395.6	100.7
江　苏	**Jiangsu**	**1656.7**	**329.4**	**220.9**	**81.7**	**2013.3**	**181.9**	**83.9**
浙　江	Zhejiang	1298.2	248.6	204.2	81.0	1471.9	100.1	36.2
安　徽	Anhui	428.0	69.2	41.1	14.0	940.2	97.6	65.1
福　建	Fujian	541.2	87.8	71.2	33.4	728.7	55.6	11.7
江　西	Jiangxi	305.5	41.2	24.7	12.4	696.4	48.9	48.6
山　东	Shandong	1356.3	242.8	148.3	45.8	1833.4	82.2	67.5
河　南	Henan	679.2	105.8	70.2	24.1	1440.1	119.2	82.8
湖　北	Hubei	476.1	77.8	47.6	19.6	1047.0	51.2	107.0
湖　南	Hunan	477.9	69.3	30.1	20.2	1064.5	72.7	102.6
广　东	Guangdong	2179.5	398.0	297.5	156.9	2553.3	272.7	49.2
广　西	Guangxi	342.6	46.9	23.5	14.7	729.5	62.2	32.0
海　南	Hainan	81.8	10.5	5.7	4.0	174.5	18.8	13.9
重　庆	Chongqing	317.7	38.7	17.2	12.2	594.3	74.7	52.8
四　川	Sichuan	607.6	84.7	54.4	26.8	1347.4	115.0	89.4
贵　州	Guizhou	226.8	38.2	21.4	11.0	610.6	41.9	27.6
云　南	Yunnan	380.0	67.5	41.3	14.5	893.6	86.1	34.2
西　藏	Tibet	14.6	1.5	0.9	0.4	200.2	58.6	5.0
陕　西	Shaanxi	362.5	73.1	34.1	13.3	824.2	72.3	69.8
甘　肃	Gansu	141.2	31.4	10.7	5.8	528.6	59.1	42.5
青　海	Qinghai	42.2	9.8	3.6	1.5	214.7	36.4	17.7
宁　夏	Ningxia	61.4	11.0	3.2	2.5	193.2	38.9	11.2
新　疆	Xinjiang	219.5	55.0	10.0	10.7	678.5	81.8	32.3

附录1－6 在岗职工平均工资（2006年）
AVERAGE WAGE OF STAFF AND WORKERS EMPLOYED（2006）

单位：元 （yuan）

地区	Region	在岗职工平均工资 Average Wage	#国有单位 State-owned Units	#城镇集体单位 Urban Collective-owned Units	#有限责任公司 Liability Co. Ltd.	#股份有限公司 Share-Holding Co. Ltd.	#港澳台商投资单位 Funded by Hong Kong Macao & Taiwan Invester	#外商投资单位 Foreign Invest-ments Units
全国	**National Total**	**21001**	**22112**	**13014**	**19509**	**25023**	**19045**	**24784**
北京	Beijing	40117	43298	17781	31375	59135	48587	58330
天津	Tianjin	28682	31240	19125	28061	38064	24000	26773
河北	Hebei	16590	17152	10337	17915	16341	17314	17341
山西	Shanxi	18300	18719	12162	20726	16318	14571	17669
内蒙古	Inner Mongolia	18469	19386	12469	17477	18259	14201	18937
辽宁	Liaoning	19624	20681	10888	19056	25312	18959	19556
吉林	Jilin	16583	17118	9787	15333	21004	13341	21875
黑龙江	Heilongjiang	16505	16374	9182	14116	24941	63747	18076
上海	Shanghai	41188	44097	25318	37987	48991	26558	42773
江苏	**Jiangsu**	**23782**	**28722**	**15550**	**20773**	**26071**	**17691**	**22233**
浙江	Zhejiang	27820	42962	22360	19968	27583	19216	20152
安徽	Anhui	17949	17755	11869	21200	21760	12990	18943
福建	Fujian	19318	23926	15695	16980	23306	15563	17085
江西	Jiangxi	15590	16491	10102	14805	17809	10925	13655
山东	Shandong	19228	22804	13132	15809	17854	15387	17346
河南	Henan	16981	17886	12483	17207	17613	17758	18016
湖北	Hubei	16048	18064	10416	14973	15265	12428	23280
湖南	Hunan	17850	18862	12883	16134	19232	15951	17400
广东	Guangdong	26186	31352	14520	28243	39601	18465	24973
广西	Guangxi	18064	18972	12428	16823	18053	12825	22328
海南	Hainan	15890	15398	9580	17453	27424	13582	19503
重庆	Chongqing	19215	21402	13522	15455	22307	16190	21487
四川	Sichuan	17852	20230	12726	13337	16778	16803	20596
贵州	Guizhou	16815	17638	12873	14422	19597	13172	15392
云南	Yunnan	18711	20017	12193	16639	20228	15005	19928
西藏	Tibet	31518	32355	11125	28311	19258		
陕西	Shaanxi	16918	17139	9086	18537	19352	14706	17410
甘肃	Gansu	17246	18108	11514	14116	22632	16712	20646
青海	Qinghai	22679	24984	11322	14232	21498	17113	11406
宁夏	Ningxia	21239	21370	19427	23003	16745	16390	21989
新疆	Xinjiang	17819	17704	14209	16777	25700	16830	17963

附录1－7 城镇居民家庭人均收支情况（2006年）
PER CAPITA INCOME AND EXPENDITURE OF URBAN HOUSEHOLD (2006)

单位：元 (yuan)

地区	Region	总收入 Total Income	#可支配收入 Disposable Income	总支出 Total Expenditure	消费性支出 Living Expenditure	非消费性支出 Non-Living Expenditure	恩格尔系数（%）Engle Coefficient (%)
全国	**National Total**	**12719**	**11759**	**11882**	**8697**	**3185**	**35.8**
北京	Beijing	22417	19978	20240	14825	5414	30.8
天津	Tianjin	15476	14283	15900	10548	5352	34.9
河北	Hebei	10887	10305	9973	7343	2629	33.9
山西	Shanxi	10794	10028	10206	7171	3035	31.4
内蒙古	Inner Mongolia	10812	10358	9884	7667	2217	30.3
辽宁	Liaoning	11230	10370	10911	7987	2923	38.8
吉林	Jilin	10245	9775	9535	7353	2183	33.4
黑龙江	Heilongjiang	9722	9182	8851	6655	2195	33.3
上海	Shanghai	22809	20668	21109	14762	6347	35.6
江苏	**Jiangsu**	**15249**	**14084**	**13793**	**9629**	**4164**	**36.0**
浙江	Zhejiang	19954	18265	18984	13349	5636	32.9
安徽	Anhui	10575	9771	10450	7295	3155	42.4
福建	Fujian	15102	13753	14319	9808	4512	39.3
江西	Jiangxi	10015	9551	8719	6646	2074	39.7
山东	Shandong	13223	12192	11717	8468	3249	32.0
河南	Henan	10339	9810	8722	6685	2037	33.1
湖北	Hubei	10533	9803	9840	7397	2442	38.8
湖南	Hunan	11146	10505	11123	8169	2954	34.9
广东	Guangdong	17726	16016	16676	12432	4243	36.2
广西	Guangxi	10624	9899	9278	6792	2486	42.1
海南	Hainan	10082	9395	9066	7127	1939	43.5
重庆	Chongqing	12549	11570	12157	9399	2758	36.3
四川	Sichuan	10117	9350	10064	7525	2539	37.7
贵州	Guizhou	9439	9117	8655	6848	1806	38.7
云南	Yunnan	10848	10070	9839	7380	2460	42.0
西藏	Tibet	9541	8941	7741	6193	1549	50.2
陕西	Shaanxi	9938	9268	10022	7553	2469	34.3
甘肃	Gansu	9586	8921	9205	6974	2231	34.5
青海	Qinghai	9803	9000	8788	6530	2258	36.2
宁夏	Ningxia	10002	9177	10582	7206	3377	33.9
新疆	Xinjiang	9689	8871	8584	6730	1854	35.5

附录 1-8 农村居民家庭人均收支情况（2006 年）
PER CAPITA INCOME AND EXPENDITURE OF RURAL HOUSEHOLD (2006)

单位:元 (yuan)

地区	Region	总收入 Total Income	#纯收入 Net Income	#现金收入 Cash Income	总支出 Total Expenditure	#生活消费支出 Living Expenditure	#现金支出 Cash Expenditure	恩格尔系数(%) Engle Coefficient (%)
全国总计	**National Total**	**5025**	**3587**	**4302**	**4485**	**2829**	**3932**	**43.0**
北京	Beijing	9821	8275	9644	7626	5725	7555	32.8
天津	Tianjin	8586	6228	8106	5812	3341	5698	36.3
河北	Hebei	5427	3802	4729	4251	2495	3913	36.7
山西	Shanxi	3993	3181	3420	3231	2253	2958	38.5
内蒙古	Inner Mongolia	5803	3342	4674	5491	2772	4657	39.0
辽宁	Liaoning	6521	4090	5784	5959	3067	5447	37.9
吉林	Jilin	5734	3641	4713	5210	2701	4755	40.1
黑龙江	Heilongjiang	6239	3552	5578	6070	2618	5634	35.3
上海	Shanghai	9818	9139	9593	9344	8006	9137	37.8
江苏	**Jiangsu**	**7267**	**5813**	**6544**	**5934**	**4135**	**5397**	**41.8**
浙江	Zhejiang	9454	7335	9093	8790	6057	8524	36.6
安徽	Anhui	4130	2969	3530	3763	2421	3325	43.2
福建	Fujian	5982	4835	5472	4910	3591	4509	45.2
江西	Jiangxi	4556	3460	3808	3976	2677	3351	49.0
山东	Shandong	6189	4368	5636	5090	3144	4712	37.9
河南	Henan	4459	3261	3537	3638	2229	3211	40.9
湖北	Hubei	4581	3419	3793	3999	2732	3267	46.8
湖南	Hunan	4737	3390	3930	4503	3013	3766	48.6
广东	Guangdong	6293	5080	5727	5205	3886	4693	48.6
广西	Guangxi	3996	2770	3253	3741	2414	3121	49.5
海南	Hainan	4507	3256	3913	3495	2232	2953	53.4
重庆	Chongqing	3814	2874	2835	3294	2205	2407	52.2
四川	Sichuan	4343	3002	3367	3883	2395	2942	50.8
贵州	Guizhou	2799	1985	2097	2629	1627	1949	51.5
云南	Yunnan	3594	2250	2665	3687	2196	2764	48.8
西藏	Tibet	3158	2435	2229	2714	2002	1928	48.2
陕西	Shaanxi	3338	2260	2833	3486	2181	3119	39.0
甘肃	Gansu	3106	2134	2402	2957	1855	2327	46.7
青海	Qinghai	3208	2358	2593	3171	2179	2495	43.1
宁夏	Ningxia	4565	2760	3729	4359	2247	3644	41.4
新疆	Xinjiang	5166	2737	4465	4758	2032	4318	39.9

注:本表现金收支不含储蓄借贷。

Note:In This table, the cash income and expenditure excluded saving deposits and loans.

附录1-9 农林牧渔业总产值和增速(2006年)

GROSS OUTPUT VALUE AND GROWTH RATE OF FARMING, FORESTRY, ANIMAL HUSBANDRY AND FISHERY (2006)

地区	Region	农林牧渔业总产值(亿元)	Gross Output Value of Farming, Forestry, Animal Husbandry and Fishery (100 million yuan) #农业 Farming	#林业 Forestry	#畜牧业 Animal Husbandry	#渔业 Fishery	农林牧渔业总产值比上年增长(%) Grouth Rate of Gross Output Value of Farming, Forestry, Animal Husbandry and Fishery Over 2005(%)
全国	**National Total**	**42424.4**	**21549.1**	**1602.0**	**13640.2**	**4433.0**	**5.4**
北京	Beijing	270.0	109.3	14.8	123.6	9.8	1.2
天津	Tianjin	271.0	105.4	2.0	104.2	38.7	3.5
河北	Hebei	2771.8	1394.7	44.3	1136.8	86.9	5.5
山西	Shanxi	512.4	304.0	15.3	150.4	3.5	5.7
内蒙古	Inner Mongolia	1085.9	532.4	41.8	487.3	8.3	6.8
辽宁	Liaoning	1841.3	715.1	52.3	654.6	366.4	7.0
吉林	Jilin	1155.5	597.0	44.3	483.5	17.0	7.5
黑龙江	Heilongjiang	1387.7	787.4	68.0	480.7	30.1	6.4
上海	Shanghai	237.0	120.0	10.4	46.3	55.3	0.7
江苏	**Jiangsu**	**2707.1**	**1389.6**	**54.2**	**571.4**	**552.2**	**4.9**
浙江	Zhejiang	1514.6	712.5	86.0	287.3	403.5	3.5
安徽	Anhui	1779.9	905.6	88.4	540.4	191.1	6.5
福建	Fujian	1496.4	628.7	105.8	279.7	463.4	3.0
江西	Jiangxi	1228.3	556.9	104.6	368.2	178.7	6.1
山东	Shandong	4056.6	2221.4	65.5	1160.4	537.7	5.2
河南	Henan	3589.7	1996.2	94.9	1299.1	44.0	7.4
湖北	Hubei	1871.0	1018.8	40.5	523.8	259.8	4.9
湖南	Hunan	2131.9	1023.5	112.5	808.3	150.5	4.9
广东	Guangdong	2678.3	1261.1	67.6	656.8	570.4	4.0
广西	Guangxi	1648.1	829.4	79.7	564.5	153.6	7.3
海南	Hainan	543.9	214.6	70.5	99.3	148.3	9.4
重庆	Chongqing	637.2	341.0	22.3	240.3	21.9	-3.9
四川	Sichuan	2602.1	1075.1	76.7	1317.4	87.2	3.7
贵州	Guizhou	610.6	354.6	25.8	207.6	12.4	4.8
云南	Yunnan	1209.8	630.2	142.6	362.9	26.3	8.4
西藏	Tibet	70.0	31.8	2.8	33.0	0.2	0.8
陕西	Shaanxi	818.7	531.6	28.9	221.9	5.6	7.3
甘肃	Gansu	561.4	395.4	15.0	135.6	1.2	4.6
青海	Qinghai	100.6	38.1	2.0	56.3	0.1	3.7
宁夏	Ningxia	152.2	89.2	5.0	49.4	4.4	6.8
新疆	Xinjiang	883.5	638.6	17.2	189.1	4.7	7.5

注:本表绝对数按当年价格计算,增速按可比价格计算。

Note: In This Table the absolute value is counted with current price, while the growth rate is counted with comparable price.

附录1－10 主要农产品产量（2006年）
OUTPUT OF MAJOR AGRICULTURAL PRODUCTS (2006)

单位：万吨 (10000 tons)

地区	Region	粮食 Grain	油料 Oil-Bearing Crops	棉花 Cotton	肉类 The Output of Meat	#猪牛羊肉 The Output of Pork, Beef and Mutton	水果 Fruit
全国	**National Total**	**49747.9**	**3059.4**	**674.6**	**8051.4**	**6416.8**	**17261.2**
北京	Beijing	109.2	2.2	0.2	59.2	35.8	114.8
天津	Tianjin	143.5	1.2	10.9	59.5	46.2	67.0
河北	Hebei	2702.8	150.3	62.8	595.5	477.6	1453.1
山西	Shanxi	1073.3	19.2	11.8	72.5	65.9	353.7
内蒙古	Inner Mongolia	1704.9	116.8	0.2	255.1	214.8	220.5
辽宁	Liaoning	1725.0	38.1	0.2	359.8	247.6	478.4
吉林	Jilin	2720.0	58.4	0.3	268.3	171.6	223.8
黑龙江	Heilongjiang	3346.4	63.1		177.8	146.0	413.8
上海	Shanghai	111.3	5.3	0.2	28.6	16.9	108.3
江苏	**Jiangsu**	**3041.4**	**218.2**	**38.1**	**351.4**	**242.1**	**628.5**
浙江	Zhejiang	884.0	47.4	2.4	170.0	134.8	650.0
安徽	Anhui	2860.7	261.6	40.8	353.8	278.7	733.6
福建	Fujian	701.5	26.9		168.3	141.2	570.8
江西	Jiangxi	1854.5	78.0	9.5	249.1	197.8	356.9
山东	Shandong	4048.8	358.2	102.3	766.1	498.4	2513.4
河南	Henan	5010.0	480.0	83.0	736.5	630.7	2005.6
湖北	Hubei	2210.1	279.8	44.9	326.9	276.6	625.2
湖南	Hunan	2706.2	149.4	24.8	539.7	481.2	607.5
广东	Guangdong	1387.6	77.6		392.8	267.6	1001.1
广西	Guangxi	1463.2	64.2	0.1	266.4	219.9	812.0
海南	Hainan	185.6	9.0		62.1	44.6	247.2
重庆	Chongqing	910.5	40.3		177.1	152.5	145.7
四川	Sichuan	2893.4	217.3	1.6	690.8	591.9	535.3
贵州	Guizhou	1122.8	89.5	0.1	175.0	160.6	109.2
云南	Yunnan	1542.2	39.0		322.0	296.1	201.9
西藏	Tibet	92.4	5.5		22.7	22.7	0.9
陕西	Shaanxi	1087.0	44.4	8.7	104.1	90.6	1053.2
甘肃	Gansu	808.1	49.0	12.8	89.3	82.6	332.8
青海	Qinghai	88.3	26.5		27.2	26.4	2.4
宁夏	Ningxia	310.9	10.4		26.7	23.9	114.2
新疆	Xinjiang	902.2	32.8	218.9	157.0	133.8	580.4

附录 1－11 规模以上工业企业主要经济指标（2006 年）

MAJOR ECONOMIC INDICATORS OF ABOVE DESIGNATED SIZE INDUSTRIAL ENTERPRISES (2006)

单位:亿元　　(100 million yuan)

地区	Region	资产合计 Total Assets	负债合计 Liabilities	主营业务收入 Major Business Revenue	#主营业务税金及附加 Major Business Tax and Extra	税金总额 Total Taxes	利润总额 Total Profits
全国	**National Total**	**285941.1**	**165181.7**	**308424.2**	**3658.2**	**13652.7**	**18783.6**
北京	Beijing	13797.6	5375.2	8649.6	62.9	289.2	407.9
天津	Tianjin	7307.9	4259.7	8782.7	99.0	313.9	690.9
河北	Hebei	11133.3	6831.6	13011.6	112.9	577.3	888.1
山西	Shanxi	8621.6	5824.5	5684.5	70.0	440.1	367.1
内蒙古	Inner Mongolia	5438.7	3309.2	4080.4	53.7	255.5	332.5
辽宁	Liaoning	13920.4	8066.6	13756.4	159.3	560.9	434.3
吉林	Jilin	5045.7	2919.1	4309.3	89.2	244.3	201.0
黑龙江	Heilongjiang	5526.6	3143.4	5685.9	89.9	457.3	1275.9
上海	Shanghai	17609.4	8812.4	19030.9	190.9	679.9	1086.7
江苏	**Jiangsu**	**30501.0**	**18477.9**	**41015.3**	**242.5**	**1261.5**	**1906.9**
浙江	Zhejiang	23491.7	14127.4	27125.4	212.3	946.1	1324.6
安徽	Anhui	6299.4	3919.4	5813.7	104.1	321.0	230.9
福建	Fujian	7959.0	4291.5	9288.5	93.1	319.0	446.6
江西	Jiangxi	3495.6	2195.1	4054.2	61.5	219.9	198.1
山东	Shandong	26251.5	15171.3	38430.5	395.4	1649.6	2634.0
河南	Henan	10910.4	6584.6	13711.3	206.7	767.3	1145.3
湖北	Hubei	9826.8	5409.3	7198.9	170.5	453.6	408.9
湖南	Hunan	5356.8	3248.7	5742.5	194.4	425.2	264.8
广东	Guangdong	33635.1	19332.0	42427.4	273.2	1236.3	1958.3
广西	Guangxi	3510.5	2146.6	3119.6	47.8	191.7	188.1
海南	Hainan	923.0	561.6	573.4	11.7	34.9	41.5
重庆	Chongqing	3646.4	2139.3	3177.4	48.9	162.0	154.7
四川	Sichuan	9033.8	5624.7	7674.3	110.3	400.9	430.7
贵州	Guizhou	3012.9	1982.0	1886.6	70.9	178.8	117.4
云南	Yunnan	4646.7	2606.6	3278.0	279.2	486.0	300.2
西藏	Tibet	109.7	28.7	27.6	0.5	3.3	3.9
陕西	Shaanxi	5976.4	3580.2	4259.8	86.4	317.1	513.6
甘肃	Gansu	3086.8	1755.7	2440.2	50.8	155.1	107.4
青海	Qinghai	1385.4	923.0	633.8	8.9	49.0	120.3
宁夏	Ningxia	1286.6	773.1	827.0	8.8	42.3	25.3
新疆	Xinjiang	3257.4	1766.9	2712.8	54.8	220.1	583.0

附录1－12　规模以上工业企业主要经济效益指标（2006年）

MAJOR INDICATORS ON ECONOMIC BENEFIT OF ABOVE DESIGNATED SIZE INDUSTRIAL ENTERPRISES (2006)

地区	Region	总资产贡献率(%) Rate of Total Funds Contribution (%)	资本保值增值率(%) Rate Between Value-Added and Assets (%)	资产负债率(%) Rate of Capital Liabilities (%)	流动资产周转次数(次) Turnover of Circulating Funds (times)	成本费用利润率(%) Rate Between Cost and Profit (%)	产品销售率(%) Rate of Product Sales (%)
全　国	**National Total**	**13.5**	**116.5**	**57.8**	**2.5**	**6.6**	**98.1**
北　京	Beijing	5.8	105.8	39.0	2.0	4.9	98.7
天　津	Tianjin	15.5	115.3	58.3	2.4	8.6	99.2
河　北	Hebei	15.6	120.6	61.4	2.8	7.4	98.2
山　西	Shanxi	11.8	126.5	67.6	1.8	7.0	97.7
内蒙古	Inner Mongolia	13.9	124.2	60.9	2.4	9.2	97.7
辽　宁	Liaoning	8.7	120.0	58.0	2.2	3.3	98.1
吉　林	Jilin	10.5	113.4	57.9	2.3	5.1	96.3
黑龙江	Heilongjiang	32.7	112.2	56.9	2.4	29.6	98.2
上　海	Shanghai	11.4	109.6	50.0	2.2	6.1	99.1
江　苏	**Jiangsu**	**12.4**	**118.7**	**60.6**	**2.7**	**4.9**	**98.5**
浙　江	Zhejiang	12.1	117.6	60.1	2.2	5.1	97.9
安　徽	Anhui	10.6	118.2	62.2	2.4	4.2	98.4
福　建	Fujian	11.7	115.8	53.9	2.4	5.1	96.9
江　西	Jiangxi	14.6	117.4	62.8	2.8	5.3	98.5
山　东	Shandong	19.3	122.1	57.8	3.4	7.4	98.5
河　南	Henan	21.0	122.7	60.4	3.1	9.3	98.5
湖　北	Hubei	10.4	115.2	55.1	2.1	6.1	98.0
湖　南	Hunan	15.3	116.5	60.7	2.9	5.1	99.7
广　东	Guangdong	11.4	113.3	57.5	2.5	4.9	97.3
广　西	Guangxi	13.1	118.5	61.2	2.3	6.5	96.3
海　南	Hainan	10.6	129.8	60.9	1.8	8.0	96.8
重　庆	Chongqing	10.6	121.0	58.7	2.0	5.2	98.4
四　川	Sichuan	11.3	114.4	62.3	2.1	6.1	97.9
贵　州	Guizhou	11.9	114.6	65.8	1.8	7.0	96.6
云　南	Yunnan	19.7	112.4	56.1	1.6	10.9	98.0
西　藏	Tibet	7.3	107.0	26.1	0.9	15.8	92.0
陕　西	Shaanxi	16.3	130.6	59.9	1.8	14.1	98.1
甘　肃	Gansu	10.1	117.3	56.9	2.2	4.8	97.8
青　海	Qinghai	15.3	130.8	66.6	1.6	23.8	96.4
宁　夏	Ningxia	7.2	125.1	60.1	1.7	3.2	97.0
新　疆	Xinjiang	27.5	115.7	54.2	2.7	29.0	98.8

附录1-13　主要工业产品产量（2006年）
OUTPUT OF MAJOR INDUSTRIAL PRODUCTS (2006)

地区 Region		原煤（万吨）Coal (10000 tons)	发电量（亿千瓦小时）Electricity (100 million kWh)	粗钢（万吨）Rough Steel (10000 tons)	钢材（万吨）Steel Products (10000 tons)	水泥（万吨）Cement (10000 tons)	农用化肥（万吨）Chemical Fertilizers (10000 tons)	汽车（万辆）Truck (10000 units)	布（亿米）Cloth (100 million meter)
全国	**National Total**	**238174**	**28344**	**42266**	**47340**	**123500**	**5592.8**	**727.9**	**550.0**
北京	Beijing	658.4	198.7	817.0	1042.6	1226.6	4.6	68.4	0.1
天津	Tianjin	0.0	359.2	1285.3	2082.9	607.3	16.3	41.2	2.8
河北	Hebei	8364.7	1451.7	9096.3	8467.1	8492.7	210.5	26.8	28.2
山西	Shanxi	58141.9	1467.4	1938.5	1663.3	2171.0	313.6	0.0	2.5
内蒙古	Inner Mongolia	30802.3	1416.4	861.1	808.5	2061.3	76.1	0.9	1.4
辽宁	Liaoning	7367.3	1013.4	3798.4	3986.9	3208.2	75.9	29.1	5.0
吉林	Jilin	2932.2	441.8	533.6	579.2	2525.0	18.7	63.3	0.8
黑龙江	Heilongjiang	10282.4	632.0	315.2	293.7	1456.3	51.1	24.4	1.2
上海	Shanghai	0.0	711.0	1902.8	2129.8	818.3	3.0	68.2	1.0
江苏	**Jiangsu**	**3047.5**	**2216.4**	**4202.3**	**5816.3**	**10880.8**	**254.7**	**27.5**	**65.0**
浙江	Zhejiang	18.3	1661.6	457.8	1143.6	9947.1	55.5	17.8	97.5
安徽	Anhui	8331.9	728.7	1293.8	1317.1	4405.5	210.1	49.0	6.0
福建	Fujian	1932.8	904.3	465.5	842.6	3343.9	64.8	7.3	19.5
江西	Jiangxi	2783.4	403.5	1163.0	1235.8	4206.3	55.8	23.4	3.4
山东	Shandong	14069.5	2314.4	3714.9	4088.4	16575.9	798.6	27.2	104.3
河南	Henan	19532.2	1590.3	1740.8	1773.0	7413.6	440.9	5.5	18.8
湖北	Hubei	1115.6	1296.4	1658.0	1689.7	5108.7	459.6	54.7	25.5
湖南	Hunan	5847.9	701.2	1191.8	1151.4	4375.5	259.2	3.7	5.0
广东	Guangdong	0.0	2358.4	902.7	1786.6	8851.1	29.4	55.5	28.5
广西	Guangxi	680.5	475.4	622.1	697.5	3545.0	94.5	51.8	0.5
海南	Hainan	0.0	94.9	0.2	14.2	577.5	64.3	8.4	0.0
重庆	Chongqing	4059.2	275.4	321.9	382.9	2533.8	127.7	52.1	3.5
四川	Sichuan	8600.0	1063.0	1225.9	1316.4	4900.2	372.4	7.0	7.8
贵州	Guizhou	11816.6	974.7	332.5	256.6	1799.4	338.8	0.1	0.5
云南	Yunnan	7339.1	692.0	634.6	578.0	3179.1	301.7	3.8	0.1
西藏	Tibet	0.0	15.2	0.0	0.0	166.7	0.0	0.0	0.0
陕西	Shaanxi	18407.6	577.3	388.6	499.8	2375.4	107.8	10.8	7.8
甘肃	Gansu	3822.8	526.3	545.3	534.8	1387.4	85.3	0.0	0.1
青海	Qinghai	628.3	277.2	79.6	76.7	371.3	205.1	0.0	0.0
宁夏	Ningxia	3273.0	388.4	0.0	21.8	699.1	77.9	0.0	0.0
新疆	Xinjiang	4318.5	331.1	388.7	408.7	1201.7	130.7	0.1	1.0

附录1－14　全社会客货运量及货物周转量（2006年）
PASSENGER AND FREIGHT TRAFFIC AND TURNOVER VOLUME OF FREIGHT TRAFFIC（2006）

地　区	Region	客运量（万人）Total Passenger Traffic（10000 persons）	#铁　路 Railway	#公　路 Highway	货运量（万吨）Total Freight Traffic（10000 tons）	#铁　路 Railway	#公　路 Highway	货物周转量（亿吨公里）Turnover Volume of Freight Traffic（100 million tons-km）	#铁　路 Railway
全　国	**National Total**	**2024158**	**125656**	**1860487**	**2037050**	**288285**	**1466347**	**88835**	**21954**
北　京	Beijing	8751	6269	2482	33008	2055	30953	653	565
天　津	Tianjin	5443	1632	3807	41939	8410	20290	12241	453
河　北	Hebei	83955	6024	77931	90830	14789	73263	5557	2756
山　西	Shanxi	42240	3760	38416	144021	65449	78513	1734	1331
内蒙古	Inner Mongolia	35307	3490	31817	80383	21405	58978	1714	1329
辽　宁	Liaoning	63942	9911	53317	105966	16306	82142	4044	1208
吉　林	Jilin	28903	4590	24198	35224	6170	28965	612	505
黑龙江	Heilongjiang	60200	8924	51023	65846	16068	48389	1211	937
上　海	Shanghai	8505	4458	2784	72381	1234	33799	13830	55
江　苏	**Jiangsu**	**161425**	**7292**	**153825**	**125114**	**5169**	**84319**	**3645**	**497**
浙　江	Zhejiang	175090	6857	165441	140892	4028	89342	4364	301
安　徽	Anhui	78938	4000	74668	74141	11095	54717	1703	913
福　建	Fujian	58883	2022	55713	44856	4209	29806	1900	199
江　西	Jiangxi	42996	4172	38454	37517	6090	27477	952	642
山　东	Shandong	109470	4755	103298	164131	15746	136750	6387	1244
河　南	Henan	107915	6465	101345	86559	15145	69898	2438	1834
湖　北	Hubei	73930	3889	69335	49304	5701	35361	1489	785
湖　南	Hunan	118466	5758	112135	85602	6251	72457	1743	914
广　东	Guangdong	186996	9356	175567	132389	7425	97461	4045	337
广　西	Guangxi	55705	2073	52609	42994	6920	30525	1221	728
海　南	Hainan	31571	23	30044	14161	693	7981	657	6
重　庆	Chongqing	61128	1528	58179	43009	2204	36254	825	119
四　川	Sichuan	194712	5776	184852	75071	8185	63719	969	613
贵　州	Guizhou	69270	2536	65786	24709	6826	17284	681	558
云　南	Yunnan	43387	1982	40861	66192	5331	60614	694	281
西　藏	Tibet	483	38	445	348	2	346	38	2
陕　西	Shaanxi	43331	4370	38606	44216	8288	35811	1082	853
甘　肃	Gansu	19083	1519	17319	28502	4624	23826	1043	896
青　海	Qinghai	5243	353	4861	7271	1407	5864	144	93
宁　夏	Ningxia	7548	357	7191	9358	3329	6029	278	206
新　疆	Xinjiang	25504	1226	24278	31163	5949	25214	893	561

附录1－15　社会消费品零售总额（2006年）
TOTAL RETAIL SALE OF CONSUMER GOODS (2006)

单位：亿元　　　　(100 million yuan)

地区	Region	社会消费品零售总额 Total Ratail Sales of Consumer Goods	市 City	县 County	县以下 County Below	批发和零售业 Wholesale and Retail Sale Trade	住宿和餐饮业 Catering	其他行业 Others
全　国	**National Total**	**76410.0**	**51542.6**	**8477.9**	**16389.5**	**64325.5**	**10345.5**	**1739.0**
北　京	Beijing	3275.2	2831.4	26.2	417.7	2865.6	362.4	47.3
天　津	Tianjin	1356.8	1275.4	44.3	37.1	1143.0	210.0	3.8
河　北	Hebei	3397.4	1612.1	680.1	1105.2	2913.1	419.4	64.9
山　西	Shanxi	1613.4	1038.6	307.8	267.1	1358.2	191.3	63.9
内蒙古	Inner Mongolia	1595.3	1080.6	326.3	188.4	1263.8	284.3	47.2
辽　宁	Liaoning	3434.6	2872.5	163.9	398.2	2870.3	513.0	51.4
吉　林	Jilin	1675.8	1304.1	127.5	244.3	1440.1	230.1	5.7
黑龙江	Heilongjiang	1997.7	1524.7	237.8	235.2	1718.6	241.2	37.9
上　海	Shanghai	3360.4	2938.7	23.9	397.8	2896.3	452.2	12.0
江　苏	**Jiangsu**	**6623.2**	**4822.9**	**413.5**	**1386.8**	**5815.8**	**746.5**	**60.9**
浙　江	Zhejiang	5325.3	3519.0	519.4	1286.9	4658.8	609.9	56.7
安　徽	Anhui	2029.4	1106.2	406.3	516.9	1719.5	283.8	26.1
福　建	Fujian	2704.2	1743.2	306.2	654.8	2324.3	329.7	50.2
江　西	Jiangxi	1428.0	748.9	312.6	366.5	1262.7	149.1	16.2
山　东	Shandong	7122.5	4534.0	788.4	1800.2	6000.1	887.2	235.3
河　南	Henan	3880.5	2119.9	753.6	1007.0	3221.6	588.7	70.2
湖　北	Hubei	3412.0	2395.6	321.0	695.4	2783.2	455.7	173.1
湖　南	Hunan	2834.2	1630.3	480.3	723.5	2386.6	404.3	43.3
广　东	Guangdong	9118.1	6472.5	383.3	2262.3	7642.3	1321.1	154.6
广　西	Guangxi	1600.8	943.8	280.1	376.9	1380.2	192.3	28.4
海　南	Hainan	308.3	221.1	22.5	64.7	241.1	55.3	11.8
重　庆	Chongqing	1403.6	833.8	187.2	382.5	1196.4	194.3	12.9
四　川	Sichuan	3421.6	1651.3	604.4	1166.0	2676.9	625.5	119.2
贵　州	Guizhou	689.8	411.5	130.7	147.6	601.7	76.1	12.0
云　南	Yunnan	1188.9	651.1	275.4	262.4	949.8	178.7	60.4
西　藏	Tibet	89.7	43.8	35.6	10.3	71.6	15.8	2.3
陕　西	Shaanxi	1522.0	992.8	272.2	257.0	1326.7	165.5	29.8
甘　肃	Gansu	717.5	462.5	114.5	140.5	579.0	116.0	22.4
青　海	Qinghai	180.1	122.8	37.7	19.6	146.0	30.3	3.9
宁　夏	Ningxia	199.0	148.4	25.5	25.1	162.9	32.8	3.3
新　疆	Xinjiang	727.6	509.2	106.9	111.5	577.8	110.7	39.1

附录 1 - 16 对外经济贸易及旅游（2006 年）
FOREIGN ECONOMY, TRADE AND TOURISM (2006)

单位：亿美元 (USD 100 million)

地 区	Region	进出口总额 Total Value of Imports and Exports Through Customs	出口 Exports	进口 Imports	国际旅游人数（万人次）Total Number of International Tourists (10000 person-times)	#外国人 Foreigners	旅游外汇收入 Earnings from International Tourism
全 国	**National Total**	**17606.9**	**9690.7**	**7916.1**	**12494.2**	**2221.0**	**339.5**
北 京	Beijing	1581.7	379.8	1201.9	390.3	338.3	40.3
天 津	Tianjin	644.8	335.0	309.8	88.1	81.2	6.3
河 北	Hebei	185.3	128.4	56.9	72.5	65.4	2.4
山 西	Shanxi	66.3	41.4	24.9	57.4	33.0	1.6
内蒙古	Inner Mongolia	59.6	21.4	38.2	123.2	122.3	4.0
辽 宁	Liaoning	483.9	283.2	200.7	161.3	137.3	9.3
吉 林	Jilin	79.1	30.0	49.2	43.5	35.4	1.4
黑龙江	Heilongjiang	128.6	84.4	44.2	106.4	99.5	4.9
上 海	Shanghai	2275.3	1135.9	1139.4	464.6	399.8	39.0
江 苏	**Jiangsu**	**2840.0**	**1604.2**	**1235.8**	**445.2**	**314.9**	**27.9**
浙 江	Zhejiang	1391.5	1009.0	382.5	426.8	281.4	21.3
安 徽	Anhui	122.6	68.4	54.2	80.4	52.6	2.3
福 建	Fujian	626.6	412.6	214.0	229.7	79.0	14.7
江 西	Jiangxi	61.9	37.5	24.4	49.7	18.4	1.4
山 东	Shandong	952.1	586.0	366.1	193.1	156.0	10.1
河 南	Henan	98.6	67.0	31.6	75.7	45.4	2.7
湖 北	Hubei	117.6	62.6	55.0	105.6	85.7	3.2
湖 南	Hunan	73.5	50.9	22.6	97.1	73.1	5.0
广 东	Guangdong	5272.2	3019.5	2252.6	2089.7	534.7	75.3
广 西	Guangxi	66.7	35.9	30.7	170.8	104.7	4.2
海 南	Hainan	28.5	13.8	14.7	61.7	46.6	2.3
重 庆	Chongqing	54.7	33.5	21.2	60.3	48.8	3.1
四 川	Sichuan	79.0	47.0	32.0	106.3	68.3	3.2
贵 州	Guizhou	16.2	10.4	5.8	32.1	10.7	1.2
云 南	Yunnan	62.3	33.9	28.4	181.0	111.2	6.6
西 藏	Tibet	3.3	2.2	1.1	15.5	13.6	0.6
陕 西	Shaanxi	53.6	36.3	17.3	106.1	83.2	5.1
甘 肃	Gansu	38.2	15.1	23.1	30.3	18.5	0.6
青 海	Qinghai	6.5	5.3	1.2	4.2	2.8	0.1
宁 夏	Ningxia	14.4	9.4	4.9	0.9	0.8	0.0
新 疆	Xinjiang	91.0	71.4	19.6	36.2	31.3	1.3

附录二

APPENDIX II

统计公报

STATISTICAL COMMUNIQUE

2006年全省及省辖市全面建设小康社会进程统计监测报告

2006年是“十一五”发展的开局之年。全省人民在省委、省政府领导下，紧紧围绕富民强省、“两个率先”目标，全面贯彻落实科学发展观和构建社会主义和谐社会的重大战略思想，坚持又好又快地推进“两个率先”，统筹发展改革稳定的各项工作，经济社会发展取得显著成绩，全面小康社会建设跃上新台阶。现根据《江苏省全面建设小康社会主要指标》，对2006年全省及各省辖市全面建设小康社会时序进度进行监测评价的结果报告如下。

一、江苏全面小康达标和时序进度完成情况

从监测结果看，2006年全省各地全面小康社会建设进程进一步加快，达标指标增加，时序进度完成情况良好，综合实现程度持续提升，全面小康建设取得重要成果。

(一)2006年全省已有18个指标达标

对照全面小康四大类18项25个指标目标值，2006年已有18个指标达标，比2005年增加6个。这表明，全省全面建设小康社会步伐呈明显加快之势。2006年达标的18个指标中，除2005年已达标的人均地区生产总值等12个指标继续达标外，新增农村人均钢筋砖木结构住房面积、恩格尔系数、R&D经费支出占GDP比重、卫生服务体系健全率、城市绿化覆盖率、环境质量综合指数等6个指标达到了目标值的要求。尚未达标的7个指标分别是：城市化水平、城镇居民人均可支配收入、农村居民人均纯收入、百户家庭电脑拥有量、居民文教娱乐服务支出占家庭消费支出比重、高中阶段教育毛入学率、森林覆盖率。

(二)2006年有23个指标达到时序进度

根据主要指标时序进度的测算方法，2003—2006年各指标完成时序进度情况是：2003年有19个，2004年19个，2005年增加到23个，2006年保持在23个。2006年未达到时序进度要求的2个指标是：农村居民人均纯收入(与时序进度仅相差8元)、居民文教娱乐服务支出占家庭消费支出比重(相差0.7个百分点)。其中农村居民人均纯收入虽已连续4年未达到时序进度，但与时序进度差距在逐年缩小，2003年相差258元，2004、2005、2006年差距分别缩小到22元、19元、8元，接近达到时序进度要求。

二、各省辖市完成时序进度和达标的具体情况

按省定实现时间及各市自定实现时间对各省辖市监测的结果显示，2006年各省辖市全面建设小康社会进展顺利，主要指标完成全面小康时序进度较好，达到目标值的指标个数明显增加，其中常州市总体上达到了全面小康指标，已达标的苏州、无锡市全面小康水平进一步提高。

(一)时序进度进展情况良好

1. 各市省定和自定实现目标时间。因苏南、苏中、苏北三大区域的发展基础不同，根据分类指导的原则，省委对三大区域实现全面小康提出了不同的时序进度，即省定时间是：苏南、苏中、苏北分别于2007年前、2012年前和2017年前总体上全面建成小康社会，宿迁市为2019年前。

省委十届五次全会后，各省辖市根据本地的具体情况提出了自定的实现目标时间。其中，与省定实现时间一致的有3个市，分别是：南京、镇江于2007年前，连云港于2017年前。其余10个市均比省定时间提前，分别是：苏南的苏州、无锡于2005年，常州于2006年；苏中的南通于2009年，扬州、泰州于2010年；苏北的徐州、盐城在2006年市党代会上将自定时间分别从原定的2014年、2013年提前到2011年，淮安于2016年，宿迁于2017年。

2. 各市完成时序进度情况。按省定实现全面小康时间，各省辖市全面小康指标中均有21个及以上指标达到时序进度要求，比2005年增加3个市。13个市的情况分别是：南京(24个)、无锡(23个)、徐州(23个)、常州(23个)、苏州(23个)、南通(22个)、连云港(23个)、淮安(23个)、盐城(21个)、扬州(25个)、镇江(22个)、泰州(24个)、宿迁(22个)。其中扬州25个指标全部达到时序进度要求，比2005年增加3个指标；镇江、泰州、宿迁3个市达到时序进度要求的指标个数分别比2005年增加3个、5个和3个，而上年达到时序进度要求的指标尚不足20个。

按各市自定实现全面小康时间，除苏州、无锡已于2005年全面达到了江苏省全面建设小康社会指标外，另有7个市按自定时间完成进度指标达到22个及以上，比2005年增加4个市。7个市的情况分别是：南京(24个)、常州(23个)、连云港(23个)、淮安(23个)、扬州(23个)、镇江(22个)、泰州(23个)。其他4个市完成时序进度指标在20个及以下，其中徐州为19个、南通18个、盐城15个、宿迁20个。其中有4个市达到时序进度要求的指标个数比上年增加3个及以上，分别是常州增加

4 个、扬州增加 3 个、镇江增加 3 个、泰州增加 5 个。

（二）各市达到目标值的指标均有增加

对照全面小康 25 个指标目标值，2006 年各省辖市中达标指标超过 20 个的有 4 个市，比 2005 年增加 2 个，分别是南京 21 个、无锡、常州、苏州各 23 个。达标指标在 10—20 个的有 5 个市，分别是徐州 10 个、南通 15 个、扬州 13 个、镇江 17 个、泰州 14 个。达标指标不足 10 个的 4 个市分别是连云港、淮安、宿迁、盐城，各有 9 个指标达到目标值。有 5 个市达标指标个数比上年增加 3 个及以上，分别是徐州、盐城、泰州增加 3 个、常州增加 7 个、扬州增加 4 个。

2006 年各地区全面小康指标时序进度情况

地区	已达标指标个数	未达标指标个数	达到时序进度指标个数		未达到时序进度指标个数	
			按省定时间	按自定时间	按省定时间	按自定时间
全　省	18	7	23	–	2	–
南　京	21	4	24	24	1	1
无　锡	23	2	23	–	2	–
徐　州	10	15	23	19	2	6
常　州	23	2	23	23	2	2
苏　州	23	2	23	–	2	–
南　通	15	10	22	18	3	7
连云港	9	16	23	23	2	2
淮　安	9	16	23	23	2	2
盐　城	9	16	21	15	4	10
扬　州	13	12	25	23	0	2
镇　江	17	8	22	22	3	3
泰　州	14	11	24	23	1	2
宿　迁	9	16	22	20	3	5

（三）常州市总体上达到了全面小康指标

对照全面建设小康社会四大类 18 项 25 条指标的要求，2006 年常州市已有 23 个指标达到或超过目标值，比 2005 年增加 7 个。全面小康核心指标中，人均 GDP、城镇居民人均可支配收入、农村居民人均纯收入均高于目标值。2 个未达标的指标为居民文教娱乐支出比重和森林覆盖率。由于绝大多数指标达到或超过目标值，特别是所有的核心指标已经达标，因此经初步评估认定：常州市以市为单位总体上达到了全面小康指标。分类指标达标情况是：

1. 经济发展。该大类的 4 项指标全部达标。2006 年常州市人均 GDP 达 37210 元（按常住人口计算），相当于目标值 24000 元的 1.55 倍。二三产业占 GDP 比重为 96.2%、城市化水平达 60.5%，分别比目标值高 4.2 个和 5.5 个百分点。城镇登记失业率 3.4%，控制在 5% 以内。

2. 生活水平。该大类 10 个指标中有 9 个达标。常州市城镇居民人均可支配收入为 16650 元，超出目标值 650 元；农村居民人均纯收入为 8001 元，略高于 8000 元的目标值。城镇人均住房建筑面积、农村人均钢筋砖木结构住房面积分别为 30 平方米和 57.2 平方米，农村行政村通灰黑公路（或航道）比重实现 100%，城镇人均拥有道路面积 18.0 平方米，百户家庭电话拥有量 262.1 部，百户家庭电脑拥有量 41.5 台，城乡恩格尔系数 36.5%，均已达标。居民文教娱乐服务支出占家庭消费支出比重为 13.4%，距离目标值尚差 4.6 个百分点。

3. 社会发展。该大类 8 个指标全部达标。R&D 经费支出占 GDP 比重达 1.63%，比目标值高 0.13 百分点。高中阶段教育毛入学率和卫生服务体系健全率均达 100%。城镇养老、失业、基本医疗保险覆盖面分别为 97.0%、97.1%、96.1%，超过 95% 的目标值。新型农村合作医疗覆盖面 97.8%，高出目标值 12.8 个百分点。人民群众对社会治安的满意率 97.3%，城镇社区居委会依法自治达标率 99.0%，农村村委会依法自治达标率 99.0%，均达到目标值要求。

4. 生态环境。该大类 3 个指标中有 2 个达标。城市绿化覆盖率 40.6%，比目标值高 0.6 个百分点。森林覆盖率为

15.3%，低于20%的目标值4.7个百分点。环境质量综合指数达80.3分，比上年提高13.9个百分点，达到目标值要求。

三、全省全面小康建设各大类指标完成情况

2006年全省各地坚持走率先发展、科学发展、和谐发展之路，实行富民优先、科教优先、环保优先、节约优先的方针，牢牢把握发展这个第一要务，加快发展先进生产力，强力推进富民目标，统筹兼顾各方利益，努力构建和谐社会，推动经济社会全面协调可持续发展，全面小康社会建设的各大类指标时序进度均取得积极进展。

（一）坚持以经济建设为中心，综合实力逐步增强

发展经济是全面建设小康社会的基础和首要任务。2006年，江苏认真贯彻落实宏观调控政策措施，经济社会发展取得新成绩，和谐社会建设收到新成效，实现了经济又好又快发展，综合实力进一步提升。"经济发展"大类的4项指标全部达到时序进度，3项指标达到目标值。全省实现生产总值突破2万亿元，达21548.36亿元，比上年增长14.9%，比全国平均增幅快4.2个百分点，自1992年以来已连续15年保持两位数增长，年均增速为14.1%，高出全国同期3.9个百分点。人均生产总值达28685元，高出目标值4685元，按当年汇率折算达3598美元。根据世界银行的划分标准，全省经济发展处于世界中等收入国家和地区的水平。经济结构调整和增长方式转变取得新进展，工业化、服务业发展加快。三次产业增加值比例调整为7.2:56.5:36.3，全省二、三产业增加值占GDP比重达92.8%，超过目标值0.8个百分点；其中服务业（包括农林牧渔服务业）增加值比重为36.6%，比上年提高0.8个百分点。城市化进程继续加快，城市化水平为51.9%，比上年提高1.4个百分点，比时序进度要求高0.5个百分点。就业再就业工作继续加强。年末全省城乡从业人员4564.76万人，比上年末增加54.64万人。通过多种途径使43.04万城镇下岗失业人员实现了再就业。年末城镇登记失业率为3.4%，比上年末下降0.2个百分点，达到了低于5%的目标。

（二）坚持富民优先发展目标，人民生活水平提高

全省坚持以人为本、富民优先的发展导向，把富民作为全面建设小康社会的核心要求，放在发展全局的优先位置。坚持发展经济与造福百姓的统一，推动自主创业和农村劳动力转移，拓宽就业渠道，提高工资和生活保障标准，城乡居民收入水平和生活质量继续提高。2006年，全省城镇居民人均可支配收入为14084元，比上年增长14.3%，剔除价格因素，实际增长12.5%；农村居民人均纯收入5813元，比上年增长10.2%，剔除价格因素，实际增长8.4%。城乡居民收入继续保持较高增速。城乡居民收入之比为2.42:1，为全国较小的省份之一。消费结构升级加速。2006年，城镇居民人均消费性支出9629元，增长11.7%；农村居民人均生活消费支出4135元，增长15.9%。居民享用型和发展型消费呈加速增长之势，家庭设备、医疗保健、交通通讯等消费支出增速快于食品、衣着、居住等生存型消费支出增幅。城乡居民食品支出占消费支出的比重即恩格尔系数为38.8%，达到全面小康目标值。居民消费已由生存型向享受型和发展型转变。居民住房条件继续改善，城镇人均住房建筑面积31.6平方米，农村人均钢筋、砖木结构住房面积40.7平方米，双双达到目标值。交通、通讯等基础实施建设力度加大，城乡居民出行条件进一步改善，居民信息化普及程度继续提高，农村行政村通灰黑公路（或航道）比重100%，城镇人均拥有道路面积18.8平方米，百户家庭电话拥有量226部，皆达到或超过目标值；百户家庭电脑拥有量29.2台，比上年增加4.3台，达到时序进度要求。

（三）坚持全面协调发展，社会事业取得新进步

随着人民群众物质生活水平的日益提高，对精神文化、健康安全、社会保障等方面的需求也日益增长，要求社会与经济更加全面协调发展。江苏在加快发展经济的同时，立足于人的全面发展，着力发展各项社会事业，政治、科技、教育、文化、卫生和社会保障等领域的建设取得明显成效。自主创新步伐加快，科技队伍迅速壮大。全省科学研究与技术开发机构3889个，从事科技活动人员36万人，其中研究与发展人员10.5万人。2006年全省研究与发展活动（R&D）经费支出330亿元，占全省生产总值（GDP）的比重1.53%，已达到1.5%的目标值。优先发展各级各类教育，加快发展职业教育，中等职业教育招生人数首次超过普通高中，高中阶段教育毛入学率继续提升，达到76.7%，完成时序进度。农村办学条件进一步改善，农村义务教育阶段学生学杂费全部免除。高等学校数、在校生人数保持全国领先地位。加强公共卫生事业建设，加大对农村卫生的扶持力度，大力发展社区卫生服务。卫生服务体系健全率90.2%，达到目标值；新型农村合作医疗覆盖面达到93.2%，超过目标值8.2个百分点。社会保障覆盖面进一步扩大。城镇企业职工基本养老保险、基本医疗保险、失业保险参保人数分别增加106.9万人、150.2万人、62.6万人，覆盖面均达92%以上。其中养老保险、失业保险覆盖面已达标，分别为97.2%和98.1%；基本医疗保险覆盖面为92.8%，达到时序进度。在全省范围内调高了最低工资标准、企业退休人员基本养老金标准、优抚对象抚恤补助标准和城乡居民最低生活保障补助水平。全省城乡"低保"实现全覆盖，148.5万困难群众实现应保尽保。加快建设"法治江苏"、"平安江苏"，人民群众对社会治安的满意率达到96.7%，比2005年又提高了0.9个百分点，超过目标值6.7个百分点，列全国第一。城镇社区居委会依法自治达标率95.4%、农村村委会依法自治达标率97.1%，均达到目标值。

（四）坚持可持续发展，生态环境逐步有所改善

针对人口密度大、矿产性资源少、环境容量小等基本省情，大力实施可持续发展战略，注重经济与人口、资源、环境的协调

发展。环境保护和生态建设走在全国前列，全国首批6家国家生态市江苏有4家，占全国的2/3。"绿色江苏"和生态省建设取得重要进展，城乡居民生存环境得到进一步改善。全省新增城市绿化覆盖面积11946万平方米，城市绿化覆盖率为41.5%，达到目标值；新增造林面积157.8万亩，森林覆盖率为15.8%，比2005年提高1.0个百分点，达到时序进度要求。环境保护工作力度加大，认真落实环保目标责任制，突出抓好重点行业和企业污染减排工作，以"三清一绿"为重点的环境整治工作完成年度目标。着力推进重点流域水污染防治、区域环境综合整治，城市水域功能区水质有了较大幅度的改善，环境质量进一步提高，全省环境质量综合指数达81.2分，比2005年增加3.7分，达到了全面小康目标值。

四、江苏全面建设小康进程中的薄弱环节

全省全面小康社会建设在顺利推进的同时，还存在一些不容忽视的薄弱环节和部分弱项，特别是仍有2个指标未达到时序进度要求，不少已经达到目标值或达到时序进度的指标尚需进一步巩固。在调整经济结构、缩小区域差距、持续增加收入、发展社会事业、改善生态环境等方面面临的难题，仍需要积极应对，并采取有效措施加以破解。

（一）农民持续增收有一定难度

农村居民人均纯收入已连续4年未达到时序进度。2003—2006年全省农村居民人均纯收入增收额分别为244元、515元、522元、537元，分别比当年时序进度要求低258元、22元、19元、8元。农村居民人均纯收入要在2010年达到目标值8000元，今后4年需年均递增8.3%，在农民收入持续增长的长效机制尚未完全建立的情况下，农民增收缺乏稳定增长的牢固基础，如期达标难度依然很大。尤其是经济薄弱地区，农民增收的渠道不多。农业综合生产能力、政策性增收、粮价上涨、劳务输出等支撑条件在未来的空间较为有限，将在一定程度上制约农民收入的持续增长。农村居民消费习惯和消费结构有待逐步改变和升级，农村居民用于"吃、穿、住"等生存型消费支出仍占较大比重，与城镇居民相比差距较大。2006年农村百户家庭电脑拥有量仅为3.62台，远低于城镇的49台；农村恩格尔系数达41.8%，超出了低于40%的目标值。由于购买汽车等耐用消费品支出、住房装修等支出大幅增加，以及在全省推行免收义务教育阶段学杂费，城乡居民文教娱乐服务支出占家庭消费支出比重提高不快，2006年为14.3%，仅比2005年增加0.1个百分点，没有达到提高0.8个百分点的时序进度要求。

（二）区域发展差距有待进一步缩小

在区域共同发展战略推动下，通过加强对区域发展的分类指导，2006年苏南、苏中、苏北经济发展步伐加快，苏南地区在高起点上继续前进，苏中、苏北工业化进程加快，多项主要经济指标的增幅高于苏南，三大区域共同发展势头良好。但从根本上缩小区域经济社会发展差距的任务仍很艰巨。从完成全面小康时序进度的情况看，各地全面建设小康社会进程逐步加快，2006年大部分省辖市达到时序进度的指标个数多于上年。但苏北、苏中部分地区进程比较缓慢。苏北的徐州、盐城和苏中的南通按省定时间达到时序进度的指标个数分别比上年减少了2个、1个和1个；连云港达到时序进度的指标个数与上年相同。部分地区按自定时间提前完成全面小康指标的难度较大。按自定时间测算，徐州、南通、盐城、宿迁达到时序进度的指标个数不超过20个，分别为19个、18个、15个和20个，徐州、盐城达到时序进度的指标个数比2005年分别减少了3个和2个（按自定实现时间为2011年测算）。

（三）社会事业发展相对滞后

近年来，全省社会发展步伐加快，经济社会发展不相协调的矛盾逐步得到缓解。但社会结构失衡、社会事业发展相对滞后的矛盾依然存在。城市化水平总体上仍落后于工业化进程，城乡二元化格局依然存在，农业的就业比重远高于其增加值比重，服务业就业比重仅为三分之一强，农村还有大量剩余劳动力，就业再就业形势依然严峻。社会保障体制尚不健全，农村社会保障体制建设滞后。城镇三大保障覆盖面基础仍不牢固，城镇基本医疗保险发展相对滞后，对非公经济就业人员、灵活就业人员、进城务工人员等群体的社会保障明显不足，尚未做到应保尽保。城乡居民收入差距进一步拉大。2006年全省城镇居民人均可支配收入增加1766元，农村居民人均纯收入增加537元，两者的增收额相差1229元；收入之比由上年的2.33扩大到2.42。教育资源不够均衡，教育机会不够均等，如中等职业教育苏南地区在办学条件、就业机会等方面有明显优势，吸引了省内外许多生源，而苏北在这方面相对不足。2006年，全省高中阶段教育毛入学率为76.7%，低于目标值13.3个百分点，徐州、连云港、淮安、泰州、宿迁5市处于全省平均水平以下，如期达标任务繁重。科技方面，省辖市中有9个市R&D经费支出占GDP比重均低于全省平均，连云港、淮安、盐城、宿迁4市比重尚不到0.7%，其中淮安、盐城、宿迁按省定和自定时间均未达到时序进度。卫生事业发展与人民群众的医疗保健需求还不相适应，主要表现医疗服务资源总量满足不了群众需求，公共卫生体系特别是社区卫生服务机构尚不够健全，看病难、看病贵等群众反映强烈的问题仍未得到根本改观。

（四）生态建设和环境保护仍需加强

由于地处相对特殊的自然地理环境，江河湖网纵横，水域面积较大，江苏森林覆盖率提高有一定难度，2006年实现15.8%，刚好达到时序进度要求。环境质量改善基础仍不稳固。2006年部分地区为改善水环境质量，提高城市水域功能区达标率，采取了调水等临时性措施和手段，对暂时改善水环境质量起到了一定的作用，但要长期保持水环境质量还需下大力气进一步加强水环境综合整治工作。

五、江苏全面建设小康社会的发展趋势

2006 年江苏全面小康社会建设取得的成就，为 2010 年左右全省总体上如期达标打下了坚实基础，也为继续前进积累了经验。实践表明，只要以科学发展观统领经济和社会发展大局，坚持“两个率先”目标不动摇，解放思想，真抓实干，下大力气攻克薄弱环节，就一定能够加快全面建设小康社会步伐。根据经济社会发展趋势和各地工作力度，预计 2007 年全省及各省辖市全面小康社会建设将继续保持加快势头，苏南部分地区可望总体上达到全面小康标准，苏中、苏北完成时序进度指标增多。

2007 年是江苏全面建设小康社会承上启下的重要一年，经济社会发展也正处在一个关键阶段。省第十一次党代会提出，今后五年全省总的奋斗目标是全面达小康、建设新江苏。要求无论是已经达到还是正在争取达到省定全面小康指标的地方，都要按照不含水分、人民群众得实惠、老百姓认可的要求，努力建设一个高水平的全面小康。各地应认真贯彻省第十一次党代会精神，以更高的标准和更高的要求，全面落实各项工作措施，完善考核方法，逐项狠抓落实，一步一个脚印地扎实推进，切实提高全面小康质量，巩固全面小康建设成果。严格坚持全面小康四大类 18 项 25 条指标进行考核，切实达到“六个更加”“一个惠及”的全面小康社会目标要求，努力建设一个高水平的全面小康。

附表：江苏省全面建设小康社会进程测算表

江苏省全面建设小康社会进程测算表

指标名称	代码	单位	目标值	2006年实现值	比上年增减值	年均应完成进度	时序进度情况
一、经济发展							
1. 人均地区生产总值	1	元	≥24000	28685	4125	—	√
2. 二、三产业增加值占GDP比重	2	%	≥92	92.8	0.8	—	√
3. 城市化水平	3	%	55	51.9	1.4	0.9	√
4. 城镇登记失业率	4	%	<5	3.4	-0.2	—	√
二、生活水平							
5. 居民收入							
(1)城镇居民人均可支配收入	5	元	≥16000	14084	1766	736	√
(2)农村居民人均纯收入	6	元	≥8000	5813	537	545	△
6. 居民住房							
(1)城镇人均住房建筑面积	7	M^2	30	31.6	1.4	—	√
(2)农村人均钢筋、砖木结构住房面积	8	M^2	40	40.7	2.5	0.4	√
7. 居民出行							
(1)农村行政村通灰黑公路(或航道)比重	9	%	100	100.0	0.0	—	√
(2)城镇人均拥有道路面积	10	M^2	12	18.8	2.5	—	√
8. 居民信息化普及程度							
(1)百户家庭电话拥有量	11	部	200	226.0	16.2	—	√
(2)百户家庭电脑拥有量	12	台	40	29.2	4.3	3.0	√
9. 居民文教娱乐服务支出占家庭消费支出比重	13	%	18	14.3	0.1	0.8	△
10. 恩格尔系数	14	%	<40	38.8	-1.8	0.1	√
三、社会发展							
11. R&D经费支出占GDP比重	15	%	≥1.5	1.53	0.05	0.00	√
12. 高中阶段教育毛入学率	16	%	≥90	76.7	5.7	3.8	√
13. 卫生服务体系健全率	17	%	≥90	90.2	4.6	0.9	√
14. 社会保障							
(1)城镇劳动保障三大保险各自覆盖面	18	%	≥95	96.0	1.0	—	√
#城镇基本养老保险		%	≥95	97.2	0.4	—	√
城镇失业保险		%	≥95	98.1	0.2	—	√
城镇基本医疗保险		%	≥95	92.8	2.4	0.9	√
(2)新型农村合作医疗覆盖面	19	%	≥85	93.2	7.7	—	√
15. 人民群众对社会治安的满意率	20	%	90	96.7	0.9	—	√
16. 城乡村(居)民依法自治							
(1)城镇社区居委会依法自治达标率	21	%	90	95.4	2.0	—	√
(2)农村村委会依法自治达标率	22	%	95	97.1	0.8	—	√
四、生态环境							
17. 绿化水平							
(1)城市绿化覆盖率	23	%	40	41.7	1.9	0.0	√
(2)森林覆盖率	24	%	20	15.8	1.0	1.0	√
18. 环境质量综合指数	25	分	80	81.2	3.7	0.5	√

注:1. 表中"—"表示该指标上年总体已达到目标值;"√"表示当年达到时序进度,总体达标视同当年达到时序进度;"△"表示未达到时序进度。

2. 全省全面建设小康社会进程按2010年为实现目标时间测算。

2006 年江苏省县级全面建设小康社会进程统计监测报告

近三年来，为贯彻党的十六大提出的全面建设小康社会的战略部署，力争全面小康建设走在全国前列，江苏围绕“两个率先”的目标，坚持率先发展，科学发展，和谐发展，全面小康建设取得显著成效。继昆山、张家港、常熟、吴江、太仓和江阴等6个县级市2005年率先实现全面小康后，2006年，省委、省政府审时度势，及时部署以县为单位全面建设小康社会工作，提出了“全面达小康，建设新江苏”战略目标，并要求不能以市域总体达标代替县县全部达标；只有以县为单位实现全面小康，才算是惠及全体人民的实实在在的全面小康。

一年来，省委、省政府大力宣传昆山等地区全面建设小康社会的先进经验，全面推进县级全面小康社会建设。全省各级党委政府高度重视、精心谋划，县（市）人民群众积极参与、奋力推进，全省县级全面小康建设迈上了新台阶。

对照《江苏省县级全面建设小康社会统计指标体系》，根据省级有关部门（省统计局、省政法委、省劳动和社会保障厅、省教育厅、省卫生厅、省建设厅、省民政厅、省交通厅、省环保厅、省林业局）对县级全面小康监测统计指标数据评审认定，结合江苏省社情民意调查中心对全面小康指标达标的县级市（区）民意调查结果，现就2006年度全省县级全面建设小康社会进程情况综合报告如下。

一、县级全面小康指标进程评价

（一）县级全面小康时序进度与达标完成情况

2006年，全省县级全面小康进程呈现稳步推进势头，各县（市）全面小康当年时序进度完成情况良好，达到全面小康目标值的指标个数稳步提高（分县（市）时序进度和达标完成情况参见附表一，统计结果不包括未经省级认定的部分县（市）的指标数据，下同）。

按省定时序进度完成情况：全省52个县（市）的省定达标年份，依照各县（市）所在省辖市的省定小康达标年份确定：即苏南地区县（市）省定时间为2007年；苏中地区县（市）为2012年；苏北地区县（市）为2017年或2019年。经综合测算，52个县（市）中，有34个县（市）完成省定时序进度指标超过20个指标，18个县（市）完成省定时序进度的指标在14－19个之间。

按自定时序进度完成情况：2006年，各县（市）相继制定了本地县级全面小康达标时间，自定时间比省定时间有所提前，进度要求相应提高。其中，自定达标时间在2007年的有3个县（市），自定达标时间在2008—2010年的有19个县（市），若加上已达标8个县（市），2010年前自定实现全面小康目标的有30个县（市）。自定达标时间在2011—2012年的有8个县（市），2013—2017年的有14个县（市）。监测统计显示：有22个县（市）完成自定时序进度指标超过20个，30个县（市）完成自定时序进度的指标在10－19个之间。

分县（市）全面小康指标达标情况：在县级全面小康25个统计指标中，达到全面小康目标值在20个指标以上的有10个县（市），比2005年增加3个县（市）；达到全面小康目标值在10到19个指标之间的有26个县（市），比2005年增加5个县（市）；达到全面小康目标值在9个指标以下的有16个县（市），比上年减少8个。县（市）全面小康指标达标分布呈现中间大，两头小的格局。

（二）宜兴市、武进区、扬中市总体上实现全面小康指标

宜兴市、武进区、扬中市多年来一直是我省县域经济社会发展较快、较均衡的地区，在2005年全国百强县排名中分别列第20位、第8位和第44位，2005年全面小康25个指标综合达标进程已位居全省52个县（市）的前列。2006年，宜兴、武进、扬中三地在巩固提升已达标指标的同时，针对全面小康建设中的薄弱环节开展扎实有效的工作，全面小康建设取得突破性成效。

1. 宜兴、武进、扬中三地2006年全面小康指标总体达标

宜兴市：2006年有23项指标达到全面小康目标值，其中，核心指标人均GDP达到35472元（按常住人口，下同），城乡居民收入分别达到16089元和8005元，均超过目标值。没有达到目标值的有二项指标，分别是百户居民家庭电脑拥有量36.8台，比目标值40台低3.2台；居民文教娱乐服务支出占家庭消费支出比重16.3%，比目标值18%低1.7个百分点。

武进区：2006年有23项指标达到全面小康目标值，其中，核心指标人均GDP达到43508元，城乡居民收入分别达到17321元和8833元，均超过目标值。没有达到小康目标值的有二项指标，分别是森林覆盖率12.3%，比目标值20%低7.7个百分点；居民文教娱乐服务支出占家庭消费支出比重17.3%，比目标值18%低0.7个百分点。

扬中市：2006年有24项指标达到全面小康目标值，其中，核心指标人均GDP达到39696元，城乡居民收入分别达到16209元和8000元，均达到或超过目标值。没有达到目标值的指标是森林覆盖率为13.1%，比目标值20%低6.9个百分点。

综上所述，宜兴市、武进区、扬中市绝大多数指标已经达到或超过全面小康目标值。仅有三项没有达标，其中：扬中、武进的森林覆盖率不达标主要是受当地水域面积比重较大等条件的限制。宜兴市、武进区的居民文教娱乐服务支出占家庭消费支出比重不达标，主要是受购买汽车等大宗消费、及近年来义务教育支出减少等影响。宜兴市的百户居民家庭电脑拥有量未达标表明当地居民的信息化水平还有待提高。鉴于当地经济社会发展和自然条件差异的特殊性，可以认定：2006 年宜兴市、武进区、扬中市监测统计指标值总体上达到省定全面小康标准。

2. 三地老百姓对当地全面小康的认可度均超过 60%

宜兴、武进、扬中三地全面小康监测统计数据在总体上达到了全面小康指标，但认定一个地区实现全面小康并不能以统计数据代替直观感受，还必须看多数老百姓是否认可达到全面小康。为贯彻省委"不能以统计数据代替老百姓直观感受"的要求，江苏省社情民意调查中心采用计算机辅助电话调查系统(CATI)，对宜兴、武进、扬中三地城乡居民进行了全面小康民意调查。调查结果显示：老百姓对本地的全面小康总体认可度分别为：宜兴 73.0%、武进 66.8%、扬中 72.2%。均达到《江苏省县级全面小康监测统计工作组织实施办法》明确的老百姓认可度要超过 60% 的规定。

鉴于宜兴市、武进区、扬中市的监测统计指标值总体上达到全面小康，老百姓对当地全面小康的总体认可度超过 60%，经省级有关部门实地调研检查，依据《江苏省县级全面小康监测统计工作组织实施办法》的有关规定评审认定：宜兴市、武进区、扬中市 2006 年总体上达到全面小康。

二、县级全面小康指标进程分析

回顾 2006 年，对照县级全面小康监测统计的 25 个指标，绝大多数指标达标的县(市)个数比上年增加。其中，包括人均 GDP、城乡居民收入等核心指标在内的 19 个指标，全省达标县(市)个数比上年增加；包括城市化率、人民群众对社会治安满意率在内的 5 个指标，全省达标县(市)个数与上年持平；而环境质量指标达标的县(市)个数比上年略有减少(县级全面小康 25 个指标的分项达标情况详见附表二)。

2006 年，我省县级全面小康各项建设在全面协调推进的同时，在增强经济实力、富民优先、强化社会保障与环境生态保护等方面重点推进，呈现以下特点：

(一)县域经济增长力求又好又快，就业规模稳步扩大

保持县域经济稳定较快增长，仍然是现阶段我省县级全面小康的物质基础。全省县域经济在科学发展观的引导下快速稳定增长。据初步测算，2006 年全省县(市)地区生产总值首次超过万亿，达到 11014 亿元，比上年增长 20.6%(现价)。人均 GDP 为 23170 元(按常住人口，下同)。全省 52 个县(市)中，人均地区生产总值达到全面小康目标值的有 16 个县(市)、比上年增加 3 个。人均 GDP 超过 24000 元的县(市)为 16 个，已占全部县(市)的 31%。其中，昆山等率先实现全面小康的 6 个县(市)，人均 GDP 已达到 53000 元以上。人均 GDP 在 8000 元以下的县(市)减少至 5 个。

在经济总量较快增长的同时，经济结构进一步改善。全省县(市)二三产业增加值占 GDP 比重为 89.7%，比上年提高 1.36 个百分点，三次产业增加值比例为 10.2:56.4:33.4。二三产业增加值占 GDP 的比重达到全面小康目标值的有 13 个县(市)，比上年增加 2 个。与经济增长密切相关的城市化水平达到 40.8%，比上年提高 1.5 个百分点。城市化水平达到全面小康目标值的县(市)为 15 个，与上年相同。

扩大就业作为政府行政的基本目标，已放在十分突出的位置。县(市)党委和政府坚持用发展经济拉动就业，市场导向引导就业，制定政策扶持就业，统筹城乡促进就业，鼓励创业带动就业，南北联动转移就业，用发展的办法和创新的举措解决就业和再就业问题。2006 年全省城镇新增就业 110.2 万人，连续两年实现新增就业突破百万人。下岗失业人员再就业 43.04 万人，其中"4050 人员"再就业 11.13 万人，全面超额完成全年任务。全省县(市)在年末城镇常住人口比上年增加 71.36 万人情况下，城镇登记失业人数仍比上年减少 1.67 万人。2006 年，各县(市)城镇登记失业率均控制在目标值 5% 以内，达到了全面小康目标值的要求。

(二)着力推进富民优先，人民生活稳步提高

富民优先是我省建设全面小康社会的核心要求。坚持发展经济与造福百姓的统一，让百姓从经济增长中得到更多的实惠。富民已成为政府的执政之要，强省之基。

城乡居民收入既是县级全面小康的核心指标，也是全面小康达标的重点和难点。2006 年全省 52 个县(市)中，城镇居民人均可支配收入达到全面小康目标值(16000 元)的有 8 个县(市)，比上年增加 2 个。人均可支配收入在 1 万元—1.6 万元的县(市)达到 19 个，比上年增加 5 个。2006 年，我省在提高城镇居民收入方面继续朝着均衡化方向发展，更加注重中低收入阶层居民的生活改善，提高最低工资标准、离退休人员的养老金、城市最低生活保障等三个方面是各地的首选着力点。另一方面，由于近两年民营经济的快速发展，城镇居民经营性净收入持续大幅度增长，在上年增长 30% 以上的基础上，2006 年再次增长 22.5%。农村居民人均纯收入达到全面小康目标值(8000 元)的有 8 个县(市)，比上年增加 2 个；人均纯收入在 5000 元—8000 元的县(市)达到 27 个，比上年增加 10 个；低于 5000 元的县(市)由上年的 29 减少到 17 个。2006 年，全省农民增收的主

要来源:一是劳务输出保持高位增长,增加工资性收入。全年新增农村劳动力转移62.60万人,其中通过对口挂钩输出的农村劳动力达10.46万人。针对农村转移的难度越来越大,省财政拿出6000万元用于促进农村劳务输出培训,特别对1011个经济薄弱村劳力的培训费提高到人均补助300元。全年对40.38万名劳力进行了转移前的技能培训。二是支持农民返乡创业致富,提高经营性收入。2006年我省2.7万进城务工农民返乡创业,创办各类企业8927个,带动9.1万农村劳动力就地转移。

通过创业致富提高城乡居民收入,2006年全面小康新达标的县(市)提供了很好的示范。在前几年积极拓展创业致富的基础上,宜兴市2006年以降低准入门槛,激活民间投资,大力扶持民营经济发展。全年新办民营工业企业913家,民营经济组织总户数达到4.32万户,比上年增长11.3%,吸纳职工23.85万人,比上年增长16.1%。扬中市2006年深入推进"千户兴业"、"千元增收"行动,出台鼓励全民创业的政策,农民创业热情高涨。全市累计新办个私企业427户,新增个体工商户1114户。针对民营企业融资难的问题,将中小企业担保基金规模扩大到4000万元、农民创业担保基金规模也达200万元,有力地拓宽了农民的增收渠道。

在城乡居民收入较快增长的基础上,生活消费水平稳步提高。城镇人均住房建筑面积达到全面小康目标值的有35个县(市),比上年增加4个。农村人均钢筋、砖木结构住房面积达到全面小康目标值的有24个县(市),比上年增加1个。城乡百户家庭电话拥有量达到全面小康目标值的有34个县(市),比上年增加9个。城乡百户家庭电脑拥有量达到全面小康目标值的有7个县(市),与上年相同。电脑拥有量偏低的原因主要是农村居民家庭电脑拥有量偏少,52个县(市)中,农村百户居民家庭的电脑拥有量超过20台的只有8个县(市)。城乡居民文教娱乐服务支出占家庭消费支出比重达到全面小康目标值的有10个县(市),比上年增加4个。城乡恩格尔系数达到全面小康目标值的有28个县(市),比上年增加12个。其中:农村居民恩格尔系数低于40%的有25个县(市),接近一半。在交通出行方面,所有县(市)的农村行政村通灰黑(或航道)比重均已达到全面小康目标值。城镇人均拥有道路面积达到全面小康目标值的有39个县(市),比上年增加9个。完善城市道路功能,不单给居民出行提供便利,也是各地在实施招商引资、进行经济建设的基础条件。各地围绕拉开城市框架,构建合理的城市道路框架体系,加大道路投资力度。据有关部门统计,2006年全省县级城市完成道路建设投资72.3亿元,占县级城市城建总投资的58.63%。

(三)以科教优先为导向、以扩大社会保障为抓手,推进可持续发展

在全面小康推进过程中,体现科教优先是我省作为人才大省、教育大省迈向全面小康社会的特质之一。由于科研院所、大专院校多集中在大城市,我省县域经济中研发经费投入主要是大中型企业。目前县域企业研发经费投入虽然基数低,但增长迅速,2006年县(市)研发经费支出首次突破百亿元达117亿,较上年增长32.2%。全省52个县(市)中,R&D经费支出占GDP比重达到全面小康目标值的有19个县(市),比上年增加2个。目前,县(市)研发经费投入较多的集中在已实现全面小康的地区。如昆山市就拥有省、市级技术中心和重点实验室21家,博士后流动站3个。拥有7个中国名牌产品、18个江苏著名商标,昆山企业累计申请专利数超过1万件。在推进县级全面建设小康社会的进程中,我省县域在普及初等教育方面起点较高,初中毕业生升学率达到全面小康目标值的有38个县(市),比上年增加16个。2006年,全省农村义务教育阶段学生学杂费已全部免除,群众反映强烈的上学贵问题得到较好的缓解。

近年来医疗、养老、失业等社会保障问题仍是百姓的后顾之忧、呼吁的热点,各级党委政府将提高社会保障水平作为全面小康推进的重点,切实履行政府的职责。2006年,医疗卫生服务体系健全率达到全面小康目标值的有32个县(市),比上年增加9个。所有县(市)的新型农村合作医疗覆盖面均已达到全面小康目标值要求。城镇三大保险(基本养老、失业、基本医疗)各自覆盖面达到全面小康目标值的有23个县(市),比上年增加2个。2006年末全省县(市)城镇企业职工基本养老参保人数420万人,较上年增加42万人,增长11.1%;城镇失业保险参保人数382万人,较上年增加36万人,增长10.4%,城镇职工基本医疗保险参保人数552万人,较上年增加73万人,增长15.1%。全省已初步建立了一套省对困难县(市)养老保险基金缺口的补助机制。2006年,省级继续安排专项补助资金,连续第六年做到了企业离退休人员养老金按时足额发放。同时,通过采取省财政安排专项资金对经济薄弱地区给予适当补助的办法,初步解决了破产、困难国有集体企业退休人员的医疗保障问题,全省破产、困难企业的42万名退休人员到去年底已基本参加医疗保险。

随着经济社会转型期带来的各种变化,保持良好的社会治安也变得更加繁重。经过近三年"平安江苏"的创建活动,2006年所有县(市)的人民群众对社会治安的满意率均已达到全面小康目标,江苏地区的安全感获得了省内外百姓的普遍认可。此外,城乡居民对社区内各项事务的监督、管理的参与感更强。城镇社区居委会依法自治达标率达到全面小康目标值的有51个县(市),比上年增加5个。农村村委会依法自治达标率达到全面小康目标值的有45个县(市),比上年增加1个。

(四)强化整治污染、改善生态环境,构建绿色城乡

我省县域经济总体上还处在工业化加速发展期,但经济快速增长与城乡居民对环境污染加重的关注、对蓝天青山绿水宁静的生活环境的向往之间,矛盾逐渐凸显,避免走先发展后治理的老路已成为全省上下的共识。

在整治环境污染方面,各地采取了多种措施:如加强建设项目审批,变招商"引资"为"选资",严格控制新污染源;关停并转一大批重污染企业;实行动态监管、提高污染处理率和达标率;加快污水处理建设步伐、大力推进河道整治等等,全省县

(市)对环境污染的整治取得了一定的成效。其中5个县市2006年由上年环境质量不达标上升为达标,其主要措施是提升城市水域功能区的水质。以武进区为例:2006年该区加大城镇生活污水处理力度和全面开展农村生态环境综合整治。采取限期治理、限期搬迁、污水截流、提标治理、控制使用化肥农药等措施,使水域功能区水质达标率上升了60%。但监测数据也显示,2006年全省环境质量综合指数达到全面小康目标值的为36个县(市),比上年减少3个。全省有8个县市的环境质量,由上年达标降为不达标,其主要原因是这些地区的城市功能区水质下降较多。

城市绿化建设是改善城市生态环境、为居民提供休闲、娱乐条件的重要手段。各地以园林城市创建为契机,大力开展园林绿化建设,尤其是苏中、苏北地区创建园林城市活动进入活跃期。率先实现小康的太仓市2006年获得"国家园林城市"称号,金坛、溧阳、邳州、射阳4个县级城市获得"省级园林城市"称号。武进区以创建全国生态区为契机,以公园和公共绿地建设为重点,全年投入绿化建设资金4.5亿元,城市绿化覆盖面增加333万平方,较上年提高62.2%。据统计,2006年我省县级城市园林绿化投资完成19.45亿元,占县级城市城建总投资的15.77%。县级城镇绿化覆盖面积47258万平方米,新增绿地6692万平方米,较上年增长16.5%。城市绿化覆盖率达到全面小康目标值的有19个县(市),比上年增加4个。

作为生态省建设的核心,大力实施造林绿化近年来得到了各级政府的高度重视和相关政策的推动。省财政以设立绿色江苏林业生态工程建设与管理专项资金,专门用于推动五项林业重点生态工程建设。各地也积极探索多种造林模式,如扬中市大力发展非公有制林业,鼓励社会资金投资林业。通过合作造林、承包造林、股份制造林、独资造林等形式,广泛吸引社会资金投资林业,森林覆盖率提升较快。全省县级造林绿化成效明显。2006年全省县级森林覆盖面积125.3万公顷,比2005年净增7.7%,其中,县(市)新增的森林覆盖面积8.93万公顷,占全省新增面积的79.8%。森林覆盖率达到全面小康目标值的有14个县(市),比上年增加3个。

三、县级全面小康建设的薄弱环节

应该看到,以县为单位实现全面小康较之以省辖市为总体的实现难度更大,实现路径也还处在探索之中,从各县(市)全面小康监测统计指标数据分析,反映出来的薄弱环节主要表现在以下几个方面。

(一)核心指标的提升难度大

人均GDP和城乡居民收入是全面小康的三大核心指标。2006年全省52个县(市)中,人均GDP未达标县(市)有36个。城镇居民人均可支配收入和农村居民人均纯收入未达全面小康目标值的有44个县(市)。江苏经济社会区域特征明显,南北地区经济社会发展差异较大,目前已达全面小康的县(市),均名列全国百强县的前50强,而未达小康的县(市)中,不少地区的人均GDP还低于全国平均水平。居民收入尤其是农民收入持续增长的长效机制尚未完全建立,部分地区特别是苏北地区的县(市)居民收入缺乏稳定增长的牢固基础。必须清醒地看到,相对省辖市,县(市)提升全面小康核心指标的难度更大,任务更艰巨。

(二)就业形势依然严峻

虽然,我省近年来城镇登记失业率控制在5%以内,城镇失业保险覆盖面达到全面小康目标值的县(市)有44个。但今后几年面临的就业形势依然严峻,保持住小康达标水平还需付出不懈的努力。据测算,"十一五"期间,每年新成长劳动力60万人左右,就业转失业人员加上结转失业人员在70万人左右,各种政策性安置人员4万人左右,被征地无业农民在内的其他人员10万人左右,农村向城镇劳务输出人员40万人左右。全省每年的劳动力供给总量在190万人左右,而每年可提供的就业岗位在140—160万个左右,劳动力供给依然存在较大的过剩。

(三)社会保障体系还不完善

目前,我省52个县(市)中,城镇基本养老保险没有达到全面小康目标值的还有23个县(市);城镇企业职工基本医疗保险没有达到全面小康目标值的还有32个县(市)。基本社会保障的覆盖面和保障水平与经济社会发展还不协调,突出的问题主要来自两个方面:

第一、参保群体不平衡。目前,国有、国有控股、外商投资企业和城镇集体企业职工已基本进入较为完善的社会保障体系,但仍有较大数量的个私经济组织因利益驱动不愿参加社会保险,灵活就业人员社会保险参保率明显偏低,农民工社会保障工作尚处于初始阶段。

第二、基金收支不平衡。以养老保险基金为例,省现行养老保险制度为县(市)级统筹,由于统筹层次过低,各统筹地区养老保险基金封闭运行,市县之间基金结余和基金不足并存,省级调剂和各级财政的压力不断增加。从近几年基金收支情况看,全省90个统筹单位,基金积累的80%以上集中在苏、锡、常三市及省行业统筹单位。随着人口老龄化趋势加剧,单纯依靠征缴收入已难以满足日益增长的支付需求。全省不少地方养老保险的当期发放困难很大,就面上而言,由于个人账户尚未做实,养老保险基金未来支付也面临着巨大的缺口。

(四)环境保护仍需强化长效机制

2006年,全省有22个县(市)的环境质量综合指数高于上年,综合指数提高的主要原因是城市水域功能区水质有了较大辐度的改善,但有部分县(市)是通过一些临时性措施和手段来改善城市水环境质量,成效难以稳定保持。

从已实现全面小康的县(市)近两年的环境质量比较,按省级环保评审标准,2006年这些县(市)综合指数得分在80-82分之间,处于小康目标值80分刚刚达线,且均比2005年下降。其中有些已达小康县(市)的环境质量综合指数降幅较大。由此可见,环境保护需要强化长效机制,即使已经达到全面小康县(市)也还需要巩固成果。

四、县级全面小康进程展望

(一)近年有望实现全面小康的县(市)情况

根据县级全面小康25个指标综合达标情况与核心指标分析,除了已实现实全面小康的8个县(市),目前处于第一方阵的县(市)有5个。这些县(市)人均GDP在23000元以上,城镇居民人均可支配收入在13000元至15000元之间,农民人均纯收入在6600元-7300元之间。这些县(市)有望在近两年实现全面小康。处于第二方阵的县(市)有8个,这些县(市)人均GDP在20000元以上,城镇居民人均可支配收入在11000元以上,农民人均纯收入多在6000元以上。这些县(市)有望于2010前实现全面小康。

以上处在第一、第二方阵的县(市)均集中在苏南、苏中地区,如果上述全面小康的目标预期得以实现,那么,我省的苏南地区将率先实现县县全面达小康,苏中地区有一半县(市)全面达小康,也有望实现总体全面达小康。如果苏北地区按时完成全面小康时序进度,有条件的县(市)努力达到全面小康,就可进而为我省在2010年左右总体上实现全面小康打下坚实的基础。

(二)县级全面小康建设步伐有望加快

随着2006年我省县级全面小康建设的全面展开,尤其是各地认真学习昆山等全面小康达标县(市)的先进经验,并注意结合本地实际情况,不断开创县级全面小康建设的新理念、新思路。各县(市、区)普遍成立了由主要领导挂帅的全面建设小康社会推进领导小组,围绕全面小康目标鼓实劲、重实效;紧扣四大类18项25条指标要求,针对薄弱环节,特别是在富民惠民,扩大社会保障、优化环境等方面积极采取切实有效的措施,取得了明显的成效。据监测分析,2007年我省苏南地区又将有部分县(市、区)迈入全面小康行列;正在争取达小康的地区将以更大的力度,更有效的举措推进全面小康建设;全面小康达标地区将在巩固小康成果的基础上,进一步提高全面小康水平。以县为单位建设全面小康将极大地激发各县(市)人民创业、创新、创优热情,县域经济社会发展将更加全面与协调,全省县级全面小康建设步伐有望进一步加快,并将有力地促进全省"两个率先"迈向更高的台阶。

(三)县级全面小康建设质量进一步提高

一方面,昆山等2005年率先实现全面小康的地区围绕建设高水平全面小康的要求,继续扎实推进全面小康社会建设,全面小康建设质量进一步提高。如昆山市,在率先实现全面小康后,围绕建设高水平全面小康的目标,从加快调整优化结构,着力提升产业层次、发挥开发开放优势,着力增强自主创新能力、完善持续增收机制,着力推进共同富裕、坚持城乡统筹发展,着力加快城市现代化和新农村建设、注重优化综合环境,着力建设"和谐昆山"等方面入手,进一步提高全面小康社会建设水平;张家港市通过改善群众生活、提高居民文明素质和培育品牌特色等方面入手,以巩固"全国文明城市"创建成果为动力,进一步坚持以人为本理念,协调推进三个文明建设,促进社会和人的全面发展,加快人文素质升级,不断提高全面小康建设质量。

另一方面,随着全面建设小康社会进程的不断推进和科学发展观的进一步落实,全面小康四大类18项25条指标已逐步深入人心,各级党委和政府对如何建设全面小康社会的认识进一步提高。全省各地围绕全面小康社会建设目标,进一步强化全面推进的理念,在发展经济的同时,普遍更加注重富民惠民,改善民生,优化环境,对群众普遍关注的社会保障、教育医疗等问题,大多数地区在提高覆盖面的基础上,开始注重增加标准,提高水平。另外,根据省第十一次党代会精神和省委的要求,在县级全面小康达标认定中除要求监测统计指标达标外,增加了民意调查,老百姓对全面小康总体认可度必须超过60%,才能认定该地区全面小康达标。这将进一步促进各级党委政府更加重视关注民生,强调和谐社会建设,从而推动我省全面小康社会建设的质量和水平不断提高。

2006年江苏省劳动和社会保障事业发展统计公报

2006年是“十一五”发展的开局之年，在省委、省政府的正确领导下，全省劳动保障系统紧紧围绕富民强省、“两个率先”目标，全面落实科学发展观，着力推进劳动和社会保障各项工作，力促城乡统筹就业工作实现新突破，社保体系建设取得新进展，劳动关系调整取得新成效，职业培训发展跃上新台阶，公共服务水平得到新提升，全面完成了年初明确的各项目标任务。

一、就业

城乡从业人数保持稳定增长。年末全省城乡从业人员总数达4564.76万人，比上年增加54.64万人，其中，第一产业从业人员1360.3万人，第二产业1588.54万人，第三产业1615.92万人，分别占全省城乡从业人员总数的29.8%、34.8%、35.4%。年末城镇单位从业人员679.37万人，城镇私营企业和个体经济组织就业人员617.16万人，社区公益岗位和灵活就业人员80.62万人。

就业再就业工作进一步加强。全年城镇新增就业110.2万人，连续两年实现新增就业突破百万人。下岗失业人员再就业43.04万人，其中“4050人员”再就业11.13万人，全面超额完成全年任务。年末城镇登记失业人数为40.4万人，城镇登记失业率为3.4%，比上年末下降0.2个百分点，连续四年持续下降。

农村劳动力外输内转继续保持良好发展态势。全年新增农村劳动力转移62.6万人，其中新增劳务输出41.5万人。全年培训农村劳动力129万人次，其中转移前职业技能培训40.38万人。全年全省农民人均劳务收入1033.48元，同比增加75.18元，增长7.9%，对农民增收贡献率达14.01%。

新一轮就业再就业优惠政策得到有效落实。2006年全省发放《再就业优惠证》27.8万本，其中“4050”人员领取14.16万本；领取优惠证再就业的下岗失业人员24.13万人（含以前年度），其中“4050”再就业10.21万人。1.1万人享受小额贷款政策，23.53万人享受税收扶持政策，58.6万人次享受社会保险补贴，补贴额4.7亿元，28.18万人次享受岗位补贴，补贴额1.97亿元。

公共职业介绍机构网络进一步健全。年末全省现有境内职业介绍机构3584个，其中劳动保障部门办的1253家，其它组织办的566家，公民个人办的1765家。全年在各类职介机构登记求职人数达319.71万人次，职业介绍成功183.51万人次，介绍成功率为58%。

职业教育培训事业发展良好。年末全省共有技工学校136所，比上年增加8所；在校学生28.88万人，比上年末增加4.34万人；招生10.64万人，毕业人数为6万人，毕业生当年总体就业率为96.3%。全年技工学校面向社会开展培训20.92万人次，比上年增长24.96%。年末全省共有民办培训机构1600个，全年共开展培训136.96万人次，比上年增长31.34%。全年共有58.97万下岗失业人员参加了再就业培训，8.2万人参加了创业培训。

年末全省共有职业技能鉴定机构294个，职业技能鉴定考评人员5314人。全年共有64.23万人参加了职业技能鉴定，比上年增长29.9%，57.22万人取得不同等级职业资格证书，比上年增长27.1%。全年职业技能鉴定平均通过率为89.07%。全年全省共培养技师、高级技师25531人。

二、社会保险

（一）基本养老保险

1. 企业职工基本养老保险

年末全省参加基本养老保险的单位24.89万家，参保职工1059.25万人，参保职工比上年末增加106.94万人，连续两年实现净增参保人数超百万。享受城镇职工基本养老保险的离退休人员302.38万人，比上年增加19.82万人。

全省企业离退休人员养老金基本做到了按时足额发放。到年末，全省企业退休人员实行社会化管理的人数达288.63万人，比年初增加了20.98万人，社会化管理率达96.5%，其中纳入社区管理的退休人员269.96万人，比年初增加33.17万人，社区管理率达93.5%。

2006年全省基本养老保险基金总收入456.36亿元，其中基金征缴收入（含清理回收历年欠费）406.31亿元，分别比上年增长28.11%和26.78%。对全省33个困难市县给予省重点补助17.05亿元。全年基金总支出355.28亿元，其中基金支出336.49亿元，分别比上年增长26.06%和26.02%。

2. 机关事业单位基本养老保险

年末全省参加机关事业单位基本养老保险单位数达 28529 个，参保职工 82.44 万人，享受机关事业单位基本养老保险的离退休人员达 25.73 万人。

2006 年全省机关事业单位养老保险基金总收入 48.68 亿元，其中基金征缴收入 47.09 亿元，分别比上年增长 6.59% 和 5.84%。全年基金总支出 44.45 亿元，比上年增长 4.32%。

（二）基本医疗保险

年末全省基本医疗保险参保人数达 1274.3 万人，比上年末增加 150.2 万人，连续六年实现净增参保人数超百万。其中参保职工 935.8 万人，参保退休人员 338.5 万人，分别比上年末增加 114.7 万人和 35.5 万人。

2006 年全省基本医疗保险基金总收入 154.62 亿元，其中基金征缴收入 143.57 亿元，分别比上年增长 31.04% 和 29.58%。全年基金总支出 107.73 亿元，其中基金支出 106.51 亿元，分别比上年增长 18.91% 和 19.89%。全年统筹基金收入 89.3 亿元，支出 56.55 亿元，分别比上年增长 38.98% 和 12.72%。

（三）失业保险

年末全省参加失业保险的人数为 901.1 万人，比上年末增加 62.6 万人。年末全省领取失业保险金人数为 22.66 万人，比上年末下降 7.52 万人。

2006 年全省失业保险基金总收入 39.23 亿元，其中基金征缴收入 35.92 亿元，分别比上年增长 18.63% 和 19.83%。全年基金支出 20.06 亿元，比上年下降 5.14%。

（四）工伤保险和生育保险

年末全省参加工伤保险人数为 812.7 万人，比上年末增加 132.5 万人，连续两年实现净增参保人数超百万。全年享受工伤保险待遇人数为 56263 人，比上年增加 19604 人。2006 年全省工伤保险基金总收入 9.05 亿元，其中基金征缴收入 8.67 亿元，分别比上年增长 35.89% 和 36.11%。全年基金支出 5.41 亿元，比上年增长 34.91%。

年末全省参加生育保险人数为 711.5 万人，比上年末增加 80.6 万人，其中女职工 309 万人。2006 年全省生育保险基金总收入 8.67 亿元，其中基金征缴收入 8.37 亿元，分别比上年增长 18.22% 和 18.44%。全年基金支出 4.96 亿元，比上年增长 14.29%。

（五）农村社会养老保险

年末全省农村社会养老保险累计参保人数达 868.97 万人，新增参保人数 43.21 万人。年末领取养老金人数达 131.71 万人。2006 年农村社会养老保险基金收入 23.52 亿元，支出 15.07 亿元，分别比上年增长 9.5% 和 6.13%。

积极稳妥地推进农民个人缴费、集体补助、政府补贴三方筹资的新型农村社会养老保险制度，年末新型农村社会养老保险覆盖人群达 189.97 万人。

（六）被征地农民基本生活保障

城市规划区内被征地农民“即征即保”机制初步形成，被征地农民基本生活保障覆盖人群不断扩大，2006 年底达到 99.73 万人。

三、工资分配和劳动关系

企业工资分配制度改革继续推进，最低工资保障制度进一步完善。2006 年全省在岗职工平均工资达 23782 元，较上年增长 13.48%。全省最低工资标准类别由四类调整为三类，调整后的一、二、三类标准分别为 750 元/月、620 元/月、520 元/月。

全面推进劳动合同制度实施三年行动计划，劳动合同制度得到较好推行，2006 年对全省 5938 家企业和个体工商户的 69394 名职工的劳动合同签订和履行情况进行了抽样调查，全省劳动合同签订率达 90% 以上，其中国有企业劳动合同签订率达 97.16%，集体企业劳动合同签订率达 91.72%，外商投资企业劳动合同签订率达 95.33%，港澳台商投资企业劳动合同签订率达 94.85%，私营企业、有雇工的个体工商户劳动合同签订率分别达 84.47%、51.86%。

2006 年全省各级劳动争议仲裁委员会共处理劳动争议案件 66073 件（立案处理案件 43984 件，案前案外调解案件 22089 件），涉及劳动者 80763 人，分别比上年上升 30.1% 和 10.8%。立案处理集体劳动争议案件 1199 件，涉及劳动者 12385 人，分别比上年下降 10% 和 14%。全年立案处理的劳动争议案件已审结 43189 件，结案率为 92.7%。

四、劳动保障法制与监察

年末全省共有劳动保障监察机构 131 个，劳动保障监察机构组建率为 100%。各级劳动保障部门配备劳动保障专职监察员 1066 人。在全省范围内重点组织开展了农民工工资支付、清理整顿劳动力市场秩序、劳动用工情况检查活动等专项检查活动，全年主动检查用人单位 8.24 万户，审查 17.34 万户用人单位报送的书面材料，接受群众举报投诉案件 4.48 万件，办结各类劳动保障违法案件2.77万件。通过劳动保障监察执法，责令用人单位为71.72万劳动者补签了劳动合同，责令用人单位为63.27万劳动者追发工资等待遇4.31亿元，其中为41.37万农民工追发工资等待遇3.23亿元，督促1.29万户用人单位补缴社会保险费2.98亿元，督促1.36万户用人单位办理了社会保险登记、申报，取缔非法职业中介机构1972户，责令用人单位退还收取劳动者的风险抵押金1021万元。

五、公共服务能力建设

金保工程建设取得新进展。大力推进全省劳动保障网络建设，实施“镇镇通”工程，信息网络不断向基层延伸，全省城域网覆盖率达到92%。数据整理和传输工作得到加强，至2006年底，已上传数据覆盖养老保险参保职工996.7万、离退休人员269万，数据准确率达91%。失业登记和失业保险监测制度在全国率先建立，向部上传全部失业人员的失业监测数据。整合业务需求、优化业务流程，统一应用软件的开发实施工作全面启动。建成了省和南京市12333信息咨询服务平台，以此为中心，进行了全省标准统一、服务规范、联动响应的12333系统的统一建设，13个省辖市都已完成了系统实施、场地建设、咨询员招聘培训、政策法规库建设等工作，其中9个市已经正式开通人工服务。“江苏劳动保障网”坚持以人为本理念，突出服务和创新，成为劳动保障政务公开和公共服务的重要平台之一。2006年全省新发行统一标准的社会保障卡102万张。

社区平台建设得到进一步加强，到年末在全省省辖市市区258个街道及156个市区乡镇及县城城关镇全部建立了劳动保障所，工作人员共1832人；并在3239个城镇社区建立了劳动保障工作站，聘用社区劳动保障工作人员4739人。

技能人才培养基地建设得到加强，全年新增省级高技能人才培养示范基地10个，累计已达30个，市级建立的培养基地达110个。

2006年江苏省旅游业发展统计公报

江苏省旅游局　江苏省统计局

二〇〇七年三月

2006年是"十一五"计划的开局之年。在省委、省政府的正确领导下,全省旅游行业认真贯彻落实富民强省、"两个率先"精神和加快服务业发展的决策部署,以科学发展观为指导,紧紧围绕建设旅游强省的目标,抢抓机遇,统筹协调,创新思路,突出重点,狠抓落实,全省旅游业取得较好成绩,旅游经济继续保持快速、健康、协调发展。

一、总体情况

全省旅游业呈现出良好发展态势,入境、出境、国内旅游三旅并进,保持稳定快速增长,主要旅游经济指标实现全面增长,实现了"十一五"良好开局。全年接待入境旅游者445.19万人次,旅游外汇收入27.87亿美元,分别比上年增长17.7%和23.3%;接待国内游客1.99亿人次,收入2012.15亿元人民币,分别增长15.7%和23.8%;旅行社组织公民自费出境旅游31.31万人次,增长21.8%。旅游总收入2284.3亿元人民币,增长23.1%。

二、入境旅游

(一)入境旅游者人数

全省接待入境旅游者445.19万人次,增长17.7%。其中,外国人314.89万人次,增长20.1%;香港同胞47.41万人次,增长14.7%;澳门同胞4.30万人次,增长17.9%;台湾同胞78.59万人次,增长10.4%。南京、苏州、无锡、扬州、镇江、常州、徐州、南通、连云港、盐城、淮安11个优秀旅游城市共接待入境旅游者440.58万人次,占全省接待入境旅游者总数的99%,增长17.6%。

(二)入境旅游者人天数

全省接待入境旅游者总人天数为1768.19万人天,增长23.1%。其中:外国人1243.55万人天,增长23.5%;香港同胞170.73万人天,增长23.0%;澳门同胞20.89万人天,增长72.4%;台湾同胞333.02万人天,增长19.4%。南京、苏州、无锡、扬州、镇江、常州、徐州、南通、连云港、盐城、淮安共接待入境旅游者人天数1714.94万人天,占全省接待入境旅游者总人天数的97%,增长22.8%。

(三)主要客源市场

外国旅游者中,亚洲182.89万人次,增长14.5%,占外国人的58.1%;欧洲65.78万人次,增长32.6%,占外国人的20.9%;美洲49.52万人次,增长27.6%,占外国人的15.7%;大洋洲11.83万人次,增长18%,占外国人的3.8%;非洲及其它4.87万人次,增长22.6%,占外国人的1.5%。主要客源国接待量位居前10位的国家依次是:(1)日本(82.88万人次、增长30.5%),(2)韩国(40.46万人次、增长14.5%),(3)美国(39.13万人次、增长29%),(4)马来西亚(22.39万人次、下降3.6%),(5)德国(16.71万人次、增长41.5%),(6)新加坡(15.52万人次、增长16.3%),(7)英国(12.52万人次、增长61.1%),(8)法国(10.65万人次、增长34.7%),(9)澳大利亚(9.27万人次、增长25.3%),(10)加拿大(8.02万人次、增长22.8%)。以上10个客源国接待量共计257.55万人次,占外国人总数的81.8%,比去年增长24.3%。

三、出境旅游

2006年全省旅行社组织公民自费出境旅游(按首站前往国家统计)31.31万人次,增长21.8%。其中出国游10.43万人次,增长14.9%;港澳游20.88万人次,增长25.7%。出境人次数列在前六位的国家和地区分别是中国香港、中国澳门、泰国、新加坡、韩国和马来西亚。

四、国内旅游

全年接待国内游客19935.79万人次,增长15.7%;其中:过夜旅游者16043.27万人次,增长10.3%,占80.5%;一日游游客3892.52万人次,增长44.9%,占19.5%。国内旅游收入2012.15亿元人民币,增长23.8%;其中:过夜旅游者花费1768.15亿元,增长18.4%,占87.9%;一日游游客花费244亿元,增长84.2%,占12.1%。

（一）花费构成

在全省2012.15亿元国内旅游收入中，长途交通费收入277.68亿元，占13.8%；住宿费收入392.37亿元，占19.5%；餐饮费收入370.24亿元，占18.4%；景点游览费收入209.26亿元，占10.4%；娱乐费收入124.75亿元，占6.2%；购物费收入484.93亿元，占24.1%；市内交通费收入46.28亿元，占2.3%；邮电通信费收入18.11亿元，占0.9%；其它花费收入88.53亿元，占4.4%。

（二）客源分布

2006年，江苏人游江苏占总数的34.6%。外省客源比重列前十位的依次是：上海（占10.3%）、浙江（占9%）、山东（占6.1%）、安徽（占5.3%）、北京（占3.6%）、广东（占3.1%）、河南（占3%）、湖北（占2.3%）、四川（占1.85%）、福建（占1.85%）。其中，比重较上年有所上升的有：上海、浙江、山东、北京、四川五省；比重较上年下降的有安徽、广东、福建、湖北、河南五省。包括本省在内，上述11个省（市）的接待量占全省国内旅游总接待量的比重达81%。

（三）出游方式

按旅游者出游方式划分，个人出游的占27.61%，单位组织的占25.04%，家庭或与亲朋结伴的占33.72%，旅行社组织的占13.63%。其中，单位组织比重较上年提高了1个百分点，旅行社组织比重提高了0.5个百分点。

（四）"黄金周"接待、收入情况

春节、"五一"、"十一"三个黄金周全省共接待国内旅游者2622.09万人次，实现国内旅游收入207.03亿元，分别占全年接待国内旅游者总人次数和收入的13.2%和10.3%。按同口径对比，春节、"五一"、"十一"三个黄金周全省接待国内旅游者人次数和国内旅游收入分别比上年同期增长16.6%和20.9%。

五、旅游产业规模情况

截止2006年底，全省拥有全国优秀旅游城市23座；旅游星级饭店799座，其中：五星级25座，四星级112座，三星级335座，二星级324座，一星级3座；旅行社1478家，其中：国际社79家，具有出境游组团资格的41家；国家等级旅游景区216家，其中：4A级63家，3A级50家，2A级100家，1A级3家；全国工农业旅游示范点94家。

六、旅游饭店接待情况

全省旅游饭店共接待入境旅游者418.62万人次，增长17.5%；接待人天数1249.1万人天，增长19.8%；全省旅游饭店平均客房出租率64.1%。

七、旅游景区接待情况

全省各类游览点全年接待游客2.77亿人次，增长14.5%。其中：年接待游客量超过100万人次的游览点58个，比上年增加5个。

八、居民出游情况

2006年全省居民出游率为119.6%。其中：城镇居民出游率为173.3%，农村居民出游率为88.4%。

注：出游率指城镇居民或农村居民出游的人次数占其人口数的比重。

2006年江苏省开发区经济发展统计公报

江苏省对外贸易经济合作厅　江苏省统计局

二〇〇七年四月三日

2006年是"十一五"开局之年，也是开发区发展的关键之年，在宏观环境偏紧、引资难度加大、区域竞争加剧的条件下，全省开发区在省委、省政府的领导下，以科学发展观统领经济和社会发展全局，坚持集约开发，在挑战中抢抓机遇，在创新中谋求发展，开发区建设保持了健康的发展态势，运行质量和效益进一步提高，对全省经济社会发展的贡献进一步加大。

一、综合

全省开发区完成业务总收入33392.31亿元、财政收入1129.68亿元、税收收入1009.41亿元，同比分别增长44.0%、34.7%和36.3%。国家级开发区完成业务总收入14654.26亿元，完成财政收入497.66亿元，完成税收收入454.70亿元，同比分别增长25.5%、30.6%和28.1%。

全省开发区期末从业人员564.13万人，其中工业从业人员436.37万人，外籍人员3.87万人，同比分别增加13.8%、24.4%和53.2%。国家级开发区期末从业人员176.31万人，其中工业从业人员138.11万人，外藉人员1.76万人，同比分别增长15.6%、28.3%和18.9%。

二、工业经济

全省开发区实现工业总产值24763.37亿元，其中规模以上工业总产值21060.53亿元，同比分别增长41.1%和47.4%。国家级开发区实现总产值10851.55亿元，其中规模以上工业总产值9714.36亿元，同比分别增长27.3%和31.3%。

全省开发区完成工业增加值5475.34亿元，其中主导产业增加值3799.03亿元，同比分别增长39.5%和47.3%。国家级开发区完成工业增加值2221.14亿元，其中主导产业增加值1550.89亿元，同比分别增长18.9%和26.5%。

三、固定资产投入

全省开发区完成全社会固定资产投资4598.0亿元，其中工业项目固定资产投资3107.55亿元，同比分别增长27.7%和58.6%；完成基础设施投入759.32亿元，同比增长19.9%。国家级开发区完成全社会固定资产投资1422.10亿元，其中工业项目固定资产投资865.31亿元，同比分别增长17.3%和22.7%；完成基础设施投入229.34亿元，同比增长12.8%。

四、投资促进

全省开发区新批外商投资企业4075家，实际到帐注册外资（商务部确认数）138.14亿美元，同比分别增长19.4%和46.6%。国家级开发区新批外商投资企业1243家，同比下降2.9%，完成实际到帐注册外资（商务部确认数）61.52亿美元，同比增长33.6%。

全省开发区新增内资企业24100家，新增内资企业注册资本981.26亿元，同比分别增长38.4%和41.7%。国家级开发区新增内资企业10069家，新增内资企业注册资本432.20亿元，同比分别下降17.6%和1.2%。

五、对外贸易

全省开发区完成进出口总额2095.71亿美元，其中出口额1132.04亿美元，同比分别增长30.4%、31.2%。国家级开发区完成进出口总额和出口额分别为1578.92亿美元和848.53亿美元，同比分别增长25.5%和32.1%。

六、科技进步

全省开发区有高新技术企业2823家，实现高新技术企业业务总收入9105.77亿元，同比分别增长49.7%和49.9%。国家级开发区有高新技术企业1270家，实现高新技术企业业务总收入5214.16亿元，同比分别增长13.6%、34.8%。

全省开发区有高新技术创业服务中心（孵化器）108家，中心（孵化器）内共有3342家企业，区内有研发中心1686家，同比分别增长86.2%、13.4%、47.4%。

七、可持续发展

全省开发区每万元工业增加值的综合能耗为1.07吨标准煤，同比下降6.1%。国家级开发区每万元工业增加值的综合能耗为0.61吨标准煤,同比下降4.7%。

全省通过ISO14000认证的开发区有66家,其中国家级开发区全部通过认证。

八、出口加工区建设

全省出口加工区基础设施投入7.58亿元,同比增长83.9%;新批外商投资企业69家,实际到帐注册外资额11.12亿美元,同比分别增长3%和107.4%;完成进出口额405.97亿美元,其中出口总额237.59亿美元,同比分别增长67.5%和73.3%。

JIANGSU STATISTICAL YEARBOOK

附录三

APPENDIX Ⅲ

单位选介

THE UNITS INTRODUCTION

2006年江苏省工业企业前一百家

（按主营业务收入排列）

江苏省电力公司
江苏沙钢集团有限公司
扬子石油化工股份有限公司
中国石油化工股份有限公司金陵分公司
江苏华西集团公司
乐金飞利浦液晶显示（南京）有限公司
南京钢铁集团有限公司
明基电通信息技术有限公司
希捷国际科技（无锡）有限公司
徐州工程机械集团有限公司
江苏三房巷集团有限公司
江苏永钢集团有限公司
中国石化仪征化纤股份有限公司
无锡夏普电子元器件有限公司
扬子石化—巴斯夫有限责任公司
纬新资通（昆山）有限公司
常州中天钢铁有限公司
江阴兴澄特钢有限公司
华芳集团有限公司
江苏阳光集团有限公司
南京爱立信熊猫通信有限公司
纬智资通（昆山）有限公司
扬子江药业集团有限公司
南京瀚宇彩欣科技有限责任公司
波司登股份有限公司
上海梅山钢铁股份有限公司
法尔胜集团公司
冠捷科技苏州飞利浦消费电子有限公司
东海粮油工业（张家港）有限公司
维维集团
东风悦达起亚汽车有限公司
纬创资通（昆山）有限公司
仁宝资讯工业（昆山）有限公司
南京汽车集团有限公司
金东纸业（江苏）有限公司
张家港联合铜业有限公司
江苏沙钢集团淮钢特钢有限公司
泰州陵光石化集团
南京卷烟厂
仁宝电子科技（昆山）有限公司
徐州矿务集团有限公司
远东控股集团有限公司
亚旭电子科技（江苏）有限公司
苏州三星电子电脑有限公司
LG同创彩色显示系统有限责任公司
苏州三星电子有限公司
海澜集团公司
江苏新长江实业集团公司
常州金源铜业有限公司
旭电（苏州）科技有限公司
华宝通讯（南京）有限公司
江苏中烟工业公司徐州卷烟厂
南京华新光电股份有限公司
奇梦达模组（苏州）有限公司
江阴市西城钢铁有限公司
日立显示器（苏州）有限公司
苏州爱普生有限公司
江苏双良集团有限公司
奇梦达科技（苏州）有限公司
仁宝信息技术（昆山）有限公司
江苏张铜集团有限公司
神讯电脑（昆山）有限公司
微盟电子（昆山）有限公司
佳能（苏州）有限公司
大亚科技集团有限公司
索尼数字产品（无锡）有限公司
江苏隆力奇集团有限公司
中国石化集团金陵石油化工有限责任公司
中国石化集团江苏石油勘探局
无锡兴达泡塑新材料有限公司
无锡市大明金属制品有限公司
益海（连云港）粮油有限公司
富士康（昆山）电脑接插件有限公司
南京夏普电子有限公司
昆达电脑科技（昆山）有限公司
江苏华宏实业集团有限公司
宝胜集团有限公司
江苏综艺集团
江阴澄星实业集团有限公司
江苏江南化纤集团有限公司
志合电脑（苏州工业园区）有限公司
江苏梦兰集团有限公司
无锡锡兴钢铁股份有限公司
江苏申特钢铁有限公司
一汽解放汽车有限公司无锡柴油机厂
索尼电子（无锡）有限公司
中外合资镇江奇美化工有限公司
天弘（苏州）有限公司
中达电子（江苏）有限公司
中国石化集团南京化学工业有限
四海电子（昆山）有限公司
高创（苏州）电子有限公司
佳能精技（苏州）办公设备有限公司
江苏亚邦化工集团有限公司
常熟科弘材料科技有限公司
泰金宝光电（苏州）有限公司
江苏常发实业集团有限公司
宜兴市意达铜业有限公司
泰州乐金电子冷机有限公司
江苏澳洋实业（集团）有限公司

2006年江苏省企业（集团）前一百家

（按营业收入排列）

江苏省电力公司
苏宁电器集团
江苏沙钢集团有限公司
中国石化集团金陵石油化工有限责任公司
中国石油化工股份有限公司江苏石油分公司
扬子石油化工股份有限公司
江苏华西集团公司
江苏省烟草公司
江苏悦达集团有限公司
南京钢铁集团
熊猫电子集团有限公司
乐金飞利浦液晶显示（南京）有限公司
希捷国际科技（无锡）有限公司
华芳集团有限公司
明基电通信息技术有限公司
徐州工程机械集团有限公司
江苏永钢集团有限公司
中国移动通信集团江苏有限公司
江苏省电信有限公司
江苏阳光集团有限公司
苏果超市有限公司
江苏三房巷集团有限公司
太平洋建设集团有限公司
江苏五星电器有限公司
江苏交通控股有限公司
中国石化集团仪征化纤股份有限公司
无锡夏普电子元器件有限公司
扬子石化－巴斯夫有限责任公司
中天钢铁集团有限公司
江苏国泰国际集团有限公司
纬新资通（昆山）有限公司
南京斯威特集团有限公司
红豆集团有限公司
海澜集团公司
江阴兴澄特种钢铁有限公司
江苏舜天国际集团有限公司
江阴澄星实业集团有限公司
江苏雨润食品产业集团有限公司
江苏文峰集团
徐州矿务集团有限公司
跃进汽车集团
法尔胜集团公司
纬智资通（昆山）有限公司
江苏新长江实业集团公司
扬子江药业集团
无锡威孚集团有限公司
南京医药产业（集团）有限责任公司
苏州创元（集团）有限公司
中国石油天然气股份有限公司江苏销售分公司
波司登股份有限公司
红星家具集团有限公司
上海梅山钢铁股份有限公司
冠捷科技苏州飞利浦消费电子有限公司
春兰集团
江苏开元国际集团有限公司
远东控股集团有限公司
东海粮油工业（张家港）有限公司
江苏省苏中建设集团
维维集团
江苏省农垦集团有限公司
纬创资通（昆山）有限公司
江苏南通二建集团
仁宝资讯工业（昆山）有限公司
江苏石油勘探局
南京物资实业集团总公司
江南百兴集团有限公司
金东纸业（江苏）有限公司
申达集团有限公司
江苏苏美达集团公司
张家港联合铜业有限公司
连云港如意集团股份有限公司
泰州陵光石化集团
江苏省第一建筑安装有限公司
苏州进出口（集团）有限公司
江苏汇鸿国际集团有限公司
恒力集团
南京卷烟厂
江阴市西城钢铁有限公司
索尼数字产品（无锡）有限公司
仁宝电子科技（昆山）有限公司
亚旭电子科技（江苏）有限公司
苏州三星电子电脑有限公司
LG同创彩色显示系统有限责任公司
苏州三星电子有限公司
江苏张铜集团有限公司
江苏双良集团有限公司
常林工程机械集团
常州金源铜业有限公司
南通四建集团有限公司
旭电（苏州）科技有限公司
宝胜集团有限公司
江苏中烟工业公司徐州卷烟厂
南京华新光电股份有限公司
中国石化集团南京化学工业有限公司
奇梦达模组（苏州）有限公司
南京纺织品进出口股份有限公司
日立显示器（苏州）有限公司
苏州爱普生有限公司
奇梦达科技（苏州）有限公司
正太集团

2006年江苏省建筑企业前五十家

（按总产值排列）

江苏省第一建筑安装有限公司
南通四建集团有限公司
江苏省苏中建设集团股份有限公司
江苏南通三建集团有限公司
江苏南通二建集团有限公司
正太集团有限公司
江苏江都建设工程有限公司
江苏中兴建设有限公司
江苏南通六建建设集团有限公司
通州建总集团有限公司
江苏江中集团有限公司
南通建筑工程总承包有限公司
江苏省华建建设股份有限公司
江苏弘盛建设工程集团有限公司
苏州二建建筑集团有限公司
南通建工集团股份有限公司
金坛市建筑安装工程公司
江苏顺通建设工程有限公司
南通五建建设工程有限公司
南通市新华建筑安装工程有限公司
江苏盐城二建集团有限公司
南通永峰建筑安装工程有限公司
龙信建设集团有限公司
江苏邗建集团有限公司
南通华新建工集团有限公司
江苏通州四建集团有限公司
苏州第一建筑集团有限公司
江苏广宇建设有限公司
锦宸集团有限公司
启东市建筑安装工程有限公司
江苏建业建筑安装工程集团有限公司
江苏省交通工程有限公司
江苏天宇建设工程有限公司
涟水县建筑工程公司
江苏武进建筑安装工程有限公司
苏州金螳螂建筑装饰股份有限公司
江苏长安建设集团有限公司
中国核工业华兴建设有限公司
南京市第六建筑安装工程有限公司
江苏金土木建设集团有限公司
中铁大桥局集团二公司
中铁大桥局集团四公司
江苏省送变电公司
江苏省建工集团有限公司
中港第二航务工程局三公司
江苏省金陵建工集团有限公司
江苏双楼建设集团有限公司
南京建工集团有限公司
江苏三兴建工集团有限公司
镇江建工建设集团有限公司

2006年江苏省房地产企业前五十家

（按销售面积排列）

南京天华百润投资发展有限责任公司
南京栖霞建设集团有限公司
明发集团南京房地产开发有限公司
南京仙林房地产开发有限公司
扬州京华城中城生活置业有限公司
南京江宁市政建设房地产开发有限公司
江苏华厦融创置地集团有限公司
南通中天房地产开发有限公司
南京浦东建设发展股份有限公司
上海绿地集团（昆山）置业有限公司
无锡万科房地产有限公司
南京西城房地产开发有限公司
江苏亚东建设发展集团有限公司
常州新城房产开发有限公司
无锡市经济适用住房管理中心
泰州市鹏欣房地产开发有限公司
江苏伟丰集团宜滨房地产开发有限公司
徐州滨湖花园房地产开发有限公司
扬州新能源有限公司
江苏中豪置业有限责任公司
中国房地产开发集团南通有限公司
苏州相城城市建设有限责任公司
江苏华西房地产开发有限公司
扬州万马房地产开发有限公司
徐州市颖都房地产开发有限公司沭阳分公司
无锡顺驰地产有限公司
无锡阳光置业有限公司
苏州工业园区建屋发展集团有限公司
南京金浦房地产开发有限责任公司
苏州江苏吴中东吴产业开发公司
苏州海发置业有限公司
常州天禄中创建设有限公司
常州市经济适用房发展中心
徐州鸿泰房地产开发有限公司
无锡虹亚房地产开发有限公司射阳分公司
南京鼎业房地产开发有限公司
姜堰市锦都房地产开发有限公司
苏州中天房地产开发有限公司靖江分公司
苏州新创建设发展有限公司
江苏天成置业有限责任公司
江苏新城房产股份有限公司
中海发展（苏州）有限公司
南通中南新世界中心开发有限公司
苏州润禾房地产开发有限公司
无锡鸿意地产发展有限公司
江苏炜赋集团建设开发有限公司
深圳市新世界集团江苏房地产有限公司
南通银洲昌诚置业有限公司
百胜麒麟南京建设发展有限公司
江阴新锦南房地产开发有限公司

2006 年江苏省贸易零售企业前一百家

（按销售额排列）

苏果超市有限公司
江苏五星电器有限公司
苏宁电器连锁集团股份有限公司
江苏无锡商业大厦集团有限公司
南京朗驰集团有限公司
南京宏图三胞企业发展有限公司
南京医药股份有限公司
江苏明都汽车摩托车有限公司
南京金鹰国际购物集团有限公司
苏州苏宁电器有限公司
南京中央商场股份有限公司
南京新街口百货商店股份有限公司
徐州医药股份有限公司
苏州人民商场股份有限公司
无锡市新纪元汽车贸易有限公司
江苏文峰大世界连锁发展股份有限公司南通文峰大世界
无锡八佰伴经济管理有限公司
昆山商厦股份有限公司
苏州礼安医药有限公司
江苏鹏润国美电器有限公司
昆山市润华商业有限公司百润发分公司
苏州市石路国际商城有限责任公司
南京福中信息产业集团有限公司
常州百货大楼股份有限公司
宜兴华地百货有限公司
苏州欧尚超市有限公司
华润万家（苏州）超市有限公司
苏州函数集团有限责任公司
江阴市全顺汽车有限公司
苏州泰华商城有限公司
苏州宏图三胞科技发展有限公司
无锡悦家商业有限公司
南京医药（淮安）天颐有限公司
无锡宝诚汽车销售服务有限公司
徐州中央百货大楼股份有限公司
无锡市第一百货（集团）有限公司
南京大洋百货有限公司
无锡德尔汽车有限公司
无锡宏图三胞科技发展有限公司
扬州金鹰国际实业有限公司
江阴市广吉汽车经销有限公司
徐州金鹰国际实业有限公司
南京悦家超市有限公司
宜兴新苏南商厦有限责任公司
中油销售江苏有限公司徐州分公司
江苏富骏汽车贸易有限公司
无锡爱莲连锁超市有限公司
常州金太阳至尊家电有限公司
常州新世纪商城有限公司
江苏中央新亚百货股份有限公司
无锡天润发超市有限公司
常州市武进药业有限公司
南通苏宁电器有限公司
南京凡德汽车销售有限公司
常熟市建发医药有限公司
昆山润华商业有限公司苏州高新区分公司
江苏雅家乐集团有限公司
江苏宏信商贸股份有限公司
南京商厦股份有限公司
苏州宝信汽车销售服务有限公司
南京福联汽车贸易有限公司
镇江百盛商城有限公司
常州商厦泰富百货有限责任公司
无锡市高尚超市有限公司
江苏盐阜人民商场有限公司
无锡国美电器有限公司
无锡三阳百盛广场有限公司
江苏华通汽车销售服务有限公司
常州九洲超市有限公司
南京利星汽车有限公司
徐州苏宁电器有限公司
南通通润发超市有限公司
南京长江丰田汽车销售服务有限公司
新合作常客隆连锁超市有限公司
无锡市华通汽车销售有限公司
常州市五星电器有限公司
泰州第一百货商店股份有限公司
常熟华联商厦有限责任公司
南京永乐生活家用电器有限公司
南通市百货大楼股份有限公司
苏州冠芝霖手机大卖场有限公司
丹阳华地百货有限公司
扬州市广润发超市有限公司
江阴华地百货有限公司
江阴市医药股份有限公司
常熟市百润发超市有限责任公司
苏州华正汽车销售服务有限公司
无锡市金城丰田汽车销售服务有限公司
苏州悦家超市有限公司
徐州（北方）宗申三轮摩托车销售有限公司
江苏省盐城药业有限公司
江苏万帮汽车有限公司
无锡市苏宁电器有限公司
南京中升丰田汽车销售有限公司
常州市武进长江石化物资有限公司
苏州三星汽车贸易有限公司
无锡天惠超市股份有限公司
常熟市常客隆购物广场有限公司
南京华诚超市有限公司
盐城商业大厦股份有限公司

2006 年江苏省外商投资企业出口前一百家

（按出口额排列）

名硕电脑（苏州）有限公司
仁宝资讯工业（昆山）有限公司
三星电子（苏州）半导体有限公司
友达光电（苏州）有限公司
希捷国际科技（无锡）有限公司
明基电通信息技术有限公司
仁宝信息技术（昆山）有限公司
苏州三星电子液晶显示器有限公司
纬新资通（昆山）有限公司
飞索半导体（苏州）有限公司
华宝通讯（南京）有限公司
无锡夏普电子元器件有限公司
迈拓科技（苏州）有限公司
纬智资通（昆山）有限公司
仁宝电子科技（昆山）有限公司
乐金飞利浦液晶显示（南京）有限公司
苏州飞利浦消费电子有限公司
亚旭电子科技（江苏）有限公司
英飞凌科技模组（苏州）有限公司
苏州三星电子电脑有限公司
索尼数字产品（无锡）有限公司
佳能（苏州）有限公司
南京 LG 同创彩色显示系统有限责任公司
苏州三星电子有限公司
神迅电脑（昆山）有限公司
志合电脑（苏州工业园区）有限公司
微盟电子（昆山）有限公司
纬创资通（昆山）有限公司
昆达电脑科技（昆山）有限公司
日立显示器件（苏州）有限公司
瑞中电子（苏州）有限公司
华映视讯（吴江）有限公司
旭电（苏州）科技有限公司

高创（苏州）电子有限公司
泰金宝光电（苏州）有限公司
南京夏普电子有限公司
仁宝电脑工业（中国）有限公司
联建（中国）科技有限公司
佳能精技（苏州）办公设备有限公司
天弘（苏州）科技有限公司
苏州爱普生有限公司
夏普办公设备（常熟）有限公司
彩晶光电科技（昆山）有限公司
无锡阿尔卑斯电子有限公司
统宝光电（南京）有限公司
罗技科技（苏州）有限公司
大同电子科技（江苏）有限公司
金东纸业（江苏）有限公司
大将科技（苏州）有限公司
牧田（昆山）有限公司
南京瀚宇彩欣科技有限责任公司
苏州富士胶片映像机器有限公司
华宇电脑（江苏）有限公司
昆山扬皓光电有限公司
苏州松下半导体有限公司
新义半导体（苏州）有限公司
英飞凌科技（苏州）有限公司
华冠通讯（江苏）有限公司
泰州乐金电子冷机有限公司
百得（苏州）科技有限公司
南通中远川崎船舶工程有限公司
中达电子（江苏）有限公司
苏州明基光电技术有限公司
芬欧汇川（常熟）纸业有限公司
索尼电子（无锡）有限公司
捷普电子（无锡）有限公司
无锡松下电池有限公司

万福阁家具（昆山）有限公司
南京乐金熊猫电器有限公司
超威半导体技术（中国）有限公司
四海电子（昆山）有限公司
乐金电子（南京）等离子有限公司
卡特彼勒（徐州）有限公司
昆山乐金微永电脑有限公司
南京爱立信熊猫通信有限公司
无锡尚德太阳能电力有限公司
海力士－意法半导体有限公司
张家港润忠钢铁有限公司
凯博电脑（昆山）有限公司
张家港宏昌钢板有限公司
江苏韩泰轮胎有限公司
南通富士通微电子股份有限公司
和舰科技（苏州）有限公司
科特拉（无锡）汽车环保科技有限公司
常熟欣瑞科技材料有限公司
好孩子儿童用品有限公司
南通新福达光电有限公司
昆山扬明光学有限公司
东方国际集装箱（连云港）有限公司
安德鲁电信器材（中国）有限公司
维讯柔性电路板（苏州）有限公司
川奇光电科技（扬州）有限公司
江阴福汇纺织有限公司
苏州光宝康电子有限公司
宜来特光电（无锡）有限公司
捷安特（中国）有限公司
无锡西姆莱斯石油专用管有限公司
江阴兴澄特种钢铁有限公司
尼康光学仪器（中国）有限公司
沪士电子股份有限公司

2006年江苏省内资企业出口前一百家

（按出口额排列）

江苏国泰国际集团有限公司
江苏舜天国际集团有限公司
江苏汇鸿国际集团有限公司
苏州进出口（集团）有限公司
江苏开元国际集团有限公司
江苏苏美达集团公司
江苏苏豪国际集团股份有限公司
江苏省海外企业集团有限公司
江苏新科电子集团有限公司
南京纺织品进出口股份有限公司
中国江苏国际经济技术合作公司
江苏三房巷集团有限公司
南京钢铁集团国际经济贸易有限公司
江苏省纺织（集团）总公司
苏州国信集团有限公司
江苏弘业国际集团有限公司
常州大华进出口（集团）有限公司
中材国际工程股份有限公司
江苏阳光集团有限公司
江苏新世纪造船股份有限公司
苏州近铁仓储有限公司
澄西船舶修造厂
南通市经济技术开发区总公司
无锡新中润国际集团有限公司
中化江苏进出口公司
吴江市外贸集团公司
金城集团进出口有限公司
连云港远泰国际贸易有限公司
徐州工程机械集团进出口有限公司
华芳集团有限公司
江苏长电科技股份有限公司
常州对外贸易有限公司
南京机械五金矿产医药保健品进出口股份公司
中国煤炭工业进出口集团连云港公司
高新张铜股份有限公司
国内贸易部口岸船舶工业公司
常州大亚进出口有限公司
法尔胜集团进出口有限公司
江苏华瑞国际实业集团有限公司
无锡小天鹅通用电器有限公司
江阴市被单厂
江苏东恒国际服务贸易集团有限公司
江阴澄星国际贸易有限公司
中设（无锡）机械设备进出口公司
江苏永钢集团有限公司
江苏华西集团公司
镇江焦化煤气集团有限公司
常州机械设备进出口有限公司
常熟市波司登进出口有限公司
江苏阳光东升进出口有限公司
无锡市金茂对外贸易有限公司
苏州工业园区中辰进出口有限公司
金龙联合汽车工业（苏州）有限公司
江苏联发进出口有限公司
小天鹅集团公司
常熟市大有进出口有限责任公司
海澜集团公司
江苏峰峰钨钼制品股份有限公司
常熟家用纺织品进出口有限责任公司
江苏江动集团进出口有限公司
宜兴市乐祺进出口有限公司?
江苏玉龙钢管有限公司
中国工艺品南京进出口公司
镇江泛华进出口有限公司
常熟三爱富中昊化工新材料有限公司
南京熊猫电子进出口有限公司
南京市对外贸易公司
黑牡丹（集团）股份有限公司
张家港市沙洲纺织印染进出口有限公司
上海梅山钢铁股份有限公司
盐城经纬国际集团有限公司
江苏天工工具股份有限公司
常熟市瀛通进出口有限责任公司
江苏省粮油食品进出口集团股份有限公司
常熟市瀛环进出口有限责任公司
常州世方国际贸易有限公司
南京市对外经贸发展有限责任公司
江苏中丹化工进出口有限公司
江苏索普（集团）有限公司
苏州宝时得电动工具有限公司
苏州高新技术产业开发区对外贸易公司（苏州新区进出口）
常熟市纺织品进出口有限责任公司
苏州市春菊电器有限公司
江苏春兰进出口公司
江苏金鼎电动工具集团有限公司
江苏省华宁国际技术贸易公司
跃进汽车集团进出口有限公司
盐城市对外贸易有限公司
江苏红豆进出口有限责任公司
无锡洛社印染有限公司
苏州得尔达国际物流有限公司
江苏亚星锚链有限公司
如东县铁链厂有限公司
南通江山农药化工股份有限公司
江苏晨风集团股份有限公司
吴江英诺时装有限公司
张家港保税区中油泰富船舶燃料供应有限公司
江苏吴中实业股份有限公司
江苏金飞达电动工具有限公司
常州老三集团进出口有限公司

2006年江苏省旅游涉外饭店前五十家

（按营业收入排列）

南京金陵饭店股份有限公司
苏州吴宫喜来登大酒店
南京中山大厦
苏州尼盛万丽酒店
苏州张家港国贸酒店
南京维景国际大酒店
常州市富都大酒店有限公司
南京玄武饭店
苏州张家港市华芳金陵国际酒店
南京侨鸿皇冠大酒店
无锡喜来登大饭店
苏州新城花园有限公司
宜兴国际饭店有限公司
江苏金丝利喜来登酒店
苏州胥城大厦有限公司
南京丁山花园酒店有限公司
南京古南都饭店
无锡太湖饭店
无锡蓝天新港餐饮娱乐有限公司
南京中心大酒店
南京国际会议大酒店
南通市文峰饭店
苏州市会议中心
无锡湖滨饭店
江苏新纪元大酒店有限公司
无锡大饭店
无锡国际饭店
苏州凯莱大酒店
南通有斐饭店
常州大酒店有限公司
苏州雅戈尔富宫大酒店
无锡锡州花园酒店
溧阳市天目湖宾馆有限公司
南京状元楼酒店
徐州开元迎宾馆
无锡锦江大酒店
苏州同里湖大饭店有限公司
苏州竹辉饭店
南京太阳宫经营有限公司
江阴国际大酒店有限公司
南京市益来名人酒店
江苏凤凰台饭店有限公司
苏州张家港市馨苑度假村
常州市金陵明都大饭店
南京饭店
苏州昆山宾馆
南通三德大酒店
苏州张家港市沙洲宾馆
扬州市京华大酒店
靖江国际大酒店有限公司

2006年江苏省旅行社前五十家

（按营业收入排列）

无锡中国旅行社
无锡中国国际旅行社
江苏中国青年旅行社有限公司
苏州文化国际旅行社有限公司
苏州中国国际旅行社有限责任公司
中国康辉苏州国际旅行社有限公司
无锡康辉旅行社有限公司
江苏华特国际旅行社有限公司
江苏水乡周庄旅游股份有限公司
南京大华旅游有限责任公司
无锡江南国际旅行社
中国康辉无锡旅行社有限责任公司
无锡海外旅游公司
江苏招商国际旅游公司
无锡青年旅行社
南京中北国际旅行社
中国康辉南京国际旅行社
江阴市中国旅行社有限公司
常州国旅旅行社有限公司
无锡二泉旅行社
苏州和平国际旅行社有限公司
江苏省中山国际旅行社
苏州青年旅行社股份有限公司
无锡假日国际旅行社
无锡春秋旅游公司
江阴市华西旅行社
无锡阳光国际旅行社
扬州中国青年旅行社
苏州职工国际旅行社有限公司
南京春秋旅行社
南京原野旅行社
港中旅国际（无锡）旅行社
无锡湖滨国际旅行社
江苏省中国旅行社
南京海外原野旅行社有限公司
苏州市东吴国际旅行社
南京禄口机场国际旅行社
江阴市友好旅行社有限公司
苏州昆山市春秋国际旅行社
无锡市旅游公司
苏州市乐乡旅行社
苏州张家港国泰国际旅行社有限公司
苏州张家港华泰国内旅行社有限公司
苏州常熟中国国际旅行社有限公司
苏州中旅国际旅行社有限公司
苏州永安国际旅行社
江苏舜天海外旅游有限公司
江苏东方航空国际旅行社有限公司
南京中国国际旅行社
江苏金陵商务国际旅行社

江苏省人口和计划生育委员会

2006年9月21日省人口计生委、省委宣传部、省妇联、省文联、省电视台联合举办"手拉手·共建和谐家园"电视文艺晚会

省人口计生委张肖敏主任参加"三下乡"慰问活动

近年来，在省委、省政府领导下，我省认真贯彻党中央、国务院关于人口和计划生育工作的部署要求，狠抓落实，开拓创新，全省人口和计划生育工作取得显著成绩。

低生育水平继续保持稳定。"十五"以来，全省人口出生率、人口自然增长率分别稳定在10‰、4‰以内，妇女总和生育率保持在1.3左右。2006年，全省人口出生率9.36‰，人口自然增长率2.28‰,计划生育率97.1%,独生子女累积率达到72.42%。实行计划生育以来，全省累计少生了4000多万人，独生子女达到1200多万人。

统筹解决人口问题取得新的进展。组织开展江苏人口发展战略研究，提出江苏人口发展战略和人口发展评价指标体系，为实现"两个率先"、构建和谐社会提供了有关人口问题的科学依据。深入开展"关爱女孩行动"，贯彻实施省人大《关于禁止非医学需要胎儿性别鉴定和选择性别人工终止妊娠的决定》,出生人口性别比升高问题专项治理取得初步成效。建立以现居住地为主的流动人口计划生育管理和服务机制，为流动人口提供计划生育免费技术服务，实行了流动人口计划生育"属地化管理、市民化服务"。

人口与计划生育管理服务体系进一步完善。加强人口和计划生育法制建设，全面推行计划生育政务公开，深入开展人口和计划生育便民维权活动，提高人口和计划生育依法行政水平，维护了群众的合法权益。创新人口和计划生育服务体系，推进计划生育"世代服务"品牌建设，全省建成50个计划生育示范服务站。切实履行人口和计划生育宣传教育、技术服务、信息咨询、人员培训、药具发放职能。2006年，全省计划生育服务机构提供随访服务1126.24万人次,随访服务率达到85.2%；提供计划生育咨询服务1774.46万人次,避孕节育方法知情选择率83%；全省出生缺陷一级干预率87.7%，育龄妇女生殖道感染防治率84.1%，群众对计划生育工作的满意度达到84%。

计划生育利益导向政策体系建设进一步加强。全面实施农村部分计划生育家庭奖励扶助制度，2006年全省奖扶对象达到21.83万人，奖励扶助总额1.31亿元。省、市、县各级建立了人口与计划生育公益金制度，用于扶助计划生育困难家庭。部分地区建立了独生子女伤残死亡家庭扶助制度。全省开展了"亲情牵手零距离服务"行动，组织志愿者32.6万人,帮扶计划生育困难家庭11.3万户。

省人口计生委张肖敏主任参加省纠风办与省广播电台联合主办的"政风热线"

江苏省

省委常委、无锡市市委书记　杨卫泽

无锡市市长　毛小平

承载千年文明，充满温情和水。江苏无锡市位于美丽富庶的太湖之滨，土地丰饶，是中国著名的鱼米之乡，享有“太湖明珠”美誉。

无锡又名“梁溪”，简称锡，是一座具有三千多年历史的江南名城，是吴文化的发祥地之一。镶嵌在古运河上，南为太湖环抱，北有长江流过，位于沪宁铁路和沪宁高速公路中段。无锡气候宜人，风景秀丽，交通发达、经济繁荣，是江南历史文化名城，是中国重要的经济中心城市、中国优秀旅游城市、国家卫生城市、国家环保模范城市、国家园林城市。被权威机构认定为“中国最具发展前途的城市”、“中国投资环境最优城市”。位列2006年最佳商业城市排行榜第四位和“中国最具竞争力城市”排行榜第七位。

2006年，全市人民在中共无锡市委领导下，以科学发展观为指导，认真贯彻落实中央宏观调控决策部署，着力提升全面小康发展质量，加快构建社会主义和谐社会，“十一五”发展实现良好开局。

2006年无锡实现地区生产总值3300亿元，继续列全国大中城市第九位。深入推进经济结构战略性调整，着力提升经济质态。大力引导科技创新创业，全力发展先进制造业，荣膺中国制造业十大最具竞争力城市称号。优先发展现代服务业，加快服务业集聚区建设；深入推

京杭大运河穿城而过

无锡市

无锡全景

进改革开放和体制创新，着力提升发展活力；提升国际化水平，优化对外贸易结构。全年到位注册外资27.52亿美元，进出口总额391.84亿美元，出口总额214.40亿美元；完善投资管理机制，强化投资调控，改善投资结构，加大高新技术产业、现代服务业和基础设施建设投入力度，第三产业投资占比达到44.8%；深入推进生态城市建设，着力提升环境质量落实节能降耗措施；深入推进区域统筹发展，着力提升城乡面貌强化规划城乡全覆盖；深入推进社会事业协调发展，着力提升文明程度统筹发展各类教育；深入推进惠民政策落实到位，着力提升民生水平，社会就业态势良好。城市居民人均可支配收入18189元，增长13.6%，农民人均纯收入8880元，增长10.9%。

无锡目前设江阴、宜兴两个县级市，市区辖崇安、南长、北塘、锡山、惠山、滨湖和新区等七个行政区，2006年常住人口584.17万人。

2007年，无锡人民将以科学发展观统领经济社会发展全局，认真落实党的十六届六中全会和省、市党代会精神，围绕“一当好三争创”目标，致力于构建高水平全面小康社会和社会主义和谐社会，加快建设科学发展先导区、和谐发展示范区，以优异成绩迎接党的十七大胜利召开。

景云立交

无锡招商城景观照明工程

崇安寺生活步行街区

江苏省

南汽厂房鸟瞰

无锡新农村

市民广场

太湖大咧咀桥夜景

环太湖公路

无锡市

便捷的交通

蠡湖风光带沿湖夜景

河埒休闲广场

江苏省徐州市

徐州经济开发区

中国矿业大学校园

徐州位于江苏省西北部，现辖2市4县5区，总人口925万、总面积11258平方公里，其中市区人口180万、面积1160平方公里。徐州是全国较大的市、国家历史文化名城、中国优秀旅游城市、全国科教兴市先进市、全国卫生城市、国家园林城市，也是省重点建设的四个特大城市和三大都市圈核心城市之一。徐州具有独特的区位条件。地处苏鲁豫皖四省接壤地区，是淮海经济区20个地级市、17万平方公里、1.2亿人口的区域内规模最大的城市，是区域性地理中心和经济中心。在全国区域经济格局中，处于东部沿海开放和中西部开发的连接带、长三角与环渤海两大经济板块的结合部，具有显著的东靠西移、南北对接、双向开放、梯度推进的战略区位特征。二是拥有显著的交通优势。徐州是全国重要的综合性交通枢纽，京沪、陇海两大铁路干线在此交汇，京沪高速铁路建成通车后，徐州到北京、上海的时间均缩短至两个多小时，并与规划建设的徐兰客运专线联结互通，将成为全国重要的高速铁路枢纽；5条国道、20条省道、5条高速公路纵横成网，京杭大运河穿境而过，观音机场已开辟15条航线，目前正在全力争取开通至香港的包机，另外鲁宁地下输油管道纵贯境内，全市已形成铁路、公路、水运、航空、管道“五通汇流”的立体交通体系。三是拥有丰富的能源资源。徐州是全国重要的煤炭产地、华东地区的电力基地，拥有煤炭、井盐、铁等30多种矿产，储量大、品位高。煤炭已探明储量达39亿吨以上，

圆桥

项羽雄风戏马台

年产量2500多万吨、占江苏省95%以上；井盐储量为220亿吨，且品位很高，发展煤化工、盐化工的资源条件十分优越；石膏年开采能力500万吨，为华东地区之首；电力能源丰富，发电装机容量已达770万千瓦。徐州农副产品资源丰富，是国家粮棉生产基地、优质农副产品生产加工出口基地和五大蔬菜产区之一，是中国银杏之乡、苹果之乡，作为全国四大胶合板加工基地之一、年生产量占全国四分之一。四是拥有优美的人文环境。徐州是华夏九州之一，古称彭城，有5000多年的悠久历史、2600年的建城史，是上古养生学家彭祖故国，汉代开国皇帝汉高祖刘邦故里，西楚霸王项羽故都，享有“千古龙飞地，一代帝王乡”的美誉。徐州是两汉文化集萃之地，文物古迹众多，汉兵马俑、汉画像石、汉墓被誉为“汉代三绝”，项羽“戏马台”、刘邦“大风歌碑”、苏轼“放鹤亭”、北魏“大石佛”、唐代“燕子楼”以及明清“城下城”遗址等名胜古迹遍布全市。徐州还是一座山水城市，形象地讲就是“山包城，城环山，山水相连”，环城72座山峦相连、碧水灵秀，云龙山留有历代名人足迹，云龙湖与杭州西湖并称“姊妹湖”。徐州科技教育发达，在全国地级城市中位居前列，现有高等院校12所、高中级职业技术院校40余所、独立科研院所31家，各类科技开发机构335家，5名中国工程院院士。五是产业体系较为健全。目前，徐州形成了具有一定规模和水平的工业体系。工程机械暨特种车辆制造业实力十分雄厚，成为徐州工业经济的主导产业；食品、纺织、板材家具等传统优势产业发展规模和层次不断提升，正逐步成为全国重要的特色食品产业基地、江苏新兴的纺织服装生产基地和全国最大的新型板材家具产业基地之一。近年来，煤化工、盐化工和光伏光电等新兴产业蓬勃兴起，正加速形成区域性化工产业基地、国内领先的光伏光电（多晶硅）产业基地。徐州市拥有全国最大的工程机械制造企业徐工集团，全国最大的汽车收放机生产企业天宝集团，全国最大的豆奶生产企业维维集团，全国最大的胰岛素生产企业万邦制药，全市有10家企业进入全国同行业百强，50余种产品产量位居全国或全省第一。我市服务业日益繁荣，城市中心商业圈集聚各类商业零售企业达1490家，成为淮海经济区第一商务中心。年成交额超百亿元的市场2个、10亿元以上的市场13个，其中徐州市区域生产资料市场是国家级市场，名列全国同业第五位、江苏省第一位。六是投资环境优越。中国社科院《2005年中国城市竞争力报告》显示，徐州城市竞争力位居大陆191个城市排行榜第36位。从2004年起连续两年荣登《福布斯》“中国大陆最佳商业城市”排行榜，2005年被评为“中国品牌经济城市”。2006年被评为中国投资环境百佳城市、浙商最佳投资城市，入围中国魅力城市20强、中国城市诚信政府排行榜30强，名列2006跨国公司眼中最具投资价值中国城市排行榜第六位。

城市面貌

扇舞晨风

老拳春秋

云龙湖景区

江苏省徐州市

华灯初上

微山湖上起芭蕾

采菱骆湖

碧水人家绕

江苏省常州市

常州市市委书记　范燕青

常州市市长　王伟成

常州，别称“龙城”，位于美丽富饶的长三角地区，下辖金坛、溧阳2个县级市和武进、新北、天宁、钟楼、戚墅堰5个区。全市总面积4375平方公里，总人口355万，其中市区面积1864平方公里，人口222万。这里经济富庶，文化昌盛，社会和谐。2006年全市实现地区生产总值1569亿元，按户籍人口计算人均GDP超过5000美元，财政总收入达到277亿元，城市居民人均可支配收入16649元，农村居民人均纯收入8001元，实现了以市为单位总体建成全面小康社会的宏伟目标。

历史悠久　人文荟萃

常州地处江南，是一座有着2500多年文字记载历史的文化古城，自古以来文风蔚然，群星荟萃。从隋唐开科取士到清末的千余年间，常州涌现出9名状元、8名榜眼、11名探花、1546名进士，数量之多，为全国罕见。明清以后，常州今文经学派、阳湖学派、常州词派、常州画派、孟河医派等“常州五学派”集群涌现，影响深远，成为中国文化史上的奇观。

近现代的常州，诞生了“常州三杰”瞿秋白、张太雷、恽代英，养育了赵元任、刘海粟、吴定良、李公仆、史良、洪深、阿甲、华罗庚、吕思勉、吴阶平等一大批名家大师。

现在，常州更是教育发达，文化繁荣。这里有高质量的基础教育、全国一流的职业教育、颇具特色的高等教育。全国第一座以高等职业教育为特色的高等职业教育基地，坐落常州。同时，常州的中等职业教育在全国也处于领先地位。

目前，常州正在积极推进学习城和动漫城建设。全市建设学习型的机关、系统、企业、社区、村镇和家庭蔚然成风，已经成为全国建设学习型城市的三大模式之一。建

高新区发展

设动漫城的氛围也日渐浓郁，中华人民共和国文化部在这里连续3年举办中国国际卡通·数码艺术周，在国际动漫界享有较高的知名度。

环境优美 生活舒适

作为国家卫生城市、全国环境保护模范城市的常州，山好水好风光好，早在2001年就被国家旅游局授予“中国优秀旅游城市”的光荣称号。全市共有中华恐龙园、天目湖、天宁寺、茅山、亚细亚影视城等5个国家AAAA级旅游景区（点），瞿秋白纪念馆、东坡公园、荆川公园等AA级以上旅游景区（点）11家，还有7家全国工农业旅游示范点。

近年来，围绕创建国家园林城市、生态城市，全市相继开展了“清水工程、蓝天工程、宁静工程”等专项整治活动，实施了以“八路八口”为重点的绿色通道和城市主要出入口绿化工程，敞开扩建了红梅公园、蔷薇生态湿地公园等园林，新建了一批大型公共绿地。现在常州市民每出行1000米，就有一片大型公共绿地，而中小型公共绿地的密度半径已在500米以内。

投资热土 掘金宝地

常州地处中国经济最活跃的长三角，东接上海，西邻南京，自古以来就是“舟车会吴越，襟带控三吴”的江南要辅。如今，沪宁铁路、高速公路、京杭运河、民航机场、长江口岸和常州信息网络等基础设施，把常州构架成一座昼夜不息的奔腾之城。

常州工业基础雄厚，具有明显的比较优势，现已拥有农业机械制造、输变电设备制造、工程机械、车辆及配件制造、新型纺织服装等四大支柱产业和电子信息设备制造及软件、生物医药及精细化工、新型材料等三大新兴产业，是国内中小功率柴油机、电子信息设备、高速内燃机车、牛仔布等产品的重要生产基地。

作为沿海和沿江开放地区的城市之一，近年来，常州按照国际化、现代化、城市化目标，先后建起了1个国家级高新技术开发区、9个省级开发区，以及环保产业园、软件产业园等一批特色园区，设立了行政审批中心和外商投资管理委员会，开通了网上审批，为市民和外商提供便捷高效的一门式审批和全方位服务。优越的投资环境使常州成为海内外投资者青睐的热点，成为国内权威机构所认可和关注的视点。2006年，常州被评为中国创新环境十优城市、中国投资环境百佳城市、中国十佳最具投资价值创意基地等。

新区大道

高速公路

常州火车站

古刹塔影

软件园

江苏省常州市

常州戚墅机车车辆厂

科教城

常州港

小松工程

商业步行街

动漫佳节

红梅秋韵

江苏省

风景如画的金山

镇江市位于长江下游南岸，地处长江运河“十字黄金水道”交汇处，是长江三角洲地区重要的港口、工贸和风景旅游城市，是国家历史文化名城、中国优秀旅游城市、国家卫生城市、国家园林城市、国家环境保护模范城市、全国科技兴市先进城市、全国双拥模范城市、全国社会治安综合治理优秀地市。总面积3847平方公里，总人口299.6万人。现辖丹阳、句容、扬中3个市，丹徒、京口、润州3个区和镇江新区。

镇江有文字记载的历史已达3000余年，是吴文化的发祥地，人文荟萃，底蕴深厚。历史上不少著名的文人雅士都在镇江留下了文章诗篇，《昭明文选》、《文心雕龙》、《梦溪笔谈》等巨著，作者或是镇江籍，或者在镇江编撰。镇江环境秀美，真山真水，素有“天下第一江山”、“城市山林”之美称。拥有金山、焦山、北固山、茅山、宝华山等著名风景区，西津渡古街区、梦溪园旧址、天下第一泉、芙蓉楼等景点也久负盛名，焦山碑林、六朝石刻等是国家一级保护文物。

镇江西距南京50公里，东距上海200公里，处于上海经济圈和南京都市圈的交汇点，区位优势突出。长江境内自然岸线长270公里，其中深水岸线87公里，已建成万吨级以上泊位28个，年吞吐量6863吨，集装箱运输23.9万标箱。镇江港是全国沿海港口之一。沪宁铁路、沪宁高速公路、312国道、104国道贯穿全境，已经通车的润扬长江公路大桥和即将建设的沪宁高速铁路、城际轻轨、镇泰过江通道，使镇江的区位优势更加明显。

镇江作为苏南经济板块的开放型新兴工业城市，拥有7个省级经济开发区和1个国家级出口加工区，已有80多个国家和地区的1200多家公司和财团在镇江投资，有23家世界500强企业落户镇江，累计实际到位外资65亿美元。总投资近20亿美元的合资项目金东纸业，是亚洲最大的造纸厂。全市已初步形成机械、化工、造纸三大主导产业，以及电子信息、新材料、电力、交通设备、食品五大优势产业。有全国最大的醋酸生产企业和铝箔包装材料定点生产基地，有亚洲最大的工程塑料PS、APS

镇江市

镇江市委书记　史和平

镇江市市长　许津荣

生产基地，有世界产能第一的生产纸机，有世界五强之一的锚链生产基地，有国内汽车行业最大的发动机缸体铸造企业华东泰克西，镇江恒顺香醋、江奎集团的DVD等产品驰名中外。2006年，镇江实现了“十一五”发展的良好开局。全市GDP突破1000亿元大关，达到1021.52亿元，增长15.2%；财政总收入突破150亿元，达到151.26亿元，增长27.7%；全社会固定资产投资达到478.54亿元，增长18.2%，其中工业性投入达到282.02亿元，增长19.4%；规模以上工业企业实现销售突破1500亿元,达到1575.9亿元，增长26.5%。全市销售超亿元企业达252家，比上年增加49家。城乡居民收入分别增长15.3%和13.5%，增幅均列全省第二。

现在，全市上下正在按照“把握一个基调、狠抓三个突出、强化四个全力推进”的思路加速奋进。一个基调，就是坚持更好更快发展，“更好”主要体现在优化经济结构、优化产业层次、优化环境质量“三个优化”上，“更快”主要体现在主要经济指标增幅高于全省平均水平、高于苏南平均水平、高于去年实绩水平“三个高于”上。三个突出，就是突出服务业发展、突出大项目建设、突出自主创新。四个全力推进，就是全力推进新农村建设、城市建设、生态建设和小康建设，2007年总体上将实现全面小康。通过五年努力，使镇江更有活力、更加富裕、更加文明、更加和谐、更加秀美，向率先基本实现现代化阔步迈进。

镇江长江路风光带

江苏省镇江市

城市山林

北固山全景

金山鸟瞰图

江中浮玉——焦山

镇江博物馆新馆

镇江新农村

中新合资镇江恒顺50万吨醋生产项目开工仪式

国投镇江港有限公司大港三期工程

江苏省江阴市

城市风景

江阴市市委书记　朱民阳

江阴市市长　王锡南

江阴市位于长江三角洲中部，区域面积988平方公里，户籍人口118万人。江阴自古钟灵毓秀，已有7000年人文史、5000年文明史和2500年文字记载的历史。明清以来，江阴涌现了地理学家徐霞客、“中国近代图书馆之父”缪荃孙、现代文学家刘半农、民族音乐家刘天华、佛学家巨赞等一大批杰出人物，拥有近百名大学校长、60多名“两院”院士和学科带头人、30多名将军。

近年来，江阴坚持科学发展、创新发展、率先发展的理念，实现了经济社会的持续、健康、协调发展。2006年，全市完成地区生产总值980亿元，财政收入140亿元。在全国万分之一的土地上，以全国千分之一的人口，创造了全国百分之一的上市公司、近二百五十分之一的地区生产总值、超三百分之一的财政收入。2006年，江阴在江苏省成为首批全面小康达标县（市）后，在中国县域经济基本竞争力排名中，再次荣膺榜首，实现四

江阴华联

连冠；建成首批国家生态市；获得中国最佳经济活力魅力城市；国家可持续发展实验区工作全国先进集体等荣誉。目前，江阴正坚持以民生为本、民富为纲、民享为先、民安为基、民强为重，建设一个幸福江阴。

华西村

江阴大桥

开发区鸟瞰

江阴港夜景

振华港机

江阴人民路学院场夜色

江苏省

市政府

黄山湖公园夜景

法尔胜利光子项目

江阴市

和谐科学发展

建设幸福江阴

徐霞客故居

江阴鸟瞰

大华文化艺术中心

城市风貌

金坛，地处江苏省南部，位居上海、南京、杭州"金三角"中心地带，于唐垂拱四年建制，至今已有1300多年历史，是著名数学家华罗庚的故乡。1993年撤县建市，现辖7个镇和一个省级经济开发区，人口54万，面积976平方公里，其中山地23万亩、水面24万亩、耕地65万亩，俗称"二山二水六分田"，素有"鱼米之乡"、"江东福地"之美誉，是一座充满江南文化气息的新兴现代城市。

金坛，以饱满的自信全方位对外开放。京沪铁路、沪宁高速和南京禄口机场等偎于身侧，常宁、扬溧高速在境内交汇，构成快速便捷的交通网络。坐拥163亿吨中国东部地区开采条件最好、综合指标最佳的大型岩盐矿床，一个资源循环利用、产品关联生产、环境设施污水处理统筹规划的盐化工产业基地正在迅速成长；作为中国出口服装制造名城、中国服装跨国采购产业基地和国家火炬计划精细化学品产业基地，纺织服装、医药化工、新型材料、机械电子等四大支柱产业构成了金坛工业经济的基础，拥有100多只国家、江苏省名牌产品，晨风服装、康美化工、中盐金坛公司、亿晶光电、盘固水泥、苏拉纺机等一批重点企业快速

江苏省金坛市

金坛市市委书记　徐惠中

金坛市市长　吴晓东

发展，与100多个国家和地区建立了经贸关系。

金坛西部是史誉“秦汉神仙府，梁唐宰相家”的苏南第一峰——茅山。作为国家4A级风景名胜区、中国三大道教圣地之一，茅山以千年道家养生文化孕育了金坛“中国名茶（绿茶）之乡”，哺造出旅游休闲度假胜地；南部浩淼13万亩洮湖碧波，是江苏省无公害标准化养殖示范基地，鱼美蟹肥，观光、美食、休闲浑然天成；挟“中华绒螯蟹之乡”、“中国食用菌之乡”等美名，金坛正全方位部署，精心酝酿一个蓬勃发展的社会主义新农村。

金坛，是中国综合实力百强县（市）、全国科技实力百强县（市）、“中国首届50家投资环境诚信安全区”、“国家卫生城市”、“国家环保模范城市”、国家生态示范区、江苏省社会治安安全市、江苏省文明城市、江苏省园林城市。

江苏省金坛市

市领导视察兰花种植基地

西气东输工程储气场

江苏省学生阳光体育运动会

廉政文化进农村

“单晶硅”生产现场

江苏省溧阳市

市委书记　高清

市长　韩立明

溧阳市位于浙江、安徽、江苏三省交界，地处中国经济增长最快、人口最密集、工业基础最雄厚、科教事业最发达的长江三角洲的几何中心，至今已有2200多年历史。全市总面积1535平方公里，总人口77.32万，辖10个镇，拥有2个省级开发区。溧阳是国家卫生城市、国家环保模范城市、中国优秀旅游城市、全国科普示范市和全国生态示范区，连续6次被评为全国农村综合实力百强县（市）和全国县域经济基本竞争力百强县(市)。2006年，国家统计局发布了2006年全国综合实力百强县（市）名单，溧阳市列第66位。溧阳山青水秀、环境优美，被誉为“江南明珠”、“绿色仙境”的天目湖是全国首批4A级旅游景区，水甜、茶香、鱼头鲜合称天目湖“三绝”，每年有数百万中外游客来此观光、旅游、度假，被中外游客誉为“中国游憩首选地”。

近年来，溧阳市坚持加大有效投入，加快结构调整，大力实施外向带动、民营赶超和服务业跨越战略。目前已基本形成机械、冶金、建材、化工、纺织、食品等支柱产业。电子信息和新材料制造两大新兴产业蓬勃发展。汽车齿轮、电线电缆、变压器、天目湖啤酒、箱包及材料等都有较高的知名度和市场覆盖面。全市拥有3只“中

四通八达的高速公路网

国家AAAA级旅游区——天目湖

国驰名商标”、3只“中国名牌产品”、6家国家级重点高新技术企业。2006年，全市实现地区生产总值217.6亿元，财政总收入27.9亿元，一般预算收入11.8亿元。2007年，溧阳市将实现全面小康。“十一五”期间，溧阳市将坚持以科学发展观统领经济社会发展全局，坚持发展第一要务，紧紧围绕力争“两个率先”、实现富民强市奋斗目标，实施工业强市、开放活市、科教兴市、环境立市、城乡统筹五大战略，全面推进经济、政治、文化和社会建设，把溧阳打造成适宜创业、生活的现代新兴中等工贸旅游城市。

布勒(常州)机械有限公司

外商独资企业——德盛食品有限公司

江苏省溧阳中学校区

江苏正昌集团

全国农业旅游示范点——大石山旅游农庄

江苏省溧阳市

市人民广场

国家重点高新技术企业——江苏华朋集团

国家重点高新技术企业——江苏上上电缆集团

中国第十届溧阳茶叶节

中共常州市委常委、武进区区委书记　沈瑞卿

武进区区长　徐伟南

武进地处我国经济最发达的长三角中心，北望长江，南枕太湖，沪宁高速、京沪铁路、京杭运河穿境而过，区位优势十分明显。全区现辖14个镇，1个街道，两个省级开发区，总面积1243平方公里，户籍人口98.6万，常住人口129.5万。武进历史悠久、文化发达、人文荟萃，有文字记载的历史2500多年，曾形成“阳湖文派”、“恽南田画派”、“常州词派”等一批具有影响力的文艺流派。

改革开放以来，武进经济迅猛发展，综合实力在全国县级区域中始终处于领先地位，在2004年、2005年、2006年全国百强县（区）评比中连续三年位列第八。在“十一五”规划的开局之年，武进牢固树立科学发展观，乘势而上，加快发展，经济社会继续保持了迅猛发展势头。综合实力持续增强。2006年实现地区生产总值572亿元，同比增长23%；财政收入78亿元，增长30.3%。工业经济量质并举。全区完成工业总产值1688亿元，产品销售收入1639亿元，分别增长29.5%和29.6%。开放型经济迅速崛起。利用外资规模不断扩大，实现协议注册外资8.59亿美元，实际到帐注册外资3.81亿美元，分别增长36.1%和90%。城乡面貌全面改善。以净化、绿化、美化、亮化为主要内容的中心城区道路、河道整治工程和镇村环境整治工程加快推进，顺利通过全国生态示范区验收；新天地城市广场、淹城森林公园、五星级酒店、大型购物中心、文化艺术中心、三甲医院等重点项目正加快实施，城市功能不断完善。和谐程度继续提高。2006年全区城镇职工人均工资24300元，农民人均纯收入9200元，人民生活更加富裕；全区城镇养老、医疗、失业三大保险基本实现了全覆盖，新型农村合作医疗保险参保率达97%，社会保障体系进一步完善；教育、卫生、科技、文化等事业取得长足发展，一批社会事业重点项目相继建成，人民群众的精神文化需求得到有效满足；慈善事业发展迅速，慈善基金达4.1亿元，居全省县级之首。

在2006年全面建成小康社会的基础上，武进区委、区政府提出了“进军现代化，建设新武进”的奋斗目标，力争在2010年率先基本实现现代化。目前，全区正以率先发展、科学发展、和谐发展为主题，以保持经济社会又好又快发展和人民生活质量不断提高为重点，积极开展“有效投入推进年”、“生态环境创建年”、“机关效能提高年”、“民心工程实施年”、“平安法治建设年”五大活动，加快推进有效投入，全力推进城市建设，不断推进改革开放，扎实推进社会主义新农村建设，努力打造实力之区、创新之区、生态之区、宜居之区、和谐之区。

常州市武进区

武进市民广场

地 址： 常州市武进区湖塘镇延政路
邮 编： 213159
电 话： 0519—6310050
传 真： 0519—6310069

座落于武进城区的全国唯一一座高等职业教育基地——常州大学城

省级武进高新技术产业开发区

鸟瞰淹城

常州市

武进文慧苑

淹城门楼

新农村建设示范点——雅浦村

武进太湖湾旅游度假区

武进区

武进高速公路

新农村建设示范点——牟家村

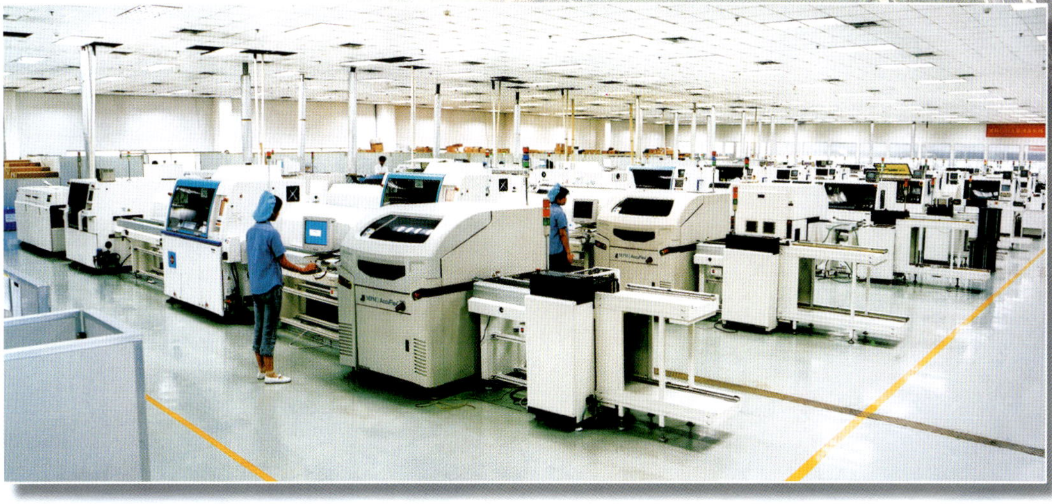

中国百强企业——江苏新科电子集团

新城区

全民运动会

太仓港现代物流园区

太仓位于江苏省东南端，东濒长江，南邻上海，总面积823平方公里，其中陆域面积649平方公里，辖太仓港经济开发区和7个镇，户籍人口46万，常住人口80多万。

魅力之城。太仓因春秋战国时期吴王和春申君在此设立粮仓而得名。郑和航海起锚地，锦绣江南金太仓。娄东文化源远流长、风格独特，自古崇文重教、名人荟萃，走出了吴健雄、朱棣文、唐文治、吴晓邦等科技文化大师和11位“两院”院士。

活力之城。2005年经济综合实力位居中国百强县(市)第9位，成为江苏省首批6个全面实现高水平小康的县(市)之一。2006年全市实现地区生产总值367亿元，同比增长23%，人均地区生产总值突破1万美元大关；财政总收入61亿元，其中一般预算收入27.6亿元，分别增长35%和46%；完成固定资产投资200亿元，增长17%；国家一类口岸太仓港实现货物吞吐量2251万吨，集装箱吞吐量60万标箱，分别增长49%和139%。

创业之城。太仓区位独特，地处长江经济带和沿

城区一瞥

江苏省太仓市

海开放带的交汇点。交通便捷发达，距上海虹桥机场仅40公里，境内每百平方公里拥有高等级公路42公里，密度在全国处于领先。拥有江苏太仓港经济开发区、江苏省现代服务业集聚区、江苏省国际服务外包基地城市、江苏台资科技创新产业园等一批功能性开发载体。形成了石油化工、电力能源、高档造纸、基础原材料、精密机械、纺织服装、电子信息、汽车配件、现代物流等支柱产业和自行车、化纤加弹、注塑、胶带等特色产业。

开放之城。全市已累计批准外商投资企业2600多家，实际利用外资35亿美元，有11家世界500强企业在太仓投资了22个项目。欧美、日韩、港台资本三足鼎立，特别是欧美企业加速集聚，德资企业已达80多家，被称为中国的“德企之乡”。2006年，实现注册外资12亿美元，实际利用外资4.4亿美元，分别增长28%和86%；进出口总额47亿美元，其中出口24亿美元，增长均超过30%。

和谐之城。2006年，城镇居民人均可支配收入和农村居民人均纯收入分别达到19091元和9285元，分别增长14.5%和12.8%；城镇失业率控制在3%以内，社会保险覆盖率达98%，被征地农民保障工作走在全国前列；城市绿化率41.3%；工业废水排放达标率和生活垃圾处理率均达100%。

中共太仓市委书记　浦荣皋

太仓市市长　谢鸣

太仓港集装箱码头

江苏省

南园（雪景）

全国综合实力十强县（市）

全国十佳节约型中小城市

全国“武术之乡”

全国首家“桥牌之乡”

全国文化先进县（市）

全国科技工作先进县（市）

国家卫生城市

国家环境保护模范城市

现代化的居住区

人口与发展南南合作伙伴组织

太仓市

城区游园

全国村民自治模范市

全国社会治安综合治理先进集体

全国科普示范市

中国优秀旅游城市

国家园林城市

全国生态示范区

全国村务公开民主管理示范单位

江苏省社会治安安全县（市）

沙溪古镇

江南丝竹演奏

中国项目办事处

太仓港口一角

江苏省

青木铸秀　笔架生辉

丹阳市市委书记　李茂川

丹阳市市长　王常生

丹阳市位于江苏省南部，地处长江三角洲、上海经济圈腹地，属苏南经济板块，东邻常州市武进区、新北区，西接句容市、镇江市丹徒区，南与金坛市接壤，北与扬中市隔江相望，全市总面积1047.44平方公里，户籍人口80.61万，是一座具有悠久历史的文化古城。1987年经国务院批准撤县建市，被列为沿海对外开放城市，是江苏省经济发展水平较高的县（市）之一。

丹阳的地理位置十分优越，东距上海200公里，西距南京68公里，京沪铁路、沪宁高速公路、312国道、京杭大运河和正在规划建设的京沪高速铁路横贯市区；常州机场坐落市境，西距南京机场80公里，东距上海虹桥机场、浦东机场2小时车程，班机直航世界各地；对外开放的长江第三大港——大港港口离市区18公里，全市已形成了铁路、公路、水路、航空综合交通运输体系。

丹阳的“三个文明”建设成绩卓越，连续被评为全国经济综合实力百强县（市），2006年经济综合实力列全国第47位，列江苏省第8位；先后被评为“全国卫生城市”、“全国环境综合整治优秀城市”、“江苏省文明城

六朝石刻

高淳县

县人民医院

双湖公路

县城夜景

购物街

江苏高淳经济开发区

江苏省高淳县

湖滨大道

高淳县位于江苏省西南端，属南京市郊县，总面积802平方公里，辖8个建制镇、1个省级经济开发区，总人口42.5万。东邻苏锡常，西接安徽的芜湖、宣州、马鞍山。区内交通便捷，生态优美。宁高高速和芜太、宁宣一级公路贯穿全境，水路西进长江黄金水道，东连太湖水网。素有“江南圣地”、“鱼米之乡”的美誉，是南京市首家国家级生态示范区、全国平原绿化达标县。

近年来，高淳围绕“工业强县、湖滨新区、边贸中心”发展定位，大力实施“工业强县、生态立县、特色兴县”三大发展战略，经济社会获得持续快速健康发展。2004年、2005年，连续两年跻身“全国综合发展百强县”行列。2006年，实现地区生产总值111.03亿元，财政收入11.4亿元，全社会固定资产投资70亿元，社会消费品零售总额38.3亿元，农民人均纯收入7048元。

工业主体地位突出。全县现有工业企业近2100家，初步形成机械电子、新型材料、绿色食品三大主导产业，药业化工、出口服装两大优势传统产业层次不断提升。拥有上市公司2家、拟上市公司1家。江苏高淳经济开发区为长三角最具投资潜力的开发区之一，规划面积29.5平方公里，建成区面积4.7平方公里，落户中外企业280家。

城市绿地

农业产业化步伐加快。形成优质“双低”油菜、特种水产、商品蔬菜、食草畜禽、经济林果和食用菌等六大农业主导产业，先后成为全国粮油生产基地县、省市重点水产品生产基地和绿色食品生产区。

商贸旅游经济蓬勃发展。培育形成水产批发市场等一批边贸综合市场和专业市场，成为苏皖商贸集散地，商贸经济综合实力列全省县(市)级前列。拥有AA级以上旅游景区5个，其中AAA级旅游景区1个。

特色经济久负盛誉。高淳是江苏省建筑之乡、国家级有机螃蟹养殖基地、中华民间造船水运第一县。国家一级资质建筑企业10家，拥有4万建筑大军。水产养殖总面积28万亩，盛产螃蟹、青虾、珍珠等特种水产，“固城湖”牌螃蟹为国内首家有机螃蟹、江苏省著名商标。拥有船舶1252艘135万吨位，造船水运专业村——武家嘴村连续12届位列“南京市综合实力百强村”榜首。

社会事业协调发展。高淳先后成为全国科技、体育工作先进县，江苏省精神文明、有线电视、计生工作先进县，被誉为“全国武术之乡”、“民俗歌舞之乡”。县城被评为国家卫生县城。拥有国家级示范学校2所、省级示范学校6所，县人民医院为基本现代化医院。

矢志存高远，盛世创伟业。大气开放的高淳人民意气风发、开拓进取，正在建设富裕和谐新高淳的康庄大道上阔步前进！

地　址：南京市高淳县淳溪镇镇兴路228号
邮　编：211300
电　话：025－57338008、57338080
传　真：025－57338002

江苏省扬中市

风光秀美的明珠湾

扬中是长江中的一个岛市，总面积332平方公里，其中陆地面积228平方公里。下辖5个镇、1个省级经济技术开发区，总人口27.39万人。2006年，扬中市坚持以科学发展观为指导，紧紧围绕率先实现全面小康的目标，高扬率先发展、科学发展、和谐发展的主旋律，经济建设和各项社会事业继续保持了快速、健康的发展势头，实现了“十一五”发展的良好开局。

全年实现地区生产总值125.5亿元，比上年增长15.5%。实现地方财政总收入15.1亿元，其中地方一般预算收入5.99亿元，比上年分别增长26.9%、31.3%。城镇居民人均可支配收入16209元，农民人均纯收入8000元，分别比上年增长11.5%、16.3%。对照省定全面小康标准，全市经济发展、生活水平、社会发展、生态环境等四大类18项25个指标中，除森林覆盖率因水域面积占比较大未能达标外，其他指标均已达到或超过省定目标值，在全省和镇江市率先建成全面小康社会。

全市规模以上工业企业实现增加值54.76亿元，增长22.1%；实现产品销售收入192.69亿元，增长26.69%；实现利税18.71亿元，增长30.54%。全年完成固定资产投资44.26亿元，增长15%。全年协议利用外资1.88亿美元，增长19.8%；实际利用外资0.83亿美元，增长38.6%。岸线开发取得突破性进展，由浙江盈都集团投资建设的镇江港扬中港区兴隆作业区码头一期工程正式开工建设，柏伦宝船业、龙源港机、苏洋船舶工程等一批投资规模超亿元的临江产业项目相继落户。

全民健身大型广场公益活动

新农村建设取得良好开局。以“千户兴业、千元增收、千河疏浚、千埭整治，万人保障、万木增绿、万家洁净、万户文明。”行动为载体，扎实推进社会主义新农村建设，农村面貌不断改善。新建农村公路35公里，累计清淤整治河道1003条；新建垃圾中转站2座，添置垃圾箱1000多座；建成社区卫生服务中心6个、社区卫生服务站60个。

社会事业协调发展。技术创新成效显著，新批国家级高新技术企业1家，认定国家级重点新产品5个，承担国家级重点火炬计划3项，国家级火炬计划9项、星火计划2项。高新技术产品销售、利税占全市工业经济比重分别达38%、73%。教育工作取得新业绩，高考万人本科率、优秀率、高分率居镇江市首位。“平安扬中”建设取得阶段性成果，连续4次被评为全省“社会治安安全市”，荣获“省级双拥模范城”五连冠、省“人民防空先进市”称号。

地 址：江苏省扬中市江洲西路8号
邮 编：212200
电 话：0511－8321657
网 址：http://www.yz.gov.cn

江苏省扬中市

成功举办2006中国扬中金秋经贸洽谈会

扬中全面小康建设成效显著

兴隆码头一期工程正式开工

魅力独具的农家楼

大全集团荣膺中国电气工业十大领军企业

具有扬中特色的社会主义新农村

南京市市长蒋宏坤视察进香河农贸市场

单景南书记、王海宏区长视察工地

南京市

南京市玄武区位于南京市的东北部，总面积80.97平方公里，户籍人口48.95万，下辖8个街道，64个社区，11个行政村。玄武区历史文化底蕴深厚。自公元229年孙权建都开始，曾是东吴、东晋和南朝宋、齐、梁、陈六朝宫阙所在地，也是明朝初期紫禁城、太平天国天王府、中华民国总统府的所在地。玄武区自然景观独特。有闻名世界的中山陵、松涛万顷的紫金山、芳菲四季的玄武湖、历经风霜的明城墙，具有融山、水、城、林为一体的秀丽风光。玄武区经济发达。有华东第一商贸商务圈新街口、集明清和民国文化于一体的长江路文化街、与中关村齐名的珠江路科技园区，以高新技术产业和商贸商务业为主体的现代服务业快速发展。“十五”期间，国内生产总值年均增长16%以上，财政收入年均增长20%以上。“十一五”期间，玄武区将以“率先发展、特色发展、科学发展”为主线，坚持“数字玄武、文化玄武、绿色玄武”发展定位，大力发展科技信息业、文化旅游业、商贸商务业三大产业，努力建成现代化国际性人文绿都标志区、全市现代服务业发展的先行区、全国重要科技中心的示范区、东部城市绿都中心的形象区、全国知名的和谐社会建设样板区。

捐助现场采访

玄武区

建设中的徐庄软件产业基地

江宁织造府奠基仪式

玄武区开展暖冬行动

市领导为江宁织造府奠基

520广场开工奠基典礼

江苏省铜山县

铜山县县委书记　周宝纯

铜山县县长　丁维和

铜山县位于江苏省西北部，地处苏鲁豫皖四省交界处和淮海经济区中心，环抱历史文化名城徐州。铜山因境内微山湖中铜山岛而得名。古称大彭氏国，秦始置县，汉列“天下九州”之一，历称大彭、彭城、铜山，迄今已有4000多年历史。

铜山县，东临沿海开放区，西接中原腹地。欧亚大陆桥横贯东西，京杭大运河穿境而过，京沪、陇海两大铁路干线在此交汇，徐州观音国际机场距县政府驻地40公里。三条高速公路（霍连、京福、宁宿徐）、四条国道（104、206、307、310国道）、六条市县一级公路及县乡公路网通达四面八方，交通十分便利。新建的京沪高速铁路将在铜山境内南北穿过。

铜山县土地总面积1856平方公里，2006年末全县总人口120.7万人。现辖20个镇、1个农场、1个省级经济开发区，312个行政村。境内资源丰富，现已探明的矿藏20多种，其中煤、铁、石灰石、白云石、大理石尤为丰富。

铜山是楚汉文化集中地，古迹众多，已发掘并被列入国家和省市重点文物保护单位的有彭祖庙、北洞山汉墓、汉画像石等文物古迹20多处。孕育出西汉刘向、东晋刘裕、南朝刘义庆、唐朝刘禹锡、宋朝陈师道以及郭影秋、李可染和喻继高等杰出人物。

2006年，全县人民在县委、县政府的正确领导下，坚持以科学发展观统领全局，围绕“苏北率先、江北领

铜山经济开发区高档居民区

铜山经济开发区主城区夜景

先、全省争先”的目标，突出招商引资、工业投入和“一区九园”建设、积极扶持支柱产业发展，呈现出经济发展全面提速、主要经济指标全省进位、运行质量明显提高的良好态势。

2006年全县实现GDP 192.65亿元，财政总收入15.68亿元，地方一般预算收入7.38亿元，分别比上年增长16.6%、34.6%和37.6%。全社会固定资产投资105亿元，比上年增长45.4%，农民人均纯收入5591元，比上年增长13.6%。主要经济指标位居徐州市各县（市）区首位，财政总收入、地方一般预算收入、城镇固定资产投资和规模以上工业增加值等指标位居苏北第一，2007年将再次跨入全国县域经济基本竞争力百强县行列。

铜山经济开发区（省级），位于徐州市区的南大门，创建于1992年，1993年被江苏省政府批准为省级开发区。铜山经济开发区经过10多年的建设，特别是近年来的快速发展，基础设施更加完善，大型商贸、服务、文化娱乐设施正加快建设。一个交通顺畅，电力充足，通信完备，科教配套，居住优雅，生活便利，环境优美，主城区面积达88平方公里，建设控制区180平方公里，城乡协调区299平方公里的综合新城区正在徐州市区南部崛起!

铜山拥有环抱徐州市区的独特区位优势，徐州都市圈和特大城市的建设，将为铜山社会经济的发展带来新的历史机遇。铜山人民热忱欢迎国内外有识之士，前来投资创业，展现才华。

铜山的明天将会更加美好。

由中央党校、徐州市委市政府主办的“建设社会主义新农村——铜山实践”高层论坛2006年11月在铜山进行

徐州市曹新平市长视察铜山重点项目建设

全国知名的工程机械制造基地

江苏省

2006年，邳州市认真落实“全面达小康、建设新江苏”的战略部署，咬定“全面领跑苏北、建成东陇海第三大市”的奋斗目标，创业创新创优，苦干实干快干，经济社会又好又快发展，主要经济指标实现领跑苏北，入选“全国中小城市综合实力100强”，第三次被省政府授予财政收入增收表彰单位，蝉联徐州市经济工作综合考核四连冠，被誉为“苏北的新昆山”。

邳州城市一角

一、发展速度发展质量同步提升。全市GDP达到149亿元，增长 16.6 %；财政总收入、一般预算收入分别达到13.1亿元、5.93亿元，增长36.7 %和31.3%，工商税收增量、增幅苏北第一；全社会固定资产投资完成108亿元，增长39.7%，实际利用市外资金达到70亿元，实际到帐注册外资4300万美元，总量、增幅苏北领先；出口总额达到2.8亿美元，增长90.5%，其中农林产品出口全省第一。24个镇有22个在徐州位次前移，运河、官湖首次进入“全国综合实力千强镇”。

邳州锦绣广扬一角

二、招大引强民营扩张两轮驱动。围绕建设“中国第一、世界第一”的家具产业基地，规划建设中国国际环保家具城、国家木制家具及人造板质量监督检验中心、家具博览中心，引进大型家具项目26个，金凤凰家具等一批家具项目建成投产；实施“板材千线扩张”，深加工生产线达到1600多条，创建成为“全国优质人造板生产基地”。食品医药、冶金机械、化工产业快速发展，工业经济全线告捷，全市竣工3000万元以上项目86个，纳税过百万元企业超过150家。开发区建成面积达到17.3平方公里，累计

邳州市

入驻项目176个，竣工103个。

三、城市实力发展环境齐头并进。加快建设“大而强富而美”的东陇海第二大市，高起点规划建设新区，高标准改造老城，加快旅游开发，推进“五城同建”，精心打造“楚韵汉风、诗意田园”的城市风格。城区面积达到50平方公里，建成区面积达到30平方公里，常住人口突破30万人，城市化率达到41%，城区绿化覆盖率达到39.8%，创建成为中国优秀旅游城市、省级园林城市。

四、产业富民环境益民成效彰显。把致富农民作为最紧迫的任务，大力发展现代农业，推进高效农业规模化。银杏、大蒜通过国家级标准化示范区验收，创建成为国家银杏GAP基地、全国大蒜定点市场，全市新增绿色食品、无公害农产品16个，规模以上农业龙头企业达到181家，农民人均纯收入达到5088元。新农村建设成效彰显，镇村建设规划全面完成，7个村达到徐州市示范村标准，15个村被省市命名为生态村。

五、关爱民生扶助弱势共享和谐。集中精力抓发展，集中财力解民忧。完成山区扶贫攻坚，建立“党员妈妈”爱心基金，1300名孤儿的健康成长，80名失去两代双亲的孤儿进入“爱心园”，2000多名老人集中赡养，640户双下岗特困职工住上了安居房。社会保障制度进一步完善，下岗职工、失地农民等弱势群体全部纳入低保，农村新型合作医疗参合率达到92.3%。在全省率先实现农民健康体检、医院挂号、孤贫儿童上学、公园公厕、农村集市临时摊点“五个免费”，城乡群众的满意度和幸福度不断提升。

徐州市副市长、邳州市委书记　李连玉

邳州市市委副书记、市长　孟铁林

邳州盛合木业有限公司

邳州市开发区一瞥

江苏省张家港市

“弘扬张家港精神，再创张家港辉煌”座谈会会场

张家港市位于中国长江三角洲腹地，是一座新兴的港口工业城市。以境内天然良港----张家港港而命名。全市总面积999平方公里，下辖8个镇和一个管理区，户籍人口88万。作为全国三个文明建设健康协调发展的先进典型，张家港的发展思路和业绩曾被《人民日报》誉为“伟大理论的成功实践”。先后荣获全国文明城市、国家生态市、国际花园城市、国家卫生城市、国家园林城市、全国文化先进市、中国人居环境奖、中国城市管理进步奖等近百项荣誉称号。在全国综合实力百强县（市）中列第三位，在全国县域经济基本竞争力排名中列第二位。

张家港市以科学发展观统领全局，推动经济社会又好又快发展。2006年，全市一、二、三产业占地区生产总值比分别为1.5%、64.5%、34%，全市完成地区生产总值841亿元，人均GDP近10000美元，财政收入136亿元，工业产品销售收入2480亿元。基本形成了规模经济、外向经济和民营经济“三足鼎立”的混合型经济发展新格局，重点发展了冶金、纺织、机电、石化、粮油、建材六大板块经济。目前，全市共有8家企业入围中国制造业500强，上市公司7家，中国名牌产品11只和国家免检产品25只。近年来，张家港市高效农业加快发展，被评为江苏省生态农业市。同时，张家港精心培育现代物流、专业市场、现代商贸和休闲旅游，全力打造“长三角”地区现代物流集散中心。

张家港博物馆

张家港公园

张家港市区人民路

ANGJIAGANGSHI

全国特大型工业企业——沙钢集团

张家港港集装箱码头

江苏省外贸企业排头兵——国泰国际集团

浦项不锈钢生产线

张家港市高新技术创业服务中心

张家港市体育馆

张家港保税物流园区

景色秀丽的暨阳湖生态园

苏州市吴中区

区委书记　金海龙

区委副书记、区长　俞杏楠

吴中区位于苏州古城南部，陆地面积742平方公里，太湖水域面积1459平方公里，辖15个镇（街道）和穹窿山风景管理区，以及1个国家级太湖旅游度假区和1个省级经济开发区，户籍人口57万。2006年，全区实现地区生产总值322亿元，完成全口径财政收入65亿元，完成全社会固定资产投资142亿元。

2007年，吴中区围绕“打造吴中新城、做美太湖山水”发展战略，坚持率先发展、科学发展、和谐发展，重点实施“做强开发区、做美度假区、做靓吴中城、做好新农村”四大工程。

吴中经济开发区是吴中先进制造业发展的核心区和主阵地，依托高水平产业载体，大力发展电子信息、生物医药、精密机械、新型建材、现代家电等五大类高科技产业，外资企业近700家，注册资本超过40亿美元，民资内资企业2000多家，注册资本109亿元。2007年，吴中出口加工区将封关运行，吴中科技创业园也将全面建成，开发区的发展空间和投资环境将进一步拓展和优化。

“太湖风光美，精华在吴中”！吴中区拥有近2/3的太湖水域，国家规划的太湖13景，吴中独占6处，仅省级以上文保单位就有20多处。2006年，度假区接待境内外游客超过600万人次。依托太湖山水的自然风光和吴文化的深厚积淀，以国家级太湖旅游度假区为龙头的环太湖旅游经济带，全力发展以“太湖山水、古镇古村、吴地文化、生态休闲”为主题的特色旅游，精心打造“太湖，苏州的绿色请柬”名片，凸显“山水苏州·人文吴中”品牌效应。

打造吴中新城，提升城市形象，实现与苏州中心城区和谐相融，是吴中区加快城市化和城市现代化建设的重点工作。目前，京杭运河南北两侧的建成区改造和东太湖越溪滨湖新城建设已经全面启动。

吴中区农村发展和改革成效显著。2006年，全区村均收入达259万元，农民人均纯收入9652元。当前，吴中区着力破解困扰农村发展的各种难题，以促进农民持续增收和实现城乡一体化为目标，不断深化农村改革，加快社会主义新农村建设步伐。

吴中，热忱邀请并欢迎海内外新老朋友和有识之士前来投资兴业、旅游观光！

太湖风光

吴中新城

甪直古韵

吴中经济开发区

吴中夜色

东吴电视塔

商务大厦

苏州市

相城中心城区

相城区设立于2001年2月，地处长江三角洲经济区腹地，是古城苏州的北大门户，苏州城市“北拓”的主空间，也是苏州市最具发展潜力的新城区之一。

相城区北与常熟市接壤，东邻苏州工业园区，西接苏州高新技术产业开发区。下辖4个镇、4个街道和1个省级经济开发区，总面积496平方公里，户籍人口35.5万，外来人口35.8万。境内河流湖泊众多，水域面积占全区总面积的39%，具有典型的江南水乡风貌。

根据苏州市的总体规划，相城区作为苏州中心城市的“北组团”，“十一五”期间承担着苏州城区北拓的重任。相城区确定了“一城两翼四镇”的分区规划，“一城”指中心城区，“两翼”指东部生态翼、西北部工业翼，“四镇”即望亭、黄埭、渭塘、阳澄湖四个中心镇。

阳澄晚景

中国珍珠（宝石）城

高港区

台七套、农民日报等新闻媒体先后报道了我区三大合作建设和三大产业的发展情况。

全年各类工业共完成现价产值135.08亿元、销售128.29亿元、利税10.66亿元、利润4.31亿元，同比分别增长28.1%、30.7%、27.9%和38.0%；规模以上企业发展加快，全年销售过亿元企业18家，其中口岸船舶工业公司首次突破10亿元大关；实施各类技术改造项目190个，当年完成投入22.93亿元，同比增长58.89%；新增私营企业387家，新增个体工商户1696户，新增注册资本11.15亿元，同比分别增长28.1%、22.9%和24.5%。经贸委被区委、区政府评为十佳“人民满意机关”、民营经济最佳服务部门、招商引资工作先进单位、创新创优二等奖；被市经贸委评为工业经济运行一等奖、商贸工作先进单位、生猪屠宰管理工作先进集体；区乡企局被市局评为优秀乡企局；何进主任被江苏省经贸委和中国人民银行南京分行评为江苏省“十五”融资洽谈活动先进工作者。

泰州市副市长、高港区委书记　张爱平

高港区委副书记、区长　王群

全区完成建筑施工总产值23.82亿元，比上年增长19.03%，分别占市交、区交指标的115.4%、106.77%；实现增加值5.94亿元，比上年增长19.28%，占市交、区交指标的118.8%、106.56%，超额完成全年各项目标任务。创省优工程3个，市优工程9个，创省级文明工地三个，市级文明工地七个。局被省表彰为“安全生产先进集体”，被区委、区政府评为“信访工作先进集体”和“建筑业工作先进集体”。

全年完成服务业增加值14.48亿元，增长15.5%，社会固定资产投资37.42亿元，增长30.2%。全区累计完成市场成交额25亿元，拥有亿元市场4个。

全区个私和私营总数达1.04万户，注册资金33.4亿元，从业人员7.51万人，其中工商联会员总数已达154户，全区非公经济实现增加值29.56亿元，占全区生产总值的68.1%，上缴利税7.91亿元，占地区财政收入的79.1%。

全区新批外资项目16个（工商登记注册投资企业13家），协议利用外资2.0966亿美元（协议利用注册外资15001万美元），实际利用外资1.0726亿美元（商务部确认数8571万美元），完成外贸出口19993万美元，同比分别增长15%、55.1%（33%）、256%；分别完成市交指标的181.8%（136%）、145.8%（119.9%）、294%。被市外经贸局表彰为泰州市外经贸工作一等奖。

高港夜景

银杏广场

古韵水岸一角

乡镇街道

建设大厦

泗阳县地处江苏省北部，中国五大淡水湖之一的洪泽湖北岸，县域总面积1418平方公里，辖16个乡镇、2个场、1个省级经济开发区，总人口96.8万。泗阳有着5000年文明史和2000年建县史，是西汉泗水王国都城所在地、中国八大名酒洋河大曲发源地、全国唯一的“中国意杨之乡”、全国著名的商品粮棉基地、棉花良种繁育基地、优质水产品基地。“泗水古国、意杨之乡、新兴纺都、生态乐园”是泗阳的城市名片。

近年来，泗阳县委、县政府按照省委书记李源潮同志“既要加快发展，更要善待百姓”的指示精神，始终把“执政为民”作为工作的出发点和落脚点，把重振淮北工业强县雄风作为经济社会发展的总定位和总目标，坚持以科学发展观为指导，在宏观调控中把握机遇，在微观调整中把握主动，在社会转型中经受锻炼，在复杂局面下提高水平，加快推进泗阳经济社会全面振兴。2006年，全县抢抓省委、省政府加快苏北振兴和帮助宿迁实现更大突破的政策机遇，顺应产业资本加速梯度转移的大好形势，以“六年振兴规划”总揽全局，以“跃升十位均量全市争第一，争当苏北振兴宿迁突破先行军”为奋斗目标，强力推进100项重点工作，广泛开展争先创优活动，全县经济社会呈现出快速发展、和谐发展、健康发展的良好态势。2006年，全县实现地区生产总值81.21亿元，同比增长15.2%，增幅全市第一；50万元以上固定资产投资47.68亿元，同比增长75.3 %；财政一般预算收入2.51亿元，同比

江苏省泗阳县

宿迁市委常委、泗阳县委书记　侍鹏

泗阳县委副书记、县长　赵深

增长54%，增幅全市第一、全省第三；农民人均纯收入4240元，同比增长10.6%；三次产业结构实现由二一三到二三一的重大突破，达到27.6：43：29.4；在全省52个县市的综合排名上升6位。在全市目标管理考核中首次夺得三县两区第1名，实现了历史性突破；列入市考核的25项指标中，人均GDP增幅、财政一般预算收入、人均财政收入增幅、50万元以上固定资产投资等14项指标排名全市第一。此外，财政、新农村建设、计划生育、平安泗阳和法治泗阳创建等工作也都取得了显著成绩，分别获得了全省“财政收入增收先进县”、“省高效农业特色县”、“全省渔业工作先进县”、“省农机服务先进单位”、“省农村河道疏浚整治工作先进县”、“全省气象科技服务先进集体”、“全国农村部分计划生育家庭奖励扶助制度和少生快富工程试点先进单位”、省“法治江苏合格县”创建工作先进单位和“社会治安综合治理先进县”等一系列荣誉称号。

北京路夜景

国际花园城市——常熟

小城镇休闲广场

虞城夜景

常熟市是一座具有3000多年历史的国家历史文化名城，也是长江三角洲中心地带新兴的港口工业城市，被联合国环境规划署评为“国际花园城市”。市域面积1264平方公里，森林覆盖率为21.4%。2006年末，全市户籍人口为105万人，暂住人口达到72万多人，城市化率达到65%。

进入新世纪以来，常熟市牢固树立富民优先、内外并举、城乡一体、亲近自然、诚信至上“五大理念”，围绕争当“两个率先”排头兵的目标，坚持加快发展不松劲，科学发展不动摇，把握工业化、城市化、服务业“三大重点”，积极构建产业、环境、文化“三大特色”,经济和社会事业实现又好又快发展，成为江苏省首批进入全面小康社会的县市之一。先后获得了“国家生态市”、“国家卫生城市”、“国家环保模范城市”、“国家园林城市”、“中国人居环境范例奖”、“中国优秀旅游城市”等30多项国家级荣誉。2006年，全市实现地区生产总值809亿元，人均GDP近10000美元，财政总收入超过100亿元。目前，全市累计注册外资超过100亿美元，到帐外资超过60亿美元；累计建办私营企业12462家，个体工商户56503户，个体、私营经济注册资本超过400亿元。全市拥有中国名牌产品15只，江苏省名牌产品81只；中国驰名商标9件，江苏省著名商标60件；拥有国家授权专利3175件，申请国际专利6件。

江苏省昆山市

城市鸟瞰

昆山市市委书记　张国华

昆山市市长　管爱国

昆山东靠上海，西邻苏州，是江苏省的东大门。1989年撤县设市，市域面积927平方公里，户籍总人口66.68万，下辖10个镇和1个国家级经济技术开发区。昆山历史悠久，人文荟萃。这里是“百戏之祖”昆曲的发源地，千年古镇周庄被誉为“中国第一水乡”，享誉海内外。昆山物产丰饶，盛产驰名中外的阳澄湖清水大闸蟹，素有江南“鱼米之乡”美称。

改革开放以来，昆山坚持从实际出发，解放思想，开拓创新，抢抓机遇，不断进取，经济社会保持了持续、快速、协调发展的良好态势，先后荣获国家卫生城市、国家环保模范城市、全国创建文明城市工作先进市、全国优秀旅游城市、国家园林城市、全国生态市等称号。近年来，昆山市认真贯彻党的十六大精神和“三个代表”重要思想，坚持以科学发展观为指导，以“两个率先”统揽全局，推动经济社会又快又好发展。2006年，全市完成GDP 932.01亿元，比上年增长24.9%；财政收入151.38亿元，其中地方一般预算收入65.37亿元，分别增长29.6%和26.6%；进出口总额427.45亿美元，增长28.7%；城镇居民人均可支配收入19016元，农民人均纯收入10508元，分别比上年增长13.1%和14.0%。在国家统计局公布的全国百强县市排名中，昆山继续蝉联第一。十个镇全部进入全国千强镇前500强，玉山镇首次名列千强镇之首。

一、加快实施产业升级，改善优化经济结构和运行质量。在保持经济较快增长的同时，把结构调整和产业升级放到更加突出的位置，大力实施外向带动、民营赶超、服务业跨越“三大战略”，加快新型工业化进程。

二、创新落实富民安民措施，着力提高城乡居民生活水平。把民营经济作为富民经济，不断加大政策扶持力度，营造放手发展的良好氛围。在此基础上，以农村为重点，积极探索具有昆山特色的富民之路

三、坚持城乡统筹发展理念，不失时机地加快城市化进程。以建设现代化中等城市、营造一流的投资创业环境和人居环境为目标，引导工业向园区集中、人口向城镇集中、住宅向社区集中，不断加快城市建设和城市化步伐，城市建成区面积已扩大到55平方公里，城市化率达到61.1%。

四、注重强化社会管理，全面推进和谐社会建设。强化政府公共管理职能，积极协调各利益关系，努力构建管理有序、治安稳定、服务高效、社会和谐的人文环境。

江苏省吴江市

吴江夜景

吴江市市委书记　朱民

吴江市市长　徐明

吴江市是江苏省南大门，地处苏浙沪两省一市交汇的长三角中心腹地，东靠上海，南接浙江，西濒太湖，北依苏州。苏嘉杭高速公路和在建的沪苏浙高速公路，318国道和227省道，京杭大运河和太浦河，十字交叉穿境而过。全市总面积1093平方公里，户籍人口78万，外来人口60万，现下辖2个省级开发区、8个镇、250个行政村。在2006年公布的全国百强县排名中，吴江位居第九；荣获2006年《福布斯》中国大陆最佳商业城市排行榜全国县级市第二名；并在第六届全国县域经济基本竞争力评比中排名第四位。

吴江别称“鲈乡”，历史悠久，人文荟萃，是著名的“鱼米之乡”、“丝绸之府”。公元909年吴江建县，1992年撤县设市。吴江全境无山可观山，六分地四分水，以世界文化遗产——同里退思园为龙头，拥有盛泽先蚕祠、震泽慈云寺和师俭堂等众多人文自然胜迹，堪称中国优秀旅游城市的江南水乡代表。

2006年，全市实现地区生产总值501亿元，完成财政一般预算收入35亿元，全社会固定资产投资额236亿元，各项主要经济指标都完成或超额完成了“十一五”规划的序时进度。

产业集群是吴江经济发展的重要特征，现已基本形成电子信息、丝绸纺织、电缆光缆3大支柱产业，缝纫机、彩钢板、羊毛衫3个特色产业，电梯制造、汽车配件、新型建材、生物医药、有色金属、日化、服装、制鞋8个成长型产业的“338”体系。

2006年吴江经济开发区、汾湖经济开发区、盛泽地区三大经济主战场实现一般预算收入21.5亿元，占全市总量的60%以上。集群产业进一步壮大，电子信息、丝绸纺织、光缆电缆三个支柱产业继续发挥主导作用，完成工业销售收入1414亿元，占全市工业销售收入的80%。规模经济支撑作用进一步凸显，规模以上企业完成销售收入1463亿元，占全市工业销售收入的81%。

吴江市在大力发展经济的同时，加快推进和谐社会进程。进一步扩大就业规模，2006年新增就业人数近8万人；进一步完善社会保障体系，社会保险覆盖面不断扩大，全市全年共有近25万人纳入城镇五大保险范围。2006年农民人均纯收入10028元，城镇居民人均可支配收入20500元。城乡环境不断改善，2006年安排62项重点建设项目，总投资143.8亿元，完成年度投资52.5亿元。吴江市荣获中国人居环境奖水环境治理优秀范例城市称号，国家生态市和国家生态园林城市创建进展顺利。

IT企业生产线

江苏省如东县

建设中的黄海大桥

10月25日如东风电二期首台机组并网发电

央视国际频道专题录播《让世界了解你——走进如东、走近洋口港》

如东县地处长江入海口北翼，东濒南黄海，南与上海、苏南一江之隔。是江苏沿海的一个重要县份，是全国首批对外开放县之一。全县总面积1872平方公里，人口107万人，下辖15个镇和两个省级经济开发区。在如东106公里绵长的海岸线上分布着两个重要的港口，一个是深水海港，一个是国家中心渔港，借助于得天独厚的海洋优势，如东将在海洋产业上奋力作为，全力争创江苏沿海开发第一县。如东的基础教育闻名全国，群众体育工作连续三年获得全国先进，是江苏省“十五”人口和计划生育示范县、省科普示范县和省“社会治安安全县”，如东还是全国民间绘画之乡和中国海鲜之乡，著名社会活动家费孝通誉之为“风水宝地，江海明珠”。

如东风电场

江苏省赣榆县

新农村农民别墅

县委书记　孙荣章

县长　王加培

赣榆县位于苏鲁两省交界，江苏省东北部海州湾畔，是江苏的北大门，素有“享山川之饶，受渔盐之利”的美誉。全县辖18个镇、2个省级开发区、424个行政村，总面积1427平方公里，总人口108万，耕地面积87万亩，境内沿海、平原、山区各占三分之一。

赣榆区位独特，发展潜力巨大。赣榆是江苏沿海经济带和东陇海产业带的东部交汇点，是连云港与岚山港的要冲腹地，紧邻大陆桥洲际铁路枢纽，距连云港民航机场30公里，距青岛流亭国际机场220公里。优越的区位、广阔的空间使赣榆发展大型临港工业、集聚重化工业具备得天独厚的条件。

赣榆基础设施完备，创业条件优越。赣榆拥有江苏赣榆经济开发区、江苏赣榆海洋经济开发区2个省级开发区以及柘汪临港工业园区和海头生物科技集聚区2个市级重点产业区。江苏省赣榆经济开发区已累计投资2.5亿元，具备了良好的项目承载条件。江苏省赣榆海洋经济开发区是省政府批准设立的全省第一家海洋经济开发区，总规划面积1.58万公顷，基础条件优越，是海洋产业发展的优良载体。柘汪临港产业园区，配套基础设施完善，是赣榆黄金岸线开发的先行区和重化工业承载区。海州湾生物科技集聚区内土地多为盐田、滩涂等，地势平坦，用地成本低。

赣榆依山傍海，城市前景广阔。徐福故里、子贡晒书、吴山望日、夹谷莺啼、文峰览柱、孔子相鲁会齐侯处等，人文与自然景观交相辉映，自成一体。目前，赣榆正大力实施新城开发战略，建设50万人口、30平方公里的现代化海滨新城。

赣榆资源丰富，物产丰饶。县内矿藏储量丰富，地下蕴藏着50亿立方米的花岗岩，储量居全省首位，另有大理石、优质黄沙、纹石、白云石、石英石、瓷石、优质矿泉水等30多种矿藏。全县已建成水产养殖基地 8 个，名列全国渔业生产百强县之列。赣榆是全国育苗之乡，全县育苗企业已达300多家。

赣榆历史悠久，人文荟萃。赣榆秦代就有建制，位于我国南北文化重合过渡地带，齐鲁文化和吴越文化在这里得到兼容并蓄和激扬沉淀，形成赣榆县勤劳淳朴、热情好客的民风民情和开拓创新、敢为人先的进取精神。

赣榆，这颗黄海之滨、海州湾畔的璀璨明珠，正在发出愈来愈耀眼的光芒。

经济开发区一角

江苏省灌云县

县城全貌

灌云县位于江苏省东北部，因南有灌河，北有云台山而得名，东临黄海，素有黄海明珠之称。县域面积1840平方公里，辖8镇、12乡，3个省市属农盐场，6个县属农林场圃，总人口107.5万。2006年完成地区生产总值54.85亿元,全社会固定资产投资64.24亿元,财政总收入4.01亿元。

灌云历史悠久、人文荟萃。秦时属朐县，民国元年建县,历代名人辈出。灌云风景秀丽、名胜众多。伊芦山风景区山林俊秀，李汝珍纪念馆历史厚重，潮河湾、新沂河、开山岛自然风光旖旎。灌云城市优美、魅力无限。灌云县城有山有水，素有“十里青山半入城”之美誉，县城镇伊山镇为江苏百家名镇，县城建成区面积达45平方公里，绿化面积达449公顷。

县城工业园区

灌云区位优越、交通便利。淮连、连徐、汾灌和沿海四条高速公路纵横境内， 204国道和324、236、242省道贯穿全境，正在规划建设的沿海铁路连接东部的燕尾港和连云港港，新沂河横穿东西，盐河纵贯南北，形成了公路、铁路、海运、水运的综合交通网络。

灌云资源丰富、优势明显。灌云县是优质农副产品的重要产区，是全国第一批商品粮生产基地县、棉花生产百强县、江苏省粮食高产示范县。境内西部地区蕴藏丰富的优质陶瓷土资源。东部沿海地区有32公里长的海岸线，42万亩滩涂，可供开发利用的岸线和土地资源十分充足。

灌云工业方兴、发展迅猛。已初步形成纺织、服装、能源、机械、食品、酿造、医药、建材等工业主导产业。县经济技术开发区为省级重点工业园区，规划建设面积40平方公里，区内基础设施完备，环境优美。燕尾港为江苏唯一的海河联运港和连云港港重要的组合港。与港口相配套的临港产业区，规划建设面积140平方公里，区内基础设施完备，已成为清洁能源、石化、机械、船舶制造等大工业、大企业重点集聚区。

灌云人民意气风发、壮志满怀。目前，全县上下紧紧围绕“实现两个进位，奋力崛起苏北”的奋斗目标，致力把灌云打造成为江苏沿海新兴的港口产业高地、苏北知名的山水城相拥的旅游生态城市、全市有位的现代制造业基地，奋力开创经济和社会跨越发展、科学发展、和谐发展的崭新局面。

彩虹桥

居民住宅小区

江苏省张家港市塘桥镇位于中国沿海和长江两大经济开发带交汇处，地处长江三角洲新兴港口城市张家港市的东南部，上海、南京、苏州、无锡、常州、南通等大中城市环列四周。东邻在建的苏通长江大桥，南接沿江高速公路，西沿苏虞张一级公路和江阴长江大桥，北濒黄金水道长江，204国道直贯南北，338省道横跨东西。全镇总面积94.4平方公里，总人口近20万人，其中户籍人口8.9万人，下辖2个办事处、3个社区居委会、14个村委会。

住宅小区一角

塘桥镇历史悠久、人杰地灵、文化底蕴深厚。境内有蔡墩、徐家湾等新石器时代遗址以及明代建筑肖家桥、弘济桥等历史遗产；镇北的古黄泗浦是唐代高僧鉴真第六次东渡成功到达日本的吉祥宝地；当代水利专家张光斗、原政协副主席钱昌照、清朝末年探花庞钟璐等名人都诞生于塘桥。

投资近亿元兴建的塘桥镇人民医院

塘桥镇经济基础雄厚，产业结构日趋合理。2006年全镇完成生产总值70.6亿元，人均GDP超过1万美元，全口径财政收入近10亿元，一般财力预算收入3.5亿元，技改投入近20亿，注册外地民资3.5亿元，进出口总额6亿美元，其中自营出口4.6亿美元。。工业是塘桥的支柱产业，全镇现有工业企业1200多家，拥有固定资产100亿元，职工9万多人，2006年实现工业开票销售225.7亿元，主要行业有纺织、电子、机械、冶金、钢管、铜管等，其中纺织产业产值超过200亿元，纺织企业近1000家，建成了规模较大的纺织产业集群，年生产精纺呢绒5000万米，列

张家港市塘桥镇

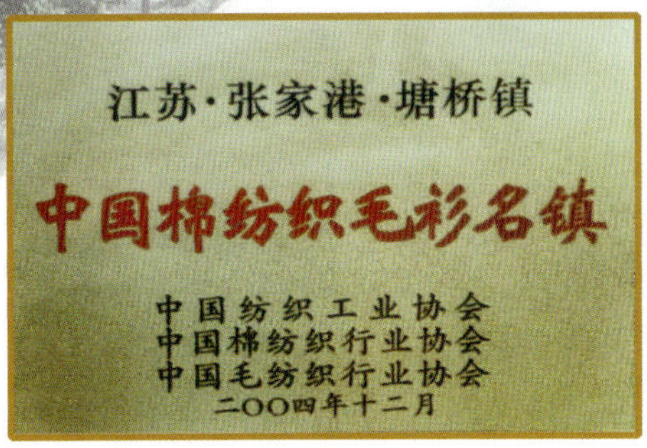

黄尧书记领取中国人居环境范例奖奖牌

全国第1，棉纱45万吨，列全国第2，羊毛衫1.5亿件，列全国第2。塘桥镇始终把农业增效、农民增收、农村稳定放在重要位置，建立了浅水养殖、花卉果品、蔬菜、苗木、奶牛、獭兔等种养特色区和无公害养殖基地。第三产业蓬勃发展，全年三产增加值20亿元。

塘桥镇城镇化水平较高，各项社会事业协调发展。近年来，以建设“充满活力、富有特色、可持续、现代化的塘桥”为指导思想，不断加快城镇规划建设步伐。先后投入5亿多元，建成了占地近10平方公里，设施较为完善配套的新城区。目前，城镇已形成“八横八纵”的道路框架，建有商业贸易区、行政服务区、文化教育区、居民住宅区和工业开发区等多个功能区，拥有一座少年文化宫、二个星级宾馆、三个街心公园、五所省级重点示范性学校等公共设施，区域性变电站、污水处理厂、热电厂等基础设施一应俱全，城区文化娱乐设施齐全、医疗卫生装备先进、供水供电充足、邮电通讯便捷，基本具备了城市功能。农民生活质量不断提高，水泥路通到村村组组，全镇每百人拥有电话45部，每7户家庭就拥有1辆私家轿车，自来水入户率达99%，有线电视全部实现光缆传输，通村入户率分别达到100%和近90%。2006年农民人均收入10189元。

塘桥素有“围棋之乡”之美称，近年来还先后获得了“国家卫生镇”、“全国首批小城镇建设示范镇”、“全国群众体育先进集体”、“全国创建文明村镇工作先进集体”、“中国棉纺织毛衫名镇”、“全国环境优美镇”、苏州地区唯一一家“全国文明镇”、“中国人居环境范例奖”等荣誉称号，综合实力排名全国千强镇第64位。

鉴真东渡纪念馆

张家港市

塘桥幼儿园

针纺城

华芳金陵五星级国际大酒店

销售超130亿的华芳集团

塘桥福沁苑（敬老院）

东渡苑全景

塘桥镇

塘桥镇人民政府

全民运动会

休闲广场一瞥

塘桥少年宫

江阴市

江苏三周庄中的现代工业重镇—江阴市周庄镇，历史悠久，人文荟萃，敢为人先，追求卓越，具有独特的区位优势、交通优势、规模工业经济优势。

周庄镇素有“三吴襟带之邦，百越舟车之会”的美誉，位于江阴市东郊，是江阴市区、张家港市区的区位中心，境内水陆交通发达，国家二级航道张家港河、沿江高速公路、省道澄杨公路、云顾公路和新建的澄东大道穿境而过。全镇总面积80平方公里，常住人口10万，新市民8万，辖15个行政村和3个社区居委。2006年，全镇地区生产总值达到105亿元，人均生产总值超过1万美元，农民人均纯收入超过1万元，工业总产值达到442亿元，工业开票销售达到440亿元，实现工业增加值85亿元，其中规模以上工业实现增加值77亿元，完成自营出口7亿美元，三产服务业增加值达到20亿元。

周庄镇在宋元时期就已成为闻名遐迩的“江南布码头”。经过长时期的发展，周庄工业经济实力雄厚，产品门类齐全，拥有江苏三房巷集团、江苏江阴模塑集团、江苏华宏集团、江苏倪家巷集团、江阴江东集团等一批充满活力的规模型企业，生产领域涵盖纺织、轻工、机械、冶金、化工、建材等十多个门类600多种产品，并形成了以涤纶化纤、人造革、纺织印染、装饰型材、汽车整车及零部件、橡塑制品为优势的七大产业，产品覆盖全国并远销海外。

工业经济的飞速发展使全镇的城镇建设日新月异，

周庄规划图

15.42亿元，连续三年位列江苏省乡镇首位；全年新增注册外资2.5亿美元，实际到账8011万美元；民营经济累计注册资本突破140亿元；拥有国家级高新技术企业6家、江苏省级高新技术企业28家、省级民营科技企业73家，中国驰名商标2只、国家免检产品8只、中国名牌产品9只、江苏省级名牌产品35只，在全省乡镇中名列前茅。

发展中的城市，日新月异的虞山，虞山人正以时不待我、责无旁贷的历史使命感和紧迫感，以只争朝夕、奋力争先的发展意识和创新精神，期待着无限美好的锦绣未来！

亮山景观工程

环境生态

急水港

牌坊全景

桃花

感受时空的记忆双桥

昆山市周庄镇

泡桐圆洞

中国第一水乡－周庄，位于江苏昆山市西南隅，东连上海，西邻苏州，交通便利。享有“上有天堂、下有苏杭、中间有个周庄”之美誉。周庄全镇镇域面积38.96平方公里，人口2.2万人，辖10个行政村，2个居委会。

经历了“十年保护”和“十年发展”，2006年，周庄进入“十年提升”阶段，全面启动“国际周庄”旅游发展战略，先后与法国阿尔勒市和美国加利福尼亚州、内华达州结成了交流与合作联盟，共同开拓旅游市场、开展文化交流活动。依托古镇旅游资源，全镇旅游经济、高新技术产业和民营经济迅猛发展。2006年，全镇实现财政收入1.7亿元，地方一般预算收入突破1亿元，农民人均收入达10551元，全年游客接待量已超过305万。被国家环保总局等11个部委联合授予“中华环境奖”以及“最值得外国人去的50个地方”、“中国十大最美村镇”、“全国旅游百强”、“中国旅游行业十大领袖品牌”等荣誉，成功创建国家首批5A级旅游景区，成为周庄新十年全面提升进程中又一重要里程碑。历史悠久、人文荟萃的周庄，其“小桥、流水、人家”的独特水乡风貌被国画大师吴冠中称赞：“黄山集中国山川之美，周庄集中国水乡之美。”；世界建筑大师贝聿铭挥毫：“周庄是国宝”。2001年，亚太经合组织贸易部长非正式会议在周庄舫召开，“中国第一水乡”的美誉传遍海内外；前国家主席江泽民、美国前总统卡特、新加坡资政李光耀等众多国内外知名政要都曾莅临周庄。2005年周庄镇被国家环保总局授予“中华环境奖”；全镇十个行政村全部通过省级生态村考核验收；美国州政府授予周庄“美国政府奖”和“世界最佳魅力水乡”称号；近日，周庄又再度入选国家文物局最新公布的“中国世界文化遗产预备名单”。2005年底，周庄达到“江苏省建设小康社会”四大类18项25条指标，为昆山率先实现高水平小康社会作出了贡献。

面向新世纪，周庄人秉执科学的发展观，坚持走保护与发展并举的可持续发展之路，成功打造了“中国第一水乡”和“传感器产业基地”两大金字招牌。1998年，周庄与中国科学院合作共建“传感器产业基地”，2000年，该基地被国家科技部批准为“国家火炬计划传感器产业基地”、“国家‘863’高新技术研究发展计划成果产业化基地”。2004年，基地又成功发起创办了江苏省传感器产业技术协会，成为全国首个省级传感器专业技术协会。目前，已吸引高新技术企业近30家，总投资15亿元，年销售收入近8亿元，年实现利税超亿元，年生产能力已达3亿只，产品95%以上销往欧美和东南亚地区，其传感器产品年销售量占全省销售总量的三分之一，占全国总量近一成。

周庄正致力于对优秀传统文化的传承与现代文明的发展，迎着世界经济潮流，紧握长三角发展之脉动，在率先建成高水平小康社会和率先基本实现现代化道路上，凸显特色，发挥优势，实现新的跨越。

农夫山庄

无锡新区鸿山镇

鸿山镇位于无锡市东南部，北依鸿山，南临望虞河。全镇行政区域面积58.6平方公里，人口5.2万，辖2个居委会、15个村委会。

区位优势独特。鸿山区位优势独特，西与无锡国家高新技术开发区无缝相接，南与苏州国家高新技术开发区隔河相望。水陆空交通便捷，南傍京杭大运河，西接无锡国际机场，紧靠312国道，沪宁高速公路、锡甘路、锡东大道穿境而过。正在规划建设中的京沪高速铁路、东干线、东环线更凸现出鸿山镇得天独厚的区位优势。

文化底蕴深厚。七千年的新石器时代遗址、庞大的越国贵族墓群再现悠久历史；至德泰伯遗风流传千古，鸿山景区成为古今寻根访祖，观光旅游之胜地；“院士之乡”的美誉蜚声中外，国学大师钱穆、物理学家钱伟长、经济学家钱俊瑞、教育家钱临照、力学家钱令希、分子生物学家邹承鲁等六位院士被列入当代世界科技文化名人。

经济潜力强劲。目前，全镇拥有规模骨干企业70家，初步形成了多元产业经济结构。国家级高新技术企业江苏双象集团和市级高新技术企业无锡银邦铝业有限公司等成为国内同行骨干企业；正在建设中的无锡机光电装备制造工业园以专业化制造为基础，以高新技术为主导，以优势品牌产品为核心，以公共服务平台为支撑，将成为一个名副其实的机械装备制造工业高地，对全镇对外开放、产业层次和区域竞争力的提升将产生极大的推动作用。

仰止阁

农业结构趋好。鸿山特色精品型农业片区被列为市六大现代都市农业主题片区，已基本形成鸿山千亩葡萄园区、鸿山奶牛园区、梁鸿花卉苗木园区等三大农业示范园区，一批特色强、市场大、品牌响的特色农产品在全市农业结构调整中崭露头角，全镇农业逐步呈现出市场农业、高效农业、生态农业的良好格局。

鸿山钟灵毓秀、人杰地灵，是历史文化名镇，同时，也是一块创新创业的热土，鸿山将创建成为经典吴越文明、现代都市农业文明、国际化工商文明交相辉映的江南名镇。

邗江区公道镇

集镇绿化大道

镇党委书记　夏元顺

公道镇地处扬州北郊，南接宁沪高速，东接京沪高速，北临高邮湖、邵伯湖，交通十分便捷，全镇陆地面积66.6平方公里，水面滩涂6.5万亩，辖11个行政村、3个居委会，常住人口4.8万人，集镇人口1万人，2006年全镇地区生产总值10.92亿元，财政收入6584万元，农民人均纯收入6818元。全镇经济社会发展指数位列全国千强镇969位，是江苏省重点中心镇，先后获得全国群众体育先进单位、江苏省卫生镇、江苏省文明镇等荣誉称号。

公道现有工业企业238家，其中规模企业32家，外资独资企业3家，2006年实现工业产值28.9亿元，机械制造、电子通讯、化工化纤、汽车配件、玩具鞋服、模具灯具等六大支柱产业齐头并进。

集镇建设按照省重点中心镇定位，加快了集镇总体规划修编，跳出老街建新街，进行了全新合理布局，形成工业、商业、居住、文教卫生、休闲娱乐等功能区。

新农村建设按照“生产发展、生活宽裕、乡风文明、村容整洁、管理民主”要求，加快完善村镇规划，加速推进农村基础设施建设，现已有1个村创成全面小康示范村，5个村正在积极创建中。全镇高效农业加快推进，以农家乐为代表的生态观光旅游业也蔚然兴起。

社会事业统筹发展。公道中学在全区农村率先创成省三星级高中，民办蓝天学校教育质量位居全市前列，小学、幼儿园均创成省级示范性实验学校，镇文化中心创成省标准文化中心，有标准场馆3000平方米，镇图书馆为省二级图书馆，藏书2万册。目前全镇群众文化设施和组织遍布各村，全镇社会保障体系健全。

“十一五”时期，公道镇以“求实创新、争先创优”的工作要求，瞄准“全面达小康，建设新公道”的工作目标，加快实施“产业强镇、环境立镇”战略步伐，全力打造文明公道、实力公道、平安公道、魅力公道。

工业集中区大道

京口区谏壁镇

农民新村

谏壁镇位于镇江市东郊，距市中心13公里，北依长江，南与丹徒区辛丰、黄墟镇接壤，东邻镇江新区，西靠丹徒镇，素有镇江“东大门”之称，为省政府确立重点发展的中心镇之一。全镇总面积31.89平方公里，耕地595公顷，现辖4个行政村，8个居委会，有谏壁发电厂等部省、市、区属企事业单位一百多家，镇大铁路及沿江公路、镇大公路、镇澄公路穿镇而过，京杭运河与长江在境内交汇，铁公水交通便捷。谏壁历史悠久，《史记》即有汉初吴王濞家在练壁聚北的记载。嘉庆年间（1796—1820）始设谏壁镇。

谏壁集镇是镇党委、政府所在地，镇政治、经济、文化、教育活动中心。集镇面积5.32平方公里，常驻人口（包括外来务工者）约四万多人。改革开放以来，谏壁镇坚持以经济建设为中心，大力开展招商引资，走集聚吸纳式发展之路。2005年实现地区生产总值90680万元，其中农业2150万元，工业83050万元，第三产业5480万元；财政收入12726万元；协议利用外资2532万美元，实际利用外资795万美元。外贸出口产品交货额660万元。农民人均纯收入6400元。近几年来，谏壁镇积极推进城市化战略，不断拉大集镇面积。谏（壁）辛（丰）公路拓宽改造、雩龙公路修复工程、谏壁复线船闸接线工程、外环线滨河公路拓宽改造工程全面完工，镇内“三纵四横”道路建成。雩北农贸市场、谏壁农贸市场二期工程、国丰大酒店、东大超市等相继建成开业。京口区文化馆、第十中学迁建全面完成，精神文明建设不断加强，多次被命名为市级文明镇、市健康教育示范镇、市食品卫生先进镇、市“创安”先进镇。连续三年荣获市双拥模范镇称号。2003年荣获镇江市“开放型经济工作先进集体”、“国土绿化先进单位”等荣誉称号，2004年通过市“双清双美”示范镇（村）验收，被授予全市“社会治安安全乡镇”。2005年被市委、市政府授予敬老模范乡镇、农民增收先进乡镇、民营经济服务先进集体、全市工业经济先进集体。

镇新农村艺术团蓬勃开展各项文艺活动

少儿文艺活动丰富多彩

区规模企业——鸿泰钢铁有限公司生产场景

江苏中烟工业公司

江苏中烟工业公司法定代表人　蒋洪喜

江苏中烟工业公司是中国烟草总公司投资的国有独资公司，拥有南京、徐州、淮阴三家卷烟生产工厂和南通烟滤嘴有限责任公司、江苏格瑞实业有限责任公司、江苏烟草原料发展有限责任公司、江苏烟草机械有限责任公司4个为卷烟工业配套的全资子公司。2006年产销卷烟168万箱，实现税利近160亿元。公司拥有职工近8000名，总资产185亿元。公司“苏烟”、“南京”、“一品梅”、“红杉树”四大主导品牌进入全国卷烟百牌号目录。其中“苏烟”被评为“烟草行业内最具成长力的自主品牌”，产销量位居全国同价位高档卷烟第二位。荣获“中国名牌”称号的“南京”牌卷烟2006年成为全国规模最大的单品牌一类卷烟。公司产品畅销全国32个省市区，并成功进入国际市场，远销加拿大、新加坡、菲律宾等国家和地区。

江苏中烟工业公司始终坚持科学发展观，不断深化内部管理体制改革，打造和谐企业，推动江苏烟草工业连续多年实现快速、协调、持续发展，为国家和地方经济建设做出了积极贡献。自江苏中……来，累计产销卷烟600余万箱，实现税利500多亿元。公司年卷烟产销量位居行业第十二位，经济效益排名全国烟草行业第四位。江苏中烟工业公司的南京、徐州、淮阴卷烟厂是当地政府的财政支柱.南京卷烟厂连续五年蝉联江苏省纳税第一名。在创建和谐企业过程中，三家卷烟厂累结硕果，南京、徐州、淮阴卷烟厂分别荣获“2005年度全国和谐劳动关系优秀企业”、“江苏省和谐劳动关系企业”和“淮安市和谐劳动关系企业”荣誉称号。在取得良好经济效益的同时，江苏中烟工业公司以奉献社会、服务大众为已任，积极履行社会责任，投身各类公益事业，社会效益显著。

新的发展形势赋予江苏中烟更大的发展责任和更高的发展目标。十一五期间，江苏中烟工业公司将始终坚持科学发展观，以创新、创业、创优为发展动力，以做大做强、跻身全国烟草行业“10多个重点骨干企业和10多个重点名优品牌”行列为发展目标，充分发挥规模优势，发挥人财物、产供销的集成优势，不断完善内部机制、优化资源配置、做精主导品牌、强化市场营销、提升管理水平、构建和谐烟草，为“全面达小康、建设新江苏”做出新的更大的贡献。

地　址：南京市中山北路406-3号
邮　编：210011
电　话：025-58590691
传　真：025-58590517

爱普生拓优科梦水晶元器件（无锡）有限公司

爱普生拓优科梦水晶元器件（无锡）有限公司是由日本爱普生拓优科梦株式会社设立的全资子公司，主要生产应用于移动通信产品、PC、PC 周边、AV 机器等光读取设备的关键元器件，这些产品具有很高的技术含量，是信息产业（IT）发展中不可或缺的。爱普生拓优科梦水晶元器件（无锡）有限公司把能够成为以水晶应用产品为核心向客户提供高质量的电子产品及其应用技术，为世界电子产业的发展做出贡献的公司作为所有经营活动的动力和目标。并将和全体员工共同承担起社会责任、通过磨炼感性、创造和挑战，追求幸福健康的社会生活。

品质/环境方针

☆品质方针：

全体员工应从顾客的角度进行考虑并行动，提供能够得到顾客满意和信赖的安全优质的商品和服务。

在所有的业务中，以 5G 主义为基础开展行动，迅速循环开展 PDCA 的活动，持续改善 QCDS.

通过对成功及失败的信息的积累、知识化及活用来预防问题的发生和再发生。

☆环境方针：

遵守法律法规，致力于持续地预防污染

改善环境、节能降耗的环境改善活动

☆环境方针的含义：

①实施环境安全的评价、削减环境负荷，努力管理节省能资源，削减化学物质的使用和废弃物的产生，防止氟离子等主要污染源对环境的污染。

②为了得到客户的满意和信赖，制定目标并贯彻实施，通过定期的修改实施具有持续性的改善。

③遵守相关法律法规所制定的规定，进一步完善本公司的基准。

④经常性业务、非经常性业务及事故等紧急状态下，贯彻实施不影响地区社会的污染防止活动。

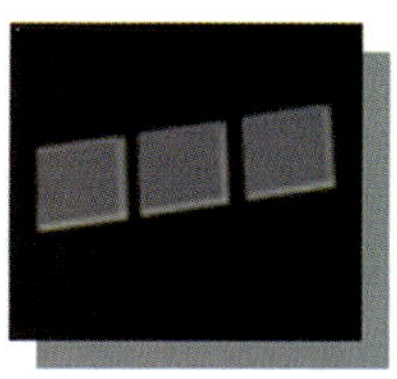

经营理念：

成为能够以水晶为核心，向客户提供高质量的电子产品及其应用技术，为世界电子产业的发展做出贡献的公司。

成为能够敏锐感知社会、环境、需求的变化、及早对应，受到信赖的「优秀公司」。

作为良好的企业市民，全体员工承担起社会责任、通过磨炼感性、创造和挑战，追求幸福健康的生活。

总经理发言：

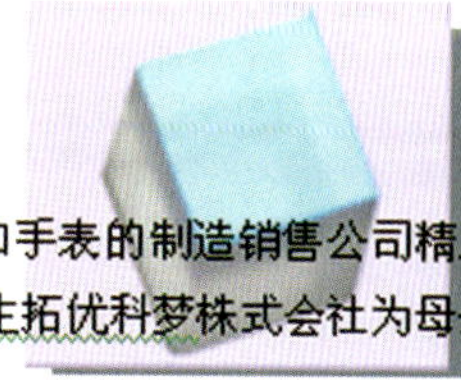

我公司是大家所熟悉的打印机和手表的制造销售公司精工爱普生集团的一员。另外也是以爱普生拓优科梦株式会社为母公司的电子产品制造公司。

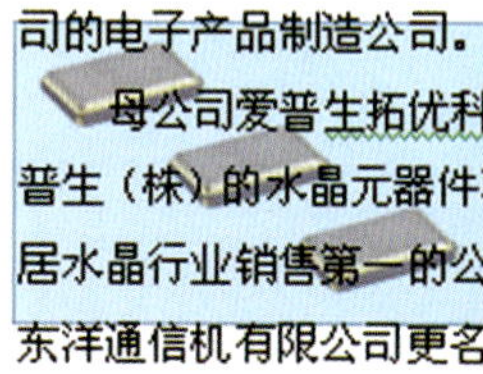

母公司爱普生拓优科梦株式会社，是去年 10 月份由精工爱普生（株）的水晶元器件事业部和东洋通信机合并后诞生的，跃居水晶行业销售第一的公司。因此，我公司也从今年一月由无锡东洋通信机有限公司更名为爱普生拓优科梦水晶元器件（无锡）有限公司。我们所生产的水晶元器件产品是驱动电子机器的核心计时元器件，就好比是人类的心脏。人们经常会这样说，半导体是电子产业的米，与此相对的水晶元器件产品就好比是电子产业的盐，因此是电子产业发展不可或缺的重要产品。

所以，为了在不远的将来实现向高信息化社会的发展，需要水晶元器件产品的不断更新，同时它的作用也将日益更加重要。另外，用于记忆媒体（DVD）的光学产品也随着信息量的扩大，蓝光等产品的日益成熟也是众所期待的。

爱普生拓优科梦作为水晶元器件行业的 NO.1，很多客户都是世界各个领域的顶尖集团公司，与客户一起共同领导着世界。

在这种形势下，爱普生拓优科梦水晶元器件（无锡）有限公司，从正式投产至今才三年的时间，加上以新区良好投资环境和优势为后盾，是今后日益发展可能性很高的先进的电子产品制造公司。我公司为了今后的壮大和发展，需要具有以公司为核心责任感和挑战精神的人才。

让我们为了自身的成长，挑战领导世界的工作吧。

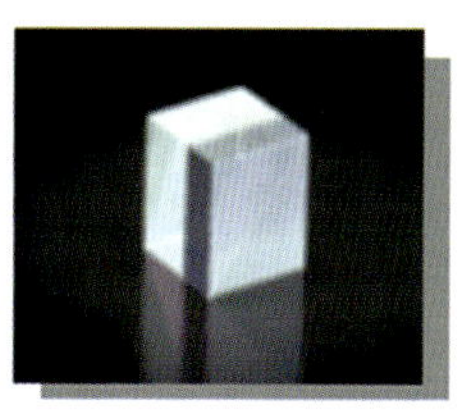

总经理：志野英男

联系人：华先生，王小姐
Email：hr2@epsontoyocom. com
地址：无锡新区长江路36号
电话：85221818-221
传真：85217713
邮编：214028

江苏雨润集团

在南京市政府召开的全市慈善动员大会上，雨润集团宣布设立2000万元慈善基金。

烟熏火腿

意大利风味萨拉米

新北京风味火腿

香辣火腿

挂炉烤肉

雨润集团总部坐落在南京市建邺区，是一家集食品、房地产、旅游、商贸、物流五大产业于一体的集团性企业，下属近60家分（子）公司，分别设立在江苏、安徽、黑龙江等28个省、直辖市。集团现有雨润、旺润、福润、大众肉联等四大品牌十大系列共1000多个品种的产品。

多年来，雨润的发展得到了社会各界的认可。早在1999年2月，雨润食品在全国肉食品行业中率先通过ISO9001国际质量体系认证；2005年，在全国民营企业工业制造业50强中，雨润集团被列入第35位；2006年，在中国企业500强中排名124位，在中国制造业500强中排名56位，在中国肉类食品加工业中排名第1位，并被国家发改委、科技部、财政部、海关总署等部委认定为国家级技术中心。

2005年10月3日，经过12年的发展，“中国雨润”在香港联交所主板正式挂牌交易，股票代码“1068”。截止目前，雨润集团已拥有东成控股（0735.HK）、A股市场的南京中央商场（600280.SH）和中国雨润（1068.HK）三家上市公司。

交通银行南京分行

南京分行夜景

交通银行始建于1908年，是中国早期四大银行之一。1986年7月24日国务院批准重新组建交通银行。1987年4月1日，重新组建后的交通银行正式对外营业，成为中国第一家全国性的国有股份制商业银行。2005年6月23日，交通银行在香港联交所正式挂牌上市，上市开盘价2.8元，股价最高较发行价增长了96%，在海外上市的国内商业银行中位居首位。2007年4月24日，交通银行A股首次公开发行圆满完成，7.90元的发行价格对应2006年底发行后市净率为3.42倍，创A股市场银行股发行估值水平之最。

交通银行南京分行重新组建于1986年，现管辖徐州、连云港、扬州、泰州、南通、镇江、常州等7家分行。近年来，南京分行以科学有效发展为主题，以深化改革为动力，加快调整资产结构、负债结构、客户结构、网点结构、产品结构，员工结构，深化经营管理体制改革，创新经营管理机制，业务逐步走上良性循环的发展轨道。通过坚持以思想解放为先导，在创新思路、创新体制、创新方法上下功夫，坚持以改革创新精神，走开拓发展之路，大力发展新兴业务，南京分行在南京金融界开创出许多第一，如第一个设立自助银行、第一个开办个人外汇买卖、第一个成立个人贷款中心、第一个开通24小时客户服务中心、第一个代销开放式基金、第一个实行综合柜员制等。同时，南京分行的创新发展还走在交行系统前列，分别被系统内选为薪酬制度改革试点行、小企业业务推广试点行等，并连续9年被总行评为A级行。

企业网银重点客户产品推介会

营业部自助区

新街口沃德财富中心

广州路支行营业厅